July 6–9, 2015
Bath, United Kingdom

Association for
Computing Machinery

Advancing Computing as a Science & Profession

ISSAC'15

Proceedings of the 2015 ACM

International Symposium on Symbolic and Algebraic Computation

Sponsored by:
ACM SIGSAM

Supported by:
London Mathematical Society & Maplesoft

Association for
Computing Machinery

Advancing Computing as a Science & Profession

The Association for Computing Machinery
2 Penn Plaza, Suite 701
New York, New York 10121-0701

ISBN: 978-1-4503-3435-8 (Digital)

ISBN: 978-1-4503-3881-3 (Print)

Additional copies may be ordered prepaid from:

ACM Order Department
PO Box 30777
New York, NY 10087-0777, USA

Phone: 1-800-342-6626 (USA and Canada)
+1-212-626-0500 (Global)
Fax: +1-212-944-1318
E-mail: acmhelp@acm.org
Hours of Operation: 8:30 am – 4:30 pm ET

Printed in the USA

Foreword

The 2015 International Symposium on Symbolic and Algebraic Computation (ISSAC 2015) is the premier conference for research in symbolic computation and computer algebra. ISSAC 2015, held at the University of Bath, U.K., is the 40th meeting in the series, which began in 1966 with the seminal ACM Symposium on Symbolic and Algebraic Manipulation. ISSAC 2015 is sponsored by the Association for Computing Machinery (ACM), in particular, the ACM Special Interest Group in Symbolic and Algebraic Manipulation (SIGSAM). The meeting is also supported by donations from the London Mathematical Society (LMS) and Maplesoft. As a scientific satellite event, the workshop Parallel Symbolic Computation (PASCO) was held in Bath immediately following ISSAC 2015.

The ISSAC conference is a showcase for original research contributions on all aspects of computer algebra and symbolic mathematical computation, including:

Algorithmic aspects:

- Exact and symbolic linear, polynomial and differential algebra
- Symbolic-numeric, homotopy, perturbation and series methods
- Computational algebraic geometry, group theory and number theory
- Computer arithmetic
- Summation, recurrence equations, integration, solution of ODEs and PDEs
- Symbolic methods in other areas of pure and applied mathematics
- Complexity of algebraic algorithms and algebraic complexity

Software aspects:

- Design of symbolic computation packages and systems
- Language design and type systems for symbolic computation
- Data representation
- Consideration for modern hardware
- Algorithm implementation and performance tuning
- Mathematical user interfaces

Application aspects:

- Applications that stretch the current limits of computer algebra algorithms or systems, use computer algebra in new areas or new ways, or apply it in situations with broad impact.

The program of ISSAC 2015 features invited talks, tutorials, contributed research presentations, a poster session and a software exhibits session. These Proceedings contain all accepted contributed papers, as well as abstracts of the invited talks and tutorials.

The ISSAC Program Committee selected 43 papers appearing in these Proceedings. All papers submitted to ISSAC 2015 were judged, and accepted or rejected, solely according to their scientific novelty and excellence. Each submitted paper was assigned to three members of the Program Committee, and two or more referee reports were obtained for each submission. We gratefully acknowledge the thorough and important work of the Program Committee Members and external reviewers, whose names appear on the following pages, and thank all the authors and lecturers for their contribution.

The success of a conference depends on the dedicated work of numerous volunteers, many of whom are listed in the following pages. To them, and to the rest of the community who contributed in various ways to the success of ISSAC 2015, we extend our thanks. We are also grateful to the sponsors of the conference, who are also listed in these pages. Finally, we thank all the members of the local organization team at the University of Bath, our host institution.

Steve Linton (General Chair)
Daniel Robertz (Proceedings Chair)
Kazuhiro Yokoyama (Program Committee Chair)

Table of Contents

ISSAC 2015 Conference Organization

General Chair: Steve Linton *(University of St Andrews, United Kingdom)*

Program Committee Chair: Kazuhiro Yokoyama *(Rikkyo University, Japan)*

Proceedings Chair: Daniel Robertz *(Plymouth University, United Kingdom)*

Local Arrangements Chair: James Davenport *(University of Bath, United Kingdom)*

Tutorial Chair: Mohab Safey El Din *(University Pierre et Marie Curie, France)*

Poster Chair: Ekaterina Shemyakova *(SUNY New Paltz, USA)*

Software Presentations Chair: Bernard Mourrain *(Inria, Sophia Antipolis Méditerranée, France)*

Treasurer: Russell Bradford *(University of Bath, United Kingdom)*

Exhibitors Chair / Webmaster: Matthew England *(Coventry University, United Kingdom)*

Program Committee:
John Abbott *(CoCoA Project, Italy)*
Xiao-Shan Gao *(KLMM, Chinese Academy of Sciences, China)*
Vladimir Gerdt *(Joint Institute for Nuclear Research, Russia)*
Grégoire Lecerf *(CNRS, France)*
Viktor Levandovskyy *(RWTH Aachen University, Germany)*
Ziming Li *(KLMM, Chinese Academy of Sciences, China)*
Marc Moreno Maza *(University of Western Ontario, Canada)*
Guénaël Renault *(University Pierre et Marie Curie, France)*
Colva M. Roney-Dougal *(University of St Andrews, United Kingdom)*
Markus Rosenkranz *(University of Kent, United Kingdom)*
Siegfried M. Rump *(Hamburg University of Technology, Germany)*
David Saunders *(University of Delaware, USA)*
Carsten Schneider *(Johannes Kepler University Linz, Austria)*
J. Rafael Sendra *(University of Alcalá, Spain)*
Thomas Sturm *(Max Planck Institute for Informatics, Germany)*
Agnes Szanto *(North Carolina State University, USA)*
Nobuki Takayama *(Kobe University, Japan)*
Jan Verschelde *(University of Illinois at Chicago, USA)*
Stephen M. Watt *(University of Waterloo, Canada)*
Kazuhiro Yokoyama *(Rikkyo University, Japan)* – **Chair**

Poster Presentation Committee:
George Labahn *(University of Waterloo, Canada)*
Elizabeth Mansfield *(University of Kent, United Kingdom)*
Manfred Minimair *(Seton Hall University, USA)*
Ekaterina Shemyakova *(SUNY New Paltz, USA)* – **Chair**
Yang Zhang *(University of Manitoba, Canada)*

Software Presentation Committee:

François Boulier *(University of Lille 1, France)*
Anton Leykin *(Georgia Tech, USA)*
Bernard Mourrain *(Inria, Sophia Antipolis Méditerranée, France)* – **Chair**

ISSAC thanks these external reviewers:

Jakob Ablinger
Sergei Abramov
Parisa Alvandi
Jennifer Balakrishnan
Saugata Basu
Prashant Batra
Benjamin Beeker
Jérémy Berthomieu
Anna Maria Bigatti
Alin Bostan
Brice Boyer
Daniel Brake
Peter Brooksbank
Christopher Brown
Laurent Busé
Jorge Caravantes
Xavier Caruso
Francisco Jesús Castro-Jiménez
Changbo Chen
Shaoshi Chen
Howard Cheng
Jin-San Cheng
Frédéric Chyzak
Thomas Cluzeau
Robert M. Corless
María Angélica Cueto
Xavier Dahan
Carlos D'Andrea
Wolfram Decker
Elie de Panafieu
Gema M. Díaz-Toca
Christian Eder
Ruyong Feng
Masaya Fujisawa
Xing Gao
Laureano González-Vega
Yoshiaki Goto
Stef Graillat
Dmitry Grigoriev
Li Guo
Mareike Haberichter
Azzam Haidar
William Hart
Albert Heinle
Christopher Hillar
Yasuaki Hiraoka
Michael Hoffman
Lei Huang
Qiaolong Huang
Zhang Huang
Hidenao Iwane
Maximilian Jaroschek
Claude-Pierre Jeannerod
David Jeffrey
Jeremy Johnson
Thomas Kahle
Manuel Kauers
Karel Klouda
Alexander Kobel
Wolfram Koepf
Marek Košta
Christoph Koutschan
George Labahn
Daniel Lazard
Wen-Shin Lee
François Lemaire
Shijun Liao
Shaowei Lin
Frank Lübeck
Christoph Lüders
Philippe Malbos
Jorge Martín-Morales
Armando Martino
Marni Mishna
Izumi Miyamoto
Antonio Montes
Guillaume Moroz
Dmitriy Morozov
Bernard Mourrain
Yayoi Nakamura
Ioana Necula
Masayuki Noro
Luca Padovani
Yanbin Pan
Ludovic Perret
Marko Petkovšek
Veronika Pillwein
Daniel Robertz
Daniel Roche
Lajos Rónyai
Mohab Safey El Din
Michael Sagraloff
Yosuke Sato
Wiland Schmale
Éric Schost
Werner M. Seiler
Takafumi Shibuta
Naoyuki Shinohara
Hakan Simsek
Michael Singer
Pierre-Jean Spaenlehauer
Arne Storjohann
Luis Tabera
Emmanuel Thomé
Blas Torrecillas
Quoc-Nam Tran
Elias Tsigaridas
Joris van der Hoeven
Mark van Hoeij
Enric Ventura
Hubert Wagner
Dingkang Wang
Chaoping Xing
Jean-Claude Yakoubsohn
Chee Yap
Masaya Yasuda
Chunming Yuan
Lihong Zhi
Konstantin Ziegler
Richard Zippel

ISSAC 2015 Sponsors & Supporters

ISSAC acknowledges the generous support of the following institutions.

sponsored by:

Association for Computing Machinery

ACM Special Interest Group in Symbolic and Algebraic Computation

supported by:

London Mathematical Society

Maplesoft

Building Bridges between Symbolic Computation and Satisfiability Checking

Erika Ábrahám
RWTH Aachen University
52056 Aachen
Germany
abraham@cs.rwth-aachen.de

ABSTRACT

The satisfiability problem is the problem of deciding whether a logical formula is satisfiable. For first-order arithmetic theories, in the early 20th century some novel solutions in form of decision procedures were developed in the area of mathematical logic. With the advent of powerful computer architectures, a new research line started to develop practically feasible implementations of such decision procedures. Since then, symbolic computation has grown to an extremely successful scientific area, supporting all kinds of scientific computing by efficient computer algebra systems.

Independently, around 1960 a new technology called SAT solving started its career. Restricted to propositional logic, SAT solvers showed to be very efficient when employed by formal methods for verification. It did not take long till the power of SAT solving for Boolean problems had been extended to cover also different theories. Nowadays, fast SAT-modulo-theories (SMT) solvers are available also for arithmetic problems.

Due to their different roots, symbolic computation and SMT solving tackle the satisfiability problem differently. We discuss differences and similarities in their approaches, highlight potentials of combining their strengths, and discuss the challenges that come with this task.

Categories and Subject Descriptors

F.4.1 [**Mathematical Logic and Formal Languages**]: Mathematical Logic; G.4 [**Mathematics of Computing**]: Mathematical Software

General Terms

Algorithms, Theory

Keywords

Arithmetic; SMT Solving; Symbolic Computation

ISSAC'15, July 6–9, 2015, Bath, United Kingdom.

DOI: http://dx.doi.org/10.1145/2755996.2756636.

1. INTRODUCTION

Formulas of *first-order logic over arithmetic theories* are logical combinations of linear or polynomial constraints over real- or integer-valued variables. This logic is a powerful modelling formalism frequently used to specify problems from the areas of scheduling, electronic design automation, product design optimisation, planning, controller synthesis, test-case generation, and the analysis of programs and probabilistic, timed, hybrid and cyber-physical systems, just to mention a few well-known examples. Once the problem is formalised, algorithms and their implementations are needed to check the validity or satisfiability of the formulas, and in case they are satisfiable, to identify satisfying solutions. Algorithms to solve this problem are called *decision procedures.*

Symbolic computation. The development of decision procedures for arithmetic theories started already in the early 20th century in mathematical logic. Though the satisfiability problem is known to be NP-hard already for the pure Boolean propositional logic (SAT) and even undecidable for non-linear integer arithmetic, the mathematical developments gave hope for practically applicable fully automated methods to solve arithmetic formulas. Therefore, an enormous effort was put into directing mathematical research towards practice, yielding powerful computer algebra systems in the area of *symbolic computation.*

Satisfiability checking. In the '60s, another line of research on *satisfiability checking* [6] for *propositional logic* started its career. The first idea used *resolution* for quantifier elimination [21], and had serious problems with the explosion of the memory requirements with increasing problem size. Another research line [20] suggested a combination of *enumeration* and *Boolean constraint propagation (BCP).* A major improvement was achieved in the '90s by *combining* the two approaches, leading to *conflict-driven clause-learning* and *non-chronological backtracking* [37]. Later on, this impressive progress was continued by novel efficient implementation techniques (e.g., sophisticated decision heuristics, two-watched-literal scheme, restarts, cache performance, etc.), resulting in numerous powerful *SAT solvers.* Also different extensions are available, e.g. QBF solvers for quantified Boolean formulas, or Max-SAT solvers to find solutions which satisfy a maximal number of clauses.

Driven by this success, big efforts were made to enrich propositional SAT-solving with solver modules for different theories. Highly interesting techniques were implemented in *SAT-modulo-theories (SMT) solvers* for checking, e.g., equality logic with uninterpreted functions, array theory, bit-vector arithmetic and quantifier-free linear real and inte-

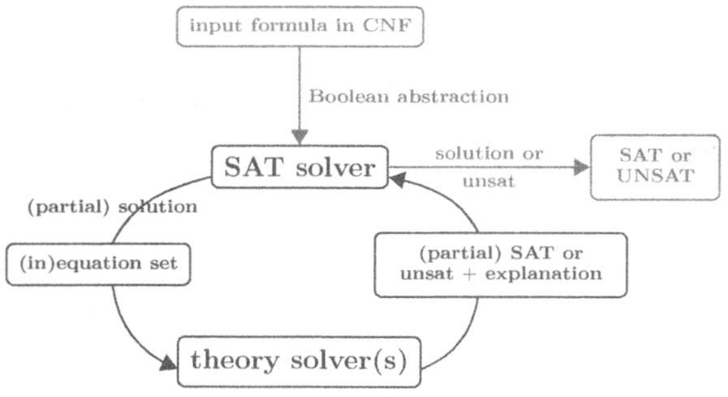

Figure 1: The functioning of SMT solvers

ger arithmetic (LRA/LIA), but the development for quantifier-free non-linear real and integer arithmetic (NRA/NIA) is still in its infancy. For further reading, see, e.g., [3, 35].

The prosperity of research on SAT- and SMT-solving is supported by a wide range of community activities. Examples are own *conferences* on satisfiability checking (the SAT conference is in its 18th edition in 2015), a forum *SatLive* to keep up-to-date with research, the development of *SMT standards*, *SAT solver competitions* since 2002, and *SMT solver competitions* since 2005.

Potentials and challenges. The research areas of SMT solving and symbolic computation are quite disconnected. On the one hand, SMT solving has its strength in efficient techniques for exploring Boolean structures, learning, combining solving techniques, and developing dedicated heuristics, but its current focus lies on easier theories and it makes use of symbolic computation results only in a rather naive way. There are fast SMT solvers available for the satisfiability check of LRA and LIA problems, but just a few can handle NRA and NIA.

On the other hand, symbolic computation is strong in providing powerful procedures for sets (conjunctions) of arithmetic constraints, but it does not exploit the achievements in SMT solving for efficiently handling logical fragments, using heuristics and learning to speed-up the search for satisfying solutions.

The SMT-solving community would definitely profit from further exploiting symbolic computation achievements and adapt and extend them to comply with the requirements on embedding in the SMT context. However, it is a highly challenging task, as it requires a deep understanding of complex mathematical problems, whose embedding in SMT solving is far from trivial and needs their adaptation and extension. Symmetrically, symbolic computation could profit from exploiting successful SMT ideas, but it requires expertise in efficient solver technologies and their implementation, like dedicated data structures, sophisticated heuristics, effective learning techniques, and approaches for incrementality and explanation generation in theory solving modules. These challenging goals could get within reach, when supported by a stronger collaboration between these research areas, creating an infrastructure for dialogue and knowledge transfer.

2. SMT SOLVING

SMT solvers were originally designed to solve *existentially quantified* (or quantifier-free) formulas. Though there are increasing activities and some SMT solvers are already able to handle quantified formulas of some theories, in the following we restrict ourselves to the solving of existential fragments of first-order logic over different theories.

SMT activities started for theories such as equality logic and uninterpreted functions, bit-vector arithmetic, and array theory. Later, these activities were further extended to (existential fragments of) arithmetic theories. The increasing variety of the theories considered by SMT solvers made an urgent need for a common input language. The `SMT-LIB` initiative [4] defined a *standard input format* for SMT solvers with a first release in 2004, and provides a large and still increasing number of *benchmarks*, systematically collected for all supported theories. `SMT-LIB` also enabled the start of *SMT competitions*; the first one took place in 2005 with 12 participating solvers in 7 divisions (theories, theory combinations, or fragments thereof) on 1360 benchmarks, which increased in 2014 to 20 solvers competing in 32 divisions on 67426 benchmarks.

The SMT-LIB standard and the competitions not only intensified the SMT research activities, but also gave visibility and acceptance for SMT solving in computer science and beyond. Once a problem is formulated in the `SMT-LIB` standard input language, the user can employ *any* SMT solver to solve his or her problem.

Modern *SMT solvers* typically combine a *SAT solver* with one or more *theory solvers* as illustrated in Figure 1. First the input formula is transformed into conjunctive normal form (CNF), a conjunction of disjunctions (clauses); this transformation can be done in linear time and space using Tseitin's transformation on the cost of additional variables. Next, the resulting CNF is abstracted to a pure Boolean propositional logic formula by replacing each theory constraint by a fresh Boolean proposition. Intuitively, the truth value of each fresh proposition defines whether the theory constraint, which it substitutes, holds. The SAT solver tries to find solutions for this propositional abstraction and during solving it consults the theory solver(s) to check the consistency of the theory constraints that should hold according to the current values of the abstraction variables. Whereas *full lazy* approaches search for a complete Boolean solution before invoking theory solvers, *less lazy* techniques consult the theory modules more frequently for partial solution candidates for the Boolean skeleton, and put special requirements on them. On the one hand the theory solvers only need to check *conjunctions (sets)* of theory constraints, instead of arbitrary Boolean combinations. On the other hand, theory solvers should have the following properties for being *SMT-compliant*:

- They should work *incrementally*, i.e., after they determine the consistency of a constraint set, they should be able to take delivery of some additional constraints and re-check the extended set, thereby making use of results from the previous check.
- In case of unsatisfiability, they should be able to return an *explanation* for inconsistency, e.g., by a preferably small inconsistent subset of the constraints.
- They should support *backtracking*, i.e., the removal of previously added constraints.

Optimally, theory solvers should also be able to provide

- a *satisfying solution*, if the problem is satisfiable, and
- a *proof of unsatisfiability* for the explanation, if the problem is unsatisfiable.

A great advantage of the SMT technology is that it can employ decision procedures not only in isolation, but also *in combination*. For example, solving non-linear arithmetic formulas can often be speeded up by first checking linear abstractions or linear problem parts using more efficient decision procedures, before applying heavier procedures. Additionally, theories can also be combined already in the input language of SMT solvers. For example, deductive program verification techniques generate verification conditions, which might refer to arrays, bit-vectors as well as integers; in such cases, dedicated SMT solvers can apply several decision procedures for different theories in combination.

When combining decision procedures, *incomplete* but *efficient* procedures are also valuable, if they guarantee termination but not necessarily return a conclusive answer. Such incomplete (but terminating) methods are frequently applied in SMT solving, a typical example being interval constraint propagation, based on interval arithmetic. Some solvers combine such incomplete methods with complete decision procedures, in order to guarantee the solution of the problem, while increasing efficiency. Other solvers even sacrifice completeness and might return a "don't know" answer, but still they are able to solve certain extremely large problems, which are out of reach for complete methods, very fast. Furthermore, incomplete procedures are the only way to support problems from undecidable theories, like formulas containing exponential or trigonometric functions.

SAT and SMT solvers are tuned for efficiency. Combining complete and incomplete decision procedures, making use of efficient heuristics, learning not only propositional facts but also (Boolean abstractions of) theory lemmas at the SAT level allow modern SMT solvers to solve relevant large-size problems with tens of thousands of variables, which could not be solved before by single decision procedures in isolation. For some example applications see, e.g., [2].

Arithmetic theories in SMT solvers. First extensions of SMT solving to arithmetic theories were designed for LRA and LIA. Some popular decision procedures to solve LRA formulas are the *simplex* algorithm, the *ellipsoid method* [34], the *Fourier-Motzkin variable elimination* algorithm, or the incomplete method of *interval constraint propagation* [30, 31].

The question whether there is a solution for an integer arithmetic formula is in general undecidable. However, its linear fragment is decidable. Some decision procedures for solving LIA are, e.g., the *Omega test* [38], *branch and bound* [26], *cutting planes* [25], *interval constraint propagation*, and *bit-blasting* [15].

Examples for solvers that can cope with LRA/LIA problems (either in a complete or in an incomplete manner) are `Alt-Ergo` [17], `CVC4` [1], `iSAT3` [29, 39], `MathSAT5` [14], `OpenSMT2` [12], `SMT-RAT` [19], `veriT` [9], `Yices2` [28], and `Z3` [24]. A further interesting SMT-approach for LIA is proposed in [10].

Much less activities can be observed for SMT solvers for NRA, which has an exponential time-complexity even for conjunctions of polynomial (in)equalities (in contrast to its linear fragment, in which conjunctions of inequalities are solvable in polynomial time). There are well-known complete as well as incomplete decision procedures for NRA, for example the *cylindrical algebraic decomposition* [16] method, methods based on *Gröbner bases* [41], the *realisation of sign conditions* [5], the *virtual substitution* [40] method, or *interval constraint propagation*.

There are some incomplete SMT-solvers for NRA like, e.g., `iSAT3`, which uses interval constraint propagation. The SMT solver `MiniSmt` [42] tries to reduce NRA problems to linear real arithmetic and can solve only satisfiable instances this way. We are aware of only two SMT solvers that are complete for non-linear real arithmetic: Firstly, the prominent `Z3` solver developed at Microsoft Research, which uses an elegant SMT-adaptation of the cylindrical algebraic decomposition method [32]. Secondly, our own SMT-solver based on our `SMT-RAT` (SMT Real-Arithmetic Toolbox) library [19], which we continuously improve and extend. The current release offers, besides some non-arithmetic components, the `CArL` [13] library for arithmetic datatypes and basic computations with them, and solver modules for simplex, the cylindrical algebraic decomposition [36], the virtual substitution method [18], Gröbner bases [33], interval constraint propagation, branch and bound, and their strategic combination [19].

Even less SMT solvers are available for NIA, which is undecidable in general. A linearisation approach was proposed in [8]. The SMT solving spin-off of `AProVE` [15] uses bit-blasting. To our knowledge, `Z3` implements a combination of linearisation and bit-blasting. `iSAT3` uses interval constraint propagation, whereas `Alt-Ergo` combines the idea of [7] with an axiom-based version of interval constraint propagation. Our `SMT-RAT`-based solver can tackle this theory using a generalised branch-and-bound technique, combined with careful selection of sample points in real-arithmetic procedures.

3. POTENTIALS AND OBSTACLES

Using arithmetic decision procedures in SMT solvers as theory modules is a promising symbiosis: highly efficient SAT solvers can handle the Boolean problem structure and learn from previous (SAT and theory) conflicts, and the expensive theory module calls only concern conjunctions of theory constraints.

The arithmetic decision procedures mentioned above are implemented in different tools. For example, a highly optimised implementation based on the cylindrical algebraic decomposition can be found in `QEPCAD` [11], whereas the `redlog` package [27] of the computer algebra system `Reduce` offers an optimised combination of the cylindrical algebraic decomposition with virtual substitution and Gröbner bases methods. *So why not use those existing implementations for SMT embedding?*

Though it sounds natural, the realisation of this idea is not at all straightforward. Available implementations of decision procedures are seldomly available as *libraries*, and even if they are, they are not SMT compliant. Thus, for SMT embedding, these mathematically complex decision procedures have to be adapted and extended before an SMT compliant implementation can be realised.

The SMT-compliant adaptation of decision procedures has to assure that the algorithms work *incrementally*, and can generate *explanations* for unsatisfiable problems. *Backtracking* is a nice-to-have property, if it can be achieved on low costs. Adapting decision procedures to be incremental can be tricky, as it requires the storage of additional bookkeeping information, and therefore a deliberate choice of efficient and well-suited data structures. Perhaps the most challenging aspect is the generation of explanations. Also this task entails the costly storage of additional information, where we need to make a careful choice of what and how to store. This leads to a healthy balance between the computational costs in space and time, and the size of the explanations we can extract from the stored information.

For the implementation of adapted algorithms, an *efficient modular library for basic computations with polynomials* is needed, which, if we want to have the door open for parallelisation, must be additionally *thread-safe*. Furthermore, on a given problem instance there might be big differences in the running times of different theory solver modules. Therefore, a *strategic combination* [23] of them should be supported.

What happens in practice is that research groups working on SMT solving do not make use of computer algebra systems, but stepwise adapt and re-implement established procedures from mathematical logic and the symbolic computation community. On the one hand, because active networking and collaboration between symbolic computation and SMT solving is still (surprisingly) quite restricted, much effort goes into re-investigation on the side of the SMT community. On the other hand, the symbolic computation community is not fully aware about the impressive achievements in SMT solving. More common projects would allow to join forces and commonly develop improvements on both sides.

4. SOME MORE CHALLENGES

SMT solvers are originally developed for checking satisfiability of existentially quantified fragments of first-order logic over different theories. However, there are further dimensions in which we could strengthen their power, and thereby increase their applicability and push forward their acceptance in other domains, including industrial applications. Research on the following extensions is interesting not only for the SMT community, but also in the context of symbolic computation.

- For the support for *linear and non-linear (global) optimisation* with respect to a possibly non-linear objective function and an arithmetic formula with an arbitrary logical structure, an interesting procedure using the cylindrical algebraic decomposition method was proposed [22], but currently available tools do not yet have optimisation functionalities.

- Another similarly complex task is the handling of *quantified arithmetic formulas*, which is already challenging for propositional logic. Though some SMT solvers like `Z3` and `CVC4` are able to handle quantified formulas, these techniques are restricted to certain logical fragments and are usually incomplete. Most SMT solvers do not support quantification at all.

- If a problem is detected to be satisfiable, SMT solvers should output *satisfying solutions*. However, solutions for non-linear real arithmetic problems might contain algebraic numbers, which can be hard to represent in a user-friendly way. This gives rise to the question, how we can aim at the generation of *user-friendly models*, at low cost. Furthermore, in some user context, not only one solution is required, but (a finite representation of) all models.

- If a problem is unsatisfiable, it is often helpful for the user to get an *unsatisfiable core*, i.e., a subset of the problem clauses that is already unsatisfiable. For example, if a formula models a realisability property, such an unsatisfiable core could explain, which parts of the system model are conflicting, and thus help to correct design errors. Furthermore, *proofs* for unsatisfiability would make the results more reliable. Last but not least, for large problems *minimal* unsatisfiable cores and proofs have a much stronger impact. Also *interpolant* generation features have great effect to extend the application domains.

- In SAT solving, some attempts were made to develop efficient *parallelisation techniques*. Unfortunately, it turned out that reaching a linear speed-up is hard to achieve. Perhaps this is the reason why parallelisation is not in the focus of the SAT- and SMT-solving communities. However, in the SMT context, parallel solutions have much more potentials. For non-linear arithmetic, even simple portfolio approaches can be very efficient, as the running times of different decision procedures or even just different heuristics might differ significantly: some procedures might succeed in milliseconds, whereas other ones might need hours or even days. Besides portfolio approaches, divide-and-conquer parallelisation inside and between theory modules, involving information exchange, are promising options. Like SAT solvers, also many theory solvers work on a tree-shaped search tree, but in the theory search space, sub-trees represent in general much harder problems. Therefore, it seems likely that additional communication effort would pay off for parallelisation. Currently available SMT parallelisation techniques mainly use the portfolio approach, as for example `CVC4` for linear arithmetic, or `SMT-RAT` for all of its modules.

- Each application has its own characteristics. Some involve symmetries; others are combined from several parts, some of which are static and others dynamically changing; sometimes single independent problems must be solved, sometimes a sequence of related problems appears. There is a wide range of possibilities to tune the solvers to be optimal for a given problem type. The applicability of SMT technology in industry could be increased by identifying typical problem patterns and implementing *dedicated SMT-solvers* for them, tuned for the given type of applications.

5. ACKNOWLEDGEMENTS

I would like to thank many of my colleagues for fruitful discussions, especially Florian Corzilius, Pascal Fontaine, Gereon Kremer, Ulrich Loup, Stefan Schupp, and Thomas Sturm.

6. REFERENCES

[1] C. Barrett, C. L. Conway, M. Deters, L. Hadarean, T. K. D. Jovanović, A. Reynolds, and C. Tinelli.

CVC4. In *Proc. CAV*, volume 6806 of *Lecture Notes in Computer Science*, pages 171–177. Springer, 2011.

[2] C. Barrett, D. Kroening, and T. Melham. Problem solving for the 21st century: Efficient solvers for satisfiability modulo theories. Technical Report 3, London Mathematical Society and Smith Institute for Industrial Mathematics and System Engineering, June 2014. Knowledge Transfer Report.

[3] C. Barrett, R. Sebastiani, S. A. Seshia, and C. Tinelli. Satisfiability modulo theories. In *Handbook of Satisfiability*, volume 185 of *Frontiers in Artificial Intelligence and Applications*, chapter 26, pages 825–885. IOS Press, 2009.

[4] C. Barrett, A. Stump, and C. Tinelli. The satisfiability modulo theories library (SMT-LIB). `www.SMT-LIB.org`, 2010.

[5] S. Basu, R. Pollack, and M. Roy. *Algorithms in Real Algebraic Geometry*. Springer, 2010.

[6] A. Biere, A. Biere, M. Heule, H. van Maaren, and T. Walsh. *Handbook of Satisfiability*, volume 185 of *Frontiers in Artificial Intelligence and Applications*. IOS Press, 2009.

[7] F. Bobot, S. Conchon, E. Contejean, A. Mahboubi, A. Mebsout, and G. Melquiond. A simplex-based extension of Fourier-Motzkin for solving linear integer arithmetic. In *Proc. IJCAR*, volume 7364 of *Lecture Notes in Computer Science*, pages 67–81. Springer, 2012.

[8] C. Borralleras, S. Lucas, R. Navarro-Marset, E. Rodriguez-Carbonell, and A. Rubio. Solving non-linear polynomial arithmetic via SAT modulo linear arithmetic. In *Proc. CADE*, volume 5663 of *Lecture Notes in Computer Science*, pages 294–305. Springer, 2009.

[9] T. Bouton, D. C. B. de Oliveira, D. Déharbe, and P. Fontaine. veriT: An open, trustable and efficient SMT-solver. In *Proc. CADE*, volume 5663 of *Lecture Notes in Computer Science*, pages 151–156. Springer, 2009.

[10] M. Bromberger, T. Sturm, and C. Weidenbach. Linear integer arithmetic revisited. *CoRR*, abs/1503.02948, 2015. Accepted at CADE-25.

[11] C. W. Brown. QEPCAD B: A program for computing with semi-algebraic sets using CADs. *SIGSAM Bulletin*, 37(4):97–108, 2003.

[12] R. Bruttomesso et al. The OpenSMT solver. In *Proc. TACAS*, volume 6015 of *Lecture Notes in Computer Science*, pages 150–153. Springer, 2010.

[13] `CArL`. Project homepage. `http://smtrat.github.io/carl/`.

[14] A. Cimatti, A. Griggio, B. Schaafsma, and R. Sebastiani. The MathSAT5 SMT solver. In *Proc. TACAS*, volume 7795 of *Lecture Notes in Computer Science*, pages 93–107. Springer, 2013.

[15] M. Codish, Y. Fekete, C. Fuhs, J. Giesl, and J. Waldmann. Exotic semi-ring constraints. In *Proc. SMT*, volume 20 of *EPiC Series*, pages 88–97. EasyChair, 2013.

[16] G. E. Collins. Quantifier elimination for real closed fields by cylindrical algebraic decomposition. In *Automata Theory and Formal Languages*, volume 33 of *Lecture Notes in Computer Science*, pages 134–183. Springer, 1975.

[17] S. Conchon, M. Iguernelala, and A. Mebsout. A collaborative framework for non-linear integer arithmetic reasoning in Alt-Ergo. In *Proc. SYNASC*, pages 161–168. IEEE Computer Society, 2013.

[18] F. Corzilius and E. Ábrahám. Virtual substitution for SMT solving. In *Proc. FCT*, volume 6914 of *Lecture Notes in Computer Science*, pages 360–371. Springer, 2011.

[19] F. Corzilius, U. Loup, S. Junges, and E. Ábrahám. SMT-RAT: An SMT-compliant nonlinear real arithmetic toolbox. In *Proc. SAT*, volume 7317 of *Lecture Notes in Computer Science*, pages 442–448. Springer, 2012.

[20] M. Davis, G. Logemann, and D. Loveland. A machine program for theorem-proving. *Communications of the ACM*, 5(7):394–397, 1962.

[21] M. Davis and H. Putnam. A computing procedure for quantification theory. *Journal of the ACM*, 7(3):201–215, July 1960.

[22] L. de Moura and G. O. Passmore. Computation in real closed infinitesimal and transcendental extensions of the rationals. In *Proc. CADE*, volume 7898 of *Lecture Notes in Computer Science*, pages 178–192. Springer, 2013.

[23] L. de Moura and G. O. Passmore. The strategy challenge in SMT solving. In *Automated Reasoning and Mathematics*, pages 15–44. Springer, 2013.

[24] L. M. de Moura and N. Bjørner. Z3: An efficient SMT solver. In *Proc. TACAS*, volume 4963 of *Lecture Notes in Computer Science*, pages 337–340. Springer, 2008.

[25] I. Dillig, T. Dillig, and A. Aiken. Cuts from proofs: A complete and practical technique for solving linear inequalities over integers. In *Proc. CAV*, volume 5643 of *Lecture Notes in Computer Science*, pages 233–247. Springer, 2009.

[26] A. G. Doig, B. H. Land, and A. G. Doig. An automatic method for solving discrete programming problems. *Econometrica*, 28:497–520, 1960.

[27] A. Dolzmann and T. Sturm. REDLOG: Computer algebra meets computer logic. *SIGSAM Bulletin*, 31(2):2–9, 1997.

[28] B. Dutertre and L. de Moura. A fast linear-arithmetic solver for DPLL(T). In *Proc. CAV*, volume 4144 of *Lecture Notes in Computer Science*, pages 81–94. Springer, 2006.

[29] M. Fränzle, C. Herde, T. Teige, S. Ratschan, and T. Schubert. Efficient solving of large non-linear arithmetic constraint systems with complex Boolean structure. *Journal on Satisfiability, Boolean Modeling and Computation*, 1(3-4):209–236, 2007.

[30] S. Gao, M. Ganai, F. Ivančić, A. Gupta, S. Sankaranarayanan, and E. M. Clarke. Integrating ICP and LRA solvers for deciding nonlinear real arithmetic problems. In *Proc. FMCAD*, pages 81–90. IEEE Computer Society, 2010.

[31] S. Herbort and D. Ratz. Improving the efficiency of a nonlinear-system-solver using a componentwise Newton method. Technical Report 2/1997, Inst. für Angewandte Mathematik, University of Karlsruhe, 1997.

[32] D. Jovanović and L. de Moura. Solving non-linear arithmetic. In *Proc. IJCAR*, volume 7364 of *Lecture Notes in Artificial Intelligence*, pages 339–354. Springer, 2012.

[33] S. Junges, U. Loup, F. Corzilius, and E. Ábrahám. On Gröbner bases in the context of satisfiability-modulo-theories solving over the real numbers. In *Proc. CAI*, volume 8080 of *Lecture Notes in Computer Science*, pages 186–198. Springer, 2013.

[34] L. C. Khačiyan. Polynomial algorithm for linear programming. *Soviet Doklady*, 244:1093–1096, 1979. Typed translation.

[35] D. Kroening and O. Strichman. *Decision Procedures: An Algorithmic Point of View.* Springer, 2008.

[36] U. Loup, K. Scheibler, F. Corzilius, E. Ábrahám, and B. Becker. A symbiosis of interval constraint propagation and cylindrical algebraic decomposition. In *Proc. CADE*, volume 7898 of *Lecture Notes in Computer Science*, pages 193–207. Springer, 2013.

[37] J. P. Marques-silva and K. A. Sakallah. Grasp: A search algorithm for propositional satisfiability. *IEEE Transactions on Computers*, 48:506–521, 1999.

[38] W. Pugh. The Omega test: A fast and practical integer programming algorithm for dependence analysis. *Communications of the ACM*, 8:4–13, 1992.

[39] K. Scheibler, S. Kupferschmid, and B. Becker. Recent improvements in the SMT solver iSAT. In *Proc. MBMV*, pages 231–241. Institut für Angewandte Mikroelektronik und Datentechnik, Fakultät für Informatik und Elektrotechnik, Universität Rostock, 2013.

[40] V. Weispfenning. Quantifier elimination for real algebra – The quadratic case and beyond. *Applicable Algebra in Engineering, Communication and Computing*, 8(2):85–101, 1997.

[41] V. Weispfenning. A new approach to quantifier elimination for real algebra. In *Quantifier Elimination and Cylindrical Algebraic Decomposition*, Texts and Monographs in Symbolic Computation, pages 376–392. Springer, 1998.

[42] H. Zankl and A. Middeldorp. Satisfiability of non-linear (ir)rational arithmetic. In *Proc. LPAR*, volume 6355 of *Lecture Notes in Artificial Intelligence*, pages 481–500. Springer, 2010.

Algorithms for Finite Field Arithmetic

Éric Schost
Computer Science Department
Western University
eschost@uwo.ca

Categories and Subject Descriptors

F.2.1 [**Theory of computation**]: Analysis of algorithms and problem complexity—*Computations in finite fields*

General Terms

Algorithms,Theory

Keywords

Finite fields, irreducible polynomials, extensions.

ABSTRACT

We review several algorithms to construct finite fields and perform operations such as field embedding. Following previous work by notably Shoup, de Smit and Lenstra or Couveignes and Lercier, as well as results obtained with De Feo and Doliskani, we distinguish between algorithms that build "towers" of finite fields, with degrees of the form $\ell, \ell^2, \ell^3, \ldots$ and algorithms for composita. We show in particular how techniques that originate from algorithms for computing with *triangular sets* can be useful in such a context.

1. INTRODUCTION

Finite fields appear in many branches of pure and applied mathematics, prominently so in areas such as number theory, cryptography and coding theory. As a result, building and computing in arbitrary finite fields is a fundamental task for any computer algebra system; for instance, the implementation available in Magma [4] remains one of the most complete known to us.

Let us have a look at two very simple computations, both in Magma. The first one,

```
k4:=GF(5^4);
k6:=GF(3^4);
a4:=Random(k4);
a6:=Random(k6);
a:=a4+a6;
 Runtime error in '+': Arguments are not compatible
 Argument types given: FldFinElt, FldFinElt
```

obviously doesn't make sense, while the second one does:

```
k4:=GF(5^4);
k6:=GF(5^6);
a4:=Random(k4);
a6:=Random(k6);
a:=a4+a6;
Parent(a);
 Finite field of size 5^12
```

In the second example, we see that the system has to be able to construct two extensions of a base field, here $\mathbb{F}_5$, build their compositum when needed, and embed elements into this compositum.

Our goal here is to present algorithms for these tasks, from results dating back to the 1980's and 1990's to more recent progress. In most of the text, we fix a prime p and we count operations in the base field $\mathbb{F}_p$ at unit cost – that is, we work in an algebraic model; another cost measure, in a boolean model, will be used at times as well.

Precisely, the questions we want to discuss are related to the construction of arbitrary extensions of $\mathbb{F}_p$: for any integer n, we want to be able to define an extension of degree n of $\mathbb{F}_p$, together with mechanisms for computing embeddings $\mathbb{F}_{p^n} \to \mathbb{F}_{p^m}$ (and invert them, when possible) in such a way that the obvious compatibility condition is satisfied.

These requirements are weaker than the framework of "compatibly embedded finite fields" used in Magma, since the latter allows for several isomorphic versions of the same finite to be present in the system. Closer to us is the construction of "standard model of finite fields" by de Smit and Lenstra [21], but as the name implies, the latter construction possesses further canonicity properties.

An outstanding question regarding the arithmetic of finite fields is whether one can construct irreducible polynomials of an arbitrary degree n over $\mathbb{F}_p$ in time polynomial in n and $\log(p)$. So far, no such result is known, although this is known to be feasible under the Extended Riemann Hypothesis [1]. Our point of view here is the following: using probabilistic algorithms (of the Las Vegas type), the questions we are considering can indeed be solved in polynomial time; then, how fast can we really do it? Can we obtain algorithms with quasi-linear cost?

As we will see, this is not known to be the case, as long as we rely on our algebraic computation model; however, in

ISSAC'15, July 6–9, 2015, Bath, United Kingdom.

978-1-4503-3435-8/15/07 ...$15.00.
DOI: http://dx.doi.org/10.1145/2755996.2756637.

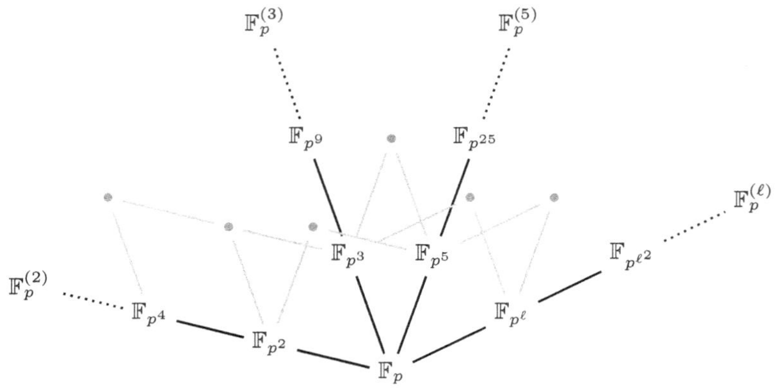

Figure 1: The algebraic closure of $\mathbb{F}_p$

a boolean model, better results can actually be obtained. Surprisingly, the main difference between these two situations is the existence of a fast algorithm due to Kedlaya and Umans [30] to perform an operation called *modular composition*.

Several previous algorithms, for instance to construct irreducible polynomials [47, 48, 15], rely on the description of $\overline{\mathbb{F}_p}$ given in Figure 1 (that figure is borrowed from [20]): in order to construct an irreducible polynomial of degree n, it is enough to factor n into prime powers, as $n = \ell_1^{e_1} \cdots \ell_s^{e_s}$, with ℓ_i's pairwise distinct primes, then construct irreducibles of degrees $\ell_1^{e_1}, \dots, \ell_s^{e_s}$, and combine them. Possibly, a coarser factorization may be used, as in [1].

The same description underlies the algorithms we describe here: instead of focusing on the construction of irreducible polynomials, we will describe algorithms for building towers of finite fields of degrees $\ell, \ell^2, \ell^3, \dots$ over $\mathbb{F}_p$, for ℓ prime, and for navigating through these towers; in a second time, we discuss the construction of composita, in order to be able to work with extensions of arbitrary degree n. First, however, we describe algorithms in a seemingly unrelated context, computations with triangular sets, and show in particular how modular composition techniques come into play.

Let us finally mention materials not discussed here: representation based on Zech logarithms or Conway polynomials [44], deterministic algorithms [1, 47], as well as the construction of irreducible polynomials with extra properties (sparseness, primitivity, ...), or of irreducibles whose degree satisfies prescribed bounds [23, 50].

2. TRIANGULAR SETS

We start with a subject that may not appear directly related to computations with finite fields: computations with *triangular sets*.

In what follows, we will call triangular set a sequence of polynomials $(T_1, \dots, T_n)$ in $\mathbb{F}_p[x_1, \dots, x_n]$, such that the following holds: for all i, T_i is in $\mathbb{F}_p[x_1, \dots, x_i]$, monic in x_i and reduced with respect to $T_1, \dots, T_{i-1}$; these polynomials form a Gröbner basis for the lexicographic order induced by $x_1 < \cdots < x_n$ (of course, the definition carries over to any base field). In addition, we will suppose that the ideal $\langle T_1, \dots, T_n \rangle$ is radical.

Such a data structure, together with more general objects called *regular chains*, has a long history in the domain of polynomial system solving. Regular chains were introduced in [27], following previous work initiated by Ritt [42] and Wu [52]. Several definitions co-exist, with contributions by Lazard [32, 33], Aubry et al. [2] and Moreno Maza [38].

The complexity of basic arithmetic. Our interest here lies not in solving polynomial systems, or computing triangular sets, but rather in computing *with* triangular sets. Indeed, the structure of a family $(T_1, \dots, T_n)$ as above shows that the quotient $\mathbb{A} = \mathbb{F}_p[x_1, \dots, x_n]/\langle T_1, \dots, T_n \rangle$ admits the natural multivariate basis $(x_1^{e_1} \cdots x_n^{e_n}$, with $0 \le e_i < d_i$ for $1 \le i \le n)$, where we write $d_i = \deg(T_i, x_i)$. Later on, we will see that questions such as the cost of arithmetic operations in such a basis appear naturally; for the moment, note that our goal is to obtain algorithms of quasi-linear cost in $\delta = d_1 \cdots d_n$, which is the dimension of $\mathbb{A}$ over $\mathbb{F}_p$.

As it turns out, we do not have good control on the complexity of these operations. Of course, addition takes linear time, but it is not known to be the case for multiplication. Indeed, the natural approach to multiplication in a multivariate basis consists in a polynomial multiplication, followed by reduction modulo $\langle T_1, \dots, T_n \rangle$. The initial product gives a polynomial of partial degrees $(2d_1 - 2, \dots, 2d_n - 2)$, so the number of its monomials, $(2d_1 - 1) \cdots (2d_n - 1)$ is not linear in δ (except of course is n is fixed).

Except in a few particular cases [5], the rather direct approach outlined above is the best known so far; it leads to an overhead of about 3^n over a linear cost in δ, see [37, 35] for details.

Change of basis. All notation being as above, let us call *primitive element* an element f of $\mathbb{A}$ such that $(1, f, \dots, f^{\delta-1})$ is an $\mathbb{F}_p$-basis of $\mathbb{A}$. In other words, knowing such an f allows us to write elements of $\mathbb{A}$ as univariate polynomials in f; this makes it possible to rely on fast FFT-based univariate polynomial arithmetic to perform computations $(+, \times)$ and $\div$ (when feasible) in $\mathbb{A}$ in quasi-linear time.

With such an approach, the main non-trivial tasks are the changes of basis, from the previous multivariate basis to the univariate one and back. As of now, no algorithm is known with a quasi-linear cost, at least in our algebraic complexity model; the best results to date take subquadratic time $C(\delta) = O\tilde{~}(\delta^{(\omega+1)/2})$ [39, 41], where ω is the exponent of linear algebra.

To illustrate the issues at hand, let us consider a seemingly trivial case, taking $n = 1$. Discarding the index

1, we are thus looking at a single polynomial T in $\mathbb{F}_p[x]$, and $\mathbb{A} = \mathbb{F}_p[x]/\langle T\rangle$; the "multivariate basis" here is simply $(1, x, \dots, x^{d-1})$. Given a primitive element f, conversion from the basis $(1, f, \dots, f^{d-1})$ to $(1, x, \dots, x^{d-1})$ amounts to taking a polynomial g in $\mathbb{F}_p[x]$ of degree less than d, and computing $g(f) \bmod T$.

This problem is known as *modular composition.* The best known algorithms for it rely on baby-step / giant-step techniques, and involve both polynomial and matrix arithmetic [10, 26]; the former reference gives an algorithm of cost $O(d^{(\omega+1)/2})$, which is $O(d^{1.686})$ for the best known value of ω [34]; in [26], this is improved to $O(d^{1.667})$, which remains far from linear time. It is worth pointing out that modular composition lies at the heart of several other important algorithms, such as polynomial factorization over finite fields [24, 49, 29, 28].

Still in the univariate case, the inverse change-of-basis amounts to taking a polynomial h of degree less than d, and finding g such that $h = g(f) \bmod T$. As it turns out, this can be done in the same cost as in the other direction: the conversion algorithm relies on the non-degeneracy of the trace $\tau : \mathbb{A} \to \mathbb{F}_p$, to (essentially) reduce the computation to computing traces of the form $\tau(h^i)$. This can in turn be done by an algorithm for *power projection* that is dual to the one for modular composition [48, 8].

Kedlaya and Umans' algorithm. In [30], Kedlaya and Umans gave an algorithm for modular composition that takes almost linear time, in a boolean model. Precisely, for any $\varepsilon > 0$, there exists an algorithm for modular composition that runs in time $O\tilde{}(d^{1+\varepsilon}\log(p))$ in a boolean RAM; this is to be compared to the bit size of the input and output, which is proportional to $d\log(p)$.

The algorithm proceeds by lifting the computation from $\mathbb{F}_p$ to $\mathbb{Z}$, which indeed requires an analysis in a boolean model; a similar algorithm for power projection can be found in [30] as well.

Going back to our conversion problems, these results allow us to handle the (rather artificial) case $n = 1$. An extension of Kedlaya and Umans' algorithms to multivariate situations is given in [40]; it makes it possible to perform the changes of basis in n variables in time $O\tilde{}(\delta^{1+\varepsilon}\log(p))$, for any $\varepsilon > 0$, still in a boolean model.

Altogether, we are able to do conversions, and thus perform arithmetic tasks in $\mathbb{A}$ in time close to linear, as long as we use a binary model. Unfortunately, the techniques involved in Kedlaya and Umans' algorithm and its extension in [40] lead to rather large constants hidden in the big-Os. As a result, as of now, there is no known implementation of these techniques that would be competitive with the baby-step / giant-step algorithm of Brent and Kung.

Back to finite fields. Recalling Figure 1, we will follow the approach below:

- For any prime ℓ, build what we will call the *ℓ-adic tower* over $\mathbb{F}_p$, that is, the extensions
$$\mathbb{F}_p \to \mathbb{F}_{p^\ell} \to \mathbb{F}_{p^{\ell^2}} \to \cdots \to \mathbb{F}_{p^{\ell^i}} \to \cdots \qquad (1)$$
of degrees $\ell, \ell^2, \dots, \ell^i, \dots$ over $\mathbb{F}_p$.
- Given any coprime degrees ℓ^i and m^j, devise a way to construct the compositum
$$\mathbb{F}_{p^{\ell^i m^j}} = \mathbb{F}_{p^{\ell^i}} \otimes \mathbb{F}_{p^{m^j}}.$$

Let us first discuss the question of data representation. Looking at the nested extensions in (1), one is led to consider polynomials $(T_{\ell,i})_{i\geq 1}$, such that for all i, $(T_{\ell,1}, \dots, T_{\ell,i})$ is a triangular set in $\mathbb{F}_p[x_1, \dots, x_i]$ with leading degrees $(\ell, \dots, \ell)$, and the ideal $\langle T_{\ell,1}, \dots, T_{\ell,i}\rangle$ is maximal; our model of the field with p^{ℓ^i} elements can then be
$$\mathbb{K}_{\ell^i} = \mathbb{F}_p[x_1, \dots, x_i]/\langle T_{\ell,1}, \dots, T_{\ell,i}\rangle.$$
Given two coprime extension degrees ℓ^i and m^j, the compositum $\mathbb{K}_{\ell^i} \otimes \mathbb{K}_{m^j}$ is simply
$$\mathbb{F}_p[x_1, \dots, x_i, y_1, \dots, y_j]/\langle T_{\ell,1}, \dots, T_{\ell,i}, T^*_{m,1}, \dots, T^*_{m,j}\rangle,$$
where the polynomials T^*'s are obtained by evaluating T's at $y_1, \dots, y_j$. In this representation, embeddings are straightforward, but as we saw before, arithmetic operations are more costly.

Lift up, push down. Assuming we can compute polynomials $T_{\ell,1}, \dots, T_{\ell,i}$, the discussion above shows that introducing a primitive element for these polynomials will allow us to reduce arithmetic operations to univariate polynomial arithmetic.

In the case at hand, it is easy to see that for all i, x_i has degree ℓ^i over $\mathbb{F}_p$, so that we can write
$$\mathbb{K}_{\ell^i} \simeq \mathbb{F}_p[x_i]/\langle Q_{\ell,i}\rangle,$$
where $Q_{\ell,i} \in \mathbb{F}_p[x_i]$ has degree ℓ^i. As per the discussion in the previous paragraphs, going from a multivariate representation to a univariate one, and back, can be done using $C(\ell^i)$ operations in $\mathbb{F}_p$, and in almost linear time in a boolean model.

Looking at two levels $i-1$ and i at once, we further have
$$\mathbb{F}_p[x_i]/\langle Q_{\ell,i}\rangle \simeq \mathbb{F}_p[x_{i-1}, x_i]/\langle Q_{\ell,i-1}, T'_{\ell,i}\rangle,$$
where $T'_{\ell,i}$ is obtained from $T_{\ell,i}$ by rewriting all expressions in $x_1, \dots, x_{i-1}$ in terms of x_{i-1} only. We call this isomorphism and its inverse *push down* and *lift up.* This equivalence is crucial: not only does it allow us to perform embeddings or compute relative traces or norms, it may also help us break down the conversion from multivariate to univariate polynomials into simpler steps, improving on the cost seen above, provided we have efficient algorithms for push down and lift up.

3. SOME USEFUL TOWERS

In addition to being one of the building blocks of algorithms for general finite field arithmetic, algorithms for computing in some specific ℓ-adic towers have found several applications. We briefly describe two of them here; both questions arise in relation to torsion subgroups of elliptic curves or Jacobians of genus 2 curves.

Quadratic extensions. The first particular case we consider is that of *quadratic extensions.* In this case, we rely on a well-known construction of such extensions [31, Th. VI.9.1], which was already put to use algorithmically in [47, 48]: if $p = 1 \bmod 4$, then for any quadratic non-residue $\alpha \in \mathbb{F}_p$, the polynomial $x^{2^k} - \alpha \in \mathbb{F}_p[X]$ is irreducible for any $k \geq 0$ (the case $p = 1 \bmod 4$ can be accommodated along the same lines, by first moving to a degree-2 extension). This allows us to define the polynomials

$$\begin{aligned}
&\vdots \\
T_{2,i} &= x_i^2 - x_{i-1} \\
&\vdots \\
T_{2,2} &= x_2^2 - x_1 \\
T_{2,1} &= x_1^2 - \alpha,
\end{aligned}$$

that define what we called the 2-adic tower. Then, for all $i \geq 1$ we have the isomorphism

$$\mathbb{F}_p[x_1, \ldots, x_i]/\langle T_{2,1}, \ldots, T_{2,i}\rangle \simeq \mathbb{F}_p[x_i]/\langle x_i^{2^i} - \alpha\rangle,$$

which maps x_j to $x_i^{2^{i-j}}$; in this case, this simply amounts to exponent arithmetic. In addition, for this very particular case, push down amounts to decomposing a polynomial $A(x_i)$ into even and odd parts, as $A(x_i) = A_0(x_i^2) + x_i A_1(x_i^2)$, and return $A_0(x_{i-1}) + x_i A_1(x_{i-1})$; lift up is the inverse operation. When these operations show up in more general towers, they are by no means as straightforward.

Computations in quadratic extensions as above were used in the algorithm of [25] that computes the cardinality of the Jacobian of a curve of genus 2, following Schoof's elliptic curve point counting algorithm [45]. The Jacobian is a group, and the point-counting algorithm involves in particular the computation of elements of 2^k-torsion in this group, by means of successive divisions by two. Such a division by two boils down to several arithmetic operations $(+, \times)$, and four square root extractions; thus, the elements we are computing are defined over the 2-adic tower over of $\mathbb{F}_p$.

At the time of writing [25], the authors relied on a variant of the Kaltofen-Shoup algorithm [29] with running time $O(d^{(\omega+1)/2})$ for an extension of degree $d = 2^k$; this was improved in [22], where fast algorithms for square root computation were given for such a tower.

Artin-Schreier extensions. Another important particular case can be highlighted: *Artin-Schreier* towers, corresponding $\ell = p$, that is, to extensions of degrees $p, p^2, \ldots$. Early results for this situation are due to Cantor [11], with a description of polynomials that can play the role of what we call $T_{p,1}, T_{p,2}, \ldots$; another family of such polynomials is given given by Adleman and Lenstra in [1], and was reused by Shoup [47, 48].

This construction is used in an algorithm due to Couveignes [13] for computing *isogenies* between elliptic curves over finite fields. Remembering that elliptic come endowed with a group law, an isogeny is simply defined as a surjective regular map between two elliptic curves that preserves the group law; in cryptology, they are the core of Elkies' improvements to the Schoof point-counting algorithm [3], and show up as well in more recent constructions [43, 51].

Couveignes' algorithm computes isogenies of degree $\sim p^k$ between two elliptic curves E and E'; it relies on the interpolation of a rational function at special points in an Artin-Schreier tower of height $O(k)$ (these points being deduced from the coordinates of points of p^k-torsion in E and E'). Since the required degree p^k can be taken arbitrarily high, we need efficient algorithms to compute the Artin-Schreier tower, but also perform other tasks such as the interpolation; the paper [14] described some algorithms in this direction, with further developments in [18, 19].

4. BUILDING GENERAL TOWERS

Using cyclotomy. To construct a tower for an arbitrary ℓ, a first approach extends directly the construction used in the quadratic case above, using ideas from Kummer theory. We first review algorithms for a similar problem, the construction of irreducible polynomials.

Suppose that $\mathbb{F}_p$ contains an ℓth root of unity, for some prime ℓ; equivalently, ℓ divides $p-1$. In order to construct an irreducible polynomial of degree ℓ in $\mathbb{F}_p$, it is enough to find a non ℓth power, say α. Then, the polynomials $x^{\ell^i} - \alpha$ are all irreducible, as was the case for quadratic extensions.

When there is no such root of unity, we can adjoin one. We follow here the approach of [47, 48]: first, compute an irreducible factor P of the ℓth cyclotomic polynomial in $\mathbb{F}_p[x]$ (call r its degree), and replace our base field $\mathbb{F}_p$ by $\mathbb{K}_0 = \mathbb{F}_p(y_0)$, where $P(y_0) = 0$. Then, proceed as in the previous case: picking a random element α in $\mathbb{K}_0$ that is not an ℓth power, we build the extension $\mathbb{K}_1 = \mathbb{K}_0(y_1)$, with $y_1^\ell = \alpha$; we can build further levels similarly.

In order to deduce an irreducible polynomial over $\mathbb{F}_p$, we compute the trace $T_{\mathbb{K}_1/\mathbb{F}_{p^\ell}}(y_1)$; its minimal polynomial over $\mathbb{F}_p$ has degree ℓ [47]. Essentially the same idea is used by de Smit and Lenstra [21], using Gauss periods to descend from $\mathbb{K}_1$.

To build the tower itself, we continue the construction above $\mathbb{K}_0$ and descend over $\mathbb{F}_p$, as illustrated in Figure 2 (which is borrowed from [16]). That reference also gives a fast algorithm for lift up and push down, allowing us to perform all conversions at level i using $O\tilde{~}(\ell^{i+2})$ operations in $\mathbb{F}_p$ (for data of size ℓ^i).

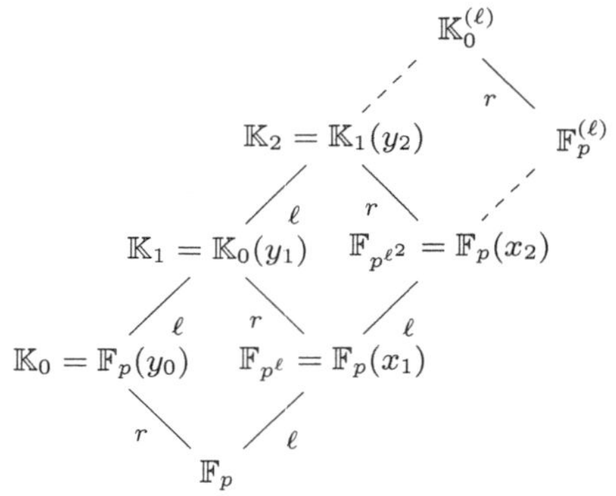

Figure 2: The ℓ-adic towers over $\mathbb{F}_p$ and $\mathbb{K}_0$.

Couveignes and Lercier's algorithm. A second workaround when roots of unity are missing is to use elliptic curves instead: this principle underlies some very well known constructions, such as Lenstra's ECM factoring algorithm [36], that is derived Pollard's $p-1$ method, as well as some other ones, such as Chudnovsky and Chudnovsky's "Fast Elliptic Number Theoretic Transform" [12], derived from the usual Fast Fourier Transform.

In the case at hand, Couveignes and Lercier [15] showed how to construct irreducible polynomials by taking fibers of isogenies (we already saw isogenies in the previous section). We will not repeat the construction here, but simply state that for well-chosen curves (with conditions on their cardinality, as often for such constructions), they showed that some particular fibers indeed give irreducible polynomials of degrees of the form ℓ^i. Note the analogy with the previous case, where we were looking at fibers of the ℓth power map.

In [16], we showed how this idea carries over to defining a whole tower; that is, how to build all polynomials defining the tower and do lift up and push down in good complexity, $O\tilde{}(\ell^i)$ operations in degree ℓ^i.

5. COMPOSITA

Finally, we look at the question of building general extensions. The basic idea already appears in [9] and was used in [47]: if a and b are elements of respective degrees $L = \ell^i$ and $M = m^j$ over $\mathbb{F}_p$, with ℓ and m coprime, then both $a+b$ and ab have degree $\ell^i m^j$.

This result was first put to use in order to compute irreducible polynomials — namely, starting from the minimal polynomials of a and b, say F and G, it is enough to compute the minimal polynomials of either $a + b$ or ab. These polynomials are often called the *composed sum* and *composed product* of F and G; they are written

$$F \oplus G = \prod_{\alpha,\beta} \left(x - (\alpha + \beta)\right) \quad \text{and} \quad F \otimes G = \prod_{\alpha,\beta} (x - \alpha\beta),$$

the products running over all the roots α of F and β of G, and have degree $D = LM$. The construction of the composed product is often credited to Selmer [46].

The polynomials $F \oplus G$ and $F \otimes G$ can be computed as resultants, namely as

$$\begin{aligned} (F \oplus G)(x) &= \mathrm{res}_y(F(x-y), G(y)) \\ (F \otimes G)(x) &= \mathrm{res}_y(y^m F(x/y), G(y)), \end{aligned} \qquad (2)$$

but it is unknown how to obtain a quasi-linear running time from these expressions. Faster algorithms were given in [6], using conversions to and from Newton sums for all these polynomials, for fields of large enough characteristics; for general cases, see the discussions in [7, 5].

The last operation we consider is embedding, and more generally change of basis. Indeed, the discussion above implies the existence of isomorphisms

$$\begin{array}{ccc} \mathbb{F}_p[x,y]/\langle F, G\rangle & \to & \mathbb{F}_p[z]/\langle F \oplus G\rangle \\ x+y & \leftarrow\!\shortmid & z \end{array}$$

and

$$\begin{array}{ccc} \mathbb{F}_p[x,y]/\langle F, G\rangle & \to & \mathbb{F}_p[z]/\langle F \otimes G\rangle \\ xy & \leftarrow\!\shortmid & z. \end{array}$$

As of now, we still do not know how to perform these operations efficiently. Of course, it is possible to use the extension of Kedlaya and Umans' algorithm mentioned before; this leads to algorithms with almost linear running time in a boolean model, but as we said above, they are difficult to put into practice. In an algebraic model, the paper [17] give two different algorithms, but none of them is quasi-linear.

6. REFERENCES

[1] L. M. Adleman and H. W. Lenstra. Finding irreducible polynomials over finite fields. In *STOC'86*, pages 350–355, New York, NY, USA, 1986. ACM.

[2] P. Aubry, D. Lazard, and M. Moreno Maza. On the theories of triangular sets. *J. Symb. Comput.*, 28(1,2):45–124, 1999.

[3] I. F. Blake, G. Seroussi, and N. P. Smart. *Elliptic curves in cryptography.* Cambridge University Press, New York, NY, USA, 1999.

[4] W. Bosma, J. Cannon, and A. Steel. Lattices of compatibly embedded finite fields. *J. Symb. Comput.*, 24(3-4):351–369, 1997.

[5] A. Bostan, M. F. I. Chowdhury, J. van der Hoeven, and É. Schost. Homotopy techniques for multiplication modulo triangular sets. *J. Symb. Comput.*, 46(12):1378-1402, 2011.

[6] A. Bostan, P. Flajolet, B. Salvy, and É. Schost. Fast computation of special resultants. *J. Symb. Comput.*, 41(1):1–29, 2006.

[7] A. Bostan, L. González-Vega, H. Perdry, and É. Schost. From Newton sums to coefficients: complexity issues in characteristic p. In *MEGA'05*, 2005.

[8] A. Bostan, G. Lecerf, and É. Schost. Tellegen's principle into practice. In *ISSAC'03*, pages 37–44. ACM, 2003.

[9] J. V. Brawley and L. Carlitz. Irreducibles and the composed product for polynomials over a finite field. *Discrete Math.*, 65(2):115–139, 1987.

[10] R. P. Brent and H.-T. Kung. Fast algorithms for manipulating formal power series. *Journal of the ACM*, 25(4):581–595, 1978.

[11] D. G. Cantor. On arithmetical algorithms over finite fields. *J. Combin. Theory Ser. A*, 50(2):285–300, 1989.

[12] D. V. Chudnovsky and G. V. Chudnovsky. Computational problems in arithmetic of linear differential equations. Some Diophantine applications. In *Number theory (New York, 1985/1988)*, volume 1383 of *Lecture Notes in Math.*, pages 12–49. Springer, Berlin, 1989.

[13] J.-M. Couveignes. Computing ℓ-isogenies using the p-torsion. In *ANTS-II*, pages 59–65, London, UK, 1996. Springer-Verlag.

[14] J.-M. Couveignes. Isomorphisms between Artin-Schreier towers. *Math. Comp.*, 69(232):1625–1631, 2000.

[15] J.-M. Couveignes and R. Lercier. Fast construction of irreducible polynomials over finite fields. *Israel J. Math.*, 194(1):77–105, 2013.

[16] L. De Feo, J. Doliskani, and É. Schost. Fast algorithms for ℓ-adic towers over finite fields. In *ISSAC'13*, pages 165–172. ACM, 2013.

[17] L. De Feo, J. Doliskani, and É. Schost. Fast arithmetic for the algebraic closure of finite fields. In *ISSAC '14*, pages 122–129. ACM, 2014.

[18] L. De Feo and É. Schost. Fast arithmetics in Artin-Schreier towers over finite fields. *J. Symb. Comput.*, 47(7):771–792, 2012.

[19] L. De Feo. Fast algorithms for computing isogenies between ordinary elliptic curves in small characteristic. *Journal of Number Theory*, 131(5):873–893, May 2011.

[20] B. de Smit and H. W. Lenstra. Standard models for finite fields: the definition, 2008.

[21] B. de Smit and H. W. Lenstra. Standard models of finite fields. In G. Mullen and D. Panario, editors, *Handbook of Finite Fields*. CRC Press, 2013.

[22] J. Doliskani and É. Schost. Computing in degree

2^k-extensions of finite fields of odd characteristic. *Des. Codes Cryptogr.*, to appear.

[23] J. von zur Gathen. Irreducible polynomials over finite fields. In *Foundations of Software Technology and Theoretical Computer Science*, volume 241 of *Lecture Notes in Computer Science*, pages 252–262. Springer Berlin Heidelberg, 1986.

[24] J. von zur Gathen and V. Shoup. Computing Frobenius maps and factoring polynomials. *Comput. Complexity*, 2:187–224, 1992.

[25] P. Gaudry and É. Schost. Point-counting in genus 2 over prime fields. *J. Symb. Comput.*, 47(4):368âĂŞ400, 2012.

[26] X. Huang and V. Y. Pan. Fast rectangular matrix multiplication and applications. *Journal of Complexity*, 14(2):257–299, 1998.

[27] M. Kalkbrener. A generalized Euclidean algorithm for computing triangular representations of algebraic varieties. *J. Symb. Comput.*, 15:143–167, 1993.

[28] E. Kaltofen and V. Shoup. Subquadratic-time factoring of polynomials over finite fields. *Math. Comp.*, 67(223):1179–1197, 1998.

[29] E. Kaltofen and V. Shoup. Fast polynomial factorization over high algebraic extensions of finite fields. In *ISSAC'97*, pages 184–188. ACM, 1997.

[30] K. S. Kedlaya and C. Umans. Fast polynomial factorization and modular composition. *SICOMP*, 40(6):1767–1802, 2011.

[31] S. Lang. *Algebra*. Springer, 3rd edition, January 2002.

[32] D. Lazard. A new method for solvong algebraic systems of positive dimension. *Disc. Appl. Math.*, 33:147–160, 1991.

[33] D. Lazard. Solving zero-dimensional algebraic systems. *J. Symb. Comput.*, 13:147–160, 1992.

[34] F. Le Gall. Powers of tensors and fast matrix multiplication. In *ISSAC'14*, pages 296–303. ACM, 2014.

[35] R. Lebreton. Relaxed Hensel lifting of triangular sets. *J. Symb. Comput.*, 68, Part 2:230–258, 2015.

[36] H. W. Lenstra. Factoring integers with elliptic curves. *Annals of Mathematics*, 126:649–673, 1987.

[37] X. Li, M. Moreno Maza, and É. Schost. Fast arithmetic for triangular sets: from theory to practice. In *ISSAC'07*, pages 269–276. ACM, 2007.

[38] M. Moreno Maza. On triangular decompositions of algebraic varieties. Technical Report TR 4/99, NAG Ltd, Oxford, UK, 1999. `http://www.csd.uwo.ca/ moreno/`.

[39] C. Pascal and É. Schost. Change of order for bivariate triangular sets. In *ISSAC'06*, pages 277–284. ACM, 2006.

[40] A. Poteaux and É. Schost. Modular composition modulo triangular sets and applications. *Comput. Complexity*, 22(3):463–516, 2013.

[41] A. Poteaux and É. Schost. On the complexity of computing with zero-dimensional triangular sets. *J. Symb. Comput.*, 50:110–138, 2013.

[42] J. F. Ritt. *Differential Algebra*. Dover Publications, 1966.

[43] A. Rostovtsev and A. Stolbunov. Public-key cryptosystem based on isogenies. Cryptology ePrint Archive, Report 2006/145, April 2006.

[44] A. Scheerhorn. Trace- and norm-compatible extensions of finite fields. *Appl. Algebra Engrg. Comm. Comput.*, 3(3):199–209, 1992.

[45] R. Schoof. Elliptic curves over finite fields and the computation of square roots mod p. *Math. Comp.*, 44(170):483–494, 1985.

[46] E. S. Selmer. *Linear recurrence relations over finite fields*. Department of Mathematics, University of Bergen, 1966.

[47] V. Shoup. New algorithms for finding irreducible polynomials over finite fields. *Math. Comp.*, 54:435–447, 1990.

[48] V. Shoup. Fast construction of irreducible polynomials over finite fields. *J. Symb. Comput.*, 17(5):371–391, 1994.

[49] V. Shoup. A new polynomial factorization algorithm and its implementation. *J. Symb. Comput.*, 20(4):363–397, 1995.

[50] I. E. Shparlinski. Finding irreducible and primitive polynomials. *Appl. Algebra Engrg. Comm. Comput.*, 4(4):263–268, 1993.

[51] E. Teske. An elliptic curve trapdoor system. *Journal of Cryptology*, 19(1):115–133, January 2006.

[52] W. T. Wu. On zeros of algebraic equations — an application of Ritt principle. *Kexue Tongbao*, 31:1–5, 1986.

Optimization Problems over Noncompact Semialgebraic Sets

Lihong Zhi
Key Laboratory of Mathematics Mechanization
Academy of Mathematics and Systems Science
Beijing 100190, China
lzhi@mmrc.iss.ac.cn

Categories and Subject Descriptors

I.1.2 [**Computing Methodologies**]: Symbolic and Algebraic Manipulation—*Algorithms*; G.1.6 [**Numerical Analysis**]: Convex programming

General Terms

Theory, Algorithms

Keywords

semidefinite representations, theta bodies, sum- s of squares, dual variety, noncompact real algebraic variety

ABSTRACT

In this talk, we will introduce some recent progress in dealing with optimization problems over noncompact semialgebraic sets. We will start with the problem of optimizing a parametric linear function over a noncompact real algebraic variety. Then we will introduce how to compute the semidefinite representation or approximation of the convex hull of a noncompact semialgebraic set. Finally, we will show how to characterize the lifts of noncompact convex sets by the cone factorizations of properly defined slack operators.

Optimizing a parametric linear function over a real algebraic variety We consider the problem of optimizing a parametric linear function over a real algebraic variety

$$c_0^* := \sup_{x \in \mathcal{V} \cap \mathbb{R}^n} \mathbf{c}^T x = \mathbf{c}_1 x_1 + \cdots + \mathbf{c}_n x_n, \qquad (1)$$

where $\mathcal{V} = \{v \in \mathbb{C}^n \mid h_1(v) = \cdots = h_m(v) = 0\}$, $h_1, \ldots, h_m \in \mathbb{R}[X_1, \ldots, X_n]$ and $\mathbf{c} = (\mathbf{c}_1, \ldots, \mathbf{c}_n)$ denotes unspecified parameters. The optimal value c_0^* can be regarded as a function of the parameters $\mathbf{c}$, i.e. the *optimal value function.* Our goal is to compute a polynomial $\Phi \in \mathbb{Q}[\mathbf{c}_0, \mathbf{c}_1, \ldots, \mathbf{c}_n]$ that defines a hypersurface in the parameters' space which contains the graph of this function.

Assuming that $\mathcal{V}$ is irreducible, smooth and compact in $\mathbb{R}^n$, Rostalski and Sturmfels showed that the optimal value function is represented by the defining equation of the irreducible hypersurface $\mathcal{V}^*$ dual to the projective closure of $\mathcal{V}$ in $\mathbb{R}^n$ [11, Theorem 5.23]. Let $C = \mathrm{cl}\,(\mathrm{co}\,(\mathcal{V} \cap \mathbb{R}^n))$ be the *closure of the convex hull* of $\mathcal{V} \cap \mathbb{R}^n$, in [5, Theorem 1.5], we proved that this conclusion is still true for a noncompact real algebraic variety $\mathcal{V} \cap \mathbb{R}^n$ when it is irreducible, smooth and the recession cone 0^+C of C is pointed (contains no lines). Although the conclusion is correct, the proof of [5, Theorem 1.5] works only if the convex hull of $\mathcal{V} \cap \mathbb{R}^n$ is closed. The new proof can be found in [4, Corollary 3.2]. Moreover, in [4], we showed $(-c_0^* : \gamma_1 : \cdots : \gamma_n) \in \mathcal{V}^*$ whenever the optimal value c_0^* is bounded at $(\gamma_1, \ldots, \gamma_n)$ and $\mathcal{V}$ is smooth. When $\mathcal{V}$ is not smooth but its real trace is compact, we constructed recursively a finite number of dual varieties such that $(-c_0^* : \gamma_1 : \cdots : \gamma_n)$ lies in the union of these dual varieties. For some special parameters' values, the representing polynomials of the dual variety $\mathcal{V}^*$ can be identically zero, which give no information on the optimal value. We designed a parametric variant of [3] that identifies those regions of the parameters' space and computed for each of these regions a new polynomial defining the optimal value over the considered region.

Semidefinite representations of semialgebraic sets We consider the semialgebraic set

$$S := \{x \in \mathbb{R}^n \mid g_1(x) \geq 0, \ldots, g_m(x) \geq 0\}, \qquad (2)$$

where $g_1, \ldots, g_m \in \mathbb{R}[X] := \mathbb{R}[X_1, \ldots, X_n]$. Let $\mathbb{R}[X]_1$ denote the subset of all linear polynomials in $\mathbb{R}[X]$, we have

$$\mathrm{cl}\,(\mathrm{co}\,(S)) = \bigcap_{p \in \mathbb{R}[X]_1, p|_S \geq 0} \{x \in \mathbb{R}^n \mid p(x) \geq 0\}. \qquad (3)$$

When S is a real algebraic variety of $I := \langle g_1, \ldots, g_m \rangle$, Ranestad and Sturmfels computed the polynomial that describes the algebraic boundary of the convex hull $\mathrm{co}\,(S)$ of S [9, 10]. In [1], Gouveia, Parrilo and Thomas defined the *k-th theta body* of I as

$$\mathrm{TH}_k(I) := \{x \in \mathbb{R}^n \mid p(x) \geq 0, \quad \forall p \in \mathcal{Q}_k(I) \cap \mathbb{R}[X]_1\}, \quad (4)$$

where $\mathcal{Q}_k(I) := \{\sigma(x) + h(x),\ \sigma \in \Sigma_{2k} \text{ and } h(x) \in I\}$ and showed that the hierarchy of theta bodies converge to $\mathrm{cl}\,(\mathrm{co}\,(S))$ when S is a compact real variety.

*This research is supported by NKBRPC 2011CB302400 and the Chinese National Natural Science Foundation under Grants:91118001

ISSAC'15, July 6–9, 2015, Bath, United Kingdom
Copyright © 2015 ACM 978-1-4503-3435-8/15/07 ...$15.00.
DOI: http://dx.doi.org/10.1145/2755996.2756638.

When S is a compact basic semialgebraic set, let $G := \{g_1, \ldots, g_m\}$, $s(k) := \binom{n+k}{n}$ and $k_j := \lceil \deg g_j/2 \rceil$,

$$\Omega_k(G) := \left\{ x \in \mathbb{R}^n \;\middle|\; \begin{array}{l} \exists y \in \mathbb{R}^{s(2k)}, \text{ s.t. } \mathscr{L}_y(1) = 1 \\ \mathscr{L}_y(X_i) = x_i, 1 \le i \le n,\ M_k(y) \succeq 0 \\ M_{k-k_j}(g_j y) \succeq 0,\ 1 \le j \le m \end{array} \right\}, \tag{5}$$

where $\mathscr{L}_y$ is the Riesz functional defined by

$$\mathscr{L}_y\left(\sum_\alpha q_\alpha X_1^{\alpha_1} \cdots X_n^{\alpha_n}\right) := \sum_\alpha q_\alpha y_\alpha, \quad \forall q(X) \in \mathbb{R}[X]_{2k},$$

$M_k(y)$ and $M_{k-d_p}(py)$ are moment matrices and localizing moment matrices respectively. Lasserre showed that the hierarchy of $\Omega_k(G)$ converges to $\mathrm{co}\,(S)$ [7].

When S is a noncompact semialgebraic set, we lift S to a cone of

$$\widetilde{S}^{\mathrm{o}} := \{\tilde{x} \in \mathbb{R}^{n+1} \mid \tilde{g}_1(\tilde{x}) \ge 0, \ldots, \tilde{g}_m(\tilde{x}) \ge 0, x_0 > 0\}, \tag{6}$$

where $\tilde{g}_i$ is the homogenized polynomial of g_i and let $\widetilde{X} := (X_0, X_1, \ldots, X_n)$. In [6], we showed that our modified hierarchies of nested theta bodies and Lasserre's relaxations corresponding to

$$\widetilde{G} := \left\{\tilde{g}_1, \ldots, \tilde{g}_m,\ X_0,\ \|\widetilde{X}\|_2^2 - 1,\ 1 - \|\widetilde{X}\|_2^2\right\} \tag{7}$$

converge to $\mathrm{cl}\,(\mathrm{co}\,(S))$ when S is closed at ∞ [8] and the convex cone $\mathrm{co}\left(\mathrm{cl}\left(\widetilde{S}^{\mathrm{o}}\right)\right)$ is closed and pointed.

Lifts of convex sets and cone factorizations Let $K \subset \mathbb{R}^m$ be a full-dimensional closed convex cone and $C \subset \mathbb{R}^n$ be a full-dimensional compact convex set that contains the origin in its interior. According to [2, Definition 1], a *K-lift* of C is a set $Q = K \cap L$ where $L \subset \mathbb{R}^m$ is an affine subspace and $\pi : \mathbb{R}^m \to \mathbb{R}^n$ is a linear map such that

$$C = \pi(K \cap L). \tag{8}$$

If L intersects the interior of K, then Q is called a *proper K-lift* of C.

Consider the operator $S : \mathbb{R}^n \times \mathbb{R}^n \longrightarrow \mathbb{R}$ defined by $S(x, y) = 1 - \langle x, y\rangle$, the *slack operator* S_C of the convex set C is the restriction of S to $\mathrm{ext}(C) \times \mathrm{ext}(C^o)$, the extreme points of C and C^o (the polar of C).

The slack operator S_C is *K-factorizable* [2, Definition 2] if there exist maps

$$A : \mathrm{ext}(C) \to K,\ B : \mathrm{ext}(C^o) \to K^* \tag{9}$$

such that $S_C(x, y) = \langle A(x), B(y)\rangle$ for all $(x, y) \in \mathrm{ext}(C) \times \mathrm{ext}(C^o)$, where K^* is the dual of K.

In [2, Theorem 1], Gouveia, Parrilo and Thomas extended Yannakakis's result [13] and showed that if C has a proper K-lift, then S_C is K-factorizable. Conversely, if S_C is K-factorizable, then C has a K-lift.

Given a noncompact convex set C, in [12], we defined the slack operator S_C and its K-factorization according to whether the convex set C is full dimensional, whether it is a translated cone and whether it contains lines. We also strengthened the condition of the *K-lift* of C by requiring

$$C = \pi(K \cap L) \text{ and } 0^+C = \pi(K \cap 0^+L). \tag{10}$$

The condition $0^+C = \pi(K \cap 0^+L)$ is not redundant and can not be deduced from the condition $C = \pi(K \cap L)$ in general. We showed that the generalized lift of a convex set can also be characterized by the cone factorization of a properly defined slack operator.

1. REFERENCES

[1] J. Gouveia, P. Parrilo, and R. Thomas. Theta bodies for polynomial ideals. *SIAM Journal on Optimization*, 20(4):2097–2118, 2010.

[2] J. Gouveia, P. Parrilo, and R. Thomas. Lifts of convex sets and cone factorizations. *Mathematics of Operations Research*, 38(2):248–264, 2013.

[3] A. Greuet and M. Safey El Din. Probabilistic algorithm for polynomial optimization over a real algebraic set. *SIAM Journal on Optimization*, 24(3):1313–1343, 2014.

[4] F. Guo, M. Safey El Din, C. Wang, and L. Zhi. Optimizing a parametric linear function over a non-compact real algebraic variety, 2015. Accepted by ISSAC 2015.

[5] F. Guo, C. Wang, and L. Zhi. Optimizing a linear function over a noncompact real algebraic variety. In *Proceedings of the 2014 Symposium on Symbolic-Numeric Computation*, SNC '14, pages 39–40, New York, NY, USA, 2014. ACM.

[6] F. Guo, C. Wang, and L. Zhi. Semidefinite representations of noncompact convex sets. *SIAM Journal on Optimization*, 25(1):377–395, 2015.

[7] J. B. Lasserre. Convex sets with semidefinite representation. *Mathematical Programming, Ser. A*, 120(2):457–477, 2009.

[8] J. Nie. An exact Jacobian SDP relaxation for polynomial optimization. *Mathematical Programming, Ser. A*, 137:225–255, 2013.

[9] K. Ranestad and B. Sturmfels. The convex hull of a variety. In P. Brändén, M. Passare, and M. Putinar, editors, *Notions of Positivity and the Geometry of Polynomials*, Trends in Mathematics, 331–344. Springer Basel, 2011.

[10] K. Ranestad and B. Sturmfels. On the convex hull of a space curve. *Advances in Geometry*, 12(1):157–178, 2012.

[11] P. Rostalski and B. Sturmfels. Dualities. In G. Blekherman, P. A. Parrilo, and R. R. Thomas, editors, *Semidefinite Optimization and Convex Algebraic Geometry*, MOS-SIAM Series on Optimization, chapter 5, pages 203–250. Society for Industrial and Applied Mathematics, Philadelphia, PA, 2012.

[12] C. Wang and L. Zhi. Lifts of non-compact convex sets and cone factorizations, 2015. Preprint available at http://arxiv.org/abs/1501.00115.

[13] M. Yannakakis. Expressing combinatorial optimization problems by linear programs. *Journal of Computer and System Sciences*, 43(3):441 – 466, 1991.

Nonnegative Matrix Factorization: Algorithms, Complexity and Applications

Ankur Moitra
Massachusetts Institute of Technology
moitra@mit.edu

ABSTRACT

How quickly can we compute the nonnegative rank (r) of an $m \times n$ matrix? This problem — and the companion problem of finding a nonnegative matrix factorization with minimum inner-dimension — has a rich history, with applications in quantum mechanics, probability theory, data analysis, communication complexity and polyhedral combinatorics. Here we will survey the recent progress on this question, that has essentially resolved its worst-case complexity.

Categories and Subject Descriptors

I.1.2 [**Symbolic and Algebraic Manipulation**]: Algorithms—*Algebraic Algorithms*; F.2.1 [**Analysis of Algorithms and Problem Complexity**]: Numerical Algorithms and Problems—*Computations on Matrices*

General Terms

Theory

Keywords

nonnegative matrix factorization; first order theory of the reals

1. INTRODUCTION

The nonnegative rank of a matrix is a fundamental parameter that arises throughout algorithms and complexity and admits many equivalent formulations. In particular, given an entry-wise nonnegative matrix M of dimension $m \times n$, its nonnegative rank is the smallest r for which:

(a) M can be written as the product of entry-wise nonnegative matrices A and W which have dimension $m \times r$ and $r \times n$ respectively

(b) M can be written as the sum of r entry-wise nonnegative rank one matrices

(c) There are r nonnegative vectors $v_1, v_2, ..., v_r$ (of length m) such that the nonnegative hull of $\{v_1, v_2, ..., v_r\}$ contains all columns in M

We will denote the nonnegative rank by $rank^+(M)$ and we will refer to a factorization $M = AW$ where A and W are nonnegative and have dimension $m \times r$ and $r \times n$ respectively as a nonnegative matrix factorization of inner-dimension r.

It is easy to see from above that $rank^+(M) \geq rank(M)$. In fact, the nonnegative rank of a matrix can and does behave much differently than its rank. The nonnegative matrix factorization problem has been independently in a wide range of settings, and for very different reasons. In the context of machine learning, it is used because a nonnegative matrix factorization is easier to interpret than one that uses negative values, and such a factorization can naturally be used to extract certain latent statistical relationships from a set of data [8, 9]. In this manner, it has been applied to problems including image segmentation, information retrieval and document clustering.

It also has applications in fields such as chemometrics [7] and biology [12] where some underlying physical model for a system has natural restrictions that components interact in a positive way without cancelation. This again results in a matrix factorization problem where each of the factors are required to be nonnegative. Finally, it plays a crucial role in various problems in theoretical computer science. In combinatorial optimization, it is known that the number of extra variables needed to succinctly describe a given polytope is precisely the nonnegative rank of some appropriately defined matrix [18]. And in communication complexity, one of the most famous open questions can be stated as a question about the relationship between the rank and the nonnegative rank of a Boolean matrix [10, 1].

With these applications in mind, the focus of this tutorial is on the following question:

Question 1. *What is the complexity of computing the nonnegative rank?*

In some cases, it is clearly easy to compute the nonnegative rank because it is just the rank — and imposing the constraint that the factorization is entry-wise nonnegative can be done without loss of generality. This is easily seen to be true when $rank(M) = 1$, but in fact holds when $rank(M) = 2$ as well [17]. However when $rank(M) > 2$ it is no longer true that the nonnegative rank of an entry-wise nonnegative matrix is necessarily equal to its rank.

A priori it is not even clear that there is any algorithm that runs in any *finite* amount of time to compute the rank.

ISSAC'15, July 6–9, 2015, Bath, United Kingdom.

DOI: http://dx.doi.org/10.1145/2755996.2756683.

However this is where the connections between nonnegative rank and systems of polynomial equations begin. It is easy to express the decision question of whether or not $rank^+(M) \leq r$ as system of polynomial inequalities [4]. We can do this by treating each entry in A and each entry in W as a variable, and thus we have $mr + nr$ variables in total. Moreover the constraint that $M = AW$ is a collection of mn quadratic equations, and the constraint that A and W are entry-wise nonnegative is itself a set of mn linear inequalities. This system of polynomial inequalities is both *sound* and *complete* in the sense that it has a solution iff $rank^+(M) \leq r$.

There are many known algorithms to decide whether a system of polynomial inequalities has a solution. This is itself a remarkable result, and the first algorithm is due to Tarski [16], and there have since been a long line of improvements to this decision procedure that each bring new algebraic tools to bear on this algorithmic problem. The best known algorithm is due to Renegar [13] and the running time of finding a solution to a system of p polynomial inequalities $f_1, f_2, ..., f_p$ with k variables $x_1, x_2, ..., x_k$ and maximum degree D is roughly $(Dp)^{O(k)}$. There are also extensions of this algorithm that not only decide whether the system has a solution, but also output an implicit representation of the solution whose values are described as roots of given polynomials in some pre-specified interval, so that one can then find the bits in the solution to an desired accuracy by binary search.

However we can see that these remarkable algorithms not only answer the question of whether the nonnegative rank can be computed in a finite amount of time, but beg us to ask an algebraic question whose answers would lead to better algorithms. The running time of the algorithm of Renegar [13] depends exponentially on the number of *variables* but polynomially on all of the other parameters, including the degree, the number of polynomial inequalities and also the bit complexity. Then the hope is that there are algebraically more efficient methods to reduce nonnegative rank to a system of polynomial inequalities:

META QUESTION 1. *Given a decision problem, how many variables are needed to encode its answer as a system of polynomial inequalities?*

In recent work, it was shown that a nonnegative matrix factorization with minimum inner-dimension could be put in a certain canonical form — based on a novel method for reducing the number of variables needed to define the associated semi-algebraic set — that expresses the decision problem for nonnegative matrix factorization using $2r^2$ distinct variables. Thus the number of variables in independent of m and n and depends only on r [2, 11]. Thus it follows that there is an $(nm)^{O(r^2)}$ time algorithm for computing the nonnegative rank. Hence for any $r = O(1)$, the nonnegative rank can be computed in polynomial time. Prior to this work it was known that the case $r = 3$ could be solved in polynomial time [5] but even the case $r = 4$ was open, and the best algorithms rank in exponential time.

These algorithms were derived from an algebraic structure theorem about nonnegative matrix factorizations. But in fact, these algorithms are nearly optimal in a complexity theoretic sense. In [17], Vavasis proved that it is NP-hard to compute the nonnegative rank. However this result only rules out an exact algorithm that runs in time polynomial in n, m and r (if $P \neq NP$). At this juncture, it could still be possible that the nonnegative rank is fixed parameter tractable and can be computed in time $f(r)\text{poly}(m, n)$. However, in recent work it was shown how to improve this reduction to show that any algorithm for computing the nonnegative rank in time $(nm)^{o(r)}$ would yield an algorithm for 3-SAT on n variables that runs in time $2^{o(n)}$. Thus under the stronger hypothesis that 3-SAT requires exponential time [6] it follows that nonnegative rank requires time $(nm)^{\Omega(r)}$.

2. REFERENCES

[1] A. Aho, J. Ullman and M. Yannakakis. On notions of information transfer in VLSI circuits. *STOC*, pp. 133–139, 1983.

[2] S. Arora, R. Ge, R. Kannan and A. Moitra. Computing a nonnegative matrix factorization - provably. *STOC* pp. 145–162, 2012.

[3] L. Blum, F. Cucker, M. Shub and S. Smale. *Complexity of Real Computations.* Springer Verlag, 1998.

[4] J. Cohen and U. Rothblum. Nonnegative ranks, decompositions and factorizations of nonnegative matices. *Linear Algebra and its Applications*, pp. 149–168, 1993.

[5] N. Gillis. Nonnegative matrix factorization: Complexity, algorithms and applications. *PhD Thesis*, Universite Catholique de Louvain, 2011.

[6] R. Impagliazzo and R. Paturi. On the complexity of k-SAT. *JCSS* pp. 367–375, 2001.

[7] W. Lawton and E. Sylvestre. Self modeling curve resolution. *Technometrics*, pp. 617– 633, 1971.

[8] D. Lee and H. Seung. Learning the parts of objects by non-negative matrix factorization. *Nature*, pp. 788-791, 1999.

[9] D. Lee and H. Seung. Algorithms for non-negative matrix factorization. *NIPS*, pp. 556–562, 2000.

[10] L. Lovász and M. Saks. Communication complexity and combinatorial lattice theory. *JCSS*, pp. 322–349, 1993. Preliminary version in *FOCS* 1988.

[11] A. Moitra. An almost optimal algorithm for nonnegative rank. *SODA*, pp. 1454–1464, 2013.

[12] P. Paatero and U. Tapper. Positive matrix factorization: a non-negative factor model with optimal utilization of error estimates of data values. *Environmetrics*, pp. 111-126, 1994.

[13] J. Renegar. On the computational complexity and geometry of the first-order theory of the reals. Journal of Symbolic Computation, pp. 255–352, 1992.

[14] J. Renegar. On the computational complexity of approximating solutions for real algebraic formulae. SIAM Journal on Computing, pp. 1008–1025,1992.

[15] A. Seidenberg. A new decision method for elementary algebra. *Annals of Math*, pp. 365–374, 1954.

[16] A. Tarski. A decision method for elementary algebra and geometry. *University of California Press*, 1951.

[17] S. Vavasis. On the complexity of nonnegative matrix factorization. *SIAM Journal on Optimization*, pp. 1364-1377, 2009.

[18] M. Yannakakis. Expressing combinatorial optimization problems by linear programs. *JCSS*, pp. 441–466, 1991. Preliminary version in *STOC* 1988.

Exact Linear Algebra Algorithmic: Theory and Practice

Clément Pernet

Univ. Grenoble Alpes, Laboratoire LIP (Inria, CNRS, UCBL, ENS de Lyon)

Clement.Pernet@imag.fr

ABSTRACT

Exact linear algebra is a core component of many symbolic and algebraic computations, as it often delivers competitive theoretical complexities and also better harnesses the efficiency of modern computing infrastructures. In this tutorial we will present an overview on the recent advances in exact linear algebra algorithmic and implementation techniques, and highlight the few key ideas that have proven successful in their design. As an illustration, we will study in more details the computation of some matrix normal forms over a finite field or the ring of polynomials, specific to computer algebra. In particular, we will give a special care to the design and implementation of parallel exact linear algebra routines, trying to emphasize the similarities and distinctness with parallel numerical linear algebra. We aim to provide the working computer algebraist with a set of best practices for the use or the design of exact linear algebra software, together with an overview on a few still unresolved algorithmic problems in the field.

Categories and Subject Descriptors

G.4 [**Mathematics and Computing**]: Mathematical Software—*Algorithm Design and Analysis*; I.1.2 [**Computing Methodologies**]: Symbolic and Algebraic Manipulation

Keywords

Exact linear algebra, Complexity reductions, Parallel computing, Software design.

1. INTRODUCTION

Exact linear algebra, over a finite field or the field of rationals is involved in many applications using intensive algebraic computations: from cryptanalysis based on algebraic sieves [21] or polynomial system solving [14], to testing conjectures in computational number theory [25] or list decoding of Reed-Solomon codes [5]... Development of both

ISSAC'15, July 6–9, 2015, Bath, United Kingdom.

Copyright is held by the owner/author(s).

ACM 978-1-4503-3435-8/15/07.

DOI: http://dx.doi.org/10.1145/2755996.2756684 .

algorithmic and efficient implementations in exact linear algebra has now reached a great level of maturity. We survey the milestones in some of these recent progresses, trying to exhibit a few general guidelines, as for example the importance of making theoretical algorithmic reductions effective, the search for trade-offs between dimension and coefficient size, and the use of recursive task based parallelization.

2. REDUCTIONS TO BUILDING BLOCKS

Since the introduction of the first sub-cubic time matrix multiplication algorithm, most problems in dense linear algebra have been reduced to the complexity of matrix multiplication: $O(n^\omega)$ field operations. Even if the asymptotically fastest algorithms [6, 22] are not practicable, matrix multiplication happens to be also the most efficient building block in practice [7, 17], thus making the reduction trees (or DAGs) from complexity theory still highly relevant in practice. The development of efficient exact linear algebra software then consists in making these reductions effective: fine tuning of the building block, taking the best advantage of the available computer arithmetic [10, 2, 1, 9, 19] and minimizing the memory footprint [3]; improving existing reductions in the leading constant of their time and space complexities [20].

A similar approach also applies to the blackbox computation model, where computing the minimal polynomial is the building block to which most problems reduce to [4, 13, 12].

3. SIZE-DIMENSION TRADE-OFFS

With coefficients of varying size, such as $\mathbb{Z}$ or $\mathbb{Z}_p[X]$, linear algebra computations reduce to linear algebra over fixed-size fields thanks to multi-modular or p-adic lifting techniques [23, 27, 28]. The recent striking reductions in the complexity of most linear algebra problems over such domains were made possible by a careful control of trade-offs between coefficient size and dimension in the course of the computation [15, 27, 28, 18, 29, 26]. Although these algorithms are most often based on recursive algorithms and geometric progressions, alternative approaches exist, such as arithmetic progression based trade-offs, used e.g. in the computation of the characteristic polynomial [24] or online update schemes in geometric progressions [16].

Multi-modular lifting, though asymptotically less efficient, remains also competitive for large scale parallel computations, as it exposes an embarrassingly parallel workload.

4. PIVOTING STRATEGIES

Contrarily to numerical linear algebra, pivoting strategies in exact linear algebra are not constrained by numerical stability issues, but on the other hand, by the nature of the computation: usual invariants being computed such as echelon forms or rank profiles strongly impact the type of pivoting and the blocking strategies permitted. A close study on the impact of pivoting [20, 8] allows one to possibly recover more information with more freedom in the blocking.

5. PARALLELIZATION

The design of parallel dense linear algebra over a finite field diverges from the well studied parallel numerical linear algebra in many ways. The use of fast matrix multiplication and of modular reductions implies that the arithmetic cost is no longer invariant with the block cutting. Hence a coarse grain parallelization with recursive tasks are to be preferred [11], giving an increased role to the scheduler of the execution runtime.

References

[1] M. Albrecht, G. Bard, and W. Hart. "Algorithm 898: Efficient Multiplication of Dense Matrices over GF(2)". In: *ACM Trans. Math. Soft.* 37.1 (Jan. 2010), 9:1–9:14. DOI: 10.1145/1644001.1644010.

[2] T. J. Boothby and R. W. Bradshaw. "Bitslicing and the Method of Four Russians Over Larger Finite Fields". In: *CoRR* arXiv:0901.1413 (2009).

[3] B. Boyer, J.-G. Dumas, C. Pernet, and W. Zhou. "Memory Efficient Scheduling of Strassen-Winograd's Matrix Multiplication Algorithm". In: *Proc. ISSAC'09.* Seoul, Corea: ACM, 2009. DOI: 10.1145/1576702.1576713.

[4] L. Chen, W. Eberly, E. Kaltofen, B. D. Saunders, W. J. Turner, and G. Villard. "Efficient matrix preconditioners for black box linear algebra". In: *Linear Algebra and its Applications* 343–344 (2002). Special Issue on Structured and Infinite Systems of Linear equations, pp. 119–146. DOI: 10.1016/S0024-3795(01)00472-4.

[5] M. Chowdhury, C. Jeannerod, V. Neiger, E. Schost, and G. Villard. "Faster Algorithms for Multivariate Interpolation With Multiplicities and Simultaneous Polynomial Approximations". In: *IEEE Trans. on Inf. Theory* 61.5 (May 2015), pp. 2370–2387. DOI: 10.1109/TIT.2015.2416068.

[6] D. Coppersmith and S. Winograd. "Matrix Multiplication via Arithmetic Progressions". In: *J. Symb. Comp.* 9.3 (Mar. 1990), pp. 251–280. DOI: 10.1016/S0747-7171(08)80013-2.

[7] J. Dongarra, J. Du Croz, I. Duff, and S. Hammarling. "A Proposal for a Set of Level 3 Basic Linear Algebra Subprograms". In: *SIGNUM Newsl.* 22.3 (July 1987), pp. 2–14. DOI: 10.1145/36318.36319.

[8] J.-G. Dumas, C. Pernet, and Z. Sultan. "Computing the Rank Profile Matrix". In: *Proc. ISSAC'15.* Bath, UK: ACM, July 2015. DOI: 10.1145/2755996.2756682.

[9] J.-G. Dumas, L. Fousse, and B. Salvy. "Simultaneous modular reduction and Kronecker substitution for small finite fields". In: *J. Symb. Comp.* 46.7 (2011), pp. 823–840. DOI: 10.1016/j.jsc.2010.08.015.

[10] J.-G. Dumas, T. Gautier, and C. Pernet. "Finite Field Linear Algebra Subroutines". In: *Proc. ISSAC'02.* Lille, France: ACM, July 7–10, 2002. DOI: 10.1145/780506.780515.

[11] J.-G. Dumas, T. Gautier, C. Pernet, and Z. Sultan. "Parallel Computation of Echelon Forms". In: *Proc. Euro-Par'14.* Vol. 8632. LNCS. Springer, 2014, pp. 499–510. DOI: 10.1007/978-3-319-09873-9_42.

[12] J.-G. Dumas, C. Pernet, and D. Saunders. "On finding multiplicities of characteristic polynomial factors of black-box matrices". In: *Proc. ISSAC'09.* Seoul, Corea: ACM, 2009. DOI: 10.1145/1576702.1576723.

[13] W. Eberly, M. Giesbrecht, P. Giorgi, A. Storjohann, and G. Villard. "Faster Inversion and Other Black Box Matrix Computations Using Efficient Block Projections". In: *Proc. ISSAC'07.* Waterloo, Ontario, Canada: ACM, 2007, pp. 143–150. DOI: 10.1145/1277548.1277569.

[14] J.-C. Faugère. "A new efficient algorithm for computing Gröbner bases without reduction to zero (F5)". In: *Proc. ISSAC'02.* Lille, France: ACM, 2002, pp. 75–83. DOI: 10.1145/780506.780516.

[15] P. Giorgi, C.-P. Jeannerod, and G. Villard. "On the Complexity of Polynomial Matrix Computations". In: *Proc. ISSAC'03.* Philadelphia, PA, USA: ACM, 2003, pp. 135–142. DOI: 10.1145/860854.860889.

[16] P. Giorgi and R. Lebreton. "Online Order Basis Algorithm and Its Impact on the Block Wiedemann Algorithm". In: *Proc. ISSAC'14.* Kobe, Japan: ACM, 2014, pp. 202–209. DOI: 10.1145/2608628.2608647.

[17] K. Goto and R. A. v. d. Geijn. "Anatomy of High-Performance Matrix Multiplication". In: *ACM Trans. Math. Soft.* 34.3 (May 2008), 12:1–12:25. DOI: 10.1145/1356052.1356053.

[18] S. Gupta, S. Sarkar, A. Storjohann, and J. Valeriote. "Triangular -basis decompositions and derandomization of linear algebra algorithms over". In: *J. Symb. Comp.* 47.4 (2012), pp. 422–453. DOI: 10.1016/j.jsc.2011.09.006.

[19] J. van der Hoeven, G. Lecerf, and G. Quintin. "Modular SIMD arithmetic in Mathemagix". In: *CoRR* arXiv:1407.3383 (2014).

[20] C.-P. Jeannerod, C. Pernet, and A. Storjohann. "Rank-profile revealing Gaussian elimination and the CUP matrix decomposition". In: *J. Symb. Comp.* 56 (2013), pp. 46–68. DOI: 10.1016/j.jsc.2013.04.004.

[21] T. Kleinjung, L. Nussbaum, and E. Thome. "Using a grid platform for solving large sparse linear systems over GF(2)". In: *Proc. GRID'10.* Oct. 2010, pp. 161–168. DOI: 10.1109/GRID.2010.5697952.

[22] F. Le Gall. "Powers of Tensors and Fast Matrix Multiplication". In: *Proc. ISSAC'14.* Kobe, Japan: ACM, 2014, pp. 296–303. DOI: 10.1145/2608628.2608664.

[23] R. Moenck and J. Carter. "Approximate algorithms to derive exact solutions to systems of linear equations". In: *In Proc. EUROSAM'79, LNCS.* Vol. 72. Springer-Verlag, 1979, pp. 65–72. DOI: 10.1007/3-540-09519-5_60.

[24] C. Pernet and A. Storjohann. "Faster algorithms for the characteristic polynomial". In: *Proc. ISSAC'07.* Waterloo, ON. Canada: ACM, 2007, pp. 307–314. DOI: 10.1145/1277548.1277590.

[25] W. Stein. *Modular forms, a computational approach.* Graduate studies in mathematics. AMS, 2007.

[26] A. Storjohann. "On the complexity of inverting integer and polynomial matrices". In: *Comp. Complexity* (2014). to appear.

[27] A. Storjohann. "High-order lifting and integrality certification". In: *J. Symb. Comp.* 36.3–4 (2003), pp. 613–648. DOI: 10.1016/S0747-7171(03)00097-X.

[28] A. Storjohann. "The Shifted Number System for Fast Linear Algebra on Integer Matrices". In: *J. Complexity* 21.4 (2005), pp. 609–650. DOI: 10.1016/j.jco.2005.04.002.

[29] W. Zhou and G. Labahn. "Efficient Algorithms for Order Basis Computation". In: *J. Symb. Comp.* 47.7 (2012), pp. 793–819. DOI: 10.1016/j.jsc.2011.12.009.

An Introduction to Finite Element Methods

Veronika Pillwein*
RISC
Johannes Kepler University
4040 Linz (Austria)
veronika.pillwein@risc.jku.at

ABSTRACT

The most common techniques for obtaining numerical solutions to partial differential equations on non-trivial domains are (high order) finite element methods. The given domain is subdivided into simple geometric objects and an approximate solution is computed as a linear combination of locally supported basis functions. In the past decade there have been several successful collaborations between mathematicians from numerical analysis and computer algebra to analyze or improve numerical methods. The applied methods include Gröbner bases, Cylindrical Algebraic Decomposition, algorithms for special functions, etc. In this tutorial we plan to present an introduction to the basic concepts of finite element methods and we want to conclude with an overview on some of those recent collaborations and the involved proof techniques.

Categories and Subject Descriptors

I.1.2 [**Computing Methodologies**]: Symbolic and Algebraic Algorithms; G.1.8 [**Mathematics of Computing**]: Partial Differential Equations

Keywords

Finite element methods, Symbolic computation, Cylindrical Algebraic Decomposition

1. OVERVIEW

Many problems in science and engineering are described by partial differential equations on non-trivial domains which, except in special cases, cannot be solved analytically. Numerical methods are required to solve these equations. In the last decades finite element methods (FEM) [6, 5, 3] have become the most popular tools for obtaining solutions of partial differential equations on complicated domains. The main advantage of finite element methods is their general applicability to a huge class of problems, linear as well as nonlinear partial differential equations, coupled systems, varying material coefficients and boundary conditions.

Finite element methods are based on the variational formulation of partial differential equations. The domain of interest is subdivided by simple geometrical objects such as triangles, quadrilaterals, tetrahedra, or hexahedra. The approximate solution is expanded in a (finite) basis of local functions, each supported on a finite number of elements in the subdivision. The discretization yields a (usually large) system of linear equations that is commonly solved using iterative methods. There are three main strategies to improve the accuracy of the approximate solution.

The classical approach is to use on each element basis functions of a fixed low polynomial degree, say $p = 1, 2$, and to increase the number of elements in the subdivision. This strategy of local or global refinement of the mesh is called the h-version of the finite element method, where h refers to the diameter of the elements in the subdivision. With this approach the approximation error decays algebraically (i.e., with polynomial rate) in the number of unknowns.

An alternative strategy is to keep the mesh fixed and to locally increase the polynomial degree p of the basis functions. This method is called the p-version of the finite element method [15, 17] and, in the case of a smooth solution, this approach leads to exponential convergence with respect to the number of unknowns. But in practical problems the solutions usually are not smooth. In this case the convergence rate of the p-method degenerates again to an algebraic one.

Exponential convergence can be regained by combining both strategies in the hp-version of the FEM [15, 11, 9]. On parts of the domain where the sought solution is smooth, few coarse elements with basis functions of high polynomial degrees are used, whereas in the presence of singularities,

*Supported by the Austrian FWF grants F50-07 and W1214.

ISSAC'15, July 6–9, 2015, Bath, United Kingdom.
Copyright © 2015 ACM 978-1-4503-3435-8/15/07 ...$15.00.
DOI: http://dx.doi.org/10.1145/2755996.2756685.

caused, e.g., by re-entrant corners, the polynomial degree is kept low and the mesh is refined locally towards the singularity. The p- and the hp-method are also referred to as high(er) order finite element methods.

Basis functions for high order finite element methods are usually constructed using certain orthogonal polynomials. For these basis functions one is interested to have recurrence relations or simplifications (closed forms) for efficient computations, as well as inequalities entering, e.g., in norm or convergence estimates. Nowadays there exist computer algebra algorithms that can assist in completing these tasks or even take them over entirely.

In the recent past there have been several successful collaborations between numerical mathematicians and computer algebraists and different symbolic methods have been applied to problems arising in the context of numerically finding approximate solutions to (systems of) partial differential equations [1, 2, 4, 7, 8, 10, 12, 13, 14, 16] (and this list is by no means complete). These applications include design, analysis and speed up of the numerical schemes. Among the applied symbolic methods we find procedures that are nowadays standard such as algorithms for symbolic summation, Gröbner basis techniques, or Cylindrical Algebraic Decomposition.

In this tutorial we plan to show with specific examples how to derive the variational formulation of a differential equation in one and two dimensions. We present a high order finite element basis that is suited for this differential equation and set up the corresponding linear system. In the second part we show more details for some of the above mentioned collaborations between symbolic and numerical mathematicians.

2. REFERENCES

[1] A. Becirovic, P. Paule, V. Pillwein, A. Riese, C. Schneider, and J. Schöberl. Hypergeometric Summation Algorithms for High Order Finite Elements. *Computing*, 78(3):235–249, 2006.

[2] S. Beuchler, V. Pillwein, J. Schöberl, and S. Zaglmayr. Sparsity optimized high order finite element functions on simplices. In U. Langer and P. Paule, editors, *Numerical and Symbolic Scientific Computing: Progress and Prospects*, pages 21–44. Springer, Wien, 2011.

[3] D. Braess. *Finite Elements: Theory, Fast Solvers and Applications in Solid Mechanics.* Cambridge University Press, Cambridge, 2007.

[4] D. Braess, V. Pillwein, and J. Schöberl. Equilibrated Residual Error Estimates are p-Robust. *Comput. Methods Appl. Mech. Engrg.*, 198:1189–1197, 2009.

[5] S. Brenner and L. Scott. *The Mathematical Theory of Finite Element Methods*, volume 15 of *Texts in Applied Mathematics.* Springer New York, 2nd edition, 2002.

[6] P. Ciarlet. *The Finite Element Method for Elliptic Problems.* North Holland, Amsterdam, 1978.

[7] T. Cluzeau, V. Dolean, F. Nataf, and A. Quadrat. Symbolic preconditioning techniques for linear systems of partial differential equations. accepted for publ. in Proceedings of 20th International Conference on Domain Decomposition Methods, 2012.

[8] T. Cluzeau, V. Dolean, F. Nataf, and A. Quadrat. Symbolic methods for developing new domain decomposition algorithms. Rapport de recherche RR-7953, INRIA, May 2012.

[9] L. Demkowicz. *Computing with hp Finite Elements I. One- and Two-Dimensional Elliptic and Maxwell Problems.* CRC Press, Taylor and Francis, 2006.

[10] H. Hong, R. Liska, and S. Steinberg. Testing stability by quantifier elimination. *J. Symbolic Comput.*, 24(2):161–187, 1997. Applications of quantifier elimination (Albuquerque, NM, 1995).

[11] G. Karniadakis and S. Sherwin. *Spectral/hp Element Methods for CFD.* Numerical Mathematics and Scientific Computation. Oxford University Press, New York, Oxford, 1999.

[12] U. Langer, S. Reitzinger, and J. Schicho. Symbolic methods for the element precondition technique. In U. Langer and F. Winkler, editors, *Proc. SNSC Hagenberg 2001*, pages 293–308. Springer, 2003.

[13] V. Pillwein. Positivity of certain sums over Jacobi kernel polynomials. *Adv. in Appl. Math.*, 41(3):365–377, 2008.

[14] V. Pillwein and S. Takacs. A local Fourier convergence analysis of a multigrid method using symbolic computation. *Journal of Symbolic Computation*, 63:1–20, 2014.

[15] C. Schwab. *p- and hp-Finite Element Methods: Theory and Applications in Solid and Fluid Mechanics.* Numerical Mathematics and Scientific Computation. Oxford University Press, Oxford, 1998.

[16] D. Sevilla and D. Wachsmuth. Polynomial integration on regions defined by a triangle and a conic. In *Proceedings of the 2010 International Symposium on Symbolic and Algebraic Computation*, ISSAC '10, pages 163–170, New York, NY, USA, 2010. ACM.

[17] B. Szabó and I. Babuška. *Finite Element Analysis.* John Wiley & Sons, 1991.

Error-Correcting Sparse Interpolation in the Chebyshev Basis

Andrew Arnold
Symbolic Computation Group
University of Waterloo
Waterloo, Ontario, Canada
a4arnold@uwaterloo.ca
www.andrewarnold.ca

Erich L. Kaltofen
Department of Mathematics,
North Carolina State University,
Raleigh, North Carolina 27695-8205, USA
kaltofen@math.ncsu.edu
www.math.ncsu.edu/ kaltofen

ABSTRACT

We present an error-correcting interpolation algorithm for a univariate black-box polynomial that has a sparse representation using Chebyshev polynomials as a term basis. Our algorithm assumes that an upper bound on the number of erroneous evaluations is given as input. Our method is a generalization of the algorithm by Lakshman and Saunders [SIAM J. Comput., vol. 24 (1995)] for interpolating sparse Chebyshev polynomials, as well as techniques in error-correcting sparse interpolation in the usual basis of consecutive powers of the variable due to Comer, Kaltofen, and Pernet [Proc. ISSAC 2012, 2014]. We prove the correctness of our list-decoder-based algorithm with a Descartes-rule-of-signs-like property for sparse polynomials in the Chebyshev basis. We show that this list decoder requires fewer evaluations than a naive *majority-rule* block decoder in the case when the interpolant is known to have at most two terms. We also give a new algorithm that reduces sparse interpolation in the Chebyshev basis to that in the power basis, thus making the many techniques for the sparse interpolation in the power basis, for instance, supersparse (lacunary) interpolation over large finite fields, available to interpolation in the Chebyshev basis. Furthermore, we can customize the randomized early termination algorithms from Kaltofen and Lee [J. Symb. Comput., vol. 36 (2003)] to our new approach.

Categories and Subject Descriptors

I.1.2 [**Symbolic and Algebraic Manipulation**]: Algorithms; E.4 [**Coding and Information Theory**]: Error control codes

General Terms: Algorithms.

Keywords: sparse polynomial interpolation; Prony's algorithm; Chebyshev polynomials; Descartes' rule of signs; orthogonal basis; error-correcting code.

ISSAC'15, July 6–9, 2015, Bath, United Kingdom.

ACM 978-1-4503-3435-8/15/07 ...$15.00.
DOI: http://dx.doi.org/10.1145/2755996.2756652.

1. INTRODUCTION

The sparse univariate interpolation problem is to reconstruct a polynomial $f(x)$ that can be sparsely represented in a given term basis from a number of evaluations that is proportionate to the number of terms t with non-zero coefficients, not the degree of the polynomial. The problem distinguishes the case where the distinct elements at which the polynomial is evaluated are chosen by the algorithm, and the case where the evaluation points cannot be adapted to the interpolation algorithm. The second case constitutes a computationally much harder problem [4], which we will not consider further in this paper. In the first case we think of the polynomial as a black-box function that can be arbitrarily probed.

We consider a black-box polynomial $f(x)$ that can be written as a t-sparse linear combination of Chebyshev polynomials

$$f(x) = \sum_{j=1}^{t} c_j T_{\delta_j}(x) \in \mathsf{K}[x], \quad 0 \le \delta_1 < \delta_2 < \cdots < \delta_t, \tag{1}$$

where K is a field of characteristic $\neq 2$, $c_j \neq 0$ for $1 \le j \le t$, and $T_n \in \mathsf{K}[x]$ is the n-th Chebyshev polynomial of the first kind, defined by:

$$T_0(x) = 1, \quad T_1(x) = x, \tag{2}$$

$$T_n(x) = 2xT_{n-1}(x) - T_{n-2}(x) \text{ for } n \ge 2. \tag{3}$$

Since $\deg(T_n) = n$ the set of Chebyshev polynomials forms a (vector-space) basis for $\mathsf{K}[x]$. We will use the following properties of Chebyshev polynomials throughout.

Fact 1.1 *Let $m, n \in \mathbb{Z}_{\ge 0}$. Then the following hold:*

i. $\begin{bmatrix} 0 & 1 \\ -1 & 2x \end{bmatrix}^n \begin{bmatrix} 1 \\ x \end{bmatrix} = \begin{bmatrix} T_n(x) \\ T_{n+1}(x) \end{bmatrix}$.

ii. $T_n(T_m(x)) = T_{mn}(x) = T_m(T_n(x))$.

iii. $T_m(x)T_n(x) = \frac{1}{2}(T_{m+n}(x) + T_{|m-n|}(x))$.

iv. $T_n(\frac{x+x^{-1}}{2}) = \frac{x^n+x^{-n}}{2}$ *for all $n \ge 0$, as an identity in the function field $\mathsf{K}(x)$.*

v. $T_n(x) = \frac{1}{2}\left(\left(x - \sqrt{x^2-1}\right)^n + \left(x + \sqrt{x^2-1}\right)^n\right)$, *as an identity in the quadratic extension of the function field $\mathsf{K}(x)$.*

vi. *For $\mathsf{K} = \mathbb{R}$ and $\xi \le -1$ or $\xi \ge 1$, $T_m(\xi) \neq 0$.*

Fact 1.1.i allows the evaluation of T_n at elements from a finite field of characteristic $\neq 2$ in $O(\log(n))$ operations by repeated squaring.

We seek to determine t, the term degrees δ_j, and the coefficients c_j from evaluations $a_i = f(\omega_i)$ where our algorithm chooses which ω_i's to use. Our objective is to require as few ω_i's as possible, and additionally allow for some of the evaluations to be incorrect, that is $a_{\lambda_\kappa} \neq f(\omega_{\lambda_\kappa})$, where λ_κ with $1 \leq \kappa \leq k$ are the indices of the error locations. No algorithm can work without having some bounds: D for the degree, $D \geq \delta_t$; B for the sparsity, $B \geq t$; and $E \geq k$ for the number of errors in the input.

1.1 Organization of paper

In Section 2 we give an overview of sparse interpolation algorithms. We also discuss previous work on error-correcting sparse interpolation in the power (i.e., monomial) basis. Furthermore, we give a simple identity test for sparse polynomials with real coefficients in the Chebyshev basis, relying on a generalization of Descartes' rule of signs [23]. This identity test allows us to verify an interpolant produced by a list-decoding interpolation procedure, such that we can identify the true interpolant.

In Section 3 we generalize the Chebyshev-basis sparse interpolation algorithm from [21]. This is for the purposes of adapting interpolation in this setting to list decoding, following previous work on list-decoding interpolation in the monomial basis [20]. We show that this gives an error-correcting interpolation procedure that requires fewer evaluations than naive "majority rule" decoding in the cases $B = 1, 2$. In Section 4 we present an alternate approach to sparse univariate polynomial interpolation in Chebyshev basis. The Fact 1.1.iv allows a reduction of the problem of interpolating a polynomial that is sparse in Chebyshev basis to interpolating a sparse Laurent polynomial in the power basis, that is, a polynomial with terms x^δ where δ can be a negative integer. We show this algorithm may be adapted to use *early termination*, such that the algorithm can probabilistically determine t and interpolate f from $2t + 2$ evaluations in the case when t is not supplied as an input.

Conclusions and discussion of future work are given in Section 5.

2. PRELIMINARIES

The algorithm by Lakshman and Saunders in [21] interpolates $f(x) \in \mathbb{R}[x]$, f given by (1), in the absence of errors. Their algorithm, given a sparsity upper bound B interpolates $f(x)$ from evaluation points $\omega_i = T_i(\xi)$ with $i = 0, 1, \ldots, 2B - 1$, for an arbitrary $\xi > 1$. The Monte-Carlo algorithm of Kaltofen and Lee [18] determines t with high probability by randomization, using $\omega_i = T_i(\xi)$ with $i = 0, 1, \ldots, 2t + 1$ in the worst case, again without errors. The bounds B and D are needed for guaranteeing an upper bound on the probability of failure. We have, for instance for K a finite field with q elements such that $q > \deg(f)$ and such that $q - 1$ has no large prime factor the bit complexity $t^2(\log(q) + \log(D) + \log(B) + \log(t))^{O(1)}$ (see also Section 4 below). In Section 3 we generalize the algorithm of Lakshman and Saunders to interpolate f from sets of evaluation points of the form

$$\omega_{|r+si|}, \quad -B \leq i < 2B,$$

provided the middle B evaluation points ($0 \leq i < B$) are distinct and $\omega_{|r+si|} > 1$ for all i. This requires τ evaluations, where $2B \leq \tau \leq 3B$, depending on how many indices $|r+si|$ overlap.

2.1 Error-correcting sparse interpolation

Suppose now that for L argument-value pairs (ω_i, a_i) we have $a_i = f(\omega_i)$ for all $i \neq \{\lambda_1, \ldots, \lambda_k\}$ and $k \leq E$ with $0 \leq i \leq L - 1$. Here the upper bound E on the number of errors is known on input, but the error locations $\lambda_1, \ldots, \lambda_k$ are not known.

Our algorithms rely on previous work on error-correcting sparse interpolation in the monomial basis. A "majority-rule" interpolation procedure is given in [8]. This is superceded by a procedure based on list-decoding in [20], which is shown to require fewer evaluations to uniquely determine the interpolant.

2.1.1 Majority-rule interpolation

If $L = (2E + 1)2B$ we can proceed as in [8]. We interpolate $2E + 1$ separate segments of $2B$ argument-value pairs $(T_i(\xi_\ell), a_{i,\ell})$ for $i = 0, 1, \ldots, 2B-1$ and $\ell = 1, 2, \ldots, 2E+1$. If all $T_i(\xi_\ell)$ are distinct and if there are no more than E pairs with $a_{i,\ell} \neq f(T_i(\xi_\ell))$, then the Lakshman-Saunders algorithm [21] applied for each ℓ separately produces the correct sparse interpolant f in Chebyshev basis at least $E+1$ times. By a majority vote we can determine the correct f. As such we refer to this method as *majority-rule* interpolation. The argument distinctness $T_{i_1}(\xi_{\ell_1}) \neq T_{i_2}(\xi_{\ell_2})$ for all $i_1 \neq i_2$ and/or $\ell_1 \neq \ell_2$ can be achieved quickly with high probability by selecting ξ_ℓ uniformly randomly from a sufficiently large finite set. Our model of black-box interpolation with errors presumes that the black box returns a single value, which can be erroneous, and multiple probes to the black box do not reveal erroneous behavior. Surprisingly, in [20] it is shown that $(2E + 1)2B$ evaluations is optimal for the Prony/Blahut algorithm: from $(2E+1)2B-1$ pairs one can obtain a second valid sparse interpolant in the power basis.

2.1.2 List-decoding interpolation

Using $E+1$ segments of $2B$ points, one can switch to list decoding (cf. [8, Theorem 3]): at least one of the valid sparse polynomials in Chebyshev basis that is computed by the Lakshman-Saunders algorithm, that is, an interpolant whose number of terms is $\leq B$ and that interpolates $\geq (E+1)2B - E$ argument-value pairs, must agree with the original black box polynomial. For certain inputs one can prove uniqueness (cf. [20, Remark 3]): if $\mathsf{K} = \mathbb{R}$ and $\xi_\ell > 1$ for all ℓ we must have by Corollary 2.4 below a unique valid interpolant.

In [20], the authors give a list-decoding-based sparse univariate polynomial interpolation algorithm for the power basis that requires $L < (E + 1)2B$ argument-value pairs (ω_i, a_i), $0 \leq i \leq L - 1$, where $\omega_i = \xi^i$ for a suitable $\xi \in \mathsf{K}$. When there are $\leq E$ erroneous values $a_i \neq f(\omega_i)$ the algorithm computes all valid interpolants, which, as stated above, in certain cases are unique. Their idea is to attempt sparse interpolation at the subsequence $(\omega_{r+si}, a_{r+si})$, $i = 0, \ldots, 2B - 1$, for all pairs (r, s) with $r \geq 0$ and $s \geq 1$ with $r + (2B - 1)s \leq L - 1$. If one subsequence avoids all erroneous a_{λ_κ} the sparse interpolant polynomial is produced from the subsequence by the Prony/Blahut algorithm.

In Section 3.2 we transfer the idea to the Chebyshev basis, using the generalization of the Lakshman-Saunders algorithm as a subroutine. In our setting we attempt sparse interpolation at subsequences $(\omega_{|r+si|}, a_{|r+si|})$, for all choices of (r, s), subject to the constraints mentioned in the first paragraph of Section 2.

2.2 A summary of sparse interpolation algorithms

Figure 1 gives a table summarizing sparse univariate polynomial interpolation algorithms in selected bases. The rows show different problem settings and whose columns select different bases. The Pochhammer basis consists of the "falling factorials" $x(x-1)\cdots(x-\delta+1)$, the shifted basis is the variable-shifted power basis $1, x-\sigma, (x-\sigma)^2, \ldots$ with a shift σ that is unknown on input. One may also consider a variable shift in the Chebyshev basis, which is done in [11]. Supersparse algorithms only make sense for coefficients from a finite field and run in time polynomial in log(degree). However, techniques from supersparse interpolation can help stabilize numerical algorithms. Errors seem difficult to correct for sparse polynomials in Pochhammer basis without interpolating the dense polynomial interpolant in power basis by a Reed-Solomon decoder, as does the algorithm for shifted basis in [5]. Interestingly, Blahut's [3] decoder for Reed-Solomon codes uses a sparse interpolation algorithm for error location, which is generalized to multivariate sparse interpolation over $\mathbb{Q}$ in [2]. George Labahn observed the connection between Prony's algorithm in [7] and those algorithms. We do not list our new algorithm from Section 4 in the numerical algorithms row, because we have not conducted the numerical analysis and experiments. Errors can be introduced in the numerical setting, where they are considered outlier evaluations. In [8] such a numerical method is formulated. Algorithms for error correction in the multivariate setting are given in [19].

2.3 Identity testing

Here we present an identity test that will allow us to uniquely identify an interpolant f given by (1), in the case where f is over $\mathsf{K} = \mathbb{R}$. Corollary 4 of [20] uses Descartes' rule of signs to give an identity test for sparse polynomials over $\mathbb{R}$ in the monomial basis (see also [4]). From this it is shown in [20] that one can verify a B-sparse interpolant f from $L = 2B + 2E$ evaluations, provided at most E evaluations are erroneous. Towards a similar result in the Chebyshev basis, we cite a generalization of Descartes' rule of signs, due to Obrechkoff, that gives an upper bound on the number of real roots ≥ 1 for polynomials over $\mathbb{R}$ with a sparse representation in the Chebyshev basis.

Theorem 2.1 (Obrechkoff, 1918) *Define the sequence of polynomials $\{\mathcal{T}_n(x)\}_{n=0}^{\infty}$ by $\mathcal{T}_{-1}(x) = 0$, $\mathcal{T}_0(x) = 1$, and the recurrence relation*

$$x\mathcal{T}_n(x) = \alpha_n \mathcal{T}_{n+1}(x) + \beta_n \mathcal{T}_n(x) + \gamma_n \mathcal{T}_{n-1}(x), \quad n \geq 0,$$

where $\alpha_n, \beta_n, \gamma_n \in \mathbb{R}$, $\alpha_n, \gamma_n > 0$. Let $(c_1, \ldots, c_t)$ be a list of nonzero real numbers with s sign changes between consecutive values, and $0 < \delta_1 < \delta_2 < \cdots < \delta_t \in \mathbb{R}$. Then $\sum_{i=1}^{t} c_i \mathcal{T}_{\delta_i}(x)$ has at most s roots in (ζ_t, ∞), where ζ_t denotes the largest real root of $\mathcal{T}_n$.

See [9] for a proof of Obrechkoff's Theorem. Combined with Fact 1.1.vi this gives the following corollary:

Corollary 2.2 *Let $\mathsf{K} = \mathbb{R}$ and $f(x) = \sum_{i=1}^{t} c_i T_{\delta_i}(x)$, with $\delta_i < \delta_j$ and $c_i \neq 0$ for $1 \leq i < j \leq t$. Then f has at most $t-1$ distinct real roots ≥ 1.*

As $T_n(\xi) > T_m(\xi)$ for $\xi > 1$ and $n > m$, we have in addition the following:

Corollary 2.3 *Let $\xi > 1$ and $f(x)$ be a t-sparse polynomial over $\mathbb{R}$ in the Chebyshev basis. Let $m_1 < m_2 < \cdots < m_B \in \mathbb{Z}_{\geq 0}$ for some $B \geq t$. If $f(T_{m_i}(\xi)) = 0$ for all i, then $f(x)$ is identically zero.*

Corollary 2.4 *Let $\xi > 1$ and $f(x), g(x)$ be two sparse polynomials over $\mathbb{R}$ in the Chebyshev basis, both of sparsity $\leq B$. Let $m_1 < m_2 < \cdots < m_{2B} \in \mathbb{Z}_{\geq 0}$. If $f(T_{m_i}(\xi)) = g(T_{m_i}(\xi))$ for all i, then $f = g$.*

From Corollary 2.3 we have a means of testing whether an interpolant produced by list-decoding interpolation is correct. In particular, if we have L distinct evaluation points $\omega_0, \ldots, \omega_{L-1} > 1$, where $L \geq 2B + 2E$, then a polynomial f comprised of at most B terms in the Chebyshev basis that disagrees with at most E of the evaluations must be the true interpolant.

Corollary 2.3 is also used to show that a linear system given by the algorithm presented in Section 3 gives a unique solution.

3. GENERALIZATION OF THE METHOD OF LAKSHMAN AND SAUNDERS

In this section we develop a generalization of the algorithm given by Lakshman and Saunders in [21] for interpolating a t-sparse polynomial in the Chebyshev basis over the rationals. This generalization will allow us to employ list-decoding interpolation in the Chebyshev basis.

Throughout Section 3 we consider $f \in \mathbb{R}[x]$ of the form given by (1). Let $\xi > 1$ and define the sequence $a_i = f(T_i(\xi))$, for $i \geq 0$. Lemma 3.1 below proves a linear relation of the a_i, taken over indices from the absolute values of an arithmetic progression. This gives us a means of solving for the coefficients. The relation is a straightforward generalization of Lemma 5 in [21], and the proof follows very similarly.

Lemma 3.1 *Fix $s \in \mathbb{Z}_{>0}$ and consider the degree-t polynomial Φ, written in the Chebyshev basis*

$$\Phi(z) = \varphi_t T_t(z) + \varphi_{t-1} T_{t-1}(z) + \cdots + \varphi_0 T_0(z), \quad (4)$$

defined by $\varphi_t = 1$ and $\Phi(T_{s\delta_\ell}(\xi)) = 0$ for $\ell = 1, \ldots, t$. Then, for $i, r \in \mathbb{Z}$,

$$\sum_{j=0}^{t} \varphi_j (a_{|s(i+j)+r|} + a_{|s(i-j)+r|}) = 0. \quad (5)$$

PROOF. Observe, using Fact 1.1.ii, that

$$\begin{aligned}\sum_{j=0}^{t} \varphi_j a_{|s(i+j)+r|} &= \sum_{j=0}^{t} \varphi_j \sum_{\ell=1}^{t} c_\ell T_{\delta_\ell}\left(T_{|s(i+j)+r|}(\xi)\right) \\ &= \sum_{\ell=1}^{t} c_\ell \sum_{j=0}^{t} \varphi_j T_{|s(i+j)+r|}(T_{\delta_\ell}(\xi)). \quad (6)\end{aligned}$$

	monomial	Chebyshev	Pochhammer	shifted power basis
bounded # of terms	Blahut (1984) [3]	Lakshman, Saunders (1995) [22]		Grigoriev, Karpinski (1993) [16]
supersparse	Kaltofen (1988) [17] Garg, Schost (2009) [10] Arnold, Giesbrecht, Roche (2014) [1]	this paper		Giesbrecht, Roche (2010) [14]
with errors	Cormer, Kaltofen, Pernet (2012) [8] Kaltofen, Pernet (2014) [20]			Boyer, Comer, Kaltofen (2014) [8]
early termination	Kaltofen, Lee (2003) [18]			Giesbrecht, Kaltofen, Lee (2004) [11]
with numerical noise	Prony (1792) Giesbrecht, Labahn, Lee (2003) [13] Giesbrecht, Roche (2011) [15]	Giesbrecht, Labahn, Lee (2004) [12]		Boyer, Comer, Kaltofen (2014) [8]

Figure 1: Selected sparse univariate interpolation algorithms

Using Facts 1.1.ii and 1.1.iii, we can rewrite the term appearing in the inner sum in (6) as

$$\begin{aligned}&\varphi_j T_{|s(i+j)+r|}(T_{\delta_\ell}(\xi))\\ &= \varphi_j\left(2T_{sj}(T_{\delta_\ell}(\xi))T_{|si+r|}(T_{\delta_\ell}(\xi)) - T_{|s(i-j)+r|}(T_{\delta_\ell}(\xi))\right)\\ &= \varphi_j\left(T_j T_{s\delta_\ell}(\xi)) \times 2T_{|si+r|}(T_{\delta_\ell}(\xi)) - T_{|s(i-j)+r|}(T_{\delta_\ell}(\xi))\right).\end{aligned}$$

Thus we can express the inner sum in (6) as

$$\underbrace{\Phi(T_{s\delta_\ell}(\xi))}_{=0} \times 2T_{|si+r|}(T_{\delta_\ell}(\xi)) - \sum_{j=0}^{t} \varphi_j T_{|s(i-j)+r|}(T_{\delta_\ell}(\xi)).$$

Thus (6) becomes

$$\begin{aligned}&-\sum_{\ell=1}^{t} c_\ell \left(\sum_{j=0}^{t} \varphi_j T_{\delta_\ell}(T_{|s(i-j)+r|}(\xi))\right)\\ &= -\sum_{j=0}^{t} \varphi_j \left(\sum_{\ell=1}^{t} c_\ell T_{\delta_\ell}(T_{|s(i-j)+r|}(\xi))\right)\\ &= -\sum_{j=0}^{t} \varphi_j a_{|s(i-j)+r|}.\end{aligned}$$

This gives

$$\sum_{j=0}^{t} \varphi_j a_{|s(i+j)+r|} = -\sum_{j=0}^{t} \varphi_j a_{|s(i-j)+r|}.$$

The identity (5) follows. ☐

For $r, s \in \mathbb{Z}$, $s \geq 1$ and taking (5) with $i = 0, 1, \ldots, t-1$, this gives us a linear system $A\varphi = -\alpha$, where

$$A = \underbrace{\left[a_{|r+(i+j)s|}\right]_{i,j=0}^{t-1}}_{\text{Hankel matrix}} + \underbrace{\left[a_{|r+(i-j)s|}\right]_{i,j=0}^{t-1}}_{\text{Toeplitz matrix}}, \tag{7}$$

$$\alpha = \left[a_{|r+(i+t)s|} + a_{|r+(i-t)s|}\right]_{i=0}^{t-1}. \tag{8}$$

Thus, provided A is nonsingular, we can obtain φ from A and α. Lemma 3.2 below is an analogue to Lemma 6 of [22]. Our proof is an immediate adaption of theirs.

Lemma 3.2 *Let $r, s \in \mathbb{Z}$, $s > 0$. If the values $|r + si|, 0 \leq i < t$ are distinct, then A is nonsingular.*

PROOF. We will show that $A = UBV$, where

$$U = \left[T_{|r+si|}(T_{\delta_{j+1}}(\xi))\right]_{i,j=0}^{t-1}, \tag{9}$$

$$V = \left[T_{sj}(T_{\delta_{i+1}}(\xi))\right]_{i,j=0}^{t-1}, \tag{10}$$

and B is a diagonal matrix with entries $2c_1, \ldots, 2c_t$. Again using Facts 1.1.ii and 1.1.iii, observe that $(UBV)_{i,j}$ is

$$\begin{aligned}&\sum_{\ell=1}^{t} 2c_\ell T_{|r+is|}(T_{\delta_\ell}(\xi))T_{js}(T_{\delta_\ell}(\xi))\\ &= \sum_{\ell=1}^{t} c_\ell \left(T_{|r+(i+j)s|}(T_{\delta_\ell}(\xi)) + T_{|r+(i-j)s|}(T_{\delta_\ell}(\xi))\right)\\ &= \sum_{\ell=1}^{t} c_\ell \left(T_{\delta_\ell}(T_{|r+(i+j)s|}(\xi)) + T_{\delta_\ell}(T_{|r+(i-j)s|}(\xi))\right)\\ &= a_{|r+(i+j)s|} + a_{|r+(i-j)s|}.\end{aligned}$$

Let b be a row vector such that $bU = \mathbf{0}$. Then

$$\sum_{i=0}^{t-1} b_i T_{|r+si|}(x)$$

is a t-sparse polynomial in the Chebyshev basis with roots $T_{\delta_1}(\xi), \ldots, T_{\delta_t}(\xi)$. By Corollary 2.3, b is necessarily zero. It follows that U is nonsingular. By a similar argument, V is nonsingular. ☐

3.1 Description of algorithm

We now give a generalization of the sparse interpolation algorithm of Lakshman and Saunders polynomials in the Chebyshev basis given in [21]. Suppose we are given a black-box polynomial $f \in \mathbb{R}[x]$, f of the form (1), with bounds B and D as described in Section 1. For the purposes of Section 3.1 we will assume our evaluations are without errors. First, we choose $\xi > 0$ and $r, s \in \mathbb{Z}$, $s > 0$, such that

$$|r + si| \neq |r + sj| \quad \text{for } 0 \leq i \neq j < B, \tag{11}$$

such that the evaluation points $T_{|r+si|}(\xi)$ are distinct for $0 \leq i < B$.

We query the black-box polynomial f for the evaluations

$$a_{|r+si|} = f(T_{|r+si|}(\xi)), \quad -B \leq i < 2B. \tag{12}$$

This can entail potentially as many as $3B$ evaluations; however, it can be as few as $2B$ in the case that the first or last B evaluations $a_{|r+si|}$ for $-B \leq i < 0$ or $B \leq i < 2B-1$ are contained in the middle B evaluations $a_{|r+si|}$ for $0 \leq i < B$, e.g., when $r = 0$. The algorithm of Lakshman and Saunders is specifically the case when $r = 0$ and $s = 1$.

If $|r| \geq |r + s(B-1)|$, then we can take $-(r + s(B-1))$ in place of r to obtain the same set of evaluation points (12). Thus without loss of generality we can choose r such that

$|r| \le |r+s(B-1)|$, or equivalently $r \ge -s(B-1)/2$. If $B \ge 3$, the distinctness criterion (11) forces $|r| \ne |r+s(B-1)|$.

Because of the column relation (5) the largest non-singular leading principal submatrix of the Hankel + Toeplitz matrix for all $t' \ge t$

$$[a_{|r+(i+j)s|}]_{i,j=0}^{t'-1} + [a_{|r+(i-j)s|}]_{i,j=0}^{t'-1} \quad (13)$$

is the matrix A in (7) for $t' = t$. By computing the determinant of the leading principal submatrices in increasing order of size, we can thus determine t.

Once we have t we solve the linear system $A\varphi = -\alpha$, where A and α are respectively given by (7) and (8). This gives us the coefficients $\varphi \in \mathbb{R}^{t+1}$ that comprise $\Phi \in \mathbb{R}[z]$ given by (4). We factor Φ to get its t roots, which are exactly the values $T_{\delta_i}(\xi)$ for $i = 1, 2, \ldots, t$. By evaluating $T_j(\xi)$ for appropriate choices of j we can discern δ_i from $T_{\delta_i}(\xi)$ and ξ for each i; see Section 3 in [21].

The coefficients $c_1, \ldots, c_t$ may be given as the solution to the linear system $U^* c = a$, where U^* is the transpose of U given by (9) and $a = (a_{|r|}, a_{|r+s|}, \ldots, a_{|r+(t-1)s|})$. This gives a representation $((c_1, \delta_1), \ldots, (c_t, \delta_t))$ of f.

3.2 A list-decoding interpolation procedure

Now we can consider interpolation in the presence of at most E erroneous evaluations. Our algorithm, on input $B \ge t$ and the sequence of evaluations (12) can determine t and f from a pair (r, s) satisfying (11) with $r \ge -s(B-1)/2$ and $s \ge 1$, provided that the evaluations are correct. We seek such a subsequence of unspoiled evaluations in $a_0, \ldots, a_{L-1}$, where L is computed sufficiently large with respect to the maximum number of errors E, which is also input, to guarantee the existence of that subsequence of at most $3B$ correct evaluations no matter where the error locations $0 \le \lambda_1 < \lambda_2 < \cdots < \lambda_k \le L-1$, with $k \le E$, occur.

We show by example that with sequence locations in arithmetic progression we can decode more errors than with error-free blocks. Since our arithmetic progressions are longer than in [20], $3B$ vs. $2B$, this is not immediately clear. It seems difficult to give an example that can be verified by hand: Let $B = 1$ and $E = 8$: the block method uses $(E+1)2B = 18$ argument-value pairs. However, as is shown in [20, Table 1: $k = 3$, $E = 8$], if in the set of $L = 17$ locations $0, 1, 2, \ldots, 16 = L-1$ we remove any 8 erroneous locations $\lambda_1, \ldots, \lambda_8$, there remains a $k = 3B = 3$-elements arithmetic progression $r, r+s, r+2s \le 16$ for integers $r \ge 0$, $s \ge 1$. Those locations constitute a sequence of the form in (12), even without wrap-around, and our algorithm produces a valid interpolant. For instance, if $\{\lambda_1, \ldots, \lambda_8\} = \{2, 5, 6, 7, 9, 12, 13, 14\}$, which makes blocks of 3 consecutive elements and blocks of 3 consecutive all even or all odd elements impossible, we have the arithmetic progression $\{0, 8, 16\}$ at good locations.

We now show that one such occurrence yields a formula for L for all E sufficiently large. If $L \ge 3B(E+1)$ we have one contiguous segment of $3B$ locations without error using $r = 3\nu B$ and $s = 1$ for some $\nu \ge 0$ (not using wrap-around). We denote by $L_{\min}(3B, E) \le 3B(E+1)$ the minimum length that suffices, without wrap-around ($r \ge Bs$, that is, $r - Bs \ge 0$). As stated in Section 1, from [20, Table 1], we have $L_{\min}(6, 8) \le 34$ ($B = 2, E = 8$).

We now consider at most $E_1 = (E_0+1)m - 1$ errors for some integer $m \ge 1$. We assume that $L_0 \ge L_{\min}(3B, E_0)$. If $L = L_0 m$, then one of the m contiguous segments of L_0 evaluations has $\le E_0$ errors, for otherwise there would be $\ge (E_0+1)m$ errors. That segment has by our assumption for L_0 an arithmetic progression of length $3B$ of locations without errors. Therefore $L_{\min}(3B, (E_0+1)m - 1) \le L_0 m$. Since $L_{\min}(3B, E) \le L_{\min}(3B, E_1)$ for $E \le E_1$ we have for $E = (E_0+1)m - (E_0+1) + \nu$ with $\nu = 0, 1, \ldots, E_0$:

$$\begin{aligned} &L_{\min}(3B, (E_0+1)m - (E_0+1) + \nu) \\ &\le L_{\min}(3B, (E_0+1)m - 1) \le L_0 m = L_0 \left\lfloor \frac{E + E_0 + 1}{E_0 + 1} \right\rfloor. \end{aligned}$$

Our objective is to have $L_0\lfloor (E+E_0+1)/(E_0+1) \rfloor < (E+1)2B$ where the latter is the length required for the block method for E errors.

From the entries in [20, Table 1] we can choose E_0 and L_0 for $B = 1$. If we choose $E_0 = 8$ and $L_0 = 17$, then $17\lfloor (E+9)/9 \rfloor < 2(E+1)$ for all $E \ge 136$. We can also choose $E_0 = 13$ and $L_0 = 23$, such that $23\lfloor (E+14)/14 \rfloor < 2(E+1)$ for all $E \ge 57$.

For $B = 2$: we can choose $E_0 = 8$ and $L_0 = 34$ such that $34\lfloor (E+9)/9 \rfloor < 4(E+1)$ for all $E \ge 136$; or $E_0 = 11$ and $L_0 = 43$ such that $43\lfloor (E+12)/12 \rfloor < 4(E+1)$ for all $E \ge 86$. This gives an algorithm in the case $B = 2$. We produce the evaluations $a_0, \ldots, a_{L-1}$ for $L = 43\lfloor (E+12)/12 \rfloor$, run the algorithm of Section 3.1 over all choices $r, s \in \mathbb{Z}$ with $r \ge -(B-1)s$ and $s \ge 1$, and for each (r, s) check whether the resulting interpolant f agrees with at least $L - E$ evaluations. We are guaranteed a pair (r, s) producing such an f exists, which by Corollary 2.4 must be the true polynomial given by our black-box.

We conjecture that for each $B \ge 3$ there exists an E_0 such that $L_0 = L_{\min}(3B, E_0) < (E_0+1)2B = L_{\text{block}}$. That implies that for all $E > (\rho(E_0+1) - 1)/(1-\rho)$ with $\rho = L_0/L_{\text{block}} < 1$ we have

$$L_0\lfloor (E+E_0+1)/(E_0+1) \rfloor < (E+1)2B. \quad (14)$$

4. AN ALTERNATE SPARSE CHEBYSHEV INTERPOLATION ALGORITHM

We can reconstruct $f \in \mathsf{K}[x]$ given by (1) when K is a field of characteristic $\ne 2$ and $c_j \ne 0$ for all $1 \le j \le t$, from the evaluations of the form

$$a_i = f(\tfrac{\omega^i + \omega^{-i}}{2}) \quad \text{for } \omega \in \mathsf{K}, \omega \ne 0, \quad (15)$$

provided that $\omega^{\delta_j} \ne \omega^{\delta_{j'}}$ for all $0 \le j < j' \le t$. We will show how to interpolate f from a worst-case $2B + 1$ evaluations. In Section 4.2 we show how to adapt the algorithm to an early termination scheme, such that only $2t + 2$ evaluations $a_0, \ldots, a_{2t+1}$ are required. Note that $a_i = f(T_i(a))$ with $a = (\omega + \omega^{-1})/2$, so the algorithms of the previous sections apply. However, $\omega^{\delta_j} \ne \omega^{\delta_{j'}}$ is not equivalent to $T_{\delta_j}(a) = (\omega^{\delta_j} + \omega^{-\delta_j})/2 \ne (\omega^{\delta_{j'}} + \omega^{-\delta_{j'}})/2 = T_{\delta_{j'}}(a)$. We have from Fact 1.1.iv,

$$g(y) \stackrel{\text{def}}{=} f(\tfrac{y+y^{-1}}{2}) = \sum_{j=1}^{t} \frac{c_j}{2}(y^{\delta_j} + y^{-\delta_j}) \in \mathsf{K}[y, y^{-1}], \quad (16)$$

which is a $(2t)$-sparse ($(2t-1)$-sparse if $\delta_1 = 0$) Laurent polynomial in power basis. Observe for $g(y)$ in (16) that

$$a_i = g(\omega^i) = a_{-i}, \quad \text{for } i \in \mathbb{Z}. \quad (17)$$

thus the evaluations $a_0, a_1, \ldots, a_\ell$ give the evaluation of g at ω^i, for $-\ell \le i \le \ell$. By the theory of sparse Prony/Blahut interpolation of Laurent polynomials (see, e.g., [8, Theorem 1]), the sequence of values (15) is linearly generated by the polynomial

$$\Gamma(z) = \prod_{j=1}^{t} \Big((z - \omega^{\delta_j})(z - \omega^{-\delta_j}) \Big). \tag{18}$$

The proof that Γ linearly generates (15) is based on the following Lemma.

Lemma 4.1 *Suppose that the infinite sequence $\{a_i\}_{i\ge 0}$ of elements $a_i \in \mathsf{K}$ is linearly generated by the minimal generator $\Lambda_1(z)$ and the infinite sequence $\{b_i\}_{i\ge 0}$ of elements $b_i \in \mathsf{K}$ is linearly generated by the minimal generator $\Lambda_2(z)$. Then the infinite sequence $\{a_i + b_i\}_{i\ge 0}$ is linearly generated by the least common multiple of Λ_1 and Λ_2, denoted by* LCM(Λ_1, Λ_2).

Note that the minimal linear generator $\Lambda(z)$ of (15) can be a non-trivial factor of (18), namely when $\omega^{\delta_j} = \omega^{-\delta_{j'}}$ for $j \neq j'$. Because our assumption $\omega^{\delta_j} \neq \omega^{\delta_{j'}}$ for all $1 \le j < j' \le t$, the factors $z - \omega^{\delta_j}$ occur in the minimal generator for all $1 \le j \le t$. We have the following lemma.

Lemma 4.2 *Let $-\delta_t \le \eta_1, \ldots, \eta_\tau \le \delta_t$ be those exponents such that $\omega^{\eta_1}, \ldots, \omega^{\eta_\tau}$ form the distinct elements of*

$$\omega^{-\delta_t}, \omega^{-\delta_{t-1}}, \ldots, \omega^{-\delta_1}, \omega^{\delta_1}, \ldots, \omega^{\delta_t}.$$

Then the minimal linear generator of (15) is

$$\Lambda(z) = \prod_{\kappa=1}^{\tau} (z - \omega^{\eta_\kappa}).$$

PROOF. The infinite sequence (15) cannot entirely be a sequence of 0's. The evaluations

$$a_i = \sum_{j=1}^{t} c_j/2 \left((\omega^{-\delta_j})^i + (\omega^{\delta_j})^i \right) \tag{19}$$

are for $0 \le i \le \tau - 1$ the entries of a $\tau \times \tau$ transposed non-singular Vandermonde matrix times a non-zero vector, which cannot be all zero. Therefore, the minimal linear generator Λ of (15) is not the constant polynomial 1. $\Lambda(z)$ is by Lemma 4.1 a factor of $\prod_{\kappa=1}^{\tau}(z-\omega^{\eta_\kappa})$, because $\{c\,\omega^{i\eta_\kappa}\}_{i\ge 1-2t}$ is linearly generated by $z - \omega^{\eta_\kappa}$. Suppose now $\Lambda(z) = \prod_{\kappa=1}^{\tau'}(z - \omega^{\eta_\kappa})$ where $\tau' < \tau$. Since Λ linearly generates all $\{c_{\ell_\kappa}/2\,\omega^{i\eta_\kappa}\}_{i\ge 1-2t}$ for $1 \le \kappa \le \tau'$, where c_{ℓ_κ} is the coefficient corresponding to the exponent η_κ in (19), and by definition linearly generates the sequence (19) for $i \ge 1 - 2t$, Λ must be a linear generator for $\{\sum_{\kappa=\tau'+1}^{\tau} c_{\ell_\kappa}/2\,\omega^{i\eta_\kappa}\}_{i\ge 1-2t}$. The latter sequence is linearly generated by $\prod_{\kappa=\tau'+1}^{\tau}(z - \omega^{\eta_\kappa})$ and by a Vandermonde matrix argument the minimal generator $\Lambda^{[2]}(z)$ must be a polynomial factor $\neq 1$. Finally, Λ must be a polynomial multiple of $\Lambda^{[2]}(z)$, which is not possible. Therefore $\tau' = \tau$. $\square$

4.1 Description of algorithm

We compute the minimal generator by a variant of the Berlekamp/Massey algorithm. Suppose on input we have an upper bound on the number of terms, $B \ge t$. One runs the Berlekamp/Massey algorithm on

$$a_{1-2B}, a_{2-2B}, \ldots, a_{2B-1}, \alpha,$$

where α is a symbolic value for a_{2B}. If $B > t$ or $\deg(\Lambda) < 2B$, e.g., when $\delta_1 = 0$, a value of α is not needed for computing Λ. The corresponding $(2B) \times (2B)$ Hankel matrix

$$H_B = \left[a_{i+j-2B-1}\right]_{i,j=0}^{2B-1} \tag{20}$$

will then have been identified by the Berlekamp/Massey algorithm as singular. If $2t = \deg(\Lambda) = 2B$, the matrix is identified as non-singular, and Λ is computed as a linear form $\Lambda_\alpha = \Lambda^{[0]} + \alpha\Lambda^{[1]}$. Since Λ then is a reciprocal polynomial, that constraint may determine the value a_{2B} for α, which, for an ω that is selected randomly from a sufficiently large finite set, can be shown to hold with high probability (see Theorem 4.3.ii below). Otherwise, we need to query the black-box polynomial f for the evaluation a_{2B} in order to finish the computation of Λ.

From Λ one computes the exponents $\delta_1, \ldots, \delta_t$ as is commonly done in all variants of the Prony/Blahut interpolation algorithm [2, 18, 13, 10, 17], and with the exponents one computes the coefficients c_j from a transposed Vandermonde system.

Remark 4.1 In order to generalize this algorithm for the purposes of error-correction, we would need to consider subsequences of the form α_{r+si}, $i = 1-2B, \ldots, 2B$, for choices of $r, s \in \mathbb{Z}, s \ge 1$. Similar to the interpolation algorithm in Section 3, this can be as few as $2B + 1$ and as many as $4B$ evaluations, depending on how many evaluations α_{r+si} are used doubly, given $\alpha_j = \alpha_{-j}$ for all j. Moreover, an error at evaluation a_i implies an error at a_{-i}, such that an erroneous evaluation of f can give us an erroneous evaluation of g at possibly two locations.

4.2 Early termination

The above approach has shortcomings compared to the early-termination algorithm in [18]. One needs $2B + 1$ evaluations in the worst case, rather than $2t + 2$. The shortcoming is fixable by adapting the arguments in [18, Proof of Theorem 4]. Let $\alpha_i = g(y^i) = f(\frac{y^i + y^{-i}}{2})$ for $i \in \mathbb{Z}$. We consider the $(2t+1) \times (2t+1)$ Hankel matrix with entries in $\mathsf{K}[y, y^{-1}]$,

$$\mathcal{H} = \begin{bmatrix} \alpha_{-2t} & \alpha_{1-2t} & \cdots & \alpha_{-1} & \alpha_0 \\ \alpha_{1-2t} & \alpha_{2-2t} & \iddots & \alpha_0 & \alpha_1 \\ \vdots & \iddots & & \vdots & \vdots \\ \alpha_0 & \cdots & & & \alpha_{2t} \end{bmatrix}. \tag{21}$$

As in [18] we will now show that the square submatrices in the right upper corner are non-singular up to the maximal dimension, with conditions for odd dimensions. By Lemma 4.2 the minimum linear generator $\prod_{j=1}^{t}(z - y^{\delta_j})(z - y^{-\delta_j})$ for $\delta_1 > 0$, and $(z-1)\prod_{j=2}^{t}(z - y^{\delta_j})(z - y^{-\delta_j})$ for $\delta_1 = 0$, produces a column relation over the field $\mathsf{K}(y)$ so for $\delta_1 > 0$ the upper-right $(2t) \times (2t)$ submatrix of $\mathcal{H}$ is non-singular, and for $\delta_1 = 0$ the right-upper $(2t-1) \times (2t-1)$ submatrix of $\mathcal{H}$ is non-singular, and $\mathcal{H}$ is singular.

Theorem 4.3 *Let $\mathcal{H}_i$ be the submatrix of $\mathcal{H}$ formed by the first i rows and the last i columns. Then the following hold:*

i. $\det(\mathcal{H}_i) \neq 0$ *for all even* $i = 2, 4, \ldots, 2t-2$; *if* $\delta_1 > 0$ *then* $\det(\mathcal{H}_{2t}) \neq 0$.

ii. $\det(\mathcal{H}_{2t-1}) \neq 0$; *for all odd* $i = 1, 3, \ldots, 2t-3$: *if* $(\sum_{\nu=1}^{t-(i-1)/2} c_\nu) \neq 0$ *then* $\det(\mathcal{H}_i) \neq 0$.

PROOF. Following Lemma 4.2 we denote

$$\begin{aligned} \eta_1 &= -\delta_t, & \eta_{2t} &= \delta_t, & \ell_1 &= \ell_{2t} = t, \\ \eta_2 &= -\delta_{t-1}, & \eta_{2t-1} &= \delta_{t-1}, & \ell_2 &= \ell_{2t-1} = t-1, \\ &\vdots & &\vdots & &\vdots \\ \eta_t &= -\delta_1, & \eta_{t+1} &= \delta_1, & \ell_t &= \ell_{t+1} = 1, \end{aligned}$$

such that $\eta_i = -\delta_{\ell_i}$ for $1 \le i \le t$, and $\eta_i = \delta_{\ell_i}$ for $t+1 \le i \le 2t$. Let $\beta_\kappa = y^{\eta_\kappa}$ for $1 \le \kappa \le 2t$. The matrix $\mathcal{H}_i$ can be factored as (see [18, Eq. (7)])

$$\mathcal{H}_i = \mathcal{B}_i C_{2t} \bar{\mathcal{B}}_i^*, \quad C_{2t} = \operatorname{diag}(c_{\ell_1}/2, c_{\ell_2}/2, \ldots, c_{\ell_{2t}}/2) \quad (22)$$

where the * is the transposition operator, with $\mathcal{B}_i, \bar{\mathcal{B}}_i \in K(y)^{i \times (2t)}$ given by

$$\mathcal{B}_i = \begin{bmatrix} 1 & 1 & \cdots & 1 \\ \beta_1 & \beta_2 & \cdots & \beta_{2t} \\ \vdots & \vdots & \ddots & \vdots \\ \beta_1^{i-1} & \beta_2^{i-1} & \cdots & \beta_{2t}^{i-1} \end{bmatrix}, \quad \bar{\mathcal{B}}_i = \begin{bmatrix} \beta_1^{1-i} & \beta_2^{1-i} & \cdots & \beta_{2t}^{1-i} \\ \beta_1^{2-i} & \beta_2^{2-i} & \cdots & \beta_{2t}^{2-i} \\ \vdots & \vdots & \ddots & \vdots \\ \beta_1^{-1} & \beta_2^{-1} & \cdots & \beta_{2t}^{-1} \\ 1 & 1 & \cdots & 1 \end{bmatrix}.$$

Let $M_{J,K}$ be the determinant of the submatrix of M consisting of rows in $J = \{j_1, \ldots, j_i\}$ and columns in $K = \{k_1, \ldots, k_i\}$. As in [18, Proof of Theorem 4], by the Binet-Cauchy formula with $I = \{1, 2, \ldots, i\}$, we can write $\det(\mathcal{H}_i)$ as

$$\begin{aligned} &\sum_J \sum_K (\mathcal{B}_i)_{I,J} (C_{2t})_{J,K} (\bar{\mathcal{B}}_i^*)_{K,I} \\ &= \sum_J 2^{-i} \left(\textstyle\prod_{m=1}^i c_{\ell_{j_m}}\right) (\mathcal{B}_i)_{I,J} (\bar{\mathcal{B}}_i^*)_{J,I} \\ &= \sum_J 2^{-i} \left(\textstyle\prod_{m=1}^i c_{\ell_{j_m}} \beta_{j_m}^{i-1}\right) \det\left(\begin{bmatrix} 1 & 1 & \cdots & 1 \\ \beta_{j_1} & \beta_{j_2} & \cdots & \beta_{j_i} \\ \vdots & \vdots & \ddots & \vdots \\ \beta_{j_1}^{i-1} & \beta_{j_2}^{i-1} & \cdots & \beta_{j_i}^{i-1} \end{bmatrix}\right)^2 \\ &= \sum_J 2^{-i} \left(\textstyle\prod_{m=1}^i c_{\ell_{j_m}} \beta_{j_m}^{i-1}\right) \prod_{1 \le v < u \le i} (\beta_{j_u} - \beta_{j_v})^2. \quad (23) \end{aligned}$$

In the expansion of the products in (23) we have the terms $\beta_{j_1}^{2i-2} \beta_{j_2}^{2i-4} \cdots \beta_{j_{i-1}}^2$ so we have a summand term $\beta_{j_1}^{i-1} \beta_{j_2}^{i-3} \times \cdots \beta_{j_{i/2}}^1 \beta_{j_{i/2+1}}^{-1} \cdots \beta_{j_{i-1}}^{3-i} \beta_{j_i}^{1-i}$. For Part i, if we set

$$\begin{aligned} j_1 &= 2t, & j_i &= 1, \\ j_2 &= 2t-1, & j_{i-1} &= 2, \\ &\vdots & &\vdots \\ j_{i/2} &= 2t - i/2 + 1, & j_{i/2+1} &= i/2, \end{aligned}$$

we obtain in the expansion of (23) the term y^D with $D = 2(i-1)\delta_t + 2(i-3)\delta_{t-1} + \cdots + 2\delta_{t-(i/2-1)}$ for even i. For $i \le 2t-2$, that is $t - (i/2 - 1) \ge 2$ and $\delta_{t-(i/2-1)} > 0$ and for $i = 2t$ and $\delta_1 > 0$ that y^D term can only occur once in the expansion, and therefore cannot cancel. We add a brief explanation to the last claim. We multiply the sum (23) by $(\beta_1 \cdots \beta_t)^{i-1}$ and expand: the terms are then of the form $\beta_{j_1}^{w_1} \cdots \beta_{j_i}^{w_i} \beta_{j_{i+1}}^{i-1} \cdots \beta_{j_t}^{i-1}$ with $\{j_1, \ldots, j_t\} = \{1, \ldots, t\}$, $w_\nu \ge 0$ and $w_1 + \cdots + w_i = i(i-1)$ and additional constraints. For instance, if $w_1 = 2i-2$ then $w_\nu \le 2i-4$ for all $\nu \ge 2$. The single maximum of the degree in y is at the assignment $w_1 = 2i-2$ and $\beta_{j_1} = y^{\delta_t}$, $w_i = 0$ and $\beta_{j_i} = y^{-\delta_t}, \ldots$, $w_{i/2} = i$ and $\beta_{j_{i/2}} = y^{\delta_{t-(i/2-1)}}$ $w_{i/2+1} = i-2$ and $\beta_{j_{i/2}} = y^{-\delta_{t-(i/2-1)}}$, which gives the largest δ_κ the largest available weights, and the smallest $-\delta_\kappa$ the smallest available weights.

For odd i in Part ii, the highest degree term $y^{D'}$ is not unique. We have the summand term in (23)

$$\beta_{j_1}^{i-1} \beta_{j_2}^{i-3} \cdots \beta_{j_{(i-1)/2}}^2 \beta_{j_{(i+1)/2}}^0 \beta_{j_{(i+3)/2}}^{-2} \beta_{j_{(i+5)/2}}^{-4} \cdots \beta_{j_i}^{1-i}.$$

If we set $j_1 = 2t, j_i = 1, j_2 = 2t-1, j_{i-1} = 2, \ldots, j_{(i-1)/2} = 2t - (i-3)/2, j_{(i+3)/2} = (i-1)/2$, and

$$j_{(i+1)/2} \in \{(i+1)/2, (i+3)/2, \ldots, 2t - (i-1)/2\},$$

we obtain in the expansion of (23) the term $y^{D'}$ with $D' = 2(i-1)\delta_t + 2(i-3)\delta_{t-1} + \cdots + 8\delta_{t-((i+1)/2-3)} + 4\delta_{t-((i+1)/2-2)}$, and only with such settings. The coefficient of $y^{D'}$ is $2^{-i} \times c_{\ell_1} c_{\ell_{2t}} \cdots c_{\ell_{(i-1)/2}} c_{\ell_{2t-(i-3)/2}} \sum_{\kappa=(i+1)/2}^{2t-(i-1)/2} c_{\ell_\kappa}$, which, by our assumption of Part ii, is non-zero ($\ell_\kappa = \ell_{2t-\kappa+1} = t - \kappa + 1$ for $1 \le \kappa \le t$); for $i = 2t-1$ we have $\sum_{\kappa=(i+1)/2}^{2t-(i-1)/2} c_{\ell_\kappa} = \sum_{\kappa=t}^{t+1} c_{\ell_\kappa} = 2c_1 \neq 0$. (Cf. [18, Proof of Theorem 11].) □

The early termination algorithm selects two random field elements $\omega, \omega' \in S$ uniformly from a sufficiently large finite set of field elements $S \subseteq \mathsf{K}$ and computes the coefficients of Λ by a linear system solver for the Toeplitz matrix

$$Z^{[\infty]} = \begin{bmatrix} a_0+\omega' & a_1+\omega' & \cdots & a_{2t-1}+\omega' & a_{2t}+\omega' & \cdots \\ a_{-1}+\omega' & a_0+\omega' & \ddots & a_{2t-2}+\omega' & a_{2t-1}+\omega' & \cdots \\ \vdots & \ddots & & \vdots & \vdots & \\ a_{1-2t}+\omega' & & \cdots & a_0+\omega' & a_1+\omega' & \cdots \\ \vdots & & & \vdots & \vdots & \ddots \end{bmatrix}. \quad (24)$$

Adding ω' changes f to $f + \omega'$ (cf. [18, Section 3.4]) and constitutes a rank 1 update in H_B in (20) that in Theorem 4.3.ii is shown to make with high probability all 1×1, $2 \times 2, \ldots, \tau \times \tau$ leading principal submatrices non-singular, where $\tau = 2t-1$ if $\delta_1 = 0$, that is if g has a non-zero constant term, and where $\tau = 2t+1$ otherwise. Although t and τ are unknown, one can now use Trench's $O(t^2)$ Toeplitz solver, or the asymptotically faster algorithms in [6] of arithmetic complexity $O(t(\log t)^2 \operatorname{loglog}(t))$, for locating the first singular leading principal submatrix and for computing Λ. The additive constant ω' can be avoided, that is setting $\omega' = 0$ in (24), if one uses Gaussian elimination or a block Toeplitz solver with 2×2 blocks.

Remark 4.2 The argument used for odd i in the proof of Lemma 4.3 relates to an old open question in [18, Footnote in the Proof of Theorem 4], where the authors interpolate the polynomial $f(x_1, \ldots, x_n) = \sum_{j=1}^t c_j x_1^{e_{j,1}} \cdots x_n^{e_{j,n}}$ with $c_j \neq 0$ from $a_i = f(\omega_1^i, \ldots, \omega_n^i)$. If we use the sequence $a_0, a_1, \ldots, a_{2t-1}$, we need to prove for indeterminate variables $y_1, \ldots, y_n$ and term values $\beta_j = y_1^{e_{j,1}} \cdots y_n^{e_{j,n}}$ the non-vanishing of the determinantal polynomial expression, for $i = 2, 3, \ldots, t$:

$$\begin{aligned} 0 \neq \sum_{J=\{j_1,\ldots,j_i\}} c_{j_1} \cdots c_{j_i} \cdot \det\left(\begin{bmatrix} 1 & 1 & \cdots & 1 \\ \beta_{j_1} & \beta_{j_2} & \cdots & \beta_{j_i} \\ \vdots & \vdots & \ddots & \vdots \\ \beta_{j_1}^{i-1} & \beta_{j_2}^{i-1} & \cdots & \beta_{j_i}^{i-1} \end{bmatrix}\right)^2 \\ = \sum_{J=\{j_1,\ldots,j_i\}} c_{j_1} \cdots c_{j_i} \cdot \prod_{1 \le v < u \le i} (\beta_{j_u} - \beta_{j_v})^2. \quad (25) \end{aligned}$$

We assume that the β_j are ordered lexicographically $\beta_1 \succ \ldots \succ \beta_t$. The difficulty is that the highest ordered term in the expansion of the products in (25) is $\beta_1^{2i-2} \cdots \beta_{i-1}^2$ and occurs with coefficients $c_1 \cdots c_{i-1} c_\nu$ where $\nu = i, \ldots, t$. As in the proof of Lemma 4.3, we may make $(\sum_{\nu=i}^{t} c_\nu) \neq 0$ by adding a random constant to f, that is, to a_i, but then we may have $t + 1$ terms. In [18, Section 3.2] the sequence is shifted by one index to $a_1, \ldots, a_{2t}$ in order to avoid the increase in the number of terms. Because we exploit the symmetry of the evaluation points in (20), we cannot utilize that shift for interpolating the Laurent polynomial (16) (see also [18, Proof of Theorem 11]). However, our Theorem 4.3.i yields early termination on all submatrices of even dimensions in any case. □

5. CONCLUSIONS AND FUTURE WORK

We presented two methods for the black-box interpolation of a sparse polynomial f in the Chebyshev basis. The first approach was a generalization of the Lakshman-Saunders algorithm [21]. This was used as part of a list-decoding interpolation procedure, which was shown to be better than majority-rule interpolation when the interpolant is known to have at most two terms. In the case that $f \in \mathbb{R}[x]$, it is shown that list-decoding interpolation will identify f.

The other interpolation procedure reduces the problem of sparse interpolation in the Chebyshev basis to sparse interpolation of a Laurent polynomial in the monomial basis. This was adapted to early termination, such that we can probabilistically determine t and f from $2t + 2$ evaluations.

We conjecture that, for any sparsity bound B and sufficiently large error bound E, one can perform error-correcting interpolation with fewer than the bound of $(2B+1)E$ errors, a naive bound due to majority-rule interpolation. We also hope to adapt our new interpolation algorithm of Section 4 to error correction.

6. ACKNOWLEDGEMENTS

We would like to thank the anonymous referees for their constructive comments, and for bringing [9] to our attention. This research was supported in part by NSERC (Arnold) and the National Science Foundation under Grants CCF-1115772 and CCF-1421128 (Kaltofen).

7. REFERENCES

[1] A. Arnold, M. Giesbrecht, and D. S. Roche. Sparse interpolation over finite fields via low-order roots of unity. In *Proc. 39th Internat. Symp. Symbolic Algebraic Comput.*, ISSAC '14, pages 27–34. ACM, 2014.

[2] M. Ben-Or and P. Tiwari. A deterministic algorithm for sparse multivariate polynomial interpolation. In *Proc. Twentieth Annual ACM Symp. Theory Comput.*, pages 301–309, New York, N.Y., 1988. ACM Press.

[3] R. E. Blahut. A universal Reed-Solomon decoder. *IBM J. Res. Develop.*, 18(2):943–959, Mar. 1984.

[4] A. Borodin and P. Tiwari. On the decidability of sparse univariate polynomial interpolation. *Computational Complexity*, 1:67–90, 1991.

[5] B. Boyer, M. Comer, and E. Kaltofen. Sparse polynomial interpolation by variable shift in the presence of noise and outliers in the evaluations. In R. Feng, W.-s. Lee, and Y. Sato, editors, *Computer Mathematics*, pages 183–197. Springer Berlin Heidelberg, 2014.

[6] R. P. Brent, F. G. Gustavson, and D. Y. Y. Yun. Fast solution of Toeplitz systems of equations and computation of Padé approximants. *J. Algorithms*, 1:259–295, 1980.

[7] C. Brezinski. *History of Continued Fractions and Padé Approximants.* Springer Verlag, Heidelberg, Germany, 1991.

[8] M. T. Comer, E. L. Kaltofen, and C. Pernet. Sparse polynomial interpolation and berlekamp/massey algorithms that correct outlier errors in input values. In *Proc. 37th Internat. Symp. Symbolic Algebraic Comput.*, ISSAC '12, pages 138–145. ACM, 2012.

[9] D. K. Dimitrov and F. R. Rafaeli. Descartes' rule of signs for orthogonal polynomials. *East J. Approx.*, 15(2):233–262, 2009.

[10] S. Garg and Éric. Schost. Interpolation of polynomials given by straight-line programs. *Theoretical Comput. Sci.*, 410(27-29):2659–2662, 2009.

[11] M. Giesbrecht, E. Kaltofen, and W.-s. Lee. Algorithms for computing sparsest shifts of polynomials in power, chebyshev, and pochhammer bases. *J. Symb. Comput.*, 36(3-4):401–424, 2003.

[12] M. Giesbrecht, G. Labahn, and W. Lee. Symbolic-numeric sparse polynomial interpolation in Chebyshev basis and trigonometric interpolation. In *Proc. Workshop on Computer Algebra in Scientific Computation (CASC)*, pages 195–205, 2004. https://cs.uwaterloo.ca/~mwg/files/triginterp.pdf.

[13] M. Giesbrecht, G. Labahn, and W. Lee. Symbolic-numeric sparse interpolation of multivariate polynomials. *J. Symbolic Comput.*, 44:943–959, 2009.

[14] M. Giesbrecht and D. Roche. Interpolation of shifted-lacunary polynomials. *Computational Complexity*, 19(3):333–354, 2010.

[15] M. Giesbrecht and D. Roche. Diversification improves interpolation. In A. Leykin, editor, *Proc. 36th Internat. Symp. Symbolic Algebraic Comput.*, pages 123–130, New York, N. Y., 2011. Association for Computing Machinery.

[16] D. Y. Grigoriev and M. Karpinski. A zero-test and an interpolation algorithm for the shifted sparse polynomials. In *Proc. AAECC-10*, volume 673 of *Lect. Notes Comput. Sci.*, pages 162–169. Springer Verlag, 1993.

[17] E. Kaltofen. Fifteen years after DSC and WLSS2 What parallel computations I do today [Invited lecture at PASCO 2010]. In *Proc. 2010 Internat. Workshop on Parallel Symbolic Comput.*, PASCO '10', pages 10–17, 2010. URL: http://www.math.ncsu.edu/~kaltofen/bibliography/10/Ka10_pasco.pdf.

[18] E. Kaltofen and W.-s. Lee. Early termination in sparse interpolation algorithms. *Journal of Symbolic Computation*, 36(3):365–400, 2003.

[19] E. Kaltofen and Z. Yang. Sparse multivariate function recovery with a high error rate in evaluations. In K. Nabeshima, editor, *Proc. 39th Internat. Symp. Symbolic Algebraic Comput.*, pages 280–287, New York, N. Y., 2014. Association for Computing Machinery. URL: http://www.math.ncsu.edu/~kaltofen/bibliography/14/KaYa14.pdf.

[20] E. L. Kaltofen and C. Pernet. Sparse polynomial interpolation codes and their decoding beyond half the minimum distance. In *Proc. 39th Internat. Symp. Symbolic Algebraic Comput.*, ISSAC '14, pages 272–279. ACM, 2014.

[21] Y. N. Lakshman and B. D. Saunders. Sparse polynomial interpolation in non-standard bases. *SIAM J. Comput.*, 24(2):387–397, 1995.

[22] Lakshman Y. N. and B. D. Saunders. Sparse shifts for univariate polynomials. *Applic. Algebra Engin. Commun. Comput.*, 7(5):351–364, 1996.

[23] N. Obrechkoff. On the roots of algebraic equations. *Annuaire University of Sofia Phys.-Math. Fac.*, 19:43–76, 1923.

Output-Sensitive Algorithms for Sumset and Sparse Polynomial Multiplication

Andrew Arnold
Symbolic Computation Group
University of Waterloo
Waterloo, Ontario, Canada
www.andrewarnold.ca

Daniel S. Roche
Computer Science Department
United States Naval Academy
Annapolis, Maryland, USA
www.usna.edu/cs/roche

ABSTRACT

We present randomized algorithms to compute the sumset (Minkowski sum) of two integer sets, and to multiply two univariate integer polynomials given by sparse representations. Our algorithm for sumset has cost softly linear in the combined size of the inputs and output. This is used as part of our sparse multiplication algorithm, whose cost is softly linear in the combined size of the inputs, output, and the sumset of the supports of the inputs. As a subroutine, we present a new method for computing the coefficients of a sparse polynomial, given a set containing its support. Our multiplication algorithm extends to multivariate Laurent polynomials over finite fields and rational numbers. Our techniques are based on sparse interpolation algorithms and results from analytic number theory.

Categories and Subject Descriptors

F.2.1 [**Analysis of algorithms and problem complexity**]: Numerical algorithms and problems—*Computations on polynomials*; G.3 [**Probability and statistics**]: Probabilistic algorithms; I.1.2 [**Symbolic and algebraic manipulation**]: Algorithms

General Terms: Algorithms.

Keywords: Polynomial multiplication; sparse interpolation, computational complexity; sumset; Minkowski sum.

1. INTRODUCTION

Sparse polynomials are a fundamental object in computer algebra. Computer algebra programs including Maple, Mathematica, Sage, and Singular use a sparse representation by default for multivariate polynomials, and there has been considerable recent work on how to efficiently store and compute with sparse polynomials [8, 10, 19, 21, 14].

However, despite the memory advantage of sparse polynomials, the alternative dense representation is still widely used for an obvious reason: speed. It is now classical [4] that two degree-D dense polynomials can be multiplied in softly linear time: $\mathcal{O}(D \log D \log\log D)$ ring operations, and even better in many cases [12]. By contrast, two size-T sparse polynomials require $\mathcal{O}(T^2)$ operations, and this excludes the potentially significant cost of exponent arithmetic.

Much of the recent work on sparse arithmetic has focused on "somewhat dense" or structured cases, where the sparsity of the product is sub-quadratic [19, 21, 14]. At the same time, sparse interpolation algorithms, which in the fastest case can learn an unknown T-sparse polynomial from $\mathcal{O}(T)$ evaluations, have gained renewed interest [7, 17, 6, 2].

Most closely related to the current work, [15] recently presented algorithms to discover the coefficients of a sparse polynomial product, provided a list of the exponents and some preprocessing. In the context of pattern matching problems, [5] gave a Las Vegas algorithm to multiply sparse polynomials with nonnegative integer coefficients whose cost is $\widetilde{\mathcal{O}}(T \log^2 D)$.

A remaining question is whether output-sensitive sparse multiplication is possible in time comparable to that of dense multiplication. This paper answers that question, with three provisos: First, our complexity is proportional to the "structural sparsity" of the output that accounts for exponent collisions but not coefficient cancellations; second, our algorithms are randomized and may produce incorrect results with controllably low probability; and third, we ignore logarithmic factors in the size of the input.

To explain the first proviso, define for a polynomial F its *support* $\mathsf{supp}(F)$ to be the set of exponents of nonzero terms in F. The *sparsity* of F, written $\#F$, is exactly $\#\,\mathsf{supp}(F)$. For two polyomials F and G, we have $\#\,\mathsf{supp}(FG) \le \#F \cdot \#G$. But in many cases the set of *possible exponents*

$$\mathsf{poss}(F, G) \overset{\text{def}}{=} \{e_F + e_G : e_F \in \mathsf{supp}(F), e_G \in \mathsf{supp}(G)\}$$

is much smaller than $\#F \cdot \#G$. This *structural sparsity* $T = \#\,\mathsf{poss}(F, G)$, is an upper bound on the actual sparsity $S = \#\,\mathsf{supp}(FG)$ of the product. Strict inequality $S < T$ occurs only in the presence of *coefficient cancellations*. Part of our algorithm's cost depends only on the actual sparsity, and part depends on the potentially-larger structural sparsity.

Our algorithms have not yet been carefully implemented, and we do not claim that they would be faster than the excellent software of [10, 20] and others for a wide range of practical problems. However, this complexity improvement indicates that the barriers between sparse and dense arithmetic may be weaker than we once thought, and we hope our work will lead to practical improvements in the near future.

ISSAC'15, July 6–9, 2015, Bath, United Kingdom.

ACM 978-1-4503-3435-8/15/07 ...$15.00.
DOI: http://dx.doi.org/10.1145/2755996.2756653.

1.1 Our contributions

Our main algorithm is summarized in Theorem 1.1. Here and throughout, we rely on a version of "soft-oh" notation that also accounts for a bound μ on the probability of failure: $\widetilde{\mathcal{O}}_\mu(\phi) \stackrel{\text{def}}{=} \mathcal{O}(\phi \cdot \mathsf{polylog}(\phi/\mu))$, for any function ϕ, where $\mathsf{polylog}$ means $\log^c$ for some fixed $c > 0$ [11, see sec. 25.7].

THEOREM 1.1. *Given $F, G \in \mathbb{Z}[x]$ with degree bound $D > \deg F + \deg G$ and height bound $C \geq \|F\|_\infty + \|G\|_\infty$, and $\mu \in (0,1)$, Algorithm SparseMultZZ correctly computes the product $H = FG$ with probability exceeding $1-\mu$, using worst-case expected $\widetilde{\mathcal{O}}_\mu(S \log C + T \log D)$ bit operations, where $S = \#\,\mathsf{supp}(FG)$ and $T = \#\,\mathsf{poss}(F,G)$ are the actual and structural sparsity of the product, respectively.*

Our algorithm relies on two subroutines, both of which are based on techniques from sparse interpolation and rely on number-theoretic results on the availability of primes.

The first subroutine Sumset$(\mathcal{A}, \mathcal{B})$ computes the *sumset* of two sets of integers $\mathcal{A}$ and $\mathcal{B}$, defined as

$$\mathcal{A} \oplus \mathcal{B} \stackrel{\text{def}}{=} \{a + b : a \in \mathcal{A}, b \in \mathcal{B}\}.$$

This algorithm, which may be of independent interest, has softly-linear complexity in the size of the output $\mathcal{A} \oplus \mathcal{B}$.

The second subroutine SparseMulCoeffs$(F, G, \mathbb{S})$ requires a set containing $\mathsf{supp}(FG)$ in order to compute FG in time softly-linear in the input and output sizes. It is based on an algorithm in [15], but is more efficient for large exponents.

The main steps of our multiplication algorithm are:

1. Use Sumset to compute $\mathsf{poss}(F, G)$.
2. Run SparseMulCoeffs with $\mathbb{S} = \mathsf{poss}(F, G)$ but with smaller coefficients, to discover the true $\mathsf{supp}(FG)$.
3. Run SparseMulCoeffs again, with the smaller exponent set $\mathsf{supp}(FG)$ but with the full coefficients.

Steps 1 and 2 work with a size-T exponent set but with small coefficients, and both contribute $\widetilde{\mathcal{O}}_\mu(T \log D)$ to the overall bit complexity. Step 3 uses the size-S true support but with the full coefficients, and requires $\widetilde{\mathcal{O}}_\mu(S(\log D + \log C))$ bit operations, for a total of $\widetilde{\mathcal{O}}_\mu(T \log D + S \log C)$.

1.2 Organization of the paper

Section 2 states our notational conventions and some standard results, and Section 3 contains the technical number theoretic results on which we base our randomizations.

Section 4 revisits and adapts our sparse interpolation algorithm from ISSAC 2014 that will be a subroutine for our sumset algorithm, presented in section 5.

Our new method to find the coefficients, once the support is known, is presented in Section 6. This is then used in concert with our sumset algorithm in Section 7 to describe fully the algorithm of Theorem 1.1, and also to explain how this can be easily extended to output-sensitive sparse multiplication over $\mathsf{R}[x_1^{\pm 1}, \ldots, x_n^{\pm 1}]$, where R is $\mathbb{Z}_m$, $\mathbb{Q}$, or $\mathsf{GF}(p^e)$.

2. BACKGROUND AND PRELIMINARIES

We count the cost of our algorithms in terms of bit complexity on a random-access machine. We state their costs using $\widetilde{\mathcal{O}}_\mu$ notation, meaning that our algorithms have a factor $\log^c \frac{1}{\mu}$ in the running time. We can make $c = 1$ by running the entire algorithm with error bound $\frac{2}{3}$ some $\mathcal{O}(\log \frac{1}{\mu})$ times, then returning the most frequent result.

Our main algorithm depends on an unknown number-theoretic constant, as discussed in Section 3. Thus we have proven only the *existence* of a Monte Carlo algorithm. We also discuss how this could be easily handled in practice.

Our randomized procedures return either the correct answer (with controllable probability $1 - \mu$), or an incorrect answer, or the symbol `Fail`. Whenever a subroutine returns `Fail`, we assume the calling procedure returns `Fail` as well.

2.1 Notation and representations

We let R denote a commutative ring with identity. For $F \in \mathsf{R}[x]$ we let $\langle F \rangle \subset \mathsf{R}[x]$ denote the ideal generated by F. For $n, m \in \mathbb{Z}$, $m > 0$, we let $n \,\overline{\mathrm{rem}}\, m$ and $n \,\mathrm{rem}\, m$ denote the integers $s \in [0, m)$ and $t \in [-m/2, m/2)$ respectively, such that $n \equiv s \equiv t \pmod m$. We write $\mathbb{Z}_m$ for $\mathbb{Z}/m\mathbb{Z}$, typically represented as $\{n \text{ rem } m | n \in \mathbb{Z}\}$.

Unless otherwise stated we assume $F \in \mathsf{R}[x]$ is of the form

$$F(x) = \textstyle\sum_{1 \leq i \leq S} c_i x^{e_i}, \tag{1}$$

with coefficients $c_i \in \mathsf{R}$ and exponents $e_i \in \mathbb{Z}_{\geq 0}$. Often we assume each $c_i \neq 0$ and the exponents are sorted $e_1 < \cdots < e_S$, but it is sometimes useful to relax these conditions.

We write $S \geq \#F$ and $D > \deg F$ for the sparsity and degree bounds. When $\mathsf{R} = \mathbb{Z}$ we write $C > \|F\|_\infty \stackrel{\text{def}}{=} \max_i |c_i|$ for the *height* of F. We also use the norm $\|F\|_1 = \sum_i |c_i|$.

More generally, we consider multivariate Laurent polynomials $F = \sum_{i=1}^{S} c_i x_1^{e_{i1}} \cdots x_n^{e_{in}} \in \mathsf{R}[x_1^{\pm 1}, \ldots, x_n^{\pm 1}]$. In the case $\mathsf{R} = \mathbb{Z}$, the *sparse representation* of F consists of a tuple (n, C, D, S), followed by a list of S tuples $(c_i, (e_{i1}, \ldots, e_{in}))$, where each c_i is stored using $\Theta(\log C)$ bits and each e_{ij} is stored using $\Theta(\log D)$ bits. The total size in this case is $\Theta(S \log C + Sn \log D)$. When R is instead a finite ring, C is omitted and each c_i is stored using $\Theta(\log |\mathsf{R}|)$ bits.

When multiplying $F, G \in \mathbb{Z}[x]$, we assume shared bounds C and D so that total input/output size is

$$\widetilde{\mathcal{O}}((\#F + \#G + \#(FG))(\log C + \log D)), \tag{2}$$

given that $\|FG\|_\infty 1 < C^2 \min(\#F, \#G)$.

The *dense representation* of an n-variate polynomial F is an n-dimensional array of D^n coefficients, where exponents are implicitly stored as array indices. In the case that $\mathsf{R} = \mathbb{Z}$ with bound C as above, this requires $\Theta(D^n \log C)$ bits.

The terms "sparse polynomial" and "dense polynomial" refer only to the choice of representation, and not to the relative number of nonzero coefficients. Typically, we assume F is sparse and reserve $\tilde{F}$ to indicate a dense polynomial. Converting between the sparse and dense representations has softly linear cost in the combined input/output size.

When computing a sumset $A \oplus B$, we assume that every integer in A or B is represented using $\Theta(\log D)$ bits, where $D > \max(\|\mathcal{A}\|_\infty, \|\mathcal{B}\|_\infty)$.

2.2 Integer and polynomial arithmetic

We cite the following results from integer and polynomial arithmetic, which we use throughout.

FACT 2.1. *[11, Ch. 8, 10] The following can be computed in softly-linear time in the bit-length of the inputs:*

- *$m \pm n$, mn, m rem n, $m \,\overline{\mathrm{rem}}\, n$, for any $m, n \in \mathbb{Z}$*
- *Arithmetic in $\mathbb{Z}_m$ for any $m \in \mathbb{Z}_{>0}$*
- *Arithmetic on dense polynomials in $\mathbb{Z}_m[x]$*
- *CRT: given integers $(v_i, m_i), \ldots, (v_N, m_N)$, determine $v \in \mathbb{Z}$, $v < \prod_i m_i$, such that $\forall i, v \equiv v_i \pmod{m_i}$.*

Procedure GetPrime(λ, μ)

Input: $\lambda \geq 21$; $\mu \in (0, 1)$.
Output: Integer $p \in (\lambda, 2\lambda]$, s.t. $\Pr[p \text{ not prime}] < \mu$.

repeat $m = \lceil (5/6) \ln \lambda \ln(1/\mu) \rceil$ **times**
  $p \leftarrow$ random odd integer from $(\lambda, 2\lambda] \cap \mathbb{Z}$
  if *p is prime* **then return** p
return Fail

Procedure GetVanishPrime(S, D, γ, μ)

Input: Integers $S, D \in \mathbb{Z}_{>0}$; $\gamma \in (0, 1]$; $\mu \in (0, 1)$.
Output: Integer p, s.t. for any set $\mathbb{S}$ satisfying $\#\mathbb{S} \leq S$ and $\|\mathbb{S}\|_\infty < D$, with probability at least $1 - \mu$, p is a γ-vanish-prime for $\mathbb{S}$.

$\lambda \leftarrow \max\left(21, \frac{10}{3\mu} \min\left(S, \frac{1}{1-\gamma}\right) \ln D\right)$
return GetPrime(λ, $\mu/2$)

Assume $F \in \mathbb{Z}[x]$ as in (1) with bounds D, S, and C as described above. Our algorithm performs arithmetic on modular images of F. For $F \in \mathbb{Z}_m[x]$, we represent $F(x) \bmod (x^p - 1) \in \mathbb{Z}_m[x]/\langle x^p - 1\rangle$ by the remainder from dividing $\mathbb{Z}_m(x)$ by $(x^p - 1)$. Note we treat $F(x) \text{ rem } (x^p - 1)$ and $F(x) \bmod (x^p - 1)$ as elements of $\mathsf{R}[x]$ and $\mathsf{R}[x]/\langle x^p - 1\rangle$ respectively. To reduce a sparse polynomial $F \bmod (x^p - 1)$, we reduce each exponent modulo p, and then add like-degree terms. By Fact 2.1, we have:

COROLLARY 2.2. *Given any $F \in \mathbb{Z}_m[x]$, we can compute $F \bmod (x^p - 1)$ using $\widetilde{\mathcal{O}}(S(\log D + \log m))$ bit operations.*

3. NUMBER-THEORETIC SUBROUTINES

3.1 Choosing primes

We first recall how to choose a random prime number.

FACT 3.1 (COROLLARY 3, [22]). *If $\lambda \geq 21$, then the number of primes in $(\lambda, 2\lambda]$ is at least $3\lambda/(5 \ln \lambda)$.*

We test if p is prime in $\mathcal{O}(\mathsf{polylog}(p))$ time via the method in [1]. This test and Fact 3.1 lead to procedure GetPrime.

LEMMA 3.2. *GetPrime(λ, μ) works as stated and has bit complexity $\widetilde{\mathcal{O}_\mu}(\mathsf{polylog}(\lambda))$.*

PROOF. The stated cost follows from fast primality testing due to [1]. The probability that any chosen p is prime is at least $6/(5 \ln \lambda)$, from Fact 3.1. Therefore, using the fact that $(1 - x) < \exp(-x)$ for any nonzero $x \in \mathbb{R}$, the probability that none of the chosen p are prime is at most $\left(1 - \frac{6}{5 \ln \lambda}\right)^m < \exp\left(\frac{-6m}{5 \ln \lambda}\right) \leq \mu$, as desired. □

It is frequently useful to choose a random prime that divides very few of the integers in some unknown finite set $\mathbb{S} \subset \mathbb{Z}$. If a fraction of γ integers in $\mathbb{S}$ do not vanish modulo p, then we call p a *γ-vanish-prime* for $\mathbb{S}$. We call a 1-vanish-prime for $\mathbb{S}$ a *good vanish-prime*. Procedure GetVanishPrime shows how to choose a random γ-vanish-prime.

LEMMA 3.3. *Procedure GetVanishPrime works as stated to produce a γ-vanish-prime p satisfying*

$$p \in \mathcal{O}\left(\frac{1}{\mu} \min\left(S, \frac{1}{1-\gamma}\right) \log D\right)$$

and has bit complexity $\mathsf{polylog}(p)$.

Procedure GetDiffPrime(S, D, γ, μ)

Input: Integers $S, D \in \mathbb{Z}_{>0}$; $\gamma \in (0, 1]$; $\mu \in (0, 1)$.
Output: Integer p, s.t. for any set $\mathbb{S}$ satisfying $\#\mathbb{S} \leq S$ and $\mathsf{diam}(\mathbb{S}) < D$, with probability at least $1 - \mu$, p is a γ-difference-prime for $\mathbb{S}$.

$\lambda \leftarrow \frac{10}{3\mu}(S - 1) \min\left(S, \frac{1}{1-\gamma}\right) \ln D$
if $\lambda < 21$ **then return** GetPrime($21, \mu/2$)
else if $\lambda > D$ **then return** GetPrime($D, \mu/2$)
else return GetPrime($\lambda, \mu/2$)

PROOF. Let $\mathbb{S}$ be any subset of integers with $\#\mathbb{S} \leq S$ and $\|S\|_\infty < D$. Write $M = \prod_{a \in \mathbb{S}} |a| < D^S$, and write k for the number of "bad primes" for which more than $(1 - \gamma)S$ elements of $\mathbb{S}$ vanish modulo p. Since each $p \geq \lambda$, this means that $\lambda^{(1-\gamma)Sk} \leq M$, and because $M < D^S$, $k < \ln D/((1 - \gamma) \ln \lambda)$ is an upper bound on the number of bad primes.

If $1 - \gamma$ is very small, we instead use a similar argument to say that the number of primes for which *any* element of $\mathbb{S}$ vanishes is at most $k < S \ln D / \ln \lambda$.

Then Fact 3.1 guarantees the prevalence of bad primes among all primes in $(\lambda, 2\lambda)$ is at most $\mu/2$, so the probability of getting a bad prime, or of erroneously returning a composite p, is bounded by μ. □

3.2 Avoiding collisions

A closely related problem is to choose p so that most integers in a finite set $\mathbb{S}$ are unique modulo p. We say that $a \in \mathbb{S}$ *collides* modulo p if there exists $b \in \mathbb{S}$ with $a \equiv b \pmod p$. We say p is a *γ-difference-prime for* $\mathbb{S}$ if the fraction of integers in $\mathbb{S}$ which do not collide modulo p is at least γ. A 1-difference-prime is called a *good difference-prime for* $\mathbb{S}$. Procedure GetDiffPrime shows how to compute difference-primes, conditioned on the *diameter* of the unknown set $\mathbb{S}$:

$$\mathsf{diam}(\mathbb{S}) \stackrel{\text{def}}{=} \max(\mathbb{S}) - \min(\mathbb{S}).$$

LEMMA 3.4. *Procedure GetDiffPrime has bit complexity $\mathsf{polylog}(p)$ and works as stated to produce a γ-difference-prime p satisfying $p \in \mathcal{O}(D)$ and*

$$p \in \mathcal{O}\left(\frac{1}{\mu} S \min\left(S, \frac{1}{1-\gamma}\right) \log D\right).$$

PROOF. Let $\mathbb{S}$ be any set as described. An element $a \in \mathbb{S}$ collides modulo p iff the product of differences $\prod_{b \in \mathbb{S}, b \neq a}(a - b)$ vanishes modulo p. If $p > D$ this can never happen. Otherwise, as each such product is at most $\mathsf{diam}(\mathbb{S})^{S-1} < D^{S-1}$, the result follows from the Lemma 3.3, setting the D of the lemma to D^{S-1}. □

Our algorithms often perform arithmetic modulo $(x^p - 1)$. Similar to the notion of collisions above for a set of integers modulo p, we say two distinct terms cx^e and $c'x^{e'}$ of $F \in \mathsf{R}[x]$ *collide* modulo $(x^p - 1)$ if $e \equiv e' \pmod p$.

Essentially, reduction modulo $(x^p - 1)$ "hashes" exponent $e \in \mathsf{supp}(F)$ to $e \,\overline{\text{rem}}\, p$. If p is a good difference-prime for $\mathsf{supp}(F)$ and q is a good vanish-prime for the coefficients of F, then $F \text{ rem } (x^p - 1)$ with coefficients reduced modulo q has the same sparsity as F itself.

3.3 Primes in arithmetic progressions

Sometimes we implicitly reduce exponents modulo p by evaluating at pth roots of unity. In such cases we need to

Procedure GetPrimRoots(D, T, C, μ)

Input: $D \geq \deg F$; $T \geq \#F$; $C \geq \|F\|_\infty$; $\mu \in (0, 1)$; where $F \in \mathbb{Z}[x]$ is fixed but unspecified.

Output: Prime p, primes $(q_1, \ldots, q_k)$, and integers $(\omega_1, \ldots, \omega_k)$; or **Fail**.

1 $m \leftarrow \lceil \lg \frac{2}{\mu} \rceil$
2 $\lambda \leftarrow \max\left(786, \lambda_0, \frac{20}{3\mu} mT(T-1)\ln D, 1.35 \ln^{3.13}(2C)\right)$
3 $a \leftarrow \lceil 1.1 \ln(2C) \ln^2 \lambda \rceil$
4 **repeat** m **times**
5     $p \leftarrow$GetPrime($\lambda, \frac{\mu}{4m}$)
6     $\mathcal{A} \leftarrow a$ distinct even integers in $[2, 2\lambda^{0.89}]$
7     $Q, W \leftarrow$ empty lists
8   **foreach** $a \in \mathcal{A}$ **do**
9         $q \leftarrow ap + 1$
10         $\zeta \leftarrow$ random nonzero element of $\mathbb{Z}_q$
11   **if** *q is prime and* $\zeta^a \bmod q \neq 1$ **then**
12   Add q to Q and $\omega = \zeta^a$ to W
13   **if** $\prod_{q \in Q} q \geq 2C$ **then return** p, Q, and W
14 **return Fail**

construct primes q such that $p|(q-1)$, and to find pth roots of unity modulo each q.

In principle, this procedure is no different than the previous ones, as there is ample practical and theoretical evidence to suggest that the prevalence of primes in arithmetic progressions without common divisors is roughly the same as their prevalence over the integers in general.

However, the closest to Fact 3.1 that we can get here is as follows, which is a special case of Lemma 7 in [9].

LEMMA 3.5. *There exists an absolute constant λ_0 such that, for all $\lambda \geq \lambda_0$, and for all but at most $\lambda/\ln^2 \lambda$ primes p in the range $(\lambda, 2\lambda]$, there are at least $\lambda^{0.89}/\ln \lambda$ primes q in the range $(\lambda^{1.89}, 2\lambda^{1.89}]$ such that $p|(q-1)$.*

PROOF. Set $K = 0.53$, which means $(1.89)^{-1} < K < \frac{17}{32}$. Fixing $s = 1$, and for any $R \geq 2$, Lemma 7 in [9] guarantees the existence of positive constants α_K and x_K such that the following holds: For all $x > \max(x_K, R^{1/K})$, and for all but $R/\ln^2 R$ integers $r \in (R, 2R]$, there are at least $\alpha_K x/(\varphi(r)\ln x)$ primes q in the range $(x, 2x]$ such that $r|(q-1)$, where $\varphi(r)$ is Euler's totient function.

Setting $\lambda_0 = \max(x_K, 3.78/\alpha_K)$, and letting $R = \lambda$, $r = p$, and $x = \lambda^{1.89}$, the statement of our lemma holds because

$$\varphi(r)\ln x = (p-1)\ln \lambda^{1.89} < 3.78\lambda \ln \lambda,$$

thus
$$\frac{\alpha_K x}{\varphi(r)\ln x} = \frac{\alpha_K \lambda^{1.89}}{(p-1)\ln \lambda^{1.89}} > \frac{\lambda^{0.89}}{\ln \lambda}. \quad \square$$

Lemma 3.5 forms the basis for Algorithm GetPrimRoots, where we assume that the constant λ_0 is given. Since this constant has not actually been computed, a reasonable strategy would be to choose some small "guess" for λ_0 and run the algorithm until it does not report failure. If the algorithm fails, it could be due to the random prime p being an "exception" in Lemma 3.5, or due to unlucky guesses for the primitive roots ζ, or due to the guessed constant λ_0 being too small. Because our primality tests are deterministic, failure due to λ_0 being too small is detectable by the algorithm returning **Fail**.

We state the running time and correctness, assuming λ_0 is sufficiently large, as follows.

LEMMA 3.6. *Procedure GetPrimRoots has worst-case bit complexity $\widetilde{\mathcal{O}}_\mu(\log C \cdot \mathsf{polylog}(T + \log D))$. With probability at least $1-\mu$, it returns a good difference-prime p for F, primes $q_1, \ldots, q_k$ such that $\prod_i q_i \geq 2C$, and pth primitive roots modulo each q_i, $\omega_1, \ldots, \omega_k$.*

PROOF. The lower bound $\lambda \geq \max(786, 1.35\ln^{3.13}(2C))$ guarantees that there are sufficiently many even integers in the range $[2, 2\lambda^{0.89}]$ in order for Step 6 to be valid, since for any $\lambda \geq 786$, we have $\lambda^{0.89} > \lambda^{.32}\ln^2 \lambda > 1.1\ln(2C)\ln^2 \lambda$.

For the running time, the outer loop does not affect the complexity in our notation because $m \in O(\log \frac{1}{\mu}) \in \widetilde{\mathcal{O}}_\mu(1)$. Observe also that

$$\log \lambda \in \mathsf{polylog}\left(\lambda_0 + T + \log D + \log C + \tfrac{1}{\mu}\right).$$

The running time is dominated by the AKS primality tests in the inner loop, which are performed $O(m \log C \mathsf{polylog}(\lambda))$ times, each at cost $O(\mathsf{polylog}(\lambda))$, giving the stated worst-case bit complexity.

All of the checks for primality of p and q_i's, as well as the test that each ω_i is a pth primitive root of unity modulo q_i, are deterministic. Therefore the only possibility that the algorithm returns an incorrect result other than **Fail** is the probability that p is not a good difference-prime for $\mathsf{supp}(F)$. According to the proof of Lemma 3.4, the condition $\lambda > \frac{20}{3\mu} mT(T-1)\ln D$, and using the union bound over all outer loop iterations, the probability that *any* of the chosen p's is not a good difference-prime is less than $\mu/2$.

Consider next a single iteration of the outer loop. This will produce a valid output unless insufficiently many good q_i's and ω_i's are found for that choice of p.

From Fact 3.1 and Lemma 3.5, the probability that p is an exception to the lemma is at most $5/(3\ln \lambda)$, which is less than $\frac{1}{4}$ from the bound $\lambda \geq 786$.

If p is not an exception, then Lemma 3.5 tells us that the probability of each q being prime is at least $\frac{1}{\ln \lambda}$. When q is prime, since prime p divides $(q-1)$, the probability that each ζ^a is a p-PRU in $\mathbb{Z}_q$ is $(p-1)/p$, easily making the total probability of successfully adding to Q and W at each loop iteration at least $0.99/(\ln \lambda)$.

Let $a \geq 1.1\ln(2C)\ln^2 \lambda$ be the size of $\mathcal{A}$. By Hoeffding's inequality ([13], Thm. 1), the probability that fewer than $0.03a/(\ln \lambda)$ integers are added to Q after all iterations of the inner loop is at most

$$\exp(-2a(0.96/\ln \lambda)^2) < \exp(-2.02\ln(2C)) < 0.25,$$

where the last inequality holds because $C \geq 1$.

Therefore, with probability at least $\frac{3}{4}$, and using again $\lambda \geq 786$, at least

$$0.03a/\ln \lambda = 0.033\ln(2C)\ln \lambda > \ln(2C)/\ln \lambda$$

integers are added to Q each time through the inner loop. Since each $q_i > \lambda$, this means $\prod_i q_i > 2C$, and the algorithm will return on Step 13.

Combining with the probability that p is an exception, we conclude that the probability the algorithm does *not* return in each iteration of the outer loop is at most $1/2$. As this is repeated $\lceil \lg \frac{2}{\mu} \rceil$ times, the probability is less than $\mu/2$ that the algorithm returns **Fail**. Using the union bound with the probability that any p is not a good difference-prime, we have the overall failure probability less than μ. $\square$

Procedure SparseInterpBB(F, G, α, r)

Input: $F, G \in \mathbb{Z}_q[x]$; $\alpha \in \mathbb{Z}_q$; $r \in \mathbb{Z}_{>0}$.
Output: $H(\alpha z) \bmod (z^r - 1)$, where $H = FG$.

```
(F̃, G̃) ← (F(αz) rem (z^r − 1), G(αz) rem (z^r − 1))
H̃ ← F̃ · G̃ rem (z^r − 1) via dense arithmetic
return sparse representation of H̃
```

Procedure BasecaseMultiply(F, G, S, μ)

Input: $F, G \in \mathbb{Z}[x]$; $S \geq \#F + \#G + \#(FG)$; $\mu \in (0, 1)$.
Output: $H \in \mathbb{Z}[x]$ such that $\Pr[H \neq FG] < \mu$.

```
q ←GetPrime(2S ‖F‖∞ ‖G‖∞ + 2 deg F + 2 deg G, μ/2)
Call procedure MajorityVoteSparseInterpolate from [3],
  with coefficient field Z_q, sparsity bound S, degree
  bound deg F + deg G, error bound μ/2, and black box
  SparseInterpBB(F, G, ·, ·).
```

4. MULTIPLYING VIA INTERPOLATION

Let $F, G \in \mathbb{Z}[x]$ be sparse polynomials with $C = \|F\|_\infty + \|G\|_\infty$ and $D = \deg F + \deg G$. The subroutine Sumset computes $\mathsf{poss}(F, G)$ by first reducing the degrees and heights of the input polynomials and then multiplying them. However, it cannot perform the multiplication using a recursive call to SparseMultZZ because the degrees are never reduced small enough to allow the use of dense arithmetic in a base case.

Instead, we present here a "base case" algorithm which, given F, G, and a bound $S \geq \#F + \#G + \#(FG)$, computes FG, in time softly linear in $S, \log C$, and $\mathsf{polylog}(D)$. Any algorithm with such running time suffices; we will use our own from [3], which is a Monte Carlo sparse interpolation algorithm for univariate polynomials over finite fields.

To adapt [3] for multiplication over $\mathbb{Z}[x]$, we first choose a "large prime" $q > \max(2C, 2D)$ and treat F, G and their product $H = FG$ as polynomials over $\mathbb{F}_q$. This size of q ensures that no extension fields are necessary. The subroutine SparseInterpBB specifies how the unknown polynomial $H = FG \in \mathbb{F}_q[x]$ will be provided to the algorithm. It exactly matches the sorts of black-box evaluations that [3] requires. The entire procedure is stated as BasecaseMultiply.

LEMMA 4.1. *The algorithm SparseInterpBB works correctly and uses $\widetilde{\mathcal{O}}(S \log D \log q + r \log q)$ bit operations.*

PROOF. Correctness is clear. To compute $F(\alpha z)$, we replace every term cx^e of F and G with $c\alpha^e x^e \in \mathbb{Z}_q$. This costs $\widetilde{\mathcal{O}}(S \log D \log q)$ by binary powering. Reducing modulo $(z^r - 1)$ costs $\widetilde{\mathcal{O}}(S(\log D + \log q))$ by Corollary 2.2. Dense arithmetic costs $\widetilde{\mathcal{O}}(r \log q)$ bit operations by Fact 2.1. Summing these costs yields $\widetilde{\mathcal{O}}(S \log D \log q + r \log q)$. □

LEMMA 4.2. *The algorithm BasecaseMultiply correctly returns the product $H = FG$ with probability at least $1 - \mu$, and has bit complexity $\widetilde{\mathcal{O}_\mu}\left(S \log^2 D \left(\log C + \log D\right)\right)$.*

PROOF. In order to use SparseInterpBB in the algorithm from [3], we simply replace the straight-line program evaluation on the first line of procedure ComputeImage with our procedure SparseInterpBB. Again, note that as the prime q was chosen with $q > 2D$, the MajorityVoteSparseInterpolate algorithm does not need to work over any extension fields.

The correctness is guaranteed by the previous lemma, as well as Theorem 1.1 in [3]. For the bit complexity, in Section 7 of [3], we see that the cost is dominated by $\widetilde{\mathcal{O}_\mu}(\log D)$ calls to the black box evaluation function, each of which is supplied $q \in \widetilde{\mathcal{O}}(C + D)$, and $r \in \widetilde{\mathcal{O}_\mu}(S \log D)$. Applying the bit complexity of Lemma 4.1 gives the stated result. □

5. SUMSET ALGORITHM

Let $\mathcal{A}, \mathcal{B} \in \mathbb{Z} \cap (-D, D)$ be nonempty, $R = \#\mathcal{A} + \#\mathcal{B}$, and $S = \#(\mathcal{A} \oplus \mathcal{B})$ throughout this section. We prove as follows:

THEOREM 5.1. *Procedure Sumset($\mathcal{A}, \mathcal{B}, \mu$) has bit complexity $\widetilde{\mathcal{O}_\mu}(S \log D)$ and produces $\mathcal{A} \oplus \mathcal{B}$ with probability at least $1 - \mu$.*

We compute the sumset $\mathcal{A} \oplus \mathcal{B}$ as $\mathsf{supp}(H)$, $H = FG \in \mathbb{Z}[x^{-1}, x]$, where $F = \sum_{a \in \mathcal{A}} x^a$ and $G = \sum_{b \in \mathcal{B}} x^b$. Here H has exponents in $(-2D, 2D)$ and $\|H\|_\infty < R$. Thus it suffices to construct the exponents of H modulo $\ell \geq 4D$. Moreover, we have $\mathsf{supp}(H) = \mathsf{poss}(F, G)$, and that

$$R - 1 \leq \#(\mathcal{A} \oplus \mathcal{B}) = S \leq R^2. \quad (3)$$

5.1 Estimating sumset output size

We first show how to compute a tighter upper bound on the true value of $S = \#H = \#(A \oplus B)$. To this end, let $p \in \mathcal{O}(D)$ be a good difference-prime for $\mathsf{supp}(H)$, using the naive bound R^2 from (3), and define the $H_1 = F_1 G_1$, where $F_1, G_1 \in \mathbb{Z}[x]$ are defined by

$$F_1 = F \text{ rem } (x^p - 1), \qquad G_1 = G \text{ rem } (x^p - 1).$$

Then $\deg H_1 < 2p$ and each term cx^e of H corresponds to either one or two terms in H_1, of degrees $e \;\overline{\text{rem}}\; p$ and $(e \;\overline{\text{rem}}\; p) + p$. Therefore

$$\#H_1/2 \leq \#H = S \leq \#H_1.$$

We will compute an approximation $S^* \approx S$ such that $S^*/2 < \#H_1 \leq S^*$, and therefore $S^*/4 < S \leq S^*$. To this end we present a test that, given S^*, always accepts if $\#H_1 \leq S^*$ and probably rejects if $\#H_1 > 2S^*$. We do this for S^* initially 2, doubling whenever the test rejects.

Given the current estimate S^*, we next choose a (1/2)-difference-prime q for the support of any $2S^*$-sparse polynomial with degree $2p > \deg H_1$, and compute $H^* = H_1 \bmod (x^q - 1)$. We work modulo $m = R^2 > \|H\|_1 \geq \|H^*\|_\infty$, such that none of the coefficients of H^* vanish modulo m. If H_1 is S^*-sparse then H^* is as well. If H_1 has $2S^*$ terms then, as fewer than S^* terms of H_1 are in collisions, H^* is *not* S^*-sparse. As no terms of H_1 vanish modulo m, additional terms in H_1 can only increase $\#H^*$.

We choose q so that the test is correct with probability at least 3/4. By iterating $\lceil 8 \ln(8/\mu) \rceil$ times, by Hoeffding's inequality, the probability is at least $1 - \mu/4$ that the test runs correctly in at least half of the iterations. As $\#H_1 < 2R^2$, it suffices that the test is correct $\lceil \log_2 R + 1 \rceil$ times.

The Sumset procedure performs this test on lines 3–7. By Corollary 2.2 the respective costs of constructing F^* and $F^* \bmod (R^2, x^q - 1)$ are $\widetilde{\mathcal{O}_\mu}(R \log D)$ and $\widetilde{\mathcal{O}_\mu}(R \log p \log R)$, and similarly for G^*. The cost of the dense arithmetic here is $\widetilde{\mathcal{O}_\mu}(q \log R)$. Given that $p \in \widetilde{\mathcal{O}_\mu}(D), q \in \widetilde{\mathcal{O}_\mu}(S \log p)$, the total bit-cost of this part is $\widetilde{\mathcal{O}_\mu}(S \log D)$.

5.2 Computing sumset

Armed with the bound $S^*/4 < S \le S^*$, we aim to compute $H = FG$. Our approach is to compute images

$$H_1 = F_1 G_1 \mod (\ell^2, x^p - 1),$$
$$H_2 = F((\ell+1)x)G((\ell+1)x) \mod (\ell^2, x^p - 1),$$

for an integer $\ell = 8D \ge \max(\deg H, \|H\|_1)$.

Since the coefficients of H_2 are scaled by powers of $(\ell+1)$, a single term cx^e in the original polynomial H becomes $cx^{e \text{ rem } p}$ in H_1 and $c(\ell+1)^e x^{e \text{ rem } p}$ in H_2, and if they are uncollided we can discover $(\ell+1)^e$ by computing their quotient. Modulo ℓ^2, this quotient $(\ell+1)^e$ is simply $e\ell+1$, from which we can obtain the exponent e. This idea is similar to the "coefficient ratios" technique suggested by [16], but working modulo ℓ^2 allows us to avoid costly discrete logarithms. Procedure Sumset contains the complete description.

Procedure Sumset($\mathcal{A}, \mathcal{B}, \mu$)

Input: $\mathcal{A}, \mathcal{B} \subseteq \mathbb{Z}$ with $\#\mathcal{A} + \#\mathcal{B} = R$ and $\max_{k \in \mathcal{A} \cup \mathcal{B}} |k| < D$; $\mu \in (0,1)$.
Output: Set $\mathbb{S} \subset \mathbb{Z}$ such that $\Pr[\mathbb{S} \ne \mathcal{A} \oplus \mathcal{B}] < \mu$.

$p \leftarrow$GetDiffPrime$(R^2, 4D, 1, \mu/4)$
$(F_1, G_1) \leftarrow \left(\sum_{a \in \mathcal{A}} x^{a \text{ rem } p}, \sum_{b \in \mathcal{B}} x^{b \text{ rem } p}\right)$
$S^* \leftarrow 2$
repeat $\lceil \max(8 \ln(8/\mu), \log_2 R + 1) \rceil$ **times**
  $q \leftarrow$GetDiffPrime$(2S^*, 2p, \frac{1}{2}, \frac{3}{4})$
  $H^* \leftarrow F_1 G_1 \bmod (R^2, x^q - 1)$, via dense arithmetic
  if $\#H^* > S^*$ **then** $S^* \leftarrow 2S^*$
$\ell \leftarrow 8D$
$(F_2, G_2) \leftarrow \left(\sum_{a \in \mathcal{A}} (a\ell+1) x^{a \text{ rem } p}, \sum_{b \in \mathcal{B}} (b\ell+1) x^{b}\right)$
$H_1 \leftarrow$BasecaseMultiply$(F_1, G_1, S^*, \mu/4)$
$H_2 \leftarrow$BasecaseMultiply$(F_2, G_2, S^*, \mu/4)$
for $j = 1, 2$ **do** $H_j \leftarrow H_j \bmod (\ell^2, x^p - 1)$
$\mathbb{S} \leftarrow$ empty list of integers
for *every nonzero term* cx^e *of* H_1 **do**
  $c' \leftarrow$ coefficient of degree-e term of H_2
  if $c \mid c'$ *and* $\ell \mid (c'/c - 1)$ *as integers* **then**
    Add $(c'/c - 1)/\ell$ to $\mathbb{S}$
  else return `Fail` //cannot reconstruct an exponent
return $\mathbb{S}$

Sumset has four steps that are probabilistic: choosing a good difference-prime p, estimating the sumset size $S = \#(\mathcal{A} \oplus \mathcal{B})$, and constructing H_1 and H_2. As each is set to fail with probability less than $\mu/4$, Sumset succeeds with probability at least $1 - \mu$.

We now analyze the total cost of this algorithm. GetDiffPrime produces p of size $\log p < \mathsf{polylog}(R + \log D + \frac{1}{\mu})$. Constructing F_1, F_2, G_1, G_2 at the beginning, and the reduction of H_1, H_2 modulo $(\ell^2, x^p - 1)$ at the end, both cost $\widetilde{\mathcal{O}}_\mu(S \log D)$ bit operations.

The search for S^* costs $\widetilde{\mathcal{O}}_\mu(S \log D)$ from the previous section. Finally, as $\|F_1\|_\infty < \ell/2$, $\deg F_1 < p$, and similarly for F_2, G_1, and G_2, the sparse multiplications due to BasecaseMultiply also costs $\widetilde{\mathcal{O}}_\mu(S \log D)$ bit operations. These dominate the complexity as stated in Theorem 5.1.

6. MULTIPLICATION WITH SUPPORT

We turn now to the problem of multiplying sparse $F, G \in \mathbb{Z}[x]$, provided some $\mathbb{S} \supseteq \mathsf{supp}(FG)$. This algorithm is used twice in our overall multiplication algorithm: first with large $\mathbb{S} = \mathsf{poss}(F, G)$ but small coefficients, then with the actual support $\mathbb{S} = \mathsf{supp}(FG)$ but full-size coefficients.

THEOREM 6.1. *Given $F, G \in \mathbb{Z}[x]$ and a set $\mathbb{S} \subset \mathbb{Z}_{\ge 0}$ such that $\mathsf{supp}(FG) \subseteq \mathbb{S}$, the product FG can be computed in time $\widetilde{\mathcal{O}}_\mu((\#F + \#G + \#\mathbb{S})(\log C + \log D))$, where $C = \|F\|_\infty + \|G\|_\infty$ and $D > \deg F + \deg G$.*

This is $\widetilde{\mathcal{O}}_\mu$-optimal, as it matches the bit-size of the inputs.

Our algorithm requires a small randomly-selected good difference-prime p with $\mathcal{O}(\log S + \log\log D)$ bits, and a series of pairs (q, ω), where each q is a slightly larger prime with $\mathcal{O}(\log p)$ bits, and ω is an order-p element in $\mathbb{Z}_q$. These numbers are provided by GetPrimRoots (Sec. 3). Our algorithm works by first reducing the exponents modulo p, then repeatedly reducing the coefficients modulo q and performing evaluation and interpolation at powers of ω. This inner loop follows exactly the algorithm of [15] and [18] for applying a transposed Vandermonde matrix and its inverse. Since p is a good difference-prime for the support of the product, there are no collisions and this gives us each coefficient modulo q. The process is then repeated $\mathcal{O}(\log C)$ times in order to recover the full coefficients via Chinese remaindering.

6.1 Comparison to prior work

Without affecting the complexity, we may assume that $\mathbb{S}$ contains the support of the inputs too, i.e., $\mathsf{supp}(F)$ and $\mathsf{supp}(G)$. We also assume that $\max \mathbb{S} = \deg FG$, such that no $e \in \mathbb{S}$ is too large to be an exponent of FG. Under these assumptions, and writing $S = \#\mathbb{S}$, the stated complexity of our algorithm is simply $\widetilde{\mathcal{O}}_\mu(S(\log C + \log D))$.

The problem of computing the coefficients of a sparse product, once the exponents of the product are given, has been recently and extensively investigated by van der Hoeven and Lecerf, where they present an algorithm whose bit complexity (in our notation) is

$$\widetilde{\mathcal{O}}_\mu\left(\left(\textstyle\sum_{e \in \mathbb{S}} \log e\right)(\log D + \log C)\right)$$

([15], Corollary 5). As $\sum_{e \in \mathbb{S}} \log e \in \mathcal{O}(S \log D)$, the algorithm here saves a factor of at most $\mathcal{O}(\log D)$ in comparison, which could be substantial if the exponents are very large.

Their algorithm is more efficient if the support superset $\mathbb{S}$ is *fixed*, in which case they can move the most expensive parts into precomputation and compute the result in the same soft-oh time as our approach, $\widetilde{\mathcal{O}}_\mu(S(\log D + \log C))$. Furthermore, the support bit-length $\sum_{e \in \mathbb{S}} \log e$ is at most $\mathcal{O}(S \log D)$, but could be as small as $\Omega(S \log S + \log D)$, for example if the support contains only a single large exponent. In such cases our savings is only on the order of $(\log D)/S$.

6.2 Transposed Vandermonde systems

Applying transposed Vandermonde systems, and their inverses, is an important subroutine in sparse interpolation algorithms, and efficient algorithms are discussed in detail by [18] and [15]. We restate the general idea here and refer the reader to those papers for more details.

If $\tilde{F}$ is a dense polynomial, it is well known that applying the Vandermonde matrix $V(\theta_1, \ldots, \theta_D)$ to a vector of coefficients from $\tilde{F}$ corresponds to evaluating $\tilde{F}$ at the points

$\theta_1 \ldots, \theta_D$. Applying the inverse Vandermonde matrix corresponds to interpolating $\tilde{F}$ from its evaluations at those points. The product tree method can perform both of these using $\widetilde{\mathcal{O}}(D)$ field operations ([11], Chapter 10).

If F is instead a sparse polynomial $F = \sum_{e \in \mathbb{S}} c_1 x^e$, evaluating F at consecutive powers of a single high-order element ω corresponds to multiplication with the transposed Vandermonde matrix:

$$V(\omega^{e_1}, \ldots, \omega^{e_S})^T (c_1, \ldots, c_S)^T = (F(1), \ldots, F(\omega^{S-1}))^T$$

The transposition principle tells us it is possible to compute the maps V^T and $(V^T)^{-1}$ in essentially the same time as dense evaluation and interpolation. In particular, if the coefficients c_i are in the modular ring $\mathbb{Z}_q$, then the transposed Vandermonde map and its inverse can be computed using $\widetilde{\mathcal{O}}(S \log q)$ bit operations [15].

6.3 Statement and analysis of the algorithm

Procedure SparseMulCoeffs($\mathbb{S}, F, G, \mu$)

Input: Exponents $\mathbb{S} = (e_1, e_2, \ldots e_S)$; coefficient lists $(f_1, \ldots, f_S)$ and $(g_1, \ldots, g_S)$, with $F, G \in \mathbb{Z}[x]$ implicitly defined as $F = \sum_{1 \le i \le S} f_i x^{e_i}$ and $G = \sum_{1 \le i \le S} g_i x^{e_i}$; error bound $\mu \in (0,1)$.

Output: $(h_1, \ldots, h_S) \in \mathbb{Z}^S$ such that, with probability least $1 - \mu$, $FG = \sum_{1 \le i \le S} h_i x^{e_i}$.

```
1  C ← (max_{1≤i≤S} |f_i|)(max_{1≤i≤S} |g_i|)S
2  p, Q, W ← GetPrimRoots(max S, #S, C, μ)
3  S_p ← (e_1 rem p, e_2 rem p, ..., e_S rem p)
4  H ← list of S empty lists of integers
5  foreach (q, ω) ∈ Q, W do
6      foreach e_ip ∈ S_p do
7          v_i ← ω^{e_ip} ∈ Z_q by binary powering
8      a ← V(v_1, ..., v_S)^T (f_1, ..., f_S)^T ∈ Z_q^S
9      b ← V(v_1, ..., v_S)^T (g_1, ..., g_S)^T ∈ Z_q^S
10     c ← (a_1 b_1, ..., a_S b_S)^T ∈ Z_q^S
11     if V(v_1, ..., v_S) is invertible then
12         (h_1p, ..., h_Sp) ← (V(v_1, ..., v_S)^T)^{-1} c ∈ Z_q^S
13         for 1 ≤ i ≤ S do Add h_ip to the list H[i]
14 for 1 ≤ i ≤ S do
15     h_i ← Chinese remaindering from images H[i]
           modulo integers in Q
16 return (h_1, ..., h_S)
```

Lemma 6.2. *Procedure SparseMulCoeffs works as stated when $\mathbb{S} \supseteq \mathsf{supp}(FG)$. In any case it has bit-complexity*

$$\widetilde{\mathcal{O}_\mu}\left(\sum_{e \in \mathbb{S}} \log e + S \log C\right).$$

Proof. We first analyze the probability of failure when $\mathbb{S} \supseteq \mathsf{supp}(FG)$. The randomization is in the choices of p, q, and ω; problems can occur if these lack the required properties.

If p is a good difference-prime for $\mathsf{supp}(FG)$, then by definition there will be no collisions in $\mathbb{S}_p$. Furthermore, if ω is a pth root of unity modulo q, then there are no collisions among the values $(v_1, \ldots, v_S)$, so $V(v_1, \ldots, v_S)$ is invertible modulo q. Algorithm GetPrimRoots ensures this is the case with high probability, and if so the algorithm here faithfully computes each coefficient h_i modulo q.

Procedure SparseMultZZ(F, G)

Input: Sparse $F, G \in \mathbb{Z}[x]$; $\mu \in (0,1)$.

Output: Sparse $H \in \mathbb{Z}[x]$, such that $\Pr[H \neq FG] < \mu$.

```
1 S_1 ← Sumset(supp(F), supp(G), μ/4)
2 C_H ← ||F||_∞ ||G||_∞ max(#F, #G)
3 p ← GetVanishPrime(#S_1, C, 1, μ/4)
4 H_1 ← SparseMulCoeffs(F rem p, G rem p, S_1, μ/4)
5 S_2 ← supp(H_1 rem p)
6 return SparseMulCoeffs(F, G, S_2, μ/4), S_2
```

Conversely, if there are no collisions in $\mathbb{S}_p$, and if no zero divisors modulo q are encountered in the application of the Vandermonde matrix and its inverse, then the algorithm correctly computes then values $h_i \bmod q$, even if p is not prime or some $\omega \in \mathbb{Z}_q$ is not actually a pth root of unity.

Therefore all failures in choosing tuples p, q, ω are either detected by the algorithm or do not affect its correctness. Since that is the only randomized step, we conclude that the entire algorithm is correct whenever the input exponent set $\mathbb{S}$ contains the support of the product.

For the complexity analysis first define $D = \deg(FG)$. Step 2 costs $\widetilde{\mathcal{O}_\mu}(\log C \cdot \mathsf{polylog}(S + \log D))$ bit operations by Lemma 3.6. Reducing each exponent e_i modulo p, on step 3, can be done for a total of $\widetilde{\mathcal{O}_\mu}(\sum_{e \in \mathbb{S}} \log e)$ bit operations.

Now we examine the cost of the for loop that begins on step 5. As the exponents are now all less than p, computing each v_i on step 7 requires only $\mathcal{O}(\log p)$ operations modulo q, for a total of $\mathcal{O}(S \log p \log q)$, which is $\widetilde{\mathcal{O}_\mu}(S \cdot \mathsf{polylog}(\log C + \log D))$ bit operations. From before we know that applying the transposed Vandermonde matrix and its inverse takes $\widetilde{\mathcal{O}_\mu}(S \log q)$, or $\widetilde{\mathcal{O}_\mu}(S \cdot \mathsf{polylog}(\log C + \log D))$ bit operations.

Because $\#Q \le \lceil \log_p(2C) \rceil$, the loop on step 5 repeats $\mathcal{O}(\log C)$ times, for a total cost of $\widetilde{\mathcal{O}_\mu}(S \log C \cdot \mathsf{polylog}(\log D))$ bit operations. This also bounds the cost of the Chinese remaindering in the final loop. □

7. MULTIPLICATION ALGORITHMS

The complete multiplication algorithm over $\mathbb{Z}[x]$ that was outlined in the introduction is presented as SparseMultZZ.

Proof of Thm. 1.1. Unless failure occurs, we have $\mathbb{S}_1 = \mathsf{poss}(F, G)$. Every coefficient in H is a sum of products of coefficients in F and G, so the value C_H computed on step 2 is an upper bound on $\|H\|_\infty$, and p is a good vanish-prime for H. Thus $\mathbb{S}_2 = \mathsf{supp}(H \text{ rem } p) = \mathsf{supp}(H)$, so the final step correctly computes the product FG.

By the union bound, Lemma 3.3, and Theorems 5.1 and 6.1, the probability of failure is less than μ.

Writing $T = \# \mathsf{poss}(F, G)$ and $S = \# \mathsf{supp}(FG)$, we see that $\log p \le \mathsf{polylog}(T + \log C + \frac{1}{\mu})$, thus steps 1 and 4 contribute $\widetilde{\mathcal{O}_\mu}(T \log D)$ to the overall cost, whereas the last step costs $\widetilde{\mathcal{O}_\mu}(S(\log D + \log C))$ bit operations. As $S \le T$, the total bit complexity is $\widetilde{\mathcal{O}_\mu}(T \log D + S \log C)$, as required. □

We now consider extensions of this algorithm to positive and negative exponents (Laurent polynomials), multiple variables, and other common coefficient rings, using Kronecker substitution. This is stated in the following theorem.

Theorem 7.1. *Let $F, G \in \mathsf{R}[x_1^{\pm 1}, \ldots, x_n^{\pm 1}]$ be sparse Laurent polynomials over R, where $\mathsf{R} = \mathbb{Z}$, $\mathbb{Z}_m$, $\mathsf{GF}(\mathsf{q}^\mathsf{e})$, or $\mathbb{Q}$.*

The product FG can be computed using $\widetilde{\mathcal{O}}_\mu(T(n \log D + B))$ bit operations, where $T = \# \mathsf{poss}(F, G)$ is the structural sparsity of the product, $D > \max_i |\deg_i(FG)|$, and B is the largest bit-length of any coefficient in the input or output.

PROOF. Write the output polynomial $H = FG$ as

$$H = \sum_{i=1}^{T} c_i x_1^{e_{i1}} x_2^{e_{i2}} \cdots x_n^{e_{in}},$$

where each $c_i \in \mathsf{R}$ and each e_{ij} satisfies $|e_{ij}| < D$.

We first apply the Kronecker substitution, providing an easily-invertible map between $\mathsf{R}[x_1^{\pm 1}, \ldots, x_n^{\pm 1}]$ and $\mathsf{R}[z^{\pm 1}]$: $x_i \mapsto z^{D^{i-1}}$ for $1 \le i \le n$. This increases the degree to D^n, such that the logarithm of this degree is $O(n \log D)$, matching the exponent bit-size in the multivariate representation.

The algorithm Sumset already handles negative exponents (i.e., Laurent polynomials) explicitly. The other primary subroutine to SparseMultZZ is SparseMulCoeffs, which only uses the exponents in the set $\mathbb{S}_p$, which are reduced modulo p and therefore cause no difficulty if they are negative. Thus the multiplication algorithms handle univariate Laurent polynomials without any changes.

To extend the multiplication algorithm and its subroutines beyond $\mathsf{R} = \mathbb{Z}$, we use that our algorithm is also softly-linear in the input *heights*. This allows us to adapt to any coefficient domain that provides a natural mapping to the integers, and to preserve softly-linear time if that mapping provides only a softly-linear increase in size.

For a modular ring $\mathsf{R} = \mathbb{Z}_m$, we can trivially treat the inputs as actual integers, then reduce modulo m after multiplying. For a finite field $\mathsf{R} = \mathsf{GF}(p^d)$, elements are typically represented as polynomials over $\mathbb{Z}_p[z]$ modulo a degree-d irreducible polynomial, so these coefficients can be converted to integers using a low-degree Kronecker substitution. For the rationals $\mathsf{R} = \mathbb{Q}$, we might choose a prime q larger than the product of the largest numerator and denominator in the output, multiply modulo q, then use rational reconstruction to recover the actual coefficients.

In all the above cases, there is growth in the bit-length of coefficients, but only in poly-logarithmic terms of input and output size, therefore not affecting the soft-oh complexity. The only downside is that we are no longer able to split the cost neatly between $T = \mathsf{poss}(F, G)$ and $S = \mathsf{supp}(FG)$ because the unreduced integer polynomial product might have nonzero coefficients which are really zeros in R. ☐

8. ACKNOWLEDGEMENTS

We thank Timothy Chan for bringing [5] to our attention, and the referees for their constructive feedback.

The first author acknowledges support from NSERC, and the second author from NSF award #1319994.

9. REFERENCES

[1] M. Agrawal, N. Kayal, and N. Saxena. Primes is in p. *Annals of mathematics*, pages 781–793, 2004.

[2] A. Arnold, M. Giesbrecht, and D. S. Roche. Faster sparse multivariate polynomial interpolation of straight-line programs. Preprint, arxiv:1412.4088 [cs.SC].

[3] A. Arnold, M. Giesbrecht, and D. S. Roche. Sparse interpolation over finite fields via low-order roots of unity. In *Proc. ISSAC '14*, pages 27–34. ACM, 2014.

[4] D. G. Cantor and E. Kaltofen. On fast multiplication of polynomials over arbitrary algebras. *Acta Inf.*, 28(7):693–701, Oct. 1991.

[5] R. Cole and R. Hariharan. Verifying candidate matches in sparse and wildcard matching. In *Proc. STOC '02*, pages 592–601. ACM, 2002.

[6] M. T. Comer, E. L. Kaltofen, and C. Pernet. Sparse polynomial interpolation and Berlekamp/Massey algorithms that correct outlier errors in input values. In *Proc. ISSAC '12*, pages 138–145. ACM, 2012.

[7] A. Cuyt and W. Lee. A new algorithm for sparse interpolation of multivariate polynomials. *Theoretical Computer Science*, 409(2):180–185, 2008.

[8] R. Fateman. Comparing the speed of programs for sparse polynomial multiplication. *SIGSAM Bull.*, 37(1):4–15, March 2003.

[9] É. Fouvry. On binary cyclotomic polynomials. *Algebra and Number Theory*, 7(5):1207–1223, 2013.

[10] M. Gastineau and J. Laskar. Highly scalable multiplication for distributed sparse multivariate polynomials on many-core systems. In *Proc. CASC 2013*, pages 100–115, New York, 2013. Springer-Verlag.

[11] J. von zur Gathen and J. Gerhard. *Modern Computer Algebra*. Cambridge University Press, New York, 3rd edition, 2013.

[12] D. Harvey, J. van der Hoeven, and G. Lecerf. Faster polynomial multiplication over finite fields. Preprint, arXiv:1407.3361v1 [cs.CC], July 2014.

[13] W. Hoeffding. Probability inequalities for sums of bounded random variables. *J. Amer. Statist. Assoc.*, 58:13–30, 1963.

[14] J. van der Hoeven and G. Lecerf. On the complexity of multivariate blockwise polynomial multiplication. In *Proc. ISSAC 2012*, pages 211–218, 2012.

[15] J. van der Hoeven and G. Lecerf. On the bit-complexity of sparse polynomial and series multiplication. *J. Symb. Comput.*, 50:227–254, 2013.

[16] J. van der Hoeven and G. Lecerf. Sparse polynomial interpolation in practice. *ACM Commun. Comput. Algebra*, 48:187–191, 2014.

[17] S. M. M. Javadi and M. Monagan. Parallel sparse polynomial interpolation over finite fields. In *Proc. PASCO '10*, pages 160–168. ACM, 2010.

[18] E. Kaltofen and L. Yagati. Improved sparse multivariate polynomial interpolation algorithms. In *Symbolic and Algebraic Computation*, volume 358 of *Lect. Notes Comput. Sc.*, pages 467–474. Springer Berlin / Heidelberg, 1989.

[19] M. Monagan and R. Pearce. Parallel sparse polynomial multiplication using heaps. In *Proc. ISSAC '09*, pages 263–270. ACM, 2009.

[20] M. Monagan and R. Pearce. POLY: A new polynomial data structure for maple 17. *ACM Commun. Comput. Algebra*, 46(3/4):164–167, Jan. 2013.

[21] D. S. Roche. Chunky and equal-spaced polynomial multiplication. *J. Symb. Comput.*, 46(7):791–806, 2011.

[22] J. B. Rosser and L. Schoenfeld. Approximate formulas for some functions of prime numbers. *Illinois J. Math.*, 6(1):64–94, 1962.

Probabilistic Algorithm for Computing the Dimension of Real Algebraic Sets*

Ivan Bannwarth, Mohab Safey El Din
Sorbonne Universités, Univ. Pierre et Marie Curie (Paris 06)
INRIA Paris Rocquencourt, POLSYS Project
LIP6 CNRS, UMR 7606
Ivan.Bannwarth@lip6.fr, Mohab.Safey@lip6.fr

ABSTRACT

Let $f \in \mathbb{Q}[X_1, \ldots, X_n]$ be a polynomial of degree D. We consider the problem of computing the real dimension of the real algebraic set defined by $f = 0$. Such a problem can be reduced to quantifier elimination. Hence it can be tackled with Cylindrical Algebraic Decomposition within a complexity that is doubly exponential in the number of variables. More recently, denoting by d the dimension of the real algebraic set under study, deterministic algorithms running in time $D^{O(d(n-d))}$ have been proposed. However, no implementation reflecting this complexity gain has been obtained and the constant in the exponent remains unspecified.

We design a probabilistic algorithm which runs in time which is essentially cubic in $D^{d(n-d)}$. Our algorithm takes advantage of genericity properties of *polar varieties* to avoid computationally difficult steps of quantifier elimination. We also report on a first implementation. It tackles examples that are out of reach of the state-of-the-art and its practical behavior reflects the complexity gain.

Categories and Subject Descriptors

I.1.2 [**Computing Methodologies**]: Symbolic and Algebraic Manipulation—*Algorithms*; F.2.2 [**Theory of Computation**]: Analysis of algorithm and problem complexity—*Non numerical algorithms and problems: Geometrical problems and computation*

Keywords

Real dimension; Real solutions; Polynomial systems; Real Geometry.

General Terms

Algorithms; Theory.

1. INTRODUCTION

This paper is devoted to the design and the implementation of an algorithm for computing the real dimension d of an algebraic set $V \cap \mathbb{R}^n$ defined by one polynomial equation $f = 0$ with rational coefficients and degree D. Recall that when $V \cap \mathbb{R}^n$ is empty, its real dimension d is -1 by convention, when it is non-empty but finite it is 0 else it is the largest integer d such that there is a projection of $V \cap \mathbb{R}^n$ over a d-dimensional affine subspace of coordinates with a non-empty interior.

Motivations. Computing the real dimension is a question of first importance since it is a basic topological invariant. It encodes the number of independent motions that are allowed on a geometric body or the number of independent parameters that may vary independently. Hence, computing the real dimension of semi-algebraic sets has many applications in engineering sciences (see e.g. [26] and references therein). It also has some algorithmic interest since the knowledge of the real dimension can be exploited to accelerate other algorithms studying real algebraic or semi-algebraic sets (see e.g. [8, Section 13.3] or [6, 7]).

State-of-the-art. Quantifier elimination (QE) over the reals plays a central role for computing the real dimension since it allows to obtain semi-algebraic descriptions of projections of semi-algebraic sets. Hence, it allows to decide if the interior of such a projection is empty. Consequently, Cylindrical Algebraic Decomposition (CAD) due to Collins [12] can be used for computing the real dimension. However, the arithmetic complexity of this algorithm is doubly exponential in the total number of variables. Several software implementing variants and improvements of CAD have been designed (Mathematica, Maple, QEPCAD, RedLog, etc.) but because of this doubly exponential complexity they are rather limited to 3 or 4 variables on a wide range of examples.

The current algorithms within the best known complexity class are due to Basu, Pollack and Roy [9] (see also [8, Chapter 14]) following previous work of Koiran [28] and Vorobjov [40]. Let $S \subset \mathbb{R}^n$ be a real algebraic set defined by a polynomial equation of degree D with rational coefficients.

These algorithms use QE techniques that essentially allow to compute the projection of S on a i-dimensional linear subspace in time $D^{O(i(n-i))}$ arithmetic operations [8, Thm 14.16]. Then, the arithmetic complexity of these algorithms is bounded by $D^{O(d(n-d))}$. These algorithms are deterministic and the complexity is output sensitive since it depends on d. They also allow to handle general semi-algebraic sets in time $(sD)^{O(d(n-d))}$ (where s is the number of inequalities). However several questions remain open.

1. What is the complexity constant hidden in the exponent of the above complexity estimates?
2. Can we obtain an efficient implementation that reflects the complexity gain compared to doubly exponential algorithms?

Main results. We provide answers to both questions: we obtain a probabilistic algorithm whose arithmetic complexity is essentially cubic in $D^{d(n-d)}$; a first implementation shows that it can tackle examples that are out of reach of the state-of-the-art. We give more details on our methodology below.

In the whole paper, let $f \in \mathbb{Q}[X_1, \ldots, X_n] \setminus \{0\}$ of degree D and let $V \subset \mathbb{C}^n$ be the algebraic set defined by $f = 0$. Our technique is still based on the investigation of projections of $V \cap \mathbb{R}^n$. Let π_i

*The authors are supported by the GEOLMI grant (ANR 2011 BS03 011 06) of the French National Research Agency.

ISSAC'15, July 6–9, 2015, Bath, United Kingdom.

DOI: http://dx.doi.org/10.1145/2755996.2756670.

be the canonical projection $(\mathbf{x}_1, \ldots, \mathbf{x}_n) \to (\mathbf{x}_1, \ldots, \mathbf{x}_i)$. Remark that in order to decide if $\pi_i(V \cap \mathbb{R}^n)$ has an empty interior, there is no need to compute a semi-algebraic description of this projection using general QE techniques. Indeed, it is sufficient to compute *(i)* a polynomial that defines a hypersurface containing the boundary of $\pi_i(V \cap \mathbb{R}^n)$, *(ii)* compute sample points in each connected component of the complementary of the real trace of that hypersurface and *(iii)* for each such sample point y, decide if the fiber $\pi_i^{-1}(y) \cap V \cap \mathbb{R}^n$ is empty. If there is no non-empty real fiber then the interior of $\pi_i(V)$ is empty.

This process has already been identified and formalized in [23, 24] where a dedicated projection step has been designed for quantifier elimination over the reals under some conditions on the input. These are regularity conditions (the algebraic set defined by $f = 0$ must be smooth) and properness conditions (for any $y \in \mathbb{R}^i$, there is a closed ball B containing y such that $\pi_i^{-1}(B) \cap V \cap \mathbb{R}^n$ is closed and bounded).

Note that when V is smooth, if $V \cap \mathbb{R}^n \neq \emptyset$, then its real dimension is $n-1$ by the implicit function theorem. Thus, in our context, this regularity condition is a strong obstruction since on all examples where the real dimension does not coincide with the complex one, this condition is not satisfied.

Moreover, the properness of the restriction of π_i to $V \cap \mathbb{R}^n$ cannot be always ensured, especially when $V \cap \mathbb{R}^n$ is not bounded and i is less than the dimension of $V \cap \mathbb{R}^n$.

Hence, results in [23, 24] are not sufficient and need to be generalized for our purpose. To do that we investigate polar varieties of a deformation V_ε of V defined by $f - \varepsilon = 0$ (where ε is an infinitesimal encoding a small perturbation of the constant coefficient in f). This allows us to retrieve a regular situation (V_ε is actually smooth). Next, we show that properness assumptions in [23, 24] can be substituted with properness assumptions on polar varieties of V_ε as in [35].

Our algorithm is probabilistic because its correctness depends on some changes of coordinates that are performed randomly. Indeed, we prove that for such a generic choice these properness assumptions on polar varieties are satisfied. Finally, letting the deformation ε tend to 0, this allows us to obtain a hypersurface defining the boundary of $\pi_i(V)$. We finally get a routine for deciding the emptiness of the interior of $\pi_i(V \cap \mathbb{R}^n)$ in generic coordinates. Also, an extra outcome of the paper is a generalization of several results in [23, 24].

These geometric steps can be eliminated using many algebraic elimination routines. To estimate the complexity we mainly rely on [17]. We use the arithmetic complexity model over $\mathbb{Q}$: we count arithmetic operations over $\mathbb{Q}$ as a unit. Below, $\tilde{O}(x)$ means $O(x \log(x)^a)$ for some $a > 0$. We can now state our main result.

THEOREM 1. *Let f be a polynomial in $\mathbb{Q}[X_1, \ldots, X_n] \setminus \{0\}$ of degree D and let d be the real dimension of the real algebraic set defined by $f = 0$. There exists a probabilistic algorithm which computes d in time $\tilde{O}(n^{16}(1+D)^{3d(n-d)+5n+5})$.*

Also, note that when a real algebraic set is defined by a polynomial system $f_1 = \cdots = f_p = 0$ with coefficients in $\mathbb{Q}$, our algorithm can be used with input $f_1^2 + \cdots + f_p^2$.

We also report on the practical performances of an implementation of our algorithm. We have used as benchmarks sums of squares of random dense polynomials, discriminants of characteristic polynomials of linear symmetric matrices and series of polynomials that are known to be non-negative over the reals. For all these polynomials, the dimensions of the real algebraic sets they define may vary. We find that our implementation allows to tackle polynomials that are out of reach of the best CAD implementations. As importantly, we emphasize that, in practice, the behaviour of our implementation is output sensitive. Indeed, for families of fixed dimension, timings seem to show a behaviour of type $D^{O(n)}$ but computations performed better when d or $n - d$ are small w.r.t $n/2$.

Related works. As already mentioned, algorithms in [8, 28, 40] are the first ones with a singly exponential complexity for computing the real dimension of semi-algebraic sets.

The use of *polar varieties* in symbolic computation appears first in [1] to compute sample points in smooth equidimensional real algebraic sets (see also [2, 3, 4, 5] and reference therein). There are also used for global optimization and for computing roadmaps (see [18, 19, 36] and references therein).

Properness properties of the restriction of a projection to a polar variety are introduced in [35] and used in [23, 24].

Our complexity estimates rely on complexity results on the geometric resolution algorithm; we refer to [17, 29, 37] and references therein for a description of these algorithms and their parametric variants.

Structure of the paper.

Section 2 is devoted to preliminaries and notation used throughout the paper. Section 3 is devoted to the description of the algorithm, the proof of its correctness and its complexity analysis. Section 4 is devoted to the proof of geometric results on which the algorithm relies. The last section reports on practical experiments.

2. PRELIMINARIES

We start with basic notions and some notation on algebraic sets.

Algebraic sets. Let $\mathbb{K}$ be a field of characteristic 0, $\overline{\mathbb{K}}$ be its algebraic closure. Let I be an ideal of $\mathbb{K}[X_1, \ldots, X_n]$ generated by $(g_1, \ldots, g_s)$. The $\mathbb{K}$-algebraic set associated to I is the $\mathbb{K}$-algebraic set defined by the polynomial equations $g_1 = \cdots = g_s = 0$; we denote it by $V(I)$.

Let $W \subset \overline{\mathbb{K}}^n$ be a $\mathbb{K}$-algebraic set defined by polynomial equations in $\mathbb{K}[X_1, \ldots, X_n]$. The dimension of W is defined as the *Krull dimension* of its associated ideal $I(W) = \{g \in \mathbb{K}[X_1, \ldots, X_n] \mid \forall x \in W, g(x) = 0\}$ (see e.g. [14]). This notion of dimension coincides with other notions inspired by differential or algebraic geometry (see e.g. [14, Part II]). Roughly speaking, it is the number of generic hypersurfaces such that their intersection with W is a finite set of points. If W' is another algebraic set and $W \subset W'$, then the dimension of W is at most the dimension of W'.

The $\mathbb{K}$-algebraic set W is said to be $\mathbb{K}$-*irreducible* if it cannot be decomposed as the union of two different $\mathbb{K}$-algebraic sets. Any $\mathbb{K}$-irreducible algebraic set W is uniquely decomposed as a finite union of $\mathbb{K}$-irreducible algebraic sets; these are called the *irreducible components* of W.

When all the irreducible components of W have the same dimension, we say that W is *equidimensional*.

Let W be an $\mathbb{K}$-algebraic set, equidimensional of co-dimension c and let $(f_1, \ldots, f_p)$ be a set of generators of its associated ideal. A point $x \in W$ is called *regular* if the Jacobian matrix $\left(\frac{\partial f_i}{\partial X_j}\right)_{\substack{1 \le i \le p \\ 1 \le j \le n}}$ associated to $(f_1, \ldots, f_p)$ has rank c at x. The kernel of this Jacobian matrix at x is the tangent space to W at x; we denote it by $T_x W$. The points in W that are not regular are *singular* by definition. An algebraic set with no singular points is *smooth*.

Algebraic sets are closed sets of the Zariski topology. Let $W \subset \overline{\mathbb{K}}^n$. The Zariski closure of W is the smallest algebraic set that contains it; we denote it by $\overline{W}$.

Most of the time, the field $\mathbb{K}$ will be clear from the context and will be omitted in the above terminology.

Fields of Puiseux series. We follow the notation of [8, Chap. 2] to define the *field of Puiseux series* $\mathbb{K}\langle\varepsilon\rangle = \{\Sigma_{i \ge i_0} a_i \varepsilon^{i/q} \mid a_i \in \mathbb{K}, q \in \mathbb{N}^*, i_0 \in \mathbb{Z}\}$ where ε is an infinitesimal over $\mathbb{K}$.

Let $S \subset \mathbb{R}^n$ be a semi-algebraic set; it is the real solution set of polynomial equations and inequalities with coefficients in $\mathbb{R}$. We denote by $\mathrm{Ext}(S, \mathbb{K}\langle\varepsilon\rangle)$ the set of solutions of this system in $\mathbb{R}\langle\varepsilon\rangle^n$.

We say that $y = \sum_{i \ge i_0} a_i \varepsilon^{i/q}$ in $\mathbb{K}\langle\varepsilon\rangle$ is *bounded over* $\mathbb{K}$ if $i_0 \ge 0$.

We say that $\mathbf{y} = (y_1, \ldots, y_n) \in \mathbb{K}\langle\varepsilon\rangle^n$ is *bounded over* $\mathbb{K}$ if each coordinate y_i is bounded over $\mathbb{K}$. Given a bounded element $y \in \mathbb{K}\langle\varepsilon\rangle$ and $\mathbf{y} \in \mathbb{K}\langle\varepsilon\rangle^n$, then $\lim_{\varepsilon \to 0}(y)$ denotes a_0 in $\mathbb{K}$ and $\lim_{\varepsilon \to 0}(\mathbf{y})$ denotes the point $(\lim_{\varepsilon \to 0}(y_1), \ldots, \lim_{\varepsilon \to 0}(y_n)) \in \mathbb{K}^n$. Given a subset $A \subset \mathbb{K}\langle\varepsilon\rangle^n$, we denote by $\lim_{\varepsilon \to 0}(A)$ the set

$$\{\lim_{\varepsilon \to 0}(y) \mid y \in A \text{ and } y \text{ is bounded.}\}$$

We say that A is bounded over $\mathbb{K}$ if evry point in A is bounded over $\mathbb{K}$. By [8, Prop 2.99] the application $\lim_{\varepsilon\to 0}$ is a ring homomorphism. We recall the following result in [31, Lemma 3.5] that we will use repeatedly in the sequel.

LEMMA 2. *[31, Lemma 3.5] Let $f \in \mathbb{Q}[X_1,\dots,X_n]$ be a non-zero polynomial, let $V_\varepsilon \subset \mathbb{C}\langle\varepsilon\rangle^n$ be algebraic sets defined by the equation $f-\varepsilon = 0$. Then, V_ε is either empty or smooth and equidimensional of codimension 1.*

Projections and Polar varieties. Let $W \subset \overline{\mathbb{K}}^n$ be an equidimensional algebraic set and let $(f_1,\dots,f_p)$ be a set of generators of the ideal associated to W. We denote by π_i the canonical projection $(x_1,\dots,x_n)\to(x_1,\dots,x_i)$ for $1\le i\le n$.
A regular point $x\in W$ is a *critical point* of the restriction of the projection π_i to W if $\pi_i(T_xW)\neq\overline{\mathbb{K}}^i$. These are the regular points of W at which the truncated Jacobian matrix $\left(\frac{\partial f_j}{\partial X_k}\right)_{\substack{1\le j\le p\\ i+1\le k\le n}}$ is rank defective.
The *polar variety* associated to π_i and W is the Zariski closure of the critical locus defined above (we refer to [36, Section 2.1]).
Consider now the polynomial $f\in\mathbb{Q}[X_1,\dots,X_n]$ that is to be given as input to our algorithm and the algebraic set $V\subset\mathbb{C}^n$ defined by $f=0$. We denote by $V_\varepsilon\subset\mathbb{C}\langle\varepsilon\rangle^n$ the algebraic set defined by $f=\varepsilon$. By Lemma 2, it is smooth. We will consider the polar varieties associated to π_i and V_ε. They are defined as the zero set in $\mathbb{C}\langle\varepsilon\rangle^n$ of

$$f-\varepsilon = \frac{\partial f}{\partial X_{i+1}} = \cdots = \frac{\partial f}{\partial X_n} = 0.$$

It will be denoted by $W_{\varepsilon,i}$.

Changes of variables and topological notions. We repeatedly use linear changes of variables and projections in the sequel.
The set of invertible matrices with entries in $\mathbb{K}$ is denoted by $\mathrm{GL}_n(\mathbb{K})$.
Let $\mathbf{A}\in\mathrm{GL}_n(\mathbb{K})$, $g\in\mathbb{K}[X_1,\dots,X_n]$. We denote by $g^{\mathbf{A}}$ the polynomial $g(\mathbf{AX})$ (with $\mathbf{X}=[X_1,\dots,X_n]$). For any set of polynomials $G\subset\mathbb{K}[\mathbf{X}]$, we denote by $G^{\mathbf{A}}$ the set $\{g^{\mathbf{A}}\mid g\in G\}$.
Let $V\subset\overline{\mathbb{K}}^n$ be an algebraic set. We denote by $V^{\mathbf{A}}\subset\overline{\mathbb{K}}^n$ the image of V by the map $x\mapsto\mathbf{A}^{-1}x$. This notation is naturally extended to semi-algebraic sets when $\mathbb{K}$ is a real closed field.
Assume that $\mathbb{K}$ is equipped with a Euclidean topology. Let U be a subset of $\mathbb{K}^n$, we denote by $\mathsf{Int}(U)$ the interior of U for the Euclidean topology. We denote by $\mathsf{Bd}(U)$ the Euclidean boundary of U defined as the closure of U without its interior.
The properness of a projection is defined as in [35, Section 1] : A map $\pi: A\subset\mathbb{K}^n\to\mathbb{K}^i$ is *proper* at $y\in\mathbb{K}^i$ if there exists a neighborhood $\mathcal{O}$ of y such that $\pi^{-1}(\overline{\mathcal{O}})$ is closed in $\mathbb{K}^n$ and bounded over $\mathbb{K}^n$, where $\overline{\mathcal{O}}$ denotes the closure of $\mathcal{O}$ for the Euclidean topology. If π is proper at every point of $\pi(A)$, we simply say that π is proper.

3. ALGORITHM

3.1 Descriptions

We start with the description of the main subroutines. The two following ones are rather standard.

HasRealSolutions: it takes as input a polynomial equation with rational coefficients. It returns true if there exists at least one real solution and false otherwise (see [32, Theorem 4]).

PointsPerComponents: it takes as input a polynomial inequation $g\neq 0$ with rational coefficients. It returns a set of points meeting each connected component of the semi-algebraic set defined by $g\neq 0$ (see [16, Section 4] and [34]).

We describe now the third subroutine. As sketched in the introduction, we need a subroutine that allows to decide if the projection of some real algebraic set has an empty interior. This third subroutine performs this task under some assumptions.

Let $f\in\mathbb{Q}[X_1,\dots,X_n]$ and $0<i<n$ an integer. Below, for $g\in\mathbb{Q}[X_1,\dots,X_n]$, we denote by $I_i(g)$ the ideal $\left\langle\frac{\partial g}{\partial X_{i+1}},\dots,\frac{\partial g}{\partial X_n}\right\rangle : \left\langle\frac{\partial g}{\partial X_1},\dots,\frac{\partial g}{\partial X_i}\right\rangle^\infty + \langle g\rangle$ (see [13, Section 4.4] for the definition of saturated ideals).

HasEmptyInterior:
Input: a polynomial $f\in\mathbb{Q}[X_1,\dots,X_n]\backslash\{0\}$, an integer i such that $0<i<n$ and a matrix $\mathbf{A}\in\mathrm{GL}_n(\mathbb{Q})$ s.t. $I_i(f^{\mathbf{A}})\cap\mathbb{Q}[X_1,\dots,X_i]$ is not empty and $\mathsf{Bd}\left(\pi_i\left(V^{\mathbf{A}}\cap\mathbb{R}^n\right)\right)\subset V(I_i(f^{\mathbf{A}})\cap\mathbb{Q}[X_1,\dots,X_i])$.
Output: true if $\mathsf{Int}(\pi_i(V^{\mathbf{A}}\cap\mathbb{R}^n))=\emptyset$, false otherwise.

1. compute $g\neq 0$ in the ideal $I_i(f^{\mathbf{A}})\cap\mathbb{Q}[X_1,\dots,X_i]$
2. let $L=$ PointsPerComponents($g\neq 0$).
3. for $(\alpha_1,\dots,\alpha_i)\in L$ do
   (a) let $f_\alpha^{\mathbf{A}}=f^{\mathbf{A}}(\alpha_1,\dots,\alpha_i,X_{i+1},\dots,X_n)$
   (b) if HasRealSolutions($f_\alpha^{\mathbf{A}}=0$) = true then return false
4. return true

We now describe our main algorithm that is called RealDimension which takes as input $f\in\mathbb{Q}[X_1,\dots,X_n]$. In the following, $\lceil\frac{n}{2}\rceil$ denotes the first integer greater than $\frac{n}{2}$. The algorithm starts by checking that the real algebraic set defined by $f=0$ has solutions. When this is the case, it chooses randomly a linear change of variables and performs successive calls to HasEmptyInterior.

Algorithm RealDimension:
Input: A polynomial $f\in\mathbb{Q}[X_1,\dots,X_n]$.
Output: The real dimension of $V\cap\mathbb{R}^n$.

1. if HasRealSolutions($f=0$) = false then return -1
2. choose a random matrix $\mathbf{A}\in\mathrm{GL}_n(\mathbb{Q})$
3. for $i=1$ to $\lceil\frac{n}{2}\rceil$ do
   (a) if HasEmptyInterior($f,i,\mathbf{A}$) = true then return $i-1$
   (b) if HasEmptyInterior($f,n-i,\mathbf{A}$) = false then return $n-i$

3.2 Correctness

Correctness of Algorithm RealDimension. The correctness proof of Algorithm RealDimension relies on the following results.

PROPOSITION 3. *[27, Section 2] Let $W\subset\mathbb{C}^n$ be an algebraic set. Assume that $W\cap\mathbb{R}^n$ has real dimension $d>0$. Then there exists a non-empty Zariski open set $\Gamma_1\subset\mathrm{GL}_n(\mathbb{C})$ such that for any $\mathbf{A}\in\Gamma_1\cap\mathrm{GL}_n(\mathbb{Q})$ and $0<i\le d$, $\mathsf{Int}(\pi_d(W^{\mathbf{A}}\cap\mathbb{R}^n))\neq\emptyset$.*

THEOREM 4. *Let $0<i<n$ be an integer. There exists a non-empty Zariski open set $\Gamma_2\subset\mathrm{GL}_n(\mathbb{C})$ such that for all $\mathbf{A}\in\Gamma_2\cap\mathrm{GL}_n(\mathbb{Q})$, HasEmptyInterior($f,i,\mathbf{A}$) returns true if $\mathsf{Int}(\pi_i(V^{\mathbf{A}}\cap\mathbb{R}^n))$ is empty and false otherwise.*

We can now prove the correctness of Algorithm RealDimension with input $f\in\mathbb{Q}[X_1,\dots,X_n]$. We denote by d the real dimension of the real algebraic set defined by $f=0$. We make the assumption that this set is non-empty (the empty case is correctly handled at Step 1). Hence, we assume that $d\ge 0$.
We make the assumption that the matrix $\mathbf{A}$ chosen at step 2 lies in $\Gamma_1\cap\Gamma_2$ where Γ_1 and Γ_2 are the non-empty Zariski open subsets of $\mathrm{GL}_n(\mathbb{C})$ defined in Proposition 3 and Theorem 4.
When the dimension d is 0, we enter in the loop at Step 3 and the call to HasEmptyInterior($f,i,\mathbf{A}$) returns true (since $\pi_1(V^{\mathbf{A}})$ is a finite set of points) and 0 is the returned value.
Assume now that $d>0$. Since $\mathbf{A}\in\Gamma_1$ by assumption, Proposition 3 implies that for any $i\le d$, $\mathsf{Int}(\pi_i(V^{\mathbf{A}}\cap\mathbb{R}^n))\neq\emptyset$. Also, by

definition of the real dimension of a real algebraic set, for any $i > d$, $\mathsf{Int}(\pi_i(V^{\mathbf{A}} \cap \mathbb{R}^n)) = \emptyset$ holds.
As long as $i \leq d$ and $n - i > d$, the calls to HasEmptyInterior in Step 3a and Step 3b return respectively false and true and the loop goes on by increasing i.
Finally if $d < \frac{n}{2}$ and $i = d + 1$, then Step 3a returns $i - 1 = d$. If $d \geq \frac{n}{2}$ and $i = n - d \leq \frac{n}{2}$, the call to HasEmptyInterior at Step 3a returns false and Step 3b returns $n - i = d$. □

Correctness of HasEmptyInterior. Assume for the moment the following proposition (we prove it in Section 4).

PROPOSITION 5. *There exists a Zariski open set $\Gamma' \subset \mathrm{GL}_n(\mathbb{C})$ such that for any $\mathbf{A} \in \Gamma' \cap \mathrm{GL}_n(\mathbb{Q})$ and for any $1 \leq i < n$, the following holds. Let $I_i(f)$ be the ideal defined in Subsection 3.1.*

1. *Let $x \in V\left(\left\langle \frac{\partial f^{\mathbf{A}}}{\partial X_{i+1}}, \ldots, \frac{\partial f^{\mathbf{A}}}{\partial X_n} \right\rangle\right) - V\left(\left\langle \frac{\partial f^{\mathbf{A}}}{\partial X_1}, \ldots, \frac{\partial f^{\mathbf{A}}}{\partial X_i} \right\rangle\right)$. Then the Jacobian matrix associated to $\left(\frac{\partial f^{\mathbf{A}}}{\partial X_{i+1}}, \ldots, \frac{\partial f^{\mathbf{A}}}{\partial X_n}\right)$ at x has maximal rank and $V(I_i(f^{\mathbf{A}}))$ is either empty or equidimensional of dimension $i - 1$.*
2. *$\mathsf{Bd}(\pi_i(V^{\mathbf{A}} \cap \mathbb{R}^n))$ is contained in $\pi_i(V(I_i(f^{\mathbf{A}})) \cap \mathbb{R}^n)$.*

We can now prove Theorem 4. As above, $f \in \mathbb{Q}[X_1, \ldots, X_n]$ is the polynomial given in the input and $V \subset \mathbb{C}^n$ is the algebraic set defined by $f = 0$.
Let $\Gamma' \subset \mathrm{GL}_n(\mathbb{C})$ be the non-empty Zariski open set defined in Proposition 5. Let $\mathbf{A} \in \Gamma' \cap \mathrm{GL}_n(\mathbb{Q})$. Then by assertion (2) of Proposition 5, $\mathsf{Bd}(\pi_i(V^{\mathbf{A}} \cap \mathbb{R}^n)) \subset \pi_i(V(I_i(f^{\mathbf{A}})) \cap \mathbb{R}^n)$.
By the elimination theorem [13], we deduce that $\mathsf{Bd}(\pi_i(V^{\mathbf{A}} \cap \mathbb{R}^n))$ is contained in $V(I_i(f^{\mathbf{A}}) \cap \mathbb{Q}[X_1, \ldots, X_i]) \cap \mathbb{R}^i$. Recall also that assertion (1) of Proposition 5 implies that $V(I_i(f^{\mathbf{A}}) \cap \mathbb{Q}[X_1, \ldots, X_i])$ has codimension ≥ 1.
So the set L computed at Step 2 contains at least one point in each connected component of the semi-algebraic set defined by $g \neq 0$. Since $\mathsf{Bd}(\pi_i(V^{\mathbf{A}} \cap \mathbb{R}^n)) \subset \pi_i(V(I_i(f^{\mathbf{A}})) \cap \mathbb{R}^n)$, L contains at least one point in each connected component of $\mathbb{R}^i - \mathsf{Bd}(\pi_i(V^{\mathbf{A}} \cap \mathbb{R}^n))$.
The final step of HasEmptyInterior decides the emptiness of $V^{\mathbf{A}} \cap \mathbb{R}^n \cap \pi_i^{-1}(\alpha)$ for every point $\alpha \in L$.
If $\mathsf{Int}(\pi_i(V^{\mathbf{A}} \cap \mathbb{R}^n)) = \emptyset$, then $\pi_i(V^{\mathbf{A}} \cap \mathbb{R}^n)$ is a subset of its boundary. Then for all $\alpha \in \mathbb{R}^i - \mathsf{Bd}(\pi_i(V^{\mathbf{A}} \cap \mathbb{R}^n))$, the set $V^{\mathbf{A}} \cap \mathbb{R}^n \cap \pi_i^{-1}(\alpha)$ is empty and HasEmptyInterior returns true as requested.
If $\mathsf{Int}(\pi_i(V^{\mathbf{A}} \cap \mathbb{R}^n)) \neq \emptyset$, then $\mathsf{Int}(\pi_i(V^{\mathbf{A}} \cap \mathbb{R}^n))$ contains at least one connected component of $\mathbb{R}^i - \mathsf{Bd}(\pi_i(V^{\mathbf{A}} \cap \mathbb{R}^n))$. So there exists $\alpha \in L$, such that α lies in this component. We deduce that α lies in the interior of $\pi_i(V^{\mathbf{A}} \cap \mathbb{R}^n)$. In other words, we have $\pi_i^{-1}(\alpha) \cap V^{\mathbf{A}} \cap \mathbb{R}^n \neq \emptyset$ and HasEmptyInterior returns false as requested. □

3.3 Complexity analysis

Our complexity analysis relies mainly on the use of algebraic elimination routines from [17]. The complexity of these routines depends polynomially on geometric degrees of algebraic sets. We investigate below the degrees of the geometric objects manipulated by our algorithm. In the whole paragraph, $f \in \mathbb{Q}[X_1, \ldots, X_n]$ denotes the input of RealDimension; it has degree D and the equation $f = 0$ defines the real algebraic set $V \cap \mathbb{R}^n$.

Degrees of algebraic sets. Let $W \subset \mathbb{C}^n$ be a non-empty irreducible algebraic set. The degree $\deg(W)$ of W is defined in [21, Section 2] as the maximal cardinality of a finite set which is obtained by intersecting W with a linear affine subspace. The degree of a reducible closed set is the sum of the degree of its irreducible components.
The complexity of RealDimension and HasEmptyInterior depends on the degree of the objects under study. Let i be an integer such that $0 < i < n$. Let $I_i(f)$ be the ideal defined in Subsection 3.1. In this paragraph we analyze the degree of the algebraic sets defined respectively by the ideal $I_i(f)$, $I_i(f) \cap \mathbb{Q}[X_1, \ldots, X_n]$ and $\pi_i^{-1}(y) \cap V \cap \mathbb{R}^n$ where y is a point returned in Step 2 of HasEmptyInterior.

LEMMA 6. *Let D be the degree of f. Then for $1 \leq i \leq n-1$, the degree of $V(I_i(f))$ and $\pi_i(V(I_i(f)))$ is bounded by D^{n-i+1} and for all $\mathbf{x}_i \in \mathbb{R}^i$, the degree of $V \cap \mathbb{R}^n \cap \pi_i^{-1}(\mathbf{x}_i)$ is bounded by D.*

PROOF. The degree of f is D so $\deg(V) \leq D$. We denote by R_i and J_i the ideals $\left\langle \frac{\partial f}{\partial X_{i+1}}, \ldots, \frac{\partial f}{\partial X_n} \right\rangle$ and $R_i : \left\langle \frac{\partial f}{\partial X_1}, \ldots, \frac{\partial f}{\partial X_i} \right\rangle^{\infty}$.
By [13, Section 4.4, Thm. 7 and Prop. 10],

$$V(J_i) = \bigcap_{l=1}^{i} \overline{V(R_i) - V\left(\left\langle \frac{\partial f}{\partial X_l} \right\rangle\right)}.$$

Then the degree of $V(J_i)$ is bounded by the product of the degrees of $\overline{V(R_i) - V\left(\left\langle \frac{\partial f}{\partial X_l} \right\rangle\right)}$, each one bounded by $\deg(V(R_i))$.
With Bezout's inequality [21], the degree of $V(R_i)$ is bounded by $\deg\left(\bigcap_{r=i+1}^{n} V\left(\left\langle \frac{\partial f}{\partial X_r} \right\rangle\right)\right) \leq D^{n-i}$.
Since $I_i(f) = J_i + \langle f \rangle$, then the degree of $V(I_i(f))$ is bounded by $D^{n-i} \cdot D = D^{n-i+1}$ and the bound holds for $\deg(\pi_i(V(I_i(f))))$.
Finally, the degree of a fiber above a point $P = (x_1, \ldots, x_i)$ is the degree of $V(\langle f, X_1 - x_1, \ldots, X_i - x_i \rangle)$ which is D. □

Complexity estimates. Our goal is to establish the following result.

THEOREM 7. *We assume that Algorithm RealDimension chooses $\mathbf{A}$ in $\Gamma_1 \cap \Gamma_2 \cap \mathrm{GL}_n(\mathbb{Q})$ where Γ_1 and Γ_2 are the non-empty Zariski open subsets of $\mathrm{GL}_n(\mathbb{C})$ defined in Proposition 3 and Theorem 4. Let d be the real dimension of $V \cap \mathbb{R}^n$, then the number of arithmetic operations needed to compute d is bounded by*

$$\tilde{O}(n^{16}(1 + D)^{3d(n-d)+5n+5}).$$

PROOF. In the sequel, we omit superscripts $\mathbf{A}$ indicating the changes of variables to keep notation simple. Also, the extra cost induced by these changes of variables are negligible compared to the cost of all other steps of the algorithm.
We start by estimating the complexity of HasEmptyInterior(f, i, Id) for an integer $0 < i < n$.
Step 1. By Proposition 5, $I_i(f)$ has dimension $i - 1$ at most. We deduce that $I_i(f) \cap \mathbb{Q}[X_1, \ldots, X_i]$ is the intersection of ideals $\tilde{I}_k$ such that $\tilde{I}_k \cap \mathbb{Q}[X_1, \ldots, X_i]$ has co-dimension k for $1 \leq k \leq i$. Below, we show how to compute $g_k \in \tilde{I}_k \cap \mathbb{Q}[X_1, \ldots, X_i]$ with $\deg(g_k) \leq \deg(V(\tilde{I}_k))$. Since $\deg(V(I_i(f))) = \sum_{k=1}^{i} \deg(V(\tilde{I}_k))$, we deduce that $g = g_1 \cdots g_i$ has degree less than or equal to D^{n-i+1} (Lemma 6). By Proposition 5, the Jacobian matrix associated to $\left(\frac{\partial f}{\partial X_{i+1}}, \ldots, \frac{\partial f}{\partial X_n}\right)$ at x has maximal rank at any point of $W = V\left(\left\langle \frac{\partial f}{\partial X_{i+1}}, \ldots, \frac{\partial f}{\partial X_n} \right\rangle\right) - V\left(\left\langle \frac{\partial f}{\partial X_1}, \ldots, \frac{\partial f}{\partial X_i} \right\rangle\right)$. This implies that we can apply lifting algorithms in [17] at points of the above constructible set. Also note that by [38, Section 6.3], for a generic point y in $\mathbb{C}^{i-1}$, $V(I_i(f)) \cap \pi_{i-1}^{-1}(y)$ is finite.
One obtains the first polynomial g_1 in the following way. We first compute generic points in $V(I_i(f)) \cap \pi_{i-1}^{-1}(y)$ where y is a generic point in $\mathbb{Q}^{i-1}$ using [17]; this is possible because Proposition 5 shows that assumptions required in [17] are satisfied. Next, we project those points on the X_i-coordinate (see e.g. [36, Lemma 10.5.5]) and repeat the process as many times as necessary to perform a multivariate interpolation. Since g_1 has degree D^{n-i+1}, we need $(D^{n-i+1} + 1)^i \leq (D+1)^{i(n-i)}$ interpolation points. Due to the lack of space, we cannot enter into the details. Combining the complexity estimates in [17] and [36, Chap. 10], we get that this is done in time $\tilde{O}(n^5 D^{i(n-i)+3n-i+4})$.
We now show how to compute g_2. Note that, choosing $y \in \mathbb{Q}^{i-2}$ generically, $V(I_i(f)) \cap \pi_{i-2}^{-1}(y)$ has dimension 1. We start by computing generic points in this set, i.e. its intersection with a hyperplane H. This is done in two steps. We first obtain a generic point W and next use the lifting procedure [17, Lemma 3] to get a lifting curve that is finally intersected with the hypersurface defined by $f = 0$ [17,

Lemma 16]. Remark that repeating the computation with a different H allows us to select, from these generic points, those who actually lie in $V(\tilde{I}_2)$. Finally we project those points who lie in $V(\tilde{I}_2)$ on the X_{i-1}-coordinate using again [36, Lemma 10.5] and use again multivariate interpolation to finally reconstruct g_2. The cost of this step is done in the same complexity bound as above.

Other polynomials g_k are obtained similarly. All in all, there are $O(n)$ such steps to perform at most.

The total cost is $\tilde{O}(n^6 D^{i(n-i)+3n-i+4})$ and $\deg(g) \leq D^{n-i+1}$.

Step 2. We estimate the complexity to compute a set L of points meeting each connected component of the semi-algebraic set defined by $g \neq 0$ in $\mathbb{R}^i$ where $g \in \mathbb{Q}[X_1, \dots, X_i]$ has degree bounded by D^{n-i+1}. To compute such a set, we take the projection over $\mathbb{R}^i$ of a set of points meeting each connected component of the real algebraic set in $\mathbb{R}^{i+1}$ defined by $gY - 1 = 0$ (where Y is a new indeterminate). The degree of this set is bounded by $(D^{n-i+1}+1)^{i+1}$. It is straightforward to see that $gY-1$ is square-free and the algebraic set it defines is smooth and equidimensional. By [35, Theorem 3], this is done using $\tilde{O}(n^{16}(D^{n-i+1}+1)^{3i+5}) \subset \tilde{O}(n^{16}(1+D)^{3(n-i)i+5n-2i+5})$ arithmetic operations in $\mathbb{Q}$ at most.

Step 3. By [32, Theorem 4], deciding the emptiness of the real algebraic set defined by $f(x_1, \dots, x_i, X_{i+1}, \dots, X_n) = 0$ where $(x_1, \dots, x_i)$ is in L is done using $O((nD^{n-i} + n^4)n^4 D^{2(n-i+1)})$ arithmetic operations in $\mathbb{Q}$ at most. By [35, Theorem 3], the number of points returned by Step 2 is bounded by $O((1+D^{n-i+1})^{i+1})$. We deduce that Step 3 uses $O(n^4(nD^n + n^4)(1+D)^{i(n-i)+3n-i+3})$ arithmetic operations in $\mathbb{Q}$ at most. Note that this step is negligible compared to the complexity of Step 2.

Finally, HasEmptyInterior(f, i, Id) runs in time

$$\tilde{O}(n^{16}(1+D)^{3i(n-i)+5n-2i+5})$$

Complexity of RealDimension. By [32, Theorem 4], one can decide the emptiness of $V \cap \mathbb{R}^n$ in Step 1 in probabilistic time $O((nD^n + n^4)n^4 D^{2(n+1)})$.

Finally, Step 3 of RealDimension is a loop from 1 to $\lceil \frac{n}{2} \rceil$ calling HasEmptyInterior with inputs (f, i, Id) and $(f, n-i, \mathrm{Id})$. These calls require respectively at most $\tilde{O}(n^{16}(1+D)^{3i(n-i)+5n-2i+5})$ and $\tilde{O}(n^{16}(1+D)^{3i(n-i)+3n+2i+5})$ arithmetic operations. Since this loop stops when i or $n-i$ is equal to d, the complexity of Step 3 and then of RealDimension is bounded by $\tilde{O}(n^{16}(1+D)^{3d(n-d)+5n+5})$. □

4. PROOF OF PROPOSITION 5

Strategy of proof. In Subsection 4.1, we prove the existence of a non-empty Zariski open subset $\Gamma_3 \subset \mathrm{GL}_n(\mathbb{C})$ such that, for any $\mathbf{A} \in \Gamma_3 \cap \mathrm{GL}_n(\mathbb{Q})$, assertion (1) of Proposition 5 holds. In Subsection 4.2, we prove the existence of a non-empty Zariski open subset $\Gamma_4 \subset \mathrm{GL}_n(\mathbb{C})$ such that, for any $\mathbf{A} \in \Gamma_4 \cap \mathrm{GL}_n(\mathbb{Q})$, assertion (2) of Proposition 5 holds. Taking $\Gamma' = \Gamma_3 \cap \Gamma_4$ ends the proof.

4.1 Proof of assertion (1) of Proposition 5

This proof is widely inspired from [1, Prop. 3].

Consider the map Φ_i defined for every $(y, \mathbf{a}) = (y, (a_{k,l})) \in \mathbb{C}^n \times \mathbb{C}^{n(n-i)}$ by $\Phi_i(y, \mathbf{a}) = \left(\sum_{k=1}^n a_{k,j} \frac{\partial f}{\partial Y_k}(y)\right)_{i+1 \leq j \leq n} \in \mathbb{C}^{n-i}$ and, for $\mathbf{a} \in \mathbb{C}^{n(n-i)}$, its restriction $\Phi_{i,\mathbf{a}} : y \in \mathbb{C}^n \to \Phi_i(y, \mathbf{a}) \in \mathbb{C}^{n-i}$.

The Jacobian matrix of Φ_i with respect to $Y_1, \dots, Y_n, a_{1,i+1}, a_{2,i+1}, \dots, a_{n,n}$ at the point $\alpha = (y, (a_{k,l}))$ is the matrix

$$\begin{pmatrix} * & \cdots & * & \frac{\partial f}{\partial Y_1} & \cdots & \frac{\partial f}{\partial Y_n} & 0 & \cdots & \cdots & 0 \\ \vdots & & \vdots & 0 & \cdots & 0 & \ddots & 0 & \cdots & 0 \\ * & \cdots & * & 0 & \cdots & \cdots & 0 & \frac{\partial f}{\partial Y_1} & \cdots & \frac{\partial f}{\partial Y_n} \end{pmatrix}.$$

Let $\mathcal{U}_i \subset \mathbb{C}^n$ be the Zariski open set defined as the set of points such that at least one of the first i partial derivatives of f does not vanish. Let α be in $(y, a) \in \mathcal{U}_i \times \mathbb{C}^{n(n-i)}$. The Jacobian matrix has maximal rank at α, since otherwise all the partial derivatives of f vanish at y and since y lies in $\mathcal{U}_i$, this is impossible. We deduce that α is a regular point of Φ_i, which implies that Φ_i is transversal to the origin $\mathbf{0}$.

By the Weak Transversality Theorem of Thom-Sard [36, Proposition 4.2.2], there exists a Zariski dense subset $\mathcal{O}_i \subset \mathbb{C}^{n(n-i)}$ such that for all $\mathbf{a} = (a_{k,l})$ in $\mathcal{O}_i \cap \mathbb{Q}^{n(n-i)}$, the map $\Phi_{i,\mathbf{a}} : \mathcal{U}_i \to \mathbb{C}^{n-i}$ is transversal to the origin.

Let Γ_3 be the non-empty Zariski subset of $\mathrm{GL}_n(\mathbb{C})$ defined as the set of matrices of $\mathrm{GL}_n(\mathbb{C})$ such that the $n-i$ last columns lie in $\mathcal{O}_i$. Let $\mathbf{A} \in \Gamma_3 \cap \mathrm{GL}_n(\mathbb{Q})$ and $\mathbf{a} \in \mathcal{O}_i$ be the $n-i$ last columns of $\mathbf{A}$.

We denote by $\mathcal{J}$ the Jacobian matrix of

$$\left(\sum_{k=1}^n a_{k,i+1}\frac{\partial f}{\partial X_k}, \dots, \sum_{k=1}^n a_{k,n}\frac{\partial f}{\partial X_k}\right).$$

Then, by the Jacobian Criterion, for all x in

$$V\left(\sum_{k=1}^n a_{k,i+1}\frac{\partial f}{\partial X_k}, \dots, \sum_{k=1}^n a_{k,i+1}\frac{\partial f}{\partial X_k}\right) - V\left(\frac{\partial f}{\partial X_1}, \dots, \frac{\partial f}{\partial X_i}\right),$$

the matrix $\mathcal{J}$ has maximal rank at x. Since $\frac{\partial f^{\mathbf{A}}}{\partial X_j} = \sum_{k=1}^n a_{k,n} \frac{\partial f}{\partial X_k} \circ \mathbf{A}$, then the Jacobian of $\left(\frac{\partial f^{\mathbf{A}}}{\partial X_{i+1}}, \dots, \frac{\partial f^{\mathbf{A}}}{\partial X_n}\right)$ equals $\mathcal{J} \cdot \mathbf{A}$.

Let y be in $V\left(\frac{\partial f^{\mathbf{A}}}{\partial X_{i+1}}, \dots, \frac{\partial f^{\mathbf{A}}}{\partial X_n}\right) - V\left(\left(\frac{\partial f}{\partial X_1}\right)^{\mathbf{A}}, \dots, \left(\frac{\partial f}{\partial X_i}\right)^{\mathbf{A}}\right)$. Without loss of generality, we assume that $\frac{\partial f}{\partial X_1}(\mathbf{A}y) \neq 0$. We now prove that $y \notin V\left(\frac{\partial f^{\mathbf{A}}}{\partial X_1}, \dots, \frac{\partial f^{\mathbf{A}}}{\partial X_i}\right)$. Otherwise, since $\frac{\partial f^{\mathbf{A}}}{\partial X_j} = \sum_{k=1}^n a_{k,j} \frac{\partial f}{\partial X_k} \circ \mathbf{A}$, for every integer $j \leq n$, $\sum_{k=1}^n a_{k,1} \frac{\partial f}{\partial X_k}(\mathbf{A}y) = 0$ with $\mathbf{A} \in \mathrm{GL}_n(\mathbb{Q})$ and $\frac{\partial f}{\partial X_1}(\mathbf{A}y) \neq 0$ which is impossible.

Let $\mathbf{A} \in \Gamma_3 \cap \mathrm{GL}_n(\mathbb{Q})$ and let K_i be the set

$$\overline{V\left(\frac{\partial f^{\mathbf{A}}}{\partial X_{i+1}}, \dots, \frac{\partial f^{\mathbf{A}}}{\partial X_n}\right) - V\left(\frac{\partial f^{\mathbf{A}}}{\partial X_1}, \dots, \frac{\partial f^{\mathbf{A}}}{\partial X_i}\right)},$$

then by the Jacobian Criterion, K_i has dimension i. So, if $K_i \cap V^{\mathbf{A}}$ is non-empty then by Krull's theorem, it has either dimension i or dimension $i-1$. We prove below that $K_i \cap V^{\mathbf{A}}$ has dimension $i-1$ or is empty. In the sequel, we omit the superscript $\mathbf{A}$ to keep simple notations. Of course, we assume that $K_i \neq \emptyset$ in the sequel.

Let $z \in K_i$ be a regular point such that $y \notin V\left(\frac{\partial f}{\partial X_1}, \dots, \frac{\partial f}{\partial X_i}\right)$. Without loss of generality, one can assume that z is the origin that we denote by $\mathbf{0}$. Since K_i has dimension i and $\mathbf{0}$ is a regular point of K_i, there exists $\{j_1, \dots, j_i\}$ such that the projection of $T_z K_i$ on the $(X_{j_1}, \dots, X_{j_i})$-space is full dimensional (hence the differential of the restriction of the projection to K_i at $\mathbf{0}$ is surjective). To keep notations as simple as possible, we assume without loss of generality that $\{j_1, \dots, j_i\} = \{1, \dots, i\}$.

By the Implicit Function Theorem, there exist two Zariski open sets $\mathcal{U} \subset \mathbb{C}^i$ and $\mathcal{V} \subset \mathbb{C}^{n-i}$ and there exists a function

$$\phi : \mathbf{x}_i \in \mathcal{U} \to (\phi_{i+1}(\mathbf{x}_i), \dots, \phi_n(\mathbf{x}_i)) \in \mathcal{V}$$

such that for every $(x_1, \dots, x_n) \in \mathcal{U} \times \mathcal{V}$, the following holds

$$(x_1, \dots, x_n) \in K_i \Leftrightarrow (x_{i+1}, \dots, x_n) = (\phi_{i+1}(\mathbf{x}_i), \dots, \phi_n(\mathbf{x}_i)).$$

We define now γ as the following map: $\mathbf{x}_i \in \mathcal{U} \to (\mathbf{x}_i, \phi(\mathbf{x}_i)) \in \mathcal{U} \times \mathcal{V}$. Remark that any point in the image of γ lies in K_i.

We deduce that for all $\mathbf{x}_i = (x_1, \dots, x_i)$,

$$f \circ \gamma(\mathbf{x}_i) = \sum_{j=1}^i \frac{\partial f \circ \gamma}{\partial X_j}(\mathbf{0}) x_j + o(\|\mathbf{x}_i\|),$$

so $f \circ \gamma(\mathbf{x}_i)$ equals to

$$\sum_{j=1}^i \left(\frac{\partial f}{\partial X_j}(\mathbf{0}) + \sum_{k=i+1}^n \frac{\partial f}{\partial X_k}(\mathbf{0}) \frac{\partial \phi_k}{\partial X_j}(\mathbf{0})\right) x_j + o(\|\mathbf{x}_i\|).$$

Now, recall that, by definition of K_i, $\frac{\partial f}{\partial X_j}(\mathbf{0}) = 0$ for every $j > i$, and that $\mathbf{0} \notin V\left(\frac{\partial f}{\partial X_1}, \dots, \frac{\partial f}{\partial X_i}\right)$. Without loss of generality, assume that $\frac{\partial f}{\partial X_1}(\mathbf{0}) \neq 0$. Setting $x_2 = \dots = x_i = 0$, we deduce that

$$f \circ \gamma(x_1, 0, \dots, 0) = \frac{\partial f}{\partial X_1}(\mathbf{0})x_1 + o(\|\mathbf{x}_i\|)$$

which implies that f is not identically 0 along the curve defined by $\gamma(x_1, 0, \dots, 0)$ with $(x_1, 0, \dots, 0) \in \mathcal{U}$. This implies that $K_i \cap V$ is either empty or it has dimension $\dim(K_i) - 1 = i - 1$.

4.2 Proof of assertion (2) of Proposition 5

It relies on the two following lemmas.

LEMMA 8. *There exists a non-empty Zariski open subset $\Gamma_5 \subset \mathrm{GL}_n(\mathbb{C})$ such that for all $\mathbf{A} \in \Gamma_5 \cap \mathrm{GL}_n(\mathbb{Q})$ the following holds. Let $y \in \mathsf{Bd}(\pi_i(V^{\mathbf{A}} \cap \mathbb{R}^n))$ and let $B_i \subset \mathbb{R}^i$ be a ball centered at y of radius $r > 0$. There exist $x \in V^{\mathbf{A}} \cap \mathbb{R}^n$ such that $\pi_i(x) = y$, a ball $B_n \subset \mathbb{R}^n$ centered at x of radius $r' > 0$ such that $\pi_i(B_n) \subset B_i$ and $y_\varepsilon \in \mathsf{Bd}(\pi_i(\mathrm{Ext}(B_n, \mathbb{R}\langle\varepsilon\rangle) \cap V_\varepsilon^{\mathbf{A}}))$ such that $\lim_{\varepsilon \to 0}(y_\varepsilon) = y$.*

Recall from Section 2 that $V_\varepsilon \in \mathbb{C}\langle\varepsilon\rangle^n$ denotes the algebraic set defined by $f - \varepsilon = 0$ and that $W_{\varepsilon,i}^{\mathbf{A}} \subset \mathbb{C}\langle\varepsilon\rangle$ denotes the polar variety defined by $f^{\mathbf{A}} - \varepsilon = \frac{\partial f^{\mathbf{A}}}{\partial X_{i+1}} = \dots = \frac{\partial f^{\mathbf{A}}}{\partial X_n} = 0$.

LEMMA 9. *There exists a non-empty Zariski open subset $\Gamma_6 \subset \mathrm{GL}_n(\mathbb{C})$ such that the following holds. For all $\mathbf{A} \in \Gamma_6 \cap \mathrm{GL}_n(\mathbb{Q})$, for any integer $1 \le i \le n-1$, the restriction of π_{i-1} to the polar variety $W_{\varepsilon,i}^{\mathbf{A}}$ is proper.*

PROOF OF ASSERTION (2) OF PROPOSITION 5. Let R_i and J_i be the ideals $\left\langle \frac{\partial f}{\partial X_{i+1}}, \dots, \frac{\partial f}{\partial X_n} \right\rangle$ and $R_i : \left\langle \frac{\partial f}{\partial X_1}, \dots, \frac{\partial f}{\partial X_i} \right\rangle^\infty$. Let $I_i(f)$ be the ideal $J_i + \langle f \rangle$. First we prove that $\lim_{\varepsilon \to 0}(W_{\varepsilon,i} \cap \mathbb{R}\langle\varepsilon\rangle^n) \subset V(I_i(f))$.
Let $(x, x_\varepsilon) \in \lim_{\varepsilon \to 0}(W_{\varepsilon,i} \cap \mathbb{R}\langle\varepsilon\rangle^n) \times W_{\varepsilon,i}$ such that $\lim_{\varepsilon \to 0}(x_\varepsilon) = x$. Since $\lim_{\varepsilon \to 0}$ is a ring homomorphism and $f \in \mathbb{Q}[X_1, \dots, X_n]$, $\lim_{\varepsilon \to 0}(f(x_\varepsilon)) = 0 = f(\lim_{\varepsilon \to 0}(x_\varepsilon)) = f(x)$.
Let $h \in J_i$; by definition of J_i, there exists $m \in \mathbb{N}^*$ such that for all $g \in \left\langle \frac{\partial f}{\partial X_1}, \dots, \frac{\partial f}{\partial X_i} \right\rangle$, the polynomial $g^m h$ lies in R_i. Since x_ε lies in $W_{\varepsilon,i}$, $g^m(x_\varepsilon)h(x_\varepsilon) = 0$ for all g in $\left\langle \frac{\partial f}{\partial X_1}, \dots, \frac{\partial f}{\partial X_i} \right\rangle$.
Since V_ε is smooth by Lemma 2, there exists $j \in \{1, \dots, i\}$ such that $\frac{\partial f}{\partial X_j}(x_\varepsilon) \neq 0$. Let g be the polynomial $\frac{\partial f}{\partial X_j}$, then $g(x_\varepsilon) \neq 0$ and $g^m(x_\varepsilon)h(x_\varepsilon) = 0$ so $h(x_\varepsilon) = 0$. Finally, since h has rational coefficients and $\lim_{\varepsilon \to 0}$ is a ring homomorphism, we deduce that $h(\lim_{\varepsilon \to 0}(x_\varepsilon)) = h(x) = 0$. Then x lies in $V(J_i + \langle f \rangle) = V(I_i(f))$. We conclude that $\lim_{\varepsilon \to 0}(W_{\varepsilon,i} \cap \mathbb{R}\langle\varepsilon\rangle^n) \subset V(I_i(f))$.
We claim that there exists a non-empty Zariski open subset $\Gamma_4 \subset \mathrm{GL}_n(\mathbb{C})$ such that for all $\mathbf{A} \in \Gamma_4 \cap \mathrm{GL}_n(\mathbb{Q})$, and for $1 \le i < n$, $\mathsf{Bd}(\pi_i(V^{\mathbf{A}} \cap \mathbb{R}^n)) \subset \pi_i(\lim_{\varepsilon \to 0}(W_{\varepsilon,i}^{\mathbf{A}} \cap \mathbb{R}\langle\varepsilon\rangle^n))$.
Since we already proved $\lim_{\varepsilon \to 0}(W_{\varepsilon,i}^{\mathbf{A}} \cap \mathbb{R}\langle\varepsilon\rangle^n) \subset V(I_i^{\mathbf{A}})$, we deduce that $\mathsf{Bd}(\pi_i(V^{\mathbf{A}} \cap \mathbb{R}^n)) \subset \pi_i(V(I_i^{\mathbf{A}}) \cap \mathbb{R}^n)$ which ends the proof of assertion (2) of Proposition 5.
Let Γ_5 be the non-empty Zariski open set of $\mathrm{GL}_n(\mathbb{C})$ defined in Lemma 8. Let Γ_6 be the non-empty Zariski open set of $\mathrm{GL}_n(\mathbb{C})$ defined in Lemma 9. We prove that taking the non-empty Zariski open set $\Gamma_4 = \Gamma_5 \cap \Gamma_6$ allows to prove our claim.
Let $\mathbf{A} \in \Gamma_4 \cap \mathrm{GL}_n(\mathbb{Q})$. Let $y \in \mathsf{Bd}(\pi_i(V^{\mathbf{A}} \cap \mathbb{R}^n))$ and $B_i \subset \mathbb{R}^i$ be the ball centered at y of radius $r > 0$. Since $\mathbf{A} \in \Gamma_5 \cap \mathrm{GL}_n(\mathbb{Q})$, there exists x, B_n and y as in Lemma 8. In particular, we have $y_\varepsilon \in \mathsf{Bd}(\pi_i(\mathrm{Ext}(B_n, \mathbb{R}\langle\varepsilon\rangle) \cap V_\varepsilon^{\mathbf{A}}))$ such that $\lim_{\varepsilon \to 0}(y_\varepsilon) = y$.
By Lemma 2, V_ε is either empty or smooth and equidimensional. By [35, Proposition 4], the set $\mathsf{Bd}(\pi_i(V_\varepsilon^{\mathbf{A}} \cap \mathbb{R}\langle\varepsilon\rangle^n))$ is a subset of $\pi_i(W_{\varepsilon,i}^{\mathbf{A}} \cap \mathbb{R}\langle\varepsilon\rangle^n)$, so $\mathsf{Bd}(\pi_i(\mathrm{Ext}(B_n, \mathbb{R}\langle\varepsilon\rangle) \cap V_\varepsilon^{\mathbf{A}}))$ is a subset of $\pi_i(\mathrm{Ext}(B_n, \mathbb{R}\langle\varepsilon\rangle) \cap W_{\varepsilon,i}^{\mathbf{A}})$. By Lemma 9, since $\mathbf{A} \in \Gamma_6 \cap \mathrm{GL}_n(\mathbb{Q})$, the restriction of π_i to $W_{\varepsilon,i}^{\mathbf{A}}$ is proper. We deduce that $\mathrm{Ext}(B_n, \mathbb{R}\langle\varepsilon\rangle)$ contains a neighborhood $\mathcal{O}$ of y_ε such that $\pi_i^{-1}(\overline{\mathcal{O}})$ is closed and bounded. In particular $\pi_i^{-1}(y_\varepsilon) \cap \mathrm{Ext}(B_n, \mathbb{R}\langle\varepsilon\rangle) \cap W_{\varepsilon,i}^{\mathbf{A}}$ is not empty. We let $x_\varepsilon \in \mathrm{Ext}(B_n, \mathbb{R}\langle\varepsilon\rangle) \cap \pi_i^{-1}(y_\varepsilon) \cap W_{\varepsilon,i}^{\mathbf{A}}$. Note that $x_\varepsilon \in \mathrm{Ext}(B_n, \mathbb{R}\langle\varepsilon\rangle)$ so it is bounded over $\mathbb{R}$; hence $x' = \lim_{\varepsilon \to 0}(x_\varepsilon)$ exists and $x' \in \lim_{\varepsilon \to 0}(\mathrm{Ext}(B_n, \mathbb{R}\langle\varepsilon\rangle) \cap W_{\varepsilon,i}^{\mathbf{A}}) = B_n \cap \lim_{\varepsilon \to 0}(W_{\varepsilon,i}^{\mathbf{A}})$.
We finish by proving that $\pi_i(x') = y$. We denote by $(x_{\varepsilon,1}, \dots, x_{\varepsilon,n})$ the coordinates of x_ε. Then $\pi_i(x')$ is the point $\pi_i(\lim_{\varepsilon \to 0}(x_\varepsilon)) = (\lim_{\varepsilon \to 0}(x_{\varepsilon,1}), \dots, \lim_{\varepsilon \to 0}(x_{\varepsilon,i}))$. So

$$\pi_i(x') = \lim_{\varepsilon \to 0}((x_{\varepsilon,1}, \dots, x_{\varepsilon,i})) = \lim_{\varepsilon \to 0}(\pi_i(x_\varepsilon))$$

which is equal to $\lim_{\varepsilon \to 0}(y_\varepsilon) = y$.
Finally, we conclude that $\mathsf{Bd}(\pi_i(V^{\mathbf{A}} \cap \mathbb{R}^n)) \subset \pi_i(\lim_{\varepsilon \to 0}(W_{\varepsilon,i}^{\mathbf{A}}) \cap B_n) \subset \pi_i(\lim_{\varepsilon \to 0}(W_{\varepsilon,i}^{\mathbf{A}} \cap \mathbb{R}\langle\varepsilon\rangle^n))$ as requested $\square$

Proof of Lemma 8. By [22, Proposition 3], there exists a non-empty Zariski open set $\Gamma_5 \subset \mathrm{GL}_n(\mathbb{C})$ such that for all $\mathbf{A} \in \Gamma_5 \cap \mathrm{GL}_n(\mathbb{Q})$ the following holds. For $1 \le i \le n-1$ and for any connected component C of $V^{\mathbf{A}} \cap \mathbb{R}^n$, $\pi_i(C)$ is closed. We prove now that Γ_5 satisfies Lemma 8. Let $\mathbf{A}$ be in $\Gamma_5 \cap \mathrm{GL}_n(\mathbb{Q})$.
Assume for the moment the following assertions. (they are proved below).

1. There exists $x \in \pi_i^{-1}(y) \cap V^{\mathbf{A}} \cap \mathbb{R}^n$ such that the ball $B_n \subset \mathbb{R}^n$ centered at x of radius $r' > 0$ satisfies $\pi_i(B_n) \subset B_i$.
2. The ball $\mathrm{Ext}(B_i, \mathbb{R}\langle\varepsilon\rangle)$ meets $\mathsf{Bd}\left(\pi_i(\mathrm{Ext}(B_n, \varepsilon) \cap V_\varepsilon^{\mathbf{A}})\right)$.

Let $x \in V^{\mathbf{A}} \cap \mathbb{R}^n$ and B_n be a ball of $\mathbb{R}^n$ as in assertion 1. For every radius $r > 0$, we denote by T_r the set $\pi_i\left(\mathrm{Ext}(B_n, \mathbb{R}\langle\varepsilon\rangle) \cap V_\varepsilon^{\mathbf{A}}\right)$. Then by assertion 2, the set $\mathsf{Bd}(T_r) \cap \mathrm{Ext}(B_i, \mathbb{R}\langle\varepsilon\rangle)$ is non-empty. It is a closed set as it is the intersections of closed sets. It is bounded over $\mathbb{R}$ since it is subset of $\mathrm{Ext}(B_i, \mathbb{R}\langle\varepsilon\rangle)$. We now consider the set T defined by $\bigcap_{r>0} \mathsf{Bd}(T_r) \cap \mathrm{Ext}(B_i, \mathbb{R}\langle\varepsilon\rangle)$. Again, the set T is closed and bounded over $\mathbb{R}$. When T is non-empty, there exists $y_\varepsilon \in T$, bounded over $\mathbb{R}$ that belongs to $\mathrm{Ext}(B_i, \mathbb{R}\langle\varepsilon\rangle)$ for any $r > 0$. Then $\lim_{\varepsilon \to 0}(y_\varepsilon)$ exists and equals y.
Now, we prove by contradiction that T is non-empty. Fix $r > 0$ and let η be the distance between y and $\mathsf{Bd}(T_r)$ (defined in [8, Section 3.1]). There are two possible cases: either the distance η is 0 or infinitesimally small (i.e $\eta \in \mathbb{R}\langle\varepsilon\rangle$ such that $0 < \eta < s$, for all $s \in \mathbb{R}$) or there exists $s' > 0$, with $s' \in \mathbb{R}$ such that $\eta > s' > 0$.
In the first case, for all $s > 0$, with $s \in \mathbb{R}$, we have $0 \le \eta < s$. Since η is the distance between y and $\mathsf{Bd}(T_r)$, there exists $y_\varepsilon \in T_r$ such that the distance η' between y and y_ε satisfies $\eta \le \eta' \le \eta + \varepsilon$. Since $\eta + \varepsilon$ is infinitesimal, then for all $s \in \mathbb{R}$ and $s > 0$, $0 < \eta + \varepsilon < s$ and y_ε lies in the ball $\mathrm{Ext}(B_i, \mathbb{R}\langle\varepsilon\rangle)$ of radius $s > 0$ and $s \in \mathbb{R}$. We deduce that $y_\varepsilon \in T$ which contradicts our assumption.
Assume now we are in the second case. By assertion 2 there exists $y_\varepsilon \in \mathsf{Bd}(T_{s'}) \cap \mathrm{Ext}(B_i', \mathbb{R}\langle\varepsilon\rangle)$, where B_i' is the ball centered at y of radius s'. So the distance η' between y and y_ε satisfies $\eta \le \eta' \le s' < \eta$ and there is a contradiction.
Finally, the two cases contradict the fact that T is empty.

It remains the prove the above assertions.
1. Since y is in the boundary of $\pi_i(V^{\mathbf{A}} \cap \mathbb{R}^n)$, the ball B_i meets $\pi_i(V^{\mathbf{A}} \cap \mathbb{R}^n)$. We deduce that there exists a connected component C of $V^{\mathbf{A}} \cap \mathbb{R}^n$ such that $\pi_i(C)$ meets B_i. Since $\mathbf{A}$ is in $\Gamma_5 \cap \mathrm{GL}_n(\mathbb{Q})$, $\pi_i(C)$ is closed. So y is in the boundary of $\pi_i(C)$ which is a subset of $\pi_i(C)$. We consider a point $x \in \pi_i^{-1}(y) \cap C$. Let $r' > 0$ be such that the ball B_n of $\mathbb{R}^n$ centered at x of radius r', satisfies $\pi_i(B_n) \subset B_i$. Then $\pi_i^{-1}(y) \cap B_n$ is not empty.

Without loss of generality, we assume that for any r', there exists a point of B_n at which f is positive (else we change f to $-f$).
2. Assume for the moment the following

(a) There exists y_ε in $\mathrm{Ext}(B_i, \mathbb{R}\langle\varepsilon\rangle)$ such that

$$\mathrm{Ext}\left(\pi_i^{-1}(y_\varepsilon) \cap B_n, \mathbb{R}\langle\varepsilon\rangle\right) \cap V_\varepsilon^{\mathbf{A}} \neq \emptyset.$$

(b) There exists y' in B_i such that

$$\mathrm{Ext}\left(\pi_i^{-1}(y') \cap B_n, \mathbb{R}\langle\varepsilon\rangle\right) \cap V_\varepsilon^{\mathbf{A}} = \emptyset.$$

On the one hand, since $\mathrm{Ext}\left(\pi_i^{-1}(y_\varepsilon) \cap B_n, \mathbb{R}\langle\varepsilon\rangle\right) \cap V_\varepsilon^{\mathbf{A}} \neq \emptyset$ by assertion (a) and $\pi_i(B_n) \subset B_i$ by assertion (1), we have

$$\mathrm{Ext}(B_i, \mathbb{R}\langle\varepsilon\rangle) \cap \pi_i\left(\mathrm{Ext}(B_n, \mathbb{R}\langle\varepsilon\rangle) \cap V_\varepsilon^{\mathbf{A}}\right) \neq \emptyset.$$

On the other hand, let U be the complementary of $\mathrm{Ext}(B_n, \mathbb{R}\langle\varepsilon\rangle) \cap V_\varepsilon^{\mathbf{A}}$ in $\mathbb{R}\langle\varepsilon\rangle^n$. Since $\mathrm{Ext}\left(\pi_i^{-1}(y') \cap B_n, \mathbb{R}\langle\varepsilon\rangle\right) \cap V_\varepsilon^{\mathbf{A}} = \emptyset$ by assertion (b) and since $\mathrm{Ext}(\pi_i^{-1}(y'), \mathbb{R}\langle\varepsilon\rangle) \neq \emptyset$ by assertion (1), we deduce that $\mathrm{Ext}\left(\pi_i^{-1}(y'), \mathbb{R}\langle\varepsilon\rangle\right) \cap U \neq \emptyset$. This implies that $\mathrm{Ext}(B_i, \mathbb{R}\langle\varepsilon\rangle) \cap \pi_i(U) \neq \emptyset$.
By [8, Prop 5.24], the set $\mathrm{Ext}(B_i, \mathbb{R}\langle\varepsilon\rangle)$ is semi-algebraically connected. It is the disjoint union of $\mathrm{Ext}(B_i, \mathbb{R}\langle\varepsilon\rangle) \cap \pi_i(U)$ and

$$\mathrm{Ext}(B_i, \mathbb{R}\langle\varepsilon\rangle) \cap \pi_i\left(\mathrm{Ext}(B_n, \mathbb{R}\langle\varepsilon\rangle) \cap V_\varepsilon^{\mathbf{A}}\right)$$

which are semi-algebraic sets, closed in $\mathrm{Ext}(B_i, \mathbb{R}\langle\varepsilon\rangle)$. So the set $\mathrm{Ext}(B_i, \mathbb{R}\langle\varepsilon\rangle)$ meets the boundary of $\pi_i(\mathrm{Ext}(B_n, \mathbb{R}\langle\varepsilon\rangle) \cap V_\varepsilon^{\mathbf{A}})$.

Finally, we prove (a) and (b).
(a). We prove that there exists a point x_ε in $\mathrm{Ext}(B_n, \mathbb{R}\langle\varepsilon\rangle) \cap V_\varepsilon^{\mathbf{A}}$. Since f is not non-positive over B_n, there exists x' in B_n such that $f^{\mathbf{A}}(x') > 0$. Since $f^{\mathbf{A}}(x') \in \mathbb{R}$, $x \in V^{\mathbf{A}} \cap \mathbb{R}^n$ and ε is an infinitesimal, we deduce that $f^{\mathbf{A}}(x) - \varepsilon < 0$ and $f^{\mathbf{A}}(x') - \varepsilon > 0$.
Let Ψ be the polynomial in $\mathbb{R}\langle\varepsilon\rangle[T]$ defined by $\Psi = f^{\mathbf{A}}(Tx + (1-T)x') - \varepsilon$. Then $\Psi(0) > 0$ and $\Psi(1) < 0$ so by [8, Thm 2.11], there exists $t_0 \in (0, 1)$ such that $\Psi(t_0) = 0$. Let x_ε be the point $t_0 x + (1 - t_0)x' \in \mathrm{Ext}(B_n, \mathbb{R}\langle\varepsilon\rangle)$, then $f^{\mathbf{A}}(x_\varepsilon) - \varepsilon = 0$. Then x_ε is in $\mathrm{Ext}(B_n, \mathbb{R}\langle\varepsilon\rangle) \cap V_\varepsilon^{\mathbf{A}}$.
Let y_ε be $\pi_i(x_\varepsilon)$, then $y_\varepsilon \in \pi_i(\mathrm{Ext}(B_n, \mathbb{R}\langle\varepsilon\rangle)) \subset \mathrm{Ext}(B_i, \mathbb{R}\langle\varepsilon\rangle)$. Then x_ε is in $\mathrm{Ext}(\pi_i^{-1}(y_\varepsilon) \cap B_n, \mathbb{R}\langle\varepsilon\rangle) \cap V_\varepsilon^{\mathbf{A}}$, so there exists y_ε in $\mathrm{Ext}(B_i, \mathbb{R}\langle\varepsilon\rangle)$ such that $\mathrm{Ext}\left(\pi_i^{-1}(y_\varepsilon) \cap B_n, \mathbb{R}\langle\varepsilon\rangle\right) \cap V_\varepsilon^{\mathbf{A}} \neq \emptyset$.

(b). Since y is in $\mathsf{Bd}(\pi_i(V^{\mathbf{A}} \cap \mathbb{R}^n))$ by assumption and since $\pi_i(B_n)$ is a neighborhood of y, there exists $y' \in \pi_i(B_n)$ such that y' is not in the Euclidean closure of $\pi_i(V^{\mathbf{A}} \cap \mathbb{R}^n)$. We deduce that the distance between y' and $\pi_i(V^{\mathbf{A}} \cap \mathbb{R}^n)$ is positive. We also deduce that the set $F = \pi_i^{-1}(y') \cap B_n$ is not empty.
The distance Δ between F and $V \cap \mathbb{R}^n$ is also positive. Indeed, otherwise, for all $\beta > 0$ there is a point $z \in F$ such that the distance between z and $V \cap \mathbb{R}^n$ is less than β. Then $\Delta < \beta$ for all $\beta > 0$. This implies that $\Delta = 0$ and F meets the closure of $V \cap \mathbb{R}^n$ which contradicts the fact that y' is not in the closure of the projection.
Since $F \subset B_n$ is closed and bounded, then the polynomial function $x \mapsto f(x)$ reach its lower bound δ at $z_0 \in F$ and its upper bound δ' at $z'_0 \in F$. Since $\Delta > 0$, either $\delta > 0$ or $\delta' < 0$.
We assume now $\delta > 0$. Then there exists $\eta > 0$, $\eta \in \mathbb{R}$ such that for all $z' \in F$, $f(z') > \eta$. If we denote the coordinates of y' by $y'_1, \ldots, y'_i$, then the semi-algebraic set F can be defined by the equations $X_1 = y'_1, \ldots, X_i = y'_i$, the polynomial inequality $d((X_1, \ldots, X_n), y) \leq r$ and both with or without the inequality $f(X_1, \ldots, X_n) > \eta$. Then by [8, Proposition 2.87], for all $z_\varepsilon \in \mathrm{Ext}(F, \mathbb{R}\langle\varepsilon\rangle)$, $f(z_\varepsilon) > \eta > 0$ with $\eta \in \mathbb{R}$. Thus f never equals to $\varepsilon < \eta$ on $\mathrm{Ext}(F, \mathbb{R}\langle\varepsilon\rangle) = \mathrm{Ext}(\pi_i^{-1}(y') \cap B_n, \mathbb{R}\langle\varepsilon\rangle)$. When $\delta' < 0$, the proof is similar. We prove that there exists $\eta' < 0$ such that f is never equals to $\varepsilon > 0 > \eta' > \delta'$ when $\delta' < 0$. In both cases, we deduce that $\mathrm{Ext}\left(\pi_i^{-1}(y') \cap B_n, \mathbb{R}\langle\varepsilon\rangle\right) \cap V_\varepsilon^{\mathbf{A}} = \emptyset$.

Proof of Lemma 9. This lemma is a generalization to $\mathbb{C}\langle\varepsilon\rangle$ of [35, Theorem 1].

PROOF. The proof of [35, Theorem 1] holds if the base field is $\mathbb{C}\langle\varepsilon\rangle$ instead of $\mathbb{C}$. This theorem can be restated as follows: *There exists a Zariski open set Γ in $\mathrm{GL}_n(\mathbb{C}\langle\varepsilon\rangle)$ such that for $\mathbf{A}$ in Γ and $i \in \{1, \ldots, n-1\}$, the restriction of π_i to the i-th polar variety $W_{\varepsilon,i}^{\mathbf{A}}$ associated to $f - \varepsilon$ is proper.* We now prove that the previous property holds over a non-empty Zariski open subset of $\mathrm{GL}_n(\mathbb{C})$.
The proof of [35, Theorem 1] uses n^2 new indeterminates denoted by $\mathcal{A}_{1,1}, \ldots, \mathcal{A}_{n,n}$, and characterizes the matrices of $\mathrm{GL}_n(\mathbb{C}\langle\varepsilon\rangle)$ which do not satisfy the properness property as the set of solutions of a polynomial system $G_1 = 0, \ldots, G_s = 0$ of $\mathbb{C}\langle\varepsilon\rangle[\mathcal{A}_{1,1}, \ldots, \mathcal{A}_{n,n}]$. Let G be the product of $G_1, \ldots, G_s$. The polynomials $G_1, \ldots, G_s$ are defined as generators of the prime components of the radical of an ideal generated by $f - \varepsilon \in \mathbb{Q}(\varepsilon)[X_1, \ldots, X_n]$ and some minors of the Jacobian matrix of $f - \varepsilon$ also in $\mathbb{Q}(\varepsilon)[X_1, \ldots, X_n]$ (see [35, Sections 2.3 and 2.4]) so their coefficients are in $\mathbb{Q}(\varepsilon)$ and the coefficients of G too. Let Ω be the non-empty Zariski open set of $\mathrm{GL}_n(\mathbb{C}\langle\varepsilon\rangle)$ defined as the complementary of this set of matrices.
If we multiply G by the least common multiple of the denominators of its coefficients, we obtain a polynomial with coefficients in $\mathbb{Q}[\varepsilon]$. Let P be the primitive part of this polynomial. Let P_0 be the polynomial with rational coefficients obtained by replacing ε by 0 in P, then $P - P_0$ can be factorized as $P - P_0 = \varepsilon^\nu P_\varepsilon$ with P_ε with coefficients in $\mathbb{Q}[\varepsilon]$ and $\nu > 0$ as large as possible. Hence, $P = P_0 + \varepsilon^\nu P_\varepsilon$.
Since the coefficients of P have non-trivial gcd, at least one of the two polynomials P_0 and P_ε is not identically 0. Indeed, if $P_0 = 0$, then since ν is maximal, $P = \varepsilon^\nu P_\varepsilon = \varepsilon^\nu(P_1 + \varepsilon^{\nu'} P_2)$ with P_1 with coefficients in $\mathbb{Q}$ and then $P_1 \neq 0$. Let $\Omega_0 \subset \mathrm{GL}_n(\mathbb{C})$ (resp. $\Omega_1 \subset \mathrm{GL}_n(\mathbb{C})$) be the non-empty Zariski open set defined by $P_0 \neq 0$ (resp. $P_1 \neq 0$).
Let $\mathbf{A}$ be in $(\Omega_0 \cup \Omega_1) \cap \mathrm{GL}_n(\mathbb{Q}) \subset \Omega$, then $P(\mathbf{A}) = P_0(\mathbf{A}) + \varepsilon^\nu P_\varepsilon(\mathbf{A}) \in \mathbb{Q}[\varepsilon]$. We now prove that $P(\mathbf{A}) \neq 0$. If $P_0(\mathbf{A}) = 0$, then $P_\varepsilon(\mathbf{A}) \neq 0$ and then $P(\mathbf{A}) = \varepsilon^\nu P_\varepsilon(\mathbf{A}) \neq 0$. If $P_0(\mathbf{A}) \neq 0$, then, since ε is transcendental, $P(\mathbf{A}) \neq 0$. Then $P(\mathbf{A}) \neq 0$ so the restriction of π_i to $W_{\varepsilon,i}^{\mathbf{A}}$ is proper. Let Γ be the set $\Omega_0 \cup \Omega_1$, then for all matrices $\mathbf{A}$ in $\Gamma \cap \mathrm{GL}_n(\mathbb{Q})$, the properness property holds. □

5. EXPERIMENTS

We report on timings obtained with a first implementation of our algorithm. This is a Maple implementation built-on the RAGlib Maple package [33] and the FGb library [15] written in C by J.-C. Faugère. RAGlib is used for deciding the emptiness of real algebraic sets and computing sample points in each of their connected components. It implements algorithms that essentially run in time $D^{O(n)}$. The library FGb is a state-of-the art library for Gröbner bases computations. We use it for all ideal-theoretic operations required by our algorithm. We also use Gröbner bases computations to check Noether position properties needed for the correctness of the algorithm. This allows us to try sparse linear changes of variables (or avoid them when unnecessary) which is crucial for practical performances.
We established that our algorithm runs in time $D^{O(d(n-d))}$ where d is the dimension of the real algebraic set under study. A first goal is to observe if the implementation has a practical behaviour that reflects this complexity. In other words computations should be "easier" when d or $n - d$ is "small" and harder when d is close to $n/2$. Another goal is to identify if such an implementation can handle examples that are out of reach of the best implementations of Cylindrical Algebraic Decomposition such as QEPCAD [10], the implementation of CAD in Maple [11] or RedLog [39] among others. We report the timings obtained with the Maple implementation of CAD (other mentioned software behave similarly on our test-suite). While it is natural to compare with CAD since it is the unique other implemented technique, remember that CAD provides much more information than the dimension.
The choice of a test-suite is often subjective. With respect to our goals, we have chosen to run the software on sums of squares of random dense polynomials because this allows us to control the dimension of the real algebraic set and identifies if the implementation reflects the $D^{O(d(n-d))}$ complexity. We also have chosen discriminants of characteristic polynomials of linear symmetric matrices (entries are chosen random dense). These are known to be sums of squares

n	s	Degrees	d	CAD	Dim	Step 1	Step 2	Step 3	Fibers
4	1	2	3	0.8 s	4.5 s	/	/	/	/
4	2	2,1	2	∞	54 s	0%	99%	1%	2
4	3	2,1,1	1	∞	41 s	25%	5%	70%	2
4	4	2,1,1,1	0	∞	14 s	12%	1%	87%	3
5	1	2	4	0.6 s	4 s	/	/	/	/
5	2	2,1	3	∞	92 s	0%	99.4%	0.6%	4
5	3	2,1,1	2	∞	94 s	6%	88%	6%	1
5	4	2,1,1,1	1	∞	54 s	7%	13%	80%	4
5	5	2,1,1,1,1	0	∞	83 s	3%	0%	97%	3
6	1	2	5	7.5 s	4.8 s	/	/	/	/
6	2	2,1	4	∞	116 s	0%	99.8%	0.2%	1
6	3	2,1,1	3	∞	140 s	2%	95%	3%	2
6	4	2,1,1,1	2	∞	190 s	3%	95%	2%	1
6	5	2,1,1,1,1	1	∞	122 s	3%	19%	78%	4
6	6	2,1,1,1,1,1	0	∞	120 s	1%	0%	99%	3
7	1	2	6	3.1 s	4.7 s	/	/	/	/
7	2	2,1	5	∞	223 s	0%	99%	1%	6
7	3	2,1,1	4	∞	2278 s	1%	96%	3%	7
7	4	2,1,1,1	3	∞	103190 s	0%	100%	0%	3
7	5	2,1,1,1,1	2	∞	2202 s	2.5%	95%	2%	4
7	6	2,1,1,1,1,1	1	∞	507 s	2%	19%	79%	5
7	7	2,1,1,1,1,1,1	0	∞	355 s	1%	0%	99%	3
8	1	2	7	24.2 s	7.6 s	/	/	/	/
8	2	2,1	6	∞	2352 s	0%	99.5%	0.5%	8
8	3	2,1,1	5	∞	∞				
8	4	2,1,1,1	4	∞	∞				
8	5	2,1,1,1,1	3	∞	∞				
8	6	2,1,1,1,1,1	2	∞	35377 s	1%	99%	0%	1
8	7	2,1,1,1,1,1,1	1	∞	1230 s	2%	36%	62%	3
8	8	2,1,1,1,1,1,1,1	0	∞	1002 s	0.2%	0%	99.8%	3
4	2	2,2	2	∞	34 s	0.1%	97%	2.9%	8
4	3	2,2,1	1	∞	54 s	10%	74%	16%	6
4	4	2,2,1,1	0	∞	25 s	19%	2%	79%	3
5	2	2,2	3	∞	79 s	0%	99.7%	.3%	1
5	3	2,2,1	2	∞	8003 s	3.8%	96.1%	.1%	8
5	4	2,2,1,1	1	∞	4773 s	3.1%	96.6%	0.3%	6
5	5	2,2,1,1,1	0	∞	284 s	15%	0%	85%	3
6	2	2,2	4	∞	2477 s	0%	100%	0%	1
6	3	2,2,1	3	∞	∞				
6	4	2,2,1,1	2	∞	∞				
6	5	2,2,1,1,1	1	∞	152500 s	3.4%	96.6%	0%	6
6	6	2,2,1,1,1,1	0	∞	6376 s	11%	0%	89%	3

Table 1: Sum of square of s random polynomials in n variables.

[25]. We finally consider sparse polynomials from [20] and [30] that are known to be non-negative over the reals but which have real roots (this implies that the dimension of the real algebraic set they define is less than $n-1$).

The computations were performed on an Intel Xeon E7540 @ 2.00 Ghz and 250GB of RAM. All timings are given in seconds. The symbol ∞ means that the computation has been stopped after 48 hours.

Random dense polynomials. Timings are given in Table 1. We consider of sums-of-squares of s n-variate polynomials. The degrees of the polynomials are given and the computed dimension as well. The column CAD indicates the timing of the Maple CAD implementation. Those for our implementation are given in the column Dim. We also give the relative part of the three main steps of HasEmptyInterior: computation of $I_i^{\mathbf{A}} \cap \mathbb{Q}[X_1, \ldots, X_i]$, computing sample points outside the zero locus of the obtained polynomial and finally decide the emptiness of fibers; we indicate their number.

It appears that the practical behaviour of our implementation reflects the complexity of our algorithm: for fixed n, timings are longer when d approaches $n/2$ while they are smaller for $d = 1$ or $n-1$.

CAD implementations don't have this behaviour and seem to be essentially sensitive to the number of variables. Hence, *on this benchmark*, our implementation tackles more examples than CAD does.

Discriminant of characteristic polynomials of linear symmetric matrices. For linear matrices of size 2, the associated polynomials have degree 2. Both our implementation and CAD manage to compute the real dimension up to more than 45 variables, and in this specific case the CAD is faster than our implementation. But in Table 2 we see that when the size of the problem increases (through the size of the matrix and hence the input degree), our implementation outperforms CAD implementations when $n > 3$. In Table 2, k is the size of the matrix, n is the number of variables, D is the degree of the polynomial, and d is the real dimension of the real algebraic set.

Other examples. We finally considered the following polynomials.

1. $g_n := (\sum_{i=1}^{n} x_i^2)^2 - 4\sum_{i=1}^{n-1} x_i^2 x_{i+1}^2 - 4x_1^2 x_n^2$, non-negative for $n \geq 4$
2. $f_n := \prod_{i=1}^{n}(x_i^2 + n - 1) - n^{n-2}(\sum_{i=1}^{n} x_i)^2$.

Timings are given in Table 5. We observe a similar behaviour than the ones already observed.

k	n	D	d	CAD	Dim	Step 1	Step 2	Step 3	Fibers
3	3	6	1	∞	8.5 s	20%	52%	28%	6
3	4	6	2	∞	81 s	3%	95%	2%	11
3	5	6	3	∞	739 s	5%	90%	5%	29
3	6	6	4	∞	28867 s	12%	87%	1%	16
4	3	12	1	∞	1816 s	21%	79%	0%	15
4	4	12	2	∞	∞				

Table 2: Discriminant of characteristic polynomials.

	n	D	d	CAD	Dim	Step 1	Step 2	Step 3	Fibers
g_3	3	4	2	0.98 s	0.18 s	/	/	/	/
g_4	4	4	3	0.54 s	2.1 s	/	/	/	/
g_5	5	4	2	24.6 s	42 s	3%	2%	95%	14
g_6	6	4	2	∞	452 s	13%	43%	44%	49
g_7	7	4		∞	∞				
f_3	3	6	1	2.68 s	0.82 s	5%	30%	65%	2
f_4	4	8	1	65 s	10 s	34%	2%	64%	2
f_5	5	10	1	∞	650 s	11%	0%	89%	2
f_6	6	12	1	∞	∞				

Table 3: Series 1 and 2.

6. REFERENCES

[1] B. Bank, M. Giusti, J. Heintz, and GM. Mbakop. Polar varieties, real equation solving, and data structures: the hypersurface case. *Journal of complexity*, 13(1):5–27, 1997.

[2] B. Bank, M. Giusti, J. Heintz, and GM. Mbakop. Polar varieties and efficient real elimination. *Mathematische Zeitschrift*, 238(1):115–144, 2001.

[3] B. Bank, M. Giusti, J. Heintz, and L.M. Pardo. Generalized polar varieties and an efficient real elimination. *Kybernetika*, 40(5):519–550, 2004.

[4] B. Bank, M. Giusti, J. Heintz, and L.M. Pardo. On the intrinsic complexity of point finding in real singular hypersurfaces. *Information Processing Letters*, 109(19):1141–1144, 2009.

[5] B. Bank, M. Giusti, J. Heintz, M. Safey El Din, and E. Schost. On the geometry of polar varieties. *Applicable Algebra in Engineering, Communication and Computing*, 21(1):33–83, 2010.

[6] S. Barone and S. Basu. Refined bounds on the number of connected components of sign conditions on a variety. *Discrete & Computational Geometry*, 47(3):577–597, 2012.

[7] S. Barone and S. Basu. On a real analogue of bezout inequality and the number of connected components of sign conditions. *ArXiv e-prints*, 2013.

[8] S. Basu, R. Pollack, and M.-F. Roy. *Algorithms in real algebraic geometry*, volume 10 of *Algorithms and Computation in Mathematics*. Springer-Verlag, Berlin, 2006 (second edition).

[9] S Basu, R Pollack, and M-F Roy. Computing the dimension of a semi-algebraic set. *Journal of Mathematical Sciences*, 134(5):2346–2353, 2006.

[10] C. Brown, H. Hong, and et al. QEPCAD B - quantifier elimination by partial cylindrical algebraic decomposition. `http://www.cs.usna.edu/\textasciitildeqepcad/B/QEPCAD.html`, 2009.

[11] C. Chen and M. Moreno Maza. Cylindrical algebraic decomposition in the regularchains library. In H. Hong and C. Yap, editors, *Mathematical Software - ICMS 2014 - 4th International Congress, Seoul, South Korea, August 5-9, 2014. Proceedings*, volume 8592 of *Lecture Notes in Computer Science*, pages 425–433. Springer, 2014.

[12] G. Collins. Quantifier elimination for real closed fields by cylindrical algebraic decompostion. In *Automata Theory and Formal Languages 2nd GI Conference Kaiserslautern, May 20–23, 1975*, pages 134–183. Springer, 1975.

[13] D. Cox, J. Little, and D. O'Shea. *Ideals, varieties and algorithms: an introduction to computational algebraic geometry and commutative algebra*. Undergraduate Texts in Mathematics. Springer-Verlag, New York, 1997.

[14] D. Eisenbud. *Commutative algebra with a view toward algebraic geometry*, volume 27. Springer New York, 1995.

[15] J.-C. Faugère. FGB: a library for computing gröbner bases. `www-polsys.lip6.fr/jcf/Software/`, 2010.

[16] J.-C. Faugère, G. Moroz, F. Rouillier, and M. Safey El Din. Classification of the perspective-three-point problem, discriminant variety and real solving polynomial systems of inequalities. In *Proceedings of the twenty-first international symposium on Symbolic and algebraic computation*, pages 79–86. ACM, 2008.

[17] M. Giusti, G. Lecerf, and B. Salvy. A gröbner free alternative for polynomial system solving. *Journal of Complexity*, 17(1):154–211, 2001.

[18] A. Greuet and M. Safey El Din. Deciding reachability of the infimum of a multivariate polynomial. In *Proceedings of the 36th international symposium on Symbolic and algebraic computation*, pages 131–138. ACM, 2011.

[19] A. Greuet and M. Safey El Din. Probabilistic algorithm for polynomial optimization over a real algebraic set. *SIAM Journal on Optimization*, 24(3):1313–1343, 2014.

[20] J. Han, L. Dai, and B. Xia. Constructing fewer open cells by gcd computation in cad projection. *arXiv preprint arXiv:1401.4953*, 2014.

[21] J. Heintz and C.-P. Schnorr. Testing polynomials which are easy to compute. In *Proceedings of the twelfth annual ACM symposium on Theory of computing*, pages 262–272. ACM, 1980.

[22] D. Henrion, S. Naldi, and M. Safey El Din. Real root finding of determinants of linear matrices. pre-print, 2014.

[23] H. Hong and M. Safey El Din. Variant real quantifier elimination: algorithm and application. In *Proceedings of the 2009 international symposium on Symbolic and algebraic computation*, pages 183–190. ACM, 2009.

[24] H. Hong and M. Safey El Din. Variant quantifier elimination. *Journal of Symbolic Computation*, 47(7):883–901, 2012.

[25] N. V. Ilyushechkin. On some identities for the elements of a symmetric matrix. *Zapiski Nauchnykh Seminarov POMI*, 303:119–144, 2003.

[26] Q. Jin and T. Yang. Overconstraint analysis on spatial 6-link loops. *Mechanism and machine theory*, 37(3):267–278, 2002.

[27] P. Koiran. Randomized and deterministic algorithms for the dimension of algebraic varieties. In *Foundations of Computer Science, 1997. Proceedings., 38th Annual Symposium on*, pages 36–45. IEEE, 1997.

[28] P. Koiran. The real dimension problem is npr-complete. *Journal of Complexity*, 15(2):227 – 238, 1999.

[29] G. Lecerf. Computing the equidimensional decomposition of an algebraic closed set by means of lifting fibers. *Journal of Complexity*, 19(4):564–596, 2003.

[30] P. A. Parrilo. *Structured semidefinite programs and semialgebraic geometry methods in robustness and optimization*. PhD thesis, Citeseer, 2000.

[31] F. Rouillier, M.-F. Roy, and M. Safey El Din. Finding at least one point in each connected component of a real algebraic set defined by a single equation. *Journal of Complexity*, 16(4):716–750, 2000.

[32] M. Safey El Din. Finding sampling points on real hypersurfaces is easier in singular situations. *MEGA (Effective Methods in Algebraic Geometry) Electronic proceedings*, 2005.

[33] M. Safey El Din. RAGlib : Real algebraic geometry library. `www-polsys.lip6.fr/~safey/RAGLib/`, 2007.

[34] M. Safey El Din. Testing sign conditions on a multivariate polynomial and applications, mathematics in computer science journal, special inaugural issue on algorithms and complexity, H. Hong and C. Yap (Guest editors), 2007.

[35] M. Safey El Din and É. Schost. Polar varieties and computation of one point in each connected component of a smooth real algebraic set. In *Proceedings of the 2003 international symposium on Symbolic and algebraic computation*, pages 224–231. ACM, 2003.

[36] M. Safey El Din and E. Schost. A nearly optimal algorithm for deciding connectivity queries in smooth and bounded real algebraic sets. *arXiv preprint arXiv:1307.7836*, 2013.

[37] E. Schost. Computing parametric geometric resolutions. *Applicable Algebra in Engineering, Communication and Computing*, 13(5):349–393, 2003.

[38] I. R. Shafarevich and K. A. Hirsch. *Basic algebraic geometry*, volume 197. Springer, 1977.

[39] T. Sturm and V. Weispfenning. Computational geometry problems in REDLOG. In *ADG*, pages 58–96, 1996.

[40] N. Vorobjov. Complexity of computing the local dimension of a semialgebraic set. *Journal of Symbolic Computation*, 27(6):565 – 579, 1999.

Formal Solutions of Linear Differential Systems with Essential Singularities in their Coefficients

Moulay A. Barkatou, Thomas Cluzeau, Achref Jalouli
University of Limoges ; CNRS ; XLIM UMR 7252
123 avenue Albert Thomas, 87060 Limoges cedex, France
{moulay.barkatou,thomas.cluzeau,achref.jalouli}@unilim.fr

ABSTRACT

The local analysis of formal meromorphic linear differential systems with coefficients in $\mathbb{C}((z))$ has been widely studied in the literature and there exist various computer algebra algorithms for computing formal solutions of such systems. In the present paper we extend the algorithm presented in [3] to allow more general systems. More precisely, we give an algorithm for computing a formal fundamental matrix of solutions around $z = 0$ of systems with coefficients in $\mathbb{C}((z))[[X]]$, where X is transcendental and hyperexponential over $\mathbb{C}((z))$.

Categories and Subject Descriptors

I.1.2 [**Symbolic and Algebraic Manipulation**]: Algorithms

General Terms

Algorithms, Experimentation, Theory

Keywords

Computer Algebra, Algorithms, Linear Differential Systems with Essential Singularities, Hyperexponential Extensions, Formal Reduction

1. INTRODUCTION

Let z be a complex variable and $\mathbb{C}[[z]]$ (resp. $\mathbb{C}((z))$) the ring (resp. field) of formal power (resp. Laurent) series in z with coefficients in the field $\mathbb{C}$ of complex numbers. Let $\mathbb{M}_n(\mathbb{C}[[z]])$ be the ring of square matrices of size $n \in \mathbb{N}^*$ with entries in $\mathbb{C}[[z]]$. In the present paper, we consider formal linear differential systems of the form

$$\frac{dY}{dz} = z^{-p}\, A(z,X)\, Y, \quad p \in \mathbb{N}^*, \tag{1a}$$

$$\frac{dX}{dz} = z^{-q}\, a(z)\, X, \quad q \geq 2, \quad a(z) \in \mathbb{C}[[z]],\ a(0) \neq 0, \tag{1b}$$

ISSAC'15, July 6–9, 2015, Bath, United Kingdom.

DOI: http://dx.doi.org/10.1145/2755996.2756669.

where $A(z,X) = \sum_{k=0}^{+\infty} A_k(z)\, X^k$ with $A_k(z) \in \mathbb{M}_n(\mathbb{C}[[z]])$ and $Y = (y_1, \dots, y_n)^T$ is a vector of unknown functions.

The conditions on the integer q and the formal power series $a(z)$ imply that $X = \exp(\int z^{-q}\, a(z)\, dz)$ is transcendental over $\mathbb{C}((z))$ (see, for example, [20, Theorem 2.4]). The coefficients of System (1a) then have an essential singularity at the origin since $z = 0$ is neither a removable singularity nor a pole.

Linear differential systems with coefficients in hyperexponential extensions appear in many applications as for example the linearization of a dynamical system defined over a base field F around a particular exponential solution ϕ. Indeed the resulting linear variational equations are linear differential systems with coefficients in $F(\phi)$ (see [1] and references therein). Moreover the study of linear differential systems with coefficients in hyperexponential extensions can be used to compute a closed form of an integral (see [6]). In computer algebra, linear differential systems (equations) with coefficients in hyperexponential extensions have been studied in [7, 8, 9]. In [10, 11], the author develops algorithms for computing closed form solutions (e.g., polynomial, rational solutions) of scalar linear differential equations with coefficients in hyperexponential extensions. More recently, the latter algorithms have been extended to handle systems directly and applied to indefinite integration in [6].

The systems (1) considered in the present paper can be viewed as a generalization of formal meromorphic linear differential systems of the form

$$\frac{dY}{dz} = z^{-p}\, A(z)\, Y, \quad p \in \mathbb{N}^*, \tag{2}$$

where $A(z) \in \mathbb{M}_n(\mathbb{C}[[z]])$ and $A(0) \neq 0$. The local analysis of formal meromorphic systems of the form (2) has been well investigated: see, e.g., [19, 18, 21, 2, 14, 3, 5, 4] and references therein. In [3], the first author gave an algorithm for computing a fundamental matrix of formal solutions of (2) of the form

$$Y = \Phi(t)\, t^{\Lambda}\, \exp(Q(1/t)), \tag{3}$$

with $z = t^r$ where $r \geq 1$ is a positive integer called *the ramification index*, $Q(1/t) = \operatorname{diag}(q_1(1/t), \dots, q_n(1/t))$ is a diagonal matrix containing polynomials in $1/t$ without constant terms, Λ is a constant matrix commuting with Q, and $\Phi(t)$ is a matrix of formal Laurent series in t.

The main contribution of the present paper is to provide an algorithm for computing a formal fundamental matrix of solutions of (1) of the form

$$Y = \left(\sum_{k=0}^{+\infty} \Phi_k(t)\, X^k \right) t^{\Lambda} \exp(Q(1/t)), \qquad (4)$$

with the notation of (3) and $\Phi_k(t) \in \mathbb{M}_n(\mathbb{C}((t)))$, for all $k \in \mathbb{N}$. Note that in the particular case $X = \exp(1/z)$, a similar form of a formal fundamental matrix of solutions can be deduced from the work of M. Bouffet in [9].

Our approach consists in viewing (1a) as a *perturbation* of the meromorphic system obtained by letting $X \to 0$ in (1a). Several cases have to be distinguished by comparing the integers p and q involved in (1). When $p < q$, we prove that (1) can be reduced via a matrix transformation $T \in \mathbb{M}_n(\mathbb{C}[[z]][[X]])$ to the formal meromorphic system $Y' = z^{-p} A_0(z)\, Y$. In the case $p = q$, one must investigate the spectrum of the leading matrix $A_0(0)$. We prove that up to an invertible transformation in $\mathbb{M}_n(\mathbb{C}[[z]][[X]])$, we can assume that the eigenvalues of $A_0(0)$ do not differ by an integer multiple of $a(0)$ and in this case, similarly to the case $p < q$, we prove that (1) can be reduced to $Y' = z^{-p} A_0(z)\, Y$. The last case $p > q$ is much more involved: by introducing, if necessary, ramifications of the form $z = t^r$, we prove that we can apply a (finite) sequence of transformations in order to reduce the problem to the case where either $p \le q$ or $n = 1$ (scalar case). Our methods are constructive and a Maple implementation will be soon available.

The paper is organized as follows. In Section 2, we introduce the different rings of coefficients considered in the sequel and we briefly review the algorithm of [3] for computing a formal fundamental matrix of solutions of formal meromorphic systems (2). In Section 3, we introduce the systems (1) considered in this paper and give an overview of our main results. Then, Section 4 handles one by one the different cases that have to be distinguished by our algorithm for computing a formal fundamental matrix of solutions of (1). In Section 5, we discuss extensions of our algorithm to a more general class of differential systems.

2. PRELIMINARIES

2.1 Rings of coefficients

In this subsection, we investigate the problem of defining the most suitable ring of coefficients for systems of the form (1).

Let z be a complex variable, $\mathbb{C}$ the field of complex numbers and consider the ring $\mathbb{C}[[z]]$ of formal power series in z with coefficients in $\mathbb{C}$ and its quotient field $\mathbb{C}((z))$, namely the field of formal Laurent series in z with coefficients in $\mathbb{C}$. The ring $\mathbb{C}[[z]]$ (resp. the field $\mathbb{C}((z))$) is endowed with a differential ring (resp. field) structure by considering the derivation $' = d/dz$. For $f \in \mathbb{C}((z))$, we denote by $v_z(f)$ the usual z-adic valuation of f, i.e., the order of f in z with $v_z(0) = +\infty$. Now let X be a transcendental element satisfying (1b), i.e., $X' = z^{-q}\, a(z)\, X$, with $q \ge 2$, $a(z) \in \mathbb{C}[[z]]$, and $a(0) \neq 0$, and consider the ring $\mathcal{R} = \mathbb{C}((z))[[X]]$ of formal power series in X with coefficients in the field of formal Laurent series in z. An element $f \in \mathcal{R}$ can be written as $f = \sum_{k=0}^{+\infty} f_k(z)\, X^k$, with $f_k(z) \in \mathbb{C}((z))$, and the derivation $' = d/dz$ extends naturally to $\mathcal{R}$ by the formula $f' = \sum_{k=0}^{+\infty} \left(f_k'(z) + k\, z^{-q}\, a(z)\, f_k(z)\right) X^k$.

LEMMA 1. *The ring of constants of the differential ring $(\mathcal{R}, d/dz)$ is $\mathbb{C}$.*

PROOF. An element $f \in \mathcal{R}$ satisfies $f' = 0$ if and only if $f_k'(z) + k\, z^{-q}\, a(z)\, f_k(z) = 0$ for all $k \ge 0$. This yields $f_0(z) \in \mathbb{C}$ and for all $k \ge 1$, we get $f_k(z) = c_k\, X^{-k}$, with $c_k \in \mathbb{C}$. Now by our hypothesis, $q \ge 2$ so that X is a transcendental element over $\mathbb{C}((z))$ (see, for example, [20, Theorem 2.4]). Consequently, since $f_k(z) \in \mathbb{C}((z))$ we necessarily have $f_k(z) = 0$ for all $k \ge 1$ and we finally get $f = f_0(z) \in \mathbb{C}$ which ends the proof. □

The coefficients of systems of the form (1a) have their z-adic valuation bounded below. However, not every system with coefficients in $\mathcal{R}$ can be written in the form (1). Therefore, let us introduce the following subset $\mathcal{A} \subsetneq \mathcal{R}$:

$$\mathcal{A} = \left\{ f = \sum_{k=0}^{+\infty} f_k(z)\, X^k \in \mathcal{R} \mid \inf_{k \in \mathbb{N}} v_z(f_k(z)) > -\infty \right\}. \qquad (5)$$

By a straightforward verification, one can show that $\mathcal{A}$ is a differential subring of $\mathcal{R}$ endowed with the derivation d/dz.

LEMMA 2. *The application $v : \mathcal{A} \to \mathbb{Z} \cup \{+\infty\}$ defined by $v(f) = \min_{k \in \mathbb{N}} v_z(f_k(z))$ for $f = \sum_{k=0}^{+\infty} f_k(z)\, X^k \in \mathcal{A}$ is a valuation of $\mathcal{A}$.*

PROOF. It is straightforward to show that, for $f_1, f_2 \in \mathcal{A}$, $v(f_1) = +\infty \Leftrightarrow f_1 = 0$, $v(f_1 + f_2) \ge \min(v(f_1), v(f_2))$ and $v(f_1\, f_2) \ge v(f_1) + v(f_2)$. It remains to prove that we have $v(f_1\, f_2) = v(f_1) + v(f_2)$. Since $f_1, f_2 \in \mathcal{A}$, we can write $f_i = p_i + z^{v(f_i)}\, \tilde{f}_i$ with $v(p_i) > v(f_i)$ and $v(\tilde{f}_i) = 0$, $i = 1, 2$. Then we have

$$f_1\, f_2 = p_1\, p_2 + p_1\, z^{v(f_2)}\, \tilde{f}_2 + p_2\, z^{v(f_1)}\, \tilde{f}_1 + z^{v(f_1)+v(f_2)}\, \tilde{f}_1\, \tilde{f}_2,$$

and inspecting the valuation of each term of the previous sum, we get the result. □

In the process of the algorithm described in Section 4, even if we start with a system with coefficients in the ring $\mathcal{A}$, it may happen, at some stage, that we get a new system whose coefficients do not belong to $\mathcal{A}$. Typically, one can obtain the formal power series $\sum_{k=0}^{+\infty} z^{-k}\, X^k$. Consequently, we need to relax a bit the condition $\inf_{k \in \mathbb{N}} v_z(f_k(z)) > -\infty$ and introduce a bigger ring.

Let $f = \sum_{k=0}^{+\infty} f_k(z)\, X^k \in \mathcal{R}$. For $k \in \mathbb{N}$, we consider the vertical half-line $l_k = \{(k, y) \mid y \ge v_z(f_k))\} \subset \mathbb{R}^2$ with $l_k = \emptyset$ if $f_k = 0$. Then we define *the Newton polygon $\mathcal{N}(f)$ of f* to be the boundary of the convex hull of $\cup_{k \in \mathbb{N}} l_k$ (see, for example, [15]). The Newton polygon is said to be *degenerate* if it is reduced to the y-axis. We now define a new ring $\mathcal{B} \supsetneq \mathcal{A}$ as follows:

$$\mathcal{B} = \{ f \in \mathcal{R} \mid \exists \alpha, \beta \in \mathbb{Q};\, \forall k,\ v_z(f_k) \ge \alpha\, k + \beta \}. \qquad (6)$$

The elements of $\mathcal{B}$ can be characterized as follows: $f \in \mathcal{B}$ if and only if $f \in \mathcal{A}$ or $\mathcal{N}(f)$ is non-degenerate and has only finitely many segments with non-positive slope. The following lemma and its proof will be very useful in Section 5.

LEMMA 3. *If $f(z, X) \in \mathcal{B}$, then there exists $c \in \mathbb{Z}$ such that $f(z, z^c\, X) \in \mathcal{A}$.*

PROOF. Let $f = \sum_{k=0}^{+\infty} f_k(z)\, X^k \in \mathcal{B}$ and, for $k \in \mathbb{N}$, $v_k = v_z(f_k)$. We then have:

$$\begin{aligned} f &= X^{\nu} \left(z^{v_0}\, \tilde{f}_0 + z^{v_1}\, \tilde{f}_1\, X + z^{v_2}\, \tilde{f}_2\, X^2 + \cdots \right), \\ &= X^{\nu} z^{v_0} \left(\tilde{f}_0 + z^{v_1 - c - v_0}\, \tilde{f}_1\, \tilde{X} + z^{v_2 - 2c - v_0}\, \tilde{f}_2\, \tilde{X}^2 + \cdots \right), \end{aligned}$$

where $\nu \geq 0$, $\tilde{f}_0 \neq 0$, $\tilde{X} = z^c X$, and for $k \in \mathbb{N}$, $v_z(\tilde{f}_k) = 0$. It is thus sufficient to prove that there exists $c \in \mathbb{Z}$ so that $v_k \geq c\,k + v_0$, for all $k \in \mathbb{N}$. Using (6), there exists $\alpha, \beta \in \mathbb{Q}$ such that $v_k \geq \alpha\,k + \beta$, for $k \in \mathbb{N}$. A straightforward calculation shows that if we take $c = \lfloor \alpha \rfloor$ if $\beta \geq v_0$, and $c = \lfloor \alpha + \beta - v_0 \rfloor$ if $\beta < v_0$, where $\lfloor a \rfloor \in \mathbb{Z}$ denotes the integer part of $a \in \mathbb{Q}$, then we have $v_k \geq \alpha\,k + \beta \geq c\,k + v_0$ which ends the proof. □

For $f \in \mathcal{B}$, let us define α_f to be the greatest α that we can take in (6). if $f \in \mathcal{A}$, then $\alpha_f = 0$ otherwise it corresponds to the greatest non-positive slope of the segments of $\mathcal{N}(f)$. Then, for $f \in \mathcal{B}$, we can define:

$$w(f) = \min_{k \in \mathbb{N}} \left(v_z(f_k) - \alpha_f\,k\right).$$

Note that geometrically, $w(f)$ corresponds to the y-coordinate of the point where the line of the greatest slope of $\mathcal{N}(f)$ crosses the y-axis. Moreover, one can check that, for all $f, g \in \mathcal{B}$,

$$w(f+g) \geq \min(w(f), w(g)), \quad w(f\,g) \geq w(f) + w(g). \quad (7)$$

For more details concerning Newton polygons in this setting, we refer to [16, 17, 15].

LEMMA 4. *Let $\mathcal{F}$ denote the quotient field of $\mathcal{B}$. Then, we have $\inf_{f \in \mathcal{F}, f \neq 0} w(f^{-1}\,f') = -q$.*

PROOF. Let $f \in \mathcal{F}$, $f \neq 0$. Using the characterization (6), we can check that f can be written as $f = X^{\nu}\,\tilde{f}$ with $\nu \in \mathbb{Z}$ and $\tilde{f} \in \mathcal{B}$. We thus obtain $f' = X^{\nu}\,(\nu\,z^{-q}\,a(z)\,\tilde{f} + \tilde{f}')$ so that $f^{-1}\,f' = \nu\,z^{-q}\,a(z) + \tilde{f}^{-1}\,\tilde{f}'$. Consequently, from (7), we have $w(f^{-1}\,f') \geq \min(-q, w(\tilde{f}') - w(\tilde{f})) \geq -q$ and the minimum is reached for $f = X$. □

We refer to [8, 4] for more explanations on the quantity computed in Lemma 4.

REMARK 1. *In our algorithms, the series of the form $f = \sum_{k=0}^{+\infty} f_k(z)\,X^k$, with $f_k(z) \in \mathbb{C}[[z]]$, are represented by their truncation up to a certain order with respect to X and z. In the sequel, the sentence "we can compute f" means that we are able to compute its truncation up to an arbitrary order.*

2.2 Meromorphic linear differential systems

In this subsection, we first recall some definitions concerning formal meromorphic linear differential systems of the form (2). Then, we review the algorithm of [3] for computing a formal fundamental matrix of solutions of the form (3). In the sequel, to simplify, we will often use the notation $[A]$ for a linear differential system $Y' = A\,Y$. Therefore System (2) is denoted by $[z^{-p}\,A]$. The integer $p - 1 \geq 0$ is then called the *Poincaré rank of* $[z^{-p}\,A]$.

If we perform a change of variables $Y = T\,Z$ with $T \in \mathrm{GL}_n(\mathbb{C}((z)))$ in a system $[A]$, then the vector in terms of new variables Z satisfies $Z' = T^{-1}(A\,T - T')\,Z$. If F denotes an algebraic field extension of $\mathbb{C}((z))$, then two formal meromorphic linear differential systems $[A]$ and $[B]$ are *equivalent over F* if there exists an invertible formal meromorphic matrix transformation $T \in \mathrm{GL}_n(F)$ such that $B = T[A] := T^{-1}(A\,T - T')$. Note that, we have $T[z^{-p}\,A] = z^{-p}\,T^{-1}(A\,T - z^p\,T')$ so that two differential systems $[z^{-p}\,A]$ and $[z^{-p}\,B]$ are equivalent over F if there exists $T \in \mathrm{GL}_n(F)$ such that $B = T^{-1}(A\,T - z^p\,T')$. Moreover if $B = T[A]$ and $Y_{[B]}$ is a formal fundamental matrix of solutions of $[B]$, then $Y_{[A]} = T\,Y_{[B]}$ is a formal fundamental matrix of solutions of $[A]$.

It is known (see, for example, [19, 21, 3]), that a formal fundamental matrix of solutions of (2) has the form (3). An algorithm to compute such a formal fundamental matrix of solutions is developed in [3]. The simplest case appears when $p \leq 1$ since in this case we have $r = 1$, $Q = 0$ and the matrices Φ and Λ can be computed by the algorithm given in [5]. When $p > 0$, then using Moser's algorithm ([18, 3]) we can reduce the system (2) to an equivalent one with minimal Poincaré rank $\tilde{p} - 1$. If $\tilde{p} = 1$, then $z = 0$ is a *regular singularity* and we can still apply the algorithm of [5] to get a formal fundamental matrix of solutions with $r = 1$ and $Q = 0$. If the minimal Poincaré rank that we can get via meromorphic transformations is not equal to 0, then we have an *irregular singularity* and we shall proceed to compute a formal fundamental matrix of solutions with an exponential part $Q \neq 0$. The technique of [3] consists in reducing the system (2) to several independent systems each of which is either a system of the form (2) with $p = 1$ or a first order scalar differential equation ($n = 1$). This is achieved as follows:

1. We apply a first transformation to split the system into a set of differential systems of the same form where each system has a leading matrix $A(0)$ with only one eigenvalue and we now consider one by one the resulting systems (of smaller size).

2. A second transformation is performed to get a new system with a nilpotent leading matrix (i.e., we shift the non-zero eigenvalues of $A(0)$ to 0) and, if its Poincaré rank is not minimal, we apply Moser's algorithm ([18, 3]) to get an equivalent system with minimal Poincaré rank.

3. If the resulting system still has a Poincaré rank strictly greater than 0 and $A(0)$ is nilpotent, then we compute its Katz' invariant κ ([14, 3]) and we perform the ramification $z = t^m$ where m is the smallest positive integer such that $m\,\kappa$ is an integer. Applying one more time Moser's algorithm ([18, 3]) yields a new system with Poincaré rank $m\,\kappa$ and $A(0)$ not nilpotent. Then, we can apply another transformation to split the system into several systems of smaller size.

4. We apply recursion.

At each step of this process, we either reduce the Poincaré rank or the size of the system so that the process ends with $p = 1$ or $n = 1$. For more details, see [3].

REMARK 2. *In the algorithm sketched above, the discussion is mainly based on the comparison between the quantities p and 1 or $-p$ and -1. Note that -1 corresponds to $\inf_{f \in \mathbb{C}((z)), f \neq 0} v_z(f^{-1}\,f')$ (see [4]). This justifies the fact that in the sequel, when we consider System (1), we compare $-p$ and $-q$ to distinguish the different cases (see Lemma 4).*

3. MAIN RESULTS

In the present paper, we study systems of the form

$$Y' = \tilde{A}(z, X)\,Y, \quad (8)$$

where $' = d/dz$, X is a transcendental element defined by (1b) and the square matrix $\tilde{A}(z, X)$ is assumed to have entries in the ring $\mathcal{A}$ defined by (5). As a consequence, we can write $\tilde{A}(z,X) = \sum_{k=0}^{+\infty} \tilde{A}_k(z)\, X^k = z^{-p}\, A(z,X)$, with

$$A(z,X) = \sum_{k=0}^{+\infty} A_k(z)\, X^k, \quad A_k(z) \in \mathbb{M}_n(\mathbb{C}[[z]]). \quad (9)$$

In the sequel, we further assume that $A(0,0) = A_0(0) \neq 0$ and $p \in \mathbb{N}^*$, so that we consider systems of the form (1) denoted by $\mathcal{S}_{A,a}^{p,q}$, namely,

$$\mathcal{S}_{A,a}^{p,q} : \begin{cases} Y' = z^{-p}\, A(z,X)\, Y, & p \in \mathbb{N}^*,\ A(0,0) \neq 0, \\ X' = z^{-q}\, a(z)\, X, & q \geq 2,\ a(z) \in \mathbb{C}[[z]],\ a(0) \neq 0, \end{cases}$$

where $A(z,X)$ is given by (9) with $A_0(0) \neq 0$. If we naturally extend the valuation v defined in Subsection 2.1 to matrices $A = (a_{i,j}) \in \mathbb{M}_n(\mathcal{A})$ by $v(A) = \min_{i,j} v(a_{i,j})$ (and we extend similarly the z-adic valuation to matrices), then the assumption $A_0(0) \neq 0$ means that

$$-p = v(\tilde{A}(z,X)) = \min_{k \in \mathbb{N}} v_z(\tilde{A}_k(z)) = v_z(\tilde{A}_0(z)).$$

The contribution of this paper consists in investigating the effective computation of a formal fundamental matrix of solutions of $\mathcal{S}_{A,a}^{p,q}$ of the form (4). See also Section 5 for extensions to more general classes of differential systems, e.g., systems with coefficients in the ring $\mathcal{B}$ defined by (6).

By analogy to the terminology used in the study of formal meromorphic linear differential systems, the systems of the form (1) can be called *X-regular* in the sense that there is no exponential part depending on X in a formal fundamental matrix of solutions. Note that this *irregular* part in X will appear when we consider systems of the form (8) but where instead of choosing the entries of $\tilde{A}(z,X)$ in $\mathcal{A}$ defined by (5), we allow terms with negative orders in X. Considering systems with poles in X is the subject of a work in progress.

The following of the paper is devoted to the construction of an algorithm for computing a formal fundamental matrix of solutions (4) of $\mathcal{S}_{A,a}^{p,q}$. We distinguish different cases by comparing the values of p and q (see Remark 2) and we shall prove that:

1. If $p < q$, $\mathcal{S}_{A,a}^{p,q}$ can be reduced to the formal meromorphic linear differential system $[z^{-p}\, A_0]$;
2. If $p = q$, $\mathcal{S}_{A,a}^{p,q}$ can first be reduced to another system of the same form $\mathcal{S}_{\tilde{A},a}^{\tilde{p},q}$ satisfying that either $\tilde{p} < q$ or $\tilde{p} = q$ and $\tilde{A}_0(0)$ does not have eigenvalues that differ by an integer multiple of $a(0)$. Moreover, in the latter case $\mathcal{S}_{\tilde{A},a}^{\tilde{p},q}$ can be reduced to the formal meromorphic linear differential system $[z^{-p}\, \tilde{A}_0]$;
3. If $p > q$, we can adapt the process of [3] reviewed in Subsection 2.2 to reduce $\mathcal{S}_{A,a}^{p,q}$ to several independent systems of the same form each of which either satisfies $p \leq q$ or $n = 1$ (scalar differential equation).

4. ALGORITHM

4.1 The case $p \leq q$

Definition 1. *We say that a system $\mathcal{S}_{A,a}^{p,q}$* satisfies the property $(\mathcal{P})$ *if either $p < q$ or $p = q$ and $A_0(0)$ has no eigenvalues that differ by an integer multiple of $a(0)$.*

The following lemma will be used in the proof of Theorem 1.

Lemma 5. *Let m be an integer such that $m \geq 2$ and $M \in \mathbb{M}_r(\mathbb{C}[[z]])$, $N \in \mathbb{M}_s(\mathbb{C}[[z]])$ be two square matrices. If $M(0)$ and $N(0)$ have no common eigenvalues, then, for every $V \in \mathbb{M}_{r\times s}(\mathbb{C}[[z]])$, there exists a unique matrix $U \in \mathbb{M}_{r\times s}(\mathbb{C}[[z]])$ such that*

$$z^m\, U' = M\, U - U\, N - V. \quad (10)$$

Proof. Let $M = \sum_{k=0}^{+\infty} M_k\, z^k$, $N = \sum_{k=0}^{+\infty} N_k\, z^k$, and $V = \sum_{k=0}^{+\infty} V_k\, z^k$. Plugging the ansatz $U = \sum_{k=0}^{+\infty} U_k\, z^k$ into (10) and identifying the coefficients in z using the fact that $m \geq 2$, we get: $M(0)\, U_0 - U_0\, N(0) = V_0$, and, for $k \geq 1$,

$$M(0)\, U_k - U_k\, N(0) = (k-m+1)\, U_{k-m+1} - \sum_{i=1}^{k} (M_i\, U_{k-i} - U_{k-i}\, N_i) + V_k,$$

with the convention $U_{-k} = 0$ for all $k > 0$. We conclude using a well known result (see for example [12, Corollary S2.3, p. 347] or [3, Remark 6]) asserting that if $M \in \mathbb{M}_r(\mathbb{C})$ and $N \in \mathbb{M}_s(\mathbb{C})$ have no common eigenvalues, then, for every matrix V in $\mathbb{M}_{r\times s}(\mathbb{C})$, we can compute a unique matrix U in $\mathbb{M}_{r\times s}(\mathbb{C})$ such that $M\, U - U\, N = V$. □

Theorem 1. *Let us consider a system $\mathcal{S}_{A,a}^{p,q}$ satisfying the property $(\mathcal{P})$. Then, $\mathcal{S}_{A,a}^{p,q}$ can be reduced to the formal meromorphic linear differential system $[z^{-p}\, A_0(z)]$. More precisely, we can compute an invertible matrix transformation*

$$T = I_n + T_1(z)\, X + T_2(z)\, X^2 + \cdots, \quad T_k(z) \in \mathbb{M}_n(\mathbb{C}[[z]]),$$

where I_n denotes the identity matrix of size n, such that $A_0 = T^{-1}(A\, T - z^p\, T')$, i.e., $z^p\, T' = A\, T - T\, A_0$.

Proof. If we take an ansatz $T = \sum_{k=0}^{+\infty} T_k(z)\, X^k$, we have:

$$z^p\, T' = \sum_{k=0}^{+\infty} (z^p\, T_k'(z) + k\, z^{p-q}\, a(z)\, T_k(z))\, X^k,$$

and

$$A\, T - T\, A_0 = \sum_{k=0}^{+\infty} \left(\sum_{m=0}^{k} (A_m\, T_{k-m}) - T_k\, A_0 \right) X^k.$$

By identification, we then obtain:

$$z^p\, T_0' = A_0\, T_0 - T_0\, A_0, \quad (11)$$

and, for $k \geq 1$,

$$z^p\, T_k' = A_0\, T_k - T_k\, (A_0 + k\, z^{p-q}\, a(z)\, \mathrm{I}_n) + \sum_{m=1}^{k} A_m\, T_{k-m}. \quad (12)$$

Multiplying (12) by z^{q-p}, we get:

$$z^q\, T_k' = (z^{q-p}\, A_0)\, T_k - T_k\, (z^{q-p}\, A_0 + k\, a(z)\, \mathrm{I}_n) + z^{q-p} \sum_{m=1}^{k} A_m\, T_{k-m}. \quad (13)$$

The matrix $T_0 = \mathrm{I}_n$ is a trivial solution of (11) and (13) can be solved using Lemma 5 below. Indeed, for all $k \geq 1$, (13) is of the form (10). Now if $p < q$, it satisfies the hypotheses of Lemma 5 since we have $q \geq 2$, $q - p > 0$ and $a(0) \neq 0$. Moreover, if $p = q$, the hypotheses of Lemma 5 are also fulfilled since $q \geq 2$ and $A_0(0)$ has no eigenvalues that differ by an integer multiple of $a(0)$. □

The proofs of Theorem 1 and Lemma 5 provide an algorithm for computing a matrix $T = \mathrm{I}_n + T_1(z)\, X + T_2(z)\, X^2 + \cdots$ such that $z^p\, T' = A\, T - T\, A_0$. Choosing the first coefficient $T_0 = \mathrm{I}_n$ ensures that the computed matrix transformation T is invertible. Moreover, from Lemma 5, we obtain unique matrices $T_k(z)$ the entries of which are formal power series, i.e., $T_k(z) \in \mathbb{M}_n(\mathbb{C}[[z]])$.

Note that when $p < q$, Theorem 1 can be applied even if $A_0(z) = 0$ in which case the matrix transformation T yields a formal fundamental matrix of solutions.

To conclude for the case $p \leq q$, it remains to consider the case when the system $\mathcal{S}^{p,q}_{A,a}$ does not satisfy the property $(\mathcal{P})$, i.e., $p = q$ and $A_0(0)$ has eigenvalues that differ by an integer multiple of $a(0)$. We have the following result:

Proposition 1. *A system $\mathcal{S}^{p,q}_{A,a}$ such that $p = q$ and $A_0(0)$ has eigenvalues that differ by an integer multiple of $a(0)$ can be reduced to a system $\mathcal{S}^{\tilde{p},q}_{\tilde{A},a}$ satisfying the property $(\mathcal{P})$.*

Proof. We adapt the process used in [21, Section 17] in a similar situation to our case. First, we arrange the eigenvalues of $A_0(0) \neq 0$ into disjoint sets, so that the elements of each set differ by an integer multiple of $a(0)$. Let $\lambda_1, ..., \lambda_s$ be the elements of such a set and sort them such that if $k_i = a(0)^{-1}(\lambda_i - \lambda_s)$, $i = 1, \ldots, s-1$, then we have $k_1 > \cdots > k_{s-1} > 0$. Let $\lambda_{s+1}, \ldots, \lambda_r$ denote the other eigenvalues of $A_0(0)$ and for $i = 1 \ldots, r$, let m_i be the multiplicity of λ_i. After applying an adequate constant matrix transformation, we may assume without loss of generality that the matrix $A_0(0)$ has the following diagonal form: $A_0(0) = \mathrm{diag}(A_0^{11}(0), A_0^{22}(0))$, and the only eigenvalue of the matrix $A_0^{11}(0)$ is λ_1. Now, since $p = q \geq 2$, and $A_0(0)$ has more than two distinct eigenvalues, the formal meromorphic linear differential system $[z^{-p}\, A_0]$ is irregular so that there exists a matrix transformation

$$P = \mathrm{I}_n + P_1\, z + P_2\, z^2 + \cdots \in \mathbb{M}_n(\mathbb{C}[[z]]), \qquad (14)$$

that splits $[z^{-p}\, A_0]$ (*Splitting lemma*: see [21, Theorem 11.1, p. 54] or [3, Theorem 2]). Note that the condition $P(0) = \mathrm{I}_n$ guarantees the fact that its inverse P^{-1} has formal power series entries so that $P^{-1}\, A_k\, P \in \mathbb{M}_n(\mathbb{C}[[z]])$ holds for all $k \in \mathbb{N}$. After applying such a *splitting transformation* P, we may assume that $A_0(z)$ has the diagonal form $A_0(z) = \mathrm{diag}(A_0^{11}(z), A_0^{22}(z))$, where $A_0^{11}(z)$ is an $m_1 \times m_1$ matrix and $A_0^{11}(0)$ has only one eigenvalue λ_1. Now, applying the transformation

$$U = \mathrm{diag}(X\, \mathrm{I}_{m_1}, \mathrm{I}_{n-m_1}), \qquad (15)$$

one can check that we get a new equivalent system $\mathcal{S}^{p,q}_{B,a}$ with

$$Y' = z^{-p}\, \underbrace{(B_0(z) + B_1(z) X + \cdots)}_{B(z,X)}\, Y,$$

where $B(z, X) = U^{-1}(A(z, X)\, U - z^p\, U')$. Now, if we partition $A_1(z) \in \mathbb{M}_n(\mathbb{C}[[z]])$ accordingly, i.e.,

$$A_1(z) = \begin{pmatrix} A_1^{11}(z) & A_1^{12}(z) \\ A_1^{21}(z) & A_1^{22}(z) \end{pmatrix}, \quad A_1^{11}(z) \in \mathbb{M}_{m_1}(\mathbb{C}[[z]]),$$

then, a straightforward calculation shows that:

$$B_0(z) = \begin{pmatrix} A_0^{11}(z) & A_1^{12}(z) \\ 0 & A_0^{22}(z) \end{pmatrix} - a(z) \begin{pmatrix} \mathrm{I}_{m_1} & 0 \\ 0 & 0 \end{pmatrix}.$$

The eigenvalues of $B_0(0)$ are thus $\lambda_1 - a(0), \lambda_2, \ldots, \lambda_r$. Thus, after $k_1 + \cdots + k_{s-1}$ steps, the eigenvalues $\lambda_1, ..., \lambda_s$ are reduced to the single eigenvalue λ_s which has multiplicity $m_1 + \cdots + m_s$. Finally, by applying the same process to the other sets of eigenvalues that differ by an integer multiple of $a(0)$, one obtains a new system $\mathcal{S}^{\tilde{p},q}_{\tilde{A},a}$ which satisfies the property $(\mathcal{P})$. $\square$

The proof of the previous proposition is constructive and provides an algorithm to compute a matrix transformation T such that $\tilde{A} = T^{-1}(A\, T - z^p\, T')$ with the notations of Proposition 1. Moreover we get a matrix $T \in \mathbb{M}_n(\mathbb{C}[[z]][[X]])$ which is invertible since it is a product of constant matrices, matrices of the form (14) and matrices of the form (15).

Remark 3. *During the process described in the proof of Proposition 1, the leading matrix $A_0(0)$ can at some stage be reduced to the zero matrix. In this case, we apply a* normalization *of the form $X \to z^m\, X$, $m \in \mathbb{Z}^*$ as explained in Section 5 to get a new system satisfying $p < q$.*

Remark 4. *Analyzing the proof of Proposition 1, we can see that for each subset of eigenvalues of $A_0(0)$ that differ by an integer multiple of $a(0)$, the number of terms needed in the X-adic expansion of the matrix $A(z, X)$ is exactly $k_1 + \cdots + k_{s-1} = a(0)^{-1}(\lambda_1 - \lambda_s)$.*

We finally get the following consequence of Theorem 1 and Proposition 1:

Theorem 2. *Let $\mathcal{S}^{p,q}_{A,a}$ be such that $p \leq q$. Then, using the above results, we can compute a formal fundamental matrix of solutions of $\mathcal{S}^{p,q}_{A,a}$ of the form*

$$Y = \left(\sum_{k=0}^{+\infty} T_k(z)\, X^k\right) \Phi(t)\, t^{\Lambda}\, \exp(Q(1/t)),$$

with the notation of (3) and $T_k(z) \in \mathbb{M}_n(\mathbb{C}[[z]])$.

Example 1. *Let us consider the Schrödinger equation with Yukawa potential given by:*

$$-\frac{\hbar^2}{2\, m}\frac{d^2 y}{dr^2} - g^2\, \frac{\mathrm{e}^{-k\, m\, r}}{r}\, y = E\, y,$$

where $\hbar, m, g$ and k are some physical constants and E is the energy eigenvalue (see [13]). This is a second order linear differential equation over $\mathbb{C}$ with an essential singularity at the point at infinity. The associated linear differential system is:

$$\frac{dY}{dr} = r^{-1}\, A(r)\, Y, \quad A(r) = \begin{pmatrix} 0 & r \\ -\frac{2\, m\, g^2}{\hbar^2}\mathrm{e}^{-k\, m\, r} - \frac{2\, m\, E}{\hbar^2}\, r & 0 \end{pmatrix}.$$

To compute the formal solutions at infinity, we perform the change of variable $z = 1/r$. Setting $X = \mathrm{e}^{-\frac{k\, m}{z}}$, we then get the system:

$$Y' = z^{-2}\, A(z, X)\, Y, \quad X' = z^{-2}\, k\, m\, X, \qquad (16)$$

where

$$A(z, X) = \begin{pmatrix} 0 & -1 \\ \dfrac{2\, m\, g^2}{\hbar^2}\, z\, X + \frac{2mE}{\hbar^2} & 0 \end{pmatrix}.$$

We thus have a system $\mathcal{S}^{2,2}_{A,a}$ with $a(z) = a(0) = k\, m$ and

$$A_0(z) = A_0(0) = \begin{pmatrix} 0 & -1 \\ \frac{2mE}{\hbar^2} & 0 \end{pmatrix}.$$

The eigenvalues of $A_0(0)$ are $\pm i \frac{\sqrt{2\,m\,E}}{\hbar}$ and the difference between them is clearly not an integer multiple of $k\,m$ so that (16) satisfies the property ($\mathcal{P}$). Then, Theorem 1 guarantees the existence of a formal matrix transformation $T = \sum_{k=0}^{+\infty} T_k(z)\,X^k$ with $T_0(z) = I_2$ and $T_k(z) \in \mathbb{M}_2(\mathbb{C}[[z]])$ such that we have $z^2\,T' = A\,T - T\,A_0$. The matrix T can be computed (up to arbitrary orders - see Remark 1) by solving Equations (13) using Lemma 5. Note that the meromorphic system $[z^{-2}\,A_0]$ is the free particle Schrödinger equation at $+\infty$. A formal fundamental matrix of solutions of $[z^{-2}\,A_0]$ is given by

$$e^{\int z^{-2}\,A_0\,dz} = \begin{pmatrix} \cos(\frac{\sqrt{2\,m\,E}}{\hbar\,z}) & \frac{\hbar}{\sqrt{2\,m\,E}}\sin(\frac{\sqrt{2\,m\,E}}{\hbar\,z}) \\ -\frac{\sqrt{2\,m\,E}}{\hbar}\sin(\frac{\sqrt{2\,m\,E}}{\hbar\,z}) & \cos(\frac{\sqrt{2\,m\,E}}{\hbar\,z}) \end{pmatrix},$$

and we get that the form of a formal fundamental matrix of solutions of (16) is $\left(\sum_{k=0}^{+\infty} T_k(z)\,X^k\right) e^{\int z^{-2}\,A_0\,dz}$.

4.2 The case $p > q$

Here, we shall adapt to our setting the strategy of the algorithm of [3] reviewed in Subsection 2.2 to study formal meromorphic linear differential systems at an irregular singularity. It consists in applying a (finite) sequence of matrix transformations and changes of variables in order to reduce to the case of a system $\mathcal{S}_{\tilde{A},a}^{\tilde{p},q}$ where either $\tilde{p} \leq q$ (Subsection 4.1) or $n = 1$ (scalar linear differential equations).

The scalar case can be handled as follows. Let $Y_0(z) = \exp(\int z^{-p}\,A_0(z)\,dz)$ be the solution of the leading equation $[z^{-p}\,A_0(z)]$. Performing the change of variables $Y = Y_0\,Z$ and using the fact that $Y_0(z)^{-1}$ satisfies $[-z^{-p}\,A_0(z)]$, we obtain that the new variable Z satisfies the differential equation $Z' = z^{-p}\,(A_1(z)\,X + A_2(z)\,X^2 + \cdots)\,Z$. Using a normalization of the form $X \to z^c\,X$ with $c \in \mathbb{Z}$, we are then reduced to a new differential equation where $p < q$ and $A_0(z) = 0$ (see Remark 6 in Section 5 below). Consequently, we can find a transformation $T \in \mathbb{C}[[z]][[X]]$ such that the equation is reduced to $[0]$. The fundamental solution is thus $Y(z, X) = Y_0(z)\,T(z, z^c\,X)$ which is of the form (4).

We first show how to split systems having a leading matrix $A_0(0)$ with at least two distinct eigenvalues.

PROPOSITION 2. *Let $\mathcal{S}_{A,a}^{p,q}$ be such that $p > q$ and assume that $A_0(0)$ has $r \geq 2$ distinct eigenvalues. Then, $\mathcal{S}_{A,a}^{p,q}$ can be split into r systems $\mathcal{S}_{A^{[i]},a}^{p,q}$, where each $A_0^{[i]}(0)$ has only one eigenvalue. More precisely, we can compute a matrix transformation*

$$T = I_n + T_1(z)\,X + T_2(z)\,X^2 + \cdots, \quad T_k(z) \in \mathbb{M}_n(\mathbb{C}[[z]]),$$

such that

$$z^p\,T' = A(z, X)\,T - T\,\mathrm{diag}(A^{[1]}(z, X), \ldots, A^{[r]}(z, X)),$$

and each $A^{[i]}(0,0)$ has only one eigenvalue.

PROOF. For simplicity, we restrict to the case $r = 2$, which will be used to prove Theorem 3 below. We mimic the strategy of [21, Chapter 4, Section 11]. Appying the splitting lemma (see [21, Theorem 11.1, p. 54] or [3, Theorem 2]) as in the proof of Proposition 1, we can first assume that $A_0(z) = \mathrm{diag}(A_0^{11}(z), A_0^{22}(z))$ and $A_0^{11}(0)$ and $A_0^{22}(0)$ have no common eigenvalues. We are going to prove that we can compute a matrix transformation T of the desired form such that we have $z^p\,T' = A(z, X)\,T - T\,\mathrm{diag}(B^{[1]}(z, X), B^{[2]}(z, X))$, where $B^{[i]}(0, 0) = A_0^{ii}(0)$ for $i = 1, 2$. Plugging an ansatz $T = \sum_{k=0}^{+\infty} T_k(z)\,X^k$, where

$$T_0(z) = \mathrm{I}_n, \quad T_k(z) = \begin{pmatrix} 0 & T_k^{12}(z) \\ T_k^{21}(z) & 0 \end{pmatrix}, \forall\, k \in \mathbb{N}^*,$$

into the relation $z^p\,T' = A(z, X)\,T - T\,B(z, X)$, we get

$$z^p\,T_0' = A_0\,T_0 - T_0\,B_0, \tag{17}$$

and, for $k \geq 1$,

$$\begin{aligned} z^p\,T_k' &= A_0\,T_k - T_k\,(B_0 + k\,z^{p-q}\,a(z)\,\mathrm{I}_n) \\ &+ \sum_{m=1}^{k-1}(A_m\,T_{k-m} - T_{k-m}\,B_m) + A_k - B_k. \end{aligned} \tag{18}$$

Now, $T_0 = \mathrm{I}_n$ and $B_0(z) = A_0(z)$ provides a trivial solution of (17). If we take the corresponding partition by blocks

$$\sum_{m=1}^{k-1}(A_m\,T_{k-m} - T_{k-m}\,B_m) + A_k = \begin{pmatrix} W_k^{11}(z) & W_k^{12}(z) \\ W_k^{21}(z) & W_k^{22}(z) \end{pmatrix},$$

and if we set $B_k(z) = \mathrm{diag}(W_k^{11}(z), W_k^{22}(z))$, then Equation (18) reduces to

$$\begin{cases} z^p\,(T_k^{12})' = A_0^{11}\,T_k^{12} - T_k^{12}\,(A_0^{22} + k\,z^{p-q}\,a(z)\,\mathrm{I}) + W_k^{12}, \\ z^p\,(T_k^{21})' = A_0^{22}\,T_k^{21} - T_k^{21}\,(A_0^{11} + k\,z^{p-q}\,a(z)\,\mathrm{I}) + W_k^{21}. \end{cases}$$

Finally, using in particular the fact that $p > q \geq 2$, the hypotheses of Lemma 5 are satisfied. This implies that both equations can be solved for matrices T_k^{12} and T_k^{21} with entries in $\mathbb{C}[[z]]$ which ends the proof. ☐

To compute a formal fundamental matrix of solutions of $\mathcal{S}_{A,a}^{p,q}$, we shall need to perform ramifications of the variable z. The following straightforward lemma shows the effect of such a ramification on a system $\mathcal{S}_{A,a}^{p,q}$.

LEMMA 6. *Let $r \in \mathbb{N}^*$ be a positive integer. Then, performing the ramification $z = t^r$ in the differential system $\mathcal{S}_{A,a}^{p,q}$ in the variable z yields a new differential system $\mathcal{S}_{\tilde{A},\tilde{a}}^{\tilde{p},\tilde{q}}$ in the variable t, where we have $\tilde{p} = r\,(p-1)+1$, $\tilde{q} = r\,(q-1)+1$, and $\tilde{A}(t, X) = r\,A(t^r, X)$, $\tilde{a}(t) = r\,a(t^r)$.*

Note that, from Lemma 6, performing a ramification on $\mathcal{S}_{A,a}^{p,q}$ does not affect the sign of the quantity $p - q$.

THEOREM 3. *Let $\mathcal{S}_{A,a}^{p,q}$ be such that $p > q$. Then, we can compute a formal fundamental matrix of solutions of $\mathcal{S}_{A,a}^{p,q}$ of the form*

$$Y = \left(\sum_{k=0}^{+\infty} \Phi_k(t)\,X^k\right) t^{\Lambda}\,\exp(Q(1/t)),$$

with the notation of (3) and $\Phi_k(t) \in \mathbb{M}_n(\mathbb{C}((t)))$.

PROOF. Let us consider the leading formal meromorphic linear differential system $[z^{-p}\,A_0(z)]$ and assume that the ramification appearing in its formal fundamental matrix of solutions of the form (3) is $z = t^r$. We first perform the ramification $z = t^r$ in the whole system $\mathcal{S}_{A,a}^{p,q}$ so that we get a new system $\mathcal{S}_{\tilde{A},\tilde{a}}^{\tilde{p},\tilde{q}}$ satisfying the relations of Lemma 6. To simplify the notation in the sequel, we still denote by $\mathcal{S}_{A,a}^{p,q}$ this ramified system and by z the variable. From the theory of formal meromorphic linear differential systems, we can compute a matrix transformation $T \in \mathrm{GL}_n(\mathbb{C}((z)))$ such that we have

$$T[z^{-p} A_0(z)] = z^{-p} \operatorname{diag}(B_1(z), \ldots, B_s(z)),$$

where, for $i = 1, \ldots, s$, $B_i(z) = \omega_i(z) I_{n_i} + z^{p-1} \Lambda_i$, with $\omega_i(z) \in \mathbb{C}[z]$ of degree $\leq (p-2)$ and $\Lambda_i \in \mathbb{M}_{n_i}(\mathbb{C})$ (see [21, 3]). Applying this matrix transformation T to the whole differential system $\mathcal{S}^{p,q}_{A,a}$, we can assume without loss of generality that in $\mathcal{S}^{p,q}_{A,a}$, we have $A_0(z) = \operatorname{diag}(B_1(z), \ldots, B_s(z))$. Then, we apply the transformation

$$T = \exp\left(\int z^{-p} \omega_1(z)\, dz\right) \mathrm{I}_n \in \mathrm{GL}_n(\mathbb{C}((z))),$$

to $\mathcal{S}^{p,q}_{A,a}$. This provides a new differential system $\mathcal{S}^{p,q}_{\tilde{A},a}$ with

$$\tilde{A}_0(z) = A_0(z) - \omega_1(z) \mathrm{I}_n = \operatorname{diag}(\tilde{B}_1(z), \ldots, \tilde{B}_s(z)),$$

with $\tilde{B}_1(z) = z^{p-1} \Lambda_1$ and

$$\tilde{B}_i(z) = \underbrace{(\omega_i(z) - \omega_1(z))}_{\tilde{\omega}_i(z)} I_{n_i} + z^{p-1} \Lambda_i, \quad i = 2, \ldots, s.$$

Let us now define the following positive integer:

$$k = \min_{i=2,\ldots,s} v_z(\tilde{\omega}_i(z)) \leq p - 2.$$

Up to a permutation (that we apply to the whole differential system $\mathcal{S}^{p,q}_{\tilde{A},a}$), we can then reorder the blocks of the matrix $\tilde{A}_0(z)$ such that $\tilde{A}_0(z) = \operatorname{diag}(\tilde{A}^{11}_0(z), \tilde{A}^{22}_0(z))$, with

$$\tilde{A}^{11}_0(z) = \operatorname{diag}(\{\tilde{B}_j(z)\}_{j \in J_1}),\ \forall j \in J_1,\ v_z(\tilde{B}_j(z)) > k,$$

$$\tilde{A}^{22}_0(z) = \operatorname{diag}(\{\tilde{B}_j(z)\}_{j \in J_2}),\ \forall j \in J_2,\ v_z(\tilde{B}_j(z)) = k,$$

so that $v_z(\tilde{A}^{11}_0(z)) > k$ and $v_z(\tilde{A}^{22}_0(z)) = k$. We now apply the normalization $X \to z^{-k} X$ which yields a new differential system $\mathcal{S}^{\bar{p},q}_{\bar{A},\bar{a}}$ satisfying the condition $\bar{p} = p - k$ and $\bar{A}_0(z) = z^{-k} \tilde{A}_0(z)$ (see Section 5). If $p - k \leq q$, then we are reduced to the case of Subsection 4.1. Otherwise we are reduced to a system $\mathcal{S}^{\bar{p},q}_{\bar{A},\bar{a}}$ satisfying both $\bar{p} > q$ and

$$\bar{A}_0(z) = \operatorname{diag}(\bar{A}^{11}_0(z), \bar{A}^{22}_0(z)),\ \bar{A}^{ii}_0(z) = z^{-k} \tilde{A}^{ii}_0(z),\ i = 1, 2.$$

Consequently, $\bar{A}^{11}_0(0) = 0$ has the sole eigenvalue 0 and $\bar{A}^{22}_0(0)$ has only non-zero eigenvalues so that we can apply Proposition 2 for $r = 2$ to split the whole differential $\mathcal{S}^{\bar{p},q}_{\bar{A},\bar{a}}$ into two uncoupled differential systems. Iterating this process on each system obtained yields the desired result. Indeed, we will necessarily end up with a differential system satisfying either $p \leq q$ (see Subsection 4.1) or $n = 1$ (scalar case). □

In our implementation, instead of proceeding as in the proof of Theorem 3 above, we rather follow the distinct steps of the algorithm of [3] applied to the leading formal meromorphic linear differential system $[z^{-p} A_0(z)]$. Namely, we apply one after the other the steps reviewed in Subsection 2.2 to $[z^{-p} A_0(z)]$ and at each step we perform the transformations needed (e.g., splitting, shift, Moser's reduction, ramification, ...) to the whole system $\mathcal{S}^{p,q}_{A,a}$.

REMARK 5. *The form (4) of a formal fundamental matrix of solutions of $\mathcal{S}^{p,q}_{A,a}$ could be confusing as one may think that no negative power in X is involved. It is not true as, for example, for all $\lambda \in \mathbb{C}^*$ and X defined by (1b), the scalar equation $Y' = \lambda z^{-q} a(z) Y$ admits the solution $Y = \exp(\int \lambda z^{-q} a(z)\, dz)$ which is exactly X^{λ}. Such a negative power of X can indeed be hidden in the part $t^{\Lambda} \exp(Q(1/t))$.*

5. WIDER CLASSES OF SYSTEMS

In this section, we show that the algorithm of Section 4 can handle a wider class of systems than $\mathcal{S}^{p,q}_{A,a}$. Consider a differential system of the form

$$\begin{cases} Y' = z^{-p} A(z, X) Y, & p \in \mathbb{N}^*,\ A(z, X) \neq 0, \\ X' = z^{-q} a(z) X,\ q \geq 2,\ a(z) \in \mathbb{C}[[z]],\ a(0) \neq 0, \end{cases} \tag{19}$$

where $A(z, X) = \sum_{k=0}^{+\infty} A_k(z) X^k$, $A_k(z) \in \mathbb{M}_n(\mathbb{C}((z)))$.

The algorithm presented in Section 4 applies to an input system $\mathcal{S}^{p,q}_{A,a}$ which is supposed to have its coefficients living in the ring $\mathcal{A}$ defined by (5) and to satisfy $A_0(0) \neq 0$. However during the reduction process described in Section 4 one naturally may obtain systems with coefficients that no longer belong to $\mathcal{A}$ (i.e., $v_z(A_k) \to -\infty$, when $k \to +\infty$). Moreover one can also be confronted to systems of the form (19) with $v_z(A_0) \neq 0$ (in particular when $A_0(0) = 0$). We show here that we can always overcome these difficulties by using *normalizations* of the form $X \to z^m X$ and allowing the coefficients of the input system to live in the ring $\mathcal{B} \supsetneq \mathcal{A}$ defined by (6). We first give the following straightforward lemma:

LEMMA 7. *Let $m \in \mathbb{Z}$ be an integer. If X satisfies*

$$X' = z^{-q} a(z) X,\ q \geq 2,\ a(z) \in \mathbb{C}[[z]],\ a(0) \neq 0,$$

then $z^m X$ satisfies the same equation where $a(z)$ is replaced by $a(z) + m z^{q-1}$. In particular, the order $q \geq 2$ of the pole $z = 0$ does not change.

PROPOSITION 3. *Consider a differential system of the form (19) with $A_0(z) \neq 0$ and $v_z(A_0) \neq 0$. If*

$$\exists c \in \mathbb{Z} \text{ such that } \forall k \in \mathbb{N}^*,\ v_z(A_k) \geq c\, k + v_z(A_0), \tag{20}$$

then the normalization $X \to z^c X$ yields a new differential system of the form (19) where p is replaced by $p - v_z(A_0)$, $v_z(A_0) = 0$, i.e., $A_0(0) \neq 0$, and $v_z(A_k) \geq 0$, for all $k \geq 1$.

PROOF. This can be deduced easily from the computation in the proof of Lemma 3. □

Note that if $v_z(A_0) = 0$ but there exists $k_0 \in \mathbb{N}^*$ with $v_z(A_{k_0}) < 0$, then the proof of Lemma 3 also shows that, if we have (20), we can perform a normalization $X \to z^c X$, $c \in \mathbb{Z}^*$ to get a new system with coefficients having all non-negative valuation.

Finally, since (20) is always satisfied when we consider systems of the form (19) where $A(z, X)$ has entries in the ring $\mathcal{B}$ defined by (6) (see the proof of Lemma 3), we have:

THEOREM 4. *The algorithm developed in Section 4 can be applied to compute a formal fundamental matrix of solutions of all systems of the form (19) with $A(z, X) \in \mathbb{M}_n(\mathcal{B})$.*

REMARK 6. *In the case where $A_0(z) = 0$ in System (19), then we can still use a normalization to come down to a system satisfying $p < q$. Indeed, let $\nu > 0$ denote the X-adic valuation of $A(z, X)$, then the normalization $X \to z^m X$ with $m = \lfloor (p-q)/\nu \rfloor + 1$ yields a new system with $p < q$. Note that, when $A_0(z) = 0$, one can also apply the change of variables $Z = X Y$ to obtain a new system for Z satisfying $A_0(z) = z^{-q} a(z) I_n \neq 0$.*

Let us illustrate the purpose of this section on an example.

EXAMPLE 2. *Let X satisfy an equation of the form (1b), i.e., $X' = z^{-q}\, a(z)\, X$ and consider the scalar equation*

$$Y' = -z^{-(q+1)} \left(\sum_{k=0}^{+\infty} A_k\, X^k \right) Y, \qquad (21)$$

with

$$A_0 = z^q, \quad \forall k \geq 1,\ A_k = z^{-(k-1)} \left(z^{q-1} - a(z) \right).$$

With the notation of the paper, we then have $p = q+1 > q$. Clearly $\inf_{k\in\mathbb{N}} v_z(A_k) = -\infty$ so that our equation does not have coefficients in the ring $\mathcal{A}$ defined by (5). However, we can check that $v_z(A_k) \geq -k+1$, for all $k \in \mathbb{N}$ so that the coefficients are in the ring $\mathcal{B}$ defined by (6) (since (6) is satisfied with $\alpha = -1$ and $\beta = 1$). This further implies that the condition (20) is fulfilled. Now $v_z(A_0) = q > 0$ so that Proposition 3 ensures that there exists $c \in \mathbb{Z}^*$ such that the normalization $X \to z^c X$ yields a new equation of the form $Y' = -z^{-1} \sum_{k=0}^{+\infty} \tilde{A}_k\, X^k$ with $\tilde{A}_0 = 1$ so that $\tilde{A}_0(0) \neq 0$, and $\tilde{A}_k \in \mathbb{M}_n(\mathbb{C}[[z]])$. From the proof of Lemma 3, since $v_z(A_0) = q > \beta = 1$, we can choose $c = \lfloor \alpha+\beta - v_z(A_0) \rfloor = -q$. The resulting equation $\mathcal{S}^{1,q}_{\tilde{A},a}$ can now be handled by our algorithm in the case $p < q$ studied in Subsection 4.1. Theorem 1 then implies that we can compute a formal power series $T = 1 + T_1\, X + T_2\, X^2 + \cdots$, with $T_k \in \mathbb{C}[[z]]$ that reduces the equation to the leading equation $y' = -z^{-1}\, \tilde{A}_0\, y = -z^{-1}\, y$ that admits the trivial solution $y = z^{-1}$. Here we find that the coefficients T_k are given by $T_k = z^{(q-1)\,k}$. A formal fundamental solution of (21) can thus be written as

$$Y = \left(\sum_{k=0}^{+\infty} z^{(q-1)\,k} \left(z^{-q}\, X \right)^k \right) z^{-1} = z^{-1} \sum_{k=0}^{+\infty} z^{-k}\, X^k.$$

The latest power series is an expansion of $(z - X)^{-1}$ which is a solution of (21).

Acknowledgment

The authors thank the anonymous referees for their valuable comments which have improved the quality of the paper.

6. REFERENCES

[1] A. Aparicio Monforte. *Méthodes effectives pour l'intégrabilité des systèmes dynamiques.* PhD thesis, Univ. de Limoges (France), 2010.

[2] D. G. Babbitt and V. S. Varadarajan. Formal reduction theory of meromorphic differential equations: a group theoretic view. *Pacific J. Math*, 109(1):1–80, 1983.

[3] M. A. Barkatou. An algorithm to compute the exponential part of a formal fundamental matrix solution of a linear differential system. *Applicable Algebra in Engineering, Communication and Computing*, 8:1–23, 1997.

[4] M. A. Barkatou, G. Broughton, and E. Pflügel. Regular systems of linear functional equations and applications. In *Proc. of ISSAC'08*, pages 15–22, Hagenberg, Austria, 2008.

[5] M. A. Barkatou and E. Pflügel. An algorithm computing the regular formal solutions of a system of linear differential equations. *J. of Symb. Comp.*, 28(4-5):569–587, 1999.

[6] M. A. Barkatou and C. Raab. Solving linear ordinary differential systems in hyperexponential extensions. In *Proc. of ISSAC'12*, pages 51–58, Grenoble, France, 2012.

[7] M. Bouffet. Un lemme de Hensel pour les opérateurs différentiels. *C. R. Acad. Sci.*, t. 331, Série I:277–280, 2000.

[8] M. Bouffet. *Théorie de Galois différentielle pour des équations différentielles linéaires dont les coefficients admettent des singularités essentielles.* PhD thesis, Univ. de Toulouse (France), 2002.

[9] M. Bouffet. Differential Galois theory for an exponential extension of $\mathbb{C}((z))$. *Bull. Soc. Math. France*, 131(4):587–601, 2003.

[10] A. Fredet. *Résolution sous forme finie d'équations différentielles linéaires et extensions exponentielles.* PhD thesis, École Polytechnique (France), 2001.

[11] A. Fredet. Linear differential equations in exponential extensions. *J. of Symb. Comp.*, 38:975–1002, 2004.

[12] I. Gohberg, P. Lancaster, and L. Rodman. *Matrix Polynomials.* Academic Press, New York, 1982.

[13] M. Hamzavi, M. Movahedi, K.-E. Thylwe, and A.-A. Rajabi. Approximate analytical solution of the Yukawa potential with arbitrary angular momenta. *Chinese Physics Letters*, 29(8), 2012.

[14] A. Hilali and A. Wazner. Un algorithme de calcul de l'invariant de katz d'un système différentiel linéaire. *Annales de l'Institut Fourier*, 36(3):67–83, 1986.

[15] D. W. Hoffmann. The Newton polygon of a product of power series. *Manuscripta Math.*, 85:109–118, 1994.

[16] M. Lazard. Les zéros d'une fonction analytique d'une variable sur un corps valué complet. *Publications Mathématiques de l'I.H.É.S.*, 14:47–75, 1962.

[17] M. Lazard. Polygone de Newton et théorème de préparation. *Séminaire Dubreuil. Algèbre*, 26, exp. 15:1–4, 1972-1973.

[18] J. Moser. The order of a singularity in Fuchs' theory. *Mathematische Zeitschrift*, 72:379–398, 1960.

[19] H. L. Turritin. Convergent solutions of ordinary linear homogeneous differential equations in the neighborhood of an irregular singular point. *Acta Math.*, 93:27–66, 1955.

[20] H. Volklein. *Groups as Galois Groups, An Introduction.* Cambridge Studies in Advanced Mathematics (53), Cambridge University Press, 1996.

[21] W. Wasow. *Asymptotic Expansions For Ordinary Differential Equations.* Dover Publi., New York, 1965.

Removing Apparent Singularities of Systems of Linear Differential Equations with Rational Function Coefficients

Moulay A. Barkatou, Suzy S. Maddah*
XLIM Institute, University of Limoges; CNRS
123, Av. A. Thomas, 87060 Limoges France
moulay.barkatou@unilim.fr, suzy.maddah@etu.unilim.fr

ABSTRACT

In this paper we present a new algorithm which, given a system of first order linear differential equations with rational function coefficients, constructs an equivalent system with rational function coefficients, whose finite singularities are exactly the non-apparent singularities of the original system. This algorithm is implemented in the computer algebra system Maple and is illustrated by examples.

Categories and Subject Descriptors

I.1.2 [**Symbolic And Algebraic Manipulation**]: Algorithms—*Algebraic algorithms*

General Terms

Algorithms, Theory

Keywords

Systems of linear ordinary differential equations, Apparent singularities, Desingularization, Computer algebra.

1. INTRODUCTION

Given a first-order differential system of size n with rational function coefficients in the complex variable z

$$[A] \qquad \partial X = A(z) X$$

where $\partial = \frac{d}{dz}$, $X = (x_1, \ldots, x_n)^t$ vector of lenght n and $A \in \mathbb{C}(z)^{n \times n}$. The finite singularities of system $[A]$ are the poles of $A(z)$ in $\mathbb{C}$. A singular point $z_0 \in \mathbb{C}$ is called an apparent singularity if there exists a fundamental matrix solution $\Phi(z)$ which is analytic at $z = z_0$. Consider, for example, the first-order differential system

$$\partial X = A(z) X, \quad A(z) = \begin{bmatrix} 0 & 1 \\ \frac{-2}{z} & 1 + \frac{2}{z}. \end{bmatrix} \qquad (1)$$

*Enrolled in a joint PhD program with the Lebanese University

ISSAC'15, July 6–9, 2015, Bath, United Kingdom.

DOI: http://dx.doi.org/10.1145/2755996.2756668.

Clearly, this system is equivalent to the second-order scalar differential equation given by the monic operator L:

$$L := \partial^2 - \frac{z+2}{z}\partial + \frac{2}{z},$$

for which e^z and $1+z+\frac{z^2}{2}$ form a basis of solutions. It follows that the point $z = 0$ is an apparent singularity of system (1). *Desingularization*, i.e. the problem of constructing another operator $\tilde{L}$ of higher order such that the solution space of $\tilde{L}(x) = 0$ contains that of $L(x) = 0$, and for which the factor z is "removed" from the denominator, is an interesting problem of research. For instance, by ABH method [2], one can compute a desingularization of order 4 given by the operator

$$\begin{aligned} \tilde{L} &= \partial^4 + (-1 + 1/4\,z)\,\partial^3 + (-1/4 - 3/8\,z)\,\partial^2 \\ &+ (1/2 + 1/8\,z)\,\partial - 1/4 \end{aligned}$$

In the scalar case, several desingularization algorithms exist for differential, difference (e.g., [2]), and more generally, Ore operators (see, e.g. [11, 10] and references therein). However, the apparent singularity of system (1) (equivalently of L) at $z = 0$, can be also removed by acting directly on it. In fact, by setting [6]

$$X = T(z)\, Y, \quad T(z) = \begin{bmatrix} 1 & 0 \\ 1 & z^2 \end{bmatrix},$$

the new variable Y satisfies the equivalent first-order differential system of the same size as the order of L, given by $[B]$ $\partial Y = B\, Y$ where

$$B := T^{-1} A T - T^{-1} \partial T = \begin{bmatrix} 1 & z^2 \\ 0 & 0 \end{bmatrix}.$$

In this paper, we shall prove that, given any system $[A]$ with rational coefficients, it can be reduced to an *equivalent* system $[B]$ with rational coefficients, such that the finite singularities of $[B]$ coincide with the non-apparent singularities of $[A]$. Our method can, in particular, be applied to the companion system of any linear differential equation with arbitrary order n. We thus have an alternative method to the standard methods for removing apparent singularities of linear differential operators. However, it is also interesting by its own since first-order linear differential systems with apparent singularities arise naturally in applications (see, e.g., [15, 16, 9] and references therein, for applications within Feynman integrals and statistical physics). Moreover, such a desingularization can serve numerical methods.

This paper is organized as follows: In Section 2 we give the notations to be used in the sequel and some preliminary definitions. In Section 3, we give our main result: We show

how apparent singularities can be detected, prove the existence of desingularizations, and develop a desingularization algorithm over $\mathbb{C}(z)$. In Section 4, we show some examples of computations compared to two desingularization algorithms designed for scalar linear differential equations. In Section 5, we give a rational version of our algorithm. And finally, we give items for further investigation in Section 6.

2. PRELIMINARIES

Given system $[A] \quad \partial X = A(z)X$. In this section, we recall the useful notion of equivalent systems and the classification of singularities.

2.1 Equivalent systems

Let $T \in \mathrm{GL}(n, \mathbb{C}(z))$, the *gauge transformation* $X = TY$, leads to a new system $[B] \quad \partial Y = B(z)Y$, where

$$B = T[A] := T^{-1}AT - T^{-1}\partial T.$$

Systems $[A]$ and $[B]$ are called *equivalent over* $\mathbb{C}(z)$.

2.2 Classification of singularities

A singular point $z_0 \in \mathbb{C}$ is called a *regular singular point* for the system $[A]$ if in a neighborhood of z_0, there exists a fundamental matrix solution of the form $X(z) = \Phi(z)(z - z_0)^{\Lambda}$ where $\Lambda \in \mathbb{C}^{n\times n}$ is a constant matrix and $\Phi(z)$ is a matrix which is analytic at z_0; otherwise z_0 is called an *irregular singular point* (see, e.g. [13, Ch 4 Sec 2 pp 111]). Hence apparent singularities of $[A]$ are among regular singularities of $[A]$.
The change of variable $z \mapsto 1/z$ permits to classify the point $z = \infty$ as an ordinary, a regular singular or an irregular singular point of the system $[A]$.
This classification, based upon knowledge of a fundamental matrix, is not immediately apparent for a given differential system. It is well known (see [3]) that if $A(z)$ has a simple pole at $z = z_0$ then the point z_0 is a regular singularity for the system $[A]$. The converse is not true: even when $A(z)$ has a multiple pole at $z = z_0$ it is still possible for z_0 to be a regular singularity. However, it was proven by Moser [19] that in the case where z_0 is a regular singularity there exists a polynomial matrix function T of $z - z_0$ which is nonsingular for $z \neq z_0$ such that the transformation $X = TY$ transforms the system $[A]$ into an equivalent system $[B] \quad \partial Y = B(z)Y$, such that z_0 is a **simple** pole of $B(z)$.
Simple poles of $A(z)$ are called *first-kind singularities* of $[A]$, poles of higher order are singularities of *second kind*. Thus, a system has a regular singularity at a point z_0 if and only if it is equivalent to a system $[B]$ with a first-kind singularity at z_0. This latter system can be constructed using the so called *Rational Moser algorithm* developed in [5]. This algorithm, establishes *partial desingularization*, as it computes for a given system $[A]$ a polynomial transformation $T(z)$ with $\det T(z) \not\equiv 0$ that leads to a system $[B]$ such that (see [5, Sec. 6]):

(i) The finite singularities of $[B]$ are among the finite singularities of $[A]$.

(ii) **Every** finite singular point of $[B]$ has a **minimal** pole order among **all** equivalent systems.

3. DETECTING AND REMOVING APPARENT SINGULARITIES

Consider a system $[A] \ \partial X = A(z)X$ with $A(z) \in \mathbb{C}(z)^{n\times n}$.

DEFINITION 1. *A system* $[\tilde{A}] \ \partial \tilde{X} = \tilde{A}(z)\tilde{X}$ *is called a desingularization of* $[A]$ *if:*

(i) There exists a **polynomial** *matrix* $T(z)$ *with* $\det T(z) \not\equiv 0$ *such that* $\tilde{A} = T[A]$*;*

(ii) The singularities of $[\tilde{A}]$ *are the singularities of* $[A]$ *that are not apparent.*

In the sequel we shall prove that desingularizations do exist and develop an algorithm that produces a desingularization of any system $[A]$ over $\mathbb{C}(z)$.
We first start by explaining how to remove one apparent singularity.

PROPOSITION 1. *If* $z = z_0$ *is a finite apparent singularity of* $[A]$ *then one can construct a polynomial matrix* $T(z)$ *with* $\det T(z) = c(z - z_0)^{\alpha}$, $c \in \mathbb{C}^*$ *and* $\alpha \in \mathbb{N}$ *such that* $T[A]$ *has at worst a simple pole at* $z = z_0$.

Proof. *(i)* An apparent singularity is a regular singularity, hence $[A]$ can be reduced to an equivalent system $T[A]$ which has z_0 as a singularity of first kind. *(ii)* The transformation T can be constructed by the algorithm in [5] and hence it has the required property (see [5, Thm 2]).

PROPOSITION 2. *Suppose that* $A(z)$ *has simple pole at* $z = z_0$ *and let*

$$A(z) = \frac{A_0}{(z - z_0)} + \sum_{i\geq 1} A_i (z - z_0)^{i-1}, \quad A_i \in \mathbb{C}^{n\times n}.$$

If z_0 *is an apparent singularity then the eigenvalues of the so-called residue matrix* A_0*, are nonnegative integers.*

Proof. Suppose that A_0 possesses at least one eigenvalue which does not belong to $\mathbb{N}$ and let μ be an eigenvalue of A_0 such that $\mu \in \mathbb{C} \setminus \mathbb{N}$ and $\Re\mu$, its real part, is maximal. Then the system $[A]$ has a nonzero local vectorial solution of the form:
$X(z) = (z - z_0)^{\mu} \sum_{k=0}^{+\infty} X_k (z - z_0)^k$ with $X_k \in \mathbb{C}^n$ and $X_0 \neq 0$, the series being convergent in a disc centered at z_0 (see, e.g. [3, Ch 2 Thm 6 pp 32]). Such a solution is not analytic at $z = z_0$ because $\mu \notin \mathbb{N}$. This implies that z_0 is a singularity which is not apparent.

PROPOSITION 3. *Suppose that* $z = z_0$ *is a simple pole of* $A(z)$ *and that* A_0 *has only nonnegative integer eigenvalues. Then there exists a polynomial matrix* $T(z)$ *with* $\det T(z) = c(z - z_0)^{\alpha}$ *for some* $c \in \mathbb{C}^*$ *and* $\alpha \in \mathbb{N}$ *such that* $B := T[A]$ *has at worst a simple pole at* $z = z_0$ *and* B_0 *has a single eigenvalue:* $B_0 = mI_n + N$ *where* $m \in \mathbb{N}$ *and* N *nilpotent. Moreover,* z_0 *is an apparent singularity iff* $N = 0$*. In this case, the gauge transformation* $Y = (z - z_0)^m \tilde{Y}$ *leads to a system for which* $z = z_0$ *is an ordinary point.*

Proof. Let $m_1, \ldots, m_s \in \mathbb{N}$ be the eigenvalues of A_0. For $i = 1, \ldots, s$, denote by ν_i the multiplicity of m_i. Suppose that $m_1 > m_2 > \ldots > m_s$ and put $\ell_i = m_i - m_{i+1} \in \mathbb{N}^*$, $i = 1, \ldots, s - 1$. By applying a constant gauge transformation we can assume that A_0 is in Jordan form:

$$A_0 = \begin{bmatrix} A_0^{11} & 0 \\ 0 & A_0^{22} \end{bmatrix}, \tag{2}$$

where A_0^{11} is an ν_1 by ν_1 matrix having one single eigenvalue m_1:

$$A_0^{11} = m_1 I_{\nu_1} + N_1$$

N_1 being a nilpotent matrix. Applying the transformation $X = UY$, where

$$U = diag((z - z_0)I_{\nu_1}, I_{n-\nu_1}) \quad (3)$$

yields the new system:

$$Y' = \tilde{A}(z)Y,$$

where

$$\tilde{A}(z) = U^{-1}A(z)U - U^{-1}U'.$$

Its residue matrix is given by:

$$\tilde{A}_0 = \left(A_0 + (z - z_0)U^{-1}A_1U - (z - z_0)U^{-1}U'\right)_{|z=z_0}.$$

Let A_1 be partitioned as A_0 :

$$A_1 = \begin{bmatrix} A_1^{11} & A_1^{12} \\ A_1^{21} & A_1^{22} \end{bmatrix}, \quad A_1^{11} \in \mathbb{C}^{\nu_1 \times \nu_1}$$

Then

$$\tilde{A}_0 = \begin{bmatrix} A_0^{11} - I_{\nu_1} & A_1^{12} \\ 0 & A_0^{22} \end{bmatrix}. \quad (4)$$

Hence the eigenvalues of $\tilde{A}_0$ are: $m_1 - 1, m_2, \ldots, m_s$, each with the same initial multiplicity ν_i.
By repeating this process ℓ_1 times where $m_1 - \ell_1 = m_2$, the eigenvalues become:

$$m_2, m_2, \ldots, m_s.$$

Thus, after $\ell_1 + \ldots + \ell_{s-1} = m_1 - m_s$ steps one gets an equivalent system $B := T[A]$ of the first kind with a residue matrix B_0 with a single eigenvalue m_s of multiplicity $\nu_1 + \ldots + \nu_s = n$. Hence the matrix $N := B_0 - m_s I_n$ is nilpotent. Moreover the matrix T is the product of matrices that are either constant or of the form (3). Hence T is a polynomial matrix of degree at most $m_1 - m_s$ and its determinant is of the form $\det T(z) = c(z - z_0)^\alpha$ for some $c \in \mathbb{C}^*$ and $\alpha \in \mathbb{N}$. Due to the form of B_0 it follows that the system $[B]$ has, in the neighborhood of z_0, a fundamental matrix solution of the form

$$Y(z) = (z - z_0)^{m_s}\Phi(z)(z - z_0)^N$$

where

$$\Phi(z) = I_n + \sum_{k=1}^{+\infty} \Phi_k(z - z_0)^k \in \mathbb{C}\{(z - z_0)\}^{n\times n},$$

Hence z_0 is an apparent singularity of $[A]$ if and only if N is the zero matrix. Finally, if we put $Y = (z - z_0)^{m_s}\tilde{Y}$ the resulting system has the above matrix $\Phi(z)$ as a fundamental matrix solution around $z = z_0$. As $\Phi(z_0) = I_n$, the point z_0 is an ordinary point for the latter system.

REMARK 1. *One can deduce from the above proof that a necessary (but not sufficient) condition for a first-kind singularity z_0 to be an apparent singularity for $[A]$ is that the residue matrix A_0 be* **diagonalizable** *with nonnegative integer eigenvalues. Indeed, if A_0 is not diagonalizable then in (2) at least one of the two blocks A_0^{11}, A_0^{22} has a nonzero nilpotent part. It follows from the form of (4) that transformation (3) cannot annihilate the nilpotent part of the residue matrix. Thus if the residue matrix A_0 of the input system (or one of the intermediate systems) is not diagonalizable then the output system $[B]$ has a residue matrix $B_0 = mI_n + N$ with $N \neq 0$.*

We thus proved the following theorem:

THEOREM 1. *If $z = z_0$ is a finite apparent singularity of $[A]$ then one can construct a polynomial matrix $T(z)$ with $\det T(z) = c(z - z_0)^\alpha$, $c \in \mathbb{C}^*$ and $\alpha \in \mathbb{N}$ such that $B(z) := T[A]$ has no pole at $z = z_0$.*

Algorithm 1 Desingularization Algorithm

Input: $A(z)$;
Output: $T(z) \in GL(n, \mathbb{C}(z))$ and $T[A]$ such that $T[A]$ is a desingularization of the input system $[A]$. And, the two sets $\mathcal{A}pp$ and Σ of apparent singularities (which are "removed") and simple poles (which are not apparent singularities) respectively.

$T \leftarrow$ Use the *Rational Moser Algorithm* of [5] to compute a polynomial matrix $T(z)$ with $\det T(z) \not\equiv 0$ such that

- The roots of $\det T(z) = 0$ belong to $\mathcal{P}(A)$ (*this implies that the poles of $T^{-1}(z)$ are among the poles of A and hence $\mathcal{P}(T[A]) \subset \mathcal{P}(A)$*)
- The orders of the poles of $T[A]$ are minimal among all equivalent systems

$A \leftarrow T[A]$;
$\mathcal{A}pp \leftarrow$ {set of simple poles of A, z_i : $1 \leq i \leq \mu$};

$\Sigma \leftarrow \{\}$;

$i \leftarrow 1$;
while $i \neq \mu + 1$ **do**

- Compute A_{z_i} the residue matrix of A at $z = z_i$
- Compute the SN decomposition of A_{z_i}, namely $A_i = S_{z_i} + N_{z_i}$ where S_{z_i} semi-simple, N_{z_i} nilpotent, and S_{z_i} and N_{z_i} commute. We remark that a rational decomposition exists (see, e.g. [17])

if $N_{z_i} \neq 0_n$ or S_{z_i} has at least one eigenvalue in $\mathbb{C} \setminus \mathbb{N}$ **then** $\mathcal{A}pp \leftarrow \mathcal{A}pp \setminus \{z_i\}$; $\Sigma \leftarrow \Sigma \cup \{z_i\}$;
else Use the method presented in the proof of Proposition 3 to compute a polynomial matrix T_{z_i} such that $T_{z_i}[A]$ has at worst a simple pole at $z = z_i$ with residue matrix of the form $A_{z_i} = m_{z_i} I_n + N_{z_i}$ where $m_{z_i} \in \mathbb{N}$ and N_{z_i} is nilpotent.
if $N_{z_i} \neq 0_n$ **then** $\mathcal{A}pp \leftarrow \mathcal{A}pp \setminus \{z_i\}$; $\Sigma \leftarrow \Sigma \cup \{z_i\}$;
else $A \leftarrow T_{z_i}[A]$; $T \leftarrow T \star (z - z_i)^{m_{z_i}} T_{z_i}$;
end if
end if

- $i \leftarrow i + 1$;

end while
return (T, A, Σ, $\mathcal{A}pp$).

Due to the form of its determinant, the gauge transformation $T(z)$ in the previous theorem does not affect the other finite singularities of $[A]$. This means that the apparent singularity at z_0 is removed without introducing new finite singularities or changing the pole order of the other finite singularties of $[A]$, as illustrated by the following simple example.

EXAMPLE 1. *Given the system* $[A]\ \partial X = A(z)X$ *where*

$$A = \begin{bmatrix} 0 & 1 \\ 2\,\frac{-1+2\,z^2}{z^2+2} & -\frac{3\,z^2-4}{z(z^2+2)} \end{bmatrix}$$

It has a simple pole at $z = 0$ *with a residue matrix*

$$A_0 = \begin{bmatrix} 0 & 0 \\ 0 & 2 \end{bmatrix}.$$

Our algorithm computes the gauge transformation given by

$$T = \begin{bmatrix} 1 & 0 \\ z & -z^2 \end{bmatrix}$$

The matrix of the new equivalent system is

$$B = T^{-1}(AT - \partial T) = \begin{bmatrix} z & -z^2 \\ 1 & -\frac{z(z^2+7)}{z^2+2} \end{bmatrix}$$

As expected it has $z = 0$ *as an ordinary point. Moreover, neither new finite singularities are introduced, nor the pole order of the other non-apparent finite singularties, i.e. the roots of* $(z^2 + 2)$, *are changed.*

Thus by successively applying Theorem 1 to each finite apparent singularity of $[A]$, we get the following:

THEOREM 2. *Given a system* $[A]$, *one can construct a polynomial matrix* $T(z)$ *which is invertible in* $\mathbb{C}(z)$ *such that the finite poles of* $B := T[A]$ *are exactly the poles of* A *that are not apparent singularities for* $[A]$.

REMARK 2. *If the point at infinity of the original system is singular regular then it will be also singular regular of the computed desingularization. However, the order of the pole at infinity may increase. This follows immediately from the fact that the two systems are gauge equivalent.*

Consider a system $[A]\ \partial X = A(z)X$ and let $\mathcal{P}(A)$ denote the set of finite poles of $A(z)$. We thus have the desingularization Algorithm 1.

4. APPLICATION: DESINGULARIZATION OF SCALAR DIFFERENTIAL EQUATION

The interest in desingularization of scalar differential equations dates back to the 19th century. Since then, several algorithms have been developed for such and more general scalar equations (see, e.g., the introductions of [2, 11] and the references therein). The desingularization algorithms developed specifically for scalar equations are based on computing a least common left multiple of the operator in question and an appropriately chosen operator. This outputs in general an equation whose solution space contains strictly the solution space of the input equation. As we mentioned in the introduction, the algorithm developed in this paper can be used as well for the desingularization of a companion system of any scalar differential equation. This desingularization is based on an adequate choice of a gauge transformation. Thus the desingularized output system is always equivalent to the input system and the dimension of the solution space is preserved. However, a scalar differential equation equivalent to the desingularized system (see, e.g., [4, 12]) would generally feature apparent singularities. Thus, when dealing with scalar differential equations, our algorithm is well-suited to situations where adhering to a scalar representation is insignificant, e.g. reduction prior to computing solutions near singularities via numerical methods.
In this section, we use Algorithm 1 to desingularize companion systems of two equations which are already treated by existing algorithms. But first we recall the definition of desingularization in the scalar case. Let $L \in \mathbb{C}(z)[\partial]$ be a monic differential operator of order n,

$$L = \partial^n + c_{n-1}(z)\partial^{n-1} + \cdots + c_0(z).$$

We denote by $S(L)$ the set of finite singularities of L, i.e. the set of the poles of the c_i's, $0 \le i \le n-1$.

DEFINITION 2. *An operator* $\tilde{L} \in \mathbb{C}[z][\partial]$ *is called a desingularization of* L *if :*

(i) $\tilde{L} = RL$ *for some* $R \in \mathbb{C}(z)[\partial]$,

(ii) $S(\tilde{L}) = \{z_0 \in S(L) \mid z_0 \text{ not apparent}\}$

An algorithm developed in [2] constructs, for a given a monic operator $L \in \mathbb{C}(z)[\partial]$ of order n, a monic operator $\tilde{L} \in \mathbb{C}(z)[\partial]$ with minimal order $m+1 \ge n$ satisfying (i) and (ii), m being the maximum of the of the set of all local exponent at the different finite apparent singularities of L. This algorithm has been implemented in Maple and is referred to in this paper by *ABH* method. The system of Example 1 is in fact the companion system of the following differential equation which we treat below by the ABH method.

EXAMPLE 2. *Consider the operator*

$$L = \partial^2 + \frac{(3z^2-4)}{z(z^2+2)}\partial + 2\frac{1-2z^2}{z^2+2}.$$

It has an apparent singularity at $z = 0$ *with local exponents* 0 *and* 3. *The desingularization computed by ABH method is the following operator of order* 4:

$$\begin{aligned} \tilde{L} &= \partial^4 + \frac{z(24+7z^2)}{2(z^2+2)}\partial^3 + \frac{(58z^2+88+27z^4)}{2(z^2+2)^2}\partial^2 \\ &- \frac{z(-4z^2+4+93z^4+28z^6)}{2(z^2+2)^3}\partial \\ &- \frac{4(44z^2+16+42z^4+7z^6)}{(z^2+2)^3} \end{aligned}$$

The classical algorithm for differential equations takes the least common left multiple of the given differential operator and a well-chosen auxiliary one (see, e.g., [14]). A "three-fold generalization" of this algorithm to more general operators is given recently in [11]. The following example has been treated therein. However, the removal of one apparent singularity, namely at $z_0 = 0$, introduces new singularities. The latter can then be removed by using a trick introduced in ABH algorithm (see [2, Thm 2 and Step 6 in Algo "t-desing"] and [11, Sec 3]). As illustrated below, Algorithm 1 removes all apparent singularities at one stroke without introducing any new ones.

EXAMPLE 3. *Let*

$$L = \partial^2 - \frac{(z^2-3)(z^2-2z+2)}{(z-1)(z^2-3z+3)z}\partial + \frac{(z-2)(2z^2-3z+3)}{(z-1)(z^2-3z+3)z}.$$

The apparent singularities of L are $z = 0$ and the roots of $z^2-3z+3 = 0$. In what follows, we seek their removal using different algorithms:
(i) A desingularization computed by the classical algorithm [11, Example 1]:

$$\begin{aligned}\tilde{L}_{Classical} &= (z-1)(z^4-z^3+3z^2-6z+6)\partial^4 \\ &- (z^5-2z^4+z^3-12z^2+24z-24)\partial^3 \\ &- (3z^3+9z^2)\partial^2+(6z^2+18z)\partial-(6z+18).\end{aligned}$$

$\tilde{L}_{Classical}$ is a desingularizaiton of L at $z = 0$ and $z^2-3z+3 = 0$. However, new apparent singularities, i.e. the roots of $z^4-z^3+3*z^2-6*z+6 = 0$, are introduced.

(ii) A desingularization computed by the probabilistic of [11], which we refer to as CKS algorithm, (see Example 7(1) *therein):*

$$\begin{aligned}\tilde{L}_{CKS} &= (z-1)(z^6-3z^5+3z^4-z^3+6)\partial^4 \\ &- (2z^6-9z^5+15z^4-11z^3+3z^2-24)\partial^3 \\ &- (z^7-4z^6+6z^5-4z^4+z^3+6z-6)\partial \\ &+ (2z^6-9z^5+15z^4-11z^3+3z^2-24).\end{aligned}$$

$\tilde{L}_{CKS}$ is a desingularizaiton of L at $z = 0$ and $z^2-3z+3 = 0$. However, new apparent singularities, i.e. the roots of $z^6-3z^5+3z^4-z^3+6 = 0$, are introduced.

(iii) The desingularization computed by ABH method:

$$\begin{aligned}\tilde{L}_{ABH} &= \partial^4 + \frac{(16z^4-55z^3+63z^2-42z+36)}{9(z-1)}\partial^3 \\ &- \frac{(64z^5-316z^4+591z^3-468z^2+123z+42)}{9(z-1)^2}\partial^2 \\ &+ \frac{\beta}{9(z-1)^3}\partial \\ &- \frac{96z^5-570z^4+1333z^3-1597z^2+993z-219}{9(z-1)^3},\end{aligned}$$

where

$$\beta = (48z^6-197z^5+148z^4+488z^3-1162z^2+999z-288).$$

(iv) The desingularization computed by algorithm 1: The companion system of L is given by:

$$[A]\quad \partial X = \begin{bmatrix} 0 & 1 \\ \frac{(z-2)(2z^2-3z+3)}{(z-1)(z^2-3z+3)z} & \frac{(z^2-3)(z^2-2z+2)}{(z-1)(z^2-3z+3)z}\end{bmatrix} X. \qquad (5)$$

The gauge transformation $X = TY$ where

$$T = \begin{bmatrix} 1 & 0 \\ 1 & (-z^2+3z-3)z^2\end{bmatrix} \qquad (6)$$

results in the following equivalent system

$$[B]\qquad \partial Y = \begin{bmatrix} 1 & -z^2(z^2-3z+3) \\ 0 & \frac{2}{1-z}\end{bmatrix} Y. \qquad (7)$$

Observe that in (iii) and (iv) no new apparent singularities are introduced while old ones are removed.

Note that, as system (5) has rational function coefficients, the transformation (6) and the equivalent system (7), computed by our algorithm, have rational function coefficients as well. In the following section, we describe how such a rationality is preserved by our algorithm.

5. RATIONAL VERSION OF THE ALGORITHM

So far, we have presented our algorithm over $\mathbb{C}$ for the sake of clarity. However, in practice, the base field can be taken as any commutative field k of characteristic zero ($\mathbb{Q} \subseteq k \subset \bar{k} \subset \mathbb{C}$). Consider now a system

$$[A]\ \partial X = A(z)X, \quad \text{with} \quad A(z) \in k(z)^{n\times n}. \qquad (8)$$

Let $\Omega = \{\alpha_1, \dots \alpha_d\} \subset \bar{k}$ be a set of conjugate simple poles of $A(z)$ over k. We aim to find an equivalent system which is a desingularization of (8) at each of the points of Ω. One possible method is the successive application of Algorithm 1 to each singularity individually. That is, we first compute a transformation T_1 such that the equivalent system $T_1[A]$ is a desingularization in α_1. We then compute a transformation T_2 such that the equivalent system $T_2[T_1[A]] = (T_2T_1)[A]$ is a desingularization in α_2. Eventually, this yields an equivalent system $(\prod_{i=1}^d T_i)[A]$ which is a desingularization of $[A]$ at all points of Ω. However, the entries of T_j and $(\prod_{i=1}^j T_i)[A]$, $1 \le j \le d$, belong to $k(\alpha_1, \dots, \alpha_j)[z]$. Thus, this individual treatment of singularities in d steps, requires an algebraic field extension $k(\alpha_1, \dots \alpha_d)$.
This section describes our "rational" algorithm, i.e. the algorithm which avoids computations with individual singularities by representing them by the irreducible polynomial $p(z)$. Consequently, it replaces d steps by only one step and the computations of intermediate steps are limited to $k(z)/(p)$. We remark however that neither the former nor the latter method require a field extension for the final output, i.e. the equivalent system and the gauge transformation.
For this purpose, we work, similar to [5], with the irreducible polynomial $p(z) = \prod_{i=1}^d (z-\alpha_i) \in k[z]$, and consider the p-adic expansions rather than Laurent series expansions at the α_i's.
Let p be an irreducible polynomial in $k[z]$, i.e. a finite "point". If f is a non-zero element of $k(z)$, we define $ord_p(f)$ (read order of f at p) to be the unique integer n such that :

$$f = \frac{a}{b}p^n, \text{ with } a, b \in k[z] \setminus \{0\}, \quad p \nmid a \text{ and } p \nmid b.$$

By convention, $ord_p(0) = +\infty$. The *local ring* at p is $\mathcal{O}_p = \{f \in k(z) \ :\ \text{ord}_p(f) \ge 0\}$. If $f \in \mathcal{O}_p$ then $f = a/b \in k(z)$, where $\gcd(a, b) = 1$ and $p \nmid b$. The residue field of $k(z)$ at p is $\mathcal{O}_p/p\mathcal{O}_p$, which is isomorphic to the field $k[z]/(p)$.
Let $f \in k(z)$ then it has a unique $p-$adic expansion given by:

$$f = p^{ord_p f}(f_{0,p} + pf_{1,p} + \cdots)$$

where the $f_{i,p}$'s are polynomials of degree $< \deg p$, and $f_{0,p} \ne 0$ is called the *leading coefficient.*
In analogy, let $A = (a_{i,j})$ be a matrix in $k(z)^{n\times n}$. We define the *order* at p of A, notation $\text{ord}_p(A)$, by

$$\underset{p}{\text{ord}}(A) = \min_{i,j}(\underset{p}{\text{ord}}(a_{i,j})).$$

We say that A has a pole at p if $\text{ord}_p(A) < 0$. Similarly, the leading coefficient is $A_{0,p} \ne 0_n$ in the p-adic expansion of A given by:

$$A = p^{\text{ord}_p(A)}(A_{0,p} + pA_{1,p} + \cdots).$$

5.1 The residue matrix at p

The following lemma leads to a definition of the *residue matrix at p*.

LEMMA 1. *Consider the system*

$$[A]\ \partial X = A(z)X, \quad \text{with} \quad A(z) \in k(z)^{n\times n}.$$

Let $\Omega = \{\alpha_1, \dots \alpha_d\} \subset \mathbb{C}$ *be a set of conjugate apparent singularities and* $p(z) = \prod_{i=1}^{d}(z-\alpha_i) \in k[z]$ *be the irreducible polynomial representing them. Consider the p-adic and* α_i*-Laurent expansions of* $A(z)$ *given respectively by*

$$A(z) = \frac{1}{p}(A_{0,p} + pA_{1,p} + \cdots)$$

$$A(z) = \frac{1}{(z-\alpha_i)}(A_{0,\alpha_i} + (z-\alpha_i)A_{1,\alpha_i} + \cdots),\ 1 \le i \le d.$$

Then we have,

$$\frac{1}{\partial p(\alpha_i)} A_{0,p}(\alpha_i) = A_{0,\alpha_i},\ 1 \le i \le d.$$

PROOF. From the above expansions, it follows that

$$\frac{A_{0,p}}{p}(z) = \sum_{i=1}^{d} \frac{A_{0,\alpha_i}}{(z-\alpha_i)} = \sum_{i=1}^{d} \frac{A_{0,\alpha_i}}{p} \prod_{1\le j\ne i\le d}(z-\alpha_j).$$

But $\partial p(\alpha_i) = \prod_{1\le j\ne i\le d}(z-\alpha_j)$, which completes the proof. □

REMARK 3. *In the following each equivalent g of* $k[x]/(p)$ *is represented by the unique polynomial of degree* $< \deg p$ *belonging to g. The operations of addition and multiplication in* $k[x]/(p)$ *are performed on the representatives considered as polynomials and the results are reduced modulo p. For inverting a nonzero element of* $k[x]/(p)$ *we use the extended Euclidean algorithm.*

Thus, the folllowing definition is well-justified.

DEFINITION 3. *The matrix given by*

$$\frac{A_{0,p}(z)}{\partial p(z)} \in (k[z]/(p))^{n\times n}$$

is called the residue matrix of $A(z)$ *at p. We shall denote by* $R_{0,p}(z)$ *its representative in* $k[z]^{n\times n}$*. The latter is of degree strictly less than d and can be computed as:* $(uA_{0,p} \bmod p)$*, where u denotes the inverse of* $(\partial p \bmod p)$.

EXAMPLE 4. *Given*

$$[A]\ \ \partial X = A(z)X = \frac{1}{1+z^2}\begin{bmatrix} 1-z & z \\ -z & 1+z \end{bmatrix} X.$$

Let $p := 1+z^2$*, then p is an irreducible polynomial over* $\mathbb{Q}[z]$ *and its roots are given by* $\pm i$ *over* $\mathbb{Q}(i)$*. Then* $u = -\frac{z}{2}$ *is the inverse of* ∂p *modp. Thus,* $R_{0,p}(z)$ *is given by* $uA_{0,p} \bmod p$ *and so we have*

$$R_{0,p}(z) = \frac{1}{2}\begin{bmatrix} 1-z & -1 \\ -1 & -1-z \end{bmatrix}.$$

Indeed, one can verify that the residue matrices at $\pm i$*, are given by*

$$\begin{bmatrix} \frac{1-i}{2i} & \frac{1}{2} \\ -\frac{1}{2} & \frac{1+i}{2i} \end{bmatrix} \quad \text{and} \quad \begin{bmatrix} \frac{-1-i}{2i} & \frac{1}{2} \\ -\frac{1}{2} & \frac{-1+i}{2i} \end{bmatrix}.$$

We now proceed to giving a rational algorithm for testing whether the eigenvalues of $R_{0,p}(z)$ are nonnegative integers or not.

5.2 Computing the integer eigenvalues of the residue matrix

Given $R_{0,p}(z) \in k[z]^{n\times n}$, we wish to compute its integer eigenvalues, in the course of reduction, to identify the nature of the singularity. Let the characteristic polynomial of $R_{0,p}(z)$ be given by

$$\chi_R(z,\lambda) = \lambda^n + a_{n-1}(z)\lambda^{n-1} + \cdots + a_0(z),$$

where $a_i(z) \in k[z]$ s.t. $deg_z(a_i) < deg_z(p) = d$. Then, $\chi_R(z,\lambda)$ can be rewritten equivalently as

$$\chi_R(z,\lambda) = \sum_{i=0}^{d-1} b_i(\lambda) z^i,$$

where $b_i(\lambda) \in k[\lambda]$, $0 \le i \le d-1$, are of maximal degree n. Let $h(\lambda) = gcd\ \{b_i(\lambda)\ ,\ 0 \le i \le d-1\}$. It follows that the set of integer roots of $h(\lambda)$ coincides with the set of integer roots of $\chi_R(z,\lambda)$.
Additionally, we remark that in order to compute the integer roots of $\chi_R(z,\lambda)$, it suffices to compute those of $det(\partial p\lambda - A_{0,p})\ mod\ p$. Similar arguments hold true for operations of Proposition 3.

5.3 Examples

In this subsection, we illustrate the rational version of our algorithm with two examples. We first treat the introductory example of [10], and then an example from [9] arising in statistical physics. We show how the corresponding systems can be desingularized by "rational" transformations at irreducible polynomials of degrees 3 and 4 respectively. A third example with an irreducible polynomial of degree 37 is available at [18].

EXAMPLE 5 (INTRODUCTION, [10]). *Consider the differential operator*

$$L = (1+z)(23-20z-z^2+2z^3)\partial^2 + 2(33-9z-3z^2-z^3)\partial - (45+25z-35z^2-z^3+2z^4).$$

whose companion system is given by:

$$[A]\quad \partial X = A(z)X$$

where

$$A(z) = \begin{bmatrix} 0 & 1 \\ \frac{(45+25z-35z^2-z^3+2z^4)}{(1+z)(23-20z-z^2+2z^3)} & -\frac{2(33-9z-3z^2-z^3)}{(1+z)(23-20z-z^2+2z^3)} \end{bmatrix}.$$

The gauge transformation $X = TY$ *where*

$$T = \begin{bmatrix} 1 & \frac{-14}{143}z^2 + \frac{3}{11}z + \frac{153}{143} \\ 0 & 1 \end{bmatrix} \begin{bmatrix} 2z^3 - z^2 - 20z + 23 & 0 \\ 0 & 1 \end{bmatrix},$$

results in the following system desingularized at $p = (23-20z-z^2+2z^3)$:

$$[B]\quad \partial Y = \begin{bmatrix} \frac{14z^3-39z^2-258z-175}{143(z+1)} & \frac{98z^2-497z-1385}{-20449(z+1)} \\ \frac{2z^4-z^3-35z^2+25z+45}{z+1} & \frac{14z^3-39z^2-258z+111}{-143(z+1)} \end{bmatrix} Y.$$

The algorithm gives as well a negative response for whether $[A]$ *can be desingularized at* $(1+z)$*. In fact, the eigenvalues of the residue matrix are* 0 *and* -2*, which is a negative integer.*

EXAMPLE 6 (THE ISING MODEL,[9]). *Given*

$$[A] \quad X = \begin{bmatrix} 0 & 1 & 0 \\ 0 & 0 & 1 \\ \frac{-4\alpha_1}{z^2(-1+16z)^3 q} & \frac{-4\alpha_2}{z^2(-1+16z)^2 q} & \frac{-2\alpha_3}{z(-1+16z)q} \end{bmatrix} X,$$

where

$$\begin{aligned} q &= (4z-1)\left(4352\,z^4 + 3607\,z^3 - 1678\,z^2 + 252\,z - 8\right) \\ \alpha_1 &= 89128960\,z^7 + 74981376\,z^6 - 97687536\,z^5 \\ &+ 33948640\,z^4 - 4652220\,z^3 + 84480\,z^2 + 9469\,z \\ &- 294 \\ \alpha_2 &= 17825792\,z^7 + 13139200\,z^6 - 16119599\,z^5 \\ &+ 5128290\,z^4 - 689440\,z^3 + 28373\,z^2 - 185\,z - 6 \\ \alpha_3 &= 1183744\,z^6 + 770128\,z^5 - 872579\,z^4 + 252146\,z^3 \\ &- 30499\,z^2 + 1172\,z - 12. \end{aligned}$$

We are interested in desingularization at

$$p = \left(4352\,z^4 + 3607\,z^3 - 1678\,z^2 + 252\,z - 8\right).$$

Our algorithm computes the gauge transformation $X = T_1 T_2 Y$ *where*

$$T_1 = \begin{bmatrix} 1 & \gamma_1\gamma_2 & \gamma_3 \\ 0 & 1 & 0 \\ 0 & 0 & 1 \end{bmatrix},$$

$$T_2 = \begin{bmatrix} p & 0 & 0 \\ 0 & 1 & 0 \\ 0 & 0 & 1 \end{bmatrix}, \quad \textit{and}$$

$$\begin{aligned} \gamma_1 &= -6128505692416\,z^3 - 5454831630087\,z^2 \\ &+ 2041133482952\,z - 215817804724 \\ \gamma_2 &= \frac{10598786\,z^3}{22324211786901375} - \frac{145270123\,z^2}{714374777180844000} \\ &- \frac{70951\,z}{71437477718084400} + \frac{79111}{44648423573802750} \\ \gamma_3 &= \frac{169580576\,z^3}{525308635} - \frac{145270123\,z^2}{1050617270} - \frac{70951\,z}{105061727} \\ &+ \frac{632888}{525308635}. \end{aligned}$$

The system is not desingularizable at any of the other polynomials. In fact, the algorithm gives as well the following information:

- $z = 0$ *is a simple pole, and a partial desingularization can be computed. However, only two of the eigenvalues of the residue matrix are nonnegative integers.*
- *The root of* $16z - 1 = 0$ *is a simple pole, and a partial desingularization can be computed. However, none of the eigenvalues of the residue matrix are nonnegative integers.*
- *The root of* $4z - 1 = 0$ *is a simple pole. However, only two of the eigenvalues of the residue matrix are nonnegative integers.*

The resulting desingularizaton at p *and the partial desingularizations at* z *and* $16z - 1$ *are available at [18].*

6. CONCLUSION

In this paper, we give a method for detecting and removing the apparent singularities of linear differential systems via a rational algorithm, i.e. an algorithm which avoids the computations with individual conjugate singularities. The Maple package is available for download at [18] with examples. Our method can be used, in particular, for the desingularization of differential operators in the scalar case.
One field of investigation is the generalization of our algorithm to treat more general systems, e.g. systems with parameters as well as investigating the case of difference systems. First steps in this direction, namely reductions in the parameter and the partial desingularization, are established in [8, 1] respectively.
Another field of investigation is the complexity study of the various algorithms existing for the scalar case, as well as this new algorithm which can be applied to the companion system, so that their efficiency can be compared. Partial results in this direction are already obtained in [7].

Acknowledgements: We thank the anonymous referees for their valuable comments.

7. REFERENCES

[1] H. ABBAS, M. A. BARKATOU AND S.S. MADDAH *On the Reduction of Singularly-Perturbed Linear Differential Systems.* In Proceedings of the 39th International Symposium on Symbolic and Algebraic Computation, pp 320-327, ACM, Japan (2014).

[2] S. ABRAMOV, M. BARKATOU AND M. VAN HOEIJ *Apparent Singularities of Linear Difference Equations with Polynomial Coefficients.* AAECC, 17:117-133, (2006).

[3] W. BALSER, *Formal power series and linear systems of meromorphic ordinary differential equations.* Springer-Verlag (2000).

[4] M. A. BARKATOU, *An Algorithm for Computing a Companion Block Diagonal Form for a System of Linear Differential Equations.* Appl. Algebra Eng. Commun. Comput. Vol. 4, Issue 3, pp 185-195, Springer (1993).

[5] M.A. BARKATOU *A Rational version of Moser's algorithm and applications.* A.H.M. Levelt (Ed.), Proceedings of the International Symposium on Symbolic and Algebraic Computation, Montreal, ACM, pp 297-302 (1995).

[6] M.A. BARKATOU *Removing Apparent Singularities of Systems of Linear Differential Equations with Rational Function Coefficients.* Extended Abstract. Second Workshop Differential Equations by Algebraic Methods, (DEAM2), Linz, Austria (2011).

[7] M.A. BARKATOU, E. PFLUEGEL *On the Moser-and super-reduction algorithms of systems of linear differential equations and their complexity.* Journal of Sym. Comput., 44 (8), 1017-1036 (2009).

[8] M. A. BARKATOU, G. BROUGHTON, E. PFLUEGEL *Regular Systems of Linear Functional Equations and Applications.* In Proceedings of the International Symposium on Symbolic and Algebraic Computation, pp 15 - 22, Waterloo (2007).

[9] A. BOSTAN, S. BOUKRAA, S. HASSANI, M. VAN HOEIJ, J.-M. MAILLARD, J.-A. WEIL, AND N.

ZENINE *The Ising model: From Elliptic Curves to ModularForms and Calabi-Yau equations.* J. Phys. A: Math. Theor., 44(4):045204, 44, (2011).

[10] S. CHEN, M. JAROSCHEK, M. KAUERS, M. F. SINGER, *Desingularization Explains Order-Degree Curves for Ore Operators.* In Proceedings of the 38th International Symposium on Symbolic and Algebraic Computation, pp 157-164, ACM, U.S.A. (2013).

[11] S. CHEN, M. KAUERS, M. F. SINGER, *Desingularization of Ore Operators.* Available at: arXiv:1408.5512v1, (2014).

[12] R.C. CHURCHILL AND J.J. KOVACIC, *Cyclic vectors.* N. Rutgers University (Ed.), In Differential Algebra and Related Topics, Proceedings of the International Workshop, pp 191- 218, World Scientific Publishing Co., River Edge, NJ (2002).

[13] E. A. CODDINGTON AND N. LEVINSON, *Theory of ordinary differential equations.* Tata McGraw-Hill Education (1955)

[14] E.L. INCE *Ordinary Differential Equations.* Dover (1926).

[15] Johannes M. HENN *Lectures on Differential Equations for Feynman Integrals.* Prepared for submission to JHEP, Available at arXiv:1412.2296v1, (2014).

[16] R. N. LEE , *Reducing differential equations for multiloop master integrals.* arXiv preprint arXiv:1411.0911 (2014).

[17] A.H.M. LEVELT, *The Semi-simple Part of a Matrix.* Algoritmen In De Algebra, The Netherlands (1993).

[18] S. S. MADDAH *http://www.unilim.fr/pages_perso/suzy.maddah/*

[19] J. MOSER *The order of a singularity in Fuch's theory.* Math. Z. 72, pp 379-398 (1960).

[20] W. WASOW, *Asymptotic Expansions for Ordinary Differential Equations.* Interscience, New York (1965).

Linear Algebra for Computing Gröbner Bases of Linear Recursive Multidimensional Sequences

Jérémy Berthomieu [a,b,c] jeremy.berthomieu@lip6.fr
Brice Boyer [a,b,c] brice.boyer@lip6.fr
Jean-Charles Faugère [c,a,b] jean-charles.faugere@inria.fr

[a] Sorbonne Universités, UPMC Univ Paris 06, Équipe PolSys, LIP6, F-75005, Paris, France
[b] CNRS, UMR 7606, LIP6, F-75005, Paris, France
[c] INRIA, Équipe PolSys, Centre Paris – Rocquencourt, F-75005, Paris, France

ABSTRACT

Sakata generalized the Berlekamp – Massey algorithm to n dimensions in 1988. The Berlekamp – Massey – Sakata (BMS) algorithm can be used for finding a Gröbner basis of a 0-dimensional ideal of relations verified by a table. We investigate this problem using linear algebra techniques, with motivations such as accelerating change of basis algorithms (FGLM) or improving their complexity.

We first define and characterize multidimensional linear recursive sequences for 0-dimensional ideals. Under genericity assumptions, we propose a randomized preprocessing of the table that corresponds to performing a linear change of coordinates on the polynomials associated with the linear recurrences. This technique then essentially reduces our problem to using the efficient 1-dimensional Berlekamp – Massey (BM) algorithm. However, the number of probes to the table in this scheme may be elevated. We thus consider the table in the *black-box* model: we assume probing the table is expensive and we minimize the number of probes to the table in our complexity model. We produce an FGLM-like algorithm for finding the relations in the table, which lets us use linear algebra techniques. Under some additional assumptions, we make this algorithm adaptive and reduce further the number of table probes. This number can be estimated by counting the number of distinct elements in a multi-Hankel matrix (a multivariate generalization of Hankel matrices); we can relate this quantity with the *geometry* of the final staircase. Hence, in favorable cases such as convex ones, the complexity is essentially linear in the size of the output. Finally, when using the LEX ordering, we can make use of fast structured linear algebra similarly to the Hankel interpretation of Berlekamp – Massey.

Categories and Subject Descriptors

I.1.2 [**Symbolic and Algebraic Manipulation**]: Algorithms

General Terms

Theory, Algorithms

Keywords

BMS and FGLM algorithms, Gröbner basis computation, 0-dimensional ideal, multidimensional linear recursive sequence

1. INTRODUCTION

A fundamental problem in Computer Science is to estimate the linear complexity of an infinite sequence S: this is the smallest length of a recurrence satisfied by S or the length of the shortest linear feedback shift register (LFSR) which generates it. From an algorithmic point of view, the Berlekamp – Massey algorithm (BM) [1, 14] solves this problem in the one dimensional case. Generalizations of linear recurrence sequences to n dimensions were proposed by several authors [3, 17, 19]. Sakata generalized the BM algorithm [19, 21] to n dimensions; in particular, the so-called BMS algorithm is able to compute a Gröbner basis [19, Lem. 5] of the ideal of relations satisfied by the input sequence.

Direct and important application of such generalization can be found in Coding Theory: the BMS algorithm can be used to decode n-dimensional cyclic codes [20] which are generalization of Reed Solomon codes. Another application is the computation of Gröbner bases since recent versions of the Sparse-FGLM algorithm [5] rely heavily on BM and BMS algorithms.

Related work

Linear Prediction dates back to Gauß in the 18th century: given a discrete set of original values $(u_i)_{i\in\mathbb{N}}$ the goal is to find the best coefficients, in the least-squares sense, $(\alpha_i)_{i\in\mathbb{N}}$ that will approximate u_i by $-\sum_{k=1}^{d}\alpha_{n-k}u_k$. This problem is equivalent to solving a linear system which is indeed a symmetric Toeplitz matrix. This problem has been extensively used in Digital Signal Processing theory and applications. In the numerical world, methods such as the Levinson – Durbin recursion can be used to solve this problem. Hence, to some extent, the original Levinson – Durbin problem in Norbert Wiener's Ph.D. thesis [13, 22] predates the Hankel interpretation of the Berlekamp – Massey algorithm (for instance [7]).

We refer to [9, 10] for a very nice classification of the BM algorithms for solving this problem and generalization to matrix sequences, see also [8]. Of particular importance for us is the solution of the underlying linear system in Toeplitz/Hankel form. Let us also mention that a call of BM on sequence $(u_0,u_1,\dots,u_{2d-1})$ will behave as the extended Euclidean algorithm with input polynomials x^{2d} and $u_0x^{2d-1}+u_1x^{2d-2}+\cdots+u_{2d-1}$ making BM a simplified version of the extended Euclidean algorithm.

BMS extends the algebraic form of BM to n dimensions [18]. In the case of 0-dimensional ideals, this algorithm can be applied for Gröbner basis computations [19].

Contributions

First of all, we define and characterize linear recurrence sequences in n dimensions. More precisely, we link them with 0-dimensional ideals and define their order as the degree of the ideal generated by the relations satisfied by the sequence (see Sec. 2). Classically, this number is also the size of the staircase of the Gröbner basis (the canonical set of generators for the residue class ring).

A first idea is to try to use the standard BM algorithm to solve the n dimensional case: we give a randomized preprocessing on the input sequence; this preprocessing will yield a new table which,

ISSAC'15, July 6–9, 2015, Bath, United Kingdom.

DOI: http://dx.doi.org/10.1145/2755996.2756673.

with good probability, will only have one linear recurrence relation (see Sec. 3). Exploiting this property yields Th. 1.

THEOREM 1. *Let $\mathbf{u} = (u_{i_1,\dots,i_n})_{i_1,\dots,i_n \in \mathbb{N}}$ be a n-dimensional linear recursive sequence over $\mathbb{K}$. Let $d \in \mathbb{N}$. When the size of $\mathbb{K}$ is large enough, we can find an equivalent basis of its relations for all $i_1 + \cdots + i_n \le 2d$ in randomized time in $O(n^{2d} + n\,\mathsf{M}(d)\log d)$ operations in $\mathbb{K}$, where $\mathsf{M}(d)$ is the complexity of multiplying two polynomials of degree at most $d-1$.*

Next, we propose two FGLM-like algorithms for computing Gröbner bases of the ideal of relations in Sec. 4 and 5. Both algorithms are based only on simple linear algebra operations: they search to extract maximal full rank submatrices of a multi-Hankel matrix (a multivariate generalization of Hankel matrices). Given a bound on the maximal degree of the elements in the final Gröbner basis, the first algorithm is able to compute it. This algorithm is efficient when the order of the sequence is relatively big. On the other hand, when the order of sequence is abnormally small we propose an output sensitive probabilistic algorithm: this time an estimate of the order of the sequence is given.

An important parameter of the complexity of the algorithms is the number of table queries. Indeed, in some applications, it is very costly to compute *one* element $u_{i_1,i_2,\dots}$ of the table; thus the number of table queries has to be minimized. For instance, in the FGLM application, each element of the table requires a matrix-vector product to be computed. This number can be estimated by counting the number of distinct elements in a multi-Hankel matrix; moreover, we can relate this quantity with the geometry of the final staircase:

THEOREM 2. *The number of queries to the table is the cardinal of set $2S = \{uv \mid (u,v) \in S^2\}$ where S is the staircase of the ideal.*

We show that in favorable cases such as convex ones, the complexity is essentially linear in the size of the output. However, we also exhibit pathological cases where the complexity grows quadratically.

In Sec. 5.2 and 5.3, to illustrate the efficiency of the proposed algorithms, we report experiments for two applications: Sparse-FGLM and the decoding of n-dimensional cyclic codes. The results of the experiments are fully in line with the theory: for instance, in coding theory, when t errors are generated randomly, they can be recovered in $O(t)$ evaluation of the syndromes.

For the LEX ordering, multi-Hankel matrices are heavily structured and can be solved with fast algorithms. In Sec. 6, we give two approaches based on the notion of displacement rank and the polynomial multiplication interpretation, we refer to [2] for both. If d_i is the maximal degree of the polynomials in x_i, then solving the mth multi-Hankel matrix can be done in $O(\mathsf{M}(2^{m-1}d_1\cdots d_m))$ operations in the base field.

Finally, we left as an open question whether our algorithms could be seen as a matrix version of BMS.

2. DEFINITION AND CHARACTERIZATION OF LINEAR RECURSIVE SEQUENCES

In Def. 2, we generalize the notion of a linear recursive sequence from the 1-dimensional case to the multidimensional case based on the terms of the sequence. We also give a characterisation of such a sequence based on the linear recurrence relations [17, Def. 21] the sequence sastifies and provide a proof in Prop. 3 that this characterization is equivalent to Def. 2. This characterization is related to but more restrictive than [3, Def. 2]. Finally, in Sec. 2.2, we adopt an FGLM viewpoint to describe a multidimensional sequence.

Let us recall that a 1-dimensional sequence $\mathbf{u} = (u_i)_{i\in\mathbb{N}}$ defined over a field $\mathbb{K}$ is linear recursive of *order* $d > 0$ if $\exists\, \alpha_0,\dots,\alpha_{d-1} \in \mathbb{K}$ s.t. for all $i \in \mathbb{N}$, $u_{i+d} + \sum_{k=0}^{d-1} \alpha_k u_{i+k} = 0$ and d is minimal. We shall denote $R(i) = u_{i+d} + \sum_{k=0}^{d-1} \alpha_k u_{i+k}$. In general, $\mathrm{Pol}_{\mathbf{u}}(R)(x) = x^d + \sum_{k=0}^{d-1} \alpha_k x^k$ is called the *characteristic polynomial* of the sequence. It is well-known that the vector space of linear sequences verifying the *linear recurrence relation* R has dimension d whose canonical basis is $(\mathbf{u}^{(0)},\dots,\mathbf{u}^{(d-1)})$ verifying $\forall i,e,\ 0 \le i,e \le d-1$, $u_i^{(e)} = \delta_{i,e}$, Kronecker's delta. Other bases are natural, let us mention the one using the roots of $\mathrm{Pol}_{\mathbf{u}}(R)$: $(\mathbf{u}^{(0,0)},\dots,\mathbf{u}^{(0,\mu_0-1)},\dots,\mathbf{u}^{(r-1,\mu_{r-1})})$ verifying $u_i^{(e,m)} = i^m \zeta_e^i$, where ζ_e is a root of multiplicity μ_e. In other words, a linear sequence of order d is uniquely determined by its characteristic polynomial, or equivalently its minimal linear recurrence relation of order d, and its d first terms.

To simplify notations, let $\mathbf{i} = (i_1,\dots,i_n) \in \mathbb{N}^n$ and $\mathbf{x} = (x_1,\dots,x_n)$. As usual, we let $\mathbf{x}^{\mathbf{i}}$ denote $x_1^{i_1}\cdots x_n^{i_n}$ and $|\mathbf{i}| = i_1 + \cdots + i_n$. We also denote e_i the ith vector of the canonical basis of $\mathbb{Z}^n$. In the following, we consider a n-dimensional sequence $\mathbf{u} = (u_{\mathbf{i}})_{\mathbf{i}\in\mathbb{N}^n}$.

As in the one-dimensional case, we can define a linear recurrence relation and its associated polynomial. Such a relation was called *n-dimensional linear recursion relation* in [17, Def. 21].

DEFINITION 1. *Let $\mathbf{u} = (u_{\mathbf{i}})_{\mathbf{i}\in\mathbb{N}^n}$ be a sequence with coefficients in $\mathbb{K}$. Let $\mathscr{K} \subset \mathbb{N}^n$ be finite. The set $\{\alpha_{\mathbf{k}},\ \mathbf{k} \in \mathscr{K}\}$ defines a* linear recurrence relation *R if for all $\mathbf{i} \in \mathbb{N}^n$, $R(\mathbf{i}) = \sum_{\mathbf{k}\in\mathscr{K}} \alpha_{\mathbf{k}} u_{\mathbf{i}+\mathbf{k}} = 0$.*

The associated polynomial *is then $\mathrm{Pol}_{\mathbf{u}}(R)(\mathbf{x}) = \sum_{\mathbf{k}\in\mathscr{K}} \alpha_{\mathbf{k}} \mathbf{x}^{\mathbf{k}}$. Conversely, from any polynomial $P \in \mathbb{K}[\mathbf{x}], P = \sum_{\mathbf{k}\in\mathscr{K}} \alpha_{\mathbf{k}} \mathbf{x}^{\mathbf{k}}$, we define the non-instantiated associated relation $\mathrm{Rel}_{\mathbf{u}}(P)(\mathbf{i}) = \sum_{\mathbf{k}\in\mathscr{K}} \alpha_{\mathbf{k}} u_{\mathbf{i}+\mathbf{k}}$.*

In the end we can always shift any polynomials so that it is enough to evaluate such a relation in $\mathbf{i} = (0,\dots,0)$, consequently we will use the following convention: $[x_1^{\alpha_1}\cdots x_n^{\alpha_n}]_{\mathbf{u}} = [x_1^{\alpha_1}\cdots x_n^{\alpha_n}] = u_{\alpha_1,\dots,\alpha_n}$, and in general $[P]_{\mathbf{u}} = [P] = u_{\mathbf{d}} + \sum_{\mathbf{k}\in\mathscr{K}} \alpha_{\mathbf{k}} u_{\mathbf{k}}$.

EXAMPLE 1. *If $P(x,y) = xy - x - 1 \in \mathbb{K}[x,y]$ then $[P] = u_{1,1} - u_{1,0} - u_{0,0}$ and $[x^2yP] = u_{3,2} - u_{3,1} - u_{2,1}$.*

We are now in a position to define a linear recursive sequence.

DEFINITION 2. *Let $\mathbf{u} = (u_{\mathbf{i}})_{\mathbf{i}\in\mathbb{N}^n}$ be a n-dimensional sequence with coefficients in $\mathbb{K}$. The sequence $\mathbf{u}$ is* linear recursive *if from a nonzero finite number of initial terms $u_{\mathbf{i}}, \mathbf{i} \in S$ and a finite number of linear recurrence relations, without any contradiction, one can compute any term of the sequence.*

For contradictions arising, we refer to Sakata's example with initial terms $\{u_{0,0}, u_{1,0}, u_{0,1}\}$ and relations $u_{i+2,j} - u_{i,j} = u_{i+1,j+1} - u_{i,j} = u_{i,j+2} - u_{i,j} = 0$, in [21, p. 147]. Indeed, one can derive a new relation $u_{i+1,j} - u_{i,j+1} = 0$ meaning that $u_{0,1}$ is determined by the knowledge of $u_{1,0}$ and the set of initial terms is only $\{u_{0,0}, u_{1,0}\}$.

In other words, a linear recursive sequence is a special case of a *holonomic* (or *P-recursive*) sequence whose recurrence relations only have constant coefficients (see [11]).

2.1 Gröbner bases and characterization of linear recursive sequences

Before giving another characterization of such sequences based on Gröbner bases, we recall some definitions and properties of Gröbner bases and admissible monomial orders.

An *admissible monomial order* $\prec$ is an order on monomials of $\mathbb{K}[\mathbf{x}]$ s.t. for any monomial $s \ne 1$, $1 \prec s$ and for any monomials t,m, s.t. $t \prec s$, $ms \prec mt$. This implies that there does not exist any infinite strictly decreasing sequences of monomials.

The leading term of a polynomial P for $\prec$, denoted $\mathrm{LT}_{\prec}(P)$ or $\mathrm{LT}(P)$ if no confusion can arise, is the greatest monomial of P multiplied by its coefficient.

Whenever an ideal I is *homogeneous*, i.e. spanned by homogeneous polynomials, a *truncated Gröbner basis of I up to degree d* for $\prec$, or *d-truncated Gröbner basis*, is a set of polynomials $\mathscr{G} = \{g_1,\dots,g_r\}$ s.t. for all $f \in I$, if $\deg f \le d$ then there exists $g_i \in \mathscr{G}$ s.t. $\mathrm{LT}(g_i)$ divides $\mathrm{LT}(f)$. This can be computed using any Gröbner basis algorithm by discarding critical pairs of degree greater than d.

For an affine ideal, we can also define a d-truncated Gröbner basis as the output of a Gröbner basis algorithm discarding critical pair of degree higher than d. That is to say, for any critical pair (f_i, f_j), if $\deg \mathrm{LT}(f_i) + \deg \mathrm{LT}(f_j) - \deg \mathrm{lcm}(\mathrm{LT}(f_i), \mathrm{LT}(f_j)) > d$, then (f_i, f_j) is not taken into account. In this situation, a truncated Gröbner basis $\mathscr{G} = \{g_1, \dots, g_r\}$ up to degree d will span the subspace of polynomials $\sum_{i=1}^{r} h_i g_i$ with $\deg h_i \leq d - \deg g_i$.

PROPOSITION 3. *Equivalently, a n-dimensional sequence defined over a field $\mathbb{K}$ is linear recursive if the ideal I spanned by all the polynomials associated to its linear recurrence relations has dimension 0, i.e. has a finite number of solutions in the algebraic closure of $\mathbb{K}$.*

PROOF. We shall prove that both definitions are equivalent. First, let us consider a sequence verifying Def. 2. Let $\prec$ be a monomial ordering. For a linear recurrence relation R with support in $\mathscr{K}$, there is a maximal element $\mathbf{d}$ in $\mathscr{K}$ for $\prec$ s.t. R is reduced to $R'(\mathbf{i}) = u_{\mathbf{i}+\mathbf{d}} + \sum_{\mathbf{k}\in\mathscr{K}} \alpha_{\mathbf{k}} u_{\mathbf{i}+\mathbf{k}} = 0, \forall \mathbf{i} \in \mathbb{N}^n$. Let $R_1, \dots, R_m$ be a set of linear recurrence relations, written as above, sufficient to compute $\mathbf{u}$ together with $\{u_{\mathbf{i}}, \mathbf{i} \in S\}$. Let us show that for all $\mathbf{i}$, there exist $\gamma_{\mathbf{i},\mathbf{k}}, \mathbf{k} \in S$ s.t. $u_{\mathbf{i}} - \sum_{\mathbf{k}\in S} \gamma_{\mathbf{i},\mathbf{k}} = 0$. Obviously, this is true if $\mathbf{i} \in S$. Let us assume this is true for any $\mathbf{k}' \prec \mathbf{i}$. As $u_{\mathbf{i}}$ can be computed from the terms before, there exists a finite set S' s.t. for all $\mathbf{k}' \in S'$, $\mathbf{k}' \prec \mathbf{i}$ and $\beta_{\mathbf{k}'} \in \mathbb{K}$ s.t. $u_{\mathbf{i}} - \sum_{\mathbf{k}'\in S'} \beta_{\mathbf{k}'} u_{\mathbf{k}'} = u_{\mathbf{i}} - \sum_{\mathbf{k}'\in S'} \beta_{\mathbf{k}'} \sum_{\mathbf{k}\in S} \gamma_{\mathbf{k}',\mathbf{k}} u_{\mathbf{k}} = 0$. This leads to I being spanned by polynomials $\mathbf{x}^{\mathbf{i}} - \sum_{\mathbf{k} S} \gamma_{\mathbf{i},\mathbf{k}} \mathbf{x}^{\mathbf{k}}$ for all $\mathbf{k} \prec \mathbf{i}$. These polynomials form a Gröbner basis for $\prec$ with a finite staircase, namely monomials $\mathbf{x}^{\mathbf{k}}, \mathbf{k} \in S$. Hence $\dim I = 0$.

Conversely, let $\mathscr{G} = \{G_1, \dots, G_m\}$ be a minimal reduced Gröbner basis of I for a monomial order $\prec$. There exists a finite subset S of $\mathbb{N}^n$ s.t. for all j, $1 \leq j \leq m$, $G_j = \mathbf{x}^{\mathbf{i}_j} - \sum_{\mathbf{k}\in S} \gamma_{\mathbf{i}_j,\mathbf{k}} \mathbf{x}^{\mathbf{k}}$ with $\gamma_{\mathbf{i}_j,\mathbf{k}} \in \mathbb{K}$. Let us prove we can set a finite number of terms of $\mathbf{u}$ and then compute any term. Let $u_{\mathbf{i}}$ be any term of the sequence. If $\mathbf{x}^{\mathbf{i}}$ is in the staircase of $\mathscr{G}$, then we set $u_{\mathbf{i}}$. Otherwise there exist j and $\mathbf{i}'$ s.t. $\mathbf{x}^{\mathbf{i}} = \mathbf{x}^{\mathbf{i}'} \mathbf{x}^{\mathbf{i}_j}$, hence $\mathbf{x}^{\mathbf{i}'} G_j = \mathbf{x}^{\mathbf{i}} - \sum_{\mathbf{k}\in S} \gamma_{\mathbf{i}_j,\mathbf{k}} \mathbf{x}^{\mathbf{i}'+\mathbf{k}} \in I$. By recurrence on the $\mathbf{x}^{\mathbf{i}'+\mathbf{k}} \prec \mathbf{x}^{\mathbf{i}}$, there exist $\alpha_{\mathbf{i},\mathbf{k}} \in \mathbb{K}$ s.t. $\mathbf{x}^{\mathbf{i}} - \sum_{\mathbf{k}\in S} \alpha_{\mathbf{i},\mathbf{k}} \mathbf{x}^{\mathbf{k}} \in I$. Therefore $u_{\mathbf{i}} - \sum_{\mathbf{k}\in S} \alpha_{\mathbf{i},\mathbf{k}} u_{\mathbf{k}} = 0$ and one can compute any $u_{\mathbf{i}}$ from a finite number of initial terms. □

In other words, if $\mathbf{u}$ is linear recursive, then $\mathbb{K}[\mathbf{x}]/I$ is a finite dimensional $\mathbb{K}$-vector space. This is related to the definition of *holonomic* function in an Ore algebra $\mathscr{A} = \mathbb{K}(\mathbf{z})\langle\partial_{\mathbf{z}}\rangle$, see [11, Def. 1]. If $\mathrm{Ann}(f)$ is the left ideal of polynomials vanishing on $f = \sum_{\mathbf{i}\in\mathbb{N}^n} u_{\mathbf{i}} \mathbf{z}^{\mathbf{i}}$, then $\mathscr{A}/\mathrm{Ann}(f)$ is a finite dimensional vector space over $\mathscr{A}$. This equivalent definition is also related to but more restrictive than [3, Def. 2], in which the author only assumes that the ideal is not reduced to zero.

EXAMPLE 2. *Consider the following sequences:*
(a) $u_{i,j} = (2^i + 3^i)5^j$ *for all* $i, j \in \mathbb{N}$ *is linear recursive of order* 2, *a minimal set of linear recurrence relations is* $\{u_{i+2,j} - 5u_{i+1,j} + 6u_{i,j} = 0, u_{i,j+1} - 5u_{i,j} = 0\}$. *The associated ideal* $\langle (x-2)(x-3), y-5 \rangle$ *has two solutions of multiplicity* 1.
(b) $u_{i,j} = (i+1)2^i 5^j$ *for all* $i, j \in \mathbb{N}$ *is linear recursive of order* 2, *a minimal set of linear recurrence relations is* $\{u_{i+2,j} - 4u_{i+1,j} + 4u_{i,j} = 0, u_{i,j+1} - 5u_{i,j} = 0\}$. *The associated ideal* $\langle (x-2)^2, y-5 \rangle$ *has one solution of multiplicity* 2.
(c) $u_{i,j} = \binom{i}{j}$ *for all* $i, j \in \mathbb{N}$ *is not* linear recursive, *however it is* holonomic. *Indeed, while calling* BMS *or our algorithms on this sequence for all* $u_{i,j}$, $i + j \leq 2d$, *one obtains relations* $u_{i+1,j+1} - u_{i,j+1} - u_{i,j} = 0$, *the famous Pascal's triangle relation, together with* $\sum_{k=0}^{d} \binom{d}{k} (-1)^k u_{i+k,j} = 0$ *and* $u_{i,j+d} = 0$. *From the polynomial point of view, they form a d-truncated Gröbner basis of* $I = \langle xy - y - 1, (x-1)^d, y^d \rangle = \langle 1 \rangle$. *Let us notice that* 1 *is reached by these polynomials only as a linear combinations of degree* $d+1$ *and the ideal* $\langle 1 \rangle$ *has not dimension* 0 *but* -1. *From the sequence point of view, one needs to add infinitely many initial conditions to compute the whole sequence.*

DEFINITION 3. *Let* $\mathbf{u} = (u_{\mathbf{i}})_{\mathbf{i}\in\mathbb{N}^n}$ *be a recursive linear sequence and* I *be its ideal of relations. The* order *of* $\mathbf{u}$ *is equivalently the minimal number of initial terms of* $\mathbf{u}$ *needed to compute any term or the degree of* I.

2.2 Matrix multiplications in the quotient ring point of view

In this section, with a FGLM point of view, we shall show that given the ideal of relations and the initial terms of a sequence, one can express all the terms of said sequence as a scalar product. This point of view will be a key for the adaptive algorithm designed in Sec. 5.

Let $\mathbf{u} = (u_{\mathbf{i}})_{\mathbf{i}\in\mathbb{N}^n}$ be a linear recursive sequence over $\mathbb{K}$. Let S be the staircase of a Gröbner basis of its ideal of relations I, then $\mathbb{K}[\mathbf{x}]/I$ is a $\mathbb{K}$-algebra whose canonical basis as a vector space is made of the monomials $\mathbf{x}^{\mathbf{i}} \in S$. Defining $T_1, \dots, T_n$ the multiplication matrices by respectively $x_1, \dots, x_n$ in $\mathbb{K}[\mathbf{x}]/I$, then $u_{\mathbf{i}} = \langle \mathbf{r}, T_1^{i_1} \cdots T_n^{i_n} \cdot \mathbf{1} \rangle$, where $\mathbf{r} = (u_{\mathbf{0}}, \dots) = (u_s, s \in S)$, the vector of initial conditions, and $\mathbf{1} = (1, 0, \dots, 0)^{\mathrm{T}}$, the vector representing 1 in the canonical basis of $\mathbb{K}[x_1, \dots, x_n]/I$.

Indeed, let $\mathbf{i} \in \mathbb{N}^n$. By definition, $T_1^{i_1} \cdots T_n^{i_n} \cdot \mathbf{1}$ is the vector representing $\mathbf{x}^{\mathbf{i}}$ in the canonical basis of $\mathbb{K}[x_1, \dots, x_n]/I$. Then, the scalar product allows one to map this vector to the corresponding linear combination of the initial terms of the sequence.

3. RANDOMIZED REDUCTION: BMS/BM

In this section, we exploit a randomized preprocessing on the table which can simplify the computation of the linear recurrence relations of the sequence. This preprocessing will yield a new table which, with good probability, will have one linear recurrence relation of the form $u_{\mathbf{i}+de_1} - \sum_{k=0}^{d-1} \alpha_k u_{\mathbf{i}+ke_1} = 0$, for all $\mathbf{i}$ and other relations of the type $u_{\mathbf{i}+e_j} - \sum_{k=0}^{d-1} \beta_{j,k} u_{\mathbf{i}+ke_1} = 0$. In other words, all the other variables can be deduced from the first one. Therefore, the bottleneck of the execution of BMS on this sequence would be the computation of the first relation. This comes down essentially to running BM on the subsequence $(u_{ie_1})_{i\in\mathbb{N}}$.

3.1 Linear Transformation of the Table

This preprocessing can be seen as a linear transformation on the variables appearing in the ideal of relations.

Let $A \in \mathrm{GL}_n(\mathbb{K})$. Let us denote $\ell_i = \sum_{j=1}^{n} a_{i,j} x^j$, the ith linear form of $A\mathbf{x}$. Then $(A\mathbf{x})^{\mathbf{i}} = \prod_{j=1}^{n} \ell_j^{i_j}$, with $\mathbf{x}^{\mathbf{i}} = x_1^{i_1} \cdots x_n^{i_j}$. We define the action of A on an n-dimensional sequence as follows.

DEFINITION 4. *Let* $\mathbf{u} = (u_{\mathbf{i}})_{\mathbf{i}\in\mathbb{N}^n}$ *be a linear recurrent sequence. We define a* change of basis *on* $\mathbf{u}$ *as an invertible matrix* $A \in \mathrm{GL}_n(\mathbb{K})$. *The sequence* $\mathbf{v} = (v_{\mathbf{i}})_{\mathbf{i}\in\mathbb{N}^n} = A \cdot \mathbf{u}$ *is defined as* $v_{\mathbf{i}} = \left[(A\mathbf{x})^{\mathbf{i}}\right]_{\mathbf{u}}$.
In other words, for instance, $v_{\mathbf{0}} = u_{\mathbf{0}}, v_{e_i} = \sum_{j=1}^{n} a_{i,j} u_{e_j}$, etc. The following proposition links the ideals of relations of $\mathbf{u}$ and $\mathbf{v}$.

PROPOSITION 4. *Let* P *be a polynomial associated to a relation of* $\mathbf{u}$. *Let* $\mathbf{v} = A \cdot \mathbf{u}$ *for* A *invertible. Then* $P(A^{-1}\mathbf{x})$ *is a polynomial associated to a relation of* $\mathbf{v}$.

PROOF. Since $v_{\mathbf{i}}$ is merely the polynomial $(A\mathbf{x})^{\mathbf{i}}$ evaluated in $\mathbf{u}$. Any polynomial $P(A^{-1}\mathbf{x})$ evaluated in $\mathbf{v}$ will yield $P(\mathbf{x})$ evaluated in $\mathbf{u}$. Therefore, $\left[P(A^{-1}\mathbf{x})\right]_{\mathbf{v}} = 0$ iff $[P(\mathbf{x})]_{\mathbf{u}} = 0$. □

3.2 Essential reduction to BM

Let $\mathbf{u} = (u_{\mathbf{i}})_{\mathbf{i}\in\mathbb{N}^n}$ be a n-dimensional linear recursive sequence. Let $\mathbf{v} = (v_{\mathbf{i},j})_{(\mathbf{i},j)\in\mathbb{N}^n\times\mathbb{N}}$ be the $(n+1)$-dimensional sequence defined by $v_{\mathbf{i},j} = u_{\mathbf{i}}$ for all $\mathbf{i} \in \mathbb{N}^n$, $j \in \mathbb{N}$. If $I \in \mathbb{K}[\mathbf{x}]$ is the ideal of relations of $\mathbf{u}$ and t is a new variable representing the last coordinate then $J = I + (t-1)$ is the ideal of relations of $\mathbf{v}$. Let us now apply the change of coordinates in which each x_i remains the same and t is mapped onto $t+\sum_{i=1}^{n} c_i x_i$ for some $c_i \in \mathbb{K}$. Generically, the minimal reduced Gröbner basis of the new ideal J' obtained from J for the LEX order with $t < x_1 < \cdots < x_n$ is in *shape position*, i.e. is $\langle f(t), x_1 - f_1(t), \dots, x_n - f_n(t)\rangle$, with $\deg f_i < \deg f$, see [6, 12]. As $f(t) = \sum_{j=0}^{d} \alpha_j t^j$ depends only on t, it is found by running BM on the subsequence $(v_{\mathbf{0},j})_{j\in\mathbb{N}}$. Each polynomial $x_i - f_i(t)$, for $1 \le i \le n$, is then found by solving the linear system $u_{e_i,k+d} - \sum_{j=0}^{d-1} \beta_{i,j} u_{e_i,k+j}$ for $0 \le k \le d-1$, whose matrix is Hankel.

Therefore, after applying a linear transformation on the table, finding its relations essentially reduces to running BM on a 1-dimensional subsequence. This is summed up in Alg. 1.

ALGORITHM 1. BM *for n-dimensional sequences*
Input: *a n-dimensional sequence* $\mathbf{u} = (u_{\mathbf{i}})_{\mathbf{i}\in\mathbb{N}^n}$
Output: *an equivalent basis of relations of* $\mathbf{u}$
Pick at random $c_1, \dots, c_n \in \mathbb{K}$
Compute $\tilde{\mathbf{v}} = (\tilde{v}_j)_{j\in\mathbb{N}}$ *with*
$\tilde{v}_j = \left[(t + c_1 x_1 + \dots + c_n x_n)^j\right]_{\mathbf{v}}$ // *with* $v_{\mathbf{i},j} = u_{\mathbf{i}}$, $\forall (\mathbf{i}, j) \in \mathbb{N}^n \times \mathbb{N}$
$\quad = \left[(1 + c_1 x_1 + \dots + c_n x_n)^j\right]_{\mathbf{u}}$
Compute f *with* BM *on* $\tilde{\mathbf{v}}$ *of degree* d.
For *i* ***from*** 1 ***to*** *n*
Solve the Hankel linear system

$$\begin{pmatrix} u_{e_i,0} & \cdots & u_{e_i,d-1} \\ \vdots & \iddots & \vdots \\ u_{e_i,d-1} & \cdots & u_{e_i,2d-2} \end{pmatrix} \begin{pmatrix} \beta_{i,0} \\ \vdots \\ \beta_{i,d-1} \end{pmatrix} = \begin{pmatrix} u_{e_i,d} \\ \vdots \\ u_{e_i,2d-1} \end{pmatrix}$$

Return $f, x_1 - \sum_{j=0}^{d-1} \beta_{1,j} t^j, \dots, x_n - \sum_{j=0}^{d-1} \beta_{n,j} t^j$.

Let us mention that one can also retrieve the relations of the original sequence, i.e. the polynomials in $x_1, \dots, x_n$ not in t, by computing a new Gröbner basis of the ideal for an order eliminating t, e.g. LEX with $x_1 < \cdots < x_n < t$. Poteaux and Schost [15] proved that there is a Las Vegas algorithm to change the order of a triangular set whose complexity is essentially that of modular composition $O(\mathsf{C}(d)) \subseteq O(d^{(\omega+1)/2})$ operations, as d is the degree of I.

3.3 Complexity results

PROPOSITION 5. *Let* $d \in \mathbb{N}$. *Computing terms* $v_{\mathbf{i}}$ *for all* $\mathbf{i} \in \mathbb{N}^n$ *such that* $|\mathbf{i}| \le d$ *can be done in* $O(n^{2d})$ *operations in* $\mathbb{K}$, $O(n^{2d})$ *memory space and* $O(n^d)$ *queries to the table elements.*

PROOF. As seen in Sec. 3.1, to compute $v_{\mathbf{i}}$, one needs to compute $\ell_1^{i_1} \cdots \ell_n^{i_n}$, where ℓ_j is the jth row of $\mathbf{Ax}$.

Let $z_0, \dots, z_n$ be new variables; expanding $(z_0 + \ell_1 z_1 + \dots + \ell_n z_n)^d$ yields terms of the form $c \ell_1^{i_1} \cdots \ell_n^{i_n} z_0^{d-|\mathbf{i}|} z_1^{i_1} \cdots z_n^{i_n}$ with $i_1, \dots, i_n \ge 0$ and s.t. $|\mathbf{i}| \le d$. This allows us to directly determine all the polynomials we need to compute $v_{\mathbf{i}}$, $|\mathbf{i}| \le d$.

Since $z_0 + \ell_1 z_1 + \dots + \ell_n z_n$ has n^2+1 monomials, its dth power has $\binom{n^2+1}{d} \in O(n^{2d})$. Using the square and multiply algorithms, one needs to perform $O(n^{2d})$ operations in $\mathbb{K}$ to compute this power. This method also needs to store every coefficient of our polynomials which is in $O(n^{2d})$.

Finally, we need to evaluate the polynomials by replacing $\mathbf{x}^{\mathbf{i}}$ by $u_{\mathbf{i}}$. For this, we only need to access each element of the table once, and update all our evaluations at the same time, hence $O(n^d)$ queries. As each of the $O(n^d)$ polynomials of degree d has $O(n^d)$ coefficients, $O(n^{2d})$ multiplications must be performed. □

PROOF OF TH. 1. Besides the change of basis in $O(n^{2d})$, we need one call of BM in $\tilde{O}(n^d)$ operations in $\mathbb{K}$. Finally, each Hankel system can be solved in $O(\mathsf{M}(d) \log d)$ operations (see [2]). □

4. MULTI-HANKEL SOLVER

This section is devoted to the design of a FGLM-like algorithm for computing the Gröbner bases of the ideal of relations of a sequence $\mathbf{u} = (u_{\mathbf{i}})_{\mathbf{i}\in\mathbb{N}^n}$, with coefficients in $\mathbb{K}$. From now on, $\mathscr{T}$ is the ordered set of terms that we can make from $x_1, \dots, x_n$. We fix $\prec$ to be an admissible monomial ordering. If $P \in \mathbb{K}[x_1, \dots, x_n]$ then $\mathscr{T}(P)$ is the set of terms composing P and $\mathrm{LT}_{\prec}(P)$ is the maximum of $\mathscr{T}(P)$. For any D, $\mathscr{T}_D$ is the set of all terms of degree $\le D$ sorted by increasing order (wrt. $\prec$). Since we want to design an algorithm we will be unable to check that a relation is valid for all $\mathbf{i} \in \mathbb{N}^n$. Indeed, at some point of the algorithm we will have a finite subset of indices $T \subset \mathbb{N}^n$ and we will try to find relations that are valid for those indices: for $\mathbf{i} \in T$, $u_{\mathbf{i}+\mathbf{d}} + \sum_{\mathbf{k}\in\mathscr{K}} \alpha_{\mathbf{k}} u_{\mathbf{i}+\mathbf{k}} = 0$.

DEFINITION 5. *Let* T *be a finite subset of* $\mathbb{N}^n$. *We say that a polynomial* $P \in \mathbb{K}[x_1, \dots, x_n]$ *is valid up to* T *if* $\mathrm{Rel}_{\mathbf{u}}(P)(\mathbf{i}) = 0$ *for all* $\mathbf{i} \in T$. *In that case we write that* $\mathrm{NF}(P, \mathbf{u}, T) = 0$.

Let T *be a finite subset of* $\mathscr{T}$. *We say that a polynomial* $P \in \mathbb{K}[x_1, \dots, x_n]$ *is valid up to* T *if* $[t\,P] = 0$ *for all* $t \in T$. *In that case we write that* $\mathrm{NF}(P, \mathbf{u}, T) = 0$.

4.1 Staircase

We assume now that $T \subset \mathscr{T}$ is a finite set of terms. Equivalently, T' is the set of exponents of all $t \in T$. Any BMS-style algorithm will generate *minimal* relations; hence when we try to establish a new relation $u_{\mathbf{i}+\mathbf{d}} + \sum_{\mathbf{k}\in\mathscr{K}} \alpha_{\mathbf{k}} u_{\mathbf{i}+\mathbf{k}}$ we must check two properties: *(a)* There are scalars $\alpha_{\mathbf{k}} \in \mathbb{K}$ so that $\forall \mathbf{i} \in T'$, $u_{\mathbf{i}+\mathbf{d}} + \sum_{\mathbf{k}\in\mathscr{K}} \alpha_{\mathbf{k}} u_{\mathbf{i}+\mathbf{k}} = 0$; *(b)* There are no nonzero relations $\sum_{\mathbf{k}\in\mathscr{K}} \beta_{\mathbf{k}} u_{\mathbf{i}+\mathbf{k}} = 0$ which are valid for all $\mathbf{i} \in T'$.

We can translate these properties in polynomial terms: *(a)* There is a monic polynomial $P \in \mathbb{K}[x_1, \dots, x_n]$ of leading term $\mathbf{x}^{\mathbf{d}}$ s.t. $\mathrm{NF}(P, \mathbf{u}, T) = 0$; *(b)* There are no nonzero relations $\sum_{t\in\mathscr{T}(P-\mathbf{x}^{\mathbf{d}})} \beta_t \mathrm{Rel}_{\mathbf{u}}(t)(\mathbf{i}) = 0$ which are valid for all $\mathbf{i} \in T'$. Equivalently, there are no nonzero relations $\sum_{t\in\mathscr{T}(P-\mathbf{x}^{\mathbf{d}})} \beta_t [m t] = 0$ which are valid for all $m \in T$.

Hence it is important to identify a set of terms for which there is *no* linear relations.

DEFINITION 6. *Let* T *be a finite subset of* $\mathscr{T}$. *We say that a finite set* $S \subset T$ *of terms is a useful staircase wrt.* $\mathbf{u}$, T *and* $\prec$ *if* $\sum_{t\in S} \beta_t [m t] = 0$, $\forall m \in S$ *implies that* $\beta_t = 0$ *for all* $t \in S$, S *is maximal for the inclusion and minimal for* $\prec$. *We compare two ordered sets for* $\prec$ *by seeing them as tuples of their elements and then comparing them lexicographically.*

Note that these "useful staircases" are not staircases in the sense of Gröbner bases since they are not always stable under division.

EXAMPLE 3. *In dimension* 2, *consider the set* $T = \{1, x, y, x^2, xy, y^2\}$ *of all degree* ≤ 2 *monomials and the table* $\mathbf{u} = \begin{pmatrix} 0 & 0 & 0 & \cdots \\ 0 & 0 & 0 & \cdots \\ 0 & 1 & 0 & \cdots \\ 0 & 0 & 0 & \ddots \end{pmatrix}$ *Then, we can check (see Ex. 4) that* $\{y, x, xy, x^2\}$ *is a useful staircase. Since* 1 *is not in this set, it is not stable under division. However, using the stability criterion, we recover the complete staircase* $\{1, x, y, xy, x^2\}$.

Alg. 2 transforms a useful staircase into a staircase.

ALGORITHM 2. *Stabilize*
Input: *S' a useful staircase*
Output: *a staircase*
$S := []$
For $s \in S'$ ***do*** $S := S \cup \{t \mid t \in \mathscr{T}$ *and* t *divides* $s\}$
Return S

4.2 Linear Algebra to find relations

We give a simple algorithm to check that a finite set $S \subset T$ is a useful staircase wrt. $\mathbf{u}$, T and $\prec$. Let us start with a simple example:

EXAMPLE 4 (EX. 3 CONT.). *We look for a relation* $P(x,y) = a_5 x^2 + a_4 xy + a_3 y^2 + a_2 x + a_1 y + a_0$ *that is to say we try to find* $a_0, \dots, a_5$ *s.t.* $[t\,P] = 0$ *for all* $t \in T$: $a_0 u_{k1,k2} + a_1 u_{k1,k2+1} + a_2 u_{k1+1,k2} + a_3 u_{i_1,i_2+2} + a_4 u_{i_1+1,i_2+1} + a_5 u_{i_1+2,i_2} = 0$, *for all* (i_1, i_2) *s.t.* $i_1 + i_2 \le 2$. *To find a useful staircase* S *it is equivalent to extracting a full rank matrix in the following multi-Hankel matrix:*

$$H_T = \begin{array}{c} \\ 1 \\ y \\ x \\ y^2 \\ xy \\ x^2 \end{array} \begin{array}{c} \begin{array}{cccccc} 1 & y & x & y^2 & xy & x^2 \end{array} \\ \begin{pmatrix} u_{0,0} & u_{0,1} & u_{1,0} & u_{0,2} & u_{1,1} & u_{2,0} \\ u_{0,1} & u_{0,2} & u_{1,1} & u_{0,3} & u_{1,2} & u_{2,1} \\ u_{1,0} & u_{1,1} & u_{2,0} & u_{1,2} & u_{2,1} & u_{3,0} \\ u_{0,2} & u_{0,3} & u_{1,2} & u_{0,4} & u_{1,3} & u_{2,2} \\ u_{1,1} & u_{1,2} & u_{2,1} & u_{1,3} & u_{2,2} & u_{3,1} \\ u_{2,0} & u_{2,1} & u_{3,0} & u_{2,2} & u_{3,1} & u_{4,0} \end{pmatrix} \end{array}$$

or equivalently

$$H_T = \begin{array}{c|cccccc} & 1 & y & x & y^2 & xy & x^2 \\ \hline 1 & 0 & 0 & 0 & 0 & 0 & 0 \\ y & 0 & 0 & 0 & 0 & 0 & 1 \\ x & 0 & 0 & 0 & 0 & 1 & 0 \\ y^2 & 0 & 0 & 0 & 0 & 0 & 0 \\ xy & 0 & 0 & 1 & 0 & 0 & 0 \\ x^2 & 0 & 1 & 0 & 0 & 0 & 0 \end{array}.$$

In this example, 1 and y^2 are clearly useless so that $S' = \{y, x, xy, x^2\}$ is the useful staircase and $\det(H_{S'}) = 1 \neq 0$. In addition we can try to find a relation $Q(x,y) = y^2 - a_3 x^2 - a_2 xy - a_1 x - a_0 y$. Again this is equivalent to finding $a_0, \ldots, a_3$ s.t. $\mathrm{Rel}(Q)(i_1, i_2) = 0$ for all (i_1, i_2) with $i_1 + i_2 \leq 2$. In turn, this reduces to solving the linear system:

$$H_{S'} \begin{pmatrix} a_0 \\ a_1 \\ a_2 \\ a_3 \end{pmatrix} = \begin{pmatrix} u_{0,3} \\ u_{1,2} \\ u_{1,3} \\ u_{2,2} \end{pmatrix} = \begin{pmatrix} 0 \\ 0 \\ 0 \\ 0 \end{pmatrix}.$$

Since $H_{S'}$ is full rank we find $a_0 = \cdots = a_3 = 0$ and the relation $Q(x,y) = y^2$.

In the general case we can now define the structured matrix associated to two lists of terms:

DEFINITION 7. *Let T and S be two finite subsets of $\mathscr{T}$. We consider the polynomial $P_S(\mathbf{x}) = \sum_{s \in S} a_s s$ and the linear equations $[t\, P_S] = 0$ for all $t \in T$. Then, we generate the coefficient matrix $H_{T,S}$ from the previous linear system of equations in the unknown variables a_s for $s \in S$:*

$$H_{T,S} = \begin{array}{c} \\ \vdots \\ t \in T \\ \vdots \end{array} \begin{array}{c} \cdots \quad s \in S \quad \cdots \\ \begin{pmatrix} \cdots & & \cdots \\ \cdots & [t\, s]_{\mathbf{u}} & \cdots \\ \cdots & & \cdots \end{pmatrix} \end{array}.$$

When $T = S$ we simply write H_T for the multi-Hankel matrix $H_{T,S}$.

These two crucial operations involve linear algebra:

(a) Checking that a finite set of terms $S \subset \mathscr{T}$ is a useful staircase wrt. T (we assume that $\#T \geqslant \#S$) is equivalent to checking that the matrix $H_{T,S}$ has full rank;

(b) Finding a monic polynomial $P \in \mathbb{K}[x_1, \ldots, x_n]$ of given support s.t. $\mathrm{NF}(P, \mathbf{u}, T) = 0$ is equivalent to solving a linear system

$$H_{T,S} \times \mathbf{a} + H_{T,\{\mathrm{LT}(P)\}} = 0$$

where $S = \mathscr{T}(P - \mathrm{LT}(P))$ is the support of the polynomial P except the leading term. If $\mathbf{a}$ is a solution then $P = \mathrm{LT}(P) + \sum_{s \in S} a_s s$ is a polynomial s.t. $\mathrm{NF}(P, \mathbf{u}, T) = 0$.

PROPOSITION 6. *Let T be a finite subset of $\mathscr{T}$. If the finite set of terms $S \subset \mathscr{T}$ is a useful staircase wrt. $\mathbf{u}$, T and $\prec$ then:*

$$\det(H_S) \neq 0 \text{ and } \operatorname{rank} H_S = \operatorname{rank} H_{T,S} = \operatorname{rank} H_T.$$

PROOF. This is another wording of Def. 6. □

The two statements of Prop. 7 are easy to prove but they are the basis of the algorithm: according to them we know that we can proceed degree by degree.

PROPOSITION 7. *If $S' \subset S$ are finite set of terms, then $\operatorname{rank} H_S \geq \operatorname{rank} H_{S'}$. Moreover, assume S is a finite subset of terms s.t. $\det(H_S) \neq 0$ and $t \in \mathscr{T} \setminus S$ then we have: $\operatorname{rank} H_{S \cup \{t\}} = \mathrm{ColRank}\, H_{S, S \cup \{t\}} = \mathrm{RowRank}\, H_{S \cup \{t\}, S}$.*

PROOF. $H_{S'}$ is a submatrix of H_S and H_S is symmetric. □

We rely on the following naive strategy to extract a full rank matrix of a multi-Hankel matrix. We start with $H_{\{\}}$ and we proceed by induction, assuming that at some point we have found a useful S s.t. H_S is full rank. Then we select the minimal $t \in \mathscr{T} \setminus S$. If $\operatorname{rank} H_{S \cup \{t\}} = \operatorname{rank} H_S + 1$ then we update $S := S \cup \{t\}$; else we have $\operatorname{rank} H_{S \cup \{t\}} = \operatorname{rank} H_S$ and we consider $t' \in \mathscr{T} \setminus (S \cup \{t\})$.

Given a useful staircase S, it is important that $2S = \{st, s, t \in S\}$ be not too big compared to S, when counting the number of table queries. We will see how to bound the cardinality of $2S$ in Sec. 5.1.

4.3 An FGLM-like Algorithm

Since the input table $\mathbf{u}$ is infinite we need a bound given by the user: $d \geq 0$ and T will be the set of all monomials of degree less than d. Accordingly, we will assume that the monomial ordering $\prec$ is an admissible ordering refined by the total degree. Since the output of the BMS algorithm is a (truncated) Gröbner basis, it is a natural idea to try to adapt existing Gröbner basis algorithms to obtain the same result. To this end, we can try to slightly modify the FGLM algorithm. However, in the scalar case, a fundamental difference is that the structure of the quotient ring (and in particular the staircase) is not known. Hence, to clarify our intention we will split the algorithm in two parts: first we derive the staircase wrt. the monomial ordering and the given bound; in a second step we compute a truncated Gröbner basis. In a real implementation, the two steps can be combined to increase the efficiency of the algorithm.

ALGORITHM 3. FGLM *for scalars.*

Input: *$\prec$ a monomial ordering, $\mathbf{u} = (u_{\mathbf{i}})_{\mathbf{i} \in \mathbb{N}^n}$ a sequence with coefficients in $\mathbb{K}$, d a given bound.*

Output: *a reduced $(d+1)$-truncated Gröbner basis wrt. $\prec$ of $\mathbf{u}$*

Build the matrix $H_{\mathscr{T}_d}$.
Find S' the useful staircase s.t. $\operatorname{rank} H_{\mathscr{T}_d} = \operatorname{rank} H_{S'}$.   // as in Sec. 4.2
$S :=$ Stabilize(S') // the staircase (stable under division)
$L := \mathscr{T}_{d+1} \setminus S$ // list of next terms to study
$G := []$ // the future Gröbner basis
While $L \neq \emptyset$ **do**
  $t := \min_{\prec}(L)$ and remove t from L
  Find $\mathbf{x}$ s.t. $H_{S'}\mathbf{x} + H_{S',\{t\}} = 0$
  $G := G \cup \left[t + \sum_{i=1}^{\#S'} x_i \cdot S'_i\right]$
  Sort L by increasing order (wrt. $\prec$) and remove multiples of $\mathrm{LT}(G)$.
Return G

EXAMPLE 5 (CONT. OF EX. 2.C). *We consider the table $\mathbf{u}$ generated by $u_{i,j} = \binom{i}{j}$ and we fix $d = 2$. We consider the matrix*

$$H = \begin{array}{c|cccccc} & 1 & y & x & y^2 & xy & x^2 \\ \hline 1 & 1 & 0 & 1 & 0 & 1 & 1 \\ y & 0 & 0 & 1 & 0 & 0 & 2 \\ x & 1 & 1 & 1 & 0 & 2 & 1 \\ y^2 & 0 & 0 & 0 & 0 & 0 & 1 \\ xy & 1 & 0 & 2 & 0 & 1 & 3 \\ x^2 & 1 & 2 & 1 & 1 & 3 & 1 \end{array}.$$

It is easy to check that the column (resp. row) xy is the sum of the first two columns (resp. rows). Hence, the useful staircase is $S' = \{1, y, x, y^2, x^2\}$. Since S' is stable under division, $S = S'$. We initialize $L = [xy, x^3, x^2y, xy^2, y^3]$ so that $t = xy$. The next step is to solve the system $H_S\mathbf{x} + [1,0,2,0,3]^{\mathrm{T}} = 0$ and we find $\mathbf{x} = [-1,-1,0,0,0]^{\mathrm{T}}$ so that $G = [xy - y - 1]$. We can update $L = [x^3, y^3]$ and by solving two other linear systems, we find $G = [xy - y - 1, x^3 - 3x^2 + 3x - 1 = (x-1)^3, y^3]$. Clearly this is not a full Gröbner basis but a 3-truncated Gröbner basis.

THEOREM 8. *The output of Alg. 3 is a $(d+1)$-truncated Gröbner basis. Moreover, if $\mathbf{u}$ is a recursive linear sequence of order D, taking $d = D$ suffices to recover a full Gröbner basis of the sequence.*

PROOF. Alg. 3 clearly terminates since the size of L decreases.

Taking the basis monomials in increasing order ensures that the set S' contains monomials of smallest degrees. Let us first show that the staircase of the ideal of u contains the useful staircase. In the following, we shall see polynomials as linear combinations of columns of $H_{\mathscr{T}_d}$. Any polynomial with leading term outside the staircase of the ideal of $\mathbf{u}$ reduces to polynomials in the staircase. Suppose that one element e of the useful staircase lies outside the staircase. Seen as linear combinations of columns of $H_{\mathscr{T}_d}$, it is then a linear combination of elements in the staircase, some of which are not in the useful staircase by linear independence. Let f be one of these particular elements: f is a linear combination of smaller elements in the useful staircase. Then e is actually a linear combination of elements in the useful staircase, which is contradictory.

Conversely, if S' does not contain a maximal (for the natural order on the table) element of the staircase for $\mathbf{u}$, then this element can be written as a linear combination of smaller terms, which contradicts the fact it belongs to the staircase. The stabilization of these maximal elements is therefore the full staircase of the ideal of $\mathbf{u}$.

The set G contains elements with leading terms that do not divide each other. Let us consider f and g in G (with leading terms in $\mathscr{T}_{d+1}$) and their S-polynomials $S(f,g)$. Then either the leading term of $S(f,g)$ is in $\mathscr{T}_{d+1} \setminus S'$ or it is in S'. In the latter case, it means there is a relation in $H_{S'}$, so it cannot be a new relation. In the former case, the relation was already found by the main loop. So no $S(f,g)$ produces a new relation. □

5. ADAPTIVE ALGORITHM

So far we have seen two algorithms to recover the relations from a table: these algorithms are efficient when the degree of the elements in the Gröbner basis G is small compared with the order of the recurrence: $\max\deg G \approx (\text{order of the recurrence})^{1/n}$.

Unfortunately, this is not always the case, especially if the monomial ordering is a lexicographical order. Using the previous algorithms on these examples would increase too much the complexity (by complexity we mean the number of accesses to the table $\mathbf{u}$). The goal of this section is to describe an adaptive algorithm to take into account the shape of the final Gröbner basis.

The main difference between Alg. 3 and the original FGLM is the following: with polynomials, when we discover a relation $f = t + \sum_{s \in S} \alpha_s\, s$ we know that $m\,f$ is still a valid relation for any $m \in \mathscr{T}$. In contrast, when we find a relation

$$[f]_{\mathbf{u}} = [t]_{\mathbf{u}} + \sum_{s \in S} \alpha_s\, [s]_{\mathbf{u}} = 0 \qquad (1)$$

it is not true in general that $[m\,f]_{\mathbf{u}} = 0$. However we know from Sec. 2.2 that any n-dimensional linear recurrence can be written as $u_{\mathbf{i}} = \langle \mathbf{r}, T_1^{i_1} \cdots T_n^{i_n} \cdot \mathbf{1} \rangle$ where $\mathbf{r}$ is a vector depending on the initial conditions and T_i are multiplication matrices associated to the Gröbner basis G. Therefore we can write $\langle \mathbf{r}, \mathrm{NormalForm}(f,G) \rangle = 0$ for relation (1). Hence, if $\mathbf{r}$ is sufficiently random we know that $\mathrm{NF}(f,G) = 0$ so that $\mathrm{NF}(m\,f,G) = 0$ for all $m \in \mathscr{T}$ which implies that $[m\,f]_{\mathbf{u}} = 0$. Note that in some applications (see for instance Sec. 5.2) it is possible to check afterwards that the relation is correct. Accordingly, we propose an FGLM algorithm to take advantage of this property. We proceed term by term and we try to discover the new staircase which is equivalent to increasing the rank of the multi-Hankel matrix by 1. We do not give any bounds on the degree of the output polynomial but we assume that an estimate of the size of order of the recurrence is given by the user. We will see later that for many applications the complexity can be reduced drastically; depending on the shape (for instance the convexity) of the final staircase, the number of queries to the table can often be linear in the order of the recurrence, similarly to the one-dimensional case. In the following algorithm, for any list of terms G, $\mathrm{MinGBasis}(G)$ is the corresponding minimal Gröbner basis.

ALGORITHM 4. *Adaptive* FGLM *for scalars (simple version)*

Input: $\prec$ *a monomial ordering,* $\mathbf{u} = (u_{\mathbf{i}})_{\mathbf{i} \in \mathbb{N}^n}$ *a sequence with coefficients in* $\mathbb{K}$*,* d *a given bound.*
$L := [1]$ *// list of next terms to study*
$S := []$ *// the useful staircase wrt. the new ordering* $\prec$
$G' := []$ *// leading terms of the final Gröbner basis*
While $L \neq \emptyset$ **do**
  $t := \mathit{first}(L)$
  If $H_{S \cup \{t\}}$ *is full rank* **then**
    $S := S \cup [t]$ *and* $L := L \cup [x_i t \mid i = 1, \ldots, n] \setminus [t]$
    Sort L (wrt. $\prec$*) and remove duplicates and multiples of* G'
    If $\#S \geq d$ **then** *// early termination*
      $G := []$ *and* $G' := \mathrm{MinGBasis}(G' \cup L \cup \mathscr{T}_{\deg(t)+1})$
      For $t \in G'$ **do**
        $G := G \cup [t + \sum_{i=1}^{\#S} x_i \cdot S_i]$ *where* $\mathbf{x}$ *s.t.* $H_S\,\mathbf{x} + H_{S,\{t\}} = 0$
      Return *S and G*
  Else $G' := G' \cup [t]$ *and remove multiples of t in L*
Error *"Run Alg. 3"*

REMARK 9. *In some applications (see e.g. Sec. 5.3 on error correcting codes), the input table is bounded:* $u_{i_1,\ldots,i_n}$ *cannot be computed or has no meaning when* $i_j > B$ *for some bound B. One can easily modify the algorithm to take this constraint into consideration.*

PROPOSITION 10. *Let S and G be the output of Alg. 4. Then S is a staircase of size* $\geq d$ *and G is a list of valid relations, that is to say* $\mathrm{NF}(f,\mathbf{u},S) = 0$ *for all* $f \in G$*.*

EXAMPLE 6. *As explained in Sec. 5.2, we consider the ideal of the vanishing ideal of the points* $\{[0,0],[0,1],[1,1]\}$*. We compute a total degree Gröbner basis in* $\mathbb{F}_{11}[x_1,x_2]$ *and we apply the Sparse-*FGLM *algorithm with a random vector* $\mathbf{r} = [10,3,5]$*. Hence, we run Alg. 4 with* $d = 3$ *on the table* $\mathbf{u} = \begin{pmatrix} 10 & 3 & 3 & \cdots \\ 5 & 5 & 5 & \\ 5 & 5 & 5 & \\ \vdots & & & \ddots \end{pmatrix}$.

Step 1: $t = 1$*; we check* $H_{[1]} = (10)$ *has rank* 1 *so that* $L = [x_2, x_1]$*.*
Step 2: $t = x_2$*; we compute the rank of* $H_{[1,x_2]} = \begin{pmatrix} 10 & 3 \\ 3 & 3 \end{pmatrix}$ *which is equal to* 2*. We update* $L = [x_2^2, x_1, x_1x_2]$ *and* $S = [1, x_2]$*.*
Step 3: $t = x_2^2$ *but obviously the rank of* $H_{[1,x_2,x_2^2]} = \begin{pmatrix} 10 & 3 & 3 \\ 3 & 3 & 3 \\ 3 & 3 & 3 \end{pmatrix}$ *is always* 2*. We set* $G' = [x_2^2]$*.*
Step 4: $t = x_1$*; we compute the rank of* $H_3 = H_{[1,x_2,x_1]} = \begin{pmatrix} 10 & 3 & 5 \\ 3 & 3 & 5 \\ 5 & 5 & 5 \end{pmatrix}$ *which is equal to* 3*. Now* $S = [1, x_2, x_1]$ *and* $L = [x_1x_2, x_1^2]$*. Since* $\#S \geq 3$ *we can stop the algorithm so that* $G' = \mathrm{MinGBasis}([x_2^2, x_1x_2, x_1^2, x_2^3, \ldots]) = [x_2^2, x_1x_2, x_1^2]$*. Lastly, we solve the* 3 *linear systems* $H_3\mathbf{x} = \mathbf{u}$ *with*

$$\mathbf{u} = H_{[x_2^2],S} = \begin{pmatrix} 3 \\ 3 \\ 5 \end{pmatrix} \text{ or } \mathbf{u} = H_{[x_1x_2],S} = \begin{pmatrix} 5 \\ 5 \\ 5 \end{pmatrix} \text{ or } \mathbf{u} = H_{[x_1^2],S} = \begin{pmatrix} 5 \\ 5 \\ 5 \end{pmatrix}$$

and we obtain $G_{\mathrm{LEX}} = [{x_2}^2 - x_2, x_1 x_2 - x_1, {x_1}^2 - x_1]$*. It is easy to compute the solutions* $\{(0,0),(0,1),(1,1)\}$*.*

5.1 Relation between the number of table queries and the geometry of the final basis

To estimate the complexity of the algorithms we have to bound the number of table queries and the complexity of the linear algebra part (this issue is addressed in Sec. 6). Indeed, in some applications computing *one* element $u_{i_1,i_2,\ldots}$ of the table is very costly (see for instance Sec. 5.2) and it is important to minimize the number of queries. Estimating this number is equivalent to counting the number of distinct elements in H_S where S can be any value of the variable in Alg. 4. We denote by S the value at the end of the algorithm. Similarly to the original FGLM algorithm we can bound the number of monomials t that we have to consider using $\#L \leq n\#S$. Hence it is crucial to bound the number of elements in H_S where S is the final staircase. Restating Th. 2, the necessary number of queries to $\mathbf{u}$ to build H_S is the cardinal of $2S = \{uv \mid (u,v) \in S^2\}$ the dilated set of S.

It is clear that $\#(2S) \leq \#S(\#S-1)/2 \leq (\#S)^2/2$ in the worst case; in many applications we have $\#(2S) \leq c\#S$ for some constant c. According to [16, Th. 1.1], sets S verifying this condition must be included in a bigger set whose elements are in arithmetical progression of dimension d and of size $C\#S$ for some constant C. In other words, S must be included in a d-dimensional parallelotope whose number of points is $C\#S$.

PROPOSITION 11. *Depending on the shape of the final Gröbner basis G, we estimate* $\#(2S)$ *when* $d \to \infty$*:*
a. *(1-dimensional case –* BM*)* $n = 1$*,* $S_d = \{1, x, \ldots, x^{d-1}\}$ *then* $\#(2S_d) = 2d - 1$ *and* $\#(2S_d)/\#S_d \approx 2$*;*
b. *(Worst 1-dimensional case)* $n = 1$*,* $S_d = \{1, x^2, x^4, \ldots, x^{2^{d-2}}\}$ *then* $\#(2S_d) = \binom{d-2}{2} + d + 1$ *and* $\#(2S_d)/S_d \approx \frac{d}{2}$*;*
c. *(Alg. 3)* $S_d = \{t \in T \mid \deg(t) \leq d\}$ *then* $\#(2S_d) = \binom{d+2}{2}$ *and* $\#(2S_d)/\#S_d \approx 2^n$*;*
d. *(Shape position) When* $G = [x_i - h_i(x_n) \mid i = 1, \ldots, n]$ *then* $S_s = \{1, x_n, \ldots, x_n^{d-1}\}$ *where* $d = \deg(h_n)$*. Again* $\#(2S_d)/\#S_d \approx 2$*;*

e. *(Worst case in dimension n)* $S_d = \bigcup_{i=1}^{n}\{1, x_i, x_i^2, ..., x_i^{d/n}\}$ *then* $\frac{\#(2S_d)}{\#S_d} \approx \frac{1}{2}\frac{n-1}{n}\#S_d$.

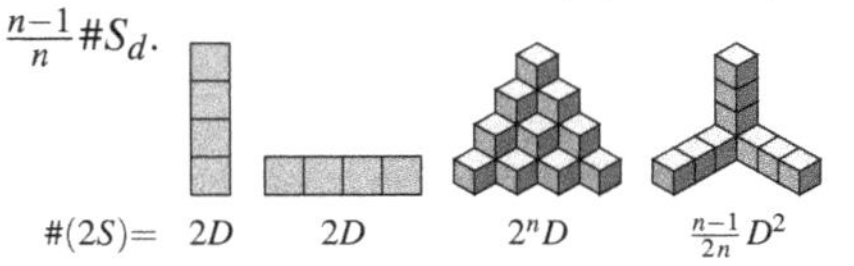

Figure 1: Behavior of $\#(2S)$ wrt. $D = \#S$ (the area in blue)

PROOF. *(a)* Clearly $2S_d = S_{2d-1}$.
(b) $S_{2d} = S_d \cup \{x^{2^i+2^j} \mid i \neq j\} \cup \{x^{2^{d-1}}\}$. Note that S_d is *not stable* under division in that case.
(c) Noticing $2S_d = S_{2d}$ and $\#S_d = \binom{d+n}{n}$, we have $\frac{\#S_{2d}}{\#S_d} = 2^n - 2^{n-1}\binom{n+1}{2}\frac{1}{d} + O(\frac{1}{d^2})$.
(d) Same as item a.
(e) We define $S'(n,d) = \bigcup_{i=1}^{n}\{x_i^j \mid j = 0, ..., d\}$ and it easy to show that $\#(2S'(n,d)) = n(n-1)d^2 + 2nd + 1$. Hence $S_d = S'(n, d/n)$ and $\#(2S_d)/\#S_d = (\frac{n-1}{2n}d^2 + 2d + 1)/(d+1) \approx \frac{1}{2}\frac{n-1}{n}d$. □

5.2 Application to the Sparse-FGLM algorithm

The Sparse-FGLM [5] is a natural application of the previous algorithm: for a 0-dimensional polynomial system we compute a first Gröbner basis (most of the time wrt. a total degree ordering). Then, we compute the $D \times D$ multiplication matrices T_i wrt. the variable x_i for all $i \in \{1, ..., n\}$. We consider the table $u_{\mathbf{i}} = \langle \mathbf{r}, T_1^{i_1} \cdots T_n^{i_n} \cdot \mathbf{1} \rangle$ where $\mathbf{r}$ is a random vector and $\mathbf{1} = [1, 0, ...]^{\mathrm{T}}$. The computation of one element of the table from the previous ones can be reduced to one matrix-vector multiplication.

REMARK 12. *Assuming that we store the vectors* $\mathbf{V_i} = T_1^{i_1} \cdots T_n^{i_n} \cdot \mathbf{1}$ *for the visited indices* $\mathbf{i}$, *any relation* $g = \sum_{s \in S} \alpha_s s \in G$ *computed by the algorithm can be easily checked:if* $\sum_{s \in S} \alpha_s \mathbf{V}_s = 0$ *then we have a proof that* $g \in I$. *Note, that in addition, we know precisely the bound d since it is the number of solutions (with multiplicities). Hence it is always possible to check the correctness of Alg. 4.*

Even if the sparsity of the multiplication matrices can be used to speed up the computation, it is important not to precompute *all* the elements of the table in advance. Hence a *black-box* representation is recommended. As shown in [5], when the lexicographical basis is in shape position, the Gröbner basis can be computed very efficiently; in particular, the number of table queries is $2D$, in this situation we can also use the change of variables designed in Sec. 3 to compute the Gröbner basis. This is why, in the experiments of the following paragraphs, we consider examples which are far from the shape position and we compute the LEX basis.

Cyclic-n problem. This is a well known benchmark; there are n equations in n variables, the ith equation is of degree i and is invariant by the action of the nth Cyclic group; since there is a linear equation, the actual number of variables is $n-1$. We report in Tab. 5.2, the number of rank computations and the normalized number of table queries (the number divided by the number of solutions). This number is always less than 2^{n-1}.

Example	n	D	Nb Ranks	#Queries/D
Cyclic 5	5	70	76	7.4
Cyclic 6	6	156	167	9.4
Cyclic 7	7	924	953	21.7

Ideal of points. Given a set $P \subset \mathbb{K}^n$ of t distinct points, we define the ideal $I_P = \{f \in \mathbb{K}[x_1, ..., x_n] \mid f(\mathbf{p}) = 0 \; \forall \mathbf{p} \in P\}$. We consider two such sets.

a. (Random) For any integer B, we generate exactly t points in $P_B \subset \mathbb{K}^n$ with coordinates randomly chosen in $\{0, ..., B-1\}$. Since B is a bound on the degree of the univariate polynomial in the LEX Gröbner basis, this basis is far from the shape position when $t \gg B$.

b. (Worst Case) $P_t = \{ie_j,\ 1 \leq i \leq n, 1 \leq j \leq t/n\}$. In both cases we report the ratio between the number of queries and the number of points. As expected in the first case, this ratio is a constant $c \in$

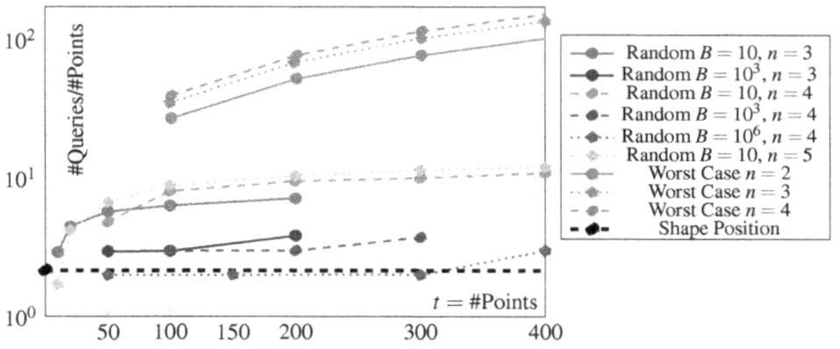

Figure 2: Number of table queries divided by number of points.

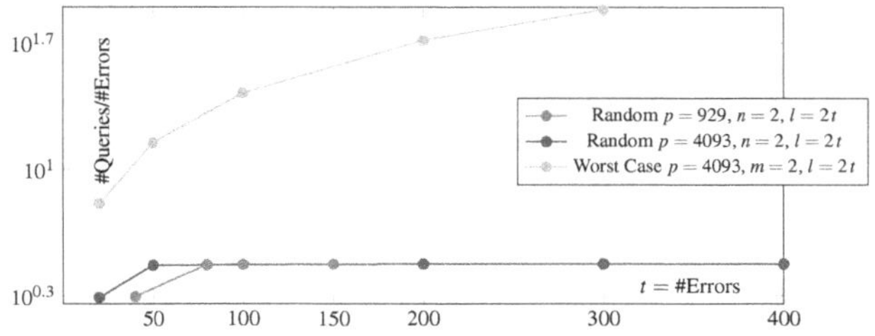

Figure 3: Number of table queries divided by number of points.

$[2, 2^n]$ depending on the value of B. In the second case, we expect a linear behavior, from Prop. 11. In Fig. 5.2 the points below the thick dashed black line correspond to Gröbner bases in shape positions.

5.3 Application to error correcting codes

In Coding Theory, n-dimensional cyclic codes with $n > 1$ are generalizations of Reed Solomon codes. We give a simplified description of such codes. Let l be an integer and $a \in \mathbb{F}_p$ such that $a^j \neq 1$ for $0 < j < p-1$. We work with polynomials in $R = \mathbb{F}_p[\mathbf{x}]/\langle x_1^{p-1} - 1, ..., x_n^{p-1} - 1\rangle$. Then we define the generating polynomials $g_i(\mathbf{x}) = \prod_{j=0}^{l-1}(x_i - a^j)$. When we send a message $\mathscr{M}$ we split this message into n blocks $\mathscr{M}^{(k)} = (c_1^{(k)}, c_2^{(k)}, ...)$ where $c_i \in \mathbb{F}_p$ and we generate n multivariate polynomials $U_k(\mathbf{x}) = c_1^{(k)} + c_2^{(k)}x_1 + c_3^{(k)}x_2 + \cdots$. The transmitter sends the encoded message $M(\mathbf{x}) = \sum_{k=1}^{n} g_k(\mathbf{x})U_k(\mathbf{x})$. The receiver interprets the received word as a multivariate polynomial $N(\mathbf{x}) = M(\mathbf{x}) + e(\mathbf{x})$ where $e(\mathbf{x}) \in R$ is the error polynomial. If the length of $e(\mathbf{x})$ is less than $t = \frac{l}{2}$ the goal is to recover it. To this end, we build the table $u_{i_1,...,i_n} := N(a^{i_1}, ..., a^{i_n}) \equiv e(a^{i_1}, ..., a^{i_n})$ in R for $0 \leq i_j < t$ and we apply Alg. 4 to obtain a LEX Gröbner basis G. It is easy to recover all the solutions in the finite field $\mathbb{F}_q$; next, by computing the discrete logarithm wrt. a of all the components we recover the position of the nonzero monomials in $e(\mathbf{x})$. Lastly, we solve a linear system to find the coefficients of $e(\mathbf{x})$.

In the experiments of Tab. 5.3, we consider two cases: (random case) we randomly generate the support and the coefficients of the error polynomial $e(\mathbf{x})$; (worst case) we take $e(\mathbf{x}) = \sum_{i=1}^{n}\sum_{j=0}^{t/n} c_{i,j}x_i^j$.

6. MULTIBLOCK HANKEL ARITHMETIC

In Alg. 3 and 4, linear systems must be solved. In this Section, we show that in fact, if $\prec$ is a LEX order, then the matrices are heavily structured as they are Hankel matrices.

Let's recall that a Gröbner basis of a 0-dimensional ideal for LEX order on $x_1, ..., x_n$ with $x_1 \prec \cdots \prec x_n$ is given in terms of non-constant polynomials $P_{1,1}(x_1)$ and $P_{i,j}(x_1, ..., x_i)$ for $i > 1$, with $\deg_{x_i} P_{i,j} \leq d_i$.

When computing $P_{1,1}$, one will only consider sets of monomials $S = \{1, x_1, ..., x_1^{d_1-1}\}$. Therefore, the matrix H_S is Hankel. When looking for $P_{2,1}, ..., P_{2,m_2}$, one needs to consider sets of monomials $S' = S \cup x_2 S_1 \cup \cdots \cup x_2^{d_2-1} S_{d_2-1}$ with $S_1, ..., S_{d_2-1} \subseteq S$. This yields the following matrix

$$H_{S'} = \begin{pmatrix} H_S & H_{x_2 S, S_1} & \cdots & H_{x_2^{d_2-1} S, S_{d_2-1}} \\ H_{x_2 S_1, S} & H_{x_2^2 S_1, S_1} & \cdots & H_{x_2^{d_2} S_1, S_{d_2-1}} \\ \vdots & \vdots & \ddots & \vdots \\ H_{x_2^{d_2-1} S_{d_2-1}, S} & H_{x_2^{d_2} S_{d_2-1}, S_1} & \cdots & H_{x_2^{2d_2-2} S_{d_2-1}, S_{d_2-1}} \end{pmatrix}$$

where each $H_{x_2^k S_i, S_j}$ is Hankel rectangular. Completing $H_{S'}$ so that each block is square, i.e. replacing each $H_{x_2^k S_i, S_j}$ by $H_{x_2^k S, S}$ makes it block Hankel with Hankel blocks. We shall say that $H_{S'}$ is *multi-block Hankel of depth* 2. Then, for $P_{3,1}, \ldots, P_{3,m_3}$ of degree at most d_3 in x_3, one will consider the matrix $H_{S''}$ that is block Hankel with blocks $H_{x_3^k S'_i, S'_j}$, $0 \le i, j \le d_3 - 1$ such that $S'_1, \ldots, S'_{d_3-1} \subseteq S'_0 = S'$. That is, they will have the same shape as $H_{S'}$ and thus can be embedded in a multiblock Hankel matrix of depth 2. The matrix $H_{S''}$ shall be called *multiblock Hankel of depth* 3. This definition extends to all $n \in \mathbb{N}^*$, with depth 1 being classical Hankel matrices.

6.1 Displacement rank

We recall that for a matrix H, a *displacement operator* φ is an operator s.t. $\varphi(H)$ has small rank. One can classically take, for H Hankel, $\varphi(H) = H - ZHZ$ with $Z = (\delta_{i-1,j})_{1 \le i,j \le d}$, where $\delta_{i,j}$ denote Kronecker's delta function. Indeed, $\varphi(H)$ has rank at most 2. This nice structure allows us to solve a linear system with a Hankel-like matrix H, i.e. a small sum of Hankel matrices, in $O(\alpha^{\omega-1} \mathsf{M}(d) \log d)$ operations if $\alpha = \operatorname{rank} \varphi(H)$ and if d is the size of H, see [2].

On block Hankel matrices, one can take the deflated operator, in which each 1 of Z is replaced by an Identity matrix of the right size. However, the expected matrix should have rank twice as much as the size of the blocks. Because our blocks are themselves Hankel, we can once again apply the displacement operator of Hankel matrices on all remaining blocks. If H is Hankel block Hankel with d_2 blocks by row or column of size d_1, then the obtained matrix has rank at most $2\min(d_1, d_2)$.

Consequently, with multiblock Hankel matrices of depth n and embedding blocks of sizes $d_1, \ldots, d_n$, one can find a displacement operator s.t. the displacement rank is at most $2\prod_{i=1}^{n} d_i / \max_{i=1}^{n} d_i$. These displacement ranks are not too small, unless e.g. all the d_i's stay constant but one that grows to infinity.

6.2 Polynomial interpretation

Fast algorithms on solving Hankel linear systems are coming from the fact that multiplying a Hankel matrix of size d with a vector can be seen as computing the middle product of univariate polynomials of sizes $2d$ and d. Solving such a system comes down to dividing a polynomial of sizes $2d$ by a polynomial of size d, which can be done in $\tilde{O}(\mathsf{M}(d))$ operations in the base field. For Hankel block Hankel linear systems with d_2 blocks of size d_1, the matrix-vector product can be seen as a generalization of the middle product of two bivariate polynomials, both of degree $d_1 - 1$ in the first variable and one of degree $d_2 - 1$ and the other $2d_2 - 1$ in the second variable. By Kronecker's trick, the complexity of solving such a system is $\tilde{O}(\mathsf{M}(2d_1 d_2))$. For multiblock Hankel of depth n system, this strategy yields a complexity in $\tilde{O}(\mathsf{M}(2^{n-1} d_1 \cdots d_n))$.

6.3 Complexity comparisons

Let us recall that d is the order of the recursive sequence $\mathbf{u}$: it is the size of the staircase of any Gröbner basis of its ideal of relations. Let also μ denote the size of the computed Gröbner basis. In [21], the complexity of BMS is given as $O(\mu d^2)$ and estimated as $O(d^3)$ with the approximation $\mu \in O(d)$. Let us remark that the only proven bound is $\mu \le nd$ [4, Cor. 2.1] making the complexity of BMS in $O(nd^3)$ operations in $\mathbb{K}$.

In the shape position situation, $d_1 = d, d_2 = \cdots = d_n = 1$; in the worst-case scenario, the staircase is a simplex with $d_1 = \cdots = d_n$ and $d_1 \cdots d_n = n!\,d$. Our complexity estimate becomes resp. $\tilde{O}(\mathsf{M}(2^{n-1} d))$ or $\tilde{O}(\mathsf{M}(2^{n-1} n!\,d))$. Both are quasi-linear in d if n is fixed.

We cannot say if one of our two algorithms could be seen as a matrix version of BMS – in which case, we would improve the complexity estimate of BMS. Finding loop invariants in these algorithms could also help make their complexities sharper and find optimal termination criteria, hence reduce the number of table queries.

Acknowledgements

We thank the anonymous referees for their careful reading and their helpful comments and Erich L. Kaltofen for valuable discussions. This work has been partly supported by the French National Research Agency ANR-11-BS02-0013 HPAC project.

7. REFERENCES

[1] E. Berlekamp. Nonbinary BCH decoding. *IEEE Trans. Inform. Theory*, 14(2):242–242, March 1968.

[2] A. Bostan, C.-P. Jeannerod, and É. Schost. Solving Toeplitz- and Vandermonde-like Linear Systems with Large Displacement Rank. In C. W. Brown, editor, *ISSAC'07*, pages 33–40. ACM Press, 2007.

[3] H. Chabanne and G. H. Norton. On the key equation for *n*-dimensional cyclic codes: applications to decoding. Tech. report INRIA RR-1796, 1992.

[4] J.-C. Faugère, P. Gianni, D. Lazard, and T. Mora. Efficient Computation of Zero-dimensional Gröbner Bases by Change of Ordering. *J. Symbolic Comput.*, 16(4):329–344, 1993.

[5] J.-C. Faugère and C. Mou. Fast Algorithm for Change of Ordering of Zero-dimensional Gröbner Bases with Sparse Multiplication Matrices. In *Proc. of the 36th ISSAC*, pages 115–122. ACM, 2011.

[6] P. Gianni and T. Mora. Algebraic solution of systems of polynomial equations using Gröbner bases. In *Proc. of AAECC-5, vol. 356 of LNCS*, pages 247–257. Springer, 1989.

[7] E. Jonckheere and C. Ma. A simple Hankel interpretation of the Berlekamp-Massey algorithm. *Linear Algebra Appl.*, 125(0):65–76, 1989.

[8] E. Kaltofen and V. Pan. Processor efficient parallel solution of linear systems over an abstract field. In *SPAA '91*, pages 180–191, New York, N.Y., 1991. ACM Press.

[9] E. Kaltofen and G. Yuhasz. A fraction free Matrix Berlekamp/Massey algorithm. *Linear Algebra Appl.*, 439(9):2515–2526, 2013.

[10] E. Kaltofen and G. Yuhasz. On the Matrix Berlekamp-Massey Algorithm. *ACM Trans. Algorithms*, 9(4):33:1–33:24, Oct. 2013.

[11] C. Koutschan. Creative Telescoping for Holonomic Functions. In C. Schneider and J. Blümlein, editors, *Computer Algebra in Quantum Field Theory*, pages 171–194. Springer Vienna, 2013.

[12] Y. N. Lakshman. On the Complexity of Computing a Gröbner Basis for the Radical of a Zero Dimensional Ideal. In *Proc. of the 22nd Annual ACM STOC*, pages 555–563. ACM, 1990.

[13] N. Levinson. The Wiener RMS (Root-Mean-Square) error criterion in the filter design and prediction. *J. Math. Phys.*, 25:261–278, 1947.

[14] J. L. Massey. Shift-register synthesis and BCH decoding. *IEEE Trans. Inform. Theory*, IT-15:122–127, 1969.

[15] A. Poteaux and É. Schost. On the complexity of computing with 0-dimensional triangular sets. *J. Symbolic Comput.*, 50(0):110–138, 2013.

[16] I. Z. Ruzsa. Generalized arithmetical progressions and sumsets. *Acta Math. Hungar.*, 65(4):379–388, 1994.

[17] K. Saints and C. Heegard. Algebraic-geometric codes and multidimensional cyclic codes: Theory and algorithms for decoding using Gröbner bases. *IEEE Trans. Inform. Theory*, 41(6):1733–1751, 1995.

[18] S. Sakata. Finding a minimal set of linear recurring relations capable of generating a given finite two-dimensional array. *J. Symbolic Comput.*, 5(3):321–337, 1988.

[19] S. Sakata. Extension of the Berlekamp-Massey algorithm to *N* Dimensions. *Inform. and Comput.*, 84(2):207–239, Feb. 1990.

[20] S. Sakata. Decoding binary 2-D cyclic codes by the 2-D Berlekamp-Massey algorithm. *IEEE Trans. Inform. Theory*, 37(4):1200–1203, 1991.

[21] S. Sakata. The BMS algorithm. In M. Sala, T. Mora, L. Perret, S. Sakata, and C. Traverso, editors, *Gröbner Bases, Coding, and Cryptography*, pages 143–163. Springer Berlin Heidelberg, 2009.

[22] N. Wiener. *Extrapolation, Interpolation, and Smoothing of Stationary Time Series.* New York Wiley, 1949. ISBN 0-262-73005-7.

A Fast Algorithm for Computing the p-Curvature

Alin Bostan
Inria (France)
alin.bostan@inria.fr

Xavier Caruso
Université Rennes 1
xavier.caruso@normalesup.org

Éric Schost
Western University
eschost@uwo.ca

ABSTRACT

We design an algorithm for computing the p-curvature of a differential system in positive characteristic p. For a system of dimension r with coefficients of degree at most d, its complexity is $O\tilde{~}(pdr^{\omega})$ operations in the ground field (where ω denotes the exponent of matrix multiplication), whereas the size of the output is about pdr^2. Our algorithm is then quasi-optimal assuming that matrix multiplication is (*i.e.* $\omega = 2$). The main theoretical input we are using is the existence of a well-suited ring of series with divided powers for which an analogue of the Cauchy–Lipschitz Theorem holds.

Categories and Subject Descriptors:
I.1.2 [**Computing Methodologies**]: Symbolic and Algebraic Manipulation – *Algebraic Algorithms*

Keywords: Algorithms, complexity, differential equations, p-curvature.

1. INTRODUCTION

We study in this article algorithmic questions related to linear differential systems in positive characteristic. Let k be an arbitrary field of prime characteristic p, and A be an $r \times r$ matrix with entries in the field $k(x)$ of rational functions over k. A simple-to-define, yet very important object attached to the differential system $Y' = AY$ is its so-called *p-curvature*. It is the p-th iterate ∂_A^p of the map $\partial_A : k(x)^r \to k(x)^r$ that sends v to $v' - Av$. It turns out that it is $k(x)$-linear. It is moreover classical that its matrix with respect to the canonical basis of $k(x)^r$ is equal to the term A_p of the recursive sequence $(A_i)_i$ defined by

$$A_1 = -A \quad \text{and} \quad A_{i+1} = A_i' - A \cdot A_i \quad \text{for} \quad i \geq 1. \qquad (1)$$

In all what follows, we will thus deliberately identify the matrix A_p with the *p-curvature of* $Y' = AY$. The above recurrence yields an algorithm for computing it, sometimes referred to as *Katz's algorithm*.

The p-curvature is related to solutions; it measures to what extent the usual Cauchy–Lipschitz theorem applies in characteristic p. More precisely, at an ordinary point, the system $Y' = AY$ admits a fundamental matrix of power series solutions in $k[[x]]$ if and only if the p-curvature A_p vanishes. In this case, the system $Y' = AY$ even admits a fundamental matrix of solutions which are rational functions in $k(x)$. More generally, the dimension of the kernel of A_p is equal to the dimension of the space of rational function solutions of $Y' = AY$.

The primary importance of the notion of p-curvature relies in its occurrence in one of the versions of the celebrated Grothendieck–Katz conjecture [19, 20, 12, 30]. This conjecture, first formulated by Alexandre Grothendieck in the late 1960s, is a local-global principle for linear differential systems, which states that a linear differential system with rational function coefficients over a function field admits a fundamental matrix of algebraic solutions if and only if its p-curvatures vanish for almost all primes p.

In computer algebra, p-curvature has been introduced by van der Put [22, 23], who popularized it as a tool for factoring differential operators in characteristic p. Cluzeau [13] generalized the approach to the decomposition of differential systems over $k(x)$. The p-curvature has also been used by Cluzeau and van Hoeij [14] as an algorithmic filter for computing exponential solutions of differential operators in characteristic zero.

Computing efficiently the p-curvature is in itself a challenging problem, especially for large values of p. Our initial motivation for studying this question emerged from concrete applications, in lattice path combinatorics [6, 7] and in statistical physics [3]. In this article, we address the question of the computation of A_p in good complexity, with respect to three parameters: the dimension r of the system $Y' = AY$, the maximum degree d of the rational function entries of A, and the characteristic p of the ground field. In terms of these quantities, the arithmetical size of A_p is generically proportional to pdr^2 if $r > 1$.

Previous work. Cluzeau [13, Prop. 3.2] observed that the direct algorithm based on recurrence (1) has complexity $O\tilde{~}(p^2dr^{\omega})$, where ω is the matrix multiplication exponent and the soft-O notation $O\tilde{~}(\,)$ hides polylogarithmic factors. Compared to the size of the p-curvature, this cost is good with respect to r and d, but not to p. The first subquadratic algorithm in p, of complexity $O\tilde{~}(p^{1+\omega/3})$, was designed in [9, §6.3]. In some special cases, additional partial results were obtained in [9], notably an algorithm of quasi-linear cost $O\tilde{~}(p)$ for certain systems of order $r = 2$. However, the question of designing a general algorithm for computing A_p with quasi-linear complexity in p remained open. In a related, but

ISSAC'15, July 6–9, 2015, Bath, United Kingdom..

ACM 978-1-4503-3435-8/15/07 ...$15.00.
http://dx.doi.org/10.1145/2755996.2756674.

different direction, the article [4] proposed an algorithm for computing the characteristic polynomial of the p-curvature in time essentially linear in $\sqrt{p}$, without computing A_p itself.

Contribution. We prove that the p-curvature A_p can be computed in quasi-linear time with respect to p. More precisely, our main result (Theorem 4.2) states that $\tilde{O}(pdr^\omega)$ operations in k are sufficient for this task. This complexity result is quasi-optimal not only with respect to the main parameter p, but also to d; with respect to the dimension r, it is as optimal as matrix multiplication. Moreover the algorithm we obtain is highly parallelizable by design. The key tools underlying the proof of Theorem 4.2 are the notion of divided power rings in characteristic p, and a new formula for the p-curvature (Propositions 4.3 and 4.4) in terms of divided power series. Crucial ingredients are the fact that a Cauchy–Lipschitz theorem for differential systems holds over divided power rings (Proposition 3.4) and the fact that Newton iteration can be used to efficiently compute (truncations of) fundamental matrices of divided power solutions.

Structure of the paper. In Section 2, we recall the main theoretical properties of the basic objects used in this article. Section 3 is devoted to the existence and the computation of solutions of differential systems in divided power rings. In Section 4, we move to the main objective of the article, the computation of the p-curvature: after relating A_p to the framework of divided powers, we describe our main algorithm for A_p, of complexity $\tilde{O}(pdr^\omega)$. We conclude in Section 5 by describing the implementation of our algorithm and some benchmarks.

Complexity measures. Throughout this article, we estimate the cost of our algorithms by counting arithmetic operations in the base ring or field at unit cost.

We use standard complexity notations. The letter ω refers to a feasible exponent for matrix multiplication (*i.e.* there exists an algorithm for multiplying $n \times n$ matrices over a ring $\mathfrak{A}$ with at most $O(n^\omega)$ operations in $\mathfrak{A}$); the best known bound is $\omega < 2.3729$ from [15]. The soft-O notation $\tilde{O}(\cdot)$ indicates that polylogarithmic factors are omitted; in particular, we will use the fact that many arithmetic operations on univariate polynomials of degree d can be done in $\tilde{O}(d)$ operations: addition, multiplication, Chinese remaindering, *etc*, the key to these results being fast polynomial multiplication [27, 26, 11, 18]. A general reference for these questions is [17].

2. THEORETICAL SETTING

We introduce and briefly recall the main properties of the theoretical objects we are going to use in this article. All the material presented in this section is classical; a general reference is [24].

Definitions and notations. Let $\mathfrak{A}$ be a commutative ring with unit. We recall that a *derivation* on $\mathfrak{A}$ is an additive map $' : \mathfrak{A} \to \mathfrak{A}$, satisfying the Leibniz rule $(fg)' = f'g + fg'$ for all $f, g \in \mathfrak{A}$. The image f' of f under the derivation is called the *derivative* of f. From now on, we assume that $\mathfrak{A}$ is equipped with a derivation. A *differential system* with coefficients in $\mathfrak{A}$ is an equation of the form $Y' = AY$ where A is a given $r \times r$ matrix with coefficients in $\mathfrak{A}$ (for a certain positive integer r), the unknown Y is a column vector of length r and Y' denotes the vector obtained from Y by taking the derivative component-wise. The integer r is called the *dimension* of the system. We recall briefly that a linear differential equation:

$$a_r y^{(r)} + \cdots + a_1 y' + a_0 y = 0 \quad (\text{with } a_i \in \mathfrak{A}) \tag{2}$$

can be viewed as a particular case of a differential system. Indeed, defining the companion matrix

$$C = \begin{pmatrix} & & & -\frac{a_0}{a_r} \\ 1 & & & -\frac{a_1}{a_r} \\ & \ddots & & \vdots \\ & & 1 & -\frac{a_{r-1}}{a_r} \end{pmatrix} \tag{3}$$

and $A = {}^tC$, the solutions of the system $Y' = AY$ are exactly the vectors of the form ${}^t(y, y', \ldots, y^{(r-1)})$ where y is a solution of (2). In this correspondence, the order of the differential equation agrees with the dimension of the associated differential system.

Differential modules. A *differential module* over $\mathfrak{A}$ is a pair (M, ∂) where M is an $\mathfrak{A}$-module and $\partial : M \to M$ is an additive map satisfying a Leibniz-like rule, which is:

$$\forall f \in \mathfrak{A}, \forall x \in M, \quad \partial(fx) = f' \cdot x + f \cdot \partial(x). \tag{4}$$

There exists a canonical one-to-one correspondence between differential systems and differential modules (M, ∂) for which $M = \mathfrak{A}^r$ for some r: to a differential system $Y' = AY$ of dimension r, we attach the differential module $(\mathfrak{A}^r, \partial_A)$ where $\partial_A : \mathfrak{A}^r \to \mathfrak{A}^r$ is the function mapping X to $X' - AX$. Under this correspondence, the solutions of $Y' = AY$ are exactly vectors in the kernel of ∂_A.

To a differential equation as (2), one can associate the *differential operator* $L = a_r\partial^r + a_{r-1}\partial^{r-1} + \cdots + a_1\partial + a_0$; it lies in the non-commutative ring $\mathfrak{A}\langle\partial\rangle$, endowed with the usual addition of polynomials and a multiplication ruled by the relation $\partial \cdot f = f \cdot \partial + f'$ for all $f \in \mathfrak{A}$ (note that, as often in the literature, we are using ∂ to denote either the structure map of a differential module, and a non-commutative indeterminate).

Then, if a_r is a unit in $\mathfrak{A}$, one can further associate to L the quotient $\mathfrak{A}\langle\partial\rangle/\mathfrak{A}\langle\partial\rangle L \simeq \mathfrak{A}^r$. The differential structure inherited from $\mathfrak{A}\langle\partial\rangle$ makes it a differential module with structure map $X \in \mathfrak{A}^r \mapsto X' + CX$, where C is the companion matrix defined above; in other words, this is the module $(\mathfrak{A}\langle\partial\rangle/\mathfrak{A}\langle\partial\rangle L, \partial_{-C})$, with the previous notation.

Scalar extension. Let $\mathfrak{A}$ and $\mathfrak{B}$ be two rings equipped with derivations and let $\varphi : \mathfrak{A} \to \mathfrak{B}$ be a ring homomorphism commuting with derivation. From a given differential system $Y' = AY$ with coefficients in $\mathfrak{A}$, one can build a differential system over $\mathfrak{B}$ by applying φ: it is $Y' = \varphi(A)Y$, where $\varphi(A)$ is the matrix obtained from A by applying φ entry-wise.

This operation admits an analogue at the level of differential modules: to a differential module (M, ∂) over $\mathfrak{A}$, we attach the differential module $(M_\mathfrak{B}, \partial_\mathfrak{B})$ over $\mathfrak{B}$ where $M_\mathfrak{B} = \mathfrak{B} \otimes_{\varphi,\mathfrak{A}} M$ and $\partial_\mathfrak{B} : M_\mathfrak{B} \to M_\mathfrak{B}$ is defined by:

$$\forall f \in \mathfrak{B}, \forall x \in M, \quad \partial_\mathfrak{B}(f \otimes x) = f' \otimes x + f \otimes \partial(x).$$

It is easily seen that if (M, ∂) is a differential module associated to the system $Y' = AY$ then $(M_\mathfrak{B}, \partial_\mathfrak{B})$ is that associated to the system $Y' = \varphi(A)Y$.

The p-curvature. Let k be any field of characteristic p. We assume here that $\mathfrak{A}$ is the field $k(x)$ — consisting of rational functions over k — equipped with the standard derivation.

The *p-curvature* of a differential module (M, ∂) over $k(x)$ is defined as the mapping $\partial^p : M \to M$. It follows from the Leibniz rule (4) and the fact that the p-th derivative of any element of $k(x)$ vanishes that the p-curvature is $k(x)$-linear.

This definition extends to differential systems as follows: the p-curvature of the system $Y' = AY$ is the $k(x)$-linear map $\partial_A^p : M_A \to M_A$ where (M_A, ∂_A) is the corresponding differential module. One can check that the matrix of ∂_A^p (in the canonical basis of M_A) is the p-th term of the recursive sequence (A_i) defined in (1).

Considering again a differential operator L and the associated differential module $(\mathfrak{A}\langle\partial\rangle/\mathfrak{A}\langle\partial\rangle L, \partial_{-C})$, for the associated companion matrix C, we obtain the usual recurrence $A_1 = C$ and $A_{i+1} = A_i' + C \cdot A_i$. The p-curvature of $\mathfrak{A}\langle\partial\rangle/\mathfrak{A}\langle\partial\rangle L$ will simply be called the p-curvature of L.

3. SERIES WITH DIVIDED POWERS

In all this section, we let ℓ be a ring in which p vanishes. We recall the definition of the divided power ring over ℓ, and its main properties — mainly, a Cauchy–Lipschitz theorem that will allow us to compute solutions of differential systems. We show how some approaches that are well-known for power series solutions carry over without significant changes in this context. Most results in this section are not new; those from §3.1 and §3.2 are implicitly contained in [1, 2], while the theoretical basis of §3.3 is similar to [21].

3.1 The ring $\ell[[t]]^{\mathrm{dp}}$

Let $\ell[[t]]^{\mathrm{dp}}$ be the ring of formal series of the form:

$$f = a_0 + a_1\gamma_1(t) + a_2\gamma_2(t) + \cdots + a_i\gamma_i(t) + \cdots \qquad (5)$$

where the a_i's are elements of ℓ and each $\gamma_i(t)$ is a symbol which should be thought of as $\frac{t^i}{i!}$. The multiplication on $\ell[[t]]^{\mathrm{dp}}$ is defined by the rule $\gamma_i(t) \cdot \gamma_j(t) = \binom{i+j}{i} \cdot \gamma_{i+j}(t)$.

Remark 3.1. *The ring $\ell[[t]]^{\mathrm{dp}}$ is not the PD-envelope in the sense of [1, 2] of $\ell[[t]]$ with respect to the ideal (t) but its completion for the topology defined by the divided powers ideals. Taking the completion is essential to have an analogue of the Cauchy–Lipschitz Theorem (*cf *Proposition 3.4).*

Invertible elements of $\ell[[t]]^{\mathrm{dp}}$ are easily described: they are exactly those for which the "constant" coefficient a_0 is invertible in ℓ. The ring $\ell[[t]]^{\mathrm{dp}}$ is moreover endowed with a derivation defined by $f' = \sum_{i=0}^{\infty} a_{i+1}\gamma_i(t)$ for $f = \sum_{i=0}^{\infty} a_i\gamma_i(t)$. It then makes sense to consider differential systems over $\ell[[t]]^{\mathrm{dp}}$. A significant difference with power series is the existence of an integral operator: it maps f as above to $\int f = \sum_{i=0}^{\infty} a_i\gamma_{i+1}(t)$ and satisfies $(\int f)' = f$ for all f.

Divided power ideals. For all positive integers N, we denote by $\ell[[t]]^{\mathrm{dp}}_{\geq N}$ the ideal of $\ell[[t]]^{\mathrm{dp}}$ consisting of series of the form $\sum_{i \geq N} a_i\gamma_i(t)$. The quotient $\ell[[t]]^{\mathrm{dp}}/\ell[[t]]^{\mathrm{dp}}_{\geq N}$ is a free ℓ-module of rank N and a basis of it is $(1, \gamma_1(t), \ldots, \gamma_{N-1}(t))$. In particular, for $N = 1$, the quotient $\ell[[t]]^{\mathrm{dp}}/\ell[[t]]^{\mathrm{dp}}_{\geq 1}$ is isomorphic to ℓ: in the sequel, we shall denote by $f(0) \in \ell$ the reduction of an element $f \in \ell[[t]]^{\mathrm{dp}}$ modulo $\ell[[t]]^{\mathrm{dp}}_{\geq 1}$. On the writing (5), it is nothing but the constant coefficient a_0 in the expansion of f.

We draw the reader's attention to the fact that $\ell[[t]]^{\mathrm{dp}}_{\geq N}$ is *not* stable under derivation, so the quotients $\ell[[t]]^{\mathrm{dp}}/\ell[[t]]^{\mathrm{dp}}_{\geq N}$ do *not* inherit a derivation.

Relationship with $\ell[t]$. There exists a natural map $\varepsilon : \ell[t] \to \ell[[t]]^{\mathrm{dp}}$ taking a polynomial $\sum_i a_i t^i$ to $\sum_{i=0}^{p-1} a_i i! \cdot \gamma_i(t)$. The latter sum stops at $i = p-1$ because $i!$ becomes divisible by p after that. Clearly, the kernel of ε is the principal ideal generated by t^p. Hence ε factors through $\ell[t]/t^p$ as follows:

$$\ell[t] \xrightarrow{\mathrm{pr}} \ell[t]/t^p \xrightarrow{\iota} \ell[[t]]^{\mathrm{dp}} \qquad (6)$$

where pr is the canonical projection taking a polynomial to its reduction modulo t^p. We observe moreover that the ideal $t^p\ell[t]$ is stable under derivation and, consequently, that the quotient ring $\ell[t]/t^p$ inherits a derivation. Furthermore, the two mappings in (6) commute with the derivation.

3.2 Computations with divided powers

It turns out that the $\gamma_n(t)$'s can all be expressed in terms of only few of them, resulting in a more flexible description of the ring $\ell[[t]]^{\mathrm{dp}}$. To make this precise, we set $t_i = \gamma_{p^i}(t)$ and first observe that $t_i^n = n! \cdot \gamma_{np^i}(t)$ for all i and n; this is proved by induction on n, using the equalities

$$t_i^{n+1} = n! \cdot \gamma_{np^i}(t) \cdot \gamma_{p^i}(t) = n! \cdot \tbinom{(n+1)p^i}{p^i}\gamma_{(n+1)p^i}(t),$$

since Lucas' Theorem shows that $\binom{(n+1)p^i}{p^i} \equiv n+1 \pmod{p}$. In particular $t_i^p = 0$ for all i.

Proposition 3.2. *Let n be a positive integer and $n = \sum_{i=0}^{s} n_i p^i$ its writing in basis p. Then:*

$$\gamma_n(t) = \gamma_{n_0}(t) \cdot \gamma_{n_1 p}(t) \cdots \gamma_{n_s p^s}(t) = \frac{t_0^{n_0}}{n_0!} \cdot \frac{t_1^{n_1}}{n_1!} \cdots \frac{t_s^{n_s}}{n_s!}.$$

Proof. The first equality is proved by induction on s using the fact that if $n = a + bp$ with $0 \leq a < p$, then $\gamma_a\gamma_{bp} = \gamma_n$, since $\binom{a+bp}{a} \equiv 1 \pmod{p}$. The second equality then follows from the relations $t_i^{n_i} = n_i! \cdot \gamma_{n_i p^i}(t)$. □

A corollary of the above proposition is that elements of $\ell[[t]]^{\mathrm{dp}}$ can be alternatively described as infinite sums of monomials $a_{n_0,\ldots,n_s} \cdot t_0^{n_0} \cdot t_1^{n_1} \cdots t_s^{n_s}$ where the n_i's are integers in the range $[0, p)$ and the coefficient $a_{n_0,\ldots,n_s}$ lies in ℓ. The product in $\ell[[t]]^{\mathrm{dp}}$ is then the usual product of series subject to the additional rules $t_i^p = 0$ for all i.

More precisely, restricting ourselves to some given precision of the form $N = np^s$, we deduce from the above discussion the following corollary.

Corollary 3.3. *For $N = np^s$, with $s \in \mathbb{N}$ and $n \in \{1, \ldots, p\}$, there is a canonical isomorphism of ℓ-algebras:*

$$\ell[[t]]^{\mathrm{dp}}/\ell[[t]]^{\mathrm{dp}}_{\geq N} \simeq \ell[t_0, \ldots, t_s]/(t_0^p, \ldots, t_{s-1}^p, t_s^n).$$

For instance, if we take $s = 0$ and $N = n$ in $\{1, \ldots, p\}$, we obtain the isomorphism $\ell[[t]]^{\mathrm{dp}}/\ell[[t]]^{\mathrm{dp}}_{\geq N} \simeq \ell[t]/t^N$.

In terms of complexity, the change of bases between left- and right-hand sides can both be done in $\tilde{O}(N)$ operations in ℓ: all the factorials we need can be computed once and for all for $O(\min(N, p))$ operations; then each monomial conversion takes $O(s) = O(\log(N))$ operations, for a total of $O(N \log(N)) = \tilde{O}(N)$.

The previous corollary is useful in order to devise a multiplication algorithm for divided powers, since it reduces this question to multivariate power series multiplication (addition takes linear time in both bases). To multiply in $\ell[t_0, \ldots, t_s]/(t_0^p, \ldots, t_{s-1}^p, t_s^n)$, one can use a direct algorithm: multiply and discard unwanted terms. Using for instance

Kronecker's substitution and FFT-based univariate arithmetic, we find that a multiplication in $\ell[[t]]^{\mathrm{dp}}$ at precision N (*i.e.* modulo $\ell[[t]]^{\mathrm{dp}}_{\geq N}$) can be performed with $\tilde{O}(2^{\log_p N} N)$ operations in k. A solution that leads to a cost $N^{1+\varepsilon}$ for any $\varepsilon > 0$ is in [28], but the former result will be sufficient.

3.3 The Cauchy–Lipschitz Theorem

A nice feature of the ring $\ell[[t]]^{\mathrm{dp}}$ — which does not hold for $\ell[[t]]$ notably — is the existence of an analogue of the classical Cauchy–Lipschitz theorem. This property will have a fundamental importance for the purpose of our paper; see for instance [21, Proposition 4.2] for similar considerations.

PROPOSITION 3.4. *Let $Y' = AY$ be a differential system of dimension r with coefficients in $\ell[[t]]^{\mathrm{dp}}$. For all initial data $V \in \ell^r$ (considered as a column vector) the following Cauchy problem has a unique solution in $\ell[[t]]^{\mathrm{dp}}$:*

$$\begin{cases} Y' = A \cdot Y \\ Y(0) = V. \end{cases}$$

PROOF. Let us write the expansions of A and Y:

$$A = \sum_{i=0}^{\infty} A_i \gamma_i(t) \quad \text{and} \quad Y = \sum_{i=0}^{\infty} Y_i \gamma_i(t)$$

where the A_i's and Y_i's have coefficients in ℓ. The Cauchy problem translates to $Y_0 = V$ and $Y_{n+1} = \sum_{i=0}^{n} \binom{n}{i} \cdot A_i \cdot Y_{n-i}$. It is now clear that it has a unique solution. □

Of course, Proposition 3.4 extends readily to the case where the initial data V is any matrix having r rows. In particular, taking $V = I_r$ (the identity matrix of size r), we find that there exists a unique $r \times r$ matrix Y with coefficients in $\ell[[t]]^{\mathrm{dp}}$ such that $Y(0) = I_r$ and $Y' = A \cdot Y$. This matrix is often called a *fundamental system of solutions.*

Finding solutions using Newton iteration. In characteristic zero, it is possible to compute power series solutions of a differential system such as $Y' = A \cdot Y$ using Newton iteration; an algorithm for this is presented on [5, Fig. 1].

One can use this algorithm to compute a fundamental system of solutions in our context. For this, we first need to introduce two notations. Given an element $f \in \ell[[t]]^{\mathrm{dp}}$ written as $f = \sum_i a_i \gamma_i(t)$ together with an integer m, we set $\lceil f \rceil^m = \sum_{i=0}^{m-1} a_i \gamma_i(t)$. Similarly, if M is a matrix with coefficients in $\ell[[t]]^{\mathrm{dp}}$, we define $\lceil M \rceil^m$ and $\int M$ by applying the corresponding operations entry-wise.

Algorithm `fundamental_solutions`
Input: a differential system $Y' = AY$, an integer N
Output: the fund. system of solutions modulo $\ell[[t]]^{\mathrm{dp}}_{\geq N}$

1. $Y = I_r + t\,A(0)$; $Z = I_r$; $m = 2$
2. **while** $m \leq N/2$:
3. $\quad Z = Z + \lceil Z(I_r - YZ) \rceil^m$
4. $\quad Y = Y - \left\lceil Y\left(\int Z \cdot (Y' - \lceil A \rceil^{2m-1} Y)\right) \right\rceil^{2m}$
5. $\quad m = 2m$
6. **return** Y

Correction is proved as in the classical case [5, Lemma 1].

Let us take $n \in \{2, \ldots, p\}$ and $s \in \mathbb{N}$ such that $n-1$ is the last digit of N written in basis p, and s the corresponding exponent; then, we have $(n-1)p^s \leq N < np^s$. Since we are only interested in costs up to logarithmic factors, we may assume that we do all operations at precision np^s (a better analysis would take into account the fact that the precision grows quadratically).

By Corollary 3.3 and the discussion that follows, arithmetic operations in $\ell[[t]]^{\mathrm{dp}} / \ell[[t]]^{\mathrm{dp}}_{\geq np^s}$ take time $\tilde{O}(2^{\log_p N} N)$. This is also the case for differentiation and integration, in view of the formulas given in the previous subsection; truncation is free. The total complexity of Algorithm `fundamental_solutions` is therefore $\tilde{O}(2^{\log_p N} N r^{\omega})$ operations in ℓ, where r is the dimension of the differential system. If $N = p^{O(1)}$, which is what we need later on, this is $\tilde{O}(N r^{\omega})$.

The case of differential operators. We now consider the case of the differential system associated to a differential operator $L = a_r \partial^r + \cdots + a_1 \partial + a_0 \in \ell[[t]]^{\mathrm{dp}}\langle\partial\rangle$. We will work under the following few assumptions: we assume that a_r is invertible, and that there exists an integer $d < p$ such that all a_i's can be written $a_i = \alpha_{i,0} + \alpha_{i,1}\gamma_1(t) + \cdots + \alpha_{i,d}\gamma_d(t)$ for some coefficients $\alpha_{i,j}$ in ℓ; thus, by assumption, $\alpha_{r,0}$ is a unit in ℓ. Our goal is still to compute a basis of solutions up to precision N; the algorithm is a direct adaptation of a classical construction to the case of divided powers.

In all that follows, we let $f_0, \ldots, f_{r-1}$ be the solutions of L in $\ell[[t]]^{\mathrm{dp}}$, such that f_i is the unique solution of the Cauchy problem (*cf* Proposition 3.4):

$$L(f_i) = 0 \quad ; \quad f_i^{(j)}(0) = \delta_{ij} \quad \text{for } 0 \leq j < r \qquad (7)$$

where δ_{ij} is the Kronecker delta. For $f = \sum_{j=0}^{\infty} \xi_j \gamma_j(t)$ in $\ell[[t]]^{\mathrm{dp}}$, a direct computation shows that the n-th coefficient of $L(f)$ is $\sum_{i=0}^{r} \sum_{j=0}^{n} \binom{n}{j} \alpha_{i,j} \xi_{n+i-j}$. Assume $L(f) = 0$. Then, extracting the term in ξ_{n+r}, and using that $\alpha_{i,j} = 0$ for $j > d$, we get $\xi_{n+r} = \frac{-1}{\alpha_{r,0}} \sum_{i=0}^{r-1} \sum_{j=0}^{d} \binom{n}{j} \alpha_{i,j} \xi_{n+i-j}$. Letting $m = i - j$, we find $\xi_{n+r} = \sum_{m=-d}^{r-1} A_m(n) \xi_{n+m}$ with

$$A_m(n) = \frac{-1}{\alpha_{r,0}} \sum_{i=0}^{r-1} \binom{n}{i-m} \alpha_{i,i-m} = \sum_{\substack{0 \leq i \leq r-1 \\ 0 \leq i-m \leq d}} \frac{-\alpha_{i,i-m}}{\alpha_{r,0}(i-m)!} n^{\underline{i-m}}$$

and $n^{\underline{i-m}} = n(n-1)\cdots(n-(i-m-1))$ is a falling factorial. The expression above for A_m is well-defined, since we assumed that $d < p$, and shows that A_m is a polynomial of degree at most d.

From this, writing the algorithm is easy. We need two subroutines: `from_falling_factorial`(F), which computes the expansion on the monomial basis of a polynomial of the form $F = \sum_{0 \leq j \leq n} f_j n^{\underline{j}}$, and `eval`$(F, N)$, which computes the values of a polynomial F at the N points $\{0, \ldots, N-1\}$. The former can be done using the divide-and-conquer algorithm of [8, Section 3] in time $\tilde{O}(n)$; the latter by the algorithm of [17, Chapter 10], in time $\tilde{O}(\deg(F) + N)$. The previous discussion leads to the algorithm `solutions_operator` below. In view of the previous discussion, the cost analysis is straightforward (at step 2., notice that all required factorials can be computed in time $O(d)$). The costs reported in the pseudo-code indicate the *total* amount of time spent at the corresponding line.

Algorithm `solutions_operator`
Input: a differential operator $L \in \ell[[t]]^{\mathrm{dp}}\langle\partial\rangle$ of bidegree (d, r), with $d < p$; an integer N
Output: the solutions $f_0, \ldots, f_{r-1}$ at precision N

1. **for** $m = -d, \dots, r-1$:
2. $\quad \hat{A}_m = \sum_{0 \le i \le r-1, 0 \le i-m \le d} \frac{-\alpha_{i,i-m}}{\alpha_{r,0}(i-m)!} \, \underline{x^{i-m}}$
   $\quad$ Cost: $O(d(r+d))$
3. $\quad A_m =$ `from_falling_factorial`$(\hat{A}_m)$
   $\quad$ Cost: $O\tilde{~}(d(r+d))$
4. $\quad$ Store `eval`$(A_m, N-r)$
   $\quad$ Cost: $O\tilde{~}((d+N)(r+d))$
5. **for** $i = 0, \dots, r-1$:
6. $\quad f_i = [0, \dots, 0, 1, 0, \dots, 0]$ (ith unit vector of length r)
   $\quad$ Cost: $O(r^2)$
7. $\quad$ **for** $n = 0, \dots, N-r-1$:
8. $\quad\quad f_{i,n+r} = \sum_{m=-d}^{r-1} A_m(n) f_{i,n+m}$
   $\quad\quad$ Cost: $O(rN(r+d))$
9. **return** $f_0, \dots, f_{r-1}$

Altogether, we obtain the following result, where we use the assumption $N > d$ to simplify slightly the cost estimate.

Lemma 3.5. *Suppose that $p < d$. Given a positive $N > d$, the classes of $f_0, \dots, f_{r-1}$ modulo $\ell[[t]]^{\mathrm{dp}}_{\ge N}$ can be computed with at most $O(rN(r+d))$ operations in ℓ.*

In particular, Algorithm `solutions_operator` has a better cost than `fundamental_solutions` when $d = O(r^{\omega-1})$.

4. COMPUTING THE P-CURVATURE

In all this section, we work over a field k of characteristic $p > 0$. We consider a differential system $Y' = AY$ of dimension r and denote by A_p the matrix of its p-curvature. We write $A = \frac{1}{f_A}\tilde{A}$, where f_A is in $k[x]$ and $\tilde{A}$ is a matrix with polynomial entries. Let $d = \max(\deg f_A, \deg \tilde{A})$, where $\deg \tilde{A}$ is the maximal degree of the entries of $\tilde{A}$. We recall ([13, Prop. 3.2], [9, Lemma 1]) a bound on the size of A_p. The bound follows from the recurrence (1), and it is tight.

Lemma 4.1. *The entries of the matrix $f_A^p \cdot A_p$ are all polynomials of degree at most dp.*

The goal of this section is to prove the following theorem.

Theorem 4.2. *There exists an algorithm (presented below) which computes the matrix of the p-curvature of the differential system $Y' = AY$ in $O\tilde{~}(pdr^\omega)$ operations in k.*

It is instructive to compare this cost with the size of the output. By Lemma 4.1, the latter is an $r \times r$ matrix whose entries are rational functions whose numerator and denominator have degree $\simeq pd$, so its size is roughly pdr^2 elements of k. Our result $O\tilde{~}(pdr^\omega)$ is quasi-optimal if we assume that matrix multiplication can be performed in quasi-optimal time.

4.1 A formula for the p-curvature

Let A_p denote the matrix of the p-curvature of the differential system $Y' = AY$ (in the usual monomial basis). The expression of A_p given at the very end of §2 is unfortunately not well-suited for fast computation. The aim of this subsection is to give an alternative formula for A_p using the framework of divided powers.

In order to relate $k(x)$ and a ring $\ell[[t]]^{\mathrm{dp}}$, we pick a separable polynomial $S \in k[x]$ which is coprime with f_A and set $\ell = k[x]/S$ (which is thus not necessarily a field). Let $a \in \ell$ be the class of x. We consider the ring homomorphism:

$$\begin{array}{rccc} \varphi_S: & k[x] & \to & \ell[t]/t^p \\ & f(x) & \mapsto & f(t+a) \bmod t^p. \end{array}$$

Regarding the differential structure, we observe that φ_S commutes with the derivation when $\ell[t]/t^p$ is endowed with the standard derivation $\frac{d}{dt}$. We furthermore deduce from the fact that S and f_A are coprime that φ_S extends to a homomorphism of differential rings $k[x][\frac{1}{f_A}] \to \ell[t]/t^p$ that we continue to denote by φ_S. We set $\psi_S = \iota \circ \varphi_S$ where ι is the canonical inclusion $\ell[t]/t^p \hookrightarrow \ell[[t]]^{\mathrm{dp}}$ (*cf* §3). As before, ψ_S commutes with the derivation. Finally, because S is separable, we can check that φ_S is surjective and its kernel is the ideal generated by S^p. Hence φ_S induces an isomorphism:

$$k[x]/S^p = k[x][\tfrac{1}{f_A}]/S^p \xrightarrow{\sim} \ell[t]/t^p. \qquad (8)$$

Let Y_S be a fundamental system of solutions of the differential system $Y' = \psi_S(A) \cdot Y$, *i.e.* Y_S is an $r \times r$ matrix with coefficients in $\ell[[t]]^{\mathrm{dp}}$ such that $Y_S(0) = I_r$ and $Y_S' = \psi_S(A) \cdot Y_S$. The existence of Y_S is guaranteed by Proposition 3.4. Moreover, the matrix Y_S is invertible because $Y_S(0) = I_r$ is.

Proposition 4.3. *Keeping the above notations, we have:*

$$\varphi_S(A_p) = -Y_S^{(p)} \cdot Y_S^{-1} \qquad (9)$$

where $Y_S^{(p)}$ is the matrix obtained from Y_S by taking the p-th derivative entry-wise.

Proof. We set $Z_S = Y_S^{-1}$ and let (M, ∂) denote the differential module over $\ell[[t]]^{\mathrm{dp}}$ associated to the differential system $Y' = \psi_S(A)Y$. Let $y_1, \dots, y_r$ denote the column vectors of Y_S. They are all solutions of the system $Y' = \psi_S(A)Y$, meaning that $\partial(y_i) = 0$ for all i. Furthermore, if $(e_1, \dots, e_r)$ is the canonical basis of $(\ell[[t]]^{\mathrm{dp}})^r$, we have the matrix relations: ${}^{\mathrm{t}}Y_S \cdot \underline{e} = \underline{y}$ and $\underline{e} = {}^{\mathrm{t}}Z_S \cdot \underline{y}$ where $\underline{y}$ (resp. $\underline{e}$) is the column vector whose coordinates are the vectors y_i's (resp. the e_i's). Applying ∂ to the above relation, we find $\partial(\underline{e}) = {}^{\mathrm{t}}Z_S' \cdot \underline{y} + {}^{\mathrm{t}}Z_S \cdot \partial(\underline{y}) = {}^{\mathrm{t}}Z_S' \cdot \underline{y}$ and iterating this p times, we deduce $\partial^p(\underline{e}) = {}^{\mathrm{t}}Z_S^{(p)} \cdot \underline{y} = {}^{\mathrm{t}}Z_S^{(p)} \cdot {}^{\mathrm{t}}Y_S \cdot \underline{e}$. On the other hand, the matrix $\psi_S(A_p)$ of the p-curvature is defined by the relation $\partial^p(\underline{e}) = {}^{\mathrm{t}}\psi_S(A_p) \cdot \underline{e}$. Therefore we get $\psi_S(A_p) = Y_S \cdot Z_S^{(p)}$. Now differentiating p times the relation $Y_S Z_S = I_r$, we find $Y_S^{(p)} Z_S + Y_S \cdot Z_S^{(p)} = 0$. Combining this with the above formula for $\psi_S(A_p)$ concludes the proof. □

In our setting, the matrix A_p has coefficients in $k[x][\frac{1}{f_A}]$ (*cf* Lemma 4.1), from which we deduce that $\psi_S(A_p)$ has actually coefficients in the subring $\ell[t]/t^p$ of $\ell[[t]]^{\mathrm{dp}}$. Therefore, using Eq. (9), one can compute $\psi_S(A_p)$ knowing only Y_S modulo the ideal $\ell[[t]]^{\mathrm{dp}}_{\ge 2p}$.

One can actually go further in this direction and establish a variant of Eq. (9) giving an expression of $\psi_S(A_p)$ which involves only the reduction of Y_S modulo $\ell[[t]]^{\mathrm{dp}}_{\ge p}$. To make this precise, we need an extra notation. Given an integer $i \in [0, p)$ and a polynomial $f \in \ell[t]/t^p$ (resp. a matrix M with coefficients in $\ell[t]/t^p$), we write $\mathrm{Coeff}(f, i)$ (resp. $\mathrm{Coeff}(M, i)$) for the coefficient in t^i in f (resp. in M).

PROPOSITION 4.4. *Keeping the above notations, we have:*

$$\psi_S(A_p) = -\bar{Y}_S \cdot Y_S^{(p)}(0) \cdot \bar{Y}_S^{-1}$$
$$= \bar{Y}_S \cdot \mathrm{Coeff}(A \cdot \bar{Y}_S,\, p{-}1) \cdot \bar{Y}_S^{-1} \qquad (10)$$

where we have set $\bar{Y}_S = Y_S \bmod \ell[[t]]^{\mathrm{dp}}_{\geq p}$.

PROOF. Differentiating p times the relation $Y_S' = \psi_S(A) \cdot Y_S$, we observe that $Y_S^{(p)}$ is solution of the same differential system $Y' = \psi_S(A)Y$. Hence, thanks to uniqueness in Cauchy–Lipschitz Theorem, we have the relation $Y_S^{(p)} = Y_S \cdot Y_S^{(p)}(0)$. The first part of the Proposition follows by plugging this in Eq. (9) and reducing the result modulo $\ell[[t]]^{\mathrm{dp}}_{\geq p}$. To establish the second part, it is now enough to notice that the relation $Y_S' = \psi_S(A) \cdot Y_S$ implies:

$$Y_S^{(p)}(0) = (A \cdot Y_S)^{(p-1)}(0) = -\mathrm{Coeff}(A \cdot \bar{Y}_S,\, p{-}1)$$

the minus sign coming from $(p-1)! \equiv -1 \pmod p$. □

REMARK 4.5. *We can rephrase Proposition 4.4 as follows: letting $y_1, \ldots, y_r$ denote the column vectors of Y_S and $\bar{y}_i \in (\ell[t]/t^p)^r$ be the reduction of y_i, the p-curvature of A modulo t^p is the linear endomorphism of $(\ell[t]/t^p)^r$ whose matrix in the basis $(\bar{y}_1, \ldots, \bar{y}_r)$ is $\mathrm{Coeff}(A \cdot \bar{Y}_S, p{-}1)$. It is worth remarking that the latter matrix has coefficients in the subring ℓ of $\ell[t]/t^p$.*

Remembering Eq. (8), we conclude that Proposition 4.4 allows us to compute the image of the p-curvature A_p modulo S^p. The strategy of our algorithm now becomes clear: we first compute A_p modulo S^p for various polynomials S and, when we have collected enough congruences, we put them together to reconstruct A_p. The first step is detailed in §4.2 just below and the second step is the subject of §4.3.

4.2 Local calculations

In all this subsection, we fix a separable polynomial $S \in k[x]$ and denote by m its degree. Our goal is to design an algorithm for computing the matrix A_p modulo S^p. After Proposition 4.4, the main remaining algorithmic issue is the effective computation of the isomorphism φ_S and its inverse.

Applying φ_S and its inverse. We remark that φ_S factors as follows:

$$\begin{array}{ccccc} k[x]/S^p & \to & k[x,t]/\langle S, (t-x)^p\rangle & \to & k[x,t]/\langle S, t^p\rangle \\ x & \mapsto & t & \mapsto & t+a. \end{array}$$

Applying the right-hand mapping, or its inverse, amounts to doing a polynomial shift in degree p with coefficients in $k[x]/S$. Using the divide-and-conquer algorithm of [16], this can be done in $O\tilde{~}(p)$ arithmetic operations in $k[x]/S$, which is $O\tilde{~}(pm)$ operations in k. Thus, we are left with the left-hand factor, say $\varphi_S^\star$. Applying it is straightforward and can be achieved in $O\tilde{~}(pm)$ operations in k. It then only remains to explain how one can apply efficiently $\varphi_S^{\star\,-1}$.

We start by determining the image of x by $\varphi_S^{\star\,-1}$; call it $y = \varphi_S^{\star\,-1}(x)$; we may identify it with its canonical preimage in $k[x]$, which has degree less than pm. Write $y = \sum_{0 \leq i < p} \zeta_i(x^p)x^i$, with every ζ_i in $k[x]$ of degree less than m (so that $\zeta_i(x^p)$ has degree less than pm). Its image through $\varphi_S^\star$ is $\sum_{0 \leq i < p} \zeta_i(t^p)t^i$, which is $\sum_{0 \leq i < p} \zeta_i(x^p)t^i$, since $x^p = t^p$ in $k[x,t]/\langle S, (t-x)^p\rangle$.

Since $\varphi_S^\star(y) = x$, we deduce that $\zeta_0(x^p) = x \bmod S$ and $\zeta_i(x^p) = 0 \bmod S$ for $i = 1, \ldots, p-1$. The first equality implies that x^p generates $k[x]/S$, so the fact that ζ_0 has degree less than m implies that ζ_0 is the unique polynomial with this degree constraint such that $\zeta_0(x^p) = x \bmod S$. The other equalities then imply that $\zeta_i = 0$ for $i = 1, \ldots, p-1$.

In order to compute ζ_0, we first compute $\nu = x^p \bmod S$, using $O\tilde{~}(m \log(p))$ operations in k. Then, we have to find the unique polynomial ζ_0 of degree less than m such that $\zeta_0(\nu) = x \bmod S$. In general, one can compute ζ_0 in $O(m^\omega)$ operations in k by solving a linear system. In the common case where $m < p$, there exists a better solution. Indeed, denote by $\mathrm{tr} : k[x]/S \to k$ the k-linear trace form and write $t_i = \mathrm{tr}(\nu^i)$ and $t_i' = \mathrm{tr}(x\nu^i)$, for $i = 0, \ldots, m-1$. Then formulas such as those in [25] allow us to recover ζ_0 from $\mathbf{t} = (t_0, \ldots, t_{m-1})$ and $\mathbf{t}' = (t_0', \ldots, t_{m-1}')$ in time $O\tilde{~}(m)$. These formulas require that $m < p$ and that S' be invertible modulo S, which is ensured by our assumption that S is separable. To compute $\mathbf{t}$ and $\mathbf{t}'$, we can use Shoup's power projection algorithm [29], which takes $O(m^{(\omega+1)/2})$ operations in k.

Once ζ_0 is known, to apply the mapping $\varphi_S^{\star\,-1}$ to an element $g(x,t)$, we proceed coefficient-wise in t. Write $g = \sum_{0 \leq i < p} g_i(x)t^i$, with all g_i of degree less than m. Then $\varphi_S^{\star\,-1}(g) = \sum_{0 \leq i < p} (g_i(\zeta_0) \bmod T)\,(x^p)\,x^i$ where T is the polynomial obtained by raising all coefficients of S to the power p, so that $S(x)^p = T(x^p)$.

Computing T takes $O(m \log(p))$ operations in k; then, computing each term $g_i(\zeta_0) \bmod T$ can be done using the Brent-Kung modular composition algorithm for $O(m^{(\omega+1)/2})$ operations in k; the total is $O(m^{(\omega+1)/2}p)$. Finally, the evaluation at x^p and the summation needed to obtain $\varphi_S^{\star\,-1}(g)$ do not involve any arithmetic operations.

REMARK 4.6. *In the case where $S = x^m - c$ (where $c \in k$ and p does not divide m), there actually exists a quite simple explicit formula for $\varphi_S^{\star\,-1}$: it takes t to x and x to $c^q x^{pn}$ where n and q are integers satisfying the Bézout's relation $pn + qm = 1$. Using this, one can compute $\varphi_S^{\star\,-1}(g)$ in $O\tilde{~}(pm)$ operations in k in this special case.*

Conclusion. Let us call `phiS` and `phiS_inverse` the two subroutines described above for computing φ_S and its inverse respectively. Proposition 4.4 leads to the following algorithm for computing the p-curvature modulo S^p.

Algorithm `local_p_curvature`
Input: a polynomial S and a matrix $A_S \in M_r(k[x]/S^p)$
Output: the p-curvature of the system $Y' = A_S\,Y$

1. $A_{S,\ell} =$ `phiS`(A_S)
   COST: $O\tilde{~}(pr^2m)$ operations in k (with $m = \deg S$)
2. compute a fund. system of solutions $Y_S \in M_r(\ell[t]/t^p)$ of the system $Y' = A_{S,\ell}Y$ at precision p.
   COST: $O\tilde{~}(pr^\omega)$ op. in ℓ using `fundamental_solutions`
   REMARK: Here $\ell = k[x]/S$
3. $A_{p,\ell} = Y_S \cdot \mathrm{Coeff}(AY_S,\, p{-}1) \cdot Y_S^{-1}$ at precision $O(t^p)$
   COST: $O\tilde{~}(pr^\omega)$ operations in ℓ
4. $A_p =$ `phiS_inverse`$(A_{p,\ell})$
   COST: $O\tilde{~}(pr^2m^\omega)$ operations in k in general
   $O\tilde{~}(pr^2m^{(\omega+1)/2})$ operations in k if $m < p$
5. **return** A_p.

To conclude with, it is worth remarking that implementing the algorithm `local_p_curvature` can be done using usual power series arithmetic: indeed, we only need to perform computations in the quotient $\ell[[t]]^{\mathrm{dp}}/\ell[[t]]^{\mathrm{dp}}_{\geq p}$ which is isomorphic to $\ell[t]/t^p$ by Corollary 3.3. Furthermore, we note that if we are using the algorithm `fundamental_solutions` at line 2, then Y_S^{-1} can be computed by performing an extra loop in `fundamental_solutions`; indeed the matrix Z we obtain this way is exactly Y_S^{-1}.

4.3 Gluing

We recall that we have started with a differential system $Y' = AY$ (with $A = \frac{1}{f_A}\tilde{A}$) and that our goal is to compute the matrix A_p of its p-curvature. Lemma 4.1 gives bounds on the size of the entries of A_p. We need another lemma, which ensures that we can find enough small "evaluation points" (lying in a finite extension of k). Let $\mathbb{F}_p$ denote the prime subfield of k.

LEMMA 4.7. *Given a positive integer D and a nonzero polynomial $f \in k[x]$, there exist pairwise coprime polynomials $S_1, \ldots, S_n \in \mathbb{F}_p[x]$ with $n \leq D$ such that:*
- $\sum_{i=1}^{n} \deg S_i \geq D$
- *for all i, the polynomial S_i is coprime with f and has degree at most $1 + \log_p(D + \deg f)$.*

PROOF. Let m be the smallest integer such that $p^m \geq D + \deg f$. Clearly $m \leq 1+\log_q(D+\deg f) \leq 1+\log_p(D+\deg f)$. Let $\mathbb{F}_{p^m}$ be an extension of $\mathbb{F}_p$ of degree m and K be the compositum of k and $\mathbb{F}_{p^m}$. Let $S_1, \ldots, S_t$ be the minimal polynomials over $\mathbb{F}_p$ (without repetition) of all elements in $\mathbb{F}_{p^m} \subset K$ which are not a root of f. We then have $\deg S_i \leq m$ for all i and $\sum_{i=1}^{t} \deg S_i \geq p^m - \deg f \geq D$. It remains now to define n as the smallest integer such that $\sum_{i=1}^{n} \deg S_i \geq D$. Minimality implies $\sum_{i=1}^{n-1} \deg S_i < D$ and thus $n \leq D$. Therefore $S_1, \ldots, S_n$ satisfy all the requirements of the lemma. □

The above proof yields a concrete algorithm for producing a sequence $S_1, \ldots, S_n$ satisfying the properties of Lemma 4.7: we run over elements in $\mathbb{F}_{p^m}$ and, for each new element, append its minimal polynomial over $\mathbb{F}_p$ to the sequence (S_i) unless it is not coprime with f. We continue this process until the condition $\sum_{i=1}^{n} \deg S_i \geq D$ holds. Keeping in mind the logarithmic bound on m, we find that the complexity of this algorithm is at most $O\tilde{~}(D + \deg f)$ operations in k. Let us call `generate_points` the resulting routine: it takes as input the parameters f and D and return an admissible sequence $S_1, \ldots, S_n$.

We are now ready to present our algorithm for computing the p-curvature:

Algorithm `p_curvature`
Input: a matrix A written as $A = \frac{1}{f_A} \cdot \tilde{A}$
Output: the p-curvature of the differential system $Y' = AY$

1. $S_1, \ldots, S_n =$ `generate_points`$(f_A, d+1)$
   COST: $O\tilde{~}(d)$ operations in k
   REMARK: we have $n = O(d)$ and $\deg S_i = O(\log d)$, $\forall i$
2. **for** $i = 1, \ldots, n$:
   $A_{i,p} =$ `local_p_curvature`$(S_i, A \bmod S_i^p)$
   COST: $O\tilde{~}(pdr^\omega)$ operations in k
3. compute $B \in M_r(k[x])$ with entries of degree $\leq pd$ such that $B \equiv f_A^p \cdot B_i \pmod{S_i^p}$ for all i
   COST: $O\tilde{~}(pdr^2)$ operations in k
4. **return** $\frac{1}{f_A^p} \cdot B$

In view of the previous discussion and Lemma 4.1, the correctness and the cost analysis of the algorithm `p_curvature` are both straightforward. Hence, Theorem 4.2 is proved.

We conclude this subsection with three remarks. First, when applying Chinese Remainder Theorem (CRT) on line 3 of Algorithm `p_curvature`, we notice that all moduli S_i^p are polynomials in x^p. This allows the following optimization. Writing $f_A^p \cdot B_i \equiv \sum_{j=0}^{p-1} B_{i,j}(x^p)x^j \pmod{S_i^p(x)}$ and denoting by C_j the unique solution of degree at most d to the congruence system:

$$B_j(x) \equiv B_{i,j}(x) \pmod{T_i(x)} \quad \text{where } T_i(x^p) = S_i^p(x)$$

we have $B = \sum_{j=0}^{p-1} B_j(x)x^j$. This basically allows us to replace one CRT with polynomials of degree dp by p CRT with polynomials of degree d. We save this way the polynomial factors in $\log(p)$ in the complexity.

Second, instead of working with n polynomials S_i, one may alternatively choose a unique polynomial S of the form $S = X^m - a$ where $m \geq d$ is an integer not divisible by p and $a \in k$ are such that S and f_A are coprime. This avoids the use of Chinese Remainder Theorem and the resulting complexity stays in $O\tilde{~}(pdr^\omega)$ provided that we use Remark 4.6 in order to compute the inverse of φ_S.

Third, we observe that the algorithm `p_curvature` is very easily parallelizable. Indeed, each iteration of the main loop (on line 2) is completely independent from the others. Thus, they all can be performed in parallel. Moreover, according to the first remark (just above), the application of the Chinese Remainder Theorem (on line 3) splits into pr^2 smaller independent problems and can therefore be efficiently parallelized as well.

4.4 The case of differential operators

To conclude with, we would like to discuss the case of a differential operator $L = a_r\partial^r + a_{r-1}\partial^{r-1} + \cdots + a_1\partial + a_0$ with $a_i \in k[x]$ for all i, of maximal degree d.

Recall that the p-curvature of L is that of the differential module $(\mathfrak{A}\langle\partial\rangle/\mathfrak{A}\langle\partial\rangle L, \partial_{-C})$, where C is the companion matrix associated to L as in (3). Applying directly the formulas in Proposition 4.4 requires the knowledge of the solutions of the system $Y' = -CY$. It is in fact easier to compute solutions for the system $X' = {}^tCX$, since we saw that these solutions are the vectors of the form ${}^t(y, y', \ldots, y^{(r-1)})$, where y is a solution of L. This is however harmless: the p-curvatures A_p and B_p of the respective systems $Y' = -CY$ and $X' = {}^tCX$ (which are so-called adjoint) satisfy $A_p = -{}^tB_p$. Thus, we can use the formulas given above to compute $\varphi_S(B_p)$, and deduce $\varphi_S(A_p)$ for a negligible cost. Equivalently, one may notice that the fundamental matrices of solutions of our two systems are transpose of one another, up to sign.

Moreover, instead of using the second formula of Proposition 4.4 to compute the local p-curvatures, we recommend using the first one, which is $\varphi_S(B_p) = -X_S \cdot X_S^{(p)}(0) \cdot \bar{X}_S^{-1}$ where X_S is a fundamental system of solutions of $X' = {}^tCX$ and $\bar{X}_S$ denotes its reduction in $M_r(\ell[t]/t^p)$. If $f_0, \ldots, f_{r-1}$ are solutions of the system (7), the (i,j)-th entry of X_S is just $f_j^{(i)}$. Hence the matrices $\bar{X}_S$ and $X_S^{(p)}(0)$ can be obtained from the knowledge of the image of f_i's modulo

	p							
	157	**281**	**521**	**983**	**1 811**	**3 433**	**6 421**	**12 007**
$d=5, \quad r=5$	0.39 s	0.71 s	1.22 s	2.34 s	4.41 s	8.93 s	18.0 s	36.1 s
	0.26 s	0.76 s	2.69 s	9.05 s	32.6 s	145 s	593 s	2 132 s
$d=5, \quad r=11$	1.09 s	2.05 s	3.65 s	7.05 s	12.6 s	26.7 s	53.3 s	109 s
	1.25 s	3.70 s	12.8 s	45.5 s	163 s	725 s	2 942 s	–
$d=5, \quad r=20$	2.93 s	5.25 s	9.52 s	17.7 s	32.5 s	68.1 s	139 s	288 s
	4.29 s	12.4 s	42.5 s	153 s	548 s	2 460 s	–	–
$d=11, \quad r=20$	6.89 s	13.3 s	22.6 s	45.0 s	80.4 s	167 s	342 s	711 s
	11.6 s	34.7 s	121 s	486 s	1 943 s	–	–	–
$d=20, \quad r=20$	14.0 s	25.1 s	49.9 s	94.0 s	176 s	357 s	733 s	1 472 s
	27.0 s	84.5 s	314 s	1 283 s	–	–	–	–

Running times obtained with Magma V2.19-4 on an AMD Opteron 6272 machine at 2GHz and 8GB RAM, running Linux.

Figure 1: Average running time on random inputs of various sizes

$\ell[[t]]^{\mathrm{dp}}_{\geq p+r}$ just by reorganizing coefficients (and possibly multiplying by some factorials depending on the representation of elements of $\ell[[t]]^{\mathrm{dp}}$ we are using).

As for the f_i's, they can be computed by the algorithm `solutions_operator` (provided its assumptions are satisfied). We need finally to compute X_S^{-1}: since $X_S(0)$ is the identity matrix, this can be done either using Newton iterator, a divide-and-conquer approach or a combination of both, which computes the inverse of X_S at a small precision, and uses divide-and-conquer techniques for higher ones (the latter being the most efficient in practice). All these remarks do speed up the execution of our algorithms when d is not too large compared to r.

Last but not least, we notice that, in the case of differential operators, the matrix A_p is easily deduced from its first column. Indeed, writing $A_p = (a_{i,j})_{0 \leq i,j < r}$ and letting $c_j = a_{r-1,j}\partial^{r-1} + \cdots + a_{1,j}\partial + a_{0,j} \in k(x)\langle\partial\rangle$ be the differential operator obtained from the j-column of A_p, it is easily checked that c_{j+1} is the remainder in the Euclidean division of ∂c_j by L. Comparing orders, we further find $c_{j+1} = \partial c_j - \frac{\mathrm{lc}(c_j)}{a_r} L$ where $\mathrm{lc}(c_j)$ is the leading coefficient of c_j. This remark is interesting because it permits to save memory: indeed, instead of storing all local p-curvatures $A_{p,\ell}$, we can just store their first column. Doing this, we can reconstruct the first column of A_p using the Chinese Remainder Theorem (*cf* §4.3) and then compute the whole matrix A_p using the recurrence.

5. IMPLEMENTATION AND TIMINGS

We implemented our algorithms in Magma in the case of differential operators; the source code is available at `https://github.com/schost`. Figure 1 gives running times for random operators of degrees (d, r) in $k[x]\langle\partial\rangle$ and compares them with running times of (a fraction free version of) Katz's algorithm which consists in computing the recursive sequence (A_i) until $i = p$. In each cell, the first line (resp. the second line) corresponds to the running time obtained with our algorithm (resp. Katz's algorithm); a dash indicates that the corresponding running time exceeded one hour. Our benchmarks rather well reflect the predicted dependence with respect to p: quasi-linear for our algorithm and quadratic for Katz's algorithm.

Larger examples (than those presented in Fig. 1) are also reachable: for instance, we computed the first column of the p-curvature of a "small" multiple of the operator $\phi_H^{(5)}$ considered in [10, Appendix B.3] modulo the prime 27449. This operator has bidegree $(d, r) = (108, 28)$. The computation took about 19 hours and the size of the output in human-readable format is about 1GB (after bzip2 compression, it decreases to about 300MB).

6. REFERENCES

[1] P. Berthelot. *Cohomologie cristalline des schémas de caractéristique $p > 0$*. Lecture Notes in Mathematics, Vol. 407. Springer-Verlag, Berlin-New York, 1974.

[2] P. Berthelot and A. Ogus. *Notes on crystalline cohomology*. Princeton University Press, Princeton, N.J.; University of Tokyo Press, Tokyo, 1978.

[3] A. Bostan, S. Boukraa, S. Hassani, J.-M. Maillard, J.-A. Weil, and N. Zenine. Globally nilpotent differential operators and the square Ising model. *J. Phys. A*, 42(12):125206, 50, 2009.

[4] A. Bostan, X. Caruso, and E. Schost. A fast algorithm for computing the characteristic polynomial of the p-curvature. In *ISSAC'14*, pages 59–66. ACM, New York, 2014.

[5] A. Bostan, F. Chyzak, F. Ollivier, B. Salvy, É. Schost, and A. Sedoglavic. Fast computation of power series solutions of systems of differential equations. In *18th ACM-SIAM Symposium on Discrete Algorithms*, pages 1012–1021, 2007. New Orleans, January 2007.

[6] A. Bostan and M. Kauers. Automatic classification of restricted lattice walks. In *FPSAC'09*, DMTCS Proc., AK, pages 201–215. 2009.

[7] A. Bostan and M. Kauers. The complete generating function for Gessel walks is algebraic. *Proc. Amer. Math. Soc.*, 138(9):3063–3078, 2010. With an appendix by Mark van Hoeij.

[8] A. Bostan and É. Schost. Polynomial evaluation and interpolation on special sets of points. *J. Complexity*, 21(4):420–446, 2005.

[9] A. Bostan and É. Schost. Fast algorithms for differential equations in positive characteristic. In *ISSAC'09*, pages 47–54. ACM, New York, 2009.

[10] S. Boukraa, S. Hassani, J.-M. Maillard, and N. Zenine. Singularities of n-fold integrals of the Ising class and the theory of elliptic curves. *J. Phys. A*, 40(39):11713–11748, 2007.

[11] D. G. Cantor and E. Kaltofen. On fast multiplication of polynomials over arbitrary algebras. *Acta Inform.*, 28(7):693–701, 1991.

[12] A. Chambert-Loir. Théorèmes d'algébricité en géométrie diophantienne (d'après J.-B. Bost, Y. André, D. & G. Chudnovsky). *Séminaire Bourbaki*, 282(886):175–209, 2002.

[13] T. Cluzeau. Factorization of differential systems in characteristic p. In *ISSAC'03*, pages 58–65. ACM Press, 2003.

[14] T. Cluzeau and M. van Hoeij. A modular algorithm for computing the exponential solutions of a linear differential operator. *J. Symbolic Comput.*, 38(3):1043–1076, 2004.

[15] F. L. Gall. Powers of tensors and fast matrix multiplication. In *ISSAC'14*, pages 296–303, 2014.

[16] J. von zur Gathen and J. Gerhard. Fast algorithms for Taylor shifts and certain difference equations. In *ISSAC'97*, pages 40–47. ACM, 1997.

[17] J. von zur Gathen and J. Gerhard. *Modern Computer Algebra*. Cambridge University Press, Cambridge, second edition, 2003.

[18] D. Harvey, J. van der Hoeven, and G. Lecerf. Faster polynomial multiplication over finite fields. http://arxiv.org/abs/1407.3361, 2014.

[19] N. M. Katz. Algebraic solutions of differential equations (p-curvature and the Hodge filtration). *Invent. Math.*, 18:1–118, 1972.

[20] N. M. Katz. A conjecture in the arithmetic theory of differential equations. *Bull. Soc. Math. France*, (110):203–239, 1982.

[21] W. F. Keigher and F. L. Pritchard. Hurwitz series as formal functions. *J. Pure Appl. Algebra*, 146(3):291–304, 2000.

[22] M. van der Put. Differential equations in characteristic p. *Compositio Mathematica*, 97:227–251, 1995.

[23] M. van der Put. Reduction modulo p of differential equations. *Indag. Mathem.*, 7(3):367–387, 1996.

[24] M. van der Put and M. Singer. *Galois theory of linear differential equations*. Springer, 2003.

[25] F. Rouillier. Solving zero-dimensional systems through the rational univariate representation. *Appl. Algebra Engrg. Comm. Comput.*, 9(5):433–461, 1999.

[26] A. Schönhage. Schnelle Multiplikation von Polynomen über Körpern der Charakteristik 2. *Acta Informatica*, 7:395–398, 1977.

[27] A. Schönhage and V. Strassen. Schnelle Multiplikation großer Zahlen. *Computing*, 7:281–292, 1971.

[28] É. Schost. Multivariate power series multiplication. In *ISSAC'05*, pages 293–300. ACM, 2005.

[29] V. Shoup. Fast construction of irreducible polynomials over finite fields. *Journal of Symbolic Computation*, 17(5):371–391, 1994.

[30] Y. Tang. Algebraic solutions of differential equations over the projective line minus three points. http://arxiv.org/abs/1412.7875, 2014.

Algebraic Diagonals and Walks

Alin Bostan
Inria
France
Alin.Bostan@inria.fr

Louis Dumont
Inria
France
Louis.Dumont@inria.fr

Bruno Salvy
Inria, Laboratoire LIP
(U. Lyon, CNRS, ENS Lyon, UCBL)
France
Bruno.Salvy@inria.fr

ABSTRACT

The diagonal of a multivariate power series F is the univariate power series $\operatorname{Diag} F$ generated by the diagonal terms of F. Diagonals form an important class of power series; they occur frequently in number theory, theoretical physics and enumerative combinatorics. We study algorithmic questions related to diagonals in the case where F is the Taylor expansion of a bivariate rational function. It is classical that in this case $\operatorname{Diag} F$ is an algebraic function. We propose an algorithm that computes an annihilating polynomial for $\operatorname{Diag} F$. Generically, it is its minimal polynomial and is obtained in time quasi-linear in its size. We show that this minimal polynomial has an exponential size with respect to the degree of the input rational function. We then address the related problem of enumerating directed lattice walks. The insight given by our study leads to a new method for expanding the generating power series of bridges, excursions and meanders. We show that their first N terms can be computed in quasi-linear complexity in N, without first computing a very large polynomial equation.

Categories and Subject Descriptors:
I.1.2 [**Computing Methodologies**]: Symbolic and Algebraic Manipulations — *Algebraic Algorithms*

General Terms: Algorithms, Theory.

Keywords: Diagonals, walks, algorithms.

1. INTRODUCTION

Context. The *diagonal* of a multivariate power series with coefficients $a_{i_1,\dots,i_k}$ is the univariate power series with coefficients $a_{i,\dots,i}$. Particularly interesting is the class of diagonals of *rational* power series (ie, Taylor expansions of rational functions). In particular, diagonals of *bivariate* rational power series are always roots of nonzero bivariate polynomials (ie, they are algebraic series) [22, 15]. Since it is also classical that algebraic series are D-finite (ie, satisfy linear differential equations with polynomial coefficients), their coefficients satisfy linear recurrences and this leads to an optimal algorithm for the computation of their first terms [11, 12, 3]. In this article, we determine the degrees of these polynomials, the cost of their computation and related applications.

Previous work. The algebraicity of bivariate diagonals is classical. The same is true for the converse; also the property persists for multivariate rational series in positive characteristic [15, 24, 13]. The first occurrence we are aware of in the literature is Pólya's article [22], which deals with a particular class of bivariate rational functions; the proof uses elementary complex analysis. Along the lines of Pólya's approach, Furstenberg [15] gave a (sketchy) proof of the general result, over the field of complex numbers; the same argument has been enhanced later [18], [26, §6.3]. Three more different proofs exist: a purely algebraic one that works over arbitrary fields of characteristic zero [17, Th. 6.1] (see also [26, Th. 6.3.3]), one based on non-commutative power series [14, Prop. 5], and a combinatorial proof [6, §3.4.1]. Despite the richness of the topic and the fact that most proofs are constructive in essence, we were not able to find in the literature any *explicit* algorithm for computing a bivariate polynomial that cancels the diagonal of a general bivariate rational function.

Diagonals of rational functions appear naturally in enumerative combinatorics. In particular, the enumeration of unidimensional walks has been the subject of recent activity, see [1] and the references therein. The algebraicity of generating functions attached to such walks is classical as well, and related to that of bivariate diagonals. Beyond this structural result, several quantitative and effective results are known. Explicit formulas give the generating functions in terms of implicit algebraic functions attached to the set of allowed steps in the case of excursions [8, §4], [17], bridges and meanders [1]. Moreover, if a and b denote the upper and lower amplitudes of the allowed steps, the bound $d_{a,b} = \binom{a+b}{a}$ on the degrees of equations for excursions has been obtained by Bousquet-Mélou, and showed to be tight for a specific family of step sets, as well as generically [7, §2.1]. From the algorithmic viewpoint, Banderier and Flajolet gave an algorithm (called the *Platypus Algorithm*) for computing a polynomial of degree $d_{a,b}$ that annihilates the generating function for excursions [1, §2.3].

Contributions. We design (Section 4) the first explicit algorithm for computing a polynomial equation for the diagonal of an arbitrary bivariate rational function. We analyze its complexity and the size of its output in Theorem 14. The algorithm has two main steps. The first step is the computation of a polynomial equation for the residues of a bivariate rational function. We propose an efficient algorithm for this task, that is a polynomial-time version of Bronstein's algorithm [9]; corresponding size and complexity bounds are given in Theorem 10. The second step is the computation of a polynomial equation for the sums of a fixed number of roots of a given polynomial. We design an additive version of the Platypus algorithm [1, §2.3] and analyze it in Theorem 12. We show in Proposition 16 that generically, the size of the minimal polynomial for the diagonal of a rational function is exponential in the degree of the input and that our algorithm computes it in quasi-optimal complexity (Theorem 14).

In the application to walks, we show how to expand to high precision the generating functions of bridges, excursions and meanders. Our main message is that pre-computing a polynomial equation for them is too costly, since that equation might have exponential size in the maximal amplitude d of the allowed steps. Our algorithms have quasi-linear complexity in the precision of the expansion, while keeping the pre-computation step in polynomial complexity in d (Theorem 18).

Structure of the paper. After a preliminary section on background

ISSAC'15, July 6–9, 2015, Bath, United Kingdom.

DOI: http://dx.doi.org/10.1145/2755996.2756663.

and notation, we first discuss several special bivariate resultants of broader general interest in Section 3. Next, we consider diagonals, the size of their minimal polynomials and an efficient way of computing annihilating polynomials in Section 4.

2. BACKGROUND AND NOTATION

In this section, that might be skipped at first reading, we introduce notation and technical results that will be used throughout the article.

2.1 Notation

In this article, $\mathbb{K}$ denotes a field of characteristic 0. We denote by $\mathbb{K}[x]_n$ the set of polynomials in $\mathbb{K}[x]$ of degree less than n. Similarly, $\mathbb{K}(x)_n$ stands for the set of rational functions in $\mathbb{K}(x)$ with numerator and denominator in $\mathbb{K}[x]_n$, and $\mathbb{K}[[x]]_n$ for the set of power series in $\mathbb{K}[[x]]$ truncated at precision n.

If P is a polynomial in $\mathbb{K}[x,y]$, then its degree with respect to x (resp. y) is denoted $\deg_x P$ (resp. $\deg_y P$), and the *bidegree* of P is the pair $\operatorname{bideg} P = (\deg_x P, \deg_y P)$. The notation deg is used for univariate polynomials. Inequalities between bidegrees are component-wise. The set of polynomials in $\mathbb{K}[x,y]$ of bidegree less than (n,m) is denoted by $\mathbb{K}[x,y]_{n,m}$, and similarly for more variables.

The *valuation* of a polynomial $F \in \mathbb{K}[x]$ or a power series $F \in \mathbb{K}[[x]]$ is its smallest exponent with nonzero coefficient. It is denoted $\operatorname{val} F$, with the convention $\operatorname{val} 0 = \infty$.

The *reciprocal* of a polynomial $P \in \mathbb{K}[x]$ is the polynomial $\operatorname{rec}(P) = x^{\deg P} P(1/x)$. If $P = c(x-\alpha_1)\cdots(x-\alpha_d)$, the notation $\mathcal{N}(P)$ stands for the generating series of the *Newton sums* of P:

$$\mathcal{N}(P) = \sum_{n \geqslant 0} (\alpha_1^n + \alpha_2^n + \cdots + \alpha_d^n) x^n.$$

A *squarefree decomposition* of a nonzero polynomial $Q \in \mathbb{A}[y]$, where $\mathbb{A} = \mathbb{K}$ or $\mathbb{K}[x]$, is a factorization $Q = Q_1^1 \cdots Q_m^m$, with $Q_i \in \mathbb{A}[y]$ squarefree, the Q_i's pairwise coprime and $\deg_y(Q_m) > 0$. The corresponding *squarefree part* of Q is the polynomial $Q^\star = Q_1 \cdots Q_m$. If Q is squarefree then $Q = Q^\star$.

The coefficient of x^n in a power series $A \in \mathbb{K}[[x]]$ is denoted $[x^n]A$. If $A = \sum_{i=0}^\infty a_i x^i$, then $A \bmod x^n$ denotes the polynomial $\sum_{i=0}^{n-1} a_i x^i$. The exponential series $\sum_n x^n/n!$ is denoted $\exp(x)$. The *Hadamard product* of two power series A and B is the power series $A \odot B$ such that $[x^n]A \odot B = [x^n]A \cdot [x^n]B$ for all n.

If $F(x,y) = \sum_{i,j \geqslant 0} f_{i,j} x^i y^j$ is a bivariate power series in $\mathbb{K}[[x,y]]$, the *diagonal* of F, denoted $\operatorname{Diag} F$ is the univariate power series in $\mathbb{K}[[t]]$ defined by $\operatorname{Diag} F(t) = \sum_{n \geqslant 0} f_{n,n} t^n$.

2.2 Bivariate Power Series

In several places, we need bounds on degrees of coefficients of bivariate rational series. In most cases, these power series belong to $\mathbb{K}(x)[[y]]$ and have a very constrained structure: there exists a polynomial $Q \in \mathbb{K}[x]$ and an integer $\alpha \in \mathbb{N}$ such that the power series can be written

$$c_0 + c_1 \frac{y}{Q} + \cdots + c_n \frac{y^n}{Q^n} + \cdots,$$

with $c_n \in \mathbb{K}[x]$ and $\deg c_n \leqslant n\alpha$, for all n. We denote by $\mathscr{E}_\alpha(Q)$ the set of such power series. Its main properties are summarized as follows.

Lemma 1 *Let $Q, R \in \mathbb{K}[x]$, $\alpha, \beta \in \mathbb{N}$ and $f \in \mathbb{K}[[y]]$.*
(1) The set $\mathscr{E}_\alpha(Q)$ is a subring of $\mathbb{K}(x)[[y]]$;
(2) Let $S \in \mathscr{E}_\alpha(Q)$ with $S(0) = 0$, then $f(S) \in \mathscr{E}_\alpha(Q)$;
(3) The products obey

$$\mathscr{E}_\alpha(Q) \cdot \mathscr{E}_\beta(R) \subset \mathscr{E}_{\max(\alpha + \deg R, \beta + \deg Q)}(QR).$$

PROOF. For *(3)*, if $A = \sum_n a_n y^n / Q^n$ and $B = \sum_n b_n y^n / R^n$ belong respectively to $\mathscr{E}_\alpha(Q)$ and $\mathscr{E}_\beta(R)$, then the nth coefficient of their product is a sum of terms of the form $a_i(x) Q^{n-i} b_{n-i}(x) R^i / (QR)^n$. Therefore, the degree of the numerator is bounded by $i(\alpha + \deg R) + (n-i)(\beta + \deg Q)$, whence *(3)* is proved. Property *(1)* is proved similarly. In Property *(2)*, the condition on $S(0)$ makes $f(S)$ well-defined. The result follows from *(1)*. □

As consequences, we deduce the following two results.

Corollary 2 *Let $Q \in \mathbb{K}[x,y]$ with $q(x) = Q(x,0)$ be such that $q(0) \neq 0$. Let $Q^\star$ be a squarefree part of Q. Then*

$$\frac{1}{Q} \in \frac{1}{q} \mathscr{E}_{\deg_x Q^\star}(Q^\star(x,0)).$$

PROOF. Write $Q = q + R$ with $R/q \in \mathscr{E}_{\deg_x Q}(q)$. Then the result when Q is squarefree ($Q = Q^\star$) follows from Part *(2)* of Lemma 1, with $f = 1/(1+y)$. The general case then follows from Parts *(1,3)*. □

Proposition 3 *Let P and Q be polynomials in $\mathbb{K}[x,y]$, with $Q(0,0) \neq 0$, $\deg_y Q > 0$ and $F = P/Q$. Then for all $n \in \mathbb{N}$,*

$$\frac{d^n F}{dy^n} = \frac{A}{Q(Q^\star)^n},$$

with $\operatorname{bideg} A \leqslant \operatorname{bideg} P + n(\deg_x Q^\star, \deg_y Q^\star - 1)$.

PROOF. The Taylor expansion of $F(x, y+t)$ has for coefficients the derivatives of F. We consider it either in $\mathbb{K}(y)[x,t]$ or in $\mathbb{K}(x)[y,t]$. Corollary 2 applies directly for the degree in x. The saving on the degree in y follows from observing that in the first part of the proof of the corollary, the decomposition $Q(x, y+t) = Q(x,y) + R(x,y,t)$ has the property that $\deg_y R \leqslant \deg_y Q - 1$. This -1 is then propagated along the proof thanks to Part *(3)* of Lemma 1. □

2.3 Complexity Estimates

We recall classical complexity notation and facts for later use. Let $\mathbb{K}$ be again a field of characteristic zero. Unless otherwise specified, we estimate the cost of our algorithms by counting arithmetic operations in $\mathbb{K}$ (denoted "ops.") at unit cost. The soft-O notation $\tilde{O}(\cdot)$ indicates that polylogarithmic factors are omitted in the complexity estimates. We say that an algorithm has quasi-linear complexity if its complexity is $\tilde{O}(d)$, where d is the maximal *arithmetic size* (number of coefficients in $\mathbb{K}$ in a dense representation) of the input and of the output. In that case, the algorithm is said to be *quasi-optimal*.

Univariate operations. Throughout this article we will use the fact that most operations on polynomials, rational functions and power series in one variable can be performed in quasi-linear time. Standard references for these questions are the books [16] and [10]. The needed results are summarized in Fact 4 below.

Fact 4 *The following operations can be performed in $\tilde{O}(n)$ ops. in $\mathbb{K}$:*
(1) addition, product and differentiation of elements in $\mathbb{K}[x]_n$, $\mathbb{K}(x)_n$ and $\mathbb{K}[[x]]_n$; integration in $\mathbb{K}[x]_n$ and $\mathbb{K}[[x]]_n$;
(2) extended gcd, squarefree decomposition and resultant in $\mathbb{K}[x]_n$;
(3) multipoint evaluation in $\mathbb{K}[x]_n$, $\mathbb{K}(x)_n$ at $O(n)$ points in $\mathbb{K}$; interpolation in $\mathbb{K}[x]_n$ and $\mathbb{K}(x)_n$ from n (resp. $2n-1$) values at pairwise distinct points in $\mathbb{K}$;
(4) inverse, logarithm, exponential in $\mathbb{K}[[x]]_n$ (when defined);
(5) conversions between $P \in \mathbb{K}[x]_n$ and $\mathcal{N}(P) \bmod x^n \in \mathbb{K}[x]_n$.

Multivariate operations. Basic operations on polynomials, rational functions and power series in several variables are hard questions from the algorithmic point of view. For instance, no general quasi-optimal algorithm is currently known for computing resultants of bivariate polynomials, even though in several important cases such algorithms are available [4]. Multiplication is the most basic non-trivial operation in this setting. The following result can be proved using Kronecker's substitution; it is quasi-optimal for fixed number of variables $m = O(1)$.

Fact 5 *Polynomials in $\mathbb{K}[x_1, \ldots, x_m]_{d_1, \ldots, d_m}$ and power series in $\mathbb{K}[[x_1, \ldots, x_m]]_{d_1, \ldots, d_m}$ can be multiplied using $\tilde{O}(2^m d_1 \cdots d_m)$ ops.*

A related operation is multipoint evaluation and interpolation. The simplest case is when the evaluation points form an m-dimensional tensor product grid $I_1 \times \cdots \times I_m$, where I_j is a set of cardinal d_j.

Fact 6 *[20] Polynomials in $\mathbb{K}[x_1,\dots,x_m]_{d_1,\dots,d_m}$ can be evaluated and interpolated from values that they take on $d_1 \cdots d_m$ points that form an m-dimensional tensor product grid using $\tilde{O}(md_1 \cdots d_m)$ ops.*

Again, the complexity in Fact 6 is quasi-optimal for fixed $m = O(1)$.

A general (although non-optimal) technique to deal with more involved operations on multivariable algebraic objects (eg, in $\mathbb{K}[x,y]$) is to use (multivariate) evaluation and interpolation on polynomials and to perform operations on the evaluated algebraic objects using Facts 4–6. To put this strategy in practice, the size of the output needs to be well controlled. We illustrate this philosophy on the example of resultant computation, based on the following easy variation of [16, Thm. 6.22].

Fact 7 *Let $P(x,y)$ and $Q(x,y)$ be bivariate polynomials of respective bidegrees (d_x^P, d_y^P) and (d_x^Q, d_y^Q). Then,*

$$\deg \mathrm{Resultant}_y(P(x,y), Q(x,y)) \leqslant d_x^P d_y^Q + d_x^Q d_y^P.$$

Lemma 8 *Let P and Q be polynomials in $\mathbb{K}[x_1,\dots,x_m,y]_{d_1,\dots,d_m,d}$. Then $R = \mathrm{Resultant}_y(P,Q)$ belongs to $\mathbb{K}[x_1,\dots,x_m]_{D_1,\dots,D_m}$, where $D_i = 1 + 2(d-1)(d_i - 1)$. Moreover, the coefficients of R can be computed using $\tilde{O}(2^m d_1 \cdots d_m d^{m+1})$ ops. in $\mathbb{K}$.*

PROOF. The degrees estimates follow from Fact 7. To compute R, we use an evaluation-interpolation scheme: P and Q are evaluated at $D = D_1 \cdots D_m$ points $(x_1,\dots,x_m)$ forming an m dimensional tensor product grid; D univariate resultants in $\mathbb{K}[y]_d$ are computed; R is recovered by interpolation. By Fact 6, the evaluation and interpolation steps are performed in $\tilde{O}(mD)$ ops. The second one has cost $\tilde{O}(dD)$. Using the inequality $D \leqslant 2^m d_1 \cdots d_m d^m$ concludes the proof. □

We conclude this section by recalling a complexity result for the computation of a squarefree decomposition of a bivariate polynomial.

Fact 9 *[19] A squarefree decomposition of a polynomial in $\mathbb{K}[x,y]_{d_x,d_y}$ can be computed using $\tilde{O}(d_x^2 d_y)$ ops.*

3. SPECIAL RESULTANTS

3.1 Polynomials for Residues

We are interested in a polynomial that vanishes at the residues of a given rational function. It is a classical result in symbolic integration that in the case of simple poles, there is a resultant formula for such a polynomial, first introduced by Rothstein [23] and Trager [27]. This was later generalized by Bronstein [9] to accommodate multiple poles as well. However, as mentioned by Bronstein, the complexity of his method grows exponentially with the multiplicity of the poles. Instead, we develop in this section an algorithm with polynomial complexity.

Let $f = P/Q$ be a nonzero element in $\mathbb{K}(y)$, where P, Q are two coprime polynomials in $\mathbb{K}[y]$. Let $Q_1 Q_2^2 \cdots Q_m^m$ be a squarefree decomposition of Q. For $i \in \{1,\dots,m\}$, if α is a root of Q_i in an algebraic extension of $\mathbb{K}$, then it is simple and the residue of f at α is the coefficient of t^{-1} in the Laurent expansion of $f(\alpha+t)$ at $t=0$. If $V_i(y,t)$ is the polynomial $(Q_i(y+t) - Q_i(y))/t$, this residue is the coefficient of t^{i-1} in the Taylor expansion at $t=0$ of the regular rational function $f(y+t)Q_i^i(y+t)/V_i^i(y,t)$, computed with rational operations only and then evaluated at $y = \alpha$. If this coefficient is denoted $S_{i-1}(y) = A_i(y)/B_i(y)$, with polynomials A_i and B_i, the residue at α is a root of $\mathrm{Resultant}_y(A_i - zB_i, Q_i)$. When $m=1$, this is exactly the Rothstein-Trager resultant. This computation leads to Algorithm 1, which avoids the exponential blowup of the complexity that would follow from a symbolic pre-computation of the Bronstein resultants.

Algorithm **AlgebraicResidues**(P/Q)

Input Two polynomials P and $Q \in \mathbb{K}[y]$
Output A polynomial in $\mathbb{K}[z]$ canceling all the residues of P/Q

Compute $Q_1 Q_2^2 \cdots Q_m^m$ a squarefree decomposition of Q;
for $i \leftarrow 1$ to m **do**
  if $\deg_y Q_i = 0$ **then** $R_i \leftarrow 1$
  else
    $U_i(y) \leftarrow Q(y)/Q_i^i(y)$;
    $V_i(y,t) \leftarrow (Q_i(y+t) - Q_i(y))/t$;
    Expand $\frac{P(y+t)}{U_i(y+t)V_i^i(y,t)} = S_0 + \cdots + S_{i-1}t^{i-1} + O(t^i)$;
    Write S_{i-1} as $A_i(y)/B_i(y)$ with A_i and B_i coprime;
    $R_i(z) \leftarrow \mathrm{Resultant}_y(A_i - zB_i, Q_i)$;
return $R_1 R_2 \cdots R_m$

Algorithm 1. Polynomial canceling the residues

Example 1. Let $d \geqslant 0$ be an integer, and let $G_d(x,y) \in \mathbb{Q}(x)[y]$ be the rational function $y^d/(y-y^2-x)^{d+1}$. The poles have order $d+1$. In this example, the algorithm can be performed by hand for arbitrary d: a squarefree decomposition has $m = d+1$ and $Q_m = y - y^2 - x$, the other Q_i's being 1. Then $V_m = 1 - 2y - t$ and the next step is to expand

$$\frac{(y+t)^d}{(1-2y-t)^{d+1}} = \frac{(y+t)^d}{(1-2y)^{d+1}\left(1 - \frac{t}{1-2y}\right)^{d+1}}.$$

Expanding the binomial series gives the coefficient of t^d as $\frac{A_m}{B_m}$, with

$$A_m = \sum_{i=0}^{d} \binom{d}{i}\binom{d+i}{i} y^i (1-2y)^{d-i}, \quad B_m = (1-2y)^{2d+1}.$$

The residues are then cancelled by $\mathrm{Resultant}_y(A_m - zB_m, Q_m)$, namely

$$(1-4t)^{2d+1}z^2 - \left(\sum_{k=0}^{\lfloor d/2 \rfloor} \binom{d}{2k}\binom{2k}{k} t^k\right)^2. \qquad (1)$$

Bounds. In our applications, as in the previous example, the polynomials P and Q have coefficients that are themselves polynomials in another variable x. Let then (d_P, e_P), (d_Q, e_Q), $(d^\star, e^\star)$ and (d_i, e_i) be the bidegrees in (x,y) of P, Q, $Q^\star$ and Q_i, where $Q^\star = Q_1 \cdots Q_m$ is a squarefree part of Q. In Algorithm 1, V_i has degree at most d_i in x and total degree $e_i - 1$ in (y,t). Similarly, $P(y+t)$ has degree d_P in x and total degree e_P in (y,t). When $e^\star > 1$, by Proposition 3, the coefficient S_j in the power series expansion of $P(y+t)/U_i(y+t)/V_i(y,t)^i$ has denominator of bidegree bounded by $(d_Q + jd^\star, e_Q - i + j(e^\star - 1))$ and numerator of bidegree bounded by $(d_P + jd^\star, e_P - j + j(e^\star - 1))$. Thus by Fact 7, $\deg_x R_i$ is at most

$$((i-1)d^\star + \max(d_P, d_Q))e_i + d_i((i-1)(e^\star - 1) - i + \max(e_P + 1, e_Q)),$$

while its degree in z is bounded by the number of residues e_i. Summing over all i leads to the bound

$$(e_Q - e^\star)d^\star + (d_Q - d^\star)(e^\star - 1) + e^\star \max(d_P, d_Q) - d_Q + d^\star \max(e_P + 1, e_Q).$$

If $e^\star = 1$, a direct computation gives the bound $\max(d_P, d_Q) + d^\star e_P$.

Theorem 10 *Let $P(x,y)/Q(x,y) \in \mathbb{K}(x,y)_{d_x+1,d_y+1}$. Let $Q^\star$ be a squarefree part of Q wrt y. Let $(d_x^\star, d_y^\star)$ be bounds on the bidegree of $Q^\star$. Then the polynomial computed by Algorithm 1 annihilates the residues of P/Q, has degree in z bounded by $d_y^\star$ and degree in x bounded by*

$$2d_x^\star(d_y+1) + (2d_y^\star - 1)d_x - 2d_x^\star d_y^\star.$$

It can be computed in $O(m^2 d_x^\star d_y^\star (m^2 + d_y^{\star 2}))$ operations in $\mathbb{K}$.

Note that both bounds above (when $e^\star > 1$ and $e^\star = 1$) are upper bounded by $2d_xd_y$, independently of the multiplicities. The complexity is also bounded independently of the multiplicities by $O(d_x^\star d_y^\star d_y^4)$.

PROOF. The bounds on the bidegree of $R = R_1R_2\cdots R_m$ are easily derived from the previous discussion.

By Fact 9, a squarefree decomposition of Q can be computed using $\tilde{O}(d_x^2 d_y)$ ops. We now focus on the computations performed inside the ith iteration of the loop. Computing U_i requires an exact division of polynomials of bidegrees at most (d_x, d_y); this division can be performed by evaluation-interpolation in $\tilde{O}(d_xd_y)$ ops. Similarly, the trivariate polynomial V_i can be computed by evaluation-interpolation wrt (x,y) in time $\tilde{O}(d_ie_i^2)$. By the discussion preceding Theorem 10, both $A_i(x,y)$ and $B_i(x,y)$ have bidegrees at most (D_i, E_i), where $D_i = d_x + id_x^\star$ and $E_i = d_y + id_y^\star$. They can be computed by evaluation-interpolation in $\tilde{O}(iD_iE_i)$ ops. Finally, the resultant $R_i(x,z)$ has bidegree at most $(d_iE_i + e_iD_i, e_i)$, and since the degree in y of $A_i - zB_i$ and Q_i is at most E_i, it can be computed by evaluation-interpolation in $\tilde{O}((d_iE_i + e_iD_i)e_iE_i)$ ops by Lemma 8. The total cost of the loop is thus $\tilde{O}(L)$, where

$$L = \sum_{i=1}^{m} \left((i + e_i^2)D_iE_i + d_ie_iE_i^2 \right).$$

Using the (crude) bounds $D_i \leqslant D_m$, $E_i \leqslant E_m$, $\sum_{i=1}^m e_i^2 \leqslant d_y^{\star 2}$ and $\sum_{i=1}^m d_ie_i \leqslant d_x^\star d_y^\star$ shows that L is bounded by

$$D_mE_m \sum_{i=1}^{m} (i + e_i^2) + E_m^2 \sum_{i=1}^{m} d_ie_i \leqslant D_mE_m(m^2 + d_y^{\star 2}) + E_m^2 d_x^\star d_y^\star,$$

which, by using the inequalities $D_m \leqslant 2md_x^\star$ and $E_m \leqslant 2md_y^\star$, is seen to belong to $O(m^2 d_x^\star d_y^\star(m^2 + d_y^{\star 2}))$.

Gathering together the various complexity bounds yields the stated bound and finishes the proof of the theorem. □

Remark. Note that one could also use Hermite reduction combined with the usual Rothstein-Trager resultant in order to compute a polynomial $\tilde{R}(x,z)$ that annihilates the residues. Indeed, Hermite reduction computes an auxiliary rational function that admits the same residues as the input, while only having simple poles. A close inspection of this approach provides the same bound $d_y^\star$ for the degree in y of $\tilde{R}(x,z)$, but a less tight bound for its degree in x, namely worse by a factor of $d_y^\star$. The complexity of this alternative approach appears to be $\tilde{O}(d_xd_y(d_y + d_y^{\star 3}))$ (using results from [2]), to be compared with the complexity bound from Theorem 10.

3.2 Sums of roots of a polynomial

Given a polynomial $P \in \mathbb{K}[y]$ of degree d with coefficients in a field $\mathbb{K}$ of characteristic 0, let $\alpha_1, \dots, \alpha_d$ be its roots in the algebraic closure of $\mathbb{K}$. For any positive integer $c \leqslant d$, the polynomial of degree $\binom{d}{c}$ defined by

$$\Sigma_c P = \prod_{i_1 < \cdots < i_c} (y - (\alpha_{i_1} + \alpha_{i_2} + \cdots + \alpha_{i_c})) \qquad (2)$$

has coefficients in $\mathbb{K}$. This section discusses the computation of $\Sigma_c P$ summarized in Algorithm 2, which can be seen as an additive analogue of the *Platypus algorithm* of Banderier and Flajolet [1].

We recall two classical formulas (see, eg, [4, §2]), the second one being valid for monic P only::

$$\mathcal{N}(P) = \frac{\operatorname{rec}(P')}{\operatorname{rec}(P)}, \qquad \operatorname{rec}(P) = \exp\left(\int \frac{d - \mathcal{N}(P)}{y}\, \mathrm{d}y \right). \qquad (3)$$

Truncating these formulas at order $d+1$ makes $\mathcal{N}(P)$ a representation of the polynomial P (up to normalization), since both conversions above can be performed quasi-optimally by Newton iteration [25,21,4]. The key for Algorithm 2 is the following variant of [1, §2.3].

Proposition 11 *Let $P \in \mathbb{K}[y]$ be a polynomial of degree d, let $\mathcal{N}(P)$ denote the generating series of its Newton sums and let S be the series $\mathcal{N}(P) \odot \exp(y)$. Let Ψ_c be the polynomial in $\mathbb{K}[t_1, \dots, t_c]$ defined by*

$$\Psi_c(t_1, \dots, t_c) = [z^c] \exp\left(\sum_{n \geqslant 1} (-1)^{n-1} t_n \frac{z^n}{n} \right).$$

Then the following equality holds

$$\mathcal{N}(\Sigma_c P) \odot \exp(y) = \Psi_c(S(y), S(2y), \dots, S(cy)).$$

PROOF. By construction, the series S is

$$S(y) = \sum_{n \geqslant 0} (\alpha_1^n + \alpha_2^n + \cdots + \alpha_d^n) \frac{y^n}{n!} = \sum_{i=1}^{d} \exp(\alpha_i y).$$

When applied to the polynomial $\Sigma_c P$, this becomes

$$\mathcal{N}(\Sigma_c P) \odot \exp(y) = \sum_{i_1 < \cdots < i_c} \exp((\alpha_{i_1} + \alpha_{i_2} + \cdots + \alpha_{i_c})y)$$
$$= [z^c] \prod_{i=1}^{d} (1 + z\exp(\alpha_i y)).$$

This expression rewrites:

$$[z^c] \exp\left(\sum_{i=1}^{d} \log(1 + z\exp(\alpha_i y)) \right)$$
$$= [z^c] \exp\left(\sum_{i=1}^{d} \sum_{m \geqslant 1} (-1)^{m-1} \exp(\alpha_i m y) \frac{z^m}{m} \right)$$
$$= [z^c] \exp\left(\sum_{m \geqslant 1} (-1)^{m-1} S(my) \frac{z^m}{m} \right),$$

and the last expression equals $\Psi_c(S(y), S(2y), \dots, S(cy))$. □

Algorithm **PureComposedSum**(P, c)

Input A polynomial P of degree d in $\mathbb{K}[y]$, a positive integer $c \leqslant d$
Output The polynomial $\Sigma_c P$ from Eq. (2)

$D \leftarrow \binom{d}{c}$
$\mathcal{N}(P) \leftarrow \operatorname{rec}(P')/\operatorname{rec}(P) \bmod y^{D+1}$
$S \leftarrow \mathcal{N}(P) \odot \exp(y) \bmod y^{D+1}$
$F \leftarrow \exp\left(\sum_{n=1}^{c} (-1)^{n-1} \frac{S(ny)}{n} z^n\right) \bmod (y^{D+1}, z^{c+1})$
$\mathcal{N}(\Sigma_c P) \leftarrow ([z^c]F) \odot \sum n! y^n \bmod y^{D+1}$
return $\operatorname{rec}\left(\exp\left(\int \frac{D - \mathcal{N}(\Sigma_c P)}{y} \mathrm{d}y\right) \bmod y^{D+1}\right)$

Algorithm 2. Polynomial canceling the sums of c roots

The correctness of Algorithm 2 follows from observing that the truncation orders $D+1$ in y and $c+1$ in z of the power series involved in the algorithm are sufficient to enable the reconstruction of $\Sigma_c P$ from its first Newton sums by (3).

Bivariate case. We now consider the case where P is a polynomial in $\mathbb{K}[x,y]$. Then, the coefficients of $\Sigma_c P$ wrt y may have denominators. We follow the steps of Algorithm 2 (run on P viewed as a polynomial in y with coefficients in $\mathbb{K}(x)$) in order to compute bounds on the bidegree of the polynomial obtained by clearing out these denominators. We obtain the following result.

Theorem 12 *Let $P \in \mathbb{K}[x,y]_{d_x+1, d_y+1}$, let c be a positive integer such that $c \leqslant d_y$ and let $D = \binom{d_y}{c}$. Let $a \in \mathbb{K}[x]$ denote the leading coefficient of P wrt y and let $\Sigma_c P$ be defined as in Eq. (2). Then $a^D \cdot \Sigma_c P$ is a polynomial in $\mathbb{K}[x,y]$ of bidegree at most (d_xD, D) that cancels all sums $\alpha_{i_1} + \cdots + \alpha_{i_c}$ of c roots $\alpha_i(x)$ of P, with $i_1 < \cdots < i_c$. Moreover, this polynomial can be computed in $\tilde{O}(cd_xD^2)$ ops.*

This result is close to optimal. Experiments suggest that for generic P of bidegree (d_x,d_y) the minimal polynomial of $\alpha_{i_1}+\cdots+\alpha_{i_c}$ has bidegree $\left(d_x\binom{d_y-1}{c-1},\binom{d_y}{c}\right)$. In particular, our degree bound is precise in y, and overshoots by a factor of d_y/c only in x. Similarly, the complexity result is quasi-optimal up to a factor of d_xd_y only.

PROOF. The Newton series $\mathcal{N}(P)$ has the form

$$\mathcal{N}(P)=\frac{a\deg_y P+yA(x,y)}{a-yB(x,y)}=\frac{a\deg_y P+yA(x,y)}{a}\sum_{n\geqslant 0}\frac{y^nB(x,y)^n}{a^n},$$

with $\deg_x A,\deg_x B\leqslant d_x$. Since both factors belong to $\mathscr{E}_{d_x}(a)$, Lemma 1 implies that $\mathcal{N}(P)\in\mathscr{E}_{d_x}(a)$. Applying this same lemma repeatedly, we get that $\Sigma_c P\in\mathscr{E}_{d_x}(a)$ (stability under the integration of Algorithm 2 is immediate). Since $\Sigma_c P$ has degree D wrt y, we deduce that $a^D\Sigma_c P$ is a polynomial that satisfies the desired bound. By evaluation and interpolation at $1+d_xD$ points, and Newton iteration for quotients of power series in $\mathbb{K}[[y]]_{1+D}$ (Fact 4), the power series $\mathcal{N}(P)$ can be computed in $\tilde{O}(d_xD^2)$ ops. The power series S is then computed from $\mathcal{N}(P)$ in $O(d_xD^2)$ ops. To compute F we use evaluation-interpolation wrt x at $1+d_xD$ points, and fast exponentials of power series (Fact 4). The cost of this step is $\tilde{O}(cd_xD^2)$ ops. Then, $\mathcal{N}(\Sigma_cP)$ is computed for $O(d_xD^2)$ additional ops. The last exponential is again computed by evaluation-interpolation and Newton iteration using $\tilde{O}(d_xD^2)$ ops. ☐

4. DIAGONALS

4.1 Algebraic equations for diagonals

The relation between diagonals of bivariate rational functions and algebraic series is classical [15,22]. We recall here the usual derivation when $\mathbb{K}=\mathbb{C}$ while setting our notation.

Let $F(x,y)$ be a rational function in $\mathbb{C}(x,y)$, whose denominator does not vanish at $(0,0)$. Then the diagonal of F is a convergent power series that can be represented for small enough t by a Cauchy integral

$$\operatorname{Diag}F(t)=\frac{1}{2\pi i}\oint F(t/y,y)\frac{\mathrm{d}y}{y},$$

where the contour is for instance a circle of radius r inside an annulus where $(t/y,y)$ remains in the domain of convergence of F. This is the basis of an algebraic approach to the computation of the diagonal as a sum of residues of the rational function

$$\frac{P(t,y)}{Q(t,y)}:=\frac{1}{y}F\left(\frac{t}{y},y\right),$$

with P and Q two coprime polynomials. For t small enough, the circle can be shrunk around 0 and only the roots of $Q(t,y)$ tending to 0 when $t\to 0$ lie inside the contour [18]. These are called the *small branches*. Thus the diagonal is given as

$$\operatorname{Diag}F(t)=\sum_{\substack{Q(t,y_i(t))=0\\ \lim_{t\to 0}y_i(t)=0}}\operatorname{Residue}\left(\frac{P(t,y)}{Q(t,y)},y=y_i(t)\right),\qquad(4)$$

where the sum is over the *distinct* roots of Q tending to 0. We call their number the number of small branches of Q and denote it by $\operatorname{Nsmall}(Q)$.

Since the y_i's are algebraic and finite in number and residues are obtained by series expansion, which entails only rational operations, it follows that the diagonal is algebraic too. Combining the algorithms of the previous section gives Algorithm 3 that produces a polynomial equation for $\operatorname{Diag}F$. The correctness of this algorithm over an arbitrary field of characteristic 0 follows from an adaptation of the arguments of Gessel and Stanley [17, Th. 6.1], [26, Th. 6.3.3].

Example 2. Let $d\geqslant 0$ be an integer, and let $F_d(x,y)$ be the rational function $1/(1-x-y)^{d+1}$. The diagonal of F_d is equal to

$$\sum_{n\geqslant 0}\binom{2n+d}{n}\binom{n+d}{d}t^n.$$

Algorithm **AlgebraicDiagonal**(A/B)

Input Two polynomials A and $B\in\mathbb{K}[x,y]$, with $B(0,0)\neq 0$
Output A polynomial $\Phi\in\mathbb{K}[t,\Delta]$ such that $\Phi(t,\operatorname{Diag}A/B)=0$

$G\leftarrow\frac{1}{y}\frac{A}{B}(\frac{t}{y},y)$
Write G as P/Q with coprime polynomials P and Q;
$R(z)\leftarrow$ **AlgebraicResidues**(P/Q)
$c\leftarrow$ number of small branches of Q
$\Phi(t,z)\leftarrow$ numer(**PureComposedSum**(R,c))
return $\Phi(t,\Delta)$

Algorithm 3. Polynomial canceling the diagonal of a rational function

By the previous argument, it is an algebraic series, which is the sum of the residues of the rational function G_d of Example 1 over its small branches (with x replaced by t). In this case, the denominator is $y-t-y^2$. It has one solution tending to 0 with t; the other one tends to 1. Thus the diagonal is cancelled by the quadratic polynomial (1).

Example 3. For an integer $d>0$, we consider the rational function

$$F_d(x,y)=\frac{x^{d-1}}{1-x^d-y^{d+1}},$$

of bidegree $(d,d+1)$. The first step of the algorithm produces

$$G_d(t,y)=\frac{t^{d-1}}{y^d-t^d-y^{2d+1}},$$

whose denominator is irreducible with d small branches. Running Algorithm 3 on this example, we obtain a polynomial Φ_d annihilating $\operatorname{Diag}F_d$, which is experimentally irreducible and whose bidegrees for $d=1,2,3,4$ are $(2,3),(18,10),(120,35),(700,126)$. From these values, it is easy to conjecture that the bidegree is given by

$$\left(d(d+1)\binom{2d-1}{d-1},\binom{2d+1}{d}\right),$$

of exponential growth in the bidegree of F_d. In general, these bidegrees do not grow faster than in this example. In Theorem 14, we prove bounds that are barely larger than the values above.

4.2 Degree Bounds and Complexity

The rest of this section is devoted to the derivation of bounds on the complexity of Algorithm 3 and on the size of the polynomial it computes, which are given in Theorem 14.

Degrees. A bound on the bidegree of Φ will be obtained from the bounds successively given by Theorems 10 and 12.

In order to follow the impact of the change of variables in the first step, we define the *diagonal degree* of a polynomial $P(x,y)=\sum_{i,j}a_{i,j}x^iy^j$ as the integer $\operatorname{ddeg}(P):=\sup\{i-j\mid a_{i,j}\neq 0\}$. We collect the properties of interest in the following.

Lemma 13 *For any P and Q in $\mathbb{K}[x,y]$,*
(1) $\operatorname{ddeg}(P)\leqslant\deg_x P$;
(2) $\operatorname{ddeg}(PQ)=\operatorname{ddeg}(P)+\operatorname{ddeg}(Q)$;
(3) there exists a polynomial $\tilde{P}\in\mathbb{K}[x,y]$, such that $P(x/y,y)=y^{-\operatorname{ddeg}(P)}\tilde{P}(x,y)$, with $\tilde{P}(x,0)\neq 0$ and

$$\operatorname{bideg}(\tilde{P})\leqslant\operatorname{bideg}(P)+(0,\operatorname{ddeg}(P));$$

(4) $\operatorname{bideg}((\tilde{P})^\star)=(\deg_x P^\star,\operatorname{ddeg}(P^\star)+\deg_y P^\star)$.

PROOF. Part *(1)* is immediate. The quantity $\operatorname{ddeg}(P)$ is nothing else than $-\operatorname{val}_y P(x/y,y)$, which makes Parts *(2)* and *(3)* clear too. From there, we get the identity $\widetilde{PQ}=\tilde{P}\tilde{Q}$ for arbitrary P and Q, whence $(\tilde{P})^\star=\widetilde{P^\star}$ and Part *(4)* is a consequence of Parts *(1)* and *(3)*. ☐

Thus, starting with a rational function $F=A/B\in\mathbb{K}(x,y)$, with (d_x,d_y) a bound on the bidegrees of A and B, and $(d_x^\star,d_y^\star)$ a bound on the bidegree of a squarefree part $B^\star$ of B, the first step of the algorithm constructs $G(t,y) = y^\alpha \frac{P}{Q}$, with polynomials P and Q and

$$\alpha = \operatorname{ddeg}(B) - \operatorname{ddeg}(A) - 1 \qquad (5)$$
$$\operatorname{bideg} P \leqslant (d_x, \operatorname{ddeg}(A) + d_y), \quad \operatorname{bideg} Q \leqslant (d_x, \operatorname{ddeg}(B) + d_y),$$
$$\operatorname{bideg} Q^\star \leqslant (d_x^\star, d_x^\star + d_y^\star).$$

These inequalities give bounds on the degrees in x of the numerator and denominator of G.

The rest of the computation depends on the sign of α. If $\alpha \geqslant 0$, then the degrees in y of $y^\alpha P$ and Q are bounded by $\operatorname{ddeg}(B) + d_y$, while if $\alpha < 0$, those of P and $y^{-\alpha} Q$ are bounded by $\operatorname{ddeg}(A) + d_y + 1$. Thus in both cases they are bounded by $d_x + d_y + \varepsilon$, where

$$\varepsilon = \begin{cases} 1 & \text{if } \alpha < 0, \\ 0 & \text{otherwise.} \end{cases} \qquad (6)$$

A squarefree part of the denominator has degree in y bounded by $d_x^\star + d_y^\star + \varepsilon$. From there, Theorem 10 yields $\operatorname{bideg} R \leqslant (D_x, D_y)$, with

$$D_x := 2d_x^\star(d_x - d_x^\star + d_y - d_y^\star + 1) + d_x(2(d_x^\star + d_y^\star + \varepsilon) - 1), \qquad (7)$$
$$D_y := d_x^\star + d_y^\star + \varepsilon.$$

Small branches. It is classical that for a polynomial $P = \sum a_{i,j} x^i y^j \in \mathbb{K}[x,y]$, the number of its solutions tending to 0 can be read off its Newton polygon. This polygon is the lower convex hull of the union of $(i,j) + \mathbb{N}^2$ for (i,j) such that $a_{i,j} \neq 0$. The number of solutions tending to 0 is given by the minimal y-coordinate of its leftmost points. Since the number of small branches counts only distinct solutions, it is thus given by

$$\operatorname{Nsmall}(P) = \operatorname{Nsmall}(P^\star) = \operatorname{val}_y([x^{\operatorname{val}_x P^\star}]P^\star). \qquad (8)$$

The change of variables $x \mapsto x/y$ changes the coordinates of the point corresponding to $a_{i,j}$ into $(i, j-i)$. This transformation maps the vertices of the original Newton polygon to the vertices of the Newton polygon of the Laurent polynomial $P(x/y, y)$. Multiplying by $y^{\operatorname{ddeg}(P)}$ yields a polynomial and shifts the Newton polygon up by $\operatorname{ddeg}(P)$, thus

$$\operatorname{Nsmall}\left(y^{\operatorname{ddeg}(P)} P(x/y, y)\right) = \operatorname{Nsmall}(P^\star) + \operatorname{ddeg}(P^\star).$$

The number of small branches of the denominator of G constructed in the first step of the algorithm is then given by

$$c := \operatorname{Nsmall}(B^\star) + \operatorname{ddeg}(B^\star) + \varepsilon. \qquad (9)$$

Complexity. We now analyze the cost of Algorithm 3. The first step does not require any arithmetic operation. Next, the computation of R takes $\tilde{O}((d_x + d_y)^6)$ ops. (see the comment after Theorem 10). The number of small branches is obtained with no arithmetic operation from a squarefree decomposition computed in Algorithm 1. Finally, Algorithm 2 uses $\tilde{O}(cD_x\binom{D_y}{c}^2)$ ops.

We now have the values required by Theorem 12, which concludes the proof of the following bounds.

Theorem 14 *Let $F = A/B$ be a rational function in $\mathbb{K}(x,y)$ with $B(0,0) \neq 0$. Let (d_x, d_y) (resp. $(d_x^\star, d_y^\star)$) be a bound on the bidegrees of A and B (resp. a squarefree part of B). Let ε, D_x, D_y, c be defined as in Eqs. (6,7,9). Then there exists a polynomial $\Phi \in \mathbb{K}[t, \Delta]$ such that $\Phi(t, \operatorname{Diag} F(t)) = 0$ and*

$$\operatorname{bideg} \Phi \leqslant \left(D_x \binom{D_y}{c}, \binom{D_y}{c}\right).$$

Algorithm 3 computes it in $\tilde{O}\left(cD_x\binom{D_y}{c}^2 + (d_x + d_y)^6\right)$ ops.

A general bound on $\operatorname{bideg} \Phi$ depending only on a bound (d,d) on the bidegree of the input can be deduced from the above as

$$\operatorname{bideg} \Phi \leqslant (d(4d+3), 1) \times \binom{2d+1}{d}.$$

4.3 Optimization

Assume that the denominator of $F(x/y)/y$ is already partially factored as $Q(y) = \tilde{Q}(y) \prod_{i=1}^k (y - y_i(x))$, where the y_i are k distinct *rational* branches among the c small branches of Q. Then their corresponding (rational) residues r_i contribute to the diagonal; therefore it is only necessary to invoke Algorithm 3 on $(\tilde{Q}, c-k)$, which produces a polynomial $\tilde{\Phi}$. Then the polynomial $\Phi(t, \Delta) = \tilde{\Phi}(t, \Delta - \sum_i r_i)$ cancels the diagonal of F.

In particular, this optimization applies systematically for the factor $y^{-\alpha}$ when $\alpha < 0$ (or equivalently $\varepsilon = 1$) in the algorithm. In this case, it yields a polynomial Φ with smaller degree than the original algorithm:

$$\deg_\Delta \Phi \leqslant \binom{d_x^\star + d_y^\star}{\operatorname{Nsmall}(B^\star) + \operatorname{ddeg}(B^\star)}.$$

(A sharper bound on the degree in t can be derived as well.)

4.4 Generic case

The bounds from Theorem 14 on the bidegree of Φ are slightly pessimistic wrt the variable t, but generically tight wrt the variable Δ, as will be proved in Proposition 16 below. We first need a lemma.

Lemma 15 *Let $\mathbb{K}$ be a field of characteristic 0, and $P \in \mathbb{K}[y]$ be a polynomial of degree d, with Galois group $\mathfrak{S}_d$ over $\mathbb{K}$. Assume that the roots $\alpha_1, \ldots \alpha_d$ of P are algebraically independent over $\mathbb{Q}$. Then, for any $c \leqslant d$, the degree $\binom{d}{c}$ polynomial $\Sigma_c P$ is irreducible in $\mathbb{K}[y]$.*

PROOF. Since $\Sigma = \alpha_1 + \cdots + \alpha_c$ is a root of $\Sigma_c P$, it suffices to prove that $\mathbb{K}(\Sigma)$ has degree $\binom{d}{c}$ over $\mathbb{K}$. The α_i's being algebraically independent, any permutation $\sigma \in \mathfrak{S}_d$ of all the α_i's that leaves Σ unchanged has to preserve $\alpha_{c+1} + \cdots + \alpha_d$ as well. It follows that $\mathbb{K}(\alpha_1, \ldots, \alpha_d)$ has degree $c!(d-c)!$ over $\mathbb{K}(\Sigma)$ and degree $d!$ over $\mathbb{K}$, so that $\mathbb{K}(\Sigma)$ has degree $\binom{d}{c}$ over $\mathbb{K}$ □

Proposition 16 *Let A be a polynomial in $\mathbb{Q}[x,y]_{d_x,d_y}$, and*

$$B(x,y) = \sum_{i \leqslant d_x, j \leqslant d_y} b_{i,j} x^i y^j \in \mathbb{Q}[(b_{i,j}); x, y],$$

where the $b_{i,j}$ are indeterminates. Then the polynomial computed by Algorithm 3 with input A/B is irreducible of degree $\binom{d_x+d_y}{d_x}$ over $\mathbb{K} = \mathbb{Q}((b_{i,j}); x)$.

PROOF. First apply the change of variables to obtain $G = P/Q$, with $Q(x,y) = \sum_{i,j} b_{i,j} x^i y^{d_x - i + j}$. Denote $d = d_x + d_y$. Then, the polynomial $Q(1,y)$ has the form $\sum_{j \leqslant d} t_j y^j$ where the t_j's are algebraically independent over $\mathbb{Q}$. Therefore, $Q(1,y)$ has Galois group $\mathfrak{S}_d$ over $\mathbb{Q}(t_0, \ldots, t_d)$ and its roots are algebraically independent over $\mathbb{Q}$ [28, §57]. This property lifts to $Q(x,y)$ [28, §61], which thus has Galois group $\mathfrak{S}_d$ and algebraically independent roots, denoted $y_1, \ldots, y_d$.

Now define the polynomial $R(x,y) = \prod_i (y - P(x,y_i)/\partial_y Q(x,y_i))$. Since Q has simple roots, this is exactly the polynomial that is computed by Algorithm 1. The family $\{P(x,y_i)/\partial_y Q(x,y_i)\}$ is algebraically independent, since any algebraic relation between them would induce one for the y_i's by clearing out denominators. In particular, the natural morphism $\operatorname{Gal}(Q/\mathbb{K}) = \mathfrak{S}_d \to \operatorname{Gal}(R/\mathbb{K})$ is injective, whence an isomorphism. (Here, $\operatorname{Gal}(P/\mathbb{K})$ denotes the Galois group of $P \in \mathbb{K}[y]$ over $\mathbb{K}$.) Since an immediate investigation of the Newton polygon of Q shows that it has d_x small branches, we conclude using Lemma 15. □

Proposition 16 implies that for a generic rational function A/B with $A \in \mathbb{K}[x,y]_{d,d}$ and $B \in \mathbb{K}[x,y]_{d+1,d+1}$, the degree of Φ in Δ is $\binom{2d}{d}$. This is indeed observed on random examples.

Example 4. We consider a rational function $F(x,y) = 1/B(x,y)$, where $B(x,y)$ is a dense polynomial of bidegree (d,d) chosen at random. For $d = 1, 2, 3, 4$, algorithm **AlgebraicDiagonal**(F) produces *irreducible* outputs with bidegrees $(2,2)$, $(16,6)$, $(108,20)$, $(640,70)$, that are matched by the formulas

$$\left(2d^2\binom{2d-2}{d-1}, \binom{2d}{d}\right), \tag{10}$$

so that the bound on $\deg_\Delta \Phi$ is tight in this case and the irreducibility of the output shows that Theorem 14 cannot be improved further.

5. WALKS

The exponential degree of the minimal polynomial of a diagonal proved in Proposition 16 concerns more generally other sums of residues, since this is the step where the exponential growth of the algebraic equations appears. This includes in particular constant terms of rational functions in $\mathbb{C}(x)[[y]]$, that can also be written as contour integrals of rational functions around the origin.

By contrast, sums of residues of a rational function always satisfy a differential equation of only polynomial size [2]. Thus, when an algebraic function appears to be connected to a sum of residues of a rational function, the use of this differential structure is much more adapted to the computation of series expansions, instead of going through a potentially large polynomial.

As an example where this phenomenon occurs naturally, we consider here the enumeration of unidimensional lattice walks, following Banderier and Flajolet [1] and Bousquet-Mélou [7]. Our goal in this section is to study, from the algorithmic perspective, the series expansions of various generating functions (for bridges, excursions, meanders) that have been identified as algebraic [1]. One of our contributions is to point out that although algebraic series can be expanded fast [11, 12, 3], the pre-computation of a polynomial equation could have prohibitive cost. We overcome this difficulty by pre-computing differential (instead of polynomial) equations that have polynomial size only, and using them to compute series expansions to precision N for bridges, excursions and meanders in time quasi-linear in N.

5.1 Preliminaries

We start with some vocabulary on lattice walks. A *simple step* is a vector $(1,u)$ with $u \in \mathbb{Z}$. A *step set* S is a finite set of simple steps. A *unidimensional walk* in the plane $\mathbb{Z}^2$ built from S is a finite sequence $(A_0, A_1, \dots, A_n)$ of points in $\mathbb{Z}^2$, such that $A_0 = (0,0)$ and $\overrightarrow{A_{k-1}A_k} = (1,u_k)$ with $(1,u_k) \in S$. In this case n is called the *length* of the walk, and S is the *step set* of the walk. The y-coordinate of the endpoint A_n, namely $\sum_{i=1}^n u_i$, is called the final altitude of the walk. The characteristic polynomial of the step set S is

$$\Gamma_S(y) = \sum_{(1,u)\in S} y^u.$$

Following Banderier and Flajolet, we consider three specific families of walks: bridges, excursions and meanders [1]. *Bridges* are walks with final altitude 0, *meanders* are walks confined to the upper half plane, and *excursions* are bridges that are also meanders.

We define the full generating power series of walks

$$W_S(x,y) = \sum_{n\geqslant 0, k\in\mathbb{Z}} w_{n,k} x^n y^k \in \mathbb{Z}[y, y^{-1}][[x]],$$

where $w_{n,k}$ is the number of walks with step set S, of length n and final altitude k. We denote by $B_S(x)$ (resp. $E_S(x)$, and $M_S(x)$) the power series $\sum_{n\geqslant 0} u_n x^n$, where u_n is the number of bridges (resp. excursions, and meanders) of length n with step set S.

We omit the step set S as a subscript when there is no ambiguity. Several properties of the power series W, B, E and M are classical:

Fact 17 *[1, §2.1-2.2] The power series W, B, E and M satisfy*
(1) $W(x,y)$ is rational and $W(x,y) = 1/(1 - x\Gamma(y))$;
(2) $B(x)$, $E(x)$ and $M(x)$ are algebraic;
(3) $B(x) = [y^0]W(x,y)$;
(4) $E(x) = \exp\left(\int (B(x)-1)/x\,\mathrm{d}x\right)$.

Our main objective in what follows is to study the efficiency of computing the power series expansions of the series B, E and M. In the next two sections, we first study two previously known methods, then we design a new one.

5.2 Expanding the generating power series

We denote by u^- (resp. u^+) the largest u such that $(1,-u) \in S$ (resp. $(1,u) \in S$) and denote by d the sum $u^- + u^+$. The integer d measures the vertical amplitude of S; this makes d a good scale for measuring the complexity of the algorithms that will follow. We assume that both u^- and u^+ are positive, since otherwise the study of the excursions and meanders becomes trivial.

The direct method. The combinatorial definition of walks yields a recurrence relation for $w_{n,k}$:

$$w_{n,k} = \sum_{(1,u)\in S} w_{n-1,k-u}, \tag{11}$$

with initial conditions $w_{n,k} = 0$ if $n,k \leqslant 0$ with $(n,k) \neq (0,0)$, and $w_{0,0} = 1$. If $\tilde{w}_{n,k}$ denotes the number of walks of length n and final altitude k that never exit the upper half plane, then $\tilde{w}_{n,k}$ also satisfies recurrence (11), but with the additional initial conditions $\tilde{w}_{n,k} = 0$ for all $k < 0$. Then the bridges (resp. excursions, meanders) are counted by the numbers $w_{n,0}$ (resp. $\tilde{w}_{n,0}$, $\sum_k \tilde{w}_{n,k}$).

One can compute these numbers by unrolling the recurrence relation (11). Each use of the recurrence costs $O(d)$ ops., and in the worst case one has to compute $O(dN^2)$ terms of the sequence (for example, if the step set is $S = \{(1,1), \dots, (1,d)\}$). This leads to the computation of each of the generating series in $O(d^2N^2)$ ops.

Using algebraic equations. Another method is suggested in [1, §2.3]. It relies on the algebraicity of B, E and M (Fact 17*(2)*). The series E and M can be expressed as products in terms of the small branches of the characteristic polynomial Γ_S (see [1, Th. 1, Cor. 1]). From there, a polynomial equation can be obtained using the Platypus algorithm [1, §2.3], which computes a polynomial canceling the products of a fixed number of roots of a given polynomial. Given a polynomial equation $P(z,E) = 0$, another one for B can be deduced from the relation $B = zE'/E + 1$ as $\mathrm{Resultant}_E((B-1)EP_E + zP_z, P)$.

Once a polynomial equation is known for one of these three series, it can be used to compute a linear recurrence with polynomial coefficients satisfied by its coefficients [11, 12, 3]. This method produces an algorithm that computes the first N terms of B, E and M in $O(N)$ ops. For this to be an improvement over the naive method for large N, the dependence on d of the constant in the $O()$ should not be too large and the precomputation not too costly.

Indeed, the cost of the pre-computation of an algebraic equation is not negligible. Generically, the minimal polynomial of E has degree $\binom{d}{u^-}$, which may be exponentially large with respect to d [7]. Empirically, the polynomials for B and M are similarly large.

The situation for differential equations and recurrences is different: B satisfies a differential equation of only polynomial size (see below), whereas (empirically), those for E and M have a potentially exponential size. These sizes then transfer to the corresponding recurrences and thereby to the constant in the complexity of unrolling them.

Example 5. With the step set $S = \{(1,d), (1,1), (1,-d)\}$ and $d \geqslant 2$, the counting series W_S equals

$$W_S(x,y) = \frac{y^d}{y^d - x(1 + y^{d+1} + y^{2d})}.$$

Experiments indicate that the minimal polynomial of $B_S(x)$ has bidegree $\left(2d\binom{2d-2}{d-1}, \binom{2d}{d}\right)$, exhibiting an exponential growth in d. On the other hand, they show that $B_S(x)$ satisfies a linear differential equation of order $2d-1$ and coefficients of degree $d^2 + 3d - 2$ for even d, and $d^2 + 3d - 4$ for odd d.

New Method. We now give a method that runs in quasi-linear time (with respect to N) and avoids the computation of an algebraic equation. Our method relies on the fact that periods of rational functions

Algorithm **Walks**(S, N)

Input A set S of simple steps and an integer N
Output $B_S, E_S, M_S \bmod x^{N+1}$

$F \leftarrow W(x,y)/y$ [case B,E] or $W(x,y)/(1-y)$ [case M]
$D \leftarrow$ **HermiteTelescoping**(F) [2, Fig. 3]
$R \leftarrow$ the recurrence of order r associated to D
$I \leftarrow [y^0]W(x,y) \bmod x^{r+1}$ [case B,E]
$[y^0]yW(x,y)/(1-y) \bmod x^{r+1}$ [case M]
$B \leftarrow [y^0]W(x,y) \bmod x^{N+1}$ (from R,I)
$A \leftarrow [y^0]yW(x,y)/(1-y) \bmod x^{N+1}$ (from R,I)
$E \leftarrow \exp(\int (B(x)-1)/x \, dx) \bmod x^{N+1}$
$M \leftarrow \exp(-\int (A(x)/x)/(1-\Gamma(1)x)\, dx) \bmod x^{N+1}$
return B,E,M

Algorithm 4. Expanding the generating functions of bridges, excursions and meanders

such as the one in Part *(3)* of Fact 17 satisfy differential equations of polynomial size in the degree of the input rational function [2]. We summarize our results in the following theorem, and then go over the proof in each case individually.

Theorem 18 *Let S be a finite set of simple steps and $d = u^- + u^+$. The series B_S (resp. E_S and M_S) can be expanded at order N in $O(d^2N)$ ops. (resp. $\tilde{O}(d^2N)$ ops.), after a pre-computation in $\tilde{O}(d^5)$ ops.*

5.3 Fast Algorithms

Bridges. To expand $B(x)$, we rely on Fact 17*(3)*. The formula can be written $B = (1/2\pi i)\oint W(x,y)\frac{dy}{y}$, the integration path being a circle inside a small annulus around the origin [1, proof of Th. 1]. Moreover, $W(x,y)/y$ is of the form P/Q, where $\operatorname{bideg} Q \leqslant (1,d)$ and $\operatorname{bideg} P \leqslant (0, d-1)$. Since P and Q are relatively prime and Q is primitive with respect to y, Algorithm **HermiteTelescoping** [2, Fig. 3] computes a telescoper for P/Q, which is also a differential equation satisfied by B, in $\tilde{O}(d^5)$ ops. The resulting differential equation has order at most d and degree $O(d^2)$. This differential equation can be turned into a recurrence of order $O(d^2)$ in quasi-optimal time (see the discussion after [5, Cor. 2]). We may use it to expand $B(x) \bmod x^N$ in $O(d^2N)$ ops, once we have a way to compute the initial conditions. But this can be done using the naive algorithm described above in $\tilde{O}(d^4)$ ops. Thus, the total cost of the pre-computation is $\tilde{O}(d^5)$, as announced.

Excursions. If $B(x) \bmod x^{N+1}$ is known, it is then possible to recover $E(x) \bmod x^{N+1}$ thanks to Fact 17*(4)*. Expanding $E(x)$ comes down to the computation of the exponential of a series, which can be performed using $\tilde{O}(N)$ ops. (Fact 4*(4)*).

Meanders. As in the case of excursions, the logarithmic derivative of $M(x)$ is recovered from a sum of residues by the following.

Proposition 19 *The series W and M are related through*

$$A(x) = [y^0]\frac{y}{1-y}W(x,y), \quad M(x) = \frac{\exp\left(-\int \frac{A(x)}{x}\, dx\right)}{1-x\Gamma(1)}.$$

PROOF. Denote by $y_1, \ldots, y_{u^-}$ the small branches of the polynomial $y^{u^-} - xy^{u^-}\Gamma(y)$. Then M is given as [1, Cor. 1]:

$$M(x) = \frac{1}{1-x\Gamma(1)}\prod_{i=1}^{u^-}(1-y_i).$$

On the other hand,

$$A(x) = \frac{1}{2\pi i}\oint \frac{W(x,y)}{1-y}\, dy$$

$$= \sum_{i=1}^{u^-} \operatorname{Residue}_{y=y_i(x)}\left(\frac{1}{(1-y)(1-x\Gamma(y))}\right) = -\sum_{i=1}^{u^-}\frac{1}{(1-y_i)x\Gamma'(y_i)},$$

where the integral has been taken over a circle around the origin and the small branches. Differentiating the equation $1 - x\Gamma(y) = 0$ with respect to x leads to $-x\Gamma'(y_i) = 1/(xy_i')$, whence $A(x) = x\sum_{i=1}^{u^-} y_i'/(1-y_i)$. Therefore, $\prod(1-y_i) = \exp(-\int A/x\, dx))$, finishing the proof. □

Thus we apply the same method as in the case of the excursions. We first compute a differential equation for $A(x)$ using the method of [2]. The computation of the initial conditions for A can also be performed naively from its definition as a constant term, by simply expanding $yW(x,y)/(1-y)$. The formula of the proposition then recovers $M(x)$. The complexity analysis goes exactly as in the previous case, giving a global cost of $\tilde{O}(d^5)$ ops.

Acknowledgements. This work has been supported in part by FastRelax ANR-14-CE25-0018-01.

6. REFERENCES

[1] C. Banderier and P. Flajolet. Basic analytic combinatorics of directed lattice paths. *TCS*, 281(1-2):37–80, 2002.

[2] A. Bostan, S. Chen, F. Chyzak, and Z. Li. Complexity of creative telescoping for bivariate rational functions. In *ISSAC'10*, pages 203–210. ACM, 2010.

[3] A. Bostan, F. Chyzak, G. Lecerf, B. Salvy, and É. Schost. Differential equations for algebraic functions. In *ISSAC'07*, pages 25–32. ACM Press, 2007.

[4] A. Bostan, P. Flajolet, B. Salvy, and É. Schost. Fast computation of special resultants. *JSC*, 41(1):1–29, 2006.

[5] A. Bostan and É. Schost. Polynomial evaluation and interpolation on special sets of points. *J. Complexity*, 21(4):420–446, 2005.

[6] M. Bousquet-Mélou. Rational and algebraic series in combinatorial enumeration. In *International Congress of Mathematicians*, pages 789–826. EMS, 2006.

[7] M. Bousquet-Mélou. Discrete excursions. *Séminaire Lotharingien de Combinatoire*, 57:Art. B57d, 23, 2006/08.

[8] M. Bousquet-Mélou and M. Petkovšek. Linear recurrences with constant coefficients: the multivariate case. *Discrete Math.*, 225(1-3):51–75, 2000.

[9] M. Bronstein. Formulas for series computations. *AAECC*, 2(3):195–206, 1992.

[10] P. Bürgisser, M. Clausen, and M. A. Shokrollahi. *Algebraic complexity theory*, volume 315 of *Grundlehren der Mathematischen Wissenschaften*. Springer, 1997.

[11] D. V. Chudnovsky and G. V. Chudnovsky. On expansion of algebraic functions in power and Puiseux series, I. *Journal of Complexity*, 2(4):271–294, 1986.

[12] D. V. Chudnovsky and G. V. Chudnovsky. On expansion of algebraic functions in power and Puiseux series, II. *Journal of Complexity*, 3(1):1–25, 1987.

[13] J. Denef and L. Lipshitz. Algebraic power series and diagonals. *Journal of Number Theory*, 26(1):46–67, 1987.

[14] M. Fliess. Sur divers produits de séries formelles. *Bull. Soc. Math. France*, 102:181–191, 1974.

[15] H. Furstenberg. Algebraic functions over finite fields. *Journal of Algebra*, 7(2):271–277, 1967.

[16] J. von zur Gathen and J. Gerhard. *Modern Computer Algebra*. Cambridge Univ. Press, second edition, 2003.

[17] I. M. Gessel. A factorization for formal Laurent series and lattice path enumeration. *JCTA*, 28(3):321–337, 1980.

[18] L. J. Hautus and D. A. Klarner. The diagonal of a double power series. *Duke Mathematical Journal*, 38:229–235, 1971.

[19] G. Lecerf. Fast separable factorization and applications. *AAECC*, 19(2):135–160, 2008.

[20] V. Y. Pan. Simple multivariate polynomial multiplication. *JSC*, 18(3):183–186, 1994.

[21] V. Y. Pan. New techniques for the computation of linear recurrence coefficients. *Finite Fields and their Applications*, 6(1):93–118, 2000.

[22] G. Pólya. Sur les séries entières, dont la somme est une fonction algébrique. *L'Enseignement Mathématique*, 22:38–47, 1921.

[23] M. Rothstein. *Aspects of symbolic integration and simplification of exponential and primitive functions*. PhD thesis, 1976.

[24] K. V. Safonov. On conditions for the sum of a power series to be algebraic and rational. *Math. Notes*, 41(3–4):185–189, 1987.

[25] A. Schönhage. The fundamental theorem of algebra in terms of computational complexity. Technical report, Tübingen, 1982.

[26] R. P. Stanley. *Enumerative Combinatorics*, volume II. Cambridge Univ. Press, 1999.

[27] B. M. Trager. Algebraic factoring and rational function integration. SYMSAC'76, pages 219–226. ACM, 1976.

[28] B. L. van der Waerden. *Modern Algebra. Vol. I*. Frederick Ungar Publ. Co., 1949.

Open Non-uniform Cylindrical Algebraic Decompositions

Christopher W. Brown
United States Naval Academy
Annapolis, Maryland, USA
wcbrown@usna.edu

ABSTRACT

This paper introduces the notion of an Open *Non-uniform Cylindrical Algebraic Decomposition* (NuCAD), and presents an efficient *model-based* algorithm for constructing an Open NuCAD from an input formula. Using a limited experimental implementation of the algorithm, we demonstrate the effectiveness of the approach. NuCAD generalizes Cylindrical Algebraic Decomposition (CAD) as defined by Collins in his seminal work from the early 1970s, and extended in concepts like Hong's partial CAD. A NuCAD, like a CAD, is a decomposition of $\mathbb{R}^n$ into cylindrical cells. But unlike a CAD, the cells in a NuCAD need not be arranged cylindrically. It is in this sense that NuCADs are not uniformly cylindrical. However, NuCADs — like CADs — carry a tree-like structure that relates different cells. It is a very different tree but, as with the CAD tree structure, it allows some operations to be performed efficiently, for example locating the containing cell for an arbitrary input point.

Categories and Subject Descriptors

G.4 [**Mathematics of Computation**]: Mathematical software—*Algorithm design and analysis*

Keywords

cylindrical algebraic decomposition; polynomial inequalities

1. INTRODUCTION

This paper[1] introduces a new *model-based* approach to constructing semi-algebraic decompositions of Euclidean space, and a new kind of semi-algebraic decomposition, the *Non-uniform Cylindrical Algebraic Decomposition* (NuCAD), that the model-based approach naturally produces. The model-based approach, building on [9] and [3], has several appealing properties . However, prior work has only applied it to a limited extent in the context of constructing semi-algebraic decompositions. Jovanovic and de Moura's work [9], which introduced the approach, uses it to determine the satisfiability of Tarski formulas. In some sense, their approach can be seen as building a CAD-like decomposition. However, what is constructed is an unstructured list of cells, which makes it unsuitable for some of what CADs are used for. Moreover, the method is not obviously parallelizable, and it doesn't take as strong advantage of the "model-based approach" as is possible. [3] shows how to make stronger use of the "model" during the construction of a single open cell. It could be plugged into Jovanovic and de Moura's algorithm to produce a superior SAT-solver for problems for which only full-dimensional regions need to be examined — solving strict inequalities, for example. The approach was extended to cells of arbitrary dimension in [5], although fallback to Jovanovic and de Moura's approach may be required when input is not *well-oriented*. These algorithms make strong use of the "model point" to produce dramatically smaller projections for the construction of a single cylindrical cell, but neither produces a decomposition. In [13], Strzebonski applies some of the ideas from Jovanovic and de Moura's work to construct CADs (more precisely *cylindrical formulas*, a distinction that is not important here) using what he calls *local projection*. It does not make strong use of the "model point" as espoused in [3], and it is essentially a mix of model-based methods and traditional CAD techniques. In particular, it has the property that a lot of projection work has to be done before any cells are produced.

This paper continues in one of the directions outlined in [3], using the strong model-based approach to construct not just a single cylindrical cell, but a whole decomposition of real space into cylindrical cells. A particularly exciting aspect of this new model-based approach is that while we construct cylindrical cells, those cells need not be cylindrically arranged with respect to one another. This frees us to construct more general decompositions than CADs, thereby representing semi-algebraic sets with fewer cells. To make use of this freedom, we introduce a new generalization of CAD, the *Open Non-uniform Cylindrical Algebraic Decomposition* (Open NuCAD), and an algorithm TI-Open-NuCAD that efficiently constructs an Open NuCAD from an input formula. As demonstrated later in the paper, the flexibility of NuCADs allows sets to be represented using fewer cells than with a CAD. Figure 1 illustrates this.

NuCADs and the model-based approach represent a dramatic departure from previous work with Cylindrical Algebraic Decomposition (CAD). NuCADs are built incrementally, not by dimension, as is usually the case in CAD, but by continually refining regions in the full space of the prob-

[1] This paper extends and improves the technical report [4].

ISSAC'15, July 6–9, 2015, Bath, United Kingdom.
ACM 978-1-4503-3435-8/15/07$15.00
DOI: http://dx.doi.org/10.1145/2755996.2756654.

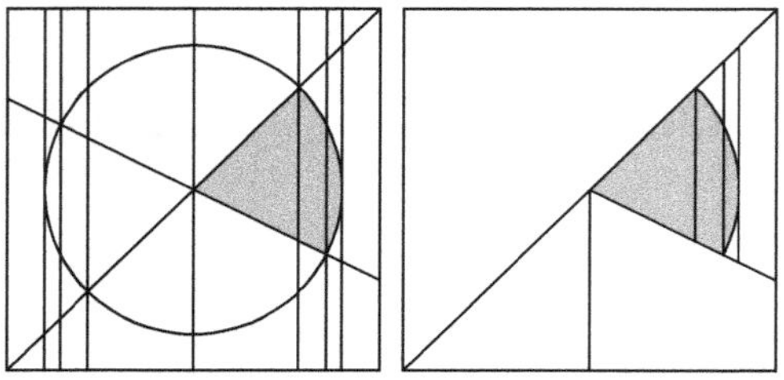

Figure 1: An open CAD (left) and NuCAD (right) representing the set $y - x < 0 \wedge 2y + x > 0 \wedge x^2 + y^2 - 1 < 0$. Note that in the CAD, each individual cell is cylindrical and, moreover, cells are arranged cylindrically — i.e. arranged in vertical strips. In the NuCAD, cells are cylindrical, but not arranged into vertical strips.

lem's dimension. This means that from the beginning of the NuCAD construction process, truth-invariant cells are produced. This is in marked contrast to CAD, where the entire projection must be done before cells are constructed. NuCADs are not generally CADs, because cells are not necessarily cylindrically arranged[2], but they retain some of the nice properties of CADs, most notably that the projection onto a lower dimension of a set represented by a NuCAD is easy to compute (once again, see Figure 1). This departure from strict cylindricity allows sets to be represented with fewer cells, as demonstrated by experiments reported later in this paper. NuCAD and the model-based construction also provide a natural way to take strong advantage of the particulars of the input formula from which the decomposition is constructed. Much of what has been done in the way of CAD research has been based on trying to do exactly this: partial CAD, equational constraints[7, 11], divide & conquer [14], and truth table invariant CAD [1], for example.

This paper's contributions are the introduction of the Open NuCAD, a model-based algorithm for efficiently constructing NuCADs along with a proof of correctness, and empirical data demonstrating how much more efficiently NuCAD represents semi-algebraic sets than CAD. The remainder of the article is laid out as follows. Section 2 defines the NuCAD data-structure. A model-based algorithm for constructing NuCADs is given in Section 3. A walkthrough of that algorithm on an example is given in Section 4, and a formal proof of correction follows in Section 5. Section 6 reports on some empirical comparisons between Open CAD and Open NuCAD and, finally, Section 7 presents further discussions, conclusions and future work.

2. NON-UNIFORM CAD

In this section we define Open Non-uniform Cylindrical Algebraic Decomposition. We assume the reader is already familiar with the usual CAD notions — like delineability, level of a polynomial, etc. Note that λ denotes the empty string in what follows, $||$ indicates concatenation, and $\pi_k(\cdot)$ denotes projection down onto $\mathbb{R}^k$. This paper deals with open cylindrical cells which, except in the trivial case of a single cell, cannot truly decompose $\mathbb{R}^n$. Instead, we say that a set of open regions defines a *weak decomposition* of $\mathbb{R}^n$ if the regions are pairwise disjoint, and the union of their closures contains $\mathbb{R}^n$. We here provide a definition of an open cylindrical cell. This is entirely in keeping with the usual definition of a cell in the CAD literature.

DEFINITION 1. *An* Open Cylindrical Cell *is a subset of* $\mathbb{R}^n$ *of the form* $\{(\alpha_1, \ldots, \alpha_n) \in B \times \mathbb{R} | f(\alpha_1, \ldots, \alpha_{n-1}) < \alpha_n < g(\alpha_1, \ldots, \alpha_{n-1})\}$ *or* $\{(\alpha_1, \ldots, \alpha_n) \in B \times \mathbb{R} | f(\alpha_1, \ldots, \alpha_{n-1}) < \alpha_n\}$ *or* $\{(\alpha_1, \ldots, \alpha_n) \in B \times \mathbb{R} | \alpha_n < g(\alpha_1, \ldots, \alpha_{n-1})\}$ *where B is an open cylindrical cell in $\mathbb{R}^{n-1}$ and the graphs of f and g over B are disjoint sections of polynomials, and () is considered an open cylindrical cell in $\mathbb{R}^0$.*

Next we define Open Non-uniform Cylindrical Algebraic Decomposition (Open NuCAD), which relaxes the requirements of the usual CAD. In particular, it is possible to have two cells whose projections onto a lower dimension are neither equal nor disjoint. In other words, while each individual cell is cylindrical, distinct cells are not necessarily organized into cylinders. A cylindrical cell with sample point α can be refined (using algorithms from [3]) to a smaller cell containing α in which a given polynomial is sign-invariant. The fundamental observation behind NuCAD is that this refined cell naturally defines a weak decomposition of the original cell. For example, consider the cell c defined by $-2 < x < 2 \wedge \mathrm{root}(2y - x + 2, 1, y) < y < 2$, with $\alpha = (-1/2, 0)$. The diagram below shows how refining c to ensure the sign-invariance of $x^2 + y^2 - 1$ naturally defines a weak decomposition of c. (On the left is c, on the right, its decomposition.)

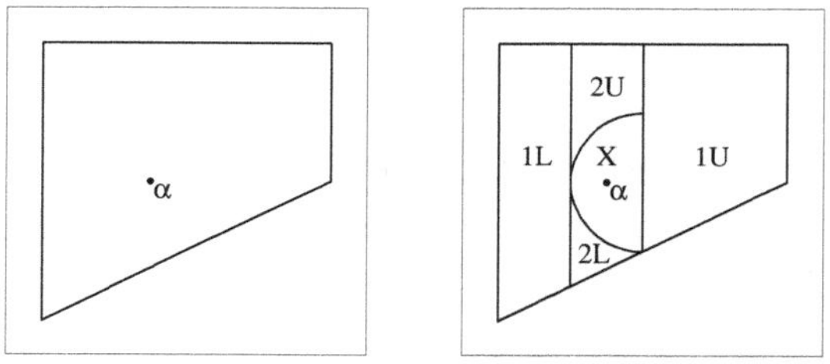

The refinement of c is labeled X, and $x^2 + y^2 - 1$ is sign-invariant in this cell. At each level i we have a cylindrical cell labeled iL, the *lower* part of c that was sliced off by refinement at level i, and one labeled iU, the *upper* part of c that was sliced off by refinement at level i. NuCADs are defined in terms of successive refinements like this (e.g. cell 1U might be refined next) and, as is seen below, this labeling scheme is an integral part of the definition of NuCAD.

DEFINITION 2. *An* Open Non-uniform Cylindrical Algebraic Decomposition *(Open NuCAD) of $\mathbb{R}^n$ is a collection C of open cylindrical cells, each of which is labeled with a unique string of the form $([0-9]+(L,U,X))*$. The relation $E = \{(C_1, C_2) | C_1, C_2$ are cells with labels lab_1 and lab_2 satisfying $lab_2 = lab_1([0-9]+(L,U,X))\}$ defines a graph on the cells such that*

1. *the graph (C, E) is a tree, rooted at cell $\mathbb{R}^n$ labeled λ,*
2. *the children of cell C_0 with label lab_0 have labels from $\{lab_0 1L, \ldots, lab_0 nL, lab_0 1U, \ldots, lab_0 nU, lab_0 nX\}$ and if C_0 has children, then one of them is labeled $lab_0 nX$,*
3. *if cell C_2 is the child of C_1 with label $lab_1 nX$, then $C_2 \subseteq C_1$ and for each $i \in \{1, \ldots, n\}$, in the cylinder over over $\pi_{i-1}(C_2)$ the section that defines the lower (resp. upper)*

[2]In a CAD, the projections of any two cells of level n onto a lower level are either identical or disjoint. In a NuCAD, this is not necessarily the case.

boundary of C_2 in x_i is either identical to or disjoint from the section that defines the lower (resp. upper) boundary of C_1 in x_i

4. *if cell C_X is the child of C_0 with label lab_0nX, then for all $i \in 1, \ldots, n$*
$$(\pi_{i-1}(C_X) \times \mathbb{R}) \cap \pi_i(C_0) - \pi_i(C_X) \quad (1)$$
consists of zero one or two open cells: the region with x_i-coordinates below $\pi_i(C_X)$ if it is non-empty, which is denoted B_L, and the region with i-coordinates above $\pi_i(C_X)$ if it is non-empty, which is denoted B_U. There is a cell with label lab_0iL if and only if B_L is non-empty and, if it exists, that cell is $(B_L \times \mathbb{R}^{n-i}) \cap C_0$. There is a cell with label lab_0iU if and only if B_U is non-empty and, if it exists, it is $(B_U \times \mathbb{R}^{n-i}) \cap C_0$.

Next we prove that NuCADs really do define decompositions of $\mathbb{R}^n$ or, more properly, Open NuCADs define weak decompositions of $\mathbb{R}^n$.

THEOREM 1. *If cell C_0 is a non-leaf node in the graph (C, E), its children form a weak decomposition of C_0.*

PROOF. What needs to be proved is that there is no open subset of C_0 having empty intersection with all of the children of C_0. Let S be an open, connected subset of C_0. Let i be the maximum element of $\{1, \ldots, n+1\}$ such that $\pi_{i-1}(S) \subseteq \pi_{i-1}(C_X)$. If $i = n+1$, then S is contained in C_X, the child that, by definition, must exist. So the theorem holds in this case.

If $i \leq n$, then we have $\pi_{i-1}(S) \subseteq \pi_{i-1}(C_X)$, but $\pi_i(S) \not\subseteq \pi_i(C_X)$. Consider the key expression (1) from Point 4 of Definition 2 with regards to i:
$$\underbrace{(\overbrace{\pi_{i-1}(C_X)}^{\pi_{i-1}(S)\subseteq} \times \mathbb{R}) \cap \pi_i(C_0)}_{\pi_i(S)\subseteq} - \underbrace{\pi_i(C_X)}_{\pi_i(S)\not\subseteq}$$
This shows that one or both of the regions B_L and B_U from Point 4 have non-empty intersection with $\pi_i(S)$, and thus is/are non-empty. Suppose $B_L \cap \pi_i(S) \neq \emptyset$ (the case for B_U is entirely analogous, and so will not be given explicitly). B_L is non-empty, so by definition C_0 has a child with label lab_0iL that is $(B_L \times \mathbb{R}^{n-i}) \cap C_0$. Since $S \subseteq C_0$ and $\pi_i(S) \cap B_L \neq \emptyset$, we have $((B_L \times \mathbb{R}^{n-i}) \cap C_0) \cap S \neq \emptyset$, which proves the theorem. □

COROLLARY 1. *The leaf cells of an Open NuCAD comprise a weak decomposition of $\mathbb{R}^n$.*

3. ALGORITHMS

In this section we define an algorithm for constructing Open NuCADs from an arbitrary input formula. The presentation in this section assumes that the reader is familiar with the material in [3]. The proof of correctness for the algorithm (Section 5) assumes familiarity with the Open McCallum projection, originally in [12], but covered in [3].

We will follow the OpenCell data structure definition provided in [3], with the following additions: *a*) each cell carries a sample point α with it *b*) each cell has an associated set P of irreducible polynomials that are known to be sign-invariant (which implies order-invariant, since these are open cells) within the cell. *c*) each cell has an associated label lab of the form described in Definition 2.

We assume the existence of a procedure OC-Merge-Set that is analogous to the procedure O-P-Merge defined in [3], except that instead of merging a single polynomial P with a given OpenCell C, it merges a set Q of polynomials with a given OpenCell C. This could be realized by simply applying O-P-Merge iteratively, or via a divide-and-conquer approach as alluded to in the final section of [3]. We will assume that this procedure manipulates OpenCell data structures with the augmentations described above. The label lab and point α for the refined cell returned by OC-Merge-Set is simply inherited from the input OpenCell C, and the associated set of polynomials is the super-set of $P \cup Q$ (where P is the set associated with C) defined by the projection factors computed during the refinement process — all of which are known to be sign-invariant in the refined OpenCell.

Note that no one method for choosing Q in Step 1 of the algorithm Split is specified. There are different ways to do this, and which one is employed may well affect practical performance quite a bit and will warrant future investigation. One point we will make, however, is that α plays a role in making this choice.

4. EXAMPLE NUCAD CONSTRUCTION

Consider the input formula $F = [16y - 16x^2 - 8x - 1 > 0 \wedge x^2 + y^2 - 1 > 0]$. We will follow the execution of Algorithm TI-Open-NuCAD on this input. In the interest of space, we will name the polynomials that will appear in the computation up front: $f_1 = 16y - 16x^2 - 8x - 1$, $f_2 = x^2 + y^2 - 1$, $f_3 = 256x^4 + 256x^3 + 352x^2 + 16x - 255$, $f_4 = x + 1$, $f_5 = x - 1$.

1. Cell $C_0 = ([\,], lab = \lambda, \alpha = (0,0), P = \{\})$ consisting of $\mathbb{R}^2$ enqueued on Q 
2. Split(C_0): $F(\alpha) = $ FALSE, choose $Q = \{f_1\}$, enqueue the following cells

$C_1 = ([y < root(f_1, 1, y)], lab = 2X, \alpha = (0,0), P = f_1)$ 

$C_2 = ([y > root(f_1, 1, y)], lab = 2U, \alpha = (0, 1/2), P = f_1)$ 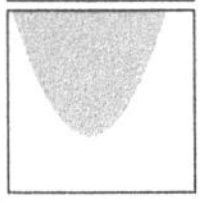

3. C_1's label ends in X, so it is not processed further
4. Split(C_2): $F(\alpha) = $ FALSE, choose $Q = \{f_2\}$, enqueue the following cells

$$C_3 = \left(\begin{array}{c} [y > root(f_1,1,y) \wedge y < root(f_2,2,y) \wedge x \\ > root(f_3,1,x) \wedge x < root(f_3,2,x)], lab = \\ 2U2X, \alpha = (0, \frac{1}{2}), P = \{f_1, f_2, f_3, f_4, f_5\} \end{array} \right)$$

$$C_4 = \left(\begin{array}{c} [y > root(f_1,1,y) \wedge x < root(f_3,1,x)], \\ lab = 2U1L, \alpha = (-\frac{3}{2}, 2), P = \{f_1, f_3\} \end{array} \right)$$

$$C_5 = \left(\begin{array}{c} [y > root(f_1,1,y) \wedge x > root(f_3,2,x)], \\ lab = 2U1U, \alpha = (\frac{3}{2}, 4), P = \{f_1, f_3\} \end{array} \right)$$

$$C_6 = \left(\begin{array}{c} [y > root(f_2,2,y) \wedge x > root(f_3,1,x) \\ \wedge x < root(f_3,2,x)], lab = 2U2U, \\ \alpha = (0,2), P = \{f_1, f_2, f_3, f_4, f_5\} \end{array} \right)$$
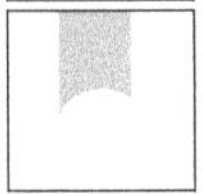

5. C_3's label ends in X, so it is not processed further
6. Split(C_4): $F(\alpha) = $ TRUE, choose $Q = \{f_2\}$, enqueue the following cells

Algorithm 1: Split(D, F)

input : OpenCell D (with point $\alpha \in \mathbb{R}^n$, projection factor set P, and label lab), Formula F

output: queue Q_{out} of OpenCells that is either empty (in which case F is truth-invariant in D), or whose elements comprise a valid set of children for D according to Definition 1 (in which case F is truth-invariant in the cell labeled $labnX$).

1 initialize Q_{out} to an empty queue
2 choose $Q \subset \mathbb{Z}[x_1, \ldots, x_n]$ such that $Q \cap P = \emptyset$ and the sign-invariance of the elements of $P \cup Q$ within a connected region containing α implies the truth-invariance of F; if $Q = \emptyset$ return Q_{out}
3 $D' = $ OC-Merge-Set(D, α, Q)
4 **if** $D' = $ (FAIL, f) **then** $\triangleleft$ perturb α
5    $L = \{f\}$, $i = $ level of f
6   **while** *at least one element of* L *is nullified at* $(\alpha_1, \ldots, \alpha_{i-1})$ **do**
7      $L = \bigcup_{g \in L}$ factors(ldcf$_{x_i}(g)$)
8      $i = i - 1$
9    $\zeta = \max(\{D[i].L\} \cup \{\beta \in \mathbb{R} \mid \beta < \alpha_i$ and $g(\alpha_1, \ldots, \alpha_{i-1}, \beta) = 0$ for some $g \in L\})$
10   choose $\gamma_i \in (\zeta, \alpha_i)$
11   **for** *j from* $i + 1$ *to* n **do**
12   choose γ_j so that $root(D[j].l(\alpha_1, \ldots, \alpha_{i-1}, \gamma_i, \ldots, \gamma_{j-1}, x_j), D[j].L.j, x_j) < \gamma_j$ and $\gamma_j < root(D[j].u(\alpha_1, \ldots, \alpha_{i-1}, \gamma_i, \ldots, \gamma_{j-1}, x_j), D[j].U.j, x_j)$
13   set $\alpha = (\alpha_1, \ldots, \alpha_{i-1}, \gamma_i, \ldots, \gamma_n)$, adjusting data-structure D accordingly. and goto Line 2
14 enqueue cell (D', α, P', lab') on Q_{out}, where P' is produced by the merge process, and $lab' = lab||nX$
15 **for** *i from 1 to* n **do**
16   **if** $D'[i].l \neq D[i].l$ **then** $\triangleleft$ i-level low bound changes
17      $D'_{iL} = D'[1], \ldots, D'[i-1], (D[i].l, D[i].L, D'[i].l, D'[i].L), D[i+1], \ldots, D[n]$
18   **for** *j from i to n* **do**
19   choose γ_j so that
20        $root(D'_{iL}[j].l(\alpha_1, \ldots, \alpha_{i-1}, \gamma_i, \ldots, \gamma_{j-1}, x_j),$ $D'_{iL}[j].L.j, x_j) < \gamma_j < root(D'_{iL}[j].u($
21        $\alpha_1, \ldots, \alpha_{i-1}, \gamma_i, \ldots, \gamma_{j-1}, x_j), D'_{iL}[j].U.j, x_j)$
22      $\alpha'_{iL} = (\alpha_1, \ldots, \alpha_{i-1}, \gamma_i, \ldots, \gamma_n)$
23      $P'_{iL} = P \cup (P' \cap \mathbb{R}[x_1, \ldots, x_{i-1}])$, where P, P' are the sign-invariant polynomial sets for D, D'
24      $lab_{iL} = lab||iL$, where lab is the label for D
25   enqueue new cell $(D'_{iL}, \alpha'_{iL}, P'_{iL}, lab_{iL})$ in Q_{out}
26   **if** $D'[i].u \neq D[i].u$ **then** $\triangleleft$ i-level up bound changes
27      $D'_{iU} = D'[1], \ldots, D'[i-1], (D[i]'.u, D'[i].U, D[i].u, D[i].U), D[i+1], \ldots, D[n]$
28   **for** *j from i to n* **do**
29   choose γ_j so that
30        $root(D'_{iU}[j].l(\alpha_1, \ldots, \alpha_{i-1}, \gamma_i, \ldots, \gamma_{j-1}, x_j),$ $D'_{iU}[j].L.j, x_j) < \gamma_j < root(D'_{iU}[j].u($
31        $\alpha_1, \ldots, \alpha_{i-1}, \gamma_i, \ldots, \gamma_{j-1}, x_j), D'_{iU}[j].U.j, x_j)$
32      $\alpha'_{iU} = (\alpha_1, \ldots, \alpha_{i-1}, \gamma_i, \ldots, \gamma_n)$
33      $P'_{iU} = P \cup (P' \cap \mathbb{R}[x_1, \ldots, x_{i-1}])$, where P, P' are the sign-invariant polynomial sets for D, D'
34      $lab_{iU} = lab||iU$, where lab is the label for D
35   enqueue new cell $D'_{iU}, \alpha'_{iU}, P'_{iU}, lab_{iU}$ in Q_{out}
36 **return** Q_{out}

Algorithm 2: TI-Open-NuCAD

input : Formula F in variables $x_1, \ldots, x_n$

output: Open-NuCAD C in the leaf cells of which F is truth invariant

1 set C_0 to the OpenCell representing $\mathbb{R}^n$, with point α chosen arbitrarily, $P = \{\}$, and label $lab = \lambda$
2 set $C = \{C_0\}$
3 set Q to a queue containing only C_0
4 **while** Q *is not empty* **do**
5   dequeue D from Q $\triangleleft$ need not actually be FIFO
6   **if** *label of* D *ends in* X **then** skip to next iteration
7    $Q' = $ Split(D, F)
8   **foreach** D' *in* Q' **do**
9   add D' to Q
10   add D' to C
11 **return** C

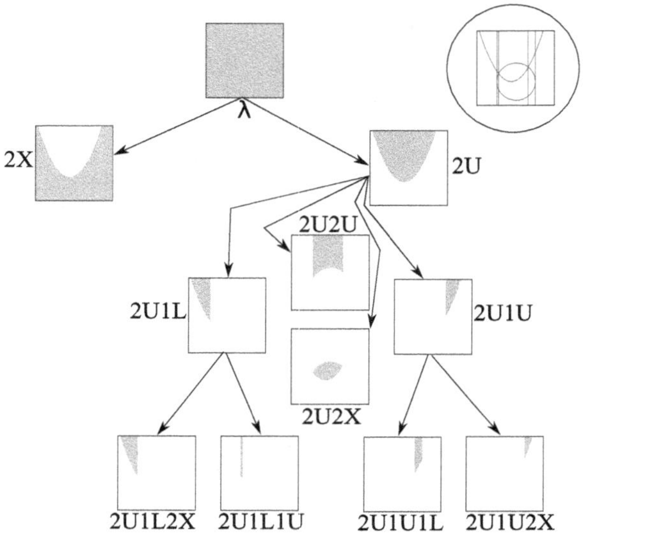

Figure 2: The graph structure produced by the example run of TI-Open-NuCAD for input formula $F = [16y - 16x^2 - 8x - 1 > 0 \wedge x^2 + y^2 - 1 > 0]$. Also shown (circled) is the truth-invariant CAD for F.

$$C_7 = \left(\begin{array}{c} [y > root(f_1, 1, y) \wedge x < -1], \\ lab = 2U1L2X, \alpha = (-\tfrac{3}{2}, 2), \\ P = \{f_1, f_2, f_3, f_4, f_5\} \end{array} \right)$$

$$C_8 = \left(\begin{array}{c} [y > root(f_1, 1, y) \wedge x > -1 \wedge \\ x < root(f_3, 1, x)], lab = 2U1L1U, \\ \alpha = (-\tfrac{15}{16}, 2), P = \{f_1, f_2, f_3, f_4, f_5\} \end{array} \right)$$

7. Split(C_5): $F(\alpha) = $ TRUE, choose $Q = \{f_2\}$, enqueue the following cells

$$C_9 = \left(\begin{array}{c} [y > root(f_1, 1, y) \wedge x > 1], \\ lab = 2U1U2X, \alpha = (\tfrac{3}{2}, 4), \\ P = \{f_1, f_2, f_3, f_4, f_5\} \end{array} \right)$$

$$C_{10} = \left(\begin{array}{c} [y > root(f_1, 1, y) \wedge x > root(f_3, 2, x) \\ \wedge x < 1], lab = 2U1U1L, \alpha = (\tfrac{15}{16}, 2), \\ P = \{f_1, f_2, f_3, f_4, f_5\} \end{array} \right)$$

8. all remaining cells in Q either have labels that end in X or, when the call to Split is made, are not split further.

Figure 2 shows the NuCAD tree resulting from the above execution of the TI-Open-NuCAD algorithm. There are seven leaf nodes, which mean $\mathbb{R}^2$ has been decomposed into seven cells. The standard truth-invariant CAD for input formula F (shown circled in Figure 2) contains 16 open cells in $\mathbb{R}^2$. The Open NuCAD fails to be an Open CAD because the projections onto $\mathbb{R}^1$ of the cell $2X$ and, for example, $2U2X$ are neither disjoint nor identical.

The primary purpose of this example is to illustrate the basic functioning of TI-Open-NuCAD, and to illustrate the Open NuCAD data structure. Hopefully it has been successful in this. There are two important limitations to this example, though. First of all, Steps 4-13, which deal with "fail" results returned by the OC-Merge-Set operation, are not illustrated. Secondly, and more importantly, because this example only involves two variables there is no opportunity to illustrate the reduction in the number and size of projection factor sets that we expect to accompany the model-based approach to CAD construction.

5. PROOF OF CORRECTNESS

In this section we sketch a proof of the correctness of TI-Open-NuCAD. TI-Open-NuCAD clearly meets its specification provided that Split meets its specification, and that termination can be proved. First we prove a lemma that is key to showing the termination of TI-Open-NuCAD.

For OpenCell D we denote the set of polynomials whose sections define the boundaries of D by bpolys(D) (note that they will be irreducible). For Tarski formula F, we use factors(F) to denote the set of irreducible factors of polynomials appearing on the left-hand-side of the atomic formulas of F when they are normalized to be of the form $f\ \sigma\ 0$.

LEMMA 1. *Suppose the call Split(D, F) produces a non-empty queue Q'. Let H be the closure under the Open McCallum projection of bpolys(D) $\cup$ factors(F). For each cell $C \in Q'$, bpolys(C) $\subseteq H$.*

PROOF. First, note that if Step 3 produces $D' = (\text{FAIL}, f)$ then although the sample point α and some of the algebraic numbers in the data-structure may change as a result of Step2 4-13, the defining formula for D and, therefore, the elements of bpolys(D) remain the same. Next we note that if Step 3 produces a cell D' (i.e. does not produce FAIL) then the specification of the O-P-Merge algorithm from [3], and by extension the OC-Merge-Set algorithm called in Step 3, guarantees that bpolys(D') is a subset of the closure under the Open McCallum projection of bpolys(D) $\cup\, Q$. Since $Q \subseteq$ factors(F), we have bpolys(D') $\subseteq H$. For any cell C enqueued on the output queue, at each level i, the boundaries of C are sections of polynomials from the set $\{D[i].l, D'[i].l, D'[i].u, D[i].u\}$, which is a subset of H. □

LEMMA 2. *The Algorithm Split(D, F) terminates and meets its specification.*

PROOF. As long as Steps 4-13 only produce new values for point α that are in the cell defined by D and Step 3 eventually produces a non-FAIL result, Split(D, F) clearly meets it specification. Moreover, if at the start of Steps 4-13 α is in the cell defined by D (which is certainly true initially), then the new value of α is also in the cell defined by D. This is clear because γ_i is chosen from the interval $(\max(\zeta, D[i].L), \alpha_i) \subset (D[i].L, D[i].U)$, and for $j \in \{i+1, \ldots, n\}$, γ_j is chosen specifically to satisfy the defining formula

$$root(D[j].l, D[j].L.j, x_j) < x_j < root(D[j].u, D[j].U.j, x_j).$$

What remains to be proven is termination, which boils down to showing that the call to OC-Merge-Set in Step 9 eventually returns a non-FAIL result. If we were assured that OC-Merge-Set would produce the same projection factors for the perturbed α as for the original, this would be clear. Unfortunately, we cannot be sure of that. Thus, we require a more subtle argument. First, we note that each perturbation (Step 13) leaves the x_kth coordinate unchanged for all $k < i$, reduces the ith coordinates α_i so that it changes from a root of $g(\alpha_1, \ldots, \alpha_{i-1}, x_i)$ to something slightly smaller (Step 9), and potentially changes the remaining coordinates.

Suppose Split does not terminate. Then there is an infinite sequence of α values and associated f's satisfying $f(\alpha) = 0$, where f is returned as (fail.f) in Step 3. Note that all the polynomials f as well as all the elements of the sets L constructed, constructed from the fs, come from the closure under the McCallum projection of bpolys(D) $\cup$ factors(F), which we'll denote P_{MC} (specifically, P_{MC} will denote the set of irreducible factors of the closure under the McCallum projection). Let $\alpha^{(0)}, \alpha^{(1)}, \ldots$ be the infinite sequence of values for α as the process progresses, let $f^{(0)}, f^{(1)}, \ldots$ be the infinite sequence of associated f's and $L^{(0)}, L^{(1)}, \ldots$ and $i^{(0)}, i^{(1)}, \ldots$ be the associated values for L and i arrived at by Steps 3-9. Let $A(m, \rho)$ be the product of the elements of $\{g \in P_{MC} | \text{level}(g) = m \wedge g(\rho_1, \ldots, \rho_{m-1}, x_m) \neq 0\}$. We note that for any k, the elements of $L^{(k)}$ all divide $A(i^{(k)}, \alpha^{(k)})$. We also note that the polynomial set $\{A(m, \rho) | m \in \{1, \ldots, n\} \wedge \rho \in \mathbb{R}^n\}$ is finite. So, for each k we have that that $i^{(k)}$th coordinate of $\alpha^{(k)}$ is a zero of some $g \in L^{(k)}$ that is not nullified at $(\alpha_1^{(k)}, \ldots, \alpha_{i^{(k)}-1}^{(k)})$ and thus is a zero of $A(i^{(k)}, \alpha^{(k)})(\alpha_1^{(k)}, \ldots, \alpha_{i^{(k)}-1}^{(k)}, x_{i^{(k)}})$. We will show that for each level r, there is a value k after which the rth coordinate of $\alpha^{(k)}$ never changes. We proceed by induction on r.

Consider the case $r = 1$. Consider the subsequence $k_1, k_2, \ldots$ of all indices k for which $i^{(k)} = 1$. For each k_j in this subsequence, $\alpha_1^{(k_j)}$ is a zero of $A(1, \alpha^{(k_j)})$. Moreover, the new value of α_1 is smaller than the previous value and, since the value of the 1st component of α is otherwise never changed, $\alpha_1^{(k)}$ is strictly decreasing over the subsequence $k_1, k_2, \ldots$. Since $A(1, \beta)$ is the same for any $\beta \in \mathbb{R}^n$, and it has finitely many roots, there are only finitely many elements of the subsequence. In particular, there is a largest index k^* in the subsequence (k^* can be taken as zero if the subsequence is empty), and α_1 is constant over all indices greater than k^*.

Suppose $r > 1$. Assume, by induction, that the result holds for all smaller values of r. Then there is an index k' such that for all $k > k'$ the first $r - 1$ components of $\alpha^{(k)}$ are constant. So, for all $k > k'$, the rth component of $\alpha^{(k)}$ is non-increasing. Consider the subsequence $k_1, k_2, \ldots$ of all indices $k > k'$ for which $i^{(k)} = r$. Note that because the rth component of α is reduced at each step for which $i^{(k)} = r$, the sequence of values $\alpha_r^{(k_1)}, \alpha_r^{(k_2)}, \ldots$ is strictly decreasing. For each k_j in the subsequence, $\alpha_r^{(k_j)}$ is a zero of $A(r, \alpha^{(k_j)})(\alpha_1^{(k_j)}, \ldots, \alpha_{r-1}^{(k_j)}, x_r)$. The polynomial $A(r, \alpha^{(k)})$ is constant for all $k > k'$, since $\alpha^{(k)} \in (\alpha_1^{(k'+1)}, \ldots, \alpha_{r-1}^{(k'+1)}) \times \mathbb{R}^{n-r+1}$, there are only finitely many elements in the subsequence. In particular, there is a largest index k^* in the subsequence (k^* can be taken as k' if the subsequence is empty), such that α_r is constant over all indices larger than k^*.

Thus, we have proven that there is an index k' such that for all $k > k'$, all coordinates of $\alpha^{(k)}$ are constant. This is a contradiction, since executing Steps 5-13 changes α, which means that our assumption that there is an input for which Split does not terminate is invalid. This completes our proof of the termination and correctness of Split. □

THEOREM 2. *TI-Open-NuCAD terminates, and meets its specification.*

PROOF. Lemma 2 shows that Split terminates and is correct. Lemma 1 shows that the boundary polynomials for the cells returned by Split are elements of the closure under the Open McCallum projection of factors(F). Thus for any cell D' in the queue returned by Split, and any cell C from the CAD produced by the Open McCallum projection for F, either $C \cap D' = \emptyset$ or $C \subseteq D'$. This means that for each each cell D enqueued on Q, we can imagine associating with D the set of cells from the CAD produced by the Open McCallum projection for F that are contained in D — we call this set M_D. Note that M_D is never empty. Recall that when a cell with label ending in X is dequeued from Q, no call to Split is made. Define X_Q to be the set of cells in Q with label ending in X. Consider the quantity

$$c_Q = |X_Q| + \sum_{E \in Q - X_Q} 2|M_E|^2. \quad (2)$$

We will show that at each iteration of the while loop in TI-Open-NuCAD the quantity c_Q is reduced. Each iteration, a cell D is dequeued from Q and one of the following occurs: 1. no new cells are enqueued — in which case one of the terms on the right-hand side of (2) gets smaller and the other term is unchanged, 2. a single cell whose label ends in X is enqueued — in which case $|X_Q|$ increases by one, but $\sum_{E \in Q - X_Q} 2|M_E|^2$ is reduced by $2|M_D|^2 > 1$, 3. more than one cell is enqueued — in which case the $|X_Q|$ term is increased by one, but in the sum the term $2|M_D|^2$ is replaced by $2|M_{D_1}|^2 + 2|M_{D_2}|^2 + \cdots + 2|M_{D_t}|^2$ where $|M_D| = |M_{D_1}| + |M_{D_2}| + \cdots + |M_{D_t}|$, $t \geq 2$. So the net change is $1 + 2|M_{D_1}|^2 + 2|M_{D_2}|^2 + \cdots + 2|M_{D_t}|^2 - 2|M_D|^2 < 0$. Thus, termination is proven and, as noted previously, correctness is then easily verified. □

6. EXAMPLE COMPUTATIONS

We have implemented a limited version of algorithm **TI-Open-NuCAD** that accepts input formulas that are conjunctions of sign-conditions on irreducible polynomials. In the "choose Q" step of the **Split** algorithm, our implementation follows the most simple-minded approach: if the formula F is satisfied at α, Q consists of all polynomials appearing in F that are not in the projection factor set of D, and if F is not satisfied at α, Q consists of the polynomial from the first inequality occurring in F that is not satisfied at α.

Despite its limitations, this implementation helps us investigate experimentally how Open-NuCAD compares to Open-CAD as the number of polynomials increases, the dimension of the problem increases, and as the degrees of polynomials in the input increase. Comparing limits us to inputs of sizes

Linear Set of Experiments			
	4 polys	5 polys	6 polys
2 vars	5.6 35.0	6.9 64.0	5.6 104.6
3 vars	21.9 271.5	24.0 1716.0	38.7 7392.0
4 vars	41.0 525.2	233.1 249149.0	≈ 8500000.0 582.2

Non-linear Set of Experiments			
vars	4 polys	5 polys	6 polys
2	9.6 59.5	10.9 111.8	11.5 185.0
3	128.4 2079.7	163.1 8535.3	176.6 30736.0
4	4147.1 446927.8	8403.4 > 8000000.0	19466.8 > 25000000.0

Figure 3: Linear and non-linear experiments.

that don't overwhelm Open-CAD. We have chosen to use randomly generated polynomials as input, so that we could create sufficiently many instances of problems, and so that we could smoothly vary the parameters of interest. However, it is well-known that algorithms for computing with real equalities and inequalities tend to behave very differently (much worse, in fact!) on random input than on inputs arising from meaningful applications. This leaves some question as to how meaningful these experimental results are, and it also leads us to consider relatively small-sized problems.

We performed two sets of experiments. In both sets we consider conjunctions of strict inequalities. For these problems, as McCallum notes in [10], an Open-CAD is sufficient for deciding satisfiability. In fact, for such input Open-CAD suffices for other problems, like finding at least one point from each connected component of the solution space. Open-NuCAD is also sufficient for these problems. In the first set of experiments we generate random, dense, linear inequalities[3], and we let the number of polynomials vary from four to six, and the number of variables vary from two to four. In the second set, we follow the same set-up except that the polynomials are non-linear — though just barely. Each is generated by first generating a dense linear polynomial, p, then randomly choosing two (not necessarily distinct) variables, v_1 and v_2, then finally substituting $v_1 v_2$ for v_1 in polynomial p. For each combination of #vars and #polys, 25 problem instances were generated. The tables report the average over the 25 problem instances of the number of open cells in the Open NuCAD vs. the Open CAD. Open CADs for each input were computed (or at least attempted) using Qepcad B [2] version 1.69. With the `measure-zero-error` option, Qepcad B produces an open CAD for the input formula. A new command, `d-number-full-dimensional-cells`, was added to report the number of full-dimensional cells in the decomposition Qepcad B produces.

The last entry in the "linear" table is only an approximate number because for all examples there was insufficient

[3]CAD is not the best tool for computing with purely linear inequalities, but the comparison between CAD and NuCAD is interesting none-the-less, because purely linear examples involve only the "combinatorial complexity" of CAD, not the "algebraic complexity".

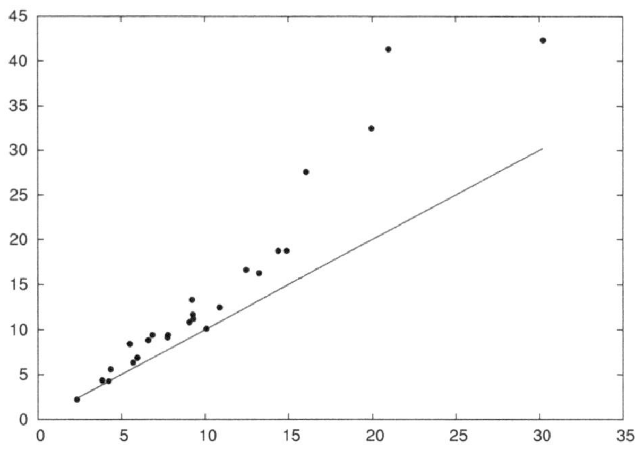

Figure 4: This plot shows how the size of the Open-McCallum projection factor set compares to the size of the set of all projection factors computed in constructing the NuCAD. Each point corresponds to a particular trial input (see text for descriptions of inputs). Its x-coordinate is the ratio of the cardinality of the Open-McCallum projection factor set to the cardinality of the set of all projection factors computed in constructing the NuCAD. The y-coordinate is the ratio of print-lengths of the projection factor sets. The line $y = x$ is shown for reference purposes.

memory to store the full Open-CAD. However, by quantifying each variable with Qepcad's `G` quantifier, Qepcad is forced to compute, but not store, all cells from the full Open-CAD. Qepcad reports how many 4-level cells were constructed, but some fraction (less than 1/2) of them are not full-dimensional. The number in the table is slightly less than 1/2 the number of 4-level cells, and thus is a lower bound on the actual number of full-dimensional cells. The actual number is less than a factor of two larger. The last two entries in the "non-linear" table are much more speculative. While Qepcad was able to compute the projection in all tested cases, there was insufficient memory for even the first lifting step. The number listed is a very conservative lower bound on the number of full-dimensional cells based on the number of projection factors.

The preceding data shows that the number of cells in a NuCAD can be (indeed, appears to usually be) dramatically smaller than the number of cells in the Open-CAD constructed from the Open-McCallum projection. Another important quantity to consider when comparing the amount of work done by the two approaches is the sizes of the projection factor sets they produce. For NuCAD, it is important to define what is meant by "the projection factor set". Each cell is constructed by repeated projections, according to the "merge" process described in [3] or to a divide-and-conquer variant of it. In general, only a small subset of the factors of resultants, discriminants and leading coefficients computed by these projections actually define the cell. However, we consider the projection factor set for a cell to be all such factors, whether they are used in defining the cell or not, and we consider the projection factor set for a NuCAD to be the union of the projection factor sets for all cells in the decomposition. To gain some insight into how the sizes of projection factor sets compare, we consider a slightly different class of problem: we consider two non-linear inequalities in six variables, along with positivity constraints for all the variables. The previous examples show that NuCAD's advantage over Open-CAD increases as the number of inequalities at the highest level increases. So by reducing the input to three inequalities at the highest level, we reduce NuCAD's advantage. The positivity assumptions are a) an extremely common kind of constraint in practice, and 2) ensure that projection doesn't "end" at one of the higher-levels: i.e. there are non-trivial projections all the way down to level 2. Our two non-linear inequalities are of the form ax_6+b and kx_6x_5+c, where a, b and c are random, dense linear polynomials in $x_1, \ldots, x_5$, and k is a random integer in $[-99, 99]$. Originally, we intended to have both be of the form $ax_6 + b$, but we were unable to complete the Open-McCallum projection for such problems (although we were able to construct NuCADs). We considered 25 such inputs, and looked at two measures of "size" for projection factor sets: cardinality (i.e. number of factors in the set), and print-length (i.e. the sum of the printed lengths of the factors in the set, where all variables have length one. Figure 6 shows the results of these experiments. For most problems, the Open-McCallum projection is 5-15 times larger in cardinality than the NuCAD's projection factor set, and 5-20 times longer in print-length. The fact that most points lie above the line $y = x$ tells us that it is not just the small projection factors that NuCAD avoids, but the larger ones too. In fact, it appears that a disproportionate number of large projection factors are avoided in many cases. It should be noted that neither the Open-McCallum nor NuCAD implementations make use of techniques to determine that projection factors are positive/negative definite, either globally or given the positivity conditions on variables. Neither implementation has such a test implemented, presumably both could benefit from doing this.

A final note about this last set of experiments concerns sizes of projection factor sets for individual cells. One might worry that there is one cell whose construction dominates the computation. This would ruin the potential for natural parallelism that seems to be a desirable trait of the model-based construction of NuCADs. In fact, this does not seem to be the case. In the 25 tests we ran, the cell with the largest projection factor set had only 1/4 or less of the total number of projection factors.

7. CONCLUSION AND FUTURE WORK

This paper has introduced the Open NuCAD and an efficient model-based procedure for constructing them. The experimental studies we report, though certainly not exhaustive, provide strong evidence that NuCADs are able to represent semi-algebraic sets far more efficiently than traditional CAD — e.g. thousands of times fewer cells in many of the examples we considered. We also report on experiments providing evidence that the set of projection factors produced while constructing an Open NuCAD is far smaller than what is produced by the Open McCallum projection when constructing a traditional open CAD — typically by a factor of 5-15 in the limited set of examples we considered. We attempted to perform experiments for larger problem sizes, but while Open NuCAD construction did fine, we were unable to even complete the projection step of traditional Open CAD construction.

It must be emphasized is that this work is a first step, a proof of concept. It shows that NuCAD and the model-based approach has promise. However, it must be expanded to construct full decompositions of Euclidean space, not just weak decomposition into open cells. There are good reasons to expect that the efficiencies to be gained are not similar to the "open" case, but far greater. Implementations that are not restricted to conjunctions need to be developed. There are sure to be many optimizations to the basic algorithm presented here — it being the first crack at the problem of constructing NuCADs. Finally, the study of how best to use NuCADs to solve problems needs to begin.

In [8], Han et al propose an algorithm, HpTwo, for constructing Open CADs that reduces the size of the projection factor set, and thus the number of cells, by computing the intersection of projections produced by different variable orders. Their algorithm produces a (weak) decomposition into regions in which the input *polynomials* have constant *sign*. NuCAD produces a (weak) decomposition into regions in which the input *formula* has constant *truth value*. Where the two problems are the same, i.e. with input of the form $f\sigma 0$, is where Open NuCAD provides the least benefit vs. the usual Open CAD. [8] provides two sets of experiments demonstrating HpTwo: first constructing sign-invariant Open CADs for polynomials generated by the Maple command `randpoly([x,y,z,w],degree=4)-1`, the second for polynomials generated by the Maple command `randpoly([seq(x[i],i=1..5)],degree=3) + add(x[i]^2,i=1..5)-1`. Compared to the usual Open CAD, it produced an average of 46% fewer cells in the first set, and 63% fewer in the second set. The reductions for Open NuCAD are more modest, 39% and 40%. However, HpTwo takes polynomials as input, not formulas, so there is no logical structure to analyze. Thus, for the examples we considered in this paper, we would expect HpTwo to behave similarly to what was observed in the two experiment sets from [8] — a reduction by a factor of approximately two rather than by factors in the 10s or 100s shown for NuCAD. In fact, it can be shown that for linear polynomials, as examined in our first set of experiments, HpTwo is the same as the usual Open CAD, so for those experiments there is no reduction at all, whereas with NuCAD there were reductions by factors greater than 1,000. However, the interesting line of inquiry is not to compare NuCAD and HpTwo, but rather to investigate whether the ideas behind HpTwo can be applied to improve the Open Cell construction algorithm from [3], which would in turn improve NuCAD construction.

Lastly, it is important to understand this work in relation to other prior work, like Jovanovic and de Moura's SAT-solving algorithm, Strzeboński's Local Projections or Bradford et al's Truth Table Invariant Decomposition (TTICAD)? For starters, none of these has an "open" variant. TTICAD falls back to traditional CAD in the full-dimensional case. One could imagine developing "open" version of Jovanovic and de Moura's SAT-solving algorithm or Strzeboński's Local Projections, but for the inputs we considered in our first two sets of experiments, both algorithms would have to deal with sample-points that would result in all input polynomials appearing in their projections, and both algorithms in such a case produce exactly the Open McCallum projection — which is what our experiments addressed. Thus, were someone to develop "open" variants of these algorithms, it seems very unlikely that they would be competitive with Open NuCAD. Finally, we mention that alternative cylindrical algebraic decomposition algorithms based on regular chains [6] similarly has no "open" variants. In fact, their advantages are precisely in dealing with cells of lower dimension. To sum up, while future versions of NuCAD that are not restricted to open cells should be compared to these other approaches, for *Open* NuCAD, the most meaningful comparisons are with Open CAD.

8. REFERENCES

[1] R. J. Bradford, J. H. Davenport, M. England, S. McCallum, and D. J. Wilson. Cylindrical algebraic decompositions for boolean combinations. In *ISSAC '13*, pages 125–132, 2013.

[2] C. W. Brown. QEPCAD B: a program for computing with semi-algebraic sets using CADs. *ACM SIGSAM Bulletin*, 37(4):97–108, 2003.

[3] C. W. Brown. Constructing a single open cell in a cylindrical algebraic decomposition. ISSAC '13, pages 133–140, New York, NY, USA, 2013. ACM.

[4] C. W. Brown. Model-based construction of open non-uniform cylindrical algebraic decompositions. *CoRR*, abs/1403.6487, 2014.

[5] W. Brown, Christopher and M. Kosta. Constructing a single cell in cylindrical algebraic decomposition. *Journal of Symbolic Computation*, Sept. 2014. To Appear.

[6] C. Chen and M. M. Maza. Quantifier elimination by cylindrical algebraic decomposition based on regular chains. ISSAC '14, pages 91–98, New York, NY, USA, 2014. ACM.

[7] G. E. Collins. Quantifier elimination by cylindrical algebraic decomposition - 20 years of progress. In B. Caviness and J. Johnson, editors, *Quantifier Elimination and Cylindrical Algebraic Decomposition*, Texts and Monographs in Symbolic Computation. Springer-Verlag, 1998.

[8] J. Han, L. Dai, and B. Xia. Constructing fewer open cells by gcd computation in cad projection. ISSAC '14, pages 240–247, New York, NY, USA, 2014. ACM.

[9] D. Jovanović and L. de Moura. Solving Non-linear Arithmetic. In B. Gramlich, D. Miller, and U. Sattler, editors, *Automated Reasoning*, volume 7364 of *Lecture Notes in Computer Science*, pages 339–354. Springer Berlin Heidelberg, 2012.

[10] S. McCallum. Solving polynomial strict inequalities using cylindrical algebraic decomposition. *The Computer Journal*, 36(5):432–438, 1993.

[11] S. McCallum. On propagation of equational constraints in CAD-based quantifier elimination. ISSAC '01, pages 223–230, 2001.

[12] A. Strzebonski. Solving systems of strict polynomial inequalities. *Journal of Symbolic Computation*, 29:471–480, 2000.

[13] A. Strzeboński. Cylindrical algebraic decomposition using local projections. ISSAC '14, pages 389–396, New York, NY, USA, 2014. ACM.

[14] A. W. Strzebonski. Divide-and-conquer computation of cylindrical algebraic decomposition. 2014.

Structure of Polyzetas and Explicit Representation on Transcendence Bases of Shuffle and Stuffle Algebras

Van Chien Bui
Hue University, Vietnam
Paris XIII University, France

Gerard H.E. Duchamp
Paris XIII University
93430 Villetaneuse, France

V. Hoang Ngoc Minh
Lille II University
59024 Lille, France

ABSTRACT

By an effective construction of pairs of bases in duality in shuffle and quasi-shuffle algebras, we identify the local coordinates of noncommutative generating series of polyzetas which are group-like. Algorithms lead to the ideal of homogeneous polynomial relations, in weight, among polyzetas and their explicit representation on irreducible elements.

Categories and Subject Descriptors

F.2.2 [**Analysis of Algorithms and Problem complexity**]: Nonnumerical Algorithms and Problems—*computations on discrete structures*; G.2.1 [**Discrete Mathematics**]: Combinatorics—*combinatorial algorithms, generating functions*

General Terms

Theory

Keywords

Poincaré-Birkhoff-Witt basis; transcendence basis; Schützenberger's factorization; noncommutative generating series; shuffle algebra; polyzetas.

1. INTRODUCTION

For any composition, $(s_1, \ldots, s_r)$, of positive integers such that $s_1 > 1$, the polyzetas [7] (also called multiple zeta values [29]), denoted by $\zeta(s_1, \ldots, s_r)$, are defined by the following convergent series

$$\zeta(s_1, \ldots, s_r) := \sum_{n_1 > \ldots > n_r > 0} \frac{1}{n_1^{s_1} \ldots n_r^{s_r}}. \quad (1)$$

Let $X = \{x_0, x_1\}$ and $Y = \{y_s\}_{s \geq 1}$ be two totally ordered alphabets[1]. The free monoid and the set of Lyndon words, over X (resp. over Y), are denoted respectively by X^* (resp. Y^*) and $\mathcal{L}ynX$ (resp. $\mathcal{L}ynY$). Let $1_{X^*}, 1_{Y^*}$ denote the neutral elements of X^*, Y^* respectively. With the definitions of shuffle and concatenation products, one constructs the bialgebra $(\mathbb{Q}\langle X \rangle, \bullet, 1_{X^*}, \Delta_{\sqcup\!\sqcup}, \mathrm{e})$ [26]. Moreover, the Poincaré-Birkhoff-Witt (PBW in the sequel) basis, $\{P_w\}_{w \in X^*}$, is expanded from $\{P_l\}_{l \in \mathcal{L}ynX}$, basis of the free Lie algebra $\mathcal{L}ie_{\mathbb{Q}}\langle X \rangle$. The dual basis (of the PBW-basis $\{P_w\}_{w \in X^*}$ [26]), $\{S_w\}_{w \in X^*}$, contains a subfamily $\{S_l\}_{l \in \mathcal{L}ynX}$, which is really a pure transcendence basis of the algebra $(\mathbb{Q}\langle X \rangle, \sqcup\!\sqcup, 1_{X^*})$. Similarly, we also constructed a basis, denoted by $\{\Pi_l\}_{l \in \mathcal{L}ynY}$ [5, 20, 21], for the (free) Lie algebra of primitive elements[2] of $\mathbb{Q}\langle Y \rangle$ and the associated PBW-basis $\{\Pi_w\}_{w \in Y^*}$ of which its dual basis [5, 20, 21], denoted by $\{\Sigma_w\}_{w \in Y^*}$, contains a subfamily $\{\Sigma_l\}_{l \in \mathcal{L}ynY}$ which is also a pure transcendence basis of the algebra $(\mathbb{Q}\langle Y \rangle, \uplus, 1_{Y^*})$.

To any multi-index $(s_1, \ldots, s_r) \in (\mathbb{N}_+)^r$, one can associate [17, 18] $x_0^{s_1-1} x_1 \ldots x_0^{s_r-1} x_1 \in X^* x_1$ or $y_{s_1} \ldots y_{s_r} \in Y^*$. We defined two non commutative generating series of polyzetas [20, 21]:

$$Z_{\sqcup\!\sqcup} := \prod_{l \in \mathcal{L}ynX \setminus X}^{\searrow} \exp(\zeta(S_l)\, P_l), \quad (2)$$

$$Z_{\uplus} := \prod_{l \in \mathcal{L}ynY \setminus \{y_1\}}^{\searrow} \exp(\zeta(\Sigma_l)\, \Pi_l). \quad (3)$$

We defined also the third noncommutative generating series of polyzetas, Z_γ [20, 21], which satisfies, via Schützenberger's factorization on the completed Hopf algebra [20, 21] ,

$$Z_\gamma = e^{\gamma y_1} Z_{\uplus}, \quad (4)$$

where γ is the Euler's constant.

In the definitions given in (2) and (3), only *convergent* polyzetas arise and these noncommutative generating series induce two following morphisms of algebras for, respectively, the shuffle and stuffle products [20, 21]

$$\zeta_{\sqcup\!\sqcup} : (\mathbb{Q}\langle X \rangle, \sqcup\!\sqcup) \longrightarrow (\mathbb{R}, .), \quad (5)$$

$$\zeta_{\uplus} : (\mathbb{Q}\langle Y \rangle, \uplus) \longrightarrow (\mathbb{R}, .), \quad (6)$$

which satisfy respectively

$$\zeta_{\sqcup\!\sqcup}(x_0) = \zeta_{\sqcup\!\sqcup}(x_1) = 0, \quad (7)$$

$$\zeta_{\uplus}(y_1) = 0 \quad (8)$$

and, for $s_1 > 1$,

$$\zeta_{\sqcup\!\sqcup}(x_0^{s_1-1} x_1 \ldots x_0^{s_r-1} x_1) = \zeta(s_1, \ldots, s_r), \quad (9)$$

$$\zeta_{\uplus}(y_{s_1} \ldots y_{s_r}) = \zeta(s_1, \ldots, s_r). \quad (10)$$

[1] By $x_0 < x_1$ and $y_1 > y_2 > y_3 > \ldots$

[2] P is a primitive element if $\Delta_{\uplus}(P) = 1_{Y^*} \otimes P + P \otimes 1_{Y^*}$.

ISSAC'15, July 6–9, 2015, Bath, United Kingdom.

DOI: http://dx.doi.org/10.1145/2755996.2756657.

Their graphs[3] then respectively read [19]

$$\sum_{w\in X^*} \zeta_{ш}(w)w = Z_{ш}, \quad (11)$$

$$\sum_{w\in Y^*} \zeta_{⧢}(w)w = Z_{⧢}. \quad (12)$$

In this work, in order to identify the local coordinates of $Z_{ш}$ (and $Z_{⧢}$), on a group of associators [20, 21], we are basing ourselves on the following comparison formula

$$Z_\gamma = \Gamma(y_1+1)\pi_Y(Z_{ш}), \quad (13)$$

where π_Y stands for the linear projection[4] from $\mathbb{Q}\oplus\mathbb{Q}\langle\langle X\rangle\rangle x_1$ to $\mathbb{Q}\langle\langle Y\rangle\rangle$ mapping $x_0^{s_1-1}x_1\ldots x_0^{s_r-1}x_1$ to $y_{s_1}\ldots y_{s_r}$ and Γ denotes the Euler Gamma function. Simultaneously, algorithms will be also given to represent polyzetas in the forms of homogeneous polynomials, in weight, of irreducible polyzetas, up to weight 12, in which the result satisfies again Zagier's dimension conjecture [29] about polyzetas.

Note that many tables of *algebraic* relations[5] had been obtained by computer up to weights 10 [17], 12 [1] and 16 [28]. These tables differ from the zig-zag relation among the moulds of formal polyzetas, *i.e.* the commutative generating series of *symbolic* polyzetas, due to Ecalle [12] (Boutet de Monvel [3] and Racinet [14] had also given equivalent relations for the noncommutative generating series of symbolic polyzetas, see also [7]). Our method is quite different from these methods which produce *linear* relations and are based on the regularized double shuffle [2, 22, 24] and from identities among associators, due to Drinfel'd [9, 10, 16].

2. BACKGROUND

2.1 Hopf algebras of shuffle and quasi-shuffle products

Let $w = y_{s_1}\ldots y_{s_k} \in Y^*$, the *length* and the *weight* of the word w are defined respectively by the numbers

$$|w| = k \quad\text{and}\quad (w) = s_1+\ldots+s_k. \quad (14)$$

Let us define[6] the commutative product over $\mathbb{Q}Y$, denoted by μ, as follows [6, 13]

$$\forall y_s, y_t \in Y, \qquad \mu(y_s,y_t) = y_{s+t}, \quad (15)$$

or its associated coproduct, Δ_+, defined by

$$\forall y_s \in Y, \qquad \Delta_+ y_s = \sum_{i=1}^{s-1} y_i\otimes y_{s-i} \quad (16)$$

satisfying,

$$\forall x,y,z\in Y, \qquad \langle\Delta_+ x \mid y\otimes z\rangle = \langle x\mid \mu(y,z)\rangle. \quad (17)$$

Let $\mathbb{Q}\langle Y\rangle$ be equipped by

1. The concatenation $\bullet$ (or by its associated coproduct, $\Delta_\bullet$).
2. The *shuffle* product, *i.e.* the commutative product defined by [26], $\forall y_s,y_t\in Y, \forall u,v,w\in Y^*$

$$w\,ш\,1_{Y^*} = 1_{Y^*}\,ш\,w = w \quad\text{and}$$
$$y_s u\,ш\,y_t v = y_s(u\,ш\,y_t v) + y_t(y_s u\,ш\,v) \quad (18)$$

or by its associated coproduct, $\Delta_{ш}$, defined, on the letters,

$$\forall y_s\in Y, \qquad \Delta_{ш} y_s = y_s\otimes 1_{Y^*} + 1_{Y^*}\otimes y_s \quad (19)$$

and extended by morphism. It satisfies

$$\forall u,v,w\in Y^*, \qquad \langle\Delta_{ш} w\mid u\otimes v\rangle = \langle w\mid u\,ш\,v\rangle. \quad (20)$$

3. The *stuffle* (or *quasi-shuffle*) product, *i.e.* the commutative product defined [22], for any $w\in Y^*$, by

$$w ⧢ 1_{Y^*} = 1_{Y^*} ⧢ w = w, \quad (21)$$

and, for any $y_s,y_t\in Y, \forall u,v\in Y^*$,

$$y_s u ⧢ y_t v = y_s(u ⧢ y_t v) + y_t(y_s u ⧢ v) + \mu(y_s,y_t)(u ⧢ v) \quad (22)$$

or by its associated coproduct, $\Delta_{⧢}$, defined, on the letters,

$$\forall y_s\in Y, \qquad \Delta_{⧢} y_s = \Delta_{ш} y_s + \Delta_+ y_s \quad (23)$$

and extended by morphism. It satisfies

$$\forall u,v,w\in Y^*, \qquad \langle\Delta_{⧢} w\mid u\otimes v\rangle = \langle w\mid u⧢ v\rangle. \quad (24)$$

Note that $\Delta_{ш}$ and $\Delta_{⧢}$ are morphisms for the concatenation (by definition) but Δ_+ is not a morphism for the product of $\mathbb{Q}\langle Y\rangle$ (concatenation) (for example $\Delta_+(y_1^2) = y_1\otimes y_1$, whereas $\Delta_+(y_1)^2 = 0$).

Hence, with the counit $\mathtt{e}$ defined by

$$\forall P\in\mathbb{Q}\langle Y\rangle, \qquad \mathtt{e}(P) = \langle P\mid 1_{Y^*}\rangle, \quad (25)$$

one gets two pairs of mutually dual bialgebras

$$\mathcal{H}_{ш} = (\mathbb{Q}\langle Y\rangle, \bullet, 1, \Delta_{ш}, \mathtt{e}),$$
$$\mathcal{H}_{ш}^\vee = (\mathbb{Q}\langle Y\rangle, ш, 1, \Delta_\bullet, \mathtt{e}) \quad (26)$$

and

$$\mathcal{H}_{⧢} = (\mathbb{Q}\langle Y\rangle, \bullet, 1, \Delta_{⧢}, \mathtt{e}),$$
$$\mathcal{H}_{⧢}^\vee = (\mathbb{Q}\langle Y\rangle, ⧢, 1, \Delta_\bullet, \mathtt{e}). \quad (27)$$

Let us then consider the following diagonal series[7]

$$\mathcal{D}_{ш} = \sum_{w\in Y^*} w\otimes w \quad\text{and}\quad \mathcal{D}_{⧢} = \sum_{w\in Y^*} w\otimes w. \quad (28)$$

Here, in $\mathcal{D}_{ш}$ and $\mathcal{D}_{⧢}$, the operation on the right factor of the tensor product is the concatenation, and the operation on the left factor is the shuffle and the quasi-shuffle, respectively.

By the Cartier-Quillen-Milnor and Moore (CQMM in the sequel) theorem [6], the connected $\mathbb{N}$-graded, co-commutative Hopf algebra $\mathcal{H}_{ш}$ is isomorphic to the enveloping algebra of the Lie algebra of its primitive elements which is isomorphic to $\mathcal{L}ie_{\mathbb{Q}}\langle Y\rangle$:

$$\mathcal{H}_{ш} \cong \mathcal{U}(\mathcal{L}ie_{\mathbb{Q}}\langle Y\rangle) \quad\text{and}\quad \mathcal{H}_{ш}^\vee \cong \mathcal{U}(\mathcal{L}ie_{\mathbb{Q}}\langle Y\rangle)^\vee. \quad (29)$$

Hence, let us consider

[3] written as series

[4] Note that, here, π_Y was extended to $\mathbb{Q}\langle\langle X\rangle\rangle$ with the convention $\pi_Y(w) = 0$ for each w ending by x_0.

[5] They form a Gröbner basis of the ideal of polynomial relations among the convergent polyzetas and the ranking of this basis is based mainly on the order of Lyndon words [1, 17, 28]. For that, this basis is also called Gröbner-Lyndon basis.

[6] $\mathbb{Q}$ being the set of rational numbers.

[7] Of course, one has (set theoretically) $\mathcal{D}_{ш} = \mathcal{D}_{⧢}$, but their structural treatment will be different.

1. the PBW-Lyndon basis $\{P_w\}_{w\in Y^*}$ for $\mathcal{U}(\mathcal{L}ie_{\mathbb{Q}}\langle Y\rangle)$ constructed recursively as follows [26]

$$\begin{cases} P_{y_s} &= y_s \quad \text{for } y_s \in Y,\\ P_l &= [P_{l_1}, P_{l_2}] \quad \text{for } l \in \mathcal{L}ynY \setminus Y,\\ P_w &= P_{l_1}^{i_1}\ldots P_{l_k}^{i_k} \quad \text{for } w = l_1^{i_1}\ldots l_k^{i_k}, \end{cases} \tag{30}$$

where (l_1, l_2) is the standard factorization[8] of l, $l_1 > \ldots > l_k$ and $l_1, \ldots, l_k \in \mathcal{L}ynY$,

2. and, by duality[9], the basis $\{S_w\}_{w\in Y^*}$ for $(\mathbb{Q}\langle Y\rangle, \sqcup\!\sqcup)$, *i.e.*

$$\forall u, v \in Y^*, \langle P_u \mid S_v\rangle = \delta_{u,v}. \tag{31}$$

It can be shown that this linear basis can be computed recursively as follows [26]

$$\begin{cases} S_{y_s} &= y_s, \quad \text{for } y_s \in Y,\\ S_l &= y_s S_u, \quad \text{for } l = y_s u \in \mathcal{L}ynY,\\ S_w &= \dfrac{S_{l_1}^{\sqcup\!\sqcup\, i_1} \sqcup\!\sqcup \ldots \sqcup\!\sqcup S_{l_k}^{\sqcup\!\sqcup\, i_k}}{i_1!\ldots i_k!} \quad \text{for } w = l_1^{i_1}\ldots l_k^{i_k}, \end{cases} \tag{32}$$

where $l_1 > \ldots > l_k$, $l_1, \ldots, l_k \in \mathcal{L}ynY$.

EXAMPLE 1.

$$\begin{aligned} P_{y_1} &= y_1,\\ P_{y_2} &= y_2,\\ P_{y_2y_1} &= y_2y_1 - y_1y_2,\\ P_{y_3y_1y_2} &= y_3y_1y_2 - y_2y_3y_1 + y_2y_1y_3 - y_1y_3y_2,\\ S_{y_1} &= y_1,\\ S_{y_2} &= y_2,\\ S_{y_2y_1} &= y_2y_1,\\ S_{y_3y_1y_2} &= y_3y_2y_1 + y_3y_1y_2. \end{aligned}$$

Hence, we get Schützenberger's factorization of $\mathcal{D}_{\sqcup\!\sqcup}$

$$\mathcal{D}_{\sqcup\!\sqcup} = \prod_{l\in\mathcal{L}ynY}^{\searrow} \exp(S_l \otimes P_l) \in \mathcal{H}_{\sqcup\!\sqcup}^{\vee} \hat{\otimes} \mathcal{H}_{\sqcup\!\sqcup}. \tag{33}$$

Similarly, by the CQMM theorem, the connected $\mathbb{N}$-graded, co-commutative Hopf algebra $\mathcal{H}_{\uplus}$ is isomorphic to the enveloping algebra of its primitive elements:

$$\mathrm{Prim}(\mathcal{H}_{\uplus}) = \mathrm{Im}(\pi_1) = \mathrm{span}_{\mathbb{Q}}\{\pi_1(w) | w \in Y^*\}, \tag{34}$$

where, for any $w \in Y^*$, $\pi_1(w)$ is obtained as follows [20, 21]

$$\begin{aligned} \pi_1(w) &= w + \sum_{k\ge2} \frac{(-1)^{k-1}}{k} \sum_{u_1,\ldots,u_k\in Y^+}\\ &\quad \langle w \mid u_1 \uplus \ldots \uplus u_k\rangle\, u_1\ldots u_k. \end{aligned} \tag{35}$$

note that the eqn. (35) is equivalent to the following identity

$$w = \sum_{k\ge0} \frac{1}{k!} \sum_{u_1,\ldots,u_k\in Y^*} \langle w \mid u_1 \uplus \ldots \uplus u_k\rangle\, \pi_1(u_1)\ldots\pi_1(u_k). \tag{36}$$

In particular, for any $y_s \in Y$, the primitive polynomial $\pi_1(y_s)$ is given by

$$\pi_1(y_s) = y_s + \sum_{i\ge2} \frac{(-1)^{i-1}}{l} \sum_{\substack{j_1,\ldots,j_i\ge1\\ j_1+\ldots+j_i=s}} y_{j_1}\ldots y_{j_i}. \tag{37}$$

As previously, (37) is equivalent to

$$y_s = \sum_{i\ge1} \frac{1}{i!} \sum_{s_1+\ldots+s_i=s} \pi_1(y_{s_1})\ldots\pi_1(y_{s_i}). \tag{38}$$

EXAMPLE 2.

$$\begin{aligned} \pi_1(y_1) &= y_1,\\ \pi_1(y_2) &= y_2 - \frac{1}{2}y_1^2,\\ \pi_1(y_3) &= y_3 - \frac{1}{2}(y_1y_2 + y_2y_1) + \frac{1}{3}y_1^3.\\ y_1 &= \pi_1(y_1),\\ y_2 &= \pi_1(y_2) + \frac{1}{2!}\pi_1(y_1)^2,\\ y_3 &= \pi_1(y_3) + \frac{1}{2!}(\pi_1(y_1)\pi_1(y_2) + \pi_1(y_2)\pi_1(y_1))\\ &+ \frac{1}{3!}\pi_1(y_1)^3. \end{aligned}$$

Introducing the new alphabet $\bar{Y} = \{\pi_1(y)\}_{y\in Y}$, one obtains

$$\mathcal{H}_{\uplus} \cong \mathcal{U}(\mathcal{L}ie_{\mathbb{Q}}\langle\bar{Y}\rangle) \cong \mathcal{U}(\mathrm{Prim}(\mathcal{H}_{\uplus})), \tag{39}$$

$$\mathcal{H}_{\uplus}^{\vee} \cong \mathcal{U}(\mathcal{L}ie_{\mathbb{Q}}\langle\bar{Y}\rangle)^{\vee} \cong \mathcal{U}(\mathrm{Prim}(\mathcal{H}_{\uplus}))^{\vee}. \tag{40}$$

Considering

1. the PBW-Lyndon basis $\{\Pi_w\}_{w\in Y^*}$ for $\mathcal{U}(\mathrm{Prim}(\mathcal{H}_{\uplus}))$ constructed recursively as follows [20, 21]

$$\begin{cases} \Pi_{y_s} &= \pi_1(y_s) \quad \text{for } y_s \in Y,\\ \Pi_l &= [\Pi_{l_1}, \Pi_{l_2}] \quad \text{for } l \in \mathcal{L}ynY \setminus Y,\\ \Pi_w &= \Pi_{l_1}^{i_1}\ldots\Pi_{l_k}^{i_k} \quad \text{for } w = l_1^{i_1}\ldots l_k^{i_k}, \end{cases} \tag{41}$$

where (l_1, l_2) is the standard factorization of l, $w = l_1^{i_1}\ldots l_k^{i_k}$, $l_1 > \ldots > l_k$, $l_1, \ldots, l_k \in \mathcal{L}ynY$,

2. and, by duality, the basis $\{\Sigma_w\}_{w\in Y^*}$ within $\mathbb{Q}\langle Y\rangle$ [10], *i.e.*

$$\forall u, v \in Y^*, \qquad \langle \Pi_u \mid \Sigma_v\rangle = \delta_{u,v} \tag{42}$$

it can be shown that this linear basis can be computed recursively as follows [5, 20, 21]

$$\begin{cases} \Sigma_{y_s} = y_s, & \text{for } y_s \in Y,\\ \Sigma_l = \displaystyle\sum_{(!)} \frac{q^{i-1}}{i!} y_{s_{k_1}+\ldots+s_{k_i}} \Sigma_{l_1\ldots l_n}, & \text{for } l = y_{s_1}\ldots y_{s_k} \in \mathcal{L}ynY,\\ \Sigma_w = \dfrac{\Sigma_{l_1}^{\uplus\, i_1} \uplus \ldots \uplus \Sigma_{l_k}^{\uplus\, i_k}}{i_1!\ldots i_k!}, & \text{for } w = l_1^{i_1}\ldots l_k^{i_k}, \text{ with } l_1 > \ldots > l_k \in \mathcal{L}ynY. \end{cases} \tag{43}$$

In (!), the sum is taken over all $\{k_1, \ldots, k_i\} \subset \{1, \ldots, k\}$ and all $l_1 \ge \ldots \ge l_n$ such that $(y_{s_1}, \ldots, y_{s_k}) \overset{*}{\Leftarrow} (y_{s_{k_1}}, \ldots, y_{s_{k_i}}, l_1, \ldots, l_n)$, where $\overset{*}{\Leftarrow}$ denotes the transitive closure of the relation on standard sequences, denoted by $\Leftarrow$ [5].

EXAMPLE 3.

$$\begin{aligned} \Pi_{y_1} &= y_1,\\ \Pi_{y_2} &= y_2 - \tfrac{1}{2}y_1^2,\\ \Pi_{y_2y_1} &= y_2y_1 - y_1y_2,\\ \Pi_{y_3y_1y_2} &= y_3y_1y_2 - \tfrac{1}{2}y_3y_1^3 - y_2y_1^2y_2\\ &+ \tfrac{1}{4}y_2y_1^4 - y_1y_3y_2 + \tfrac{1}{2}y_1y_3y_1^2 + \tfrac{1}{2}y_1^2y_2^2 - \tfrac{1}{2}y_1^2y_2y_1^2\\ &- y_2y_3y_1 + \tfrac{1}{2}y_2^2y_1^2 + y_2y_1y_3 + \tfrac{1}{2}y_1^2y_3y_1 - \tfrac{1}{2}y_1^3y_3 + \tfrac{1}{4}y_1^4y_2,\\ \Sigma_{y_1} &= y_1,\\ \Sigma_{y_2} &= y_2,\\ \Sigma_{y_2y_1} &= y_2y_1 + \tfrac{1}{2}y_3,\\ \Sigma_{y_3y_1y_2} &= y_3y_2y_1 + y_3y_1y_2 + y_3^2 + \tfrac{1}{2}y_4y_2 + \tfrac{1}{3}y_6 + \tfrac{1}{2}y_5y_1. \end{aligned}$$

---

[8]This is the factorization of $l = l_1l_2$ in two Lyndon words such that l_2 is of maximal length.

[9]The dual family, *i.e.* the set of coordinate forms a basis lies in the algebraic dual which is here the space of noncommutative series, but as the enveloping algebra under consideration is graded in finite dimensions (by the multidegree), these series are in fact multihomogeneous polynomials.

[10]Same remark as previously, the grading being here provided by the weight.

We get the following extension of Schützenberger's factorization for $\mathcal{D}_{\boxplus}$ [5, 20, 21]

$$\mathcal{D}_{\boxplus} = \prod_{l\in\mathcal{L}ynY}^{\searrow} \exp(\Sigma_l \otimes \Pi_l) \in \mathcal{H}^{\vee}_{\boxplus}\hat{\otimes}\mathcal{H}_{\boxplus}. \tag{44}$$

2.2 Regularizations of shuffle and quasi-shuffle products

Put

$$\begin{aligned}
\mathcal{H}_1 &:= \mathbb{Q} \oplus \mathbb{Q}\langle X\rangle x_1 \simeq \mathbb{Q}\langle Y\rangle, & (45)\\
\mathcal{H}_2 &:= \mathbb{Q} \oplus x_0\mathbb{Q}\langle X\rangle x_1 \simeq \mathbb{Q} \oplus (Y \smallsetminus \{y_1\})\mathbb{Q}\langle Y\rangle, & (46)\\
L_1 &:= \mathcal{L}ynX \smallsetminus \{x_0\} \simeq \mathcal{L}ynY, & (47)\\
L_2 &:= \mathcal{L}ynX \smallsetminus \{x_0, x_1\} \simeq \mathcal{L}ynY \smallsetminus \{y_1\}. & (48)
\end{aligned}$$

Then $\mathcal{H}_1$ and $\mathcal{H}_2$ are closed by concatenation and shuffle products.

PROPOSITION 1 ([17, 18]). *One has the isomorphisms*

$$\mathcal{H}_1 \simeq \mathbb{Q}[L_1] \quad \textit{and} \quad \mathcal{H}_2 \simeq \mathbb{Q}[L_2].$$

Through the definitions of $Z_{\sqcup\!\sqcup}$ and $Z_{\boxplus}$ at (2) and (3), we have the following properties.

PROPOSITION 2 ([19]). *The noncommutative generating series $Z_{\sqcup\!\sqcup}$ and $Z_{\boxplus}$ are group-like for the coproducts $\Delta_{\sqcup\!\sqcup}$ and $\Delta_{\boxplus}$, respectively, i.e. they are not zero and :*

$$\Delta_{\sqcup\!\sqcup}(Z_{\sqcup\!\sqcup}) = Z_{\sqcup\!\sqcup} \otimes Z_{\sqcup\!\sqcup} \quad \textit{and} \quad \Delta_{\boxplus}(Z_{\boxplus}) = Z_{\boxplus} \otimes Z_{\boxplus}.$$

From (4) and (13), by *cancellation*, we established the identity between the noncommutative generating series of polyzetas, as global regularization[11] [20, 21]

$$Z_{\boxplus} = B'(y_1)\pi_Y Z_{\sqcup\!\sqcup}, \tag{49}$$

where [8]

$$B'(y_1) = \exp\left(\sum_{k\geq 2} \frac{(-1)^{k-1}\zeta(k)}{k} y_1^k\right). \tag{50}$$

We will rewrite this expression on the same bases and, thanks to the graded property, identify the local coordinates to find the structure of polyzetas.

To end this Section, let us note that we get on the one hand, by (2) and (3),

$$\begin{aligned}
\forall u, v \in \mathcal{L}ynX \smallsetminus X, &\quad \zeta(u)\zeta(v) = \zeta(u \sqcup\!\sqcup v), & (51)\\
\forall u, v \in \mathcal{L}ynY \smallsetminus \{y_1\}, &\quad \zeta(u)\zeta(v) = \zeta(u \boxplus v). & (52)
\end{aligned}$$

and on the other hand, by (49), for any $l \in \mathcal{L}ynX \smallsetminus X$ and for any $l' \in \mathcal{L}ynY \smallsetminus \{y_1\}$,

1. $\zeta_{\sqcup\!\sqcup}(x_1 \sqcup\!\sqcup l - x_1 l) = -\zeta_{\sqcup\!\sqcup}(x_1 l) = -\langle Z_{\sqcup\!\sqcup} \mid x_1 l\rangle$,
2. $\zeta_{\boxplus}(y_1 \boxplus l' - y_1 l') = -\zeta_{\boxplus}(y_1 l') = -\langle Z_{\boxplus} \mid y_1 l'\rangle$,
3. $\langle B'(y_1) \mid y_1\rangle = 0$.

This means that the identity (49), which is equivalent to (13) [20, 21], yields immediately the family of regularized double shuffle relations considered in [1, 2, 14, 17, 24, 28] (see also [3, 7, 22, 23, 27]).

[11]In [3, 7, 23, 27], the authors suggest the simultaneous regularizations, with respect to the shuffle and quasi-shuffle, to the indeterminate T and then to specialize $T = 0$.

3. STRUCTURE OF POLYZETAS

3.1 Representations of polynomials on bases

The aim of this subsection is to provide a method to represent any polynomial of $\mathbb{Q}\langle X\rangle$ (reps. $\mathbb{Q}\langle Y\rangle$) in terms of the bases $\{P_w\}_{w\in X^*}$ or $\{S_w\}_{w\in X^*}$ (resp. $\{\Pi_w\}_{w\in Y^*}$ or $\{\Sigma_w\}_{w\in Y^*}$).

Recall that, the bases $\{P_w\}_{w\in X^*}$ and $\{\Pi_w\}_{w\in Y^*}$ are homogeneous and upper triangular, the bases $\{S_w\}_{w\in X^*}$ and $\{\Sigma_w\}_{w\in Y^*}$ are homogeneous and lower triangular[12]. Without loss of generality we can assume that $P \in \mathbb{Q}\langle Y\rangle$ is a homogeneous polynomial of weight n, we now represent P in terms of the basis $\{\Sigma_w\}_{w\in Y^*}$ by the following algorithm.

Algorithm 1

INPUT: A homogeneous polynomial P of weight n.
OUTPUT: The representation of P on the basis $\{\Sigma_w\}_{w\in Y^*}$.

Step 1. Choose the leading term[13] of P, rewrite the word, without coefficient, called w_1, of this monomial as follows

$$w_1 = \Sigma_{w_1} + \sum_{v<w_1,(v)=n} \alpha_v v. \tag{53}$$

After that, replace w_1 with this expression in P and re-put the coefficients

$$P = \lambda_{w_1}\Sigma_{w_1} + \sum_{v<w_1,(v)=n} \beta_v v. \tag{54}$$

Step 2. Assign now P the sum $\sum_{v<w_1,(v)=n} \beta_v v$ in (54) and repeat the **Step 1.** until the last monomial which admits the smallest word of weight n, y_n, and we really have $y_n = \Sigma_{y_n}$. At last, by re-putting the coefficients, we will obtain the representation of the original

$$P = \sum_{v\leq w_1,(v)=n} \lambda_v \Sigma_v. \tag{55}$$

EXAMPLE 4. $P := 2y_1y_2 - \frac{1}{2}y_3$.
Step 1. Since $\Sigma_{y_1y_2} = y_1y_2 + y_2y_1 + y_3$ *we replace* y_1y_2 *with* $\Sigma_{y_1y_2} - y_2y_1 - y_3$ *in* P

$$P = 2\Sigma_{y_1y_2} - 2y_2y_1 - \frac{5}{2}y_3.$$

Step 2.

- *Since* $\Sigma_{y_2y_1} = y_2y_1 + \frac{1}{2}y_3$ *we replace* y_2y_1 *with* $\Sigma_{y_2y_1} - \frac{1}{2}y_3$ *in* P

$$P = 2\Sigma_{y_1y_2} - 2\Sigma_{y_2y_1} - \frac{3}{2}y_3.$$

- *Since* $y_3 = \Sigma_{y_3}$, *we thus get*

$$P = 2\Sigma_{y_1y_2} - 2\Sigma_{y_2y_1} - \frac{3}{2}\Sigma_{y_3}.$$

Follow the above algorithm, we imply the following consequence.

COROLLARY 1. *For any $u \in X^*, v \in Y^*$, we can represent*

$$\begin{aligned}
u &= P_u + \sum_{w>u,|w|=|u|} \alpha_w^1 P_w &= S_u + \sum_{w<u,|w|=|u|} \alpha_w^2 S_w,\\
v &= \Pi_v + \sum_{w>v,(w)=(v)} \beta_w^1 \Pi_w &= \Sigma_v + \sum_{w<v,(w)=(v)} \beta_w^2 \Sigma_w.
\end{aligned}$$

[12]w.r.t the basis of words, for example, with the alphabet Y, one has $\Sigma_w = w + \sum_{v<w,(v)=(w)} \alpha_v v$.

[13]This term stands for the greatest word of the support of P (for the lexicographic ordering).

3.2 Identifying the local coordinates

Now, we will rewrite the formula (49) on the same bases as the coordinates choosen for their representation. First, we expand $B'(y_1)$ as follows.

LEMMA 1. *Let us consider the expression*

$$B'(y_1) = 1 + \sum_{m \ge 2} B^{(m)} y_1^m.$$

We have

$$B^{(m)} = \sum_{i=1}^{\lfloor m/2 \rfloor} \sum_{\substack{k_1,\ldots,k_i \ge 2 \\ k_1+\ldots+k_i = m}} (-1)^{m-i} \frac{\zeta(k_1)\ldots\zeta(k_i)}{k_1 \ldots k_i},$$

where $\lfloor m/2 \rfloor$ is the largest integer not greater than $m/2$.

PROOF.

$$\begin{aligned}
B'(y_1) &= \exp\left(\sum_{k \ge 2} \frac{(-1)^{k-1}\zeta(k)}{k} y_1^k \right) \\
&= \sum_{n \ge 0} \frac{1}{n!} \left(\sum_{k \ge 2} \frac{(-1)^{k-1}\zeta(k)}{k} y_1^k \right)^n \\
&= \sum_{n \ge 0} \frac{1}{n!} \\
&\quad \sum_{k_1,\ldots,k_n \ge 2} \frac{(-1)^{k_1+\ldots+k_n-n}\zeta(k_1)\ldots\zeta(k_n)}{k_1 \ldots k_n} y_1^{k_1+\ldots+k_n} \\
&= 1 + \sum_{m \ge 2} \\
&\quad \left(\sum_{n=1}^{\lfloor m/2 \rfloor} \frac{1}{n!} \sum_{\substack{k_1,\ldots,k_n \ge 2 \\ k_1+\ldots+k_n = m}} \frac{(-1)^{m-n}\zeta(k_1)\ldots\zeta(k_n)}{k_1 \ldots k_n} \right) y_1^m \\
&= 1 + \sum_{m \ge 2} B^{(m)} y_1^m.
\end{aligned}$$

□

EXAMPLE 5.

$$\begin{aligned}
B^{(2)} &= -\frac{\zeta(2)}{2}, \\
B^{(3)} &= \frac{\zeta(3)}{3}, \\
B^{(4)} &= -\frac{\zeta(4)}{4} + \frac{\zeta(2)^2}{2^2}, \\
B^{(5)} &= \frac{\zeta(5)}{5} - 2\frac{\zeta(2)}{2}\frac{\zeta(3)}{3}.
\end{aligned}$$

3.2.1 *Identifying on the basis* $\{\Pi_w\}_{w \in Y^*}$

By using the duality of the bases, we rewrite (49) as follows

$$\sum_{v \in Y^*} \zeta_{\uplus}(\Sigma_v)\Pi_v = B'(y_1) \sum_{v \in Y^*} \zeta_{\sqcup\!\sqcup}(\pi_X(\Sigma_v))\Pi_v, \qquad (56)$$

where π_X denotes the inverse of π_Y (restricted to $\mathbb{Q} \oplus \mathbb{Q}\langle X \rangle x_1$). Moreover, we see that $B'(y_1)$ is a series of a single letter (like a sigle variable), y_1, and

$$y_1^k \Pi_v = \Pi_{y_1}^k \Pi_v = \Pi_{y_1^k v}, \quad \forall k \ge 1, v \in Y^*.$$

We can then identify the coefficients in (56) and obtain that:

PROPOSITION 3. *i) For any $v \in Y^* \setminus y_1 Y^*$, we have*[14]

$$\zeta(\Sigma_v) = \zeta(\pi_X \Sigma_v). \qquad (57)$$

[14]Note that the notation $\zeta(P)$ is used to replace $\zeta_{\sqcup\!\sqcup}(P)$ or $\zeta_{\uplus}(P)$ if the polynomial P only contains words in the forms $x_0 X^* x_1$ or $Y^* \setminus y_1 Y^*$ respectively.

ii) For any $v = y_1^k w \in Y^*, k \ge 1, w \in Y^* \setminus y_1 Y^*$, we have

$$\zeta_{\sqcup\!\sqcup}(\pi_X \Sigma_v) + \sum_{m=2}^{k} B^{(m)} \zeta_{\sqcup\!\sqcup}(\pi_X \Sigma_{y_1^{k-m} w}) = 0. \qquad (58)$$

EXAMPLE 6. *With $v = y_2$:*

$$\zeta(\Sigma_{y_2}) = \zeta(S_{x_0 x_1}).$$

With $v = y_2 y_3$:

$$\zeta(\Sigma_{y_2 y_3}) = \zeta(S_{x_0 x_1 x_0^2 x_1}) - 2\zeta(S_{x_0^2 x_1 x_0 x_1}) - 2\zeta(S_{x_0^3 x_1^2}) + \zeta(S_{x_0^4 x_1}).$$

With $v = y_1^3$:

$$-\frac{1}{2}\zeta(S_{x_0 x_1^2}) + \frac{1}{6}\zeta(S_{x_0^2 x_1}) + B^{(3)} = 0.$$

With $v = y_1^2 y_2$:

$$\zeta(S_{x_0 x_1^3}) - \zeta(S_{x_0^2 x_1^2}) + \frac{1}{2}\zeta(S_{x_0^3 x_1}) + B^{(2)} = 0.$$

3.2.2 *Identifying on the basis* $\{P_w\}_{w \in X^*}$

Let denote[15] $\{P'_w\}_{w \in X^* x_1}$ the reductions of $\{P_w\}_{w \in X^* x_1}$ on $\mathbb{Q} \oplus \mathbb{Q}\langle X \rangle x_1$. By applying the mapping π_X on the two sides of (56) and using the duality of the bases, we can rewrite the regularization as follows

$$B'(x_1) \sum_{u \in X^* x_1} \zeta_{\sqcup\!\sqcup}(S_u) P'_u = \sum_{u \in X^* x_1} \zeta_{\uplus}(\pi_Y S_u) P'_u. \qquad (59)$$

Similarly, by the remark that $B'(x_1)$ is a series of a single letter, x_1, and

$$x_1^k P_u = P_{x_1}^k P_u = P_{x_1^k u}, \quad \forall k \ge 1, u \in X^*,$$

we can identify the coefficients in (59) and then obtain that:

PROPOSITION 4. *i) For any $u \in X^* \setminus x_1 X^*$, we have*

$$\zeta(S_u) = \zeta(\pi_Y S_u). \qquad (60)$$

ii) For any $u \in x_1 X^* \setminus x_1^2 X^*$, we have

$$\zeta_{\uplus}(\pi_Y S_u) = 0. \qquad (61)$$

iii) For any $u = x_1^k w \in X^*, k \ge 2, w \in X^* \setminus x_1 X^*$, we have

$$B^{(k)} \zeta(S_w) = \zeta_{\uplus}(\pi_Y S_u). \qquad (62)$$

EXAMPLE 7. *With $u = x_0 x_1$:*

$$\zeta(S_{x_0 x_1}) = \zeta(\Sigma_{y_2}).$$

With $u = x_0 x_1 x_0^2 x_1$:

$$\zeta(S_{x_0 x_1 x_0^2 x_1}) = \zeta(\Sigma_{y_2 y_3}) + 2\zeta(\Sigma_{y_3 x_2}) + 6\zeta(\Sigma_{y_4 x_1}) - 5\zeta(\Sigma_{y_5}).$$

With $u = x_1 x_0 x_1$:

$$\zeta(\Sigma_{y_2 y_1}) - \frac{3}{2}\zeta(\Sigma_{y_3}) = 0.$$

With $u = x_1^2 x_0 x_1$:

$$B^{(2)} \zeta(S_{x_0 x_1}) = 2\zeta(\Sigma_{y_4}) - \zeta(\Sigma_{y_2})^2 - \zeta(\Sigma_{y_3 y_1}).$$

[15]They are defined by $P'_w = \pi_X(\pi_Y P_w)$, $\forall w \in X^*$. Note that $\pi_Y P_w = \pi_Y w = 0$, $\forall w \in X^* x_0$.

3.3 Algorithms to represent the structure of polyzetas

We really have relations among polyzetas represented on the bases $\{S_w\}_{w\in X^*}$ and $\{\Sigma_w\}_{w\in Y^*}$. In fact, from the formulas (32) and (43) we can easily represent these relations on the pure transcendence bases $\{S_l\}_{l\in\mathcal{L}ynX}$ or $\{\Sigma_l\}_{l\in\mathcal{L}ynY}$ respectively. In the two following algorithms, one uses these relations and the other one uses as well the structures of shuffle and stuffle products, we will eliminate these relations, in weight, to find the structure of polyzetas represented on the bases $\{S_l\}_{l\in\mathcal{L}ynX}$ and $\{\Sigma_l\}_{l\in\mathcal{L}ynY}$. These two algorithms return the same result which will be shown in the next subsection.

Algorithm 2

INPUT: A positive integer N.
OUTPUT: Representations of polyzetas, up to weight N, in the forms of polynomial relations of irreducible elements on the transcendence basis $\{\Sigma_l\}_{l\in\mathcal{L}ynY}$ (resp. $\{S_l\}_{l\in\mathcal{L}ynX}$).

Step 1. Find all words and Lyndon words, of weight[16] N of X^* and Y^*.

Step 2. Use Proposition 4 and *Algorithm* 1 to establish relations among polyzetas on the basis $\{\Sigma_l\}_{l\in\mathcal{L}ynY}$ (resp. use Proposition 3 and *Algorithm* 1 to establish relations among polyzetas on the basis $\{S_l\}_{l\in\mathcal{L}ynX}$).

Step 3. Eliminate these relations to find representations of polyzetas in the forms of a polynomial of irreducible elements.

The next lemma will show one other way to find the relations among the family $\{\zeta_{⧢}(S_w)\}_{w\in X^*}$ and the family $\{\zeta_{⧢\!\!\!\!\!+}(\Sigma_w)\}_{w\in Y^*}$.

LEMMA 2. *i) For any Lyndon words $l_1,l_2\in\mathcal{L}ynX\setminus X$ (resp. $l_1,l_2\in\mathcal{L}ynY\setminus\{y_1\}$), we have*

$$\zeta(S_{l_1}⧢ S_{l_2}) = \zeta(\pi_Y(S_{l_1}) \uplus \pi_Y(S_{l_2})),$$
$$(\textit{resp. } \zeta(\Sigma_{l_1}\uplus\Sigma_{l_2}) = \zeta(\pi_X(\Sigma_{l_1}) ⧢ \pi_X(\Sigma_{l_2}))).$$

ii) For any $w\in x_0X^*x_1$ or $w\in x_1x_0X^*x_1$ (resp. $w\in Y^*\setminus y_1^2Y^*$), we have

$$\zeta_{⧢}(S_w) = \zeta_{\uplus}(\pi_Y(S_w)),$$
$$(\textit{resp. } \zeta_{\uplus}(\Sigma_w) = \zeta_{⧢}(\pi_X(\Sigma_w))).$$

PROOF. Remark that $S_w = w + \sum_{v<w}\alpha_v v, \forall w\in X^*$ and if $l\in\mathcal{L}ynX\setminus X$ then $l\in x_0X^*x_1$. Basing ourselves on properties of polyzetas on words [21] $\zeta(l_1⧢ l_2)=\zeta(\pi_Y(l_1)\uplus\pi_Y(l_2))$ and $\zeta_{⧢}(x_1⧢ l)=\zeta_{\uplus}(y_1\uplus\pi_Y(l))$, we easily prove the desired solutions of the lemma. □

EXAMPLE 8. *With $l_1=x_0x_1, l_2=x_0^2x_1^2$ (in $\mathcal{L}ynX$):*

$$\zeta(S_{x_0x_1})\zeta(S_{x_0^2x_1^2}) = \zeta(\Sigma_{y_2})\zeta(\Sigma_{y_3y_1}) - \frac{1}{2}\zeta(\Sigma_{y_2})\zeta(\Sigma_{y_4}).$$

With $l_1=y_2, l_2=y_3y_1$ (in $\mathcal{L}ynY$):

$$\zeta(\Sigma_{y_2})\zeta(\Sigma_{y_3y_1}) = \zeta(S_{x_0x_1})\zeta(S_{x_0^2x_1^2}) + \frac{1}{2}\zeta(S_{x_0x_1})\zeta(S_{x_0^3x_1}).$$

With $w=x_1x_0^2x_1$ (in $x_1x_0X^*x_1$):

$$0 = \frac{1}{2}\zeta(\Sigma_{y_2})^2 + \zeta(\Sigma_{y^3y_1}) - 2\zeta(\Sigma_{y_4}).$$

With $w=y_1y_3$ (in y_1Y^*):

$$0 = -\frac{1}{2}\zeta(S_{x_0x_1})^2 + \zeta(S_{x_0^2x_1^2}) + \zeta(S_{x_0^3x_1}).$$

[16]In the alphabet X, the weight of a word is understood as the length of that word.

Algorithm 3

INPUT: A positive integer N.
OUTPUT: Representations of polyzetas, up to weight N, in the forms of polynomial relations of irreducible elements on the transcendence basis $\{\Sigma_l\}_{l\in\mathcal{L}ynY}$ (resp. $\{S_l\}_{l\in\mathcal{L}ynX}$).

Step 1. Find all words and Lyndon words, of weight N of X^* and Y^*.

Step 2. Use Lemma 2 and *Algorithm* 1 to establish relations among polyzetas on the basis $\{\Sigma_l\}_{l\in\mathcal{L}ynY}$ (resp. $\{S_l\}_{l\in\mathcal{L}ynX}$).

Step 3. Eliminate these relations to find representations of polyzetas in the forms of polynomials of irreducible elements.

3.4 Results

Representations of polyzetas in the forms of homogeneous polynomials of irreducible elements on the basis $\{\Sigma_l\}_{l\in\mathcal{L}ynY\setminus\{y_1\}}$:
Weight $n=3$

$$\zeta(\Sigma_{y_2y_1}) = \frac{3}{2}\zeta(\Sigma_{y_3}) \quad (63)$$

Weight $n=4$

$$\zeta(\Sigma_{y_4}) = \frac{2}{5}\zeta(\Sigma_{y_2})^2 \quad (64)$$
$$\zeta(\Sigma_{y_3y_1}) = \frac{3}{10}\zeta(\Sigma_{y_2})^2 \quad (65)$$
$$\zeta(\Sigma_{y_2y_1^2}) = \frac{2}{3}\zeta(\Sigma_{y_2})^2 \quad (66)$$

Weight $n=5$

$$\zeta(\Sigma_{y_3y_2}) = 3\zeta(\Sigma_{y_3})\zeta(\Sigma_{y_2}) - 5\zeta(\Sigma_{y_5}) \quad (67)$$
$$\zeta(\Sigma_{y_4y_1}) = -\zeta(\Sigma_{y_3})\zeta(\Sigma_{y_2}) + \frac{5}{2}\zeta(\Sigma_{y_5}) \quad (68)$$
$$\zeta(\Sigma_{y_2^2y_1}) = \frac{3}{2}\zeta(\Sigma_{y_3})\zeta(\Sigma_{y_2}) - \frac{25}{12}\zeta(\Sigma_{y_5}) \quad (69)$$
$$\zeta(\Sigma_{y_3y_1^2}) = \frac{5}{12}\zeta(\Sigma_{y_5}) \quad (70)$$
$$\zeta(\Sigma_{y_2y_1^3}) = \frac{1}{4}\zeta(\Sigma_{y_3})\zeta(\Sigma_{y_2}) + \frac{5}{4}\zeta(\Sigma_{y_5}) \quad (71)$$

Weight $n=6$

$$\zeta(\Sigma_{y_6}) = \frac{8}{35}\zeta(\Sigma_{y_2})^3 \quad (72)$$
$$\zeta(\Sigma_{y_4y_2}) = \zeta(\Sigma_{y_3})^2 - \frac{4}{21}\zeta(\Sigma_{y_2})^3 \quad (73)$$
$$\zeta(\Sigma_{y_5y_1}) = \frac{2}{7}\zeta(\Sigma_{y_2})^3 - \frac{1}{2}\zeta(\Sigma_{y_3})^2 \quad (74)$$
$$\zeta(\Sigma_{y_3y_1y_2}) = -\frac{17}{30}\zeta(\Sigma_{y_2})^3 + \frac{9}{4}\zeta(\Sigma_{y_3})^2 \quad (75)$$
$$\zeta(\Sigma_{y_3y_2y_1}) = 3\zeta(\Sigma_{y_3})^2 - \frac{9}{10}\zeta(\Sigma_{y_2})^3 \quad (76)$$
$$\zeta(\Sigma_{y_4y_1^2}) = \frac{3}{10}\zeta(\Sigma_{y_2})^3 - \frac{3}{4}\zeta(\Sigma_{y_3})^2 \quad (77)$$
$$\zeta(\Sigma_{y_2^2y_1^2}) = \frac{11}{63}\zeta(\Sigma_{y_2})^3 - \frac{1}{4}\zeta(\Sigma_{y_3})^2 \quad (78)$$
$$\zeta(\Sigma_{y_3y_1^3}) = \frac{1}{21}\zeta(\Sigma_{y_2})^3 \quad (79)$$
$$\zeta(\Sigma_{y_2y_1^4}) = \frac{17}{50}\zeta(\Sigma_{y_2})^3 + \frac{3}{16}\zeta(\Sigma_{y_3})^2 \quad (80)$$
$$\vdots$$

Representations of polyzetas in the forms of homogeneous polynomials of irreducible elements on the basis $\{S_l\}_{l\in\mathcal{L}ynX\setminus X}$:

Weight $n = 3$

$$\zeta(S_{x_0x_1^2}) = \zeta(S_{x_0^2x_1}) \tag{81}$$

Weight $n = 4$

$$\begin{aligned}
\zeta(S_{x_0^3x_1}) &= \frac{2}{5}\zeta(S_{x_0x_1})^2 && (82)\\
\zeta(S_{x_0^2x_1^2}) &= \frac{1}{10}\zeta(S_{x_0x_1})^2 && (83)\\
\zeta(S_{x_0x_1^3}) &= \frac{2}{5}\zeta(S_{x_0x_1})^2 && (84)
\end{aligned}$$

Weight $n = 5$

$$\begin{aligned}
\zeta(S_{x_0^3x_1^2}) &= -\zeta(S_{x_0^2x_1})\zeta(S_{x_0x_1}) + 2\zeta(S_{x_0^4x_1}) && (85)\\
\zeta(S_{x_0^2x_1x_0x_1}) &= -\frac{3}{2}\zeta(S_{x_0^4x_1}) + \zeta(S_{x_0^2x_1})\zeta(S_{x_0x_1}) && (86)\\
\zeta(S_{x_0^2x_1^3}) &= -\zeta(S_{x_0^2x_1})\zeta(S_{x_0x_1}) + 2\zeta(S_{x_0^4x_1}) && (87)\\
\zeta(S_{x_0x_1x_0x_1^2}) &= \frac{1}{2}\zeta(S_{x_0^4x_1}) && (88)\\
\zeta(S_{x_0x_1^4}) &= \zeta(S_{x_0^4x_1}) && (89)
\end{aligned}$$

Weight $n = 6$

$$\begin{aligned}
\zeta(S_{x_0^5x_1}) &= \frac{8}{35}\zeta(S_{x_0x_1})^3 && (90)\\
\zeta(S_{x_0^4x_1^2}) &= \frac{6}{35}\zeta(S_{x_0x_1})^3 - \frac{1}{2}\zeta(S_{x_0^2x_1})^2 && (91)\\
\zeta(S_{x_0^3x_1x_0x_1}) &= \frac{4}{105}\zeta(S_{x_0x_1})^3 && (92)\\
\zeta(S_{x_0^3x_1^3}) &= \frac{23}{70}\zeta(S_{x_0x_1})^3 - \zeta(S_{x_0^2x_1})^2 && (93)\\
\zeta(S_{x_0^2x_1x_0x_1^2}) &= \frac{2}{105}\zeta(S_{x_0x_1})^3 && (94)\\
\zeta(S_{x_0^2x_1^2x_0x_1}) &= -\frac{89}{210}\zeta(S_{x_0x_1})^3 + \frac{3}{2}\zeta(S_{x_0^2x_1})^2 && (95)\\
\zeta(S_{x_0^2x_1^4}) &= \frac{6}{35}\zeta(S_{x_0x_1})^3 - \frac{1}{2}\zeta(S_{x_0^2x_1})^2 && (96)\\
\zeta(S_{x_0x_1x_0x_1^3}) &= \frac{8}{21}\zeta(S_{x_0x_1})^3 - \zeta(S_{x_0^2x_1})^2 && (97)\\
\zeta(S_{x_0x_1^5}) &= \frac{8}{35}\zeta(S_{x_0x_1})^3 && (98)\\
&\vdots
\end{aligned}$$

From these representations, we easily deduce lists of irreducible polyzetas viewed as algebraic generators of the algebra of convergent polyzetas up to weight 12:

1. Irreducible polyzetas represented on the basis $\{\Sigma_l\}_{l\in\mathcal{L}ynY}$: $\zeta(\Sigma_{y_2})$, $\zeta(\Sigma_{y_3})$, $\zeta(\Sigma_{y_5})$, $\zeta(\Sigma_{y_7})$, $\zeta(\Sigma_{y_3y_1^5})$, $\zeta(\Sigma_{y_9})$, $\zeta(\Sigma_{y_3y_1^7})$, $\zeta(\Sigma_{y_{11}})$, $\zeta(\Sigma_{y_2y_1^9})$, $\zeta(\Sigma_{y_3y_1^9})$, $\zeta(\Sigma_{y_2^2y_1^8})$.

2. Irreducible polyzetas represented on the basis $\{S_l\}_{l\in\mathcal{L}ynX}$: $\zeta(S_{x_0x_1})$, $\zeta(S_{x_0^2x_1})$, $\zeta(S_{x_0^4x_1})$, $\zeta(S_{x_0^6x_1})$, $\zeta(S_{x_0x_1^2x_0x_1^4})$, $\zeta(S_{x_0^8x_1})$, $\zeta(S_{x_0x_1^2x_0x_1^6})$, $\zeta(S_{x_0^{10}x_1})$, $\zeta(S_{x_0x_1^3x_0x_1^7})$, $\zeta(S_{x_0x_1^2x_0x_1^8})$, $\zeta(S_{x_0x_1^4x_0x_1^6})$.

Let us now denote by $\mathcal{Z}_n$ the $\mathbb{Q}$-vector space generated by polyzetas of weight n, d_n its dimension. Here again, the result satisfies the Zagier's dimension conjecture[17] meaning that the two previous families of irreducible polyzetas are algebraically independent if and only if this conjecture holds up to weight 12.

[17] *i.e.*, $d_1 = 0,\ d_2 = d_3 = 1$ and $\forall n \geq 4, d_n = d_{n-2} + d_{n-3}$.

- $n = 2, d_2 = 1$,

$$\begin{aligned}
\mathcal{Z}_2 &= span\{\zeta(\Sigma_{y_2})\}\\
&= span\{\zeta(S_{x_0x_1})\}
\end{aligned}$$

- $n = 3, d_3 = 1$,

$$\begin{aligned}
\mathcal{Z}_3 &= span\{\zeta(\Sigma_{y_3})\}\\
&= span\{\zeta(S_{x_0^2x_1})\}
\end{aligned}$$

- $n = 4, d_4 = 1$,

$$\begin{aligned}
\mathcal{Z}_4 &= span\{\zeta(\Sigma_{y_2})^2\}\\
&= span\{\zeta(S_{x_0x_1})^2\}
\end{aligned}$$

- $n = 5, d_5 = 2$,

$$\begin{aligned}
\mathcal{Z}_5 &= span\{\zeta(\Sigma_{y_5}), \zeta(\Sigma_{y_2})\zeta(\Sigma_{y_3})\}\\
&= span\{\zeta(S_{x_0^4x_1}), \zeta(S_{x_0x_1})\zeta(S_{x_0^2x_1})\}
\end{aligned}$$

- $n = 6, d_6 = 2$,

$$\begin{aligned}
\mathcal{Z}_6 &= span\{\zeta(\Sigma_{y_2})^3, \zeta(\Sigma_{y_3})^2\}\\
&= span\{\zeta(S_{x_0x_1})^3, \zeta(S_{x_0^2x_1})^2\}
\end{aligned}$$

- $n = 7, d_7 = 3$,

$$\begin{aligned}
\mathcal{Z}_7 &= span\{\zeta(\Sigma_{y_7}), \zeta(\Sigma_{y_2})\zeta(\Sigma_{y_5}), \zeta(\Sigma_{y_2})^2\zeta(\Sigma_{y_3})\}\\
&= span\{\zeta(S_{x_0^6x_1}), \zeta(S_{x_0x_1})\zeta(S_{x_0^4x_1}), \zeta(S_{x_0x_1})^2\zeta(S_{x_0^2x_1})\}
\end{aligned}$$

- $n = 8, d_8 = 4$,

$$\begin{aligned}
\mathcal{Z}_8 &= span\{\zeta(\Sigma_{y_2})^4, \zeta(\Sigma_{y_3y_1^5}), \zeta(\Sigma_{y_3})\zeta(\Sigma_{y_5}),\\
&\quad \zeta(\Sigma_{y_3})^2\zeta(\Sigma_{y_2})\}\\
&= span\{\zeta(S_{x_0x_1})^4, \zeta(S_{x_0^2x_1})\zeta(S_{x_0^4x_1}),\\
&\quad \zeta(S_{x_0x_1})\zeta(S_{x_0^2x_1})^2, \zeta(S_{x_0x_1^2x_0x_1^4})\}
\end{aligned}$$

- $n = 9, d_9 = 5$,

$$\begin{aligned}
\mathcal{Z}_9 &= span\{\zeta(\Sigma_{y_9}), \zeta(\Sigma_{y_2})^2\zeta(\Sigma_{y_5}), \zeta(\Sigma_{y_2})\zeta(\Sigma_{y_7}),\\
&\quad \zeta(\Sigma_{y_2})^3\zeta(\Sigma_{y_3}), \zeta(\Sigma_{y_3})^3\}\\
&= span\{\zeta(S_{x_0^8x_1}), \zeta(S_{x_0x_1})^2\zeta(S_{x_0^4x_1}), , \zeta(S_{x_0^2x_1})^3\\
&\quad \zeta(S_{x_0x_1})\zeta(S_{x_0^6x_1}), \zeta(S_{x_0x_1})^3\zeta(S_{x_0^2x_1})\}
\end{aligned}$$

- $n = 10, d_{10} = 7$,

$$\begin{aligned}
\mathcal{Z}_{10} &= span\{\zeta(\Sigma_{y_2})^5, \zeta(\Sigma_{y_5})^2, \zeta(\Sigma_{y_3y_1^7}), \zeta(\Sigma_{y_2})^2\zeta(\Sigma_{y_3})^2,\\
&\quad \zeta(\Sigma_{y_2})\zeta(\Sigma_{y_3})\zeta(\Sigma_{y_5}), \zeta(\Sigma_{y_3})\zeta(\Sigma_{y_7}), \zeta(\Sigma_{y_2})\zeta(\Sigma_{y_3y_1^5})\}\\
&= span\{\zeta(S_{x_0^4x_1})^2, \zeta(S_{x_0^4x_1})\zeta(S_{x_0^2x_1})\zeta(S_{x_0x_1}),\\
&\quad \zeta(S_{x_0x_1})^2\zeta(S_{x_0^2x_1})^2, \zeta(S_{x_0x_1})^5, \zeta(S_{x_0x_1^3x_0x_1^5}),\\
&\quad \zeta(S_{x_0^6x_1})\zeta(S_{x_0^2x_1}), \zeta(S_{x_0x_1})\zeta(S_{x_0x_1^2x_0x_1^4})\}
\end{aligned}$$

- $n = 11, d_{11} = 9$,

$$\begin{aligned}
\mathcal{Z}_{11} &= span\{\zeta(\Sigma_{y_{11}}), \zeta(\Sigma_{y_2})^2\zeta(\Sigma_{y_7}), \zeta(\Sigma_{y_2})\zeta(\Sigma_{y_9}),\\
&\quad \zeta(\Sigma_{y_2})^3\zeta(\Sigma_{y_5}), \zeta(\Sigma_{y_3})^2\zeta(\Sigma_{y_5}), \zeta(\Sigma_{y_2})\zeta(\Sigma_{y_3})^3,\\
&\quad \zeta(\Sigma_{y_2})^2\zeta(\Sigma_{y_7}), \zeta(\Sigma_{y_3})\zeta(\Sigma_{y_3y_1^5}), \zeta(\Sigma_{y_2y_1^9})\}\\
&= span\{\zeta(S_{x_0^{10}x_1}), \zeta(S_{x_0^4x_1})\zeta(S_{x_0^2x_1})^2,\\
&\quad \zeta(S_{x_0x_1^2x_0x_1^2x_0x_1^4}), \zeta(S_{x_0^2x_1})\zeta(S_{x_0x_1})^3\zeta(S_{x_0x_1}),\\
&\quad \zeta(S_{x_0^8x_1})\zeta(S_{x_0x_1}), \zeta(S_{x_0^2x_1})\zeta(S_{x_0x_1})^4,\\
&\quad \zeta(S_{x_0^4x_1})\zeta(S_{x_0x_1})^3, \zeta(S_{x_0^6x_1})\zeta(S_{x_0x_1})^2,\\
&\quad \zeta(S_{x_0^2x_1})\zeta(S_{x_0x_1^2x_0x_1^4})\}
\end{aligned}$$

• $n = 12, d_{12} = 12$,

$$\begin{aligned}\mathcal{Z}_{12} &= span\{\zeta(\Sigma_{y_2})^6, \zeta(\Sigma_{y_3})^4, \zeta(\Sigma_{y_2})\zeta(\Sigma_{y_5})^2, \\ &\zeta(\Sigma_{y_3}\Sigma_{y_1^9}), \zeta(\Sigma_{y_2})\zeta(\Sigma_{y_3})\zeta(\Sigma_{y_7}), \zeta(\Sigma_{y_2^2}\Sigma_{y_1^8}), \\ &\zeta(\Sigma_{y_2})^3\zeta(\Sigma_{y_3})^2, \zeta(\Sigma_{y_3})\zeta(\Sigma_{y_9}), \zeta(\Sigma_{y_5})\zeta(\Sigma_{y_7}), \\ &\zeta(\Sigma_{y_2})^2\zeta(\Sigma_{y_3})\zeta(\Sigma_{y_5}), \zeta(\Sigma_{y_2})\zeta(\Sigma_{y_3}\Sigma_{y_1^7}), \\ &\zeta(\Sigma_{y_2})^2\zeta(\Sigma_{y_3}\Sigma_{y_1^5})\}\end{aligned}$$

4. CONCLUSION

In the classical theory of (finite-dimensional) Lie groups, every ordered basis of the Lie algebra provides a system of local coordinates of a suitable neighbourhood of the unity (of the group) via an ordered product of the one parameter groups corresponding to the (ordered) basis. Here, we get a perfect analogue of this geometrical picture for the Hausdorff groups (in shuffle and stuffle Hopf algebras) through Schützengerger's factorization, this doesn't depend on the regularization of shuffle and quasi-shuffle. Moreover, through the bridge equation (13) which relates two elements on these groups and an identification of the local coordinates of their L.H.S. and R.H.S. of (49) which involve only convergent polyzetas as local coordinates, we get a confirmation of Zagier's conjecture, up to weight 12, which is not due to the regularized double-shuffle relations.

5. REFERENCES

[1] M. Bigotte– *Etude symbolique et algorithmique des fonctions polylogarithmes et des nombres d'Euler-Zagier colorés*, doctor thesis, Lille, 2000.

[2] J. Blümlein, D. J. Broadhurst, J. A. M. Vermaseren– *The multiple zeta values data mine*, Computer Physics Communications, 181 (3), pp. 582 - 625, 2010.

[3] L. Boutet de Monvel– *Remark on divergent multizeta series*, in Microlocal Analysis and Asymptotic Analysis, RIMS workshop 1397, pp. 1-9, 2004.

[4] V.C. Bui– *Hopf algebras of shuffle and quasi-shuffle & Construction of dual bases*, Master thesis at LIPN , 2012.

[5] V.C. Bui, G. H. E. Duchamp, Hoang Ngoc Minh– *Schützenberger's factorization on the (completed) Hopf algebra of q−stuffle product*, Journal of Algebra, Number Theory and Applications, pp 191 - 215, 30, No. 2 ,2013.

[6] V.C. Bui, G. H. E. Duchamp, N. Hoang, Hoang Ngoc Minh, C. Tollu– *Combinatorics of ϕ-deformed quasi-shuffle Hopf algebras*, (in preparation).

[7] P. Cartier– *Fonctions polylogarithmes, nombres polyzetas et groupes pro-unipotents*, Sém BOURBAKI, $53^{\text{ème}}$, $n°885$, 2000-2001.

[8] C. Costermans, Hoang Ngoc Minh– *Noncommutative algebra, multiple harmonic sums and applications in discrete probability*, Journal of Symbolic Computation, pp. 801-817, 2009.

[9] Drinfel'd– *Quasi-Hopf Algebras*, Leningrad Math. J., 1, 1419-1457, 1990.

[10] Drinfel'd– *On quasitriangular quasi-hopf algebra and a group closely connected with gal($\bar{q}/q$)*, Leningrad Math. J., 4, 829-860, 1991.

[11] G. H. E. Duchamp and C. Tollu– *Sweedler's dual and Schützenberger's calculus*, In K. Ebrahimi-Fard, M. Marcolli and W. van Suijlekom (eds), Combinatorics and Physics, p. 67 - 78, Amer. Math. Soc. (Contemporary Mathematics), arXiv:0712.0125v3 [math.CO], vol. 539, 2011.

[12] J. Ecalle– *ARI/GARI, la dimorphie et l'arithmétique des multizêtas : un premier bilan*, J. Th. des nombres de Bordeaux, 15, pp. 411-478, 2003.

[13] J.Y. Enjalbert, Hoang Ngoc Minh– *Combinatorial study of Hurwitz colored polyzêtas*, Discrete Mathematics, pp. 3489-3497, 1. 24 no. 312, 2012.

[14] M. Espie, J.-C. Novelli, G. Racinet– *Formal Computations About Multiple Zeta Values*, in From Combinatorics to Dynamical Systems (Strasbourg, 2002), F. Fauvet and C. Mitschi (eds.), IRMA Lect. Math. Theor. Phys. 3, de Gruyter, Berlin, pp. 1-16, 2003.

[15] Ph. Flajolet & B. Salvy– *Euler sums and contour integral representations*, Experimental Macthemaics, 1998.

[16] Furusho, H– *The multiple zeta value algebra and the stable derivation algebra*, Publ. Res. Inst. Math. Sci., pp. 695-720, Vol 39. no 4, 2003.

[17] Hoang Ngoc Minh, M.Petitot– *Lyndon words, polylogarithms and the Riemann ζ function*, Discrete Mathematics, pp. 273 - 292, 2000.

[18] Hoang Ngoc Minh, Jacob G., N.E. Oussous, M. Petitot.– *Aspects combinatoires des polylogarithmes et des sommes d'Euler-Zagier*, journal électronique du Séminaire Lotharingien de Combinatoire, B43e, 2000.

[19] Hoang Ngoc Minh, Jacob G., N.E. Oussous, M. Petitot.– *De l'algèbre des ζ de Riemann multivariées à l'algèbre des ζ de Hurwitz multivariées*, journal électronique du Séminaire Lotharingien de Combinatoire, 44, 2001.

[20] Hoang Ngoc Minh– *On a conjecture by Pierre Cartier about a group of associators*, Acta Math. Vietnamica, pp. 339-398, 38, Issue 3, 2013.

[21] Hoang Ngoc Minh– *Structure of polyzetas and Lyndon words*, Vietnamese Math. J., pp. 409-450, 41, Issue 4, 2013.

[22] M. Hoffman.– *Quasi-shuffle products*, J. of Alg. Cominatorics, pp. 49-68, 11, 2000.

[23] K. Ihara, M. Kaneko & D. Zagier.– *Derivation and double shuffle relations for multiple zetas values*, Compositio Math. 142, pp. 307-338, 2006.

[24] M. Kaneko, M. Noro, and K. Tsurumaki,– *On a conjecture for the dimension of the space of the multiple zeta values*, in Software for Algebraic Geometry, M. Stillman et. al (eds.), IMA Volumes in Mathematics and its Applications 148, Springer, New York, pp. 47-58, 2008.

[25] J.W. Milnor, J.C. Moore– *On the structure of Hopf algebras*, The Annals of Mathematics, second series, pp. 211 - 264, Vol 81, No 2, 1965.

[26] C. Reutenauer– *Free Lie Algebras*, London Math. Soc. Monographs, New Series-7, Oxford Sc. Pub., 1993.

[27] M. Waldschmidt– *Hopf Algebra and Transcendental numbers, Zeta-functions*, Topology and Quantum Physics 2003, Kinki : Japan, 2003.

[28] El Wardi.– Mémoire de DEA, Lille, 1999.

[29] D. Zagier.– *Values of zeta functions and their applications*, in "First European Congress of Mathematics", vol. 2, Birkhäuser, pp. 497-512, 1994.

p-Adic Stability In Linear Algebra

Xavier Caruso
Université Rennes 1
xavier.caruso@normalesup.org

David Roe
University of British Columbia
roed.math@gmail.com

Tristan Vaccon
Université Rennes 1
tristan.vaccon@univ-rennes1.fr

ABSTRACT

Using the differential precision methods developed previously by the same authors, we study the p-adic stability of standard operations on matrices and vector spaces. We demonstrate that lattice-based methods surpass naive methods in many applications, such as matrix multiplication and sums and intersections of subspaces. We also analyze determinants, characteristic polynomials and LU factorization using these differential methods. We supplement our observations with numerical experiments.

Categories and Subject Descriptors

I.1.2 [**Computing Methodologies**]: Symbolic and Algebraic Manipulation – *Algebraic Algorithms*

General Terms

Algorithms, Theory

Keywords

p-adic precision; linear algebra; ultrametric analysis

1. INTRODUCTION

For about twenty years, the use of p-adic methods in symbolic computation has been gaining popularity. Such methods were used to compute composed products of polynomials [2], to produce hyperelliptic curves of genus 2 with complex multiplication [4], to compute isogenies between elliptic curves [8] and to count points on varieties using p-adic cohomology theories (*cf.* [5, 7] and many followers). However, a general framework allowing a precise study of p-adic precision — the main issue encountered when computing with p-adic numbers — was designed only recently in [3].

In [3], we advocate the use of lattices to track the precision of vectors and points on p-adic manifolds. The main result of *loc. cit.*, recalled in Proposition 2.1, allows for the propagation of precision using differentials. While representing precision by lattices carries a high cost in space and time requirements, the reduced precision loss can sometimes overwhelm these costs within a larger algorithm. In this paper, we apply the ideas of [3] to certain linear algebraic tasks.

Main Results. We give a number of contexts where lattice-based precision methods outperform the standard coordinate-wise methods. The two most striking examples are an analysis of matrix multiplication and of sums and intersections of subspaces. In Proposition 3.1, we give a formula for the lattice-precision of the product of two matrices. In Figure 2, we describe the precision loss in multiplying n matrices, which appears linear in n when using standard methods and logarithmic in n when using lattice methods. We also give an example in Figure 4 where lattice methods actually yield an *increase* in precision as the computation proceeds.

Organization of the paper. Section 2.1 recalls the theory of precision developed in [3] and defines a notion of diffuse precision for comparing to coordinate-wise methods. In particular, we recall Proposition 2.1, which allows the computation of precision using differentials. Proposition 2.5 in Section 2.2 is a technical result that will be used to determine the applicability of Proposition 2.1.

In Section 3.1, we analyze matrix multiplication and report on experiments that demonstrate the utility of lattice-based precision tracking. Section 3.2 finds the precision of the determinant of a matrix, and Section 3.3 applies the resulting formula to characteristic polynomials. We define the precision polygon of a matrix, which gives a lower bound on the precision of the characteristic polynomial. This polygon lies above the Hodge polygon of the matrix; we give statistics on the difference and the amount of diffuse precision. Finally, we apply Proposition 2.1 to LU factorization and describe experiments with lattice-based precision analysis. Section 4.1 reviews the geometry of Grassmannians, which we apply in Section 4.2 to differentiating the direct image, inverse image, sum and intersection maps between Grassmannians. We then report in Section 4.3 on tracking the precision of subspace arithmetic in practice. In the appendix, we give a proof of Proposition 2.4.

The code used to make experiments presented in this paper is available at `https://github.com/CETHop/padicprec`.

Notation. Throughout the paper, K will refer to a complete discrete valuation field. Usual examples are finite extensions of $\mathbb{Q}_p$ and Laurent series fields over a field. We denote by $\mathrm{val} : K \twoheadrightarrow \mathbb{Z} \cup \{+\infty\}$ the valuation on K, by $\mathcal{O}_K$ the ring of integers and by $\pi \in K$ an element of valuation 1. We let $\|\cdot\|$ be the norm associated to val.

ISSAC'15, July 6–9, 2015, Bath, United Kingdom.

DOI: http://dx.doi.org/10.1145/2755996.2756655.

2. THE THEORY OF P-ADIC PRECISION

The aim of this section is to briefly summarize the content of [3] and fill in certain details.

2.1 Lattices as precision data

In [3], we suggest the use of lattices to represent the precision of elements in K-vector spaces. We shall contrast this approach with the *coordinate-wise method* used in Sage, where the precision of an element is specified by giving the precision of each coordinate separately and is updated after each basic operation.

Consider a finite dimensional[1] normed vector space E defined over K. We use the notation $\|\cdot\|_E$ for the norm on E and $B_E^-(r)$ (resp. $B_E(r)$) for the open (resp. closed) ball of radius r centered at the origin. A *lattice* $L \subset E$ is a sub-$\mathcal{O}_K$-module which generates E over K. Since we are working in a ultrametric world, the balls $B_E(r)$ and $B_E^-(r)$ are examples of lattices. Actually, lattices should be thought of as special neighborhoods of 0 and therefore are good candidates to model precision data. Moreover, as revealed in [3], they behave quite well under (strictly) differentiable maps:

Proposition 2.1. *Let E and F be two finite dimensional normed vector spaces over K and $f : U \to F$ be a function defined on an open subset U of E. We assume that f is differentiable at some point $v_0 \in U$ and that the differential $f'(v_0)$ is surjective. Then, for all $\rho \in (0, 1]$, there exists a positive real number δ such that, for all $r \in (0, \delta)$, any lattice H such that $B_E^-(\rho r) \subset H \subset B_E(r)$ satisfies:*

$$f(v_0 + H) = f(v_0) + f'(v_0)(H). \tag{1}$$

This proposition enables the *lattice method* of tracking precision, where the precision of the input is specified as a lattice H and precision is tracked via differentials of the steps within a given algorithm. The equality sign in Eq. (1) shows that this method yields the optimum possible precision. We refer to [3, §4.1] for a more complete exposition.

In [3], we also explained that if f is locally analytic, then the constant δ appearing in Proposition 2.1 can be expressed in terms of the growing function $\Lambda(f)$ defined by

$$\Lambda(f)(v) = \log\left(\sup_{h \in B_E^-(e^v)} \|f(h)\|\right)$$

with the convention that $\Lambda(f)(v) = +\infty$ if f does not converge on $B_E^-(e^v)$. We refer to [3, Proposition 3.12] for the precise statement. We state here the case of integral polynomial functions. A function $f : E \to F$ is said to be *integral polynomial* if it is given by multivariate polynomial functions with coefficients in $\mathcal{O}_K$ in any (equivalently all) system of coordinates associated to a $\mathcal{O}_K$-basis of $B_E(1)$.

Proposition 2.2. *We keep the notation of Proposition 2.1 and assume in addition that f is integral polynomial. Let C be a positive real number such that $B_F(1) \subset f'(v_0)(B_E(C))$. Then Proposition 2.1 holds with $\delta = C \cdot \rho^{-1}$.*

In [3, Appendix A], the theory is extended to manifolds over K, where the precision datum at some point x is a lattice in the tangent space at x. Propositions 2.1 and 2.2 have analogues obtained by working in charts. We use this extension to compute with vector spaces in §4.

[1]The framework of [3] is actually those of Banach spaces. However, we will not need infinite dimensional spaces here.

We will use the following definition in contrasting lattice and coordinate-wise methods. Suppose E is equipped with a basis $(e_1, \ldots, e_n)$ and write $\pi_i : E \to Ke_i$ for the projections.

Definition 2.3. Let $H \subset E$ be a lattice. The number of *diffused digits of precision* of H is the length of H_0/H where $H_0 = \pi_1(H) \oplus \cdots \oplus \pi_n(H)$.

If H represents the actual precision of some object, then H_0 is the smallest diagonal lattice containing H. Since coordinate-wise methods cannot yield a precision better than H_0, k provides a lower bound on the number of p-adic digits gained by lattice methods over standard methods.

2.2 A bound on a growing function

In the next sections, we will compute the derivative of several standard operations and sometimes give a simple expression in term of the input and the output. In other words, the function f modeling such an operation satisfies a differential equation of the form $f' = g \circ (f, \mathrm{id})$ where g is a given — and hopefully rather simple — function. The aim of this subsection is to study this differential equation and to derive from it certain bounds on the growing function $\Lambda(f)$. *We will assume that K has characteristic* 0.

Let E, F and G be finite-dimensional normed vector spaces with $U \subseteq E$ and $V \subseteq F$ and $W \subset G$ open subsets. Generalizing the setting above, we consider the differential equation:

$$f' = g \circ (f, h). \tag{2}$$

Here $g : V \times W \to \mathrm{Hom}(E, F)$ and $h : U \to W$ are known locally analytic functions and $f : U \to V$ is the unknown locally analytic function. In what follows, we always assume that V and W contain the origin, $f(0) = 0$, $h(0) = 0$ and $g(0) \neq 0$. These assumptions are harmless for two reasons: first, we can always shift f and h (and g accordingly) so that they both vanish at 0, and second, in order to apply Proposition 2.2 the derivative $f'(0)$ needs to be surjective and therefore *a fortiori* nonzero.

We assume that we are given in addition two nondecreasing convex functions Λ_g and Λ_h such that $\Lambda(g) \leq \Lambda_g$ and $\Lambda(h) \leq \Lambda_h$. We suppose further that there exists ν such that Λ_g is constant on the interval $(-\infty, \nu]$[2]. We introduce the functions τ_ν and Λ_f defined by:

$$\tau_\nu(x) = \begin{cases} x & \text{if } x \leq \nu, \\ +\infty & \text{otherwise;} \end{cases}$$

$$\text{and } \Lambda_f(x) = \tau_\nu \circ (\mathrm{id} + \Lambda_g \circ \Lambda_h)(x + \alpha),$$

where α is a real number satisfying $\|n!\| \geq e^{-\alpha n}$ for all n. If p is the characteristic of the residue field, a suitable value for α is $\alpha = -\frac{p}{p-1} \cdot \log \|p\|$ if $p > 0$ and $\alpha = 0$ if $p = 0$. The next Proposition is proved in Appendix A.

Proposition 2.4. *We have $\Lambda(f) \leq \Lambda_f$.*

Figure 1 illustrates Proposition 2.4. The blue plain line represents the graph of the function Λ_f. A quick computation shows that, on a neighborhood of $-\infty$, this function is given by $\Lambda_f(x) = x + \alpha + \mu$ where μ is the value that Λ_g takes on the interval $(-\infty, \nu]$. Proposition 2.4 says that the graph of $\Lambda(f)$ lies below the plain blue line. Moreover, we remark that the Taylor expansion of $f(z)$ starts

[2]We note that this assumption is fulfilled if we take $\Lambda_g = \Lambda(g)$ because we have assumed that $g(0)$ does not vanish.

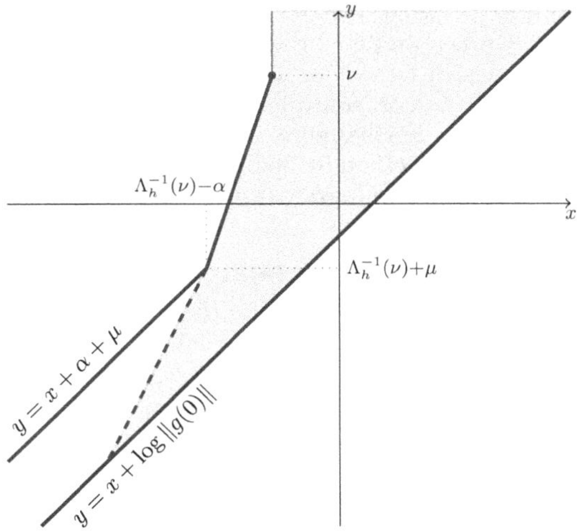

Figure 1: Admissible region for the graph of $\Lambda(f)$

with the term $g(0)z$. Hence, on a neighborhood of $-\infty$, we have $\Lambda(f)(x) = x + \log\|g(0)\|$. Using convexity, we get: $\Lambda(f)(x) \geq x + \log\|g(0)\|$ for all $x \in \mathbb{R}$. In other words, the graph of $\Lambda(f)$ lies above the brown line. Furthermore, we know that the slopes of $\Lambda(f)$ are all integral because f is locally analytic. Hence, $\Lambda(f)$ cannot lie above the dashed blue line defined as the line of slope 2 passing through the first break point of the blue plain line, which has coordinates $(y_0 - \alpha - \mu, y_0)$ with $y_0 = \min(\Lambda_h^{-1}(\nu) + \mu, \nu)$. As a conclusion, we have proved that the graph of $\Lambda(f)$ must coincide with the brown line until it meets the dashed blue line and then has to stay in the green area.

As a consequence, we derive the following proposition, which can be combined with Proposition 3.12 of [3]. Following [3], if φ is a convex function and $v \in \mathbb{R}$, we define

$$\varphi_{\geq v} : x \mapsto \inf_{y \geq 0} \big(\varphi(x+y) - vy\big).$$

It is the highest convex function with $\varphi_{\geq v} \leq \varphi$ and $\varphi'_{\geq v} \geq v$.

Proposition 2.5. *Keeping the above notation, we have:*

$$\Lambda(f)_{\geq 2}(x) \leq 2(x + \alpha + \mu) - \min(\Lambda_h^{-1}(\nu) + \mu,\ \nu)$$

for all $x \leq \min(\Lambda_h^{-1}(\nu) - \alpha,\ \nu - \mu - \alpha)$.

PROOF. The inequality follows from the fact that $y = 2(x+\alpha+\mu) - y_0$ is the equation of the dashed blue line. □

Remark 2.6. In certain situations, it may happen that the function f is solution of a simpler differential equation of the form $f' = g \circ f$. If this holds, Proposition 2.5 gives the bound $\Lambda(f)_{\geq 2}(x) \leq 2(x + \alpha + \mu) - \nu$ for $x \leq \nu - \mu - \alpha$.

Beyond this particular case, we recommend choosing the function h by endowing F with the second norm $\|x\|'_F = e^{\mu} \cdot \|x\|_F$ ($x \in F$) and taking $h : (F, \|\cdot\|_F) \to (F, \|\cdot\|'_F)$ to be the identity on the underlying vector spaces. The function $\Lambda(h) : \mathbb{R} \to \mathbb{R}$ then maps x to $x + \mu$ and we can choose $\Lambda_h = \Lambda(h)$.

3. MATRICES

Let $M_{m,n}(K)$ denote the space of $m \times n$ matrices over K. We will repeatedly use the Smith decomposition for $M \in M_{m,n}(K)$, which is $M = U_M \cdot \Delta_M \cdot V_M$ with U_M and V_M unimodular and Δ_M diagonal. Write $\sigma_i(M)$ for the valuation of the (i,i)-th entry of Δ_M, and by convention set $\sigma_i(M) = +\infty$ if $i > \min(m,n)$. Order the $\sigma_i(M)$ so that $\sigma_i(M) \leq \sigma_{i+1}(M)$.

3.1 Multiplication

To begin with, we want to study the behavior of the precision when performing a matrix multiplication. Let r, s and t be three positive integers and assume that we want to multiply a matrix $A \in M_{r,s}(K)$ by a matrix $B \in M_{s,t}(K)$. This operation is of course modeled by the integral polynomial function:

$$\begin{array}{rccl} \mathcal{P}_{r,s,t} : & M_{r,s}(K) \times M_{s,t}(K) & \to & M_{r,t}(K) \\ & (A,B) & \mapsto & AB. \end{array}$$

According to Proposition 2.1, the behavior of the precision when computing AB is governed by $\mathcal{P}'_{r,s,t}(A,B)$, the linear mapping that takes a pair (dA, dB) to $A \cdot dB + dA \cdot B$.

To fix ideas, let us assume from now that the entries of A and B all lie in $\mathcal{O}_K$ and are known at the same precision $O(\pi^N)$. In order to apply Propositions 2.1 and 2.2, we then need to compute the image of the standard lattice $\mathcal{L}_0 = M_{r,s}(\mathcal{O}_K) \times M_{s,t}(\mathcal{O}_K)$ under $\mathcal{P}'_{r,s,t}(A,B)$. It is of course contained in $M_{r,t}(\mathcal{O}_K)$; this reflects the obvious fact that each entry of the product AB is also known with precision at least $O(\pi^N)$. Nonetheless, it may happen that the above inclusion is strict, meaning that we are *gaining* precision in those cases.

Set $a_i = \sigma_i(A)$ and $b_i = \sigma_i(B)$, and define $M_{r,t}((a_i),(b_j))$ as the sublattice of $M_{r,t}(\mathcal{O}_K)$ consisting of matrices $M = (M_{i,j})$ such that $\mathrm{val}(M_{i,j}) \geq \min(a_i, b_j)$ for all (i,j).

Proposition 3.1. *With the above notation, we have*

$$\mathcal{P}'_{r,s,t}(A,B)(\mathcal{L}_0) = U_A \cdot M_{r,t}((a_i),(b_j)) \cdot V_B$$

$$\text{and} \quad \mathrm{length}\Big(\tfrac{M_{r,t}(\mathcal{O}_K)}{\mathcal{P}'_{r,s,t}(A,B)(\mathcal{L}_0)}\Big) = \sum_{i,j} \min(a_i, b_j)$$

PROOF. We write $A \cdot dB + dA \cdot B = U_A \cdot M \cdot V_B$ with

$$M = \Delta_A \cdot V_A \cdot dA \cdot V_B^{-1} + U_A^{-1} \cdot dB \cdot U_B \cdot \Delta_B.$$

When dA varies in $M_{a,b}(\mathcal{O}_K)$ so does $V_A \cdot dA \cdot V_B^{-1}$ and therefore the first summand in M varies in the subspace of $M_{r,t}(\mathcal{O}_K)$ consisting of matrices whose entries on the i-th row have valuation at least a_i. Arguing similarly for the second summand, we deduce the first statement of the Proposition. The second statement is now clear. □

From the perspective of precision, the second statement of Proposition 3.1 means that the computation of AB gains $\sum_{i,j} \min(a_i, b_j)$ significant digits in absolute precision[3] as soon as $N > \min(a_r, b_t)$ (*cf.* Proposition 2.2). However, many of these digits are diffused in the sense of Definition 2.3. To change bases in order to make this increased precision visible with coordinates, write $AB = U_A \cdot P \cdot V_B$ with $P = \Delta_A \cdot V_A \cdot U_B \cdot \Delta_B$. Tracking precision in the usual way, the (i,j)-th entry of P is known at precision $O(\pi^{N+\min(a_i,b_j)})$. Multiplication by U_A and V_B then diffuses the precision across the entries of AB.

[3]We note that, on the other side, the valuation of the entries of AB may increase, meaning that we are also losing some significant digits if we are reasoning in relative precision.

d	n	Average loss of precision	
		Coord-wise method	Lattice method
2	10	2.8	2.4
2	100	16.7	5.0
2	1000	157.8	7.9
3	10	2.2	1.9
3	100	12.8	4.0
3	1000	122.5	7.0

Results for a sample of 1000 random inputs in $M_{d,d}(\mathbb{Z}_2)^n$

Figure 2: Average loss of precision in Algorithm 1

We now consider the impact of tracking this diffuse precision. Although the benefit is not substantial for a single product of matrices, it accumulates as we multiply a large number of matrices. We illustrate this phenomenon with the following simple example.

Algorithm 1: `example_product`
Input: a list $(M_1, \dots, M_n)$ of square matrices of size d.
1. Set P to the identity matrix of size d
2. **for** $j = 1, \dots, n$ **do compute** $P = PM_i$
3. **return** the top left entry of P

Figure 2 compares the number of significant digits in *relative* precision we are losing on the output of Algorithm 1 when we are using, on the one hand, a standard coordinate-wise track of precision and, on the other hand, a lattice-based method to handle precision. We observe that, in the first case, the number of lost digits seems to grow linearly with respect to the number of multiplications we are performing (that is n) whereas, in the second case, the growth seems to be only logarithmic. It would be nice to have a precise formulation (and proof) of this heuristic.

Note that multiplication of many random matrices plays a central role in the theory of random walks on homogeneous spaces [1]. Better stability in computing such products helps estimate Lyapunov exponents in that context.

3.2 Determinant

The computation of the differential of $\det : M_{n,n}(K) \to K$ is classical: at a point M it is the linear map

$$\det{}'(M) : dM \mapsto \mathrm{Tr}(\mathrm{Com}(M) \cdot dM),$$

where $\mathrm{Com}(M)$ stands for the comatrix of M, which is $\det(M)M^{-1}$ when M is invertible. If $\mathrm{rank}(M) < n-1$, then $\det{}'(M)$ is not surjective and we cannot apply Proposition 2.1. Therefore, we suppose that $\mathrm{rank}(M) \geq n-1$ for the rest of this section.

As with matrix multiplication, we first determine the image of the standard lattice $\mathcal{L}_0 = M_{n,n}(\mathcal{O}_K)$ under $\det{}'(M)$.

Proposition 3.2. *Setting* $v = \sigma_1(M) + \dots + \sigma_{n-1}(M)$, *we have* $\det{}'(M)(\mathcal{L}_0) = \pi^v \mathcal{O}_K$.

PROOF. From the description of $\det{}'(M)$, we see that it is enough to prove that the smallest valuation of an entry of $\mathrm{Com}(M)$ is v or, equivalently, that the ideal of $\mathcal{O}_K$ generated by all minors of M of size $(n-1)$ is $\pi^v\mathcal{O}_K$. But this ideal remains unchanged when we multiply M on the left or on the right by a unimodular matrix. Thus we may assume that $M = \Delta_M$, and the result becomes clear. □

In terms of precision, Proposition 3.2 implies that if M is given at flat precision $O(\pi^N)$ with $N > v$, then $\det(M)$ is known at precision $O(\pi^{N+v})$. Thus we are gaining v digits in absolute precision or, equivalently, losing $\sigma_n(M)$ digits of relative precision. Furthermore, one may compute $\det(M)$ with this optimal precision by finding an approximate Smith decomposition with Δ_M known at precision $O(\pi^N)$ and multiplying its diagonal entries.

3.3 Characteristic polynomials

Write $\mathrm{char} : M_{n,n}(K) \to K[X]$ for the characteristic polynomial, and $K_{<n}[X] \subset K[X]$ for the subspace consisting of polynomials of degree less than n. Then the differential of char at a point M is

$$\mathrm{char}'(M) : dM \mapsto \mathrm{Tr}(\mathrm{Com}(X - M) \cdot dM).$$

The image is the K-span of the entries of $\mathrm{Com}(X-M)$, which is clearly contained within $K_{<n}[X]$. In fact, the image will equal $K_{<n}[X]$ as long as M does not have two Jordan blocks with the same generalized eigenvalue. For now on, we make this assumption.

Recall that the *Newton polygon* $\mathrm{NP}(f)$ of a polynomial $f(X) = \sum_i a_i X^i$ is the lower convex hull of the points $(i, \mathrm{val}(a_i))$ and the *Newton polygon* $\mathrm{NP}(M)$ of a matrix M is $\mathrm{NP}(\mathrm{char}(M))$. The *Hodge polygon* $\mathrm{HP}(M)$ of M is the lower convex hull of the points $(i, \sum_{j=1}^{n-i} \sigma_j(M))$. For any matrix M, the polygon $\mathrm{NP}(M)$ lies above $\mathrm{HP}(M)$ [6, Thm. 4.3.11].

Such polygons arise naturally in tracking the precision of polynomials [3, §4.2]. Any such polygon P yields a lattice $\mathcal{L}_P$ in $K_{<n}[X]$ consisting of polynomials whose Newton polygons lie above P. This lattice is generated by monomials $a_i X^i$, where $\mathrm{val}(a_i)$ is the ceiling of the height of P at i. These polygons are used in a coordinate-wise precision tracking for polynomial arithmetic. We now introduce another polygon, bounded between $\mathrm{NP}(M)$ and $\mathrm{HP}(M)$, that will provide an estimate on the precision of $\mathrm{char}(M)$.

Definition 3.3. The *precision polygon* $\mathrm{PP}(M)$ of M is the lower convex hull of the Newton polygon of the entries of $\mathrm{Com}(X-M)$.

It is clear from the definition $\mathcal{L}_{\mathrm{PP}(M)} \subset \mathrm{char}'(M)(\mathcal{L}_0)$ where $\mathcal{L}_0$ is the standard lattice $M_{n,n}(\mathcal{O}_K)$. More precisely, $\mathrm{PP}(M)$ is the smallest polygon P for which the inclusion $\mathcal{L}_P \subset \mathrm{char}'(M)(\mathcal{L}_0)$ holds. By Proposition 2.1, the precision polygon determines the minimal precision losses possible when encoding polynomial precision using polygons.

It turns out that the precision polygon is related to the Hodge and Newton polygons. If a polygon P has vertices (x_i, y_i), we let $T_n(P)$ be the translated polygon with vertices $(x_i - n, y_i)$.

Proposition 3.4. *The precision polygon* $\mathrm{PP}(M)$ *lies between* $T_1(\mathrm{HP}(M))$ *and* $\mathrm{NP}(M)$.

Moreover, $\mathrm{PP}(M)$ *and* $T_1(\mathrm{HP}(M))$ *meet at* 0 *and* $n-1$.

PROOF. The coefficients of $\mathrm{char}(M)$ can be expressed as traces of exterior powers: the coefficient of X^i is $\mathrm{Tr}(\Lambda^i(M))$, which is $\mathrm{Tr}(\Lambda^i(U_M)\Lambda^i(\Delta_M)\Lambda^i(V_M))$. Computing $\Lambda^i(\Delta_M)$, we get the first statement of the Proposition. For $i = 1$, we further find that $\mathrm{PP}(M)$ vanishes at the abscissa $n-1$. By definition so does $T_1(\mathrm{HP}(M))$. The fact that $\mathrm{PP}(M)$ and $T_1(\mathrm{HP}(M))$ meet at abscissa 0 follows from Proposition 3.2.

It remains to prove the comparison with the Newton polygon. Set $f = \mathrm{char}(M)$, set $m_{i,j}$ as the (i,j)-th entry of

M, $f_{i,j}$ as the (i,j)-th entry of $\mathrm{Com}(X-M)$ and $\mu_{i,j} = \mathrm{val}(m_{i,j})$. We write $f[k]$ for valuation of the coefficient of X^k in f, and set $f[-1] = +\infty$. The equation $(X-M) \cdot \mathrm{Com}(X-M) = f \cdot I$ yields, for all i and k,

$$\begin{aligned} f[k] &\geq \inf(f_{i,i}[k-1], \mu_{i,0} + f_{0,i}[k], \ldots, \mu_{i,n} + f_{n,i}[k]) \\ &\geq \inf(f_{i,i}[k-1], f_{j,i}[k]), \end{aligned}$$

with the infimum over j. Taking lower convex hulls and noting that $\mathrm{PP}(M)$ is nonincreasing, which follows from the comparison with the Hodge polygon, we get the result. □

Remark 3.5. Experiments actually support the following stronger result: $\mathrm{PP}(M)$ is bounded above by $T_1(\mathrm{NP}(M))$.

For many matrices, $\mathrm{PP}(M) = T_1(\mathrm{HP}(M))$. For random matrices over $\mathbb{Z}_2$, the 2-adic precision polygon is equal to the Hodge polygon in 99.5% of cases in dimension 4, down to 99.1% in dimension 8. Over $\mathbb{Z}_3$, the fraction rises to 99.98%, with no clear dependence on dimension. Empirically, $\mathrm{PP}(M)$ seems most likely to differ from $T_1(\mathrm{HP}(M))$ at 1, corresponding to the precision of the linear term of the characteristic polynomial.

Of course, the precision lattice $\mathcal{E} = \mathrm{char}'(M)(\mathcal{L}_0)$ may contain diffuse precision which is not encapsulated in $\mathrm{PP}(M)$. Diffuse precision arises in 11% of cases in dimension 3, up to 15% of cases in dimension 8. This percentage increases as $\mathrm{val}(\det(M))$ increases, reaching 34% in dimension 9 for matrices constrained to have determinant with 2-adic valuation 12. Moreover, one can construct examples with arbitrarily large amounts of diffuse precision. Suppose the $\sigma_i(M)$ are large. Proposition 3.4 implies that $\mathcal{E}$ is contained within $\mathcal{O}_{K,<n}[X]$ with index at least $\sum_{i=1}^{n-1} \sigma_i(M)$. The precision lattice of $1+M$ is obtained from $\mathcal{E}$ via the transformation $X \mapsto 1+X$, but $\mathrm{PP}(1+M)$ is now flat with height 0.

For randomly chosen matrices, approximating $\mathcal{E}$ using the Hodge polygon loses only a small amount of precision. However, if the $\sigma_i(M)$'s are large or if M is a translate of such a matrix, using lattice precision can be very useful.

3.4 LU factorization

In this section, we denote by $\|\cdot\|$ the subordinate matrix norm on $M_n(K)$ and, given a positive real number C, we let $B(C)$ be the closed ball in $M_n(K)$ centered at the origin of radius C. We consider the following subsets of $M_n(K)$:

- O_n is the open subset of matrices whose principal minors do not vanish (we recall that the latest condition implies the existence and the uniqueness of a LU factorization);
- U_n is the sub-vector space of upper-triangular matrices;
- L_n^0 (resp. L_n^u) is the sub-affine space of nilpotent (resp. unipotent) lower-triangular matrices.

Calculus and precision. We choose to normalize the LU factorization by requiring that L is unipotent and denote by $D : O_n \to L_n^u \times U_n$ the function modeling this decomposition. The computation of the differential of D has already been done in [3, Appendix B]. For $M \in \mathcal{O}_n$ with $D(M) = (L, U)$, the linear mapping $D'(M)$ is given by:

$$dM \mapsto (L \cdot \mathrm{low}(dX), \mathrm{up}(dX) \cdot U) \text{ with } dX = L^{-1} \cdot dM \cdot U^{-1}$$

where low (resp. up) denotes the canonical projection of $M_n(K)$ onto L_n^0 (resp. U_n). It is easily checked that $D'(M)$ is bijective with inverse given by $(A, B) \mapsto AU + LB$.

We now want to apply Proposition 2.5 in order to derive a concrete result on precision. *We then assume that K has characteristic* 0. We pick $M_0 \in O_n$ and write $D(M_0) = (L_0, U_0)$. We consider the translated function f taking M to $D(M_0 + M) - D(M_0)$. We then have $f(0) = 0$ and $f'(M) = D'(M_0 + M)$. Using the explicit description of the inverse of $D'(M_0+M)$, we find $B(1) \subset f'(0) \cdot B(C)$ for $C = \max(\|U_0\|, \|L_0\|)$. Moreover, f satisfies the differential equation $f' = g \circ f$ where g is defined by:

$$\begin{aligned} g(A,B)(X) = \big((L_0 + A) \cdot \mathrm{low}(Y), \mathrm{up}(Y) \cdot (U_0 + B)\big) \\ \text{with } Y = (L_0 + A)^{-1} \cdot X \cdot (U_0 + B)^{-1}. \end{aligned} \quad (3)$$

Let $\kappa(S) = \|S\| \cdot \|S^{-1}\|$ denote the condition number of a matrix S. Remarking that $\|S+T\| = \|S\|$ if $\|T\| < \|S\|$ and $\|(S+T)^{-1}\| = \|S^{-1}\|$ if $\|T\| < \|S^{-1}\|^{-1}$, we deduce from (3) that $\|g(A,B)\| \leq \max\big(\kappa(L_0)\|U_0^{-1}\|, \kappa(U_0)\|L_0^{-1}\|\big)$ provided that $\|A\| < \|L_0^{-1}\|^{-1}$ and $\|B\| < \|U_0^{-1}\|^{-1}$. Combining this with Proposition 2.5 and [3, Proposition. 3.12], we finally find that Eq. (1) holds as soon as

$$\begin{aligned} \frac{\rho}{r} > \|p\|^{-\frac{2p}{p-1}} \cdot \max(\|L_0\|, \|U_0\|) \cdot \max(\|L_0^{-1}\|, \|U_0^{-1}\|) \cdot \\ \max\big(\kappa(L_0)\|U_0^{-1}\|, \kappa(U_0)\|L_0^{-1}\|\big)^2. \end{aligned}$$

Numerical experiments. Let $B_n = (E_{i,j})_{1 \leq i,j \leq n}$ be the canonical basis of $M_n(K)$. It can be naturally seen as a basis of $L_n^0 \times U_n$ as well. For a given $M \in O_n$, let us abuse notation and write $D'(M)$ for the matrix of this linear mapping in the above basis. We remark that $D'(M)$ is lower-triangular in this basis. Projecting $D'(M)$ onto each coordinate, we find the best coordinate-wise loss of precision we can hope for the computation of D is given by $\sum_u (\max_v (\mathrm{val}(D'(M)_{u,v})))$. This number should be compared to $\mathrm{val}(\det(D'(M)))$, which is precision lost in the lattice method. The number of diffused digits of precision of $D'(M)(M_{n,n}(\mathcal{O}_K))$ is then the difference between these two numbers. Figure 3 summarizes the mean and standard deviation of those losses for a sample of 2000 random matrices in $M_{d,d}(\mathbb{Z}_2)$.

matrix size	Loss of precision in LU decomposition			
	coord-wise method		lattice method	
	mean	deviation	mean	deviation
2	3.0	5	1.5	1.4
3	9.4	11	2.3	2.3
4	20	20	3.8	3.1

Results for a sample of 2000 instances

Figure 3: Loss of precision for LU factorization

4. VECTOR SPACES

Vector spaces are generally represented as subspaces of K^n for some n and hence naturally appear as points on Grassmannians. Therefore, one can use the framework of [3, Appendix A] to study p-adic precision in this context.

4.1 Geometry of Grassmannians

Given E, a finite dimensional vector space over K, and d, an integer in the range $[0, \dim E]$, we write $\mathrm{Grass}(E,d)$ for the Grassmannian of d-dimensional subspaces of E. It is well-known that $\mathrm{Grass}(E,d)$ has the natural structure of a K-manifold. The aim of this subsection is to recall standard facts about its geometry. In what follows, we set $n = \dim E$ and equip E with a distinguished basis $(e_1, \ldots, e_n)$.

Description and tangent space. Let V denote a fixed subspace of E of dimension d. The Grassmannian $\mathrm{Grass}(E,d)$ can be viewed as the quotient of the set of linear embeddings $f : V \hookrightarrow E$ modulo the action (by precomposition) of $\mathrm{GL}(V)$: the mapping f represents its image $f(V)$. It follows from this description that the tangent space of $\mathrm{Grass}(E,d)$ is canonically isomorphic to $\mathrm{Hom}(V,E)/\mathrm{End}(V)$, which is $\mathrm{Hom}(V,E/V)$.

Charts. Let V and V^c be two complementary subspaces of E (*i.e.* $V \oplus V^c = E$). We assume that V has dimension d and denote by π the projection $E \to V$ corresponding to the above decomposition. We introduce the set $\mathcal{U}_{V,V^c}$ of all embeddings $f : V \hookrightarrow E$ such that $\pi \circ f = \mathrm{id}_V$. Clearly, it is an affine space over $\mathrm{Hom}(V,V^c)$. Furthermore, we can embed it into $\mathrm{Grass}(E,d)$ by taking f as above to its image. This way, $\mathcal{U}_{V,V^c}$ appears as an open subset of $\mathrm{Grass}(E,d)$ consisting exactly of those subspaces W such that $W \cap V^c = 0$. As a consequence, the tangent space at each such W becomes isomorphic to $\mathrm{Hom}(V,V^c)$. The identification $\mathrm{Hom}(V,V^c) \to \mathrm{Hom}(W,E/W)$ is given by $du \mapsto (du \circ f^{-1}) \bmod W$ where $f : V \xrightarrow{\sim} W$ is the linear mapping defining W.

When the pair (V,V^c) varies, the open subsets $\mathcal{U}_{V,V^c}$ cover the whole Grassmannian and define an atlas. When implementing vector spaces on a computer, we usually restrict ourselves to the subatlas consisting of all charts of the form (V_I, V_{I^c}) where I runs over the family of subsets of $\{1,\dots,n\}$ of cardinality d and V_I is the subspace spanned by the e_i's with $i \in I$. A subspace $W \in E$ then belongs to at least one $\mathcal{U}_{V_I,V_{I^c}}$ and, given a family of generators of W, we can determine such an I together with the corresponding embedding $f : V_I \hookrightarrow E$ by row reducing the matrix of generators of W.

A variant. Alternatively, one can describe $\mathrm{Grass}(E,d)$ as the set of linear surjective morphisms $f : E \to E/V$ modulo the action (by postcomposition) of $\mathrm{GL}(E/V)$. This identification presents the tangent space at a given point V as the quotient $\mathrm{Hom}(E,E/V)/\mathrm{End}(E/V) \simeq \mathrm{Hom}(V,E/V)$. Given a decomposition $E = V \oplus V^c$ as above, we let $\mathcal{U}^\star_{V,V^c}$ denote the set of surjective linear maps $f : E \to V^c$ whose restriction to V^c is the identity. It is an affine space over $\mathrm{Hom}(V,V^c)$ which can be identified with an open subset of $\mathrm{Grass}(E,d)$ *via* the map $f \mapsto \ker f$.

It is easily seen that $\mathcal{U}_{V,V^c}$ and $\mathcal{U}^\star_{V,V^c}$ define the same open subset in $\mathrm{Grass}(E,d)$. Indeed, given $f \in \mathcal{U}_{V,V^c}$, one can write $f = \mathrm{id}_V + h$ with $h \in \mathrm{Hom}(V,V^c)$ and define the morphism $g = \mathrm{id}_E - h \circ \pi \in \mathcal{U}^\star_{V,V^c}$. The association $f \mapsto g$ then defines a bijection $\mathcal{U}_{V,V^c} \to \mathcal{U}^\star_{V,V^c}$ which commutes with the embeddings into the Grassmannian.

Duality. If E is a finite dimensional vector space over K, we use the notation $E^\star$ for its dual (*i.e.* $E^\star = \mathrm{Hom}(E,K)$). If we are also given a subspace $V \subset E$, we denote by $V^\perp$ the subspace of $E^\star$ consisting of linear maps that vanish on V. We recall that the dual of $V^\perp$ (resp. $E^\star/V^\perp$) is canonically isomorphic to E/V (resp. V). For all d, the association $V \mapsto V^\perp$ defines a continuous morphism $\psi_E : \mathrm{Grass}(E,d) \to \mathrm{Grass}(E^\star, n-d)$. The action of ψ_E on tangent spaces is easily described. Indeed, the differential of ψ_E at V is nothing but the canonical identification between $\mathrm{Hom}(V,E/V)$ and $\mathrm{Hom}(V^\perp, E^\star/V^\perp)$ induced by transposition. Furthermore, we observe that ψ_E respects the charts we have defined above, in the sense that it maps bijectively $\mathcal{U}_{V,V^c}$ to $\mathcal{U}^\star_{V^\perp,(V^c)^\perp} \simeq \mathcal{U}_{V^\perp,(V^c)^\perp}$.

4.2 Differential computations

In this subsection, we compute the differential of various operations on vector spaces. For brevity, we skip the estimation of the corresponding growing functions (but this can be done using Proposition 2.5 as before if $\mathrm{char}(K) = 0$).

Direct images. Let E and F be two finite dimensional K-vector spaces of dimension n and m, respectively. Let d be an integer in $[0,n]$. We are interested in the direct image function DI defined on $\mathcal{M} = \mathrm{Hom}(E,F) \times \mathrm{Grass}(E,d)$ that takes the pair (f,V) to $f(V)$. Since the dimension of $f(V)$ may vary, the map DI does not take its values in a well-defined Grassmannian. We therefore stratify $\mathcal{M}$ as follows: for each integer $r \in [0,d]$, let $\mathcal{M}_r \subset \mathcal{M}$ be the subset of pairs (f,V) for which $f(V)$ has dimension r. The $\mathcal{M}_r$'s are locally closed in $\mathcal{M}$ and are therefore submanifolds. Moreover, DI induces differentiable functions $\mathrm{DI}_r : \mathcal{M}_r \to \mathrm{Grass}(F,r)$.

We would like to differentiate DI_r around some point $(f,V) \in \mathcal{M}_r$. To do so, we use the first description of the Grassmannians we gave above: we see points in $\mathrm{Grass}(E,d)$ (resp. $\mathrm{Grass}(F,d)$) as embeddings $V \hookrightarrow E$ (resp. $W \hookrightarrow F$) modulo the action of $\mathrm{GL}(V)$ (resp. $\mathrm{GL}(W)$). The point $V \in \mathrm{Grass}(E,d)$ is then represented by the canonical inclusion $v : V \to E$ whereas a representative w of W satisfies $w \circ \varphi = f \circ v$ where $\varphi : V \to W$ is the linear mapping induced by f. The previous relation still holds if (f,v) is replaced by a pair $(f',v') \in \mathcal{M}_r$ sufficiently close to (f,v). Differentiating it and passing to the quotient we find, first, that the tangent space of $\mathcal{M}_r$ at (f,v) consists of pairs $(df,dv) \in \mathrm{Hom}(E,F) \times \mathrm{Hom}(V,E/V)$ such that

$$d\tilde{w} = \big((df \circ v + f \circ dv) \bmod W\big) \in \mathrm{Hom}(V, F/W)$$

factors through φ (*i.e.* vanishes on $\ker \varphi = V \cap \ker f$) and, second, that the differential of DI_r at (f,V) is the linear mapping sending (df,dv) as above to the unique element $dw \in \mathrm{Hom}(W,F/W)$ such that $dw \circ \varphi = d\tilde{w}$.

Inverse images. We now consider the inverse image mapping II sending a pair $(f,W) \in \mathcal{W} = \mathrm{Hom}(E,F) \times \mathrm{Grass}(F,d)$ to $f^{-1}(W)$. As before, this map does not take values in a single Grassmannian, so we need to stratify $\mathcal{W}$ in order to get differentiable functions. For each integer $s \in [0,n]$, we introduce the submanifold $\mathcal{W}_s$ of $\mathcal{W}$ consisting of those pairs (f,W) such that $\dim f^{-1}(W) = s$. For all s, II induces a continuous function $\mathrm{II}_s : \mathcal{W}_s \to \mathrm{Grass}(E,s)$. Pick $(f,W) \in \mathcal{W}_s$. Set $V = f^{-1}(W)$ and denote by $w : F \to F/W$ the canonical projection. Similarly to what we have done for direct images, one can prove that the tangent space of $\mathcal{W}_s$ at some point $(f,W) \in \mathcal{W}_s$ is the subspace of $\mathrm{Hom}(E,F) \times \mathrm{Hom}(W,F/W)$ consisting of pairs (df,dw) such that $d\tilde{v} = (w \circ df + dw \circ f)_{|W}$ factors through the linear mapping $\varphi : E/V \to F/W$ induced by f. Furthermore II_s is differentiable at (f,W) and its differential is the linear mapping that takes (df,dw) as above to the unique element $dv \in \mathrm{Hom}(V,E/V)$ satisfying $\varphi \circ dv = d\tilde{v}$.

Direct images and inverse images are related by duality as follows: if $f : E \to F$ is any linear map and W is a subspace of F, then $f^\star(W^\perp) = f^{-1}(W)^\perp$. We can thus deduce the differentials of DI_s from those of II_s and *vice versa*.

Sums and intersections. Let d_1 and d_2 be two nonnegative integers. We consider the function Σ defined on the manifold $\mathcal{C} = \mathrm{Grass}(E,d_1) \times \mathrm{Grass}(E,d_2)$ by $\Sigma(V_1,V_2) = V_1 + V_2$. As before, in order to study Σ, we stratify $\mathcal{C}$ according to the dimension of the sum: for each integer $d \in [0, d_1 +$

$d_2]$, we define $\mathcal{C}_d$ as the submanifold of $\mathcal{C}$ consisting of those pairs (V_1, V_2) such that $\dim(V_1 + V_2) = d$. We get a well-defined mapping $\mathcal{C}_d \to \text{Grass}(E, d)$ whose differential can be computed as before. The tangent space of $\mathcal{C}_d$ at a given point (V_1, V_2) consists of pairs $(dv_1, dv_2) \in \text{Hom}(V_1, E/V_1) \times \text{Hom}(V_2, E/V_2)$ such that $dv_1 \equiv dv_2 \pmod{V_1 + V_2}$ on the intersection $V_1 \cap V_2$, and the differential of Σ at (V_1, V_2) maps (dv_1, dv_2) to $dv \in \text{Hom}(V, E/V)$ (with $V = V_1 + V_2$) defined by $dv(v_1 + v_2) = dv_1(v_1) + dv_2(v_2)$ ($v_1 \in V_1$, $v_2 \in V_2$).

Using duality, we derive a similar result for the mapping $(V_1, V_2) \mapsto V_1 \cap V_2$ (left to the reader).

4.3 Implementation and experiments

Standard representation of vector spaces. One commonly represents subspaces of K^n using the charts $\mathcal{U}_{V_I, V_{I^c}}$ (where I is a subset of $\{1, \dots, n\}$) introduced above. More concretely, a subspace $V \subset K^n$ is represented as the span of the rows of a matrix G_V having the following extra property: there exists some $I \subset \{1, \dots, n\}$ such that the submatrix of G_V obtained by keeping only columns with index in I is the identity matrix. We recall that such a representation always exists and, when the set of indices I is fixed, at most one G_V satisfies the above condition. Given a family of generators of V, one can compute G_V and I as above by performing standard row reduction. Choosing the first non-vanishing pivot at every stage provides a canonical choice for I, but in the context of inexact base fields, choosing the pivot with the maximal norm yields a more stable algorithm.

The dual representation. Of course, one may alternatively use the charts $\mathcal{U}^\star_{V_I, V_{I^c}}$. Concretely, this means that we represent V as the left kernel of a matrix H_V having the following extra property: there exists some $I \subset \{1, \dots, n\}$ such that the submatrix of H_V obtained by *deleting* rows with index in I is the identity matrix. As above, we can then compute I and H_V by performing column reduction.

Note that switching representations is cheap and stable. If $I = \{1, \dots, d\}$ with $d = \dim V$ and I_d is the identity matrix of size d, the matrix G_V has the form $(I_d \;\; G'_V)$. One can represent V with the same I and the matrix $H_V = \begin{pmatrix} -G'_V \\ I_{n-d} \end{pmatrix}$. A similar formula exists for general I.

Operations on vector spaces. The first representation we gave is well suited for the computation of direct images and sums. For instance, to compute $f(V)$ we apply f to each row of G_V, obtaining a family of generators of $f(V)$, and then row reduce. Dually, the second representation works well for computing inverse images, including kernels, and intersections. Since translating between the two dual representations is straightforward, we get algorithms for solving both problems using either representation.

Some experiments. Let us consider the example computation given in the following algorithm.

Algorithm 2: `example_vector_space`
Input: two integers n and N

1. Set $L_0 = \langle (1 + O(2^N), O(2^N), O(2^N)) \rangle \subset \mathbb{Q}_2^3$
2. **for** $i = 0, \dots, n-1$
3. pick randomly $\alpha, \beta, \gamma, \delta \in M_{3,3}(\mathbb{Z}_2)$ with high precision
4. **compute** $L_{i+1} = \big(\alpha(L_i) + \beta(L_i)\big) \cap \big(\gamma(L_i) + \delta(L_i)\big)$
5. **return** L_n

n	Average loss of precision		
	Coord-wise method	Lattice method	
		Projected	Diffused
10	7.3	2.7	-2.4×2
20	14.8	5.5	-4.7×2
50	38.6	13.1	-12.0×2
100	78.1	26.5	-23.5×2

Results for a sample of 1000 executions (with $N \gg n$)

Figure 4: Average loss of precision in Algorithm 2

The expression *high precision* on line 3 means that the precision on α, β, γ and δ is set in such a way that it does not affect the resulting precision on L_{i+1}. Figure 4 shows the losses of precision when executing Algorithm 2 with various inputs n (the input N is always chosen sufficiently large so that it does not affect the behavior of precision). The *Coord-wise* column corresponds to the standard way of tracking precision. On the other hand, in the two last columns, the precision is tracked using lattices. The *Diffused* column gives the amount of diffused precision, factored to be comparible to the Coord-wise column. The fact that only negative numbers appear in this column means that we are actually always gaining precision with this model! Finally, the *Projected* column gives the precision loss after projecting the lattice precision onto coordinates.

APPENDIX

A. PROOF OF PROPOSITION 2.4

We prove Proposition 2.4 in the slightly more general context of K-Banach spaces.

A.1 Composite of locally analytic functions

Let U, V and W be three open subsets in K-Banach spaces E, F and G, respectively. We assume that $0 \in U$, $0 \in V$. Let $f : U \to V$ and $g : V \to W$ be two locally analytic functions around 0 with $f(0) = 0$. The composition $h = g \circ f$ is then locally analytic around 0 as well. Let $f = \sum_{n \ge 0} f_n$ $g = \sum_{n \ge 0} g_n$ and $h = \sum_{n \ge 0} h_n$ be the analytic expansions of f, g and h. Here f_n, g_n and h_n are the restrictions to the diagonal of some symmetric n-linear forms F_n, G_n and H_n, respectively. The aim of this subsection is to prove the following intermediate result.

Proposition A.1. *With the above notation, we have*

$$\|h_r\| \le \sup_{m, (n_i)} \|g_m\| \cdot \|f_{n_1}\| \cdots \|f_{n_m}\|$$

for all nonnegative integers r, where the supremum is taken over all pairs $(m, (n_i))$ where m is a nonnegative integer and $(n_i)_{1 \le i \le m}$ is a sequence of length m of nonnegative integers such that $n_1 + \ldots + n_m = r$.

A computation gives the following expansion for $g \circ f$:

$$\sum \binom{m}{k_1 \;\cdots\; k_\ell} G_m(f_{n_1}, \dots, f_{n_1}, \dots, f_{n_\ell}, \dots, f_{n_\ell}) \quad (4)$$

where $\binom{m}{k_1 \;\cdots\; k_\ell}$ denotes the multinomial coefficient and the sum runs over:
(a) all finite sequences (k_i) of positive integers whose length (resp. sum) is denoted by ℓ (resp. m), and

(b) all finite sequences (n_i) of positive integers of length ℓ. Moreover, in the argument of G_m, the variable f_{n_i} is repeated k_i times.

The degree of $G_m(f_{n_1}, \dots, f_{n_1}, \dots, f_{n_\ell}, \dots, f_{n_\ell})$ is $r = k_1 n_1 + \ldots + k_\ell n_\ell$ and then contributes to h_r. As a consequence h_r is equal to (4) where the sum is restricted to sequences (k_i), (n_i) such that $k_1 n_1 + \ldots + k_\ell n_\ell = r$. Proposition A.1 now follows from the next lemma.

Lemma A.2. *Let E be a K-vector space. Let $\varphi : E^m \to K$ be a symmetric m-linear form and $\psi : E \to K$ defined by $\psi(x) = \varphi(x, x, \dots, x)$. Given positive integers $k_1, \dots, k_\ell$ whose sum is m and $x_1, \dots, x_\ell \in E$, we have*

$$\left\| \binom{m}{k_1\ k_2\ \cdots\ k_\ell} \cdot \varphi(x_1, \dots, x_1, \dots, x_\ell, \dots, x_\ell) \right\| \leq \|\psi\| \cdot \|x_1\|^{k_1} \cdots \|x_\ell\|^{k_\ell}$$

where, in the LHS, the variable x_i is repeated k_i times.

PROOF. It is enough to prove that

$$\left\| \binom{m}{k_1\ k_2\ \cdots\ k_\ell} \cdot \varphi(x_1, \dots, x_1, \dots, x_\ell, \dots, x_\ell) \right\| \leq \|\psi\|$$

provided that all the x_i's have norm at most 1. We proceed by induction on ℓ. The $\ell = 1$ case follows directly from the definition of $\|\psi\|$. We now pick $(\ell + 1)$ integers $k_1, \dots, k_{\ell+1}$ whose sum equals m, together with $(\ell + 1)$ elements $x_1, \dots, x_{\ell+1}$ lying in the unit ball of E. We also consider a new variable λ varying in $\mathcal{O}_K$. We set $x'_i = x_i$, $k'_i = k_i$ when $i < \ell$ and $x'_\ell = x_\ell + \lambda x_{\ell+1}$ and $k'_\ell = k_\ell + k_{\ell+1}$. By the induction hypothesis, we know that the inequality

$$\left\| \binom{m}{k'_1\ \cdots\ k'_\ell} \cdot \varphi(x'_1, \dots, x'_1, \dots, x'_\ell, \dots, x'_\ell) \right\| \leq \|\psi\|$$

holds for all $\lambda \in K$. Furthermore, the LHS of the inequality is a polynomial $P(\lambda)$ of degree k'_ℓ whose coefficient in λ^j is

$$\binom{m}{k'_1\ \cdots\ k'_\ell} \cdot \binom{k'_\ell}{j} \cdot \varphi(\underline{x}_j) = \binom{m}{k_1\ \cdots\ k_{\ell-1}\ j} \cdot \varphi(\underline{x}_j)$$

with $\underline{x}_j = (x_1, \dots, x_1, \dots, x_{\ell+1}, \dots, x_{\ell+1})$ where x_i is repeated k_i times if $i < \ell$ and x_ℓ (resp. $x_{\ell+1}$) is repeated j times (resp. $k'_\ell - j$ times). Since $\|P(\lambda)\| \leq \|\psi\|$ for all λ in the unit ball, the norm of all its coefficients must also be at most $\|\psi\|$. From the coefficient of λ^{k_ℓ}, the result follows. □

A.2 Bounding a growing function

We return to the setting of Proposition 2.4. Let $f = \sum_{n \geq 0} f_n$, $g = \sum_{n \geq 0} g_n$ and $h = \sum_{n \geq 0} h_n$ be the analytic expansions of f, g and h. Here f_n, g_n and h_n are the restrictions to the diagonal of some symmetric n-linear forms F_n, G_n and H_n, respectively. We recall that $\Lambda(f)$ is the Legendre transform of the Newton polygon $\mathrm{NP}(f)$ defined in Section 3 [3, Proposition 3.9], and that α is a real number such that $\|n!\| \geq e^{-\alpha n}$ for all positive integers n.

Lemma A.3. *We keep the above notation. If (a, b) satisfies $b \geq a + \Lambda(g)\big(\max(b, \Lambda(h)(a))\big)$ then $b \geq \Lambda(f)(a - \alpha)$.*

PROOF. We have $f' = \sum_{n \geq 0} f'_n$ where

$$f'_n : U \to \mathcal{L}(E, F), \quad x \mapsto \big(h \mapsto n \cdot F_n(h, x, x, \dots, x)\big).$$

Taking $h = x$, we find $\|f'_n\| \geq \|n f_n\| = \|n\| \cdot \|f_n\|$. Combining this with Proposition A.1, we get

$$\|(r+1) f_{r+1}\| \leq \sup_{m, (n_i)} \|g_m\| \cdot \prod_{i=1}^{m} \max(\|f_{n_i}\|, \|h_{n_i}\|)$$

for all nonnegative integers r, where the supremum runs over all pairs $(m, (n_i))$ where m is a nonnegative integer and $(n_i)_{1 \leq i \leq m}$ is a sequence of length m of nonnegative integers such that $n_1 + \ldots + n_m = r$. We set $u_r = \|r! f_r\|$. Multiplying the above inequality by $\|r!\|$, we obtain:

$$u_{r+1} \leq \sup_{m, (n_i)} \|g_m\| \cdot \prod_{i=1}^{m} \max(u_{n_i}, \|n_i! h_{n_i}\|) \qquad (5)$$

since the multinomial coefficient $\binom{r}{n_1\ \cdots\ n_m}$ is an integer and hence has norm at most 1. We now pick two real numbers a and b satisfying the hypothesis of the Lemma. Set $d = \Lambda(h)(a)$. Going back to the definitions of $\Lambda(h)$ and Legendre transform, we get $\|h_n\| \leq e^{-an+d}$ for all n. Similarly, from our hypothesis on (a, b), we find $\|g_m\| \leq e^{-\max(b,d) \cdot m + b - a}$ for all m. We are now ready to prove $u_r \leq e^{-ar+b}$ by induction on r. When $r = 0$, it is obvious because u_0 vanishes. Otherwise, the induction follows from

$$\begin{aligned} u_{r+1} &\leq \sup_{m, (n_i)} e^{-\max(b,d) \cdot m + b - a + \sum_{i=1}^{m}(-a n_i + \max(b,d))} \\ &= e^{b - a - ar} = e^{-a(r+1)+b}. \end{aligned}$$

From the definition of u_r, we obtain $\|f_r\| \leq u_r \cdot \|r!\|^{-1} \leq e^{-(a-\alpha)r+b}$. Thus $b \geq \Lambda(f)(a - \alpha)$. □

We can now conclude the proof of Proposition 2.4 as follows. Given $a \in \mathbb{R}$ and $b = a + \Lambda_g \circ \Lambda_h(a)$, we have to prove that $\Lambda(f)(a - \alpha) \leq b$ provided that $b \leq \nu$. Thanks to Proposition 2.4, it is enough to check that such pairs (a, b) satisfy the hypothesis of Lemma A.3. Clearly: $b \geq a + \Lambda(g) \circ \Lambda(h)(a)$ since $\Lambda_g \geq \Lambda(g)$, $\Lambda_h \geq \Lambda(h)$ and Λ_g is nondecreasing. Furthermore, from $b \leq \nu$, we get $\Lambda_g(b) = \min_{x \in \mathbb{R}} \Lambda_g(x) \leq \Lambda_g \circ \Lambda_h(a)$, from which we derive $a + \Lambda_g(b) \leq a + \Lambda_g \circ \Lambda_h(a) = b$.

References

[1] Yves Benoist and Jean-Francois Quint, *Introduction to random walks on homogeneous spaces*, Japanese Journal of Mathematics **7** (2012), no. 2, 135–166.

[2] Alin Bostan, Laureano González-Vega, Hervé Perdry, and Éric Schost, *From Newton sums to coefficients: complexity issues in characteristic p*, MEGA'05, 2005.

[3] Xavier Caruso, David Roe, and Tristan Vaccon, *Tracking p-adic precision*, LMS Journal of Computation and Mathematics **17** (2014), no. A, 274–294.

[4] Pierrick Gaudry, Thomas Houtmann, Annegret Weng, Christophe Ritzenthaler, and David Kohel, *The 2-adic CM method for genus 2 curves with application to cryptography*, Asiacrypt 2006, 2006, pp. 114–129.

[5] Kiran S. Kedlaya, *Counting points on hyperelliptic curves using monsky–washnitzer cohomology*, J. Ramanujan Math. Soc. **16** (2001), 323–338.

[6] ______, *p-adic differential equations*, Cambridge Studies in Advanced Mathematics, vol. 125, Cambridge UP, Cambridge, UK, 2010.

[7] Alan Lauder, *Deformation theory and the computation of zeta functions*, Proc. London Math. Soc. **88** (2004), no. 3, 565–602.

[8] Reynald Lercier and Thomas Sirvent, *On Elkies subgroups of ℓ-torsion points in elliptic curves defined over a finite field*, J. Théorie des Nombres des Bordeaux **20** (2008), 783–797.

On $\mathfrak{p}$-adic Expansions of Algebraic Integers

Hsing-Hau Chen
Department of Computer Science
University of Southern California
Los Angeles, CA 90089
hsinghau.chen@usc.edu

Ming-Deh Huang
Department of Computer Science
University of Southern California
Los Angeles, CA 90089
mdhuang@usc.edu

ABSTRACT

It is well known that every rational integer has a finite or periodic p-adic expansion. In this paper a more general notion of $\mathfrak{p}$-adic expansion is introduced for algebraic integers, where given a number field K and a principal prime ideal $\mathfrak{p}$ in K, a different choice of generator for $\mathfrak{p}$ is allowed in each stage of the expansion. With the notion of $\mathfrak{p}$-adic expansion, we prove that there is always a finite or periodic $\mathfrak{p}$-adic expansion for every algebraic integer. Moreover, we prove a bound on the periodicity of the $\mathfrak{p}$-adic expansion that depends only on the number field K and the prime ideal $\mathfrak{p}$. The proof yields an algorithm for constructing such a $\mathfrak{p}$-adic expansion for elements in the ring $\mathcal{O}$ of algebraic integers of K, through finding an approximation to the closest vector on the lattice spanned by the unit group of $\mathcal{O}$.

As a special case we prove that, similar to rational integers, Gaussian integers are finite or periodic not only in $\mathfrak{p}$-adic expansion but also in π-adic expansion, where a fixed generator π for $\mathfrak{p}$ is used in each stage of the expansion. Moreover, the time complexity of finding a π-adic expansion for a Gaussian integer is polynomial in the length of input, the period, and p, where p is the rational prime contained in $\mathfrak{p}$. We implement the algorithm for some quadratic number fields and provide examples which illustrate that the $\mathfrak{p}$-adic expansion of the elements in $\mathcal{O}$ is either finite or periodic.

Categories and Subject Descriptors

F.2.1 [**Analysis of Algorithms and Problem Complexity**]: Numerical Algorithms and Problems—*Number-theoretic computations (e.g., factoring, primality testing)*

General Terms

Theory, Algorithms

Keywords

$\mathfrak{p}$-adic expansions, algebraic integers, lattice-based algorithms

ISSAC'15, July 6–9, 2015, Bath, United Kingdom.

ACM 978-1-4503-3435-8/15/07 ...$15.00.
DOI: http://dx.doi.org/10.1145/2755996.2756675.

1. INTRODUCTION

The concept of p-adic numbers was introduced by Kurt Hensel in 1897 [8] primarily as an attempt to bring the ideas and techniques of power series methods into number theory. By now the influence of p-adic numbers and p-adic analysis have extended far beyond the original scope. It is an independent field of study as well as an integral part of number theory. In the context of computation, some problems and algorithms are p-adic by nature, such as polynomial factorization with Hensel's Lemma [9] and Kedlaya's counting-point algorithm on hyperelliptic curves with p-adic cohomology [10]. Completion and deformation techniques come up in many areas of symbolic and analytic computations, such as polynomial factorization, polynomial or differential system solving, and analytic continuation, with an intensive use of power series and p-adic integers [4, 3, 5]. The p-adic arithmetic allows error-free representation of fractions and error-free arithmetic using fractions [13, 12, 11].

In this paper, we are interested in $\mathfrak{p}$-adic expansions of algebraic integers, where $\mathfrak{p}$ is a prime ideal of a number field. We first look at a special case of number field, $\mathbb{Q}$, the set of rational numbers.

Let a be an element in $\mathbb{N}$, the set of natural numbers. Let $p \in \mathbb{N}$ be a rational prime. Then a can be written as a p-adic expansion of the form

$$a = \sum_{i=k}^{m} r_i p^i,$$

where $k \geq 0$ and $r_i \in R = \{0, 1, \dots, p-1\}$ for all i. Consider writing a negative integer, e.g. -1, as a p-adic expansion using the same residue class representative set R, we have $-1 = \sum_{i=0}^{\infty} (p-1)\, p^i$, as an element in the ring $\mathbb{Z}_p$ of p-adic integers. It is known that for any $a \in \mathbb{Z}$, the set of rational integers, the p-adic expansion of a is either finite or periodic [6, 16].

Let K be a number field and $\mathcal{O}$ its ring of integers. Let $\mathfrak{p} \subset \mathcal{O}$ be a prime ideal. A natural question arises as follows. Is there always a finite or periodic $\mathfrak{p}$-adic expansion for $\alpha \in \mathcal{O}$? Our results give an affirmative answer in the case where $\mathfrak{p}$ is a principal ideal, provided a different choice of generator for $\mathfrak{p}$ is allowed in each stage of the expansion. To the best of our knowledge, our result is the first positive general result to this open problem.

Let $\mathfrak{p}$ be a principal ideal and Γ a set of representatives of the residue field $\mathcal{O}/\mathfrak{p}\mathcal{O}$. Let α be an element in $\mathcal{O}$. Then $\alpha \equiv \gamma_0 \bmod \mathfrak{p}$ with $\gamma_0 \in \Gamma$, and since $\mathfrak{p}$ is principal, we can write

$$\alpha = \alpha_1 \pi_1 + \gamma_0, \tag{1.1}$$

where $\alpha_1 \in \mathcal{O}$ and $\pi_1 \mathcal{O} = \mathfrak{p}$. Likewise, we can write $\alpha_1 = \alpha_2\pi_2 + \gamma_1$, where $\alpha_2 \in \mathcal{O}$, $\pi_2\mathcal{O} = \mathfrak{p}$ and $\gamma_1 \in \Gamma$. Substituting for α_1 in (1.1), we obtain

$$\alpha = \gamma_0 + \gamma_1\pi_1 + \alpha_2\pi_1\pi_2.$$

Inductively, we obtain

$$\alpha = \gamma_0 + \gamma_1\omega_1 + \gamma_2\omega_2 + \gamma_3\omega_3 + \cdots + \gamma_i\omega_i + \alpha_{i+1}\omega_{i+1},$$

where $\omega_i = \prod_{k=1}^{i} \pi_k$. Let

$$\beta_i = \gamma_0 + \gamma_1\omega_1 + \gamma_2\omega_2 + \gamma_3\omega_3 + \cdots + \gamma_i\omega_i.$$

Then $\alpha \equiv \beta_i \mod \mathfrak{p}^{i+1}$ since $\omega_i\mathcal{O} = \mathfrak{p}^i$, hence

$$(\beta_i) \in \varprojlim_i \mathcal{O}/\mathfrak{p}^i\mathcal{O} = \mathcal{O}_\mathfrak{p}.$$

That is, as i tends to infinity, (β_i) gives a $\mathfrak{p}$-adic expansion of α as an element in $\mathcal{O}_\mathfrak{p}$. A $\mathfrak{p}$-adic expansion is *finite* when $\alpha_i = 0$ for some $i \in \mathbb{N}$. A $\mathfrak{p}$-adic expansion is *periodic* when $\alpha_i = \alpha_j \neq 0$ for some $i > j$. Let π be a generator for $\mathfrak{p}$. A $\mathfrak{p}$-adic expansion is a π-adic expansion if $\pi_i = \pi$, hence $\omega_i = \pi^i$, for all i.

With the notion of $\mathfrak{p}$-adic expansion, we prove the following:

Theorem 1.2. *Let K be a number field, and $\mathcal{O}$ its ring of integers. Let $\mathfrak{p}$ be a principal prime ideal of K and $\mathrm{N}(\mathfrak{p}) > 2^{[K:\mathbb{Q}]}$. Then for any $\alpha \in \mathcal{O}$, there is always a periodic or finite $\mathfrak{p}$-adic expansion.*

Theorem 3.7, a more detailed version of Theorem 1.2, is stated and proved in §3.1 where a bound on periodicity is also given. Theorem 1.2 yields an algorithm for constructing a $\mathfrak{p}$-adic expansion of elements in $\mathcal{O}$ (see §3.2). In order to prove Theorem 1.2, we prove an upper bound on the length of the closest vector in a lattice in §2.1 and apply this upper bound to the lattice spanned by the unit group of the ring of integers of a number field in §2.2.

In §4, we apply the theorem and the associated algorithm on two specific number fields, $\mathbb{Q}(i)$ and $\mathbb{Q}(\sqrt{2})$, and provide some concrete numeric examples. For the case of $\mathbb{Q}(i)$, we show the following:

Theorem 1.3. *Let $K = \mathbb{Q}(i)$ be a number field, and $\mathcal{O} = \mathbb{Z}[i]$ its ring of integers. Let $\mathfrak{p} = \pi\mathcal{O}$ be a prime ideal (which is principal since K is a PID). There is an algorithm that, for any $\alpha \in \mathcal{O}$, finds a periodic or finite π-adic expansion for α in time polynomial in the length of input, the period and p, where p is the rational prime contained in $\mathfrak{p}$.*

2. PRELIMINARIES

2.1 Upper Bounding the Closest Vector

In this subsection we examine the closest vector problem of a lattice $\mathcal{L}$, and deduce an upper bound on the length of the closest vector. We denote the rank of $\mathcal{L}$ as $\mathrm{rk}(\mathcal{L})$, the determinant of $\mathcal{L}$ as $\det(\mathcal{L})$, and the length of the shortest non-zero vector in the lattice as $\lambda(\mathcal{L})$.

A full lattice in $\mathbb{R}^n$ (where $\mathbb{R}$ is the set of real numbers) is any set of the form

$$\mathcal{L} = \mathcal{L}(b_1, \dots, b_n) = \left\{ \sum_{i=1}^{n} \lambda_i b_i \mid \lambda_i \in \mathbb{Z}, i = 1, \dots, n \right\}$$

where $\{b_1, \dots, b_n\}$ is a basis of $\mathbb{R}^n$ (see [15] for more detailed notions about lattices). The *closest vector problem* is as follows: given n linearly independent vectors $a_1, \dots, a_n \in \mathbb{R}^n$, and a vector $b \in \mathbb{R}^n$, find a vector $v \in \mathcal{L}(a_1, \dots, a_n)$ with $\|b - v\|$ minimal. The closest vector problem along with the shortest vector problem arise in many fields of computational mathematics and computer science [7, 17, 2]. To derive an upper bound on the length of the closest vector, we adapt the procedure of approximating the closest vector using Lenstra-Lenstra-Lovász lattice basis reduction algorithm (LLL algorithm) [14, 1]. First, we recall that the result of *Gram-Schmidt orthogonalization* of an ordered basis $(b_1, \dots, b_n)$ of $\mathbb{R}^n$ is another ordered basis $(b_1^*, \dots, b_n^*)$ whose vectors b_i^*'s are pairwise orthogonal, and each vector b_j can be expressed as a linear combination of the vectors $b_1^*, \dots, b_j^*$ as follows:

$$b_j = \sum_{i=1}^{j} \mu_{ji} b_i^* \ (j = 1, \dots, n), \tag{2.1}$$

and that in this formula $\mu_{jj} = 1$. With the definition of Gram-Schmidt orthogonalization, the *Lovász-reduced basis* is defined as follows.

Definition 2.2 (Lovász-Reduced Basis). Let $\mathcal{L}$ be a lattice, $(b_1, \dots, b_n)$ an ordered basis of $\mathcal{L}$, and $(b_1^*, \dots, b_n^*)$ its Gram-Schmidt orthogonalization; let the number μ_{ij} be defined by (2.1). We say that the basis $(b_1, \dots, b_n)$ is a *Lovász-reduced basis*, if the following two conditions hold:

(a) $|\mu_{ji}| \leq \frac{1}{2}$ for every $1 \leq i < j \leq n$;

(b) $\left\| b_{j+1}^* + \mu_{j+1,j} b_j^* \right\|^2 \geq \frac{3}{4} \left\| b_j^* \right\|^2$ for $j = 1, \dots, n-1$.

We then find the lower bound on the length of the shortest vector among the Gram-Schmidt orthogonalization of a Lovász-reduced basis:

Lemma 2.3. *Let $\mathcal{L}$ be a lattice in $\mathbb{R}^n$ and $(b_1, \dots, b_n)$ a reduced basis of $\mathcal{L}$. Let $(b_1^*, \dots, b_n^*)$ be the Gram-Schmidt orthogonalization of $(b_1, \dots, b_n)$. Then*

$$\min\{\|b_1^*\|, \dots, \|b_n^*\|\} \geq 2^{\frac{(1-n)}{2}} \|b_1\| \geq 2^{\frac{(1-n)}{2}} \lambda(\mathcal{L}).$$

Proof. By property (b) in the definition of a reduced basis (Definition 2.2), we have

$$\frac{3}{4}\left\|b_j^*\right\|^2 \leq \left\|b_{j+1}^* + \mu_{j+1,j} b_j^*\right\|^2 = \left\|b_{j+1}^*\right\|^2 + \mu_{j+1,j}^2 \left\|b_j^*\right\|^2.$$

By property (a), we have $\mu_{j+1,j}^2 \leq \frac{1}{4}$, and thus

$$\left\|b_{j+1}^*\right\|^2 \geq \frac{1}{2}\left\|b_j^*\right\|^2 \ (1 \leq j \leq n-1).$$

It follows by induction that

$$\left\|b_j^*\right\|^2 \geq 2^{i-j}\left\|b_i^*\right\|^2 \ (1 \leq i < j \leq n).$$

Hence

$$\|b_j^*\| \geq 2^{\frac{1-j}{2}} \|b_1^*\| = 2^{\frac{1-j}{2}} \|b_1\|$$
$$\geq 2^{\frac{1-n}{2}} \|b_1\| \geq 2^{\frac{1-n}{2}} \lambda(\mathcal{L}) \ (1 \leq j \leq n),$$

which proves the lemma. ■

For any lattice $\mathcal{L}$, the LLL algorithm constructs a reduced basis in a finite number of steps. Moreover, if the initial basis vectors have rational coordinates, then the reduced basis is constructed in polynomial time. We describe the result as follows.

Proposition 2.4 (Lenstra et al. (1982) [14]). *For any given linearly independent vectors $a_1, \ldots, a_n \in \mathbb{R}^n$, there exists a reduced basis of the lattice $\mathcal{L} = \mathcal{L}(a_1, \ldots, a_n)$. Moreover, there is a polynomial time algorithm that, for any given linearly independent vectors $a_1, \ldots, a_n \in \mathbb{Q}^n$, finds a reduced basis of the lattice $\mathcal{L}(a_1, \ldots, a_n)$.*

To prove the upper bound on the length of the approximated closest vector found using LLL algorithm, Babai proved the following:

Proposition 2.5 (Babai (1986) [1]). *Let $a_1, \ldots, a_n \in \mathbb{R}^n$ be linearly independent vectors. Let $(b_1, \ldots, b_n)$ be a reduced basis of $\mathcal{L}(a_1, \ldots, a_n)$, and $(b_1^*, \ldots, b_n^*)$ its Gram-Schmidt orthogonalization. For any given $b \in \mathbb{R}^n$, there exists a lattice vector $v \in \mathcal{L}$ such that*

$$b - v = \sum_{i=1}^{n} \lambda_i b_i^*, \ |\lambda_i| \leq \frac{1}{2} \ (i = 1, \ldots, n). \tag{2.6}$$

Moreover, there is a polynomial time algorithm that, for any given linearly independent vectors $a_1, \ldots, a_n \in \mathbb{Q}^n$ and $b \in \mathbb{Q}^n$, finds a lattice vector $v \in \mathcal{L}(a_1, \ldots, a_n)$ satisfying (2.6).

With the lower bound on the length of the shortest vector among the Gram-Schmidt orthogonalization of a reduced basis and the above two Propositions, we then derive the upper bound on the length of the closest vector.

Theorem 2.7. *Let $a_1, \ldots, a_n \in \mathbb{R}^n$ be linearly independent vectors. Let $(b_1, \ldots, b_n)$ be a reduced basis of $\mathcal{L}(a_1, \ldots, a_n)$. Then for any given $b \in \mathbb{R}^n$, there exists $v \in \mathcal{L}(a_1, \ldots, a_n)$ such that*

$$\|b - v\|^2 \leq \frac{2^{(n-1)^2} n (\det(\mathcal{L}))^2}{4 (\|b_1\|)^{2(n-1)}}.$$

Proof. Let $(b_1^*, \ldots, b_n^*)$ be the Gram-Schmidt orthogonalization of $(b_1, \ldots, b_n)$. By Proposition 2.5, there exists $v \in \mathcal{L}(a_1, \ldots, a_n)$ such that

$$b - v = \sum_{i=1}^{n} \lambda_i b_i^*, \ |\lambda_i| \leq \frac{1}{2} \ (i = 1, \ldots, n).$$

It follows that

$$\|b - v\|^2 = \left\| \sum_{i=1}^{n} \lambda_i b_i^* \right\|^2 = \sum_{i=1}^{n} |\lambda_i|^2 \|b_i^*\|^2 \leq \frac{1}{4} \sum_{i=1}^{n} \|b_i^*\|^2. \tag{2.8}$$

Since

$$\det(\mathcal{L}) = |\det(b_1, \ldots, b_n)| = |\det(b_1^*, \ldots, b_n^*)| = \prod_{i=1}^{n} \|b_i^*\|$$
$$\geq \left(\min_{1 \leq i \leq n} \|b_i^*\| \right)^{n-1} \max_{1 \leq i \leq n} \|b_i^*\|,$$

substituting for $\min_{1 \leq i \leq n} \|b_i^*\|$ using the inequality in Lemma 2.3, we obtain

$$\max_{1 \leq i \leq n} \|b_i^*\| \leq \frac{\det(\mathcal{L})}{\left(2^{\frac{1-n}{2}} \|b_1\|\right)^{n-1}} = \frac{2^{\frac{(n-1)^2}{2}} \det(\mathcal{L})}{(\|b_1\|)^{n-1}}.$$

Thus by (2.8),

$$\|b - v\|^2 \leq \frac{1}{4} \sum_{i=1}^{n} \|b_i^*\|^2 \leq \frac{n}{4} \max_{1 \leq i \leq n} \|b_i^*\|^2 = \frac{2^{(n-1)^2} n (\det(\mathcal{L}))^2}{4 (\|b_1\|)^{2(n-1)}}.$$

■

Note if the initial basis vectors $a_1, \ldots, a_n$ and the given vector b all have rational coordinates, then such a vector can be constructed in polynomial time.

2.2 Lattice Spanned by the Unit Group

In this subsection we apply the upper bound deduced in Section 2.1 on the lattice spanned by the unit group of the ring of integers of a number field.

Let K be a number field, and $\mathcal{O}$ its ring of integers. Let $\mathcal{U}$ be the group of units of $\mathcal{O}$. Let $\{\sigma_1, \ldots, \sigma_r\}$ be the real embeddings and $\{\sigma_{r+1}, \bar{\sigma}_{r+1}, \ldots, \sigma_{r+s}, \bar{\sigma}_{r+s}\}$ be the complex embeddings. Since

$$|\mathrm{N}(\alpha)| = |\sigma_1(\alpha)| \cdots |\sigma_r(\alpha)| \, |\sigma_{r+1}(\alpha)|^2 \cdots |\sigma_{r+s}(\alpha)|^2,$$

we define the homomorphism

$$\mathrm{Log} : K^{\times} \to \mathbb{R}^{r+s}$$
$$\mathrm{Log}(\alpha) = (\log|\sigma_1(\alpha)|, \ldots, \log|\sigma_r(\alpha)|,$$
$$2\log|\sigma_{r+1}(\alpha)|, \ldots, 2\log|\sigma_{r+s}(\alpha)|).$$

Proposition 2.9 (Dirichlet's Unit Theorem, 1846). *The image $\mathcal{L} = \mathrm{Log}(\mathcal{U})$ is a full lattice in the hyperplane*

$$\mathcal{H} = \{(x_1, \ldots, x_{r+s}) : x_1 + \cdots + x_{r+s} = 0\}.$$

Therefore it has rank $r + s - 1$.

Theorem 2.10. *Let $\alpha \in K$ and $n = [K : \mathbb{Q}]$. Let $\mathcal{L} = \mathrm{Log}(\mathcal{U})$ and b_1 be the shortest vector among a reduced basis of $\mathcal{L}$. Let $a = \frac{|\mathrm{N}(\alpha)|^{\frac{1}{n}}}{\alpha}$. Then $\mathrm{Log}(a)$ is contained in $\mathcal{H}$, and there exists $u \in \mathcal{U}$ such that*

$$\|\mathrm{Log}(u) - \mathrm{Log}(a)\|^2 < \varepsilon,$$

where $\varepsilon = \frac{2^{(\mathrm{rk}(\mathcal{L})-1)^2}(\mathrm{rk}(\mathcal{L})+1)(\det(\mathcal{L}))^2}{4(\|b_1\|)^{2(\mathrm{rk}(\mathcal{L})-1)}}$.

Proof. For $1 \leq i \leq r + s$, since σ_i's are homomorphisms, we have

$$\log\left|\sigma_i\left(\frac{|\mathrm{N}(\alpha)|^{\frac{1}{n}}}{\alpha}\right)\right| = \log\left|\sigma_i\left(|\mathrm{N}(\alpha)|^{\frac{1}{n}}\right)\right| - \log|\sigma_i(\alpha)|.$$

It follows by the definition of Log that

$$\mathrm{Log}(a) = \mathrm{Log}\left(|\mathrm{N}(\alpha)|^{\frac{1}{n}}\right) - \mathrm{Log}(\alpha).$$

Since $|\mathrm{N}(\alpha)| = \left(\prod_{i=1}^{r} |\sigma_i(\alpha)|\right) \cdot \left(\prod_{i=r+1}^{r+s} |\sigma_i(\alpha)|^2\right)$, taking logs of both sides gives

$$\log|\mathrm{N}(\alpha)| = \sum_{i=1}^{r} \log|\sigma_i(\alpha)| + 2\sum_{i=r+1}^{r+s} \log|\sigma_i(\alpha)|.$$

Since $n = r + 2s$, it follows that

$$\sum_{i=1}^{r} \left(\frac{1}{n} \log |\mathrm{N}(\alpha)| - \log |\sigma_i(\alpha)| \right) + \sum_{i=r+1}^{r+s} 2 \left(\frac{1}{n} \log |\mathrm{N}(\alpha)| - \log |\sigma_i(\alpha)| \right)$$

$$= \frac{r+2s}{r+2s} \log |\mathrm{N}(\alpha)| - \left(\sum_{i=1}^{r} \log |\sigma_i(\alpha)| + 2 \sum_{i=r+1}^{r+s} \log |\sigma_i(\alpha)| \right)$$

$$= 0$$

Thus $\mathrm{Log}(a) = \mathrm{Log}\left(|\mathrm{N}(\alpha)|^{\frac{1}{n}} \right) - \mathrm{Log}(\alpha)$ is contained in $\mathcal{H}$.

By Proposition 2.9, since $\mathcal{L} = \mathrm{Log}(\mathcal{U})$ has rank $r+s-1$, we define the following $r+s-1$ homomorphisms with rank $r+s-1$

$\mathrm{Log}_i : K^\times \to \mathbb{R}^{r+s-1}$

$\mathrm{Log}_i(\alpha) = \mathrm{Log}(\alpha)$ with the ith embedding dropped

Each of these homomorphisms has a set of linearly independent vectors of size $r+s-1$ and shares the same determinant. Thus, by Theorem 2.7, we have

$$\|\mathrm{Log}(u) - \mathrm{Log}(a)\|^2 \leq \mathrm{UB}(r+s-1) + |\log|\sigma_i(u)| - \log|\sigma_i(a)||^2$$

for $i = 1, \ldots, r$, and

$$\|\mathrm{Log}(u) - \mathrm{Log}(a)\|^2 \leq \mathrm{UB}(r+s-1) + 4\,|\log|\sigma_i(u)| - \log|\sigma_i(a)||^2$$

for $i = r+1, \ldots, r+s$, where $\mathrm{UB}(k) = \dfrac{2^{(k-1)^2} k (\det(\mathcal{L}))^2}{4(\|b_1\|)^{2(k-1)}}$.

Adding up all these $r+s$ inequalities, we obtain

$$(r+s)\,\|\mathrm{Log}(u) - \mathrm{Log}(a)\|^2 \leq (r+s)\,\mathrm{UB}(r+s-1) + \|\mathrm{Log}(u) - \mathrm{Log}(a)\|^2.$$

Hence,

$$\|\mathrm{Log}(u) - \mathrm{Log}(a)\|^2 \leq \frac{r+s}{r+s-1} \mathrm{UB}(r+s-1) = \frac{2^{(\mathrm{rk}(\mathcal{L})-1)^2} (\mathrm{rk}(\mathcal{L})+1)(\det(\mathcal{L}))^2}{4(\|b_1\|)^{2(\mathrm{rk}(\mathcal{L})-1)}}$$

which proves the Theorem. ■

3. π-ADIC EXPANSION WITH MULTIPLICATION BY UNITS

3.1 A Constructive Proof

In this subsection we provide a constructive proof to show the existence of either a finite or a periodic $\mathfrak{p}$-adic expansion for every algebraic integer.

Let K be a number field, $\mathcal{O}$ its ring of integers. Let $\mathcal{U}$ be the group of units of $\mathcal{O}$. Let $\mathfrak{p}$ be a principal prime ideal in K. Recall that provided a different choice of generator π_i for $\mathfrak{p}$ is allowed in each stage of the expansion, we can write $\alpha \in \mathcal{O}$ in the following form:

$$\alpha = \gamma_0 + \gamma_1\omega_1 + \gamma_2\omega_2 + \gamma_3\omega_3 + \cdots + \gamma_i\omega_i + \alpha_{i+1}\omega_{i+1},$$

where $\omega_i = \prod_{k=1}^{i} \pi_k$ and $\gamma_i \in \Gamma$, a residue class representative set for each i. Fix a generator π for $\mathfrak{p}$. Since π_i and π are associated (off by a unit) for each i, we have

$$\omega_i = \pi_1\pi_2\cdots\pi_i = (u_1\pi)(u_2\pi)\cdots(u_i\pi) = \mu_i\pi^i,$$

where $u_i \in \mathcal{U}$ for all i and $\mu_i = u_1u_2\cdots u_i \in \mathcal{U}$. With the notion of $\mathfrak{p}$-adic expansion, we define the *periodic π-adic expansion with multiplication by units* as follows.

Definition 3.1. Let K be a number field, $\mathcal{O}$ its ring of integers and $\mathcal{U}$ its unit group. Let $\mathfrak{p}$ be a principal prime ideal of K and $\Gamma = \mathcal{O}/\mathfrak{p}\mathcal{O}$ a residue class representative set. Let π be a generator of $\mathfrak{p}$, then an infinite *periodic π-adic expansion with multiplication by units* for $\alpha \in \mathcal{O}$ is a π-adic expansion that can be placed in the form

$$\alpha = \gamma_0 + \sum_{i=1}^{k} \gamma_i\mu_i\pi^i + \sum_{i=k+1}^{k+m} \gamma_i\mu_i\pi^i + \nu\pi^m \sum_{i=k+1}^{k+m} \gamma_i\mu_i\pi^i + (\nu\pi^m)^2 \sum_{i=k+1}^{k+m} \gamma_i\mu_i\pi^i + \cdots$$

$$= \gamma_0 + \sum_{i=1}^{k} \gamma_i\mu_i\pi^i + \frac{1}{1-\nu\pi^m} \sum_{i=k+1}^{k+m} \gamma_i\mu_i\pi^i$$

where $\gamma_0, \ldots, \gamma_{k+m} \in \Gamma$ and $\nu, \mu_1, \ldots, \mu_{k+m} \in \mathcal{U}$.

A periodic $\mathfrak{p}$-adic expansion allowing a different choice of generator for $\mathfrak{p}$ and a periodic π-adic expansion with multiplication by units are essentially the same. We define the latter to facilitate the proof of existence of either a finite or a periodic $\mathfrak{p}$-adic expansion for every algebraic integer. A sketch of the proof is as follows.

We iteratively find $\gamma_i \in \Gamma$ such that $\gamma_i \equiv \alpha_i \bmod \mathfrak{p}$ to construct the $\mathfrak{p}$-adic expansion. Given $\mathfrak{p}$ principal, we fix a generator π of $\mathfrak{p}$. We use the field norm as a metric. For $|\mathrm{N}(\alpha_i)|$ not smaller than a certain threshold τ, given $\mathrm{N}(\mathfrak{p})$ large enough, we prove that $u_i \in \mathcal{U}$, $\alpha_{i+1} \in \mathcal{O}$ and $\gamma_i \in \Gamma$ can be found such that $u_i\alpha_i = \alpha_{i+1}\pi + \gamma_i$ and $|\mathrm{N}(\alpha_{i+1})|$ is strictly smaller than $|\mathrm{N}(\alpha_i)|$. Then in finitely many steps a dividend α_j such that $|\mathrm{N}(\alpha_j)|$ is smaller than the threshold τ will be found. For $|\mathrm{N}(\alpha_j)|$ smaller than threshold, we show that $|\mathrm{N}(\alpha_{j+1})|$ is bounded. Then, if $|\mathrm{N}(\alpha_{j+1})|$ becomes larger than the threshold, since it is bounded, in another finitely many steps another dividend will be again smaller than the threshold. Proving that the number of algebraic integers with norm smaller than the threshold is finite up to units, unless the $\mathfrak{p}$-adic expansion is finite, two associated algebraic integers with norm smaller than the threshold, α_i and α_j, where $j > i$ must be found in finitely many iterations. We first prove the lemma that there exists α_{i+1} such that $|\mathrm{N}(\alpha_{i+1})|$ is smaller than $|\mathrm{N}(\alpha_i)|$ when $|\mathrm{N}(\alpha_i)|$ is not smaller than the threshold τ.

Lemma 3.2. *Let K be a degree n number field and $\mathcal{O}$ its ring of integers. Let $\mathcal{U}$ be the group of units of $\mathcal{O}$. Let $\mathfrak{p} = \pi\mathcal{O}$ be a principal prime of K where $\mathrm{N}(\mathfrak{p}) > 2^n$. Let $\Gamma = \mathcal{O}/\mathfrak{p}\mathcal{O}$ be a residue class representative set, and $\Delta = \max_{1\leq i\leq n, r\in\Gamma} |\sigma_i(r)|$. Let $\mathcal{L}$ be the lattice spanned by $\mathcal{U}$, and ε as in Theorem 2.10. Then for any $\alpha \in \mathcal{O}$, $|\mathrm{N}(\alpha)| \geq \tau = \left(e^{\sqrt{\varepsilon}}\Delta\right)^n$ there exist $u \in \mathcal{U}$ and $\delta \in \mathcal{O}$ such that $u\alpha - \delta\pi \in \Gamma$ and $|\mathrm{N}(\delta)| < |\mathrm{N}(\alpha)|$.*

Proof. Let $a = \frac{|\mathrm{N}(\alpha)|^{\frac{1}{n}}}{\alpha}$. Then by Theorem 2.10, there exists $u \in \mathcal{U}$ such that

$$\|\mathrm{Log}(u) - \mathrm{Log}(a)\|^2 < \varepsilon.$$

It follows that for each embedding σ_i,

$$|\log|\sigma_i(u)| - \log|\sigma_i(a)||^2 < \|\mathrm{Log}(u) - \mathrm{Log}(a)\|^2 < \varepsilon$$
$$\Rightarrow -\sqrt{\varepsilon} < \log\frac{|\sigma_i(u)|}{|\sigma_i(a)|} < \sqrt{\varepsilon}$$
$$\Rightarrow e^{-\sqrt{\varepsilon}}|\sigma_i(a)| < |\sigma_i(u)| < e^{\sqrt{\varepsilon}}|\sigma_i(a)|. \quad (3.3)$$

Since $|\sigma_i(a)| = \frac{\left|\sigma_i\left(|\mathrm{N}(\alpha)|^{\frac{1}{n}}\right)\right|}{|\sigma_i(\alpha)|}$, substituting for $|\sigma_i(a)|$ in (3.3), we obtain

$$e^{-\sqrt{\varepsilon}}\frac{\left|\sigma_i\left(|\mathrm{N}(\alpha)|^{\frac{1}{n}}\right)\right|}{|\sigma_i(\alpha)|} < |\sigma_i(u)| < e^{\sqrt{\varepsilon}}\frac{\left|\sigma_i\left(|\mathrm{N}(\alpha)|^{\frac{1}{n}}\right)\right|}{|\sigma_i(\alpha)|}$$
$$\Rightarrow e^{-\sqrt{\varepsilon}}\cdot|\mathrm{N}(\alpha)|^{\frac{1}{n}} < |\sigma_i(u\alpha)| < e^{\sqrt{\varepsilon}}\cdot|\mathrm{N}(\alpha)|^{\frac{1}{n}}. \quad (3.4)$$

Given $|\mathrm{N}(\alpha)| \geq \tau = \left(e^{\sqrt{\varepsilon}}\Delta\right)^n$, we have

$$|\sigma_i(u\alpha)| > e^{-\sqrt{\varepsilon}}\cdot|\mathrm{N}(\alpha)|^{\frac{1}{n}} \geq e^{-\sqrt{\varepsilon}}\cdot\left(\left(e^{\sqrt{\varepsilon}}\Delta\right)^n\right)^{\frac{1}{n}} = \Delta.$$

Let $u\alpha \equiv \gamma \bmod \mathfrak{p}$, where $\gamma \in \Gamma$. Since $\mathfrak{p}$ is principal, we can find $\delta \in \mathcal{O}$ such that $u\alpha - \delta\pi = \gamma$. Then for each embedding σ_i $(1 \leq i \leq n)$, we have

$$|\sigma_i(\delta)||\sigma_i(\pi)| = |\sigma_i(u\alpha - \gamma)| \leq |\sigma_i(u\alpha)| + |\sigma_i(\gamma)|$$
$$\leq |\sigma_i(u\alpha)| + \Delta < 2|\sigma_i(u\alpha)|.$$

Hence, given the field norm is the product of all the embeddings σ_i $(1 \leq i \leq n)$, we have

$$|\mathrm{N}(\delta\pi)| = \prod_{i=1}^{n}|\sigma_i(\delta\pi)| < \prod_{i=1}^{n}2|\sigma_i(u\alpha)| = 2^n|\mathrm{N}(u\alpha)|, \quad (3.5)$$

which proves the lemma given $\mathrm{N}(\pi) = \mathrm{N}(\mathfrak{p}) > 2^n$ and $\mathrm{N}(u) = 1$. ∎

Next we show that the number of algebraic integers with norm smaller than the threshold τ is finite up to units.

Lemma 3.6. *Let K be a number field and $\mathcal{O}$ its ring of integers. Then the set $B = \{b \in \mathcal{O} \mid |\mathrm{N}(b)| < \tau\}$ is finite up to units.*

Proof. Since $b \in B$ is an element in $\mathcal{O}$, $|\mathrm{N}(b)|$ must be a natural number. Since $|\mathrm{N}(b)| < \tau$, we have $|\mathrm{N}(b)| \in \{0, 1, \ldots, \lfloor\tau\rfloor\}$. That is, there are only $\lfloor\tau\rfloor + 1$ different values of $|\mathrm{N}(b)|$.

We now explore the relation between x and y given that $|\mathrm{N}(x)| = |\mathrm{N}(y)|$ and $x \neq y$. Let $|\mathrm{N}(x)| = |\mathrm{N}(y)|$ decompose into $p_1^{e_1}p_2^{e_2}\cdots p_z^{e_z}$, where p_i is a rational prime and $e_i \in \mathbb{N}$ for each i. If p_i is either inert or ramified for all i, then x and y are associated. If more than one p_i splits, x and y may not be associated. However, since a splitting p_i splits into at most the degree of K many different prime ideals, the number of decompositions of b for certain $|\mathrm{N}(b)|$ value is finite. Thus, $B = \{b \in \mathcal{O} \mid |\mathrm{N}(b)| < \tau\}$ is finite up to units. ∎

Given B is finite up to units, we can compute a representative set $\mathcal{B}$ of B by first decomposing (in the ring of algebraic integers) of each natural number smaller than τ, then choosing a single representative of each decomposition. In the next theorem we prove by construction the existence of either a finite or a periodic π-adic expansion with multiplication by units for every algebraic integer.

Theorem 3.7. *Let K be a number field of degree n and $\mathcal{O}$ its ring of integers. Let $\mathcal{U}$ be the group of units of $\mathcal{O}$. Let $\mathfrak{p} = \pi\mathcal{O}$ be a principal prime of K where $\mathrm{N}(\mathfrak{p}) > 2^n$. Let $\Gamma = \mathcal{O}/\mathfrak{p}\mathcal{O}$ be a residue class representative set, and $\Delta = \max_{1\leq i\leq n, r\in\Gamma}|\sigma_i(r)|$. Let $\mathcal{B}$ be a representative set of $B = \{b \in \mathcal{O} \mid |\mathrm{N}(b)| < \tau\}$, τ as in Lemma 3.2, and $\Xi = \max_{1\leq i\leq n, b\in\mathcal{B}}|\sigma_i(b)|$. Then for any $\alpha \in \mathcal{O}$ either we can find a periodic π-adic expansion with multiplication by units or the π-adic expansion with multiplication by units is finite. Moreover, the periodicity is bounded by $|\mathcal{B}|\cdot\frac{2^n}{(\mathrm{N}(\mathfrak{p}))^2}(\Xi + \Delta)^n$.*

Proof. When $\alpha \in \Gamma$, $\gamma_0 = \alpha$ is the finite π-adic expansion. When $\alpha = \alpha_1\pi + \gamma_0$, $\gamma_0, \alpha_1 \in \Gamma$, $\gamma_0 + \alpha_1\pi$ is the finite π-adic expansion.

When $\alpha_1 \notin \Gamma$, we start to iteratively find $v_i \in \mathcal{U}$, $\alpha_{i+1} \in \mathcal{O}$ and $\gamma_i \in \Gamma$, such that $v_i\alpha_i = \alpha_{i+1}\pi + \gamma_i$ for each $\alpha_i \notin \Gamma$. First, v_i is chosen depending on whether $|\mathrm{N}(\alpha_i)|$ is not smaller than τ. Then since $\mathfrak{p} = \pi\mathcal{O}$ is principal, $\alpha_{i+1} \in \mathcal{O}$ and $\gamma_i \in \Gamma$ are determined. If at some point α_i is in Γ, then the π-adic expansion with multiplication by units is finite

We now examine the first case when $|\mathrm{N}(\alpha_i)| \geq \tau$. By Lemma 3.2, given $|\mathrm{N}(\alpha_i)| \geq \tau$, there exist $v_i \in \mathcal{U}$, $\alpha_{i+1} \in \mathcal{O}$ and $\gamma_i \in \Gamma$ such that $v_i\alpha_i = \alpha_{i+1}\pi + \gamma_i$ and $|\mathrm{N}(\alpha_{i+1})| < |\mathrm{N}(\alpha_i)|$. By (3.5), $|\mathrm{N}(\alpha_i)|$ decreases at a ratio larger than $\frac{\mathrm{N}(\mathfrak{p})}{2^n} > 1$. Thus, $|\mathrm{N}(\alpha_i)|$ decreases until $|\mathrm{N}(\alpha_j)|$ becomes smaller than τ for some $j > i$ in finitely many iterations.

When $|\mathrm{N}(\alpha_i)| < \tau$, $v_i \in \mathcal{U}$ such that $v_i\alpha_i \in \mathcal{B}$ can be found by first decomposing $|\mathrm{N}(\alpha_i)|$ and then comparing the decomposition with the decomposition of those representatives in $\mathcal{B}$ with the same value of field norm. For $\mathfrak{p} = \pi\mathcal{O}$ is principal, there exist $\alpha_{i+1} \in \mathcal{O}$ and $\gamma_i \in \Gamma$ such that $v_i\alpha_i = \alpha_{i+1}\pi + \gamma_i$. Consider the absolute value of each embedding σ of α_{i+1}, we have

$$|\sigma(\alpha_{i+1})| = \left|\sigma\left(\frac{v_i\alpha_i - \gamma_i}{\pi}\right)\right|$$
$$\leq \frac{1}{|\sigma(\pi)|}(|\sigma(v_i\alpha_i)| + |\sigma(\gamma_i)|) < \frac{1}{|\sigma(\pi)|}(\Xi + \Delta).$$

It follows that $|\mathrm{N}(\alpha_{i+1})| < \frac{1}{\mathrm{N}(\mathfrak{p})}(\Xi + \Delta)^n$. Thus, if $|\mathrm{N}(\alpha_{i+1})|$ is again not smaller than τ, given the decreasing ratio larger than $\frac{\mathrm{N}(\mathfrak{p})}{2^n}$, in $\frac{2^n}{(\mathrm{N}(\mathfrak{p}))^2}(\Xi + \Delta)^n$ iterations $|\mathrm{N}(\alpha_j)| < \tau$ for some $j > i + 1$ can be found.

For the following 4 reasons, if we do not find some $\alpha_i \in \Gamma$ (this results in a finite π-adic expansion with multiplication by units), we must have $\alpha_j = \alpha_i$ for some $j > i$:

- Given the same $\alpha \in \mathcal{O}$ we yield the same $\delta \in \mathcal{O}$ and $\gamma \in \Gamma$ such that $\alpha = \delta\pi + \gamma$.
- When $|\mathrm{N}(\alpha_i)| \geq \tau$, $|\mathrm{N}(\alpha_i)|$ decreases until $|\mathrm{N}(\alpha_j)| < \tau$ for some $j > i$ in finitely many iterations (Lemma 3.2).
- When $|\mathrm{N}(\alpha_i)| < \tau$, the value of $|\mathrm{N}(\alpha_{i+1})|$ is bounded (proved above).
- Set $\mathcal{B}$ is finite (Lemma 3.6).

Since we must have $\alpha_j = \alpha_i$ for some $j > i$ (if the expansion is not finite) before the set of $v_i\alpha_i$'s covers all the elements in $\mathcal{B}$, the periodicity is bounded by $|\mathcal{B}|\cdot\frac{2^n}{(\mathrm{N}(\mathfrak{p}))^2}(\Xi+\Delta)^n$. ■

Remark 3.8. By properly choosing the representative sets Γ and $\mathcal{B}$, the upper bound on the periodicity $|\mathcal{B}|\cdot\frac{2^n}{(\mathrm{N}(\mathfrak{p}))^2}(\Xi+\Delta)^n$ will depend only on the number field K and the prime ideal $\mathfrak{p}$.

Below we discuss how this can be done.

Using the same technique to get (3.4) as in the proof of Lemma 3.2, for any $\alpha \in \mathcal{O}$, there exists $u \in \mathcal{U}$ such that $|\sigma(u\alpha)| < e^{\sqrt{\varepsilon}} \cdot |\mathrm{N}(\alpha)|^{\frac{1}{n}}$ for each embedding σ. Thus, by properly choosing the representative set $\Gamma = \mathcal{O}/\mathfrak{p}\mathcal{O}$, we have

$$\Delta = \max_{1\le i\le n, r\in\Gamma} |\sigma_i(r)| < \max_{r\in\Gamma}\left(e^{\sqrt{\varepsilon}}\cdot|\mathrm{N}(r)|^{\frac{1}{n}}\right) < e^{\sqrt{\varepsilon}}\cdot|\mathrm{N}(\mathfrak{p})|^{\frac{1}{n}}.$$

By the same token, we have

$$\Xi = \max_{1\le i\le n, b\in\mathcal{B}} |\sigma_i(b)| < \max_{b\in\mathcal{B}}\left(e^{\sqrt{\varepsilon}}\cdot|\mathrm{N}(b)|^{\frac{1}{n}}\right)$$
$$< e^{\sqrt{\varepsilon}}\cdot\tau^{\frac{1}{n}} = e^{2\sqrt{\varepsilon}}\Delta < e^{3\sqrt{\varepsilon}}\cdot|\mathrm{N}(\mathfrak{p})|^{\frac{1}{n}}.$$

Given $\mathcal{B}$ is the representative set of $B = \{b \in \mathcal{O} \mid |\mathrm{N}(b)| < \tau\}$, $|\mathcal{B}|$ has a rough upper bound of $n\tau^2 = n\left(e^{\sqrt{\varepsilon}}\Delta\right)^{2n}$.

Let $\varepsilon' = \frac{2^{(\mathrm{rk}(\mathcal{L})-1)^2}(\mathrm{rk}(\mathcal{L})+1)(\det(\mathcal{L}))^2}{4(\lambda(\mathcal{L}))^{2(\mathrm{rk}(\mathcal{L})-1)}}$. Then we have $\varepsilon' \ge \varepsilon$ for $\varepsilon = \frac{2^{(\mathrm{rk}(\mathcal{L})-1)^2}(\mathrm{rk}(\mathcal{L})+1)(\det(\mathcal{L}))^2}{4(\|b_1\|)^{2(\mathrm{rk}(\mathcal{L})-1)}}$ and $\|b_1\| \ge \lambda(\mathcal{L})$. Therefore we can replace ε with ε' and the above upper bounds on Δ, Ξ, and $|\mathcal{B}|$ still hold. Since ε' is a constant depending only on the number field K, these upper bounds then depend only on the number field K and the prime ideal $\mathfrak{p}$.

In the algorithm, we use $\|b_1\|$ instead of $\lambda(\mathcal{L})$ when setting the bound ε since $\lambda(\mathcal{L})$ is difficult to compute.

3.2 Algorithm

The proof of Theorem 3.7 yields an algorithm constructing a π-adic expansion with multiplication by units, as described in Algorithm 1.

In our algorithm, we need to work with the units in the ring of integers and the lattice spanned by the unit group $\mathcal{L} = \mathrm{Log}(\mathcal{U})$. Since the Log homomorphism takes its values in $\mathbb{R}^{r+s}$ and we can not really compute with real numbers but only with rationals, we refer to [19] on how to represent the units so that unit lattice can be represented by its q-approximation where $q \in \mathbb{N}$. A rational number z' is called a *q-approximation to a real number z* if $|z - z'| < 2^{-q-1}$. Also refer to [19, Definitions 4.1.2-4.1.7] for definitions of q-approximations to vectors, matrices, and so on.

Let $K = \mathbb{Q}(\alpha)$ be represented by a monic irreducible polynomial $f \in \mathbb{Z}[x]$ where $f(\alpha) = 0$. In polynomial time, this representation can be transformed into description of the multiplication in K on a $\mathbb{Q}$-basis of K. The description can be encoded as a multiplication table of the basis Ω, denoted $\mathrm{MT}(\Omega)$. With $\mathrm{MT}(\Omega)$, using algorithm FUNDAMENTAL [19, Algorihtm 7.2.14], a system of fundamental units can be represented. Then, $\mathrm{Log}(\mathcal{U})$ can be represented with its q-approximation.

To ensure the correctness of our algorithm, we must have enough precision to find a correct v_i in line 15 of Algorithm 1. Using the tools provided by Thiel's dissertation [19], given ε, we are able to determine the precision q so that we can find the coordinates of $v = \mathrm{Log}(v_i)$ on $\mathcal{L}$ such that $\|b - v\| < \varepsilon$ by finding the coordinates of its approximation v' on $\mathcal{L}'$ where $\mathcal{L}'$ is a q-approximation of $\mathcal{L}$ and b' is a q-approximation of $b = \mathrm{Log}(a_i)$.

Algorithm 1 Constructing a π-adic Expansion with Multiplication by Units

Precondition:
K, $\mathcal{O}$, $\mathcal{U}$, $\mathfrak{p} = \pi\mathcal{O}$, Γ, $\mathcal{B}$ and n as in Theorem 3.7
$\mathcal{L}$, ε, and τ as in Lemma 3.2
$\alpha \in \mathcal{O}$

1: **function** CONSTRUCTION($\alpha, K, \mathcal{O}, \mathcal{U}, \pi, \Gamma, \mathcal{B}, n, \mathcal{L}, \varepsilon, \tau$)
2:   **if** $\alpha \in \Gamma$ **then**
3:     **return** α
4:   **else**
5:     Find $\gamma_0 \in \Gamma$ such that $\gamma_0 \equiv \alpha \bmod \mathfrak{p}$
6:     $\alpha_1 \leftarrow \frac{\alpha - \gamma_0}{\pi}$
7:     **if** $\alpha_1 \in \Gamma$ **then**
8:       **return** $\gamma_0 + \alpha_1\pi$
9:     **else**
10:       $\mu_0 \leftarrow 1$
11:       $i \leftarrow 1$
12:       **repeat**
13:         **if** $|\mathrm{N}(\alpha_i)| \ge \tau$ **then**
14:           $a_i \leftarrow \frac{|\mathrm{N}(\alpha_i)|^{\frac{1}{n}}}{\alpha_i}$
15:           Find $v_i \in \mathcal{U}$ such that $\|\mathrm{Log}(v_i) - \mathrm{Log}(a_i)\|^2 < \varepsilon$
16:         **else**
17:           Find $v_i \in \mathcal{U}$ such that $v_i\alpha_i \in \mathcal{B}$
18:         **end if**
19:         Find $\gamma_i \in \Gamma$, such that $\gamma_i \equiv v_i\alpha_i \bmod \mathfrak{p}$
20:         $\alpha_{i+1} \leftarrow \frac{v_i\alpha_i - \gamma_i}{\pi}$
21:         $\mu_i \leftarrow \frac{\mu_{i-1}}{v_i}$
22:         $i \leftarrow i + 1$
23:       **until** $\alpha_i \in \{\alpha_1, \ldots, \alpha_{i-1}\} \cup \Gamma$
24:     **end if**
25:     **if** $\alpha_i \in \Gamma$ **then**
26:       **return** $\sum_{k=0}^{i-1} \gamma_k\mu_k\pi^k + \alpha_i\mu_{i-1}\pi^i$
27:     **else**
28:       Find $j < i$ such that $\alpha_j = \alpha_i$.
29:       $\nu \leftarrow \frac{\mu_{i-1}}{\mu_{j-1}}$
30:       **return** $\sum_{k=0}^{j-1} \gamma_k\mu_k\pi^k + \frac{1}{1-\nu\pi^{i-j}}\sum_{k=j}^{i-1} \gamma_k\mu_k\pi^k$
31:     **end if**
32:   **end if**
33: **end function**

4. EXAMPLES

In this section, we apply the theorem and the associated algorithm on two specific number fields, the Gaussian rationals, $\mathbb{Q}(i)$, and $\mathbb{Q}(\sqrt{2})$, and provide some concrete numeric examples.

4.1 Gaussian Rationals

Let $K = \mathbb{Q}(i) = \{a + bi \mid a, b \in \mathbb{Q}\}$, the set of Gaussian rationals. The Gaussian integers $\mathbb{Z}[i]$ form the ring of integers of $\mathbb{Q}(i)$. The two embeddings are $\sigma_1(a + bi) =$

$a+bi$ and $\sigma_2(a+bi) = a - bi$. The field norm $\mathrm{N}(a+bi) = \sigma_1(a+bi)\,\sigma_2(a+bi) = a^2 + b^2$ is the square of its Euclidean norm. For any $\alpha \in K$, $|\sigma_1(\alpha)| = |\sigma_2(\alpha)| = \sqrt{\mathrm{N}(\alpha)}$. The units of $\mathbb{Z}[i]$ are those elements with norm 1, i.e. the set $\{\pm 1, \pm i\}$. For the rank of unit spanned lattice is 0 and the embeddings are both equal, Lemma 3.2 can be restated as follows.

Lemma 4.1. *Let $K = \mathbb{Q}(i)$ and $\mathcal{O} = \mathbb{Z}[i]$ its ring of integers. Let $\mathfrak{p} = \pi\mathcal{O}$ be a prime of K. Let $\Gamma = \mathcal{O}/\mathfrak{p}\mathcal{O}$ be a residue class representative set, and $\Delta = \max_{r\in\Gamma} \mathrm{N}(r)$. Then for $\alpha = \delta\pi + \gamma$, $\gamma \in \Gamma$ and $\mathrm{N}(\alpha) > \Delta$, we have $\mathrm{N}(\delta) < \mathrm{N}(\alpha)$.*

Proof. $\mathrm{N}(\delta)\,\mathrm{N}(\pi) \le \mathrm{N}(\alpha) + \mathrm{N}(\gamma) < 2\,\mathrm{N}(\alpha)$. Since for any $\mathfrak{p} \subset K$, $\mathrm{N}(\mathfrak{p}) \ge 2$, we have $\mathrm{N}(\delta) < \mathrm{N}(\alpha)$. ∎

Since the group of units is finite, we can restate Lemma 3.6 as follows.

Lemma 4.2. *Let $K = \mathbb{Q}(i)$, and Δ as in Lemma 4.1. Then the set $B = \{b \in \mathcal{O} = \mathbb{Z}[i] \mid |\mathrm{N}(b)| < \Delta\}$ is finite.*

Using the lemma and following the proof of Theorem 3.7, we see that for any $\alpha \in \mathbb{Z}[i]$ either we can find a periodic π-adic expansion or the π-adic expansion is finite. Note that adjustment using multiplication by units is not even required since the unit group is finite. We then can write the periodic π-adic expansion of $\alpha \in \mathbb{Z}[i]$ in the following form:

$$\alpha = \gamma_0 + \sum_{i=1}^{k} \gamma_i \pi^i + \frac{1}{1-\pi^m} \sum_{i=k+1}^{k+m} \gamma_i \pi^i.$$

For each stage of π-adic expansion, at most $\mathrm{N}(\pi)$ many divisions of Gaussian integers are required. Note that $\mathrm{N}(\pi)$ is polynomial in p, the rational prime contained in $\mathfrak{p}$. Consider two Gaussian integers $a+bi$ and $c+di$. The division of $a+bi$ over $c+di$ is

$$\frac{a+bi}{c+di} = \frac{(a+bi)\cdot(c-di)}{(c+di)\cdot(c-di)} = \frac{ac+bd}{c^2+d^2} + i\frac{bc-ad}{c^2+d^2}.$$

Evaluating naively, 6 integer multiplications and 2 integer divisions are required. The time complexity of each of these arithmetic operation is polynomial in the length of input. Since there are exactly the period many stage of expansions, the time complexity of finding a π-adic expansion for a Gaussian integer is polynomial in the length of input, the period, and p.

With a toy implementation in Sage [18] of our algorithm for quadratic number fields, we then provide some concrete numeric examples for each type of prime in $K = \mathbb{Q}(i)$. To present the concrete numeric examples in a simpler and clearer way, we denote

$$\alpha = \gamma_0 + \sum_{i=1}^{k} \gamma_i \pi^i + \frac{1}{1-\pi^m} \sum_{i=k+1}^{k+m} \gamma_i \pi^i$$

as

$$\alpha = [\gamma_0, \gamma_1, \ldots, \gamma_k, \overline{\gamma_{k+1}, \ldots, \gamma_{k+m}}],$$

where $\overline{\gamma_{k+1}, \ldots, \gamma_{k+m}}$ is the periodic part of α.

4.1.1 $\mathfrak{p}$ is ramified

The only ramified prime in $\mathbb{Q}(i)$ is $\mathfrak{p} = \langle 1+i \rangle$. Let $\Gamma = \{0, 1\}$ representing $\mathcal{O}/\mathfrak{p}\mathcal{O} \cong \mathbb{F}_2$. Here are some numeric examples.

$\alpha \in \mathcal{O}$	$\alpha \in \mathcal{O}_{1+i}$
i	$[\overline{1}]$
$1-i$	$[0,1,1,0,\overline{1}]$
$2+7i$	$[1,1,1,0,1,1,0,\overline{1}]$
$-8+3i$	$[1,1,0,1,0,0,1,1,0,\overline{1}]$
$31+53i$	$[0,1,1,1,0,0,0,0,1,1,1]$
$15-59i$	$[0,1,1,1,0,0,0,0,1,0,0,0,\overline{1}]$
$-89+99i$	$[0,1,0,1,0,0,1,1,1,1,1,0,1,1,1,0,\overline{1}]$
$-41-67i$	$[0,1,1,1,0,0,0,1,1,0,0,0,0,1]$
$-361+686i$	$[1,0,0,1,1,1,0,0,1,1,1,0,0,0,0,1,1,1,1,0,1]$

4.1.2 $\mathfrak{p}$ splits

The splitting primes in $\mathbb{Q}(i)$ are those $\mathfrak{p} = \langle a+bi \rangle$ with $a^2+b^2 = p$, $a > |b| > 0$ where $p \equiv 1 \bmod 4$ is a rational prime.

Let $p = 5$. Then $\mathfrak{p} = \langle 2+i \rangle$ or $\langle 2-i \rangle$. Take $\mathfrak{p} = \langle 2+i \rangle$. Let $\Gamma_{\mathfrak{p}} = \{0,1,2,3,4\}$ representing $\mathcal{O}/\mathfrak{p}\mathcal{O} \cong \mathbb{F}_5$. Also let $q = 97$. Then $\mathfrak{q} = \langle 9+4i \rangle$ or $\langle 9-4i \rangle$. Take $\mathfrak{q} = \langle 9-4i \rangle$. Let $\Gamma_{\mathfrak{q}} = \{0,1,\ldots,96\}$ representing $\mathcal{O}/\mathfrak{q}\mathcal{O} \cong \mathbb{F}_{97}$. Here are some numeric examples for $\mathcal{O}_{\mathfrak{p}}$ and $\mathcal{O}_{\mathfrak{q}}$.

$\alpha \in \mathcal{O}$	$\alpha \in \mathcal{O}_{2+i}$	$\alpha \in \mathcal{O}_{9-4i}$
i	$[3,\overline{2}]$	$[75,59,\overline{60}]$
$1-i$	$[3,4,1,\overline{2}]$	$[23,\overline{20}]$
$2+7i$	$[3,0,4,\overline{2}]$	$[42,18,\overline{20}]$
$-8+3i$	$[1,1,0,3,\overline{2}]$	$[23,19,\overline{20}]$
$31+53i$	$[0,3,2,1,3,4,1,\overline{2}]$	$[29,82,58,\overline{60}]$
$15-59i$	$[3,0,0,4,4,3,\overline{4}]$	$[52,56,61,\overline{60}]$
$-89+99i$	$[3,2,0,2,3,4,\overline{2}]$	$[61,13,19,\overline{20}]$
$-41-67i$	$[3,0,1,2,1,0,3,\overline{2}]$	$[75,40,62,\overline{60}]$
$-361+686i$	$[2,3,3,0,1,4,4,1,4,1,\overline{2}]$	$[67,84,28,\overline{40}]$

4.1.3 $\mathfrak{p}$ is inert

The inert primes in $\mathbb{Q}(i)$ are those $\mathfrak{p} = \langle p \rangle$, where $p \equiv 3 \bmod 4$ is a rational prime.

Let $\mathfrak{p} = \langle 3 \rangle$ and $\Gamma = \{0, 1, 2, i, 1+i, 2+i, 2i, 1+2i, 2+2i\}$ be the representation of $\mathcal{O}/\mathfrak{p}\mathcal{O} \cong \mathbb{F}_{3^2}$. Here are some numeric examples.

$\alpha \in \mathcal{O}$	$\alpha \in \mathcal{O}_3$
i	$[i]$
$1-i$	$[1+2i,\overline{2i}]$
$2+7i$	$[2+i,2i]$
$-8+3i$	$[1,i,\overline{2}]$
$31+53i$	$[1+2i,1+2i,2i,1+i]$
$15-59i$	$[i,2+i,1+2i,0,\overline{2i}]$
$-89+99i$	$[1,0,2+2i,2,1+i,\overline{2}]$
$-41-67i$	$[1+2i,1+i,1+i,1,\overline{2+2i}]$
$-361+686i$	$[2+2i,2,1+i,1+i,1+2i,1+2i,\overline{2}]$

We can tell from the examples when p is inert, $a+bi \equiv \overline{a} + \overline{b}i \bmod p$. That is, the result is actually applying modulo operations to the real and to the imaginary part respectively, then adding up those two parts.

4.2 Real Quadratic Integers

Let $K = \mathbb{Q}(\sqrt{2})$, then its ring of integers $\mathcal{O} = \mathbb{Z}[\sqrt{2}]$. Here we provide some concrete numeric examples for each type of prime in $K = \mathbb{Q}(\sqrt{2})$.

4.2.1 $\mathfrak{p}$ is ramified

The only ramified prime in $\mathbb{Q}(\sqrt{2})$ is $\mathfrak{p} = \langle \sqrt{2} \rangle$. Let $\Gamma = \{0, 1\}$ representing $\mathcal{O}/\mathfrak{p}\mathcal{O} \cong \mathbb{F}_2$. Here are some numeric examples.

$\alpha \in \mathcal{O}$	$\alpha \in \mathcal{O}_{\sqrt{2}}$
-1	$[\overline{1, 0}]$
$1 + \sqrt{2}$	$[1, 1]$
$2 + 7\sqrt{2}$	$[0, 1, 1, 1, 0, 1]$
$-8 + 3\sqrt{2}$	$[0, 1, 0, 1, 0, \overline{0, 1}]$
$31 + 53\sqrt{2}$	$[1, 1, 1, 0, 1, 1, 1, 0, 1, 1, 0, 1]$
$15 - 59\sqrt{2}$	$[1, 1, 1, 0, 1, 1, 1, 0, 0, 0, 0, 0, , \overline{0, 1}]$
$-89 + 99\sqrt{2}$	$[1, 1, 1, 1, 1, 0, 0, 0, 0, 0, 1, 1, 0, 1, \overline{1, 0}]$
$-41 - 67\sqrt{2}$	$[1, 1, 1, 0, 1, 1, 0, 1, 1, 1, 0, 1, 1, 0, \overline{1}]$
$-361 + 686\sqrt{2}$	$[1, 0, 1, 1, 1, 0, 0, 0, 1, 1, 0, 0, 0, 1, 1, 0, 0, 1, 1, 0, \overline{1}]$

4.2.2 *p splits*

The splitting primes in $\mathbb{Q}\left(\sqrt{2}\right)$ are those $\mathfrak{p} = \langle a + b\sqrt{2} \rangle$ with $a^2 - 2b^2 = p$, $a > |b| > 0$ where $p \equiv 1$ or $7 \bmod 8$ is a rational prime.

Let $p = 7$. Then $\mathfrak{p} = \langle 3 + \sqrt{2} \rangle$ or $\langle 3 - \sqrt{2} \rangle$. Take $\mathfrak{p} = \langle 3 + \sqrt{2} \rangle$. Let $\Gamma_{\mathfrak{p}} = \{0, 1, 2, 3, 4, 5, 6\}$ representing $\mathcal{O}/\mathfrak{p}\mathcal{O} \cong \mathbb{F}_7$. Also let $q = 97$. Then $\mathfrak{q} = \langle 13 + 6\sqrt{2} \rangle$ or $\langle 13 - 6\sqrt{2} \rangle$. Take $\mathfrak{q} = \langle 13 - 6\sqrt{2} \rangle$. Let $\Gamma_{\mathfrak{q}} = \{0, 1, \ldots, 96\}$ representing $\mathcal{O}/\mathfrak{q}\mathcal{O} \cong \mathbb{F}_{97}$. Here are some numeric examples for $\mathcal{O}_{\mathfrak{p}}$ and $\mathcal{O}_{\mathfrak{q}}$.

$\alpha \in \mathcal{O}$	$\alpha \in \mathcal{O}_{3+\sqrt{2}}$	$\alpha \in \mathcal{O}_{13-6\sqrt{2}}$
-1	$[6, 1, \overline{2}]$	$[96, 71, \overline{72}]$
$1 + \sqrt{2}$	$[5, \overline{2}]$	$[84, 59, \overline{60}]$
$2 + 7\sqrt{2}$	$[2, 3, 5, \overline{4}]$	$[1, 84, 59, \overline{60}]$
$-8 + 3\sqrt{2}$	$[4, \overline{6}]$	$[47, 35, \overline{36}]$
$31 + 53\sqrt{2}$	$[5, 2, 0, 0, 1, 5, \overline{4}]$	$[65, 29, 11, \overline{12}]$
$15 - 59\sqrt{2}$	$[3, 5, 1, 6, 2, 1, 4, 6, 1, \overline{2}]$	$[65, 43, 61, \overline{60}]$
$-89 + 99\sqrt{2}$	$[6, 1, 6, 0, 1, 2, 1, 3, 0, 5, \overline{4}]$	$[77, 45, 35, \overline{36}]$
$-41 - 67\sqrt{2}$	$[6, 2, 4, 1, 1, 4, 6, 1, \overline{2}]$	$[24, 68, 85, \overline{84}]$
$-361 + 686\sqrt{2}$	$[3, 3, 6, 6, 3, 0, 3, 2, 5, 1, 1, 3, 0, 5, \overline{4}]$	$[26, 51, 88, 46, \overline{48}]$

4.2.3 *p is inert*

The inert primes in $\mathbb{Q}\left(\sqrt{2}\right)$ are those $\mathfrak{p} = \langle p \rangle$ where where $p \equiv 3$ or $5 \bmod 8$ is a rational prime.

Let $\mathfrak{p} = \langle 3 \rangle$ and $\Gamma = \{0, 1, 2, \sqrt{2}, 1 + \sqrt{2}, 2 + \sqrt{2}, 2\sqrt{2}, 1 + 2\sqrt{2}, 2 + 2\sqrt{2}\}$ representing $\mathcal{O}/\mathfrak{p}\mathcal{O} \cong \mathbb{F}_{3^2}$. Here are some numeric examples.

$\alpha \in \mathcal{O}$	$\alpha \in \mathcal{O}_3$
-1	$[\overline{2}]$
$1 + \sqrt{2}$	$[1 + \sqrt{2}]$
$2 + 7\sqrt{2}$	$[2 + \sqrt{2}, 2\sqrt{2}]$
$-8 + 3\sqrt{2}$	$[1, \sqrt{2}, \overline{2}]$
$31 + 53\sqrt{2}$	$[1 + 2\sqrt{2}, 1 + 2\sqrt{2}, 2\sqrt{2}, 1 + \sqrt{2}]$
$15 - 59\sqrt{2}$	$[\sqrt{2}, 2 + \sqrt{2}, 1 + 2\sqrt{2}, 0, \overline{2\sqrt{2}}]$
$-89 + 99\sqrt{2}$	$[1, 0, 2 + 2\sqrt{2}, 2, 1 + \sqrt{2}, \overline{2}]$
$-41 - 67\sqrt{2}$	$[1 + 2\sqrt{2}, 1 + \sqrt{2}, 1 + \sqrt{2}, 1, \overline{2 + 2\sqrt{2}}]$
$-361 + 686\sqrt{2}$	$[2 + 2\sqrt{2}, 2, 1 + \sqrt{2}, 1 + \sqrt{2}, 1 + 2\sqrt{2}, 1 + 2\sqrt{2}, \overline{2}]$

Similar to the case when p is inert in $K = \mathbb{Q}(i)$, we can tell from the examples, $a + b\sqrt{2} \equiv \overline{a} + \overline{b}\sqrt{2} \bmod p$.

5. CONCLUSION AND FUTURE WORK

In this paper we prove that for K a number field and $\mathcal{O}$ its ring of integers there is always a periodic or finite $\mathfrak{p}$-adic expansion for $\alpha \in \mathcal{O}$ where $\mathfrak{p}$ is a principal prime ideal of K. The proof yields an algorithm for finding such a $\mathfrak{p}$-adic expansion. Since the $\mathfrak{p}$-adic expansion found is either periodic or finite, it provides an exact $\mathfrak{p}$-adic expression, which may be useful for applications involving p-adic analysis or a local completion of number fields.

It will be interesting to construct more efficient algorithms for finding finite or periodic $\mathfrak{p}$-adic expansion, generalize the notion of $\mathfrak{p}$-adic expansion as well as the characterization of finite or periodic expansion beyond the case of principal prime ideals, and explore applications of such expansions.

6. ACKNOWLEDGMENTS

We would like to thank the reviewers for their insightful comments on the paper, as these comments lead us to an improvement of the work.

7. REFERENCES

[1] L. Babai. On Lovász' lattice reduction and the nearest lattice point problem. *Combinatorica*, 6(1):1–13, 1986.

[2] A. Becker, N. Gama, and A. Joux. A sieve algorithm based on overlattices. In *Proc. of ANTS XI*, pages 49–70. London Math. Soc., 2014.

[3] J. Berthomieu and R. Lebreton. Relaxed p-adic Hensel lifting for algebraic systems. In *Proc. of ISSAC '12*, pages 59–66. ACM, 2012.

[4] J. Berthomieu, J. van der Hoeven, and G. Lecerf. Relaxed algorithms for p-adic numbers. *J. Théor. Nombres Bordeaux*, 23(3):541–577, 2011.

[5] X. Caruso, D. Roe, and T. Vaccon. Tracking p-adic precision. In *Proc. of ANTS XI*, pages 274–294. London Math. Soc., 2014.

[6] C. Frougny and K. Klouda. Rational base number systems for p-adic numbers. *RAIRO–Theor. Inform. Appl.*, 46(1):87–106, 2012.

[7] G. Hanrot, X. Pujol, and D. Stehlé. Algorithms for the shortest and closest lattice vector problems. In *Proc. of IWCC 2011*, pages 159–190. Springer, 2011.

[8] K. Hensel. Über eine neue Begründung der Theorie der algebraischen Zahlen. *Jahresber. Dtsch. Math.-Ver.*, 6(3):83–88, 1897.

[9] K. Hensel. Eine neue Theorie der algebraischen Zahlen. *Math. Z.*, 2(3-4):433–452, 1918.

[10] K. S. Kedlaya. Counting points on hyperelliptic curves using Monsky-Washnitzer cohomology. *J. Ramanujan Math. Soc.*, 16:323–338, 2001.

[11] Ç. K. Koç. A tutorial on p-adic arithmetic. Technical report, Oregon State University, 2002.

[12] E. V. Krishnamurthy. Matrix processors using p-adic arithmetic for exact linear computations. *IEEE Trans. Comput.*, C-26(7):633–639, 1977.

[13] E. V. Krishnamurthy, T. M. Rao, and K. Subramanian. Finite segment p-adic number systems with applications to exact computation. *Proc. Indian Acad. Sci.*, 81 A(2):58–79, 1975.

[14] A. K. Lenstra, H. W. Lenstra, Jr., and L. Lovász. Factoring polynomials with rational coefficients. *Math. Ann.*, 261(4):515–534, 1982.

[15] H. W. Lenstra, Jr. Lattices. In *Algorithmic Number Theory*, volume 44 of *Math. Sci. Res. Inst. Publ.*, pages 127–181. Cambridge Univ. Press, 2008.

[16] C. Lu, X. Li, and L. Shan. Periodicity of the p-adic expansion after arithmetic operations in p-adic field. In *Proc. of ICIS 2012*, pages 8–13. IEEE, 2012.

[17] P. Q. Nguyen. Lattice reduction algorithms: Theory and practice. In *Proc. of EUROCRYPT 2011*, pages 2–6. Springer, 2011.

[18] W. A. Stein et al. *Sage Mathematics Software (Version 6.4.1)*. The Sage Development Team, 2014.

[19] C. Thiel. *On the complexity of some problems in algorithmic algebraic number theory*. PhD thesis, Universität des Saarlandes, 1995.

A Modified Abramov-Petkovšek Reduction and Creative Telescoping for Hypergeometric Terms*

Shaoshi Chen[1], Hui Huang[1,2], Manuel Kauers[2], Ziming Li[1]
[1]KLMM, AMSS, Chinese Academy of Sciences, Beijing 100190, (China)
[2]RISC, Johannes Kepler University, Linz A-4040, (Austria)
schen, huanghui@amss.ac.cn
mkauers@risc.jku.at, zmli@mmrc.iss.ac.cn

ABSTRACT

The Abramov-Petkovšek reduction computes an additive decomposition of a hypergeometric term, which extends the functionality of the Gosper algorithm for indefinite hypergeometric summation. We modify the Abramov-Petkovšek reduction so as to decompose a hypergeometric term as the sum of a summable term and a non-summable one. The outputs of the Abramov-Petkovšek reduction and our modified version share the same required properties. The modified reduction does not solve any auxiliary linear difference equation explicitly. It is also more efficient than the original reduction according to computational experiments. Based on this reduction, we design a new algorithm to compute minimal telescopers for bivariate hypergeometric terms. The new algorithm can avoid the costly computation of certificates.

Categories and Subject Descriptors

I.1.2 [**Computing Methodologies**]: Symbolic and Algebraic Manipulation—*Algebraic Algorithms*

General Terms

Algorithms, Theory

Keywords

Abramov-Petkovšek reduction, Hypergeometric term, Telescoper, Summability

*S. Chen was supported in part by the NSFC grant 11371143 and by President Fund of Academy of Mathematics and Systems Science, CAS (2014-cjrwlzx-chshsh), H. Huang by the Austrian Science Fund (FWF) grant W1214-13, M. Kauers by the Austrian Science Fund (FWF) grants Y464-N18 and F50-04, H. Huang and Z. Li by two NSFC grants (91118001, 60821002/F02) and a 973 project (2011CB302401).

ISSAC'15, July 6–9, 2015, Bath, United Kingdom.

DOI: http://dx.doi.org/10.1145/2755996.2756648.

1. INTRODUCTION

Creative telescoping is a staple of symbolic summation. Its main use is to construct recurrence equations that have a prescribed definite sum among their solutions. By using other algorithms applicable to recurrence equations, it is then possible to derive interesting facts about the original definite sum, such as closed forms or asymptotic expansions.

The computational problem of creative telescoping is to construct, for a given term $f(x, y)$, polynomials $\ell_0, \ldots, \ell_r$ in x only, not all zero, and another term $g(x, y)$ s.t.

$$\ell_0(x)f(x, y) + \cdots + \ell_r(x)f(x + r, y) = g(x, y + 1) - g(x, y).$$

The number r may or may not be part of the input.

We can distinguish four generations of creative telescoping algorithms. The first generation was based on elimination techniques [15, 22, 19, 14]. The second generation started with what is now known as Zeilberger's algorithm [21, 5, 23, 19]. The algorithms of this generation use the idea of augmenting an algorithm for indefinite summation (or integration) by additional parameters $\ell_0, \ldots, \ell_r$ that are carried along during the calculation and are finally instantiated, if at all possible, such as to ensure the existence of a term g as needed for the right-hand side. See [19] for details about the first two generations.

The third generation was initiated by Apagodu and Zeilberger [17, 6]. In a sense, they applied a second-generation algorithm by hand to a generic input and worked out the resulting linear system of equations for the parameters ℓ_i and the coefficients inside the desired term g. Their algorithm then merely consists in solving this system. This approach is interesting not only because it is easier to implement and tends to run faster than earlier algorithms, but also because it is easy to analyze. In fact the analysis of algorithms from this family gives rise to the best output size estimates for creative telescoping known so far [11, 12, 13]. A disadvantage is that these algorithms may not always find the smallest possible output.

The fourth generation of creative telescoping algorithms originates from [7]. The basic idea behind these algorithms is to bring each term $f(x + i, y)$ of the left-hand side into some kind of normal forms modulo all terms that are differences of other terms. Then to find $\ell_0, \ldots, \ell_r$ amounts to finding a linear dependence among these normal forms. The key advantage of this approach is that it separates the computation of the ℓ_i from the computation of g. This is desirable in the typical situation where we are only interested in the ℓ_i and their size is much smaller than the size of g. With previous algorithms there was no way to obtain ℓ_i without also computing g, but with fourth generation algorithms there is. So far this approach has only been worked out for several instances in the differential case [7, 9, 8]. The goal of the present paper is to give a fourth-generation algorithm for the discrete case, namely for the classical setting of hypergeometric telescoping.

Our starting point is the Abramov-Petkovšek reduction for hypergeometric terms introduced in [3] and summarized in Section 3 below. Unfortunately the reduced forms obtained by this reduction are not sufficiently "normal" for our purpose. Therefore, in Sections 4 and 5 we present a refined variant of the reduction process and show that the corresponding normal forms are well-behaved with respect to taking linear combinations. Then in Section 6 we describe the creative telescoping algorithm obtained from this reduction. The final section contains an experimental comparison between this algorithm and the built-in algorithm of Maple.

2. PRELIMINARIES

Throughout the paper, we let $\mathbb{F}$ be a field of characteristic zero, and $\mathbb{F}(y)$ be the field of rational functions in y over $\mathbb{F}$. Let σ_y be the automorphism that maps $r(y)$ to $r(y+1)$ for every $r \in \mathbb{F}(y)$. The pair $(\mathbb{F}(y), \sigma_y)$ is called a difference field. A difference ring extension of $(\mathbb{F}(y), \sigma_y)$ is a ring $\mathbb{D}$ containing $\mathbb{F}(y)$ together with a distinguished endomorphism $\sigma_y \colon \mathbb{D} \to \mathbb{D}$ whose restriction to $\mathbb{F}(y)$ agrees with the automorphism defined before. An element $c \in \mathbb{D}$ is called a constant if $\sigma_y(c) = c$. For a nonzero polynomial $p \in \mathbb{F}[y]$, its degree and leading coefficient are denoted by $\deg_y(p)$ and $\operatorname{lc}_y(p)$, respectively.

Definition 2.1. *Let $\mathbb{D}$ be a difference ring extension of $\mathbb{F}(y)$. A nonzero element $T \in \mathbb{D}$ is called a* hypergeometric term *over $\mathbb{F}(y)$ if $\sigma(T) = rT$ for some $r \in \mathbb{F}(y)$. We call r the* shift quotient *of T w.r.t. y.*

The product of hypergeometric terms is again hypergeometric. Two hypergeometric terms T_1, T_2 are called *similar* if there exists a rational function $r \in \mathbb{F}(y)$ s.t. $T_1 = rT_2$. By Proposition 5.6.2 in [19], the sum of similar hypergeometric terms is either hypergeometric or zero.

A univariate hypergeometric term T is called *hypergeometric summable* if there exists another hypergeometric term G s.t. $T = \Delta_y(G)$, where Δ_y denotes the difference of σ_y and the identity map. We abbreviate "hypergeometric summable" as "summable" in this paper.

Given a hypergeometric term T, we let $\mathbb{U}_T$ be the union of $\{0\}$ and the set of summable hypergeometric terms that are similar to T. Then $\mathbb{U}_T$ is an $\mathbb{F}$-linear subspace of $\mathbb{D}$. Note that $\mathbb{U}_T = \mathbb{U}_H$ if H is a hypergeometric term similar to T.

Recall [3, §1] that a nonzero polynomial in $\mathbb{F}[y]$ is said to be *shift-free* if it is coprime with any of its nontrivial shifts. A nonzero rational function is said to be *shift-reduced* if its numerator is coprime with any shift of its denominator.

A basic property of shift-reduced rational functions is given below.

Lemma 2.2. *Let $f \in \mathbb{F}(y)$ be shift-reduced and unequal to one. If there exists $r \in \mathbb{F}[y]$ s.t. $f\sigma_y(r) - r = 0$, then $r = 0$.*

Proof. Suppose that $r \neq 0$. Then $f = r/\sigma_y(r)$. Since f is unequal to one, r does not belong to $\mathbb{F}$. It follows that f is not shift-reduced, a contradiction. □

According to [3, 4], every hypergeometric term T has a multiplicative decomposition SH, where S is in $\mathbb{F}(y)$ and H is another hypergeometric term whose shift quotient is shift-reduced. We call the shift quotient $K := \sigma_y(H)/H$ a *kernel* of T w.r.t. y and S the corresponding *shell*. Note that $K = 1$ if and only if T is a rational function, which is then equal to cS for some element $c \in \mathbb{D}$ with $\sigma_y(c) = c$.

Let $T = SH$ be a multiplicative decomposition, where S is a rational function and H a hypergeometric term with a kernel K. Assume that $T = \Delta_y(G)$ for some hypergeometric term G. A straightforward calculation shows that G is similar to T. So there exists $r \in \mathbb{F}(y)$ s.t. $G = rH$. One can easily verify that

$$SH = \Delta_y(rH) \iff S = K\sigma_y(r) - r. \tag{1}$$

Let $\mathbb{V}_K = \{K\sigma_y(r) - r \mid r \in \mathbb{F}(y)\}$, which is an $\mathbb{F}$-linear subspace of $\mathbb{F}(y)$. Then (1) translates into

$$SH \equiv 0 \bmod \mathbb{U}_H \iff S \equiv 0 \bmod \mathbb{V}_K. \tag{2}$$

These congruences enable us to shorten expressions.

3. ABRAMOV-PETKOVŠEK REDUCTION

Reduction algorithms have been developed for computing additive decompositions of rational functions [1], hyperexponential functions [8], and hypergeometric terms [3, 4]. These algorithms can be viewed as generalizations of the Gosper algorithm [16, 19] and its differential analogue [5].

The Abramov-Petkovšek reduction [3, 4] is fundamental for this paper. To describe it concisely, we need a notational convention and a technical definition.

Convention 3.1. *Let T be a hypergeometric term whose kernel is K and the corresponding shell is S. Then $T = SH$, where H is a hypergeometric term whose shift quotient is K. Assume that K is unequal to one. Moreover, write $K = u/v$, where u, v are polynomials in $\mathbb{F}[y]$ with $\gcd(u, v) = 1$.*

Definition 3.2. *A nonzero polynomial p in $\mathbb{F}[y]$ is said to be* strongly prime *with K if $\gcd\left(p, \sigma_y^{-i}(u)\right) = \gcd\left(p, \sigma_y^{i}(v)\right) = 1$ for all $i \geq 0$.*

The proof of Lemma 3 in [3] contains a reduction algorithm whose inputs and outputs are given below.

AbramovPetkovšekReduction: Given K and S as defined in Convention 3.1, compute a rational function $S_1 \in \mathbb{F}(y)$ and polynomials $b, w \in \mathbb{F}[y]$ s.t. b is shift-free and strongly prime with K, and the following equation holds:

$$S = K\sigma_y(S_1) - S_1 + \frac{w}{b \cdot \sigma_y^{-1}(u) \cdot v}. \tag{3}$$

The algorithm contained in the proof of Lemma 3 in [3] is described as pseudo code on page 4 of the same paper, in which the last ten lines are to make the denominator of the rational function V in its output minimal in some technical sense. We shall not execute these lines. Then the algorithm will compute two rational functions U_1 and U_2. They correspond to S_1 and $w/\left(b\sigma_y^{-1}(u)v\right)$ in (3), respectively.

We slightly modify the output of the Abramov-Petkovšek reduction. Note that K is shift-reduced and b is strongly prime with K. Thus, b, $\sigma_y^{-1}(u)$ and v are pairwise coprime. By partial fraction decomposition, (3) can be rewritten as

$$S = K\sigma_y(S_1) - S_1 + \left(\frac{a}{b} + \frac{p_1}{\sigma_y^{-1}(u)} + \frac{p_2}{v}\right),$$

where $a, p_1, p_2 \in \mathbb{F}[y]$. Furthermore, we set $r = p_1/\sigma_y^{-1}(u)$. A direct calculation yields $r = K\sigma_y(-r) - (-r) + \sigma_y(p_1)/v$. Update S_1 to be $S_1 - r$ and set p to be $\sigma_y(p_1) + p_2$. Then

$$S = K\sigma_y(S_1) - S_1 + \frac{a}{b} + \frac{p}{v}. \tag{4}$$

This modification leads to shell reduction specified below.

ShellReduction: Given K and S as defined in Convention 3.1, compute a rational function $S_1 \in \mathbb{F}(y)$ and polynomials $a, b, p \in \mathbb{F}[y]$ s.t. b is shift-free and strongly prime with K, and that (4) holds.

Shell reduction provides us with a necessary condition on summability.

Proposition 3.3. *With Convention 3.1, assume that a, b, p are polynomials in $\mathbb{F}[y]$ s.t. b is shift-free and strongly prime with K. Assume further that (4) holds. If T is summable, then a/b belongs to $\mathbb{F}[y]$.*

Proof. Recall that $T = SH$ by Convention 3.1 and it has a kernel K and the corresponding shell S. It follows from (2) and (4) that $T \equiv (a/b + p/v)\,H \bmod \mathbb{U}_H$. Thus, T is summable if and only if $(a/b + p/v)\,H$ is summable.

Set $H' = (1/v)H$, which has a kernel $K' = u/\sigma_y(v)$. Note that b is also strongly prime with K'. We can apply Theorem 11 in [4] to $(av/b + p)\,H'$, which equals $(a/b + p/v)\,H$. Thus, a/b is a polynomial because b is coprime with v. □

Example 3.4. *Let $T = y^2 y!/(y+1)$. Then the term has a kernel $K = y + 1$ and the shell $S = y^2/(y+1)$. Shell reduction yields $S \equiv -1/(y+2) + y/v \bmod \mathbb{V}_K$ where v=1. By Proposition 3.3, T is not summable.*

Note that $a/b + p/v$ in (4) can be nonzero for a summable T.

Example 3.5. *Let $T = y \cdot y!$ whose kernel is $K = y+1$ and shell is $S = y$. Then $S \equiv y/v \bmod \mathbb{V}_K$, where $v = 1$. But T is summable as it is equal to $\Delta_y(y!)$.*

The above example illustrates that neither shell reduction nor the Abramov-Petkovšek reduction can decide summability directly. One way to proceed is to find a polynomial solution of an auxiliary first-order linear difference equation [4]. We show how this can be avoided in the next section.

4. MODIFICATIONS

After the shell reduction described in (4), it remains to check the summability of $(a/b + p/v)\,H$. In the rational case, i.e. when the kernel K is one, $a/b + p/v$ in (4) can be further reduced to a/b with $\deg_y(a) < \deg_y(b)$, because all polynomials are rational summable. However, a hypergeometric term with a polynomial shell is not necessarily summable, for example, $y!$ has a polynomial shell but it is not summable.

We define the notion of discrete residual forms for rational functions, and present a discrete variant of the polynomial reduction for hyperexponential functions given in [8]. This variant not only leads to a direct way to decide summability, but also reduces the number of terms of p in (4).

4.1 Discrete residual forms

With Convention 3.1, we define an $\mathbb{F}$-linear map ϕ_K from $\mathbb{F}[y]$ to itself by sending p to $u\sigma_y(p) - vp$ for all $p \in \mathbb{F}[y]$. We call ϕ_K the *map for polynomial reduction w.r.t. K.*

Lemma 4.1. *Let*

$$\mathbb{W}_K = \operatorname{span}_{\mathbb{F}}\left\{y^\ell \mid \ell \in \mathbb{N}, \ell \neq \deg_y(p) \textit{ for all } p \in \operatorname{im}(\phi_K)\right\}.$$

Then $\mathbb{F}[y] = \operatorname{im}(\phi_K) \oplus \mathbb{W}_K$.

Proof. By the definition of $\mathbb{W}_K$, $\operatorname{im}(\phi_K) \cap \mathbb{W}_K = \{0\}$. The same definition also implies that, for every non-negative integer m, there exists a polynomial $f_m \in \operatorname{im}(\phi_K) \cup \mathbb{W}_K$ s.t. the degree of f_m is equal to m. The set $\{f_0, f_1, f_2, \ldots\}$ forms an $\mathbb{F}$-basis of $\mathbb{F}[y]$. Thus $\mathbb{F}[y] = \operatorname{im}(\phi_K) \oplus \mathbb{W}_K$. □

In view of the above lemma, we call $\mathbb{W}_K$ the *standard complement of* $\operatorname{im}(\phi_K)$. A polynomial $p \in \mathbb{F}$ can be uniquely decomposed as $p = p_1 + p_2$ with $p_1 \in \operatorname{im}(\phi_K)$ and $p_2 \in \mathbb{W}_K$.

Lemma 4.2. *With Convention 3.1, let p be a polynomial in $\mathbb{F}[y]$. Then there exists $q \in \mathbb{W}_K$ s.t. $p/v \equiv q/v \bmod \mathbb{V}_K$.*

Proof. Let q be the projection of p on $\mathbb{W}_K$. Then there exists f in $\mathbb{F}[y]$ s.t. $p = \phi_K(f) + q$, that is, $p = u\sigma_y(f) - vf + q$. So $p/v = K\sigma_y(f) - f + q/v$, that is, $p/v \equiv q/v \bmod \mathbb{V}_K$. □

Remark 4.3. *Replacing p in the above lemma by vp, we see that, for every polynomial $p \in \mathbb{F}[y]$, there exists $q \in \mathbb{W}_K$ s.t. $p \equiv q/v \bmod \mathbb{V}_K$.*

By Lemma 4.2 and Remark 4.3, (4) implies that

$$S \equiv \frac{a}{b} + \frac{q}{v} \bmod \mathbb{V}_K, \tag{5}$$

where $a, b, q \in \mathbb{F}[y]$, $\deg_y(a) < \deg_y(b)$, b is shift-free and strongly prime with K, and $q \in \mathbb{W}_K$. The congruence (5) motivates us to translate the notion of (continuous) residual forms in [8] into the discrete setting.

Definition 4.4. *With Convention 3.1, we further let f be a rational function in $\mathbb{F}(y)$. Another rational function r in $\mathbb{F}(y)$ is called a* (discrete) residual form *of f w.r.t. K if there exist a, b, q in $\mathbb{F}[y]$ s.t.*

$$f \equiv r \bmod \mathbb{V}_K \quad \textit{and} \quad r = \frac{a}{b} + \frac{q}{v},$$

where $\deg_y(a) < \deg_y(b)$, b is shift-free and strongly prime with K, and q belongs to $\mathbb{W}_K$. For brevity, we just say that r is a residual form *w.r.t. K if f is clear from the context.*

Residual forms help us decide summability, as shown in the next proposition.

Proposition 4.5. *With Convention 3.1, we further assume that r is a nonzero residual form w.r.t. K. The hypergeometric term rH is not summable.*

Proof. Suppose that rH is summable. Let $r = a/b + q/v$, where $\deg_y(a) < \deg_y(b)$, b is shift-free and strongly prime with K, and q belongs to $\mathbb{W}_K$. By Proposition 3.3, a/b is a polynomial. Since $\deg_y(a) < \deg_y(b)$, $a = 0$. Thus, $(q/v)H$ is summable. It follows from (1) that there exists w in $\mathbb{F}(y)$ s.t. $u\sigma_y(w) - vw = q$. Thus, $w \in \mathbb{F}[y]$ by Theorem 5.2.1 in [19, page 76]. So q belongs to $\operatorname{im}(\phi_K)$. But q also belongs to $\mathbb{W}_K$. By Lemma 4.1, $q = 0$, a contradiction. □

With Convention 3.1, let r be a residual form of the shell S. Then $SH \equiv rH \bmod \mathbb{U}_H$ by (2) and (5). By Proposition 4.5, SH is summable if and only if $r = 0$. Thus, determining the summability of a hypergeometric term T amounts to computing a residual form of the corresponding shell w.r.t. a kernel of T, which is studied below.

4.2 Polynomial reduction

To compute a residual form of a rational function, we project a polynomial on $\mathrm{im}(\phi_K)$ and on its standard complement $\mathbb{W}_K$, both defined in the previous subsection.

Let $\mathbb{B}_K = \{\phi_K(y^i) \mid i \in \mathbb{N}\}$. The $\mathbb{F}$-linear map ϕ_K is injective by Lemma 2.2. So $\mathbb{B}_K$ is an $\mathbb{F}$-basis of $\mathrm{im}(\phi_K)$, which allows us to construct an echelon basis. By an echelon basis, we mean an $\mathbb{F}$-basis in which distinct elements have distinct degrees. We can easily project a polynomial using an echelon basis and linear elimination.

To construct an echelon basis, we rewrite $\mathrm{im}(\phi_K)$ as

$$\mathrm{im}(\phi_K) = \{u\Delta_y(p) - (v-u)p \mid p \in \mathbb{F}[y]\}.$$

Set $\alpha_1 = \deg_y(u), \alpha_2 = \deg_y(v)$, and $\beta = \deg_y(v-u)$. Moreover, set $\tau_K = \mathrm{lc}_y(v-u)/\mathrm{lc}_y(u)$, which is nonzero due to Convention 3.1 and let p be a nonzero polynomial in $\mathbb{F}[y]$.

We make the following case distinction.

Case 1. $\beta > \alpha_1$. Then $\beta = \alpha_2$, and

$$\phi_K(p) = -\mathrm{lc}_y(v-u)\,\mathrm{lc}_y(p) y^{\alpha_2 + \deg_y(p)} + \text{lower terms}.$$

So $\mathbb{B}_K$ is an echelon basis of $\mathrm{im}(\phi_K)$, in which $\deg_y(\phi_K(y^i))$ is equal to $\alpha_2 + i$ for all $i \in \mathbb{N}$. Accordingly, $\mathbb{W}_K$ has an echelon basis $\{1, y, \ldots, y^{\alpha_2 - 1}\}$ and $\dim(\mathbb{W}_K) = \alpha_2$.

Case 2. $\beta = \alpha_1$. Then

$$\phi_K(p) = -\mathrm{lc}_y(v-u)\,\mathrm{lc}_y(p) y^{\alpha_1 + \deg_y(p)} + \text{lower terms}.$$

So $\mathbb{B}_K$ is an echelon basis of $\mathrm{im}(\phi_K)$, in which $\deg_y(\phi_K(y^i))$ is equal to $\alpha_1 + i$ for all $i \in \mathbb{N}$. Accordingly, $\mathbb{W}_K$ has an echelon basis $\{1, y, \ldots, y^{\alpha_1 - 1}\}$ and $\dim(\mathbb{W}_K) = \alpha_1$.

Case 3. $\beta < \alpha_1 - 1$. If $\deg_y(p) = 0$, then $\phi_K(p) = (u-v)p$. Otherwise, we have

$$\phi_K(p) = \deg_y(p)\,\mathrm{lc}_y(u)\,\mathrm{lc}_y(p) y^{\alpha_1 + \deg_y(p) - 1} + \text{lower terms}.$$

It follows that $\mathbb{B}_K$ is an echelon basis of $\mathrm{im}(\phi_K)$, in which $\deg_y(\phi_K(1)) = \beta$ and

$$\deg_y(\phi_K(y^i)) = \alpha_1 + i - 1 \quad \text{for all } i \geq 1.$$

So $\mathbb{W}_K$ has an echelon basis $\{1, \ldots, y^{\beta-1}, y^{\beta+1}, \ldots, y^{\alpha_1 - 1}\}$, and $\dim(\mathbb{W}_K) = \alpha_1 - 1$.

Case 4. $\beta = \alpha_1 - 1$ and τ_K is not a positive integer. Then

$$\phi_K(p) = \left(\deg_y(p)\,\mathrm{lc}_y(u) - \mathrm{lc}_y(v-u)\right)\mathrm{lc}_y(p) y^{\alpha_1 + \deg_y(p) - 1} + \text{lower terms}. \quad (6)$$

So $\mathbb{B}_K$ is an echelon basis of $\mathrm{im}(\phi_K)$, in which, for all $i \in \mathbb{N}$, $\deg_y(\phi_K(y^i)) = \alpha_1 + i - 1$. Accordingly, $\mathbb{W}_K$ is spanned by an echelon basis $\{1, y, \ldots, y^{\alpha_1 - 2}\}$, and has dimension $\alpha_1 - 1$.

Case 5. $\beta = \alpha_1 - 1$ and τ_K is a positive integer. It follows from (6) that for $i \neq \tau_K$, $\deg_y(\phi_K(y^i)) = \alpha_1 + i - 1$. Moreover, for every polynomial p of degree τ_K, $\phi_K(p)$ is of degree less than $\alpha_1 + \tau_K - 1$. So any echelon basis of $\mathrm{im}(\phi_K)$ does not contain a polynomial of degree $\alpha_1 + \tau_K - 1$. Set

$$\mathbb{B}'_K = \left\{\phi_K(y^i) \mid i \in \mathbb{N}, i \neq \tau_K\right\}.$$

Reducing $\phi_K(y^{\tau_K})$ by the polynomials in $\mathbb{B}'_K$, we obtain a polynomial p' with $\deg_y(p') < \alpha_1 - 1$. Since $\mathbb{B}_K$ is an $\mathbb{F}$-basis and $\mathbb{B}'_K \subset \mathbb{B}_K$, $p' \neq 0$. So $\mathbb{B}'_K \cup \{p'\}$ is an echelon basis of $\mathrm{im}(\phi_K)$. Consequently, $\mathbb{W}_K$ is spanned by an echelon basis $\left\{1, y, \ldots, y^{\deg_y(p')-1}, y^{\deg_y(p')+1}, \ldots, y^{\alpha_1 - 2}, y^{\alpha_1 + \tau_K - 1}\right\}$. The dimension of $\mathbb{W}_K$ is equal to $\alpha_1 - 1$.

Example 4.6. *Let $K = (y^4+1)/(y+1)^4$, which is shift-reduced. Then $\tau_K = 4$. According to Case 5,* $\mathrm{im}(\phi_K)$ *has an echelon basis*

$$\{\phi_K(p)\} \cup \{\phi_K(y^m) \mid m \in \mathbb{N}, m \neq 4\},$$

where $p = y^4 + y/3 + 1/2$, $\phi_K(p) = (5/3)y^2 + 2y + 4/3$, and $\phi_K(y^m) = (m-4)y^{m+3}$ + lower terms. Therefore, $\mathbb{W}_K$ has a basis $\{1, y, y^7\}$.

From the above case distinction and example, one observes that, although the degree of a polynomial in the standard complement depends on τ_K, which may be arbitrarily high, the number of its terms depends merely on the degrees of u and v. We record this observation in the next proposition.

Proposition 4.7. *With the Convention 3.1, we further let*

$$\alpha_1 = \deg_y(u), \quad \alpha_2 = \deg_y(v), \quad \text{and} \quad \beta = \deg_y(v-u).$$

Then there exists $\mathcal{P} \subset \{y^i \mid i \in \mathbb{N}\}$ with

$$|\mathcal{P}| \leq \max\{\alpha_1, \alpha_2\} - [\![\beta \leq \alpha_1 - 1]\!]$$

s.t. every polynomial in $\mathbb{F}[y]$ can be reduced modulo $\mathrm{im}(\phi_K)$ to an $\mathbb{F}$-linear combination of the elements in $\mathcal{P}$. Note that here $[\![\beta \leq \alpha_1 - 1]\!]$ equals 1 if $\beta \leq \alpha_1 - 1$, otherwise it is 0.

Proof. By the above case distinction, $\dim(\mathbb{W}_K)$ is no more than $\max\{\alpha_1, \alpha_2\} - [\![\beta \leq \alpha_1 - 1]\!]$. The lemma follows. □

The above case distinction enables one to find an infinite sequence $p_0, p_1, \ldots$ in $\mathbb{F}[y]$ s.t.

$$\mathbb{E}_K = \{\phi_K(p_i) | i \in \mathbb{N}\} \text{ with } \deg_y \phi_K(p_i) < \deg_y \phi_K(p_{i+1}),$$

is an echelon basis of $\mathrm{im}(\phi_K)$. This basis allows us to project a polynomial on $\mathrm{im}(\phi_K)$ and $\mathbb{W}_K$, respectively. In the first four cases, the p_i's can be chosen as powers of y. But in the last case, one of the p_i's is not necessarily a monomial as shown in Example 4.6.

PolynomialReduction: Given $p \in \mathbb{F}[y]$, compute $f \in \mathbb{F}[y]$ and $q \in \mathbb{W}_K$ s.t. $p = \phi_K(f) + q$.

1. If $p = 0$, then set $f = 0$ and $q = 0$; return.
2. Set $d = \deg_y(p)$. Find the subset $\mathbb{P} = \{p_{i_1}, \ldots, p_{i_s}\}$ consisting of the preimages of all polynomials in the echelon basis $\mathbb{E}_K$ whose degrees are at most d.
3. For $k = s, s-1, \ldots, 1$, perform linear elimination to find $c_s, c_{s-1}, \ldots, c_1 \in \mathbb{F}$ s.t. $p - \sum_{k=1}^{s} c_k \phi_K(p_{i_k}) \in \mathbb{W}_K$.
4. Set $f = \sum_{k=1}^{s} c_k p_{i_k}$ and $q = p - \phi_K(f)$; and return.

We now present a modified version of the Abramov-Petkovšek reduction, which determines summability without solving any auxiliary difference equations explicitly.

ModifiedAbramovPetkovšekReduction: Given an irrational hypergeometric term T over $\mathbb{F}(y)$, compute a hypergeometric term H with a kernel K, and two rational functions $f, r \in \mathbb{F}(y)$ s.t. r is a residual form w.r.t. K, and

$$T = \Delta_y(fH) + rH. \quad (7)$$

1. Find a kernel K and the corresponding shell S of T;

2. Apply shell reduction to S w.r.t. K to find $b, s, t \in \mathbb{F}[y]$ and $g \in \mathbb{F}(y)$ s.t. b is shift-free and strongly prime with K; and

$$T = \Delta_y(gH) + \left(\frac{s}{b} + \frac{t}{v}\right)H, \tag{8}$$

where $\sigma_y(H)/H = K$ and v is the denominator of K.

3. Set p and a to be the quotient and remainder of s and b, respectively.
4. Apply polynomial reduction to $vp + t$ to find $h \in \mathbb{F}[y]$ and $q \in \mathbb{W}_K$ s.t. $vp + t = \phi_K(h) + q$.
5. Set $f := g+h$ and $r := a/b+q/v$ and return H, f and r.

Theorem 4.8. *With Convention 3.1, the modified version of the Abramov-Petkovšek reduction computes a rational function f in $\mathbb{F}(y)$ and a residual form r w.r.t. K s.t. (7) holds. Moreover, T is summable if and only if $r = 0$.*

Proof. Recall that $T = SH$, where H has a kernel K and S is a rational function. Applying shell reduction to S w.r.t. K yields (8), which can be rewritten as

$$T = \Delta_y(gH) + \left(\frac{a}{b} + \frac{vp+t}{v}\right)H,$$

where a and p are given in step 3 of the modified Abramov-Petkovšek reduction. The polynomial reduction in step 4 yields that $vp + t = u\sigma_y(h) - vh + q$. Substituting this into (8), we see that

$$\begin{aligned} T &= \Delta_y(gH) + (K\sigma_y(h) - h)H + \left(\frac{a}{b} + \frac{q}{v}\right)H \\ &= \Delta_y((g+h)H) + rH, \end{aligned}$$

where $r = a/b+q/v$. Thus, (7) holds. By Proposition 4.5, T is summable if and only r is equal to zero. □

Example 4.9. *Let T be the same hypergeometric term as in Example 3.4. Then $K = y + 1$ and $S = y^2/(y+1)$. Set $H = y!$. By the shell reduction in Example 3.4,*

$$T = \Delta_y\left(\frac{-1}{y+1}H\right) + \left(\frac{-1}{y+2} + \frac{y}{v}\right)H,$$

where $v = 1$. Applying the polynomial reduction to $(y/v)H$ yields $(y/v)H = \Delta_y(1 \cdot H)$. Combining the above steps, we decompose T as $T = \Delta_y(y/(y+1)H) - (1/(y+2))H$. So the input term T is not summable.

Example 4.10. *Let T be the same hypergeometric term as in Example 3.5. Then $K = y+1$ and $S = y$. Set $H = y!$. By the shell reduction in Example 3.5, $T = yH$. The polynomial reduction yields $yH = \Delta_y(y!)$, hence $T = \Delta_y(y!)$.*

Remark 4.11. *With the notation given in the step 5 of the modified version, we can rewrite rH as $(s_1/s_2)G$, where $s_1 = av + bq$, $s_2 = b$, and $G = H/v$. It follows from the case distinction at the beginning of this section that the degree of s_1 is bounded by λ given in [3, Theorem 8]. The polynomial s_2 is equal to b in (3) whose degree is minimal by [3, Theorem 3]. Moreover, $\sigma_y(G)/G$ is shift-reduced, because $\sigma_y(H)/H$ is. These are exactly the same required properties of the output of the original version [3].*

5. SUM OF TWO RESIDUAL FORMS

To compute telescopers for bivariate hypergeometric terms by the modified Abramov-Petkovšek reduction, we are confronted with the difficulty that the sum of two residual forms is not necessarily a residual form. This is because the least common multiple of two shift-free polynomials is not necessarily shift-free.

The goal of this section is to show that the sum of two residual forms is congruent to a residual form modulo $\mathbb{V}_K$.

Example 5.1. *Let $K=1/y$, $r=1/(2y+1)$ and $s=1/(2y+3)$. Then both r and s are residual forms w.r.t. K, but their sum is not, because the denominator $(2y+1)(2y+3)$ is not shift-free. However, we can still find an equivalent residual form. For example, we have $r+s \equiv -1/(2(2y+1))+1/2y \bmod \mathbb{V}_K$. Note that the residual form is not unique. Another possible choice is $r + s \equiv 1/(3(2y+3)) + 1/3y \bmod \mathbb{V}_K$.*

Let f and g be two nonzero polynomials in $\mathbb{F}[y]$. We say that f and g are *shift-coprime* if $\gcd\left(f, \sigma_y^{\ell}(g)\right) = 1$ for all nonzero integer ℓ. Assume that both f and g are shift-free. By polynomial factorization and dispersion computation, one can uniquely decompose

$$g = \tilde{g}\sigma_y^{\ell_1}(p_1^{m_1}) \cdots \sigma_y^{\ell_k}(p_k^{m_k}), \tag{9}$$

where $\tilde{g}$ is shift-coprime with f, $p_1, \ldots, p_k$ are distinct, monic and irreducible factors of f, $\ell_1, \ldots, \ell_k$ are nonzero integers, $m_1, \ldots, m_k$ are multiplicities of $\sigma_y^{\ell_1}(p_1), \ldots, \sigma_y^{\ell_k}(p_k)$ in g, respectively. We refer to (9) as the *shift-coprime decomposition* of g w.r.t. f.

Remark 5.2. *The factors $\tilde{g}, \sigma_y^{\ell_1}(p_1^{m_1}), \ldots, \sigma_y^{\ell_k}(p_k^{m_k})$ in (9) are pairwise coprime, since f and g are shift-free.*

To construct a residual form congruent to the sum of two given residual ones, we need three technical lemmas. The first one corresponds to the kernel reduction in [8].

Lemma 5.3. *With Convention 3.1, assume that p_1, p_2 are in $\mathbb{F}[y]$ and m in $\mathbb{N}$. Then there exist q_1, q_2 in $\mathbb{W}_K$ s.t.*

$$\frac{p_1}{\prod_{i=0}^{m}\sigma_y^i(v)} \equiv \frac{q_1}{v} \bmod \mathbb{V}_K \text{ and } \frac{p_2}{\prod_{j=1}^{m}\sigma_y^{-j}(u)} \equiv \frac{q_2}{v} \bmod \mathbb{V}_K.$$

Proof. To prove the first congruence, let $w_m = \prod_{i=0}^{m}\sigma_y^i(v)$. We proceed by induction on m. If $m = 0$, then the conclusion holds by Lemma 4.2. Assume that the lemma holds for $m - 1$. Consider the equality

$$\frac{p_1}{w_m} = K\sigma_y\left(\frac{s}{w_{m-1}}\right) - \frac{s}{w_{m-1}} + \frac{t}{w_{m-1}},$$

where $s, t \in \mathbb{F}[y]$ are to be determined. This equality holds if and only if $\sigma_y(s)u + (t-s)\sigma_y^m(v) = p_1$. Since u and $\sigma_y^m(v)$ are coprime, such s and t can be computed by the extended Euclidean algorithm. Thus, $p_1/w_m \equiv t/w_{m-1} \bmod \mathbb{V}_K$. Consequently, p_1/w_m has a required residual form by the induction hypothesis.

To prove the second congruence, we use the identity

$$\frac{p_2}{\sigma_y^{-1}(u)} = K\sigma_y\left(-\frac{p_2}{\sigma_y^{-1}(u)}\right) - \left(-\frac{p_2}{\sigma_y^{-1}(u)}\right) + \frac{\sigma_y(p_2)}{v},$$

which implies that $p_2/\sigma_y^{-1}(u) \equiv \sigma_y(p_2)/v \bmod \mathbb{V}_K$. By Lemma 4.2, there exists $q_2 \in \mathbb{W}_K$ s.t. q_2/v is a residual form of $p_2/\sigma_y^{-1}(u)$ w.r.t. K. Assume that the congruence holds for $m - 1$. The induction can be completed as in the proof for p_1/w_m. □

The next lemma provides us with flexibility to rewrite a rational function modulo $\mathbb{V}_K$.

Lemma 5.4. *Let $K \in \mathbb{F}(y)$ be nonzero and shift-reduced. Then, for every $f \in \mathbb{F}(y)$ and every $\ell \in \mathbb{Z}^+$,*

$$f \equiv \sigma_y^\ell(f) \prod_{i=0}^{\ell-1} \sigma_y^i(K) \equiv \sigma_y^{-\ell}(f) \prod_{i=1}^{\ell} \sigma_y^{-i}\left(\frac{1}{K}\right) \bmod \mathbb{V}_K.$$

Proof. Let us show the first congruence by induction on ℓ. For $\ell = 1$, the identity $f = K\sigma_y(-f) - (-f) + \sigma_y(f)K$ implies that f is congruent to $\sigma_y(f)K$ modulo $\mathbb{V}_K$. Assume that it holds for $\ell - 1$. Set $w_\ell = \prod_{i=0}^{\ell-1} \sigma_y^i(K)$. Then f is congruent to $\sigma_y^{\ell-1}(f)w_{\ell-1}$ modulo $\mathbb{V}_K$ by the induction hypothesis. Moreover, $\sigma_y^{\ell-1}(f)w_{\ell-1}$ is congruent to $\sigma_y^\ell(f)w_\ell$ by the induction base, in which f is replaced with $\sigma_y^{\ell-1}(f)w_{\ell-1}$. Hence, f is congruent to $\sigma_y^\ell(f)w_\ell$ modulo $\mathbb{V}_K$.

The second congruence can be shown similarly. For $\ell = 1$, the identity $f = K\sigma_y(r) - r + r$ with $r = \sigma_y^{-1}(f)\sigma_y^{-1}(1/K)$ implies that f is congruent to r modulo $\mathbb{V}_K$. We can then proceed as in the proof of the first congruence. □

Lemma 5.5. *With Convention 3.1, let $a, b \in \mathbb{F}[y]$ with $b \neq 0$. Assume that b is shift-free and strongly prime with K. Assume further that $\sigma_y^\ell(b)$ is strongly prime with K for some integer ℓ, then a/b has a residual form $c/\sigma_y^\ell(b) + q/v$ w.r.t. K, where $c \in \mathbb{F}[y]$ with $\deg_y(c) < \deg_y(b)$ and $q \in \mathbb{W}_K$.*

Proof. First, consider the case in which $\ell \geq 0$. If $\ell = 0$, then there exist $c, p \in \mathbb{F}$ with $\deg_y(c) < \deg_y(b)$ s.t. $a/b = c/b + p$. The lemma follows from Remark 4.3.

Assume that $\ell > 0$. By the first congruence of Lemma 5.4,

$$\frac{a}{b} \equiv \sigma_y^\ell\left(\frac{a}{b}\right)\left(\prod_{i=0}^{\ell-1} \sigma_y^i(K)\right) = \frac{\sigma_y^\ell(a) \prod_{i=0}^{\ell-1} \sigma_y^i(u)}{\sigma_y^\ell(b) \prod_{i=0}^{\ell-1} \sigma_y^i(v)} \bmod \mathbb{V}_K.$$

Note that $\sigma_y^\ell(b)$ is strongly prime with v by assumption. Then it is coprime with the product $v\sigma_y(v) \cdots \sigma_y^{\ell-1}(v)$. By partial fraction decomposition, we get

$$\frac{a}{b} \equiv \frac{\tilde{a}}{\sigma_y^\ell(b)} + \frac{\tilde{q}}{\prod_{i=0}^{\ell-1} \sigma_y^i(v)} \bmod \mathbb{V}_K.$$

By the first congruence of Lemma 5.3, the second summand in the right-hand side of the above congruence can be replaced by a residual form whose denominator is equal to v. The first assertion holds.

The case in which $\ell < 0$ can be handled in the same way, in which the second congruences of Lemmas 5.4 and 5.3 will be used instead of the first ones in these lemmas. □

We are ready to present the main result of this section.

Theorem 5.6. *With Convection 3.1, let r and s be two residual forms w.r.t. K. Then there exists a residual form t congruent to s modulo $\mathbb{V}_K$ s.t., for all $\lambda, \mu \in \mathbb{F}$, $\lambda r + \mu t$ is a residual form w.r.t. K congruent to $\lambda r + \mu s$ modulo $\mathbb{V}_K$.*

Proof. Let $r = a/f + p/v$ and $s = b/g + q/v$, where $a, f, b, g \in \mathbb{F}[y]$, $\deg_y(a) < \deg(f)$, $\deg_y(b) < \deg_y(g)$, $p, q \in \mathbb{W}_K$, and f, g are shift-free and strongly prime with K.

Assume that (9) is the shift-coprime decomposition of g w.r.t. f. Set $P_i = \sigma_y^{\ell_i}(p_i)$ for $i = 1, \ldots, k$. By Remark 5.2 and partial fraction decomposition, we have

$$\frac{b}{g} = \frac{b_0}{\tilde{g}} + \sum_{i=1}^{k} \frac{b_i}{P_i^{m_i}}, \tag{10}$$

where $b_0, b_1, \ldots, b_k \in \mathbb{F}[y]$. Note that $p_i = \sigma_y^{-\ell_i}(P_i)$, which is a factor of f. Thus it is strongly prime with K. So we can apply Lemma 5.5 to each fraction $b_i/P_i^{m_i}$ in (10) to get

$$\frac{b}{g} \equiv \frac{b_0}{\tilde{g}} + \sum_{i=1}^{k} \frac{b_i'}{p_i^{m_i}} + \frac{q'}{v} \bmod \mathbb{V}_K, \tag{11}$$

where $b_1', \ldots, b_k' \in \mathbb{F}[y]$ and $q' \in \mathbb{W}_K$.

Set $h = \tilde{g} \prod_{i=1}^{k} p_i^{m_i}$. Then h is shift-free and strongly prime with K as both f and g are. Since f is shift-free, all its factors are shift-coprime with f, so are the p_i's, and so is h. Let t be the sum of q/v and the rational function in the right-hand side of (11). Then there exist b^* in $\mathbb{F}[y]$ with $\deg_y(b^*) < \deg_y(h)$ and q^* in $\mathbb{W}_K$ s.t. $t = b^*/h + q^*/v$. Since f and h are shift-coprime, their least common multiple is shift-free. Therefore, $\lambda r + \mu t$ is a residual form w.r.t. K, and $\lambda r + \mu t$ is congruent to $\lambda r + \mu s$ mod $\mathbb{V}_K$. □

6. TELESCOPING VIA REDUCTIONS

Let $\mathcal{C}$ be a field of characteristic zero, and $\mathcal{C}(x, y)$ be the field of rational functions in x and y over $\mathcal{C}$. Let σ_x, σ_y be the shift operators w.r.t. x and y, respectively, defined by,

$$\sigma_x(f(x, y)) = f(x + 1, y) \text{ and } \sigma_y(f(x, y)) = f(x, y + 1),$$

for any $f \in \mathcal{C}(x, y)$. Then the pair $(\mathcal{C}(x, y), \{\sigma_x, \sigma_y\})$ forms a partial difference field.

Definition 6.1. *Let $\mathbb{D}$ be a partial difference ring extension of $\mathcal{C}(x, y)$. A nonzero element $T \in \mathbb{D}$ is called a* hypergeometric term *over $\mathcal{C}(x, y)$ if there exist $f, g \in \mathcal{C}(x, y)$ s.t. $\sigma_x(T) = fT$ and $\sigma_y(T) = gT$. We call f, g the* shift quotients *of T w.r.t. x and y, respectively.*

An irreducible polynomial $p \in \mathcal{C}[x, y]$ is said to be *integer-linear* over $\mathcal{C}$ if there exist $f \in \mathcal{C}[z]$, $m, n \in \mathbb{Z}$ with $n \geq 0$ and $\gcd(m, n) = 1$, s.t. $p = f(mx + ny)$. A polynomial in $\mathcal{C}[x, y]$ is said to be *integer-linear* over $\mathcal{C}$ if all of its irreducible factors are integer-linear. A rational function in $\mathcal{C}(x, y)$ is said to be *integer-linear* over $\mathcal{C}$ if its denominator and numerator are integer-linear.

Let $\mathbb{F}$ be the field $\mathcal{C}(x)$, and $\mathbb{F}\langle S_x \rangle$ be the ring of linear recurrence operators in x, in which the commutation rule is that $S_x r = \sigma_x(r) S_x$ for all $r \in \mathbb{F}$. The application of an operator $L = \sum_{i=0}^{\rho} \ell_i S_x^i$ to a hypergeometric term T is defined as $L(T) = \sum_{i=0}^{\rho} \ell_i \sigma_x^i(T)$.

Definition 6.2. *Let T be a hypergeometric term over $\mathbb{F}(y)$. A nonzero operator $L \in \mathbb{F}\langle S_x \rangle$ is called a* telescoper *for T if there exists a hypergeometric term G s.t. $L(T) = \Delta_y(G)$. We call G the* certificate *of L.*

For hypergeometric terms, telescopers do not always exist. Abramov presented a criterion for determining the existence of telescopers in [2, Theorem 10]. Let $K = u/v$ be a kernel of $\sigma_y(T)/T$ and S the corresponding shell. Applying the modified Abramov-Petkovšek reduction w.r.t. y to T yields $T = \Delta_y(uH) + rH$, where $u \in \mathbb{F}(y)$, $H = T/S$, and $r = a/b + q/v$ is the residual form of S w.r.t. K. By Abramov's criterion, T has a telescoper if and only if b is integer-linear over $\mathcal{C}$. When telescopers exist, Zeilberger's algorithm [21] constructs a telescoper for T by iteratively using the Gosper algorithm to detect the summability of $L(T)$ for an ansatz $L = \sum_{i=0}^{\rho} \ell_i S_x^i \in \mathbb{F}\langle S_x \rangle$.

Following the creative telescoping algorithms based on Hermite reductions [7, 10, 9, 8] in the continuous case, we use the modified Abramov-Petkovšek reduction to develop a telescoping algorithm, which is outlined below.

ReductionCT: Given a hypergeometric term T with shift quotients $f = \sigma_x(T)/T$ and $g = \sigma_y(T)/T$ in $\mathbb{F}(y)$, compute a telescoper of minimal order for T and its certificate if telescopers exist.

1. Find a kernel K and shell S of T w.r.t. y s.t. $T = SH$ with $K = \sigma_y(H)/H$.
2. Apply the modified Abramov-Petkovšek reduction to T to get
$$T = \Delta_y(u_0 H) + r_0 H. \quad (12)$$
If $r_0 = 0$, then return $(1, u_0 H)$.
3. If the denominator of r_0 is not integer-linear, return "No telescoper exists!".
4. Set $N := \sigma_x(H)/H$ and $R := \ell_0 r_0$, where ℓ_0 is an indeterminate.

   For $i = 1, 2, \ldots$, do

   4.1. View $\sigma_x(r_{i-1})NH$ as a hypergeometric term with kernel K and shell $\sigma_x(r_{i-1})N$. Using shell reduction w.r.t. K and polynomial reduction w.r.t. K, find $u_i' \in \mathbb{F}$ and a residual form $\tilde{r}_i$ w.r.t. K s.t. $\sigma_x(r_{i-1})NH = \Delta_y(u_i' H) + \tilde{r}_i H$.

   4.2. Set $\tilde{u}_i = \sigma_x(u_{i-1})N + u_i'$, so that
$$\sigma_x^i(T) = \Delta_y(\tilde{u}_i H) + \tilde{r}_i H. \quad (13)$$

   4.3. Follow the proof of Theorem 5.6 to compute u_i and r_i in $\mathbb{F}(y)$ s.t. $r_i \equiv \tilde{r}_i \bmod \mathbb{V}_K$,
$$\sigma_x^i(T) = \Delta_y(u_i H) + r_i H, \quad (14)$$
and that $R + \ell_i r_i$ is a residual form w.r.t. K, where ℓ_i is an indeterminate.

   4.4. Update R to be $R + \ell_i r_i$.

   4.5. Find $\ell_j \in \mathbb{F}$ s.t. $R = 0$ by solving a linear system in $\ell_0, \ldots, \ell_i$ over $\mathbb{F}$. If there is a nontrivial solution, return $\left(\sum_{j=0}^{i} \ell_j S_x^j, \sum_{j=0}^{i} \ell_j u_j H\right)$.

Theorem 6.3. *Let T be a hypergeometric term over $\mathbb{F}(y)$. If T has a telescoper, then the algorithm* **ReductionCT** *terminates and returns a telescoper of minimal order for T.*

Proof. By Theorem 4.8, $r_0 = 0$ implies that 1 is a telescoper for T of minimal order.

Let r_0 obtained from step 2 be of the form $a_0/b_0 + q_0/v$, where $a_0, b_0, v \in \mathbb{F}[y]$, $\deg_y(a_0) < \deg_y(b_0)$, b_0 is strongly prime with K, $q_0 \in \mathbb{W}_K$, and v is the denominator of K. By Ore-Sato's theorem [18, 20] on hypergeometric terms, K is integer-linear and so is v. It follows that b_0 is integer-linear if and only if $b_0 v$ is. By Abramov's criterion, T has a telescoper if and only if the denominator of r_0 is integer-linear. Thus, steps 2 and 3 are correct.

It follows from (12) and $\sigma_x(r_0 H) = \sigma_x(r_0)NH$ that (13) holds for $i = 1$. By Theorem 5.6, there exists a residual form r_1 w.r.t. K with $r_1 \equiv \tilde{r}_1 \bmod \mathbb{V}_K$ s.t. $R + \ell_1 r_1$ is again a residual form for all $\ell_0, \ell_1 \in \mathbb{F}$. Indeed, the proofs of the lemmas and Theorem 5.6 enable us to obtain not only r_1 but also a rational function g_1 s.t. $\tilde{r}_1 = K\sigma_y(g_1) - g_1 + r_1$. Setting $u_1 = \tilde{u}_1 + g_1$, we see that (14) holds for $i = 1$. By a direct induction on i, (14) holds in the loop of step 4.

Assume that $L = \sum_{i=0}^{\rho} c_i S_x^i$ is a telescoper of minimal order for T with $c_i \in \mathbb{F}$ and $c_\rho \neq 0$. Then $L(T)$ is summable. By Theorem 4.8, $\sum_{i=0}^{\rho} c_i r_i$ is equal to zero. Thus, the linear homogeneous system (over $\mathbb{F}$) obtained by equating $\sum_{i=0}^{\rho} \ell_i r_i$ to zero has a nontrivial solution, which yields a telescoper of minimal order. □

Remark 6.4. *The algorithm* **ReductionCT** *separates the computation of minimal telescopers from that of certificates. In applications where the certificates are irrelevant, we can drop step 4.2 and in step 4.3 compute u_i and r_i with $r_i \equiv \tilde{r}_i \bmod \mathbb{V}_K$ and $\sigma_x^i(r_{i-1})NH = \Delta_y(u_i H) + r_i H$ and that $R + \ell_i r_i$ is a residual form w.r.t. K, where ℓ_i is an indeterminate. The rational function u_i can be discarded, and we do not need to calculate $\sum_{j=0}^{i} \ell_j u_j H$ in the end.*

Remark 6.5. *Instead of applying the modified Abramov-Petkovšek reduction to $\sigma_x(r_{i-1})NH$ in step 4.1, it is also possible to apply the reduction to $\sigma_x^i(T)$, but our experiments suggest that this variant takes considerably more time.*

Example 6.6. *Let $T = \binom{x}{y}^3$. Set f and g to be $\sigma_x(T)/T$ and $\sigma_y(T)/T$, respectively. Since g is shift-reduced w.r.t. y, its kernel is equal to g itself, and the corresponding shell is equal to 1. In step 4, we obtain $\sigma_y^i(T) \equiv (q_i/v)H \bmod \mathbb{U}_H$, where i=0, 1, 2, $v = (y+1)^3$, H has shift quotient g w.r.t. y,*

$$q_0 = \tfrac{1}{2}(x+1)(x^2-x+3y(y-x+1)+1), \quad q_1 = (x+1)^3, \quad \textit{and}$$
$$q_2 = \frac{(x+1)^3}{(x+2)^2}\left(11x^2 - 12xy + 17x + 20 + 12y + 12y^2\right).$$

By finding an $\mathbb{F}$-linear dependency among q_0, q_1, q_2, we get

$$L := (x+2)^2 S_x^2 - (7x^2 + 21x + 16)S_x - 8(x+1)^2$$

is a telescoper of minimal order for T.

7. IMPLEMENTATION AND TIMINGS

We have implemented our algorithms in Maple. In order to get an idea about their efficiency, we compared their runtime and memory requirements to the performance of known algorithms. All timings are measured in seconds on a Linux computer with 388Gb RAM and twelve 2.80GHz Dual core processors.

For the first comparison, we considered univariate hypergeometric terms of the form

$$T = \frac{f(y)}{g_1(y)g_2(y)} \frac{\Gamma(y-\alpha)}{\Gamma(y-\beta)},$$

where $f \in \mathbb{Z}[y]$ of degree 20, $g_i = p_i \sigma_y^\lambda(p_i) \sigma_y^\mu(p_i)$ with $p_i \in \mathbb{Z}[y]$ of degree 10, $\lambda, \mu \in \mathbb{N}$, and $\alpha, \beta \in \mathbb{Z}$. For a selection of random terms of this type for different choices of μ and λ, Table 1 compares the timings of Maple's implementation of the classical Abramov-Petkovšek reduction (AP) and our modified version (MAP). We apply the algorithms to T as well as to the summable terms $\sigma_y(T) - T$.

For the second comparison, we considered bivariate hypergeometric terms of the form

$$T = \frac{f(x,y)}{g_1(x+y)g_2(2x+y)} \frac{\Gamma(2\alpha x + y)}{\Gamma(x + \alpha y)}$$

(λ,μ)	T AP	T MAP	$\sigma_y(T)-T$ AP	$\sigma_y(T)-T$ MAP
$(0,0)$	0.45	0.30	4.41	2.29
$(5,5)$	5.94	1.21	10.19	2.40
$(5,10)$	14.69	2.20	15.67	3.30
$(10,10)$	17.22	2.31	17.98	2.77
$(10,20)$	57.05	6.20	38.03	3.80
$(10,30)$	316.51	15.73	74.55	3.73
$(10,40)$	514.84	32.64	134.29	3.99

Table 1: Comparison of the Abramov-Petkovšek reduction and the modified version for a collection of non-summable terms T and summable terms $\sigma_y(T)-T$.

with $f\in\mathbb{Z}[x,y]$ of degree n, $g_i=p_i\sigma_z^{\lambda}(p_i)\sigma_z^{\mu}(p_i)$ with $p_i\in\mathbb{Z}[z]$ of degree m, and $\alpha,\lambda,\mu\in\mathbb{N}$. For a selection of random terms of this type for different choices of n,m,α,μ,λ, Table 2 compares the timings of Maple's implementation of Zeilberger's algorithm (Z) and two variants of the algorithm **ReductionCT** from Section 6: For the column RCT_1 we computed both the telescoper and certificate, and for RCT_2 we only compute the telescoper. The difference between these two variants comes mainly from the time needed to bring the rational function u in the certificate uH on a common denominator. When it is acceptable to keep the certificate as an unnormalized linear combination of rational functions, the timings are virtually the same as for RCT_2.

(m,n,α,λ,μ)	Z	RCT_1	RCT_2	order
$(1,0,1,5,5)$	17.12	5.00	1.80	4
$(1,0,2,5,5)$	74.91	26.18	5.87	6
$(1,0,3,5,5)$	445.41	92.74	17.34	7
$(1,8,3,5,5)$	649.57	120.88	23.59	7
$(2,0,1,5,10)$	354.46	58.01	4.93	4
$(2,0,2,5,10)$	576.31	363.25	53.15	6
$(2,0,3,5,10)$	2989.18	1076.50	197.75	7
$(2,3,3,5,10)$	3074.08	1119.26	223.41	7
$(2,0,1,10,15)$	2148.10	245.07	11.22	4
$(2,0,2,10,15)$	2036.96	1153.38	153.21	6
$(2,0,3,10,15)$	11240.90	3932.26	881.12	7
$(2,5,3,10,15)$	10163.30	3954.47	990.60	7
$(3,0,1,5,10)$	18946.80	407.06	43.01	6
$(3,0,2,5,10)$	46681.30	2040.21	465.88	8
$(3,0,3,5,10)$	172939.00	5970.10	1949.71	9

Table 2: Comparison of Zeilberger's algorithm to reduction-based telescoping with and without construction of a certificate

8. REFERENCES

[1] S. A. Abramov. The rational component of the solution of a first-order linear recurrence relation with a rational right side. *USSR Comp. Math. Math. Phys.*, 15(4):216–221, 1975.

[2] S. A. Abramov. When does Zeilberger's algorithm succeed? *Adv. in Appl. Math.*, 30(3):424–441, 2003.

[3] S. A. Abramov and M. Petkovšek. Minimal decomposition of indefinite hypergeometric sums. In *Proc. of ISSAC'01*, pp. 7–14, 2001. ACM.

[4] S. A. Abramov and M. Petkovšek. Rational normal forms and minimal decompositions of hypergeometric terms. *J. Symbolic Comput.*, 33(5):521–543, 2002.

[5] G. Almkvist and D. Zeilberger. The method of differentiating under the integral sign. *J. Symbolic Comput.*, 10:571–591, 1990.

[6] M. Apagodu and D. Zeilberger. Multi-variable Zeilberger and Almkvist-Zeilberger algorithms and the sharpening of Wilf-Zeilberger theory. *Adv. in Appl. Math.*, 37(2):139–152, 2006.

[7] A. Bostan, S. Chen, F. Chyzak, and Z. Li. Complexity of creative telescoping for bivariate rational functions. In *Proc. of ISSAC '10*, pp. 203–210, 2010. ACM.

[8] A. Bostan, S. Chen, F. Chyzak, Z. Li, and G. Xin. Hermite reduction and creative telescoping for hyperexponential functions. In *Proc. of ISSAC'13*, pp. 77–84, 2013. ACM.

[9] A. Bostan, P. Lairez, and B. Salvy. Creative telescoping for rational functions using the Griffith-Dwork method. In *Proc. of ISSAC'13*, pp. 93–100, 2013. ACM.

[10] S. Chen. *Some applications of differential-difference algebra to creative telescoping.* PhD thesis, École Polytechnique, Palaiseau, 2011.

[11] S. Chen and M. Kauers. Order-degree curves for hypergeometric creative telescoping. In *Proc. of ISSAC'12*, pp. 122–129, 2012. ACM.

[12] S. Chen and M. Kauers. Trading order for degree in creative telescoping. *J. Symbolic Comput.*, 47(8):968–995, 2012.

[13] S. Chen, M. Kauers, and C. Koutschan. A generalized Apagodu-Zeilberger algorithm. In *Proc. of ISSAC'14*, pp. 107–114, 2014. ACM.

[14] F. Chyzak and B. Salvy. Non-commutative elimination in Ore algebras proves multivariate identities. *J. Symbolic Comput.*, 26:187–227, 1998.

[15] M. C. Fasenmyer. Some generalized hypergeometric polynomials. *Bull. Amer. Math. Soc.*, 53:806–812, 1947.

[16] R. W. Gosper, Jr. Decision procedure for indefinite hypergeometric summation. *Proc. Nat. Acad. Sci. U.S.A.*, 75(1):40–42, 1978.

[17] M. Mohammed and D. Zeilberger. Sharp upper bounds for the orders of the recurrences output by the Zeilberger and q-Zeilberger algorithms. *J. Symbolic Comput.*, 39(2):201–207, 2005.

[18] O. Ore. Sur la forme des fonctions hypergéométriques de plusieurs variables. *J. Math. Pures Appl. (9)*, 9(4):311–326, 1930.

[19] M. Petkovšek, H. S. Wilf, and D. Zeilberger. *A = B*. A K Peters Ltd., Wellesley, MA, 1996.

[20] M. Sato. Theory of prehomogeneous vector spaces (algebraic part). *Nagoya Math. J.*, 120:1–34, 1990.

[21] D. Zeilberger. A fast algorithm for proving terminating hypergeometric identities. *Discrete Math.*, 80:207–211, 1990.

[22] D. Zeilberger. A holonomic systems approach to special functions identities. *J. Comput. Appl. Math.*, 32:321–368, 1990.

[23] D. Zeilberger. The method of creative telescoping. *J. Symbolic Comput.*, 11:195–204, 1991.

Computer Algebra Applied to a Solitary Waves Study

Didier Clamond
Université de Nice-Sophia Antipolis
Laboratoire de Mathématiques
Parc Valrose 06108 Nice cedex 02, France.
didier.clamond@unice.fr

Denys DUTYKH
Université de Savoie Mont Blanc
LAMA, UMR 5127 CNRS
Campus Scientifique, 73376 Le Bourget-du-Lac Cedex, France.
Denys.Dutykh@univ-savoie.fr

André Galligo*
Université de Nice-Sophia Antipolis (and INRIA)
Laboratoire de Mathématiques
Parc Valrose 06108 Nice cedex 02, France.
galligo@unice.fr

ABSTRACT

We apply computer algebra techniques, such as algebraic computations of resultants and discriminants, certified drawing (with a guaranteed topology) of plane curves, to a problem in fluid dynamics: We investigate "capillary-gravity" solitary waves in shallow water, relying on the framework of the Serre-Green-Naghdi equations. So, we deal with two-dimensional surface waves, propagating in a shallow water of constant depth. By a differential elimination process, the study reduces to describing the solutions of an ordinary non linear first order differential equation, depending on two parameters. The paper is illustrated with examples and pictures computed with the computer algebra system Maple.

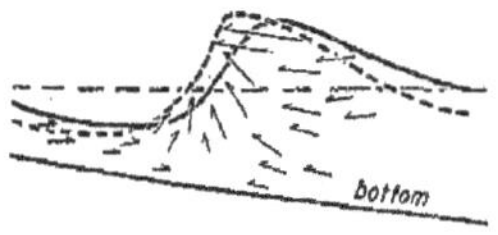

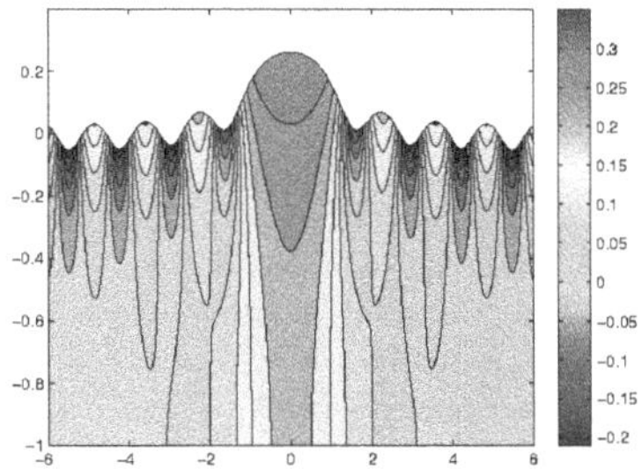

Figure 1: Water wave Figure 2: $x-$velocity

Categories and Subject Descriptors

I.1.2 [**Computing Methodologies**]: Symbolic and Algebraic Manipulation; J.6 [**Computer Applications**]: [Fluid Mechanics]

General Terms

Theory

Keywords

solitary waves; peakon; non linear differential equation; differential elimination; plane phase analysis; resultants; discriminants; plane curves; certified drawing; classification

1. INTRODUCTION

In this paper we apply computer algebra techniques such as algebraic computations of resultants and discriminants, certified drawing (with a guaranteed topology) of plane curves, to a problem in fluid dynamics. More precisely, we investigate "capillary-gravity" solitary waves in shallow water, relying on the framework of the Serre-Green-Naghdi equations. So, we deal with two-dimensional surface waves, propagating in a shallow water of constant depth (without assuming small wave amplitudes), see [6, 7, 11, 23]. Figure 1 represents two successive positions of a water wave, the bottom level and the still water level are emphasized (in our study the bottom will be horizontal), the velocities are indicated by small arrows. Beside the kinematic energy, the governing equations take into account an effect of capillarity pressure quantified by a Bond number $\mathcal{B}$ (depending on a tension surface coefficient) and an effect of gravity force, jointly quantified by a (squared) Froude number $\mathcal{F}$, which also indicates the wave phase velocity. To ease the presentation and for physical reasons, we can concentrate on the cases where $\mathcal{F} \in [0, 2]$ and $\mathcal{B} \in [-1, 2]$. The variable x indicates the abscissa in the channel, the principal unknowns are the elevation $h(x)$ of the free surface above x, and $\bar{u}(x)$ the depth-averaged horizontal velocity. The height of the surface at rest is denoted by d; $h = d$ is therefore a trivial solution. To illustrate some typical features of a water wave we have shown, in Figure 2, a color representation of the (normalized) variations of the horizontal component of the velocity $u(x, y)$, the coordinates x, and y are also normalized. The bottom surface is assumed horizontal, and we only consider a (vertical) section of the wave. One can also see the graph of $y = h(x)$ which forms the elevation curve. It is called free curve (or more generally free surface) because unlike the bottom it is not prescribed.

The primitive equations of the general motion were established already in the 18th century by the great mathe-

*corresponding author

ISSAC'15, July 6–9, 2015, Bath, United Kingdom.

DOI: http://dx.doi.org/10.1145/2755996.2756659.

maticians Euler, Bernoulli and d'Alembert relying on physical conservative laws: conservations of mass and energy. However these non linear partial differential equations are difficult to solve and need to be contextualized (e.g. in the shallow water regime). Usually, the physicists consider that some quantity is small and replace the equations by the first terms of a Taylor approximation, see e.g. [20] for a mathematical general presentation. Here we follow the path opened by Lord Kelvin and his followers, and choose the equations of gravity waves first derived by Serre [23] in 1953, and later rediscovered by Green and Naghdi [11], which uses the depth-averaged horizontal velocity. As in [8], we generalize these equation by adding a term which takes into account the tension forces induced by capillarity. So the PDEs depend on the gravity g and a surface tension coefficients τ. In the second section, we present these non linear differential equations with boundary conditions and we explain that by considering a mobile frame, we are reduced to investigate their steady waves. Then, by a first integration and a simple substitution eliminating the variable $\bar{u}(x)$, the study reduces to describing the solutions of a system of ordinary differential equations depending on two parameters, $\mathcal{F}$ and $\mathcal{B}$. By a differential elimination process, inspired by physics considerations, we were able to reduces it further to a non linear first order differential equation. In this paper, we concentrate on the description of solitary waves, the steady waves which decay to a constant value at infinity. Solitary waves play a central role in nonlinear sciences, see [21]. For some special PDEs, such as KdV, NLS and classical Serre-Green-Naghdi equations, the solitary waves can be found analytically; this is not the case for the equations, with capillarity effects, that we consider. But we will get certified qualitative results. In the third section, we review the different kinds of solutions of differential equations and emphasize the interest of singular solutions, first investigated algebraically by Hamburger in 1893 [12] and studied more recently in computer algebra by Hubert [13, 14, 15] in a more general framework. The angular solitons were first considered by Stokes in 1880 [24] and received a renewed interest with the many studies on Camassa–Holmes "peakons" [3], see also [19]. Then, we explain our phase plane analysis: to the first order non linear ODE, depending on two parameters, we associate a family of plane curves; and we translate the solution of the fluid mechanics problem into a geometrical problem. In the fourth section, we make judicious use of resultants and discriminants computations to get a cell decomposition of the parameter space to classify the different behaviors of the (generalized) solutions.

2. FORMULATION OF THE PROBLEM

The flow is assumed to be two-dimensional and irrotational, we neglect viscosity and compressibility of the fluid. The bottom is assumed to be horizontal. We will take a coordinate system (x, y) moving with the wave at the same speed. The x-coordinate is taken horizontally to the right and the y-coordinate is taken vertically upward, the bottom equation is $y = 0$. In this moving frame, the wave profile is stationary and there is an underlying flow traveling in the opposite direction. Let us recall that following Newton's law of motion, the description of the flow is governed by the Euler equations in the plane which express mass and energy conservations. They are constraints on the velocity (u, v) and the pressure p. The pressure can be replaced by $p = p_0 + \tau K$, where p_0 is the pressure of the air above the free boundary, τ is the surface tension coefficient and K is the curvature of the free boundary.

2.1 Approximation in shallow water regime

In shallow water regime, following Serre, Green and Naghdi, we assume that the horizontal velocity $u(x, y)$ can be approximated by its averaged value $\bar{u}(x)$ over the water column, so in Euler equations $u(x, y)$ is replaced by $\bar{u}(x)$; $\bar{u}_x$ denotes the derivative with respect to x (more generally a subscript denotes a derivative). Applying the incompressibility hypothesis, we can also replace the vertical velocity $v(x, y)$ by $-y\,\bar{u}_x$. Finally, the new variables characterizing the flow are the elevation of the free surface $h(x)$ and the averaged horizontal velocity $\bar{u}(x)$. Time dependent Euler equations are also approximated and become the following two PDEs, called (gravity-capillarity) Serre-Green-Naghi equations:

$$h_t + [h\,\bar{u}]_x = 0,$$

$$[h\,\bar{u}]_t + \left[h\,\bar{u}^2 + \tfrac{1}{2}g\,h^2 + \tfrac{1}{3}h^2\gamma - \tau R\right]_x = 0, \qquad (1)$$

g being the acceleration due to gravity and

$$R = h\,h_{xx}\left(1 + h_x^2\right)^{-3/2} + \left(1 + h_x^2\right)^{-1/2},$$

$$\gamma = h\,(\bar{u}_x^2 - \bar{u}_{xt} - \bar{u}\,\bar{u}_{xx}),$$

γ being the vertical acceleration of the fluid at the free surface.

In the second equation, which expresses energy conservation, we note that γ contains a derivative in t. To concentrate all such derivatives in the first bracket, we consider two conservation laws of other momentums. Formally this amounts to add and subtract in equation (1) a third of $(h^3\bar{u}_x)_{xt}$ to $h\bar{u}$ in order to get the following equation (2).

$$\left[h\bar{u} - \frac{(h^3\bar{u}_x)_x}{3}\right]_t + \qquad (2)$$

$$\left[h\bar{u}^2 + \frac{gh^2}{2} - \frac{2h^3\bar{u}_x^2}{3} - \frac{h^3\bar{u}\bar{u}_{xx}}{3} - h^2h_x\bar{u}\bar{u}_x - \tau R\right]_x = 0,$$

$$\left[\bar{u} - \frac{(h^3\bar{u}_x)_x}{3\,h}\right]_t + \qquad (3)$$

$$\left[\frac{\bar{u}^2}{2} + g\,h - \frac{h^2\,\bar{u}_x^2}{2} - \frac{\bar{u}\,(h^3\bar{u}_x)_x}{3\,h} - \frac{\tau\,h_{xx}}{(1 + h_x^2)^{3/2}}\right]_x = 0.$$

Similarly considering the derivative of the similar quantity divided out by h, we get equation (3). Equations (2) and (3) also imply energy conservation, so we can replace the second equation of (1) by equations (2) and (3).

Since our aim is to study steady waves, for now on, we set to zero all derivatives with respect to t. Integrating the first equation of (1), we obtain a constant that we set to $-cd$. For a physical interpretation, we consider a $2L$-periodic solution, we have:

$$d = \frac{1}{2L}\int_{-L}^{L} h\,\mathrm{d}x, \qquad -c\,d = \frac{1}{2L}\int_{-L}^{L} h\,\bar{u}\,\mathrm{d}x, \qquad (4)$$

thus c is the wave phase velocity observed in the frame of reference without mean flow. This extends to the case of solitary waves, by letting L tend to infinity. The values c, g and τ serve to define three constants used, in fluid mechanics, to classify the waves: the (squared) Froude number $\mathcal{F} = c^2/gd$, the Bond number $\mathcal{B} = \tau/gd^2$ and the Weber number $\mathcal{W} = \frac{\mathcal{B}}{\mathcal{F}} = \tau/c^2d$.

The mass conservation of (1) yields

$$\bar{u} = -cd/h, \tag{5}$$

hence

$$\bar{u}_x = \frac{cd}{h^2}, \quad \bar{u}_{xx} = -2\frac{cd}{h^3}. \tag{6}$$

Then, replacing R by its value, substitutions of $\bar{u}$ and its derivatives into (2) and (3), followed by an integration, give

$$\frac{\mathcal{F}d}{h} + \frac{h^2}{2d^2} + \frac{\gamma h^2}{3gd^2} - \frac{\mathcal{B}hh_{xx}}{(1+h_x^2)^{\frac{3}{2}}} - \frac{\mathcal{B}}{(1+h_x^2)^{\frac{1}{2}}} = \mathcal{F} + \frac{1}{2} - \mathcal{B} + K_1. \tag{7}$$

$$\frac{\mathcal{F}d^2}{2h^2} + \frac{h}{d} + \frac{\mathcal{F}d^2h_{xx}}{3h} - \frac{\mathcal{F}d^2h_x^2}{6h^2} - \frac{\mathcal{B}dh_{xx}}{(1+h_x^2)^{\frac{3}{2}}} = \frac{\mathcal{F}}{2} + 1 + \frac{\mathcal{F}K_2}{2}, \tag{8}$$

with

$$\gamma/g = \mathcal{F}d^3h_{xx}/h^2 - \mathcal{F}d^3h_x^2/h^3, \tag{9}$$

the K_1 and K_2 are integration constants.

In the case of solitary waves, which interest us here, all these derivations remain correct with $K_1 = K_2 = 0$.

2.2 Solitary waves

Letting $K_1 = K_2 = 0$, in equations (7) and (8), we obtain two nonlinear differential equations governing the solitary waves solutions.

A key remark is that once we replace γ by its value, the terms in h_{xx} of these two equations are similar.

Computing (7)$-(h/d)\times$(8) in order to eliminate h_{xx} between (7) and (8), one obtains

$$\frac{\mathcal{F}d}{2h} - \frac{h^2}{2d^2} - \frac{\mathcal{F}dh_x^2}{6h} - \frac{\mathcal{B}}{(1+h_x^2)^{\frac{1}{2}}} = \mathcal{F} + \frac{1}{2} - \mathcal{B} - \frac{(\mathcal{F}+2)h}{2d}, \tag{10}$$

that is a first-order differential equation for h.

Normalizing d to $d = 1$, writing $h' = \frac{\mathrm{d}h(x)}{\mathrm{d}x}$ and multiplying by h, equation (10) becomes

$$F(h',h) := \frac{\mathcal{F}h'^2}{3} + \frac{2\mathcal{B}h}{\left(1+h'^2\right)^{\frac{1}{2}}} - \mathcal{F}$$

$$+ (2\mathcal{F}+1-2\mathcal{B})h - (\mathcal{F}+2)h^2 + h^3 = 0. \tag{11}$$

Notice that, by taking the derivative of this equation with respect to x, assuming that h is twice derivable, we obtain a system equivalent to the system formed by equations (7) and (8). In other words, starting from the first equations (1) in their steady solitary wave form, our manipulations amount to perform a differential elimination but directed by a physical intuition.

Now, we are reduced to a mathematical problem: study the solutions of the nonlinear first order differential equation $F(h',h) = 0$.

In a strict physical interpretation only the twice derivable functions $h(x)$ (such that the curvature of the wave, thence the capillarity force are well defined) should be considered. However in the next section, we will see that it is worthwhile to also consider less regular solutions of this equation; they are sometimes called singular solutions.

3. GENERALIZED SOLUTIONS

3.1 Corner waves

The theory of corner waves goes back to G.G. Stokes [24] who, in 1880, conjectured that finite amplitude crest gravity waves are limited by a wave with a corner at its crest; he proved that this corner has a 120 degrees angle. It also can be proved that the two branches at the crest of this highest corner wave have vanishing curvature. In other words, if $y = h(x)$ is the equation of the free surface and the crest occurs at $x = 0$ then $h'(0_-) = -h'(0_+) = \frac{\sqrt{3}}{3}$ and $h''(0_-) = h''(0_+) = 0$ (see Figure 3). For a presentation of Stokes waves see [10] and Wikipedia or another encyclopedia for a brief introduction.

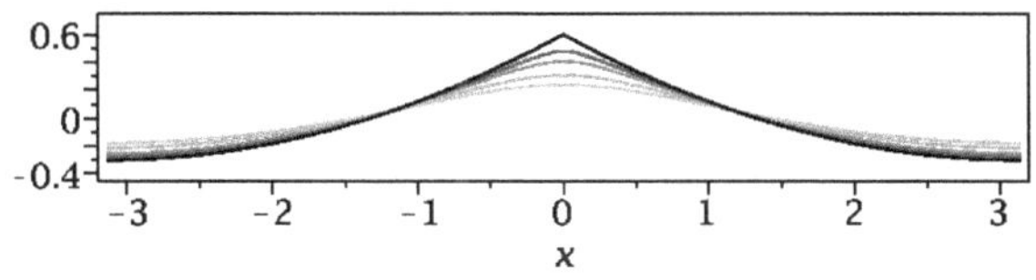

Figure 3: Stokes' limit wave

More recently, a famous equation was introduced by Camassa and Holm [3] to provide another simple model for waves in shallow water,

$$u_t + 2\kappa u_x - u_{xxt} + 3uu_x = 2u_xu_{xx} + uu_{xxx}.$$

It depends on a parameter κ which, in this context, should be positive so that the solitary wave solutions are smooth solitons.

When κ is zero, the Camassa–Holm this equation has so-called "peakon" solitary wave solutions. The wave slope at the peak does not vanish but jumps from one value to the opposite value. In other words, they are shaped like the graph of the function $h(x) = \exp(-|x|)$. Moreover, explicit formulas for the peakon interactions are known, [22]. There is an extensive literature on Camassa–Holm equation.

In 2013, a unified wave model for progressive gravity waves in finite water depth was proposed by Liao [19]. Based on the symmetry and the exact wave equations, it admits not only all traditional smooth periodic solitary waves but also the peaked solitary waves including the famous peaked solitary waves of Camassa–Holm equation mentioned above.

In all these cases, the corner wave can be viewed as a limit of a sequence of regular functions $h_\kappa(x)$ solutions of a differential equation depending on κ.

3.2 Singular solutions

Singular solutions of an ordinary differential equation of the form $G(x, y, dy/dx) = 0$ are not always clearly defined. As written in [17], in the classical treaties (see [16]) the answer is informal: a "general solution" is defined to be a one parameter family of solutions and a singular solution is a solution which is not contained in that family, see also [5]. Clearly if G depends on a parameter λ the envelope or the limit of the graphs of a family of solutions will be the graphs of general solutions. Note that these functions need not have singular points. These are the generalized solutions usually admitted under the vocable of singular solutions. See [17] for a formalization of these concepts and also the book of V. Arnol'd [1].

In computer algebra, the works of E. Hubert [13, 14, 15] present a computational view on general as well as singular solutions, that have enveloping properties of polynomial ordinary differential equations. We can also cite the work initiated by M. Hamburger already in 1893 [12].

Here, we consider another kind of generalized solutions which could also be called singular.

3.3 Our generalized solutions

The differential equations governing the steady waves of the (gravity-capillarity) Serre-Green-Naghi equations, (7) and (8) presented in Section 2, involve the derivative h_x only by its square. Since these equations express the conservative laws, the non regular solutions $h(x)$ such that the derivative jumps at some points, but such that $h_x(x)^2$ and $h_{xx}(x)$ are continuous have a physical interest.

More precisely, in the sequel of this paper, we will investigate both the regular solutions and the "peakon" or angular solutions $h(x)$ such that h_x is differentiable except for a finite number of values x_i, $i = 1..N$, at which only $h_x(x)^2$ is continuous and differentiable and $h_{xx}(x_i) = 0$.

Unlike the singular solutions of the previous subsection, these peakon solutions are not isolated and we do not know yet if they are limit solutions of a system of differential equation generalizing the Serre-Green-Naghi equations and involving more parameters.

3.4 Phase plane analysis

In order to investigate the number and behavior of the solutions and peakon solutions (defined in the previous subsection) of the differential equation $F_{\mathcal{F},\mathcal{B}}(h,h') = 0$, with respect to the pair of parameters $(\mathcal{F},\mathcal{B}) \in [-1,2]^2$, our approach is to describe graphically the variations of h and h', through the corresponding family of real algebraic curves $C_{\mathcal{F},\mathcal{B}} \in \mathbf{R}^2$. The algebraic implicit equation of $C_{\mathcal{F},\mathcal{B}}$ is $F_{\mathcal{F},\mathcal{B}}(h,h') = 0$. We will decompose the parameters space $(\mathcal{F},\mathcal{B})$, with our restriction to the square $[0,2]^2$, into sub-domains where the plane curves $C_{\mathcal{F},\mathcal{B}}$ have the same "shape" (in particular the same topology). Some sub-domains can be very small, to overcome this computational difficulty, the study of the curves delimiting the sub-domains will be performed with a certified topology (see, e.g. [9] or [4] and the references therein).

Let us illustrate our approach with an example: the phase plane description for some values of the parameters that we chose randomly, $\mathcal{F} = 0.4$ and $\mathcal{B} = 0.9$. The corresponding curve $C_{0.4,0.9}$ is shown on the left of Figure 4. It can be plotted by simply using a discretization, e.g. using Mathlab or drawn with a guaranteed topology using specialized programs such as the a algebraic curves package of Maple or Axel [2]. In particular, this means that ovals of whatever size are preliminary detected relying on exact (given certain precision) numerical and algebraic computations.

After computing the points of the curve with a horizontal tangent and the singular points, we can decompose the curve into a finite number N of portions of of graphs $\Gamma_j, j = 1..N$ of type $h = \phi_j(h')$, for some differentiable functions $\phi_j, j = 1..N$. Moreover, since when h' is positive (resp. negative), h should increase (resp. decrease), so each Γ_j can be oriented. See Figure 4 where there are $N = 6$ oriented portions of graphs. The points with a horizontal tangent or a singular point satisfy the condition $\partial F/\partial h' = 0$.

Then, on each branch, the corresponding differential equation $dx = \frac{dh}{\phi(h)}$ can be solved numerically. It provides, on the corresponding interval, an approximate solution $h(x)$ which is qualitatively correct.

In this example, there are four points such that $\partial F/\partial h' = 0$: $A_1 = (0,1)$, $A_2 = (0,0.4)$, $A_3 \approx (2.1,1.955)$ and $A_4 \approx (-2.1,1.955)$. Call B_1 and B_2 the intersections of the curve with the h'-axis. Then, we get the following going up branches: Γ_1 from B_1 to A_3, Γ_2 from A_2 to A_1 (on the right side) and Γ_3 from A_1 to A_3. Symmetrically, the down-going branches $\Gamma_j, j = 4,5,6$ are in the left half-plane $h' < 0$.

Constrained by the asymptotic conditions, we only consider loops starting from A_1 and arriving at A_1. In this example, the only continuous one is going down on Γ_5 from A_1 to A_2 (on the left side), then going up on Γ_2 from A_2 to A_1 (on the right side). It will correspond to the unique differentiable solution $h(x)$ of the differential equation.

As we said in the previous subsection, we will also consider other solutions that we call **angular solutions**.

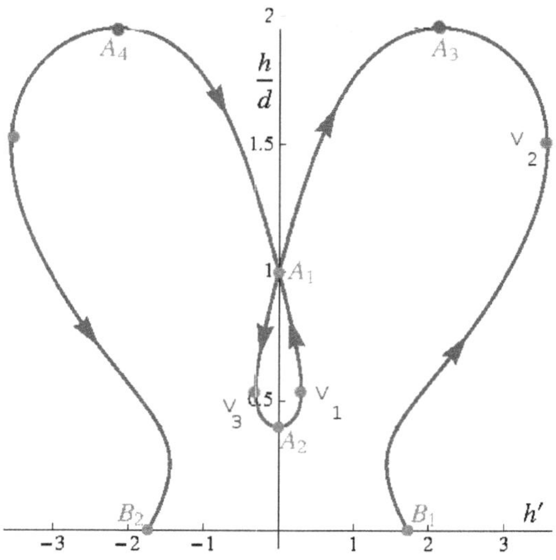

Figure 4: Curve $C_{0.4,0.9}$ of Example1

Note that there are 6 points of the curve $C_{0.4,0.9}$ with a vertical tangent, they are symmetric with respect to the h-axis. We call V_1, V_2, V_3 three of these 6 points, their coordinates are approximately $V_1 = (0.3, 0.5)$, $V_2 = (3.5, 1.5)$, $V_1 = (-0.3, 0.5)$. The two semi second derivatives at these points are zero. The points V_2 belongs to Γ_1 which is not connected to A_1, so we do not consider it; but V_1 and V_3 are connected to A_1 by respectively Γ_2 and Γ_5. So, we can form a discontinuous symmetrical loop going down from A_1 to V_3 (on Γ_5), jumping from V_3 to V_1, then going up from V_1 to A_1 (on Γ_2). It corresponds to an interesting new solitary wave with an angle, a "peakon", $h(x)$ which satisfies all the conservative laws. We can as well consider a loop

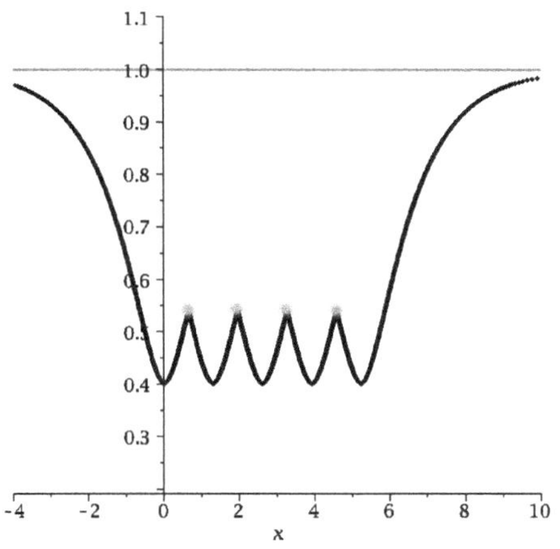

Figure 5: Multiangular wave

going down from A_1 to A_2 (on the left side), then going up from A_2 to V_1 , then jumping from V_1 to V_3, then cycling through V_3, A_2, V_1, V_3, then going up from A_2 to A_1. The corresponding wave has several "peaks", see Figure 5. The angular points are emphasized by green solid disks.

4. A FAMILY OF PLANE CURVES

By the discussion in the previous section, we are led to study and classify the family of curves $\mathcal{C}_{\mathcal{F},\mathcal{B}}$, in the real (k, h) plane, defined by the algebraic (but non polynomial) equation $F(k, h) = 0$ with exact coefficients

$$F(k,h) = \frac{\mathcal{F}k^2}{3} + \frac{2\mathcal{B}h}{(1+k^2)^{\frac{1}{2}}} - \mathcal{F}$$

$$+ (2\mathcal{F} + 1 - 2\mathcal{B})h - (\mathcal{F}+2)h^2 + h^3 = 0, \qquad (12)$$

To compute the points with horizontal or vertical tangent and the singular points, we will use resultants after changes of coordinate.

We have the following partial derivatives of F with respect to h and k

$$F_h = \frac{2\,\mathcal{B}}{(1+k^2)^{\frac{1}{2}}} + (2\mathcal{F}+1-2\mathcal{B}) - 2\,(\mathcal{F}+2)\,h + 3\,h^2,$$

$$F_k = \frac{2\,\mathcal{F}\,k}{3} + (\frac{2\,\mathcal{B}\,k\,h}{(1+k^2)^{\frac{3}{2}}}.$$

4.1 Points on the h-axis

The points on the h-axis are important; to determine them it suffices to substitute $k = 0$ and solve the univariate equation $F_{\mathcal{F},\mathcal{B}}(0, h) = 0$, which gives either $h = 1$ with multiplicity 2, or $h = \mathcal{F}$. Call A_1 and A_2 the points of coordinates $(0, 1)$ and $(0, \mathcal{F})$.

In order to investigate the local behavior at A_1, we compute the second-order Taylor expansion of F at that point

$$(\mathcal{F} - 3\mathcal{B})\,k^2 - 3\,(\mathcal{F}-1)\,(h-1)^2 = 0.$$

Therefore, if $(\mathcal{F} - 1)(\mathcal{F} - 3\mathcal{B}) < 0$, A_1 is an isolated point of the curve $C_{\mathcal{F},\mathcal{B}}$; this implies that the only solution is the trivial one $h = 1$. If $(\mathcal{F} - 1)(\mathcal{F} - 3\mathcal{B}) > 0$, A_1 is a double point corresponding to the crossing of two branches of $C_{\mathcal{F},\mathcal{B}}$; hence there is no obstruction (at the level of this preliminary local analysis) for the existence of a solitary wave. If $\mathcal{F} = 1$, then $A_1 = A_2$ and we must consider the third-order Taylor expansion

$$(1 - 3\mathcal{B})\,k^2 + 3\,(h-1)^3 - (h-1)\,k^2 = 0.$$

Therefore if $3\mathcal{B} > 1$, (resp. $3\mathcal{B} < 1$), $C_{\mathcal{F},\mathcal{B}}$ admits at A_1 a cusp above (resp. below) A_1; while if $3\mathcal{B} = 1$, the Taylor expansion corresponds to three lines including $h = 1$; i.e., no obstruction (at this local analysis) for the existence of a (non constant) solitary wave.

Now, a Taylor expansion of F at the point A_2, i.e. $(k = 0, h = \mathcal{F})$, yields

$$3\,(\mathcal{F}-1)^2\,(h-\mathcal{F}) = \mathcal{F}\,(3\mathcal{B}-1)\,k^2.$$

So, when $\{\mathcal{F} \neq 1, 3\mathcal{B} \neq 1\}$, we get a point with an horizontal tangent; it is of convex type if $3\mathcal{B} > 1$ and concave if $3\mathcal{B} < 1$. Therefore, if $\mathcal{F} < 1$ and $3\mathcal{B} > 1$, or if $\mathcal{F} > 1$ and $3\mathcal{B} < 1$, there is no obstruction (at this local analysis level) for the existence of a solitary wave. While if $\mathcal{F} < 1$ and $\mathcal{F} < 3\mathcal{B} < 1$, or if $\mathcal{F} > 1$ and $\mathcal{F} > 3\mathcal{B} > 1$, this local analysis only permits an angular solitary wave.

When $\mathcal{F} \neq 1$ and $3\mathcal{B} = 1$, the Taylor expansion of F at the point A_2 yields

$$\mathcal{F}(h'^4 \sim 4(\mathcal{F}-1)^2(h-d).$$

In other words, the curve has a flat point (the curvature vanishes).

Notice that at the end of this first local analysis, our discussion partitioned the parameter plane $(\mathcal{F}, \mathcal{B})$ into domains delimited by the three lines $\mathcal{F} = 1$, $\mathcal{B} = \frac{1}{3}$ and $\mathcal{F} - 3\mathcal{B} = 0$, and discarded the domain defined by $(\mathcal{F} - 1)(\mathcal{F} - 3\mathcal{B}) < 0$.

4.1.1 *Points with a horizontal tangent*

These points satisfy the two equations $F = 0$ and $\partial F/\partial k = 0$. For $k \neq 0$, the second equation vanishes when $\mathcal{F}^2(1 + k^2)^3 = (3\mathcal{B}h)^2$. From which we express k^2 as a function in h and replace this expression into the equation $F = 0$. We get an equation depending only on h, but with a cubic root operator. To get rid of it, and deal with polynomials, we introduce a new variable Y such that $h = (\mathcal{F}/3\mathcal{B})Y^3$, thence $k^2 = Y^2 - 1$ with $Y \geq 1$. We are led to the following polynomial equation in Y

$$f(Y) = \mathcal{F}^2 Y^9 - (3\mathcal{F}-2)\mathcal{F}\mathcal{B}Y^6$$

$$+ 9\mathcal{B}^2(1 + 2\mathcal{F} - 2\mathcal{B})Y^3 + 27\mathcal{B}^3 Y^2 - 36\mathcal{B}^3 = 0. \qquad (13)$$

The adapted tool to discuss the number of real roots of f is its discriminant $D_1(\mathcal{F}, \mathcal{B})$.

The real trace of the discriminant locus $\mathcal{D}_1$ is an algebraic curve in the $(\mathcal{F}, \mathcal{B})$-plane, it characterizes the values of $(\mathcal{F}, \mathcal{B})$ where $f(Y)$ has (real or complex) multiple roots. A key property, for our analysis, is that this curve $\mathcal{D}_1$ divides the parametric plane into domains where f has a constant number of real roots. However, since we do not have a necessary and sufficient condition, two adjacent domains delimited by $\mathcal{D}_1$ may correspond to the same number of real roots, they should be merged to form only one domain. The sub-domains of these domains delimited by the implicit curve defined by $f_{\mathcal{F},\mathcal{B}}(1) = 0$, in the parametric plane, have a constant number of real roots greater than 1. Also, two adjacent sub-domains may have the same number of real roots greater than 1 and should be merged. Eventually, we explicitly construct a partition into connex domains. In each such domain the number of local extrema of h on $C_{\mathcal{F},\mathcal{B}}$ is fixed, and we are able to classify the possible shapes of $C_{\mathcal{F},\mathcal{B}}$.

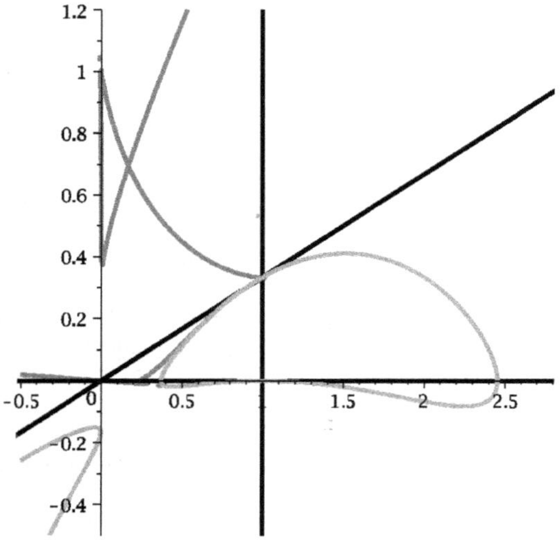

Figure 6: Discriminant loci

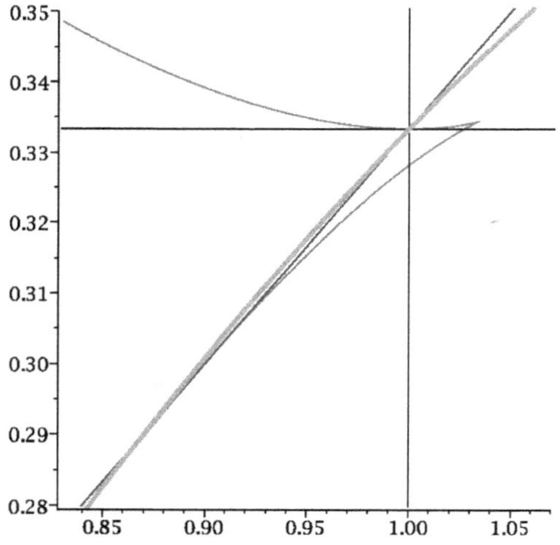

Figure 7: Zoom on a detail

4.1.2 Points with a vertical tangent

We follow roughly the same method to study the points of $C_{(\mathcal{F},\mathcal{B})}$ with a vertical tangent. They satisfy the two equations $F = 0$ and $\partial F/\partial h = 0$. Combining these equations, and introducing a new variable Z such that $k^2 = Z^2 - 1$ thence $\mathcal{F}(Z^2 - 1) = 3(h-1)(2h^2 - h - 1)$. Eliminating h by the computation of a resultant, we get a polynomial $g(Z, \mathcal{F}, \mathcal{B})$, of degree 6 in Z, which plays the same role than the polynomial $f(Y)$ in the previous paragraph.

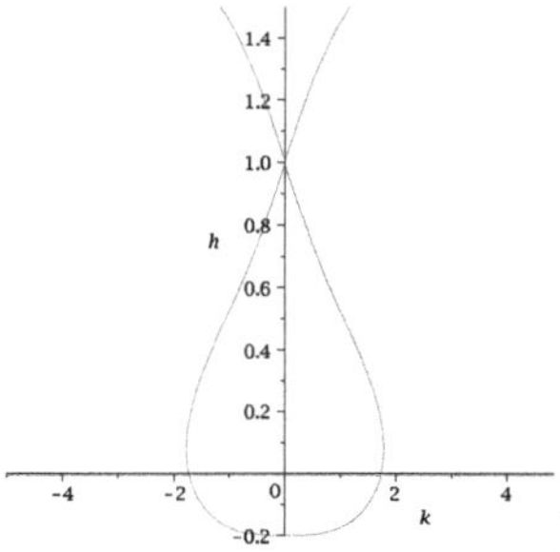

Figure 8: $C_{-02,032}$

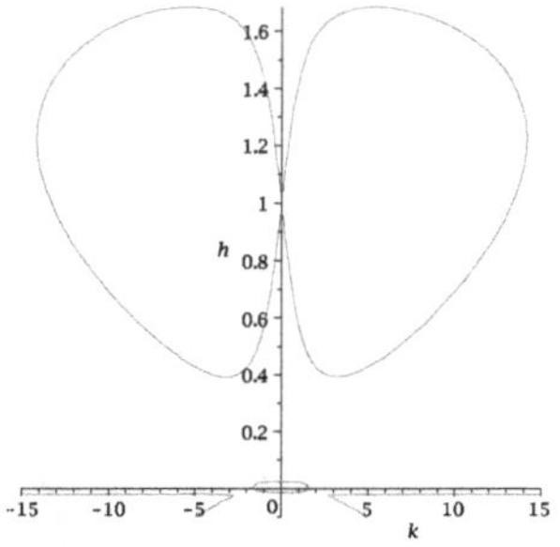

Figure 9: $C_{01,032}$

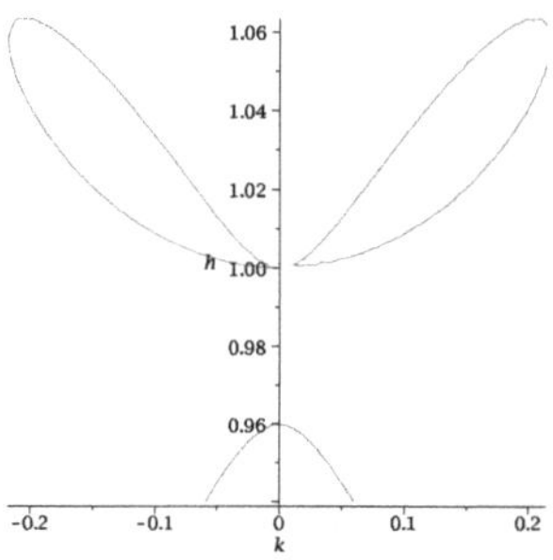

Figure 10: $C_{096,032}$

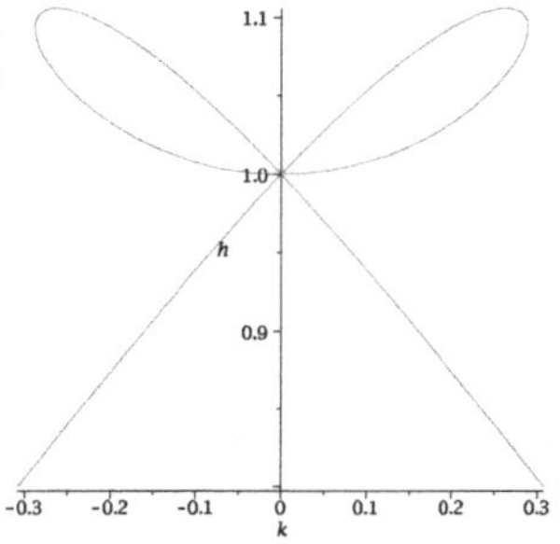

Figure 11: Extremal curve

Then we compute the discriminant polynomial of g with respect to Z, we find a polynomial $D_2(\mathcal{F}, \mathcal{B})$. As explained above, it allows to decompose the parameters space into domains where the number of points with a vertical tangent is constant. We also require that these points satisfy $h \geq 0$.

Then we take the intersection of the two families of sub-domains defined by $D_1(\mathcal{F}, \mathcal{B})$ and by $D_2(\mathcal{F}, \mathcal{B})$.

Eventually, we explicitly construct a "cell decomposition". In each such cell the number of local extrema of h and the number of local extrema of k on $C_{\mathcal{F},\mathcal{B}}$ is fixed, and we are able to classify the possible shapes of $C_{\mathcal{F},\mathcal{B}}$, with respect to admissible paths connecting A_1 either to a point with $k = 0$ or to a point with a vertical tangent.

4.1.3 Pictures

Using the commands *discrim*() and *factor*() of the computer algebra system Maple, we decompose the discriminant polynomial D_1 into the product of a square $(\mathcal{F} - 3\mathcal{B})^2$ by another polynomial D of degree 10 in $(\mathcal{F}, \mathcal{B})$. The zero locus of D (in red) together with the lines $\mathcal{B} = \frac{1}{3}$, $3\mathcal{B} = \mathcal{F}$ and $\mathcal{F} = 1$ are shown in Figure 6.

We also decompose the other discriminant polynomial D_2, with respect to Z. We find the product of the same polynomial D by powers of $\mathcal{F}$, powers of $\mathcal{B}$, and by the cube of another polynomial $D_3(\mathcal{F}, \mathcal{B})$. The zero locus of D_3 is shown in green in Figure 6.

The line defined by the equation $\mathcal{F} - 3\mathcal{B} = 0$ is of special interest since it corresponds to a double root at a fixed value $Y = 1$, which corresponds to the double point at $h = 1$ and $k = 0$, and another simple solution $Y(\mathcal{B})$.

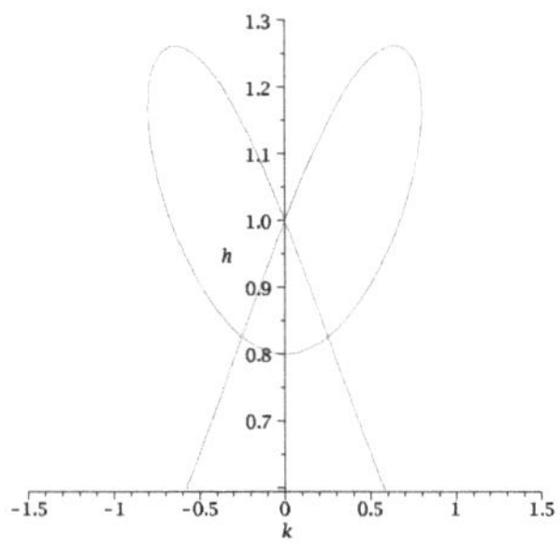

Figure 12: Curve $C_{08,03538}$ from the discriminant locus

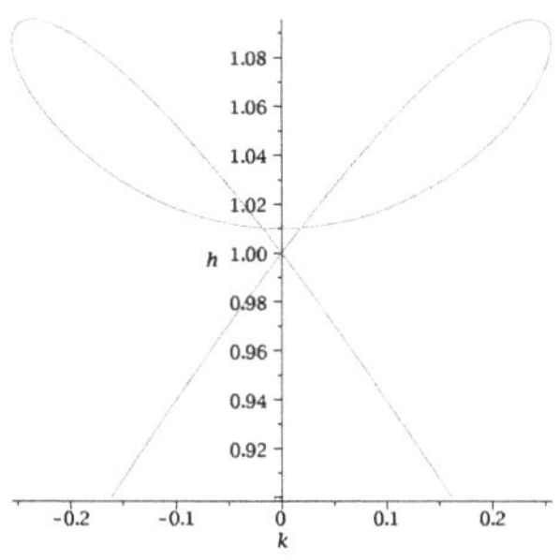

Figure 13: Semi extremal curve

4.1.4 *Classification and special behaviors*

Considering each of the delimited domains, allow to classify all the possible curves $C_{\mathcal{F},\mathcal{B}}$, by the relative location of their points with horizontal tangent, vertical tangent, singularity. For each such type of curve, we analyzed all the possible admissible paths (with respect to the orientation) departing from A_1 and arriving to a point with a vertical tangent, or to a point of the line $k = 0$. To each of them is associated a regular or an angular solitary wave.

We found only two types of regular solitary waves: a crest when $\mathcal{F} > 1$ and a through when $\mathcal{F} < 1$, they appear for some sub-domain of the square. For $(\mathcal{F}, \mathcal{B})$ in another sub-domain, we may have a multi angular solitary wave, they correspond to curves similar to the one in Figure 4.

Then in another parameter domain, we find curves similar to $C_{-0.2,0.32}$, see Figure 8 which allow only one angular solitary wave as in Figure 15. Here is a list of additional extremal behaviors.

1. The limiting case where $(\mathcal{F}, \mathcal{B})$ belongs to a branch of the discriminant locus e.g. when $(\mathcal{F} = 0.8, \mathcal{B} = .3538557)$ approximately, we obtain the curve shown in Figure 12. There is a a connex path but with an angle going from A_1 to a lower point on $h' = 0$. It gives rise to a weak regular wave shown in Figure 16, which has two points where the regularity is only C^1 (we represented them by changing the colors of the branches).

2. A tiny branch of the discriminant with $\mathcal{F} > \infty$ gives rise to another interesting type of "semi extremal curve" e.g. $C_{1.01,0.33341215}$, shown in Figure 13 , it corresponds to (multi) angular weak crests, shown in Figure 17. The angles are indicated with a red bullet and the weak defect of regularity is indicated with a green bullet.

3. The most extremal curve is $C_{1,\frac{1}{3}}$ (see Figure 11) since it has a branch with an horizontal tangent passing through the point A_1 which means that the decreases at infinity is algebraic and not exponential. It admits a symmetric single angular solitary wave.

5. CONCLUSION

In this paper, we have presented for the computer algebra community, an actual problem coming from the fluid mechanics community. Indeed, the discovery of giant ocean waves, sometimes called freak or rogue waves, renewed the interest of that community in classical water wave problems and their "mathematical" aspects. We explained how the deep understanding of the solitary capillary-gravity waves in shallow water, including the investigation of singular or "angular" waves, could benefit from the mathematical description of the shapes of a family of plane real algebraic curves depending on two real parameters.

Then, relying on computer algebra techniques (adapted coordinates changes, geometric interpretation and computations of resultants and discriminants, certified graph drawing) we were able to list all the possible shapes of the phase diagram curves and all possible regular or "angular" solitary waves.

Of course, much work remains to be done. In particular, it would be worthwhile to investigate all the periodic steady waves. It would also be very interesting to derive from the primitive equation of motion, a set of equations depending on more (physical) parameters such that the angular solutions described here appear as limit of regular solutions of this new set of equations. Then, our angular solutions will become singular solutions in the more usual sense.

6. REFERENCES

[1] ARNOLD, V. I., Geometrical Methods In The Theory Of Ordinary Differential Equations, *Springer-Verlag* (1988).

[2] See HTTP://AXEL.INRIA.FR.

[3] CAMASSA, R.; HOLM, D.D., An integrable shallow water equation with peaked solitons, *Phys. Rev. Lett. 71 (11): 1661–1664*, (1993),

[4] CHENG,J ET AL.., On the topology of real algebraic plane curves. *Mathematics in Computer Science, Springer, 4 (1), pp.113–137.* (2010), https://hal.inria.fr/inria-0051717.

[5] COHN, R. The general solution of a first order differential polynomial. Proceedings of the American Mathematical Society 55,1, 14–16. (1976).

[6] DUTYKH, D., CLAMOND, D., MILEWSKY, P. & MITSOTAKIS, M., An implicit-explicit finite volume scheme for fully nonlinear Serre equations. *Eur. J. App. Math.* **24**, 761–787, (2013).

[7] DUTYKH, D. AND CLAMOND, D., Efficient computation of steady solitary gravity waves. *Wave Motion* **51**, 86–99, (2014).

[8] CLAMOND, D., DUTYKH, D. AND AND GALLIGO, A, Extreme solitary capillarity-gravity waves in shallow water. *In preparation*, (2015).

[9] GONZALEZ-VEGA, L. & NECULA, I., Efficient topology determination of implicitly defined algebraic plane curves. *Computer Aided Geometric Design* **19**, **9**, 719–743, (2002).

[10] GRANT, M.A., Standing Stokes waves of maximum height, *Journal of Fluid Mechanics* 60 (3): 593âĂŞ604, (1973).

[11] GREEN, A.E AND NAGHDI, P.M, A derivation of equations for wave propagation of water of variable depth. *J. of Fluid Mechanics*, 78, 237–246, (1976).

[12] HAMBURGER, M. Ueber die singulären lösungen der algebraischen differentialgleichungen erster ordnung. *J. Reine Ang. Math.*, 112, 205–246, (1893).

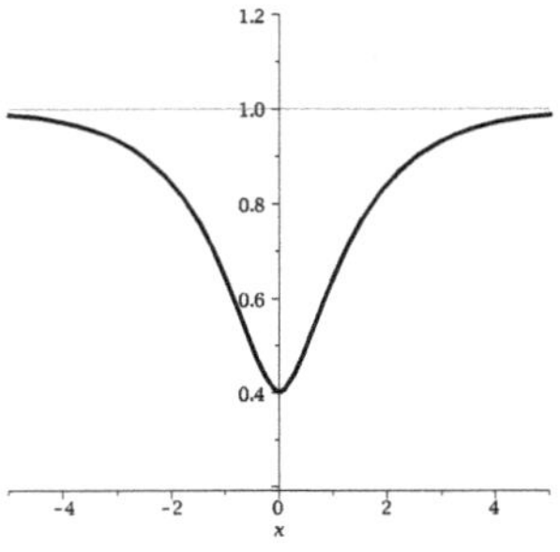

Figure 14: Regular

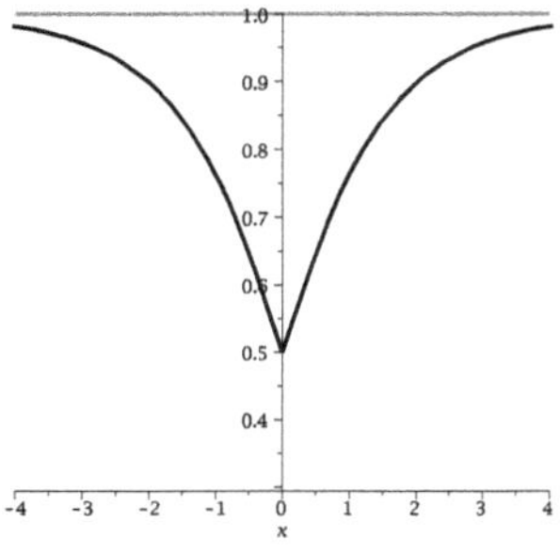

Figure 15: Angular

[13] HUBERT, E., The general solution of an ordinary differential equation. *In ISSAC'96.* ACM Press. (1996).

[14] HUBERT, E., Detecting Degenerate Behaviors in Non-Linear Differential Equations of First order Algebraic Differential Equations. *Theoretical Computer Science*, vol 187 (1-2), pages 7–25, (1997).

[15] HUBERT, E. (1998), Essential components of an algebraic differential equation. *Journal of Symbolic Computations*, volume 28(4-5), 657–680, (1999).

[16] INCE, E., Ordinary Differential Equations. Dover (1956).

[17] IZUMIYA, S. AND YU, J. How to define singular solutions. Kodai Math. J.16 , 227–234, (1993).

[18] LANG, S, Algebra. Chapter 5. em Addison-Wesley, (1984).

[19] LIAO, S.J., Do peaked solitary water waves indeed exist?, *Communications in Nonlinear Science and Numerical Simulation*, 19:1792–1821, (2014).

[20] OKAMOTO, I. AND SHOJI, M., The mathematical theory of permanent progressive water-waves. *Adv. Ser. Nonlin. Dyn.*, 20. Worlds Scientific. (2001).

[21] OSBORN, A., Nonlinear ocean waves and the inverse scattering transform. *Academic Press.*, 97, Elsevier (2010).

[22] PARKER, A., On the Camassa–Holm equation and a direct method of solution. III. N-soliton solutions, *Proc. R. Soc. Lond. Ser. A Math. Phys. Eng. Sci.* 461: 3893–3911, (2005).

[23] SERRE, F., Contribution à l'étude des écoulements permanents et variables dans les canaux. *Houille Blanche*, 8, 374–388, (1953).

[24] STOKES, G.G., Supplement to a paper on the theory of oscillatory waves, *Mathematical and Physical Papers, Volume I, Cambridge University Press*, pp. 314–326, (1880).

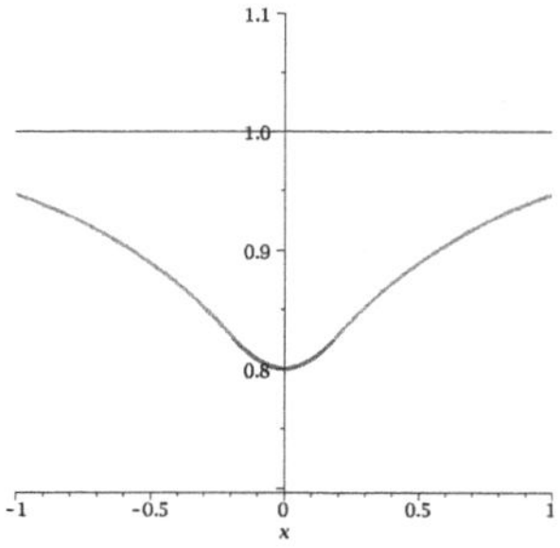

Figure 16: Weak regular wave

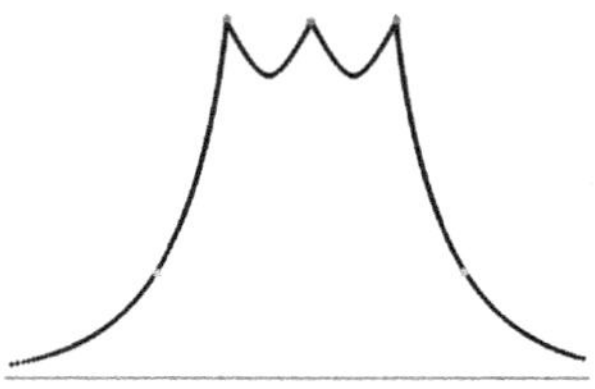

Figure 17: Weak multi angular crest wave

Graph-Coloring Ideals: Nullstellensatz Certificates, Gröbner bases for Chordal Graphs, and Hardness of Gröbner Bases

Jesús A. De Loera
University of California, Davis
deloera@math.ucdavis.edu

Susan Margulies
United States Naval Academy
margulie@usna.edu

Michael Pernpeintner
Technische Universität München
michaelpernpeintner@gmail.com

Eric Riedl
Harvard University
ebriedl@math.harvard.edu

David Rolnick
Massachusetts Institute of Technology
drolnick@math.mit.edu

Gwen Spencer
Smith College
gspencer@smith.edu

Despina Stasi
University of Cyprus and Illinois Institute of Technology
despina.stasi@gmail.com

Jon Swenson
University of Washington
jmswen@math.washington.edu

ABSTRACT

We consider a well-known family of polynomial ideals encoding the problem of graph-k-colorability. Our paper describes how the inherent combinatorial structure of the ideals implies several interesting algebraic properties. Specifically, we provide lower bounds on the difficulty of computing Gröbner bases and Nullstellensatz certificates for the coloring ideals of general graphs. We revisit the fact that computing a Gröbner basis is NP-hard and prove a robust notion of hardness derived from the inapproximability of coloring problems. For chordal graphs, however, we explicitly describe a Gröbner basis for the coloring ideal and provide a polynomial-time algorithm to construct it.

Categories and Subject Descriptors

I.1.2 [**SYMBOLIC AND ALGEBRAIC MANIPULATION**]: Algebraic algorithms; F.2.1 [**ANALYSIS OF ALGORITHMS AND PROBLEM COMPLEXITY**]: Computations on polynomials, Computations in finite fields

Keywords

Groebner basis, coloring ideal, graph coloring, Nullstellensatz, infeasibility certificate, inapproximability

1. INTRODUCTION

Many authors in computer algebra and complexity theory have studied the complexity of Gröbner bases (see e.g., [19, 23, 34, 35, 39] and references therein) and the difficulty of Hilbert's Nullstellensatz (see [5, 6, 7, 12, 28, 29, 33]). With few exceptions authors have concentrated on proving worst-case upper bounds. In this paper we look instead at the behavior of Gröbner bases and Hilbert Nullstellensätze in a concrete combinatorial family of polynomials. Our key point is to study how the structure of graph coloring problems provides lower bounds on the difficulty of finding Gröbner bases and Nullstellensatz certificates, providing a counterpart to lower and upper bound theorems for general polynomial systems.

Many authors have studied the rich connection between graphs and polynomials (see e.g., [2, 3, 13, 26, 30, 32, 37]). Our starting point is Bayer's theorem for 3-colorings [4], further generalized in [15, 17] to k-coloring over a finite field. Suppose we wish to check whether a graph $G = (V, E)$ is k-colorable, and set $n = |V|$. For fields $\mathbb{K}$ of characteristic not dividing k, we define the *k-coloring ideal* $\mathcal{I}_k(G) \subset \mathbb{K}[x_1, \ldots, x_n]$ (also denoted by $\mathcal{I}_G$ if the number of colors is clear) to be the ideal generated by the *vertex polynomials* $\nu_i := x_i^k - 1$, for $1 \leq i \leq n$, and the *edge polynomials* $\eta_{i,j} := \sum_{l=0}^{k-1} x_i^l x_j^{k-1-l}$, for $\{i, j\} \in E$. The set of all vertex and edge polynomials of a graph G is denoted by $\mathcal{F}_G$.

THEOREM 1.1 (SEE [15, 17]). *The graph G is k-colorable if and only if $\mathcal{I}_k(G)$ has a common root in the algebraic closure of $\mathbb{K}$. In other words, G is not k-colorable if and only if $\mathcal{I}_k(G) = \langle 1 \rangle = \mathbb{K}[x_1, \ldots, x_n]$. Moreover, the dimension of the vector space $\mathbb{K}[x_1, \ldots, x_n]/\mathcal{I}_k(G)$ equals $k!$ times the number of distinct k-colorings of G.*

The ideal $\mathcal{I}_k(G)$ has been used for interesting applications to graph theory (see [26] and references there). From the well-known Hilbert Nullstellensatz [10], one can derive *certificates* that a system of polynomials has no solution (i.e., in our case, that a graph does not have a k-coloring).

THEOREM 1.2 (HILBERT'S NULLSTELLENSATZ [10]). *Suppose that $f_1, \ldots, f_m \in \mathbb{K}[x_1, \ldots, x_n]$. Then, there are no*

ISSAC'15, July 6–9, 2015, Bath, United Kingdom.

DOI: http://dx.doi.org/10.1145/2755996.2756639.

solutions to the system $\{f_i = 0\}$ *in the algebraic closure of* $\mathbb{K}$*, if and only if there exist* $\alpha_i \in \mathbb{K}[x_1, \ldots, x_n]$ *such that*

$$\alpha_1 f_1 + \cdots + \alpha_m f_m = 1.$$

We refer to the set $\{\alpha_i\}$ as a *Nullstellensatz certificate*, and measure the complexity of a certificate by its *degree*, defined as the maximum degree of any α_i. If a system is known to have a Nullstellensatz certificate of small constant degree (over a finite field), one can simply find this certificate by a series of linear algebra computations [14, 15, 16]. There are well-known *upper bounds* for the degrees of the coefficients α_i in the Nullstellensatz certificate for *general* systems of polynomials that grow with the number of variables [28]. Furthermore, these bounds turn out to be sharp for some pathological instances.

Connections between complexity theory and the Gröbner bases and Nullstellensätze of coloring ideals have been made in [5, 30, 31]. These include the result that unless NP = coNP, there must exist an infinite family of non-3-colorable graphs for which the minimum degree of a Hilbert Nullstellensatz certificate grows arbitrarily large [16, 31]. We remark that for an ideal I for which the set of zeroes is finite, the vector space dimension of the quotient ring obtained from I is finite, too (see §2.2 of [11]). Zero-dimensional ideals admit special algorithms (see e.g. [20]). Cifuentes and Parrilo [9] identify graph structure within an arbitrary polynomial system and show that this yields faster algorithms for solving systems of polynomials. Our coloring ideals are quite unique as they both have unique structure inherent from the graph relating the polynomials and are zero-dimensional.

This article offers three new contributions in the structure and complexity of Gröbner bases and Nullstellensätze of coloring ideals.

(1) In Section 2.1, we show that the minimal degree of Nullstellensatz certificates of coloring ideals satisfies certain modular constraints and that it grows at least linearly in the number of colors (similar results were observed for other ideals in [8]). We indicate that the field of coefficients has some intriguing influence upon the complexity and propose a conjecture.

(2) It is well-known that many combinatorial problems are hard to solve even approximately. For instance, Khanna et al. [27] have shown it is NP-hard to 4-color a 3-colorable graph. More strongly, even if one is allowed to ignore a particular small (but non-zero) fraction of nodes, it is NP-hard to properly 4-color the remaining nodes.

In Section 2.2, we demonstrate how one can transfer inapproximability results for graphs to inapproximability results for polynomial rings. We prove that it is hard to compute a Gröbner basis for an ideal even if we are allowed to ignore a large subset of the generators for our ideal. Thus the coloring ideal provides a sense of "robust" hardness for the computation of Gröbner bases.

(3) Despite hardness in the general case of computing a Gröbner basis, we might hope that some algorithm could find Gröbner bases efficiently, particularly if we restrict our focus to some special class of systems of polynomials. In Section 3, we prove that computing a Gröbner basis can be done in polynomial time when the associated graph is *chordal*. We describe explicitly the structure of such a Gröbner basis.

For background on the material presented in this paper, we direct the interested reader to the books [1, 10, 11, 22].

2. LOWER BOUNDS ON HARDNESS: GRÖBNER BASES & NULLSTELLENSÄTZE

Deciding whether a graph is k-colorable is an NP-complete problem, and we encoded it as the solution of a multivariate polynomial system (see e.g., [4, 17, 13]). It is clear that if the system of equations in the coloring ideal can be solved in polynomial time (in the input size) for 3-coloring ideals, then P = NP. What makes this very interesting is that one can see (or at least try to see) algebraic phenomena that are produced by the separation of complexity classes. For example, assuming that P $\neq$ NP then the degree of Nullstellensatz certificates for systems of equations coming from non-3-colorable graphs must show some growth in the degree. Now we discuss two ways in which the hardness of solving the coloring problem algebraically is made concrete. We note that in [8], prior similar work was done on a different family of zero-dimensional ideals.

2.1 Nullstellensätze

In this section, we consider $N_{k,\mathbb{K}}(G)$, the minimal Nullstellensatz degree for the k-coloring ideal of a graph G over the field $\mathbb{K}$. We show that $N_{k,\mathbb{K}}(G)$ grows at least linearly with respect to k, and provide evidence that the growth is, in fact, faster. Note that $N_{k,\mathbb{K}}(G)$ is defined for all graphs G that are *not* k-colorable, and for all fields $\mathbb{K}$ for which the characteristic does not divide k. Our main result is the following:

THEOREM 2.1. $N_{k,\mathbb{K}}(G) \equiv 1 \pmod k$*, for all* $k, \mathbb{K}, G$*. Furthermore* $N_{k,\mathbb{K}}(G) \geq k+1$ *if* $k > 3$*.*

PROOF. Let $G = (V, E)$, and let $\mathcal{I}_G$ denote the k-coloring ideal of G. Then, $\mathcal{I}_G$ is generated by vertex polynomials $\nu_i = x_i^k - 1$ (for $i \in V(G)$) and edge polynomials $\eta_{ij} = (x_i^k - x_j^k)/(x_i - x_j)$ (for $(i,j) \in E(G)$). We note that $\mathcal{I}_G$ has a Nullstellensatz certificate over $\mathbb{K}[x_1, \ldots, x_n]$ if and only if it has such a certificate over $\mathbb{K}[x_1, \ldots, x_n]/\langle x_1^k - 1, \ldots, x_n^k - 1\rangle$. Therefore, we may consider only the edge polynomials η_{ij} and assume that degrees of variables are taken modulo k, that is, $x_i^k = 1$ for every i.

Suppose that $\{\alpha_{ij}\}$ is a Nullstellensatz certificate of degree d, so that $\sum_{ij \in E} \alpha_{ij}\eta_{ij} = 1$. We write $\alpha_{ij} = \sum_t \alpha_{t,ij}$, where $\alpha_{t,ij}$ is homogeneous of degree t. Equating terms of like degree, we conclude:

$$\sum_{ij \in E, t \equiv 1} \alpha_{t,ij}\eta_{ij} = 1 \quad \text{and}$$

$$\sum_{ij \in E} \alpha_{t,ij}\eta_{ij} = 0, \quad \text{for every } t \not\equiv 1 \pmod k$$

Hence, letting $\beta_{ij} = \sum_{t \equiv 1} \alpha_{t,ij}$, observe that $\{\beta_{ij}\}$ is a Nullstellensatz certificate with degree congruent to 1 modulo k. We conclude that $N_{k,\mathbb{K}}(G) \equiv 1 \pmod k$.

Now consider $k > 3$ and suppose towards a contradiction that there exists a Nullstellensatz certificate $\{\alpha_{ij}\}$ of degree at most 1. By our logic above, we need only consider terms in α_{ij} for which the degree is 1 modulo k. Suppose therefore that $\alpha_{ij} = \sum_h c_{h,ij}x_h$, so that

$$\sum_{h \in V,\, ij \in E} c_{h,ij}x_h\eta_{ij} = 1.$$

Notice that $c_{h,ij}x_h\eta_{ij}$ can contain a constant term only when h equals i or j, in which case $x_h(x_i^{k-1})$ or $x_h(x_j^{k-1})$ equals

1. We conclude that

$$1 = \sum_{ij \in E} (c_{i,ij} + c_{j,ij}). \qquad (1)$$

Observe that $c_{i,ij} x_i \eta_{ij}$ contains a term of the form $c_{i,ij} x_i^{k-2} x_j^2$. Since $k > 3$, the monomial $x_i^{k-2} x_j^2$ occurs for only one other choice of h' and $i'j'$, namely $i' = i$ and $h' = j' = j$. In order for this term to cancel in the final sum, therefore, we must have $c_{j,ij} = -c_{i,ij}$ for all $ij \in E$. However, this contradicts (1). We conclude that for $k > 3$, no Nullstellensatz certificate exists of degree 1, and therefore that $N_{k,\mathbb{K}}(G) \geq k + 1$. □

We observe that Theorem 2.1 is a generalization of Lemmas 4.0.48 and 4.0.49 of [31], which only deals with the graph-3-colorability case.

EXAMPLE 2.2. *Consider the following* ***incomplete*** *degree four certificate for non-3-colorability over* $\mathbb{F}_2$. *Observe that the coefficient for the vertex polynomial* $(x_1^3 + 1)$ *contains only monomials of degree zero and degree three, whereas the coefficient for the edge polynomial* $(x_1^2 + x_1x_3 + x_3^2)$ *contains only monomials of degree one or degree four. This certificate demonstrates the modular degree grouping of the monomials in the certificates, as described by Theorem 2.1. We do not display the full certificate here due to space considerations.*

$$\begin{aligned}
1 = {} & (1 + x_1x_3x_5 + x_1x_3x_7 + x_1x_4x_5 + x_1x_4x_6 + x_1x_5x_6 \\
& + x_1x_5x_7 + x_2^2x_5 + x_2^2x_7 + x_2x_4x_5 + x_2x_4x_6 + x_2x_6x_7 \\
& + x_3x_4x_5 + x_3x_4x_7 + x_4x_6x_7 + x_5x_6x_7)(x_1^3 + 1) \\
& + (x_2 + x_4 + x_5 + x_1^2x_2x_5 + x_1^2x_2x_7 + x_1^2x_3x_5 + x_1^2x_3x_7 \\
& + x_1^2x_4x_5 + x_1^2x_4x_6 + x_1^2x_6x_7 + x_1x_2x_4x_5 + x_1x_2x_4x_7 \\
& + x_1x_3x_4x_5 + x_1x_3x_4x_7 + x_1x_3x_5x_6 + x_1x_3x_5x_7 \\
& + x_1x_3x_6x_7 + x_1x_4x_5x_6 + x_1x_4x_5x_7 + x_1x_4x_6x_7 \\
& + x_1x_5x_6x_7 + x_2x_4x_5x_6 + x_2x_4x_5x_7 + x_2x_5x_6x_7 \\
& + x_3x_4x_5x_6 + x_3x_4x_5x_7)(x_1^2 + x_1x_2 + x_2^2) + \cdots
\end{aligned}$$

2.1.1 Experiments on change of coefficient field

In Table 1, we display experimental data on minimum-degree Nullstellensatz certificates for various cases of graph-k-colorability and various finite fields. This data was found via the high-performance computing cluster at the US Naval Academy (and the NulLa software [15]). Observe that the Nullstellensatz certificate computed by testing the complete graph K_7 for non-6-colorability is **not** the minimum degree seven, instead the minimum-degree certificate is the next higher residue class (degree thirteen). Additionally we performed many more experiments not presented in Table 1. We tested non-3-colorability for K_4 for the first 1,000 prime finite fields. The certificate degree was degree one for finite fields $\mathbb{F}_2$ and $\mathbb{F}_5$, changed to the next highest degree (degree four) at $\mathbb{F}_7$, and then remained degree four for the next 997 primes (up to $\mathbb{F}_{7919}$). We also tested non-4-colorability for K_5 for the first 1,000 primes: the minimum-degree remained five for the entire series of computations. In general, Table 1 suggests that the bound $N_{k,\mathbb{K}}(G) \geq k + 1$ for $k \geq 4$ is not tight for large k. We propose the following conjecture:

CONJECTURE 2.3. *For every field* $\mathbb{K}$ *and for every positive integer* m, *there exists a constant* k_0 *with the following property. For each* $k > k_0$ *and* G *a non-k-colorable graph, every Nullstellensatz certificate of the k-coloring ideal of G has degree at least* $mk + 1$.

Graph	k	Theorem 2.1 Possible degrees	$\mathbb{F}_2$	$\mathbb{F}_3$	$\mathbb{F}_5$	$\mathbb{F}_7$
K_4	3	$1, 4, 7, 10, \ldots$	1	–	4	4
K_5	4	$5, 9, 13, \ldots$	–	5	5	5
K_6	5	$6, 11, 16, \ldots$	6	6	–	11
K_7	6	$7, 13, 19, \ldots$	–	–	13	13
K_8	7	$8, 15, 22, \ldots$	8	≥ 15	≥ 15	–
K_9	8	$9, 17, 25, \ldots$	–	≥ 17	≥ 17	≥ 17
K_{10}	9	$10, 19, 28, \ldots$	≥ 19	–	≥ 19	≥ 19
K_{11}	10	$11, 21, 31, \ldots$	–	≥ 21	–	≥ 21

Table 1: The minimum degree of Nullstellensatz certificates for complete graphs over $\mathbb{F}_p$. Note that computations are only possible when k and p are relatively prime (incompatible pairs (k, p) are denoted by –).

2.2 The Robust Hardness of Colorful Gröbner Bases

We know it is NP-hard to compute Gröbner bases. It is even known the problem is EXPSPACE-complete (see [23, 33]), and the maximum degree of the basis can become very large. In [24, 36, 35] the authors presented bounds for the degree of a reduced Gröbner basis for an ideal whose generators have degree bounded by d. E.g., the authors of [35] show that a Gröbner basis of an r-dimensional ideal has degree at most $2\left(\frac{1}{2}d^{n-r} + d\right)^{2^r}$. For the case of general zero-dimensional ideals, this bound reduces to $2\left(\frac{1}{2}d^n + d\right)$. In [39], a lower bound of d^n for zero-dimensional ideals is given by a suitable example. Finally from the work of Lazard and Brownawell [6, 29] it follows an $n(d-1)$ bound on zero-dimensional ideals with generators having no common zeros at infinity. These include our coloring ideals, $\mathcal{I}_k(G)$.

On the other hand, it is well-known that some combinatorial problems are even hard to approximate or it is hard to find partial solutions. Here we discuss how the hardness of finding suboptimal or approximate solutions to graph k-coloring can be translated into similar results for the computation of Gröbner bases, therefore showing some kind of "robust hardness" for Gröbner bases computation. We will use the following theorem.

THEOREM 2.4 (SEE [27]). *It is NP-hard to color a 3-colorable graph with 4 colors. More generally, for every* $k \geq 3$ *it is NP-hard to color a k-chromatic graph with at most* $k + 2\left\lfloor \frac{k}{3} \right\rfloor - 1$ *colors.*

We now translate this theorem into a statement about Gröbner bases. Having additional colors to work with allows us to ignore certain vertices of our graph and color these later using our extra colors. Algebraically, this corresponds to ignoring certain variables and computing a Gröbner basis for the partial coloring ideal on the remaining variables.

DEFINITION 2.5. *Given a set of polynomials* $\mathcal{F} \subseteq \mathbb{K}[x_1, \ldots, x_n]$, *we say that a subset* X *of the variables* $x_1, \ldots, x_n$ *is* independent *on* $\mathcal{F}$ *if no two variables in* X *appear together in any element of* $\mathcal{F}$.

Clearly independent sets in our coloring ideal generators correspond to independent sets of vertices of the graph.

DEFINITION 2.6. *Define the* strong c-partial Gröbner *problem as follows. Given as input, a set $\mathcal{F}$ of polynomials on a set X of variables, output the following:*

- *disjoint $X_1, \ldots, X_b \subseteq X$, such that $b \leq c$ and each X_i is an independent set of variables,*
- *$X' \subseteq X$, where $X' = X \setminus (\bigcup_i X_i)$ (i.e., we have taken away at most c independent sets of variables),*
- *$\mathcal{F}' \subseteq \mathcal{F}$ such that $\mathcal{F}'$ consists of all polynomials in $\mathcal{F}$ involving only variables in X',*
- *a Gröbner basis for $\langle \mathcal{F}' \rangle$ over X' (where the monomial order on X is restricted to a monomial order on X').*

THEOREM 2.7. *Suppose that we are working over a polynomial ring $\mathbb{K}[x_1, \ldots, x_n]$ under some elimination order on the variables (such as lexicographic order).*

Let $k \geq 3$ be an integer, and set $c = 2\lfloor \frac{k}{3} \rfloor - 1$. Unless P = NP, there is no polynomial-time algorithm $\mathcal{A}$ that solves the strong c-partial Gröbner problem (even if we restrict to sets of polynomials of degree at most k).

The following lemma will be useful in our proof.

LEMMA 2.8. *Suppose that we are given a Gröbner basis $\mathcal{G}$ for the k-coloring ideal $\mathcal{I}_G$ of a graph G, with respect to a given elimination order. Assuming the variety $\mathcal{V}(\mathcal{I}_G)$ is non-empty, there is an algorithm that finds some solution $x \in \mathcal{V}(\mathcal{I}_G)$ in time polynomial in the encoding length of $\mathcal{G}$, and therefore identifies a k-coloring of G.*

PROOF. Suppose without loss of generality that our elimination order gives $x_n > x_{n-1} > \cdots > x_1$. We may enumerate the elements of $\mathcal{G}$: $g_1, g_2, \ldots, g_n$, so that g_1 is univariate in x_1, the polynomial g_2 is bivariate (or univariate) in x_1 and x_2, etc. See [10, Chap. 3] for more details.

As always with coloring ideals, we assume that k is not divisible by the characteristic of $\mathbb{K}$. Hence, in a standard result of Galois theory, there exists a primitive kth root of unity over $\mathbb{K}$, and so the kth cyclotomic polynomial Φ_k over $\mathbb{K}$ must be nontrivial. In order to find Φ_k, we repeatedly divide the polynomial $x^k - 1$ by its greatest common factors with polynomials $x^\ell - 1$ for $\ell < k$; these gcd's can be found by the Euclidean algorithm. The time required may be exponential in k but is obviously independent of $\mathcal{G}$.

Note that every proper k-coloring of G must correspond to a solution to all polynomials in $\mathcal{G}$. Thus, if some collection of roots of unity forms a solution, any permutation of those roots of unity must also. Therefore, every root of Φ_k must also be a root of g_1, that is, Φ_k divides g_1.

The Elimination Theorem [10, Chap. 3] now guarantees that any solution to g_1 and g_2 extends to a solution for all $\mathcal{G}$. For each i with $1 \leq i \leq k$, we set $x_1 = \omega$ and $x_2 = \omega^i$. We then test, using the Euclidean algorithm, whether there exists a common solution to $g_1(x_1)$, $g_2(x_1, x_2)$, and $\Phi_k(x_1)$, considered as polynomials in ω. If so, then every primitive root ω gives us a common solution of g_1, g_2.

Having identified i, set $i_2 = i$ and $i_1 = 1$, so that $x_1 = \omega^{i_1}$, $x_2 = \omega^{i_2}$ is a partial solution. We proceed as above to check each i_3 satisfying $1 \leq i_3 \leq k$. Using the Euclidean algorithm, we test if there is a common solution ω to $g_1(x_1)$, $g_2(x_1, x_2)$, $g_3(x_1, x_2, x_3)$, $\Phi_k(x_1)$, if we set $x_1 = \omega^{i_1}$, $x_2 = \omega^{i_2}$, $x_3 = \omega^{i_3}$. This enables us to find a partial solution for x_1, x_2, x_3. Continuing in this fashion, we find a complete solution for all variables. □

PROOF OF THEOREM 2.7. The proof is by contradiction. Let $G = (V, E)$ be a k-colorable graph and assume such a polynomial-time algorithm $\mathcal{A}$ exists. We will give a method for producing a proper $(k + c)$-coloring of G. This contradicts Theorem 2.4 under the assumption that P $\neq$ NP, as mentioned above.

Let us apply the algorithm $\mathcal{A}$ to our coloring polynomials $\mathcal{F}_G$ for the graph G, giving us a Gröbner basis $\mathcal{G}$. Note that the input consists of $|V| + |E|$ polynomials with degree $\leq k$ and length $\leq k$. Thus, $\mathcal{F}_G$ has polynomial size in k and the encoding length of G, and by assumption $\mathcal{A}$ terminates in time which is polynomial in both of these quantities.

Observe that the variables in $\mathcal{F}_G$ correspond to vertices of G, and an independent set of variables corresponds to an independent set of vertices. Assume that the independent sets of variables which were ignored by $\mathcal{A}$ are $X_1, X_2, \ldots, X_b$ for $b \leq c$. Let $I_1, I_2, \ldots, I_b$ be the corresponding independent sets of vertices. The Gröbner basis $\mathcal{G}$ corresponds to proper k-colorings of $G' = G \setminus (\cup_i I_i)$. Therefore, Lemma 2.8 implies that we can identify some proper coloring of G' using the colors $1, \ldots, k$. Note that in order to apply this lemma, we must be working with an elimination order over our restricted polynomial ring; this is true since the restriction of an elimination order to a smaller set of variables is also an elimination order.

Now color the independent sets $I_1, \ldots, I_b$ in the colors $k + 1, \ldots, k + b$. This gives us a proper coloring of G using at most

$$k + b \leq k + c = k + 2\left\lfloor \frac{k}{3} \right\rfloor - 1$$

colors. By Theorem 2.4, this is impossible to construct in polynomial time, giving us a contradiction, as desired. □

Theorem 2.7 demonstrates how results on coloring graphs translate effectively to results on Gröbner bases. For reference, a weaker result may be proven without recourse to the full power of the coloring ideal.

DEFINITION 2.9. *Define the* weak c-partial Gröbner *problem as follows. Given, as input, a set $\mathcal{F}$ of polynomials on a set X of variables, output the following:*

- *$X' \subseteq X$ such that $|X'| \geq |X| - c$,*
- *$\mathcal{F}' \subseteq \mathcal{F}$ such that $\mathcal{F}'$ consists of all polynomials in $\mathcal{F}$ involving only variables in X',*
- *a Gröbner basis for $\langle \mathcal{F}' \rangle$ over X' (where the monomial order on X is restricted to a monomial order on X').*

THEOREM 2.10. *For constant c, there is no polynomial-time algorithm to solve the weak c-partial Gröbner problem, unless P=NP. This holds even if we restrict to sets of polynomials of degree at most 3.*

Our proof will use the following lemma.

LEMMA 2.11. *Suppose that $\mathcal{F}_1, \mathcal{F}_2, \ldots, \mathcal{F}_m$ are sets of polynomials on disjoint sets of variables (that is, no variable appears both in a polynomial of $\mathcal{F}_i$ and in a polynomial of $\mathcal{F}_j$). Then, the reduced Gröbner basis of $\langle \cup_i \mathcal{F}_i \rangle$ is the union of the reduced Gröbner bases for the individual $\langle \mathcal{F}_i \rangle$.*

PROOF. Let $\mathcal{G}_i$ be the reduced Gröbner bases for the $\langle \mathcal{F}_i \rangle$, respectively, and set $\mathcal{G} := \cup_i \mathcal{G}_i$. For a set S of polynomials, we use $\mathcal{L}(S)$ to denote the ideal generated by the leading terms of elements of S.

Note first that every leading term of $\langle \cup_i \mathcal{F}_i \rangle$ is also a leading term of some $\langle \mathcal{F}_i \rangle$ and hence is contained in $\mathcal{L}(\mathcal{G})$. Conversely, every leading term of $\mathcal{G}$ is also a leading term of $\langle \mathcal{F}_i \rangle$, for some i, and therefore is contained in $\langle \cup_i \mathcal{F}_i \rangle$. We conclude that

$$\langle \cup_i \mathcal{F}_i \rangle = \mathcal{L}(\mathcal{G}),$$

and therefore $\mathcal{G}$ is a Gröbner basis of $\cup_i \langle \mathcal{F}_i \rangle$. □

PROOF OF THEOREM 2.10. Suppose that there exists an algorithm $\mathcal{A}$ for c-partial Gröbner that runs in time at most $p(s)$, where s is the size of the input. Let $\mathcal{F}$ be a system of polynomials in $\mathbb{K}[x_1, \ldots, x_n]$ with input size s, such that the degree of every polynomial in $\mathcal{F}$ is at most 3. We show how to use $\mathcal{A}$ to compute a Gröbner basis for $\langle \mathcal{F} \rangle$ in polynomial time, which will lead to a contradiction.

Construct copies $\mathcal{F}_1, \mathcal{F}_2, \ldots, \mathcal{F}_{c+1}$ of $\mathcal{F}$ on disjoint sets of variables, so that $\mathcal{F}_i$ includes polynomials over the variables $x_{i,1}, x_{i,2}, \ldots, x_{i,n}$. The size of $\cup_i \mathcal{F}_i$ is obviously $(c+1)s$. Now run $\mathcal{A}$ on $\cup_i \mathcal{F}_i$, removing at most c variables from $\cup_i \mathcal{F}_i$. In the process, we remove certain polynomials from $\mathcal{F}_i$ to yield sets $\mathcal{F}_i'$ of polynomials. The output of $\mathcal{A}$ is a Gröbner basis $\mathcal{G}$ for $\langle \cup_i \mathcal{F}_i' \rangle$.

Now, since there are $c+1$ disjoint sets of variables $\{x_{i,1}, x_{i,2}, \ldots, x_{i,n}\}$, there must exist at least one i such that we have not removed any variable in $\{x_{i,1}, x_{i,2}, \ldots, x_{i,n}\}$. For this value of i, we have $\mathcal{F}_i' = \mathcal{F}_i$. Transforming $\mathcal{G}$ to a reduced Gröbner basis is routine and can be performed in polynomial time. Applying Lemma 2.11, we see that the restriction of $\mathcal{G}$ to $\{x_{i,1}, x_{i,2}, \ldots, x_{i,n}\}$ gives a reduced Gröbner basis for $\mathcal{F}_i' = \mathcal{F}_i$. This immediately gives us a reduced Gröbner basis for $\langle \mathcal{F} \rangle$.

Observe that $(c+1)s$ is the size of our input $\cup_i \mathcal{F}_i$ to $\mathcal{A}$. Therefore, the time required by our algorithm is at most $p((c+1)s) \leq (c+1)^{\deg(p)} p(s)$. Since $\mathcal{F}$ was chosen arbitrarily, this implies that for every family of polynomials of input size s, a Gröbner basis can be found in polynomial time at most $(c+1)^{\deg(p)} p(s)$. However, since 3-coloring is NP-hard, the general problem of finding a Gröbner basis cannot be performed in polynomial time, even if we assume that every $f \in \mathcal{F}$ has degree at most 3. Thus we have a contradiction, and conclude that the algorithm $\mathcal{A}$ cannot exist. □

Comparing Theorems 2.7 and 2.10, we see that the latter allows us to remove only a constant number of individual variables, not a constant number of independent sets. Furthermore, the set of polynomials constructed in Theorem 2.10 is *disconnected*, according to the following Definition 2.12, while the set of polynomials constructed in Theorem 2.7 is *connected*. It appears more natural to consider connected sets of polynomials, which occur in many applications.

DEFINITION 2.12. *We say that a set $\mathcal{F}$ of polynomials is* disconnected *if we can partition $\mathcal{F}$ into $\mathcal{F}_1, \mathcal{F}_2$ such that the variables for $\mathcal{F}_1$ and $\mathcal{F}_2$ are disjoint. Otherwise, we say that $\mathcal{F}$ is* connected.

3. GRÖBNER BASES FOR CHORDAL GRAPHS

Even though graph coloring is hard for general graphs, the problem can be solved in linear time for chordal graphs (see e.g. [25]). Taking advantage of the structure of chordal graphs, we develop a polynomial time algorithm that computes a Gröbner basis for the k-coloring ideal $\mathcal{I}_G$ of a given chordal graph G. The monomial order we consider is related to the perfect elimination ordering of G.

We begin with some basic definitions in graph theory (see also e.g. [18].) Recall that a graph $G = (V, E)$ is *chordal* if every cycle of length more than 3 has a chord, or equivalently, every induced cycle in the graph has length 3. A vertex $v \in V$ is *simplicial* if its neighbors form a clique. A graph is *recursively simplicial* if it contains a simplicial vertex v such that the induced graph $G[V \setminus \{v\}]$ produced by removing v and its incident edges, is recursively simplicial[1]. If G is recursively simplicial, there exists an ordering on V, called a *perfect elimination ordering*, such that when the vertices of G are removed in that order, each vertex will be simplicial at the time of removal.

PROPOSITION 3.1 ([21]). *Let $G = (V, E)$ be a graph. Then G is chordal if and only if it is recursively simplicial.*

For a vertex $v \in V$, the neighborhood of v in G is the set $\mathcal{N}(v) = \{w \in V : (v, w) \in E(G)\}$. If $U \subseteq V$ is a subset of the vertices forming a clique in G, then we define

$$G^{+U} := \big(V \cup \{n+1\}, E \cup \{(j, n+1) : j \in U\}\big)$$

to be the graph obtained by adding a new vertex and connecting it to all $u \in U$. Note that this operation is the inverse of deleting a simplicial vertex of G, and, by Proposition 3.1, every chordal graph can be constructed in this way.

Algorithm 1 constructs a Gröbner basis $\mathcal{G}$ for a chordal graph G, building up the graph one vertex at a time according to the reverse elimination order. Each newly added vertex adds a polynomial to $\mathcal{G}$. At any point, having constructed the graph $G' \subseteq G$, the set of polynomials added will form a Gröbner basis for the coloring ideal of G'.

3.1 Preliminaries

Recall the following definitions. The *kth elementary symmetric polynomial* $\sigma_k(x_1, \ldots, x_n)$ over n variables is

$$\sigma_k(x_1, \ldots, x_n) := \sum_{1 \leq j_1 < \cdots < j_k \leq n} x_{j_1} \cdots x_{j_k} \quad .$$

The *kth complete homogeneous symmetric polynomial* $S_k(x_1, \ldots, x_n)$ over n variables is given by

$$S_k(x_1, \ldots, x_n) := \sum_{1 \leq j_1 \leq \cdots \leq j_k \leq n} x_{j_1} \cdots x_{j_k} \quad .$$

Note that both polynomials are degree-k-homogeneous, but the monomials of σ_k are by definition square-free, while S_k can contain higher powers of a variable.

LEMMA 3.2. *For a positive integer k, let $\zeta_1, \zeta_2, \ldots, \zeta_k$ be the kth roots of unity in some order. Then, for every $k > r$,* $S_{k-r}(\zeta_1, \zeta_2, \ldots, \zeta_r, x) = (x - \zeta_{r+1})(x - \zeta_{r+2}) \cdots (x - \zeta_k)$.

[1] The graph on zero vertices is recursively simplicial.

PROOF. It suffices to prove

$$S_{k-r}(\zeta_1, \zeta_2, \dots, \zeta_r, x) \cdot (x - \zeta_1) \cdots (x - \zeta_r) = x^k - 1 \ .$$

Consider the degree d-homogeneous polynomial $\sigma_i(\zeta_1, \dots, \zeta_r) S_{d-i}(\zeta_1, \dots, \zeta_r)$. For every monomial x^α with $|\alpha| = d$ and $\mathrm{supp}(\alpha) = m$ (the number of non-zero elements in α equals m), its coefficient is the number of square-free factors of degree i, that is, $\binom{m}{i}$. Summing up these coefficients over d with alternating signs gives that the coefficient of x^α in

$$\sum_{i=0}^{d} (-1)^{d-i} \sigma_i(\zeta_1, \dots, \zeta_r) S_{d-i}(\zeta_1, \dots, \zeta_r)$$

equals

$$\sum_{i=0}^{m} (-1)^{d-i} \binom{m}{i} = 0 \ .$$

Therefore,

$$\sum_{i=0}^{d} (-1)^{d-i} \sigma_i(\zeta_1, \dots, \zeta_r) S_{d-i}(\zeta_1, \dots, \zeta_r) = 0,$$

for every $d \in \{0, \dots, k-1\}$. Now, since $\zeta_1, \dots, \zeta_k$ are the roots of unity, we know that, for every $d \in \{1, \dots, k-1\}$:

$$\sum_{i=0}^{d} \sigma_i(\zeta_1, \dots, \zeta_r) \sigma_{d-i}(\zeta_{r+1}, \dots, \zeta_k) = \sigma_d(\zeta_1, \dots, \zeta_k) = 0.$$

We now have identical recursions for $S_d(\zeta_1, \dots, \zeta_r)$ and $(-1)^d \sigma_d(\zeta_{r+1}, \dots, \zeta_k)$. In the base case, $S_0(\zeta_1, \dots, \zeta_r) = 1 = (-1)^0 \sigma_0(\zeta_{r+1}, \dots, \zeta_k)$. We conclude that for all d,

$$S_d(\zeta_1, \dots, \zeta_r) = (-1)^d \sigma_d(\zeta_{r+1}, \dots, \zeta_k).$$

Therefore,

$$\begin{aligned} & S_{k-r}(\zeta_1, \dots, \zeta_r, x) \cdot \prod_{i=1}^{r} (x - \zeta_i) \\ &= \sum_{d=0}^{k-r} S_d(\zeta_1, \dots, \zeta_r) x^{k-r-d} \cdot \prod_{i=1}^{r} (x - \zeta_i) \\ &= \sum_{d=0}^{k-r} (-1)^d \sigma_d(\zeta_{r+1}, \dots, \zeta_k) x^{k-r-d} \cdot \prod_{i=1}^{r} (x - \zeta_i) \\ &= \prod_{i=r+1}^{k} (x - \zeta_i) \cdot \prod_{i=1}^{r} (x - \zeta_i) = x^k - 1. \end{aligned}$$

□

3.2 The Algorithm

BuildGröbnerBasis (Algorithm 1) successively tests vertices of a chordal graph G for simpliciality and obtains a perfect elimination order while concurrently adding new polynomials to a set $\mathcal{G}$. At termination, $\mathcal{G}$ is a Gröbner basis for $\mathcal{I}_G$ with respect to the lexicographic order with variables ordered according to a perfect elimination order of G.[2]

For a clique $U = \{u_1, u_2, \dots, u_r\}$ and vertex v in our graph, we will use the notation $S_{k-r}(U, v)$ to denote the polynomial $S_{k-r}(x_{u_1}, x_{u_2}, \dots, x_{u_r}, x_v)$.

[2]The existence of this algorithm was first conjectured by experimental work of Pernpeintner [38].

Algorithm 1 Produces a Gröbner basis for the k-coloring ideal $\mathcal{I}_G$ for G chordal

```
function BuildGröbnerBasis(G. k)
Input: A chordal graph G, integer k
Output: A Gröbner basis for I_G
    G_n ← G
    𝒢 ← ∅
    for all i ∈ {n − 1, ..., 1} do
        for all v ∈ V_{i+1} do
            if IsSimplicial(v, G_{i+1}) then
                v_i ← v
                U_i ← N(v)
                if |U_i| ≥ k then
                    return {1}
                end if
                G_i ← G_{i+1} − v
                𝒢 ← 𝒢 ∪ {S_{k−|U_i|}(U_i, v_i)}
            end if
        end for
    end for
    return 𝒢
end function
function IsSimplicial(v, G)
Input: A vertex v of the graph G and the graph G itself
Output: True if v is simplicial in G; False otherwise
    d ← deg(v)
    for all w ∈ N(v) do
        if |N(v) ∩ N(w)| < d − 1 then
            return false
        end if
    end for
    return true
end function
```

As we have seen above, exactly one polynomial is added to $\mathcal{G}$ for every vertex of G. From the definition of $S_k(x_1, \dots, x_n)$, we see that its length is $\binom{k+n-1}{n-1}$ and its degree is k. So the polynomials S_i added to $\mathcal{G}$ have length $\binom{k}{|U_i|}$ and degree $(k - |U_i|)$. Both quantities are polynomial in k and constant for a constant number k of colors.

Finally let us discuss an important aspect of our algorithm. If G is not k-colorable, then in the process of **BuildGröbnerBasis** we would intuitively expect the constant polynomial 1 to appear somewhere in the set $\mathcal{G}$. This can be shown formally: Assume that $\chi(G) = \chi > k$, and we try to find a Gröbner basis for the k-coloring ideal of G. Since G is chordal, it is also perfect, and thus has a χ-clique $\{v_1, \dots, v_\chi\}$. We assume without loss of generality that these vertices are ordered ascendingly with respect to the perfect elimination order from the algorithm.

In the step, where v_{k+1} is removed from the graph, we have $\{v_1, \dots, v_k\} \subseteq \mathcal{N}(v_{k+1})$, and therefore, we add the complete polynomial of degree 0

$$S_{k-k}(x_{v_1}, \dots, x_{v_k}, x_{v_{k+1}}) = 1 \ .$$

Hence, BuildGröbnerBasis detects non-k-colorability on the fly. This observation allows us to do the following: If we find a simplicial vertex of degree $\geq k$, then we can stop immediately and return the trivial Gröbner basis $\mathcal{G} = \{1\}$. On the other hand, we can be sure that if there is no such forbidden vertex, then G is k-colorable.

3.3 Correctness

LEMMA 3.3 (LEMMA 2.2 FROM [26]). *Let G be a graph. Then $\mathcal{I}_G$ is a radical ideal.*

PROPOSITION 3.4 ([10] 2.9 PROPOSITION 4). *Let $P \subset \mathbb{K}[x_1, \ldots, x_n]$ be a finite set, and let $p_1, p_2 \in P$ be such that*

$$lcm(LM(p_1), LM(p_2)) = LM(p_1) \cdot LM(p_2) ,$$

where LM denotes the leading monomial of a polynomial. Then,

$$S\text{-}pair(p_1, p_2) \to_P 0.$$

Recall that $v_i \in \mathcal{I}_G$, and $\eta_{ij} \in \mathcal{I}_G$ are the vertex and edge polynomials, respectively.

LEMMA 3.5. *Let G be a chordal graph on n vertices, and let $\succ$ be a term order. Let $U = \{u_1, \ldots, u_r\}$ be an r-clique in G, and choose a Gröbner basis $\mathcal{G}$ of $\mathcal{I}_G$. Set $p = S_{k-r}(x_{u_1}, \ldots, x_{u_r}, x_{n+1})$. Then,*

$$\langle \mathcal{G}, p\rangle = \langle \mathcal{G}, \nu_{n+1}, \eta_{u_1,n+1}, \ldots, \eta_{u_r,n+1}\rangle = \mathcal{I}_{G+U} .$$

PROOF. We show that $\langle \mathcal{G}, p\rangle$ is a radical ideal, and that both ideals generate the same variety. Then the claim follows from the bijection between varieties and radical ideals [10, §4.2, Theorem 7].

Consider some setting of the variables $x_{u_1}, \ldots, x_{u_r}$ to distinct kth roots of unity $\zeta_1, \ldots, \zeta_r$, and suppose that $\zeta_{r+1}, \ldots, \zeta_k$ are the other kth roots of unity, in some order. By Lemma 3.2, we have $p = \prod_{i=r+1}^{k}(x_{n+1} - \zeta_i)$. This implies that $p(x_{u_1}, x_{u_2}, \ldots, x_{u_r}, x_{n+1})$ is a square-free polynomial so $\langle p\rangle$ is a radical ideal. The ideal $\langle \mathcal{G}\rangle$ is also radical, since it is the coloring ideal of a graph (Lemma 3.3). But then

$$\begin{aligned}\text{rad}(\langle \mathcal{G}, p\rangle) &= \text{rad}(\langle \mathcal{G}\rangle \cap \langle p\rangle) = \text{rad}(\langle \mathcal{G}\rangle) \cap \text{rad}(\langle p\rangle)\\ &= \langle \mathcal{G}\rangle \cap \langle p\rangle = \langle \mathcal{G}, p\rangle\end{aligned}$$

as claimed. The second equality is [10, §4.3, Proposition 16],

Now consider $\mathbf{x} = (x_1, \ldots, x_{n+1}) \in \mathcal{V}(\langle \mathcal{G}, p\rangle)$. Since $u_1, \ldots, u_r$ form a clique, we know that x_{u_i} are distinct kth roots of unity. Then, by Lemma 3.2, x_{n+1} is a kth root of unity, and so $\nu_{n+1} = 0$. Moreover, $x_{n+1} \neq x_{u_i}\ \forall\ i \in \{1, \ldots, r\}$, which implies that $\eta_{u_i,n+1} = 0$. We conclude that $\mathbf{x} \in \mathcal{V}(\mathcal{I}_{G+U})$.

Conversely, consider $\mathbf{x} = (x_1, \ldots, x_{n+1}) \in \mathcal{V}(\mathcal{I}_{G+U})$. The generator polynomials $\nu_1, \ldots, \nu_r, \nu_{n+1}$ and $\eta_{u_1,n+1}, \ldots, \eta_{u_r,n+1}$ ensure that $x_{u_1}, \ldots, x_{u_r}, x_{n+1}$ are distinct kth roots of unity. Hence $p(\mathbf{x}) = 0$ and $\mathbf{x} \in \mathcal{V}(\langle \mathcal{G}, p\rangle)$. □

LEMMA 3.6. *Given a chordal graph G, every Gröbner basis $\mathcal{G}$ of $\mathcal{I}_G$ with respect to $\succ$, $\mathcal{G} \cup \{p\}$ is a Gröbner basis of $\mathcal{I}_{G+U}$ with respect to an extended term order $\succ'$, where p is again defined as in Lemma 3.5.*

PROOF. Lemma 3.5 shows that $\langle \mathcal{G}, p\rangle = \mathcal{I}_{G+U}$. Hence, it is left to show that all S-polynomials in $\mathcal{G} \cup \{p\}$ reduce to 0. We only have to consider S-pairs that involve the new polynomial p.

By definition of $\succ'$, we have that $\text{LM}_{\succ'}(p) = x_{n+1}^{k-r}$, which is relatively prime to all $g \in \mathcal{G}$, since x_{n+1} does not appear in this basis. Therefore, for all $g \in \mathcal{G}$, S-pair$(g, p) \to_{\mathcal{G}\cup\{p\}} 0$ by Proposition 3.4. This is sufficient for $\mathcal{G}' := \mathcal{G} \cup \{p\}$ to be a Gröbner Basis. □

THEOREM 3.7. *For G chordal, the set $\mathcal{G}$ output by* BUILDGRÖBNERBASIS(G) *is a Gröbner basis for $\mathcal{I}_G$ under the Lex order, with variables ordered according to the perfect elimination order of G established in the algorithm.*

PROOF. Note that $\{p_1 := \nu_n\}$ is a Gröbner basis for G_1. By Lemma 3.6, this basis can be extended in $n - 1$ steps by adding p_i as constructed in the algorithm. Therefore, $\mathcal{G} = \{p_1, \ldots, p_n\}$ is a Gröbner basis of $G_n = G$ with respect to the extended vertex order, which concludes the proof. □

3.4 Complexity

The function ISSIMPLICIAL consists of an outer loop with exactly n iterations, each of which calculates the intersection of two subsets of V. This intersection is computed in time $O(n)$ and, hence, the function runs in time $O(n^2)$.

In the main function BUILDGRÖBNERBASIS, the two nested **for**-loops are traversed $O(n)$ times each, and every time ISSIMPLICIAL is called. The main part of the **if**-case is the assignment of $\mathcal{G}$. If $r = |U_i|$, then building the polynomial $S_{k-|U_i|}(U_i, v_i)$ takes $(k-r)\cdot\binom{k}{r}$ steps, which is clearly in $O(kn^k)$. The remaining statements can be neglected, since they have running time $O(n^2)$. Finally, putting the pieces together, we obtain a total running time of $O(kn^{k+2})$, which is polynomial in n for fixed k.

It is evident that our implementation is not optimal with respect to running time. For instance, finding a simplicial vertex can be done in linear time [40], giving a linear-time procedure that establishes a perfect elimination order on G. Nevertheless, our algorithm shows that finding the Gröbner basis for a chordal graph is polynomial-time solvable, and it describes explicitly the structure of this basis.

4. ACKNOWLEDGEMENTS

The authors wish to thank Hannah Alpert for her extremely helpful thoughts. We acknowledge partial support by the National Science Foundation under Grant No. DMS-1321794 and Grant No. 1122374. We are very grateful to the AMS Mathematical Research Communities program, and especially Ellen J. Maycock, for their support of this project. We are also grateful to the Simons Institute and would like to thank Agnes Szanto and Pablo Parrilo for their constructive comments. Finally we thank the anonymous referees for many helpful suggestions.

5. REFERENCES

[1] W. Adams and P. Loustaunau, "An introduction to Gröbner bases", *American Mathematical Society*, Providence, Rhode Island, 1994.

[2] N. Alon, "Combinatorial Nullstellensatz" *Combin. Prob. and Comput.* 8, pg. 7–29, 1999.

[3] N. Alon and M. Tarsi, "Colorings and orientations of graphs", *Combinatorica*, 12, pg. 125–134, 1992.

[4] D. A. Bayer, "The Division Algorithm and the Hilbert Scheme", Ph.D Thesis, Harvard University, 1982.

[5] P. Beamer, R. Impagliazzo, J. Krajicek, T. Pitassi, and P. Pudlák, "Lower bounds on Hilbert's Nullstellensatz and propositional proofs", *Proc. of the London Math. Soc.*, 73, pg. 1–26, 1996.

[6] W. D. Brownawell, "Bounds for the degrees in the Nullstellensatz", *Annals of Mathematics*, 126(3), pg. 577–591, 1987.

[7] S. Buss and T. Pitassi, "Good degree bounds on Nullstellensatz refutations of the induction principle", *IEEE Conference on Computational Complexity*, pg. 233–242, 1996.

[8] S. Buss, D. Grigoriev, R. Impagliazzo, T. Pitassi, "Linear Gaps Between Degrees for the Polynomial Calculus Modulo Distinct Primes." *J. Comput. Syst. Sci.*, 2001, vol. 62, pg. 267–289.

[9] D. Cifuentes and P. Parrilo, "Chordal Structure and Polynomial Systems", manuscript available from math ArXiv:1411.1745.

[10] D. Cox, J. Little and D. O'Shea, "Ideals,Varieties and Algorithms", *Springer Undergraduate texts in Mathematics*, Springer-Verlag, New York, 1992.

[11] D. Cox, J. Little and D. O'Shea, "Using Algebraic Geometry", *Springer Graduate Texts in Mathematics*, 185, 1998.

[12] C. D'Andrea, T. Krick, M.Sombra: "Heights of varieties in multiprojective spaces and arithmetic Nullstellensätze". Annales Scientifiques de l'Ecole Normale Supérieure 46 (2013) 549–627.

[13] J. A. De Loera, "Gröbner bases and graph colorings", *Beitrage zur Algebra und Geometrie*, 36(1), pg. 89–96, 1995.

[14] J. A. De Loera, P. Malkin, and P. Parrilo "Computation with Polynomial Equations and Inequalities arising in Combinatorial Optimization", in "Mixed Integer Non-Linear Programming" (J. Lee and S. Leyffer eds.), IMA Volumes in Mathematics and its Applications, Vol. 154. 1st Edition., 2011, X, 660 p.

[15] J. A. De Loera, J. Lee, P. N. Malkin, S. Margulies, "Hilbert's Nullstellensatz and an Algorithm for Proving Combinatorial Infeasibility", *Interntl. Symposium on Symbolic and Algebraic Computation*, ISSAC 2009.

[16] J. A. De Loera, J. Lee, P. N. Malkin, S. Margulies, "Computing Infeasibility Certificates for Combinatorial Problems through Hilbert's Nullstellensatz", *Journal of Symbolic Computation*, 46(11), pg. 1260–1283, 2011.

[17] J. A. De Loera, J. Lee, S. Margulies and S. Onn, "Expressing combinatorial optimization problems by systems of polynomial equations and the Nullstellensatz", *Combinatorics, Probability and Computing*, 18, pg. 551–582, 2009.

[18] R. Diestel, "Graph theory", *Springer Graduate Texts in Mathematics*, 173, 2005.

[19] T. W. Dubé, "The structure of polynomial ideals and Gröbner bases", SIAM Journal on Computing, v.19 n.4, p.750–773, Aug. 1990

[20] J. Faugere, P. Gianni, D. Lazard and T. Mora, "Efficient computation of zero dimensional Gröbner bases by change of ordering". *Journal of Symbolic Computation*, 1989.

[21] D. R. Fulkerson and O. A. Gross, "Incidence matrices and interval graphs", *Pacific J. Math*, 15, pg. 835–855, 1965.

[22] S. Garey and D. Johnson, "Computers and Intractability: A Guide to the Theory of NP-Completeness", *W.H. Freeman and Company*, 1979.

[23] J. von zur Gathen, J. Gerhard, "Modern Computer Algebra", *Cambridge University Press*, 3rd ed., 2013.

[24] M. Giusti, Some effectivity problems in polynomial ideal theory. EUROSAM 84 (Cambridge, 1984), 159–171, Lecture Notes in Comput. Sci., 174, Springer, Berlin, 1984.

[25] M. C. Golumbic, "Algorithmic graph theory and perfect graphs", *Academic Press*, 1980.

[26] C. J. Hillar and T. Windfeldt, "An algebraic characterization of uniquely vertex colorable graphs", *Journal of Combinatorial Theory, Series B*, 98(2), pg 400–414, March 2008.

[27] S. Khanna, N. Linial, S. Safra, "On the hardness of approximating the chromatic number". *Proceedings of the 2nd Israel Symposium on Theory and Computing Systems*, pg. 250–260, 1993.

[28] J. Kollar, "Sharp effective Nullstellensatz", *J. of the AMS*, 1(4), 963–975, 1988.

[29] D. Lazard, "Algèbre linéaire sur $\mathbb{K}[x_1, \ldots, x_n]$ et elimination". *Bulletin de las S.M.F*, 105:165–190, 1977.

[30] L. Lovász, "Stable sets and Polynomials", *Discrete Mathematics*, 124, 137–153, 1994.

[31] S. Margulies, Computer Algebra, Combinatorics and Complexity Theory: Hilbert's Nullstellensatz and NP-complete problems. Ph.D. thesis, UC Davis, 2008.

[32] Yu. V. Matiyasevich. "Some algebraic methods for calculation of the number of colorings of a graph" (in Russian). *Zapiski Nauchnykh Seminarov POMI*, 293, pg. 193–205 (available via www.pdmi.ras.ru), 2001.

[33] E. W. Mayr "Some Complexity Results for Polynomial Ideals" Journal of Complexity Volume 13, Issue 3, 1997, 303–325.

[34] E. W. Mayr and A. Meyer. "The complexity of the word problems for commutative semigroups and polynomial ideals". Advances in Mathematics, 46(3):305–329, 1982.

[35] E. W. Mayr, S. Ritscher, "Degree bounds for Gröbner bases of low-dimensional polynomial ideals", In Proceedings of the 2010 International Symposium on Symbolic and Algebraic Computation (ISSAC '10) 21–27.

[36] M.H. Möller, and T. Mora, "Upper and lower bounds for the degree of Groebner bases". EUROSAM 84 (Cambridge, 1984), 172–183, Lecture Notes in Comput. Sci., 174, Springer, Berlin, 1984.

[37] M. Mnuk, "Representing graph properties by polynomial ideals". In V. G. Ganzha, E. W. Mayr, and E. V. Vorozhtsov, editors, Computer Algebra in Scientific Computing, CASC 2001. *Proceedings of the Fourth International Workshop on Computer Algebra in Scientific Computing*, Konstanz, pages 431–444. Springer-Verlag, September 2001.

[38] M. Pernpeintner, On the Structure of Gröbner Bases for Graph Coloring Ideals. Masters thesis, TU Munich, 2014.

[39] S. Ritscher, "Degree Bounds for Zero-dimensional Gröbner Bases", Master's Thesis, 2009.

[40] R. Tarjan, M. Yannakakis, "Simple linear-time algorithms to test chordality of graphs, test acyclicity of hypergraphs, and selectively reduce acyclic hypergraphs", *SIAM J.Comput.*, 13, pg. 566–579, 1984.

Amenability of Schreier Graphs and Strongly Generic Algorithms for the Conjugacy Problem

Volker Diekert
FMI, Universität Stuttgart
Stuttgart, Germany

Alexei G. Myasnikov
Stevens Institute of Technology
Hoboken, NJ, USA

Armin Weiß
FMI, Universität Stuttgart
Stuttgart, Germany

ABSTRACT

In various occasions the conjugacy problem in finitely generated amalgamated products and HNN extensions can be decided efficiently for elements which cannot be conjugated into the base groups. This observation asks for a bound on how many such elements there are. Such bounds can be derived using the theory of amenable graphs:

In this work we examine Schreier graphs of amalgamated products and HNN extensions. For an amalgamated product $G = H \star_A K$ with $[H : A] \geq [K : A] \geq 2$, the Schreier graph with respect to H or K turns out to be non-amenable if and only if $[H : A] \geq 3$. Moreover, for an HNN extension of the form $G = \langle H, b \mid bab^{-1} = \varphi(a), a \in A \rangle$, we show that the Schreier graph of G with respect to the subgroup H is non-amenable if and only if $A \neq H \neq \varphi(A)$.

As application of these characterizations we show that under certain conditions the conjugacy problem in fundamental groups of finite graphs of groups with free abelian vertex groups can be solved in polynomial time on a strongly generic set. Furthermore, the conjugacy problem in groups with more than one end can be solved with a strongly generic algorithm which has essentially the same time complexity as the word problem. These are rather striking results as the word problem might be easy, but the conjugacy problem might be even undecidable. Finally, our results yield another proof that the set where the conjugacy problem of the Baumslag group $\mathbf{G}_{1,2}$ is decidable in polynomial time is also strongly generic.

Categories and Subject Descriptors: F.2.2 [**Nonnumerical Algorithms and Problems**]: Computations on discrete structures; G.2.m [**Discrete Mathematics**]: Miscellaneous

General Terms: Algorithmic group theory

Keywords: generic case complexity, amenability, Schreier graph, HNN extension, amalgamated product, conjugacy problem

ISSAC'15, July 6–9, 2015, Bath, United Kingdom.

ACM 978-1-4503-3435-8/15/07 ...$15.00.
DOI: http://dx.doi.org/10.1145/2755996.2756644.

1. INTRODUCTION

The conjugacy problem of a group G asks on input of two words x, y over some set of generators whether there exists some group element z such that $zxz^{-1} = y$ as equality in G. In recent years, conjugacy played an important role in non-commutative cryptography, see e. g. [16, 27]. These applications are based on the idea that it is easy to create elements which are conjugated, but to check whether two given elements are conjugated might be difficult.

The conjugacy problem is inherently more difficult than the word problem (which asks whether some word represents the identity). Miller's group [22] is a famous example for that: its word problem is solvable in polynomial time (actually in logspace), but the conjugacy problem is undecidable. In [3] Borovik, Myasnikov, and Remeslennikov showed that, nevertheless, the conjugacy problem is decidable in polynomial time on a strongly generic set. This means that the probability to find an "undecidable" input decreases exponentially in its length – with other words conjugacy is decidable for "almost all" inputs.

Bogopolski, Martino, and Ventura constructed another example in [2]: an HNN extension of $\mathbb{Z}^4$ with several stable letters, which is actually a $\mathbb{Z}^4$-by-free group. For this group the decidability of the word problem is immediate by the standard algorithm for HNN extensions, but, again, the conjugacy problem is undecidable. Our results show that the conjugacy problem is strongly generically decidable in polynomial time, Corollary 4.

Even if the conjugacy problem is decidable, there might be a non-elementary gap between the complexities. Perhaps, the most striking example so far (for a not-on-purpose construction) is the Baumslag group $\mathbf{G}_{1,2}$. It is an HNN extension of the structural much simpler Baumslag-Solitar group $\mathbf{BS}_{1,2}$, which is defined with two (group) generators a and t and one defining relation $tat^{-1} = a^2$. Now, $\mathbf{G}_{1,2}$ is defined as the HNN extension of $\mathbf{BS}_{1,2}$ with stable letter b and the additional relation $bab^{-1} = t$.

It has a non-elementary Dehn function and was a prominent candidate for having the most difficult word problem among all one-relator groups until Myasnikov, Ushakov, and Won showed in [24] that the word problem of the Baumslag group is solvable in polynomial time! However, there are strong indications that this does not transfer to the conjugacy problem for the group $\mathbf{G}_{1,2}$. We conjectured in [9] that the conjugacy problem for $\mathbf{G}_{1,2}$ is non-elementary on average. Nevertheless, having a non-elementary time complexity on average does not prevent the set of "difficult instances" to be extremely sparse: we could use the techniques developed in [24] to show that the conjugacy problem can be solved in polynomial time for elements which cannot be conjugated into $\mathbf{BS}_{1,2}$. Moreover, we showed that this is a strongly generic set by deriving some explicit bounds; thus, we established a strongly generic polynomial time algorithm to solve the conjugacy problem for $\mathbf{G}_{1,2}$ [9].

The present paper extends the results on the Baumslag group by considering any finitely generated group G which is either an amalgamated product $G = H \star_A K$ with $H \neq A \neq K$ or an HNN extension $G = \langle H, t \mid tat^{-1} = \varphi(a) \text{ for } a \in A \rangle$ with stable letter t and an isomorphism $\varphi : A \to B$ for subgroups A and B of H. We characterize precisely when the Schreier graph $\Gamma(G, P, \Sigma)$ is non-amenable, see Theorem 2 and Theorem 3.

The notion of strongly generic sets is closely related to non-amenability. In Theorem 1 we derive that under certain conditions the words which cannot be conjugated into the base groups of the HNN extension (resp. amalgamated product) form a strongly generic set. This gives us another proof that the words in the Baumslag group which cannot be conjugated into the Baumslag-Solitar group form a strongly generic set. We present two more applications of our results:

First, we show in Corollary 4 that the conjugacy problem of the $\mathbb{Z}^4$-by-free group from [2] – and more generally, in fundamental groups of finite graphs of groups with finitely generated free abelian vertex groups – is decidable on a strongly generic set.

The second result is about finitely generated groups with more than one end. These groups have a characterization as amalgamated product or HNN extension where A is finite. We show that in this case in a strongly generic setting the conjugacy problem has essentially the same difficulty as the word problem, see Corollary 5. At first glance, this result is quite surprising because the word problem in G can be easy and the conjugacy problem can be undecidable. However, Corollary 5 affirms that in practice we might spend a hard time to find difficult instances for the conjugacy problem at all.

2. NOTATION

Words. An *alphabet* is a (finite) set Σ; an element $a \in \Sigma$ is called a *letter*. The the free monoid over Σ is denoted by Σ^*, its elements are called *words*. The length of a word w is denoted by $|w|$, and Σ^n forms the set of words of length n. The empty word is denoted by 1. Let $a \in \Sigma$ be a letter and $w \in \Sigma^*$; the number of occurrences of a in w is denoted by $|w|_a$. If w, p, x, q are words such that $w = pxq$, then we call p a *prefix*, x a *factor*, and q a *suffix* of w. We also say that $w = uxv$ is a *factorization.*

Involutions. An involution on a set S is a mapping $x \mapsto \overline{x}$ such that $\overline{\overline{x}} = x$. If S is a semigroup, then we additionally demand that $\overline{xy} = \overline{y}\,\overline{x}$. If S is a monoid, then it follows $\overline{1} = 1$. Moreover, every group is viewed as a monoid with involution by $g \mapsto g^{-1}$. Thus, in groups we always have $\overline{g} = g^{-1}$.

Groups. We consider groups G together with a finite subset of monoid generators $\Sigma \subseteq G$. Whenever convenient we demand $1 \notin \Sigma$. Every word $w \in \Sigma^*$ is simultaneously viewed as the corresponding group element in G under the canonical homomorphism $\eta : \Sigma^* \to G$, which is induced by the inclusion $\Sigma \subseteq G$. Frequently we write $w =_G w'$ as a shorthand of $\eta(w) = \eta(w')$. Thus, $w =_G w'$ means that w and w' represent the same element in the group G. If $\Sigma = \Sigma^{-1}$, then we call Σ *symmetric.* A symmetric set of generators is a set with the involution $a \mapsto \overline{a} = a^{-1}$.

Let $w \in \Sigma^*$ and Σ be symmetric. We say that w is *reduced* if there is no factor $a\overline{a}$ for any letter $a \in \Sigma$. It is called *cyclically reduced* if ww is reduced. For words (or group elements) we write $x \sim_G y$ to denote conjugacy, i. e., $x \sim_G y$ if and only if there exists some $z \in G$ such that $zx\overline{z} =_G y$.

The paper is about finitely generated groups which are either amalgamated products or HNN extensions. A group G is an amalgamated product if

$$G = H \star_A K = \langle H, K \mid \varphi(a) = \psi(a) \text{ for } a \in A \rangle$$

for groups H and K with a common subgroup A where φ and ψ are the inclusions of A in H and K. An HNN extension is of the form

$$G = \langle H, t \mid tat^{-1} = \varphi(a) \text{ for } a \in A \rangle$$

with a stable letter t and an isomorphism $\varphi : A \to B$ for subgroups A and B of H.

According to the more general notion of *graph of groups*, we refer to the groups H, K as "vertex groups" and to A as "edge group". Elements of G which are conjugate to some element in one of the vertex groups are called *elliptic*, the others are called *hyperbolic*[1]. Thus, if G is an amalgamated product, then the set of elliptic elements is $\bigcup_{g \in G} g(H \cup K)g^{-1}$; if G is an HNN extension, then the set of elliptic elements is $\bigcup_{g \in G} gHg^{-1}$. With $[H : A]$ we denote the index of the subgroup A in H.

Graphs. For the notation of graphs we follow Serre's book [26]. A *directed graph* $\Gamma = (V, E, \iota, \tau)$ is given by the following data: A set of *vertices* $V = V(\Gamma)$ and a set of *edges* $E = E(\Gamma)$ together with two mappings $\iota, \tau : E \to V$. The vertex $\iota(e)$ is the *initial* vertex (or *source*) of e, and $\tau(e)$ is the *target* of e. If $\tau(e) = u$ (resp. $\iota(e) = u$), we call e an *incoming edge* (resp. *outgoing edge*) of u. The *in-degree* (resp. *out-degree*) of a vertex is the number of incoming edges (resp. outgoing edges); Γ is called *locally finite* if the in-degrees and out-degrees of all vertices are finite. If both the in-degrees and out-degrees of all vertices are equal to some constant, then Γ is called *regular*; and if the degree is d, then it is *d-regular.*

An *undirected graph* is a directed graph Γ such that the set of edges E is equipped with an involution $e \mapsto \overline{e}$ without fixed points such that $\iota(e) = \tau(\overline{e})$. In particular, we have $\overline{\overline{e}} = e$ and $\overline{e} \neq e$ for all $e \in E$. Every undirected graph is also a directed graph by forgetting the involution.

For simplicity of notation, we often suppress the incidence functions (and involution): we mostly write $\Gamma = (V, E)$ for a (directed) graph Γ knowing that the incidence functions (and involution) are implicitly part of the specification.

Schreier and Cayley graphs. Let G be a group and P be a subgroup of G. The *Schreier graph* $\Gamma = \Gamma(G, P, \Sigma)$ of G with respect to P and set of monoid generators $\Sigma \subseteq G$ is defined as follows: The vertex set $V(\Gamma)$ is the set of right

[1]The distinction between elliptic and hyperbolic elements stems from group actions on trees. The group G acts naturally on a tree: its Bass-Serre tree corresponding to the splitting. The "elliptic" elements of G are those which fix a vertex of the tree. These are in turn exactly those elements which are conjugates of elements in H or K. The "hyperbolic" elements are those which act without fixed points.

cosets $P\backslash G = \{Pg \mid g \in G\}$ and the edge set $E(\Gamma)$ is the set $P\backslash G \times \Sigma$ with $\iota(Pg, a) = Pg$ and $\tau(Pg, a) = Pga$. For $|\Sigma| = d$ it is a directed d-regular graph. If Σ is symmetric and $1 \notin \Sigma$ (i. e., $1 \notin \Sigma = \Sigma^{-1}$), then $\Gamma(G, P, \Sigma)$ is an undirected graph thanks to the involution $\overline{(Pg, a)} = (Pga^{-1}, a^{-1})$.

If P is the trivial group, then $\Gamma(G, P, \Sigma)$ is the called the *Cayley graph* of G.

Strongly generic algorithms. In algorithmic problems the inputs are taken from some specific domain D; and in most cases the domain D comes as disjoint union $D = \bigcup \left\{ D^{(n)} \;\middle|\; n \in \mathbb{N} \right\}$ such that each $D^{(n)}$ is finite. For example, $D^{(n)}$ is the set of words of length n or the set of reduced words of length n or the set of integers having a binary representation with n bits, etc. A set $N \subseteq D$ is called *strongly negligible* if

$$\frac{\left|N \cap D^{(n)}\right|}{\left|D^{(n)}\right|} \in 2^{-\Omega(n)}.$$

A set $L \subseteq D$ is called *strongly generic* if its complement $D \backslash L$ is strongly negligible. Thus, as soon as L is strongly generic, if a random process chooses an element uniformly among all elements from $D^{(n)}$, then, for all practical purposes, we can ignore with increasing n the event that it finds an element outside L. A problem $\mathcal{P}$ is solved by a *strongly generic algorithm* $\mathcal{A}$ if there is a strongly generic set L such that the following three conditions hold:

(i) $\mathcal{A}$ solves $\mathcal{P}$ correctly on all inputs from L.

(ii) $\mathcal{A}$ may refuse to give an answer or it might not terminate, but only on inputs outside L.

(iii) If $\mathcal{A}$ gives an answer, then the answer *must* be correct.

The (time) complexity is the worst case behavior measured only on elements of L: for inputs in L we count the maximal number of steps until the algorithm stops with the correct answer.

3. RESULTS

Let G be a finitely generated group and $\eta : \Sigma^* \to G$ be a finite monoid presentation. In case that $\Sigma = \Sigma^{-1} \subseteq G$ is symmetric, let Δ denote the subset of cyclically reduced words in Σ^*.

THEOREM 1. *Let*

- $G = H \star_A K$ *be an amalgamated product such that* $[H : A] \geq 3$ *and* $[K : A] \geq 2$, *or let*
- $G = \left\langle H, t \;\middle|\; tat^{-1} = \varphi(a) \text{ for } a \in A \right\rangle$ *be an HNN extension with* $[H : A] \geq 2$ *and* $[H : \varphi(A)] \geq 2$.

Then the following holds:

(i) *The set of words representing hyperbolic elements in* G *is strongly generic in* Σ^*.

(ii) *If* Σ *is symmetric, then the set of cyclically reduced words representing hyperbolic elements in* G *is strongly generic in* Δ, *too.*

The proof of Theorem 1 relies on the notion of an *amenable graph* given below in Section 4 and the following two results about amenable Schreier graphs.

THEOREM 2. *Let* $G = H \star_A K$ *with* $[H : A] \geq [K : A] \geq 2$ *and* $P \in \{H, K\}$ *and let* Σ *be a symmetric set of generators. Then the Schreier graph* $\Gamma(G, P, \Sigma)$ *is non-amenable if and only if* $[H : A] \geq 3$.

THEOREM 3. *Let* $G = \left\langle H, t \;\middle|\; tat^{-1} = \varphi(a) \text{ for } a \in A \right\rangle$ *be an HNN extension and let* Σ *be a symmetric set of generators of* G. *Then the Schreier graph* $\Gamma(G, H, \Sigma)$ *is non-amenable if and only if both* $[H : A] \geq 2$ *and* $[H : \varphi(A)] \geq 2$.

Example 1. Let $\mathbf{BS}_{p,q} = \left\langle a, t \;\middle|\; ta^pt^{-1} = a^q \right\rangle$ the Baumslag-Solitar group with $1 \leq p \leq q$. Furthermore, let H be the subgroup generated by a. Then the Schreier graph $\Gamma(\mathbf{BS}_{p,q}, H, \{a, \bar{a}, t, \bar{t}\})$ is amenable if and only if $p = 1$.

Actually, even the Cayley graph of $\mathbf{BS}_{1,q}$ is amenable, see [31, Thm. 15.14]. $\diamond$

Example 2. Let $\mathbf{G}_{1,2} = \left\langle \mathbf{BS}_{1,2}, b \;\middle|\; bab^{-1} = t \right\rangle$ the Baumslag group. We have shown in [9] that the Schreier graph $\Gamma(\mathbf{G}_{1,2}, \mathbf{BS}_{1,2}, \{a, \bar{a}, b, \bar{b}\})$ is non-amenable. This fact is now a special case of Theorem 3. $\diamond$

We postpone the proofs of Theorem 2 and 3 and present two more applications of these theorems: The first corollary shows that also the conjugacy problem of the $\mathbb{Z}^4$-by-free group of [2] (with undecidable conjugacy problem) is strongly generically decidable in polynomial time.

COROLLARY 4. *If one of the following three cases holds*

- $G = H \star_A K$ *is an amalgamated product with* H, K *free abelian and* $[H : A] \geq 3$, $[K : A] \geq 2$,
- $G = \left\langle H, t \;\middle|\; tat^{-1} = \varphi(a) \text{ for } a \in A \right\rangle$ *is an HNN extension with* H *free abelian and both* $[H : A] \geq 2$ *and* $[H : \varphi(A)] \geq 2$,
- G *is a fundamental group of a reduced finite graph of groups*[2] *with free abelian vertex groups and at least two edges,*

then the conjugacy problem of G *is decidable in polynomial time on a strongly generic set.*

By [1, Thm. 1.4.7] the conjugacy problem is decidable for words representing hyperbolic elements. Hence, by Theorem 1 the result follows when we replace "decidable in polynomial time" by "decidable". The polynomial time bound can be derived using the results of [12, 30] that systems of linear integer equations can be solved in polynomial time. For details we refer to the full version on arXiv [10].

The next corollary is about the conjugacy problem in groups with more than one end[3]. It shows that in a strongly generic setting the conjugacy problem is essentially as difficult as the word problem. Note that we do not require anything about the conjugacy problem at all!

COROLLARY 5. *Let* G *be a finitely generated group with more than one end. If the word problem of* G *is decidable in polynomial time (resp. in time* $\mathcal{O}(t(n))$ *with* $t(n) \geq n$), *then there is a strongly generic algorithm which solves the conjugacy problem of* G *in polynomial time (resp. in time* $\mathcal{O}(nt(n + \mathcal{O}(1))))$ *– in particular, the conjugacy problem of* G *is decidable on a strongly generic set.*

[2]For a definition we refer to [26].

[3]A group has more than one end if its Cayley graph can be split into two infinite connected components by removing some finite set of vertices. A more thorough definition can be found e. g. in the survey [23].

Proof. Due to Stallings' structure theorem [29], we have to consider two situations: either G is an amalgamated product $G = H \star_A K$ with $H \neq A \neq K$ or G is an HHN extension $G = \langle H, t \mid tat^{-1} = \varphi(a) \text{ for } a \in A \rangle$ where in both cases the edge group A is finite. If $G = H \star_A K$ with $[H : A] = [K : A] = 2$ or $G = \langle H, t \mid tat^{-1} = \varphi(a) \text{ for } a \in A \rangle)$ with $A = H$ (and thus $H = \varphi(A)$), then the group G is virtually cyclic [6, Thm. IV.6.12]. For virtually cyclic groups the conjugacy problem is very easy: it can be solved in linear time. (In fact, all virtually free groups have conjugacy problem solvable in linear time, see e.g. [8, Prop. 6.1]).

Thus, we can assume that either we have $[H : A] \geq 3$ and $[K : A] \geq 2$ (if $G = H \star_A K$) or we have $[H : A] \geq 2$ (if $G = \langle H, t \mid tat^{-1} = \varphi(a) \text{ for } a \in A \rangle$). Hence, by Theorem 1 over any finite alphabet the set of words representing hyperbolic elements is strongly generic.

We now describe an algorithm to solve the conjugacy problem which gives an answer as long as one of the input words is hyperbolic. We choose a finite symmetric generating set Σ such that $A \subseteq \Sigma$ and $\Sigma \subseteq H \cup K$ (if $G = H \star_A K$) respectively $A, \varphi(A) \subseteq \Sigma$ and $\Sigma \subseteq H \cup \{t, \bar{t}\}$ (if $G = \langle H, t \mid tat^{-1} = \varphi(a) \text{ for } a \in A \rangle$).

Let $u, v \in \Sigma^*$ be input words with $|uv| = n$. The question is whether u and v are conjugate. First, we apply Britton reductions to both words leading to Britton-reduced words u' and v'. This means that either the number of alternations between H and K is minimized or the number of letters from $\{t, \bar{t}\}$ is minimized. If the word problem of G is decidable in time $t(n)$, we can perform Britton reductions for a word w with $|w| \leq n$ in time at most $\mathcal{O}(nt(n))$. Indeed, if we see, for example, a factor tpt^{-1} where $p \in \Sigma^*$ with $p =_G a$ for some $a \in A$, then we can replace the factor tpt^{-1} by $\varphi(a)$, which is a word of length one. The other situations are similar.

Next, in the HNN case, we write $u' = u_1' u_2'$ such that $\left| |u_1'|_t + |u_1'|_{\bar{t}} - |u_2'|_t - |u_2'|_{\bar{t}} \right| \leq 1$ and u_1' ends in t or $\bar{t}$; then we apply Britton reductions to the word $u_2' u_1'$. Likewise, we proceed for v'. This leads to cyclically Britton-reduced words u'' and v'' such that $u \sim_G u''$ and $v \sim_G v''$. In the case of an amalgam, $u' = u_1' u_2'$ is factorized such that the number of alternations between the factors H and K in u_1' and in u_2' differ by at most one and u_1' ends with letters from the other factor than u_2' starts with – then we proceed as for HNN extensions.

Collins' Lemma (see e.g. [21]) tells us several things: u is hyperbolic if and only if u'' does not belong to a vertex group – the same assertion holds for v and v''. By the very definition, hyperbolic elements are never conjugate to elliptic elements. Thus, if say u is elliptic and v is hyperbolic, then u and v are not conjugate. If both are elliptic, then the algorithm refuses the answer. Thus, without restriction, henceforth u and v are both hyperbolic. In this case Collins' Lemma tells us that u and v are conjugate if and only if there is a cyclic permutation $u_2'' u_1''$ of $u'' = u_1'' u_2''$ and some $a \in A$ such that $a u_2'' u_1'' =_G v'' a$. This can be checked with at most $n\,|A|$ calls to the word problem (with inputs of length $n + 2$). We need time $\mathcal{O}(nt(n + \mathcal{O}(1)))$ to perform the entire algorithm. □

4. PROOFS FOR THEOREMS 1, 2, AND 3

4.1 Random walks and amenability

There is large body of literature on amenable groups, graphs, and metric spaces as well as on different notions for random walks. In this section we review some of the known characterizations of amenability for undirected d-regular graphs and the consequences for return probabilities of random walks in (directed) Schreier graphs. We consider d-regular graphs $\Gamma = (V, E)$, only. This means for each $v \in V$ there are exactly d outgoing edges and d incoming edges. We allow self-loops and multiple edges. As a consequence, there are exactly d^n different paths of length n starting at a fixed vertex. Recall that undirected graphs are special cases of directed graphs.

Random Walks. The *random walk* on a directed graph is as follows: it starts at some vertex, chooses an outgoing edge uniformly at random and goes to the target vertex of this edge, then it chooses the next edge and so on. With $p^{(n)}(u, v)$ we denote the probability that the random walk on Γ ends after n steps in v when starting in u. Thus,

$$p^{(n)}(u, v) = \frac{\text{number of paths from } u \text{ to } v}{d^n}.$$

Similarly we can define the *random walk without backtracking* on an undirected graph: it starts by choosing an edge starting at u uniformly at random. For the following steps the inverse of the previous edge is excluded, i.e., there are only $d - 1$ possible choices each of which has equal probability. We obtain the following probability for $n \geq 1$:

$$q^{(n)}(u, v) = \frac{\#\text{paths without backtracking from } u \text{ to } v}{d \cdot (d-1)^{n-1}}.$$

We say that the random walk has *exponentially decreasing return probability* if there are constants $c, \varepsilon > 0$ such that for all $n \in \mathbb{N}$ and $u, v \in V$ we have $p^{(n)}(u, v) \leq c 2^{-\varepsilon n}$.

Spectral Radius. We can think of V as a subset of $\mathbb{R}^V$ by identifying a vertex $u \in V$ with its characteristic function x_u. (Thus, $x_u(v) = 1$ if $u = v$ and $x_u(v) = 0$ otherwise.) We restrict our attention to the Hilbert space of functions $x : V \to \mathbb{R}$ such that $\|x\| = \sqrt{\sum_{v \in V} x(u)^2} < \infty$. The inner product is as usual $\langle x, y \rangle = \sum_{u \in V} x(u) y(v)$.

The unit vectors x_u span a dense vector space in the Hilbert space and Γ defines a *random walk operator* R_Γ by letting

$$R_\Gamma(x_u) = \frac{1}{d} \sum \left\{ x_{\tau(e)} \mid e \in E \wedge \iota(e) = u \right\}.$$

It is clear that $R_\Gamma^n(x_u)$ describes exactly the probability distribution of the random walk on Γ of length n starting in vertex u. The *spectral radius* $\rho(\Gamma)$ is defined as

$$\rho(\Gamma) = \sup \left\{ \langle x, R_\Gamma(x) \rangle \mid \|x\| = 1 \right\}.$$

Let R be any linear operator on the Hilbert space. Its *norm* $\|R\|$ is defined by

$$\|R\| = \sup \left\{ \sqrt{|\langle Rx, Rx \rangle|} \;\middle|\; \|x\| = 1 \right\}.$$

We have $\rho(\Gamma) \leq \|R_\Gamma\| \leq 1$. Indeed, $\rho(\Gamma) \leq \|R_\Gamma\|$ follows immediately by Cauchy-Schwarz. A slightly more complicated calculation shows that $\|R_\Gamma\| \leq 1$, see [28, Lem. I.3.12].

Distance and k-th neighborhood. Let $\Gamma = (V, E)$ be an undirected graph. The *distance* $d(u, v)$ between vertices u and v is defined by the length of a shortest path connecting u and v, if there is such a path. Otherwise, we let $d(u, v) = \infty$.

For $k \in \mathbb{N}$ the k-th neighborhood $\mathcal{N}^k(U)$ of a set of vertices $U \subseteq V$ is defined by

$$\mathcal{N}^k(U) = \{ v \in V \mid \exists u \in U : d(u, v) \leq k \}.$$

Amenability and return probabilities. The following proposition well-known. For Cayley graphs it goes back to Kesten [19, 20]. The generalization to arbitrary graphs of bounded degree appeared in [13]. Condition (i) is due to Gromov (see [17, Condition $0.5.C_1''$]). The result about random walks without backtracking was shown independently by Cohen [5] and Grigorchuk [15] for Cayley graphs of finitely generated groups. They used the notion of *cogrowth*. The generalization to arbitrary d-regular graphs was proven by Northshield [25]. Proofs of conditions (i)–(iv) can also be found in Thm. 32 and Thm. 51 of [4] and Thm. 4.27 of [28].

PROPOSITION 6. *Let $\Gamma = (V, E)$ be a d-regular undirected graph. Then the following statements are equivalent:*

(i) Γ *satisfies the* Gromov condition*: there exists a map $f : V \to V$ such that $\sup_{v \in V} d(f(v), v) < \infty$ and $\left|f^{-1}(v)\right| \geq 2$ for all $v \in V$.*

(ii) Γ *satisfies the* doubling condition*: there exists some $k \in \mathbb{N}$ such that for every finite $U \subseteq V$ we have*
$$\left|\mathcal{N}^k(U)\right| \geq 2\,|U|\,.$$

(iii) *The spectral radius is less than one: $\rho(\Gamma) < 1$.*

(iv) *The random walk on Γ has exponentially decreasing return probability.*

(v) *The random walk on Γ without backtracking has exponentially decreasing return probability.*

Definition 1. A graph is called *non-amenable* if it satisfies one of the equivalent conditions of Proposition 6. Otherwise, it is called *amenable*.

A finitely generated group is called *non-amenable* (resp. *amenable*) if it has a non-amenable (resp. amenable) Cayley graph with respect to some finite symmetric generating set.

Sometimes non-amenable graph are also called *infinite expanders* because in finite graph theory an undirected d-regular graph is an expander if and only if the second largest eigenvalue of its random walk matrix is strictly less than 1. Condition (iii) plays an analogue role for infinite graphs.

The notion of amenability is originally for groups, where it was first defined via invariant means. Using the Følner condition [11] (a slight modification of the doubling condition (ii)), it can be seen that this definition coincides with Definition 1. Moreover, it is well-known that amenability is a property of the group and does not depend on its symmetric generating set. This can be generalized to Schreier graphs:

COROLLARY 7. *Let G be a finitely generated group and P be a subgroup of G. Let Σ_1 and Σ_2 be two finite symmetric generating sets of G. Then, $\Gamma(G, P, \Sigma_1)$ is amenable if and only if $\Gamma(G, P, \Sigma_2)$ is amenable.*

Proof. This is trivial consequence of Proposition 6 because the Gromov condition (i) is invariant under the change of finite generating sets. □

Clearly, Corollary 7 has been known before. For example it can be found in [18, Prop 6.2] which in turn refers to [4, Prop. 38]. Unfortunately, [4, Prop. 38] is not correct as it is stated there. We give a counter example in Example 6. Still, the mistake did not affect the correctness of the proof in [18] as only a special case of the statement is used.

It is a classical fact that groups of subexponential growth are amenable, see e. g. [4, Thm. 66]. As a direct consequence, all virtually nilpotent and, in particular, all abelian groups are amenable. On the other hand, non-abelian free groups are non-amenable. This can be verified for example using the Gromov condition (i). The function f can be defined by deleting the last letter of a reduced word and letting $f(1)$ arbitrary.

Condition (iv) of Proposition 6 can be defined for all directed Schreier graphs (not only undirected ones). However, (iv) depends on the chosen set of monoid generators. Moreover, Example 3 shows that, in general, for directed graphs conditions (iii) and (iv) in Proposition 6 are not equivalent.

Example 3. Let $G = \mathbb{Z}$. Compare the following two directed and different Cayley graphs with respect to the letters $a = -1$, $\bar{a} = 1$, and $b = 2$.

The Cayley graph of G with respect to the symmetric generating set $\Sigma = \{a, \bar{a}\}$ is amenable; and the random walk has a return probability in $\Omega(\frac{1}{\sqrt{n}})$ which is not exponentially decreasing. For $\Sigma' = \{a, b\}$ we obtain directed 2-regular Cayley graph. The random walk on $\Gamma(G, \{1\}, \Sigma')$ has exponentially decreasing return probability. More precisely, the return probability is at most $\binom{n}{\lceil n/3 \rceil}2^{-n}$. On the other hand, we have $\rho(\Gamma) = 1$. To see this define $x_n(v) = \frac{1}{\sqrt{n}}$ if $v \in \{1, \ldots, n\}$ and $x_n(v) = 0$ otherwise for $n \geq 1$. Then we have $\|x_n\| = 1$ and $\lim_{n\to\infty} \langle x_n,\, R_\Gamma x_n\rangle = 1$. ◇

For a directed graph $\Gamma = (V, E)$, we can construct an undirected graph $\Gamma' = (V, E \cup \overline{E})$, where $\overline{E}$ is a disjoint copy of E, and $\iota(\bar{e}) = \tau(e), \tau(\bar{e}) = \iota(e)$ for $\bar{e} \in \overline{E}$. If Γ is d-regular, then Γ' is $2d$-regular. We call Γ' the *undirected version* of Γ. Concerning random walks on directed graphs, we obtain Lemma 8, which is a special case of [31, Thm. 10.6]. As the statement in [31] is slightly different, we give a proof in [10].

LEMMA 8. *Let $\Gamma = (V, E)$ be a d-regular directed graph with random walk operator R. If we have $\rho(\Gamma) < 1$ (the spectral radius is less than 1), then the undirected version $\Gamma' = (V, E \cup \overline{E})$ of Γ is non-amenable.*

Moreover, if Γ' is non-amenable, then the random walk on Γ has exponentially decreasing return probability.

Note that the converse of Lemma 8 is not true, in general, (even not under the stronger assumption of Γ being strongly connected) as we have seen in Example 3.

Next, we combine Corollary 7 (independence of the symmetric generating set) with Lemma 8:

PROPOSITION 9. *Let G be a finitely generated group and P be a subgroup of G. Let Σ be a finite symmetric generating set of G. If $\Gamma(G, P, \Sigma)$ is non-amenable and Σ' is a finite monoid generating set of G, then the random walk on $\Gamma(G, P, \Sigma')$ has exponentially decreasing return probability.*

4.2 Amenability of Schreier graphs for amalgams

The aim of this section is to prove Theorem 2. Thus, we consider an amalgamated product $G = H \star_A K$ with vertex groups H and K and edge group A. We start by choosing transversals $C \subseteq H$ and $D \subseteq K$ for cosets of A in H and in

K with $1 \in C \cap D$ such that there are unique decompositions $H = AC$ and $K = AD$. The following lemma is easy to see, c.f. [7, Sec. 7.4]).

LEMMA 10. *Every group element $g \in G$ can be uniquely written as*

$$g =_G x_0 \cdots x_k$$

for some $k \in \mathbb{N}$, $x_0 \in H \cup K$ such that for all $1 \le i \le k$ we have

$$x_i \in C \cup D \setminus \{1\};$$
$$x_{i-1} \in H \iff x_i \in K.$$

Example 4. Let $G = H \star_A K$ with $[H : A] = [K : A] = 2$ and $P \in \{H, K\}$, $\Sigma \subseteq A \cup \{h, k\}$ a finite generating set with $h \in H$ and $k \in K$. Then we have

$$p^{(2n)}(P, P) \in \Theta(n^{-1/2}).$$

As A is normal in both H and K, we can rewrite any word $w \in \Sigma^*$ to a unique normal form $x_0 \cdots x_\ell$ for some $\ell \in \mathbb{N}$ such that $x_0 \in H \cup K$, $x_i \in \{h, k\}$ for $i > 0$ and letters h and k always alternate.

Let $P \in \{H, K\}$ one of the vertex groups. Up to self-loops the Schreier graph $\Gamma(G, P, \Sigma)$ is isomorphic to the Cayley graph $\Gamma_{\mathbb{Z}}$ of $\mathbb{Z}$ with respect to the natural symmetric generating set $\{\pm 1\}$. The return probability in $\Gamma_{\mathbb{Z}}$ (without self-loops) is $\binom{n}{n/2} 2^{-n}$ for n even; an easy estimation shows that $p^{(2n)}(P, P) \in \Theta(n^{-1/2})$ whether or not there are self-loops. ◇

Proof of Theorem 2. For the only-if direction we assume $[H : A] = [K : A] = 2$. Then the Schreier graph $\Gamma(G, P, \Sigma)$ is amenable due to Example 4 and Proposition 6.

For the other direction let $[H : A] \ge 3$. We show condition (i) in Proposition 6. In order to do so, we define a function $f : P\backslash G \to P\backslash G$ as follows: We fix $c, c' \in C$ with $c \ne 1 \ne c'$ and $c \ne c'$ and some $1 \ne d \in D$. For a normal form w (according to Lemma 10) with $w = vcd$ or $w = vc'd$ for some word v, set $f(Pw) = Pv$. Likewise, for a normal form w with $w = vdc$ or $w = vdc'$, set $f(Pw) = Pv$. Otherwise, set $f(Pw) = Pw$. Due to Lemma 10, the function f is well-defined. Let $k \in \mathbb{N}$ be some number which is large enough such that c, c', and d can be written with at most k letters from Σ. Then we obtain $\sup\{d(f(Pw), Pw) \mid Pw \in P\backslash G\} \le 2k < \infty$. For every normal form w, either wcd and $wc'd$ or wdc and wdc' are normal forms. Hence, we have $\left|f^{-1}(Pw)\right| \ge 2$ for all $w \in G$. □

4.3 Amenability of Schreier graphs for HNN extensions

The aim of this section is to prove Theorem 3. Thus, let

$$G = \left\langle H, t \mid tat^{-1} = \varphi(a) \text{ for } a \in A \right\rangle$$

be an HNN extension of H with an isomorphism $\varphi : A \to B$ of subgroups A, B of H. We can prove an analog result as for amalgamated products by the same strategy: first, we define certain normal forms, second, we show that the Schreier graph is amenable if $H = A$, and third, we show, using again the Gromov condition, that it is non-amenable for $A \ne H \ne \varphi(A)$.

To begin with, we choose transversals for cosets of A and $B = \varphi(A)$ in H; that is $C, D \subseteq H$ with $1 \in C \cap D$ such that there are unique decompositions $H = AC$ and $H = BD$. The next lemma is easy to see again, c.f. [7, Sec. 7.3]. It is the analogue of Lemma 10. We write t^{-1} for the letter $\bar{t}$.

LEMMA 11. *Every group element $g \in G$ can be uniquely factorized (as a word over $H \cup \{t, \bar{t}\}$) as*

$$g =_G x_0 t^{\varepsilon_1} x_1 \cdots t^{\varepsilon_k} x_k$$

such that $k \in \mathbb{N}$, $x_0 \in H$, and for all $1 \le i \le k$ we have:

- *$x_i \in C \cup D$ and $\varepsilon_i \in \{\pm 1\}$;*
- *if $\varepsilon_i = 1$, then $x_i \in C$; if $\varepsilon_i = -1$, then $x_i \in D$;*
- *if $\varepsilon_i = -\varepsilon_{i+1}$ and $i < k$, then $x_i \ne 1$.*

Example 5. Let $G = \left\langle H, t \mid tat^{-1} = \varphi(a), a \in A \right\rangle$ with $A = H \ne \{1\}$ (and $B = H$ or $B \ne H$). Let $\Sigma \subseteq H \cup \{t, \bar{t}\}$ be a finite generating set of G. Then we have

$$p^{(n)}(H, H) \in \Omega(n^{-3/2}).$$

Let $0 \le m \le n/2$. Consider a word $w \in \Sigma^*$ of length n with $m = |w|_t = |w|_{\bar{t}}$ such that every prefix w' of w satisfies $|w'|_t \ge |w'|_{\bar{t}}$. Then we have $w \in H$. This is because always some Britton reduction can be applied (replacing $ta\bar{t}$ by $\varphi(a)$), and hence the word can be reduced to some word in H. Restricted to $\{t, \bar{t}\}$, these words are exactly the Dyck words of length $2m$. The number of Dyck words of length $2m$ is the m-th Catalan number $\frac{1}{m+1}\binom{2m}{m}$, see e. g. [14]. We have $\frac{1}{m+1}\binom{2m}{m} \in \Theta(m^{-3/2} \cdot 4^m)$. As $m \le n$ we obtain the desired result. ◇

Proof of Theorem 3. The case $A = H$ leads to an amenable Schreier graph as we calculated in Example 5.

For the other direction, let $[H : A] \ge 2$ and $[H : B] \ge 2$. We show condition (i) in Proposition 6. In order to do so, we define a function $f : H\backslash G \to H\backslash G$ as follows: We fix $1 \ne c \in C$ and $1 \ne d \in D$. (Note that we cannot exclude $c = d$.) Let $w = x_0 t^{\varepsilon_1} x_1 \cdots t^{\varepsilon_k} x_k$ be in normal form according to Lemma 11. If w ends with $x_k = 1$, then there is some $\gamma \in \{c, d\}$ (depending on ε_k) such that both $w\gamma t$ and $w\gamma\bar{t}$ are in normal form (we identify $1 \in H$ with the empty word); and we set $f(Hw\gamma t) = f(Hw\gamma\bar{t}) = Hw$. If w ends with $x_k \ne 1$, then wtc and $w\bar{t}d$ are both in normal form, and we set $f(Hwtc) = f(Hw\bar{t}d) = Hw$. Furthermore, we set $f(Hw') = Hw'$ for words w' in normal form which are not of the above form. Because of Lemma 11, the function f is well-defined. Let $k \in \mathbb{N}$ some number which is large enough that c, d, t and $\bar{t}$ can we written with at most k letters from Σ. Then we obtain $\sup\{d(f(Hw), Hw) \mid Hw \in H\backslash G\} \le 2k < \infty$. Moreover, we have $\left|f^{-1}(Hw)\right| \ge 2$ for all $w \in G$. □

4.4 Proof of Theorem 1

The aim of this section is to prove Theorem 1 using Theorem 2 for amalgams and Theorem 3 for HNN extensions. In the following we say a word over a set of generators is *elliptic* if it represents an elliptic element in the generated group. This is the complement of the words representing hyperbolic group elements. Therefore, Theorem 1 is a consequence of the following two assertions:

(i) The set of elliptic words is strongly negligible in Σ^*.

(ii) The set of cyclically reduced, elliptic words is strongly negligible in Δ (recall that Δ denotes the set of cyclically reduced words).

We only state the proof of Theorem 1 for HNN extensions. The proof for amalgamated products is an almost verbatim translation of the proof for HNN extensions. Details are left to the reader.

First, let us consider another finite set of generators Σ' with some additional properties. Without restriction we may assume that, first, Σ' is symmetric and, second, $t, \bar{t} \in \Sigma'$ and $\Sigma' \subseteq H \cup \{t, \bar{t}\}$. Part of the difficulty in the proof is due to the fact that encoding Σ^* into Σ'^* turns Σ^* into a strongly negligible set inside Σ'^*, in general. This makes the proof a little bit tedious.

Recall that we do not require Σ to be symmetric. Every letter $a \in \Sigma$ can be written as a word $u_a \in \Sigma'^*$. We need also the somehow other direction. For every letter $a \in \Sigma$ and every factorization $u_a = p_a q_a$ (with $q_a \neq 1$) we assign a pair of words $(P_a, Q_a) \in \Sigma^* \times \Sigma^*$ with $P_a =_G p_a$ and $Q_a =_G q_a$. We let $c \in \mathbb{N}$ be a constant with $|P_a Q_a| \leq c$ and $|u_a| \leq c$ for all $a \in \Sigma$ and all factorizations $u_a = p_a q_a$. We obtain a list $\mathcal{L} = \{(P_a, Q_a, a) \mid a \in \Sigma\}$ containing at most $c\,|\Sigma|$ tuples.

Proof of (i). The idea is now to label certain words in Σ^* such that at the end all elliptic words are labeled and that the set of words having a label is strongly negligible.

By Theorem 3 the Schreier graph $\Gamma(G, H, \Sigma \cup \Sigma^{-1})$ is non-amenable. Thus, by Proposition 9, the random walk on $\Gamma(G, H, \Sigma)$ has exponentially decreasing return probability. Therefore, we can label all words in Σ^* which represent elements in H – now the set of words with a label is strongly negligible. But of course, there are many more elliptic elements. Hence, we have to label more words.

Next, for every $(P_a, Q_a, a) \in \mathcal{L}$ and every word of the form $Q_a v P_a$ which has a label, we label the word $w = av$, too. The length of words $Q_a v P_a$ is between $|w|$ and $|w| + c$ and for every v there are at most $c \cdot |\Sigma|$ of the form (Q_a, P_a). Hence, the set of labeled words remains strongly negligible.

In one more round we label all words $w_2 w_1$ where $w_1 w_2$ has a label. Still the set of words with label is strongly negligible.

We claim that all elliptic elements are labeled now. To see this, let $w = a_1 \cdots a_n$ be a word with $a_i \in \Sigma$ such that w is conjugate to some element in H. Then the same is true for the word $w' = u_{a_1} \cdots u_{a_n} \in \Sigma'^*$ because $w =_G w'$. Recall that we have $\Sigma' \subseteq H \cup \{t, \bar{t}\}$. Hence, by Collins' Lemma, we can factorize $w' = w_1' w_2'$ such that $w_2' w_1'$ represents an element in H. Therefore, we find some index i and a factorization $u_{a_i} = p_{a_i} q_{a_i}$ with $q_{a_i} \neq 1$ such that

$$\begin{aligned} w_2' w_1' &= q_{a_i} u_{a_{i+1}} \cdots u_{a_n} u_{a_1} \cdots u_{a_{i-1}} p_{a_i} \\ &=_G Q_{a_i} a_{i+1} \cdots a_n a_1 \cdots a_{i-1} P_{a_i} = Q_{a_i} v P_{a_i}. \end{aligned}$$

The word $Q_{a_i} v P_{a_i}$ got a label because it is a word representing an element in H. This puts a label on $a_i v$, too. Finally, w is a transposition of $a_i v$. Hence, latest in the last step, w got a label. □

Proof of (ii). Recall that Δ denotes the subset of cyclically reduced words and that Σ is assumed to be symmetric (otherwise we did not define the notion of reduced word). Let Δ' denote the subset of reduced words. Hence, we have

$$\Delta \subseteq \Delta' \subseteq \Sigma^*.$$

We have $\Sigma \geq 4$ (otherwise G is a cyclic group); hence, the degree d of the Schreier graph $\Gamma(G, H, \Sigma)$ is at least 4. Moreover, $\Delta' \cap \Sigma^n = d(d-1)^{n-1}$ and $\Delta \cap \Sigma^n \geq d(d-2)(d-1)^{n-2}$ for all $n \geq 1$. Since $\frac{|\Delta' \cap \Sigma^n|}{|\Delta \cap \Sigma^n|} \leq \frac{d-1}{d-2}$, the proof of (ii) is reduced to show the following lemma.

LEMMA 12. *The set of cyclically reduced, elliptic words is strongly negligible in the set of reduced words Δ'.*

Proof. Again we label words in Δ' such that at the end all elliptic words are labeled and that the set of words with label is strongly negligible.

We start to label all reduced words in Σ^* which have length at most $4c$. Next, for each $(P_a, Q_a, a) \in \mathcal{L}$ we consider all words of the form $W = Q_a v P_a$ where, first, av is reduced, second, $|v| \geq 2c$, and third, $Q_a v P_a$ represents an element in H. In particular, W is elliptic. Since v is reduced and long enough, we obtain a reduced word $W' = Q_a' u P_a'$ such that $W =_G W'$, Q_a' is a prefix of Q_a, and P_a' is a suffix of P_a. We label W'. It represents an element in H. Thus, the set of reduced words with a label is strongly negligible in Δ' by Proposition 6 (v).

In the next round we label all words av where there exists some $(P_a, Q_a, a) \in \mathcal{L}$ such that $Q_a v P_a$ reduces to some reduced word W' which is labeled. Now, we can recover av if we know the following four data:

$$W',\ (P_a, Q_a, a) \in \mathcal{L},\ |Q_a'|,\ \text{and}\ |P_a'|. \tag{1}$$

Thus, each labeled W' can produce at most $c\,|\Sigma|\,(c+1)^2 \in \mathcal{O}(1)$ new labels. Hence, the set of reduced words with label is still strongly negligible. Note that now all words representing elements of H are labeled.

Finally, as above, we label all words $w_2 w_1$ where $w_1 w_2$ has a label; and the set of reduced words with label remains strongly negligible.

It remains to show that all cyclically reduced elliptic words are labeled. This is true for all words of length at most $4c$. Hence, let $n > 4c$ and $w = a_1 \cdots a_n$ be a cyclically reduced word with $a_i \in \Sigma$ such that w is conjugate to some element in H. As above we switch to the corresponding word $w' = u_{a_1} \cdots u_{a_n} \in \Sigma'^*$. By Collins' Lemma, we can factorize $w' = w_1' w_2'$ such that $w_2' w_1'$ represents an element in H. Again, we find some index i and $(P_{a_i}, Q_{a_i}, a_i) \in \mathcal{L}$ together with a factorization $w_2' w_1' = q_{a_i} u_{a_{i+1}} \cdots u_{a_n} u_{a_1} \cdots u_{a_{i-1}} p_{a_i}$ and $u_{a_i} = p_{a_i} q_{a_i}$. Now, since w is cyclically reduced, the word $a_i v = a_i a_{i+1} \cdots a_n a_1 \cdots a_{i-1}$ is reduced. Moreover,

$$w_2' w_1' =_G Q_{a_i} a_{i+1} \cdots a_n a_1 \cdots a_{i-1} P_{a_i} = Q_{a_i} v P_{a_i} \in H.$$

According to our procedure the reduced word $a_i v$ got a label. Finally, w is a transposition of $a_i v$. Hence, latest in the last step, w got a label. □

A counterexample for Prop. 38 of [4]

The fact that amenability of Schreier graphs does not depend on the symmetric generating set can be derived easily from [4, Prop. 38], see [18, Prop 6.2]. However, the proposition does not hold in full generality as stated in [4], see Example 6 below. (It still holds for graphs of bounded degree and the proof in [18, Prop 6.2] is therefore not affected.) We need the notion of quasi-isometry:

Definition 2. A *quasi-isometry* between graphs $\Gamma = (V, E)$ and $\Gamma' = (V', E')$ is a function $f : V \to V'$ such that there is some constant $C > 0$ satisfying the following conditions:

- $\frac{1}{C} \cdot d_\Gamma(x, y) - C \leq d_{\Gamma'}(f(x), f(y)) \leq C \cdot d_\Gamma(x, y) + C$ for all $x, y \in V$.
- For every $y \in V'$ there exists some $x \in V$ such that $d_{\Gamma'}(y, f(x)) \leq C$.

[4, Prop. 38] asserts that condition (i) of Proposition 6 is a quasi-isometry invariant for discrete metric spaces; thus, in particular, for arbitrary locally finite undirected graphs. However this is not true, in general. There are locally finite graphs satisfying Proposition 6 (i) and which are quasi-isometric to amenable graphs:

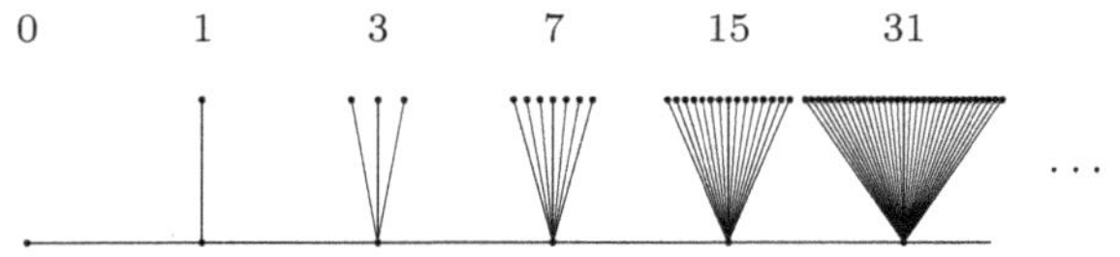

Figure 1: Counterexample for [4, Prop. 38].

Example 6. Consider an infinite sequence of rooted trees T_k each with 2^k nodes of which $2^k - 1$ are leaves for $k = 0, 1, 2, \ldots$. Connect the root of T_k with the root of T_{k+1}, see Figure 1 for the resulting undirected graph Γ (the numbers displayed there are the numbers of leaves of the trees T_k). Since there is a two-to-one mapping of T_{k+1} onto T_k the graph satisfies the Gromov condition from Proposition 6 (i). On the other hand, mapping all leaves to their roots we obtain a quasi-isometry onto a graph which is amenable.

5. REFERENCES

[1] B. Beeker. *Problèmes géométriques et algorithmiques dans des graphes de groupes.* PhD thesis, Université de Caen Basse-Normandie, 2011.

[2] O. Bogopolski, A. Martino, and E. Ventura. Orbit decidability and the conjugacy problem for some extensions of groups. *Trans. Amer. Math. Soc.*, 362(4):2003–2036, 2010.

[3] A. V. Borovik, A. G. Myasnikov, and V. N. Remeslennikov. Generic Complexity of the Conjugacy Problem in HNN-Extensions and Algorithmic Stratification of Miller's Groups. *IJAC*, 17(5/6):963–997, 2007.

[4] T. Ceccherini-Silberstein, R. I. Grigorchuk, and P. de la Harpe. Amenability and paradoxical decompositions for pseudogroups and discrete metric spaces. *Tr. Mat. Inst. Steklova*, 224:68–111, 1999.

[5] J. M. Cohen. Cogrowth and amenability of discrete groups. *J. Funct. Anal.*, 48(3):301–309, 1982.

[6] W. Dicks and M. J. Dunwoody. *Groups acting on graphs.* Cambridge University Press, 1989.

[7] V. Diekert, A. J. Duncan, and A. G. Myasnikov. Geodesic rewriting systems and pregroups. In O. Bogopolski et al. editors, *Combinatorial and Geometric Group Theory*, Trends in Mathematics, pages 55–91. Birkhäuser, 2010.

[8] V. Diekert, A. J. Duncan, and A. G. Myasnikov. Cyclic rewriting and conjugacy problems. *Groups Complexity Cryptology*, 4(2):321–355, 2012.

[9] V. Diekert, A. G. Myasnikov, and A. Weiß. Conjugacy in Baumslag's Group, Generic Case Complexity, and Division in Power Circuits. In A. Pardo and A. Viola, editors, *LATIN*, vol. 8392 of *LNCS*, pages 1–12. Springer, 2014.

[10] V. Diekert, A. G. Myasnikov, and A. Weiß. Amenability of Schreier graphs and strongly generic algorithms for the conjugacy problem. *ArXiv e-prints*, abs/1501.05579, 2015.

[11] E. Følner. On groups with full Banach mean value. *Math. Scand.*, 3:243–254, 1955.

[12] M. A. Frumkin. Polynomial time algorithms in the theory of linear Diophantine equations. In *Fundamentals of computation theory (Proc. Internat. Conf., Poznań-Kórnik, 1977)*, volume 56 of *LNCS*, pages 386–392. Springer, Berlin, 1977.

[13] P. Gerl. Random walks on graphs with a strong isoperimetric property. *J. Theoret. Probab.*, 1(2):171–187, 1988.

[14] R. L. Graham, D. E. Knuth, and O. Patashnik. *Concrete Mathematics: A Foundation for Computer Science.* Addison-Wesley, 1994.

[15] R. I. Grigorchuk. Symmetric random walks on discrete groups. *Uspehi Mat. Nauk*, 32(6(198)):217–218, 1977.

[16] D. Grigoriev and V. Shpilrain. Authentication from matrix conjugation. *Groups Complexity Cryptology*, 1:199–205, 2009.

[17] M. Gromov. Asymptotic invariants of infinite groups. In *Geometric group theory, Vol. 2 (Sussex, 1991)*, volume 182 of *London Math. Soc. Lecture Note Ser.*, pages 1–295. Cambridge Univ. Press, 1993.

[18] I. Kapovich, A. G. Miasnikov, P. Schupp, and V. Shpilrain. Generic-case complexity, decision problems in group theory and random walks. *J. Algebra*, 264:665–694, 2003.

[19] H. Kesten. Full Banach mean values on countable groups. *Math. Scand.*, 7:146–156, 1959.

[20] H. Kesten. Symmetric random walks on groups. *Trans. Amer. Math. Soc.*, 92:336–354, 1959.

[21] R. Lyndon and P. Schupp. *Combinatorial Group Theory.* Classics in Mathematics. Springer, 2001. First edition 1977.

[22] C. F. Miller III. *On group-theoretic decision problems and their classification*, volume 68 of *Annals of Mathematics Studies.* Princeton Univ. Press, 1971.

[23] R. G. Möller. Groups acting on locally finite graphs—a survey of the infinitely ended case. In *Groups '93 Galway/St. Andrews, Vol. 2*, volume 212 of *London Math. Soc. Lecture Note Ser.*, pages 426–456. Cambridge Univ. Press, Cambridge, 1995.

[24] A. G. Myasnikov, A. Ushakov, and D. W. Won. The Word Problem in the Baumslag group with a non-elementary Dehn function is polynomial time decidable. *Journal of Algebra*, 345:324–342, 2011.

[25] S. Northshield. Cogrowth of regular graphs. *Proc. Amer. Math. Soc.*, 116(1):203–205, 1992.

[26] J.-P. Serre. *Trees.* Springer, 1980. French original 1977.

[27] V. Shpilrain and G. Zapata. Combinatorial group theory and public key cryptography. *Appl. Algebra Engrg. Comm. Comput.*, 17:291–302, 2006.

[28] P. M. Soardi. *Potential theory on infinite networks*, volume 1590 of *Lecture Notes in Mathematics.* Springer-Verlag, Berlin, 1994.

[29] J. Stallings. *Group theory and three-dimensional manifolds.* Yale Univ. Press, New Haven, Conn., 1971.

[30] J. von zur Gathen and M. Sieveking. A bound on solutions of linear integer equalities and inequalities. *Proc. Amer. Math. Soc.*, 72(1):155–158, 1978.

[31] W. Woess. *Random Walks on Infinite Graphs and Groups.* Cambridge University Press, 2000.

Computing the Rank Profile Matrix*

Jean-Guillaume Dumas
Univ. Grenoble Alpes
Laboratoire LJK
CNRS, Univ. Grenoble Alpes
51, av. des Mathématiques,
F38041 Grenoble, France
Jean-Guillaume.Dumas@imag.fr

Clément Pernet
Univ. Grenoble Alpes
Laboratoire LIP
Inria, CNRS, UCBL, ENS de Lyon
46, Allée d'Italie, F69364 Lyon
Cedex 07, France
Clement.Pernet@imag.fr

Ziad Sultan
Univ. Grenoble Alpes
Laboratoires LJK and LIG
Inria, CNRS, Univ. Grenoble Alpes
Inovallée, 655, av. de l'Europe,
F38334 St Ismier Cedex,
France
Ziad.Sultan@imag.fr

ABSTRACT

The row (resp. column) rank profile of a matrix describes the stair-case shape of its row (resp. column) echelon form. In an ISSAC'13 paper, we proposed a recursive Gaussian elimination that can compute simultaneously the row and column rank profiles of a matrix, as well as those of all of its leading sub-matrices, in the same time as state of the art Gaussian elimination algorithms. Here we first study the conditions making a Gaussian elimination algorithm reveal this information. We propose the definition of a new matrix invariant, the rank profile matrix, summarizing all information on the row and column rank profiles of all the leading sub-matrices. We also explore the conditions for a Gaussian elimination algorithm to compute all or part of this invariant, through the corresponding PLUQ decomposition. As a consequence, we show that the classical iterative CUP decomposition algorithm can actually be adapted to compute the rank profile matrix. Used, in a Crout variant, as a base-case to our ISSAC'13 implementation, it delivers a significant improvement in efficiency. Second, the row (resp. column) echelon form of a matrix are usually computed via different dedicated triangular decompositions. We show here that, from some PLUQ decompositions, it is possible to recover the row and column echelon forms of a matrix and of any of its leading sub-matrices thanks to an elementary post-processing algorithm.

Categories and Subject Descriptors

G.4 [**Mathematics and Computing**]: Mathematical Software—*Algorithm Design and Analysis*; I.1.2 [**Computing Methodologies**]: Symbolic and Algebraic Manipulation

General Terms

Algorithms, Experimentation, Performance

*This work is partly funded by the HPAC project of the French Agence Nationale de la Recherche (ANR 11 BS02 013).

ISSAC'15, July 6–9, 2015, Bath, United Kingdom.

DOI: http://dx.doi.org/10.1145/2755996.2756682.

Keywords

Gaussian elimination, Rank profile, Echelon form, PLUQ decomposition.

1. INTRODUCTION

Triangular matrix decompositions are widely used in computational linear algebra. Besides solving linear systems of equations, they are also used to compute other objects more specific to exact arithmetic: computing the rank, sampling a vector from the null-space, computing echelon forms and rank profiles.

The *row rank profile* (resp. *column rank profile*) of an $m \times n$ matrix A with rank r, denoted by RowRP(A) (resp. ColRP(A)), is the lexicographically smallest sequence of r indices of linearly independent rows (resp. columns) of A. An $m \times n$ matrix has generic row (resp. column) rank profile if its row (resp. column) rank profile is $(1, .., r)$. Lastly, an $m \times n$ matrix has generic rank profile if its r first leading principal minors are non-zero. Note that if a matrix has generic rank profile, then its row and column rank profiles are generic, but the converse is false: the matrix $\left[\begin{smallmatrix} 0 & 1 \\ 1 & 0 \end{smallmatrix}\right]$ does not have generic rank profile even if its row and column rank profiles are generic. The row support (resp. column support) of a matrix A, denoted by RowSupp(A) (resp. ColSupp(A)), is the subset of indices of its non-zero rows (resp. columns).

We recall that the row echelon form of an $m \times n$ matrix A is an upper triangular matrix $E = TA$, for a non-singular matrix T, with the zero rows of E at the bottom and the non-zero rows in stair-case shape: $\min\{j : a_{i,j} \neq 0\} < \min\{j : a_{i+1,j} \neq 0\}$. As T is non singular, the column rank profile of A is that of E, and therefore corresponds to the column indices of the leading elements in the staircase. Similarly the row rank profile of A is composed of the row indices of the leading elements in the staircase of the column echelon form of A.

Rank profile and triangular matrix decompositions.

The rank profiles of a matrix and the triangular matrix decomposition obtained by Gaussian elimination are strongly related. The elimination of matrices with arbitrary rank profiles gives rise to several matrix factorizations and many algorithmic variants. In numerical linear algebra one often uses the PLUQ decomposition, with P and Q permutation matrices, L a lower unit triangular matrix and U an upper triangular matrix. The LSP and LQUP variants of [8] are used to reduce the complexity rank deficient Gaussian elimination to that of matrix multiplication. Many other algorithmic decompositions exist allowing fraction free computations [10], in-place computations [4, 9] or sub-cubic rank-sensitive time complexity [13, 9]. In [5] we proposed a Gaussian elimination algorithm with a recursive splitting of both row and column dimensions, and replacing row and column transpositions by rotations. This elimination can compute simultaneously the row and column rank profile while preserving the sub-cubic rank-sensitive time complexity and keeping the computation in-place.

In this paper we first study the conditions a PLUQ decomposition algorithm must satisfy in order to reveal the rank profile structure of a matrix. We introduce in section 2 the rank profile matrix $\mathcal{R}_A$, a normal form summarizing all rank profile information of a matrix and of all its leading sub-matrices. We then decompose, in section 3, the pivoting strategy of any PLUQ algorithm into two types of operations: the search of the pivot and the permutation used to move it to the main diagonal. We propose a new search and a new permutation strategy and show what rank profiles are computed using any possible combination of these operations and the previously used searches and permutations. In particular we show three new pivoting strategy combinations that compute the rank profile matrix and use one of them, an iterative Crout CUP with rotations, to improve the base case and thus the overall performance of exact Gaussian elimination. Second, we show that preserving both the row and column rank profiles, together with ensuring a monotonicity of the associated permutations, allows us to compute faster several other matrix decompositions, such as the LEU and Bruhat decompositions, and echelon forms.

In the following, $0_{m\times n}$ denotes the $m \times n$ zero matrix and $A_{i..j,k..l}$ denotes the sub-matrix of A of rows between i and j and columns between k and l. To a permutation $\sigma : \{1,\dots,n\} \to \{1,\dots,n\}$ we define the associated permutation matrix P_σ, permuting rows by left multiplication: the rows of $P_\sigma A$ are that of A permuted by σ. Reciprocally, for a permutation matrix P, we denote by σ_P the associated permutation.

2. THE RANK PROFILE MATRIX

We start by introducing in Theorem 1 the rank profile matrix, that we will use throughout this document to summarize all information on the rank profiles of a matrix. From now on, matrices are over a field K and a valid pivot is a non-zero element.

DEFINITION 1. *An r-sub-permutation matrix is a matrix of rank r with only r non-zero entries equal to one.*

LEMMA 1. *An $m \times n$ r-sub-permutation matrix has at most one non-zero entry per row and per column, and can be written* $P\begin{bmatrix} I_r & \\ & 0_{(m-r)\times(n-r)} \end{bmatrix} Q$ *where P and Q are permutation matrices.*

THEOREM 1. *Let $A \in \mathrm{K}^{m\times n}$. There exists a unique $m\times n$ rank(A)-sub-permutation matrix $\mathcal{R}_A$ of which every leading sub-matrix has the same rank as the corresponding leading sub-matrix of A. This sub-permutation matrix is called the* rank profile matrix *of A.*

PROOF. We prove existence by induction on the row dimension of the leading submatrices.

If $A_{1,1..n} = 0_{1\times n}$, setting $\mathcal{R}^{(1)} = 0_{1\times n}$ satisfies the defining condition. Otherwise, let j be the index of the leftmost invertible element in $A_{1,1..n}$ and set $\mathcal{R}^{(1)} = e_j^T$ the j-th n-dimensional row canonical vector, which satisfies the defining condition.

Now for a given $i \in \{1,\dots,m\}$, suppose that there is a unique $i\times n$ rank profile matrix $\mathcal{R}^{(i)}$ such that $\mathrm{rank}(A_{1..i,1..j}) = \mathrm{rank}(\mathcal{R}_{1..i,1..j})$ for every $j \in \{1..n\}$. If $\mathrm{rank}(A_{1..i+1,1..n}) = \mathrm{rank}(A_{1..i,1..n})$, then $\mathcal{R}^{(i+1)} = \begin{bmatrix} \mathcal{R}^{(i)} \\ 0_{1\times n}\end{bmatrix}$. Otherwise, consider k, the smallest column index such that $\mathrm{rank}(A_{1..i+1,1..k}) = \mathrm{rank}(A_{1..i,1..k}) + 1$ and set $\mathcal{R}^{(i+1)} = \begin{bmatrix} \mathcal{R}^{(i)} \\ e_k^T\end{bmatrix}$. Any leading sub-matrix of $\mathcal{R}^{(i+1)}$ has the same rank as the corresponding leading sub-matrix of A: first, for any leading subset of rows and columns with less than i rows, the case is covered by the induction; second define $\begin{bmatrix} B & u \\ v^T & x \end{bmatrix} = A_{1..i+1,1..k}$, where u, v are vectors and x is a scalar. From the definition of k, v is linearly dependent with B and thus any leading sub-matrix of $\begin{bmatrix} B \\ v^T \end{bmatrix}$ has the same rank as the corresponding sub-matrix of $\mathcal{R}^{(i+1)}$. Similarly, from the definition of k, the same reasoning works when considering more than k columns, with a rank increment by 1.

Lastly we show that $\mathcal{R}^{(i+1)}$ is a r_{i+1}-sub-permutation matrix. Indeed, u is linearly dependent with the columns of B: otherwise, $\mathrm{rank}([B\ u]) = \mathrm{rank}(B) + 1$. From the definition of k we then have $\mathrm{rank}(\begin{bmatrix} B & u \\ v^T & x \end{bmatrix}) = rank([B\ u]) + 1 = \mathrm{rank}(B)+2 = \mathrm{rank}(\begin{bmatrix} B \\ v^T \end{bmatrix})+2$ which is a contradiction. Consequently, the k-th column of $\mathcal{R}^{(i)}$ is all zero, and $\mathcal{R}^{(i+1)}$ is a r-sub-permutation matrix.

To prove uniqueness, suppose there exist two distinct rank profile matrices $\mathcal{R}^{(1)}$ and $\mathcal{R}^{(2)}$ for a given matrix A and let (i,j) be some coordinates where $\mathcal{R}^{(1)}_{1..i,1..j} \neq \mathcal{R}^{(2)}_{1..i,1..j}$ and $\mathcal{R}^{(1)}_{1..i-1,1..j-1} = \mathcal{R}^{(2)}_{1..i-1,1..j-1}$. Then, $\mathrm{rank}(A_{1..i,1..j}) = \mathrm{rank}(\mathcal{R}^{(1)}_{1..i,1..j}) \neq \mathrm{rank}(\mathcal{R}^{(2)}_{1..i,1..j}) = \mathrm{rank}(A_{1..i,1..j})$ which is a contradiction. □

EXAMPLE 1. $A = \begin{bmatrix} 2&0&3&0\\1&0&0&0\\0&0&4&0\\0&2&0&1 \end{bmatrix}$ *has* $\mathcal{R}_A = \begin{bmatrix} 1&0&0&0\\0&0&1&0\\0&0&0&0\\0&1&0&0 \end{bmatrix}$ *for rank profile matrix over* $\mathbb{Q}$.

REMARK 1. *The matrix E introduced in Malaschonok's LEU decomposition [12, Theorem 1], is in fact the rank profile matrix. There, the existence of this decomposition was only shown for $m = n = 2^k$, and no connection was made to the relation with ranks and rank profiles. This connection was made in [5, Corollary 1], and the existence of E generalized to arbitrary dimensions m and n. Finally, after proving its uniqueness here, we propose this definition as a new matrix normal form.*

The rank profile matrix has the following properties:

LEMMA 2. *Let A be a matrix.*

1. *$\mathcal{R}_A$ is* diagonal *if A has* generic rank profile.
2. *$\mathcal{R}_A$ is a* permutation *matrix if A is* invertible
3. *RowRP(A) = RowSupp($\mathcal{R}_A$); ColRP(A) = ColSupp($\mathcal{R}_A$).*

Moreover, for all $1 \le i \le m$ and $1 \le j \le n$, we have:

4. *RowRP($A_{1..i,1..j}$) = RowSupp($(\mathcal{R}_A)_{1..i,1..j}$)*
5. *ColRP($A_{1..i,1..j}$) = ColSupp($(\mathcal{R}_A)_{1..i,1..j}$),*

These properties show how to recover the row and column rank profiles of A and of any of its leading sub-matrix.

3. INGREDIENTS OF A PLUQ DECOMPOSITION ALGORITHM

Over a field, the LU decomposition generalizes to matrices with arbitrary rank profiles, using row and column permutations (in some cases such as the CUP, or LSP decompositions, the row permutation is embedded in the structure of the C or S matrices). However such PLUQ decompositions are not unique and not all of them will necessarily reveal rank profiles and echelon forms. We will characterize the conditions for a PLUQ decomposition algorithm to reveal the row or column rank profile or the rank profile matrix.

We consider the four types of operations of a Gaussian elimination algorithm in the processing of the k-th pivot:

Pivot search: finding an element to be used as a pivot,

Pivot permutation: moving the pivot in diagonal position (k,k) by column and/or row permutations,

Update: applying the elimination at position (i,j): $a_{i,j} \leftarrow a_{i,j} - a_{i,k}a_{k,k}^{-1}a_{k,j}$,

Normalization: dividing the k-th row (resp. column) by the pivot.

Choosing how each of these operation is done, and when they are scheduled results in an elimination algorithm. Conversely, any Gaussian elimination algorithm computing a PLUQ decomposition can be viewed as a set of specializations of each of these operations together with a scheduling.

The choice of doing the normalization on rows or columns only determines which of U or L will be unit triangular. The scheduling of the updates vary depending on the type of algorithm used: iterative, recursive, slab or tiled block splitting, with right-looking, left-looking or Crout variants [2]. Neither the normalization nor the update impact the capacity to reveal rank profiles and we will thus now focus on the pivot search and the permutations.

Choosing a search and a permutation strategy fixes the matrices P and Q of the PLUQ decomposition obtained and, as we will see, determines the ability to recover information on the rank profiles. Once these matrices are fixed, the L and the U factors are unique. We introduce the pivoting matrix.

Definition 2. *The pivoting matrix of a PLUQ decomposition $A = PLUQ$ of rank r is the r-sub-permutation matrix*

$$\Pi_{P,Q} = P \begin{bmatrix} I_r & \\ & 0_{(m-r)\times(n-r)} \end{bmatrix} Q.$$

The r non-zero elements of $\Pi_{P,Q}$ are located at the initial positions of the pivots in the matrix A. Thus $\Pi_{P,Q}$ summarizes the choices made in the search and permutation operations.

Pivot search.

The search operation vastly differs depending on the field of application. In numerical dense linear algebra, numerical stability is the main criterion for the selection of the pivot. In sparse linear algebra, the pivot is chosen so as to reduce the fill-in produced by the update operation. In order to reveal some information on the rank profiles, a notion of precedence has to be used: a usual way to compute the row rank profile is to search in a given row for a pivot and only move to the next row if the current row was found to be all zeros. This guarantees that each pivot will be on the first linearly independent row, and therefore the row support of $\Pi_{P,Q}$ will be the row rank profile. The precedence here is that the pivot's coordinates must minimize the order for the first coordinate (the row index). As a generalization, we consider the most common preorders of the cartesian product $\{1,\dots m\} \times \{1,\dots n\}$ inherited from the natural orders of each of its components and describe the corresponding search strategies, minimizing this preorder:

Row order: $(i_1,j_1) \preceq_{\text{row}} (i_2,j_2)$ iff $i_1 \le i_2$: *search for any invertible element in the first non-zero row.*

Column order: $(i_1,j_1) \preceq_{\text{col}} (i_2,j_2)$ iff $j_1 \le j_2$. *search for any invertible element in the first non-zero column.*

Lexicographic order: $(i_1,j_1) \preceq_{\text{lex}} (i_2,j_2)$ iff $i_1 < i_2$ or $i_1 = i_2$ and $j_1 \le j_2$: *search for the leftmost non-zero element of the first non-zero row.*

Reverse lexicographic order: $(i_1,j_1) \preceq_{\text{revlex}} (i_2,j_2)$ iff $j_1 < j_2$ or $j_1 = j_2$ and $i_1 \le i_2$: *search for the topmost non-zero element of the first non-zero column.*

Product order: $(i_1,j_1) \preceq_{\text{prod}} (i_2,j_2)$ iff $i_1 \le i_2$ and $j_1 \le j_2$: *search for any non-zero element at position (i,j) being the only non-zero of the leading (i,j) sub-matrix.*

Example 2. *Consider the matrix $\begin{bmatrix} 0&0&0&a&b\\ 0&c&d&e&f\\ g&h&i&j&k\\ l&m&n&o&p \end{bmatrix}$, where each literal is a non-zero element. The minimum non-zero elements for each preorder are the following:*

Row order	a, b
Column order	g, l
Lexicographic order	a
Reverse lexic. order	g
Product order	a, c, g

Pivot permutation.

The pivot permutation moves a pivot from its initial position to the leading diagonal. Besides this constraint all possible choices are left for the remaining values of the permutation. Most often, it is done by row or column transpositions, as it clearly involves a small amount of data movement. However, these transpositions can break the precedence relations in the set of rows or columns, and can therefore prevent the recovery of the rank profile information. A pivot permutation that leaves the precedence relations unchanged will be called k-monotonically increasing.

Definition 3. *A permutation of $\sigma \in \mathcal{S}_n$ is called k-monotonically increasing if its last $n-k$ values form a monotonically increasing sequence.*

In particular, the last $n-k$ rows of the associated row-permutation matrix P_σ are in row echelon form. For example, the cyclic shift between indices k and i, with $k < i$ defined as $R_{k,i} = (1,\dots,k-1,i,k,k+1,\dots,i-1,i+1,\dots,n)$, that we will call a (k,i)-rotation, is an elementary k-monotonically increasing permutation.

Example 3. *The $(1,4)$-rotation $R_{1,4} = (4,1,2,3)$ is a 1-monotonically increasing permutation. Its row permutation matrix is $\begin{bmatrix} 0&&&1\\ 1&&&\\ &1&&\\ &&1&0 \end{bmatrix}$. In fact, any (k,i)-rotation is a k-monotonically increasing permutation.*

Monotonically increasing permutations can be composed as stated in Lemma 3.

Lemma 3. *If $\sigma_1 \in \mathcal{S}_n$ is a k_1-monotonically increasing permutation and $\sigma_2 \in \mathcal{S}_{k_1} \times \mathcal{S}_{n-k_1}$ a k_2-monotonically increasing permutation with $k_1 < k_2$ then the permutation $\sigma_2 \circ \sigma_1$ is a k_2-monotonically increasing permutation.*

PROOF. The last $n-k_2$ values of $\sigma_2 \circ \sigma_1$ are the image of a sub-sequence of $n-k_2$ values from the last $n-k_1$ values of σ_1 through the monotonically increasing function σ_2. □

Therefore an iterative algorithm, using rotations as elementary pivot permutations, maintains the property that the permutation matrices P and Q at any step k are k-monotonically increasing. A similar property also applies with recursive algorithms.

4. HOW TO REVEAL RANK PROFILES

A PLUQ decomposition reveals the row (resp. column) rank profile if it can be read from the first r values of the permutation matrix P (resp. Q). Equivalently, by Lemma 2, this means that the row (resp. column) support of the pivoting matrix $\Pi_{P,Q}$ equals that of the rank profile matrix.

DEFINITION 4. *The decomposition $A = PLUQ$ reveals:*
1. *the row rank profile if $RowSupp(\Pi_{P,Q}) = RowSupp(\mathcal{R}_A)$,*
2. *the col. rank profile if $ColSupp(\Pi_{P,Q}) = ColSupp(\mathcal{R}_A)$,*
3. *the rank profile matrix if $\Pi_{P,Q} = \mathcal{R}_A$.*

EXAMPLE 4. $A = \begin{bmatrix} 2&0&3&0\\1&0&0&0\\0&0&4&0\\0&2&0&1\end{bmatrix}$ *has* $\mathcal{R}_A = \begin{bmatrix}1&0&0&0\\0&0&1&0\\0&0&0&0\\0&1&0&0\end{bmatrix}$ *for rank profile matrix over $\mathbb{Q}$. Now the pivoting matrix obtained from a PLUQ decomposition with a pivot search operation following the row order (any column, first non-zero row) could be the matrix* $\Pi_{P,Q} = \begin{bmatrix}0&0&1&0\\1&0&0&0\\0&0&0&0\\0&1&0&0\end{bmatrix}$. *As these matrices share the same row support, the matrix $\Pi_{P,Q}$ reveals the row rank profile of A.*

REMARK 2. *Example 4, suggests that a pivot search strategy minimizing row and column indices could be a sufficient condition to recover both row and column rank profiles at the same time, regardless the pivot permutation. However, this is unfortunately not the case. Consider for example a search based on the lexicographic order (first non-zero column of the first non-zero row) with transposition permutations, run on the matrix:* $A = \left[\begin{smallmatrix}0&0&1\\2&3&0\end{smallmatrix}\right]$. *Its rank profile matrix is* $\mathcal{R}_A = \left[\begin{smallmatrix}0&0&1\\1&0&0\end{smallmatrix}\right]$ *whereas the pivoting matrix could be* $\Pi_{P,Q} = \left[\begin{smallmatrix}0&0&1\\0&1&0\end{smallmatrix}\right]$, *which does not reveal the column rank profile. This is due to the fact that the column transposition performed for the first pivot changes the order in which the columns will be inspected in the search for the second pivot.*

We will show that if the pivot permutations preserve the order in which the still unprocessed columns or rows appear, then the pivoting matrix will equal the rank profile matrix. This is achieved by the monotonically increasing permutations.

Theorem 2 shows how the ability of a PLUQ decomposition algorithm to recover the rank profile information relates to the use of monotonically increasing permutations. More precisely, it considers an arbitrary step in a PLUQ decomposition where k pivots have been found in the elimination of an $\ell \times p$ leading sub-matrix A_1 of the input matrix A.

THEOREM 2. *Consider a partial PLUQ decomposition of an $m \times n$ matrix A:*

$$A = P_1 \begin{bmatrix} L_1 & \\ M_1 & I_{m-k}\end{bmatrix} \begin{bmatrix} U_1 & V_1 \\ & H\end{bmatrix} Q_1$$

where $\begin{bmatrix} L_1 \\ M_1 \end{bmatrix}$ *is $m \times k$ lower triangular and* $\begin{bmatrix} U_1 & V_1\end{bmatrix}$ *is $k \times n$ upper triangular, and let A_1 be some $\ell \times p$ leading sub-matrix of A, for $\ell, p \geq k$. Let $H = P_2L_2U_2Q_2$ be a PLUQ decomposition of H. Consider the PLUQ decomposition*

$$A = \underbrace{P_1 \begin{bmatrix} I_k & \\ & P_2\end{bmatrix}}_{P} \underbrace{\begin{bmatrix} L_1 & \\ P_2^T M_1 & L_2\end{bmatrix}}_{L} \underbrace{\begin{bmatrix} U_1 & V_1 Q_2^T \\ & U_2\end{bmatrix}}_{U} \underbrace{\begin{bmatrix} I_k & \\ & Q_2\end{bmatrix} Q_1}_{Q}.$$

Consider the following clauses:
(i) $RowRP(A_1) = RowSupp(\Pi_{P_1,Q_1})$
(ii) $ColRP(A_1) = ColSupp(\Pi_{P_1,Q_1})$
(iii) $\mathcal{R}_{A_1} = \Pi_{P_1,Q_1}$
(iv) $RowRP(H) = RowSupp(\Pi_{P_2,Q_2})$
(v) $ColRP(H) = ColSupp(\Pi_{P_2,Q_2})$
(vi) $\mathcal{R}_H = \Pi_{P_2,Q_2}$
(vii) P_1^T is k-monotonically increasing or (P_1^T is ℓ-monotonically increasing and $p = n$)
(viii) Q_1^T is k-monotonically increasing or (Q_1^T is p-monotonically increasing and $\ell = m$)

Then,
(a) if (i) or (ii) or (iii) then $H = \begin{bmatrix} 0_{(\ell-k)\times(p-k)} & * \\ * & * \end{bmatrix}$
(b) if (vii) then ((i) and (iv)) ⇒ $RowRP(A) = RowSupp(\Pi_{P,Q})$;
(c) if (viii) then ((ii) and (v)) ⇒ $ColRP(A) = ColSupp(\Pi_{P,Q})$;
(d) if (vii) and (viii) then (iii) and (vi) ⇒ $\mathcal{R}_A = \Pi_{P,Q}$.

PROOF. Let $P_1 = \begin{bmatrix} P_{11} & E_1\end{bmatrix}$ and $Q_1 = \begin{bmatrix} Q_{11} \\ F_1\end{bmatrix}$ where E_1 is $m \times (m-k)$ and F_1 is $(n-k)\times n$. On one hand we have

$$A = \underbrace{\begin{bmatrix} P_{11} & E_1\end{bmatrix} \begin{bmatrix} L_1 \\ M_1\end{bmatrix} \begin{bmatrix} U_1 & V_1\end{bmatrix} \begin{bmatrix} Q_{11} \\ F_1\end{bmatrix}}_{B} + E_1 H F_1. \quad (1)$$

On the other hand,

$$\begin{aligned}\Pi_{P,Q} &= P_1 \begin{bmatrix} I_k & \\ & P_2\end{bmatrix} \begin{bmatrix} I_r & \\ & 0_{(m-r)\times(n-r)}\end{bmatrix} \begin{bmatrix} I_k & \\ & Q_2\end{bmatrix} Q_1 \\ &= P_1 \begin{bmatrix} I_k & \\ & \Pi_{P_2,Q_2}\end{bmatrix} Q_1 = \Pi_{P_1,Q_1} + E_1 \Pi_{P_2,Q_2} F_1.\end{aligned}$$

Let $\overline{A}_1 = \begin{bmatrix} A_1 & 0 \\ 0 & 0_{(m-\ell)\times(n-p)}\end{bmatrix}$ and denote by B_1 the $\ell \times p$ leading sub-matrix of B.

(a) The clause (i) or (ii) or (iii) implies that all k pivots of the partial elimination were found within the $\ell \times p$ sub-matrix A_1. Hence $\text{rank}(A_1) = k$ and we can write $P_1 = \begin{bmatrix} P_{11} & E_1 \\ 0_{(m-\ell)\times k} & \end{bmatrix}$ and $Q_1 = \begin{bmatrix} Q_{11} & 0_{k\times(n-p)} \\ & F_1\end{bmatrix}$, and the matrix A_1 writes

$$A_1 = \begin{bmatrix} I_\ell & 0\end{bmatrix} A \left[\begin{smallmatrix} I_p \\ 0\end{smallmatrix}\right] = B_1 + \begin{bmatrix} I_\ell & 0\end{bmatrix} E_1 H F_1 \left[\begin{smallmatrix} I_p \\ 0\end{smallmatrix}\right]. \quad (2)$$

Now $\text{rank}(B_1) = k$ as a sub-matrix of B of rank k and since

$$\begin{aligned} B_1 &= \begin{bmatrix} P_{11} & \begin{bmatrix} I_\ell & 0\end{bmatrix} \cdot E_1\end{bmatrix} \begin{bmatrix} L_1 \\ M_1\end{bmatrix} \begin{bmatrix} U_1 & V_1\end{bmatrix} \begin{bmatrix} Q_{11} \\ F_1 \cdot \left[\begin{smallmatrix} I_p \\ 0\end{smallmatrix}\right]\end{bmatrix} \\ &= P_{11}L_1U_1Q_{11} + \begin{bmatrix} I_\ell & 0\end{bmatrix} E_1 M_1 \begin{bmatrix} U_1 & V_1\end{bmatrix} Q_1 \left[\begin{smallmatrix} I_p \\ 0\end{smallmatrix}\right]\end{aligned}$$

where the first term, $P_{11}L_1U_1Q_{11}$, has rank k and the second term has a disjoint row support.

Finally, consider the term $\begin{bmatrix} I_\ell & 0\end{bmatrix} E_1 H F_1 \left[\begin{smallmatrix} I_p \\ 0\end{smallmatrix}\right]$ of equation (2). As its row support is disjoint with that of the pivot rows of B_1, it has to be composed of rows linearly dependent with the pivot rows of B_1 to ensure that $\text{rank}(A_1) = k$. As its column support is disjoint with that of the pivot columns of B_1, we conclude that it must be the zero matrix. Therefore the leading $(\ell-k)\times(p-k)$ sub-matrix of E_1HF_1 is zero.

(b) From (a) we know that $A_1 = B_1$. Thus $\text{RowRP}(B) = \text{RowRP}(A_1)$. Recall that $A = B + E_1HF_1$. No pivot row of B can be made linearly dependent by adding rows of E_1HF_1, as the column position of the pivot is always zero in the latter matrix. For the same reason, no pivot row of E_1HF_1 can be made linearly dependent by adding rows of B. From (i), the set of pivot rows of B is $\text{RowRP}(A_1)$, which shows that

$$\text{RowRP}(A) = \text{RowRP}(A_1) \cup \text{RowRP}(E_1HF_1). \quad (3)$$

Let $\sigma_{E_1} : \{1..m-k\} \to \{1..m\}$ be the map representing the sub-permutation E_1 (i.e. such that $E_1[\sigma_{E_1}(i), i] = 1\ \forall i$). If P_1^T is k-monotonically increasing, the matrix E_1 has full column rank and is in column echelon form, which implies that

$$\begin{aligned}\text{RowRP}(E_1HF_1) &= \sigma_{E_1}(\text{RowRP}(HF_1)) \\ &= \sigma_{E_1}(\text{RowRP}(H)), \quad (4)\end{aligned}$$

since F_1 has full row rank. If P_1^T is ℓ monotonically increasing, we can write $E_1 = \begin{bmatrix} E_{11} & E_{12}\end{bmatrix}$, where the $m\times(m-\ell)$ matrix E_{12} is in column echelon form. If $p = n$, the matrix H writes $H = \begin{bmatrix} 0_{(\ell-k)\times(n-k)} \\ H_2 \end{bmatrix}$. Hence we have $E_1HF_1 = E_{12}H_2F_1$ which also implies

$$\text{RowRP}(E_1HF_1) = \sigma_{E_1}(\text{RowRP}(H)).$$

From equation (2), the row support of $\Pi_{P,Q}$ is that of $\Pi_{P_1,Q_1} + E_1\Pi_{P_2,Q_2}F_1$, which is the union of the row support of these two terms as they are disjoint. Under the conditions of point (b), this row support is the union of $\text{RowRP}(A_1)$ and $\sigma_{E_1}(\text{RowRP}(H))$, which is, from (4) and (3), $\text{RowRP}(A)$.

(c) Similarly as for point (b).

(d) From (a) we have still $A_1 = B_1$. Now since $\text{rank}(B) = \text{rank}(B_1) = \text{rank}(A_1) = k$, there is no other non-zero element in $\mathcal{R}_B$ than those in $\mathcal{R}_{\overline{A}_1}$ and $\mathcal{R}_B = \mathcal{R}_{\overline{A}_1}$. The row and column support of $\mathcal{R}_B$ and that of E_1HF_1 are disjoint. Hence

$$\mathcal{R}_A = \mathcal{R}_{\overline{A}_1} + \mathcal{R}_{E_1HF_1}. \quad (5)$$

If both P_1^T and Q_1^T are k-monotonically increasing, the matrix E_1 is in column echelon form and the matrix F_1 in row echelon form. Consequently, the matrix E_1HF_1 is a copy of the matrix H with k zero-rows and k zero-columns interleaved, which does not impact the linear dependency relations between the non-zero rows and columns. As a consequence

$$\mathcal{R}_{E_1HF_1} = E_1\mathcal{R}_HF_1. \quad (6)$$

Now if Q_1^T is k-monotonically increasing, P_1^T is ℓ-monotonically increasing and $p = n$, then, using notations of point (b), $E_1HF_1 = E_{12}H_2F_1$ where E_{12} is in column echelon form. Thus $\mathcal{R}_{E_1HF_1} = E_1\mathcal{R}_HF_1$ for the same reason. The symmetric case where Q_1^T is p-monotonically increasing and $\ell = m$ works similarly. Combining equations (2), (5) and (6) gives $\mathcal{R}_A = \Pi_{P,Q}$. □

5. ALGORITHMS FOR RANK PROFILES

Using Theorem 2, we deduce what rank profile information is revealed by a PLUQ algorithm by the way the Search and the Permutation operations are done. Table 1 summarizes these results, and points to instances known in the literature, implementing the corresponding type of elimination. More precisely, we first distinguish in this table the ability to compute the row or column rank profile or the rank profile matrix, but we also indicate whether the resulting PLUQ decomposition preserves the monotonicity of the rows or columns. Indeed some algorithm may compute the rank profile matrix, but break the precedence relation between the linearly dependent rows or columns, making it unusable as a base case for a block algorithm of higher level.

5.1 Iterative algorithms

We start with iterative algorithms, where each iteration handles one pivot at a time. Here Theorem 2 is applied with $k = 1$, and the partial elimination represents how one pivot is being treated. The elimination of H is done by induction.

Row and Column order Search.

The row order pivot search operation is of the form: *any non-zero element in the first non-zero row*. Each row is inspected in order, and a new row is considered only when the previous row is all zeros. With the notations of Theorem 2, this means that A_1 is the leading $\ell \times n$ sub-matrix of A, where ℓ is the index of the first non-zero row of A. When permutations P_1 and Q_1, moving the pivot from position (ℓ, j) to (k, k) are transpositions, the matrix Π_{P_1,Q_1} is the element $E_{\ell,j}$ of the canonical basis. Its row rank profile is (ℓ) which is that of the $\ell \times n$ leading sub-matrix A_1. Finally, the permutation P_1 is ℓ-monotonically increasing, and Theorem 2 case (b) can be applied to prove by induction that any such algorithm will reveal the row rank profile: $\text{RowRP}(A) = \text{RowSupp}(\Pi_{P,Q})$. The case of the column order search is similar.

Lexicographic order based pivot search.

In this case the Pivot Search operation is of the form: *first non-zero element in the first non-zero row*. The lexicographic order being compatible with the row order, the above results hold when transpositions are used and the row rank profile is revealed. If in addition column rotations are used, $Q_1 = R_{1,j}$ which is 1-monotonically increasing. Now $\Pi_{P_1,Q_1} = E_{\ell,j}$ which is the rank profile matrix of the $\ell \times n$ leading sub-matrix A_1 of A. Theorem 2 case (d) can be applied to prove by induction that any such algorithm will reveal the rank profile matrix: $\mathcal{R}_A = \Pi_{P,Q}$. Lastly, the use of row rotations, ensures that the order of the linearly dependent rows will be preserved as well. Algorithm 1 is an instance of Gaussian elimination with a lexicographic order search and rotations for row and column permutations.

The case of the reverse lexicographic order search is similar. As an example, the algorithm in [13, Algorithm 2.14] is based on a reverse lexicographic order search but with transpositions for the row permutations. Hence it only reveals the column rank profile.

Product order based pivot search.

The search here consists in finding any non-zero element $A_{\ell,p}$ such that the $\ell \times p$ leading sub-matrix A_1 of A is all

Search	Row Perm.	Col. Perm.	Reveals	Monotonicity	Instance
Row order	Transposition	Transposition	RowRP		[8, 9]
Col. order	Transposition	Transposition	ColRP		[11, 9]
	Transposition	Transposition	RowRP		[13]
Lexicographic	Transposition	Rotation	RowRP, ColRP, $\mathcal{R}$	Col.	here
	Rotation	Rotation	RowRP, ColRP, $\mathcal{R}$	Row, Col.	here
	Transposition	Transposition	ColRP		[13]
Rev. lexico.	Rotation	Transposition	RowRP, ColRP, $\mathcal{R}$	Row	here
	Rotation	Rotation	RowRP, ColRP, $\mathcal{R}$	Row, Col.	here
	Rotation	Transposition	RowRP	Row	here
Product	Transposition	Rotation	ColRP	Col	here
	Rotation	Rotation	RowRP, ColRP, $\mathcal{R}$	Row, Col.	[5]

Table 1: Pivoting Strategies revealing rank profiles

zeros except this coefficient. If the row and column permutations are the rotations $R_{1,\ell}$ and $R_{1,p}$, we have $\Pi_{P_1,Q_1} = E_{\ell,p} = \mathcal{R}_{A_1}$. Theorem 2 case (d) can be applied to prove by induction that any such algorithm will reveal the rank profile matrix: $\mathcal{R}_A = \Pi_{P,Q}$. An instance of such an algorithm is given in [5, Algorithm 2]. If P_1 (resp. Q_1) is a transposition, then Theorem 2 case (c) (resp. case (b)) applies to show by induction that the columns (resp. row) rank profile is revealed.

5.2 Recursive algorithms

A recursive Gaussian elimination algorithm can either split one of the row or column dimension, cutting the matrix in wide or tall rectangular slabs, or split both dimensions, leading to a decomposition into tiles.

Slab recursive algorihtms.

Most algorithms computing rank profiles are slab recursive [8, 11, 13, 9]. When the row dimension is split, this means that the search space for pivots is the whole set of columns, and Theorem 2 applies with $p = n$. This corresponds to a either a row or a lexicographic order. From case(b), one shows that, with transpositions, the algorithm recovers the row rank profile, provided that the base case does. If in addition, the elementary column permutations are rotations, then case (d) applies and the rank profile matrix is recovered. Finally, if rows are also permuted by monotonically increasing permutations, then the PLUQ decomposition also respects the monotonicity of the linearly dependent rows and columns. The same reasoning holds when splitting the column dimension.

Tile recursive algorithms.

Tile recursive Gaussian elimination algorithms [5, 12, 6] are more involved, especially when dealing with rank deficiencies, and we refer to [5] for a detailed description of such an algorithm. Here, the search area A_1 has arbitrary dimensions $\ell \times p$, often specialized as $m/2 \times n/2$. As a consequence, the pivot search can not satisfy neither row, column, lexicographic or reverse lexicographic orders. Now, if the pivots selected in the elimination of A_1 minimizes the product order, then they necessarily also respect this order as pivots of the whole matrix A. Now, from (a), the remaining matrix H writes $H = \begin{bmatrix} 0_{(\ell-k)\times(p-k)} & H_{12} \\ H_{21} & H_{22} \end{bmatrix}$ and its elimination is done by two independent eliminations on the blocks H_{12} and H_{21}, followed by some update of H_{22} and a last elimination on it. Here again, pivots minimizing the row order on H_{21} and H_{12} are also pivots minimizing this order for H, and so are those of the fourth elimination. Now the block row and column permutations used in [5, Algorithm 1] to form the PLUQ decomposition are r-monotonically increasing. Hence, from case (d), the algorithm computes the rank profile matrix and preserves the monotonicity. If only one of the row or column permutations are rotations, then case (b) or (c) applies to show that either the row or the column rank profile is computed.

6. RANK PROFILE MATRIX BASED TRIANGULARIZATIONS

6.1 LEU decomposition

The LEU decomposition introduced in [12] involves a lower triangular matrix L, an upper triangular matrix U and a r-sub-permutation matrix E.

THEOREM 3. *Let $A = PLUQ$ be a PLUQ decomposition revealing the rank profile matrix ($\Pi_{P,Q} = \mathcal{R}_A$). Then an LEU decomposition of A with $E = \mathcal{R}_A$ is obtained as follows (only using row and column permutations):*

$$A = \underbrace{P \begin{bmatrix} L & 0_{m\times(n-r)} \end{bmatrix} P^T}_{\overline{L}} \underbrace{P \begin{bmatrix} I_r & \\ & 0 \end{bmatrix} Q}_{E} \underbrace{Q^T \begin{bmatrix} U \\ 0_{(n-r)\times n} \end{bmatrix} Q}_{\overline{U}} \quad (7)$$

PROOF. First $E = P \begin{bmatrix} I_r & \\ & 0 \end{bmatrix} Q = \Pi_{P,Q} = \mathcal{R}_A$. Then there only needs to show that $\overline{L}$ is lower triangular and $\overline{U}$ is upper triangular. Suppose that $\overline{L}$ is not lower triangular, let i be the first row index such that $\overline{L}_{i,j} \neq 0$ for some $i < j$. First $j \in \text{RowRP}(A)$ since the non-zero columns in $\overline{L}$ are placed according to the first r values of P. Remarking that $A = P \begin{bmatrix} L & 0_{m\times(n-r)} \end{bmatrix} \begin{bmatrix} U \\ 0 & I_{n-r} \end{bmatrix} Q$, and since right multiplication by a non-singular matrix does not change row rank profiles, we deduce that $\text{RowRP}(\Pi_{P,Q}) = \text{RowRP}(A) = \text{RowRP}(\overline{L})$. If $i \notin \text{RowRP}(A)$, then the i-th row of $\overline{L}$ is linearly dependent with the previous rows, but none of them has a non-zero element in column $j > i$. Hence $i \in \text{RowRP}(A)$.

Let (a, b) be the position of the coefficient $\overline{L}_{i,j}$ in L, that is $a = \sigma_P^{-1}(i), b = \sigma_P^{-1}(j)$. Let also $s = \sigma_Q(a)$ and $t = \sigma_Q(b)$ so that the pivots at diagonal position a and b in L respectively correspond to ones in $\mathcal{R}_A$ at positions (i, s) and (j, t). Consider the $\ell \times p$ leading sub-matrices A_1 of A where $\ell = \max_{x=1..a-1}(\sigma_P(x))$ and $p = \max_{x=1..a-1}(\sigma_Q(x))$. On one hand (j, t) is an index position in A_1 but not (i, s), since otherwise $\text{rank}(A_1) = b$. Therefore, $(i, s) \not\prec_{prod} (j, t)$, and $s > t$ as $i < j$. As coefficients (j, t) and (i, s) are pivots in $\mathcal{R}_A$ and $i < j$ and $t < s$, there can not be a non-zero element above (j, t) at row i when it is chosen as a pivot. Hence $\overline{L}_{i,j} = 0$ and $\overline{L}$ is lower triangular. The same reasoning applies to show that $\overline{U}$ is upper triangular. □

REMARK 3. *Note that the LEU decomposition with $E = \mathcal{R}_A$ is not unique, even for invertible matrices. As a counter-example, the following decomposition holds for any $a \in \mathrm{K}$:*

$$\begin{bmatrix} 0 & 1 \\ 1 & 0 \end{bmatrix} = \begin{bmatrix} 1 & 0 \\ a & 1 \end{bmatrix} \begin{bmatrix} 0 & 1 \\ 1 & 0 \end{bmatrix} \begin{bmatrix} 1 & -a \\ 0 & 1 \end{bmatrix} \quad (8)$$

6.2 Bruhat decomposition

The Bruhat decomposition, that has inspired Malaschonok's LEU decomposition [12], is another decomposition with a central permutation matrix [1, 7].

THEOREM 4 ([1]). *Any invertible matrix A can be written as $A = VPU$ for V and U uppper triangular invertible matrices and P a permutation matrix. The latter decomposition is called the* Bruhat decomposition *of A.*

It was then naturally extended to singular square matrices by [7]. Corollary 1 generalizes it to matrices with arbitrary dimensions, and relates it to the PLUQ decomposition.

COROLLARY 1. *Any $m \times n$ matrix of rank r has a VPU decomposition, where V and U are upper triangular matrices, and P is a r-sub-permutation matrix.*

PROOF. Let J_n be the unit anti-diagonal matrix. From the LEU decomposition of J_nA, we have $A = \underbrace{J_nLJ_n}_{V}\underbrace{J_nE}_{P}U$ where V is upper triangular. □

6.3 Relation to LUP and PLU decompositions

The LUP decomposition $A = LUP$ only exists for matrices with generic row rank profile (including matrices with full row rank). Corollary 2 shows upon which condition the permutation matrix P equals the rank profile matrix $\mathcal{R}_A$. Note that although the rank profile A is trivial in such cases, the matrix $\mathcal{R}_A$ still carries important information on the row and column rank profiles of all leading sub-matrices of A.

COROLLARY 2. *Let A be an $m \times n$ matrix.*

If A has generic column rank profile, then any PLU decomposition $A = PLU$ computed using reverse lexicographic order search and row rotations is such that $\mathcal{R}_A = P \left[\begin{smallmatrix} I_r & \\ & 0 \end{smallmatrix}\right]$. In particular, $P = \mathcal{R}_A$ if $r = m$.

If A has generic row rank profile, then any LUP decomposition $A = LUP$ computed using lexicographic order search and column rotations is such that $\mathcal{R}_A = \left[\begin{smallmatrix} I_r & \\ & 0 \end{smallmatrix}\right] P$. In particular, $P = \mathcal{R}_A$ if $r = n$.

PROOF. Consider A has generic column rank profile. From table 1, any PLUQ decomposition algorithm with a reverse lexicographic order based search and rotation based row permutation is such that $\Pi_{P,Q} = P \left[\begin{smallmatrix} I_r & \\ & \end{smallmatrix}\right] Q = \mathcal{R}_A$. Since the search follows the reverse lexicographic order and the matrix has generic column rank profile, no column will be permuted in this elimination, and therefore $Q = I_n$. The same reasoning hold for when A has generic row rank profile. □

Note that the L and U factors in a PLU decomposition are uniquely determined by the permutation P. Hence, when the matrix has full row rank, $P = \mathcal{R}_A$ and the decomposition $A = \mathcal{R}_A LU$ is unique. Similarly the decomposition $A = LU\mathcal{R}_A$ is unique when the matrix has full column rank. Now when the matrix is rank deficient with generic row rank profile, there is no longer a unique PLU decomposition revealing the rank profile matrix: any permutation applied to the last $m - r$ columns of P and the last $m - r$ rows of L yields a PLU decomposition where $\mathcal{R}_A = P \left[\begin{smallmatrix} I_r & \\ & \end{smallmatrix}\right]$.

Lastly, we remark that the only situation where the rank profile matrix $\mathcal{R}_A$ can be read directly as a sub-matrix of P or Q is as in corollary 2, when the matrix A has generic row or column rank profile. Consider a PLUQ decomposition $A = PLUQ$ revealing the rank profile matrix ($\mathcal{R}_A = P \left[\begin{smallmatrix} I_r & \\ & \end{smallmatrix}\right] Q$) such that $\mathcal{R}_A$ is a sub-matrix of P. This means that $P = \mathcal{R}_A + S$ where S has disjoint row and column support with $\mathcal{R}_A$. We have $\mathcal{R}_A = (\mathcal{R}_A + S) \left[\begin{smallmatrix} I_r & \\ & \end{smallmatrix}\right] Q = (\mathcal{R}_A + S) \left[\begin{smallmatrix} Q_1 \\ 0_{(n-r)\times n} \end{smallmatrix}\right]$. Hence $\mathcal{R}_A(I_n - \left[\begin{smallmatrix} Q_1 \\ 0_{(n-r)\times n} \end{smallmatrix}\right]) = S \left[\begin{smallmatrix} Q_1 \\ 0_{(n-r)\times n} \end{smallmatrix}\right]$ but the row support of these matrices are disjoint, hence $\mathcal{R}_A \left[\begin{smallmatrix} 0 \\ I_{n-r} \end{smallmatrix}\right] = 0$ which implies that A has generic column rank profile. Similarly, one shows that $\mathcal{R}_A$ can be a sub-matrix of Q only if A has a generic row rank profile.

7. IMPROVEMENTS IN PRACTICE

In our previous contribution [5], we identified the ability to recover the rank profile matrix via the use of the product order search and of rotations. Hence we proposed an implementation combining a tile recursive algorithm and an iterative base case, using these search and permutation strategies.

The analysis of sections 4 and 5 shows that other pivoting strategies can be used to compute the rank profile matrix, and preserve the monotonicity. We present here a new base case algorithm and its implementation over a finite field that we wrote in the `FFLAS-FFPACK` library[1]. It is based on a lexicographic order search and row and column rotations. Moreover, the schedule of the update operations is that of a Crout elimination, for it reduces the number of modular reductions, as shown in [3, § 3.1]. Algorithm 1 summarizes this variant.

Algorithm 1 Crout variant of PLUQ with lexicographic search and column rotations

```
1: k ← 1
2: for i = 1 ... m do
3:     A_{i,k..n} ← A_{i,k..n} − A_{i,1..k−1} × A_{1..k−1,k..n}
4:     if A_{i,k..n} = 0 then
5:         Loop to next iteration
6:     end if
7:     Let A_{i,s} be the left-most non-zero element of row i.
8:     A_{i+1..m,s} ← A_{i+1..m,s} − A_{i+1..m,1..k−1} × A_{1..k−1,s}
9:     A_{i+1..m,s} ← A_{i+1..m,s}/A_{i,s}
10:    Bring A_{*,s} to A_{*,k} by column rotation
11:    Bring A_{i,*} to A_{k,*} by row rotation
12:    k ← k + 1
13: end for
```

In the following experiments, we measured the real time of the computation averaged over 10 instances (100 for $n <$

[1] FFLAS-FFPACK revision 1193, `http://linalg.org/projects/fflas-ffpack`, linked against OpenBLAS-v0.2.8.

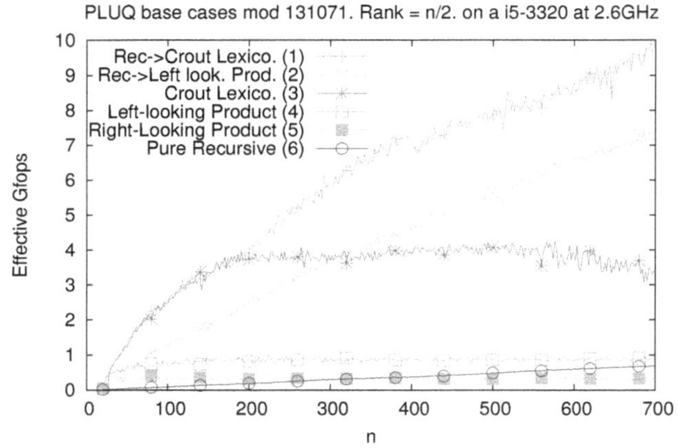

Figure 1: Computation speed of PLUQ decomposition base cases.

500) of $n \times n$ matrices with rank $r = n/2$ for any even integer value of n between 20 and 700. In order to ensure that the row and column rank profiles of these matrices are uniformly random, we construct them as the product $A = L\mathcal{R}U$, where L and U are random non-singular lower and upper triangular matrices and $\mathcal{R}$ is an $m \times n$ r-sub-permutation matrix whose non-zero elements positions are chosen uniformly at random. The effective speed is obtained by dividing an estimate of the arithmetic cost $(2mnr + 2/3r^3 - r^2(m+n))$ by the computation time.

Figure 1 shows its computation speed (3), compared to that of the pure recursive algorithm (6), and to our previous base case algorithm [5], using a product order search, and either a left-looking (4) or a right-looking (5) schedule. At $n = 200$, the left-looking variant (4) improves over the right looking variant (5) by a factor of about 2.14 as it performs fewer modular reductions. Then, the Crout variant (3) again improves variant (4) by a factor of about 3.15. Lastly we also show the speed of the final implementation, formed by the tile recursive algorithm cascading to either the Crout base case (1) or the left-looking one (2). The threshold where the cascading to the base case occurs is experimentally set to its optimum value, i.e. 200 for variant (1) and 70 for variant (2). This illustrates that the gain on the base case efficiency leads to a higher threshold, and improves the efficiency of the cascade implementation (by an additive gain of about 2.2 effective Gfops in the range of dimensions considered).

8. COMPUTING ECHELON FORMS

Usual algorithms computing an echelon form [13, 9] use a slab block decomposition (with row or lexicographic order search), which implies that pivots appear in the order of the echelon form. The column echelon form is simply obtained as $C = PL$ from the PLUQ decomposition. Using product order search, this is no longer true, and the order of the columns in L may not be that of the echelon form. Algorithm 2 shows how to recover the echelon form in such cases. Note that both the row and the column echelon forms can thus be computed from the same PLUQ decomposition. Lastly, the column echelon form of the $i \times j$ leading sub-matrix, is computed by removing rows of PL below index i and filtering out the pivots of column index greater than j. The latter is achieved by replacing line 2 by $(p_1, .., p_s) = \text{Sort}(\{\sigma_P(i) : \sigma_Q(i) \leq j\})$.

Algorithm 2 Echelon form from a PLUQ decomposition

Input: P, L, U, Q, a PLUQ decomp. of A with $\mathcal{R}_A = \Pi_{P,Q}$
Output: C: the column echelon form of A
1: $C \leftarrow PL$
2: $(p_1, .., p_r) = \text{Sort}(\sigma_P(1), .., \sigma_P(r))$
3: **for** $i = 1..r$ **do**
4: $\quad \tau = (\sigma_P^{-1}(p_1), .., \sigma_P^{-1}(p_r), r+1, .., m)$
5: **end for**
6: $C \leftarrow CP_\tau$

References

[1] N. Bourbaki. *Groupes et Algègres de Lie.* Elements of mathematics Chapters 4–6. Springer, 2008.

[2] J. J. Dongarra, L. S. Duff, D. C. Sorensen, and H. A. V. Vorst. *Numerical Linear Algebra for High Performance Computers.* SIAM, 1998.

[3] J.-G. Dumas, T. Gautier, C. Pernet, and Z. Sultan. "Parallel Computation of Echelon Forms". In: *Euro-Par 2014 Parallel Proc.* LNCS (8632). Springer, 2014, pp. 499–510. DOI: 10.1007/978-3-319-09873-9_42.

[4] J.-G. Dumas, P. Giorgi, and C. Pernet. "Dense Linear Algebra over Prime Fields". In: *ACM TOMS* 35.3 (Nov. 2008), pp. 1–42. DOI: 10.1145/1391989.1391992.

[5] J.-G. Dumas, C. Pernet, and Z. Sultan. "Simultaneous computation of the row and column rank profiles". In: *Proc. ISSAC'13.* Ed. by M. Kauers. ACM Press, 2013. DOI: 10.1145/2465506.2465517.

[6] J.-G. Dumas and J.-L. Roch. "On parallel block algorithms for exact triangularizations". In: *Parallel Computing* 28.11 (Nov. 2002), pp. 1531–1548. DOI: 10.1016/S0167-8191(02)00161-8.

[7] D. Y. Grigor'ev. "Analogy of Bruhat decomposition for the closure of a cone of Chevalley group of a classical serie". In: *Soviet Mathematics Doklady* 23.2 (1981), pp. 393–397.

[8] O. H. Ibarra, S. Moran, and R. Hui. "A Generalization of the Fast LUP Matrix Decomposition Algorithm and Applications". In: *J. of Algorithms* 3.1 (1982), pp. 45–56. DOI: 10.1016/0196-6774(82)90007-4.

[9] C.-P. Jeannerod, C. Pernet, and A. Storjohann. "Rank-profile revealing Gaussian elimination and the CUP matrix decomposition". In: *J. Symbolic Comput.* 56 (2013), pp. 46–68. DOI: 10.1016/j.jsc.2013.04.004.

[10] D. J. Jeffrey. "LU factoring of non-invertible matrices". In: *ACM Comm. Comp. Algebra* 44.1/2 (July 2010), pp. 1–8. DOI: 10.1145/1838599.1838602.

[11] W. Keller-Gehrig. "Fast algorithms for the characteristic polynomial". In: *Th. Comp. Science* 36 (1985), pp. 309–317. DOI: 10.1016/0304-3975(85)90049-0.

[12] G. I. Malaschonok. "Fast generalized Bruhat decomposition". In: *CASC'10.* Vol. 6244. LNCS. Tsakhkadzor, Armenia: Springer-Verlag, 2010, pp. 194–202.

[13] A. Storjohann. "Algorithms for Matrix Canonical Forms". PhD thesis. ETH-Zentrum, Zürich, Switzerland, Nov. 2000. DOI: 10.3929/ethz-a-004141007.

Minkowski Decomposition and Geometric Predicates in Sparse Implicitization

Ioannis Z. Emiris
University of Athens,Greece
emiris@di.uoa.gr

Christos Konaxis
University of Athens,Greece
ckonaxis@di.uoa.gr

Zafeirakis Zafeirakopoulos
University of Athens,Greece
zafeirakopoulos@gmail.com

ABSTRACT

Based on the computation of a polytope Q, called the predicted polytope, containing the Newton polytope P of the implicit equation, implicitization of a parametric hypersurface is reduced to computing the nullspace of a numeric matrix. Polytope Q may contain P as a Minkowski summand, thus jeopardizing the efficiency of sparse implicitization. Our contribution is twofold. On one hand we tackle the aforementioned issue in the case of 2D curves and 3D surfaces by Minkowski decomposing Q thus detecting the Minkowski summand relevant to implicitization: we design and implement in `Sage` a new, public domain, practical, potentially generalizable and worst-case optimal algorithm for Minkowski decomposition in 3D based on integer linear programming. On the other hand, we formulate basic geometric predicates, namely membership and sidedness for given query points, as rank computations on the interpolation matrix, thus avoiding to expand the implicit polynomial. This approach is implemented in `Maple`.

Categories and Subject Descriptors

I.1.2 [**Symbolic and Algebraic Manipulation**]: Algorithms—*Algebraic algorithms*; J.6 [**Computer-aided engineering**]: Computer-aided design

General Terms

Algorithms, Theory

Keywords

matrix representation; sparse implicitization; Newton polytope; interpolation; Minkowski decomposition; integer linear programming; membership; sidedness

1. INTRODUCTION

A fundamental question in changing representation of geometric objects is implicitization, namely the process of changing the representation of a geometric object from parametric to implicit. It is a basic operation with several applications in computer-aided geometric design (CAGD) and geometric modeling. There have been numerous approaches for implicitization, including resultants, Gröbner bases, moving lines and surfaces, and interpolation techniques.

In this work, we restrict attention to hypersurfaces and exploit a matrix representation of hypersurfaces without developing the actual implicit equation. Our approach is based on potentially interpolating the unknown coefficients of the implicit polynomial, but we shall avoid actually computing these coefficients when defining our geometric predicates. The basis of this approach is a sparse interpolation matrix, sparse in the sense that it is constructed when one is given a superset of the monomials in the implicit polynomial.

We call the support and the Newton polytope of the implicit equation, *implicit support* and *implicit polytope*, respectively. Its vertices are called *implicit vertices*. The implicit polytope is computed from the Newton polytope of the sparse (or toric) resultant, or *resultant polytope*, of polynomials defined by the parametric equations, thus exploiting the input and output sparseness, in other words, the structure of the parametric equations as well as the implicit polynomial. Under certain genericity assumptions, the implicit polytope coincides with a projection of the resultant polytope, which we call *predicted polytope*, see Section 2. In general, the predicted polytope contains the Minkowski sum of the implicit polytope and an extraneous polytope, which may be a single point. The set of lattice points in the predicted polytope, called the predicted support, is a superset of the implicit support, modulo the Minkowski summand.

The predicted support is used to build a numerical matrix whose kernel is, ideally, 1-dimensional, thus yielding (up to a nonzero scalar multiple) the coefficients corresponding to the predicted implicit support. This is a standard case of *sparse interpolation* of the polynomial from its values. When dealing with hypersurfaces of high dimension, or when the support contains a large number of lattice points, then exact solving is expensive. Since the kernel can be computed numerically, our approach also yields an approximate sparse implicitization method. Our results also apply when the hypersurface is given as a point cloud but in this case a d-simplex is used as the predicted polytope, where d is an estimation of the total degree of the implicit equation.

Contribution.

The contribution of this work is twofold: first we show the usefulness of Minkowski decomposition of the predicted polytope to improve the efficiency of interpolating the im-

ISSAC'15, July 6–9, 2015, Bath, United Kingdom.

DOI: http://dx.doi.org/10.1145/2755996.2756661.

plicit equation. A full-dimensional indecomposable Minkowski summand of the predicted polytope, when it exists, may be the exact implicit polytope. We offer an algorithm, and a public-domain implementation in Sage, for computing the 1-skeleton and the V-representation of such summand in $\mathbb{R}^2$ and $\mathbb{R}^3$, by using integer linear programming (ILP), while excluding homothetic summands. Second, we utilize sparse interpolation matrices to formulate some geometric problems as questions in numerical linear algebra. In particular, we reduce the membership test $p(q) = 0$, for a query point q and a hypersurface defined implicitly by $p(x) = 0$, to a rank test on an interpolation matrix for $p(x)$. Moreover, when this matrix is non-singular, we use the (nonzero) sign of its determinant to decide sidedness for query points q with nonzero coordinates that do not lie on the surface $p(x) = 0$. We have implemented these algorithms in Maple 14. A beta-version is publicly available[1].

The rest of the paper is organized as follows: Next, we overview previous work. Section 2 describes the overall approach. Section 3 presents an algorithm for Minkowski decomposition, focusing on the 3-dimensional case. Section 4 presents matrix constructions that reduce membership and sidedness predicates to numerical linear algebra. We conclude with future work and open questions.

Previous work.

If S is a superset of the implicit support, then the most direct method to reduce implicitization to linear algebra is to construct a $|S| \times |S|$ matrix M, indexed by monomials with exponents in S evaluated at $|S|$ different values. Then the vector of coefficients of the implicit equation is in the kernel of M. This idea was used in [4, 10, 14]; it is also the starting point of this paper.

Our method of sparse implicitization was introduced in [4], where the overall algorithm was presented together with a preliminary implementation, including the case of approximate sparse implicitization. The emphasis of that work was on sampling and oversampling the parametric object so as to create a numerically stable matrix, and examined evaluating the monomials at random integers, random complex numbers of modulus 1, and complex roots of unity.

One issue was that the kernel of the matrix might be of high dimension, in which case the equation obtained may be a multiple of the implicit equation. In [5] they show that if the kernel is not 1-dimensional then the predicted polytope is the Minkowski sum of the implicit polytope and an extraneous one. The true implicit polynomial is obtained as the greatest common divisor (GCD) of the polynomials corresponding to at least two and at most all of the kernel vectors, or via multivariate polynomial factoring.

There are methods for the computing the implicit polytope based on tropical geometry [13, 14], cf. [3]. Sparse implicitization relies on computing the Newton polytope of the sparse resultant or its orthogonal projection along a given direction [6], implemented in ResPol[2].

Matrix representations in geometric modeling are not new. A major current direction is based on the theory of moving curves and surfaces. In [2], they use generalized matrix-based representations of parameterized surfaces in order to represent the intersection curve of two such surfaces as the zero set of a matrix determinant. In [1] they introduce a new implicit representation of rational Bézier curves and surfaces in $\mathbb{R}^3$, namely a matrix whose entries depend on the space variables and whose rank drops exactly on this curve or surface.

Previous work on Minkowski decomposition algorithms mainly focuses on $\mathbb{R}^2$. In [8] the authors give an algorithm deciding decomposability in $\mathbb{R}^2$ (in pseudo-polynomial time) and a generalization in higher dimensions. A subset-sum based pseudo-polynomial time algorithm for decomposition of polygons is given in [7]. Smilansky [12] offers decomposability criteria by considering the space of affine dependences of the vertices of the dual polytope. In [9] they reduce the problem of deciding absolute irreducibility of multivariate polynomials to Minkowski decomposability of a lattice polytope which in turn is reduced to ILP. Our approach differs in the construction of the ILP: we exclude homothetic summands and favor balanced-size summands. Moreover, we employ a combinatorial algorithm to obtain a V-representation of the summand.

2. IMPLICITIZATION BY SUPPORT PREDICTION

This section describes how sparse elimination can be used to compute the implicit polytope by exploiting sparseness and how this can reduce implicitization to linear algebra. We also discuss how the quality of the predicted support affects the implicitization algorithm and develop the necessary constructions that allow us to formulate the membership and sidedness criteria in the next sections.

A *parameterization* of a geometric object of co-dimension one, in a space of dimension $n+1$, can be described by a set of parametric functions:

$$x_i = f_i(t_1, \dots, t_n) : \Omega \to \mathbb{R}$$

where $i = 0, 1, 2, \dots, n$, $\Omega := \Omega_1 \times \cdots \times \Omega_n$, $\Omega_i \subseteq \mathbb{R}$ and $t := (t_1, t_2, \dots, t_n)$ is the vector of parameters and $f := (f_0, \dots, f_n) : \Omega \to \mathbb{R}^{n+1}$ is a vector of continuous functions, also called *coordinate functions*, including polynomial, rational, and trigonometric functions.

The *implicitization problem* asks for the smallest algebraic variety containing the closure of the image of the parametric map $f : \mathbb{R}^n \to \mathbb{R}^{n+1} : t \mapsto f(t)$. Implicitization of planar curves and surfaces in three dimensional space corresponds to $n = 1$ and $n = 2$ respectively. The image of f is contained in the variety defined by the ideal of all polynomials $p(x_0, \dots, x_n)$ such that $p(f_0(t), \dots, f_n(t)) = 0$, for all t in Ω. We restrict ourselves to the case when this is a principal ideal, and we wish to compute its unique (up to a constant multiple) defining polynomial $p(x_0, \dots, x_n) \in \mathbb{R}[x_0, \dots, x_n]$, given its Newton polytope $P = N(p) \subset \mathbb{R}^{n+1}$. We can regard the variety in question as the (closure of the) projection of the graph of map f to the last $n+1$ coordinates. Assuming the rational parameterization

$$x_i = f_i(t)/g_i(t), \ i = 0, \dots, n, \qquad (1)$$

implicitization is reduced to eliminating t from the polynomials in $(\mathbb{R}(x_0, \dots, x_n))[t, y]$:

$$F_i := x_i g_i(t) - f_i(t), \ i = 0, \dots, n, \qquad (2)$$
$$F_{n+1} := 1 - y g_0(t) \cdots g_n(t),$$

[1] http://ergawiki.di.uoa.gr/index.php/Implicitization
[2] http://sourceforge.net/projects/respol

where y is a new variable and F_{i+1} assures that all $g_i(t) \neq 0$. If one omits F_{n+1}, the generator of the corresponding (principal) ideal would be a multiple of the implicit equation. Then the extraneous factor corresponds to the g_i. Eliminating t, y is done by the *resultant* of the polynomials in (2).

Let $A_i \subset \mathbb{Z}^{n+1}$, $i = 0, \ldots, n+1$ be the supports of the polynomials F_i and consider the generic polynomials

$$F'_0, \ldots, F'_n, F'_{n+1} \tag{3}$$

with the same supports A_i and symbolic coefficients c_{ij}.

DEFINITION 1. *Their sparse resultant $Res(F'_0, \ldots, F'_{n+1})$ is a polynomial in the c_{ij} with integer coefficients, namely*

$$\mathcal{R} \in \mathbb{Z}[c_{ij} : i = 0, \ldots, n+1, j = 1, \ldots, |A_i|],$$

which is unique up to sign and vanishes if and only if the system $F'_0 = F'_1 = \cdots = F'_{n+1} = 0$ has a common root in a specific variety. This variety is the projective variety $\mathbb{P}^n$ over the algebraic closure of the coefficient field in the case of projective (or classical) resultants, or the toric variety defined by the A_i's.

The implicit equation of the parametric hypersurface defined in (2) equals the resultant $\mathrm{Res}(F_0, \ldots, F_{n+1})$, provided that the latter does not vanish identically. $\mathrm{Res}(F_0, \ldots, F_{n+1})$ can be obtained from $\mathrm{Res}(F'_0, \ldots, F'_{n+1})$ by specializing the symbolic coefficients of the F'_i's to the actual coefficients of the F_i's, provided that this specialization is generic enough. Then the implicit polytope P equals the projection Q of the resultant polytope to the space of the implicit variables, i.e. the Newton polytope of the specialized resultant, up to some translation. We shall call Q the *predicted (implicit) polytope*. When the specialization of the c_{ij} is not generic enough, then Q contains a translate of P. This follows from the fact that the method computes the same resultant polytope as the tropical approach, see [13, Prop.5.3]. Note that there is no exception even in the presence of base points.

Our method is based on computing the predicted polytope Q, given the Newton polytopes of the polynomials in (2). Then the implicit support is a subset of the set of lattice points contained in the predicted polytope, modulo the Minkowski summand. For computing Q we employ [6] and software `ResPol`.

EXAMPLE 1. *Eight-surface parameterization:*

$$\left(\frac{4s(-1+t^2)(-1+s^2)}{(1+t^2)(1+s^2)^2}, \frac{-8st(-1+s^2)}{(1+t^2)(1+s^2)^2}, \frac{2s}{(1+s^2)} \right).$$

`ResPol` predicts a polytope Q with vertices $(0,0,8)$, $(0,0,12)$, $(0,2,2)$, $(0,4,0)$, $(0,4,4)$, $(2,2,0)$, $(4,0,4)$. The true polytope of the implicit equation $-4x_2^2 + x_1^2 + x_0^2 + 4x_2^4$ is smaller.

Sparse elimination theory works over the ring of Laurent polynomials $\mathbb{C}[t_1^{\pm 1}, \ldots, t_n^{\pm 1}]$ which means that points in the supports of the polynomials may have negative coordinates. As a consequence, evaluation points of polynomials cannot have zero coordinates. In the sequel we assume that P and Q are translated to the positive orthant and have non-empty intersection with all coordinate axes. This allows us to consider points with zero coordinates.

Let $S := \{s_1, \ldots, s_{|S|}\}$ be the set of lattice points in Q. S is used in our implicitization algorithm to construct a numerical matrix M: each $s_j = (s_{j0}, \ldots, s_{jn})$, $j = 1, \ldots, |S|$ is an exponent of a (potential) monomial $m_j := x^{s_j} = x_0^{s_{j0}} \cdots x_n^{s_{jn}}$ of the implicit polynomial, where x_i is defined in (1). We denote by $\boldsymbol{m} = (m_1, \ldots, m_{|S|})$ the vector of potential monomials and evaluate m_j at *generic* points $\tau_k \in \mathbb{C}^n$, $k = 1, \ldots, \mu$, $\mu \geq |S|$, avoiding values that make the denominators of the parametric expressions close to 0. Let

$$m_j|_{t=\tau_k} := \prod_{i=0}^{n} \left(\frac{f_i(\tau_k)}{g_i(\tau_k)} \right)^{s_{ji}}, \quad j = 1, \ldots, |S|$$

denote the evaluated j-th monomial m_j at τ_k. Thus, we construct an $\mu \times |S|$ matrix M with rows indexed by $\tau_1, \ldots, \tau_\mu$ and columns by $m_1, \ldots, m_{|S|}$:

$$M = \begin{bmatrix} m_1|_{t=\tau_1} & \cdots & m_{|S|}|_{t=\tau_1} \\ \vdots & \cdots & \vdots \\ m_1|_{t=\tau_\mu} & \cdots & m_{|S|}|_{t=\tau_\mu} \end{bmatrix}. \tag{4}$$

The vectors in the kernel of M contain the coefficients of the monomials with exponents in S in multiples of the implicit polynomial $p(x)$, where $x := (x_0, \ldots, x_n)$.

To cope with numerical issues, especially when computation is approximate, we let $\mu \geq |S|$; this overconstrained system increases numerical stability and reduces the probability of obtaining an empty or higher dimensional kernel due to a bad sampling, see below.

When constructing matrix M we assume that the parametric hypersurface is sampled sufficiently generically by evaluating the parametric expressions at random points $\tau_k \in \mathbb{C}^n$. It is possible to check a-posteriori the genericity of the sampling by testing the evaluated matrix. Using more than $|S|$ sample points we reduce the probability that another polynomial vanishes at those points. Let $G \subset \Omega$ be the sampling space, typically the set of lattice points in a hypercube in $\mathbb{R}^n$ of size $|S|^2$, and by abuse of notation, let τ_k, $k = 1 \ldots, \mu$, denote the parameter value and its image via the parameterization (1). Let $h(x)$ be a nonzero polynomial in the basis S, of total degree $d \leq |S|^{2n}$. By the Schwartz-Zippel lemma [11]:

$$Prob[h(\tau_k) = 0] \leq d/|G| = d/|S|^{2n},$$

hence for μ (independently chosen) lattice sample points

$$Prob[h(\tau_k) = 0, \text{ for all } k = 1, \ldots, \mu] \leq \left(d/|S|^2\right)^\mu.$$

It follows that we can obtain a good sample by choosing suitable values for μ and $|G|$. Hence:

LEMMA 2. [5] *Any polynomial in the basis of monomials S indexing M, with coefficient vector in the kernel of M, is a multiple of the implicit polynomial $p(x)$.*

As in [4], one of the main difficulties is to build M whose corank, or kernel dimension, equals 1, i.e. its rank is 1 less than its column dimension. For some inputs we obtain a matrix of corank > 1 when the predicted polytope Q is significantly larger than P. It can be explained by the nature of our method: we rely on a *generic* resultant to express the implicit equation, whose symbolic coefficients are then specialized to the actual coefficients of the parametric equations. If this specialization is not generic, then the implicit equation divides the specialized resultant. The following theorem establishes the relation between the dimension of the kernel of M and the accuracy of the predicted support. It remains valid even in the presence of base points. In fact, it also accounts for them since then P is expected to be much smaller than Q.

THEOREM 3. [5] *Let $P = N(p(x))$ be the implicit polytope, and Q be the predicted polytope. Assuming M has been built using sufficiently generic evaluation points, the dimension of its kernel equals $r = \#\{a \in \mathbb{Z}^{n+1} : a + P \subseteq Q\} = \#\{a \in \mathbb{Z}^{n+1} : N(x^a \cdot p(x)) \subseteq Q\}$. In particular, corank$(M) \geq 1$.*

The formula for the corank of the matrix also implies that the coefficients of the polynomials $x^a p(x)$ such that $N(x^a p(x)) \subseteq Q$, form a basis of the kernel of M (see [5, Proof of Thm. 10]). This observation will be useful in Lem. 14 but also implies the following.

COROLLARY 4. [5] *Let M be the matrix from (4), built with sufficiently generic evaluation points, and suppose the specialization of the polynomials in (3) to the parametric equations is sufficiently generic. Let $\{\mathbf{c_1}, \ldots, \mathbf{c_\lambda}\}$ be a basis of the kernel of M and $g_1(x), \ldots, g_\lambda(x)$ be the polynomials obtained as the inner product $g_i = \mathbf{c_i} \cdot \mathbf{m}$. Then the greatest common divisor (GCD) of $g_1(x), \ldots, g_\lambda(x)$ equals the implicit equation up to a monomial factor x^e.*

REMARK 5. *The extraneous monomial factor x^e in the previous corollary is always a constant when the predicted polytope Q is of the form $Q = P + E$ and, as we assume throughout this paper, it is translated to the positive orthant and touches the coordinate axes. However, it is possible that Q strictly contains $P + E$ and the extraneous polytope E is a point $e \in \mathbb{R}^{n+1}$, or it is the Minkowski sum of point e and a polytope E' which touches the axis. Let $\sum_\beta c_\beta x^\beta$ be the GCD of the polynomials g_i in Cor. 4, and let $\gamma = (\gamma_0, \ldots, \gamma_n)$, where $\gamma_i = \min_\beta(\beta_i)$, $i = 0, \ldots, n$. We can efficiently remove the extraneous monomial x^e by dividing $\sum_\beta c_\beta x^\beta$ with x^γ, i.e. the GCD of monomials x^β.*

3. MINKOWSKI DECOMPOSITION

In this section, we develop a method for Minkowski decomposition in $\mathbb{R}^3$, which also works in $\mathbb{R}^2$. A predicted polytope may correspond to a polynomial containing extraneous factors whose Newton polytope may be Minkowski summands of the predicted polytope. We shall briefly examine the case where $P + E \subsetneq Q$ later in this section.

Given two polytopes A and B in $\mathbb{R}^d$, we define their Minkowski sum by

$$A + B = \{a + b \mid a \in A, \in B\} \subseteq \mathbb{R}^d;$$

A and B are called Minkowski summands.

PROBLEM 6 (MINKOWSKI DECOMPOSITION). *Given a polytope $Q \in \mathbb{R}^d$, find polytopes A and B in $\mathbb{R}^d$, such that $A + B = Q$ and neither A nor B are homothetic to Q.*

A polytope $Q \in \mathbb{R}^d$ is homothetic to the polytope $A \in \mathbb{R}^d$ if there exist $\lambda \in \mathbb{R}$ and $t \in \mathbb{R}^d$ such that $Q = t + \lambda A$.

In general polytope Q may be written as a sum of more than two summands and one may examine decomposition into indecomposable summands. By applying recursion, it suffices to consider decomposition into two summands.

Let us restrict to 3-dimensional polytopes: $d = 3$. Our goal is to construct an ILP expressing Minkowski decomposition so as to compute the 1-skeleton of a summand and its V-representation.

We represent polytopes by a combination of their face lattice and a list of primitive edges. Since the face lattice contains no information about coordinates, we will use the primitive edges for the computation of the V-representation of the polytope. For representing edges we follow a classical method, cf. [8, 9]. Let Q be a lattice polytope and $V = [v_1, v_2, \ldots, v_m]$ its vertices. For every edge $\mathcal{E}_i = (v_{i,1}, v_{i,2})$, where $v_{i,j} \in V$, denote by e'_i the vector $v_{i,2} - v_{i,1}$. Let ℓ_i, called the integer length of $\mathcal{E}_i$, be the gcd of the entries in e'_i, and let e_i be the primitive vector obtained by dividing each entry of e'_i by ℓ_i. Any facet F of Q is a polygon in $\mathbb{R}^2$, determined by a set of primitive vectors and their integer lengths.

Determining the edges of a summand.

The following lemma is the starting point of the algorithm.

LEMMA 7. *Given a Minkowski summand A of a polytope Q, for every facet $F = \langle (e_1, \ell_1), (e_2, \ell_2), \ldots (e_k, \ell_k) \rangle$ of Q there exist a_i with $0 \leq a_i \leq \ell_i$ for $i = 1, 2, \ldots, k$, such that $F' = \langle (e_1, a_1), (e_2, a_2), \ldots (e_k, a_k) \rangle$ is a face of A. Moreover, every facet of A can be obtained from a facet of Q by an appropriate choice of a_i's.*

PROOF. If F is a facet of Q, there are 3 cases:

- $F' = F$ is a facet both of Q and A. Then $a_i = \ell_i$ for all i.
- Only 0-dimensional faces of A appear as Minkowski summands of F. Then $a_i = 0$ for all i.
- Face F' of A is a Minkowski summand of F. Then there is a choice of a_i such that $F' = \langle (e_1, a_1), (e_2, a_2), \ldots (e_k, a_k) \rangle$, due to the theory of Minkowski decomposition in $\mathbb{R}^2$.

By the construction of Minkowski sum, every facet of A, appears as a Minkowski summand of a facet of Q. □

The previous lemma considers a single facet at a time. But we fix the integers a_i globally, i.e., if an edge $\ell_i e_i$ appears in facets F_1 and F_2 of Q, then fixing a_i means that $a_i e_i$ appears in both F'_1 and F'_2, possibly with opposite sign. We call this sign the orientation of the edge in the face and illustrate it in Figure1, showing the development in $\mathbb{R}^2$ of 3 adjacent oriented facets of a unit cube intersecting on a vertex. Note that at least one edge (e.g., the one shown in red/grey in the electronic/printed version) will have inconsistent orientation in the two facets it belongs to, i.e., the signs of this edge in the two facets are opposite.

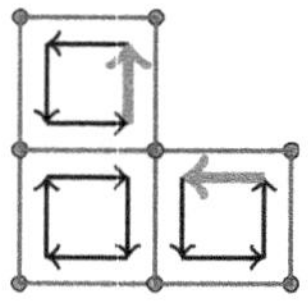

Figure 1: Edge orientation.

For a face $F \subset Q$, we call a face $F' \subset A$ the corresponding face if F' is obtained by F through an appropriate choice of a_i's. Since the a_i are global, we obtain:

LEMMA 8 (PRESERVING ADJACENCY). *Let F_1, F_2 be adjacent, i.e., they have a non-empty intersection, facets of Q and F'_1 and F'_2 be corresponding faces in A, a Minkowski summand of P. Then either F'_1 and F'_2 are adjacent faces in A or they are 0-dimensional and $F'_1 = F'_2$.*

Due to Lem. 7, given Q, we know that any facet of a Minkowski summand is obtained by a facet of Q. Moreover, every facet $F \subset Q$ is a 2D polygon, thus $\sum_{i \text{ s.t. } e_i \in F} \sigma_{i,F} \ell_i e_i = 0$, where $\sigma_{i,F}$ is the sign of e_i and depends on the orientation of the edge $\ell_i e_i$ in the facet F. Similarly, every facet $F' = \langle (e_1, a_1), (e_2, a_2), \ldots (e_k, a_k) \rangle$ of A corresponding to facet $F = \langle (e_1, \ell_1), (e_2, \ell_2), \ldots (e_k, \ell_k) \rangle$ of Q, needs to satisfy the same condition, i.e.,

$$\sum_{i \text{ s.t. } e_i \in F} \sigma_{i,F} a_i e_i = 0 \tag{5}$$

Lem. 8 implies that the edges of a Minkowski summand A are obtained by choosing integers $0 \leq a_i \leq \ell_i$ satisfying relations (5) for every facet of Q. In other words, the set of edges $\mathcal{E}_A = [a_1 e_1, a_2 e_2, \ldots, a_n e_n]$ corresponds to the set of edges of a polytope.

In the definition of Minkowski decomposition, we exclude summands homothetic to Q. In order to avoid such summands we require that the ratios a_i/ℓ_i are not all equal, i.e., $\sum_{i \neq j} (a_i \ell_j - a_j \ell_i) r_i \neq 0$ for some sufficiently random $r_i \in \mathbb{R}^*$. More formally, we have:

THEOREM 9. *Let Q be a polytope given as a set of M facets, where each facet is a list of edges denoted by pairs (e_i, ℓ_i). Let N be the total number of edges. Then there exists a linear Diophantine system with $N+1$ variables and $M+2$ inequalities such that:*

- *The system is infeasible iff there is no non-homothetic Minkowski summand of Q, i.e., Q is indecomposable.*
- *Substituting ℓ_i by a_i in the facet representation of Q, where $(a_1, a_2, \ldots, a_N)$ is a solution to the system, we obtain the facet representation of a (non-homothetic) Minkowski summand of Q.*

In particular, one such linear Diophantine system is:

$$x_i \in \mathbb{N}, \quad b \in \{0,1\}, \tag{6}$$

$$\sum_{i e_i \in F} \sigma_{i,F} x_i e_{i,k} = 0 \text{ for every facet } F \text{ and } k = 1,2,3, \tag{7}$$

$$bM + \sum_{i \geq j} (a_i \ell_j - a_j \ell_i) r_i \geq \epsilon, \tag{8}$$

$$bM + \sum_{i \geq j} (a_i \ell_j - a_j \ell_i) r_i \leq M - \epsilon, \tag{9}$$

where M bounds the absolute value of $\sum_{i \geq j} (a_i \ell_j - a_j \ell_i) r_i$.

PROOF. Conditions (7) ensure that for every facet $F \subset Q$, by substituting ℓ_i with a_i we obtain a 2D polygon. By construction, if an edge (e_i, ℓ_i) of Q is taken as (a_i, ℓ_i), then it has the same length in both faces it appears. By Lem. 8, if two facets are adjacent in Q, the respective faces after substitution are either adjacent or the same 0-dimensional face. Thus, after substituting ℓ_i by a_i in the facets of Q, we obtain facets of A. By Lem. 7 and the discussion following it, if A is a Minkowski summand of Q, then the face list we obtained contains the list of facets of A. Conditions (8)- (9) guarantee that the Minkowski summand A is not homothetic to Q. □

We recurse the decomposition procedure until we obtain lower dimensional or indecomposable summands. Let the size of a summand be the sum of integer length over its edges, i.e., the sum of all a_i's. A heuristic we use is to try obtain balanced summands, i.e., we favor summands with almost equal size. This reduces the depth of the recursion tree. Thus we add to the system of Thm. 9 the constraint $\sum_{i=1}^{n} a_i \leq \frac{1}{2} \sum_{i=1}^{n} \ell_i$ and consider the optimization problem maximizing over the linear functional $\sum_{i=1}^{n} a_i$.

Reconstruction.

From the previous discussion, we can obtain a set of pairs (e_i, a_i) that are edges of a polytope. This is neither an H-representation nor a V-representation of the polytope. We choose to construct a V-representation.

LEMMA 10. *Solving the ILP above we obtain a list $\mathcal{F} = [[(e_i, a_i) \mid a_i \neq 0, (e_i, \ell_i) \in F] \mid F \text{ a facet of } Q]$. Then every $F' \in \mathcal{F}$ belongs to one of three types:*

1. *F' is 0-dimensional (has cardinality 0).*
2. *F' is 1-dimensional (has cardinality 2).*
3. *F' is 2-dimensional (has cardinality more than 2).*

PROOF. Due to the constraint corresponding to F' in the ILP, if F' is not 0-dimensional, then it contains at least 2 edges. If it contains exactly 2 edges, then they must have opposite directions, the same length and correspond to the same edge $\mathcal{E}_i$, i.e., they define an edge. There is no way to choose more than 2 edges of a 2D polygon such that they constitute a polytope of dimension < 2. □

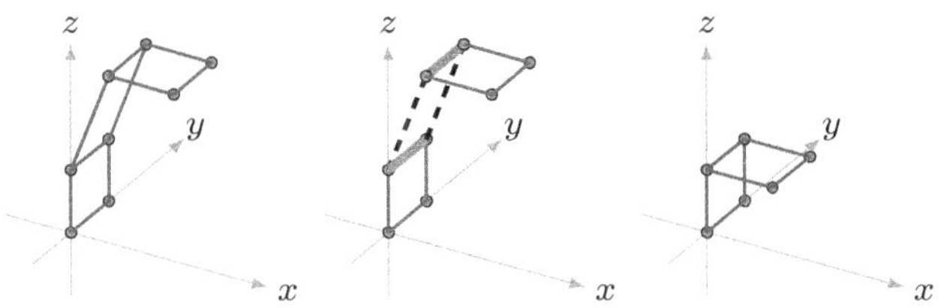

Figure 2: Identifying edges.

Due to Lem. 10, we use possible faces of cardinality 2, in order to "glue" the faces of A together. In Fig. 2 we illustrate a case of cardinality-2 face. Essentially we collapse all edges except the two bold ones, i.e., we collapse two sequences of edges (the ones shown dashed). In the figure, each sequence consists of exactly one edge. From Lem. 10, we have that the two bold edges define the same edge in the polytope we are constructing. Thus we translate one of the facets accordingly, so that the two edges coincide.

More generally, assume we are given a list of faces $L' = \{F_1, F_2, \ldots, F_k\}$. Let $\mathcal{I}$ be the set of all pairs (e_i, e_j) such that there exists an F_k containing only edges corresponding to e_i and e_j. Let $\mathcal{D}$ be a dictionary mapping any e_i appearing in any F_k in L' to a pair of points. This dictionary fixes the endpoints of an edge in the coordinate system. In order to obtain a polytope, we require that edges corresponding to a pair in $\mathcal{I}$, are mapped to the same pair of points in $\mathcal{D}$. Now let L be the list containing all elements of L' with cardinality greater than 2. Let $F = [(e_1, a_1), (e_2, a_2), \ldots, (e_n, a_n)]$ be an element of L. Starting from the origin, fix the endpoints of e_1, i.e., put in the dictionary the key-value pair $(e_1 : [(0,0,0), a_1 e_1])$. We call e_1 a fixed edge, since its endpoints have fixed coordinates. Continue with e_2 starting from the point $a_1 e_1$, and so on for all e_i's in F. Since this is the description of a 2-dimensional face, the endpoint will be the origin. Remove F from L.

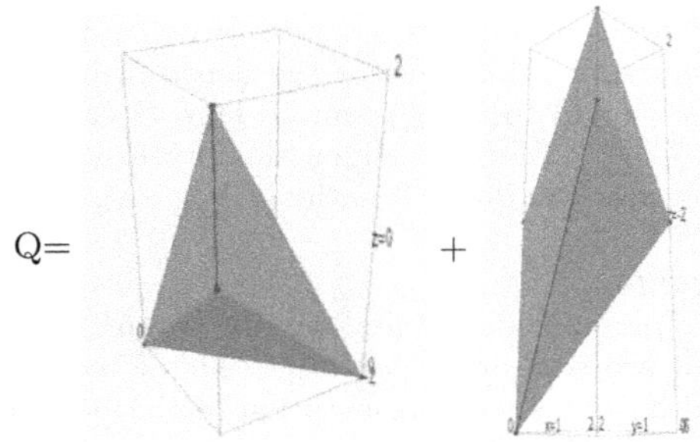

Figure 3: The decomposition of polytope Q in Exam. 2 into indecomposable summands.

Pick an element of L that contains an e_i already mapped via the dictionary $\mathcal{D}$. If this is not possible, pick an element of L containing an e_j, such that there exists a pair (e_i, e_j) (or (e_j, e_i)) in $\mathcal{I}$ with e_i already mapped via $\mathcal{D}$. Repeat the procedure as above, using as starting point the starting point of e_i given by the dictionary instead of the origin. Note that orientation needs to be taken care of, i.e., if e_k is backwards, then use as starting point the endpoint of e_k as fixed in the dictionary. The procedure described will produce all vertices of a polytope defined by the faces described in L. Actually, it will also produce all edges, i.e., the 1-skeleton of the polytope. Thus, it allows for a recursive application of the algorithm in order to obtain indecomposable factors.

EXAMPLE 2 (CONT'D FROM EXAM. 1). *Given the predicted polytope Q, we construct an ILP in 12 variables and 22 constraints. Our method obtains the decomposition (see Fig. 3):*

$$
\begin{aligned}
Q &= CH\,((0,0,6),(0,0,8),(0,2,0),(0,2,4),(2,0,4)) \\
&+ CH\,((0,2,0),(2,0,0),(0,0,2),(0,0,4)),
\end{aligned}
$$

where CH denotes convex hull. Both summands are indecomposable; the second one is the exact implicit polytope P. Using Q in the implicitization algorithm yields a 67×67 matrix, while P a 10×10 matrix.

REMARK 11. *Minkowski decomposition fails to extract the implicit polytope P from the predicted polytope Q, if $Q \subsetneq P + E$. Then Q might be indecomposable, see Exam. 3, or less often, Q is decomposable but none of the summands is exactly P. We can address these cases by either taking smaller homothetic copies of Q and trying to decompose them, or by removing a few vertices from Q and using the resulting polytope as input to our algorithm.*

EXAMPLE 3. *For the Bohemian Dome*

$$
\left(\frac{1-t^2}{1+t^2}, \frac{1+2t+t^2-s^2-s^2t^2+2ts^2}{(1+t^2)(1+s^2)}, \frac{2s}{(1+s^2)}\right)
$$

***ResPol** predicts a polytope with vertices $(0,0,0)$, $(0,0,4)$, $(0,4,0)$, $(4,0,0)$, $(4,0,4)$, while the true implicit polytope has vertices $(0,0,4)$, $(0,4,0)$, $(4,0,0)$, $(0,2,0)$. The predicted polytope is indecomposable.*

Analysis.

Let Q be given by M facets, where each facet is a list of edges denoted by pairs (e_i, ℓ_i) and let N be the total number of edges. Our algorithm has two steps.

Algorithm 1: Minkowski Decomposition

Input : A polytope Q, given as a list of its facets $[F_1, F_2, \dots, F_k]$ where F_i is a list of pairs (ℓ_i, e_i) (length, primitive edge)
Output: A V-rep of a Minkowski summand of Q.

$f \leftarrow$ MAXIMIZE$(\sum_{i=1}^n x_i)$
Choose random r_i
$B \leftarrow \sum_{i \geq j} (\ell_j^2 - \ell_i)\, r_i$
$C \leftarrow 0 < \sum_{i=1}^n x_i < \frac{1}{2} \sum_{i=1}^n \ell_i$
for $i \leftarrow 1$ **to** $|F|$ **do**
  $C \leftarrow \sum_{i \text{ s.t. } e_i \in F} \sigma_{i,F} a_i e_i = 0$
$C \leftarrow bB + \sum_{i \geq j} (a_i \ell_j - a_j \ell_i)\, r_i \geq \epsilon$
$C \leftarrow bB + \sum_{i \geq j} (a_i \ell_j - a_j \ell_i)\, r_i \leq B - \epsilon$
a = solution to the ILP given by (f, C)
for $f \in F$ **do**
  $L \leftarrow f|_{\ell_i = a_i}$
$\mathcal{I}$ = the set of (e_i, e_j) such that there exists $F_k \in L$ containing only edges corresponding to e_i and e_j
$\mathcal{D}$ = an empty dictionary.
Remove from L all elements of cardinality less than 3
F = the first element of L ; startpoint=$(0,0,0)$
while *true* **do**
  for $i \leftarrow 1$ **to** $|F|$ **do**
    if $e_i \notin \mathcal{D}$ **then**
      if $e_i \in \mathcal{I}$ **then** $e = e_j$ such that (e_i, e_j) in $\mathcal{I}$
      else e=e_i
      endpoint= startpoint+ $a_i e$
      $\mathcal{D}$ $[e_i]$ = [startpoint , endpoint]
      startpoint=endpoint
    else startpoint= $\mathcal{D}$ $[e_i][2]$
  if $L \neq \emptyset$ **then**
    Pick F containing an edge either fixed or in $\mathcal{I}$
  else Break
A = the convex hull of all points where $\mathcal{D}$ is mapping to
return A

The first consists in defining and solving an ILP. In order to define the program, we need a number of operations in $O(M)$. We then solve a system in $N+1$ variables with $M+2$ inequalities. ILP is strongly NP-complete, thus we cannot expect a pseudo-polynomial algorithm. Nevertheless, there exist very efficient implementations.

The second step concerns the computation of a V-representation of a Minkowski summand, given a solution of the ILP. In Alg 1, we use a dictionary and the complexity becomes $\mathcal{O}(NM^2)$. A detailed analysis of further data-structures and optimizations to increase performance is out of scope.

4. GEOMETRIC OPERATIONS

In this section we formulate the membership and sidedness operations on the hypersurface $p(x) = 0$ as matrix operations. This is done by modifying slightly the construction of the interpolation matrix M in Section 2 to obtain matrix $M(x)$ which is numeric except for its last row.

Recall S is the predicted support and $\boldsymbol{m}$ the row vector of predicted monomials. Fix a set of *generic* distinct values τ_k, $k = 1, \dots, |S|-1$ and recall that $m_j|_{t=\tau_k}$ denotes the j-th monomial m_j evaluated at τ_k. Let M' be the $(|S|-1) \times |S|$

numeric matrix obtained by evaluating $\boldsymbol{m}$ at the $|S|-1$ points τ_k, i.e., M' is obtained from M in (4) for $\mu = |S|-1$. Finally, let $M(x)$ be the $|S| \times |S|$ matrix obtained by appending row vector $\boldsymbol{m}$ to matrix M':

$$M(x) = \begin{bmatrix} M' \\ \boldsymbol{m} \end{bmatrix}. \qquad (10)$$

Given a point $q \in \mathbb{R}^{n+1}$, let $M(q) = \begin{bmatrix} M' \\ \boldsymbol{m}|_{x=q} \end{bmatrix}$, where $\boldsymbol{m}_{x=q}$ denotes vector $\boldsymbol{m}$ evaluated at q. We assume that $q \neq x(\tau_k)$, for all $k = 1, \ldots, |S|-1$, which implies that the rows of $M(q)$ are distinct. This can be checked efficiently. Obviously, when $p(q) = 0$, $M(q)$ is equivalent to matrix M in (4) in the sense that they both have the same kernel.

REMARK 12. *Let M be a matrix as in (4) and $\boldsymbol{c}$ be a vector in the kernel of M. Since the kernel is a vector space, then $\lambda\boldsymbol{c}$ is also in the kernel of M, for any $0 \neq \lambda \in \mathbb{R}$. This also follows from the fact that the implicit polynomial is defined up to a non-zero scalar multiple. Hence we can set an arbitrary non-zero coordinate of $\boldsymbol{c}$ equal to 1. As a consequence the matrices M', M and $M(q)$, for $p(q) = 0$, have the same kernel of corank r, where r is given in Thm. 3.*

Matrix $M(x)$ has an important property:

LEMMA 13. *Assuming M' is of full rank, the $\det M(x)$ equals the implicit polynomial $p(x)$ up to a constant.*

PROOF. Suppose that M' is of full rank equal to $|S|-1$. Then there exists a non-singular $(|S|-1)\times(|S|-1)$ submatrix of M'. Without loss of generality we assume that it is the submatrix $M'' = M'_{-|S|}$ obtained from M' by removing its last column. By Rmk 12, M' and M have the same kernel consisting of a single vector $\boldsymbol{c} = (c_1, \ldots, c_{|S|})$, where we can assume that $c_{|S|} = 1$. Let N denote $|S|$, then

$$\begin{bmatrix} m_1|_{t=\tau_1} & \cdots & m_N|_{t=\tau_1} \\ \vdots & \cdots & \vdots \\ m_1|_{t=\tau_{N-1}} & \cdots & m_N|_{t=\tau_{N-1}} \end{bmatrix} \begin{bmatrix} c_1 \\ \vdots \\ c_{N-1} \\ 1 \end{bmatrix} = \mathbf{0} \Leftrightarrow \qquad (11)$$

$$\begin{bmatrix} m_1|_{t=\tau_1} & \cdots & m_{N-1}|_{t=\tau_1} \\ \vdots & \cdots & \vdots \\ m_1|_{t=\tau_{N-1}} & \cdots & m_{N-1}|_{t=\tau_{N-1}} \end{bmatrix} \begin{bmatrix} c_1 \\ \vdots \\ c_{N-1} \\ 1 \end{bmatrix} = - \begin{bmatrix} m_k|_{t=\tau_1} \\ \vdots \\ m_k|_{t=\tau_{N-1}} \end{bmatrix},$$

which, by applying Cramer's rule yields

$$c_k = \det M''_k / \det M'', \quad k = 1, \ldots, N-1, \qquad (12)$$

where M''_k is the matrix obtained by replacing the kth column of M'' by the $|S|$th column of M', which plays the role of the constant vector in (11). Note that M''_k equals (up to reordering of the columns) M'_{-k}, where M'_{-k} is the matrix obtained by removing the kth column of M'. Hence, $\det M''_k$ equals (up to sign) $\det M'_{-k}$.

Now, the assumption that M' is of full rank in conjunction with Thm. 3 and Cor. 4 implies that

$$p(x) = \boldsymbol{m} \cdot \boldsymbol{c} = \sum_{i=1}^{|S|} m_i \cdot c_i = \sum_{i=1}^{|S|-1} m_i \cdot c_i + m_{|S|},$$

which combined with (12) gives

$$p(x) = \sum_{i=1}^{|S|-1} m_i \cdot \frac{\det M''_k}{\det M''} + m_{|S|}$$

$$= \pm \sum_{i=1}^{|S|-1} m_i \cdot \frac{\det M'_{-k}}{\det M'_{-|S|}} + m_{|S|} - = \pm \frac{\det M(x)}{\det M'_{-|S|}}. \quad \square$$

Membership predicate.

Given parameterization (1) and query point $q \in \mathbb{R}^{n+1}$, we wish to decide whether $p(q) = 0$ or not, where $p(x)$ is the unknown implicit equation of the parametric hypersurface. We formulate this using the interpolation matrix in (10).

Working with matrices instead of polynomials, we cannot utilize Cor. 4 and Rmk 5 to process the kernel polynomials. To avoid false positives we restrict membership testing to points $q \in (\mathbb{R}^*)^{n+1}$, where $\mathbb{R}^* = \mathbb{R} \setminus \{0\}$.

LEMMA 14. *Let $M(x)$ be as in (10) and $q = (q_0, \ldots, q_n)$ be a query point in $(\mathbb{R}^*)^{n+1}$. Then q lies on the hypersurface defined by $p(x) = 0$ if and only if corank$(M(q))$ = corank(M').*

PROOF. For every point q, since M' is an $(|S|-1) \times |S|$ submatrix of the $|S| \times |S|$ matrix $M(q)$, we have that $\text{rank}(M(q)) \geq \text{rank}(M')$ which implies that $\text{corank}(M(q)) \leq \text{corank}(M')$. Moreover, it holds that

$$\text{kernel}(M(q)) \subseteq \text{kernel}(M'). \qquad (13)$$

($\rightarrow$) Assume that q lies on the hypersurface defined by p, hence $p(q) = 0$. Then by Rmk 12 the matrices $M(q)$ and M' have the same corank.
($\leftarrow$) Suppose that $\text{corank}(M(q)) = \text{corank}(M')$. Then the last row $\boldsymbol{m}|_{x=q}$ of $M(q)$ is linearly dependent on the first $|S|-1$ rows, hence there exist $l_k \in \mathbb{R}, k = 1, \ldots, |S|$, not all zero, such that $\boldsymbol{m}|_{x=q} = \sum_{k=1}^{|S|} l_k \boldsymbol{m}|_{t=\tau_k}$. Let $\boldsymbol{c} \in \text{kernel}(M')$. Then $\boldsymbol{m}|_{x=q} \cdot \boldsymbol{c} = (\sum_{i=k}^{|S|} l_k \boldsymbol{m}|_{t=\tau_k}) \cdot \boldsymbol{c} = \sum_{i=k}^{|S|} l_k (\boldsymbol{m}|_{t=\tau_k} \cdot \boldsymbol{c}) = 0$, so $\boldsymbol{c} \in \text{kernel}(M(q))$, which, given relation (13), implies that M' and $M(q)$ have the same kernel.

Every vector $\boldsymbol{c}$ in the kernel of M', hence, also of $M(q)$, is a linear combination of the coefficient vectors of the polynomials $x^a p(x)$, where $a \in \mathbb{Z}^{n+1}$ such that $N(x^a p(x)) \subseteq Q$, (see also the discussion following Thm. 3). So we have $\boldsymbol{m}|_{x=q} \cdot \boldsymbol{c} = \sum_a \lambda_a q^a p(q) = 0$, where $\lambda_a \in \mathbb{R}$ are not all equal to zero, which, since $q \in (\mathbb{R}^*)^{n+1}$, implies that $p(q) = 0$. $\square$

Lemma 14 readily yields an algorithm that reduces the membership test $p(q) = 0$ for a query point $q \in (\mathbb{R}^*)^{n+1}$, to the comparison of the ranks of the matrices M' and $M(q)$. Note that the lemma is valid even if corank(M')>1.

Sidedness predicate.

The sidedness operation is defined as follows.

DEFINITION 15. *Given a hypersurface in $\mathbb{R}^{n+1}$ with defining equation $p(x) \in \mathbb{R}[x]$, and a point $q \in \mathbb{R}^{n+1}$ such that $p(q) \neq 0$, we define side(q) = sign$(p(q)) \in \{-1, 1\}$.*

See Fig. 4 for an example of applying Def. 15 to the Eight-curve defined by $x^4 - x^2 + y^2 = 0$.

We use matrix $M(x)$ defined in (10) to reduce sidedness as in Def. 15, to the computation of the sign of a numerical determinant. First we show that this determinant is non-zero for relevant inputs.

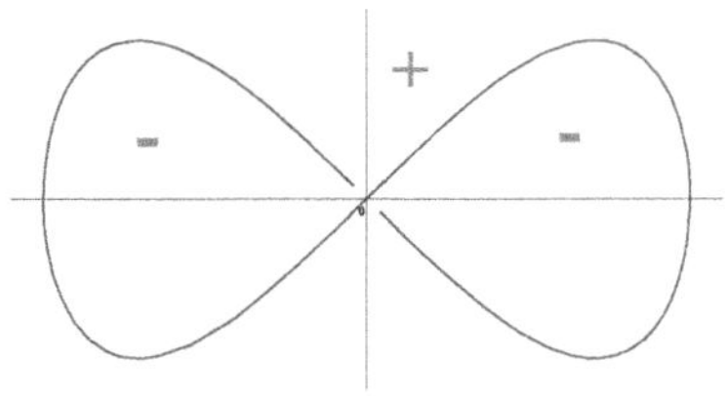

Figure 4: The sign of the Eight-curve polynomial.

LEMMA 16. *Suppose that the predicted polytope Q contains only one translate of the implicit polytope P. Let $M(x)$ be a matrix as in (10) and let $q \in (\mathbb{R}^*)^{n+1}$ such that $p(q) \neq 0$. Then* $\det M(q) \neq 0$.

PROOF. Since Q contains only one translate of the implicit polytope P, Thm. 3 implies that corank$(M) = 1$ and by Rmk 12 this means that corank$(M') = 1$, where matrix M is defined in (4). Then since $p(q) \neq 0$, from Lem. 14 we have that corank$(M') \neq$ corank$(M(q))$, which implies that the matrix $M(q)$ is of full rank equal to $|S|$. Hence $\det M(q) \neq 0$. □

Next we show that, given matrix $M(x)$ and a point $q \in (\mathbb{R}^*)^{n+1}$ such that $p(x) \neq 0$, the sign of $\det(M(q))$ is consistent with side(q) in the following sense: for every pair of query points q_1, q_2, whenever side(q_1) = side(q_2), we have that sign$(\det M(q_1))$ = sign$(\det M(q_2))$.

THEOREM 17. *Let $M(x)$ be as in (10) and q_1, q_2 be two query points in $(\mathbb{R}^*)^{n+1}$ not lying on the hypersurface defined by $p(x) = 0$. Assuming that Q contains only one translate of the implicit polytope P, then side(q_1) = side(q_2) if and only if sign$(\det M(q_1))$ = sign$(\det M(q_2))$, where sign$(\cdot)$ is an integer in $\{-1, 1\}$.*

PROOF. For points q_1, q_2 as in the statement of the theorem, we have from Lem. 16 that $\det M(q_1))$ and $\det M(q_2))$ are non-zero, hence their sign is an integer in $\{-1, 1\}$. We need to show that sign$(p(q_1))$ = sign$(p(q_2))$ if and only if sign$(\det M(q_1))$ = sign$(\det M(q_2))$. But this is an immediate consequence from Lem. 13, since $\det M(x)$ equals $p(x)$ up to a constant factor. □

We thus obtain an algorithm for deciding sidedness for any two query points. The rank test can be avoided if we directly compute sign$(\det M(q_i))$ and proceed depending on whether this sign equals 0 (i.e., $\det M(q_i) = 0$) or not.

5. FUTURE WORK

We currently work on further operations on the matrix representation of a hypersurface, most notably ray shooting, either in exact or approximate form. This boils down to computing the smallest positive root of a univariate polynomial in matrix form. We plan to employ state of the art real solvers which rely on evaluating the polynomial in hand.

We plan to study the structure of our matrices, which generalizes Vandermonde: columns are indexed by monomials and rows by values where the monomials are evaluated. To gain an order of magnitude in complexity, though, we need fast multivariate interpolation and evaluation over arbitrary points, for which there are many open questions.

We are currently enhancing our method and code by also interpolating the normal vector to the curve or surface: We add rows to the interpolation matrix expressing the fact that the normal to the parametric hypersurface and the gradient of the implicit equation must be parallel. We thus add new constraints at the same evaluation points.

Acknowledgement. This research has been co-financed by the European Union (European Social Fund - ESF) and Greek national funds through the Operational Program "Education and Lifelong Learning" of the National Strategic Reference Framework (NSRF) - Research Funding Program: THALIS-UOA (MIS 375891).

6. REFERENCES

[1] L. Busé. Implicit matrix representations of rational Bézier curves and surfaces. *J. CAD*, 46:14–24, 2014.

[2] L. Busé and T. Luu Ba. The surface/surface intersection problem by means of matrix based representations. *J. CAGD*, 29(8):579–598, 2012.

[3] C. D'Andrea and M. Sombra. Rational parametrizations, intersection theory and Newton polytopes. In *Nonlinear Comp. Geom.*, volume 151 of *Volumes in Math. & Appl.*, pages 35–50. IMA, 2009.

[4] I. Emiris, T. Kalinka, C. Konaxis, and T. Luu Ba. Implicitization of curves and surfaces using predicted support. *Theor. Comp. Science*, 479:81–98, 2013.

[5] I. Emiris, T. Kalinka, C. Konaxis, and T. Luu Ba. Sparse implicitization by interpolation: Characterizing non-exactness and an application to computing discriminants. *J. CAD*, 45(2):252–261, 2013.

[6] I. Z. Emiris, V. Fisikopoulos, C. Konaxis, and L. Peñaranda. An oracle-based, output-sensitive algorithm for projections of resultant polytopes. *Int. J. Comp. Geom. App., Special Issue*, 23:397–423, 2013.

[7] I. Z. Emiris and E. P. Tsigaridas. Minkowski decomposition of convex lattice polygons. In M. Elkadi, B. Mourrain, and R. Piene, eds., *Algebraic geometry and geometric modeling*. Springer, 2005.

[8] S. Gao and A. Lauder. Decomposition of polytopes and polynomials. *Disc. Comp. Geom*, 26:89–104, 2001.

[9] D. Kesh and S. K. Mehta. Polynomial irreducibility testing through minkowski summand computation. In *Proc. Canadian Conf. Comp. Geom.*, 2008.

[10] A. Marco and J. Martinez. Implicitization of rational surfaces by means of polynomial interpolation. *J. CAGD*, 19:327–344, 2002.

[11] J. T. Schwartz. Fast probabilistic algorithms for verification of polynomial identities. *J. ACM*, 27(4):701–717, 1980.

[12] Z. Smilansky. Decomposability of polytopes and polyhedra. *Geometriae Dedicata*, 24(1):29–49, 1987.

[13] B. Sturmfels, J. Tevelev, and J. Yu. The Newton polytope of the implicit equation. *Moscow Math. J.*, 7(2), 2007.

[14] B. Sturmfels and J. Yu. Tropical implicitization and mixed fiber polytopes. In *Software for Algebraic Geometry*, volume 148 of *IMA Volumes in Math. & its Applic.*, pages 111–131. Springer, New York, 2008.

Improving the Use of Equational Constraints in Cylindrical Algebraic Decomposition

Matthew England
Coventry University
Matthew.England@coventry.ac.uk

Russell Bradford
University of Bath
R.J.Bradford@bath.ac.uk

James H. Davenport
University of Bath
J.H.Davenport@bath.ac.uk

ABSTRACT

When building a cylindrical algebraic decomposition (CAD) savings can be made in the presence of an equational constraint (EC): an equation logically implied by a formula.

The present paper is concerned with how to use multiple ECs, propagating those in the input throughout the projection set. We improve on the approach of McCallum in ISSAC 2001 by using the reduced projection theory to make savings in the lifting phase (both to the polynomials we lift with and the cells lifted over). We demonstrate the benefits with worked examples and a complexity analysis.

Categories and Subject Descriptors

I.1.2 [**Symbolic and Algebraic Manipulation**]: Algorithms—*Algebraic algorithms, Analysis of algorithms*

General Terms

Algorithms, Experimentation, Theory

Keywords

cylindrical algebraic decomposition, equational constraint

1. INTRODUCTION

A *cylindrical algebraic decomposition* (CAD) splits $\mathbb{R}^n$ into cells arranged *cylindrically*, meaning the projections of any pair are either equal or disjoint, and such that each can be described with a finite sequence of polynomial constraints.

Introduced by Collins for quantifier elimination in real closed fields, applications of CAD include: derivation of optimal numerical schemes [18], parametric optimisation [19], epidemic modelling [9], theorem proving [27], reasoning with multi-valued functions [13], and much more.

CAD has complexity doubly exponential in the number of variables [14]. For some applications there exist algorithms with better complexity (see [2]), but CAD implementations remain the best general purpose approach for many. This may be due to the many extensions and optimisations of CAD since Collins including: partial CAD (to lift only when necessary for quantifier elimination); symbolic-numeric lifting schemes [29, 22]; local projection approaches [8, 30]; and decompositions via complex space [11, 3]. Collins original algorithm is described in [1] while a more detailed summary of recent developments can be found, for example, in [5].

ISSAC'15, July 6–9, 2015, Bath, United Kingdom.
ACM 978-1-4503-3435-8/15/07.
DOI: http://dx.doi.org/10.1145/2755996.2756678.

1.1 CAD computation and terminology

We describe the computation scheme and terminology that most CAD algorithms share. We assume a set of input polynomials (possibly derived from formulae) in ordered variables $\boldsymbol{x} = x_1 \prec \ldots \prec x_n$. The *main variable* of a polynomial (mvar) is the greatest variable present under the ordering.

The first phase of CAD, *projection*, applies projection operators repeatedly, each time producing another set of polynomials in one fewer variables. Together these contain the *projection polynomials* used in the second phase, *lifting*, to build the CAD incrementally. First $\mathbb{R}$ is decomposed into cells which are points and intervals according to the real roots of polynomials univariate in x_1. Then $\mathbb{R}^2$ is decomposed by repeating the process over each cell with the bivariate polynomials in (x_1, x_2) evaluated at a sample point. This produces *sections* (where a polynomial vanishes) and *sectors* (the regions between) which together form the *stack* over the cell. Taking the union of these stacks gives the CAD of $\mathbb{R}^2$ and this is repeated until a CAD of $\mathbb{R}^n$ is produced.

At each stage cells are represented by (at least) a sample point and an *index*. The latter is a list of integers, with the kth describing variable x_k according to the ordered real roots of the projection polynomials in $(x_1, \ldots, x_k)$. If the integer is $2i$ the cell is over the ith root (counting from low to high) and if $2i+1$ over the interval between the ith and $(i+1)$th (or the unbounded intervals at either end).

The projection operator is chosen so polynomials are *delineable* in a cell: the portion of their zero set in the cell consists of disjoint sections. A set of polynomials are *delineable* if each is individually, and the sections of different polynomials are identical or disjoint. If all projection polynomials are delineable then the input polynomials must be *sign-invariant*: have constant sign in each cell of the CAD.

1.2 Equational constraints

Most applications of CAD require *truth-invariance* for logical formulae, meaning each formula has constant boolean truth value on each cell. Sign-invariance for the polynomials in a formula gives truth-invariance, but we can obtain the latter more efficiently by using equational constraints.

Definition 1. *We use* QFF *to denote a quantifier free Tarski formula: Boolean combinations* $(\wedge, \vee, \neg)$ *of statements about the signs* $(= 0, > 0, < 0)$ *of integral polynomials.*

An equational constraint *(EC) is a polynomial equation logically implied by a QFF. If an atom of the formula it is said to be* explicit *and is otherwise* implicit.

Collins first suggested that the projection phase of CAD could be simplified in the presence of an EC [12]. He noted that a CAD sign-invariant for the defining polynomial of an EC, and sign-invariant for any others only on sections of that polynomial, would be sufficient. An intuitive approach to produce this is to consider resultants of the EC polynomial with the other polynomials, in place of them. This approach was first formalised and verified in [24].

A recent complexity analysis [5] showed that using an EC in this way reduces the double exponent in the complexity bound for CAD by 1. A natural question is whether this can be repeated in the presence of multiple ECs. An algorithm for CAD in the presence of two ECs was detailed in [25]. The main idea was to observe that the resultant of the polynomials defining two ECs is itself an EC, and so the same ideas could be applied for the second projection as for the first. However, this approach was complicated as the key result verifying [24] could not be applied recursively.

1.3 Contribution and plan

This paper discusses how we can extend the theory of ECs to produce CADs more efficiently. In Section 2.1 we revise key components of the theory for reduced projection in the presence of an EC from [24, 25]. Then in Section 2.2 we explain how it can also give reductions in the lifting phase, allowing us to propose and verify a new algorithm in Section 3 for making use of multiple ECs. This breaks with the tradition of producing CADs sign-invariant for EC polynomials, instead guaranteeing only invariance for the truth of their conjunction. We demonstrate our contributions in Sections 4 and 5 with a worked example and complexity analysis.

All experiments in Maple were conducted using Maple 18. All code and data created for this paper is openly available from `http://dx.doi.org/10.15125/BATH-00071`.

2. CAD WITH MULTIPLE EQUATIONAL CONSTRAINTS

2.1 Key theory from [23, 24, 25]

We recall some of the key theory behind McCallum's operators. Let cont, prim, disc, coeff and ldcf denote the content, primitive part, discriminant, coefficients and leading coefficient of polynomials respectively (in each case taken with respect to a given mvar). Let res denote the resultant of a pair of polynomials. When applied to a set of polynomials we interpret these as producing sets of polynomials, e.g.

$$\operatorname{res}(A) = \{\operatorname{res}(f_i, f_j) \mid f_i \in A, f_j \in A, f_j \neq f_i\}.$$

Recall that a set $A \subset \mathbb{Z}[\mathbf{x}]$ is an *irreducible basis* if the elements of A are of positive degree in the mvar, irreducible and pairwise relatively prime. Throughout this section suppose B is an irreducible basis for a set of polynomials, that every element of B has mvar x_n and that $F \subseteq B$. Define

$$P(B) := \operatorname{coeff}(B) \cup \operatorname{disc}(B) \cup \operatorname{res}(B), \tag{1}$$

$$P_F(B) := P(F) \cup \{\operatorname{res}(f, g) \mid f \in F, g \in B \setminus F\}, \tag{2}$$

$$P_F^*(B) := P_F(B) \cup \operatorname{disc}(B \setminus F), \tag{3}$$

as the projection operators introduced respectively in [23, 24, 25]. In the general case with A a set of polynomials and $E \subseteq A$ we proceed with projection by: letting B and F be irreducible basis of the primitive parts of A and E respectively; applying the operators as defined above; and then taking the union of the output with cont(A).

The theorems in this section validate the use of these operators for CAD. They use the condition of *order-invariance*, meaning each polynomial has constant order of vanishing within each cell, which of course implies sign-invariance. We say that a polynomial with mvar x_k is *nullified* over a cell in $\mathbb{R}^{k-1}$ if it vanishes identically throughout.

Theorem 1 ([23]). *Let S be a connected submanifold of $\mathbb{R}^{n-1}$ in which each element of $P(B)$ is order-invariant.*

Then on S, each element of B is either nullified or analytic delineable (a variant on delineability, see [23]). Further, the sections of B not nullified are pairwise disjoint, and each element of such B is order-invariant on such sections.

Suppose we apply P repeatedly to generate projection polynomials. Repeated use of Theorem 1 concludes that a CAD produced by lifting with respect to these projection polynomial is order-invariant so long as no projection polynomial with mvar x_k is nullified over a cell in the CAD of $\mathbb{R}^{k-1}$ (a condition known as *well-orientedness* which can be checked during lifting). If this condition is not satisfied then P cannot be used (and we should restart the CAD construction using a different projection operator, such as Hong's [20]).

Theorem 2 ([24]). *Let f and g be integral polynomials with mvar x_n, $r(x_1, \ldots, x_{n-1})$ be their resultant, and suppose $r \neq 0$. Let S be a connected subset of $\mathbb{R}^{n-1}$ on which f is delineable and r order-invariant.*

Then g is sign-invariant in every section of f over S.

Suppose A was derived from a formula with EC defined by $E = \{f\}$, and that we apply $P_E(A)$ once and then P repeatedly to generate a set of projection polynomials. Assuming the input is well-oriented, we can use Theorem 1 to conclude the CAD of $\mathbb{R}^{n-1}$ order invariant for $P_E(A)$. The CAD of $\mathbb{R}^n$ is then sign-invariant for E using Theorem 1 and sign-invariant for A in the sections of E using Theorem 2. Hence the CAD is truth-invariant for the formula.

What if there are multiple ECs? We could designate one for special use and treat the rest as any other constraint (heuristics can help with the choice [6]). But this does not gain any more advantage than one EC gives. However, we cannot simply add multiple polynomials into E at the top level as this would result in a CAD truth-invariant for the disjunction of the ECs, not the conjunction.

Suppose we have a formula with a second EC. If this has a lower mvar then we may consider applying the reduced projection operator again at this lower level. In fact, even if the second EC is also in the mvar of the system we can *propagate* it to the lower level by noting that the resultant of the two ECs is itself an EC in one fewer variable.

So we consider applying first the operator $P_E(A)$ where E defines the first EC and then $P_{E'}(A')$ where $A' = P_E(A)$ and $E' \subseteq A'$ contains the EC in one variable fewer. Unfortunately, Theorem 2 does not validate this approach. While it could be applied once for the CAD of $\mathbb{R}^{n-1}$ it cannot then

Figure 1: The polynomials from Example 1.

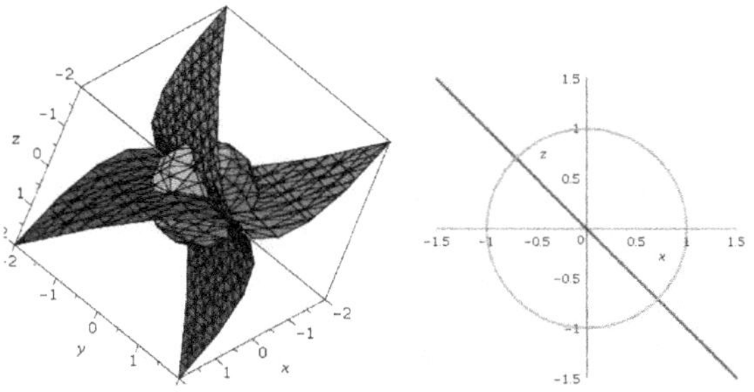

validate the CAD of $\mathbb{R}^n$ because the first application of the theorem provided sign-invariance while the second requires the stronger condition of order invariance. Note however, that this approach is acceptable if $n = 3$ (since in two variables the conditions are equivalent for squarefree bases).

EXAMPLE 1. *The following are graphed in Figure 1, with g the sphere, f_1 the upper surface and f_2 the lower:*

$$f_1 = x + y^2 + z, \quad f_2 = x - y^2 + z, \quad g = x^2 + y^2 + z^2 - 1.$$

We consider the formula $\phi = f_1 = 0 \wedge f_2 = 0 \wedge g \geq 0$. The surfaces f_1 and f_2 only meet on the plane $y = 0$ and this projection is on the right of Figure 1). From this it is clear the solution requires $|x| \geq \sqrt{2}/2$ and $z = -x$.

How could this be ascertained using CAD? With variable ordering $z \succ y \succ x$ a sign-invariant CAD for (f_1, f_2, g) has 1487 cells using QEPCAD *[7]. We could then test a sample point of each cell to identify the ones where ϕ is true.*

It is preferable to use the presence of ECs. Declaring an EC to QEPCAD *will ensure it uses the algorithm in [24] based on a single use of $P_E(A)$ followed by P. Either choice results in 289 cells. In particular, the solution set is described using 8 cells: all have $y = 0, z = -x$ but the x-coordinate unnecessarily splits cells at $\frac{1}{2}(1 \pm \sqrt{6})$. This is identified due to the projection polynomial $d = \mathrm{disc}_y(\mathrm{res}_z(f_i, g))$.*

If we declare both ECs to QEPCAD *then it will use the algorithm in [25] applying $P_E(A)$ twice (allowed since $n = 3$) to produce a CAD with 133 cells. The solution set is now described using only 4 cells (the minimum possible). Note that d was no longer produced as a projection polynomial.*

For problems with $n > 3$ it is still possible to make use of multiple ECs. However, we must include the extra information necessary to provide order-invariance of the non-EC polynomials in the sections of ECs. The following theorem may be used to conclude that $P_E^*(A)$ is appropriate.

THEOREM 3 ([25]). *Let f and g be integral polynomials with mvar x_n, $r = \mathrm{res}(f, g)$, $d = disc(g)$, and suppose $r, d \neq 0$. Let S be a connected subset of $\mathbb{R}^{n-1}$ on which f is analytic delineable, g is not nullified and r and d are order-invariant.*

Then g is order-invariant in each section of f over S.

Suppose we have a formula with two ECs, one with mvar x_n and the other with mvar x_{n-1}. The second could be explicit in the formula or implicit (a resultant as described earlier). Theorem 3 allows us to use a reduced operator twice. We first calculate $A' = P_E(A)$ where E contains the defining polynomial of the first EC, and then $P_{E'}^*(A')$ where E' contains the defining polynomial of the other. Subsequent projections simply use P. When lifting we use Theorem 1 to verify the CAD of $\mathbb{R}^{n-2}$ as order-invariant for $P_{E'}^*(A')$; Theorem 1 to verify the CAD of $\mathbb{R}^{n-1}$ order-invariant for E' everywhere and Theorem 3 to verify it order-invariant for A' in the sections of E'; and Theorem 1 and 2 to verify the CAD of $\mathbb{R}^n$ order-invariant for E and sign-invariant for A in those cells that are both sections of E and E'.

2.2 Reductions in the lifting phase

The main contribution of the present paper is to realise that the theorems above also allow for significant savings in the lifting phase of CAD. However, to implement these we must discard two embedded principles of CAD:

1. That the projection polynomials are a fixed set.
2. That the invariance structure of the final CAD can be expressed in terms of sign-invariance of polynomials.

Abandoning the first is key to recent work in [11, 3], while the second was also investigated in [10, 26].

2.2.1 Minimising the polynomials when lifting

Consider Theorem 2: it allows us to conclude that g is sign-invariant in the sections of f produced over a CAD of $\mathbb{R}^{n-1}$ order-invariant for $P_{\{f\}}(\{f, g\})$. Therefore, it is sufficient to perform the final lift with respect to f only (decompose cylinders according to the roots of f but not g). The decomposition imposes sign-invariance for f while Theorem 2 guarantees it for g in the cells where it matters.

EXAMPLE 2. *We return to Example 1. Recall that designating either EC and using [24] produced a CAD with 289 cells. If we follow this approach but lift only with respect to the designated EC at the final step (implemented in our* MAPLE *package [17]) we obtain a CAD with 141 cells.*

This improved lifting follows from the theorems in [24], but was only noticed 15 years later during the generalisation of [24] to the case of multiple formulae in [4, 5]. Experiments there demonstrated its importance, particularly for problems with many constraints (see Section 8.3 of [5]).

When we apply a reduced operator at two levels then we can make such reductions at both the corresponding lifts.

EXAMPLE 3. *We return to the problem from Example 1. Set $A = \{f_1, f_2, g\}$ and $E = \{f_1\}$. Then project out z using*

$$P_E(A) = \{y^2, y^4 + 2xy^2 + 2x^2 + y^2 - 1\}.$$

These are the resultants of f_1 with f_2 and g. The discriminant of f_1 was a constant and so could be discarded, as was its leading coefficient (meaning no further coefficients were required). We set $A' = P_E(A)$, $E' = \mathrm{res}_z(f_1, f_2) = y^2$ and

$$R = \mathrm{res}_y(y^2, y^4 + 2xy^2 + 2x^2 + y^2 - 1) = (2x^2 - 1)^2.$$

We have $P_{E'}(A') = \{R\}$ since the other possible entries (the discriminants and coefficients from E') are all constants. We hence build a 5 cell CAD of the real line with respect to the two real roots of R. We then lift above each cell with respect to y^2 only, in each case splitting the cylinder into three cells about $y = 0$, to give a CAD of $\mathbb{R}^2$ with 15 cells.

Finally, we lift over each of these 15 cells with respect to f_1 to give 45 cells of $\mathbb{R}^3$. This compares to 133 from QEPCAD*, which used reduced projection but then lifted with all projection polynomials. No polynomials were nullified, so using Theorems 1 and 2, the output is truth-invariant for ϕ.*

The additional lifting that QEPCAD performed does not provide any further structure. For example, if we had lifted with respect to f_2 at the final stage in Example 3 then we would be doing so without the knowledge that it is delineable. Hence splitting the cylinder at the sample point offers no guarantee that the cells produced are sign-invariant away from that point. So the extra work does not allow us to conclude that f_2 is sign-invariant (except on sections of f_1).

Note that using fewer projection polynomials for lifting not only decreases output size (and computation time) but also the risk of failure from non well-oriented input: we only need worry about nullification of polynomials we lift with.

2.2.2 Minimising the cells for stack generation

We can achieve still more savings from the theory in Section 2.1 by abandoning the aim of producing a CAD sign-invariant with respect to any polynomial, instead insisting only on truth-invariance for the formula. We may then lift trivially to cylinders over cells already known to be false, only identifying sections of projection polynomials if there is a possibility the formula may be true. The idea of avoiding computations over false cells was presented in [28]. Our contribution is to explain how such cells can easily be identified in the presence of ECs. We demonstrate with our example.

EXAMPLE 4. *Return to the problem from Examples 1 – 3 and in particular the CAD of $\mathbb{R}^2$ produced with 15 cells in Example 3. On 5 of these 15 cells the polynomial R is zero and on the others it is either positive or negative throughout.*

Now, ϕ can only be satisfied above the 5 cells, as elsewhere the two EC defining polynomials cannot share a root and thus vanish together. We can already conclude the truth value for the 10 cells (false) and thus we do not need to lift over them, except in the trivial sense of extending them to a cylinder in $\mathbb{R}^3$. Lifting over the 5 cells where $R = 0$ with respect to f_1 gives 15 cells, which combined with the 10 cylinders gives a CAD of $\mathbb{R}^3$ with 25 cells that is truth-invariant for ϕ.

This 25 cell CAD is not sign-invariant for f_1. The cylinders above the 10 cells in $\mathbb{R}^2$ where $R \neq 0$ may have f_1 varying sign, but since f_1 can never equal zero at the same time as f_2 in these cells it does not affect the truth of ϕ.

Identifying the 5 cells where $R = 0$ in the CAD of $\mathbb{R}^2$ was trivial since they are simply the sections of the second lift, and hence those cells with second entry even in the cell index. Those sections produced in the third lift are similarly all cells where f_1 is zero, however, we cannot conclude that f_2 is also zero on these. Theorem 2 only guarantees that f_2 is sign-invariant on such cells, so to determine those signs we must still evaluate the polynomials at the sample point.

Reducing the number of cells for stack generation clearly decreases output size, and since the cells can be identified using only a parity check on an integer, computation time decreases also. As with the improvements in Section 2.2.1, this also decreases the risk of non well-oriented input: we only need worry about nullification over these identified cells.

3. ALGORITHM

We present Algorithm 1 to build a truth-invariant CAD for a formula in the presence of multiple ECs. We assume that the ECs are already identified as input to the algorithm (they may have been first computed through propagation as described in Section 2). We assume further that each EC is primitive, and that all the ECs have different mvar (so in practice a choice of designation may have been made).

Algorithm 1: CAD using multiple ECs

Input : A formula ϕ in variables $x_1, \ldots, x_n$, and a sequence of sets $\{E_k\}_{k=1}^{n}$; each either empty or containing a single primitive polynomial with mvar x_k which defines an EC for ϕ.

Output: Either: $\mathcal{D}$, a truth-invariant CAD of $\mathbb{R}^n$ for ϕ (described by lists I and S of cell indices and sample points); or **FAIL**, if not well-oriented.

1 Extract from ϕ the set of defining polynomials A_n;
2 **for** $k = n, \ldots, 2$ **do**
3   Set B_k to the finest squarefree basis for prim(A_k);
4   Set C to cont(A_k);
5   Set F_k to the finest squarefree basis for E_k;
6   **if** *F_k is empty* **then**
7   Set $A_{k-1} := C \cup P(B_k)$;
8   **else**
9   **if** *$k = n$ or $k = 2$* **then**
10   Set $A_{k-1} := C \cup P_{F_i}(B_i)$;
11   **else**
12   Set $A_{k-1} := C \cup P^*_{F_i}(B_i)$;
13 If E_1 is not empty then set p to be its element; otherwise set p to the product of polynomials in A_1;
14 Build $\mathcal{D}_1 := (I_1, S_1)$ according to the real roots of p;
15 **if** $n = 1$ **then**
16   **return** $\mathcal{D}_1$;
17 **for** $k = 2, \ldots, n$ **do**
18   Initialise $\mathcal{D}_k = (I_k, S_k)$ with I_k and S_k empty sets;
19   **if** *F_k is empty* **then**
20   Set $L := B_k$;
21   **else**
22   Set $L := F_k$;
23   **if** *E_{k-1} is empty* **then**
24   Set $\mathcal{C}_a := \mathcal{D}_{k-1}$ and $\mathcal{C}_b$ empty;
25   **else**
26   Set $\mathcal{C}_a$ to be cells in $\mathcal{D}_{k-1}$ with $I_{k-1}[-1]$ even;
27   Set $\mathcal{C}_b := \mathcal{D}_{k-1} \setminus \mathcal{C}_a$;
28   **for** *each cell $c \in \mathcal{C}_a$* **do**
29   **if** *An element of L is nullified over c* **then**
30   **return** FAIL;
31   Generate a stack over c with respect to the polynomials in L, adding cell indices and sample points to I_k and S_k;
32   **for** *each cell $c \in \mathcal{C}_b$* **do**
33   Extend to a single cell in $\mathbb{R}^k$ (cylinder over c), adding index and sample point to I_k and S_k;
34 **return** $\mathcal{D}_n = (I_n, S_n)$.

Steps 1 – 12 run the projection phase of the algorithm. Each projection starts by identifying contents and primitive parts. When there is no declared EC (E_i is empty) the projection operator (1) is used (step 7). Otherwise the operator (3) is used (step 12), unless it is the very first or very last projection (step 10) when we use (2). In each case the output of the projection operator is combined with the contents to form the next layer of projection polynomials.

Steps 13 – 16 construct a CAD for the real line (and return it if the input was univariate). This is sometimes referred to in the literature as the *base phase*. If there is a declared EC in the smallest variable then the real line is decomposed according to its roots, otherwise according to the roots of all the univariate projection polynomials.

Steps 17 – 33 run the lifting phase, incrementally building CADs of $\mathbb{R}^k$ for $k = 2, \ldots, n$. For each k there are two considerations. First, whether there is a declared EC with mvar x_k. If so we lift only with respect to this (step 22) and if not we use all projection polynomials with mvar x_k (step 20). Second, whether there is a declared EC with mvar x_{k-1}. If so we restrict stack generation to those cells where the EC was satisfied. These are simply those with $I_{k-1}[-1]$ (last entry in the cell index) even (step 26). We lift the other cells trivially to a cylinder in step 33.

Algorithm 1 clearly terminates. We will verify that it produces a truth-invariant CAD for the formula so long as the input is well-oriented, as defined below.

DEFINITION 2. *For $k = 2, \ldots, n$ define sets:*

- L_k – *the* lifting polynomials*: the defining polynomial of the declared EC with mvar x_k if one exists, or all projection polynomials with mvar x_k otherwise.*
- $\mathcal{C}_k$ – *the* lifting cells*: those cells in the CAD of $\mathbb{R}^{k-1}$ in which the designated EC with mvar x_{k-1} vanishes if it exists, and all cells in that CAD otherwise.*

The input of Algorithm 1 is well-oriented *if for $k = 2, \ldots, n$ no element of L_k is nullified over an element of $\mathcal{C}_k$.*

THEOREM 4. *Algorithm 1 satisfies its specification.*

PROOF. We must show the CAD is truth-invariant for ϕ, unless the input is not well-oriented when FAIL is returned.

First consider the case where $n = 1$. The projection phase would not run, with the algorithm jumping to the CAD construction in step 13, returning the output in step 16. If there was no declared EC then the CAD is sign-invariant for all polynomials defining ϕ and thus every cell is truth invariant for ϕ. If there was a declared EC then the output is sign-invariant for its defining polynomial. Cells would either be intervals where the formula must be false; or points, where the EC is satisfied, and the formula either identically true or false depending on the signs of the other polynomials.

Next suppose that the input were not well-oriented (Definition 2). For a fixed k, the conditional in steps 19 – 22 sets the lifting polynomials L_k to L and the conditional in steps 23 – 27 the lifting cells $\mathcal{C}_k$ to $\mathcal{C}_a$. Thus it is exactly the conditions of Definition 2 which are checked by step 29, returning FAIL in step 30 when they are not satisfied. If the lifting phase completes then the input is well-oriented.

From now on we suppose $n > 1$ and the input is well-oriented. For a fixed k define *admissible* cells to be those in the induced CAD of $\mathbb{R}^{k-1}$ where all declared ECs with mvar smaller than x_k are satisfied, or to be all cells in that induced CAD if there are no such ECs. Then let $I(k)$ be the following statement for the CADs produced by Algorithm 1. *Over admissible cells (in $\mathbb{R}^{k-1}$) the CAD of $\mathbb{R}^k$ is:*

(a) order-invariant for any EC with mvar x_k;
(b) order- (sign- if $k = n$) invariant for all projection polynomials with mvar x_k on sections of the EC over admissible cells, or over all admissible cells if no EC exists.

We have already proved $I(1)$, and $I(n)$ may be proved by induction. To assert the truth of $I(k)$ we note the following:

- When E_k is empty we use Theorem 1 to assert all projection polynomials with mvar x_k are order-invariant in the stacks over admissible cells giving (a) and (b).
- When E_k is not empty and $k = 2$ we used the projection operator (2). Theorem 2 allows us to conclude (b) and that the EC is sign-invariant in admissible cells. The stronger property of order-invariance follows automatically since the lifting polynomials form a squarefree basis in two variables.
- When E_k is not empty and $k = n$ we used the projection operator (2). Theorem 2 allows us to conclude (b), but also (a) since in the case $k = n$ the statement requires only sign-invariance.
- When E_k is not empty and $2 < k < n$ we used the projection operator (3). Theorem 3 then allows us to conclude the statement.

In each case the assumptions of the theorems are met by the inductive hypothesis, exactly over admissible cells as defined according to whether E_{k-1} was empty or not.

From the definition of admissible cells, we know that ϕ is false (and thus trivially truth invariant) upon all cells in the CAD of $\mathbb{R}^n$ built over an inadmissible cell of $\mathbb{R}^k$, $k < n$. Coupled with the truth of (a) for $k = 1, \ldots, n$, this implies the CAD of $\mathbb{R}^n$ is truth-invariant for the conjunction of ECs (although it may not be truth-invariant for any one individually). The truth of (b) implies that on those cells where all ECs are satisfied, the other polynomials in ϕ are sign-invariant and thus ϕ is truth-invariant. □

4. WORKED EXAMPLE

Assume variable ordering $z \succ y \succ x \succ u \succ v$ and define

$$f_1 := x - y + z^2, \quad f_2 := z^2 - u^2 + v^2 - 1, \quad g := x^2 - 1,$$
$$f_3 := x + y + z^2, \quad f_4 := z^2 + u^2 - v^2 - 1, \quad h := z.$$

We consider the formula

$$\phi = f_1 = 0 \wedge f_2 = 0 \wedge f_3 = 0 \wedge f_4 = 0 \wedge g \geq 0 \wedge h \geq 0.$$

The solution can be found manually by decomposing the system into blocks. The surfaces f_1 and f_3 are graphed in (x, y, z)-space on the left of Figure 2. They meet only on the plane $y = 0$ and this projection is shown on the right. The surfaces f_2 and f_4 are graphed in (z, u, v)-space on the left of Figure 3 and meet only when $z = \pm 1$. We consider only $z = +1$ due to $h \geq 0$, with this projection plotted on the right. We thus see that the solution set is given by

$$\{u = \pm v, x = -1, y = 0, z = 1\}.$$

To ascertain this by Algorithm 1 we must first propagate and designate ECs. We choose to use f_1 first, calculate

$$\mathrm{res}_z(f_1, f_2) = (-u^2 + v^2 - x + y - 1)^2$$

and assign r_1 to be the square root: the defining polynomial for an EC with mvar y. Similarly consider

$$\mathrm{res}_y\left(r_1, \mathrm{res}_z(f_1, f_3)\right) = 16(u^2 - v^2 + x + 1)^4,$$
$$\mathrm{res}_y\left(r_1, \mathrm{res}_z(f_1, f_4)\right) = 4(u^2 - v^2)^2$$

and assign $r_2 := u^2 - v^2 + x + 1$, $r_3 := u^2 - v^2$: defining polynomials for ECs with mvar x and u respectively. There is no series of resultants that leads to an EC with mvar u. We hence have $\{E_j\}_{k=1}^n := \{f_1\}, \{r_1\}, \{r_2\}, \{r_3\}, \{\,\}$ as input for Algorithm 1, along with ϕ.

Figure 2: The polynomials f_1 and f_3 from Section 4.

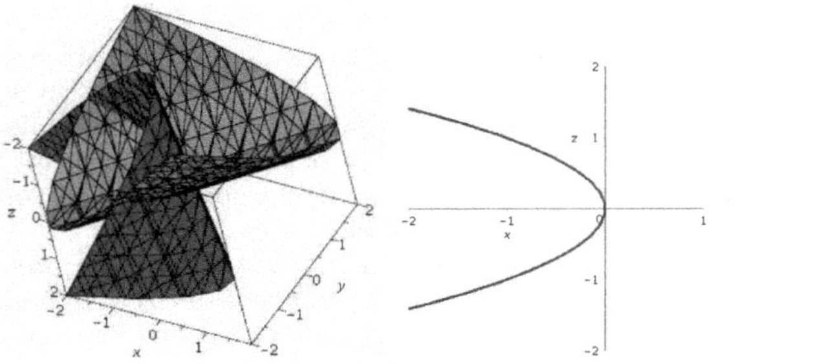

Figure 3: The polynomials f_2 and f_4 from Section 4.

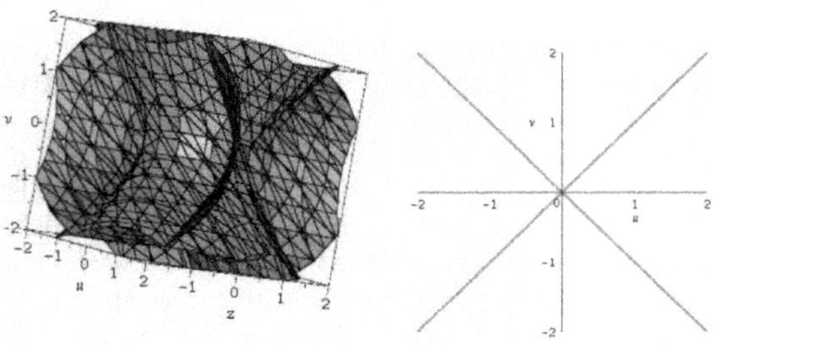

The algorithm starts by extracting the defining polynomials $A_5 = \{f_1, f_2, f_3, f_4, g, h\}$ and finds $B_5 = A_5, F_5 = E_5$ (in fact $F_i = E_i$ for all $i = 1, \ldots, 5$). There is a declared EC for the first projection so we use the operator (2) to derive

$$A_4 := P_{F_5}(B_5) = \{(x^2-1)^2, (-u^2+v^2-x+y-1)^2, (u^2-v^2-x+y-1)^2, 4y^2, x-y\}.$$

Hence $C := \{x^2 - 1\}$ and

$$B_4 := \{y, y-x, -u^2+v^2-x+y-1, u^2-v^2-x+y-1\}.$$

For the next projection we must use operator (3), giving

$$A_3 := C \cup P^*_{F_4}(B_4) = \{x^2-1, u^2-v^2+x+1, u^2-v^2, u^2-v^2+1\}$$

noting that for this example the extra discriminants in (3) all evaluated to constants and so could be discarded. Then

$$B_3 := \{x^2-1, u^2-v^2+x+1\}, \quad C := \{u^2-v^2, u^2-v^2+1\},$$

and the next projection also uses (3) to produce

$$A_2 := \{u^2-v^2, u^2-v^2+1, u^4-2u^2v^2+v^4+2u^2-2v^2\}.$$

For the final projection there is no EC and so we use operator (1) to find $A_1 := \{v^2\}$. The base phase of the algorithm hence produces a 3-cell CAD of the real line isolating 0.

For the first lift we have $L = \{u^2 - v^2\}$ and C_a containing all 3 cells. Above the two intervals we split into 5 cells by the curves $u = \pm v$, while above $v = 0$ we split into three cells about the origin. From these 13 cells of $\mathbb{R}^2$ we select the 5 which were sections of $u^2 - v^2$ for C_a. These are lifted with respect to $L = \{r_2\}$, and the other 8 are simply extended to cylinders in $\mathbb{R}^3$. Together this gives a CAD of $\mathbb{R}^3$ with 23 cells. The next two lifts are similar, producing first a CAD of $\mathbb{R}^4$ with 53 cells and finally a CAD of $\mathbb{R}^5$ with 113 cells. The entire calculation takes less than a second in MAPLE.

Choice in EC designation

Algorithm 1 could have been initialised with alternative EC designations. There were the 4 explicit ECs with mvar z, and by taking repeated resultants we discover the following implicit ECs, organised in sets with decreasing mvar:

$$\{y^2, u^2-v^2+x-y+1, -u^2+v^2+x-y+1, u^2-v^2+x+y+1, -u^2+v^2+x+y+1\},$$
$$\{x+1, -u^2+v^2+x+1, u^2-v^2+x+1\}, \quad \{u^2-v^2\}.$$

There are hence 60 possible permutations of EC designation, but they lead to only 3 different outputs, with 113, 103 and 93 cells. Heuristics for other questions of CAD problem formulation [15, 6, 21, 31] could likely be adapted to assist here. We note that 93 cells is not a minimal truth invariant CAD for ϕ as it splits the CAD of $\mathbb{R}^1$ at $v = 0$ (identified from the discriminant of the only EC with mvar u).

Comparison with other CAD implementations

A sign-invariant CAD of $\mathbb{R}^5$ for the 6 polynomials in the example could be produced by QEPCAD with 1,118,205 cells. Neither the `RegularChains` Library in MAPLE [11] nor our MAPLE package [17] could produce one in under an hour.

Our implementation of [24], which uses operator (2) once but also performs the final lift with respect to the EC only, can produce a CAD with either 3023, 10935 or 48299 (twice) cells depending on which EC is designated. The QEPCAD implementation of [24] gives 11961, 30233, 158475, or 158451 cells. Comparing these sets of figures we see the dramatic improvements from just a single reduced lift.

Allowing QEPCAD to propagate the 4 ECs (so a similar projection phase as Algorithm 1 but then a normal CAD lifting phase) produces a CAD with 21079 cells. By declaring only a subset of the 4 (which presumably changes the designations of implicit ECs) a CAD with 5633 cells can be produced, still much more than using Algorithm 1.

The `RegularChains` Library can also make use of multiple ECs, as detailed in [3]. The version in MAPLE 18 times out after an hour, however, with the development version a CAD can be produced instantly. There are choices (with analogies to designation [16]) but they all lead to a 137 cell output. In particular, they all have an induced CAD of the real line which splits at $v = \pm 1$ as well as $v = 0$.

5. COMPLEXITY ANALYSIS

We build on recent work in [5] to measure the dominant term in bounds on the number of CAD cells produced. Numerous studies have shown this to be closely correlated to the computation time. We assume input with m polynomials of maximum degree d in any one of n variables.

DEFINITION 3. *Consider a set of polynomials p_j. The* combined degree *of the set is the maximum degree (taken with respect to each variable) of the product of all the polynomials in the set:* $\max_i(\deg_{x_i}(\prod_j p_j))$.

The set has the (m,d)-property *if it may be partitioned into m subsets, each with maximum combined degree d.*

For example, $\{y^2 - x, y^2 + 1\}$ has combined degree 4 and thus the $(1, 4)$-property, but also the $(2, 2)$-property.

This property (introduced in McCallum's thesis) can measure growth in the projection phase. In [5] we proved that if A has the (m, d)-property then $P(A) \cup \mathrm{cont}(A)$ has the $(M, 2d^2)$-property with $M = \lfloor \frac{1}{2}(m+1)^2 \rfloor$. When $m > 1$, we can bound M by m^2 (but we need $2m^2$ to cover $m = 1$).

If A has the (m,d)-property then so does its squarefree basis. Hence applying this result recursively (as in Table 1) measures the growth in (m,d)-property during projection under operator (1). After the first projection there are multiple polynomials and so the tighter bound for M is used.

The number of real roots in a set with the (m,d)-property is at most md. The number of cells in the CAD of $\mathbb{R}^1$ is thus bounded by twice the product of the final two entries, plus 1. Similarly, the total number of cells in the CAD of $\mathbb{R}^n$ by

$$(2md+1)\prod_{r=1}^{n-1}\left[2\left(2^{2^{r-1}}m^{2^r}\right)\left(2^{2^r-1}d^{2^r}\right)+1\right]. \quad (4)$$

Omitting the +1s will leave us with the dominant term of the bound, which evaluates to give the following result.

THEOREM 5. *The dominant term in the bound on the number of CAD cells in $\mathbb{R}^n$ produced using (1) is*

$$(2d)^{2^n-1}m^{2^n-1}2^{2^{n-1}-1}. \quad (5)$$

From now on assume ℓ ECs, $0<\ell\leq\min(m,n)$, all with different mvar. For simplicity we assume these variables are $x_n,\dots,x_{n-\ell+1}$ (the first ℓ projections are reduced).

LEMMA 6. *Suppose A is a set with the (m,d)-property and $E\subset A$ has the $(1,d)$-property. Then $\mathrm{cont}(A)\cup P_E^*(A)$ has the $(2m,2d^2)$-property.*

PROOF. In [5] we proved that applying $P_E(A)\cup\mathrm{cont}(A)$ gives a set of $\lfloor\frac{1}{2}(3m+1)\rfloor$ polynomials of combined degree $2d^2$. The extra $m-1$ discriminants required by operator (3) will each have degree at most $d(d-1)$, so pairing them we have $\lceil\frac{1}{2}(m-1)\rceil$ sets of combined degree at most $2d^2$. Then

$$\lfloor\tfrac{1}{2}(3m+1)\rfloor+\lceil\tfrac{1}{2}(m-1)\rceil=m+\lfloor\tfrac{1}{2}(m+1)\rfloor+\lfloor\tfrac{m}{2}\rfloor$$

and since $m\in\mathbb{Z}$ this always equals $2m$. □

We apply this recursively in the top half of Table 2, with the bottom derived via the process for P, as in Table 1.

Define d_i and m_i as the entries in the Number and Degree columns of Table 2 from the row with i Variables. We can bound the number of real roots of projection polynomials in i variables by $m_i d_i$. If we lifted with respect to all these projection polynomials, the cell count would be bounded by

$$\prod_{i=1}^{n}[2m_id_i+1]=\prod_{s=0}^{\ell}\left[2\left(2^sm2^{2^s-1}d^{2^s}\right)+1\right]$$
$$\cdot\prod_{r=1}^{n-\ell-1}\left[2\left(2^{2^r\ell}m^{2^r}2^{2^{\ell+r}-1}d^{2^{\ell+r}}\right)+1\right]. \quad (6)$$

Omitting the +1 from each product allows us to calculate the dominant term of the bound explicitly as

$$(2d)^{2^n-1}m^{2^{n-\ell}+\ell-1}2^{\ell 2^{n-\ell}+\ell(\ell-3)/2}. \quad (7)$$

Now we consider the benefit of improved lifting. Start by considering the CAD of $\mathbb{R}^{n-(\ell+1)}$. There can be no reduced lifting until this point and so the cell count bound is given by the second product in (6), which we will denote by †. The lift to $\mathbb{R}^{n-\ell}$ will involve stack generation over all cells, but only with respect to the EC. This can have at most $d_{n-\ell}$ real roots and so the CAD at most $[2d_{n-\ell}+1](\dagger)$ cells.

The next lift, to $\mathbb{R}^{n-\ell-1}$, will lift the sections with respect to the EC, and the sectors only trivially (to produce the same number of cylinders). Hence the cell count bound is $[2d_{n-(\ell-1)}+1]d_{n-\ell}(\dagger)+(d_{n-\ell}+1)(\dagger)$ with dominant term $2d_{n-(\ell-1)}d_{n-\ell}(\dagger)$. Subsequent lifts follow the same pattern and so $2d_nd_{n-1}\dots d_{n-(\ell-1)}d_{n-\ell}(\dagger)$ is the dominant term in the bound for $\mathbb{R}^n$. This evaluates to give the following result.

Table 1: Projection under operator (1).

Variables	Number	Degree
n	m	d
$n-1$	$2m^2$	$2d^2$
$n-2$	$4m^4$	$8d^4$
$\vdots$	$\vdots$	$\vdots$
$n-r$	$2^{2^r-1}m^{2^r}$	$2^{2^r-1}d^{2^r}$
$\vdots$	$\vdots$	$\vdots$
1	$2^{2^{n-2}}m^{2^{n-1}}$	$2^{2^{n-1}-1}d^{2^{n-1}}$

Table 2: Projection with (3) ℓ times and then (1).

Variables	Number	Degree
n	m	d
$n-1$	$2m$	$2d^2$
$\vdots$	$\vdots$	$\vdots$
$n-\ell$	$2^\ell m$	$2^{2^\ell-1}d^{2^\ell}$
$n-(\ell+1)$	$2^{2\ell}m^2$	$2^{2^{\ell+1}-1}d^{2^{\ell+1}}$
$\vdots$	$\vdots$	$\vdots$
$n-(\ell+r)$	$2^{2^r\ell}m^{2^r}$	$2^{2^{\ell+r}-1}d^{2^{\ell+r}}$
$\vdots$	$\vdots$	$\vdots$
1	$2^{2^{(n-1-\ell)}\ell}m^{2^{n-1-\ell}}$	$2^{2^{n-1}-1}d^{2^{n-1}}$

THEOREM 7. *Consider the CAD of $\mathbb{R}^n$ produced using Algorithm 1 in the presence of ECs in the top ℓ variables. The dominant term in the bound on the number of cells is*

$$2\prod_{s=0}^{\ell}\left[2^{2^s-1}d^{2^s}\right]\prod_{r=1}^{n-\ell-1}\left[2\left(2^{2^r\ell}m^{2^r}2^{2^{\ell+r}-1}d^{2^{\ell+r}}\right)\right]$$
$$=(2d)^{2^n-1}m^{2^{n-\ell}-2}2^{\ell 2^{n-\ell}-3\ell}. \quad (8)$$

The bound in Theorem 7 is strictly less than the one in Theorem 5. The double exponent of m has decreased by the number of ECs; the result of the improved projection in (7). Improved lifting reduced the single exponents further still.

6. CONCLUSIONS AND FUTURE WORK

We have explained how the existing theory for CAD projection using ECs can also be leveraged for significant savings in the lifting phase. We can reduce both the projection polynomials used for lifting and the cells over which stacks are generated. We have formalised these ideas in Algorithm 1, verified their use in Theorem 4, and demonstrated the benefit with a worked example and complexity analysis.

A key question is how to best deal with non-primitive ECs? Consider $\phi := zy = 0\wedge\varphi$. Under ordering $\dots\succ z\succ y\succ\dots$ the EC $zy=0$ is not primitive, so Algorithm 1 cannot use it. We may be tempted to take $E=\{z\}$ as the primitive part, project with operator (2) and include the content y in the first projection. The CAD of $(y,\dots)$-space would be sign-invariant for y and thus the CAD of $(z,y,\dots)$-space truth invariant for the EC (over admissible cells). But we can no longer say only sections are admissible for the next lift as there may be cells with $z\neq 0$ and $y=0$. We could instead lift over all cells. Alternatively we might rewrite ϕ as $\phi := (z=0\wedge\varphi)\vee(y=0\wedge\varphi)$, so each clause has its own EC. The theory of truth-table invariant CADs [4, 5] is designed to deal with such input, but would require its own extension to use beyond the first projection. Of course, this extension would also be valuable in its own right.

Acknowledgements

Thanks to the the referees for their helpful comments. This work was supported by EPSRC grant: EP/J003247/1.

7. REFERENCES

[1] D. Arnon, G.E. Collins, and S. McCallum. Cylindrical algebraic decomposition I: The basic algorithm. *SIAM J. of Computing*, 13:865–877, 1984.

[2] S. Basu, R. Pollack, and M.F. Roy. Algorithms in Real Algebraic Geometry. (Volume 10 of Algorithms and Computations in Mathematics). Springer-Verlag, 2006.

[3] R. Bradford, C. Chen, J.H. Davenport, M. England, M. Moreno Maza, and D. Wilson. Truth table invariant cylindrical algebraic decomposition by regular chains. In *Computer Algebra in Scientific Computing* (LNCS 8660), pages 44–58. Springer, 2014.

[4] R. Bradford, J.H. Davenport, M. England, S. McCallum, and D. Wilson. Cylindrical algebraic decompositions for boolean combinations. In *Proc. ISSAC '13*, pages 125–132. ACM, 2013.

[5] R. Bradford, J.H. Davenport, M. England, S. McCallum, and D. Wilson. Truth table invariant cylindrical algebraic decomposition. *Submitted for Publication.* Preprint: `arXiv:1401.0645`, 2015.

[6] R. Bradford, J.H. Davenport, M. England, and D. Wilson. Optimising problem formulations for cylindrical algebraic decomposition. In *Intelligent Computer Mathematics* (LNCS 7961), pages 19–34. Springer Berlin Heidelberg, 2013.

[7] C.W. Brown. QEPCAD B: A program for computing with semi-algebraic sets using CADs. *ACM SIGSAM Bulletin*, 37(4):97–108, 2003.

[8] C.W. Brown. Constructing a single open cell in a cylindrical algebraic decomposition. In *Proc. ISSAC '13*, pages 133–140. ACM, 2013.

[9] C.W. Brown, M. El Kahoui, D. Novotni, and A. Weber. Algorithmic methods for investigating equilibria in epidemic modelling. *J. Symbolic Computation*, 41:1157–1173, 2006.

[10] C.W. Brown and S. McCallum. On using bi-equational constraints in CAD construction. In *Proc. ISSAC '05*, pages 76–83. ACM, 2005.

[11] C. Chen, M. Moreno Maza, B. Xia, and L. Yang. Computing cylindrical algebraic decomposition via triangular decomposition. In *Proc. ISSAC '09*, pages 95–102. ACM, 2009.

[12] G.E. Collins. Quantifier elimination by cylindrical algebraic decomposition – 20 years of progress. In *Quantifier Elimination and Cylindrical Algebraic Decomposition*, pages 8–23. Springer-Verlag, 1998.

[13] J.H. Davenport, R. Bradford, M. England, and D. Wilson. Program verification in the presence of complex numbers, functions with branch cuts etc. In *Proc. SYNASC '12*, pages 83–88. IEEE, 2012.

[14] J.H. Davenport and J. Heintz. Real quantifier elimination is doubly exponential. *J. Symbolic Computation*, 5(1-2):29–35, 1988.

[15] A. Dolzmann, A. Seidl, and T. Sturm. Efficient projection orders for CAD. In *Proc. ISSAC '04*, pages 111–118. ACM, 2004.

[16] M. England, R. Bradford, C. Chen, J.H. Davenport, M. Moreno Maza, and D. Wilson. Problem formulation for truth-table invariant cylindrical algebraic decomposition by incremental triangular decomposition. In *Intelligent Computer Mathematics* (LNAI 8543), pages 45–60. Springer, 2014.

[17] M. England, D. Wilson, R. Bradford, and J.H. Davenport. Using the Regular Chains Library to build cylindrical algebraic decompositions by projecting and lifting. *Mathematical Software - ICMS 2014* (LNCS 8592), pages 458–465. Springer Heidelberg, 2014.

[18] M. Erascu and H. Hong. Synthesis of optimal numerical algorithms using real quantifier elimination (Case Study: Square root computation). In *Proc. ISSAC '14*, pages 162–169. ACM, 2014.

[19] I.A. Fotiou, P.A. Parrilo, and M. Morari. Nonlinear parametric optimization using cylindrical algebraic decomposition. In *Proc. CDC-ECC '05*, pages 3735–3740, 2005.

[20] H. Hong. An improvement of the projection operator in cylindrical algebraic decomposition. In *Proc. ISSAC '90*, pages 261–264. ACM, 1990.

[21] Z. Huang, M. England, D. Wilson, J.H. Davenport, L. Paulson, and J. Bridge. Applying machine learning to the problem of choosing a heuristic to select the variable ordering for cylindrical algebraic decomposition. In *Intelligent Computer Mathematics* (LNAI 8543), pages 92–107. Springer, 2014.

[22] H. Iwane, H. Yanami, H. Anai, and K. Yokoyama. An effective implementation of a symbolic-numeric cylindrical algebraic decomposition for quantifier elimination. In *Proc. SNC '09*, pages 55–64, 2009.

[23] S. McCallum. An improved projection operation for cylindrical algebraic decomposition. In *Quantifier Elimination and Cylindrical Algebraic Decomposition*, pages 242–268. Springer-Verlag, 1998.

[24] S. McCallum. On projection in CAD-based quantifier elimination with equational constraint. In *Proc. ISSAC '99*, pages 145–149. ACM, 1999.

[25] S. McCallum. On propagation of equational constraints in CAD-based quantifier elimination. In *Proc. ISSAC '01*, pages 223–231. ACM, 2001.

[26] S. McCallum and C.W. Brown. On delineability of varieties in CAD-based quantifier elimination with two equational constraints. In *Proc. ISSAC '09*, pages 71–78. ACM, 2009.

[27] L.C. Paulson. Metitarski: Past and future. In *Interactive Theorem Proving* (LNCS 7406), 1–10. Springer, 2012.

[28] A. Seidl. Cylindrical decomposition under application-oriented paradigms. PhD Thesis (University of Passau, Germany), 2006.

[29] A. Strzeboński. Cylindrical algebraic decomposition using validated numerics. *J. Symbolic Computation*, 41(9):1021–1038, 2006.

[30] A. Strzeboński. Cylindrical algebraic decomposition using local projections. In *Proc. ISSAC '14*, pages 389–396. ACM, 2014.

[31] D. Wilson, M. England, J.H. Davenport, and R. Bradford. Using the distribution of cells by dimension in a cylindrical algebraic decomposition. *Proc. SYNASC '14*, pages 53–60. IEEE, 2014.

Real Quantifier Elimination by Computation of Comprehensive Gröbner Systems

Ryoya Fukasaku
Tokyo University of Science
Kagurazaka 1-3, Shinjuku,
Tokyo, Japan
1414704@ed.tus.ac.jp

Hidenao Iwane
National Institute of Informatics
Fujitsu Laboratories Ltd
2-1-2 Hitotsubashi,
Chiyoda-ku, Tokyo, Japan
iwane@jp.fujitsu.com

Yosuke Sato
Tokyo University of Science
Kagurazaka 1-3, Shinjuku,
Tokyo, Japan
ysato@rs.kagu.tus.ac.jp

ABSTRACT

A real quantifier elimination method based on the theory of real root counting and the computation of comprehensive Gröbner systems introduced by V. Weispfenning is studied in more detail. We introduce a simpler and more intuitive algorithm which is shown to be an improvement of the original algorithm. Our algorithm is implemented on the computer algebra system Maple using a recent algorithm to compute comprehensive Gröbner systems together with several simplification techniques. According to our computation experiments, our program is superior to other existing implementations for many examples which contain many equalities.

Categories and Subject Descriptors

G.0 [**Mathematics of Computing**]: GENERAL

General Terms

Algorithm Theory

Keywords

comprehensive Gröbner system, real quantifier elimination

1. INTRODUCTION

The motivation of our work has its roots in the ongoing research project of artificial intelligence 'Todai Robot Project' by National Institute of Informatics, Japan [26]. The purpose of the project is to develop software which automatically produces an answer sheet for an entrance examination of Todai (The University of Tokyo which is the highest rank university in Japan) that can obtain a sufficient score to pass. The authors are involved in the mathematics team of the project. Our goal consists of two steps. The first one is to develop a special first order language such that the translated sentences from a mathematics problem written in a natural language can be handled by a computer algebra system. The second one is to develop a program of a computer algebra system which can solve the translated problems in a realistic length of time [1, 10, 14]. The authors are mainly working on the second one. In our experience, most problems which are theoretically solvable by real quantifier elimination (QE) can be handled by existing software such as the Mathematica package Reduce or Resolve if we convert them into optimal forms using some mathematical heuristics. Unfortunately, it is extremely difficult to have those heuristics as a program. The translated sentences into our language often contain many unnecessary equalities. There are many such examples which cannot be solved by any of the existing real QE implementations. We need to establish a practical implementation of real QE for quantified formulas with many equalities.

The cylindrical algebraic decomposition (CAD) algorithm introduced in [6] has been the most efficient method for real QE up to the present date together with the improvements by many successive works. When the given quantified formula contains many equalities, however, the original algorithm often executes useless computations on unnecessary cells. Though there have been done several works such as [15, 16] to avoid such unpleasant computations, it does not seem that there is a way to detect and use all equalities implicitly contained in the given formula as long as we use a CAD based real QE algorithm.

An alternative real QE algorithm based on the real root counting theorem introduced in [27] mainly consists of computations of comprehensive Gröbner systems (CGSs). It eliminates all quantifiers by handling underlying ideals, hence it essentially uses every equality which is (even implicitly) contained in the given quantified formula. His algorithm was implemented in Redlog [21] as the command rlhqe [7]. Unfortunately we cannot say that it achieves pre-eminent performance over CAD based real QE implementations even for quantified formulas with many equalities, although a more practical approach is reported in [7] for a restricted QE. We think the main reason is that there was not an efficient algorithm to compute a CGS at that time.

By the new algorithm introduced in [22] together with its improvements by [12, 13, 17], we can now have a powerful implementation. In this paper, we report on our real QE method based on the new algorithm to compute a CGS. Using the obvious equivalent relation $h > 0 \Leftrightarrow \exists z\ z^2h = 1$,

ISSAC'15, July 6–9, 2015, Bath, United Kingdom.

DOI: http://dx.doi.org/10.1145/2755996.2756646.

we give a natural algorithm for handling inequalities. We will show that our algorithm is actually an improvement of Weispfenning's algorithm. In order to achieve a practical implementation, our algorithm does not handle a quantified formula consisting only of inequalities. More precisely, our algorithm divides a QE procedure into several branches of independent computations. In case the algorithm cannot remove all quantifiers in some branch, it always produces a equivalent quantified formula consisting only of inequalities. Our implementation uses a CAD algorithm for such a quantified formula. By contrast, Weispfenning's algorithm is applied even for such a quantified formula by an ingenious technique. For such a case, however, a CAD based QE algorithm is more efficient in most cases. We implemented our algorithm on the computer algebra system Maple together with several simplification techniques. Our program is satisfactorily efficient for our purpose. It can solve many examples which cannot be solved by any other existing real QE implementations.

The paper is organized as follows. In Section 2, we give a quick review of the real root counting theorem independently found in [3, 19]. We introduce a simple method to extend the theorem so that we can handle many inequalities. We show that it is actually an improvement of the method introduced in [27]. In Section 3, we give a short description of a CGS. Our main algorithm is presented in Section 4 on a primitive level. Section 5 is devoted to several implementation issues such as a simplification technique we use. Some computation data we have obtained with our implementation are given in Section 6.

2. REAL ROOT COUNTING

In the rest of the paper, R denotes a real closed field, C its algebraic closed extension and K a computable subfield of R. The reader may consider R as the field of real numbers $\mathbb{R}$, C as the field of complex numbers $\mathbb{C}$ and K as the field of rational numbers $\mathbb{Q}$. $\bar{X}$ denotes some variables $X_1, \ldots, X_n$. $T(\bar{X})$ denotes the set of all terms consisting of variables in $\bar{X}$. For an ideal $I \subset K[\bar{X}]$, $V_R(I)$ and $V_C(I)$ denote the varieties of I in R and C respectively, i.e., $V_R(I) = \{\bar{c} \in R^n | \forall f \in I\ f(\bar{c}) = 0\}$ and $V_C(I) = \{\bar{c} \in C^n | \forall f \in I\ f(\bar{c}) = 0\}$.

Let I be a zero dimensional ideal in a polynomial ring $K[\bar{X}]$. Considering the residue class ring $K[\bar{X}]/I$ as a vector space over K, let $v_1, \ldots, v_d$ be its basis. For an arbitrary $h \in K[\bar{X}]/I$ and each i, j $(1 \leqslant i, j \leqslant d)$ we define a linear map $\theta_{h,i,j}$ from $K[\bar{X}]/I$ to $K[\bar{X}]/I$ by $\theta_{h,i,j}(f) = hv_iv_jf$ for $f \in K[\bar{X}]/I$. Let $q_{h,i,j}$ be the trace of $\theta_{h,i,j}$ and M_h^I be a symmetric matrix such that the (i,j)-th component is given by $q_{h,i,j}$. The characteristic polynomial of M_h^I is denoted by $\chi_h^I(X)$. The signature of M_h^I denoted $\sigma(M_h^I)$ is the number of positive eigenvalues of M_h^I minus the number of negative eigenvalues of M_h^I, in another word the number of positive roots of $\chi_h^I(X) = 0$ minus the number of negative roots of $\chi_h^I(X) = 0$. The real root counting theorem found independently in [3, 19] is the following assertion.

Theorem 1 $\sigma(M_h^I) = \#(\{\bar{c} \in V_R(I) | h(\bar{c}) > 0\}) - \#(\{\bar{c} \in V_R(I) | h(\bar{c}) < 0\})$.

We have the following corollary.

Corollary 2 $\sigma(M_1^I) = \#(V_R(I))$.

Using the equivalent relation $h > 0 \Leftrightarrow \exists z\ z^2h = 1$, we have the following obvious fact.

Lemma 3 Let $h_1, \ldots, h_l$ be polynomials in $K[\bar{X}]$ and $\bar{Z} = Z_1, \ldots, Z_l$ be new variables. Using the same notations as above, let J be an ideal in $K[\bar{X}, \bar{Z}]$ defined by $J = I + \langle Z_1^2h_1 - 1, \ldots, Z_l^2h_l - 1\rangle$. Then the following equation holds.

$$\#(V_R(J)) = 2^l \#(\{\bar{c} \in V_R(I) | h_1(\bar{c}) > 0, \ldots, h_l(\bar{c}) > 0\}).$$

Since $\#(V_R(J)) = \sigma(M_1^J)$, we can compute the number $\#(\{\bar{c} \in V_R(I) | h_1(\bar{c}) > 0, \ldots, h_l(\bar{c}) > 0\})$.
Furthermore, the next lemma together with the following theorem enables us to compute the characteristic polynomial $\chi_1^J(X)$ of the symmetric matrix M_1^J using only the structure of the elimination ideal $J \cap K[\bar{X}]$ in $K[\bar{X}]$.

Lemma 4 Using the same notations as the above lemma, let I' be the elimination ideal $J \cap K[\bar{X}]$. Then either $I' = \langle 1 \rangle$ or h_i is invertible in $K[\bar{X}]/I'$ for every $i = 1, \ldots, l$. In the latter case, let h_i' be the inverse of h_i for each $i = 1, \ldots, l$. Then $J = I' + \langle Z_1^2 - h_1', \ldots, Z_l^2 - h_l'\rangle$.

(See Lemma 1 of [23] for example.)

Theorem 5 Let I be a zero dimensional ideal of $K[\bar{X}]$ and $J = I + \langle Z_1^2 - h_1, \ldots, Z_l^2 - h_l\rangle$ be an ideal of $K[\bar{X}, \bar{Z}]$ with polynomials $h_1, \ldots, h_l \in K[\bar{X}]$. Let k be a dimension of $K[\bar{X}]/I$ and $\{t_1, \ldots, t_k\} \subset T(\bar{X})$ be a basis of the vector space $K[\bar{X}]/I$, then $\{t_1Z_1^{e_1}Z_2^{e_2}\cdots Z_l^{e_l}, \ldots, t_kZ_1^{e_1}Z_2^{e_2}\cdots Z_l^{e_l} | (e_1, e_2, \ldots, e_l) \in \{0,1\}^l\}$ forms a basis of the vector space $K[\bar{X}, \bar{Z}]/J$. Let M_g^J denote a symmetric matrix and χ_g^J denote its characteristic polynomial for a polynomial $g \in K[\bar{X}]$ induced by the above basis of $K[\bar{X}, \bar{Z}]/J$. Let M_g^I denote a symmetric matrix and χ_g^I denote its characteristic polynomial for a polynomial $g \in K[\bar{X}]$ induced by the above basis of $K[\bar{X}]/I$. Then we have the following equation for some non-zero constant c.

$$\chi_g^J(2^lX) = c\Pi_{(e_1,e_2,\ldots,e_l)\in\{0,1\}^l}\chi^I_{gh_1^{e_1}h_2^{e_2}\cdots h_l^{e_l}}(X).$$

PROOF. The first assertion is obvious. For the second assertion, we first give a proof for $l = 1$. We simply write Z for Z_1 and h for h_1. Let $t_{k+1} = t_1Z, t_{k+2} = t_2Z, \ldots, t_{2k} = t_kZ$. Let $\theta_{g,i,j}^I$ denote the induced linear map of $K[\bar{X}]/I$ and $\theta_{g,i,j}^J$ denote the induced linear map of $K[\bar{X}, \bar{Z}]/J$, that is $\theta_{g,i,j}^I(f) = gt_it_jf$ for $f \in K[\bar{X}]/I$ and $1 \leqslant i, j \leqslant k$, $\theta_{g,i,j}^J(f) = gt_it_jf$ for $f \in K[\bar{X}, \bar{Z}]/J$ and $1 \leqslant i, j \leqslant 2k$. Let $B_{g,i,j}^I$ denote the representing matrix of $\theta_{g,i,j}^I$ for $1 \leqslant i, j \leqslant k$ and $B_{g,i,j}^J$ denote the representing matrix of $\theta_{g,i,j}^J$ for $1 \leqslant i, j \leqslant 2k$. Then the following equations hold for each i, j $(1 \leqslant i, j \leqslant k)$. (Note that $Z^2 = h$ in $K[\bar{X}, Z]/J$.)

$$B_{g,i,j}^J = \begin{pmatrix} B_{g,i,j}^I & 0 \\ 0 & B_{g,i,j}^I \end{pmatrix},$$

$$B_{g,i+k,j+k}^J = \begin{pmatrix} B_{gh,i,j}^I & 0 \\ 0 & B_{gh,i,j}^I \end{pmatrix},$$

$$B_{g,i+k,j}^J = B_{g,i,j+k}^J = \begin{pmatrix} 0 & B_{g,i,j}^I \\ B_{gh,i,j}^I & 0 \end{pmatrix}.$$

Hence $\mathrm{trace}(B_{g,i,j}^J) = 2\mathrm{trace}(B_{g,i,j}^I)$, $\mathrm{trace}(B_{g,i+k,j+k}^J) = 2\mathrm{trace}(B_{gh,i,j}^I)$ and $\mathrm{trace}(B_{g,i+k,j}^J) = \mathrm{trace}(B_{g,i,j+k}^J) = 0$ for each i, j $(1 \leqslant i, j \leqslant k)$.

Therefore, we have the equation $M_g^J = 2\begin{pmatrix} M_g^I & 0 \\ 0 & M_{gh}^I \end{pmatrix}$, from which we have $\chi_g^J(2X) = 2^{2k}\chi_g^I(X)\chi_{gh}^I(X)$.
For the case $l > 1$, let $I_1 = I + \langle Z_1^2 - h_1\rangle, \ldots, I_l = I_{l-1} + \langle Z_l^2 - h_l\rangle = J$. Applying the above equation to I_r and I_{r-1} ($l \geqslant r \geqslant 2$), we have $\chi_g^{I_l}(2^l X) = c_l \chi_g^{I_{l-1}}(2^{l-1}X)\chi_{gh_l}^{I_{l-1}}(2^{l-1}X) = c_{l-1}\chi_g^{I_{l-2}}(2^{l-2}X)\chi_{gh_{l-1}}^{I_{l-2}}(2^{l-2}X)\chi_{gh_l}^{I_{l-2}}(2^{l-2}X)\chi_{gh_l h_{l-1}}^{I_{l-2}}(2^{l-2}X) = \cdots = c_1 \Pi_{(e_1,e_2,\ldots,e_l)\in\{0,1\}^l}\chi^I_{gh_1^{e_1}h_2^{e_2}\cdots h_l^{e_l}}(X)$ for some non-zero constants $c_l, c_{l-1}, \ldots, c_1$. □

Note that the theorem is actually a generalization of the method introduced in [27]. In his method, the elimination ideal I' is not computed but the characteristic polynomial $\Pi_{(e_1,e_2,\ldots,e_l)\in\{1,2\}^l}\chi^I_{gh_1^{e_1}h_2^{e_2}\cdots h_l^{e_l}}(X)$ is directly computed. As long as I' is equal to I, there is not much difference between both polynomials, however, when I' is bigger than I there may be significant difference.

Example 6 Let $I = \langle (X^2 - Y^2)(X + 2Y - 1), (3X + Y - 1)^2\rangle \subset \mathbb{Q}[X, Y]$ and $h_1 = X - Y, h_2 = X + Y$. The reduced Gröbner basis of $\langle (X^2 - Y^2)(X + 2Y - 1), (3X + Y - 1)^2, Z_1^2 h_1 - 1, Z_2^2 h_2 - 1\rangle$ w.r.t. the lexicographic term order such that $Z_1 > Z_2 > X > Y$ is $\{25Y^2 - 20Y + 4, X + 2Y - 1, 9Z_2^2 - 25Y - 5, Z_1^2 - 75Y + 35\}$. Let $I' = (I + \langle Z_1^2 h_1 - 1, Z_2^2 h_2 - 1\rangle) \cap \mathbb{Q}[X, Y] = \langle 25Y^2 - 20Y + 4, X + 2Y - 1\rangle$ and $h_1' = 15Y - 7, h_2' = 5Y + 1$. The polynomial $\chi^I_{h_1^2 h_2^2}(X)\chi^I_{h_1 h_2^2}(X)\chi^I_{h_1^2 h_2}(X)\chi^I_{h_1 h_2}(X)$ has a degree 24, whereas $\chi_1^{I'}(X)\chi_{h_1'}^{I'}(X)\chi_{h_2'}^{I'}(X)\chi_{h_1' h_2'}^{I'}(X)$ has a degree 8.

If we use a primary decomposition of I, we can certainly remove the unnecessary portion $\langle X^2 - Y^2, (3X + Y - 1)^2\rangle$ from I, however, for parametric polynomial ideals, which we have to handle for real QE in this paper, this computation or even factorization of a polynomial becomes a significantly heavy computation.

Using the equivalent relation $h \neq 0 \Leftrightarrow \exists z\ zh = 1$, we also have the following obvious similar fact as Lemma 3.

Lemma 7 Let I be a zero dimensional ideal and $h_1, \ldots, h_l$ be polynomials of $K[\bar{X}]$. For new variables $\bar{Z} = Z_1, \ldots, Z_l$ let J be an ideal of $K[\bar{X}, \bar{Z}]$ defined by $J = I + \langle Z_1 h_1 - 1, \ldots, Z_l h_l - 1\rangle$. Then the following equation holds.

$$\#(V_R(J)) = \#(\{\bar{c} \in V_R(I) | h_1(\bar{c}) \neq 0, \ldots, h_l(\bar{c}) \neq 0\}).$$

We also have the following fact which is essentially same as Lemma 4.

Lemma 8 Using the same notations as the above lemma, let I' be the elimination ideal $J \cap K[\bar{X}]$. Then either $I' = \langle 1\rangle$ or h_i is invertible in $K[\bar{X}]/I'$ for every $i = 1, \ldots, l$. In the latter case, let h_i' be the inverse of h_i for each $i = 1, \ldots, l$. Then $J = I' + \langle Z_1 - h_1', \ldots, Z_l - h_l'\rangle$.

We conclude this section with the following fact which is also obvious.

Lemma 9 Let I be a zero dimensional ideal of $K[\bar{X}]$ and $J = I + \langle Z_1^2 - h_1, \ldots, Z_l^2 - h_l\rangle$ be an ideal of $K[\bar{X}, \bar{Z}]$ with polynomials $h_1 \ldots, h_l \in K[\bar{X}]$. Using the same notations above, the following equivalent relation holds.

$$\sigma(M_1^J) > 0 \Leftrightarrow \#(\{\bar{c} \in V_R(I) | h_1(\bar{c}) \geqslant 0, \ldots, h_l(\bar{c}) \geqslant 0\}) > 0.$$

3. CGS

In the rest of the paper, the symbol $>$ denotes an admissible term order. A term order on $T(\bar{X}, \bar{Y})$ such that each variable of $\bar{X}$ is greater than any term of $T(\bar{Y})$ is denoted by $\bar{X} \gg \bar{Y}$. Given a term order, $LM(f)$, $LT(f)$ and $LC(f)$ denotes the leading monomial, the leading term and the leading coefficient of a polynomial f, respectively. (Note that $LM(f) = LC(f)LT(f)$.) When $f \in K[\bar{Y}, \bar{X}]$ and $>$ is a term order on $T(\bar{X})$, we regard f as a polynomial of $(K[\bar{Y}])[\bar{X}]$. Hence, $LC(f) \in K[\bar{Y}]$ and $LT(f) \in T(\bar{X})$.

Definition 10 Let S be a subset of an affine space C^n for some natural number n. A finite set $\{\mathcal{S}_1, \ldots, \mathcal{S}_t\}$ of non-empty subsets of S is called an algebraic partition of S if it satisfies the following properties 1, 2 and 3:

1. $\cup_{i=1}^t \mathcal{S}_i = S$.
2. $\mathcal{S}_i \cap \mathcal{S}_j = \emptyset$ if $i \neq j$.
3. For each i, $\mathcal{S}_i = V_C(I_1)\backslash V_C(I_2)$ for some ideals I_1, I_2 of $K[\bar{Y}]$.

Each $\mathcal{S}_i$ is called a segment.

Definition 11 Let S be a subset of C^n. Let $>$ be a term order on $T(\bar{X})$. For a finite subset F of $K[\bar{Y}, \bar{X}]$, a finite set $\mathcal{G} = \{(\mathcal{S}_1, G_1), \ldots, (\mathcal{S}_s, G_s)\}$ satisfying the following properties 1, 2, 3 and 4 is called a comprehensive Gröbner system (CGS) of F over S with parameters $\bar{Y}$ w.r.t. $>$:

1. Each G_i is a finite subset of $K[\bar{Y}, \bar{X}]$.
2. $\{\mathcal{S}_1, \ldots, \mathcal{S}_s\}$ is an algebraic partition of S.
3. For each $\bar{c} \in \mathcal{S}_i$, $G_i(\bar{c}) = \{g(\bar{c}, \bar{X}) | g(\bar{Y}, \bar{X}) \in G_i\}$ is a Gröbner basis of the ideal $\langle F(\bar{c})\rangle$ in $C[\bar{X}]$ with respect to $>$, where $F(\bar{c}) = \{f(\bar{c}, \bar{X}) | f(\bar{Y}, \bar{X}) \in F\}$
4. For each $\bar{c} \in \mathcal{S}_i$, $LC(g)(\bar{c}) \neq 0$ for any element g of G_i.

In addition, if each $G_i(\bar{c})$ is a minimal (reduced) Gröbner basis, $\mathcal{G}$ is said to be minimal (reduced). Being monic is not required. When $\mathcal{S}$ is a whole space C^n, the words "over $\mathcal{S}$" is usually omitted.

For applying a CGS to our real QE, we need the property 4 for the computation of normal forms to produce a symmetric matrix. The set of leading terms of $G_i(\bar{c})$ is invariant for each $\bar{c} \in \mathcal{S}_i$, hence the dimension of the ideal $\langle G_i(\bar{c})\rangle$ is also invariant. A minimal CGS is desirable for their computation.

4. MAIN ALGORITHM

We describe our algorithm for the following basic quantified formula on a primitive level, practical implementations are discussed in the next section.

$$\begin{aligned} \exists \bar{X}(f_1(\bar{Y}, \bar{X}) = 0 \wedge \cdots \wedge f_r(\bar{Y}, \bar{X}) = 0 \wedge \\ p_1(\bar{Y}, \bar{X}) > 0 \wedge \cdots \wedge p_s(\bar{Y}, \bar{X}) > 0 \wedge \\ q_1(\bar{Y}, \bar{X}) \neq 0 \wedge \cdots \wedge q_t(\bar{Y}, \bar{X}) \neq 0). \end{aligned} \quad (1)$$

$$f_1, \ldots, f_r, p_1, \ldots, p_s, q_1, \ldots, q_t \in \mathbb{Q}[\bar{Y}, \bar{X}],$$
$$f_1, \ldots, f_r, p_1, \ldots, p_s, q_1, \ldots, q_t \notin \mathbb{Q}[\bar{Y}].$$

The following fact is a direct consequence of Descartes' rule which is used in the real QE algorithm of [27].

Lemma 12 Let M be a real symmetric $d \times d$ matrix and $\chi(X)$ be its characteristic polynomial of degree d. Let $\chi(X) = X^d + a_{d-1}X^{d-1} + \cdots + a_0$ and $\chi(-X) = (-1)^d X^d + b_{d-1}X^{d-1} + \cdots + b_0$. So, $b_i = a_i$ if i is even, $b_i = -a_i$

if i is odd. Let S_+ be the number of sign changes in the sequence $(1, a_{d-1}, \ldots, a_0)$, S_- be the number of sign changes in the sequence $((-1)^d, b_{d-1}, \ldots, b_0)$. (0 is ignored.) Then the following equations hold:

1. $S_+ = \#(\{c \in \mathbb{R} | c > 0 \wedge \chi(c) = 0\})$.
2. $S_- = \#(\{c \in \mathbb{R} | c < 0 \wedge \chi(c) = 0\})$.

Corollary 13 Let I be a zero dimensional ideal in a polynomial ring over $\mathbb{Q}$. Using the same notations as in Section 2, let S_+ and S_- be defined from the symmetric matrix M_1^I as in the above lemma. Then the following property holds.

$$\#(V_{\mathbb{R}}(I)) = \sigma(M_1^I) > 0 \Leftrightarrow S_+ \neq S_-.$$

Definition 14 Considering $a_0, \ldots, a_{d-1}$ as variables, we can write $S_+ \neq S_-$ as a quantifier free first order formula. We denote such a formula by $I_d(a_0, \ldots, a_{d-1})$.

Definition 15 Let $\mathcal{S} = V_{\mathbb{C}}(I_1) \backslash V_{\mathbb{C}}(I_2)$ be a segment of some CGS with ideals I_1 and I_2 in a polynomial ring $\mathbb{Q}[\bar{Y}]$ such that $I_1 = \langle f_1, \ldots, f_k \rangle, I_2 = \langle g_1, \ldots, g_l \rangle$. The defining formula of $\mathcal{S}$ denoted $\mathcal{F}(\mathcal{S})$ is the following formula:

$$f_1(\bar{X}) = 0 \wedge \cdots \wedge f_k(\bar{X}) = 0 \wedge (g_1(\bar{X}) \neq 0 \vee \cdots \vee g_l(\bar{X}) \neq 0).$$

Let $(\mathcal{S}, G)$ be an element of a minimal CGS w.r.t. a term order $>$ with main variables $\bar{X}$. **MaxIndVar**$(\bar{X}, G, >)$ denotes some maximal independent set of variables among $\bar{X}$ w.r.t. an ideal $\langle G(\bar{c}) \rangle$ for $\bar{c} \in \mathcal{S}$. Remember that the set of leading terms of $G(\bar{c})$ is invariant for each $\bar{c} \in \mathcal{S}$ and easily computed from G.

Free$(\psi, \bar{X})$ and **NonFree**$(\psi, \bar{X})$ denote the free part and non-free part of ψ w.r.t. the variables $\bar{X}$, respectively. More precisely, let $\psi = \phi_1 \wedge \cdots \wedge \phi_s \wedge \varphi_1 \wedge \cdots \wedge \varphi_t$ for atomic formulas $\phi_1, \ldots, \phi_s, \varphi_1, \ldots, \varphi_t$ such that each ϕ_i contains no variables in $\bar{X}$ and each φ_i contains at least one variable in $\bar{X}$, then **Free**$(\psi, \bar{X}) = \phi_1 \wedge \cdots \wedge \phi_s$ and **NonFree**$(\psi, \bar{X}) = \varphi_1 \wedge \cdots \wedge \varphi_t$. Note that $\exists \bar{X} \psi \Leftrightarrow$ **Free**$(\psi, \bar{X}) \wedge \exists \bar{X}$**NonFree**$(\psi, \bar{X})$.

Now we are ready to write our algorithm.

Algorithm 1 MainQE

Input: a basic quantified formula $\exists \bar{X} \phi$ in a form of (1);
Output: an equivalent quantifier free formula ψ;
1: $\bar{Z} = Z_1, \ldots, Z_s, \bar{W} = W_1 \ldots, W_t \leftarrow$ new variables;
$> \leftarrow$ a term order of $T(\bar{X}, \bar{Z}, \bar{W})$ such that $\bar{Z}, \bar{W} \gg \bar{X}$;
2: $\mathcal{G} \leftarrow$ a minimal CGS of $\{f_1, \ldots, f_r, Z_1^2 p_1 - 1, \ldots, Z_s^2 p_s - 1, W_1 q_1 - 1, \ldots, W_t q_t - 1\}$ w.r.t. $>$ with parameters $\bar{Y}$;
3: $\psi \leftarrow false$;
4: **while** $\mathcal{G} \neq \emptyset$ **do**
5: $(\mathcal{S}, G) \leftarrow$ an element of $\mathcal{G}$; $\mathcal{G} \leftarrow \mathcal{G} \backslash \{(\mathcal{S}, G)\}$;
6: **if** $G(\bar{c}, \bar{X})$ is $\{0\}$ for $\bar{c} \in \mathcal{S}$ **then**
7: $\psi \leftarrow \psi \vee \mathcal{F}(\mathcal{S})$;
8: **else**
9: **if** $\langle G(\bar{c}, \bar{X}) \rangle$ is zero dimensional for $\bar{c} \in \mathcal{S}$ **then**
10: $\psi \leftarrow \psi \vee$ **ZeroDimQE**$(\mathcal{S}, G, >)$;
11: **else**
12: $\psi \leftarrow \psi \vee$ **NonZeroDimQE**$(\phi, \mathcal{S}, G, >)$;
13: **end if**
14: **end if**
15: **end while**
16: **return** ψ;

Algorithm 2 ZeroDimQE

Input: a component $(\mathcal{S}, G)$ of a CGS in $\mathbb{Q}[\bar{Y}, \bar{X}, \bar{Z}, \bar{W}]$ w.r.t. a term order $>$ of $T(\bar{X}, \bar{Z}, \bar{W})$ produced in Algorithm 1 such that $\langle G(\bar{c}, \bar{X}) \rangle$ is zero dimensional for $\bar{c} \in \mathcal{S}$;
Output: a quantifier free formula ψ s.t. $\mathcal{F}(\mathcal{S}) \wedge \exists \bar{X} \phi \Leftrightarrow \psi$;
1: **if** $\langle G(\bar{c}, \bar{X}) \rangle$ is $\langle 1 \rangle$ for $\bar{c} \in \mathcal{S}$ **then**
2: $\psi \leftarrow false$;
3: **else**
4: G has a form $\{f'_1, \ldots, f'_{r'}, u_1 Z_1^2 - p'_1, \ldots, u_s Z_s^2 - p'_s, v_1 W_1 - q'_1, \ldots, v_t W_s - q'_t\}$ for $u_1, \ldots, u_s, v_1, \ldots, v_t \in \mathbb{Q}[\bar{Y}]$ and $f'_1, \ldots, f'_{r'}, p'_1, \ldots, p'_s, q'_1, \ldots, q'_t \in \mathbb{Q}[\bar{Y}, \bar{X}]$. {Consider $\bar{Y}$ as parameters in the following.}
5: $I \leftarrow \langle f'_1, \ldots, f'_{r'} \rangle \subset \mathbb{Q}[\bar{X}]$;
6: $\chi(X) \leftarrow \Pi_{(e_1, e_2, \ldots, e_s) \in \{0,1\}^s} \chi^I_{h_1^{e_1} h_2^{e_2} \cdots h_s^{e_s}}(X)$
with $h_i = p'_i / u_i$ for $i = 1, \ldots, s$;
7: Let $\chi(X) = X^d + a_{d-1} X^{d-1} + \cdots + a_0$
for $a_{d-1}, \ldots, a_0 \in \mathbb{Q}(\bar{Y})$.
8: $\psi \leftarrow \psi \vee (\mathcal{F}(\mathcal{S}) \wedge I_d(a_0, \ldots, a_{d-1}))$;
9: **end if**
10: **return** ψ;

Remark For the construction of symmetric matrices, we need to use rational functions $\mathbb{Q}(\bar{Y})$. By the property 4 of CGSs, any denominator of them does not vanish on $\mathcal{S}$, so the denominator of each a_i does not vanish on them either. Note also that we can easily transform the formula $I_d(a_0, \ldots, a_{d-1})$ into a formula using only polynomials.

Algorithm 3 NonZeroDimQE

Input: a basic quantified formula $\exists \bar{X} \phi$ in a form of (1) and a component $(\mathcal{S}, G)$ of a CGS in $\mathbb{Q}[\bar{Y}, \bar{X}, \bar{Z}, \bar{W}]$ w.r.t. a term order $>$ of $T(\bar{X}, \bar{Z}, \bar{W})$ produced in Algorithm 1;
Output: a quantifier free formula ψ s.t. $\mathcal{F}(\mathcal{S}) \wedge \exists \bar{X} \phi \Leftrightarrow \psi$;
1: $\bar{U} \leftarrow$ **MaxIndVar**$(\bar{X}, G, >)$;
2: **if** $\bar{U} = \bar{X}$ **then**
3: **return** **OtherQE**$(\mathcal{F}(\mathcal{S}) \wedge \exists \bar{X} \phi)$;
4: **else**
5: $\bar{X}' \leftarrow \bar{X} \backslash \bar{U}$;
6: $\phi_1 \leftarrow$ **Free**$(\phi, \bar{X}')$; $\phi_2 \leftarrow$ **NonFree**$(\phi, \bar{X}')$;
7: $\varphi \leftarrow \phi_1 \wedge$**MainQE**$(\exists \bar{X}' \phi_2)$;
8: Let $\varphi_1 \vee \cdots \vee \varphi_l$ be a disjunctive normal form of φ.
9: **for** $1 \leqslant i \leqslant l$ **do**
10: $\varphi_i^1 \leftarrow$ **Free**$(\varphi_i, \bar{U})$; $\varphi_i^2 \leftarrow$ **NonFree**$(\varphi_i, \bar{U})$;
11: $\psi_i \leftarrow \varphi_i^1 \wedge$**MainQE**$(\exists \bar{U} \varphi_i^2)$;
12: **end for**
13: $\psi \leftarrow \mathcal{F}(\mathcal{S}) \wedge (\psi_1 \vee \cdots \vee \psi_l)$;
14: **return** ψ;
15: **end if**

Remark **OtherQE** denotes another real QE algorithm. Note that this procedure is called only when ϕ contains no equalities. For such a case, a CAD based real QE algorithm is more practical in general, we use a CAD based algorithm of SyNRAC [25, 11] in our implementation.

Theorem 16 The algorithm **MainQE** terminates and computes an equivalent quantifier free formula.

Proof. The algorithm **MainQE** consists of a recursive call of itself. In the first recursive call at the line 7 of

NonZeroDimQE, $\#(\bar{X}') < \#(\bar{X})$ since $\langle G(\bar{c}, \bar{X})\rangle$ is not zero dimensional for each $\bar{c} \in \mathcal{S}$. In the second recursive call at the line 11 of **NonZeroDimQE**, it is obvious that $\#(\bar{U}) < \#(\bar{X})$. Hence, the algorithm terminates. For proving its correctness, it suffices to show the correctness of the algorithm **ZeroDimQE**. The assertion of the line 4 follows from Lemma 4 and Lemma 8 together with the properties of a minimal CGS. The correctness of the next procedures follows from Theorem 5, Corollary 2, Lemma 3 and Lemma 7 together with Corollary 13. $\square$

5. IMPLEMENTATION

We presented our algorithm in a very naive form. There are several issues to be considered for a practical implementation. In this section we discuss them on two aspects. One is a simplification method to produce a compact size of a quantifier free formula. Another one is several refinements of the algorithm for efficient computations. All of them are employed in our implementation.

5.1 Simplification

Simplification of the output quantifier free formula is of great importance in any QE algorithm. In our algorithm, a simple representation of formula $I_d(a_0, \ldots, a_{d-1})$ is specially important. In the algorithm **NonZeroDimQE**, we transform the formula produced by the recursive call of **MainQE** at line 7 into a disjunctive normal form with $l-1$ many disjunctions, then we produce a final output formula containing a formula with $l-1$ many disjunctions at line 13. For a simple representation of the output formula, we need to reduce the number l as far as possible. If we get a representation of formula $I_d(a_0, \ldots, a_{d-1})$ as a disjunctive normal form with a minimum number of disjunctions, we can reduce the number l. Using a simplification method by Boolean function manipulation introduced in [9], we computed a disjunctive normal form of $I_d(a_0, \ldots, a_{d-1})$ with a minimal number of disjunctions for $d = 2, \ldots, 12$. Note that when d is an odd number any characteristic polynomial of a symmetric real matrix has only real roots, hence $I_d(a_0, \ldots, a_{d-1})$ is equivalent to $a_0 \neq 0 \vee I_{d-1}(a_1, \ldots, a_{d-1})$.
The followings are obtained formulas for $d = 2, 4, 6$ and 8. We omit I_{10}, I_{12} since they are much longer.

$$
\begin{aligned}
I_2(a_0, a_1) \ &: \ (0 \leqslant a_0 \wedge a_1 \neq 0) \\
I_4(a_0, \ldots, a_3) \ &: \ (a_0 \leqslant 0 \wedge a_1 \neq 0) \vee \\
&\quad (0 \leqslant a_1 \wedge 0 \leqslant a_2 \wedge 0 < a_3) \vee \\
&\quad (a_1 \leqslant 0 \wedge 0 \leqslant a_2 \wedge a_3 < 0) \\
I_6(a_0, \ldots, a_5) \ &: \ (0 \leqslant a_0 \wedge a_1 \neq 0) \vee \\
&\quad (0 \leqslant a_2 \wedge 0 \leqslant a_3 \wedge 0 \leqslant a_4 \wedge 0 < a_5) \vee \\
&\quad (0 \leqslant a_2 \wedge a_3 \leqslant 0 \wedge 0 \leqslant a_4 \wedge a_5 < 0) \vee \\
&\quad (0 \leqslant a_1 \wedge a_2 \leqslant 0 \wedge 0 \leqslant a_4 \wedge a_5 < 0) \vee \\
&\quad (0 \leqslant a_1 \wedge a_2 \leqslant 0 \wedge 0 < a_3 \wedge a_4 \leqslant 0) \vee \\
&\quad (a_1 \leqslant 0 \wedge a_2 \leqslant 0 \wedge 0 \leqslant a_4 \wedge 0 < a_5) \vee \\
&\quad (a_1 \leqslant 0 \wedge a_2 \leqslant 0 \wedge a_3 < 0 \wedge a_4 \leqslant 0)
\end{aligned}
$$

$$
\begin{aligned}
I_8(a_0, \ldots, a_7) \ &: \ (a_0 \leqslant 0 \wedge a_1 \neq 0) \vee \\
&\quad (0 \leqslant a_3 \wedge 0 \leqslant a_4 \wedge 0 \leqslant a_5 \wedge 0 \leqslant a_6 \wedge 0 < a_7) \vee \\
&\quad (a_3 \leqslant 0 \wedge 0 \leqslant a_4 \wedge a_5 \leqslant 0 \wedge 0 \leqslant a_6 \wedge a_7 < 0) \vee \\
&\quad (a_2 \leqslant 0 \wedge 0 \leqslant a_3 \wedge a_5 \leqslant 0 \wedge 0 \leqslant a_6 \wedge a_7 < 0) \vee \\
&\quad (a_2 \leqslant 0 \wedge 0 \leqslant a_3 \wedge a_4 \leqslant 0 \wedge 0 \leqslant a_6 \wedge a_7 < 0) \vee \\
&\quad (a_2 \leqslant 0 \wedge 0 \leqslant a_3 \wedge a_4 \leqslant 0 \wedge 0 < a_5 \wedge a_6 \leqslant 0) \vee \\
&\quad (a_2 \leqslant 0 \wedge a_3 \leqslant 0 \wedge 0 \leqslant a_5 \wedge 0 \leqslant a_6 \wedge 0 < a_7) \vee \\
&\quad (a_2 \leqslant 0 \wedge a_3 \leqslant 0 \wedge a_4 \leqslant 0 \wedge a_5 < 0 \wedge 0 \leqslant a_7) \vee \\
&\quad (a_2 \leqslant 0 \wedge a_3 \leqslant 0 \wedge a_4 \leqslant 0 \wedge a_5 < 0 \wedge a_6 \leqslant 0) \vee \\
&\quad (0 \leqslant a_1 \wedge 0 \leqslant a_2 \wedge 0 \leqslant a_5 \wedge 0 \leqslant a_6 \wedge 0 < a_7) \vee \\
&\quad (0 \leqslant a_1 \wedge 0 \leqslant a_2 \wedge a_4 \leqslant 0 \wedge a_5 < 0 \wedge 0 \leqslant a_7) \vee \\
&\quad (0 \leqslant a_1 \wedge 0 \leqslant a_2 \wedge a_4 \leqslant 0 \wedge a_5 < 0 \wedge a_6 \leqslant 0) \vee \\
&\quad (0 \leqslant a_1 \wedge 0 \leqslant a_2 \wedge 0 < a_3 \wedge a_5 \leqslant 0 \wedge 0 \leqslant a_7) \vee \\
&\quad (0 \leqslant a_1 \wedge 0 \leqslant a_2 \wedge 0 < a_3 \wedge a_5 \leqslant 0 \wedge a_6 \leqslant 0) \vee \\
&\quad (0 \leqslant a_1 \wedge 0 \leqslant a_2 \wedge 0 < a_3 \wedge 0 < a_4 \wedge 0 \leqslant a_5) \vee \\
&\quad (a_1 \leqslant 0 \wedge 0 \leqslant a_2 \wedge a_5 \leqslant 0 \wedge 0 \leqslant a_6 \wedge a_7 < 0) \vee \\
&\quad (a_1 \leqslant 0 \wedge 0 \leqslant a_2 \wedge a_4 \leqslant 0 \wedge 0 < a_5 \wedge a_6 \leqslant 0) \vee \\
&\quad (a_1 \leqslant 0 \wedge 0 \leqslant a_2 \wedge a_4 < 0 \wedge 0 \leqslant a_5 \wedge a_7 \leqslant 0) \vee \\
&\quad (a_1 \leqslant 0 \wedge 0 \leqslant a_2 \wedge a_3 < 0 \wedge 0 \leqslant a_5 \wedge a_7 \leqslant 0) \vee \\
&\quad (a_1 \leqslant 0 \wedge 0 \leqslant a_2 \wedge a_3 < 0 \wedge 0 \leqslant a_5 \wedge a_6 \leqslant 0) \vee \\
&\quad (a_1 \leqslant 0 \wedge 0 \leqslant a_2 \wedge a_3 < 0 \wedge 0 < a_4 \wedge a_5 \leqslant 0)
\end{aligned}
$$

The following table contains some data of their structures. The second row $\vee$ means the number of the disjunctions, i.e., the number of the logic symbol $\vee$ contained in the disjunctive normal form of I_d. The third row $\wedge$ means the maximum number of the logic symbol $\wedge$ which appears in some conjunction.

Table 1: Simplified I_d

d	2	4	6	8	10	12
$\vee$	0	2	6	20	40	142
$\wedge$	1	2	3	4	5	6

Similar simplification of I_d is also discussed in [27]. They give a simplified formula for $d = 1, \ldots, 6$. (Actually they give a simplified formula for its negation $\neg I_d(a_0, \ldots, a_{d-1})$.) Though it is not fair to compare their formulas with ours in our measure since their aim is not same as ours, the disjunctive normal form of $I_d(a_0, \ldots, a_{d-1})$ transformed from their simplified formula of its negation contains 5 disjunction symbols for $d = 4$ and 27 disjunction symbols for $d = 6$.

5.2 Refinements

We describe several methods to refine our algorithm.

5.2.1 Parameter Space

In the algorithms **ZeroDimQE** and **NonZeroDimQE**, we do not check the feasibility of $\mathcal{F}(\mathcal{S})$ in $\mathbb{R}$, i.e., we do not check whether $\exists \bar{Y} \in \mathbb{R}^m \mathcal{F}(\mathcal{S})$ holds, meanwhile its feasibility in $\mathbb{C}$ is always guaranteed by the CGS algorithm. Since both computations are useless unless it is feasible, we have to check it before the computation. Our algorithm **MainQE** is also applicable to it. In our implementation, we always apply **MainQE** beforehand. It not only avoids useless computations but also produces a simpler formula.

5.2.2 Weak Inequality

In order to use our algorithm, a weak inequality $f \geqslant g$ always needs to be transformed into the equivalent form $f > g \vee f = g$. Using Lemma 9, however, we can directly handle it without using this transformation. When the majority of inequalities in a given quantified formula are weak inequalities, this treatment is more efficient according to our computation experiments.

5.2.3 Practical Computations of CGS

In the algorithm **MainQE**, we do not need the inverses of $q_1, \ldots, q_t$. We can replace $W_1 q_1 - 1, \ldots, W_t q_t - 1$ with $W q_1 \cdots q_t$ using only one variable W. In our experience, this computation tends to be faster when $q_1, \ldots, q_t$ are small size of polynomials. In our implementation, we prepare an option for it.

In our CGS computation algorithm, for the computation of $(V_{\mathbb{C}}(I_1) \backslash V_{\mathbb{C}}(I_2), G)$, we first obtain I_1 and I_2 then compute G. The feasibility of $\mathcal{S} = V_{\mathbb{C}}(I_1) \backslash V_{\mathbb{C}}(I_2)$ is checked throughout of the computation of G. Since we have to check the feasibility of $\mathcal{S} = V_{\mathbb{R}}(I_1) \backslash V_{\mathbb{R}}(I_2)$ as described above, we had better check it before or parallel to the computation of G.

6. COMPUTATION DATA

Using our implementation we have computed many real QE problems, not only problems from 'Todai Robot Project' but also example problems treated in several published papers. In the following, we show some interesting data from them. The first problem **Example 1** is the example problem treated in the section 6.4 of [27], the next 3 problems **Example 2-4** are the example problems given in the section 6 of [5], the next 6 problems **Example 5-10** are from 'Todai Robot Project'. They are also put on the website `www.mi.kagu.tus.ac.jp/~fukasaku/issac2015/data/` with more detailed information. Table 2 contains the data of their computation time not only by our implementation but also by other existing real QE implementations. **O** is our implementation, **SN** is a CAD based QE program of SyNRAC, **Reg** is a real QE program in RegularChains package of Maple 18 [5], **Res** and **Red** are Resolve and Reduce of Mathematica 9, **QC** is QEPCAD, **hqe** is rlhqe of Redlog and **rqe** is the regular QE rlqe of Redlog. All the computations were done by the same computer environment with an Intel CORE i7 CPU 2.40 GHz with 64 GB memory OS Ubuntu14.04. Computing time is written in second. '0' means that the computation time is within 1 second, '>1' means that the computation does not terminate within 1 hour, 'm' means memory exhaust and 'er' means the computation was crashed with some error.

Example 1

$\forall x \forall y (b^2(x-c)^2 + a^2y^2 = a^2b^2 \Rightarrow x^2 + y^2 \leqslant 1)$

Example 2

$\exists x \exists y \exists z ((1/200)xs(1-(1/400)x) + ys(1-(1/400)x) - (35/2)x = 0 \wedge 250xs(1-(1/600)y)(z+(3/250)) - (55/2)y = 0 \wedge 500(y + (1/20)x)(1-(1/700)z) - 5z = 0)$

Example 3

$\exists c_2 \exists s_2 \exists c_1 \exists s_1 (r - c_1 + l(s_1s_2 - c_1c_2) = 0 \wedge z - s_1 - l(s_1c_2 + s_2c_1) = 0 \wedge s_1^2 + c_1^2 - 1 = 0 \wedge s_2^2 + c_2^2 - 1 = 0)$

Example 4

$\exists y \exists z (x^2 + y^2z + z^3 = 0 \wedge 3x^2 + 3y^2 + z^2 - 1 = 0 \wedge x^2 + z^2 - y^3(y-1)^3 < 0)$

Example 5

$\exists x \exists y \exists z (xy + axz + yz - 1 = 0 \wedge xyz + xz + xy = a \wedge xz + yz - az - x - y - 1 = 0 \wedge axy = byz \wedge ayz = bzx)$

Example 6

$\exists x \exists y \exists z (xy + axz + yz - 1 = 0 \wedge xyz + xz + xy = b \wedge xz + yz - az - x - y - 1 = 0)$

Example 7

$\exists x_0 \exists x_2 \exists x_3 (x_0 + 2x_2 \neq 5 \wedge x_0x_2 - 1 = 0 \wedge x_0^2 - 2x_0x_1 + x_2^2 - 2x_2x_3 - x_4 = 0 \wedge -16x_1x_4^2 - 800x_3^3 - 1240x_3^2x_4 - 408x_3x_4^2 - 40x_4^3 + 240x_1x_3 - 532x_1x_4 - 17720x_3^2 - 6214x_3x_4 - 550x_4^2 - 4480x_1 + 25240x_3 + 5695x_4 + 1050 = 0 \wedge 32x_1^2 + 168x_1x_3 + 40x_1x_4 + 8x_3^2 + 20x_3x_4 + 4x_4^2 - 270x_1 - 390x_3 - 105x_4 + 450 = 0 \wedge 320x_1x_3x_4 + 32x_1x_4^2 + 16x_3x_4^2 + 8320x_1x_3 + 264x_1x_4 + 240x_3^2 - 372x_3x_4 - 140x_4^2 - 14840x_1 - 23380x_3 - 2575x_4 + 36750 = 0)$

Example 8

$\exists x_0 \exists x_1 \exists x_2 \exists x_3 \exists x_4 \exists x_5 \exists x_6 \exists x_7 (x_2 \neq 0 \wedge x_3 \neq 0 \wedge x_4 = 0 \wedge x_5 = 0 \wedge x_2 - x_3 \neq 0 \wedge x_0x_8 + x_1x_9 - 1 = 0 \wedge 2x_0x_2 + 2x_1x_3 + 2x_4x_5 - x_0 - x_1 - x_4 = 0 \wedge x_0x_6 + x_0x_7 - x_1x_7 - x_4x_6 - x_0 + x_8 = 0 \wedge x_2x_6 + x_2x_7 - x_3x_7 - x_5x_6 - x_2 + x_9 = 0 \wedge 2x_0x_2 - 2x_0x_4 + 2x_1x_3 - 2x_1x_5 - x_2^2 - x_3^2 + x_4^2 + x_5^2 = 0 \wedge x_0^2 + x_1^2 - x_2^2 - x_3^2 + x_4^2 - x_5^2 + x_2 + x_3 + x_5 = 0 \wedge 14x_9^3 + 2x_8^2 - 12x_8x_9 - 16x_9^2 + 4x_8 + 17x_9 - 10 = 0 \wedge 14x_8x_9^2 - 3x_8^2 - 10x_8x_9 - 11x_9^2 + x_8 + 20x_9 - 6 = 0 \wedge 14x_8^2x_9 - 6x_8^2 - 20x_8x_9 + 20x_9^2 + 16x_8 - 9x_9 + 2 = 0 \wedge 14x_8^3 - 19x_8^2 + 58x_8x_9 + 5x_9^2 - 17x_8 - 32x_9 + 46 = 0)$

Example 9

$\exists x_0 \exists x_2 \exists x_5 \exists x_3 \exists x_1 \exists x_4 ((\exists x_{10} \exists x_9 (0 = (x_5 - x_0)(1/2x_0 + 1/2x_5 - x_{10}) + (x_3 - x_2)(1/2x_2 + 1/2x_3 - x_9) \wedge 0 = (x_1 - x_5)(1/2x_5 + 1/2x_1 - x_{10}) + (x_4 - x_3)(1/2x_3 + 1/2x_4 - x_9) \wedge ((x_{10} - x_0)^2 + (x_9 - x_2)^2)^{1/2} = 1 \wedge 0 < ((x_{10} - x_0)^2 + (x_9 - x_2)^2)^{1/2})) \wedge (0 \leqslant x_0x_3 - x_0x_4 + x_1x_2 - x_1x_3 - x_2x_5 + x_4x_5 \wedge 0 \leqslant (x_5 - x_0)(x_4 - x_2) - (x_3 - x_2)(x_1 - x_0)) \wedge 3 \leqslant |x_0x_3 - x_0x_4 + x_1x_2 - x_1x_3 - x_2x_5 + x_4x_5|/((x_1 - x_0)(x_5 - x_0) + (x_4 - x_2)(x_3 - x_2)) \wedge 3 \leqslant |x_0x_3 - x_0x_4 + x_1x_2 - x_1x_3 - x_2x_5 + x_4x_5|/((x_0 - x_5)(x_1 - x_5) + (x_2 - x_3)(x_4 - x_3)) \wedge x_8 = |x_0x_3 - x_0x_4 + x_1x_2 - x_1x_3 - x_2x_5 + x_4x_5|/((x_1 - x_0)(x_5 - x_0) + (x_4 - x_2)(x_3 - x_2)) \wedge x_7 = |x_0x_3 - x_0x_4 + x_1x_2 - x_1x_3 - x_2x_5 + x_4x_5|/((x_0 - x_5)(x_1 - x_5) + (x_2 - x_3)(x_4 - x_3)) \wedge x_6 = 1/2|(x_5 - x_0)(x_4 - x_2) - (x_3 - x_2)(x_1 - x_0)|)$

Example 10

$\exists x_0 \exists x_1 \exists x_7 (x_5x_7 - x_6x_7 + x_1 - x_5 = 0 \wedge x_0^2 + x_1^2 - 1 = 0 \wedge x_3^4x_7^2 - 4x_3^3x_4x_7^2 + 6x_3^2x_4^2x_7^2 + 2x_3^2x_5^2x_7^2 - 4x_3^2x_5x_6x_7^2 + 2x_3^2x_6^2x_7^2 - 4x_3x_4^3x_7^2 - 4x_3x_4x_5^2x_7^2 + 8x_3x_4x_5x_6x_7^2 - 4x_3x_4x_6^2x_7^2 + x_4^4x_7^2 + 2x_4^2x_5^2x_7^2 - 4x_4^2x_5x_6x_7^2 + 2x_4^2x_6^2x_7^2 + x_5^4x_7^2 - 4x_5^3x_6x_7^2 + 6x_5^2x_6^2x_7^2 - 4x_5x_6^3x_7^2 + x_6^4x_7^2 + 2x_0x_3^3x_7 - 6x_0x_3^2x_4x_7 + 6x_0x_3x_4^2x_7 + 2x_0x_3x_5^2x_7 - 4x_0x_3x_5x_6x_7 + 2x_0x_3x_6^2x_7 - 2x_0x_4^3x_7 - 2x_0x_4x_5^2x_7 + 4x_0x_4x_5x_6x_7 - 2x_0x_4x_6^2 x_7 + 2x_1x_3^2x_5x_7 - 2x_1x_3^2x_6x_7 - 4x_1x_3x_4x_5x_7 + 4x_1x_3x_4x_6x_7 + 2x_1x_4^2x_5x_7 - 2x_1x_4^2x_6x_7 + 2x_1x_5^3x_7 - 6x_1x_5^2x_6x_7 + 6x_1x_5x_6^2x_7 - 2x_1x_6^3x_7 - 2x_3^4x_7 + 6x_3^3x_4x_7 - 6x_3^2x_4^2x_7 - 4x_3^2x_5^2x_7 + 6x_3^2x_5x_6x_7 - 2x_3^2x_6^2x_7 + 2x_3x_4^3x_7 + 6x_3x_4x_5^2x_7 - 8x_3x_4x_5 x_6x_7 + 2x_3x_4x_6^2x_7 - 2x_4^2x_5^2x_7 + 2x_4^2x_5x_6x_7 - 2x_5^4x_7 + 6x_5^3x_6x_7 - 6x_5^2x_6^2x_7 + 2x_5x_6^3x_7 + x_0^2x_3^2 - 2x_0^2x_3x_4 + x_0^2x_4^2 + 2x_0x_1x_3x_5 - 2x_0x_1x_3x_6 - 2x_0x_1x_4x_5 + 2x_0x_1x_4x_6 - 2x_0x_3^3 + 4x_0x_3^2x_4 - 2x_0x_3x_4^2 - 2x_0x_3x_5^2 + 2x_0x_3x_5x_6 + 2x_0x_4x_5^2 - 2x_0x_4x_5x_6 + x_1^2x_5^2 - 2x_1^2x_5x_6 + x_1^2x_6^2 - 2x_1x_3^2x_5 + 2x_1x_3^2x_6 + 2x_1x_3x_4x_5 - 2x_1x_3x_4x_6 - 2x_1x_5^3 + 4x_1x_5^2x_6 - 2x_1x_5x_6^2 + x_3^4 - 2x_3^3x_4 + x_3^2x_4^2 + 2x_3^2x_5^2 - 2x_3^2x_5x_6 - x_3^2x_8^2 - 2x_3x_4x_5^2 + 2x_3x_4x_5x_6 + 2x_3x_4x_8^2 - x_4^2x_8^2 + x_5^4 - 2x_5^3x_6 + x_5^2x_6^2 - x_5^2x_8^2 + 2x_5x_6x_8^2 - x_6^2x_8^2 = 0)$

Table 2: Computation Time

	O	SN	Reg	Res	Red	QC	hqe	rqe
1	2	2	285	0	1	2	>1	0
2	1	>1	4	0	30	er	>1	>1
3	1	1	29	0	>1	>1	0	>1
4	1	1	1	0	0	er	95	>1
5	0	er	>1	250	>1	>1	>1	>1
6	10	>1	>1	>1	>1	m	>1	er
7	2	er	>1	586	587	>1	420	>1
8	1	>1	m	>1	>1	>1	>1	>1
9	791	>1	>1	>1	>1	er	>1	>1
10	83	>1	>1	>1	>1	>1	>1	>1

The following are the output formulas obtained by our implementation.

Example 1: $(-a \leqslant 0 \vee c < 1) \wedge (-a^2 + 2b^2 + c^2 < 1 \vee -a^2b^2 + b^4 + b^2c^2 + a^2 - b^2 \leqslant 0) \wedge a \neq 0 \wedge b \neq 0 \wedge -c < 1 \wedge a + c \leqslant 1 \wedge a - c \leqslant 1 \wedge c - a \leqslant 1 \wedge -c - a \leqslant 1)$

Example 2: *true*

Example 3: $(l = 0 \wedge r^2 + z^2 - 1 = 0) \vee (l - 1 = 0 \wedge z = 0 \wedge r = 0) \vee (l + 1 = 0 \wedge z = 0 \wedge r = 0) \vee (l \neq 0 \wedge r \neq 0 \wedge l^2 - r^2 - z^2 - 2l + 1 = 0 \wedge l^4 - 2l^2r^2 - 2l^2z^2 + r^4 + 2r^2z^2 + z^4 - 6l^2 - 2r^2 - 2z^2 + 1 \neq 0) \vee (l \neq 0 \wedge r \neq 0 \wedge l^2 - r^2 - z^2 + 2l + 1 = 0 \wedge l^4 - 2l^2r^2 - 2l^2z^2 + r^4 + 2r^2z^2 + z^4 - 6l^2 - 2r^2 - 2z^2 + 1 \neq 0) \vee (l \neq 0 \wedge r \neq 0 \wedge -l^2 + r^2 + z^2 - 2l \leqslant 1 \wedge l^2 - r^2 - z^2 - 2l \leqslant -1 \wedge l^4 - 2l^2r^2 - 2l^2z^2 + r^4 + 2r^2z^2 + z^4 - 6l^2 - 2r^2 - 2z^2 + 1 \neq 0) \vee (l \neq 0 \wedge r \neq 0 \wedge -l^2 + r^2 + z^2 + 2l \leqslant 1 \wedge l^2 - r^2 - z^2 + 2l \leqslant -1 \wedge l^4 - 2l^2r^2 - 2l^2z^2 + r^4 + 2r^2z^2 + z^4 - 6l^2 - 2r^2 - 2z^2 + 1 \neq 0) \vee (r = 0 \wedge l \neq 0 \wedge z \neq 0 \wedge l^4 - 2l^2z^2 + z^4 - 6l^2 - 2z^2 + 1 \neq 0 \wedge l^6 - 2l^4z^2 + l^2z^4 - 2l^4 - 2l^2z^2 + l^2 \leqslant 0)$

The obtained formula is simpler than the one of **Res**, but **Reg** produces a much simpler formula.

Example 4: $x = 0 \vee 387420489x^{36} + 473513931x^{34} + 1615049199x^{32} - 5422961745x^{30} + 2179233963x^{28} - 14860773459x^{26} + 43317737551x^{24} - 45925857657x^{22} + 60356422059x^{20} - 126478283472x^{18} + 164389796305x^{16} - 121571730573x^{14} + 54842719755x^{12} - 16059214980x^{10} + 3210573925x^8 - 446456947x^6 + 43657673x^4 - 1631864x^2 < 40328$

Example 5: $(a = 0 \wedge b = 0) \vee (b = 0 \wedge a + 1 = 0)$

Example 6: Though the input formula has only two free variables, the obtained output formula is too long to be presented here.

Example 7: The output formula is very long, but the output by **Res**, **Red** or **hqe** is more complicated.

Example 8: $(933310015536x_8^2 - 1180364661893x_8x_9 - 2789612317005x_9^2 - 1647908788394x_8 + 3796484222917x_9 \leqslant 1116708327190 \wedge 15957579805003x_8^2 - 77903808369439x_8x_9 + 49112832908310x_9^2 + 43189770064463x_8 - 25506604039134x_9 - 22204848564870 \neq 0 \wedge 14x_9^3 + 2x_8^2 - 12x_8x_9 - 16x_9^2 + 4x_8 + 17x_9 - 10 = 0 \wedge -14x_8x_9^2 + 3x_8^2 + 10x_8x_9 + 11x_9^2 - x_8 - 20x_9 + 6 = 0 \wedge 14x_8^2x_9 - 6x_8^2 - 20x_8x_9 + 20x_9^2 + 16x_8 - 9x_9 + 2 = 0 \wedge 14x_8^3 - 19x_8^2 + 58x_8x_9 + 5x_9^2 - 17x_8 - 32x_9 + 46 = 0) \vee (-15957579805003x_8^2 + 77903808369439x_8x_9 - 49112832908310x_9^2 - 43189770064463x_8 + 25506604039134x_9 \leqslant -22204848564870 \wedge -9268258341646x_8^2 + 39858124637223x_8x_9 - 34100541512895x_9^2 - 22211179355616x_8 + 22376128132763x_9 \leqslant -6000263098390 \wedge -7946417x_8^2 + 34970121x_8x_9 - 27286046x_9^2 - 14715105x_8 + 16566738x_9 < -2049566 \wedge 14x_9^3 + 2x_8^2 - 12x_8x_9 - 16x_9^2 + 4x_8 + 17x_9 - 10 = 0 \wedge -14x_8x_9^2 + 3x_8^2 + 10x_8x_9 + 11x_9^2 - x_8 - 20x_9 + 6 = 0 \wedge 14x_8^2x_9 - 6x_8^2 - 20x_8x_9 + 20x_9^2 + 16x_8 - 9x_9 + 2 = 0 \wedge 14x_8^3 - 19x_8^2 + 58x_8x_9 + 5x_9^2 - 17x_8 - 32x_9 + 46 = 0) \vee (-9268258341646x_8^2 + 39858124637223x_8x_9 - 34100541512895x_9^2 - 22211179355616x_8 + 22376128132763x_9 \leqslant -6000263098390 \wedge 7946417x_8^2 - 34970121x_8x_9 + 27286046x_9^2 + 14715105x_8 - 16566738x_9 < 2049566 \wedge 15957579805003x_8^2 - 77903808369439x_8x_9 + 49112832908310x_9^2 + 43189770064463x_8 - 25506604039134x_9 \leqslant 22204848564870 \wedge 14x_9^3 + 2x_8^2 - 12x_8x_9 - 16x_9^2 + 4x_8 + 17x_9 - 10 = 0 \wedge -14x_8x_9^2 + 3x_8^2 + 10x_8x_9 + 11x_9^2 - x_8 - 20x_9 + 6 = 0 \wedge 14x_8^2x_9 - 6x_8^2 - 20x_8x_9 + 20x_9^2 + 16x_8 - 9x_9 + 2 = 0 \wedge 14x_8^3 - 19x_8^2 + 58x_8x_9 + 5x_9^2 - 17x_8 - 32x_9 + 46 = 0)$

Example 9: $x_6 = (2x_7x_8(x_7 + x_8))/((1 + x_7^2)(1 + x_8^2)) \wedge x_7 \geqslant 3 \wedge x_8 \geqslant 3$
The actual output formula is rather complex. The original problem requires the free variables x_7 and x_8 to be integers. The above output formula is equivalent to the input formula for integer values of x_7, x_8.

Example 10: The input formula is produced in the process of solving some original problem. It contains only three but very complicated polynomial equations. For such a problem our algorithm is most adequate to apply. The output formula is too long to be presented here.

We put our program as open software on the website `www.mi.kagu.tus.ac.jp/~fukasaku/issac2015/program/` together with information how to get an old version of SyNRAC. By a regulation of the company one of us belongs, we cannot open the recent SyNRAC. Since the old version of SyNRAC is much slower than the recent one, computations of some examples do not terminate in a standard computer.

7. CONCLUSION AND REMARKS

Our algorithm using the relation $h > 0 \Leftrightarrow \exists z\ z^2h = 1$ is so natural that anybody may come up with Lemma 3. For the computation of a characteristic polynomial χ_1^J, however, we have to compute a symmetric matrix M_1^J of the size $k\ 2^l \times k\ 2^l$. Our theoretical result Theorem 5 drastically reduces its size to $k \times k$. As explained after the theorem together with Example 6, the algorithm gives us a possibility to reduce the size of the underling matrix, whereas the algorithm of [23] does not. Theorem 5 also gives us a simple but essential proof to Weispfenning's rather tricky method for handling inequalities presented in the section 3 of [23].

In order to handle a quantified formula with equations which form a non-zero dimensional ideal, Weispfenning's algorithm presented below Step M2 of [23] does not address a practical computation, Algorithm 3 together with a simplified formula $I_d(a_0, \ldots, a_{d-1})$ enables us to handle such a formula. Example 9 is a typical such example.

When a quantified formula contains no equations, our algorithm simply gives up, while Weispfenning's algorithm tries to convert it to equational forms by an ingenious technique as presented in Step M1 of [23]. That is we can consider our algorithm as a preprocessing. This observation is important. Our algorithm can be viewed as a complete preprocessing. It transforms any quantified formula with equations into a form with no equations eliminating all possible quantifiers, whereas any other approach such as [4, 28] does not have this completeness. As a result, **SN**, **Res** or **Red** which contains some of these preprocessing method by Gröbner bases cannot solve a rather simple example such as Example 6. CGS is an ideal tool which completely handles parametric equations. Example 7 is a typical example of zero-dimensional equations, **hqe** with a rather slow CGS program can solve it faster than **Res**, **Red**. For a quantified formula containing only strict inequalities, a CAD based algorithm such as the one introduced in [24] is more practical.

For the computation of the signature $\sigma(M_1^J)$, we do not use the factorization structure of a characteristic polynomial $\chi_1^J(2^lX) = c\Pi_{(e_1,e_2,\ldots,e_l)\in\{0,1\}^l}\chi^I_{h_1^{e_1}h_2^{e_2}\cdots h_l^{e_l}}(X)$. It is probably possible to combine all signatures $\sigma(M^I_{h_1^{e_1}h_2^{e_2}\cdots h_l^{e_l}})$ to compute a simpler representation of I_d.

By the recent works of real effective algebraic geometry such as [2, 8], we have theoretically good algorithms to decide emptiness of the variety $V_{\mathbb{R}}(I)$ for a given (even a non-zero dimensional) polynomial ideal I. These algorithms enable us to have an alternative algorithm to handle the basic quantified formula (1). When the formula has no free variable, i.e., $\bar{Y}$ is empty, the algorithm is theoretically better than ours. Otherwise, however, we have to handle parametric ideals. We need several heavy manipulations such as a computation of the radical ideal of a parametric ideal. In fact, the software [20] which is based on the above work cannot handle a quantified formula with free variables. Our (also Weispfenning's) algorithm does not need such a heavy computation, we need only CGS computations.

8. REFERENCES

[1] Arai, N.H., Matsuzaki, T., Iwane, H. and Anai, H.: Mathematics by Machine, Proceedings of International Symposium on Symbolic and Algebraic Computation, pp. 1-8, ACM, 2014.

[2] Aubry, P., Rouillier, F. and Safey El Din, M. : Real Solving for Positive Dimensional Systems, J. Symb. Comput. 34, no. 6, pp. 543-560, 2002.

[3] Becker, E. and Wörmann, T.: On the trace formula for quadratic forms. Recent advances in real algebraic geometry and quadratic forms (Berkeley, CA, 1990/1991; San Francisco, CA, 1991), pp. 271-291, Contemp. Math., 155, Amer. Math. Soc., Providence, RI, 1994.

[4] Buchberger, B. and Hong, H. : Speeding-up Quantifier Elimination by Gröbner Bases. Technical Report 91-06, 1991.

[5] Chen, C. and Maza, M, M. : Quantifier Elimination by Cylindrical Algebraic Decomposition Based on Regular Chains. Proceedings of International Symposium on Symbolic and Algebraic Computation, pp. 91-98, ACM, 2014.

[6] Collins, G, E. : Quantifier elimination for real closed fields by cylindrical algebraic decomposition. Automata theory and formal languages (Second GI Conf., Kaiserslautern, 1975), pp. 134-183. Lecture Notes in Comput. Sci., Vol. 33, Springer, Berlin, 1975.

[7] Dolzmann, A. and Gilch, L. : Generic Hermitian Quantifier Elimination. Proceedings of the Artificial Intelligence and Symbolic Computation, pp. 80-93, Springer, 2004.

[8] Bank, B., Giusti, M. and Heintz, J. : Point searching in real singular complete intersection varieties - algorithms of intrinsic complexity, Math. Comp. 83, pp. 873-897, 2014

[9] Iwane, H., Higuchi, H. and Anai, H. : An Effective Implementation of a Special Quantifier Elimination for a Sign Definite Condition by Logical Formula Simplification. Proceedings of CASC2013, pp. 194-208, Springer, 2013.

[10] Iwane, H., Matsuzaki, T., Arai, N., Anai, H. : Automated Natural Language Geometry Math Problem Solving by Real Quantifier Elimination. Proceedings of the 10th International Workshop on Automated Deduction in Geometry (ADG 2014), pp. 75-84, 2014.

[11] Iwane, H.,Yanami, H. and Anai, H.: A Toolbox for Solving Real Algebraic Constraints, Proceedings of 4th International Congress of Mathematical Software, pp. 518-522, Springer, 2014.

[12] Kapur, D., Sun, Y., and Wang, D. : A New Algorithm for Computing Comprehensive Gröbner Systems. Proceedings of International Symposium on Symbolic and Algebraic Computation, pp. 29-36, ACM, 2010.

[13] Kurata, Y. : Improving Suzuki-Sato's CGS Algorithm by Using Stability of Gröbner Bases and Basic Manipulations for Efficient Implementation. Communications of the Japan Society for Symbolic and Algebraic Computation, Vol. 1, pp. 39-66, JSSAC, 2011.

[14] Matsuzaki, T., Iwane, H., Anai, H. and Arai, N.H. : The Most uncreative Examinee: A First Step toward Wide Coverage Natural Language Math Problem Solving, Proceedings of the Twenty-Eighth AAAI Conference on Artificial Intelligence, pp. 1098-1104, 2014.

[15] McCallum, S. : On Projection in CAD-Based Quantifier Elimination with Equational Constraint. Proceedings of the International Symposium on Symbolic and Algebraic Computation, pp. 145-149, ACM,1999.

[16] McCallum, S. : On Propagation of Equational Constraints in CAD-Based Quantifier Elimination. Proceedings of the International Symposium on Symbolic and Algebraic Computation, pp. 223-231, ACM,2001.

[17] Nabeshima, K. : A Speed-Up of the Algorithm for Computing Comprehensive Gröbner Systems. Proceedings of the International Symposium on Symbolic and Algebraic Computation, pp. 299-306, ACM, 2007.

[18] Nabeshima, K. : Stability Conditions of Monomial Bases and Comprehensive Gröbner systems. Lecture Notes in Computer Science, Vol. 7442, pp. 248-259, Springer, 2012.

[19] Pedersen, P., Roy, M.-F., and Szpirglas, A. : Counting real zeroes in the multivariate case. Proceedings of the Effective Methods in Algebraic Geometry, pp. 203-224, Springer, 1993.

[20] RAGLIB: A library for real solving polynomial systems of equations and inequalities. `http://www-salsa.lip6.fr/~safey/RAGLib/`

[21] Redlog: an integral part of the interactive computer algebra system Reduce. `http://www.redlog.eu/`

[22] Suzuki, A. and Sato, Y. : A Simple Algorithm to Compute Comprehensive Gröbner Bases Using Gröbner Bases. Proceedings of International Symposium on Symbolic and Algebraic Computation, pp. 326-331, ACM, 2006.

[23] Sato, Y. and Suzuki, A.: Computation of Inverses in Residue Class Rings of Parametric Polynomial Ideals, Proceedings of International Symposium on Symbolic and Algebraic Computation, pp. 311-315, ACM, 2009.

[24] Strzebonski, A.: Solving Systems of Strict Polynomial Inequalities, J. Symb. Comput. 29, no. 3, pp. 471-480, 2000.

[25] SyNRAC: a software package for quantifier elimination. `http://jp.fujitsu.com/group/labs/en/techinfo/freeware/synrac/`

[26] Todai Robot Project. `http://21robot.org/About/?lang=english`

[27] Weispfenning, V. : A New Approach to Quantifier Elimination for Real Algebra. Quantifier Elimination and Cylindrical Algebraic Decomposition, pp. 376-392, Springer, 1998.

[28] Wilson, D. J., Bradford, R. J. and Davenport, J. H. : Speeding Up Cylindrical Algebraic Decomposition by Gröbner Bases. Lecture Notes in Computer Science 7362 (Proceedings of CICM 2012), pp. 280-294, Springer, 2012.

Computation of Dimension in Filtered Free Modules by Gröbner Reduction

Christoph Fürst*
Research Institute for Symbolic Computation
Johannes Kepler University Linz
A-4040, Linz, Austria
Christoph.Fuerst@risc.jku.at

Günter Landsmann
Research Institute for Symbolic Computation
Johannes Kepler University Linz
A-4040, Linz, Austria
Guenter.Landsmann@risc.jku.at

ABSTRACT

We present an axiomatic approach to Gröbner basis techniques in free multi-filtered modules over a not necessarily commutative multi-filtered ring. It is shown that classical Gröbner basis concepts can be viewed as models of our axioms. Within this theory it is possible to prove a general theorem about the dimension of filter spaces in multi-filtered modules. We use these ideas for computing the Hilbert function of finitely generated multi-filtered modules over difference-differential rings. Thus the presented method allows to compute a multivariate generalization of the univariate and the bivariate dimension polynomial considered in the papers of Winkler and Zhou.

Categories and Subject Descriptors

I.1.2 [**Symbolic and Algebraic Manipulation**]: Algorithms – *Algebraic algorithms*

General Terms

Algorithms

Keywords

Filtered free modules; difference and differential operators; Gröbner bases

1. INTRODUCTION

Gröbner bases, as introduced in [1], are a well established algorithmic concept for solving problems occurring in polynomial ideal theory, that is, performing computations in finitely generated modules over $K[x_1, \ldots, x_n]$. As the theory and its applications evolved, increasing interest came up in generalizing the notion of Gröbner bases to modules over more general rings.

*Partially support by Austrian Science Fund (FWF): W1214-N15, project DK11

ISSAC'15, July 6–9, 2015, Bath, United Kingdom.
Copyright © 2015 ACM 978-1-4503-3435-8/15/07 ...$15.00.
DOI: http://dx.doi.org/10.1145/2755996.2756680.

In [10] Winkler and Zhou introduced the concept of Gröbner bases in difference-differential modules.

Already in 1964 Kolchin formulated a fundamental theorem on univariate differential dimension polynomials [3] and ([4], Sect. II.12. Thm. 6). In 2007, by using serveral term orders, Levin was able to extend the computation of univariate and bivariate dimension polynomials to multivariate dimension polynomials [7]. In 2008, Winkler and Zhou extended their 2006-approach to the notion of relative Gröbner bases and applied it to the computation of difference-differential dimension polynomials [12]. Splitting the set of derivations and the set of automorphisms, they provided algorithms for the univariate and the bivariate case [11, 12].

In his 2013 paper, C. Dönch pointed out that the algorithm which generates a relative Gröbner basis out of a finite set of generators, as formulated in [12], might not terminate [2].

Different viewpoints on the computation and applications of dimension polynomials are presented in [5].

The backbone of Gröbner basis techniques in a module is the existence of monomials. In case that the set of monomials is appropriately contained in some monoid $\mathbb{N}^n$ we always may find an admissible linear extension of the product order in $\mathbb{N}^n$ (a monomial order). Then the usual Gröbner basis algorithms terminate, i.e., the classical concepts apply. There are but situations where this is not the case. For example, in rings of difference-differential operators, the set of monomials is isomorphic to $\mathbb{N}^m \times \mathbb{Z}^n$, and it is not obvious how to design a reduction process in a way that unique normal forms are produced. Several methods to overcome this problem have been developed, each with its own facet of technical difficulties, e.g. in [12] the set of monomials is covered by finitely many subsets in each of which reduction terminates, while in [6] characteristic sets are used to come to a solution.

In any case there is some filtration present derived naturally from the respective type of monomials and such that the reduction process is compatible with it.

Carefully inspecting the procedures provided by the papers mentioned above we gained increasing evidence that the interplay of filtrations and Gröbner bases must have a key role. Thus we tried to set up a general theory of reduction in a free module that takes into account a given filtration inherited naturally from the basic ring. The resulting computational tool is applicable to general filtered rings including polynomial rings $K[x_1,\dots,x_n]$ as well as modules of difference-differential operators as special cases.

2. FILTERED MODULES

$\mathbb{N}$, $\mathbb{Z}$ and $\mathbb{Q}$ denote the sets of non-negative integers, integers and rational numbers respectively. Throughout, the letter K will denote a field, and R will be an associative ring with 1, such that $K \subseteq R$. All modules over R are assumed to be left modules without further mention. The field K is not assumed to be central, so R is not necessarily an algebra in the classical sense. In addition we always assume given a distinguished basis Λ of the K-vector space R whose members are called monomials. We will indicate this by writing $R = K^{(\Lambda)}$ when necessary. Thus, elements $a \in R$ admit a unique representation $a = \sum_{\lambda\in\Lambda} a_\lambda \lambda$ as a K-linear combination of monomials.

The basis Λ extends naturally to a basis of free modules: let $F = Re_1 \oplus \cdots \oplus Re_q$ be the free R-module on the set $E = \{e_1,\dots,e_q\}$. Then the set $\Lambda E = \{\lambda e \colon \lambda \in \Lambda \wedge e \in E\}$ is a K-basis of F. Again we will call its members monomials, and elements $f \in F$ are represented uniquely as K-linear combinations of monomials.

As we will work over fields exclusively, we do not distinguish formally between monomials and terms. So we write $\mathrm{T}(f)$ for the set of terms of f, i.e., the set of all monomials which appear with a non-zero coefficient in a standard representation of f

$$\mathrm{T}(\sum_{t\in\Lambda E} f_t t) = \{t \in \Lambda E \colon f_t \neq 0\}.$$

This applies in particular to elements of the ring R. Also we will write $\mathrm{lt}(f)$ and $\mathrm{lc}(f)$ for the leading term and leading coefficient in contexts where these notions apply, so that, in such a situation, each $f \neq 0$ has a representation

$$f = \mathrm{lc}(f) \cdot \mathrm{lt}(f) + \text{lower order terms}.$$

Obviously we have that $\mathrm{T}(f \pm g) \subseteq \mathrm{T}(f) \cup \mathrm{T}(g)$.

One object of particular interest is the ring D of difference-differential operators, defined over a field K, and its finitely generated (left) modules. On K there are assumed two distinguished finite sets Δ, Σ where $\Delta = \{\delta_1,\dots,\delta_m\}$ consists of derivations and $\Sigma = \{\sigma_1,\dots,\sigma_n\}$ contains automorphisms of K, all commuting with one another (a difference-differential field, cf. [12]). The ring D is then constructed as the free K-vector space on the set of formal expressions

$$\delta_1^{k_1}\cdots\delta_m^{k_m}\sigma_1^{l_1}\cdots\sigma_n^{l_n} \ (k_i \in \mathbb{N},\, l_j \in \mathbb{Z}) \tag{1}$$

and a product that reflects the properties of derivations and automorphisms, that is

$$\delta_i \cdot a = a\delta_i + \delta_i(a) \text{ and } \sigma_j \cdot a = \sigma_j(a)\sigma_j \ (a \in K). \tag{2}$$

In the ring D the natural K-basis is the set Λ of all expressions (1). Note that the elements $\lambda \in \Lambda$ involve negative exponents in the automorphisms σ_j, and from (2) one derives that Λ is a multiplicative monoid that is isomorphic to $\mathbb{N}^m \times \mathbb{Z}^n$. The elements of D, called **difference-differential operators**, are thus finite K-linear combinations

$$\sum_{(k,l)\in\mathbb{N}^m\times\mathbb{Z}^n} a_{k,l}\delta^k\sigma^l.$$

A left module over D is also called a **difference-differential module** (over K) or a $\Delta - \Sigma$ module.

In the sequel, the letter D will be reserved for the ring of difference-differential operators, whereas R may denote an arbitrary ring of the type mentioned above.

For $r, s \in \mathbb{N}^p$ set $r \leq_\pi s \iff r_i \leq s_i$ $(1 \leq i \leq p)$. By a (p-fold) filtration of R we mean a family of additive subgroups $R_r \subseteq R$, indexed by $\mathbb{N}^p$, such that

- $R_r \cdot R_s \subseteq R_{r+s} \quad (r, s \in \mathbb{N}^p)$;
- $R_r \subseteq R_s \quad (r \leq_\pi s \in \mathbb{N}^p)$;
- $R = \bigcup_{r\in\mathbb{N}^p} R_r$;
- $1 \in R_0$.

R together with such a filtration will be called a **multi-filtered ring**. In a filtered ring R, R_0 is a subring and each R_r is a left and a right R_0-module.

DEFINITION 1. *A filtration of R is called* **monomial** *iff*

$$R_0 = K \text{ and } \forall r \in \mathbb{N}^p\, \forall f\, (f \in R_r \Rightarrow \mathrm{T}(f) \subseteq R_r).$$

EXAMPLE 1. *For a monomial $\lambda = \delta^k\sigma^l$ in D we set*

$$|\lambda|_1 := k_1 + \cdots + k_m \text{ and } |\lambda|_2 := |l_1| + \cdots + |l_n|.$$

For a general operator $a = \sum_{\lambda\in\Lambda} a_\lambda\lambda$ in D we define the order functions $|a|_\nu := \max\{|\lambda|_\nu \colon a_\lambda \neq 0\}$ $(\nu = 1, 2)$. Then, for $r, s \in \mathbb{N}$, the sets

$$D_{r,s} := \{a \in D \colon |a|_1 \leq r \wedge |a|_2 \leq s\}$$

define a (bivariate) monomial filtration. We call it the **standard filtration** *of D (see [12]).*

Let M be a left R-module. A (p-fold) filtration of M w.r.t. the (p-fold) filtered ring R is a family $(M_r)_{r\in\mathbb{N}^p}$ of additive subgroups $M_r \subseteq M$ with the properties

- $R_r \cdot M_s \subseteq M_{r+s} \quad (r, s \in \mathbb{N}^p)$;
- $M_r \subseteq M_s \quad (r \leq_\pi s \in \mathbb{N}^p)$;
- $M = \bigcup_{r\in\mathbb{N}^p} M_r$.

M together with such a filtration is called a **filtered module** (over the filtered ring R). Plainly, each M_r is an R_0-module. If in addition we have $M_r = R_r M_0\ \forall r$, the filtration is called **standard**. Note that the filtration on the ring D is standard.

NOTATION 1. *If X is an arbitrary subset of a filtered module $M = \bigcup_{r\in\mathbb{N}^p} M_r$ we set $X_r = X \cap M_r$.*

A (p-fold) filtration of R extends naturally to a (p-fold) filtration of free modules: Let R be a filtered ring, and $F = Re_1 \oplus \cdots \oplus Re_q$ the free R-module on the set $E = \{e_1,\dots,e_q\}$. Then

$$F_r := R_r e_1 \oplus \cdots \oplus R_r e_q \quad (r \in \mathbb{N}^p)$$

defines a filtration on F. If the filtration of R is monomial (w.r.t. the basis Λ) then so is the extended filtration of F (w.r.t. ΛE), meaning that always $f \in F_r \Rightarrow \mathrm{T}(f) \subseteq F_r$.

Example 2. *We extend the order functions of the difference-differential ring D to the free module $F = D^q$: For $\lambda e \in \Lambda E$ and $\nu = 1, 2$ let $|\lambda e|_\nu := |\lambda|_\nu$ and for a module element $f = \sum_{t \in \Lambda E} f_t t \in F$ let $|f|_\nu := \max\{|t|_\nu : t \in \mathrm{T}(f)\}$. This gives the extended filtration on F - for $r, s \in \mathbb{N}$*

$$F_{r,s} = D_{r,s}e_1 \oplus \cdots \oplus D_{r,s}e_q = \{f \in F : |f|_1 \le r \wedge |f|_2 \le s\}.$$

From $|e_j|_\nu = 0$ it is clear that $E \subseteq F_{0,0}$ whence $(F_{r,s})$ is a standard filtration. We will call it **the standard filtration of** F*. Since the ring filtration is monomial, the extended filtration is so too. Obviously*

$$f \in F_{r,s} \iff \forall t \in \mathrm{T}(f) : |t|_1 \le r \wedge |t|_2 \le s \iff \mathrm{T}(f) \subseteq F_{r,s}.$$

Let the ring R be a filtered ring, and M, N filtered R-modules. An R-homomorphism $\varphi \colon M \longrightarrow N$ is called a **morphism** if it respects the filter structure, that is, if

$$\varphi(M_r) \subseteq N_r, \ \forall r \in \mathbb{N}^p.$$

A morphism induces R_0-linear maps $M_r \longrightarrow N_r \ \forall r \in \mathbb{N}^p$.

Lemma 1. *Let R be a filtered ring and $\varphi \colon M \longrightarrow N$ a homomorphism of R-modules.*

1. *If M is filtered over R then $\mathrm{im}(\varphi)$ is filtered by setting $\mathrm{im}(\varphi)_r = \varphi(M_r)$. φ is then a morphism $M \longrightarrow \mathrm{im}(\varphi)$.*
2. *If N is filtered over R then M is filtered by setting $M_r = \varphi^{-1}(N_r)$. φ is then a morphism $M \longrightarrow N$.*

Thus, each finitely generated R-module $M = Rh_1 + \cdots + Rh_q$ inherits a filtration by first extending the family R_r to the free module $F \cong R^q$ and then pushing down with a map

$$\pi \colon F \longrightarrow M, \ e_i \mapsto h_i. \tag{3}$$

By specializing Lemma 1 to inclusion $N \hookrightarrow M$ any submodule $N \subseteq M$ naturally inherits a filtration from M via

$$N_r = N \cap M_r.$$

3. REDUCTION RELATIONS

Let X be a set and $\rho \subseteq X \times X$ a binary relation. We write $f \longrightarrow h$ to indicate that $(f, h) \in \rho$, and $f \longrightarrow^\star h$ when there is a chain of finite length

$$f = f_0 \longrightarrow f_1 \longrightarrow \cdots \longrightarrow f_k = h \quad (k \in \mathbb{N})$$

from f to h, that is

$$f \longrightarrow^\star h \iff (f, h) \in \rho^\star = \bigcup_{k \in \mathbb{N}} \rho^k.$$

With I we denote the set of ρ-irreducible elements, that is

$$I = \{x \in X \mid \nexists y \in X \text{ such that } x \longrightarrow y\}.$$

A subset $Y \subseteq X$ is called ρ-**stable** if $y \in Y$ and $y \longrightarrow z$ implies that $z \in Y$.

If $\rho \subseteq M \times M$ is a relation on a **module** M then, for $k \in \mathbb{N}$ we set

$$Z_k = \{f \mid (f, 0) \in \rho^k\}, \ Z_{\le k} = \bigcup_{l \le k} Z_l \text{ and } Z = \bigcup_{k=0}^{\infty} Z_k.$$

It is plain that $Z = \bigcup_{k=0}^{\infty} Z_{\le k} = \{f \in M : f \longrightarrow^\star 0\}$.

We consider a list of axioms which make a relation appropriate for reducing module elements to normal forms.

Definition 2. *Let M be a module, $N \subseteq M$ a submodule and ρ a binary relation on M. ρ is called a* **(weak) reduction** *for N provided that*

1. *ρ is noetherian, i.e., every sequence*
$$f_1 \longrightarrow f_2 \longrightarrow \cdots$$
terminates;
2. *I is a monomial K-linear subspace of M, that is, I is a vector space and*
$$\forall f \in M \, (f \in I \Rightarrow \mathrm{T}(f) \subseteq I);$$
3. *$f \longrightarrow h \Rightarrow f \equiv h \mod N$;*

ρ is a **strong reduction** *for N if it satisfies in addition*

4. *$I \cap N = 0$ that is, every non-zero element in N is reducible.*

We will refer to these items as axioms 1 to 4. A relation satisfying Axiom 2 is used only when M is a free module, so that the passage 'monomial' does make sense.

Lemma 2. *Let $N \subseteq M$ be a submodule, and the relation $\rho \subseteq M \times M$ be such that it satisfies axioms 1. and 3. Then we have*

1. *$M = N + I$;*
2. *$I \cap N \subseteq 0 \iff Z = N$.*

Consequently, if F is a free module and ρ is a strong reduction for $N \subseteq F$ then

$$F = N \oplus I \text{ and } Z = N.$$

Proof. By axioms 1. and 3., $Z \subseteq N$. Assume $I \cap N \subseteq 0$. Let $n \in N$. Then there is an irreducible element $r \in N$ with $n \longrightarrow^\star r$. Thus $r \in I \cap N \subseteq 0$ and so $n \longrightarrow^\star 0$, i.e., $n \in Z$.

Conversely, assume that $Z = N$. Then, for $x \in I \cap N$, $x \longrightarrow^\star 0$ and x is irreducible. Therefore $x = 0$. Consequently $I \cap N \subseteq 0$. □

Note that a relation satisfying axioms 1 - 4 is noetherian and confluent. If F is a free module we will write $\mathrm{NF}(f)$ for the unique normal form of $f \in F$. Thus we always have $f \longrightarrow^\star \mathrm{NF}(f)$.

Theorem 1. *Let $M = Rm_1 + \cdots + Rm_q$ be a finitely generated R-module with free presentation*

$$0 \longrightarrow N \longrightarrow F \xrightarrow{\pi} M \longrightarrow 0$$

where $F = R^q$. Assume given a strong reduction for N with set of irreducibles I. Let $V \subseteq F$ be a monomial K-linear subspace that is ρ-stable and let U be the set of irreducible monomials in V. Then $\pi(U)$ is a K-vector space basis for $\pi(V)$. In particular we obtain that

$$\dim_K \pi(V) = |\pi(U)| = |U|.$$

Proof. Let $f, h \in I$. Then $\pi(f) = \pi(h)$ implies that $f - h \in N \cap I = 0$ whence $\pi|I$ is injective. Since $U = I \cap \Lambda E \cap V \subseteq I$ it is plain that $\pi|U$ is injective, whence $|\pi(U)| = |U|$. Let

$$\sum_j c_j \pi(\mu_j) = 0 \ (c_j \in K, \ \mu_j \in I \cap \Lambda E).$$

Then $\sum_j c_j\mu_j \in N \cap I = 0$. Therefore $c_j = 0\ \forall j$. This demonstrates that $\pi(I \cap \Lambda E)$ is K-linearly independent. Thus $\pi(U) \subseteq \pi(I \cap \Lambda E)$ is linearly independent. Now we may reduce elements $f \in F$ until an irreducible r is reached. Doing this for elements $f \in V$ and taking into account that the reduction stays inside V we obtain an irreducible $r \in V$. Thus

$$\forall f \in V\ \exists r \in I \cap V \text{ with } \pi(r) = \pi(f).$$

Now take $m \in \pi(V)$. $\exists f \in V$ with $m = \pi(f)$. Choose $r \in I \cap V$ with $\pi(r) = \pi(f)$,

$$r = \sum_j c_j\mu_j\ (c_j \in K, \mu_j \in \Lambda E).$$

Since V is monomial, all μ_j are in V and because $r \in I$, all terms of r must be in I. Therefore

$$\mu_j \in V \cap \Lambda E \cap I = U\ \forall j.$$

Consequently

$$m = \pi(r) = \sum_j c_j\pi(\mu_j) \in K \cdot \pi(U).$$

So $\langle \pi(U) \rangle_K = \pi(V)$ and $\pi(U)$ is a K-basis. □

4. GRÖBNER REDUCTION

We return to a monomially filtered ring $R = \bigcup_{r \in \mathbb{N}^p} R_r$ and a finitely generated free R-module F with extended filtration.

DEFINITION 3. *Let $N \subseteq F$ be a submodule. A strong reduction $\rho \subseteq F \times F$ for N is called a* **Gröbner reduction** *for N if it satisfies the axiom*

5. F_r is ρ-stable $\forall r \in \mathbb{N}^p$.

PROPOSITION 1. *Let $N \subseteq F$ be a submodule, $\rho \subseteq F \times F$ be a relation satisfying axioms 1, 3, 5. Then*

$$F_r = N_r + I_r\ \forall r \in \mathbb{N}^p. \tag{4}$$

Consequently, if ρ is a Gröbner reduction for N then

$$F = N \oplus I \text{ and } \forall r \in \mathbb{N}^p\ F_r = N_r \oplus I_r \tag{5}$$

PROOF. Let $f \in F_r$. Reduce f to normal form $f \longrightarrow^* z$. $f \equiv z \mod N$ whence $f - z = n \in N$. By axiom 5, $z \in F_r$. Thus $z \in I \cap F_r = I_r$. As both f and z are in F_r, so is n. Therefore $f = n + z \in N_r + I_r$. □

Equation (4) of Proposition 1 corresponds to 'division with remainder' in the classical theory. Similar, equation (5) describes 'uniqueness of normal forms' in Gröbner basis computations.

For classical monomials it is easy to deal with monomial submodules:

PROPOSITION 2. *Assume that the set Λ of monomials in R satisfies $\Lambda\Lambda \subseteq \Lambda$. Let $N \subseteq F$ be a monomial submodule. Choose a monomial K-linear complement I of N in F (e.g., $I = KS$ where $S = \{t \in \Lambda E : t \notin N\}$). Let p_I denote projection $N \oplus I \longrightarrow I$ and let $\rho \subset F \times F$ be the relation*

$$\rho = p_I|_{F \setminus I}.$$

Then, with arbitrary monomial filtration, ρ is a Gröbner reduction for N.

PROOF. Let N be generated by $X \subseteq \Lambda E$. The general element of N is $n = \sum_{x \in X} a_x x$. The elements $a_x \in R$ are

$$a_x = \sum_{\lambda \in \Lambda} a_x^\lambda \lambda\ (a_x^\lambda \in K) \text{ whence } n = \sum_{x \in X}\sum_{\lambda \in \Lambda} a_x^\lambda \lambda x. \tag{6}$$

Since $\Lambda\Lambda \subseteq \Lambda$, the expressions λx are monomials in ΛE. After (possibly) some cancellations, equation (6) results in the unique representation of n as K-linear combination of ΛE. Since each surviving term is a (monomial) multiple of a generator monomial of N, it is in N, this means, N is a monomial module.

Let $S = \{t \in \Lambda E : t \notin N\}$, and let $I = KS$, the vector space generated by elements from S. By construction, I is a **monomial** subspace of F.

Evidently $N \cap I = 0$.

Write $f \in F$ as K-linear combination of elements of ΛE. We may split this expression as

$$f = \sum_{t \in S} f_t t + \sum_{t \notin S} f_t t \quad (f_t \in K)$$

which shows that $f \in I + N$. Consequently $F = N \oplus I$. The relation ρ results in

$$\rho : f \longrightarrow h \iff f \in F \setminus I \wedge h = p_I(f)$$

Thus, with exception of elements in I, every $f \in F$ reduces to normal form in 1 step. If $f \longrightarrow h$ then $f \in F \setminus I$ and $h = p_I(f) = p_I(n + r) = r$; thus, $f - h = n \in N$, i.e., $f \equiv h \mod N$. Consequently ρ is a strong reduction for N.

Let $f \in F_r$ and $f \longrightarrow h$. By monomiality of F_r, $T(f) \subseteq F_r$. Because $f = n + h$ is a direct decomposition, it follows that $T(h) \subseteq F_r$. Consequently $h \in F_r$ and ρ is a Gröbner reduction. □

The following example is less artificial.

EXAMPLE 3. *$R = K[x_1, \dots, x_n]$, $N \trianglelefteq R$ an ideal, $R_s = \{f \in R \mid \deg f \leq s\}$. Then R is monomially filtered ($p = 1$). The reduction relation coming from a Gröbner basis of N w.r.t a degree lexicographic order obeys axioms 1. to 5. Consequently such a Gröbner basis induces a Gröbner reduction.*

This filtration is not appropriate for arbitrary term orders. For instance in $R = K[x, y]$ with lexicographic order $x \succ y$ and ideal $N = \langle x - y^2 \rangle \triangleleft R$, the polynomial x reduces by means of the Gröbner basis $\{x - y^2\}$ to y^2, thereby leaving the filter space R_1. For arbitrary term orders we have the following.

PROPOSITION 3. *If $N \trianglelefteq R = K[x_1, \dots, x_n]$ is an ideal and G a Gröbner basis of N w.r.t. any term order $\prec$, then for $r \in \mathbb{N}^n$*

$$R_r := \{f \in K[x_1, \dots, x_n] : \forall m \in \mathrm{T}(f) : m \preceq x_1^{r_1} \cdots x_n^{r_n}\}$$

defines a monomial filtration with the additional property

$$m \in R_r \wedge n \preceq m \Rightarrow n \in R_r.$$

Consequently $\longrightarrow_G$ is a Gröbner-reduction w.r.t. $(R_r)_{r \in \mathbb{N}^n}$.

NOTATION 2. *If $\prec$ is a (partial) order on ΛE (of any kind whatsoever), $\lambda \in \Lambda$ and $f \in F$, we will write $f \prec \lambda$ to indicate that $t \prec \lambda\ \forall t \in \mathrm{T}(f)$. In particular, if $\prec$ is a term order, we have $f \preceq \lambda \iff \mathrm{lt}_\preceq(f) \preceq \lambda$.*

5. RELATIVE REDUCTION OVER DIFFERENCE DIFFERENTIAL FIELDS

For details within this section we refer to the paper [12]. As before, we treat the ring D of difference-differential operators on the field K with given derivations $\delta_1, \ldots, \delta_m$ and automorphisms $\sigma_1, \ldots, \sigma_n$, and the finitely generated free D-module F on the set $E = \{e_1, \ldots, e_q\}$. In the paper [12], the troubles caused by negative exponents in reduction relations are solved by introducing the notion of **orthant decomposition**. This is a finite family of monoid homomorphisms $\phi_u \colon \mathbb{N}^n \longrightarrow \mathbb{Z}^n$ each of whose images generate the group $\mathbb{Z}^n$ and being such that

$$\bigcup_u \mathrm{im}(\phi_u) = \mathbb{Z}^n.$$

The decomposition extends naturally to the set

$$\Lambda E \cong \mathbb{N}^m \times \mathbb{Z}^n \times E.$$

Consequently the set of monomials ΛE of F is covered by finitely many isomorphic copies of $\mathbb{N}^m \times \mathbb{N}^n \times E$ in which term orders are well founded and reduction is supposed to behave well. Remark that only the $\mathbb{Z}$-part contributes to the orthant of a monomial $t = \delta^k \sigma^l e_i$, i.e., the position of $l = (l_1, \ldots, l_n)$ in $\bigcup_u \mathrm{im}(\phi_u)$ determines the orthant of t. The orthant decomposition concept provides the basis for a special type of order:

DEFINITION 4. *Given an orthant decomposition on ΛE. A* **generalized term order** *is a total order $\prec$ on ΛE such that*

1. *e_i is the smallest element in Λe_i $(1 \leq i \leq q)$;*
2. *if $\lambda e_i \prec \mu e_j$ and $\nu \in \Lambda$ is in the same orthant as μ then $\nu\lambda e_i \prec \nu\mu e_j$.*

In [10] it is proved that a generalized term order is always a well order.

In [12] the following orders $\prec$ and $\prec'$ on ΛE are considered:

For monomials $t = \delta^k \sigma^l e_i$ in ΛE, $\prec$ is given lexicographically by $(|t|_2, |t|_1, e_i, k, |l|, l)$ and $\prec'$ by $(|t|_1, |t|_2, e_i, k, |l|, l)$. Precisely, for $\lambda = \delta_1^{k_1} \ldots \delta_m^{k_m} \sigma_1^{l_1} \ldots \sigma_n^{l_n}$, $\mu = \delta_1^{r_1} \ldots \delta_m^{r_m} \sigma_1^{s_1} \ldots \sigma_n^{s_n}$

$$\begin{aligned}\lambda e_i \prec \mu e_j \quad :\Longleftrightarrow \quad & (|\lambda|_2, |\lambda|_1, e_i, k_1, \ldots, k_m, |l_1|, \ldots, |l_n|, l_1, \ldots, l_n) \\ & <_{\mathrm{lex}} \\ & (|\mu|_2, |\mu|_1, e_j, r_1, \ldots, r_m, |s_1|, \ldots, |s_n|, s_1, \ldots, s_n)\end{aligned}$$

respectively

$$\begin{aligned}\lambda e_i \prec' \mu e_j \quad :\Longleftrightarrow \quad & (|\lambda|_1, |\lambda|_2, e_i, k_1, \ldots, k_m, |l_1|, \ldots, |l_n|, l_1, \ldots, l_n) \\ & <_{\mathrm{lex}} \\ & (|\mu|_1, |\mu|_2, e_j, r_1, \ldots, r_m, |s_1|, \ldots, |s_n|, s_1, \ldots, s_n)\end{aligned}$$

where the set E of basis elements is assumed ordered by $e_i < e_j \iff i < j$. Both, $\prec$ and $\prec'$ are generalized term orders w.r.t. the canonical orthant decomposition, ($\mathbb{Z}^n$ covered by several arrangements of cartesian products of $\mathbb{N}$ and $-\mathbb{N}$).

Relative reduction, invented in [12] and called **$\prec$-reduction relative to $\prec'$** amounts to the following.

Let $f, g, h \in F$. Then $f \xrightarrow{\mathrm{rel}}_g h$ iff $\exists \lambda \in \Lambda$ such that

$$\mathrm{lt}_\prec(\lambda g) = \mathrm{lt}_\prec(f) \wedge \mathrm{lt}_{\prec'}(\lambda g) \preceq' \mathrm{lt}_{\prec'}(f) \wedge h = f - \frac{\mathrm{lc}_\prec(f)}{\mathrm{lc}_\prec(\lambda g)} \lambda g.$$

Therefore, writing $\longrightarrow_g$ for ordinary leading term reduction w.r.t. $\prec$ by g, we obtain

$$f \xrightarrow{\mathrm{rel}}_g h \iff f \longrightarrow_g h \wedge \mathrm{lt}_{\prec'}(\lambda g) \preceq' \mathrm{lt}_{\prec'}(f).$$

For a set $G \subseteq F$ relative reduction is defined as

$$f \xrightarrow{\mathrm{rel}}_G h \iff \exists g \in G \text{ with } f \xrightarrow{\mathrm{rel}}_g h.$$

PROPOSITION 4. *Let $F_{r,s}$ denote standard filtration of the free D-module F. Then*

$$f \xrightarrow{\mathrm{rel}}_g h \text{ and } f \in F_{r,s} \Rightarrow h \in F_{r,s}$$

that is, $\prec$-reduction relative to $\prec'$ is a reduction compatible with the filtration $(F_{r,s})$. Consequently $\xrightarrow{\mathrm{rel}}_G$ gives rise to a Gröbner reduction.

PROOF. Assume $f \xrightarrow{\mathrm{rel}}_g h$ and $f \in F_{r,s}$. Thus $|f|_1 \leq r$ and $|f|_2 \leq s$. We set

$$u := \mathrm{lt}_\prec(f) = \mathrm{lt}_\prec(\lambda g), u' := \mathrm{lt}_{\prec'}(f), c = \mathrm{lc}_\prec(\lambda g).$$

Thus we may write

$$\begin{aligned} f &= f_u u + \varphi = f_{u'} u' + \varphi' \\ \lambda g &= cu + \psi. \end{aligned}$$

From the assumption we obtain that $\lambda g \preceq' u'$ and

$$h = f - \frac{\mathrm{lc}_\prec(\mathrm{f})}{\mathrm{lc}_\prec(\lambda g)} \lambda g = f_u u + \varphi - \frac{f_u}{c}(cu + \psi) = \varphi - \frac{f_u}{c}\psi.$$

Therefore

$$\mathrm{T}(h) \subseteq \mathrm{T}(\varphi) \cup \mathrm{T}(\psi) = \big(\mathrm{T}(f) \cup \mathrm{T}(\lambda g)\big) \setminus \{u\}.$$

Take $\mu \in \mathrm{T}(h)$. If $\mu \in \mathrm{T}(f)$ then $|\mu|_1 \leq r \wedge |\mu|_2 \leq s$. If $\mu \in \mathrm{T}(\lambda g)$ then, since $\lambda g \preceq' u'$, we obtain $\mu \preceq' u'$ and therefore $|\mu|_1 \leq |u'|_1 \leq r$. Because $u = \mathrm{lt}_\prec(\lambda g)$ we obtain $\mu \prec u$ and thus $|\mu|_2 \leq |u|_2 \leq s$. So in any case we obtain $|\mu|_1 \leq r \wedge |\mu|_2 \leq s$, that is, $|h|_1 \leq r \wedge |h|_2 \leq s$. Therefore $h \in F_{r,s}$. Obviously $f \xrightarrow{\mathrm{rel}}_g h$ implies that $\mathrm{lt}_\prec(h) \prec \mathrm{lt}_\prec(f)$. Consequently $\xrightarrow{\mathrm{rel}}_G$ is a noetherian reduction compatible with the filtration. □

6. EXISTENCE OF GRÖBNER REDUCTION AND ALGORITHMIC ASPECTS

We return to the general setting of a free module F over a ring R of the type introduced in Section 2.

PROPOSITION 5. *Let N be an arbitrary submodule of F. Then there is a strong reduction for N.*

PROOF. Assume that $N \subset F$ whence $\Lambda E \not\subseteq N$. Choose a set S being maximal in the non-empty inductively ordered set $\{T \subseteq \Lambda E \mid KT \cap N = 0\}$. Put $C = KS$. Obviously $F = K^{(\Lambda E)} = N \oplus C$, so consider projection $p_C \colon N \oplus C \longrightarrow C$ and define a reduction relation

$$\rho = \{(f, h) \in F \times F \colon f \notin C \wedge h = p_C(f)\}.$$

It is clear that ρ terminates. The set I of ρ-irreducible elements is C which is a monomial K-linear space. If $f \longrightarrow h$ then $f = n + c \in N \oplus C$ and $h = c$ which shows that $f \equiv h$ mod N. Finally, $I \cap N = C \cap N = 0$, and thus ρ is a strong reduction for N. □

Whereas the situation in Proposition 2 is decidable as long as we know which monomials are in N, the present construction is totally non-constructive. Comparing this with the reduction relation induced by an ordinary Gröbner basis computation we see that, in order to be algorithmically applicable, a Gröbner reduction $\tau \subseteq F \times F$ for N has to be an extension of ρ (i.e. such that $\rho^\star \subseteq \tau^\star$) being strong enough to be decidable but weak enough to terminate. It depends on the nature of the ring R how to design such a reduction for algorithmic purposes. The same remark applies to the choice of a filtration. In our examples they have been selected with the aim to weaken usual Gröbner basis reduction w.r.t. a term order.

Now assume we are concerned with two rings and modules joined by a homomorphism, precisely, consider a ring $R = K^{(\Lambda)}$, a free module $F = Re_1 \oplus \cdots \oplus Re_q$ and a submodule $N \subseteq F$. Let $S = K^{(\Omega)}$ be another such ring and let $\varphi\colon S \longrightarrow R$ denote a surjective homomorphism of rings such that $\varphi(K) = K$ and $\varphi(\Omega) = \Lambda$. Further let $G = Se_1 \oplus \cdots \oplus Se_q$ be the free S-module (with rank S = rank R). We extend the map φ to a homomorphism of S-modules denoted by the same symbol

$$\varphi\colon G \longrightarrow F, \quad \sum_{i=1}^{q} r_i e_i \mapsto \sum_{i=1}^{q} \varphi(r_i) e_i.$$

Proposition 6. *If $\sigma \subseteq G \times G$ is a strong reduction for $\varphi^{-1}(N)$ then there is a strong reduction $\rho \subseteq F \times F$ such that*

$$\varphi(\mathrm{NF}(g)) = \mathrm{NF}(\varphi(g)).$$

Further, if σ is a Gröbner reduction for $\varphi^{-1}(N)$ w.r.t. a monomial filtration $S = \bigcup_{r \in \mathbb{N}^p} S_r$ then ρ is a Gröbner reduction for N w.r.t. filtration $R = \bigcup_{r \in \mathbb{N}^p} \varphi(S_r)$.

Proof. Let $I = \{g \in G : \nexists z \text{ with } g \longrightarrow z\}$ denote the monomial subspace of irreducibles in G. By Proposition 1 we have that $G = \varphi^{-1}(N) \oplus I$. Then $F = N \oplus \varphi(I)$. Let $\pi\colon F \longrightarrow \varphi(I)$ denote projection. We define the relation $\rho \subseteq F \times F$ by

$$f \longrightarrow_\rho h \iff f \notin \varphi(I) \wedge h = \pi(f).$$

It is clear that ρ is noetherian. $\varphi(I)$ is the K-space of ρ-irreducibles. $\varphi(I)$ is monomial. Indeed, if $f = \varphi(i) \in \varphi(I)$ with $i = \sum_{t \in \Omega E} i_t t \in I$ then

$$f = \sum_{t \in \Omega E} \varphi(i_t)\varphi(t). \tag{7}$$

By monomiality of I we know that all monomials t occuring in this sum are in I and so the corresponding $\varphi(t)$ are in $\varphi(I)$. Since $\varphi(\Omega E) = \Lambda E$, i.e., φ maps monomials in G onto monomials in F, by collecting terms in (7) we see, that $\mathrm{T}(f) \subseteq \varphi(I)$ demonstrating Axiom 2. Axiom 3 and 4 are obvious.

Take $g \in G$ and let $i = \mathrm{NF}(g)$ w.r.t. σ. Then $g \longrightarrow_\sigma^\star i$ and $g - i = \nu \in \varphi^{-1}(N)$ (according to Ax 3 for σ). $\varphi(g) = \varphi(\nu) + \varphi(i) \in N \oplus \varphi(I)$. If $\nu \in \ker\varphi$ then $\varphi(g) = \varphi(i)$ equals its own normal form. If $\nu \notin \ker\varphi$ then $\varphi(g) \longrightarrow_\rho \varphi(i)$. In both cases we derive $\varphi(i) = \mathrm{NF}(\varphi(g))$ w.r.t. ρ.

Now assume that $S = \bigcup_{r \in \mathbb{N}^p} S_r$ is a filtration and that σ is a Gröbner reduction w.r.t. the extended filtration $G_r = S_r e_1 \oplus \cdots \oplus S_r e_q$. Then Proposition 1 assures that $G_r = \varphi^{-1}(N)_r \oplus I_r \ \forall r \in \mathbb{N}^p$. By Lemma 1, $R_r = \varphi(S_r)$ is a filtration on R and $F_r = \varphi(G_r)$ yields the extended filtration $F = \bigcup_{r \in \mathbb{N}^p} F_r$. Let $f \longrightarrow_\rho h$ and $f \in F_r$. There is a $g \in G_r$ with $\varphi(g) = f$. Let $i = \mathrm{NF}(g)$. Then $i \in G_r$ and so $\varphi(i) \in \varphi(G_r) = F_r$. But $\varphi(i) = \mathrm{NF}(f)$ and therefore we see that $h \in F_r$. Consequently ρ is a Groebner reduction. $\square$

Applying the last proposition to the ring D provides an alternative method for constructing a Gröbner reduction in free D-modules.

Corollary 1. *Consider the ring D (as mentioned on page 2) and let S be the ring constructed from the same data as D but using positive exponents exclusively. More precisely, set $\tau_j = \sigma_j^{-1}$ and let S be the free K-vector space on the set of expressions*

$$\delta_1^{k_1} \cdots \delta_m^{k_m} \sigma^{l_1} \cdots \sigma_n^{l_n} \tau_1^{p_1} \cdots \tau_n^{p_n} \quad (k_i, l_j, p_j \in \mathbb{N})$$

with product being formally the same as the one in D (cf. Equation (2)). Let φ be the K-linear map $S \longrightarrow D$ defined on basis elements

$$\varphi(\delta^k \sigma^l \tau^p) = \delta^k \sigma^{l-p} \quad (k \in \mathbb{N}^m, l, p \in \mathbb{N}^n).$$

Then φ is a surjective homomorphism of rings and Proposition 6 applies. That is, given a submodule N of a finitely generated free D-module F, we may derive a Gröbner reduction for N by means of one constructed in a corresponding free module over S.

Of course the purpose is to represent the ring D as the quotient of S by $\ker\varphi$

$$D \cong S / \langle \sigma_1\tau_1 - 1, \ldots, \sigma_n\tau_n - 1 \rangle$$

This construction can be used to execute computational tasks over D omitting negative exponents.

7. DIMENSION OF FILTER SPACES AND THE HILBERT POLYNOMIAL

In the general situation consider a finitely generated module M over an arbitrary monomially filtered ring R

$$R = \bigcup_{r \in \mathbb{N}^p} R_r \quad M = Rm_1 + \cdots + Rm_q.$$

Choose a free presentation

$$0 \longrightarrow N \longrightarrow F \xrightarrow{\pi} M \longrightarrow 0$$

with $F = R^q$. We get the following corollary.

Corollary 2. *Let F be equipped with extended filtration from R and consider M with the filtration $M_r = \pi(F_r)$. For $r \in \mathbb{N}^p$ let U_r be the set of irreducible monomials in the filter space F_r. Assume given a Gröbner reduction for N. Then the sets $\pi(U_r)$ provide K-vector space bases for the spaces M_r. In particular*

$$\dim_K M_r = |\pi(U_r)| = |U_r| \quad (r \in \mathbb{N}^p).$$

Proof. Apply Theorem 1 with $V = F_r$. $\square$

Combining this corollary with Proposition 2 gives:

Corollary 3. *Assume that the monomials in R satisfy $\Lambda\Lambda \subseteq \Lambda$ and let $N \subseteq F$ be a monomial submodule. Let $S = \{t \in \Lambda E : t \notin N\}$. Then, for arbitrary monomial filtration $R = \bigcup_{r \in \mathbb{N}^p} R_r$ and extended filtration $F = \bigcup_{r \in \mathbb{N}^p} F_r$, we have*

$$\dim_K (F/N)_r = |S_r|.$$

PROOF. Let $I = KS$. Then $I \cap \Lambda E = S$ und thus $I \cap \Lambda E \cap F_r = S \cap F_r = S_r$. Using Corollary 2 proves the assertion. $\square$

We may now determine the Hilbert function for filtered modules. This is most simple for monomial modules.

EXAMPLE 4. *Let $R = K[x, y]$ and N the ideal*

$$N = \langle x^4y^3,\ x^2y^5,\ 2x^5y^2 - 4x^3y^5 \rangle.$$

It is easy to see that N is generated by the set

$$G = \{x^4y^3, x^2y^5, x^5y^2\}.$$

Thus, N is a monomial ideal and G is a Gröbner basis for N (w.r.t. arbitrary term-order).

Thus, Corollary 3 is applicable. For example when

$$R_k = \{f \in D\colon \deg(f) \le k\} \text{ and}$$

$$R_{r,s} = \{f \in D\colon \deg_x(f) \le r \wedge \deg_y(f) \le s\}$$

counting irreducible monomials that are not multiples of elements in G produces the dimensions in R/N. Let

$$\begin{array}{rcl} p_1(k) & = & \#\text{ irred. monomials in } R_k \\ p_2(r,s) & = & \#\text{ irred. monomials in } R_{r,s} \end{array}$$

k	7	8	9	10	11	12
$p_1(k)$	33	37	41	45	49	53

For example, there are $\binom{8+2}{2} = 45$ monomials in 2 variables of total degree ≤ 8. From this 45 monomials, 37 monomials are irreducible, leaving 8 reducible elements w.r.t. graded lexicographic order. They are given by:

$$R_8 \setminus I = \{x^5y^2, x^6y^2, x^4y^3, y^3x^5, x^4y^4, x^2y^5, x^3y^5, x^2y^6\}.$$

From the 8 elements in $R_8 \setminus I$ there are 3 elements of degree 7, hence, in two variables, there are in total $\binom{7+2}{2} = 36$ monomials of degree 7, 3 of them reducible modulo G, giving us the value 33.

Since the degree of the Hilbert polynomial is bounded by the number of variables, interpolation gives

$$\begin{array}{rcl} p_1(k) & = & 4k + 5 \ (k \ge 7) \\ p_2(r,s) & = & 2r + 2s + 7 \ ((r,s) \ge_\pi (4,4)). \end{array}$$

From this we see that the growth of elements is linear *by increasing the degree in one direction. Moreover p_2 is symmetric ($p_2(r,s) = p_2(s,r)$) which shows that the growth of dimension is the same in x and y direction.*

An obvious relation between $R_{r,s}$ and R_{r+s} is

$$\forall\,(r,s) \in \mathbb{N}^2\colon R_{r,s} \subseteq R_{r+s}.$$

A less obvious relation is the following. We have that

$$\begin{array}{rcl} \#\text{ irred. elements in } R_{k,k} & = & p_2(k,k) = 4k + 7 \\ \#\text{ irred. elements in } R_{k+k} & = & p_1(k+k) = 8k + 5. \end{array}$$

Consequently $p_2(k,k) \le p_1(k+k)$ for $k \ge 1$.

8. COMPUTATION OF MULTIVARIATE DIFFERENCE DIFFERENTIAL DIMENSION POLYNOMIALS

In the general case, Corollary 2 applies. We will generalize the dimension polynomial computed in [12].

For example, using Corollary 2 to a finitely generated module over the ring D using relative reduction, the resulting sets U_r coincide with those computed in [12]. We will now set up a refined filtration of the ring D, controlled by a partition of the basic operators in the difference-differential field K. After designing a Gröbner reduction for a submodule, Corollary 2 will give us an improved picture of the filter spaces in the quotient.

Consider the sets $\Delta = \{\delta_1, \ldots, \delta_m\}$, $\Sigma = \{\sigma_1, \ldots, \sigma_n\}$ of the difference-differential field K.

We divide Δ and Σ into p respectively q pairwise disjoint subsets

$$\Delta = \Delta_1 \cup \cdots \cup \Delta_p \text{ and } \Sigma = \Sigma_1 \cup \cdots \cup \Sigma_q \tag{8}$$

where

$$\begin{aligned} \Delta_1 &= \{\delta_1, \ldots, \delta_{m_1}\} \\ \Delta_k &= \{\delta_{m_1+\cdots+m_{k-1}+1}, \ldots, \delta_{m_1+\cdots+m_k}\}, \quad (2 \le k \le p) \end{aligned}$$

and $m_1 + \cdots + m_p = m$. Similar for Σ

$$\begin{aligned} \Sigma_1 &= \{\sigma_1, \ldots, \sigma_{n_1}\} \\ \Sigma_k &= \{\sigma_{n_1+\cdots+n_{k-1}+1}, \ldots, \sigma_{n_1+\cdots+n_k}\}, \quad (2 \le k \le q) \end{aligned}$$

where $n_1 + \cdots + n_q = n$.

DEFINITION 5. *For a monomial*

$$\lambda = \delta_1^{k_1} \cdots \delta_m^{k_m} \sigma_1^{l_1} \cdots \sigma_n^{l_n} \in \Lambda$$

we define

$$\begin{aligned} |\lambda|_{\Delta_j} &= \sum_{\delta_i \in \Delta_j} k_i \quad (1 \le j \le p) \\ |\lambda|_{\Sigma_j} &= \sum_{\sigma_i \in \Sigma_j} |l_i| \quad (1 \le j \le q) \end{aligned}$$

For a general difference-differential operator

$$a = \sum_{\lambda \in \Lambda} a_\lambda \lambda \in D$$

we set

$$|a|_\Phi := \max\{|\lambda|_\Phi\colon \lambda \in T(a)\},$$

with $\Phi \in \{\Delta_1, \ldots, \Delta_p, \Sigma_1, \ldots, \Sigma_q\}$.

The following device defines a $p+q$-variate filtration on D. For $r \in \mathbb{N}^{p+q}$ set

$$D_r = \{u \in D\colon \forall_{1 \le i \le p}\ |u|_{\Delta_i} \le r_i \wedge \forall_{1 \le j \le q}\ |u|_{\Sigma_j} \le r_{p+j}\}. \tag{9}$$

DEFINITION 6. *Let M be a Δ-Σ module over a Δ-Σ field with m derivations and n automorphisms, partitioned as given in (8) and set $s = p + q$. The numerical polynomial $p(t_1, \ldots, t_s)$ is called difference-differential dimension polynomial associated to M, if*

1. $\deg(p) \le m + n$

2. $p(r_1,\dots,r_s) = \dim_K M_{r_1,\dots,r_s}$ *for all* $(r_1,\dots,r_s) \in \mathbb{N}^s$ *large enough.*

By a change of the vector space basis of polynomials of degree less than or equal to s to the Newton basis p admits a canonical representation of the form

$$\sum_{i_1=0}^{n_1}\sum_{i_2=0}^{n_2}\cdots\sum_{i_s=0}^{n_s} a_{i_1,i_2,\dots,i_s}\binom{t_1+i_1}{i_1}\binom{t_2+i_2}{i_2}\cdots\binom{t_s+i_s}{i_s},$$

s.t. $a_{i_1,i_2,\dots,i_s} \in \mathbb{Z}$, *the dimension polynomial mentioned in [8, 9].*

THEOREM 2. *Let K be a* $\Delta-\Sigma$ *field and M a finitely generated difference-differential module. Produce a partition of the sets* Δ, Σ *as described in (8) and equip the operator ring D with the filtration described in (9). Extend the filtration to the finite free presentation*

$$0 \longrightarrow N \longrightarrow F \stackrel{\pi}{\longrightarrow} M \longrightarrow 0$$

where F has K-basis E, and let $\prec$ *be a generalized term order on* ΛE*. If G is a Gröbner basis of N then the cardinality of the sets*

$$U_r = \{t \in \Lambda E \cap F_r : \forall_{g\in G}\forall_{\lambda\in\Lambda} \\ (t = \mathrm{lt}_\prec(\lambda g) \Rightarrow \exists_i\, |\lambda g|_{\Delta_i} > r_i \vee \exists_j\, |\lambda g|_{\Sigma_j} > r_{p+j})\}$$

provide the values of the Hilbert function of M, i.e.,

$$\dim_K M_r = |U_r| \quad \forall r \in \mathbb{N}^{p+q}.$$

PROOF. The relation

$$f \longrightarrow h \iff \exists_{g\in G}\,\exists_{\lambda\in\Lambda}\ \mathrm{lt}_\prec(\lambda g) = \mathrm{lt}_\prec(f)\wedge \\ \forall_{1\le i\le p}\,|\lambda g|_{\Delta_i} \le |f|_{\Delta_i} \wedge \forall_{1\le j\le q}\,|\lambda g|_{\Sigma_j} \le |f|_{\Sigma_j}\wedge \\ h = f - \frac{\mathrm{lc}_\prec(f)}{\mathrm{lc}_\prec(\lambda g)}\lambda g$$

defines a Gröbner reduction for N and Corollary 2 is applicable. □

9. CONCLUSIONS

We have set up a theory of reduction intended to extend Gröbner basis computations to modules over (possibly) noncommutative rings which contain a field as a subring. This applies in particular to rings of difference-differential operators. Assuming a multivariate filtration in the ground ring compatible with a given vector space basis, we have formulated natural axioms such a reduction should obey. It was possible to demonstrate that relative reduction as introduced in [12] as well as the reduction relations defined by classical Gröbner bases in polynomial rings or free modules over them can be viewed as an instance of our axioms. Further we have proved a general theorem on the dimension of filter spaces in finitely generated modules over such rings. The concepts have been demonstrated to be applicable to the computation of the Hilbert polynomial of multivariate difference-differential modules.

So far we have not given a general algorithm for computing such a reduction relation in nontrivial instances. In a continuing paper we plan to refine our approach and by giving additional features to the data of the ground ring, to formulate Buchberger criteria for such reductions. In doing so we try to make our approach suitable for actual computations in such general rings.

10. ACKNOWLEDGMENTS

The authors would like to thank the professors Meng Zhou and Franz Winkler for their helpful hints and support. Many thanks also to the reviewers for their valuable hints.

11. REFERENCES

[1] B. Buchberger. *Ein Algorithmus zum Auffinden der Basiselemente des Restklassenringes nach einem nulldimensionalen Polynomideal (An Algorithm for Finding the Basis Elements in the Residue Class Ring Modulo a Zero Dimensional Polynomial Ideal).* PhD thesis, Mathematical Institute, University of Innsbruck, Austria, 1965. English translation in J. of Symbolic Computation, Special Issue on Logic, Mathematics, and Computer Science: Interactions. Vol. 41, Number 3-4, Pages 475–511, 2006.

[2] C. Dönch. Characterization of relative Gröbner bases. *Journal of Symbolic Computation*, 55:19–29, 2013.

[3] E. R. Kolchin. *The notion of dimension in the theory of algebraic differential equationes. Bull. Amer. Math. Soc.* 70, 570–573, 1964.

[4] E. R. Kolchin. *Differential Algebra and Algebraic Groups.* Academic Press Inc, June 1973.

[5] M. V. Kondratieva, A. B. Levin, M. A.V., and P. E. V. *Differential and Difference Dimension Polynomials.* Mathematics and Its Applications. Springer, 1998.

[6] A. Levin. Reduced Gröbner bases, free difference-differential modules and difference-differential dimension polynomials. *Journal of Symbolic Computation*, 30(4):357–382, 2000.

[7] A. Levin. Gröbner bases with respect to several term orderings and multivariate dimension polynomials. In *Proceedings of the 2007 International Symposium on Symbolic and Algebraic Computation*, ISSAC '07, pages 251–260, New York, NY, USA, 2007. ACM.

[8] A. Levin. Multivariate Difference-Differential Dimension Polynomials. *ArXiv e-prints*, July 2012.

[9] A. Levin. Multivariate Difference-Differential Dimension Polynomials and New Invariants of Difference-Differential Field Extensions. *ArXiv e-prints*, Feb. 2013.

[10] M. Zhou and F. Winkler. Gröbner bases in difference-differential modules. In *Proceedings of the 2006 international symposium on Symbolic and algebraic computation*, ISSAC '06, pages 353–360, New York, NY, USA, 2006. ACM.

[11] M. Zhou and F. Winkler. Computing difference-differential Groebner Bases and difference-differential dimension polynomials. RISC Report Series 07-01, Research Institute for Symbolic Computation (RISC), Johannes Kepler University Linz, Schloss Hagenberg, 4232 Hagenberg, Austria, January 2007.

[12] M. Zhou and F. Winkler. Computing difference-differential dimension polynomials by relative Gröbner bases in difference-differential modules. *Journal of Symbolic Computation*, 43(10):726–745, 2008.

Separable Automorphisms on Matrix Algebras over Finite Field Extensions: Applications to Ideal Codes*

José Gómez-Torrecillas
Universidad de Granada
Dept. of Algebra and CITIC
gomezj@ugr.es

F. J. Lobillo
Universidad de Granada
Dept. of Algebra and CITIC
jlobillo@ugr.es

Gabriel Navarro
Universidad de Granada
Dept. of Computer Science and A. I., and CITIC
gnavarro@ugr.es

ABSTRACT

Let $\mathbb{F} \subseteq \mathbb{K}$ an extension of finite fields and $A = \mathcal{M}_n(\mathbb{K})$ be the ring of square matrices of order n over $\mathbb{K}$ viewed as an algebra over $\mathbb{F}$. Given an $\mathbb{F}$–automorphism σ on A, the Ore extension $A[z;\sigma]$ may be used to built certain convolutional codes, namely, the ideal codes. We provide an algorithm to decide if the automorphism σ on A is a separable returning the corresponding separability element p. In this case p is also a separability element for the extension $\mathbb{F}[z] \subseteq A[z;\sigma]$, and as a consequence ideal codes are generated by idempotents in $A[z;\sigma]$, which can be computed applying previous algorithms of the authors.

Categories and Subject Descriptors

E.4 [**Data**]: Coding and Information Theory—*error control codes*

General Terms

Algorithms, Theory

Keywords

Ideal code; separability element; Ore polynomial

1. INTRODUCTION, BASIC NOTIONS, AND STATEMENT OF THE PROBLEM

Convolutional codes are error correcting codes widely used in engineering. They can be understood as direct summands of free modules of finite rank over a polynomial ring $\mathbb{F}[z]$ where $\mathbb{F} = \mathbb{F}_q$ is a finite field, see [10] for details. A straightforward extension of the notion of cyclic linear codes to convolutional codes is not enough as the pioneer work [15] shows. It is necessary to enrich the algebraic structure of convolutional codes with non–commutative multiplication. Concretely, given a (possibly non commutative) $\mathbb{F}$–algebra A of finite dimension m, and $\sigma \in \mathrm{Aut}_{\mathbb{F}}(A)$, an algebra automorphism, we can built the ring $A[z;\sigma]$ of Ore polynomials over A. The elements of $A[z;\sigma]$ are polynomials in z with coefficients on the right, and the multiplication is derived from the rule $az = z\sigma(a)$ for all $a \in A$. The action given by left multiplication of $\mathbb{F}[z]$ on $A[z;\sigma]$ makes $A[z;\sigma]$ a free $\mathbb{F}[z]$–module of rank m. Recall from [13] that an ideal code is a left ideal $I \leq A[z;\sigma]$ such that I is a direct summand of $A[z;\sigma]$ as an $\mathbb{F}[z]$–module. So, ideal codes are convolutional codes. This additional algebraic structure has been studied from the perspective of cyclic convolutional codes in [3, 13, 6], where the separability hypothesis on the ground algebra A plays, implicitly in [3, 13], a prominent role.

A central problem is to decide whether a given ideal code I is generated as a left ideal of $A[z;\sigma]$ by an idempotent element, and how to compute it. This problem is addressed in [6, 5] by mean of a new systematic approach based on the notion of a separable ring extension. Recall from [7] that a ring extension $C \subseteq B$ is called separable if the multiplication map $\mu : B \otimes_C B \to B$ is a split epimorphism of B–bimodules, i.e. if there exists a homomorphism of B–bimodules $\beta : B \to B \otimes_C B$ such that $\mu\beta(f) = f$ for all $f \in B$. Equivalently there exists $p \in B \otimes_C B$ satisfying $rp = pr$ for all $r \in B$, and $\mu(p) = 1$. Obviously, in this case, $\beta(1) = p$. The element p is called a *separability element* of the extension. If C is a subring of the center of B, then the extension $C \subseteq B$ is separable if and only if B is a separable C–algebra in the sense of [2].

By [6, Proposition 17], if $\mathbb{F}[z] \subseteq A[z;\sigma]$ is a separable ring extension then each ideal code is a direct summand as left ideal of $A[z;\sigma]$, and therefore it is generated by an idempotent, which can be computed using [6, Algorithm 1] once a separability element is known. One way to prove that $\mathbb{F}[z] \subseteq A[z;\sigma]$ is separable is to lift a separability element of the extension $\mathbb{F} \subseteq A$, if it is exists. This can be done as a consequence of [6, Theorem 6]: let $\sigma^{\otimes} = \sigma \otimes \sigma : A \otimes_{\mathbb{F}} A \to A \otimes_{\mathbb{F}} A$ and let p be a separability element of the extension $\mathbb{F} \subseteq A$, if $\sigma^{\otimes}(p) = p$ then p is a separability element for the extension $\mathbb{F}[z] \subseteq A[z;\sigma]$. An automorphism is called separable if there exists a separability element $p \in A \otimes_{\mathbb{F}} A$ such that $\sigma^{\otimes}(p) = p$. This leads to a computational problem.

> Is it possible to decide if a given $\sigma \in \mathrm{Aut}_{\mathbb{F}}(A)$ is separable?

In [4] we give a complete answer for the case $A = \mathcal{M}_n(\mathbb{F})$

*Research partially supported by grants MTM2013-41992-P and TIN2013-41990-R from Ministerio de Economía y Competitividad of the Spanish Government and from FEDER

ISSAC'15, July 6–9, 2015, Bath, United Kingdom.

ACM 978-1-4503-3435-8/15/07 ...$15.00.
DOI: http://dx.doi.org/10.1145/2755996.2756671.

by means of an algorithm that computes, if it exists, a separability element p of A over $\mathbb{F}$ such that $\sigma^{\otimes}(p) = p$. In this paper we deal with the case of the $\mathbb{F}$–algebra $A = \mathcal{M}_n(\mathbb{K})$, where $\mathbb{F} \subseteq \mathbb{K}$ is a finite field extension of degree t, and σ is any $\mathbb{F}$–automorphism of A. The examples of Section 3 have been implemented by using the mathematical software SageMath [16].

We refer to [12] for properties and notation of finite fields, which are going to be used without further mention. The extension $\mathbb{F} \subseteq A$ is separable because $\mathbb{K}$ is a separable algebra over $\mathbb{F}$ (by, e.g., [11, Proposition III.3.4]) and $\mathbb{K} \subseteq A$ is separable [2, Example II], and [2, Proposition II.1.12] applies. Hence the main result of this paper (Theorem 1) is an algorithm to decide whether a given automorphism $\sigma \in \mathrm{Aut}_{\mathbb{F}}(A)$ is separable, and compute the corresponding separability idempotent if it exists. This algorithm is based on the description of all separability elements of A over $\mathbb{F}$ provided in Proposition 1. The key of this description is the analysis of the center of the A–bimodule $A \otimes_{\mathbb{F}} A$, which is done by means of Artin-Wedderburn's Theory, since these algebras are semi-simple. We refer to [14, Chapter 3] as a source of information for the theory of semi-simple algebras, and to [2] for separable algebras.

Let us fix some notation for this paper. Given any finite dimensional vector space V, we denote $\mathfrak{v}(v)$ the coordinates of $v \in V$ with respect to a fixed basis. From now on we fix a normal basis $\{\alpha^{q^0}, \ldots, \alpha^{q^{t-1}}\}$ of $\mathbb{K}$ as $\mathbb{F}$–vector space, and we denote $\{\beta^{q^0}, \ldots, \beta^{q^{t-1}}\}$ its dual basis. By using the properties of the trace function, it follows that, for all $\gamma \in \mathbb{K}$,

$$\mathfrak{v}(\gamma) = (\mathrm{Tr}_{\mathbb{K}/\mathbb{F}}(\gamma\beta^{q^0}), \ldots, \mathrm{Tr}_{\mathbb{K}/\mathbb{F}}(\gamma\beta^{q^{t-1}}))$$

are the coordinates of γ. Let V be a $\mathbb{K}$–vector space with basis $B = \{e_i \mid 0 \leq i \leq n-1\}$. Then V is an $\mathbb{F}$–vector space with basis $\widetilde{B} = \{\alpha^{q^k} e_i \mid 0 \leq k \leq t-1, 0 \leq i \leq n-1\}$, which is ordered lexicographically. We use the same notation

$$\mathfrak{v} : V \to \mathbb{K}^n, \qquad \mathfrak{v} : V \to \mathbb{F}^{nt}$$

to denote the linear map which associates to each vector its coordinates with respect to B and $\widetilde{B}$ respectively. It will be clear from the context which coordinates we are using.

Let $\gamma \in \mathbb{K}$. The map $\rho_\gamma : \mathbb{K} \to \mathbb{K}$ defined by $\rho_\gamma(\delta) = \gamma\delta$ is $\mathbb{F}$–linear, hence there exists an unique matrix $\mathfrak{m}(\gamma) \in \mathcal{M}_t(\mathbb{F})$ such that $\mathfrak{v}(\gamma\delta) = \mathfrak{v}(\delta)\mathfrak{m}(\gamma)$. The map

$$\begin{aligned} \mathfrak{m} : \mathbb{K} &\to \mathcal{M}_t(\mathbb{F}) \\ \gamma &\mapsto \mathfrak{m}(\gamma) \end{aligned}$$

is an injective homomorphism of $\mathbb{F}$–algebras. By linear algebra

$$\mathfrak{m}(\gamma) = \begin{pmatrix} \mathfrak{v}(\alpha^{q^0}\gamma) \\ \vdots \\ \mathfrak{v}(\alpha^{q^{t-1}}\gamma) \end{pmatrix} = \begin{pmatrix} \mathrm{Tr}_{\mathbb{K}/\mathbb{F}}(\alpha^{q^0}\gamma\beta^{q^0}) & \ldots & \mathrm{Tr}_{\mathbb{K}/\mathbb{F}}(\alpha^{q^0}\gamma\beta^{q^{t-1}}) \\ \vdots & \ddots & \vdots \\ \mathrm{Tr}_{\mathbb{K}/\mathbb{F}}(\alpha^{q^{t-1}}\gamma\beta^{q^0}) & \ldots & \mathrm{Tr}_{\mathbb{K}/\mathbb{F}}(\alpha^{q^{t-1}}\gamma\beta^{q^{t-1}}) \end{pmatrix}.$$

Since $\mathfrak{v}(1)\mathfrak{m}(\gamma) = \mathfrak{v}(\gamma)$, it follows that the map

$$\begin{aligned} \mathfrak{f} : \mathcal{M}_t(\mathbb{F}) &\to \mathbb{K} \\ \Gamma &\mapsto \mathfrak{v}(1)\Gamma\left(\alpha^{q^0}, \ldots, \alpha^{q^{t-1}}\right)^{\mathrm{T}} \end{aligned}$$

is an $\mathbb{F}$–linear left inverse of $\mathfrak{m}$.

Let $M = (m_{ij}) \in \mathcal{M}_{r\times s}(\mathbb{K})$ and consider the $\mathbb{K}$–linear map $\cdot M : \mathbb{K}^r \to \mathbb{K}^s$ given by right multiplication. Let B and B' be the canonical bases of $\mathbb{K}^r$ and $\mathbb{K}^s$ respectively. Let us also call

$$\begin{aligned} \mathfrak{m} : \mathcal{M}_{r\times s}(\mathbb{K}) &\to \mathcal{M}_{rt\times st}(\mathbb{F}) \\ (m_{ij}) &\mapsto \mathfrak{m}\big(m_{ij}\big) = \big(\mathfrak{m}(m_{ij})\big) \end{aligned}$$

the componentwise extension of $\mathfrak{m}$ to $\mathcal{M}_{r\times s}(\mathbb{K})$. As before we can define an $\mathbb{F}$–linear left inverse of $\mathfrak{m}$: given $M \in \mathcal{M}_{rt\times st}(\mathbb{F})$, we can represent it as the block matrix

$$M = \begin{pmatrix} M_{0,0} & \cdots & M_{0,s-1} \\ \vdots & \ddots & \vdots \\ M_{r-1,0} & \cdots & M_{r-1,s-1} \end{pmatrix}$$

where $M_{i,j} \in \mathcal{M}_t(\mathbb{F})$, hence

$$\begin{aligned} \mathfrak{f} : \mathcal{M}_{rt\times st}(\mathbb{F}) &\to \mathcal{M}_{r\times s}(\mathbb{K}) \\ M &\mapsto (\mathfrak{f}(M_{i,j}))_{r\times s} \end{aligned}$$

is the corresponding left inverse. Observe that if we have two matrices M, N of appropriate sizes, we have

$$\mathfrak{m}(MN) = \mathfrak{m}(M)\mathfrak{m}(N),$$

so in particular

$$\mathfrak{m} : A \to \mathcal{M}_{nt}(\mathbb{F})$$

is a monomorphism of $\mathbb{F}$–algebras. Since

$$\alpha^{q^k} e_i M = \begin{pmatrix} & 0 & \\ & \vdots & \\ \alpha^{q^k} m_{i,0} & \cdots & \alpha^{q^k} m_{i,s-1} \\ & \vdots & \\ & 0 & \end{pmatrix},$$

the following lemma follows easily.

Lemma 1. *The matrix associated to the $\mathbb{F}$–linear map $\cdot M$ with respect to the bases $\widetilde{B}$ and $\widetilde{B'}$ is the block matrix*

$$\mathfrak{m}(M) = \big(\mathfrak{m}(m_{ij})\big)_{r\times s} \in \mathcal{M}_{rt\times st}(\mathbb{F}).$$

Let $M \in \mathcal{M}_{n\times m}(\mathbb{K})$ and $N \in \mathcal{M}_{u\times v}(\mathbb{K})$. The Kronecker product $M \boxtimes N$ is the matrix

$$\begin{pmatrix} m_{0,0}N & m_{0,1}N & \cdots & m_{0,m-1}N \\ m_{1,0}N & m_{1,1}N & \cdots & m_{1,m-1}N \\ \vdots & \vdots & \ddots & \vdots \\ m_{n-1,0}N & m_{n-1,1}N & \ldots & m_{n-1,m-1}N \end{pmatrix} \in \mathcal{M}_{nu\times mv}(\mathbb{K}).$$

We refer to [8, Chapter 4] as a source of well known properties of the Kronecker product that we will use. For the convenience of the reader, we summarize two of them.

1. Let M, N, P, Q be matrices over $\mathbb{K}$ of appropriate sizes to allow products. Then
$$MPN = Q \iff \mathfrak{v}(P)(M^{\mathrm{T}} \boxtimes N) = \mathfrak{v}(Q). \qquad (1)$$
2. Let $f : \mathbb{K}^n \to \mathbb{K}^m$ and $g : \mathbb{K}^u \to \mathbb{K}^v$ be linear maps represented by the matrices $M \in \mathcal{M}_{n\times m}(\mathbb{K})$ and $N \in \mathcal{M}_{u\times v}(\mathbb{K})$. The matrix representing $f \otimes g$ with respect to the canonical bases of $\mathbb{K}^n \otimes \mathbb{K}^u$ and $\mathbb{K}^m \otimes \mathbb{K}^v$ is $M \boxtimes N$.

Remark 1. As observed for example in [9, Proposition 4.10], $\mathcal{M}_r(\mathbb{F}) \otimes \mathcal{M}_s(\mathbb{F})$ is isomorphic to $\mathcal{M}_{rs}(\mathbb{F})$ via the Kronecker product. We denote by $K_{r,s}$ the matrix associated to this isomorphism in the canonical bases. This is a permutation matrix and it is possible to provide a general description of $K_{r,s}$, albeit it is quite tedious.

We denote by $\tau : \mathbb{K} \to \mathbb{K}$ the Frobenius automorphism, i.e $\tau(\gamma) = \gamma^q$, where q is the number of elements of $\mathbb{F}$. Let $A = \mathcal{M}_n(\mathbb{K})$ and let $\sigma \in \mathrm{Aut}_{\mathbb{F}}(A)$. By [1, Theorem 2.4] there exists a regular matrix $U \in A$ and $0 \leq h \leq t-1$ such that $\sigma = \sigma_U \circ \widehat{\tau^h}$, where σ_U is the inner automorphism associated to U, i.e. $\sigma_U(a) = UaU^{-1}$, and $\widehat{\tau^h}$ is the componentwise extension of τ^h to A. Next lemmas describe the matrices over $\mathbb{F}$ associated to σ_U and $\widehat{\tau^h}$.

LEMMA 2. *The matrix associated to the* $\mathbb{F}$*–linear map* $\sigma_U : A \to A$ *is* $M_{\sigma_U} = \mathfrak{m}(U^{\mathrm{T}} \boxtimes U^{-1})$.

PROOF. Using the basic properties of the Kronecker product, concretely (1), the matrix associated to σ_U as $\mathbb{K}$–linear map is $U^{\mathrm{T}} \boxtimes U^{-1}$, hence the result follows from Lemma 1. □

For each $0 \leq h \leq t-1$, let

$$P_h = \left(\begin{array}{c|c} 0 & I_{t-h} \\ \hline I_h & 0 \end{array} \right).$$

LEMMA 3. *The matrix associated to the* $\mathbb{F}$*–linear map* $\widehat{\tau^h} : A \to A$ *is* $\widehat{P_h} = I_{n^2} \boxtimes P_h$.

PROOF. It is an easy computation once it is easily checked that P_h is the matrix associated to τ^h. □

Observe that

$$I_{n^2} \boxtimes P_h = \begin{pmatrix} P_h & & \\ & \ddots & \\ & & P_h \end{pmatrix}_{n^2 \times n^2} \in \mathcal{M}_{n^2 t}(\mathbb{F}).$$

We finish this section with the description of the $\mathbb{F}$–linear maps $\mathfrak{m}$ and $\mathfrak{f}$ as matrices. Let $\{E_{ij} : 0 \leq i, j \leq n-1\}$ be the set of all matrix units of size $n \times n$.

LEMMA 4. *Let us fix the bases* $\{\alpha^{q^k} E_{ij} \mid 0 \leq k \leq t-1, 0 \leq i, j \leq n-1\}$ *and* $\{E_{ij} \mid 0 \leq i, j \leq nt-1\}$ *of* A *and* $\mathcal{M}_{nt}(\mathbb{F})$ *respectively.*

1. *The matrix associated to the linear map* $\mathfrak{m} : A \to \mathcal{M}_{nt}(\mathbb{F})$ *is*

$$M_{\mathfrak{m}} = I_n \boxtimes \left(\; I_n \boxtimes \mathfrak{m}(\alpha^{q^0}) \; \middle| \; \cdots \; \middle| \; I_n \boxtimes \mathfrak{m}(\alpha^{q^{t-1}}) \; \right)$$

2. *The matrix associated to the linear map* $\mathfrak{f} : \mathcal{M}_{nt}(\mathbb{F}) \to A$ *is*

$$M_{\mathfrak{f}} = I_n \boxtimes \begin{pmatrix} \mathrm{Tr}_{\mathbb{K}/\mathbb{F}}(\beta^{q^0}) \\ \vdots \\ \mathrm{Tr}_{\mathbb{K}/\mathbb{F}}(\beta^{q^{t-1}}) \end{pmatrix} \boxtimes I_{nt}$$

PROOF. The proof is long but straightforward. It requires to compute carefully the images of the basis elements. But there aren't additional difficulties. □

2. MAIN RESULT

Let A be an $\mathbb{F}$–algebra. For any A–bimodule M, the notation M^A stands for the *center* of the bimodule M, namely, the $\mathbb{F}$–vector space

$$M^A = \{m \in M \mid am = ma, \; \forall a \in A\}$$

If we consider the algebra A as an A–bimodule in the canonical way, then A^A becomes the usual center $C(A)$ of A as an algebra.

Observe that $A \otimes_{\mathbb{F}} A$ is an A–bimodule and the multiplication map $\mu : A \otimes_{\mathbb{F}} A \to A$ is an A–bimodule map.

We shall need the following interpretation of the center of a bimodule in terms of homomorphisms from [2, Chapter II]. Every A–bimodule M may be seen as a left module over the enveloping algebra A^e of A. Recall that $A^e = A \otimes_{\mathbb{F}} A^{op}$, where A^{op} is the opposite algebra of A. In this way, A^e is the vector space $A \otimes_{\mathbb{F}} A$ endowed with the multiplication $(a \otimes b) \cdot (a' \otimes b') := aa' \otimes b'b$. Now, every A–bimodule M becomes a left A^e–module via the action $(a \otimes b) \cdot m = amb$, for all $a \otimes b \in A^e$, $m \in M$. With this interpretation of bimodules, the homomorphisms of A–bimodules are exactly the homomorphisms of left A^e–modules. A straightforward computation shows that the map

$$\hom_{A^e}(A, M) \to M^A, \quad f \mapsto f(1) \tag{2}$$

is an isomorphism of $\mathbb{F}$–vector spaces, where $\hom_{A^e}(A, M)$ denotes de set (that becomes a vector space) of all homomorphisms of left A^e–modules from A to M.

LEMMA 5. *Let* A *be a simple algebra separable over its center* $\mathbb{K}$*. Then the canonical map* $\pi : A \otimes_{\mathbb{F}} A \to A \otimes_{\mathbb{K}} A$ *sending* $a \otimes_{\mathbb{F}} b$ *onto* $a \otimes_{\mathbb{K}} b$ *induces an isomorphism of* $\mathbb{F}$*–vector spaces* $(A \otimes_{\mathbb{F}} A)^A \cong (A \otimes_{\mathbb{K}} A)^A$.

PROOF. Let J denote the kernel of π. We have an exact sequence of A–bimodules

$$0 \longrightarrow J \longrightarrow A \otimes_{\mathbb{F}} A \xrightarrow{\pi} A \otimes_{\mathbb{K}} A \longrightarrow 0 \tag{3}$$

Since A is a separable algebra over $\mathbb{F}$, its enveloping algebra $A^e_{\mathbb{F}}$ becomes a separable algebra by [2, Proposition II.1.6] and, hence, a semi-simple algebra [2, Corollary II.2.4]. Therefore, the exact sequence of left $A^e_{\mathbb{F}}$–modules (3) is split. Therefore, we have a split exact sequence of $\mathbb{F}$–vector spaces

$$\begin{aligned} 0 \longrightarrow \hom_{A^e_{\mathbb{F}}}(A, J) \longrightarrow \hom_{A^e_{\mathbb{F}}}(A, A \otimes_{\mathbb{F}} A) \\ \longrightarrow \hom_{A^e_{\mathbb{F}}}(A, A \otimes_{\mathbb{K}} A) \longrightarrow 0 \end{aligned} \tag{4}$$

In view of the isomorphism (2) we just need to prove that $\hom_{A^e_{\mathbb{F}}}(A, J) = 0$. To this end, let us denote by $A^e_{\mathbb{K}}$ the enveloping algebra of A considered as a $\mathbb{K}$–algebra, and observe that the map π may be considered as a (surjective) homomorphism of rings $\pi : A^e_{\mathbb{F}} \to A^e_{\mathbb{K}}$, so that J becomes a twosided ideal of $A^e_{\mathbb{F}}$. Being $A^e_{\mathbb{F}}$ semi-simple, we get from Artin-Wedderburn's Theorem that $A^e_{\mathbb{F}} = J \oplus I$, for a twosided ideal I of $A^e_{\mathbb{F}}$ isomorphic to $A^e_{\mathbb{K}}$ as an $A^e_{\mathbb{F}}$–bimodule. On the other hand, $\hom_{A^e_{\mathbb{F}}}(A, A) \cong C(A) = \mathbb{K}$, which implies that A is simple as a left $A^e_{\mathbb{F}}$–module. We the deduce, from the block decomposition of $A^e_{\mathbb{F}}$ given by Artin-Wedderburn's Theorem, that either $\hom_{A^e_{\mathbb{F}}}(A, I) = 0$

or $\hom_{A^e_{\mathbb{F}}}(A, J) = 0$. But

$$\hom_{A^e_{\mathbb{F}}}(A, I) \cong \hom_{A^e_{\mathbb{F}}}(A, A^e_{\mathbb{K}}) = \\ = \hom_{A^e_{\mathbb{F}}}(A, A \otimes_{\mathbb{K}} A) \cong (A \otimes_{\mathbb{K}} A)^A \neq 0,$$

since any separability element of the extension $\mathbb{K} \subseteq A$ belongs to $(A \otimes_{\mathbb{K}} A)^A$. Therefore, $\hom_{A^e_{\mathbb{F}}}(A, J) = 0$, and we get the desired isomorphism $(A \otimes_{\mathbb{F}} A)^A \cong (A \otimes_{\mathbb{K}} A)^A$. □

LEMMA 6. *Let* $\lambda = \sum_{h=0}^{t-1} \alpha^{q^h} \otimes \beta^{q^h} \in \mathbb{K} \otimes_{\mathbb{F}} \mathbb{K}$. *An* $\mathbb{F}$*–basis of* $(\mathbb{K} \otimes_{\mathbb{F}} \mathbb{K})^{\mathbb{K}}$ *is* $\{\alpha^{q^k}\lambda \mid 0 \leq k \leq t-1\}$.

PROOF. It is well known that λ is a separability element (see e.g. [6, Example 7]), and hence $\lambda \in (\mathbb{K} \otimes_{\mathbb{F}} \mathbb{K})^{\mathbb{K}}$. In fact for all $\gamma \in \mathbb{K}$,

$$\begin{aligned} \gamma\lambda &= \sum_i \gamma\alpha^{q^i} \otimes \beta^{q^i} \\ &= \sum_{i,j} \mathrm{Tr}_{\mathbb{K}/\mathbb{F}}(\beta^{q^j}\gamma\alpha^{q^i})\alpha^{q^j} \otimes \beta^{q^i} \\ &= \sum_{i,j} \alpha^{q^j} \otimes \mathrm{Tr}_{\mathbb{K}/\mathbb{F}}(\beta^{q^j}\gamma\alpha^{q^i})\beta^{q^i} \\ &= \sum_j \alpha^{q^j} \otimes \beta^{q^j}\gamma = \lambda\gamma \end{aligned}$$

as desired. Moreover, by Lemma 5 applied to $A = \mathbb{K}$, the restriction of the multiplication map $\mu : (\mathbb{K} \otimes_{\mathbb{F}} \mathbb{K})^{\mathbb{K}} \to \mathbb{K}$ is an $\mathbb{F}$–linear isomorphism such that $\mu(\lambda) = 1$. Via this bijection $\{\alpha^{q^k}\lambda \mid 0 \leq k \leq t-1\}$ is mapped to $\{\alpha^{q^k} \mid 0 \leq k \leq t-1\}$. Therefore the lemma follows. □

For the rest of this paper $A = \mathcal{M}_n(\mathbb{K})$. We want to describe $(A \otimes_{\mathbb{F}} A)^A$. For each $0 \leq i, j \leq n-1$ and all $0 \leq k \leq t-1$, we denote

$$p_{ijk} = \sum_{l=0}^{n-1} \sum_{h=0}^{t-1} E_{li}\alpha^{q^k}\alpha^{q^h} \otimes \beta^{q^h} E_{jl} \in A \otimes_{\mathbb{F}} A.$$

LEMMA 7. *The dimension of* $(A \otimes_{\mathbb{F}} A)^A$ *as an* $\mathbb{F}$*–vector space is* n^2t. *An* $\mathbb{F}$*–basis for* $(A \otimes_{\mathbb{F}} A)^A$ *is* $\{p_{ijk} \mid 0 \leq i, j \leq n-1, 0 \leq k \leq t-1\}$.

PROOF. We know, by [4, Proposition 4.1], that the dimension of $(A \otimes_{\mathbb{K}} A)^A$ as a vector space over $\mathbb{K}$ is n^2. We thus deduce from Lemma 5 that $\dim_{\mathbb{F}}(A \otimes_{\mathbb{F}} A)^A = n^2t$. In order to check that $p_{ijk} \in (A \otimes_{\mathbb{F}} A)^A$, it is enough to check that $ap_{ijk} = p_{ijk}a$ for matrix units and elements in $\mathbb{K}$. But $E_{hl}p_{ijk} = p_{ijk}E_{hl}$ is an easy computation, and $\gamma p_{ijk} = p_{ijk}\gamma$ for all $\gamma \in \mathbb{K}$ follows from Lemma 6. Since the elements $E_{ij}\alpha^{q^k} \otimes \beta^{q^l}E_{i'j'}$ form an $\mathbb{F}$–basis for $A \otimes_{\mathbb{F}} A$, the linear independence of $\{p_{ijk} \mid i, j, k\}$ follows. □

Let

$$E_0 = \{p \in (A \otimes_{\mathbb{F}} A)^A \mid \mu(p) = 0\}$$

and

$$E_1 = \{p \in (A \otimes_{\mathbb{F}} A)^A \mid \mu(p) = 1\}.$$

Then E_1 is the set of all separability elements of the extension $\mathbb{F} \subseteq A$. Let $p_1 = \sum_{k=0}^{t-1} \mathrm{Tr}_{\mathbb{K}/\mathbb{F}}(\beta)p_{00k}$.

PROPOSITION 1. *E_0 is an $\mathbb{F}$–vector subspace of $(A \otimes_{\mathbb{F}} A)^A$ and E_1 is an affine subspace of $(A \otimes_{\mathbb{F}} A)^A$ both of dimension $(n^2-1)t$. An $\mathbb{F}$–basis of E_0 is $\mathcal{E} = \{p_{ijk} \mid 0 \leq i \neq j \leq n-1, 0 \leq k \leq t-1\} \cup \{p_{00k} - p_{iik} \mid 1 \leq i \leq n-1, 0 \leq k \leq t-1\}$. Moreover $E_1 = \{p_1 + q \mid q \in E_0\}$.*

PROOF. First observe that

$$\begin{aligned} \mu(p_{ijk}) &= \sum_{l=0}^{n-1} \sum_{h=0}^{t-1} \alpha^{q^k}\alpha^{q^h}\beta^{q^h}E_{li}E_{jl} \\ &= \alpha^{q^k} \sum_{h=0}^{t-1} (\alpha\beta)^{q^h} \sum_{l=0}^{n-1} \delta_{ij}E_{ll} \\ &= \alpha^{q^k}\,\mathrm{Tr}_{\mathbb{K}/\mathbb{F}}(\alpha\beta)\delta_{ij}I_n \\ &= \alpha^{q^k}\delta_{ij}I_n, \end{aligned} \tag{5}$$

where $E_{li}E_{jl} = \delta_{ij}E_{ll}$ by properties of the product of matrix units and $\mathrm{Tr}_{\mathbb{K}/\mathbb{F}}(\alpha\beta) = 1$ because $\{\alpha^{q^k} \mid k\}$ and $\{\beta^{q^k} \mid k\}$ are dual bases. Hence it follows that $\mathcal{E} \subseteq E_0$ and $\mathbb{K} \subseteq \mu((A \otimes_{\mathbb{F}} A)^A)$. For all $p \in (A \otimes_{\mathbb{F}} A)^A$, $\mu(p)$ is a scalar matrix because $a\mu(p) = \mu(ap) = \mu(pa) = \mu(p)a$ for $a \in A$, i.e. $\mu((A \otimes_{\mathbb{F}} A)^A) \subseteq \mathbb{K}$ and equality holds. Since $\dim_{\mathbb{F}} \mathbb{K} = t$ and $E_0 = \ker(\mu_{|(A \otimes_{\mathbb{F}} A)^A})$ it follows that E_0 is a vector subspace of dimension $n^2t - t$. E_1 is non empty because

$$\begin{aligned} \mu(p_1) &= \sum_{k=0}^{t-1} \mathrm{Tr}_{\mathbb{K}/\mathbb{F}}(\beta)\mu(p_{00k}) \\ &= \sum_{k=0}^{t-1} \mathrm{Tr}_{\mathbb{K}/\mathbb{F}}(\beta^{q^k})\alpha^{q^k}\delta_{00}I_n \\ &= I_n, \end{aligned}$$

by (5) and properties of the trace function. From the linearity of μ, it follows that $E_1 = \{p_1 + q \mid q \in E_0\}$, hence $\dim_{\mathbb{F}} E_1 = n^2t - t$. □

The description of E_1 provided in Proposition 1 is the key of Algorithm 1.

We can now prove the main result of this paper.

THEOREM 1. *Algorithm 1 correctly decides if $\sigma \in \mathrm{Aut}_{\mathbb{F}}(A)$ is a separable automorphism. If it is, it also correctly returns a separability element invariant under $\sigma^{\otimes}$.*

PROOF. Recall that the map $\mathfrak{m} : A \to \mathcal{M}_{nt}(\mathbb{F})$ is an $\mathbb{F}$–algebra monomorpshim with left inverse $\mathfrak{f}$. Hence for every $\mathbb{F}$–linear map $\phi : A \to A$, the map $\mathfrak{m}\phi\mathfrak{f} : \mathcal{M}_{nt}(\mathbb{F}) \to \mathcal{M}_{nt}(\mathbb{F})$ satisfies $(\mathfrak{m}\phi\mathfrak{f})\mathfrak{m} = \mathfrak{m}\phi$.

By [9, Proposition 4.10], the map

$$\begin{aligned} \Phi : A \otimes_{\mathbb{F}} A &\to \mathcal{M}_{n^2t^2}(\mathbb{F}) \\ a \otimes b &\mapsto (\mathfrak{m}(a) \boxtimes \mathfrak{m}(b))K_{nt,nt} \end{aligned}$$

is a monomorphism of $\mathbb{F}$–algebras. By Lemma 2, $M_{\sigma_U} = \mathfrak{m}(U^{\mathrm{T}} \boxtimes U^{-1})$ is the matrix associated to the $\mathbb{F}$–linear map σ_U. By Lemma 3, $\widehat{P_h} = I_{n^2} \boxtimes P_h$ is the matrix associated to $\widehat{\tau^h}$ as $\mathbb{F}$–linear map. Hence $M_\sigma = M_{\mathfrak{f}}\widehat{P_h}M_{\sigma_U}M_{\mathfrak{m}}$ is the matrix associated to $\mathfrak{m}\sigma\mathfrak{f}$. Using the properties of the Kronecker product, the restriction of the linear map given by $M_{\sigma^{\otimes}} = K_{nt,nt}^{-1}(M_\sigma \boxtimes M_\sigma)K_{nt,nt}$ to the image of Φ corresponds to $\sigma^{\otimes}$.

Now σ is a separable automorphism if and only if there exists $p \in E_1$ such that $\sigma^{\otimes}(p) = p$. This is equivalent to

Algorithm 1 `Separable Automorphism`

Input: An automorphism $\sigma \in \mathrm{Aut}_{\mathbb{F}}(A)$, given as $\sigma = \sigma_U \widehat{\tau^h}$, where σ_U is the inner automorphism associated to regular matrix $U \in A$, $0 \leq h \leq t-1$, τ is the Frobenius automorphism and $\widehat{\tau^h}$ is the canonical componentwise extension of τ^h to A

Output: A separability element invariant under $\sigma^{\otimes}$ if σ is a separable automorphism. 0 otherwise.

1: **for** $0 \leq i, j \leq n-1$ **do**
2: $\quad p_{ijk} = \sum_{l=0}^{n-1} \sum_{h=0}^{t-1} \mathfrak{m}(\alpha^{q^k} \alpha^{q^h} E_{li}) \boxtimes \mathfrak{m}(\beta^{q^h} E_{jl})$
3: $\mathcal{E} = \{\ \}$
4: **for** $0 \leq i, j \leq n-1$ **do**
5: $\quad$ **for** $0 \leq k \leq t-1$ **do**
6: $\quad\quad$ **if** $i \neq j$ **then**
7: $\quad\quad\quad \mathcal{E} = \mathcal{E} \cup \{p_{ijk}\}$
8: $\quad\quad$ **else if** $i \neq 0$ **then**
9: $\quad\quad\quad \mathcal{E} = \mathcal{E} \cup \{p_{00k} - p_{iik}\}$
10: $p_1 = \sum_{k=0}^{t-1} \mathrm{Tr}_{\mathbb{K}/\mathbb{F}}(\beta) p_{00k}$
11: Let $\widehat{P_h}, M_{\sigma_U}, M_{\mathfrak{m}}, M_{\mathfrak{f}}$ be as in Lemmas 2, 3 and 4.
12: $M_\sigma = M_{\mathfrak{f}} \widehat{P_h} M_{\sigma_U} M_{\mathfrak{m}}$
13: $M_{\sigma^{\otimes}} = K_{nt,nt}^{-1} (M_\sigma \boxtimes M_\sigma) K_{nt,nt}$
14: $\mathcal{G} = \{\ \}$
15: **for all** $q \in \mathcal{E}$ **do**
16: $\quad \mathcal{G} = \mathcal{G} \cup \{\mathfrak{v}(q) \cdot (I_{n^4t^4} - M_{\sigma^{\otimes}})\}$
17: **if** $\mathfrak{v}(p_1) \cdot (M_{\sigma^{\otimes}} - I_{n^4t^4}) \in \langle \mathcal{G} \rangle$ **then**
18: $\quad$ Compute $\{\alpha_{ijk} \mid 0 \leq i \neq j \leq n-1, 0 \leq k \leq t-1\} \cup \{\alpha_{ik} \mid 1 \leq i \leq n-1, 0 \leq k \leq t-1\} \subseteq \mathbb{F}$ such that

$$\mathfrak{v}(p_1) \cdot (M_{\sigma^{\otimes}} - I_{n^4t^4}) =$$
$$= \sum_{i \neq j} \sum_k \alpha_{ijk} \left(\mathfrak{v}(p_{ijk}) \cdot (I_{n^4t^4} - M_{\sigma^{\otimes}})\right)$$
$$+ \sum_i \sum_k \alpha_{ik} \left(\mathfrak{v}(p_{00k} - p_{iik}) \cdot (I_{n^4t^4} - M_{\sigma^{\otimes}})\right)$$

19: $\quad$ **return** $p_1 + \sum_{i \neq j} \sum_k \alpha_{ijk} p_{ijk} + \sum_i \sum_k \alpha_{ik}(p_{00k} - p_{iik})$
20: **else**
21: $\quad$ **return** 0

the existence of $q \in E_0$ such that $\sigma^{\otimes}(p_1 + q) = p_1 + q$, i.e. $(\sigma^{\otimes} - \mathrm{id})(p_1) \in (\mathrm{id} - \sigma^{\otimes})(E_0)$.

Since $\mathcal{E}$ is a basis for E_0 by Proposition 1, $\mathcal{G}$ is a generator set for $(\mathrm{id} - \sigma^{\otimes})(E_0)$. We conclude that σ is a separable automorphism if and only if $\mathfrak{v}(p_1) \cdot (M_{\sigma^{\otimes}} - I_{n^4t^4}) \in \langle \mathcal{G} \rangle$.

If

$$\mathfrak{v}(p_1) \cdot (M_{\sigma^{\otimes}} - I_{n^4t^4}) =$$
$$= \sum_{i \neq j} \sum_k \alpha_{ijk} \left(\mathfrak{v}(p_{ijk}) \cdot (I_{n^4t^4} - M_{\sigma^{\otimes}})\right)$$
$$+ \sum_i \sum_k \alpha_{ik} \left(\mathfrak{v}(p_{00k} - p_{iik}) \cdot (I_{n^4t^4} - M_{\sigma^{\otimes}})\right),$$

it follows that $p = \sum_{i \neq j} \sum_k \alpha_{ijk} p_{ijk} + \sum_i \sum_k \alpha_{ik}(p_{00k} - p_{iik}) \in E_0$ satisfies $\sigma^{\otimes}(p_1 + p) = p_1 + p$, hence Algorithm 1 works correctly. $\square$

Remark 2. The complexity of Algorithm 1 is bounded by the theoretical efficiency of solving the linear system stated in Line 18. The coefficient matrix of the system has size n^4t^4, so the run-time belongs to $\mathcal{O}(n^{12}t^{12})$. Although the degree of the polynomial is not very small, this algorithm is a preprocessing step which has to be computed only once. If such separability element is computed, then it allows us to calculate a generating idempotent of any ideal code of the extension [5, 6]. Additionally, in this case, we give a positive answer to the question posed in [13]: is any ideal code a direct summand, as a left ideal, of the working algebra $A[z;\sigma]$?

3. EXAMPLES

Let us consider the field extension $\mathbb{F} = \mathbb{F}_2 \subset \mathbb{F}_4 = \mathbb{K}$, where $\mathbb{K}$ is viewed as the quotient ring $\frac{\mathbb{F}_2[a]}{(a^2+a+1)}$ and its elements are represented as $\{0, 1, a, a^2\}$. Let $A = \mathcal{M}_2(\mathbb{K})$ be the algebra of 2×2 matrices over $\mathbb{K}$ and $\sigma : A \to A$ the automorphism given by $\sigma = \sigma_U \widetilde{\tau}$, where $U = \left(\begin{smallmatrix} 1 & a \\ a^2 & a \end{smallmatrix}\right)$ and τ is the Frobenius automorphism. Let us apply Algorithm 1 in order to check if σ is separable. We first establish a normal basis $\mathcal{B} = \{a, a^2\}$, which is also self-dual. In this case, a basis of A as an $\mathbb{F}$-vector space is given by the matrices $\{E_{ij}^k\}_{i,j,k=0,1}$, where E_{ab}^c is the 2×2-matrix whose entries are zero except in the position i, j, which has the element $a^{q^c} \in \mathbb{K}$. We may then compute the elements p_{ijk} described in Line 2 of Algorithm 1. For instance, p_{001}, viewed as an element in $\mathcal{M}_2(\mathbb{K}) \otimes_{\mathbb{F}} \mathcal{M}_2(\mathbb{K})$, can be written as the following element:

$$p_{001} = \begin{pmatrix} 1 & 0 \\ 0 & 0 \end{pmatrix} \otimes \begin{pmatrix} a & 0 \\ 0 & 0 \end{pmatrix} + \begin{pmatrix} a & 0 \\ 0 & 0 \end{pmatrix} \otimes \begin{pmatrix} a^2 & 0 \\ 0 & 0 \end{pmatrix} + \begin{pmatrix} 0 & 0 \\ 1 & 0 \end{pmatrix} \otimes \begin{pmatrix} 0 & a \\ 0 & 0 \end{pmatrix} + \begin{pmatrix} 0 & 0 \\ a & 0 \end{pmatrix} \otimes \begin{pmatrix} 0 & a^2 \\ 0 & 0 \end{pmatrix}.$$

However, in order to use mathematical software, it is convenient to see the elements in $\mathcal{M}_{16}(\mathbb{F})$ via the embedding $\Phi = \boxtimes(\mathfrak{m} \otimes \mathfrak{m}) : \mathcal{M}_2(\mathbb{K}) \otimes_{\mathbb{F}} \mathcal{M}_2(\mathbb{K}) \to \mathcal{M}_{16}(\mathbb{F})$. For instance,

$$p_{001} = \begin{pmatrix}
0 & 1 & 0 & 0 & 1 & 1 & 0 & 0 & 0 & 0 & 0 & 0 & 0 & 0 & 0 & 0 \\
1 & 1 & 0 & 0 & 1 & 0 & 0 & 0 & 0 & 0 & 0 & 0 & 0 & 0 & 0 & 0 \\
0 & 0 & 0 & 0 & 0 & 0 & 0 & 0 & 0 & 0 & 0 & 0 & 0 & 0 & 0 & 0 \\
0 & 0 & 0 & 0 & 0 & 0 & 0 & 0 & 0 & 0 & 0 & 0 & 0 & 0 & 0 & 0 \\
1 & 1 & 0 & 0 & 1 & 0 & 0 & 0 & 0 & 0 & 0 & 0 & 0 & 0 & 0 & 0 \\
1 & 0 & 0 & 0 & 0 & 1 & 0 & 0 & 0 & 0 & 0 & 0 & 0 & 0 & 0 & 0 \\
0 & 0 & 0 & 0 & 0 & 0 & 0 & 0 & 0 & 0 & 0 & 0 & 0 & 0 & 0 & 0 \\
0 & 0 & 0 & 0 & 0 & 0 & 0 & 0 & 0 & 0 & 0 & 0 & 0 & 0 & 0 & 0 \\
0 & 0 & 0 & 1 & 0 & 0 & 1 & 1 & 0 & 0 & 0 & 0 & 0 & 0 & 0 & 0 \\
0 & 0 & 1 & 1 & 0 & 0 & 1 & 0 & 0 & 0 & 0 & 0 & 0 & 0 & 0 & 0 \\
0 & 0 & 0 & 0 & 0 & 0 & 0 & 0 & 0 & 0 & 0 & 0 & 0 & 0 & 0 & 0 \\
0 & 0 & 0 & 0 & 0 & 0 & 0 & 0 & 0 & 0 & 0 & 0 & 0 & 0 & 0 & 0 \\
0 & 0 & 1 & 1 & 0 & 0 & 1 & 0 & 0 & 0 & 0 & 0 & 0 & 0 & 0 & 0 \\
0 & 0 & 1 & 0 & 0 & 0 & 0 & 1 & 0 & 0 & 0 & 0 & 0 & 0 & 0 & 0 \\
0 & 0 & 0 & 0 & 0 & 0 & 0 & 0 & 0 & 0 & 0 & 0 & 0 & 0 & 0 & 0 \\
0 & 0 & 0 & 0 & 0 & 0 & 0 & 0 & 0 & 0 & 0 & 0 & 0 & 0 & 0 & 0
\end{pmatrix}$$

In this case, the basis

$$\mathcal{E} = \{p_{010}, p_{011}, p_{100}, p_{101}, p_{000} - p_{110}, p_{001} - p_{111}\}$$

and

$$p_1 = \sum_{k=0}^{t-1} \mathrm{Tr}_{\mathbb{K}/\mathbb{F}}(a) p_{00k} = p_{000} + p_{001} =$$

$$= \begin{pmatrix}
1 & 1 & 0 & 0 & 1 & 0 & 0 & 0 & 0 & 0 & 0 & 0 & 0 & 0 & 0 & 0 \\
1 & 0 & 0 & 0 & 0 & 1 & 0 & 0 & 0 & 0 & 0 & 0 & 0 & 0 & 0 & 0 \\
0 & 0 & 0 & 0 & 0 & 0 & 0 & 0 & 0 & 0 & 0 & 0 & 0 & 0 & 0 & 0 \\
0 & 0 & 0 & 0 & 0 & 0 & 0 & 0 & 0 & 0 & 0 & 0 & 0 & 0 & 0 & 0 \\
1 & 0 & 0 & 0 & 0 & 1 & 0 & 0 & 0 & 0 & 0 & 0 & 0 & 0 & 0 & 0 \\
0 & 1 & 0 & 0 & 1 & 1 & 0 & 0 & 0 & 0 & 0 & 0 & 0 & 0 & 0 & 0 \\
0 & 0 & 0 & 0 & 0 & 0 & 0 & 0 & 0 & 0 & 0 & 0 & 0 & 0 & 0 & 0 \\
0 & 0 & 0 & 0 & 0 & 0 & 0 & 0 & 0 & 0 & 0 & 0 & 0 & 0 & 0 & 0 \\
0 & 0 & 1 & 1 & 0 & 0 & 1 & 0 & 0 & 0 & 0 & 0 & 0 & 0 & 0 & 0 \\
0 & 0 & 1 & 0 & 0 & 0 & 0 & 1 & 0 & 0 & 0 & 0 & 0 & 0 & 0 & 0 \\
0 & 0 & 0 & 0 & 0 & 0 & 0 & 0 & 0 & 0 & 0 & 0 & 0 & 0 & 0 & 0 \\
0 & 0 & 0 & 0 & 0 & 0 & 0 & 0 & 0 & 0 & 0 & 0 & 0 & 0 & 0 & 0 \\
0 & 0 & 1 & 0 & 0 & 0 & 0 & 1 & 0 & 0 & 0 & 0 & 0 & 0 & 0 & 0 \\
0 & 0 & 0 & 1 & 0 & 0 & 1 & 1 & 0 & 0 & 0 & 0 & 0 & 0 & 0 & 0 \\
0 & 0 & 0 & 0 & 0 & 0 & 0 & 0 & 0 & 0 & 0 & 0 & 0 & 0 & 0 & 0 \\
0 & 0 & 0 & 0 & 0 & 0 & 0 & 0 & 0 & 0 & 0 & 0 & 0 & 0 & 0 & 0
\end{pmatrix}.$$

Now, the matrix of the automorphism σ,

$$M_\sigma = \begin{pmatrix}
0&1&0&1&1&1&1&1&1&0&1&0&0&1&0&1\\
1&0&1&0&0&1&0&1&1&1&1&1&1&0&1&0\\
1&1&1&0&1&0&0&1&0&1&1&1&1&1&1&0\\
0&1&1&1&1&1&1&0&1&0&0&1&0&1&1&1\\
0&1&0&1&1&1&1&1&1&0&1&0&0&1&0&1\\
1&0&1&0&0&1&0&1&1&1&1&1&1&0&1&0\\
1&1&1&0&1&0&0&1&0&1&1&1&1&1&1&0\\
0&1&1&1&1&1&1&0&1&0&0&1&0&1&1&1\\
1&1&1&1&1&0&1&0&1&1&1&1&1&0&1&0\\
0&1&0&1&1&1&1&1&0&1&0&1&1&1&1&1\\
1&0&0&1&0&1&1&1&1&0&0&1&0&1&1&1\\
1&1&1&0&1&0&0&1&1&1&1&0&1&0&0&1\\
1&1&1&1&1&0&1&0&1&1&1&1&1&0&1&0\\
0&1&0&1&1&1&1&1&0&1&0&1&1&1&1&1\\
1&0&0&1&0&1&1&1&1&0&0&1&0&1&1&1\\
1&1&1&0&1&0&0&1&1&1&1&0&1&0&0&1
\end{pmatrix},$$

is the key to compute the linear system for deciding if $(\sigma^{\otimes} - \mathrm{id})(p_1) \in (\mathrm{id} - \sigma^{\otimes})(E_0)$. In this case, the coefficients in $\mathbb{F}$ of the vectors $\{\mathfrak{v}(q) \cdot (I_{n^4t^4} - M_{\sigma^{\otimes}})\}_q$ yields a 256×256 matrix whose rank equals the rank of the extended matrix by $\{\mathfrak{v}(p_1) \cdot (M_{\sigma^{\otimes}} - I_{n^4t^4})\}$. Hence, following Algorithm 1, the automorphism is separable. A solution to the homogeneous system is given by the coefficients $(0,0,1,0,1,0)$ in the basis $\mathcal{E}$, so $p = p_1 + p_{100} + p_{000} + p_{110} = p_{100} + p_{110} + p_{001}$ is the desired separability element. Concretely,

$$p = \begin{pmatrix}
0&1&0&0&1&1&0&0&1&0&0&0&0&1&0&0\\
1&1&0&0&1&0&0&0&0&1&0&0&1&1&0&0\\
0&0&0&0&0&0&0&0&1&0&0&0&0&1&0&0\\
0&0&0&0&0&0&0&0&0&1&0&0&1&1&0&0\\
1&1&0&0&1&0&0&0&0&1&0&0&1&1&0&0\\
1&0&0&0&0&1&0&0&1&1&0&0&1&0&0&0\\
0&0&0&0&0&0&0&0&0&1&0&0&1&1&0&0\\
0&0&0&0&0&0&0&0&1&1&0&0&1&0&0&0\\
0&0&0&1&0&0&1&1&0&0&1&0&0&0&0&1\\
0&0&1&1&0&0&1&0&0&0&0&1&0&0&1&1\\
0&0&0&0&0&0&0&0&0&0&1&0&0&0&0&1\\
0&0&0&0&0&0&0&0&0&0&0&1&0&0&1&1\\
0&0&1&1&0&0&1&0&0&0&0&1&0&0&1&1\\
0&0&1&0&0&0&0&1&0&0&1&1&0&0&1&0\\
0&0&0&0&0&0&0&0&0&0&0&1&0&0&1&1\\
0&0&0&0&0&0&0&0&0&0&1&1&0&0&1&0
\end{pmatrix},$$

or, viewed as a tensor product of matrices in $\mathcal{M}_2(\mathbb{K})$,

$$\begin{aligned}
p &= \begin{pmatrix}0&a^2\\0&0\end{pmatrix} \otimes \begin{pmatrix}a&0\\0&0\end{pmatrix} + \begin{pmatrix}0&1\\0&0\end{pmatrix} \otimes \begin{pmatrix}a^2&0\\0&0\end{pmatrix}\\
&+ \begin{pmatrix}0&0\\0&a^2\end{pmatrix} \otimes \begin{pmatrix}0&a\\0&0\end{pmatrix} + \begin{pmatrix}0&0\\0&1\end{pmatrix} \otimes \begin{pmatrix}0&a^2\\0&0\end{pmatrix}\\
&+ \begin{pmatrix}0&a^2\\0&0\end{pmatrix} \otimes \begin{pmatrix}0&0\\a&0\end{pmatrix} + \begin{pmatrix}0&1\\0&0\end{pmatrix} \otimes \begin{pmatrix}0&0\\a^2&0\end{pmatrix}\\
&+ \begin{pmatrix}0&0\\0&a^2\end{pmatrix} \otimes \begin{pmatrix}0&0\\0&a\end{pmatrix} + \begin{pmatrix}0&0\\0&1\end{pmatrix} \otimes \begin{pmatrix}0&0\\0&a^2\end{pmatrix}\\
&+ \begin{pmatrix}1&0\\0&0\end{pmatrix} \otimes \begin{pmatrix}a&0\\0&0\end{pmatrix} + \begin{pmatrix}a&0\\0&0\end{pmatrix} \otimes \begin{pmatrix}a^2&0\\0&0\end{pmatrix}\\
&+ \begin{pmatrix}0&0\\1&0\end{pmatrix} \otimes \begin{pmatrix}0&a\\0&0\end{pmatrix} + \begin{pmatrix}0&0\\a&0\end{pmatrix} \otimes \begin{pmatrix}0&a^2\\0&0\end{pmatrix}.
\end{aligned}$$

Once we have found the separability element fixed under $\sigma^{\otimes}$, we may apply [6, Algorithm 1] for computing a generating idempotent of a given ideal code . For instance, let

$$g = z\begin{pmatrix}0&1\\0&a\end{pmatrix} + \begin{pmatrix}1&0\\1&0\end{pmatrix} \in A[z;\sigma] = R$$

be a generator of the ideal code $I = Rg$. Hence, its generator matrix is given by

$$M_g = \begin{pmatrix}
1&0&z&z&0&0&0&z\\
0&1&0&z&0&0&z&0\\
1&0&z&z&0&0&0&z\\
0&1&0&z&0&0&z&0\\
0&0&z&0&1&0&z&0\\
0&0&z&z&0&1&z&z\\
0&0&z&0&1&0&z&0\\
0&0&z&z&0&1&z&z
\end{pmatrix},$$

whose Smith form decomposition is $H = PM_gQ$, where $H = \left(\begin{smallmatrix}I_4&0\\0&0\end{smallmatrix}\right)$ and

$$Q = \begin{pmatrix}
1&0&0&0&z&z&0&z\\
0&1&0&0&0&z&z&0\\
0&0&0&0&1&0&0&0\\
0&0&0&0&0&1&0&0\\
0&0&1&0&z&0&z&0\\
0&0&0&1&z&z&z&z\\
0&0&0&0&0&0&1&0\\
0&0&0&0&0&0&0&1
\end{pmatrix}.$$

Hence, I is an ideal code of dimension 4 and length 8. Following [6, Algorithm 1], the generating idempotent $q = 1 - \sum_i p_i^1 \mathfrak{p}(\mathfrak{v}(p_i^2) \cdot QVV^tQ^{-1})$, where $V = \left(\begin{smallmatrix}0\\I_4\end{smallmatrix}\right)$ and our separability element is written as $p = \sum_i p_i^1 \otimes p_i^2$. Indeed,

$$q = z\begin{pmatrix}0&a\\0&1\end{pmatrix} + \begin{pmatrix}1&0\\0&0\end{pmatrix}.$$

Unfortunately, we cannot always ensure that the above procedure finds a separability element of the extension $\mathbb{F}[z] \subset A[z;\sigma]$. For instance, let $\mathbb{F}_2 \subset \mathbb{F}_8$, where $\mathbb{F}_8$ is viewed as the quotient ring $\frac{\mathbb{F}_2[a]}{(a^3+a+1)}$. Let $A = \mathcal{M}_2(\mathbb{F}_8)$ be the algebra of 2×2 matrices over $\mathbb{F}_8$ and $\sigma : A \to A$ the automorphism given by $\sigma = \sigma_U \widehat{\tau}$, where $U = \left(\begin{smallmatrix}a+1&1\\1&a^2+1\end{smallmatrix}\right)$ and τ is the Frobenius automorphism. In this case, applying Algorithm 1, we get that σ is not separable. Therefore, any separability element of $\mathbb{F}_2[z] \subset A[z;\sigma]$, if it exists, could not be derived from a separability element of $\mathbb{F}_2 \subset A$.

4. REFERENCES

[1] G. Cauchon and J. Robson. Endomorphisms, derivations, and polynomial rings. *Journal of Algebra*, 53(1):227–238, 1978.

[2] F. DeMeyer and E. Ingraham. *Separable Algebras over Commutative Rings*, volume 181 of *Lecture Notes in Mathematics*. Springer-Verlag, 1971.

[3] H. Gluesing-Luerssen and W. Schmale. On cyclic convolutional codes. *Acta Applicandae Mathematica*, 82(2):183–237, 2004.

[4] J. Gómez-Torrecillas, F. J. Lobillo, and G. Navarro. Dual codes of ideal codes in skew polynomials over matrix algebras, 2014.

[5] J. Gómez-Torrecillas, F. J. Lobillo, and G. Navarro. Generating idempotents in ideal codes. In W.-S. Lee, editor, *ISSAC 2014 Poster Abstract*, volume 48, number 3, issue 189 of *ACM Communications in Computer Algebra*. ACM-SIGSAM, 2014.

[6] J. Gómez-Torrecillas, F. J. Lobillo, and G. Navarro. Ideal codes over separable ring extensions. arXiv:1408.1546, 2014.

[7] K. Hirata and K. Sugano. On semisimple extensions and separable extensions over non commutative rings. *Journal of the Mathematical Society of Japan*, 18(4):360–373, 10 1966.

[8] R. A. Horn and C. R. Johnson. *Topics in matrix analysis*. Cambridge University Press, 1994.

[9] N. Jacobson. *Basic Algebra: II*. W.H. Freeman & Company, 1980.

[10] R. Johannesson and K. S. Zigangirov. *Fundamentals of Convolutional Coding*. Wiley-IEEE Press, 1999.

[11] M. Knus and M. Ojanguren. *Théorie de la Descente et Algèbres d'Azumaya*, volume 389 of *Lecture Notes in Mathematics*. Springer-Verlag, 1974.

[12] R. Lidl and H. Niederreiter. *Finite Fields*. Number V. 20, part 1 in Encyclopedia of Mathematics and its Applications. Cambridge University Press, 1997.

[13] S. R. López-Permouth and S. Szabo. Convolutional codes with additional algebraic structure. *Journal of Pure and Applied Algebra*, 217(5):958 – 972, 2013.

[14] R. Pierce. *Associative algebras*. Graduate texts in mathematics. Springer-Verlag, 1982.

[15] P. Piret. Structure and constructions of cyclic convolutional codes. *IEEE Transactions on Information Theory*, 22(2):147–155, 1976.

[16] W. A. Stein et al. Sage Mathematics Software (Version 6.3), The Sage Development Team, 2014, http://www.sagemath.org.

Randomized Root Finding over Finite FFT-fields using Tangent Graeffe Transforms

Bruno Grenet
Laboratoire d'informatique, de robotique et de microélectronique de Montpellier
LIRMM, UMR 5506 CNRS, CC477
Université de Montpellier
161, rue Ada
34095 Montpellier Cedex 5, France
bruno.grenet@lirmm.fr

Joris van der Hoeven, Grégoire Lecerf
Laboratoire d'informatique de l'École polytechnique
LIX, UMR 7161 CNRS
Campus de l'École polytechnique
1, rue Honoré d'Estienne d'Orves
Bâtiment Alan Turing, CS35003
91120 Palaiseau, France
{vdhoeven,lecerf}@lix.polytechnique.fr

ABSTRACT

Consider a finite field $\mathbb{F}_q$ whose multiplicative group has smooth cardinality. We study the problem of computing all roots of a polynomial that splits over $\mathbb{F}_q$, which was one of the bottlenecks for fast sparse interpolation in practice. We revisit and slightly improve existing algorithms and then present new randomized ones based on the Graeffe transform. We report on our implementation in the MATHEMAGIX computer algebra system, confirming that our ideas gain by a factor ten at least in practice, for sufficiently large inputs.

Categories and Subject Descriptors

F.2.1 [**Analysis of algorithms and problem complexity**]: Numerical Algorithms and Problems—*Computations in finite fields*; G.4 [**Mathematical software**]: Algorithm design and analysis

General Terms

Algorithms, Theory

Keywords

Finite fields; polynomial root finding; algorithm; Mathemagix

1. INTRODUCTION

Let $\mathbb{F}_q$ represent the finite field with $q = p^k$ elements, where p is a prime number, and $k \geqslant 1$. Throughout this article, such a field is supposed to be described as a quotient of $\mathbb{F}_p[x]$ by a *monic* irreducible polynomial. Let $f \in \mathbb{F}_q[x]$ represent a *separable monic polynomial* of degree $d \geqslant 1$ which *splits* over $\mathbb{F}_q$, which means that all its irreducible factors have degree one and multiplicity one. In this article we are interested in computing all the roots of f.

ISSAC'15, July 6–9, 2015, Bath, United Kingdom.

ACM 978-1-4503-3435-8/15/07 ...$15.00.
DOI: http://dx.doi.org/10.1145/2755996.2756647.

Notice that for a general polynomial f, which does not split over $\mathbb{F}_q$, our algorithms will not apply. Nevertheless this hypothesis is not restrictive since the set of roots of f in $\mathbb{F}_q$ coincides with the set of roots of $\gcd(f(x), x^q - x)$, which actually splits over $\mathbb{F}_q$, and which can be computed efficiently.

1.1 Motivation

One of our interests in root finding came from the recent design of efficient algorithms to interpolate, into the standard monomial basis, polynomials that are given through evaluation functions. This task is briefly called *sparse interpolation*, and root finding often turns out to be a bottleneck, as reported in [19, 20]. In fact, in this case, the ground field can be chosen to be $\mathbb{F}_p$ with $p = M\,2^m + 1$, and where 2^m is taken to be much larger than the number of terms to be discovered. In practice, to minimize the size of p, so that it fits a machine register, we take $M = O(\log p)$ as small as possible. A typical example is $p = 7 \cdot 2^{26} + 1$. We informally refer to such primes as *FFT primes*.

Root finding over prime finite fields critically occurs during the computation of integer and rational roots of polynomials in $\mathbb{Q}[x]$, both for dense and lacunary representations. Yet other applications concern cryptography and error correcting codes. Nevertheless, practical root finding has received only moderate attention so far, existing algorithms with good average complexity bounds often being sufficient [21, 22].

In this article, we focus on fast randomized root finding algorithms, targeting primarily FFT prime fields and, more generally, finite fields whose multiplicative group has $O(\log q)$-smooth cardinality, which means that all the prime factors of $q - 1$ are in $O(\log q)$. Smoothness assumptions will be made more precise for each situation in the sequel. At a second stage, we report on practical efficiency of our new algorithms within the MATHEMAGIX computer algebra system [18].

1.2 Notations and prerequisites

The *multiplicative group* $\mathbb{F}_q \setminus \{0\}$ of $\mathbb{F}_q$ is written $\mathbb{F}_q^*$. In order to simplify the presentation of complexity bounds, we use the *soft-Oh* notation: $f(n) \in \tilde{O}(g(n))$ means that $f(n) = g(n) \log^{O(1)} g(n)$ (we refer the reader to [11, Chapter 25, Section 7] for technical details). The least integer larger or equal to x is written $\lceil x \rceil$. The largest integer smaller or equal to x is written $\lfloor x \rfloor$. The *remainder* of g in the division by f is denoted by $g \operatorname{rem} f$.

We write $\mathsf{M}\colon \mathbb{N} \to \mathbb{Z}$ for a function that bounds the total cost of a polynomial product algorithm in terms of the number of ring operations performed independently of the coefficient ring, assuming a unity is available. In other words, two polynomials of degrees at most d over such a ring $\mathbb{A}$ can be multiplied with at most $\mathsf{M}(d)$ arithmetic operations in $\mathbb{A}$. The schoolbook algorithm allows us to take $\mathsf{M}(d) = O(d^2)$. On the other hand the fastest known algorithm, due to Cantor and Kaltofen [7], provides us with $\mathsf{M}(d) = O(d \log d \log \log d)$. In order to simplify the cost analysis of our algorithms we make the customary assumption that $\mathsf{M}(d_1) / d_1 \leqslant \mathsf{M}(d_2) / d_2$ for all $0 < d_1 \leqslant d_2$. Notice that this assumption implies the *super-additivity* of M, namely $\mathsf{M}(d_1) + \mathsf{M}(d_2) \leqslant \mathsf{M}(d_1 + d_2)$ for all $d_1 \geqslant 0$ and $d_2 \geqslant 0$.

For operations in $\mathbb{Z}$ and in finite fields, we are interested in the *Turing machine model*, with a sufficiently large number of tapes. In short, we use the terms *bit-cost* and *bit-complexity* to refer to this model whenever the context is not clear. For *randomized algorithms*, we endow Turing machines with an additional instruction which generates random bits with a uniform distribution [29]. Readers unfamiliar with Turing machines may also freely interpret our results in the *random-access machine model* used in [11].

Our *randomized algorithms* always return a correct output, but their computation times vary according to internal random choices. For a given input, the *average time* (also called *expected time*) is the average of the execution times taken over all the possible executions, and for a uniform distribution over the set of random bits. Our algorithms will thus always terminate in practice whenever using *non-repeating* pseudo-random generators.

We write $\mathsf{I}(n)$ for a function that bounds the bit-cost of an algorithm which multiplies two integers of bit-sizes at most n, viewed in classical binary representation. Recently, the best bound for $\mathsf{I}(n)$ has been improved to $\mathsf{I}(n) = O(n \log n\, 8^{\log^* n})$, where $\log^*$ represents the *iterated logarithm* function [16]. Again, we make the customary assumption that $\mathsf{I}(n_1) / n_1 \leqslant \mathsf{I}(n_2) / n_2$ for all $0 < n_1 \leqslant n_2$. We freely use the following classical facts: ring operations in $\mathbb{F}_p$ cost $O(\mathsf{I}(\log p))$ and one division or inversion in $\mathbb{F}_p$ costs $O(\mathsf{I}(\log p) \log \log p)$ [11, Chapter 11].

For polynomial operations over $\mathbb{F}_q$, we let $\mathsf{M}_q(d)$ represent a function that bounds the bit-cost of an algorithm that multiplies two polynomials of degrees at most d, with the same kind of assumptions as for M and I. According to [17], we may take $\mathsf{M}_q(d) = O(d \log q \log(d \log q)\, 8^{\log^*(d \log q)})$. The ring operations in $\mathbb{F}_q$ cost at most $O(\mathsf{M}_p(k))$, and inversions take at most $O(\mathsf{M}_p(k) \log k + \mathsf{I}(\log p) \log \log p)$. For convenience, m_q and d_q will respectively denote cost functions for the product and the inverse in $\mathbb{F}_q$.

Let us recall that the gcd of two polynomials of degrees at most d over $\mathbb{F}_q$ can be computed in time $O(\mathsf{M}_q(d) \log d)$: One can for instance use pseudo-remainders in [11, Algorithm 11.4], *mutatis mutandis*. Given monic polynomials f and $g_1, \ldots, g_l$ with $\deg f = d$ and $\deg g_1 + \cdots + \deg g_l = O(d)$, all the remainders $f \operatorname{rem} g_i$ can be computed in time $O(\mathsf{M}_q(d) \log l)$ using a *subproduct tree* [11, Chapter 10]. The inverse problem, called *Chinese remaindering*, can be solved within a similar cost $O(\mathsf{M}_q(d) \log l + d\, \mathsf{d}_q)$.

In this article, when needed, we consider that the factorization of $q - 1$ and a primitive element of $\mathbb{F}_q^*$ have been precomputed once, and we discard the necessary underlying costs. In practice, if the factorization of $q - 1$ is given, then it is straightforward to verify whether a given element is primitive. For known complexity bounds and historical details on these tasks, we refer the reader to [1, 27, 33].

1.3 Related work and our contributions

Seminal algorithms for polynomial factorization over finite fields are classically attributed to Berlekamp [2, 3], and Cantor and Zassenhaus [8], but central earlier ideas can be found in works of Gauss, Galois, Arwins, Faddeev and Skopin. Cantor–Zassenhaus' algorithm is randomized and well suited to compute roots of polynomials of degree d that split over $\mathbb{F}_q$ in average time $O(\mathsf{M}_q(d)\, (\log q + \log d) \log d + d\, \mathsf{d}_q)$. Of course, if $q = O(d)$ then an exhaustive search can be naively performed in time $O(\mathsf{M}_q(d) \log d)$ (the factor $\log d$ can be discarded if a primitive element of $\mathbb{F}_q^*$ is given, by means of [6, Proposition 3]), so that the cost of root finding simplifies to $O(\mathsf{M}_q(d)\, \log q\, \log d + d\, \mathsf{d}_q)$. This classical approach is for instance implemented in the NTL library written by Shoup [34]. However neither Berlekamp's nor Cantor–Zassenhaus' algorithm seems to benefit from particular prime numbers such as FFT primes. Instead, alternative approaches have been proposed by Moenck [26], von zur Gathen [10], Mignotte and Schnorr [25], and then by Rónyai [31].

In Section 2, for the sake of comparison, we first revisit Cantor–Zassenhaus' approach and propose a practical trick to slightly speed it up. We also briefly recall the complexity bound of Mignotte–Schnorr's algorithm [25].

We then design and analyze fast randomized algorithms based on tangent Graeffe transforms, leading to an important speed-up for FFT primes. The practical efficiency of the new algorithms is discussed on the basis of implementations in the MATHEMAGIX computer algebra system [18], thus revealing that our fastest variant gains an order of magnitude over other existing software. In addition our algorithms turn out to be very useful for applications to sparse interpolation.

Let us finally mention that our present randomized algorithms admit deterministic counterparts which are studied in [14].

2. KNOWN ALGORITHMS REVISITED

In this section we revisit efficient root finding algorithms previously described in the literature, and slightly improve their complexity analysis. The first stream, followed by Berlekamp [3], Rabin [30], Cantor and Zassenhaus [8], consists in splitting the input polynomial by computing suitable modular exponentiations and gcds. The second stream, followed by Moenck [26], and Mignotte and Schnorr [25], takes advantage of the smoothness of $q - 1$.

2.1 Cantor–Zassenhaus' algorithm

In this subsection we suppose that q has the form $q = \chi\, \rho + 1$, with $\chi \geqslant 2$. The following randomized algorithm extends Cantor–Zassenhaus' one, which corresponds to $\chi = 2$, when q is odd. We need a primitive root ξ of unity of order χ.

Randomized algorithm 1.

Input. $f\in\mathbb{F}_q[x]$ of degree $d\geqslant 1$, monic, separable, which splits over $\mathbb{F}_q$, and such that $f(0)\neq 0$; a primitive root ξ of unity of order χ.

Output. The roots of f.

1. If $d=O(\chi)$ then compute the roots of f by calling a fallback root finding algorithm.
2. Pick $g\in\mathbb{F}_q[x]$ at random of degree at most $d-1$.
3. Compute $h:=g^\rho \operatorname{rem} f$, and set $f_0:=f$.
4. For all i from 1 to $\chi-1$, compute $f_i:=\gcd(h-\xi^i, f_0)$, make it monic, and replace f_0 by f_0/f_i.
5. Recursively call the algorithm with those of $f_0,\ldots,f_{\chi-1}$ which are not constant, and return the disjoint union of the sets of their roots.

In the classical case when $\chi=2$, then we recall that step 3 costs $O(\mathsf{M}_q(d)\log q)$ and step 4 takes $O(\mathsf{M}_q(d)\log d)$ plus one inversion in $\mathbb{F}_q$. Since the average depth of the recursion is in $O(\log d)$ [9], the total average cost amounts to $O(\mathsf{M}_q(d)(\log q+\log d)\log d+d\,\mathsf{d}_q)$.

For the case of arbitrary χ, we propose an informal discussion, so as to justify the interest in the algorithm. If α is a root of f, then $h(\alpha)=g(\alpha)^\rho$ has order dividing χ, hence is a power of ξ, or zero with a very small probability. Therefore we have $f=f_0\,f_1\cdots f_{\chi-1}$. Since g is taken at random, we might expect that the values of $h(\alpha)$ are distributed uniformly among the powers of ξ (we discard cases when $h(\alpha)=0$). In other words, the depth of the recursive calls is expected to be in $O(\log d/\log\chi)$.

If we further assume that $\log\chi=o(\log q)$, then step 3 takes approximately $C_1\,\mathsf{M}_q(d)\log q$ for a certain constant C_1, and step 4 costs $C_2\,\chi\,\mathsf{M}_q(d)\log d$. Discarding the cost of the inversions, and compared to the case $\chi=2$, we achieve an approximate speed-up of

$$\frac{(C_1\log q+2\,C_2\log d)\,\mathsf{M}_q(d)\,(\log d)/\log 2}{(C_1\log q+\chi\,C_2\log d)\,\mathsf{M}_q(d)\,(\log d)/\log\chi}=\frac{\log\chi}{\log 2}\,\frac{C_1\log q/\log d+2\,C_2}{C_1\log q/\log d+\chi\,C_2}.$$

Whenever $C_1\log q/\log d\gg\chi\,C_2$, this speed-up is of order $\log\chi/\log 2$. In general, the speed-up is maximal if $\chi(\log\chi-1)=\frac{C_1\log q}{C_2\log d}$.

2.2 Mignotte–Schnorr's algorithm

Assuming given a primitive element of $\mathbb{F}_q^*$, Mignotte and Schnorr proposed a general deterministic root finding algorithm in [25], that is efficient when $q-1$ is smooth. For a fair comparison with our new algorithm presented in the next section (and since their article is written in French) we recall their method in a different and concise manner.

Let $\pi_1,\ldots,\pi_m$ be integers $\geqslant 2$, such that $q-1=\rho\,\pi_1\cdots\pi_m$, and let $\chi=\pi_1\cdots\pi_m$ and $\sigma=\pi_1+\cdots+\pi_m$. For instance, if the irreducible factorization of $q-1=p_1^{m_1}\cdots p_r^{m_r}$ is known, then we may take $\rho=1$ and $\pi_1=\pi_2=\cdots=\pi_{m_1}=p_1$, $\pi_{m_1+1}=\pi_{m_1+2}=\cdots=\pi_{m_1+m_2}=p_2$, ..., and set $m=m_1+\cdots+m_r$. In order to split f into factors of degrees at most ρ, we may use the following algorithm.

Algorithm 2.

Input. $f\in\mathbb{F}_q[x]$ of degree $d\geqslant 1$, monic, separable, which splits over $\mathbb{F}_q$, and such that $f(0)\neq 0$; a primitive root ξ of unity of order χ.

Output. $(f_1,e_1),\ldots,(f_s,e_s)$ in $(\mathbb{F}_q[x]\setminus\mathbb{F}_q)\times\{0,\ldots,\chi-1\}$ such that $f=f_1\cdots f_s$, and the f_i are monic, separable, and divide $x^\rho-\xi^{e_i}$, for all i.

1. Let $h_0(x):=x^\rho\operatorname{rem} f(x)$, and compute $h_i(x):=h_{i-1}(x)^{\pi_i}\operatorname{rem} f(x)$, for all $1\leqslant i\leqslant m-1$.
2. Initialize F with the list $[(f,0)]$.
3. For i from m down to 1 do
   a. Compute $h_{i-1}\operatorname{rem} g$ for all pairs (g,e) in F using a subproduct tree.
   b. Initialize G with the empty list, and for all j from 0 to π_i-1 do
      For each pair (g,e) in F do
         Compute $g_j:=\gcd((h_{i-1}\operatorname{rem} g)-\xi^{(e+j\chi)/\pi_i}, g)$.
         If g_j is not constant, then make it monic and append $(g_j,(e+j\chi)/\pi_i)$ to G.
      Let $F:=G$.
4. Return F.

Lemma 3. *Algorithm 2 is correct and executes in time* $O(\sigma\,\mathsf{M}_q(d)\log d+\mathsf{M}_q(d)\log q+m\,d\,\mathsf{I}(\log\chi)+m\,\mathsf{m}_q\,d\log\chi+d\,\mathsf{d}_q)=\sigma\,\tilde{O}(d\log q)+\tilde{O}(d\log^3 q)$.

Proof. We prove the correctness by descending induction on i from m down to 1. In fact, at the end of iteration i of the loop of step 3, we claim that $f=\prod_{(g,e)\in F} g$, that g divides $x^{\rho\pi_1\cdots\pi_{i-1}}-\xi^e$ for all $(g,e)\in F$, and that the integers e in F are divisible by $\pi_1\cdots\pi_{i-1}$ and bounded by $\chi-1$. By construction, these properties are all true with $i=m+1$ when entering step 3, so that by induction we can assume that these properties hold for $i+1$ when entering the loop at level i. Let $(g,e)\in F$, and let α be a root of g. From $\alpha^{\rho\pi_1\cdots\pi_i}=\xi^e$, since e is divisible by π_i, there exists $j\in\{0,\ldots,\pi_i-1\}$ such that $\alpha^{\rho\pi_1\cdots\pi_{i-1}}=\xi^{\frac{e+j\chi}{\pi_i}}$. We are done with the correctness.

As to the complexity, we can compute the χ/π_i for $i\in\{1,\ldots,m\}$ in time $O(m\,\mathsf{I}(\log\chi))$ as follows: we first compute π_1, $\pi_1\,\pi_2$, $\pi_1\,\pi_2\,\pi_3$, ..., $\pi_1\,\pi_2\cdots\pi_{m-1}$, and π_m, $\pi_{m-1}\,\pi_m$, $\pi_{m-2}\,\pi_{m-1}\,\pi_m$, ..., $\pi_2\cdots\pi_{m-1}\,\pi_m$, and then deduce each χ/π_i by multiplying $\pi_1\cdots\pi_{i-1}$ and $\pi_{i+1}\cdots\pi_m$.

Step 1 requires time $O(\mathsf{M}_q(d)\log q)$. In step 3.a, since the sum of the degrees of the polynomials in F is at most d, and since these polynomials are monic, this step can be done in time $O(\mathsf{M}_q(d)\log d)$. The cost of the gcds in step 3.b is $O(\pi_i\,\mathsf{M}_q(d)\log d)$ by the super-additivity of M_q. We compute all the e/π_i in time $O(d\,\mathsf{I}(\log\chi))$, and then all the ξ^{e/π_i} and ξ^{χ/π_i} by means of $O(d\log\chi)$ operations in $\mathbb{F}_q$. Deducing all the $\xi^{(e+j\chi)/\pi_i}$ takes $O(\pi_i\,d)$ additional products in $\mathbb{F}_q$.

Since the cardinality of F cannot exceed d, the total number of proper factors g_j in step 3.b is at most d. Therefore, we need $O(d)$ inversions in order to make all the polynomials in F monic. □

Notice that the dependence on σ is good when $q-1$ is smooth. For example, if $\rho=1$ and $\sigma=O(\log q)$, then the cost of root finding *via* the latter proposition drops to $\tilde{O}(d\log^3 q)$. This is higher than the average $\tilde{O}(d\log^2 q)$ bit-cost of Cantor–Zassenhaus' algorithm. Nevertheless since the term $\tilde{O}(d\log^3 q)$ corresponds to $O(d\log^2 q)$ products in $\mathbb{F}_q$, with a small constant hidden in the O, Mignotte–Schnorr's algorithm is competitive for small values of $\log q$.

In the original work of Mignotte and Schnorr [25], the cost of the algorithm was estimated to be $O(\mathsf{M}(d) \sum_{i=1}^{r} m_i (\log q + p_i \log d))$ operations in $\mathbb{F}_q$, if $q - 1 = p_1^{m_1} \cdots p_r^{m_r}$. Our presentation slightly differs by the use of a subproduct tree in step 3.a.

Let us briefly mention that a better bound for splitting f was achieved in [10]. Nevertheless, for finding all the roots, the method of [10] does not seem competitive in general.

2.3 Moenck's algorithm

Moenck's algorithm [26] deals with the special case when $q-1=\rho 2^m$. Let ζ be a primitive root of $\mathbb{F}_q^*$. Let $1 \leqslant i \leqslant m$, let f be a polynomial whose roots have orders dividing $\rho 2^i$, and let $\alpha \in \mathbb{F}_q^*$ be one of these roots. Then either this order divides $\rho\, 2^{i-1}$, or we have $\alpha^{\rho 2^{i-1}} + 1 = 0$, since $x^{\rho 2^i} - 1 = (x^{\rho 2^{i-1}} + 1)(x^{\rho 2^{i-1}} - 1)$. In the latter case, we obtain $(\alpha / \zeta^{2^{m-i}})^{\rho 2^{i-1}} = 1$. The polynomials $f_1 = \gcd(x^{\rho 2^{i-1}} - 1, f)$ and $f_2(x) = (f / f_1)(\zeta^{2^{m-i}} x)$ have all their roots of order dividing $\rho 2^{i-1}$. In this way, the roots of f can be computed inductively starting from $i=m$ down to $i=1$. At the end, we are reduced to finding roots of several polynomials whose orders divide ρ. If ρ is small, then an exhaustive search easily completes the computations. Otherwise we may use a fallback algorithm. Moenck's algorithm summarizes as follows.

Algorithm 4.

Input. $f \in \mathbb{F}_q[x]$ of degree $d \geqslant 1$, monic, separable, which splits over $\mathbb{F}_q$, and such that $f(0) \neq 0$; a primitive element ζ of $\mathbb{F}_q^*$.

Output. $(f_1, \gamma_1), \ldots, (f_s, \gamma_s)$ in $(\mathbb{F}_q[x] \setminus \mathbb{F}_q) \times \mathbb{F}_q$ such that $f = f_1 \cdots f_s$, the f_i are monic, separable, and the roots of $f_i(\gamma_i x)$ have orders dividing ρ.

1. Compute $h_i(x) := x^{\rho 2^i} \operatorname{rem} f(x)$ for all $i \in \{0, \ldots, m-1\}$.
2. Initialize F with the list $[(f, 1)]$.
3. For i from m down to 1 do
   a. Compute the remainders of $h_{i-1} \operatorname{rem} g$ for all triples (g, γ) in F using a subproduct tree.
   b. Initialize G as an empty list.
   c. For all (g, γ) in F do
      i. Compute $g_1(x) := \gcd((h_{i-1} \operatorname{rem} g)(x) - \gamma^{\rho 2^{i-1}}, g(x))$. If g_1 is not constant then make it monic and append (g_1, γ) to G.
      ii. Compute $g_2 := g / g_1$. If g_2 is not constant then make it monic, and append $(g_2, \gamma \zeta^{2^{m-i}})$ to G.
   d. Replace F by G.
4. Return F.

Our presentation differs from [26]. We also introduced step 3.a, which yields a slight theoretical speed-up, similarly to Mignotte–Schnorr's algorithm. In fact Moenck's and Mignotte–Schnorr's algorithms are quite similar from the point of view of the successive splittings of f, and the intermediate operations. We thus leave out the details on correctness and cost analysis. As an advantage, the logarithms of the successive roots are not needed. Nevertheless computing all the powers of γ in steps 3.c amounts to a bit-cost $\tilde{O}(d \log^3 q)$.

3. USING GRAEFFE TRANSFORMS

One advantage of Cantor–Zassenhaus' algorithm is its average depth in the recursive calls in $O(\log d)$. This is to be compared to the $O(\log q)$ iterations of Algorithms 2 and 4. In this section we propose a new kind of root finder based on the tangent Graeffe transform, which takes advantage of a FFT prime field, with an average cost not exceeding the one of Cantor–Zassenhaus.

3.1 Generalized Graeffe transforms

Classically, the *Graeffe transform* of a polynomial $g \in \mathbb{F}_q[x]$ of degree d is the unique polynomial $h \in \mathbb{F}_q[x]$ satisfying $h(x^2) = g(x)\, g(-x)$. If $g(x) = \prod_{i=1}^{d} (\alpha_i - x)$, then $h(x) = \prod_{i=1}^{d} (\alpha_i^2 - x)$. This construction can be extended to higher orders as follows: the *generalized Graeffe transform* of g of order π, written $G_\pi(g)$, is defined as the resultant

$$G_\pi(g)(x) = (-1)^{\pi d} \operatorname{Res}_z(g(z), z^\pi - x).$$

If $g = \prod_{i=1}^{d} (\alpha_i - x)$, then $G_\pi(g)(x) = \prod_{i=1}^{d} (\alpha_i^\pi - x)$. Equivalently, $G_\pi(g)$ is the characteristic polynomial of multiplication by x^π in $\mathbb{F}_q[x] / (g)$ (up to the sign). For our root finding algorithms, the most important case is when $q-1$ is smooth and the order π of the generalized Graeffe transform divides $q-1$.

Proposition 5. *Let $\pi_1, \ldots, \pi_m$ be integers $\geqslant 2$, such that $\chi = \pi_1 \cdots \pi_m$ divides $q-1$, and let ξ_i be given primitive roots of unity of orders π_i, for all $i \in \{1, \ldots, m\}$. If g is a monic polynomial in $\mathbb{F}_q[x]$ of degree d, then the generalized Graeffe transforms of orders $\pi_1, \pi_1 \pi_2, \pi_1 \pi_2 \pi_3, \ldots, \chi$ of g can be computed in time $O(m\, \mathsf{M}_q(\mu\, d))$ or $O(\mathsf{M}_q(\sigma\, d))$, where $\mu = \max(\pi_1, \ldots, \pi_m)$ and $\sigma = \pi_1 + \cdots + \pi_m$.*

Proof. Writing $g(x) = c \prod_{j=1}^{d} (\alpha_j - x)$ in an algebraic closure of $\mathbb{F}_q$, the Graeffe transform of g of order π_i is $h_i(x) = c^{\pi_i} \prod_{j=1}^{d} (\alpha_j^{\pi_i} - x)$. Consequently this leads to $h_i(x^{\pi_i}) = g(x)\, g(\xi_i\, x)\, g(\xi_i^2\, x) \cdots g(\xi_i^{\pi_i - 1}\, x)$. Using the latter formula, by Lemma 6 below, the transform can be obtained in time $O(\mathsf{M}_q(\pi_i\, d))$. Taking the sum over i concludes the proof. □

Lemma 6. *Let g be a polynomial of degree $d \geqslant 1$ in $\mathbb{F}_q[x]$, let $\alpha \in \mathbb{F}_q$, and let l be an integer. Then the product $P_l(x) = g(x)\, g(\alpha\, x)\, g(\alpha^2\, x) \cdots g(\alpha^{l-1}\, x)$ can be computed in time $O(\mathsf{M}_q(l\, d))$.*

Proof. Let $h := \lfloor l / 2 \rfloor$. If l is even, then we have $P_l(x) = P_h(x)\, P_h(\alpha^h\, x)$, otherwise we have $P_l(x) = P_h(x)\, P_h(\alpha^h\, x)\, g(\alpha^{l-1}\, x)$. These formulas lead to an algorithm with the claimed cost. □

Let us mention that good complexity bounds for Graeffe transforms for general finite fields can be found in [14].

3.2 Tangent Graeffe transforms

Introducing a formal parameter ε with $\varepsilon^2 = 0$, we define the *generalized tangent Graeffe transform* of g of order π as being $G_\pi(g(x + \varepsilon)) \in (\mathbb{F}_q[\varepsilon] / (\varepsilon^2))[x]$. For any ring R, computations with "tangent numbers" in $R[\varepsilon] / (\varepsilon^2)$ can be done with constant overhead with respect to computations in R (in the FFT model, the overhead is asymptotically limited to a factor of two). Whenever a Graeffe transform preserves the number of distinct simple roots, the tangent Graeffe transform can be used to directly recover the original simple roots from the transformed polynomial, as follows:

LEMMA 7. *Let $g \in \mathbb{F}_q[x]$ be separable of degree d, let π be coprime to p, and let $h(x) + \bar{h}(x)\,\varepsilon + O(\varepsilon^2) = G_\pi(g(x+\varepsilon))$. A nonzero root β of h is simple if, and only if, $\bar{h}(\beta) \neq 0$. For such a root, $\pi\,\beta\, h'(\beta)/\bar{h}(\beta)$ is the unique root α of g such that $\alpha^\pi = \beta$.*

PROOF. Let α be a root of g in an algebraic closure of $\mathbb{F}_q$. The lemma follows from the formula $\bar{h}(\alpha^\pi) = \pi\,\alpha^{\pi-1}\,h'(\alpha^\pi)$, obtained by direct calculation. □

In the context of the Graeffe method, the tangent transform is classical (for instance, see [24, 28] for history, references, and use in numerical algorithms). The generalized tangent Graeffe transform can also be seen as the *tangent characteristic polynomial* of x^π modulo $g(x+\varepsilon)$, and this construction is often attributed to Kronecker in algebraic geometry [23].

3.3 Overview of our methods

Let us write $q - 1 = \rho\,\pi_1 \cdots \pi_m$. Let $h_0 := f$, and let $h_1, \ldots, h_m$ be the Graeffe transforms of orders $\pi_1, \pi_1\,\pi_2, \ldots, \pi_1 \cdots \pi_m$ of f. The roots of h_m are to be found among the elements of order ρ. One may then find the roots of h_{m-1} among the π_m-th roots of the roots of h_m, and, by induction, the roots of h_{i-1} are to be found among the π_i-th roots of the roots of h_i. This is the starting point of the efficient deterministic algorithm designed in [14]. But in order to make it much more efficient than Cantor–Zassenhaus' algorithm we introduce and analyze two types of randomizations in the next sections. First we avoid computing π_i-th roots by combining random variable shifts and tangent transforms. Second we analyze the behaviour for random polynomials, which leads us to a very efficient heuristic algorithm.

3.4 A randomized algorithm

Our randomized algorithms can be competitive to Cantor–Zassenhaus' algorithm only for very smooth values of $q - 1$. For simplicity we focus on the important case of an FFT field where $q = M\,2^m + 1$, with $M = O(\log q)$.

We introduce the parameter $\tau \in \mathbb{F}_q$. Let $\chi = M\,2^{m-l}$ be a divisor of $q-1$, and let $\rho = (q-1)/\chi = 2^l$. Let $\alpha_1, \ldots, \alpha_d$ denote the roots of f. The Graeffe transform g_τ of $f(x-\tau)$ of order ρ equals $\prod_{i=1}^{d} ((\alpha_i + \tau)^\rho - x)$.

Given a pair of distinct roots α_i and α_j of f, we have $(\tau + \alpha_i)^\rho \neq (\tau + \alpha_j)^\rho$ for all but at most ρ values of τ. Therefore for all but at most $\frac{d(d-1)}{2}\,\rho$ values of τ, the polynomial g_τ has no multiple root. Considering that τ is taken uniformly at random in $\mathbb{F}_q$, the probability that g_τ has multiple roots is at most $\frac{d(d-1)}{2}\,\frac{1}{\chi}$. This yields the following randomized algorithm.

Randomized algorithm 8.

Input. $f \in \mathbb{F}_q[x]$ of degree $d \geqslant 1$, monic, separable, which splits over $\mathbb{F}_q$, and such that $f(0) \neq 0$; a primitive root ζ of $\mathbb{F}_q^*$.

Output. The roots of f.

1. If $d\,(d-1) \geqslant q$ then set l to 0. Otherwise set l to the largest integer in $\{0, \ldots, m\}$ such that $d\,(d-1) \leqslant M\,2^{m-l}$. Compute $\chi := M\,2^{m-l}$ and $\rho := (q-1)/\chi = 2^l$.
2. Pick $\tau \in \mathbb{F}_q$ uniformly at random, and compute $h_0(x) + \varepsilon\,\bar{h}_0(x) := f(x - \tau + \varepsilon)$, where $\varepsilon^2 = 0$.
3. Recursively compute the Graeffe transform $h_i + \varepsilon\,\bar{h}_i$ of order 2 of $h_{i-1} + \varepsilon\,\bar{h}_{i-1}$, for all $1 \leqslant i \leqslant m$.
4. Compute the list $E := [j\;2^m|\; j \in \{0, \ldots, M-1\}, h_m(\zeta^{j\,2^m}) = 0]$ of ζ-logarithms of the roots of h_m.
5. For i from m down to $l+1$ do
   a. Replace E by the concatenation of $[(e + j\,\chi)/2 |\, e \in E]$ for $j \in \{0, 1\}$.
   b. If E has cardinality more than d then remove the elements e from E such that $h_{i-1}(\zeta^e) \neq 0$.
6. If $l = 0$ then return $\{\zeta^e - \tau |\, e \in E\}$.
7. Compute $E_1 := [e |\, e \in E, \bar{h}_l(\zeta^e) \neq 0]$.
8. Compute $Z_1 := [2^l\,\zeta^e\,h_l'(\zeta^e)/\bar{h}_l(\zeta^e) - \tau |\, e \in E_1]$. Add τ to Z_1 if $f(\tau) = 0$.
9. Compute $f_2(x) := f(x)/\prod_{a \in Z_1}(x - a)$.
10. Compute recursively the roots Z_2 of f_2.
11. Return $Z_1 \cup Z_2$.

PROPOSITION 9. *Algorithm 8 is correct, and takes an average time $\tilde{O}(d\,\log^2 q)$, if $d < q$ and $q = M\,2^m + 1$ with $M = O(\log q)$.*

PROOF. The correctness follows from Lemma 7, which asserts that Z_1 is a subset of the roots of f.

Step 3 takes $\tilde{O}(d\,\log^2 q)$ by Proposition 5. Steps 2, 5.a, 5.b, 6, 7, 8, 9 execute in time $\tilde{O}(d\,\log^2 q)$. Step 4 costs $\tilde{O}((d+M)\,\log q) = \tilde{O}(d\,\log q + \log^2 q)$. If $d\,(d-1) \geqslant q$ then the number of iterations in step 5 is $m = O(\log q) = O(\log d)$. Otherwise the number of iterations is $m - l = O(\log d)$. Consequently, the total cost of all steps but step 10 is $\tilde{O}(d\log^2 q)$. From the choice of l, we have already seen that the degree of f_2 equals 0 with probability at least 1/2. Writing $T(d)$ for the average execution time, we thus have $T(d) \leqslant \tilde{O}(d\,\log^2 q) + \frac{1}{2}\,T(d)$, which implies $T(d) = \tilde{O}(d\log^2 q)$. □

Since the base field supports FFTs it is important to perform all intermediate computations by taking advantage of sharing transforms. This technique was popularized within the NTL library for many algorithms. In addition we notice that the first few iterates of the loop of step 5 can be reduced to direct FFT computations instead of generic multi-point evaluations.

3.5 Random polynomials which split over $\mathbb{F}_q$

Taking a monic random polynomial of degree d which splits over $\mathbb{F}_q$, for a uniform distribution, is equivalent to taking its d roots at random in $\mathbb{F}_q$. Let $\alpha_1, \ldots, \alpha_d$ represent the roots of f. We examine the behavior of tangent Graeff e transforms of such random polynomials.

Let $P_{d,i}$ be the number of monic polynomials of degree d which split over $\mathbb{F}_q$ and have i distinct nonzero roots of order dividing χ. Such a polynomial uniquely corresponds to the choice of i distinct values among χ, namely the roots, and then of the multiplicities of these roots with sum d.

Therefore we have $P_{d,i} = \binom{\chi}{i}\binom{d-1}{i-1}$. One can check that $\sum_{i=0}^{d} P_{d,i} = \binom{\chi+d-1}{\chi-1}$, which corresponds to choosing a multiplicity in $\{0, \ldots, d\}$ for each element of order dividing χ, under the constraint that the sum of the multiplicities is exactly d. The average number of roots of such polynomials is

$$\frac{\sum_{i=0}^{d} i\, P_{d,i}}{\sum_{i=0}^{d} P_{d,i}} = \frac{\chi\binom{\chi+d-2}{\chi-1}}{\binom{\chi+d-1}{\chi-1}} = \frac{d}{1+(d-1)/\chi}.$$

The latter formulas are direct consequences of the classical Chu–Vandermonde identity. Assuming that $\chi \geqslant d$, the average number of distinct roots is at least $d/2$. When χ is much greater than d then this lower bound is getting close to d.

PROPOSITION 10. *Let ρ be a fixed divisor of $q-1$, and let $\chi = (q-1)/\rho$. Let $f \in \mathbb{F}_q[x]$ be a monic separable polynomial of degree $d \leqslant q-1$, which splits over $\mathbb{F}_q$, and such that $f(0) \neq 0$. Let g be the Graeffe transform of f of order ρ. The average number of simple roots of g over all such polynomials f endowed with a uniform distribution is at least $d\frac{1-d/\chi}{1+d/\chi}$.*

Moreover, assuming that $\chi > 3d$ the probability that g has at least $\left(2 - \frac{1+d/\chi}{1-d/\chi}\right)d$ simple roots is at least $1/2$.

PROOF. The polynomial g is uniformly distributed in the set of monic polynomials with roots of order χ. Let s and m be the respective numbers of simple and multiple roots of g, so that $d \geqslant s + 2m$. We have just seen that the average number $s+m$ of distinct roots of g is at least $\frac{d}{1+d/\chi}$. Hence, $s + (d-s)/2 \geqslant \frac{d}{1+d/\chi}$ and $s \geqslant \frac{2d}{1+d/\chi} - d = d\frac{1-d/\chi}{1+d/\chi}$.

Setting $K = \frac{1-d/\chi}{1+d/\chi}$ and assuming that $\chi > 3d$, so that $2 > 1/K > 1$, let P be the probability that g has less than $(2-K)\,d$ simple roots. Then the average number of roots $K\,d$ is at most $P\,(2-1/K)\,d + (1-P)\,d$, whence $(K-1)\,d \leqslant P\,(1-1/K)\,d$. We conclude that $P \geqslant (K-1)/(1-1/K) = K > 1/2$. □

3.6 A heuristic randomized algorithm

Let χ be a divisor of $q-1$, $\rho = (q-1)/\chi$ and consider a polynomial $f \in \mathbb{F}_q[x]$ of degree d. In Section 3.4, we have shown that for all but at most $\frac{d(d-1)}{2}\rho$ values of τ, the Graeffe transform g_τ of order ρ of $f(x-\tau)$ has no multiple root. Taking $\chi > d^2$, this implies that g_τ has no multiple roots with probability at least $1/2$, when picking τ at random. Now Proposition 10 implies that at least one third of the roots remain simple with probability at least $1/2$ under the weaker condition that $\chi > 4d$ and for random f. It is an interesting question whether this fact actually holds for any f if τ is randomly chosen:

HEURISTIC. *Let $q - 1 = \rho\chi$ with $\chi > 4d$ and let $f \in \mathbb{F}_q[x]$ be a monic, separable polynomial of degree d which splits over $\mathbb{F}_q$. Then there exist at least $q/2$ elements $\tau \in \mathbb{F}_q[x]$ such that the Graeffe transform of order ρ of $f(x-\tau)$ has at least $d/3$ simple roots.*

From now on, assume that f is picked at random or that the above heuristic holds and τ is chosen at random. Taking $\chi > 4\,d$, we may then find the roots of g_τ by computing a few discrete Fourier transforms of length $O(d)$, instead of more expensive multi-point evaluations. Using tangent Graeffe transforms, the simple roots can be lifted back for almost no cost. These considerations lead to the following efficient randomized algorithm.

Randomized algorithm 11.

Input. $f \in \mathbb{F}_q[x]$ of degree $d \geqslant 1$, monic, separable, which splits over $\mathbb{F}_q$, and such that $f(0) \neq 0$; a primitive element ζ of $\mathbb{F}_q^*$.

Output. The roots of f.

1. If $d \geqslant M\,2^{m-3}$ then evaluate f on all the elements of $\mathbb{F}_q^*$, and return the roots.
2. Otherwise set l to be the largest integer in $\{1, \ldots, m-2\}$ such that $d < M\,2^{m-l-2}$. Compute $\chi := M\,2^{m-l}$ and $\rho := (q-1)/\chi = 2^l$.
3. Pick a random τ in $\mathbb{F}_q$, and compute the Graeffe transform $h_l(x) + \varepsilon\,\bar{h}_l(x)$ of order ρ of $f(x-\tau+\varepsilon)$ with $\varepsilon^2 = 0$.
4. Compute $[h_l(\zeta^{j2^l}) \mid j \in \{0, \ldots, \chi-1\}]$, $[h_l'(\zeta^{j2^l}) \mid j \in \{0, \ldots, \chi-1\}]$, $[\bar{h}_l(\zeta^{j2^l}) \mid j \in \{0, \ldots, \chi-1\}]$.
5. Compute $Z_1 := [2^l\,\zeta^{j2^l}\,h_l'(\zeta^{j2^l})/\bar{h}_l(\zeta^{j2^l}) - \tau \mid j \in \{0, \ldots, \chi-1\}, h_l(\zeta^{j2^l}) = 0, \bar{h}_l(\zeta^{j2^l}) \neq 0]$. Add τ to Z_1 if $f(\tau) = 0$.
6. Compute $f_2(x) := f(x)/\prod_{a \in Z_1}(x-a)$.
7. Compute recursively the roots Z_2 of f_2.
8. Return $Z_1 \cup Z_2$.

PROPOSITION 12. *Assume the heuristic or that f is chosen at random among the monic, separable polynomials with $f(0) \neq 0$ and which split over $\mathbb{F}_q$. Then Algorithm 11 takes an average time $O(\mathsf{M}_q(d)\,\log\,q) = \tilde{O}(d\,\log^2 q)$, whenever $d < q$ and $q = M\,2^m + 1$ with $M = O(\log q)$.*

PROOF. Of course if $d > M\;2^{m-3}$ then the cost is $O(\mathsf{M}_q(d)\log d)$. Now suppose we arrive in step 2. The roots of h_l have order dividing χ, and we have $\chi/2 \leqslant 4\,d < \chi$. If the algorithm terminates then it is correct by the same arguments as for Algorithm 8.

The cost of step 3 is bounded by $O(\mathsf{M}_q(d)\,\log\,d)$ (and even by $O(\mathsf{M}_q(d))$ if $p > d$ according to [4, Chapter 1, Section 2]). When computing h_l using l tangent Graeffe transforms of order 2, the cost of step 3 is bounded by $O(\mathsf{M}_q(d)\,l) = O(\mathsf{M}_q(d)\,\log\,q)$. Steps 4 and 5 can be done in time $O(\mathsf{M}_q(d)\,\log\,d)$. The average execution time $T(d)$ thus satisfies

$$T(d) \leqslant O(\mathsf{M}_q(d)\log q) + P\,T(d) + (1-P)\,T(2d/3),$$

where $P \leqslant 1/2$ is the probability that Z_2 contains more than $2\,d/3$ elements in step 7. It follows that $T(d) = O(\mathsf{M}_q(d)\,\log\,q) + T(2\,d/3)$, whence $T(d) = O(\mathsf{M}_q(d)\log q)$. □

The main bottleneck for Algorithm 11 is step 3. It would be possible to improve our complexity bound if a better algorithm were known to compute Graeffe transforms of order 2^l. In the FFT model, the tangent Graeffe transform of a polynomial of degree d can be computed in time $(4/3 + o(1))\;\mathsf{M}_q(d)$. In practice, this means that the asymptotic complexity of Algorithm 11 is equivalent to $4/3\,\mathsf{M}_q(d)\log_2 q$.

In order to reduce the cost of the Graeffe transforms, it is relevant to choose l such that $M\, 2^{m-l-\eta-1} < d \leqslant M\, 2^{m-l-\eta}$ for some small $\eta \geqslant 2$, which is to be determined in practice as a function of d and q. In this way more time is spent in multi-point evaluations. For the multi-point evaluations in step 4, one may use M FFTs of size 2^{m-l} for small values of M, or appeal to Bluestein's chirp transform [5].

4. TIMINGS

In this section we report on timings for the algorithms presented above. We use a platform equipped with an INTEL® CORE™ *i7-4770* CPU at 3.40 GHz, and 8 GB of *1600 MHz DDR3*. It runs the JESSIE GNU DEBIAN® operating system with a LINUX® kernel version 3.14 in 64 bit mode. We compile with GCC [12] version 4.9.1.

We use revision 9738 of MATHEMAGIX. For the sake of comparison to other software, we installed the NTL library version 8.0.0 [34] (configured to benefit from GMP [13] version 6.0.0), and FLINT version 2.4.4 [15]. For our benchmark family we simply build polynomials f of degree d from random pairwise distinct roots.

Table 1 shows timings for the FFT prime field $\mathbb{F}_q = \mathbb{F}_p$ with $p = 7 \cdot 2^{26} + 1$. The row NTL corresponds to the function `FindRoots`, which contains an optimization with respect to Algorithm 1 with $\chi = 2$: in fact, the polynomials g in step 2 are taken of degree 1 (see [20, 30, 32] for details). We implemented the same optimization in our versions of Cantor–Zassenhaus in MATHEMAGIX. The row FLINT corresponds to the function `nmod_poly_factor_equal_deg`, that does not take advantage of this optimization, which mainly explains a loss of efficiency. The rows "Alg. 1" to "Alg. 11" correspond to our own implementations in MATHEMAGIX of the above algorithms (see files `algebramix/polynomial_modular_int.hpp` and `algebramix/bench/polynomial_modular_int_bench.cpp`). Our modified version of Cantor–Zassenhaus' algorithm, with $\chi > 2$, does not reveal to be of practical interest for this prime size.

Concerning the deterministic algorithms, let us precise that we take $\pi_1 = \cdots = \pi_{m-1} = 2$ and $\pi_m = M$ in Algorithm 2. In addition, in our implementation of Algorithm 4, when g and i are small, for efficiency reasons, we compute $h_{i-1} \operatorname{rem} g$ using binary powering instead of simultaneous remainders. These deterministic methods turn out to be quite competitive.

Our Table 2 is similar to Table 1 for the FFT prime field $\mathbb{F}_q = \mathbb{F}_p$ with $p = 5 \cdot 2^{55} + 1$. Nevertheless NTL does not support this larger prime within its type `zz_p`. This larger prime starts to reveal the interest in our modified version of Cantor–Zassenhaus with $\chi > 2$. The speed-up measured with the modified version even more increases with larger primes: With $p = 7 \cdot 2^{120} + 1$, it reaches a factor 1.6 in size 2^{14}.

Using Graeffe transforms as in Algorithm 8 is not very competitive. However, in final, it is satisfactory to observe that our Algorithm 11, exploiting the tangent transform, gains by an order of magnitude over other existing methods in both tables.

$d+1$	2^8	2^9	2^{10}	2^{11}	2^{12}	2^{13}	2^{14}	2^{15}	2^{16}	2^{17}	2^{18}
NTL	0.0065	0.015	0.037	0.090	0.20	0.48	1.1	2.5	5.4	12	26
FLINT	0.0093	0.025	0.065	0.17	0.45	1.2	3.0	8.0	22	63	250
Alg. 1, Cantor–Zassenhaus, $\chi = 2$	0.010	0.020	0.043	0.092	0.20	0.42	0.90	1.9	4.0	8.6	18
Alg. 1, Cantor–Zassenhaus, modified	0.009	0.018	0.036	0.091	0.20	0.41	0.96	2.1	4.4	10	22
Alg. 2, Mignotte–Schnorr	0.063	0.12	0.25	0.51	1.0	2.0	3.9	7.8	15	31	62
Alg. 4, Moenck	0.025	0.051	0.10	0.21	0.44	0.91	1.9	3.9	8.2	17	35
Alg. 8, Graeffe, randomized	0.003	0.006	0.021	0.074	0.25	0.70	1.7	3.6	7.5	15	29
Alg. 11, Graeffe, heuristic	0.001	0.002	0.003	0.007	0.015	0.031	0.065	0.13	0.24	0.59	1.4

Table 1. Randomized root finding in degree d over $\mathbb{F}_p$, with $p = 7 \cdot 2^{26} + 1$, time in seconds.

$d+1$	2^8	2^9	2^{10}	2^{11}	2^{12}	2^{13}	2^{14}	2^{15}	2^{16}	2^{17}	2^{18}
FLINT	0.032	0.084	0.22	0.58	1.5	3.8	9.5	23	58	150	470
Alg. 1, Cantor–Zassenhaus, $\chi = 2$	0.035	0.075	0.16	0.37	0.78	1.7	3.8	8.6	19	41	90
Alg. 1, Cantor–Zassenhaus, modified	0.025	0.055	0.11	0.28	0.63	1.3	3.1	7.0	14	33	76
Alg. 2, Mignotte–Schnorr	0.22	0.46	0.96	2.0	4.2	8.7	18	39	83	180	370
Alg. 4, Moenck	0.89	0.18	0.37	0.76	1.6	3.4	7.2	16	33	72	150
Alg. 8, Graeffe, randomized	0.011	0.038	0.14	0.56	1.1	2.6	6.8	16	40	92	210
Alg. 11, Graeffe, heuristic	0.005	0.007	0.016	0.032	0.067	0.14	0.29	0.61	1.3	2.7	5.6

Table 2. Randomized root finding in degree d over $\mathbb{F}_p$, with $p = 5 \cdot 2^{55} + 1$, time in seconds.

Coming back to our initial motivation for sparse polynomial interpolation, let us mention that plugging Algorithm 11 into our implementations reported in [19] leads to quite good speed-ups. The total time for Example 1 of [19], concerning the product of random sparse polynomials, decreases from 12 s to 7.6 s with the "coefficient ratios" technique. In fact, the time spent in root finding decreases from 50 % to 8 % during the sole determination of the support.

Example 2 of [19] concerns the sparse interpolation of the determinant of the generic $n \times n$ matrix. For $n = 8$, the time for the "Kronecker substitution" technique with a prime of 68 bits decreases from 95 s to 43 s. The time elapsed in root finding during the sole determination of the support drops from 70 % to 20 %. Thanks to additional optimizations, the "coefficient ratios" technique now runs this example in 46 s.

Acknowledgements

Bruno Grenet was partially supported by a LIX–Qualcomm®–Carnot postdoctoral fellowship.

5. REFERENCES

[1] E. Bach. Comments on search procedures for primitive roots. *Math. Comp.*, 66:1719–1727, 1997.

[2] E. R. Berlekamp. Factoring polynomials over finite fields. *Bell System Tech. J.*, 46:1853–1859, 1967.

[3] E. R. Berlekamp. Factoring polynomials over large finite fields. *Math. Comp.*, 24:713–735, 1970.

[4] D. Bini and V. Y. Pan. *Polynomial and matrix computations. Vol. 1. Fundamental algorithms*. Progress in Theoretical Computer Science. Birkhäuser, 1994.

[5] L. I. Bluestein. A linear filtering approach to the computation of discrete Fourier transform. *IEEE Transactions on Audio and Electroacoustics*, 18(4):451–455, 1970.

[6] A. Bostan and É. Schost. Polynomial evaluation and interpolation on special sets of points. *J. Complexity*, 21(4):420–446, 2005.

[7] D. G. Cantor and E. Kaltofen. On fast multiplication of polynomials over arbitrary algebras. *Acta Infor.*, 28(7):693–701, 1991.

[8] D. G. Cantor and H. Zassenhaus. A new algorithm for factoring polynomials over finite fields. *Math. Comp.*, 36(154):587–592, 1981.

[9] Ph. Flajolet and J.-M. Steyaert. A branching process arising in dynamic hashing, trie searching and polynomial factorization. In M. Nielsen and E. M. Schmidt, editors, *Automata, Languages and Programming. Proceedings of the 9th ICALP Symposium*, volume 140 of *Lecture Notes in Comput. Sci.*, pages 239–251. Springer Berlin Heidelberg, 1982.

[10] J. von zur Gathen. Factoring polynomials and primitive elements for special primes. *Theoret. Comput. Sci.*, 52(1-2):77–89, 1987.

[11] J. von zur Gathen and J. Gerhard. *Modern computer algebra*. Cambridge University Press, 2nd edition, 2003.

[12] GCC, the GNU Compiler Collection. Software available at `http://gcc.gnu.org`, from 1987.

[13] T. Granlund et al. GMP, the GNU multiple precision arithmetic library, from 1991. Software available at `http://gmplib.org`.

[14] B. Grenet, J. van der Hoeven, and G. Lecerf. Deterministic root finding over finite fields using Graeffe transforms. `http://hal.archives-ouvertes.fr/hal-01081743`, 2015.

[15] W. Hart, F. Johansson, and S. Pancratz. FLINT: Fast Library for Number Theory, 2014. Version 2.4.4, `http://flintlib.org`.

[16] D. Harvey, J. van der Hoeven, and G. Lecerf. Even faster integer multiplication. `http://arxiv.org/abs/1407.3360`, 2014.

[17] D. Harvey, J. van der Hoeven, and G. Lecerf. Faster polynomial multiplication over finite fields. `http://arxiv.org/abs/1407.3361`, 2014.

[18] J. van der Hoeven et al. Mathemagix, from 2002. `http://www.mathemagix.org`.

[19] J. van der Hoeven and G. Lecerf. Sparse polynomial interpolation in practice. *ACM Commun. Comput. Algebra*, 48(4), 2014. In section "ISSAC 2014 Software Presentations".

[20] E. Kaltofen. Fifteen years after DSC and WLSS2, what parallel computations I do today. Invited lecture at PASCO 2010. In *Proceedings of the 4th International Workshop on Parallel and Symbolic Computation*, PASCO '10, pages 10–17. ACM Press, 2010.

[21] E. Kaltofen and V. Shoup. Subquadratic-time factoring of polynomials over finite fields. *Math. Comp.*, 67(223):1179–1197, 1998.

[22] K. S. Kedlaya and C. Umans. Fast modular composition in any characteristic. In A. Z. Broder et al., editors, *49th Annual IEEE Symposium on Foundations of Computer Science 2008 (FOCS '08)*, pages 146–155. IEEE, 2008.

[23] L. Kronecker. Grundzüge einer arithmetischen Theorie der algebraischen Grössen. *J. reine angew. Math.*, 92:1–122, 1882.

[24] G. Malajovich and J. P. Zubelli. Tangent Graeffe iteration. *Numer. Math.*, 89(4):749–782, 2001.

[25] M. Mignotte and C. Schnorr. Calcul déterministe des racines d'un polynôme dans un corps fini. *C. R. Acad. Sci. Paris Sér. I Math.*, 306(12):467–472, 1988.

[26] R. T. Moenck. On the efficiency of algorithms for polynomial factoring. *Math. Comp.*, 31:235–250, 1977.

[27] G. L. Mullen and D. Panario. *Handbook of Finite Fields*. Discrete Mathematics and Its Applications. Chapman and Hall/CRC, 2013.

[28] V. Pan. Solving a polynomial equation: Some history and recent progress. *SIAM Rev.*, 39(2):187–220, 1997.

[29] C. H. Papadimitriou. *Computational Complexity*. Addison-Wesley, 1994.

[30] M. O. Rabin. Probabilistic algorithms in finite fields. *SIAM J. Comput.*, 9(2):273–280, 1980.

[31] L. Rónyai. Factoring polynomials modulo special primes. *Combinatorica*, 9(2):199–206, 1989.

[32] V. Shoup. A fast deterministic algorithm for factoring polynomials over finite fields of small characteristic. In S. M. Watt, editor, *ISSAC '91: Proceedings of the 1991 International Symposium on Symbolic and Algebraic Computation*, pages 14–21. ACM Press, 1991.

[33] V. Shoup. Searching for primitive roots in finite fields. *Math. Comp.*, 58:369–380, 1992.

[34] V. Shoup. *NTL: A Library for doing Number Theory*, 2014. Software, version 8.0.0. `http://www.shoup.net/ntl`.

Optimizing a Parametric Linear Function over a Non-compact Real Algebraic Variety

Feng Guo
School of Mathematical Sciences
Dalian University of Technology
Dalian, 116024, China
fguo@dlut.edu.cn

Mohab Safey El Din
Sorbonne Universités, UPMC, Univ Paris 06
INRIA Paris-Rocquencourt
POLSYS project-team
CNRS LIP6 UMR 7606
Mohab.Safey@lip6.fr

Chu Wang and Lihong Zhi
Key Lab. of Mathematics Mechanization
AMSS, Beijing 100190, China
{cwang,lzhi}@mmrc.iss.ac.cn

ABSTRACT

We consider the problem of optimizing a parametric linear function over a non-compact real trace of an algebraic set $\mathcal{V}$. Our goal is to compute a representing polynomial which defines a hypersurface containing the graph of the optimal value function. Rostalski and Sturmfels showed that when $\mathcal{V}$ is irreducible and smooth with a compact real trace, then the least degree representing polynomial is given by the defining polynomial of the irreducible hypersurface dual to the projective closure of the $\mathcal{V}$.

First, we generalize this approach to non-compact situations. We prove that the graph of the opposite of the optimal value function is still contained in the affine cone over a dual variety similar to the one considered in compact case. In consequence, we present an algorithm for solving the considered parametric optimization problem for generic parameters' values. For some special parameters' values, the representing polynomials of the dual variety can be identically zero, which give no information on the optimal value. We design a dedicated algorithm that identifies those regions of the parameters' space and computes for each of these regions a new polynomial defining the optimal value over the considered region.

Categories and Subject Descriptors

I.1.2 [**Computing Methodologies**]: Symbolic and Algebraic Manipulation—*Algorithms*; G.1.6 [**Numerical Analysis**]: Global optimization

Keywords

Dual variety; polynomial optimization; recession pointed cone

1. INTRODUCTION

Parametric optimization problems widely arise in both theoretical problems and practical applications, like the maximum likelihood estimation and the model predictive control [5]. It is worthwhile to express the optimal value as an explicit or implicit function of the parameters in the region of interest.

In this paper, we consider the problem of optimizing a parametric linear function over a real algebraic variety

$$c_0^* := \sup_{x\in\mathbb{R}^n} \quad \mathbf{c}^T x = \mathbf{c}_1 x_1 + \cdots + \mathbf{c}_n x_n \qquad \text{s.t.} \quad h_1(x) = \cdots = h_p(x) = 0, \tag{1}$$

where $h_1, \ldots, h_p \in \mathbb{R}[X_1, \ldots, X_n]$ are polynomials in the decision variables $(X_1, \ldots, X_n)$ and $\mathbf{c} = (\mathbf{c}_1, \ldots, \mathbf{c}_n)$ denotes unspecified parameters.

The optimal value c_0^* can be regarded as a function of the parameters $\mathbf{c}$, i.e. the *optimal value function*. Our goal is to compute a polynomial that defines a hypersurface in the parameters' space which contains the graph of this function.

Typically, the *cylindrical algebraic decomposition* (CAD) [8] can be applied to solve (1).

More precisely, by introducing the Boolean operators $\wedge$ (and), we associate (1) with a Boolean expression

$$(h_1(X) = 0) \wedge \cdots \wedge (h_p(X) = 0) \wedge (\mathbf{c}_0 - \mathbf{c}^T X \geq 0) \tag{2}$$

with $X = (X_1, \ldots, X_n)$.

Indeed, recall that a CAD can be used to describe the projection of a semi-algebraic set (which is equivalent to eliminating one block of quantifiers).

By computing the CAD of the semi-algebraic set in $\mathbb{R}^{2n+1}$ defined by (2) with an ordering where the X-variables are larger than the $\mathbf{c}$-variables, the *projection phase* provides us a set of polynomials in $\mathbb{R}[\mathbf{c}_0, \mathbf{c}, X]$, called *projection level factors*, which defines the boundaries of *cells* in the parameters' space $\mathbb{R}^n$. However, the complexity of CAD algorithms is doubly exponential in the number of variables which limits its practical application to nontrivial problems involving 4 variables at most and this general approach may return numerous irrelevant polynomials.

In the last decade, several approaches have been developed to design dedicated algebraic techniques for polynomial optimization (see [31, 17, 16, 18, 2, 34] and references therein). In the non-parametric case, they allow to compute polynomials defining the optimum of a polynomial optimization problem whose degrees are singly exponential in the number of decision variables.

Here, our goal is to extend these techniques to the parametric case. We denote by $\Phi \in \mathbb{Q}[\mathbf{c}_0, \mathbf{c}_1, \ldots, \mathbf{c}_n]$ a polynomial defining a hypersurface in the parameters' space which contains the graph of the optimal value function.

The smallest possible degree for Φ in the variable $\mathbf{c}_0$ is called the *algebraic degree* of the optimization problem (1). This number measures the complexity of (1). Therefore, a lot of interest has been attracted on finding the polynomial Φ and the algebraic degree [6, 15, 20, 24, 25, 27, 30].

We denote $\mathbf{h} = \{h_1, \ldots, h_p\}$ the sequence of polynomials appearing in (1) and let

$$\mathcal{V} = \{v \in \mathbb{C}^n \mid h_1(v) = \cdots = h_p(v) = 0\}. \tag{3}$$

*Feng Guo is supported by the Fundamental Research Funds for the Central Universities, the Chinese National Natural Science Foundation under grants 11401074. Lihong Zhi and Chu Wang are supported by NKBRPC 2011CB302400, the Chinese National Natural Science Foundation under grants 91118001. Mohab Safey El Din is supported by the GEOLMI grant (ANR 2011 BS03 011 06) of the French National Research Agency. The authors are supported by CNRS and INRIA through the ECCA project at LIAMA.

ISSAC'15, July 6–9, 2015, Bath, United Kingdom.

DOI: http://dx.doi.org/10.1145/2755996.2756666.

We assume below that $\mathbf{h}$ generates a radical and equidimensional ideal. The *regular points* of $\mathcal{V}$ are those points at which the rank of Jacobian matrix associated to $\mathbf{h}$ is the codimension of $\mathcal{V}$.

We let $\mathcal{V}^*$ be the dual variety associated with $\mathcal{V}$, which is the Zariski closure of the vectors in the projective space tangent to the projective closure of $\mathcal{V}$ at its regular points. Its defining polynomials can be seen as polynomials with coefficients in $\mathbb{Q}[\mathbf{c}_0, \mathbf{c}_1, \ldots, \mathbf{c}_n]$. Rostalski and Sturmfels in [30, Theorem 5.23] show that, when $\mathcal{V}$ is irreducible, compact in $\mathbb{R}^n$ and smooth, the optimal value function Φ is represented by the defining polynomial of $\mathcal{V}^*$. Therefore, when $\mathcal{V}$ is compact in $\mathbb{R}^n$, the defining polynomial of $\mathcal{V}^*$ can fulfill our goal mentioned above. The compactness in the assumption is included to ensure that the optimum c_0^* is well-defined and achieved which are essential in the proof of [30, Theorem 5.23].

However, when $\mathcal{V} \cap \mathbb{R}^n$ is *non-compact*, the optimal value c_0^* for some $(\gamma_1, \ldots, \gamma_n) \in \mathbb{R}^n$ could be infinite or finite but can not be attained, i.e. c_0^* is an *asymptotic critical value* at infinity [21, 22, 26]. Hence, the proof of [30, Theorem 5.23] is not valid in this case. Another issue with the defining polynomials of $\mathcal{V}^*$ is that they might vanish on a Zariski closed set of parameters' values $(\gamma_1, \ldots, \gamma_n) \in \mathbb{R}^n$. In other words, they give no information about the optimal values for these parameters' values. We aim to explore the treatment of the above difficulties.

Main contributions. We consider the problem of optimizing a parametric linear function over a non-compact real trace of an algebraic set $\mathcal{V}$. Supposing $\mathcal{V}$ is smooth, we show that the graph of the opposite of the optimal value function is contained in the affine cone over a dual variety $\mathcal{V}^*$, i.e. $(-c_0^* : \gamma_1 : \cdots : \gamma_n) \in \mathcal{V}^*$ whenever the optimal value c_0^* is bounded at $(\gamma_1, \ldots, \gamma_n)$. We design an algorithm for solving the optimization problem (1) for generic parameters' values. It returns a set of two polynomials (Φ, Z) such that

- $\Phi \in \mathbb{Q}[\mathbf{c}_0, \mathbf{c}]$ and $Z \in \mathbb{Q}[\mathbf{c}]$;
- for any $\gamma = (\gamma_1, \ldots, \gamma_n) \notin \mathbf{V}(Z)$, if the associated optimum c_0^* of (1) is bounded, then $\Phi(\mathbf{c}_0, \gamma)$ is not zero and its set of roots contains the optimum c_0^* of (1).

If $\mathcal{V}$ is irreducible, smooth and the closure of the convex hull of $\mathcal{V} \cap \mathbb{R}^n$ contains no lines, then similar to [30, Theorem 5.23], we show that $\mathcal{V}^*$ is an irreducible hypersurface and its defining polynomial represents the optimal value function of (1).

When $\mathcal{V}$ is not smooth but its real trace is compact, we construct recursively a finite number of dual varieties such that $(-c_0^* : \gamma_1 : \cdots : \gamma_n)$ lies in the union of these dual varieties. We design an algorithm which returns a finite sequence of (Φ_i, Z_i) with the property that for any $\gamma = (\gamma_1, \ldots, \gamma_n)$ whose associated optimum c_0^* is bounded, there exists an i, if $Z_i(\gamma) \neq 0$, then c_0^* is contained in the roots of $\Phi_i(\mathbf{c}_0, \gamma)$.

It may happen that for some special parameters' values, the polynomials obtained with the above approach are identically 0. Then, they provide no information on the optimization problem when the parameters are instantiated to these values.

We design a parametric variant of [18] that solves this problem. Under the assumption that $\mathcal{V}$ is smooth and when the parameters are instantiated, the algorithm in [18] allows to obtain a polynomial of degree singly exponential in the number of decision variables X whose set of roots contains the global optimum of the instantiated polynomial optimization problem.

We use the algebraic nature of the algorithm in [18] to design a parametric variant that returns a list of triples

$$(\Phi_1, Z_1, \mathbf{P}_1), \ldots, (\Phi_k, Z_k, \mathbf{P}_k)$$

such that

- $\Phi_i \in \mathbb{Q}[\mathbf{c}_0, \mathbf{c}]$, $Z_i \in \mathbb{Q}[\mathbf{c}]$ and $\mathbf{P}_i \subset \mathbb{Q}[\mathbf{c}]$ generates a prime ideal for $1 \leq i \leq k$;
- $\cup_{i=1}^k \mathbf{V}(\mathbf{P}_i)$ is the whole parameters' space and $\mathbf{V}(\mathbf{P}_i) - \mathbf{V}(Z_i)$ is not empty for $1 \leq i \leq k$;
- for any $\gamma = (\gamma_1, \ldots, \gamma_n) \in \mathbb{R}^n$ such that $\gamma \in \mathbf{V}(\mathbf{P}_i) - \mathbf{V}(Z_i)$, the set of roots of $\Phi(\mathbf{c}_0, \gamma_1, \ldots, \gamma_n)$ contains the global optimum of the polynomial optimization problem (1) when $\mathbf{c}_1, \ldots, \mathbf{c}_n$ are instantiated to $\gamma_1, \ldots, \gamma_n$.

This paper is organized as follows. In Section 2, we recall some background in convex analysis, algebraic geometry and dual varieties needed in this paper. In Section 3, we investigate the relation between the graph of the optimal value function and the dual variety $\mathcal{V}^*$ when the algebraic variety $\mathcal{V}$ is not compact in $\mathbb{R}^n$ or not smooth. In Section 4, we present the parametrized variant of [18].

2. PRELIMINARIES

2.1 Convex sets and cones

We first present some ingredients from convex analysis [28]. A non-empty subset $C \subseteq \mathbb{R}^n$ is said to be *convex* if $(1-\lambda)x + \lambda y \in C$ whenever $x \in C$, $y \in C$ and $0 < \lambda < 1$. We denote $\mathbf{cl}\,(C)$ and $\mathbf{int}\,(C)$ as the *closure* and *interior* of C, respectively. The *affine hull* of a convex set C, denoted by $\mathbf{aff}(C)$, is the unique smallest affine set containing C. The *relative interior* of a convex set $C \subseteq \mathbb{R}^n$, denoted by $\mathbf{ri}\,(C)$, is defined as the interior of C regarded as a subset of $\mathbf{aff}(C)$. For an arbitrary set $C \subseteq \mathbb{R}^n$, denote $\mathbf{co}\,(C)$ as its convex hall.

The *polar* of a non-empty convex set $C \subseteq \mathbb{R}^n$ is a closed convex set defined as

$$C^{\circ} = \{x \in \mathbb{R}^n \mid \forall y \in C, \langle x, y \rangle \leq 1\}.$$

We have $C^{\circ\circ} = \mathbf{cl}\,(\mathbf{co}\,(C \cup \{0\}))$.

A subset $K \subseteq \mathbb{R}^n$ is called a *cone* if it is closed under positive scalar multiplication, i.e. $\lambda x \in K$ for all $x \in K$ and $\lambda > 0$. A convex cone K is *pointed* if it is closed and $K \cap -K = \{0\}$. The *polar* of a non-empty convex cone K is defined as

$$K^{\circ} = \{x \in \mathbb{R}^n \mid \forall y \in K, \langle x, y \rangle \leq 0\}.$$

The *recession cone* 0^+C of a non-empty convex set C is the set including all vectors y satisfying $x + \lambda y \in C$ for every $\lambda > 0$ and $x \in C$. Importantly, a closed convex set $C \subseteq \mathbb{R}^n$ is bounded if and only if 0^+C consists of the zero vector alone. A closed and unbounded convex set C contains *no* lines if and only if 0^+C is pointed.

Let f be a function whose domain is a subset $S \subseteq \mathbb{R}^n$ and values are real or $\pm\infty$. The *epigraph* of f is defined as

$$\mathbf{epi}(f) = \{(x, \mu) \in \mathbb{R}^{n+1} \mid x \in S,\ \mu \in \mathbb{R},\ \mu \geq f(x)\}.$$

We say that f is a *convex function* on S if $\mathbf{epi}(f)$ is convex as a subset of $\mathbb{R}^{n+1}$. The effective domain of a convex function f on S is the projection of $\mathbf{epi}(f)$ on $\mathbb{R}^n$:

$$\begin{aligned}\mathbf{dom}(f) &= \{x \in \mathbb{R}^n \mid \exists \mu \in \mathbb{R} \text{ s.t. } (x, \mu) \in \mathbf{epi}(f)\} \\ &= \{x \in \mathbb{R}^n \mid f(x) < +\infty\}.\end{aligned}$$

THEOREM 2.1. [19, Theorem 1.2] *Let $C \subseteq \mathbb{R}^n$ be a closed and unbounded convex set, then*

1. $(0^+C)^{\circ}$ *is an n-dimensional convex set;*
2. $\mathbf{int}\,((0^+C)^{\circ}) \subseteq \mathbf{dom}(c_0^*(\mathbf{c} \mid C)) \subseteq (0^+C)^{\circ}$. *Moreover, we have $f(x) = a^T x$ attains its supremum on C for every $a \in \mathbf{int}\,((0^+C)^{\circ})$.*

2.2 Dual varieties

Denote $X = (X_1, \ldots, X_n)$. For any ideal (homogeneous ideal) I in $\mathbb{R}[X]$ ($\mathbb{R}[X_0, X]$), denote $\mathbf{V}(I)$ as the affine (projective) variety defined by I in $\mathbb{C}^n$ ($\mathbb{P}^n(\mathbb{C})$). Now let us review some background about dual varieties in $\mathbb{P}^n(\mathbb{C})$ [29, 30]. In the following, we abbreviate $\mathbb{P}^n(\mathbb{C})$ as $\mathbb{P}^n$ for convenience. Let $I = \langle f_1, \ldots, f_p \rangle$ be a homogeneous radical ideal in the polynomial ring $\mathbb{R}[X_0, X]$ and $V = \mathbf{V}(I) \subseteq \mathbb{P}^n$. The *singular locus* $\mathrm{sing}(V)$ is defined by the vanishing of the $c \times c$ minors of the $p \times (n+1)$ Jacobian matrix $\mathsf{Jac}(I) = (\partial f_i / \partial X_j)$, where $c = \mathrm{codim}(V)$. Let $V_{\mathrm{reg}} = V \backslash \mathrm{sing}(V)$ denote the set of regular points in V. The projective variety V is smooth if $V = V_{\mathrm{reg}}$.

A point $u = (u_0 : u_1 : \cdots : u_n)$ in the dual projective space $(\mathbb{P}^n)^*$ represents the hyperplane $\{x \in \mathbb{P}^n \mid \sum_{i=0}^n u_i x_i = 0\}$. We say that u is *tangent* to V at a regular point $x \in V_{\text{reg}}$ if x lies in the hyperplane $\sum_{i=0}^n u_i x_i = 0$ and its representing vector $(u_0, u_1, \ldots, u_n)$ lies in the row space of the Jacobian matrix $\mathsf{Jac}(I)$ at the point x. The *conormal variety* $\text{CN}(V)$ is the closure of the set

$$\{(x, u) \in \mathbb{P}^n \times (\mathbb{P}^n)^* \mid x \in V_{\text{reg}} \text{ and } u \text{ is tangent to } V \text{ at } x\}.$$

The *dual variety* V^* is the projection of $\text{CN}(V)$ onto the second factor. More precisely, the dual variety is the closure of the set

$$\{u \in (\mathbb{P}^n)^* \mid u \text{ is tangent to } V \text{ at some regular point}\}.$$

2.3 Generalized critical values

For a vector $v \in \mathbb{R}^n$, $\|v\|$ denotes the standard Euclidean norm of v. Let V be a smooth affine variety, and let $f : V \to \mathbb{R}$ be a polynomial dominant mapping. Denote $K_0(f, V)$ as the critical values of f on V. The set of *asymptotic critical values* at infinity [21, 22, 26] of f on V is defined as

$$K_\infty(f, V) = \left\{ y \in \mathbb{R} \;\middle|\; \begin{array}{l} \exists\, x^{(k)} \in V, \text{ s.t. } x^{(k)} \to \infty, \\ f(x^{(k)}) \to y,\ \|x^{(k)}\|\nu(d_{x^{(k)}} f) \to 0 \end{array} \right\},$$

where $d_{x^{(k)}} f$ stands for the differential of f evaluated at $x^{(k)}$ and ν stands for the distance of $d_{x^{(k)}} f$ to the space of degenerate linear maps on the tangent space to V at $x^{(k)}$. The set of generalized critical values of f is defined as

$$K(f, V) = K_0(f, V) \cup K_\infty(f, V).$$

It has been shown in [22, Theorem 3.1] and [21, Theorem 3.3, Corollary 4.1] that $K(f, V)$ is a finite set.

THEOREM 2.2. [21, 26] *If f is bounded above, i.e. $f^* = \sup_{x \in V} f(x)$ is finite, then $f^* \in K(f, V)$.*

3. DUALITY IN NON-COMPACT CASE

For the algebraic variety $\mathcal{V}$ defined in (3), let

$$C_{\mathbf{h}} = \mathbf{cl}\left(\mathbf{co}\left(\mathcal{V} \cap \mathbb{R}^n\right)\right),$$

i.e. the closure of the convex hull of $\mathcal{V} \cap \mathbb{R}^n$. Then, the problem (1) is equivalent to

$$c_0^* = \sup\ \mathbf{c}^T x \quad \text{s.t. } x \in C_{\mathbf{h}}. \tag{4}$$

Let $\mathcal{V}^*$ be the dual variety to the projective closure of $\mathcal{V}$. When $C_{\mathbf{h}}$ contains no lines, i.e. $0^+ C_{\mathbf{h}}$ is pointed, the relation between the optimal value function of (1) and the defining polynomial of $\mathcal{V}^*$ is investigated in [19]. Now we prove the correctness of some results therein without the assumption of pointedness. It will yield an algorithm for solving parametric optimization problem (1) with generic parameters.

3.1 Smooth Case

In this subsection, we assume the algebraic variety $\mathcal{V}$ in (3) is smooth. Recall that $\mathbf{dom}(c_0^*(\mathbf{c} \mid C_{\mathbf{h}}))$ denotes the collection of the parameters' values $\gamma \in \mathbb{R}^n$ such that the supremum of $\gamma^T x$ on $C_{\mathbf{h}}$ is finite. We generalize Rostalski and Sturmfels' result [30, Theorem 5.23] to the non-compact case as follows.

THEOREM 3.1. *Suppose that $\mathcal{V}$ in (3) is smooth, then*

$$(-c_0^* : \gamma_1 : \cdots : \gamma_n) \in \mathcal{V}^* \tag{5}$$

for every $\gamma \in \mathbf{dom}(c_0^*(\mathbf{c} \mid C_{\mathbf{h}}))$.

PROOF. Fix a $\gamma \in \mathbf{dom}(c_0^*(\mathbf{c} \mid C_{\mathbf{h}}))$. By the definition, the supremum c_0^* of $f(X) = \gamma^T X$ on $\mathcal{V} \cap \mathbb{R}^n$ is finite. For the case when c_0^* is a critical value which can be attained, see the proof of [30, Theorem 5.23]. Now by Theorem 2.2, we suppose that c_0^* is an asymptotic critical value of f over $\mathcal{V} \cap \mathbb{R}^n$. Then, there exists a sequence $\{x^{(k)}\} \subseteq \mathcal{V} \cap \mathbb{R}^n$ such that $\|x^{(k)}\| \to \infty$, $f(x^{(k)}) \to c_0^*$ and $\|x^{(k)}\|\nu(d_{x^{(k)}} f) \to 0$. By [36, Lemma 2.1], for each $x^{(k)}$, we can find a vector $\gamma^{(k)}$ in the normal space of $\mathcal{V}$ at $\{x^{(k)}\}$ such that $\|\gamma^{(k)} - \gamma\| = \nu(d_{x^{(k)}} f)$. Then, $\|x^{(k)}\|\|\gamma^{(k)} - \gamma\| \to 0$, which implies $\|\gamma^{(k)} - \gamma\| \to 0$ and $(\gamma^{(k)})^T x^{(k)} \to c_0^*$. It can be checked that

$$(-(\gamma^{(k)})^T x^{(k)} : \gamma_1^{(k)} : \cdots : \gamma_n^{(k)}) \in \mathcal{V}^*.$$

Since $\mathcal{V}^*$ is closed, we have $(-c_0^* : \gamma_1 : \cdots : \gamma_n) \in \mathcal{V}^*$. □

COROLLARY 3.2. *If $\mathcal{V}$ is irreducible, smooth and $C_{\mathbf{h}}$ contains no lines, then $\mathcal{V}^*$ is an irreducible hypersurface and its defining polynomial represents the optimal value function of (1).*

PROOF. Since $C_{\mathbf{h}}$ contains no lines, $0^+(C_{\mathbf{h}})$ is pointed. According to Theorem 2.1, $(0^+ C_{\mathbf{h}})^{\text{o}}$ is a n-dimensional convex set and $\mathbf{int}\left((0^+ C_{\mathbf{h}})^{\text{o}}\right)$ is contained in $\mathbf{dom}(c_0^*(\mathbf{c} \mid C_{\mathbf{h}}))$. Therefore, the affine cone of the Zariski closure of

$$\left\{(-c_0^* : \gamma_1 : \cdots : \gamma_n) \in (\mathbb{P}^n)^* \mid \gamma \in \mathbf{int}\left((0^+ C_{\mathbf{h}})^{\text{o}}\right)\right\} \tag{6}$$

has dimension $\geq n$. By [9, Theorem 12 (i), §3, Chpt. 9], the Zariski closure of (6) is of dimension $\geq n - 1$. By Theorem 3.1 and [30, Proposition 5.10], we have $\dim(\mathcal{V}^*) = n - 1$. As $\mathcal{V}$ is irreducible, $\mathcal{V}^*$ is an irreducible hypersurface [13, Proposition 1.3], and coincides with the Zariski closure of (6) according to [9, Proposition 10 (ii), §4, Chpt. 9]. Then, the conclusion follows. □

In the sequel, we say that a property depending on some indeterminates is *generic* if there exists a non-empty Zariski open subset of the space endowed by these indeterminates over which the property holds (we will also say that the property holds for generic values of these indeterminates).

An algorithm can be derived from Theorem 3.1 for solving the parametric optimization (1) for generic parameter as described below. Denote $\mu = (\mu_1, \ldots, \mu_p)$. Let $\mathsf{J} \subseteq \mathbb{Q}[\mathbf{c}_0, \mathbf{c}, \mu, X]$ be the ideal generated by

$$\mathbf{c}^T X - \mathbf{c}_0,\ h_1, \ldots, h_p,\ \mathbf{c}_i - \sum_{j=1}^p \mu_j \frac{\partial h_j}{\partial X_i},\ i = 1, \ldots, n.$$

Since $\mathbf{h}$ generates a radical ideal, for any $(c_0^*, \gamma, \bar{\mu}, \bar{x}) \in \mathbf{V}(\mathsf{J})$, c_0^* is a critical value of the function $\gamma^T X$ on $\mathcal{V}$ at a critical point $\bar{x}$.

ALGORITHM 3.1. $\mathsf{GenericParametricOptimization}(\mathbf{h})$
Input: $h_1, \ldots, h_p \in \mathbb{Q}[X]$ *which generate a radical ideal*
Output: (Φ, Z) *such that*

- $\Phi \in \mathbb{Q}[\mathbf{c}_0, \mathbf{c}]$ *and* $Z \in \mathbb{Q}[\mathbf{c}]$
- *For any* $\gamma \in \mathbf{dom}(c_0^*(\mathbf{c} \mid C_{\mathbf{h}}))$ *such that* $Z(\gamma) \neq 0$, $\Phi(\mathbf{c}_0, \gamma)$ *is not zero and its set of roots contains the optimum* c_0^* *of* (1).

Step 1 *Compute the reduced Gröbner basis G of $\mathsf{J} \cap \mathbb{Q}[\mathbf{c}_0, \mathbf{c}]$ with block lex order $X \succ \mu \succ \mathbf{c} \succ \mathbf{c}_0$.*
Step 2 *Set Γ to be the set of polynomials in G containing the variable $\mathbf{c}_0$.*
Step 3 *Set Φ to be the polynomial in Γ with the lowest degree in $\mathbf{c}_0$.*
Step 4 *Set Z to be the sum of squares of all coefficients of Φ in view of $\mathbb{Q}[\mathbf{c}_1, \ldots, \mathbf{c}_n][\mathbf{c}_0]$.*

THEOREM 3.3. *In Algorithm 3.1, we have $\Gamma \neq \emptyset$, $\mathcal{V}^* = \mathbf{V}(\Gamma)$ and the algorithm is correct.*

PROOF. By the definition of dual varieties and Theorem 3.1, it suffices to show that $\Gamma \neq \emptyset$. Let $\pi_{n+1}(\mathbf{V}(\mathsf{J}))$ be the projection of points in $\mathbf{V}(\mathsf{J})$ on their first $n+1$ coordinates, then G is the corresponding elimination ideal. By the Closure Theorem [9], $\pi_{n+1}(\mathbf{V}(\mathsf{J})) \subseteq \mathbf{V}(G)$ and there exists a subvariety $W \subsetneq \mathbf{V}(G)$ such that $\mathbf{V}(G) \backslash W \subseteq \pi_{n+1}(\mathbf{V}(\mathsf{J}))$. Fix a point $(c_0^*, \gamma) \in \mathbf{V}(G)$. Suppose to the contrary that $\Gamma = \emptyset$, then $\mathbb{C} \times \gamma \subseteq \mathbf{V}(G)$. By Sard's Theorem, $\mathbb{C} \times \gamma \cap \pi_{n+1}(\mathbf{V}(\mathsf{J}))$ is an empty set or a finite set. Therefore, $\mathbb{C} \times \gamma \subseteq \mathbf{V}(G) \backslash \pi_{n+1}(\mathbf{V}(\mathsf{J})) \subseteq W$ except for at most finitely many points in $\mathbb{C} \times \gamma$. Since W is closed, $\mathbb{C} \times \gamma \subseteq W$. In particular, $(c_0^*, \gamma) \in W$ which means $\mathbf{V}(G) = W$, a contradiction. □

REMARK 3.1. *As proved in Corollary 3.2, when $\mathcal{V}$ is irreducible, smooth and $C_{\mathbf{h}}$ contains no lines, there is only one polynomial in the set Γ in Algorithm 3.1. If $C_{\mathbf{h}}$ contains lines, Γ might consist of more than one polynomial and $\mathcal{V}^*$ may not be the Zariski closure of the set (6), see Example 3.1.*

Similar to [31, Theorem 6], with Algorithm 3.1 and procedures of deciding the emptiness of real algebraic varieties, we can determine whether a generic γ ($\gamma \notin \mathbf{V}(Z)$) belongs to $\mathbf{dom}(c_0^*(\mathbf{c} \mid C_{\mathbf{h}}))$ and the associated optimum c_0^* if it does.

EXAMPLE 3.1. *Consider the algebraic variety $\mathcal{V}$ defined by*

$$h(X_1, X_2) = X_1^2 X_2 - 1$$

which is irreducible, smooth, non-compact in $\mathbb{R}^2$ and $C_{\mathbf{h}}$ contains lines. Let $\gamma = (0, -1)$, then clearly $c_0^* = 0$. Running Algorithm 3.1, we get $\Gamma = \{4\mathbf{c}_0^3 + 27\mathbf{c}_1^2\mathbf{c}_2\}$ and hence

$$\Phi = 4\mathbf{c}_0^3 + 27\mathbf{c}_1^2\mathbf{c}_2, \qquad \mathbf{V}(Z) = \emptyset.$$

Hence, $\mathcal{V}^* = \mathbf{V}(\Gamma) \subseteq \mathbb{P}^2$ and $(0 : 0 : -1) \in \mathcal{V}^*$.

Since $\mathbf{dom}(c_0^*(\mathbf{c} \mid C_{\mathbf{h}})) = \{\gamma \in \mathbb{R}^2 \mid \gamma_1 = 0, \gamma_2 < 0\}$ and $c_0^* = 0$ for any $\gamma \in \mathbf{dom}(c_0^*(\mathbf{c} \mid C_{\mathbf{h}}))$, the Zariski closure of

$$\{(-c_0^* : \gamma_1 : \gamma_2) \in (\mathbb{P}^2)^* \mid \gamma \in \mathbf{dom}(c_0^*(\mathbf{c} \mid C_{\mathbf{h}}))\} \qquad (7)$$

is $\{(0 : 0 : \gamma_2) \in (\mathbb{P}^2)^* \mid \gamma_2 \in \mathbb{C}\}$ which is of dimension 0. Since we have $\dim \mathcal{V}^* = 1$, $\mathcal{V}^*$ is not the Zariski closure of the set (7).

3.2 Singular case

Now we suppose that $\mathcal{V}$ is irreducible, compact in $\mathbb{R}^n$ but is *not* smooth. We point out that the inclusion (5) might not hold in this case.

EXAMPLE 3.2. *Consider the astroid which is a real locus of a plane algebraic curve $\mathcal{V}$ defined by*

$$h(X_1, X_2) = \left(X_1^2 + X_2^2 - 1\right)^3 + 27X_1^2X_2^2.$$

It is obvious that for any linear function on $\mathcal{V} \cap \mathbb{R}^2$, its optimizer is one of the four singular points $\{(\pm 1, 0), (0, \pm 1)\}$. We have $\mathcal{V}^* = \mathbf{V}(\Gamma)$ where

$$\Gamma = \{-\mathbf{c}_1^2\mathbf{c}_2^2 + \mathbf{c}_0^2\mathbf{c}_1^2 + \mathbf{c}_2^2\mathbf{c}_0^2\}.$$

For a given $\gamma \in \mathbb{R}^2$, we have $c_0^* = \max\{|\gamma_1|, |\gamma_2|\} > 0$. It is easy to check $(-c_0^* : \gamma_1 : \gamma_2) \notin \mathcal{V}^*$ when $\gamma_1 \neq 0$ or $\gamma_2 \neq 0$, i.e. (5) does not hold.

Next we recursively construct a finite number of dual varieties such that (5) holds for the union of these varieties. For similar treatment, see [35]. The following algorithm has the same input as Algorithm 3.1 and returns a finite sequence of (Φ_k, Z_k) with the property that for any $\gamma \in \mathbf{dom}(c_0^*(\mathbf{c} \mid C_{\mathbf{h}}))$, there exists a k, such that if $Z_k(\gamma) \neq 0$, then c_0^* is contained in the roots of $\Phi_k(\mathbf{c}_0, \gamma)$.

ALGORITHM 3.2. SingularParametricOptimization($\mathbf{h}$)

Step 1 *Let $k = 1$ and $V_k = \mathcal{V}$.*

Step 2 *Compute an equidimensional decomposition $V_k = \cup_i V_{k,i}$ with $V_{k,i} = \mathbf{V}(I_{k,i})$ and each $I_{k,i}$ is a radical ideal.*

Step 3 *Run* GenericParametricOptimization($I_{k,i}$) *for each i and set $(\mathcal{V}^{(k)})^* = \cup_i V_{k,i}^*$.*

Step 4 *Compute the set $\Gamma_k \subseteq \mathbb{Q}[\mathbf{c}_0, \mathbf{c}]$ such that $\mathbf{V}(\Gamma_k) = (\mathcal{V}^{(k)})^*$.*

Step 5 *Set Φ_k to be the polynomial in Γ_k with the lowest degree in $\mathbf{c}_0$.*

Step 6 *Set Z_k to be the sum of squares of all coefficients in Φ_k in view of $\mathbb{Q}[\mathbf{c}_1, \ldots, \mathbf{c}_n][\mathbf{c}_0]$.*

Step 7 *Compute the singular locus $\widetilde{V}_{k,i}$ of each $V_{k,i}$ and set $V_{k+1} = \cup_i \widetilde{V}_{k,i}$. If $V_{k+1} \neq \emptyset$, then let $k = k + 1$ and go to Step 2.*

The next theorem shows the correctness of Algorithm 3.2.

THEOREM 3.4. *The algorithm terminates in a finite number of steps and for every $\gamma \in \mathbb{R}^n$, we have*

$$(-c_0^* : \gamma_1 : \cdots : \gamma_n) \subseteq \cup_{k=1}^{l} (\mathcal{V}^{(k)})^*.$$

PROOF. Since $\widetilde{V}_{k,i}$ is the singular locus of $V_{k,i}$, $\dim(\widetilde{V}_{k,i}) < \dim(V_{k,i})$ and then the algorithm terminates in a finite number of steps. Since $\mathcal{V}$ is compact in $\mathbb{R}^n$, for every parameter γ, the optimum c_0^* is finite and attainable. If the optimizer x^* is a smooth point, by Theorem 3.1, $(-c_0^* : \gamma_1 : \ldots : \gamma_n) \in \mathcal{V}^*$. If x^* is a singular point of $\mathcal{V}$. Then there exist k and i such that x^* is regular in $V_{k,i}$ and $(-c_0 : \gamma_1 : \ldots : \gamma_n) \in V_{k,i}^*$. □

EXAMPLE 3.2 (CONTINUED) The singular locus of $\mathcal{V}$ is defined by

$$\{h, X_1^5 - X_1, X_1^3X_2 + X_1X_2, 3X_1^4 - X_1^2 + 2X_2^2 - 2\},$$

and has four real points $\{(\pm 1, 0), (0, \pm 1)\}$. Running Algorithm 3.2, we get Γ_1 consisting of

$$(\mathbf{c}_0 - \mathbf{c}_2)(\mathbf{c}_0 + \mathbf{c}_2)(\mathbf{c}_0 - \mathbf{c}_1)(\mathbf{c}_0 + \mathbf{c}_1)(\mathbf{c}_0^2 + \mathbf{c}_1^2 - 2\mathbf{c}_1\mathbf{c}_2 + \mathbf{c}_2^2)$$
$$(\mathbf{c}_0^2 + \mathbf{c}_1^2 + 2\mathbf{c}_1\mathbf{c}_2 + \mathbf{c}_2^2).$$

By the discussion in Example 3.2, it is easy to check that $(-c_0^* : \gamma_1 : \gamma_2) \in \mathbf{V}(\Gamma_1) = (\mathcal{V}^{(1)})^*$ for every $\gamma \in \mathbb{R}^2$.

3.3 "Bad" parameters

It is clear that the polynomial Φ in Algorithm 3.1 gives no information about the optimal value of (1) with parameters belonging to $\mathbf{V}(Z)$. In particular, it might happen for the problem (1) reformulated from a general polynomial optimization problem by introducing a new variable.

Consider the polynomial optimization problem

$$f^* := \max_{x \in \mathbb{R}^n} f(x) \quad \text{s.t. } h_1(x) = \cdots = h_p(x) = 0,$$

where $f \in \mathbb{R}[X]$. If f is bounded from above on $\mathcal{V} \cap \mathbb{R}^n$, then we have $f^* \in K(f, \mathcal{V} \cap \mathbb{R}^n)$. Let

$$\mathcal{V}_{\mathbf{h},f} = \{(x, x_{n+1}) \in \mathbb{C}^{n+1} \mid x \in \mathcal{V}, x_{n+1} - f(x) = 0\}.$$

By Theorem 3.1, we have $(-f^* : 0 : \cdots : 0 : 1) \in \mathcal{V}_{\mathbf{h},f}^*$.

EXAMPLE 3.3. *[22, Example 2.1] Let $f = (X_1 + X_1^2X_2 + X_1^4X_2X_3)^2$. Running Algorithm 3.1 for $\mathcal{V}_{\mathbf{h},f}$ with $p = 0$, we get $\Gamma = \{\Phi\}$ where*

$$\begin{aligned}\Phi =& 1073741824\mathbf{c}_0^{12}\mathbf{c}_2^4\mathbf{c}_4^2 + 268435456\mathbf{c}_0^{11}\mathbf{c}_1^2\mathbf{c}_2^4\mathbf{c}_4 - \\ &+ 9865003008\mathbf{c}_0^{10}\mathbf{c}_2^4\mathbf{c}_3\mathbf{c}_4^3 + \cdots + 520093696\mathbf{c}_0^9\mathbf{c}_1\mathbf{c}_2^3\mathbf{c}_3^2\mathbf{c}_4^3.\end{aligned}$$

We have $\Phi(\mathbf{c}_0, 0, 0, 0, 1) \equiv 0$ which gives no information about f^*. In fact, we have $\mathbf{V}(Z) = \mathbf{V}(\mathbf{c}_2\mathbf{c}_4, \mathbf{c}_3\mathbf{c}_4, \mathbf{c}_3\mathbf{c}_2\mathbf{c}_1)$. Hence, for $\mathbf{c}_2 = 0, \mathbf{c}_3 = 0$, we always have $\Phi(\mathbf{c}_0, \mathbf{c}_1, 0, 0, \mathbf{c}_4) \equiv 0$, i.e. $\mathbf{c}_0$ can be arbitrary values.

In next section, we aim to design a complete algorithm to solve this problem.

4. COMPLETE ALGORITHM

4.1 Overview

As above, let $\mathbf{h} = (h_1, \ldots, h_p) \subset \mathbb{Q}[X_1, \ldots, X_n]$ that generates a radical and equidimensional ideal and $\mathcal{V}$ be the algebraic set defined by $h_1 = \cdots = h_p = 0$; we assume that $\mathcal{V}$ is smooth and denote by r its codimension.

It might happen that for some "bad" parameters' values $\gamma = (\gamma_1, \ldots, \gamma_n)$, the defining polynomials of the dual variety $\mathcal{V}^*$ become identically zero. For such values, this gives no information about the optimum c_0^* of the map $x \to \gamma^T x$ on $\mathcal{V} \cap \mathbb{R}^n$. For instance, in Example 3.3, the polynomial Φ is a zero polynomial for any $\gamma = (\gamma_1, 0, 0, \gamma_4)$, $\gamma_1, \gamma_4 \in \mathbb{R}$. In this section, we describe an algorithm that allows to avoid this problem. It can be seen as a parametric version of [18] that provides a complete algorithm for polynomial optimization.

Our algorithm starts by computing a couple of the form $(\Phi, Z, \mathbf{P})$ where $\Phi \in \mathbb{Q}[\mathbf{c}_0, \mathbf{c}]$, $\mathbf{P} \subset \mathbb{Q}[\mathbf{c}]$ and $Z \in \mathbb{Q}[\mathbf{c}] - \langle \mathbf{P} \rangle$ such that for any $(\gamma_1, \ldots, \gamma_n) \in \mathbf{V}(\mathbf{P}) - \mathbf{V}(Z)$, $\Phi(\mathbf{c}_0, \gamma_1, \ldots, \gamma_n)$ is not identically 0 and the optimum of the restriction of the map $x \to \gamma^T x$ to $\mathcal{V} \cap \mathbb{R}^n$ is a root of $\Phi(\mathbf{c}_0, \gamma_1, \ldots, \gamma_n)$. Next, the algorithm is called recursively to study the parametric optimization problem under each constraint $\mathbf{P}_i$ which is a prime component of $\sqrt{\langle \mathbf{P} \rangle + \langle Z \rangle}$. Hence, we are led to run our algorithm over an integral domain $\mathbb{Q}[\mathbf{c}_1, \ldots, \mathbf{c}_n]/\mathcal{P}$ where $\mathcal{P} \subset \mathbb{Q}[\mathbf{c}_1, \ldots, \mathbf{c}_n]$ is a prime ideal. Since the domain on which the computations are performed is integral, all operations that we need to manipulate polynomial ideals are available; the only difference is that we need to compute pseudo-inverse of polynomials modulo $\mathcal{P}$, hence simulating computations over the fraction field of $\mathbb{Q}[\mathbf{c}_1, \ldots, \mathbf{c}_n]/\mathcal{P}$.

The routine that handles these computations over these integral rings is called BasicParametricOptimization. It is a parametric variant of Algorithm SetContainingLocalExtrema in [18, Section 3]. One of its advantages is that in the fraction field of the integral domains $\mathbb{Q}[\mathbf{c}_1, \ldots, \mathbf{c}_n]/\mathcal{P}$, it performs a number of operations that is singly exponential in n (see [18, Section 6, Lemma 6.8]) to be compared with the doubly exponential complexity in n that is needed by Cylindrical Algebraic Decomposition.

Note that one can also use lazy representations of ideals and dynamic evaluation techniques (see e.g. [10, 23]) to work with these parameters as well as comprehensive Gröbner bases or comprehensive triangular sets (see e.g. [7, 37] and references therein). The description below is done assuming that our domain is integral for simplicity; this allows us to focus more on objects and properties related to polynomial optimization and introduced in [18].

Before describing in detail the recursive procedure that is sketched above, let us describe the objects and subroutines that we need and which are extracted from [18].

4.2 Basic objects and properties

We start with polar varieties (see e.g. [1, 3] and references therein) and their Noether position properties (see [32]). Let $\mathbf{P} \subset \mathbb{Q}[\mathbf{c}]$ be a finite polynomial sequence generating a prime ideal $\mathcal{P}$ and let $\mathbb{A} = \mathbb{Q}[\mathbf{c}]/\mathcal{P}$. Hence $\mathbb{A}$ is an integral ring.

For $\gamma \in \mathbf{V}(\mathbf{P})$, we consider the canonical projections $\pi_i : (x_1, \ldots, x_n) \to (x_1, \ldots, x_i)$ for $1 \leq i \leq n$ and the following projections

$$\pi_\gamma : x = (x_1, \ldots, x_n) \to \gamma^T x = \gamma_1 x_1 + \cdots + \gamma_n x_n$$

and for $1 \leq i \leq \dim(\mathcal{V}) = n - r$,

$$\pi_{\gamma,i} : x = (x_1, \ldots, x_n) \to (\gamma^T x, x_1, x_2, \ldots, x_i).$$

For $\vartheta \in \mathbb{C}$, we denote by $\mathcal{V}_{\gamma,\vartheta}$ the algebraic set defined by $\mathcal{V} \cap \pi_\gamma^{-1}(\vartheta)$. We consider

- the set of all $(r+1)$-minors of the truncated Jacobian matrix $\mathsf{Jac}([h_{i_1}, \ldots, h_{i_r}, \gamma^T X], \mathbf{X}_{>i})$ (columns corresponding to partial derivatives w.r.t $X_1, \ldots, X_i$ are omitted) for all subsets $\{i_1, \ldots, i_r\} \subset \{1, \ldots, p\}$ for $1 \leq i \leq n-r-1$; we denote it by $\mathsf{M}(\mathbf{h}, \gamma, i)$. For convenience, let $\mathsf{M}(\mathbf{h}, \gamma, n-r) = \emptyset$.

  When the entries of γ are parameters $\mathbf{c} = (\mathbf{c}_1, \ldots, \mathbf{c}_n)$, the set of minors is denoted by $\mathsf{M}(\mathbf{h}, \mathbf{c}, i)$.

- the set of all $(r+1)$-minors of the Jacobian matrix $\mathsf{Jac}([h_{i_1}, \ldots, h_{i_r}, \gamma^T X])$ for all subsets $\{i_1, \ldots, i_r\} \subset \{1, \ldots, p\}$; we denote it by $S(\mathbf{h}, \gamma)$.

  When the entries of γ are parameters $\mathbf{c} = (\mathbf{c}_1, \ldots, \mathbf{c}_n)$, the set of minors is denoted by $\mathsf{S}(\mathbf{h}, \mathbf{c})$.

Let $\gamma \in \mathbb{C}^n - \{\mathbf{0}\}$ and $\vartheta \in \mathbb{C}$. Assume that $\mathcal{V}_{\gamma,\vartheta}$ is smooth and that the ideal $\langle \mathbf{h}, \gamma^T X - \vartheta \rangle$ is radical and equidimensional. The polar variety $W(\mathbf{h}, \gamma, \vartheta, i)$ associated to $\mathcal{V}_{\gamma,\vartheta}$ and $\pi_{\gamma,i}$ is the critical locus of the restriction to $\mathcal{V}_{\gamma,\vartheta}$ of π_i. It is defined by the vanishing of the polynomials in $\mathbf{h}$ and $\mathsf{M}(\mathbf{h}, \gamma, i)$ and the polynomial $\gamma^T X - \vartheta$.

We will denote by $W(\mathbf{h}, \gamma, i)$ the algebraic set defined by the vanishing of the polynomials in $\mathbf{h}$ and $\mathsf{M}(\mathbf{h}, \gamma, i)$, for $1 \leq i \leq n-r$.

The polar variety $C(\mathbf{h}, \gamma)$ associated to $\mathcal{V}$ and π_γ is the critical locus of the restriction to $\mathcal{V}$ of π_γ. It is defined by the vanishing of the polynomials in $\mathbf{h}$ and $\mathsf{S}(\mathbf{h}, \gamma)$.

In the sequel, we will use some properties of polar varieties that hold under generic changes of coordinates.

For $\mathbf{A} \in \mathrm{GL}_n(\mathbb{C})$ and $S \subset \mathbb{C}^n$, we denote by $S^{\mathbf{A}}$ the image of S by the map $x \to \mathbf{A}^{-1} x$.

Let $\mathbf{A} \in \mathrm{GL}_n(\mathbb{Q})$, we are interested in the parameters' values $\gamma \in \mathbf{V}(\mathbf{P})$ such that there exists a non-empty Zariski open set $\mathcal{O} \subset \mathbb{C}$ such that for any $\vartheta \in \mathcal{O}$, the following holds:

> $\mathfrak{P}_1$: $(\mathbf{h}, \gamma^T X - \vartheta)$ is radical and equidimensional and $\mathcal{V}_{\gamma,\vartheta}$ is smooth; note that by the Jacobian criterion, this is equivalent to saying that at any point of $\mathcal{V}_{\gamma,\vartheta}$, the rank of $(\mathbf{h}, \gamma^T X - \vartheta)$ is $r+1$.
>
> $\mathfrak{P}_2(\mathbf{A})$: for $1 \leq i \leq n-r$, the polar variety $W(\mathbf{h}^{\mathbf{A}}, \gamma, \vartheta, i)$ is in Noether position with respect to the projection π_{i-1}.

For those parameters' values for which $\mathfrak{P}_1$ and $\mathfrak{P}_2(\mathbf{A})$ hold, we simply say that $\mathfrak{P}(\mathbf{A})$ holds.

We recall now the statement of [18, Proposition 4.2]. It emphasizes the interest of these properties for polynomial optimization.

PROPOSITION 4.1. *[18, Proposition 4.2] Let $\mathbf{A} \in \mathrm{GL}_n(\mathbb{C})$ and let $\gamma \in \mathbb{C}^n - \{\mathbf{0}\}$ such that $\mathfrak{P}(\mathbf{A})$ holds. Then the following holds:*

- *the algebraic set $\mathcal{C}_\gamma^{\mathbf{A}}$ defined as the Zarsiki closure of*

$$\cup_{i=1}^{n-r} \left(\left(W(\mathbf{h}^{\mathbf{A}}, \gamma, i) - C(\mathbf{h}^{\mathbf{A}}, \gamma) \right) \cap \pi_{i-1}^{-1}(\mathbf{0}) \right)$$

  has dimension at most 1;

- *the union of $\pi_\gamma(C(\mathbf{h}^{\mathbf{A}}, \gamma))$ and the set of non-properness of the restriction of π_γ to $\mathcal{C}_\gamma^{\mathbf{A}}$ is finite and contains the extremum of the restriction of the map π_γ to $\mathcal{V} \cap \mathbb{R}^n$.*

From [18, Proposition 4.3], for any $\gamma \in \mathbf{V}(\mathbf{P})$ there exists a non-empty Zariski open set $\mathscr{A} \subset \mathrm{GL}_n(\mathbb{C})$ such that for any $\mathbf{A} \in \mathscr{A} \cap \mathrm{GL}_n(\mathbb{Q})$, $\mathfrak{P}(\mathbf{A})$ holds.

However, note that in order to use Proposition 4.1 for parametric optimization, we need to prove a stronger statement: there exists a non-empty Zariski open subset $\mathscr{A} \subset \mathrm{GL}_n(\mathbb{C})$ such that the following holds. For any $\mathbf{A} \in \mathscr{A} \cap \mathrm{GL}_n(\mathbb{Q})$, there exists a Zariski dense subset $U \subset \mathbf{V}(\mathbf{P})$ such that for $\gamma \in U$, $\mathfrak{P}(\mathbf{A})$ holds.

Basically, our algorithm BasicParametricOptimization identifies a polynomial Z such that $\mathbf{V}(\mathbf{P}) - \mathbf{V}(Z)$ is non-empty and computes a polynomial $\Phi(\mathbf{c}_0, \mathbf{c})$ such that for any $\gamma \in \mathbf{V}(\mathbf{P}) - \mathbf{V}(Z)$, $\Phi(\mathbf{c}_0, \gamma)$ defines the union of the finite algebraic sets in the second item of Proposition 4.1.

This is what we prove below but before doing that we introduce the data-structure and subroutines used by our algorithm.

4.3 Data-structures and subroutines

From now on, $\mathbf{P} \subset \mathbb{Q}[\mathbf{c}]$ is a polynomial sequence that generates a prime ideal $\mathcal{P}$. We denote by $\mathbb{A}$ the integral ring $\mathbb{Q}[\mathbf{c}]/\mathcal{P}$, by $\mathbb{K}$ the fraction field of $\mathbb{A}$ and by $\bar{\mathbb{K}}$ the algebraic closure of $\mathbb{K}$.

Data-structures. Let $\mathbf{F} \subset \mathbb{Q}[X_1, \ldots, X_n]$ that defines a finite algebraic set V in $\mathbb{C}^n$. Then, V can be encoded with a zero-dimensional rational parametrization which is a sequence of polynomials $\mathbf{Q} = (q, q_0, q_1, \ldots, q_n) \subset \mathbb{Q}[U]$, i.e. V is defined by

$$q(U) = 0,\ X_i = q_i(U)/q_0(U),\ q_0(U) \neq 0 \quad \text{for } 1 \leq i \leq n,$$

with $\gcd(q, q_0) = 1$ and q is unitary and its degree is the cardinality of V.

When $\mathbf{F}$ defines an algebraic curve $V \subset \mathbb{C}^n$, then a rational parametrization for V is a sequence of polynomials $\mathbf{Q} = (q, q_0, q_1, \ldots, q_n) \subset \mathbb{Q}[U, T]$ such that V is the algebraic closure of the set defined by

$$q(U,T) = 0,\ X_i = \frac{q_i(U,T)}{q_0(U,T)},\ q_0(U,T) \neq 0 \quad \text{for } 1 \leq i \leq n$$

with q unitary in U and T, its degree is the degree of the algebraic curve V and $\gcd(q, q_0) = 1$.

Below, we will also consider polynomial systems in the ring $\mathbb{A}[X_1, \ldots, X_n]$ where $\mathbb{A}$ is an integral ring. We denote by $\mathbb{K}$ the fraction field of $\mathbb{A}$ and by $\overline{\mathbb{K}}$ the algebraic closure of $\mathbb{K}$. Hence, the algebraic sets defined by these polynomial systems lie in $\overline{\mathbb{K}}^n$; whenever they define finite algebraic sets or algebraic curves, they can be encoded with rational parametrizations with coefficients in $\mathbb{K}$, which up to normalization can be turned into rational parameterizations with coefficients in $\mathbb{A}$.

Basic routines. We need to introduce the following routines.

The routine SingularMinors takes as input $\mathbf{h}$ and $\mathbf{P}$ and it returns $\tilde{\mathbf{G}} = (\mathbf{h}, \mathsf{S}(\mathbf{h}, \mathbf{c}))$.

The routine SpecialCurve takes as input $\mathbf{h}$ and $\mathbf{P}$ and returns $\tilde{\mathbf{F}} = (\tilde{\mathbf{F}}_1, \ldots, \tilde{\mathbf{F}}_{n-r})$ such that for $1 \leq i \leq n-r$, $\tilde{\mathbf{F}}_i$ is $\mathbf{h}, \mathsf{M}(\mathbf{h}, \mathbf{c}, i), X_1, \ldots, X_{i-1}$.

These systems will allow us to compute parametrized representations of the sets $\mathcal{C}_\gamma$ for γ lying in a Zariski dense subset.

The routine PointsPerComponents takes as input $\mathbf{h} \in \mathbb{Q}[X_1, \ldots, X_n]$ and it returns a zero-dimensional rational parametrization that encodes a finite set of points contained in $\mathcal{V} = \mathbf{V}(\mathbf{h})$ and meeting all the connected components of $\mathcal{V} \cap \mathbb{R}^n$.

The routine ValuesTakenByPoly takes as input a zero-dimensional rational parametrization $\mathbf{Q} \subset \mathbb{Q}[U]$ that encodes a finite set of points V in $\mathbb{C}^n$, the sequence of polynomials $\mathbf{P} \subset \mathbb{Q}[\mathbf{c}]$. It returns $\Phi \subset \mathbb{Q}[\mathbf{c}_0, \mathbf{c}]$ and a polynomial $Z \in \mathbb{Q}[\mathbf{c}] - \langle \mathbf{P} \rangle$ such that for $\gamma \in \mathbf{V}(\mathbf{P}) - \mathbf{V}(Z)$, $\Phi(\mathbf{c}_0, \gamma)$ defines the set $\{\gamma^T x \mid x \in V\}$. It essentially consists of substituting the parametrization in the polynomial $\mathbf{c}^T X - \mathbf{c}_0$, clearing the denominators and eliminating the variable U with a resultant computation to get Φ. Note that these computations are done modulo $\mathbf{P}$ (hence in $\mathbb{A}$). Keeping track of exact divisions performed during the resultant computation needed to do this computation (or using specialization theorems, see e.g. [12]) yields the polynomial Z. Note that Z does not belong to $\mathbf{P}$ (else we wouldn't use its factors for performing divisions).

As above, the routine ParametricValuesTakenByPoly takes as input a zero-dimensional rational parametrization $\mathbf{Q}$ but with coefficients in $\mathbb{A}$, the sequence of polynomials $\mathbf{P} \subset \mathbb{Q}[\mathbf{c}]$. The parametrization $\mathbf{Q}$ encodes a finite set of points V in $\overline{\mathbb{K}}^n$. It returns $\Phi \subset \mathbb{Q}[\mathbf{c}_0, \mathbf{c}]$ and a polynomial $Z \in \mathbb{Q}[\mathbf{c}] - \langle \mathbf{P} \rangle$ such that for $\gamma \in \mathbf{V}(\mathbf{P}) - \mathbf{V}(Z)$, $\Phi(\mathbf{c}_0, \gamma)$ defines the set $\{\gamma^T x \mid x \in V\}$. As ValuesTakenByPoly does, this routine works using substitutions and resultant computations.

The following lemma is immediate.

LEMMA 4.2. *Let $\mathbf{Q}$ and $\mathbf{P}$ be as above and (Φ, Z) be the output of* ParametricValuesTakenByPoly$(\mathbf{Q}, \mathbf{P})$. *Then, $Z \notin \langle \mathbf{P} \rangle$.*

Properness. We describe now a routine CheckProperness that takes as input $\mathbf{h}$, a matrix $\mathbf{A} \in \mathrm{GL}_n(\mathbb{Q})$ and $\mathbf{P} \subset \mathbb{Q}[\mathbf{c}]$ as above.

When there are no generic parameters' values in $\mathbf{V}(\mathbf{P})$ for which $\mathfrak{P}(\mathbf{A})$ holds, the routine CheckProperness simply returns (0). Else it returns $Z \in \mathbb{Q}[\mathbf{c}] - \langle \mathbf{P} \rangle$ such that for any $\gamma \in \mathbf{V}(\mathbf{P}) - \mathbf{V}(Z)$, property $\mathfrak{P}(\mathbf{A})$ holds.

Roughly speaking, the above routine identifies those parameters' values γ for which $\mathfrak{P}(\mathbf{A})$ holds.

LEMMA 4.3. *We use the above notation and assumptions. Then, there exists a non-empty Zariski open set $\mathscr{A} \subset \mathrm{GL}_n(\mathbb{C})$ such that for any $\mathbf{A} \in \mathscr{A} \cap \mathrm{GL}_n(\mathbb{Q})$ the following holds.*

Let Z be the output of CheckProperness$(\mathbf{h}, \mathbf{A}, \mathbf{P})$. *Then, $\mathbf{V}(\mathbf{P}) - \mathbf{V}(Z)$ is Zariski dense in $\mathbf{V}(\mathbf{P})$ and for $\gamma \in \mathbf{V}(\mathbf{P}) - \mathbf{V}(Z)$, property $\mathfrak{P}(\mathbf{A})$ holds.*

PROOF. Note that by construction, under our assumptions, $Z \notin \langle \mathbf{P} \rangle$. Hence, since $\langle \mathbf{P} \rangle$ is prime, $\mathbf{V}(\mathbf{P}) - \mathbf{V}(Z)$ is Zariski dense in $\mathbf{V}(\mathbf{P})$.

It remains to prove that there exists a non-empty Zariski open set $\mathscr{A} \subset \mathrm{GL}_n(\mathbb{C})$ such that for any $\mathbf{A} \in \mathscr{A} \cap \mathrm{GL}_n(\mathbb{Q})$ and $\gamma \in \mathbf{V}(\mathbf{P}) - \mathbf{V}(Z)$, property $\mathfrak{P}(\mathbf{A})$ holds.

By [18, Proposition 4.3], for any $\gamma \in \mathbf{V}(\mathbf{P})$, there exists a non-empty Zariski open set $\mathscr{A} \in \mathrm{GL}_n(\mathbb{C})$ such that $\mathfrak{P}(\mathbf{A})$ holds for γ.

We prove below that there exists $Z \notin \langle \mathbf{P} \rangle$ such that for any $\mathbf{A} \in \mathscr{A}$ and $\gamma' \in \mathbf{V}(\mathbf{P}) - \mathbf{V}(Z)$, $\mathfrak{P}(\mathbf{A})$ holds for γ'.

Consider a minimal Gröbner basis G of the ideal generated by $\langle \mathbf{h}, \mathbf{c}^T X - \mathbf{c}_0 \rangle$ and all $(r+1)$-minors of $\mathsf{Jac}(\mathbf{h}, \mathbf{c}^T X - \mathbf{c}_0)$ with $\mathbb{K}(\mathbf{c}_0)$ as a ground field. We claim that G is (1). Indeed, if it was not the case, this would imply that for any $\gamma \in \mathbf{V}(\mathbf{P})$ which does not cancel the finitely many denominators that appear in a computation of G, $\mathfrak{P}_1$ does not hold; hence a contradiction. We deduce that G is (1) as claimed and let Z' be the product of all denominators appearing during the computation of G.

Now let $\mathfrak{A}$ be an $n \times n$ matrix with entries $\mathfrak{A}_{i,j}$ as indeterminates.

By [33], one can ensure Noether position properties by setting the non-vanishing of some denominators of a minimal reduced Gröbner basis of the ideals generated by

$$\mathbf{h}^{\mathfrak{A}}, \mathsf{M}(\mathbf{h}^{\mathfrak{A}}, \mathbf{c}, i), \mathbf{c}^T \mathfrak{A} X - \mathbf{c}_0$$

with $\mathbb{K}(\mathfrak{A}_{i,j})$ as a ground field. The coefficients of these denominators lie in $\mathbb{K}$ which contains $\mathbb{Q}$. Now, we define the Zariski open set $\mathscr{A} \subset \mathrm{GL}_n(\mathbb{C})$ by the non-vanishing of the coefficients of the monomials in $\mathbf{c}, \mathbf{c}_0$. This set is non-empty because, as above, it would contradict that for any $\gamma \in \mathbf{V}(\mathbf{P})$, $\mathfrak{P}(\mathbf{A})$ holds for $\mathbf{A}$ generic.

Now, remark that for $\mathbf{A} \in \mathscr{A}$, one can define Z'' as the denominators that appear in the computation of the minimal reduced Gröbner basis of the ideals generated by

$$\mathbf{h}^{\mathbf{A}}, \mathsf{M}(\mathbf{h}^{\mathbf{A}}, \mathbf{c}, i), \mathbf{c}^T \mathbf{A} X - \mathbf{c}_0$$

with $\mathbb{K}$ as a ground field.

Taking $Z = Z'Z''$ ends the proof. □

Rational parametrizations. Consider a sequence of polynomials polynomials $\mathbf{F} = (f_1, \ldots, f_s)$ and $\mathbf{G} = (g_1, \ldots, g_k)$ in $\mathbb{A}[X_1, \ldots, X_n]$ and $I \subset \mathbb{K}[X_1, \ldots, X_n]$ be the saturation of $\langle \mathbf{F} \rangle$ by $\langle \mathbf{G} \rangle$; we denote it by $\langle \mathbf{F} \rangle : \langle \mathbf{G} \rangle^\infty$. We assume that I has dimension 1 and is equidimensional.

We are interested in studying the complex solutions of $\mathbf{F}$ that are not solutions of $\mathbf{G}$ where the admissible values for the parameters $\mathbf{c}$ lie in the irreducible algebraic set associated to $\mathcal{P}$. We consider a routine ParametricCurveRepresentation that takes as input $\mathbf{F}$, $\mathbf{G}$ and $\mathbf{P}$ and which returns a finite sequence of polynomials $\mathbf{Q} = (q, q_0, q_1, \ldots, q_n) \subset \mathbb{K}[U, T]$ and a polynomial Z in $\mathbb{Q}[\mathbf{c}] - \mathcal{P}$ such that for any $\gamma = (\gamma_1, \ldots, \gamma_n) \in \mathbf{V}(\mathbf{P}) - \mathbf{V}(Z)$ the curve associated to $\langle \mathbf{F}_\gamma \rangle : \langle \mathbf{G} \rangle^\infty$ is the Zariski closure of the set defined by

$$q_\gamma(U, T) = 0, \quad X_i = q_{i,\gamma}(U, T)/q_{0,\gamma}(U, T), \quad q_{0,\gamma}(U, T) \neq 0$$

for $1 \leq i \leq n$ (where q_γ and $q_{i,\gamma}$ denote the polynomials of $\mathbf{Q}$ obtained by instantiating $\mathbf{c}$ to γ in q and $q_{i,\gamma}$ for $i \in \{0, \ldots, n\}$).

LEMMA 4.4. *Let $\mathbf{F}$ and $\mathbf{G}$ be as above and let $(\mathbf{Q}, Z)$ be the output of* ParametricCurveRepresentation$(\mathbf{F}, \mathbf{G}, \mathbf{P})$. *Then the Krull dimension of $\langle \mathbf{P} \rangle + \langle Z \rangle$ is less than the Krull dimension of $\langle \mathbf{P} \rangle$.*

PROOF. Without loss of generality, one can assume that we are in generic coordinates. Using Gröbner bases with $\mathbb{K}$ as ground field and linear algebra in $\mathbb{K}(X_1)[X_2, \ldots, X_n]$ one can compute a rational parametrization of I (see e.g. [11, 4]). During this computation, some polynomials (which are not 0 modulo $\mathcal{P}$ by construction) are used to perform divisions. Taking Z as the product of these polynomials is a valid output and since these polynomials are not 0 modulo $\mathcal{P}$, Z is not. Since $\mathcal{P}$ is prime, we deduce that $\mathcal{P} + \langle Z \rangle$ has dimension less than the dimension of $\mathcal{P}$. □

Reusing the above notations and ParametricCurveRepresentation, it is straightforward to obtain a routine UnionParametricCurve that takes as input a sequence of sequences of polynomials $\mathbf{F} = (\mathbf{F}_1, \ldots, \mathbf{F}_l)$ a sequence of polynomials $\mathbf{G}$ and $\mathbf{P}$ such that the ideal $\langle \mathbf{F}_k \rangle : \langle \mathbf{G} \rangle^\infty \subset \mathbb{K}[X_1, \ldots, X_n]$ has dimension 1 and is equidimensional for $1 \leq k \leq l$. It returns a finite sequence of polynomials $\mathbf{Q} = (q, q_0, q_1, \ldots, q_n) \subset \mathbb{K}[U, T]$ and a polynomial Z in $\mathbb{Q}[\mathbf{c}] - \mathcal{P}$ such that for any $\gamma = (\gamma_1, \ldots, \gamma_n) \in \mathbf{V}(\mathbf{P}) - \mathbf{V}(Z)$ the curve associated to $\bigcap_{k=1}^{l} \langle \mathbf{F}_{k\gamma} \rangle : \langle \mathbf{G} \rangle^\infty$ is the Zariski closure of the set defined by

$$q_\gamma(U, T) = 0, \quad X_i = q_{i,\gamma}(U, T)/q_{0,\gamma}(U, T) \quad q_{0,\gamma}(U, T) \neq 0$$

for $1 \leq i \leq n$ (where q_γ and $q_{i,\gamma}$ denotes the polynomials of $\mathbf{Q}$ obtained by instantiating $\mathbf{c}$ to γ in q and $q_{i,\gamma}$ for $i \in \{0, \ldots, n\}$). The following lemma is an immediate consequence of Lemma 4.4.

LEMMA 4.5. *Let* $\mathbf{F}$ *and* $\mathbf{G}$ *be as above and let* $(\mathbf{Q}, Z)$ *be the output of* UnionCurveParametric$(\mathbf{F}, \mathbf{G}, \mathbf{P})$. *Then the Krull dimension of* $\langle \mathbf{P} \rangle + \langle Z \rangle$ *is less than the Krull dimension of* $\langle \mathbf{P} \rangle$.

Intersection of a curve with a variety. We describe now the routine ParametricIntersection which takes as input a one-dimensional rational parametrization $\mathbf{Q}$ of a curve $C \subset \bar{\mathbb{K}}^n$, a polynomial sequence $\mathbf{G} \in \mathbb{A}[X_1, \ldots, X_n]$ and $\mathbf{P}$. The sequence $\mathbf{G}$ defines an algebraic set H in $\bar{\mathbb{K}}^n$. Assume that the intersection of C and H is finite. Then, following [14] one can compute a parametric zero-dimensional rational parametrization $\mathbf{Q}'$ that encodes $C \cap H$. This is done by substituting in $\mathbf{G}$ the parametrizations of the X_i's hence reducing the computation to computing the intersection defined by the vanishing of two bivariate polynomials with coefficients in $\mathbb{K}$ (using resultant computations). Again, keeping track of the denominators appearing during the computation or using specialization theorems, one can finally return a parametric zero-dimensional parametrization $\mathbf{Q}$ and a polynomial $Z \notin \langle \mathbf{P} \rangle$ such that for any $\gamma \in \mathbf{V}(\mathbf{P}) - \mathbf{V}(Z)$, $\mathbf{Q}'_\gamma$ encodes $C_\gamma \cap H_\gamma$.

LEMMA 4.6. *Let* $\mathbf{Q}$, $\mathbf{G}$ *and* $\mathbf{P}$ *as above and* (Φ, Z) *be the output of* ParametricIntersection$(\mathbf{Q}, f, \mathbf{P})$. *Then,* $\dim(\langle \mathbf{P} \rangle + \langle Z \rangle) < \dim(\mathbf{P})$.

Computing a set of non-properness. Let $\mathbf{Q}$ be a one dimensional rational parametrization with coefficients in $\mathbb{A}$; it defines an algebraic curve $C_1 \subset \bar{\mathbb{K}}^n$. Then, there exists a Zariski dense subset U of $\mathbf{V}(\mathbf{P})$ such that for $\gamma \in U$, $V(\mathbf{Q}_\gamma)$ defines an algebraic curve C_γ.

The routine ParametricSetOfNonProperness computes (Φ, Z) such that $\mathbf{V}(\mathbf{P}) - \mathbf{V}(Z) \subset U$ and is non-empty and such that for $\gamma \in \mathbf{V}(\mathbf{P}) - \mathbf{V}(Z)$, $\Phi(\mathbf{c}_0, \gamma)$ is not 0 and its set of roots contains the set of non-properness of the restriction of the map $x \rightarrow \gamma^T x$ to C_γ.

We denote by C_2 the algebraic curve $\{(\gamma_0, x) \mid x \in C_1$ and $\gamma_0 = \mathbf{c}^T x\}$. We also denote by $\mathfrak{C}_1$ the projective closure of C_1 in $\mathbb{P}^n(\bar{\mathbb{K}})$. For $x = (x_0 : x_1 : \cdots : x_n) \in \mathfrak{C}_1$ with $x_0 \neq 0$, we denote by $\tilde{x}$ the point $\left(\frac{x_1}{x_0}, \ldots, \frac{x_n}{x_0}\right)$ and by $\mathfrak{C}_2$ the quasi-projective set $\{(\gamma_0, x) \mid x \in \mathfrak{C}_1$ and $\mathbf{c}^T \tilde{x} = \gamma_0\}$.

Following algorithm given in [9] our routine reduces to the following steps:

- compute a representation of the projective closure $\mathfrak{C}_2$; this can be done using Gröbner bases with $\mathbb{K}$ as a ground field;
- compute the intersection of $\mathfrak{C}_2$ with the hyperplane at infinity defined by $X_0 = 0$; this is a finite set of points and again it can be done using Gröbner bases with $\mathbb{K}$ as a ground field.

Keeping track of all denominators that appear during the computations yields the polynomial $Z \notin \langle \mathbf{P} \rangle$ as above.

The following lemma is immediate.

LEMMA 4.7. *Let* $\mathbf{Q}$ *and* $\mathbf{P}$ *be as above and let* (Φ, Z) *be the output of* ParametricSetOfNonProperness$(\mathbf{Q}, \mathbf{P})$. *Then* $\dim(\langle \mathbf{P} \rangle + \langle Z \rangle) < \dim(\mathbf{P})$.

4.4 Basic routine for parametric optimization

We describe now our basic subroutine BasicParametricOptimization. It can be seen as a parametrized version of Algorithm SetContainingLocalExtrema in [18].

This latter algorithm consists in reducing the problem of computing the optimum of a polynomial function restricted to a real algebraic set $\mathcal{V} \cap \mathbb{R}^n$ to the problem of computing the optimum of the same polynomial function restricted to a curve. Obviously, this is done in such a way that both optimization problems share the same optimum.

We describe the main steps and refer to the steps of algorithm BasicParametricOptimization corresponding to their parametric variants. The algorithm starts by computing sample points in $\mathcal{V} \cap \mathbb{R}^n$ and gets *(i)* the values attained by the polynomial function to optimize at those points (this corresponds to Steps 1-2). Next, it computes representations of linear sections of polar varieties that define algebraic curves (Step 5-6). Finally, it computes *(ii)* the set of non-properness of the restriction of the considered function to the curve (Step 7) and gets *(iii)* the critical values of this function restricted to the curve (Step 8-9). All this is done in such a way that the optimum lies in the set of values *(i)*, *(ii)* and *(iii)*.

Input: $\mathbf{h} = (h_1, \ldots, h_p) \subset \mathbb{Q}[X_1, \ldots, X_n]$ and $\mathbf{P} \subset \mathbb{Q}[\mathbf{c}]$

Properties: $\mathbf{P}$ generates a prime ideal and $\langle h_1, \ldots, h_p \rangle$ generates a radical equidimensional ideal defining a smooth algebraic set.

Output: (Φ, Z) such that

- $\Phi \in \mathbb{Q}[\mathbf{c}_0, \mathbf{c}]$ and $Z \in \mathbb{Q}[\mathbf{c}]$;
- Z is not 0 modulo $\langle \mathbf{P} \rangle$;
- For any $\gamma \in \mathbf{V}(\mathbf{P}) - \mathbf{V}(Z)$ such that $Z(\gamma) \neq 0$, $\Phi(\mathbf{c}_0, \gamma)$ is not zero and its set of roots contains the optimum of the restriction of π_γ to $\mathcal{V} \cap \mathbb{R}^n$.

BasicParametricOptimization$(\mathbf{h}, \mathbf{P})$

1. $R =$ PointsPerComponents$(\mathbf{h})$
2. $(\Phi_0, Z_0) =$ ValuesTakenByPoly$(R, \mathbf{c}^T X, \mathbf{P})$
3. Choose randomly $\mathbf{A} \in \mathrm{GL}_n(\mathbb{C})$
4. $Z'_0 =$ CheckProperness$(\mathbf{h}, \mathbf{A}, \mathbf{P})$
5. $\tilde{\mathbf{F}} =$ SpecialCurve$(\mathbf{h}^{\mathbf{A}}, \mathbf{P})$, $\tilde{\mathbf{G}} =$ SingularMinors$(\mathbf{h}^{\mathbf{A}}, \mathbf{P})$
6. $(R_1, Z_1) =$ UnionParametricCurve$(\tilde{\mathbf{F}}, \tilde{\mathbf{G}}, \mathbf{P})$
7. $(\Phi_1, Z'_1) =$ ParametricSetofNonProperness$(R_1, \mathbf{P}, \mathbf{c}^T X)$
8. $R_2 =$ ParametricIntersection$(R_1, \tilde{\mathbf{G}}, \mathbf{P})$
9. $(\Phi_2, Z_2) =$ ParametricValuesTakesByPoly$(R_2, \mathbf{c}^T X, \mathbf{P})$
10. Take $Z = Z_0 Z'_0 Z_1 Z'_1 Z_2$ and $\Phi = \Phi_0 \Phi_1 \Phi_2$
11. return (Φ, Z)

THEOREM 4.8. *Let* $\mathbf{h}$ *and* $\mathbf{P}$ *be as above and* (Φ, Z) *be the output of* BasicParametricOptimization$(\mathbf{h}, \mathbf{P})$. *Then,* $Z \notin \langle \mathbf{P} \rangle$ *and its output is correct.*

PROOF. The fact that $Z \notin \langle \mathbf{P} \rangle$ is an immediate consequence of the fact that $\langle \mathbf{P} \rangle$ is prime and that its factors Z_0, Z'_0, Z_1, Z'_1 and Z_2 do not belong to $\langle \mathbf{P} \rangle$ from Lemmata 4.2, 4.3, 4.5, 4.6 and 4.7.

It remains to prove the correctness of the output. Since $\mathbf{A}$ is chosen at random at Step 3, one can assume that $\mathbf{A}$ belongs to the non-empty Zariski open set $\mathscr{A}$ defined in Lemma 4.3.

Now, remark that for any $\gamma \in \mathbf{V}(\mathbf{P}) - \mathbf{V}(Z)$. By Lemma 4.3, property $\mathfrak{P}(\mathbf{A})$ holds.

Hence, without loss of generality one can assume that algorithm SetContainingLocalExtrema in [18] runs by choosing the matrix $\mathbf{A}$ selected at Step 3 of BasicParametricOptimization. On input $\gamma^T X$ and $\mathbf{h}$ the output of SetContainingLocalExtrema is a polynomial $\varphi \in \mathbb{Q}[\mathbf{c}_0]$ whose set of roots contains the optimum of the restriction of the map $x \rightarrow \gamma^T x$ to $\mathcal{V} \cap \mathbb{R}^n$. From Lemmata 4.2, 4.5, 4.6 and 4.7 this polynomial φ is exactly $\Phi(\mathbf{c}_0, \gamma)$. Hence, correctness of algorithm SetContainingLocalExtrema [18, Proposition 4.2] implies the one of BasicParametricOptimization. □

4.5 Recursive procedure

We present now our recursive procedure. It uses the routine BasicParametricOptimization presented above. It also uses a routine PrimeDecomposition which takes as input a polynomial family $\mathbf{P} \subset \mathbb{Q}[\mathbf{c}]$ and a polynomial $Z \in \mathbb{Q}[\mathbf{c}]$. It returns polynomial families $\mathbf{P}_1, \ldots, \mathbf{P}_k$ such that

$$\sqrt{\langle \mathbf{P} \rangle + \langle Z \rangle} = \cap_{i=1}^k \langle \mathbf{P}_i \rangle$$

and $\langle \mathbf{P}_i \rangle$ is prime for $1 \leq i \leq k$.

Input: $\mathbf{h} = (h_1, \ldots, h_p) \subset \mathbb{Q}[X_1, \ldots, X_n]$ and $\mathbf{P}_0 \subset \mathbb{Q}[\mathbf{c}]$
Properties: $\mathbf{P}_0$ generates a prime ideal and $\langle h_1, \ldots, h_p\rangle$ generates a radical equidimensional ideal defining a smooth algebraic set.
Output: a list of triples $(\Phi, Z, \mathbf{P})$ such that

- $\mathbf{P} \subset \mathbb{Q}[\mathbf{c}]$ generates a prime ideal; $Z \in \mathbb{Q}[\mathbf{c}] - \langle \mathbf{P}\rangle$ and $\Phi \in \mathbb{Q}[\mathbf{c}_0, \mathbf{c}]$;
- for any $\gamma \in \mathbf{V}(\mathbf{P}) - \mathbf{V}(Z)$, $\Phi(\mathbf{c}_0, \gamma)$ is not identically 0 and its set of roots contains the optimum of the restriction of the map $x \to \gamma^T x$ to $\mathcal{V} \cap \mathbb{R}^n$

and the union of the algebraic sets defined by the families $\mathbf{P}$ in the output is $\mathbf{V}(\mathbf{P}_0)$.

When calling this recusive algorithm with input $\mathbf{h}$ and $(0) \in \mathbb{Q}[\mathbf{c}]$ we get a list of triples $(\Phi_i, Z_i, \mathbf{P}_i)$ for $1 \le i \le k$ such that $\cup_{i=1}^k \mathbf{V}(\mathbf{P}_i)$ is the whole parameters' space. Remark that with the above properties of the output, given $\gamma \in \mathbb{C}^n$, the optimum of the restrition of the map $x \to \gamma^T x$ is a root of the non-zero polynomial $\Phi_i(\mathbf{c}_0, \gamma)$ if $\gamma \in \mathbf{V}(\mathbf{P}_i) - \mathbf{V}(Z_i)$.

$\mathsf{ParametricOptimizationRec}(\mathbf{h}, \mathbf{P}_0)$

1. if $\langle \mathbf{P}_0\rangle = \langle 1\rangle$ then return []
2. $(\Phi, Z) = \mathsf{BasicParametricOptimization}(\mathbf{h}, \mathbf{P}_0)$
3. $(\mathbf{P}_1, \ldots, \mathbf{P}_k) = \mathsf{PrimeDecomposition}(\mathbf{P}, Z)$
4. Let $\mathbf{L}_i = \mathsf{ParametricOptimizationRec}(\mathbf{h}, \mathbf{P}_i)$ for $1 \le i \le k$
5. return the union of $(\Phi, Z, \mathbf{P}_0)$ with $\mathbf{L}_1, \ldots, \mathbf{L}_i$

THEOREM 4.9. *Algorithm* ParametricOptimizationRec *terminates and is correct.*

PROOF. Correctness follows straightforwardly from an induction on the depth of the recursion and the correctness of BasicParametricOptimization (see Theorem 4.8).

We prove now termination. Using again Theorem 4.8, note that the polynomial Z obtained at Step 2 is such that $\dim(\langle \mathbf{P}_0\rangle + \langle Z\rangle) < \dim(\mathbf{P}_0)$ since $\mathbf{P}_0$ is prime and $Z \notin \langle \mathbf{P}_0\rangle$. We deduce that at each recursive call, the dimension decreases which ends the proof. □

EXAMPLE 3.3 (CONTINUED) Since $\langle \mathbf{c}_2\mathbf{c}_4, \mathbf{c}_3\mathbf{c}_4, \mathbf{c}_3\mathbf{c}_2\mathbf{c}_1\rangle$ represents the bad parameters' values for Algorithm 3.1, we need to consider its prime components $\langle \mathbf{c}_1, \mathbf{c}_4\rangle, \langle \mathbf{c}_2, \mathbf{c}_4\rangle, \langle \mathbf{c}_3, \mathbf{c}_4\rangle$ and $\langle \mathbf{c}_2, \mathbf{c}_3\rangle$ in our recursive procedure described above. Due to the limit of space, we do not provide all details. We only present the results obtained with $\mathbf{P} = \langle \mathbf{c}_2, \mathbf{c}_3\rangle$, especially those of Step 7 in the subroutine BasicParametricOptimization but all the computations take a few minutes using Macaulay2 while the best implementations of CAD don't tackle this example. Following the paragraph on computing sets of non-properness, we obtain that the square-free parts of Φ_1 and $Z_1 Z_1'$ are respectively $\mathbf{c}_0\mathbf{c}_1\mathbf{c}_4$ and $\mathbf{c}_1\mathbf{c}_4$. Thus, we need recursive routines with $\mathbf{P}_1 = \langle \mathbf{c}_1, \mathbf{c}_2, \mathbf{c}_3\rangle$ and $\mathbf{P}_2 = \langle \mathbf{c}_2, \mathbf{c}_3, \mathbf{c}_4\rangle$, repectively. In both cases, all parameters are instantiated; the objective function is X_4 in the case of $\mathbf{P}_1$ and X_1 in the case of $\mathbf{P}_2$. In the case of $\mathbf{P}_1$, the problem is reduced to the non-parametric optimization problem with the objective X_4. Running the algorithm in [18], we get $\Phi_1 = \mathbf{c}_0$ which represents the asymptotic optimum that we are concerned about.

5. REFERENCES

[1] B. Bank, M. Giusti, J. Heintz, and L.-M. Pardo. Generalized polar varieties: Geometry and algorithms. *Journal of complexity*, 21(4):377–412, 2005.

[2] B. Bank, M. Giusti, J. Heintz, and M. Safey El Din. Intrinsic complexity estimates in polynomial optimization. *J. Complexity*, 30(4):430–443, 2014.

[3] B. Bank, M. Giusti, J. Heintz, M. Safey El Din, and E. Schost. On the geometry of polar varieties. *Applicable Algebra in Engineering, Communication and Computing*, 21(1):33–83, 2010.

[4] E. Becker, T. Mora, M. G. Marinari, and C. Traverso. The shape of the shape lemma. In *Proceedings of the international symposium on Symbolic and algebraic computation*, pages 129–133. ACM, 1994.

[5] D. P. C. Garcia and M. Morari. Model predictive control: theory and practice - a survey. *Automatica*, 25:335 – 348, 1989.

[6] F. Catanese, S. Hosten, A. Khetan, and B. Sturmfels. The maximum likelihood degree. *American Journal of Mathematics*, 128(3):671–677, 2006.

[7] C. Chen, O. Golubitsky, F. Lemaire, M. M. Maza, and W. Pan. Comprehensive triangular decomposition. In *Computer Algebra in Scientific Computing, 10th International Workshop, CASC 2007, Bonn, Germany, September 16-20, 2007, Proceedings*, pages 73–101, 2007.

[8] G. Collins. Quantifier elimination for real closed fields by cylindrical algebraic decompostion. volume 33 of *Lecture Notes in Computer Science*, pages 134–183. 1975.

[9] D. Cox, J. Little, and D. O'Shea. *Ideals, Varieties, and Algorithms: An Introduction to Computational Algebraic Geometry and Commutative Algebra*. Undergraduate Texts in Mathematics. Springer, Springer Science+Business Media, LLC, 233 Spring Street, New York, NY 10013, USA, 3rd edition, 2007.

[10] J. Della Dora, C. Discrescenzo, and D. Duval. About a new method method for computing in algebraic number fields. In *EUROCAL 85 Vol. 2*, volume 204 of *LNCS*, pages 289–290. Springer, 1985.

[11] J.-C. Faugère, P. Gianni, D. Lazard, and T. Mora. Efficient computation of zero-dimensional Gröbner bases by change of ordering. *Journal of Symbolic Computation*, 16(4):329–344, 1993.

[12] J. v. Gathen and J. Gerhard. *Modern computer algebra*. Cambridge University Press, 1999.

[13] I. Gelfand, I. Gelfand, M. Kapranov, and A. Zelevinsky. *Discriminants, Resultants, and Multidimensional Determinants*. Mathematics (Birkhäuser). Birkhäuser Boston, 2008.

[14] M. Giusti, G. Lecerf, and B. Salvy. A Gröbner-free alternative for polynomial system solving. *Journal of Complexity*, 17(1):154–211, 2001.

[15] H.-C. Graf von Bothmer and K. Ranestad. A general formula for the algebraic degree in semidefinite programming. *Bulletin of the London Mathematical Society*, 41(2):193–197, 2009.

[16] A. Greuet, F. Guo, M. Safey El Din and L. Zhi. Global optimization of polynomials restricted to a smooth variety using sums of squares. *Journal of Symbolic Computation*, 47(5), 503-518, 2012.

[17] A. Greuet and M. Safey El Din. Deciding reachability of the infimum of a multivariate polynomial. In Proceedings of the 36th international symposium on Symbolic and algebraic computation, ISSAC '11, pages 131–138, New York, NY, USA, 2011. ACM.

[18] A. Greuet and M. Safey El Din. Probabilistic algorithm for polynomial optimization over a real algebraic set. *SIAM Journal on Optimization*, 24(3):1313–1343, 2014.

[19] F. Guo, C. Wang, and L. Zhi. Optimizing a linear function over a noncompact real algebraic variety. In *Proceedings of the 2014 Symposium on Symbolic-Numeric Computation*, SNC '14, pages 39–40, New York, NY, USA, 2014. ACM.

[20] S. Hosten, A. Khetan, and B. Sturmfels. Solving the likelihood equations. *Foundations of Computational Mathematics*, 5(4):389–407, 2005.

[21] Z. Jelonek and K. Kurdyka. Quantitative generalized bertini-sard theorem for smooth affine varieties. *Discrete & Computational Geometry*, 34(4):659–678, 2005.

[22] K. Kurdyka, P. Orro, and S. Simon. Semialgebraic sard theorem for generalized critical values. *Journal Differential Geom*, 56(1):67–92, 2000.

[23] X. Li, M. M. Maza, and W. Pan. Computations modulo regular chains. In J. R. Johnson, H. Park, and E. Kaltofen, editors, *Symbolic and Algebraic Computation, International Symposium, ISSAC 2009, Seoul, Republic of Korea, July 29-31, 2009, Proceedings*, pages 239–246. ACM, 2009.

[24] J. Nie and K. Ranestad. Algebraic degree of polynomial optimization. *SIAM Journal on Optimization*, 20(1):485–502, 2009.

[25] J. Nie, K. Ranestad, and B. Sturmfels. The algebraic degree of semidefinite programming. *Mathematical Programming*, 122(2):379–405, 2010.

[26] P. J. Rabier. Ehresmann fibrations and Palais-Smale conditions for morphisms of Finsler manifolds. *Annals of Mathematics*, 146(3):647–691, 1997.

[27] K. Ranestad. Algebraic degree in semidefinite and polynomial optimization. In M. F. Anjos and J. B. Lasserre, editors, *Handbook on Semidefinite, Conic and Polynomial Optimization*, volume 166 of *International Series in Operations Research & Management Science*, pages 61–75. Springer US, 2012.

[28] R. Rockafellar. *Convex Analysis*. Convex Analysis. Princeton University Press, 1970.

[29] P. Rostalski and B. Sturmfels. Dualities in convex algebraic geometry. *Rendiconti di Matematica, Serie VII*, 30:285–327, 2010.

[30] P. Rostalski and B. Sturmfels. Dualities. In G. Blekherman, P. A. Parrilo, and R. R. Thomas, editors, *Semidefinite Optimization and Convex Algebraic Geometry*, MOS-SIAM Series on Optimization, chapter 5, pages 203–250. Society for Industrial and Applied Mathematics, Philadelphia, PA, 2012.

[31] M. Safey El Din. Computing the global optimum of a multivariate polynomial over the reals. In *Proceedings of ISSAC 2008*, pages 71–78, 2008.

[32] M. Safey El Din and E. Schost. Polar varieties and computation of one point in each connected component of a smooth real algebraic set. In J. Sendra, editor, *Proceedings of ISSAC 2003*, pages 224–231. ACM Press, aug 2003.

[33] M. Safey El Din and E. Schost. Properness defects of projections and computation of at least one point in each connected component of a real algebraic set. *Discrete & Computational Geometry*, 32(3):417–430, 2004.

[34] M. Safey El Din and L. Zhi. Computing rational points in convex semialgebraic sets and sum of squares decompositions. *SIAM Journal on Optimization*, 20(6):2876–2889, 2010.

[35] R. Sinn. Algebraic boundaries of convex semi-algebraic sets. 2014. URL http://arxiv.org/pdf/1405.7822v2.pdf.

[36] H. Vui and P. Sòn. Representations of positive polynomials and optimization on noncompact semialgebraic sets. *SIAM Journal on Optimization*, 20(6):3082–3103, 2010.

[37] V. Weispfenning. Comprehensive Gröbner bases. *Journal of Symbolic Computation*, 14(1):1–29, 1992.

Certifying isolated singular points and their multiplicity structure

Jonathan D. Hauenstein*
University of Notre Dame
hauenstein@nd.edu

Bernard Mourrain
INRIA Sophia Antipolis
bernard.mourrain@inria.fr

Agnes Szanto†
North Carolina State University
aszanto@ncsu.edu

ABSTRACT

This paper presents two new constructions related to singular solutions of polynomial systems. The first is a new deflation method for an isolated singular root. This construction uses a single linear differential form defined from the Jacobian matrix of the input, and defines the deflated system by applying this differential form to the original system. The advantages of this new deflation is that it does not introduce new variables and the increase in the number of equations is linear instead of the quadratic increase of previous methods. The second construction gives the coefficients of the so-called inverse system or dual basis, which defines the multiplicity structure at the singular root. We present a system of equations in the original variables plus a relatively small number of new variables. We show that the roots of this new system include the original singular root but now with multiplicity one, and the new variables uniquely determine the multiplicity structure. Both constructions are "exact" in that they permit one to treat all conjugate roots simultaneously and can be used in certification procedures for singular roots and their multiplicity structure with respect to an exact rational polynomial system.

Categories and Subject Descriptors

[**Mathematics of computing**]: Computations on polynomials

General Terms

Theory, Algorithms

Keywords

isolated point, root deflation, dual space, multiplicity structure, inverse system, local algebra, multiplication operator

1. INTRODUCTION

One issue when using numerical methods for solving polynomial systems is the ill-conditioning and possibly erratic behavior of Newton's method near singular solutions. Regularization (deflation) techniques remove the singular structure to restore local quadratic convergence of Newton's method.

Our motivation for the current work is twofold. On one hand, in a recent paper [1], two of the co-authors of the present paper studied a certification method for approximate roots of exact overdetermined and singular polynomial systems, and wanted to extend the method to certify the multiplicity structure at the root as well. Since all these problems are ill-posed, in [1] a hybrid symbolic-numeric approach was proposed, that included the exact computation of a square polynomial system that had the original root with multiplicity one. In certifying singular roots, this exact square system was obtained from a deflation technique that added subdeterminants of the Jacobian matrix to the system iteratively. However, since the multiplicity structure is destroyed by this deflation technique, it remained an open question how to certify the multiplicity structure of singular roots of exact polynomial systems.

Our second motivation is to find a method that simultaneously refines the accuracy of a singular root and a small number of parameters describing the multiplicity structure at the root. The knowledge of the multiplicity structure can be useful in many contexts. For instance, it can be used to analyze the number of branches of an algebraic curve at a singular point [20]. Coupled with subdivision methods [2], it provides an efficient method to certify the topology of curves or surfaces.

In previous numerical approaches which both describe the multiplicity structure and restore the quadratic convergence of Newton's method, the number of parameters is large which can make computation and certification difficult. Therefore, a method which uses a small number of parameters describing the multiplicity structure, and which uses Newton's method to simultaneously approximate the coordinates of the singular root and the parameters, will improve certification of singular roots and their multiplicity structure.

Related work. The treatment of singular roots is a critical issue for numerical analysis with a large literature on methods that transform the problem into a new one for which Newton-type methods converge quadratically to the root.

Deflation techniques which add new equations in order to reduce the multiplicity were considered in [25, 26]. By triangulating the Jacobian matrix at the (approximate) root, new minors of the polynomial Jacobian matrix are added to the initial system in order to reduce the multiplicity of the singular solution.

A similar approach is used in [10] and [8], where a maximal invertible block of the Jacobian matrix at the (approximate)

*Research partly supported by DARPA YFA, NSF grant ACI-1460032, and Sloan Research Fellowship.

†Research partly supported by NSF grant CCF-1217557.

ISSAC'15, July 6–9, 2015, Bath, United Kingdom.
ACM 978-1-4503-3435-8/15/07.
DOI: http://dx.doi.org/10.1145/2755996.2756645.

root is computed and minors of the polynomial Jacobian matrix are added to the initial system. For example, when the Jacobian matrix at the root vanishes, all first derivatives of the input polynomials are added to the system in both of these approaches. Moreover, it is shown in [10] that deflation can be performed at nonisolated solutions in which the process stabilizes to so-called *isosingular sets*. At each iteration of this deflation approach, the number of added equations can be taken to be $(N-r)\cdot(n-r)$, where N is the number of input polynomials, n is number of variables, and r is the rank of the Jacobian at the root.

These methods repeatedly use their constructions until a system with a simple root is obtained.

In [12], a triangular presentation of the ideal in a good position and derivations with respect to the leading variables are used to iteratively reduce the multiplicity. This process is applied for p-adic lifting with exact computation.

In other approaches, new variables and new equations are introduced simultaneously. For example, in [31], new variables are introduced to describe some perturbations of the initial equations and some differentials which vanish at the singular points. This approach is also used in [18], where it is shown that this iterated deflation process yields a system with a simple root.

In [20], perturbation variables are also introduced in relation with the inverse system of the singular point to obtain directly a deflated system with a simple root. The perturbation is constructed from a monomial basis of the local algebra at the multiple root.

In [13, 14], only variables for the differentials of the initial system are introduced. The analysis of this deflation is improved in [5], where it is shown that the number of steps is bounded by the order of the inverse system. This type of deflation is also used in [17], for the special case where the Jacobian matrix at the multiple root has rank $n-1$ (the breadth one case).

In these methods, at each step, both the number of variables and equations are increased, but the new equations are linear in the newly added variables.

The aforementioned deflation techniques usually break the structure of the local ring at the singular point. The first method to compute the inverse system describing this structure is due to F.S. Macaulay [19] and known as the dialytic method. More recent algorithms for the construction of inverse systems are described in [21] which reduces the size of the intermediate linear systems (and exploited in [28]) and further improved in [23] and more recently in [20] using a formal integration method.

The computation of inverse systems has also been used to approximate a multiple root. The dialytic method is used in [32] and the relationship between the deflation approach and the inverse system is analyzed, exploited and implemented in [11]. In [27], a minimization approach is used to reduce the value of the equations and their derivatives at the approximate root, assuming a basis of the inverse system is known. In [7], the certification of a multiple root with breadth one is obtained using α-theorems. In [30], the inverse system is constructed via Macaulay's method, tables of multiplications are deduced, and their eigenvalues are used to improve the approximated root. They show that the convergence is quadratic at the multiple root. In [16], they show that in the breadth one case the parameters needed to describe the inverse system is small, and use it to compute the singular roots in [15]. The inverse system has further been exploited in deflation techniques in [20]. This is the closest to our approach as it computes a perturbation of the initial polynomial system with a given inverse system, deduced from an approximation of the singular solution. The inverse system is used to transform directly the singular root into a simple root of an augmented system.

Singular solutions of polynomial systems have been studied by analyzing multiplication matrices (e.g.,[4, 22, 9]) via non-local methods, which apply to the zero-dimensional case.

Contributions. In the present paper, we first give an improved version of a deflation method that can be used in the certification algorithm of [1]. This method reduces the number of added equations at each deflation iteration from quadratic to linear. We prove that applying a single linear differential form to the input system corresponding to a generic kernel element of the Jacobian matrix reduces both the multiplicity and the depth of the singular root. The deflated system does not involve any approximate coefficients and can therefore be used in certification methods as in [1].

Secondly, to approximate efficiently both the singular point and its multiplicity structure, we propose a new deflation which involves a small number of new variables compared to other approaches that rely on Macaulay multiplication matrices. It is based on a new characterization of the isolated singular point together with its multiplicity structure via inverse systems. The deflated polynomial system exploits the nilpotent and commutation properties of the multiplication matrices in the local algebra of the singular point. We prove that the polynomial system we construct has a root corresponding to the singular root but now with multiplicity one, and the new added coordinates describe the multiplicity structure. In particular, this system completely deflates the system in one step. Moreover, the number of variables and equations in this construction is at most $n+n\delta(\delta-1)/2$ and $N\delta+n(n-1)(\delta-1)(\delta-2)/4$, respectively, where N is the number of input polynomials, n is the number of variables, and δ is the multiplicity of the singular point. This construction is the first approach that completely deflates a singular root and has polynomial number of equations and variables in the input size and the multiplicity. Again, the deflated system does not involve any approximate coefficients and thus can handle conjugate roots simultaneously and also be used in certification techniques of exact polynomials as in [1].

2. PRELIMINARIES

Let $\mathbf{f} := (f_1, \ldots, f_N) \in \mathbb{K}[\mathbf{x}]^N$ where $\mathbf{x} = (x_1, \ldots, x_n)$ for some field $\mathbb{K} \subset \mathbb{C}$ and $I = (f_1, \ldots, f_N) \subset \mathbb{K}[\mathbf{x}]$. Suppose that $\xi = (\xi_1, \ldots, \xi_n) \in \mathbb{C}^n$ is an isolated multiple root of $\mathbf{f}$, $\mathfrak{m}_\xi$ is the maximal ideal at ξ, and Q is the primary component of I at ξ, i.e., $\sqrt{Q} = \mathfrak{m}_\xi$.

Let $\mathbb{C}[[\boldsymbol{\partial}_\xi]] := \mathbb{C}[[\partial_{1,\xi}, \ldots, \partial_{n,\xi}]]$ be the ring of power series. We will use the notation for $\beta = (\beta_1, \ldots, \beta_n) \in \mathbb{N}^n$:

$$\boldsymbol{\partial}_\xi^\beta := \partial_{1,\xi}^{\beta_1} \cdots \partial_{n,\xi}^{\beta_n}.$$

We identify $\mathbb{C}[[\boldsymbol{\partial}_\xi]]$ with the dual space $\mathbb{C}[\mathbf{x}]^*$ by considering $\boldsymbol{\partial}_\xi^\beta$ as derivations and evaluations at ξ, defined by

$$\boldsymbol{\partial}_\xi^\beta(p) := \boldsymbol{\partial}^\beta(p)\Big|_\xi := \frac{d^{|\beta|}p}{dx_1^{\beta_1}\cdots dx_n^{\beta_n}}(\xi) \quad \text{for } p \in \mathbb{C}[\mathbf{x}]. \quad (1)$$

The derivation on $\mathbb{C}[[\boldsymbol{\partial}_\xi]]$ with respect to the variable $\partial_{i,\xi}$ is denoted $d_{\partial_{i,\xi}}$ for $i = 1, \ldots, n$. Note that

$$\frac{1}{\beta!}\boldsymbol{\partial}_\xi^\beta((\mathbf{x}-\xi)^\alpha) = \begin{cases} 1 & \text{if } \alpha = \beta, \\ 0 & \text{otherwise} \end{cases}$$

where $\beta! = \beta_1! \cdots \beta_n!$.

For $p \in \mathbb{C}[\mathbf{x}]$ and$\Lambda \in \mathbb{C}[[\boldsymbol{\partial}_\xi]] = \mathbb{C}[\mathbf{x}]^*$, let

$$p \cdot \Lambda : q \mapsto \Lambda(pq).$$

We check that $p = (x_i - \xi_i)$ acts as a derivation on $\mathbb{C}[[\boldsymbol{\partial}_\xi]]$:

$$(x_i - \xi_i) \cdot \boldsymbol{\partial}_\xi^\beta = d_{\partial_{i,\xi}}(\boldsymbol{\partial}_\xi^\beta).$$

For an ideal $I \subset \mathbb{C}[\mathbf{x}]$, consider

$$I^\perp = \{\Lambda \in \mathbb{C}[[\boldsymbol{\partial}_\xi]] \mid \forall p \in I, \Lambda(p) = 0\}.$$

The vector space $I^\perp$ is naturally identified with the dual space of $\mathbb{C}[\mathbf{x}]/I$. One can easily show that $I^\perp$ is a vector subspace of $\mathbb{C}[[\boldsymbol{\partial}_\xi]]$ which is stable by the derivations $d_{\partial_{i,\xi}}$. Since Q is the $\mathfrak{m}_\xi$-primary of I, we have the following classical result:

Lemma 2.1. *If Q is a $\mathfrak{m}_\xi$-primary component of I, then $Q^\perp = I^\perp \cap \mathbb{C}[\boldsymbol{\partial}_\xi]$.*

This lemma shows that to compute $Q^\perp$, it suffices to compute all polynomials of $\mathbb{C}[\boldsymbol{\partial}_\xi]$ which are in $I^\perp$. Let us denote this set $\mathscr{D} = I^\perp \cap \mathbb{C}[\boldsymbol{\partial}_\xi]$. It is a vector space stable under the derivations $d_{\partial_{i,\xi}}$. Its dimension is the dimension of $Q^\perp$ or $\mathbb{C}[\mathbf{x}]/Q$, that is the *multiplicity* of ξ, denoted by $\delta_\xi(I)$ or simply by δ if ξ and I are clear from the context.

For an element $\Lambda(\boldsymbol{\partial}_\xi) \in \mathbb{C}[\boldsymbol{\partial}_\xi]$ we define the *order*, denoted by $o(\Lambda)$, to be the maximal $|\beta|$ such that $\boldsymbol{\partial}_\xi^\beta$ appears in $\Lambda(\boldsymbol{\partial}_\xi)$ with a non-zero coefficient. For $t \in \mathbb{N}$, let $\mathscr{D}_t$ be the elements of $\mathscr{D}$ of order $\leq t$. As $\mathscr{D}$ is of dimension δ, there exists a smallest $t \geq 0$ such that $\mathscr{D}_{t+1} = \mathscr{D}_t$. Let us call this smallest t, the *nil-index* of $\mathscr{D}$ and denote it by $o_\xi(I)$, or simply by o. As $\mathscr{D}$ is stable by the derivations $d_{\partial_{i,\xi}}$, we easily check that for $t \geq o_\xi(I)$, $\mathscr{D}_t = \mathscr{D}$ and that $o_\xi(I)$ is the maximal degree of the elements in $\mathscr{D}$.

3. DEFLATION USING FIRST DIFFERENTIALS

To improve the numerical approximation of a root, one usually applies a Newton-type method to converge quadratically from a nearby solution to the root of the system, provided it is simple. In the case of multiple roots, deflation techniques are employed to transform the system into another one which has an equivalent root with a smaller multiplicity or even with multiplicity one.

We describe here a construction, using differentials of order one, which leads to a system with a simple root. This construction improves the constructions in [13, 5] since no new variables are added. It also improves the constructions presented in [10] and the "kerneling" method of [8] by adding a smaller number of equations at each deflation step. Note that, in [8], there are smart preprocessing and postprocessing steps which could be utilized in combination with our method. In the preprocessor, one adds directly partial derivatives of polynomials which are zero at the root. The postprocessor extracts a square subsystem of the completely deflated system for which the Jacobian has full rank at the root.

Consider the Jacobian matrix $J_\mathbf{f}(\mathbf{x}) = [\partial_j f_i(\mathbf{x})]$ of the initial system $\mathbf{f}$. By reordering properly the rows and columns (i.e., polynomials and variables), it can be put in the form

$$J_\mathbf{f}(\mathbf{x}) := \begin{bmatrix} A(\mathbf{x}) & B(\mathbf{x}) \\ C(\mathbf{x}) & D(\mathbf{x}) \end{bmatrix} \tag{2}$$

where $A(\mathbf{x})$ is an $r \times r$ matrix with $r = \operatorname{rank} J_\mathbf{f}(\xi) = \operatorname{rank} A(\xi)$.

Suppose that $B(\mathbf{x})$ is an $r \times c$ matrix. The c columns

$$\det(A(\mathbf{x})) \begin{bmatrix} -A^{-1}(\mathbf{x})B(\mathbf{x}) \\ \mathrm{Id} \end{bmatrix}$$

(for $r = 0$ this is the identity matrix) yield the c elements

$$\Lambda_1^\mathbf{x} = \sum_{i=1}^n \lambda_{1,j}(\mathbf{x})\partial_j, \quad \ldots, \quad \Lambda_c^\mathbf{x} = \sum_{i=1}^n \lambda_{c,j}(\mathbf{x})\partial_j.$$

Their coefficients $\lambda_{i,j}(\mathbf{x}) \in \mathbb{K}[\mathbf{x}]$ are polynomial in the variables $\mathbf{x}$. Evaluated at $\mathbf{x} = \xi$, they generate the kernel of $J_\mathbf{f}(\xi)$ and form a basis of $\mathscr{D}_1$.

Definition 3.1. The family $D_1^\mathbf{x} = \{\Lambda_1^\mathbf{x}, \ldots, \Lambda_c^\mathbf{x}\}$ is the *formal* inverse system of order 1 at ξ. For $\boldsymbol{i} = \{i_1, \ldots, i_k\} \subset \{1, \ldots, c\}$ with $|\boldsymbol{i}| \neq 0$, the $\boldsymbol{i}$*-deflated system* of order 1 of $\mathbf{f}$ is

$$\{\mathbf{f}, \Lambda_{i_1}^\mathbf{x}(\mathbf{f}), \ldots, \Lambda_{i_k}^\mathbf{x}(\mathbf{f})\}.$$

By construction, for $i = 1, \ldots, c$,

$$\Lambda_i^\mathbf{x}(\mathbf{f}) = \sum_{j=1}^n \partial_j(\mathbf{f})\lambda_{i,j}(\mathbf{x}) = \det(A(\mathbf{x}))J_\mathbf{f}(\mathbf{x})[\lambda_{i,j}(\mathbf{x})]$$

has $n - c$ zero entries. Thus, the number of non-trivial new equations added in the $\boldsymbol{i}$-deflated system is $|\boldsymbol{i}| \cdot (N - n + c)$. The construction depends on the choice of the invertible block $A(\xi)$ in $J_\mathbf{f}(\xi)$. By a linear invertible transformation of the initial system and by computing a $\boldsymbol{i}$-deflated system, one obtains a deflated system constructed from any $|\boldsymbol{i}|$ linearly independent elements of the kernel of $J_\mathbf{f}(\xi)$.

Example 3.2. Consider the multiplicity 2 root $\xi = (0, 0)$ for the system $f_1(\mathbf{x}) = x_1 + x_2^2$ and $f_2(\mathbf{x}) = x_1^2 + x_2^2$. Then,

$$J_\mathbf{f}(\mathbf{x}) = \begin{bmatrix} A(\mathbf{x}) & B(\mathbf{x}) \\ C(\mathbf{x}) & D(\mathbf{x}) \end{bmatrix} = \begin{bmatrix} 1 & 2x_2 \\ 2x_1 & 2x_2 \end{bmatrix}.$$

The corresponding vector $[-2x_2 \;\; 1]^T$ yields the element
$\Lambda_1^\mathbf{x} = -2x_2\partial_1 + \partial_2$.

Since$\Lambda_1^\mathbf{x}(f_1) = 0$, the $\{1\}$-deflated system of order 1 of $\mathbf{f}$ is

$$\{x_1 + x_2^2, \;\; x_1^2 + x_2^2, \;\; -4x_1x_2 + 2x_2\}$$

which has a multiplicity 1 root at ξ.

We use the following to analyze this deflation procedure.

Lemma 3.3 (Leibniz rule)**.** *For $a, b \in \mathbb{K}[\boldsymbol{x}]$,*

$$\boldsymbol{\partial}^\alpha(a\,b) = \sum_{\beta \in \mathbb{N}^n} \frac{1}{\beta!}\boldsymbol{\partial}^\beta(a)d_{\boldsymbol{\partial}}^\beta(\boldsymbol{\partial}^\alpha)(b).$$

Proposition 3.4. *Let r be the rank of $J_\mathbf{f}(\xi)$. Assume that $r < n$. Let $\boldsymbol{i} \subset \{1, \ldots, n\}$ with $0 < |\boldsymbol{i}| \leq n - r$ and $\mathbf{f}^{(1)}$ be the $\boldsymbol{i}$-deflated system of order 1 of $\mathbf{f}$. Then, $\delta_\xi(\mathbf{f}^{(1)}) \geq 1$ and $o_\xi(\mathbf{f}^{(1)}) < o_\xi(\mathbf{f})$, which also implies that $\delta_\xi(\mathbf{f}^{(1)}) < \delta_\xi(\mathbf{f})$.*

Proof. By construction, for $i \in \boldsymbol{i}$, the polynomials $\Lambda_i^{\mathbf{x}}(\mathbf{f})$ vanish at ξ, so that $\delta_\xi(\mathbf{f}^{(1)}) \geq 1$. By hypothesis, the Jacobian of $\mathbf{f}$ is not injective yielding $o_\xi(\mathbf{f}) > 0$. Let $\mathscr{D}^{(1)}$ be the inverse system of $\mathbf{f}^{(1)}$ at ξ. Since $(\mathbf{f}^{(1)}) \supset (\mathbf{f})$, we have $\mathscr{D}^{(1)} \subset \mathscr{D}$. In particular, for any non-zero element $\Lambda \in \mathscr{D}^{(1)} \subset \mathbb{K}[\boldsymbol{\partial}_\xi]$ and $i \in \boldsymbol{i}$, $\Lambda(\mathbf{f}) = 0$ and $\Lambda(\Lambda_i^{\mathbf{x}}(\mathbf{f})) = 0$.

Using Leibniz rule, for any $p \in \mathbb{K}[\mathbf{x}]$, we have

$$\begin{aligned}\Lambda(\Lambda_i^{\mathbf{x}}(p)) &= \Lambda\left(\sum_{j=1}^{n} \lambda_{i,j}(\mathbf{x})\partial_j(p)\right)\\ &= \sum_{\beta\in\mathbb{N}^n}\sum_{j=1}^{n}\frac{1}{\beta!}\boldsymbol{\partial}_\xi^{\beta}(\lambda_{i,j}(\mathbf{x}))d^{\beta}_{\partial_\xi}(\Lambda)\partial_{j,\xi}(p)\\ &= \sum_{\beta\in\mathbb{N}^n}\sum_{j=1}^{n}\frac{1}{\beta!}\boldsymbol{\partial}_\xi^{\beta}(\lambda_{i,j}(\mathbf{x}))\boldsymbol{\partial}_{j,\xi}d^{\beta}_{\partial_\xi}(\Lambda)(p)\\ &= \sum_{\beta\in\mathbb{N}^n}\Delta_{i,\beta}d^{\beta}_{\partial_\xi}(\Lambda)(p)\end{aligned}$$

where

$$\Delta_{i,\beta} = \sum_{j=1}^{n}\lambda_{i,j,\beta}\partial_{j,\xi} \in \mathbb{K}[\boldsymbol{\partial}_\xi] \text{ and } \lambda_{i,j,\beta} = \frac{1}{\beta!}\partial_\xi^{\beta}(\lambda_{i,j}(\mathbf{x})) \in \mathbb{K}.$$

The term $\Delta_{i,\mathbf{0}}$ is $\sum_{j=1}^{n}\lambda_{i,j}(\xi)\partial_{j,\xi}$ which has degree 1 in $\boldsymbol{\partial}_\xi$ since $[\lambda_{i,j}(\xi)]$ is a non-zero element of $\ker J_{\mathbf{f}}(\xi)$. For simplicity, let $\phi_i(\Lambda) := \sum_{\beta\in\mathbb{N}^n}\Delta_{i,\beta}d^{\beta}_{\partial}(\Lambda)$.

For any $\Lambda \in \mathbb{C}[\boldsymbol{\partial}_\xi]$, we have

$$\begin{aligned}d_{\partial_{j,\xi}}(\phi_i(\Lambda)) &= \sum_{\beta\in\mathbb{N}^n}\lambda_{i,j,\beta}d^{\beta}_{\partial}(\Lambda) + \Delta_{i,\beta}d^{\beta}_{\partial}(d_{\partial_{j,\xi}}(\Lambda))\\ &= \sum_{\beta\in\mathbb{N}^n}\lambda_{i,j,\beta}d^{\beta}_{\partial}(\Lambda) + \phi_i(d_{\partial_{j,\xi}}(\Lambda)).\end{aligned}$$

Moreover, if $\Lambda \in \mathscr{D}^{(1)}$, then by definition $\phi_i(\Lambda)(\mathbf{f}) = 0$. Since $\mathscr{D}$ and $\mathscr{D}^{(1)}$ are both stable by derivation, it follows that $\forall\Lambda \in \mathscr{D}^{(1)}$, $d_{\partial_{j,\xi}}(\phi_i(\Lambda)) \in \mathscr{D}^{(1)} + \phi_i(\mathscr{D}^{(1)})$. Since $\mathscr{D}^{(1)} \subset \mathscr{D}$, we know $\mathscr{D} + \phi_i(\mathscr{D}^{(1)})$ is stable by derivation. For any element Λ of $\mathscr{D} + \phi_i(\mathscr{D}^{(1)})$, $\Lambda(\mathbf{f}) = 0$. We deduce that $\mathscr{D} + \phi_i(\mathscr{D}^{(1)}) = \mathscr{D}$. Consequently, the order of the elements in $\phi_i(\mathscr{D}^{(1)})$ is at most $o_\xi(\mathbf{f})$. The statement follows since ϕ_i increases the order by 1, therefore $o_\xi(\mathbf{f}^{(1)}) < o_\xi(\mathbf{f})$. □

We consider now a sequence of deflations of the system $\mathbf{f}$. Let $\mathbf{f}^{(1)}$ be the $\boldsymbol{i}_1$-deflated system of $\mathbf{f}$. We construct inductively $\mathbf{f}^{(k+1)}$ as the $\boldsymbol{i}_{k+1}$-deflated system of $\mathbf{f}^{(k)}$ for some choices of $\boldsymbol{i}_j \subset \{1, \ldots, n\}$.

Proposition 3.5. *There exists $k \leq o_\xi(\mathbf{f})$ such that ξ is a simple root of $\mathbf{f}^{(k)}$.*

Proof. By Proposition 3.4, $\delta_\xi(\mathbf{f}^{(k)}) \geq 1$ and $o_\xi(\mathbf{f}^{(k)})$ is strictly decreasing with k until it reaches the value 0. Therefore, there exists $k \leq o_\xi(I)$ such that $o_\xi(\mathbf{f}^{(k)}) = 0$ and $\delta_\xi(\mathbf{f}^{(k)}) \geq 1$. This implies that ξ is a simple root of $\mathbf{f}^{(k)}$. □

To minimize the number of equations added at each deflation step, we take $|\boldsymbol{i}| = 1$. Then, the number of non-trivial new equations added at each step is at most $N - n + c$.

We described this approach using first order differentials arising from the Jacobian, but this can be easily extended to use higher order differentials.

4. THE MULTIPLICITY STRUCTURE

Before describing our results, we start this section by recalling the definition of pairs of primal-dual bases for the space $\mathbb{C}[\mathbf{x}]/Q$ and its dual $\mathscr{D}$.

Definition 4.1 (Primal-dual basis pair). Let $\mathbf{f}$, ξ, Q, $\mathscr{D}$, $\delta = \delta_\xi(\mathbf{f})$ and $o = o_\xi(\mathbf{f})$ be as above. A primal-dual basis pair is a basis of $\mathbb{C}[\mathbf{x}]/Q$ of the form

$$B = \{(\mathbf{x}-\xi)^{\alpha_1}, (\mathbf{x}-\xi)^{\alpha_2}, \ldots, (\mathbf{x}-\xi)^{\alpha_\delta}\} \quad (3)$$

with $\alpha_1 = 0$, and a dual basis D of $\mathscr{D}$ of the form:

$$\begin{aligned}\Lambda_{\alpha_1} &= \boldsymbol{\partial}_\xi^{\alpha_1} = 1_\xi\\ \Lambda_{\alpha_2} &= \frac{1}{\alpha_2!}\boldsymbol{\partial}_\xi^{\alpha_2} + \sum_{\substack{|\beta|\leq o\\ \beta\notin E}}\frac{\nu_{\alpha_2,\beta}}{\beta!}\boldsymbol{\partial}_\xi^{\beta}\\ &\vdots\\ \Lambda_{\alpha_\delta} &= \frac{1}{\alpha_\delta!}\boldsymbol{\partial}_\xi^{\alpha_\delta} + \sum_{\substack{|\beta|\leq o\\ \beta\notin E}}\frac{\nu_{\alpha_\delta,\beta}}{\beta!}\boldsymbol{\partial}_\xi^{\beta}.\end{aligned} \quad (4)$$

where $E = \{\alpha_1, \ldots, \alpha_\delta\} \subset \mathbb{N}^n$. Let $E^+ := \bigcup_{i=1}^{n}(E + \mathbf{e}_i)$ where $E + \mathbf{e}_i := \{(\gamma_1, \ldots, \gamma_i + 1, \ldots, \gamma_n) : \gamma \in E\}$, and $\partial(E) := E^+ \setminus E$.

We may assume that primal-dual basis pair is such that B is *connected to 1* (c.f. [24]) with the orders satisfying $0 = o(\Lambda_{\alpha_1}) \leq \cdots \leq o(\Lambda_{\alpha_\delta})$ (see, e.g., [20]).

Throughout this section we assume that we are given a fixed primal basis B for $\mathbb{C}[\mathbf{x}]/Q$. Note that a primal basis B connected to 1 can be computed numerically from an approximation of ξ as in [6, 11, 23, 20].

Given the primal basis B, the dual basis D can be computed by Macaulay's dialytic method which can be used to deflate the root ξ as in [14]. This method would introduce $n + (\delta - 1)\left(\binom{n+o}{n} - \delta\right)$ new variables, which is not polynomial in o. Below, we give a construction of a polynomial system that only depends on at most $n + n\delta(\delta-1)/2$ variables. These variables correspond to the entries of the *multiplication matrices* that we define next.

Let

$$\begin{aligned}M_i : \mathbb{C}[\mathbf{x}]/Q &\to \mathbb{C}[\mathbf{x}]/Q\\ p &\mapsto (x_i - \xi_i)\,p\end{aligned}$$

be the multiplication operator by $x_i - \xi_i$ in $\mathbb{C}[\mathbf{x}]/Q$. Its transpose operator is

$$\begin{aligned}M_i^t : \mathscr{D} &\to \mathscr{D}\\ \Lambda &\mapsto \Lambda \circ M_i = (x_i - \xi_i)\cdot\Lambda = \frac{d}{d\partial_{i,\xi}}(\Lambda) = d_{\partial_{i,\xi}}(\Lambda)\end{aligned} \quad (5)$$

where $\mathscr{D} = Q^\perp \subset \mathbb{C}[\boldsymbol{\partial}_\xi]$. The matrix of M_i in the basis B of $\mathbb{C}[\mathbf{x}]/Q$ is denoted $\mathtt{M}_i$.

As B is a basis of $\mathbb{C}[\mathbf{x}]/Q$, we can identify the elements of $\mathbb{C}[\mathbf{x}]/Q$ with the elements of the vector space $\mathrm{span}_{\mathbb{C}}(B)$. We define the normal form $N(p)$ of a polynomial p in $\mathbb{C}[\mathbf{x}]$ as the unique element b of $\mathrm{span}_{\mathbb{C}}(B)$ such that $p - b \in Q$. Hereafter, we are going to identify the elements of $\mathbb{C}[\mathbf{x}]/Q$ with their normal form in $\mathrm{span}_{\mathbb{C}}(B)$.

For any polynomial $p(x_1, \ldots, x_n) \in \mathbb{C}[\mathbf{x}]$, let $p(\mathbf{M})$ be the operator of $\mathbb{C}[\mathbf{x}]/Q$ obtained by replacing $x_i - \xi_i$ by M_i. By definition of a dual basis, we have the following property:

Lemma 4.2. *For any $p \in \mathbb{C}[\mathbf{x}]$, the normal form of p is $N(p) = p(\mathbf{M})(1)$ and we have*

$$p(\mathbf{M})(1) = \Lambda_{\alpha_1}(p)\, 1 + \Lambda_{\alpha_2}(p)\, (\mathbf{x}-\xi)^{\alpha_2} + \cdots + \Lambda_{\alpha_d}(p)\, (\mathbf{x}-\xi)^{\alpha_\delta}.$$

This shows that the coefficient vector $[p]$ of $N(p)$ in the basis B is $[p] = (\Lambda_{\alpha_i}(p))_{1\le i\le\delta}$.

The following lemma is well-known, but we include a proof.

Lemma 4.3. *The values of the coefficients $\nu_{\alpha,\beta}$ for $(\alpha,\beta) \in E\times\partial(E)$ appearing in the dual basis (4) uniquely determine the system of pairwise commuting multiplication matrices $\mathtt{M}_i$, namely, for $i = 1,\ldots,n$,*

$$\mathtt{M}_i^t = \begin{bmatrix} 0 & \nu_{\alpha_2,\mathbf{e}_i} & \nu_{\alpha_3,\mathbf{e}_i} & \cdots & \nu_{\alpha_\delta,\mathbf{e}_i} \\ 0 & 0 & \nu_{\alpha_3,\alpha_2+\mathbf{e}_i} & \cdots & \nu_{\alpha_\delta,\alpha_2+\mathbf{e}_i} \\ \vdots & \vdots & & & \vdots \\ 0 & 0 & 0 & \cdots & \nu_{\alpha_\delta,\alpha_{\delta-1}+\mathbf{e}_i} \\ 0 & 0 & 0 & \cdots & 0 \end{bmatrix}. \quad (6)$$

Moreover,

$$\nu_{\alpha_i,\alpha_k+\mathbf{e}_j} = \begin{cases} 1 & \text{if } \alpha_i = \alpha_k + \mathbf{e}_j \\ 0 & \text{if } \alpha_k + \mathbf{e}_j \in E, \alpha_i \ne \alpha_k + \mathbf{e}_j. \end{cases}$$

Proof. As M_i^t acts as a derivation on $\mathscr{D}$ (see (5)) and as the elements Λ_{α_i} are numbered by increasing order, the matrix M_i^t in this basis of $\mathscr{D}$ has an upper triangular form with zero (blocks) on the diagonal.

For an element Λ_{α_j} of order k, its image by M_i^t is

$$\begin{aligned} M_i^t(\Lambda_{\alpha_j}) &= (x_i - \xi_i)\cdot\Lambda_{\alpha_j} \\ &= \sum_{o(\Lambda_{\alpha_l})<k} \Lambda_{\alpha_j}((x_i-\xi_i)(\mathbf{x}-\xi)^{\alpha_l})\Lambda_{\alpha_l} \\ &= \sum_{o(\Lambda_{\alpha_l})<k} \Lambda_{\alpha_j}((\mathbf{x}-\xi)^{\alpha_l+\mathbf{e}_i})\,\Lambda_{\alpha_l} = \sum_{o(\Lambda_{\alpha_l})<k} \nu_{\alpha_j,\alpha_l+\mathbf{e}_i}\Lambda_{\alpha_l}. \end{aligned}$$

This shows that $\mathtt{M}_i^t$ is upper triangular with zeroes on the diagonal, and the entries of $\mathtt{M}_i$ are the coefficients of the dual basis elements corresponding to exponents in $E\times\partial(E)$. The second claim is clear from the definition of $\mathtt{M}_i$. □

The previous lemma shows that the dual basis uniquely defines the system of multiplication matrices for $i = 1,\ldots,n$, so we can combine Lemmas 4.2 and 4.3 to get

$$\mathtt{M}_i^t = \begin{bmatrix} \Lambda_{\alpha_1}(x_i-\xi_i) & \cdots & \Lambda_{\alpha_\delta}(x_i-\xi_i) \\ \Lambda_{\alpha_1}((\mathbf{x}-\xi)^{\alpha_2+\mathbf{e}_i}) & \cdots & \Lambda_{\alpha_\delta}((\mathbf{x}-\xi)^{\alpha_2+\mathbf{e}_i}) \\ \vdots & & \vdots \\ \Lambda_{\alpha_1}((\mathbf{x}-\xi)^{\alpha_\delta+\mathbf{e}_i}) & \cdots & \Lambda_{\alpha_\delta}((\mathbf{x}-\xi)^{\alpha_\delta+\mathbf{e}_i}) \end{bmatrix}$$

$$= \begin{bmatrix} 0 & \nu_{\alpha_2,\mathbf{e}_i} & \nu_{\alpha_3,\mathbf{e}_i} & \cdots & \nu_{\alpha_\delta,\mathbf{e}_i} \\ 0 & 0 & \nu_{\alpha_3,\alpha_2+\mathbf{e}_i} & \cdots & \nu_{\alpha_\delta,\alpha_2+\mathbf{e}_i} \\ \vdots & \vdots & & & \vdots \\ 0 & 0 & 0 & \cdots & \nu_{\alpha_\delta,\alpha_{\delta-1}+\mathbf{e}_i} \\ 0 & 0 & 0 & \cdots & 0 \end{bmatrix}.$$

Note that these matrices are nilpotent by their upper triangular structure with all eigenvalues equal to zero. As o is the maximal order of the elements of $\mathscr{D}$, $\mathtt{M}^\gamma = 0$ for $|\gamma| > o$.

Conversely, the system of multiplication matrices $\mathtt{M}_1,\ldots,\mathtt{M}_n$ uniquely defines the dual basis as follows. Consider $\nu_{\alpha_i,\gamma}$ for some (α_i,γ) such that $|\gamma| \le o$ but $\gamma \notin E^+$. We can uniquely determine $\nu_{\alpha_i,\gamma}$ from $\{\nu_{\alpha_j,\beta} : (\alpha_j,\beta) \in E\times\partial(E)\}$ using the following identities:

$$\nu_{\alpha_i,\gamma} = \Lambda_{\alpha_i}((\mathbf{x}-\xi)^\gamma) = [\mathtt{M}_{(\mathbf{x}-\xi)^\gamma}]_{1,i} = [\mathtt{M}^\gamma]_{1,i}. \quad (7)$$

The next definition defines the *parametric multiplication matrices* that we use in our construction.

Definition 4.4 (Parametric multiplication matrices)**.** Let $E = \{\alpha_1,\ldots,\alpha_\delta\} \subset \mathbb{N}^n$ be as above. We define the array μ consisting of 0's, 1's and the variables $\mu_{\alpha_i,\beta}$ as follows: for all $\alpha_i,\alpha_k \in E$ and $j \in \{1,\ldots,n\}$ the corresponding entry is

$$\mu_{\alpha_i,\alpha_k+\mathbf{e}_j} = \begin{cases} 1 & \text{if } \alpha_i = \alpha_k + \mathbf{e}_j \\ 0 & \text{if } \alpha_k + \mathbf{e}_j \in E, \alpha_i \ne \alpha_k + \mathbf{e}_j \\ \mu_{\alpha_i,\alpha_k+\mathbf{e}_j} & \text{if } \alpha_k + \mathbf{e}_j \in \partial(E) \end{cases} \quad (8)$$

The number of variables in μ is $|E\times\partial(E)| \le n\delta(\delta-1)/2$. For $i = 1,\ldots,n$, the *parametric multiplication matrices* are:

$$\mathtt{M}_i^t(\mu) := \begin{bmatrix} 0 & \mu_{\alpha_2,\mathbf{e}_i} & \mu_{\alpha_3,\mathbf{e}_i} & \cdots & \mu_{\alpha_\delta,\mathbf{e}_i} \\ 0 & 0 & \mu_{\alpha_3,\alpha_2+\mathbf{e}_i} & \cdots & \mu_{\alpha_\delta,\alpha_2+\mathbf{e}_i} \\ \vdots & \vdots & & & \vdots \\ 0 & 0 & 0 & \cdots & \mu_{\alpha_\delta,\alpha_{\delta-1}+\mathbf{e}_i} \\ 0 & 0 & 0 & \cdots & 0 \end{bmatrix}. \quad (9)$$

We denote by

$$\mathtt{M}(\mu)^\gamma := \mathtt{M}_1(\mu)^{\gamma_1}\cdots\mathtt{M}_n(\mu)^{\gamma_n},$$

and note that for general parameter values μ, the matrices $\mathtt{M}_i(\mu)$ do not commute, so we fix their order by their indices in the above definition of $\mathtt{M}(\mu)^\gamma$.

Remark 4.5. Note that we can reduce the number of free parameters in the parametric multiplication matrices by exploiting the commutation rules of the multiplication matrices corresponding to a given primal basis B. For example, consider the breadth one case, where we can assume that $E = \{\mathbf{0}, \mathbf{e}_1, 2\mathbf{e}_1, \ldots, (\delta-1)\mathbf{e}_1\}$. In this case the only free parameters appear in the first columns of $\mathtt{M}_2(\mu),\ldots,\mathtt{M}_n(\mu)$, the other columns are shifts of these. Thus, it is enough to introduce $(n-1)(\delta-1)$ free parameters, similarly as in [17]. In Section 5 we present a modification of [17, Example 3.1] which has breadth two, but also uses at most $(n-1)(\delta-1)$ free parameters.

Definition 4.6 (Parametric normal form)**.** Let $\mathbb{K} \subset \mathbb{C}$ be a field. We define

$$\begin{aligned} \mathcal{N}_{\mathbf{z},\mu} : \mathbb{K}[\mathbf{x}] &\to \mathbb{K}[\mathbf{z},\mu]^\delta \\ p &\mapsto \mathcal{N}_{\mathbf{z},\mu}(p) := \sum_{\gamma\in\mathbb{N}^n} \frac{1}{\gamma!}\boldsymbol{\partial}_{\mathbf{z}}^\gamma(p)\,\mathtt{M}(\mu)^\gamma[1]. \end{aligned}$$

where $[1] = [1,0,\ldots,0]$ is the coefficient vector of 1 in the basis B. This sum is finite since for $|\gamma| \ge \delta$, $\mathtt{M}(\mu)^\gamma = 0$, so the entries of $\mathcal{N}_{\mathbf{z},\mu}(p)$ are polynomials in μ and $\mathbf{z}$.

Note that for the specialization at $(\mathbf{z},\mu) = (\xi,\nu)$ the matrices $\mathtt{M}_i(\mu)$ $(i = 1,\ldots,n)$ are commuting and we have

$$\mathcal{N}_{\xi,\nu}(p) = [\Lambda_{\alpha_1}(p),\ldots,\Lambda_{\alpha_\delta}(p)]^t \in \mathbb{C}^\delta.$$

4.1 The multiplicity structure equations of a singular point

We can now characterize the multiplicity structure by polynomial equations.

Theorem 4.7. *Let $\mathbb{K} \subset \mathbb{C}$ be any field, $\mathbf{f} \in \mathbb{K}[\mathbf{x}]^N$ and let $\xi \in \mathbb{C}^n$ be an isolated solution of $\mathbf{f}$. Let $\mathtt{M}_i(\mu)$ for $i = 1,\ldots n$ be the parametric multiplication matrices as in (9) and $\mathcal{N}_{\xi,\mu}$*

be the parametric normal form as in Defn. 4.6 at $\mathbf{z} = \xi$. *Then the ideal* J_ξ *of* $\mathbb{C}[\mu]$ *generated by the polynomial system*

$$\begin{cases} \mathcal{N}_{\xi,\mu}(f_k) & \text{for } k = 1,\ldots,N, \\ \mathtt{M}_i(\mu)\cdot \mathtt{M}_j(\mu) - \mathtt{M}_i(\mu)\cdot \mathtt{M}_i(\mu) & \text{for } i,j = 1,\ldots,n \end{cases} \quad (10)$$

is the maximal ideal

$$\mathfrak{m}_\nu = (\mu_{\alpha,\beta} - \nu_{\alpha,\beta}, (\alpha,\beta) \in E \times \partial(E))$$

where $\nu_{\alpha,\beta}$ *are the coefficients of the dual basis defined in (4).*

Proof. As before, the system (10) has a solution $\mu_{\alpha,\beta} = \nu_{\alpha,\beta}$ for $(\alpha,\beta) \in E \times \partial(E)$. Thus $J_\xi \subset \mathfrak{m}_\nu$.

Conversely, let $C = \mathbb{C}[\mu]/J_\xi$ and consider the map

$$\Phi : C[\mathbf{x}] \to C^\delta, \quad p \mapsto \mathcal{N}_{\xi,\mu}(p).$$

Let K be its kernel. Since the matrices $\mathtt{M}_i(\mu)$ are commuting modulo J_ξ, we can see that K is an ideal. As $f_k \in K$, we have $\mathcal{I} := (f_k) \subset K$.

Next we show that $Q \subset K$. By construction, for any $\alpha \in \mathbb{N}^n$ we have modulo J_ξ

$$\mathcal{N}_{\xi,\mu}((\mathbf{x}-\xi)^\alpha) = \sum_{\gamma\in\mathbb{N}^n} \frac{1}{\gamma!}\boldsymbol{\partial}_\xi^\gamma((\mathbf{x}-\xi)^\alpha)\,\mathtt{M}(\mu)^\gamma[1] = \mathtt{M}(\mu)^\alpha[1].$$

Using the previous relation, we check that $\forall p,q \in C[\mathbf{x}]$,

$$\Phi(pq) = p(\xi + \mathtt{M}(\mu))\Phi(q) \quad (11)$$

where $p(\xi + \mathtt{M}(\mu))$ is obtained by replacing $x_i - \xi_i$ by $\mathtt{M}_i(\mu)$. Let $q \in Q$. As Q is the $\mathfrak{m}_\xi$-primary component of $\mathcal{I}$, there exists $p \in \mathbb{C}[\mathbf{x}]$ such that $p(\xi) \neq 0$ and $p\,q \in \mathcal{I}$. By (11), we have

$$\Phi(p\,q) = p(\xi + \mathtt{M}(\mu))\Phi(q) = 0.$$

Since $p(\xi) \neq 0$ and $p(\xi + \mathtt{M}(\mu)) = p(\xi)Id + N$ with N lower triangular and nilpotent, $p(\xi+\mathtt{M}(\mu))$ is invertible. We deduce that $\Phi(q) = p(\xi + \mathtt{M}(\mu))^{-1}\Phi(pq) = 0$ and $q \in K$.

Let us show now that Φ is surjective and more precisely, that $\phi((\mathbf{x}-\xi)^{\alpha_k}) = \mathbf{e}_k$ (abusing the notation as here $\mathbf{e}_k$ has length δ not n). Since B is connected to 1, either $\alpha_k = 0$ or there exists $\alpha_j \in E$ such that $\alpha_k = \alpha_j + \mathbf{e}_i$ for some $i \in \{1,\ldots,n\}$. Thus the jth column of $\mathtt{M}_i(\mu)$ is $\mathbf{e}_k$ by (8). As $\{\mathtt{M}_i(\mu) : i = 1,\ldots,n\}$ are pairwise commuting, we have $\mathtt{M}(\mu)^{\alpha_k} = \mathtt{M}_j(\mu)\mathtt{M}(\mu)^{\alpha_j}$, and if we assume by induction on $|\alpha_j|$ that the first column of $\mathtt{M}(\mu)^{\alpha_j}$ is $\mathbf{e}_j$, we obtain $\mathtt{M}(\mu)^{\alpha_k}[1] = \mathbf{e}_k$. Thus, for $k = 1,\ldots,\delta$, $\Phi((\mathbf{x}-\xi)^{\alpha_k}) = \mathbf{e}_k$.

We can now prove that $\mathfrak{m}_\nu \subset J_\xi$. As $M_i(\nu)$ is the multiplication by $(x_i-\xi_i)$ in $\mathbb{C}[\mathbf{x}]/Q$, for any $b \in B$ and $i = 1,\ldots,n$, we have $(x_i - \xi_i)\,b = M_i(\nu)(b) + q$ with $q \in Q \subset K$. We deduce that for $k = 1,\ldots,\delta$,

$$\Phi((x_i-\xi_i)\,(\mathbf{x}-\xi)^{\alpha_k}) = \mathtt{M}_i(\mu)\Phi((\mathbf{x}-\xi)^{\alpha_k}) = \mathtt{M}_i(\mu)(\mathbf{e}_k) = \mathtt{M}_i(\nu)(\mathbf{e}_k).$$

This shows that $\mu_{\alpha,\beta} - \nu_{\alpha,\beta} \in J_\xi$ for $(\alpha,\beta) \in E \times \partial(E)$ and that $\mathfrak{m}_\nu = J_\xi$. □

In the proof of the next theorem we need to consider cases when the multiplication matrices do not commute. We introduce the following definition:

Definition 4.8. Let $\mathbb{K} \subset \mathbb{C}$ be any field. Let $\mathcal{C}$ be the ideal of $\mathbb{K}[\mathbf{z},\mu]$ generated by entries of the commutation relations: $\mathtt{M}_i(\mu)\cdot\mathtt{M}_j(\mu) - \mathtt{M}_j(\mu)\cdot\mathtt{M}_i(\mu) = 0$, $i,j = 1,\ldots,n$. We call $\mathcal{C}$ the *commutator ideal.*

Lemma 4.9. *For any field* $\mathbb{K} \subset \mathbb{C}$, $p \in \mathbb{K}[\mathbf{x}]$, *and* $i = 1,\ldots,n$, *we have*

$$\mathcal{N}_{\mathbf{z},\mu}(x_ip) = x_i\mathcal{N}_{\mathbf{z},\mu}(p) + \mathtt{M}_i(\mu)\,\mathcal{N}_{\mathbf{z},\mu}(p) + O_{i,\mu}(p). \quad (12)$$

where $O_{i,\mu} : \mathbb{K}[\mathbf{x}] \to \mathbb{K}[\mathbf{z},\mu]^\delta$ *is linear with image in the commutator ideal* $\mathcal{C}$.

Proof. $\mathcal{N}_{\mathbf{z},\mu}(x_ip) = \sum_\gamma \frac{1}{\gamma!}\,\partial_\mathbf{z}^\gamma(x_ip)\,\mathtt{M}(\mu)^\gamma[1]$

$$\begin{aligned}
&= x_i \sum_\gamma \frac{1}{\gamma!}\partial_\mathbf{z}^\gamma(p)\,\mathtt{M}(\mu)^\gamma[1] + \sum_\gamma \frac{1}{\gamma!}\gamma_i\,\partial_\mathbf{z}^{\gamma-e_i}(p)\,\mathtt{M}(\mu)^\gamma[1] \\
&= x_i \sum_\gamma \frac{1}{\gamma!}\partial_\mathbf{z}^\gamma(p)\,\mathtt{M}(\mu)^\gamma[1] + \sum_\gamma \frac{1}{\gamma!}\partial_\mathbf{z}^\gamma(p)\,\mathtt{M}(\mu)^{\gamma+e_i}[1] \\
&= x_i\,\mathcal{N}_{\mathbf{z},\mu}(p) + \mathtt{M}_i(\mu)\left(\sum_\gamma \frac{1}{\gamma!}\partial_\mathbf{z}^\gamma(p)\,\mathtt{M}(\mu)^\gamma[1]\right) \\
&\quad + \sum_\gamma \frac{1}{\gamma!}\,\partial_\mathbf{z}^\gamma(p)\,O_{i,\gamma}(\mu)[1]
\end{aligned}$$

where $O_{i,\gamma} = \mathtt{M}_i(\mu)\mathtt{M}(\mu)^\gamma - \mathtt{M}(\mu)^{\gamma+e_i}$ is a $\delta\times\delta$ matrix with coefficients in $\mathcal{C}$. Therefore, $O_{i,\mu} : p \mapsto \sum_\gamma \frac{1}{\gamma!}\partial_\mathbf{z}^\gamma(p)\,O_{i,\gamma}(\mu)[1]$ is a linear functional of p with coefficients in $\mathcal{C}$. □

The next theorem proves that the system defined as in (10) for general $\mathbf{z}$ has (ξ,ν) as a simple root.

Theorem 4.10. *Let* $\mathbf{f} \in \mathbb{K}[\mathbf{x}]^N$ *and* $\xi \in \mathbb{C}^n$ *be as above. Let* $\mathtt{M}_i(\mu)$ *for* $i = 1,\ldots n$ *be the parametric multiplication matrices defined in (9) and* $\mathcal{N}_{\mathbf{x},\mu}$ *be the parametric normal form as in Defn. 4.6. Then* $(\mathbf{z},\mu) = (\xi,\nu)$ *is an isolated root with multiplicity one of the polynomial system in* $\mathbb{K}[\mathbf{z},\mu]$*:*

$$\begin{cases} \mathcal{N}_{\mathbf{z},\mu}(f_k) = 0 & \text{for } k = 1,\ldots,N, \\ \mathtt{M}_i(\mu)\cdot\mathtt{M}_j(\mu) - \mathtt{M}_j(\mu)\cdot\mathtt{M}_i(\mu) = 0 & \text{for } i,j = 1,\ldots,n. \end{cases} \quad (13)$$

Proof. For simplicity, let us denote the (non-zero) polynomials appearing in (13) by

$$P_1,\ldots,P_M \in \mathbb{K}[\mathbf{z},\mu],$$

where $M \leq N\delta + n(n-1)(\delta-1)(\delta-2)/4$. To prove the theorem, it is sufficient to prove that the columns of the Jacobian matrix of the system $[P_1,\ldots,P_M]$ at $(\mathbf{z},\mu) = (\xi,\nu)$ are linearly independent. The columns of this Jacobian matrix correspond to the elements in $\mathbb{C}[\mathbf{z},\mu]^*$

$$\partial_{1,\xi},\ldots,\partial_{n,\xi}, \text{ and } \partial_{\mu_{\alpha,\beta}} \quad \text{for } (\alpha,\beta) \in E \times \partial(E),$$

where $\partial_{i,\xi}$ defined in (1) for $\mathbf{z}$ replacing $\mathbf{x}$, and $\partial_{\mu_{\alpha,\beta}}$ is defined by

$$\partial_{\mu_{\alpha,\beta}}(q) = \frac{dq}{d\mu_{\alpha,\beta}}\,|_{(\mathbf{z},\mu)=(\xi,\nu)} \qquad \text{for } q \in \mathbb{C}[\mathbf{z},\mu].$$

Suppose there exist $a_1,\ldots,a_n$, and $a_{\alpha,\beta} \in \mathbb{C}$ for $(\alpha,\beta) \in E \times \partial(E)$ not all zero such that

$$\Delta := a_1\partial_{1,\xi} + \cdots + a_n\partial_{n,\xi} + \sum_{\alpha,\beta} a_{\alpha,\beta}\partial_{\mu_{\alpha,\beta}} \in \mathbb{C}[\mathbf{z},\mu]^*$$

vanishes on all polynomials $P_1,\ldots,P_M$ in (13). In particular, for an element $P_i(\mu)$ corresponding to the commutation relations and any polynomial $Q \in \mathbb{C}[\mathbf{x},\mu]$, using the product rule for the linear differential operator Δ we get

$$\Delta(P_iQ) = \Delta\,(P_i)Q(\xi,\nu) + P_i(\nu)\Delta(Q) = 0$$

since $\Delta(P_i) = 0$ and $P_i(\nu) = 0$. By the linearity of Δ, for any polynomial C in the commutator ideal $\mathcal{C}$, we have $\Delta(C) = 0$.

Furthermore, since $\Delta(\mathcal{N}_{\mathbf{z},\mu}(f_k)) = 0$ and

$$\mathcal{N}_{\xi,\nu}(f_k) = [\, \Lambda_{\alpha_1}(f_k), \ldots, \Lambda_{\alpha_\delta}(f_k)]^t,$$

we get that

$$(a_1\partial_{1,\xi}+\cdots, a_n\partial_{n,\xi})\cdot\Lambda_{\alpha_\delta}(f_k) + \sum_{|\gamma|\leq|\alpha_\delta|} p_\gamma(\nu)\, \partial_{\gamma,\xi}(f_k) = 0 \quad (14)$$

where $p_\gamma \in \mathbb{C}[\mu]$ are some polynomials in the variables μ that do not depend on f_k. If $a_1, \ldots, a_n$ are not all zero, we have an element $\tilde{\Lambda}$ of $\mathbb{C}[\boldsymbol{\partial}_\xi]$ of order strictly greater than $\operatorname{ord}(\Lambda_{\alpha_\delta}) = o$ that vanishes on $f_1, \ldots, f_N$.

Let us prove that this higher order differential also vanishes on all multiples of f_k for $k = 1, \ldots, N$. Let $p \in \mathbb{C}[\mathbf{x}]$ such that $\mathcal{N}_{\xi,\nu}(p) = 0$, $\Delta(\mathcal{N}_{\mathbf{z},\mu}(p)) = 0$. By (12), we have

$$\begin{aligned}&\mathcal{N}_{\xi,\nu}((x_i - \xi_i)p)\\ &\quad= (x_i - \xi_i)\mathcal{N}_{\xi,\nu}(p) + \mathtt{M}_i(\nu)\mathcal{N}_{\xi,\nu}(p) + O_{i,\nu}(p) = 0\end{aligned}$$

and $\Delta(\mathcal{N}_{\mathbf{z},\mu}((x_i - \xi_i)p))$

$$\begin{aligned}&= \Delta((x_i - \xi_i)\mathcal{N}_{\mathbf{z},\mu}(p)) + \Delta(\mathtt{M}_i(\mu)\mathcal{N}_{\mathbf{z},\mu}(p)) + \Delta(O_\mu(p))\\ &= \Delta(x_i - \xi_i)\mathcal{N}_{\xi,\nu}(p) + (\xi_i - \xi_i)\Delta(\mathcal{N}_{\mathbf{z},\mu}(p))\\ &\qquad + \Delta(\mathtt{M}_i(\mu))\mathcal{N}_{\xi,\mu}(p) + \mathtt{M}_i(\nu)\Delta(\mathcal{N}_{\mathbf{z},\mu}(p))\\ &\qquad + \Delta(O_{i,\mu}(p))\\ &= 0.\end{aligned}$$

As $\mathcal{N}_{\xi,\nu}(f_k) = 0$, $\Delta(\mathcal{N}_{\mathbf{z},\mu}(f_k)) = 0$, $i = 1, \ldots, N$, we deduce by induction on the degree of the multipliers and by linearity that for any element f in the ideal I generated by $f_1, \ldots, f_N$, we have

$$\mathcal{N}_{\xi,\nu}(f) = 0 \quad \text{and} \quad \Delta(\mathcal{N}_{\mathbf{z},\mu}(f)) = 0,$$

which yields $\tilde{\Lambda} \in I^\perp$. Thus we have $\tilde{\Lambda} \in I^\perp \cap \mathbb{C}[\boldsymbol{\partial}_\xi] = Q^\perp$ (by Lemma 2.1). As there is no element of degree strictly bigger than o in $Q^\perp$, this implies that

$$a_1 = \cdots = a_n = 0.$$

Then, by specialization at $\mathbf{x} = \xi$, Δ yields an element of the kernel of the Jacobian matrix of the system (10). By Theorem 4.7, this Jacobian has a zero-kernel, since it defines the simple point ν. We deduce that $\Delta = 0$ and (ξ, ν) is an isolated and simple root of the system (13). □

The following corollary applies the polynomial system defined in (13) to refine the precision of an approximate multiple root together with the coefficients of its Macaulay dual basis. The advantage of using this, as opposed to using the Macaulay multiplicity matrix, is that the number of variables is much smaller, as was noted above.

Corollary 4.11. *Let $\mathbf{f} \in \mathbb{K}[\mathbf{x}]^N$ and $\xi \in \mathbb{C}^n$ be as above, and let $\Lambda_{\alpha_0}(\nu), \ldots, \Lambda_{\alpha_{d-1}}(\nu)$ be its dual basis as in (4). Let $E \subset \mathbb{N}^n$ be as above. Assume that we are given approximates for the singular roots and its inverse system as in (4)*

$$\tilde{\xi} \cong \xi \ \ \text{and} \ \ \tilde{\nu}_{\alpha_i,\beta} \cong \nu_{\alpha_i,\beta} \ \ \forall \alpha_i \in E, \beta \notin E, \ |\beta| \leq o.$$

Consider the overdetermined system in $\mathbb{K}[\mathbf{z}, \mu]$ from (13). Then a random square subsystem of (13) will have a simple root at $\mathbf{z} = \xi$, $\mu = \nu$ with high probability. Thus, we can apply Newton's method for this square subsystem to refine $\tilde{\xi}$ and $\tilde{\nu}_{\alpha_i,\beta}$ for $(\alpha_i, \beta) \in E \times \partial(E)$. For $\tilde{\nu}_{\alpha_i,\gamma}$ with $\gamma \notin E^+$ we can use (7) for the update.

Example 4.12. Reconsider the setup from Ex. 3.2 with primal basis $\{1, x_2\}$ and $E = \{(0,0), (0,1)\}$. We obtain

$$\mathtt{M}_1(\mu) = \begin{bmatrix} 0 & 0 \\ \mu & 0 \end{bmatrix} \quad \text{and} \quad \mathtt{M}_2(\mu) = \begin{bmatrix} 0 & 0 \\ 1 & 0 \end{bmatrix}.$$

The resulting deflated system in (13) is $F(z_1, z_2, \mu) = [z_1 + z_2^2,\ \mu + 2z_2, z_1^2 + z_2^2, 2\mu z_1 + 2z_2]^t$ which has a nonsingular root at $(z_1, z_2, \mu) = (0, 0, 0)$ corresponding to the origin with multiplicity structure $\{\partial_1, \partial_{x_2}\}$.

5. EXAMPLES

Computations for the following examples, as well as several other systems, along with MATLAB code can be found at `www.nd.edu/~jhauenst/deflation/`.

5.1 A family of examples

We first consider a modification of [17, Example 3.1]. For any $n \geq 2$, the following system has n polynomials, each of degree at most 3, in n variables:

$$x_1^3 + x_1^2 - x_2^2,\ x_2^3 + x_2^2 - x_3, \ldots, x_{n-1}^3 + x_{n-1}^2 - x_n,\ x_n^2.$$

The origin is a multiplicity $\delta := 2^n$ root having breadth 2 (i.e., the corank of Jacobian at the origin is 2).

We apply our parametric normal form method described in § 4. Similarly as in Remark 4.5, we can reduce the number of free parameters to be at most $(n-1)(\delta-1)$ using the structure of the primal basis $B = \{x_1^a x_2^b : a < 2^{n-1},\ b < 2\}$.

The following table shows the multiplicity, number of variables and polynomials in the deflated system, and the time (in seconds) it took to compute this system (on a iMac, 3.4 GHz Intel Core i7 processor, 8GB 1600Mhz DDR3 memory). Note that when comparing our method to an approach using the null spaces of Macaulay multiplicity matrices (see for example [6, 14]), we found that for $n \geq 4$ the deflated system derived from the Macaulay multiplicity matrix was too large to compute. This is because the nil-index at the origin is 2^{n-1}, so the size of the Macaulay multiplicity matrix is $n \cdot \binom{2^{n-1}+n-1}{n-1} \times \binom{2^{n-1}+n}{n}$.

		New approach			Null space		
n	mult	vars	poly	time	vars	poly	time
2	4	5	9	1.476	8	17	2.157
3	8	17	31	5.596	192	241	208
4	16	49	100	19.698	7189	19804	> 76000
5	32	129	296	73.168	*N/A*	*N/A*	*N/A*
6	64	321	819	659.59	*N/A*	*N/A*	*N/A*

5.2 Caprasse system

We consider the Caprasse system [3, 29]:

$$f(x_1, x_2, x_3, x_4) = \begin{bmatrix} x_1{}^3 x_3 - 4\,x_1 x_2{}^2 x_3 - 4\,x_1{}^2 x_2 x_4 - 2\,x_2{}^3 x_4 - 4\,x_1{}^2 + \\ \quad 10\,x_2{}^2 - 4\,x_1 x_3 + 10\,x_2 x_4 - 2, \\ x_1 x_3{}^3 - 4\,x_2 x_3{}^2 x_4 - 4\,x_1 x_3 x_4{}^2 - 2\,x_2 x_4{}^3 - 4\,x_1 x_3 + \\ \quad 10\,x_2 x_4 - 4\,x_3{}^2 + 10\,x_4{}^2 - 2, \\ x_2{}^2 x_3 + 2\,x_1 x_2 x_4 - 2\,x_1 - x_3, \\ x_4{}^2 x_1 + 2\,x_2 x_3 x_4 - 2\,x_3 - x_1 \end{bmatrix}$$

at the multiplicity 4 root $\xi = (2, -\sqrt{-3}, 2, \sqrt{-3})$.

We first consider simply deflating the root. Using the approaches of [6, 10, 13], one iteration suffices. For example, using an extrinsic and intrinsic version of [6, 13], the resulting system consists of 10 and 8 polynomials, respectively, and 8 and 6 variables, respectively. Following [10], using all minors results in a system of 20 polynomials in 4 variables which can be reduced to a system of 8 polynomials in 4 variables using the 3×3 minors containing a full rank 2×2 submatrix. The approach of § 3 using an $|\boldsymbol{i}| = 1$ step creates a deflated system consisting of 6 polynomials in 4 variables. In fact, since the null space of the Jacobian at the root is 2 dimensional, adding two polynomials is necessary and sufficient.

Next, we consider the computation of both the point and multiplicity structure. Using an intrinsic null space approach via a second order Macaulay matrix, the resulting system consists of 64 polynomials in 37 variables. In comparison, using the primal basis $\{1, x_1, x_2, x_1x_2\}$, the approach of § 4 constructs a system of 30 polynomials in 19 variables.

5.3 Examples with multiple iterations

In our last set of examples, we consider simply deflating a root of the last three systems from [6, § 7] and a system from [12, § 1], each of which required more than one iteration to deflate. These four systems and corresponding points are:

1: $\{x_1^4 - x_2x_3x_4, x_2^4 - x_1x_3x_4, x_3^4 - x_1x_2x_4, x_4^4 - x_1x_2x_3\}$ at $(0, 0, 0, 0)$ with $\delta = 131$ and $o = 10$;

2: $\{x^4, x^2y + y^4, z + z^2 - 7x^3 - 8x^2\}$ at $(0, 0, -1)$ with $\delta = 16$ and $o = 7$;

3: $\{14x + 33y - 3\sqrt{5}(x^2 + 4xy + 4y^2 + 2) + \sqrt{7} + x^3 + 6x^2y + 12xy^2 + 8y^3, 41x - 18y - \sqrt{5} + 8x^3 - 12x^2y + 6xy^2 - y^3 + 3\sqrt{7}(4xy - 4x^2 - y^2 - 2)\}$ at $Z_3 \approx (1.5055, 0.36528)$ with $\delta = 5$ and $o = 4$;

4: $\{2x_1 + 2x_1^2 + 2x_2 + 2x_2^2 + x_3^2 - 1, (x_1 + x_2 - x_3 - 1)^3 - x_1^3, (2x_1^3 + 5x_2^2 + 10x_3 + 5x_3^2 + 5)^3 - 1000x_1^5\}$ at $(0, 0, -1)$ with $\delta = 18$ and $o = 7$.

We compare using the following four methods: (A) intrinsic slicing version of [6, 13]; (B) isosingular deflation [10] via a maximal rank submatrix; (C) "kerneling" method in [8]; (D) approach of § 3 using an $|\boldsymbol{i}| = 1$ step. We performed these methods without the use of preprocessing and postprocessing as mentioned in § 3 to directly compare the number of nonzero distinct polynomials, variables, and iterations for each of these four deflation methods.

	Method A			Method B			Method C			Method D		
	Poly	Var	It	Poly	Var	It	Poly	Var	It	Poly	Var	It
1	16	4	2	22	4	2	22	4	2	16	4	2
2	24	11	3	11	3	2	12	3	2	12	3	3
3	32	17	4	6	2	4	6	2	4	6	2	4
4	96	41	5	54	3	5	54	3	5	22	3	5

For breadth one singular points as in system 3, methods B, C, and D yield the same deflated system. Except for methods B and C on the second system, all four methods required the same number of iterations to deflate the root. For the first and third systems, our new approach matched the best of the other methods and resulted in a significantly smaller deflated system for the last one.

6. REFERENCES

[1] T.A. Akoglu, J.D. Hauenstein, and A. Szanto. Certifying solutions to overdetermined and singular polynomial systems over $\mathbb{Q}$. Preprint, http://arxiv.org/abs/1408.2721, 2014.

[2] L. Alberti, B. Mourrain, and J. Wintz. Topology and arrangement computation of semi-algebraic planar curves. *Computer Aided Geometric Design*, 25(8):631–651, 2008.

[3] H. Caprasse, J. Demaret, E. Schrüfer: Can EXCALC be used to Investigate High-Dimensional Cosmological Models with Non-Linear Lagrangians? ISSAC 1988: 116-124.

[4] R.M. Corless, P.M. Gianni, and B.M. Trager. A reordered Schur factorization method for zero-dimensional polynomial systems with multiple roots. In *ISSAC 1997*, ACM, New York, 1997, pp. 133–140.

[5] B.H. Dayton, T.-Y. Li, and Z. Zeng. Multiple zeros of nonlinear systems. *Math. Comput.*, 80(276):2143–2168, 2011.

[6] B.H. Dayton and Z. Zeng. Computing the multiplicity structure in solving polynomial systems. In *ISSAC'05*, ACM, New York, 2005, pp. 116–123.

[7] M. Giusti, G. Lecerf, B. Salvy, and J.-C. Yakoubsohn. On location and approximation of clusters of zeros: Case of embedding dimension one. *Foundations of Computational Mathematics*, 7:1–58, 2007.

[8] M. Giusti and J.-C. Yakoubsohn. Multiplicity hunting and approximating multiple roots of polynomial systems. *Contemp. Math.*, 604:105–128, 2013.

[9] S. Graillat and P. Trébuchet. A new algorithm for computing certified numerical approximations of the roots of a zero-dimensional system. In *ISSAC2009*, pages 167–173, 2009.

[10] J.D. Hauenstein and C. Wampler. Isosingular sets and deflation. *Found. Comput. Math.*, 13(3):371–403, 2013.

[11] W. Hao, A.J. Sommese, and Z. Zeng. Algorithm 931: an algorithm and software for computing multiplicity structures at zeros of nonlinear systems. *ACM Trans. Math. Software*, 40(1):Art. 5, 2013.

[12] G. Lecerf. Quadratic newton iterarion for systems with multiplicity. *Found. Comput. Math.*, (2):247–293, 2002.

[13] A. Leykin, J. Verschelde, and A. Zhao. Newton's method with deflation for isolated singularities of polynomial systems. *Theor. Comput. Sci.*, 359(1-3):111–122, 2006.

[14] ——. Higher-order deflation for polynomial systems with isolated singular solutions. In A. Dickenstein, F.-O. Schreyer, and A. Sommese, editors, *Algorithms in Algebraic Geometry*, volume 146 of *The IMA Volumes in Mathematics and its Applications*, Springer, New York, 2008, pp. 79–97.

[15] N. Li and L. Zhi. Computing isolated singular solutions of polynomial systems: case of breadth one. *SIAM J. Numer. Anal.*, 50(1):354–372, 2012.

[16] ——. Computing the multiplicity structure of an isolated singular solution: case of breadth one. *J. Symbolic Comput.*, 47(6):700–710, 2012.

[17] ——. Verified error bounds for isolated singular solutions of polynomial systems: Case of breadth one. *Theor. Comput. Sci.*, 479:163–173, 2013.

[18] ——. Verified error bounds for isolated singular solutions of polynomial systems. *SIAM J. Numer. Anal.*, 52(4):1623–1640, 2014.

[19] F.S. Macaulay. *The Algebraic Theory of Modular Systems.* Cambridge Univ. Press, 1916.

[20] A. Mantzaflaris and B. Mourrain. Deflation and certified isolation of singular zeros of polynomial systems. In *ISSAC 2011*, ACM, New York, 2011, pp. 249–256.

[21] M.G. Marinari, T. Mora, and H. Möller. Gröbner duality and multiplicities in polynomial system solving. In *ISSAC '95*, ACM, New York, 1995, pp. 167–179.

[22] H.M. Möller and H.J. Stetter. Multivariate polynomial equations with multiple zeros solved by matrix eigenproblems. *Numer. Math.*, 70(3):311–329, 1995.

[23] B. Mourrain. Isolated points, duality and residues. *J. Pure Appl. Alg.*, 117-118:469–493, 1997.

[24] ——. A new criterion for normal form algorithms. *LNCS*, 1719:430–443, 1999.

[25] T. Ojika. Modified deflation algorithm for the solution of singular problems. I. a system of nonlinear algebraic equations. *J. Math. Anal. Appl.*, 123(1):199–221, 1987.

[26] T. Ojika, S. Watanabe, and T. Mitsui. Deflation algorithm for the multiple roots of a system of nonlinear equations. *J. Math. Anal. Appl.*, 96(2):463–479, 1983.

[27] S. Pope and A. Szanto. Nearest multivariate system with given root multiplicities. *J. Symb. Comput.*, 44(6):606–625, 2009.

[28] H.J. Stetter. Analysis of zero clusters in multivariate polynomial systems. In *ISSAC '96*, ACM, New York, 1996, pp. 127–136.

[29] C. Traverso. The posso test suite. with complement by D. Bini & B. Mourrain, 1993. www-sop.inria.fr/saga/POL/index.html.

[30] X. Wu and L. Zhi. Determining singular solutions of polynomial systems via symbolic-numeric reduction to geometric involutive form. *J. Symb. Comput.*, 27:104–122, 2008.

[31] N. Yamamoto. Regularization of solutions of nonlinear equations with singular jacobian matrices. *J. Inform. Proc.*, 7(1):16–21, 1984.

[32] Z. Zeng. Computing multiple roots of inexact polynomials. *Math. Comput.*, 74:869–903, 2005.

Real Root Finding for Rank Defects in Linear Hankel Matrices*

Didier Henrion
CNRS, LAAS, 7 avenue du colonel Roche, F-31400 Toulouse; France
Université de Toulouse; LAAS, F-31400 Toulouse, France
Faculty of Electrical Engineering, Czech Technical University in Prague, Czech Republic.
henrion@laas.fr

Simone Naldi
CNRS, LAAS, 7 avenue du colonel Roche, F-31400 Toulouse; France
Université de Toulouse; LAAS, F-31400 Toulouse, France
naldi@laas.fr

Mohab Safey El Din
Sorbonne Universités
Univ. Pierre et Marie Curie (Paris 06)
INRIA Paris Rocquencourt, POLSYS Project
LIP6 CNRS, UMR 7606
Institut Universitaire de France
Mohab.Safey@lip6.fr

ABSTRACT

Let $H_0, \dots, H_n$ be $m \times m$ matrices with entries in $\mathbb{Q}$ and Hankel structure, i.e. constant skew diagonals. We consider the linear Hankel matrix $H(\mathbf{x}) = H_0 + x_1 H_1 + \cdots + x_n H_n$ and the problem of computing sample points in each connected component of the real algebraic set defined by the rank constraint $\mathsf{rank}(H(\mathbf{x})) \leq r$, for a given integer $r \leq m-1$. Computing sample points in real algebraic sets defined by rank defects in linear matrices is a general problem that finds applications in many areas such as control theory, computational geometry, optimization, etc. Moreover, Hankel matrices appear in many areas of engineering sciences. Also, since Hankel matrices are symmetric, any algorithmic development for this problem can be seen as a first step towards a dedicated exact algorithm for solving semi-definite programming problems, i.e. linear matrix inequalities. Under some genericity assumptions on the input (such as smoothness of an incidence variety), we design a probabilistic algorithm for tackling this problem. It is an adaptation of the so-called critical point method that takes advantage of the special structure of the problem. Its complexity reflects this: it is essentially quadratic in specific degree bounds on an incidence variety. We report on practical experiments and analyze how the algorithm takes advantage of this special structure. A first implementation outperforms existing implementations for computing sample points in general real algebraic sets: it tackles examples that are out of reach of the state-of-the-art.

Categories and Subject Descriptors

I.1.2 [**Computing Methodologies**]: Symbolic and algebraic manipulation — *Exact arithmetic algorithms*

Keywords

linear matrix inequalities; Hankel matrix; real root finding; low rank

1. INTRODUCTION

Problem statement and motivation. Let $\mathbb{Q}, \mathbb{R}, \mathbb{C}$ be respectively the fields of rational, real and complex numbers, and let m, n be positive integers. Given $m \times m$ matrices $H_0, H_1, \dots, H_n$ with entries in $\mathbb{Q}$ and Hankel structure, i.e. constant skew diagonals, we consider the *linear Hankel matrix* $H(\mathbf{x}) = H_0 + x_1 H_1 + \ldots + x_n H_n$, denoted H for short, and the algebraic set

$$\mathsf{H}_r = \{\mathbf{x} \in \mathbb{C}^n : \operatorname{rank} H(\mathbf{x}) \leq r\}.$$

The goal of this paper is to provide an efficient algorithm for computing at least one sample point per connected component of the real algebraic set $\mathsf{H}_r \cap \mathbb{R}^n$. Such an algorithm can be used to solve the matrix rank minimization problem for H. Matrix rank minimization mostly consists of minimizing the rank of a given matrix whose entries are subject to constraints defining a convex set. These problems arise in many engineering or statistical modeling applications and have recently received a lot of attention. Considering Hankel structures is relevant since it arises in many applications (e.g. for model reduction in linear dynamical systems described by Markov parameters, see [16, Section 1.3]). Moreover, an algorithm for computing sample points in each connected component of $\mathsf{H}_r \cap \mathbb{R}^n$ can also be used to decide the emptiness of the feasibility set $S = \{\mathbf{x} \in \mathbb{R}^n : H(\mathbf{x}) \succeq 0\}$. Indeed, considering the minimum rank r attained in the boundary of S, it is easy to prove that one of the connected components of $\mathsf{H}_r \cap \mathbb{R}^n$ is actually contained in S. Note also that such feasibility sets, called Hankel spectrahedra, have attracted some attention (see e.g. [3]).

The intrinsic algebraic nature of our problem makes relevant the design of exact algorithms to achieve reliability. On the one hand, we aim at exploiting algorithmically the special Hankel structure to gain efficiency. On the other hand, the design of a special algorithm for the case of linear Hankel matrices can bring the foundations of a general approach to e.g. the symmmetric case which is important for semi-definite programming, i.e. solving linear matrix inequalities.

Related works and state-of-the-art. Our problem consists of computing sample points in real algebraic sets. The first algorithm for this problem is due to Tarski but its complexity was not elementary recursive [23]. Next, Collins designed the Cylindrical Algebraic Decomposition algorithm [5]. Its complexity is doubly exponential in the number of variables which is far from being optimal since the number of connected components of a real algebraic set defined by n-variate polynomial equations of degree $\leq d$ is upper bounded by $O(d)^n$. Next, Grigoriev and Vorobjov [12] introduced the first algorithm based on critical point computations computing sample point in real algebraic sets within $d^{O(n)}$ arithmetic operations. This work has next been improved and generalized (see [2] and references therein) from the complexity viewpoint. We may apply these algorithms to our problem by computing all $(r+1)$-minors of the Hankel matrix and compute sample points in the real algebraic set defined by the vanishing of these minors. This is done in time $(\binom{m}{r+1}\binom{n+r}{r})^{O(1)} + r^{O(n)}$ however since the constant in the exponent is rather high, these algorithms

*The authors are supported by the GEOLMI grant (ANR 2011 BS03 011 06) of the French National Research Agency.

ISSAC'15, July 6–9, 2015, Bath, United Kingdom.

DOI: http://dx.doi.org/10.1145/2755996.2756667.

did not lead to efficient implementations in practice. Hence, another series of works, still using the critical point method but aiming at designing algorithms that combine asymptotically optimal complexity and practical efficiency has been developed (see e.g. [1, 19, 11] and references therein).

Under regularity assumptions, these yield probabilistic algorithms running in time which is essentially $O(d^{3n})$ in the smooth case and $O(d^{4n})$ in the singular case (see [18]). Practically, these algorithms are implemented in the library RAGLIB which uses Gröbner bases computations (see [10, 22] about the complexity of computing critical points with Gröbner bases).

Observe that determinantal varieties such as H_r are generically singular (see [4]). Also the aforementioned algorithms do not exploit the structure of the problem. In [14], we introduced an algorithm for computing real points at which a *generic* linear square matrix of size m has rank $\leq m-1$, by exploiting the structure of the problem. However, because of the requested genericity of the input linear matrix, we cannot use it for linear Hankel matrices. Also, it does not allow to get sample points for a given, smaller rank deficiency.

Methodology and main results. Our main result is an algorithm that computes sample points in each connected component of $\mathsf{H}_r \cap \mathbb{R}^n$ under some genericity assumptions on the entries of the linear Hankel matrix H (these genericity assumptions are made explicit below). Our algorithm exploits the Hankel structure of the problem. Essentially, its complexity is quadratic in a multilinear Bézout bound on the number of complex solutions. Moreover, we find that, heuristically, this bound is less than $\binom{m}{r+1}\binom{n+r}{r}\binom{n+m}{r}$. Hence, for subfamilies of the real root finding problem on linear Hankel matrices where the maximum rank allowed r is fixed, the complexity is essentially in $(nm)^{O(r)}$.

The very basic idea is to study the algebraic set $\mathsf{H}_r \subset \mathbb{C}^n$ as the Zariski closure of the projection of an incidence variety, lying in $\mathbb{C}^{n+r+1}$. This variety encodes the fact that the kernel of H has dimension $\geq m-r$. This lifted variety turns out to be generically smooth and equidimensional and defined by quadratic polynomials with multilinear structure. When these regularity properties are satisfied, we prove that computing one point per connected component of the incidence variety is sufficient to solve the same problem for the variety $\mathsf{H}_r \cap \mathbb{R}^n$. We also prove that these properties are generically satisfied. We remark that this method is similar to the one used in [14], but in this case it takes strong advantage of the Hankel structure of the linear matrix, as detailed in Section 2. This also reflects on the complexity of the algorithm and on practical performances.

Let C be a connected component of $\mathsf{H}_r \cap \mathbb{R}^n$, and and Π_1, π_1 be the canonical projections $\Pi_1 : (x_1, \ldots, x_n, y_1, \ldots, y_{r+1}) \to x_1$ and $\pi_1 : (x_1, \ldots, x_n) \to x_1$. We prove that in generic coordinates, either *(i)* $\pi_1(C) = \mathbb{R}$ or *(ii)* there exists a critical point of the restriction of Π_1 to the considered incidence variety. Hence, after a generic linear change of variables, the algorithm consists of two main steps: *(i)* compute the critical points of the restriction of Π_1 to the incidence variety and *(ii)* instantiating the first variable x_1 to a generic value and perform a recursive call following a geometric pattern introduced in [19].

This latter step *(i)* is actually performed by building the Lagrange system associated to the optimization problem whose solutions are the critical points of the restriction of π_1 to the incidence variety. Hence, we use the algorithm in [15] to solve it. One also observes heuristically that these Lagrange systems are typically zero-dimensional.

However, we were not able to prove this finiteness property, but we prove that it holds when we restrict the optimization step to the set of points $\mathbf{x} \in \mathsf{H}_r$ such that $\operatorname{rank} H(\mathbf{x}) = p$, for any $0 \leq p \leq r$. However, this is sufficient to conclude that there are finitely many critical points of the restriction of π_1 to $\mathsf{H}_r \cap \mathbb{R}^n$, and that the algorithm returns the output correctly.

When the Lagrange system has dimension 0, the complexity of solving its equations is essentially quadratic in the number of its complex solutions. As previously announced, by the structure of these systems one can deduce multilinear Bézout bounds on the number of solutions that are polynomial in nm when r is fixed, and polynomial in n when m is fixed. This complexity result outperforms the state-of-the-art algorithms. We finally remark that the complexity gain is reflected also in the first implementation of the algorithm, which allows to solve instances of our problem that are out of reach of the general algorithms implemented in RAGLIB.

Structure of the paper. The paper is structured as follows. Section 2 contains preliminaries about Hankel matrices and the basic notation of the paper; we also prove that our regularity assumptions are generic. In Section 3 we describe the algorithm and prove its correctness. This is done by using preliminary results proved in Sections 5 and 6. Section 4 contains the complexity analysis and bounds for the number of complex solutions of the output of the algorithm. Finally, Section 7 presents the results of our experiments on generic linear Hankel matrices, and comparisons with the state-of-the-art algorithms for the real root finding problem.

2. NOTATION AND PRELIMINARIES

Basic notations. We denote by $\mathrm{GL}(n, \mathbb{Q})$ (resp. $\mathrm{GL}(n, \mathbb{C})$) the set of $n \times n$ non-singular matrices with rational (resp. complex) entries. For a matrix $M \in \mathbb{C}^{m \times m}$ and an integer $p \leq m$, one denotes with minors(p, M) the list of determinants of $p \times p$ sub-matrices of M. We denote by M' the transpose matrix of M.

Let $\mathbb{Q}[\mathbf{x}]$ be the ring of polynomials on n variables $\mathbf{x} = (x_1, \ldots, x_n)$ and let $\mathbf{f} = (f_1, \ldots, f_p) \in \mathbb{Q}[\mathbf{x}]^p$ be a polynomial system. The common zero locus of the entries of $\mathbf{f}$ is denoted by $\mathsf{Z}(\mathbf{f}) \subset \mathbb{C}^n$, and its dimension with $\dim \mathsf{Z}(\mathbf{f})$. The ideal generated by $\mathbf{f}$ is denoted by $\langle \mathbf{f} \rangle$, while if $\mathsf{V} \subset \mathbb{C}^n$ is any set, the ideal of polynomials vanishing on V is denoted by $I(\mathsf{V})$, while the set of regular (resp. singular) points of V is denoted by $\operatorname{reg} \mathsf{V}$ (resp. $\operatorname{sing} \mathsf{V}$). If $\mathbf{f} = (f_1, \ldots, f_p) \subset \mathbb{Q}[\mathbf{x}]$, we denote by $D\mathbf{f} = (\partial f_i / \partial x_j)$ the Jacobian matrix of $\mathbf{f}$. We denote by $\operatorname{reg}(\mathbf{f}) \subset \mathsf{Z}(\mathbf{f})$ the subset where $D\mathbf{f}$ has maximal rank.

A set $\mathscr{E} \subset \mathbb{C}^n$ is locally closed if $\mathscr{E} = \mathsf{Z} \cap \mathscr{O}$ where Z is a Zariski closed set and $\mathscr{O}$ is a Zariski open set.

Let $\mathsf{V} = \mathsf{Z}(\mathbf{f}) \subset \mathbb{C}^n$ be a smooth equidimensional algebraic set, of dimension d, and let $\mathbf{g} \colon \mathbb{C}^n \to \mathbb{C}^p$ be an algebraic map. The set of critical points of the restriction of $\mathbf{g}$ to V is the solution set of $\mathbf{f}$ and of the $(n-d+p)-$minors of the matrix $D(\mathbf{f}, \mathbf{g})$, and it is denoted by $\operatorname{crit}(\mathbf{g}, \mathsf{V})$. Finally, if $\mathscr{E} \subset \mathsf{V}$ is a locally closed subset of V, we denote by $\operatorname{crit}(\mathbf{g}, \mathscr{E}) = \mathscr{E} \cap \operatorname{crit}(\mathbf{g}, \mathsf{V})$.

Finally, for $M \in \mathrm{GL}(n, \mathbb{C})$ and $f \in \mathbb{Q}[\mathbf{x}]$, we denote by $f^M(\mathbf{x}) = f(M\mathbf{x})$, and if $\mathbf{f} = (f_1, \ldots, f_p) \subset \mathbb{Q}[\mathbf{x}]$ and $\mathsf{V} = \mathsf{Z}(\mathbf{f})$, by $\mathsf{V}^M = \mathsf{Z}(\mathbf{f}^M)$ where $\mathbf{f}^M = (f_1^M, \ldots, f_p^M)$.

Hankel structure. Let $\{h_1, \ldots, h_{2m-1}\} \subset \mathbb{Q}$. The matrix $H = (h_{i+j-1})_{1 \leq i,j \leq m} \in \mathbb{Q}^{m \times m}$ is called a Hankel matrix, and we use the notation $H = \mathsf{Hankel}(h_1, \ldots, h_{2m-1})$. The structure of a Hankel matrix induces structure on its kernel. By [13, Theorem 5.1], one has that if H is a Hankel matrix of rank at most r, then there exists a non-zero vector $\mathbf{y} = (y_1, \ldots, y_{r+1}) \in \mathbb{Q}^{r+1}$ such that the columns of the $m \times (m-r)$ matrix

$$Y(\mathbf{y}) = \begin{bmatrix} \mathbf{y} & 0 & \ldots & 0 \\ 0 & \mathbf{y} & \ddots & \vdots \\ \vdots & \ddots & \ddots & 0 \\ 0 & \ldots & 0 & \mathbf{y} \end{bmatrix}$$

generate a $(m-r)-$dimensional subspace of the kernel of H. We observe that $HY(\mathbf{y})$ is also a Hankel matrix.

The product $HY(\mathbf{y})$ can be re-written as a matrix-vector product $\tilde{H}y$, with $\tilde{H}$ a given rectangular Hankel matrix. Indeed, let $H = \mathsf{Hankel}(h_1, \ldots, h_{2m-1})$. Then, as previously observed, $HY(\mathbf{y})$ is a rectangular Hankel matrix, of size $m \times (m-r)$, whose entries coincide with the entries of

$$\tilde{H}\mathbf{y} = \begin{bmatrix} h_1 & \ldots & h_{r+1} \\ \vdots & & \vdots \\ h_{2m-r-1} & \ldots & h_{2m-1} \end{bmatrix} \begin{bmatrix} y_1 \\ \vdots \\ y_{r+1} \end{bmatrix}.$$

Let $H(\mathbf{x})$ be a linear Hankel matrix. From [6, Corollary 2.2] we deduce that, for $p \leq r$, then the ideals $\langle \text{minors}(p+1, H(\mathbf{x}))\rangle$ and $\langle \text{minors}(p+1, \tilde{H}(\mathbf{x}))\rangle$ coincide. One deduces that $\mathbf{x} = (x_1, \ldots, x_n) \in \mathbb{C}^n$ satisfies $\operatorname{rank} H(\mathbf{x}) = p$ if and only if it satisfies $\operatorname{rank} \tilde{H}(\mathbf{x}) = p$.

Basic sets. We first recall that the linear matrix $H(\mathbf{x}) = H_0 + x_1 H_1 + \ldots + x_n H_n$, where each H_i is a Hankel matrix, is also a Hankel matrix. It is identified by the $(2m-1)(n+1)$ entries of the matrices H_i. Hence we often consider H as an element of $\mathbb{C}^{(2m-1)(n+1)}$. For $M \in \mathrm{GL}(n, \mathbb{Q})$, we denote by $H^M(\mathbf{x})$ the linear matrix $H(M\mathbf{x})$.

We define in the following the main algebraic sets appearing during the execution of our algorithm, given $H \in \mathbb{C}^{(2m-1)(n+1)}$, $0 \leq p \leq r$, $M \in \mathrm{GL}(n, \mathbb{C})$ and $\mathbf{u} = (u_1, \ldots, u_{p+1}) \in \mathbb{Q}^{p+1}$.

Incidence varieties. We consider the polynomial system

$$\mathbf{f}(H^M, \mathbf{u}, p): \quad \begin{array}{ccc} \mathbb{C}^n \times \mathbb{C}^{p+1} & \longrightarrow & \mathbb{C}^{2m-p-1} \times \mathbb{C} \\ (\mathbf{x}, \mathbf{y}) & \longmapsto & \left((\tilde{H}(M\mathbf{x})\mathbf{y})', \mathbf{u}'\mathbf{y} - 1\right) \end{array}$$

where $\tilde{H}$ has been defined in the previous section. We denote by $\mathsf{J}(H^M, \mathbf{u}, p) = \mathsf{Z}(\mathbf{f}_p(H^M, \mathbf{u})) \subset \mathbb{C}^{n+p+1}$ and simply $\mathsf{J} = \mathsf{J}(H^M, \mathbf{u}, p)$ and $\mathbf{f} = \mathbf{f}(H^M, \mathbf{u}, p)$ when p, H, M and $\mathbf{u}$ are clear. We also denote by $\mathsf{K}(H^M, \mathbf{u}, p) = \mathsf{J}(H^M, \mathbf{u}, p) \cap \{(\mathbf{x}, \mathbf{y}) \in \mathbb{C}^{n+p+1} : \operatorname{rank} H(x) = p\}$.

Fibers. Let $\alpha \in \mathbb{Q}$. We denote by $\mathbf{f}_\alpha(H^M, \mathbf{u}, p)$ (or simply $\mathbf{f}_\alpha$) the polynomial system obtained by adding $x_1 - \alpha$ to $\mathbf{f}(H^M, \mathbf{u}, p)$. The resulting algebraic set $\mathsf{Z}(\mathbf{f}_\alpha)$, denoted by J_α, equals $\mathsf{J} \cap \mathsf{Z}(x_1 - \alpha)$.

Lagrange systems. Let $\mathbf{v} \in \mathbb{Q}^{2m-p}$. Let $D_1\mathbf{f}$ denote the matrix of size $c \times (n+p)$ obtained by removing the first column of $D\mathbf{f}$ (the derivative w.r.t. x_1), and define $\mathbf{l} = \mathbf{l}(H^M, \mathbf{u}, \mathbf{v}, p)$ as the map

$$\mathbf{l}: \quad \begin{array}{ccc} \mathbb{C}^{n+2m+1} & \to & \mathbb{C}^{n+2m+1} \\ (\mathbf{x}, \mathbf{y}, \mathbf{z}) & \mapsto & (\tilde{H}(M\mathbf{x})\mathbf{y}, \mathbf{u}'\mathbf{y} - 1, \mathbf{z}' D_1 \mathbf{f}, \mathbf{v}'\mathbf{z} - 1) \end{array}$$

where $\mathbf{z} = (z_1, \ldots, z_{2m-p})$ stand for Lagrange multipliers. We finally define $\mathsf{Z}(H^M, \mathbf{u}, \mathbf{v}, p) = \mathsf{Z}(\mathbf{l}(H^M, \mathbf{u}, \mathbf{v}, p)) \subset \mathbb{C}^{n+2m+1}$.

Regularity property G. We say that a polynomial system $\mathbf{f} \in \mathbb{Q}[x]^c$ satisfies Property G if the Jacobian matrix $D\mathbf{f}$ has maximal rank at any point of $\mathsf{Z}(\mathbf{f})$. We remark that this implies that:

1. the ideal $I(\mathbf{f})$ is radical;
2. the set $\mathsf{Z}(\mathbf{f})$ is either empty or smooth and equidimensional of co-dimension c.

We say that $\mathbf{l}(H^M, \mathbf{u}, \mathbf{v}, p)$ satisfies G over $\mathsf{K}(H^M, \mathbf{u}, p)$ if the following holds:
for $(\mathbf{x}, \mathbf{y}, \mathbf{z}) \in \mathsf{Z}(H^M, \mathbf{u}, \mathbf{v}, p)$ such that $(\mathbf{x}, \mathbf{y}) \in \mathsf{K}(H^M, \mathbf{u}, p)$, the matrix $D(\mathbf{l}(H^M, \mathbf{u}, \mathbf{v}, p))$ has maximal rank at $(\mathbf{x}, \mathbf{y}, \mathbf{z})$.

Let $\mathbf{u} \in \mathbb{Q}^{p+1}$. We say that $H \in \mathbb{C}^{(2m-1)(n+1)}$ satisfies Property G if $\mathbf{f}(H, \mathbf{u}, p)$ satisfies Property G for all $0 \leq p \leq r$. The first result essentially shows that G holds for $\mathbf{f}(H^M, \mathbf{u}, p)$ (resp. $\mathbf{f}_\alpha(H^M, \mathbf{u}, p)$) when the input parameter H (resp. α) is generic enough.

Proposition 1 *Let $M \in \mathrm{GL}(n, \mathbb{C})$.*

(a) There exists a non-empty Zariski-open set $\mathscr{H} \subset \mathbb{C}^{(2m-1)(n+1)}$ such that, if $H \in \mathscr{H} \cap \mathbb{Q}^{(2m-1)(n+1)}$, for all $0 \leq p \leq r$ and $\mathbf{u} \in \mathbb{Q}^{p+1} - \{\mathbf{0}\}$, $\mathbf{f}(H^M, \mathbf{u}, p)$ satisfies Property G;

(b) for $H \in \mathscr{H}$, and $0 \leq p \leq r$, if $\mathsf{J}(H^M, \mathbf{u}, p) \neq \emptyset$ then $\dim \mathsf{H}_p \leq n - 2m + 2p + 1$;

(c) For $0 \leq p \leq r$ and $\mathbf{u} \in \mathbb{Q}^{p+1}$, if $\mathbf{f}(H^M, \mathbf{u}, p)$ satisfies G, there exists a non-empty Zariski open set $\mathscr{A} \subset \mathbb{C}$ such that, if $\alpha \in \mathscr{A}$, the polynomial system $\mathbf{f}_\alpha$ satisfies G;

PROOF. Without loss of generality, we can assume that $M = \mathrm{I}_n$. We let $0 \leq p \leq r$, $\mathbf{u} \in \mathbb{Q}^{p+1} - \{\mathbf{0}\}$ and recall that we identify the space of linear Hankel matrices with $\mathbb{C}^{(2m-1)(n+1)}$. This space is endowed by the variables $\mathfrak{h}_{k,\ell}$ with $1 \leq k \leq 2m-1$ and $0 \leq \ell \leq n$; the generic linear Hankel matrix is then given by $\mathfrak{H} = \mathfrak{H}_0 + x_1 \mathfrak{H}_1 + \cdots + x_n \mathfrak{H}_n$ with $\mathfrak{H}_i = \mathsf{Hankel}(\mathfrak{h}_{1,i}, \ldots, \mathfrak{h}_{2m-1,i})$.

We consider the map

$$q: \quad \begin{array}{ccc} \mathbb{C}^{n+(p+1)+(2m-1)(n+1)} & \longrightarrow & \mathbb{C}^{2m-p} \\ (\mathbf{x}, \mathbf{y}, H) & \longmapsto & \mathbf{f}(H, \mathbf{u}, p) \end{array}$$

and, for a given $H \in \mathbb{C}^{(2m-1)(n+1)}$, its section-map $q_H : \mathbb{C}^{n+(p+1)} \to \mathbb{C}^{2m-p}$ sending $(\mathbf{x}, \mathbf{y})$ to $q(\mathbf{x}, \mathbf{y}, H)$. We also consider the map $\tilde{q}$ which associates to $(\mathbf{x}, \mathbf{y}, H)$ the entries of $\tilde{H}\mathbf{y}$ and its section map $\tilde{q}_H$; we consider these latter maps over the open set $O = \{(\mathbf{x}, \mathbf{y}) \in \mathbb{C}^{n+p+1} \mid \mathbf{y} \neq \mathbf{0}\}$. We prove below that $\mathbf{0}$ is a regular value for both q_H and $\tilde{q}_H$.

Suppose first that $q^{-1}(\mathbf{0}) = \emptyset$ (resp. $\tilde{q}^{-1}(\mathbf{0})$). We deduce that for all $H \in \mathbb{C}^{(2m-1)(n+1)}$, $q_H^{-1}(\mathbf{0}) = \emptyset$ (resp $\tilde{q}_H^{-1}(\mathbf{0}) = \emptyset$) and $\mathbf{0}$ is a regular value for both maps q_H and $\tilde{q}_H$. Note also that taking $\mathscr{H} = \mathbb{C}^{(2m-1)(n+1)}$, we deduce that $\mathbf{f}(H, \mathbf{u}, p)$ satisfies G.

Now, suppose that $q^{-1}(\mathbf{0})$ is not empty and let $(\mathbf{x}, \mathbf{y}, H) \in q^{-1}(0)$. Consider the Jacobian matrix Dq of the map q with respect to the variables $\mathbf{x}, \mathbf{y}$ and the entries of H, evaluated at $(\mathbf{x}, \mathbf{y}, H)$. We consider the submatrix of Dq by selecting the column corresponding to:

- the partial derivatives with respect to $\mathfrak{h}_{1,0}, \ldots, \mathfrak{h}_{2m-1,0}$;
- the partial derivatives with respect to $y_1, \ldots, y_{p+1}$.

We obtain a $(2m-p) \times (2m+p)$ submatrix of Dq; we prove below that it has full rank $2m-p$.

Indeed, remark that the $2m-p-1$ first lines correspond to the entries of $\tilde{H}\mathbf{y}$ and last line corresponds to the derivatives of $\mathbf{u}'\mathbf{y} - 1$. Hence, the structure of this submatrix is as below

$$\begin{bmatrix} y_1 & \ldots & y_{p+1} & 0 & \ldots & 0 & 0 & \cdots & 0 \\ 0 & y_1 & \ldots & y_{p+1} & \ldots & 0 & & & \\ \vdots & & \ddots & & \ddots & & \vdots & & \vdots \\ \vdots & & & y_1 & \ldots & y_{p+1} & 0 & & 0 \\ 0 & & \ldots & & \ldots & 0 & u_1 & \cdots & u_{p+1} \end{bmatrix}$$

Since this matrix is evaluated at the solution set of $\mathbf{u}'\mathbf{y} - 1 = 0$, we deduce straightforwardly that one entry of $\mathbf{u}$ and one entry of $\mathbf{y}$ are non-zero and that the above matrix is full rank and that $\mathbf{0}$ is a regular value of the map q.

We can do the same for $D\tilde{q}$ except the fact that we do not consider the partial derivatives with respect to $y_1, \ldots, y_{p+1}$. The $(2m-p-1) \times (2m-1)$ submatrix we obtain corresponds to the upper left block containing the entries of $\mathbf{y}$. Since $\tilde{q}$ is defined over the open set O in which $\mathbf{y} \neq \mathbf{0}$, we also deduce that this submatrix has full rank $2m-p-1$.

By Thom's Weak Transversality Theorem one deduces that there exists a non-empty Zariski open set $\mathscr{H}_p \subset \mathbb{C}^{(2m-1)(n+1)}$ such that if $H \in \mathscr{H}_p$, then $\mathbf{0}$ is a regular value of q_H (resp. $\tilde{q}_H$). We deduce that for $H \in \mathscr{H}_p$, the polynomial system $\mathbf{f}(H, \mathbf{u}, p)$ satisfies G and using the Jacobian criterion [7, Theorem 16.19], $\mathsf{J}(H, \mathbf{u}, p)$ is either empty or smooth equidimensional of dimension $n - 2m + 2p + 1$. This proves assertion (a), with $\mathscr{H} = \bigcap_{0 \leq p \leq r} \mathscr{H}_p$.

Similarly, we deduce that $\tilde{q}_H^{-1}(\mathbf{0})$ is either empty or smooth and equidimensional of dimension $n - 2m + 2p + 2$. Let $\Pi_{\mathbf{x}}$ be the canonical projection $(\mathbf{x}, \mathbf{y}) \to \mathbf{x}$; note that for any $\mathbf{x} \in \mathsf{H}_r$, the dimension of $\Pi_{\mathbf{x}}^{-1}(x) \cap \tilde{q}_H^{-1}(\mathbf{0})$ is ≥ 1 (by homogeneity of the $\mathbf{y}$-variables). By the Theorem on the Dimension of Fibers [21, Sect.6.3,Theorem 7], we deduce that $n - 2m + 2p + 2 - \dim(\mathsf{H}_p) \geq 1$. We deduce that for $H \in \mathscr{H}$, $\dim(\mathsf{H}_p) \leq n - 2m + 2p + 1$ which proves assertion (b).

It remains to prove assertion (c). We assume that $\mathbf{f}(H, \mathbf{u}, p)$ satisfies G. Consider the restriction of the map $\Pi_1 : \mathbb{C}^{n+p+1} \to \mathbb{C}$, $\Pi_1(\mathbf{x}, \mathbf{y}) = x_1$, to $\mathsf{J}(H, \mathbf{u}, p)$, which is smooth and equidimensional by assertion (a).

By Sard's Lemma [20, Section 4.2], the set of critical values of the restriction of Π_1 to $\mathsf{J}(H, \mathbf{u}, p)$ is finite. Hence, its complement $\mathscr{A} \subset \mathbb{C}$ is a non-empty Zariski open set. We deduce that for $\alpha \in \mathscr{A}$, the Jacobian matrix of $\mathbf{f}_\alpha(H, \mathbf{u}, p)$ satisfies G. □

3. ALGORITHM AND CORRECTNESS

3.1 Description

Data representation. The algorithm takes as *input* (H, r) where $H = (H_0, H_1, \ldots, H_n)$ encodes $m \times m$ Hankel matrices with entries in $\mathbb{Q}$, defining the linear matrix $H(\mathbf{x})$, and $0 \le r \le m-1$.

The *output* is represented by a rational parametrization, that is a polynomial system

$$\mathbf{q} = (q_0(t), q_1(t), \ldots, q_n(t), q(t)) \subset \mathbb{Q}[t]$$

of univariate polynomials, with $gcd(q, q_0) = 1$. The set of solutions of

$$x_i - q_i(t)/q_0(t) = 0, \; i = 1 \ldots n \qquad q(t) = 0$$

is clearly finite and expected to contain at least one point per connected component of the algebraic set $\mathsf{H}_r \cap \mathbb{R}^n$.

Main subroutines and formal description. We start by describing the main subroutines we use.

ZeroDimSolve. It takes as input a polynomial system defining an algebraic set $\mathsf{Z} \subset \mathbb{C}^{n+k}$ and a subset of variables $\mathbf{x} = (x_1, \ldots, x_n)$. If Z is finite, it returns a rational parametrization of the projection of Z on the $\mathbf{x}$-space else it returns an empty list.

ZeroDimSolveMaxRank. It takes as input a polynomial system $\mathbf{f} = (f_1, \ldots, f_c)$ such that $\mathsf{Z} = \{\mathbf{x} \in \mathbb{C}^{n+k} \mid \mathsf{rank}(D\mathbf{f}(\mathbf{x})) = c\}$ is finite and a subset of variables $\mathbf{x} = (x_1, \ldots, x_n)$ that endows $\mathbb{C}^n$. It returns fail: the assumptions are not satisfied if assumptions are not satisfied, else it returns a rational parametrization of the projection of Z on the $\mathbf{x}$-space.

Lift. It takes as input a rational parametrization of a finite set $\mathsf{Z} \subset \mathbb{C}^N$ and a number $\alpha \in \mathbb{C}$, and it returns a rational parametrization of $\{(\alpha, \mathbf{x}) : \mathbf{x} \in \mathsf{Z}\}$.

Union. It takes as input two rational parametrizations encoding finite sets $\mathsf{Z}_1, \mathsf{Z}_2$ and it returns a rational parametrization of $\mathsf{Z}_1 \cup \mathsf{Z}_2$.

ChangeVariables. It takes as input a rational parametrization of a finite set $\mathsf{Z} \subset \mathbb{C}^N$ and a non-singular matrix $M \in \mathrm{GL}(N, \mathbb{C})$. It returns a rational parametrization of Z^M.

The algorithm LowRankHankel is recursive, and it assumes that its input H satisfies Property G.

LowRankHankel(H, r):

1. If $n < 2m - 2r - 1$ then return [].
2. Choose randomly $M \in \mathrm{GL}(n, \mathbb{Q})$, $\alpha \in \mathbb{Q}$ and $\mathbf{u}_p \in \mathbb{Q}^{p+1}$, $\mathbf{v}_p \in \mathbb{Q}^{2m-p}$ for $0 \le p \le r$.
3. If $n = 2m - 2r - 1$ then return ZeroDimSolve$(\mathbf{f}(H, \mathbf{u}_r, r), \mathbf{x})$).
4. Let P = ZeroDimSolve$(\mathbf{l}(\mathbf{f}(H, \mathbf{u}_r, r), \mathbf{v}))$
5. If P = [] then for p from 0 to r do
   (a) P′ = ZeroDimSolveMaxRank$(\mathbf{l}(H^M, \mathbf{u}_p, \mathbf{v}_p), \mathbf{x})$;
   (b) P = Union(P, P′)
6. Q = Lift(LowRankHankel(Subs$(x_1 = \alpha, H^M), r), \alpha)$;
7. return(ChangeVariables(Union(Q, P), M^{-1})).

3.2 Correctness

The correctness proof is based on the two following results that are proved in Sections 5 and 6.

The first result states that when the input matrix H satisfies G and that, for a generic choice of M and $\mathbf{v}$, and for all $0 \le p \le r$, the set of solutions $(\mathbf{x}, \mathbf{y}, \mathbf{z})$ to $\mathbf{l}(H^M, \mathbf{u}, \mathbf{v}, p)$ at which $\operatorname{rank} \tilde{H}(x) = p$ is finite and contains $\operatorname{crit}(\pi_1, \mathsf{K}(H^M, \mathbf{u}, p))$.

Proposition 2 *Let $\mathscr{H}$ be the set defined in Proposition 1 and let $H \in \mathscr{H}$ and $\mathbf{u} \in \mathbb{Q}^{p+1} - \{\mathbf{0}\}$ for $0 \le p \le r$. There exist non-empty Zariski open sets $\mathscr{M}_1 \subset \mathrm{GL}(n, \mathbb{C})$ and $\mathscr{V} \subset \mathbb{C}^{2m-p}$ such that if $M \in \mathscr{M}_1 \cap \mathbb{Q}^{n \times n}$ and $\mathbf{v} \in \mathscr{V} \cap \mathbb{Q}^{2m-p}$, the following holds:*

(a) $\mathbf{l}(H^M, \mathbf{u}, \mathbf{v}, p)$ satisfies G over $\mathsf{K}(H^M, u, p)$;

(b) the projection of $\operatorname{reg}(\mathbf{l}(H^M, \mathbf{u}, \mathbf{v}, p))$ on the $(\mathbf{x}, \mathbf{y})$-space contains $\operatorname{crit}(\Pi_1, \mathsf{K}(H^M, \mathbf{u}, p))$

Proposition 3 *Let $H \in \mathscr{H}$, $0 \le p \le r$ and $d_p = n - 2m + 2p + 1$ and C be a connected component of $\mathsf{H}_p \cap \mathbb{R}^n$. Then there exist non-empty Zariski open sets $\mathscr{M}_2 \subset \mathrm{GL}(n, \mathbb{C})$ and $\mathscr{U} \subset \mathbb{C}^{p+1}$ such that for any $M \in \mathscr{M}_2 \cap \mathbb{Q}^{n \times n}$, $\mathbf{u} \in \mathscr{U} \cap \mathbb{Q}^{p+1}$, the following holds:*

(a) for $i = 1, \ldots, d_p$, $\pi_i(C^M)$ is closed;

(b) for any $\alpha \in \mathbb{R}$ in the boundary of $\pi_1(C^M)$, $\pi_1^{-1}(\alpha) \cap C^M$ is finite;

(c) for any $\mathbf{x} \in \pi_1^{-1}(\alpha) \cap C^M$ and p such that $\operatorname{rank} \tilde{H}_p(\mathbf{x}) = p$, there exists $(\mathbf{x}, \mathbf{y}) \in \mathbb{R}^n \times \mathbb{R}^{p+1}$ such that $(\mathbf{x}, \mathbf{y}) \in \mathsf{J}(H^M, \mathbf{u}, p)$.

Our algorithm is probabilistic and its correctness depends on the validity of the choices that are made at Step 2. We make this assumption that we formalize below.

We need to distinguish the choices of $M, \mathbf{u}$ and $\mathbf{v}$ that are made in the different calls of LowRankHankel; each of these parameter must lie in a non-empty Zariski open set defined in Propositions 1, 2 and 3.

We assume that the input matrix H satisfies G; we denote it by $H^{(0)}$, where the super script indicates that no recursive call has been made on this input; similarly $\alpha^{(0)}$ denotes the choice of α made at Step 2 on input $H^{(0)}$. Next, we denote by $H^{(i)}$ the input of LowRankHankel at the i-th recursive call and by $\mathscr{A}^{(i)} \subset \mathbb{C}$ the non-empty Zariski open set defined in Proposition 1 applied to $H^{(i)}$. Note that if $\alpha^{(i)} \in \mathscr{A}^{(i)}$, we can deduce that $H^{(i+1)}$ satisfies G.

Now, we denote by $\mathscr{M}_1^{(i)}, \mathscr{M}_2^{(i)}$ and $\mathscr{U}^{(p,i)}, \mathscr{V}^{(p,i)}$ the open sets defined in Propositions 1, 2 and 3 applied to $H^{(i)}$, for $0 \le p \le r$ and where i is the depth of the recursion.

Finally, we denote by $M^{(i)} \in \mathrm{GL}(n, \mathbb{Q})$, $\mathbf{u}_p^{(i)} \in \mathbb{Q}^{p+1}$ and $\mathbf{v}_p^{(i)}$, for $0 \le p \le r$, respectively the matrix and the vectors chosen at Step 2 of the i-th call of LowRankHankel.

Assumption A. We say that A is satisfied if $M^{(i)}$, $\alpha^{(i)}$, $\mathbf{u}_p^{(i)}$ and $\mathbf{v}_p^{(i)}$ satisfy:

- $M^{(i)} \in (\mathscr{M}_1^{(i)} \cap \mathscr{M}_2^{(i)}) \cap \mathbb{Q}^{i \times i}$;
- $\alpha^{(i)} \in \mathscr{A}^{(i)}$.
- $\mathbf{u}_p^{(i)} \in \mathscr{U}^{(p,i)} \cap \mathbb{Q}^{p+1} - \{\mathbf{0}\}$, for $0 \le p \le r$;
- $\mathbf{v}_p^{(i)} \in \mathscr{V}^{(p,i)} \cap \mathbb{Q}^{2m-p} - \{\mathbf{0}\}$ for $0 \le p \le r$;

Theorem 4 *Let H satisfy* G. *Then, if* A *is satisfied,* LowRankHankel *with input (H, r), returns a rational parametrization that encodes a finite algebraic set in H_r meeting each connected component of $\mathsf{H}_r \cap \mathbb{R}^n$.*

PROOF. The proof is by decreasing induction on the depth of the recursion.

When $n < 2m - 2r - 1$, H_r is empty since the input H satisfies G (since A is satisfied). In this case, the output defines the empty set.

When $n = 2m - 2r - 1$, since A is satisfied, by Proposition 1, either $\mathsf{H}_r = \emptyset$ or $\dim \mathsf{H}_r = 0$. Suppose $\mathsf{H}_r = \emptyset$. Hence $\mathsf{J}_r = \emptyset$, since the projection of J_r on the $\mathbf{x}-$space is included in H_r. Suppose now that $\dim \mathsf{H}_r = 0$: Proposition 3 guarantees that the output of the algorithm defines a finite set containing H_r.

Now, we assume that $n > 2m - 2r - 1$; our induction assumption is that for any $i \ge 1$ LowRankHankel$(H^{(i)}, r)$ returns a rational parametrization that encodes a finite set of points in the algebraic set defined by $\mathsf{rank}(H^{(i)}) \le r$ and that meets every connected component of its real trace.

Let C be a connected component of $\mathsf{H}_r \cap \mathbb{R}^n$. To keep notations simple, we denote by $M \in \mathrm{GL}(n, \mathbb{Q})$, $\mathbf{u}_p$ and $\mathbf{v}_p$ the matrix and vectors chosen at Step 2 for $0 \le p \le r$. Since A holds one can apply Proposition 3. We deduce that the image $\pi_1(C^M)$ is closed. Then, either $\pi_1(C^M) = \mathbb{R}$ or it is a closed interval.

Suppose first that $\pi_1(C^M) = \mathbb{R}$. Then for $\alpha \in \mathbb{Q}$ chosen at Step 2, $\pi_1^{-1}(\alpha) \cap C^M \neq 0$. Remark that $\pi_1^{-1}(\alpha) \cap C^M$ is the union of some connected components of $\mathsf{H}_r^{(1)} \cap \mathbb{R}^{n-1} = \{\mathbf{x} = (x_2,\dots,x_n) \in \mathbb{R}^{n-1} : \operatorname{rank} H^{(1)}(\mathbf{x}) \leq r\}$. Since A holds, assertion (c) of Proposition 1 implies that $H^{(1)}$ satisfies G. We deduce by the induction assumption that the parametrization returned by Step 6 where LowRankHankel is called recursively defines a finite set of points that is contained in H_r and that meets C.

Suppose now that $\pi_1(C^M) \neq \mathbb{R}$. By Proposition 3, $\pi_1(C^M)$ is closed. Since C^M is connected, $\pi_1(C^M)$ is a connected interval, and since $\pi_1(C^M) \neq \mathbb{R}$ there exists β in the boundary of $\pi_1(C^M)$ such that $\pi_1(C^M) \subset [\beta, +\infty)$ or $\pi_1(C^M) \subset (-\infty, \beta]$. Suppose without loss of generality that $\pi_1(C^M) \subset [\beta, +\infty)$, so that β is the minimum value attained by π_1 on C^M.

Let $\mathbf{x} = (\beta, x_2, \dots, x_n) \in C^M$, and suppose that $\operatorname{rank}(\tilde{H}(\mathbf{x})) = p$. By Proposition 3 (assertion (c)), there exists $\mathbf{y} \in \mathbb{C}^{p+1}$ such that $(\mathbf{x},\mathbf{y}) \in \mathsf{J}(H,\mathbf{u},p)$. Note that since $\operatorname{rank}(\tilde{H}(\mathbf{x})) = p$, we also deduce that $(\mathbf{x},\mathbf{y}) \in \mathsf{K}(H,\mathbf{u},p)$.

We claim that there exists $\mathbf{z} \in \mathbb{C}^{2m-p}$ such that $(\mathbf{x},\mathbf{y},\mathbf{z})$ lies on $\operatorname{reg}(\mathbf{l}(H^M,\mathbf{u},\mathbf{v},p))$.

Since A holds, Proposition 2 implies that $\mathbf{l}(H^M,\mathbf{u},\mathbf{v},p)$ satisfies G over $\mathsf{K}(H^M,\mathbf{u},p)$. Also, note that the Jacobian criterion implies that $\operatorname{reg}(\mathbf{l}(H^M,\mathbf{u},\mathbf{v},p))$ has dimension at most 0. We conclude that the point $\mathbf{x} \in C^M$ lies on the finite set encoded by the rational parametrization P obtained at Step 5 of LowRankHankel and we are done.

It remains to prove our claim, i.e. there exists $\mathbf{z} \in \mathbb{C}^{2m-p}$ such that $(\mathbf{x},\mathbf{y},\mathbf{z})$ lies on $\operatorname{reg}(\mathbf{l}(H^M,\mathbf{u},\mathbf{v},p))$.

Let C' be the connected component of $\mathsf{J}(H,\mathbf{u},p)^M \cap \mathbb{R}^{n+m(m-r)}$ containing $(\mathbf{x},\mathbf{y})$. We first prove that $\beta = \pi_1(\mathbf{x},\mathbf{y})$ lies on the boundary of $\pi_1(C')$. Indeed, suppose that there exists $(\widetilde{\mathbf{x}},\widetilde{\mathbf{y}}) \in C'$ such that $\pi_1(\widetilde{\mathbf{x}},\widetilde{\mathbf{y}}) < \beta$. Since C' is connected, there exists a continuous semi-algebraic map $\tau\colon [0,1] \to C'$ with $\tau(0) = (\mathbf{x},\mathbf{y})$ and $\tau(1) = (\widetilde{\mathbf{x}},\widetilde{\mathbf{y}})$. Let $\varphi : (\mathbf{x},\mathbf{y}) \to \mathbf{x}$ be the canonical projection on the $\mathbf{x}$-space.

Note that $\varphi \circ \tau$ is also continuous and semi-algebraic (it is the composition of continuous semi-algebraic maps), with $(\varphi \circ \tau)(0) = \mathbf{x}$, $(\varphi \circ \tau)(1) = \widetilde{\mathbf{x}}$. Since $(\varphi \circ \tau)(\theta) \in \mathsf{H}_p$ for all $\theta \in [0,1]$, then $\widetilde{\mathbf{x}} \in C$. Since $\pi_1(\widetilde{\mathbf{x}}) = \pi_1(\widetilde{\mathbf{x}},\widetilde{\mathbf{y}}) < \alpha$ we obtain a contradiction. So $\pi_1(\mathbf{x},\mathbf{y})$ lies on the boundary of $\pi_1(C')$.

By the Implicit Function Theorem, and the fact that $\mathbf{f}(H,\mathbf{u},p)$ satisfies Property G, one deduces that $(\mathbf{x},\mathbf{y})$ is a critical point of the restriction of $\Pi_1 : (x_1,\dots,x_n,y_1,\dots,y_{r+1}) \to x_1$ to $\mathsf{J}(H,\mathbf{u},p)$.

Since $\operatorname{rank}(H^M(\mathbf{x})) = p$ by construction, we deduce that $(\mathbf{x},\mathbf{y})$ is a critical point of the restriction of Π_1 to $\mathsf{K}(H^M,\mathbf{u},p)$ and that, by Proposition 2, there exists $\mathbf{z} \in \mathbb{C}^{2m-p}$ such that $(\mathbf{x},\mathbf{y},\mathbf{z})$ belongs to the set $\operatorname{reg}(\mathbf{l}(H^M,\mathbf{u},\mathbf{v},p))$, as claimed. □

4. DEGREE BOUNDS AND COMPLEXITY

We first remark that the complexity of subroutines Union, Lift and ChangeVariables (see [20, Chap. 10]) are negligible with respect to the complexity of ZeroDimSolveMaxRank. Hence, the complexity of LowRankHankel is at most n times the complexity of the routine ZeroDimSolveMaxRank, which is computed below.

Let (H,r) be the input, and let $0 \leq p \leq r$. We estimate the complexity of ZeroDimSolveMaxRank with input $(H^M,\mathbf{u}_p,\mathbf{v}_p)$. It depends on the algorithm used to solve zero-dimensional polynomial systems. We choose the one of [15] that can be seen as a symbolic homotopy taking into account the sparsity structure of the system to solve. More precisely, let $\mathbf{p} \subset \mathbb{Q}[x_1,\dots,x_n]$ and $s \in \mathbb{Q}[x_1,\dots,x_n]$ such that the common complex solutions of polynomials in $\mathbf{p}$ at which s does not vanish is finite. The algorithm in [15] builds a system $\mathbf{q}$ that has the same monomial structure as $\mathbf{p}$ has and defines a finite algebraic set. Next, the homotopy system $\mathbf{t} = t\mathbf{p} + (1-t)\mathbf{q}$ where t is a new variable is built. The system $\mathbf{t}$ defines a 1-dimensional constructible set over the open set defined by $s \neq 0$ and for generic values of t. Abusing notation, we denote by $Z(\mathbf{t})$ the curve defined as the Zariski closure of this constructible set.

Starting from the solutions of $\mathbf{q}$ which are encoded with a rational parametrization, the algorithm builds a rational parametrization for the solutions of $\mathbf{p}$ which do not cancel s. Following [15, Prop.6.1], the complexity of the algorithm essentially depends on the number δ of isolated solutions of $\mathbf{p}$, and δ', the degree of $Z(\mathbf{t})$ defined by $\mathbf{t}$.

Below, we estimate these degrees when the input is a Lagrange system as the ones we consider.

Degree bounds. We let $((\tilde{H}\,\mathbf{y})', \mathbf{u}_p{}'\mathbf{y} - 1)$, with $\mathbf{y} = (y_1,\dots,y_{p+1})'$, defining $\mathsf{J}_p(H,\mathbf{u}_p)$. Since $\mathbf{y} \neq 0$, one can eliminate w.l.o.g. y_{p+1}, and the linear form $\mathbf{u}_p{}'\mathbf{y} - 1$, obtaining a system $\tilde{\mathbf{f}} \in \mathbb{Q}[\mathbf{x},\mathbf{y}]^{2m-p-1}$. We recall that if $\mathbf{x}^{(1)},\dots,\mathbf{x}^{(c)}$ are c groups of variables, and $f \in \mathbb{Q}[\mathbf{x}^{(1)},\dots,\mathbf{x}^{(c)}]$, we say that the multidegree of f is $(d_1,\dots,d_c)$ if its degree with respect to the group $\mathbf{x}^{(j)}$ is d_j, for $j = 1,\dots,c$.

Let $\mathbf{l} = (\tilde{\mathbf{f}},\tilde{\mathbf{g}},\tilde{\mathbf{h}})$ be the corresponding Lagrange system, where

$$(\tilde{\mathbf{g}},\tilde{\mathbf{h}}) = (\tilde{g}_1,\dots,\tilde{g}_{n-1},\tilde{h}_1,\dots,\tilde{h}_p) = \mathbf{z}' D_1 \tilde{\mathbf{f}}$$

with $\mathbf{z} = [1, z_2, \dots, z_{2m-p-1}]$ a non-zero vector of Lagrange multipliers (we let $z_1 = 1$ w.l.o.g.). One obtains that $\mathbf{l}$ is constituted by *(i)* $2m-p-1$ polynomials of multidegree bounded by $(1,1,0)$ with respect to $(\mathbf{x},\mathbf{y},\mathbf{z})$, *(ii)* $n-1$ polynomials of multidegree bounded by $(0,1,1)$ with respect to $(\mathbf{x},\mathbf{y},\mathbf{z})$, and *(iii)* p polynomials of multidegree bounded by $(1,0,1)$ with respect to $(\mathbf{x},\mathbf{y},\mathbf{z})$, that is by $n+2m-2$ polynomials in $n+2m-2$ variables.

Lemma 5 *With the above notations, the number of isolated solutions of* $\mathsf{Z}(\mathbf{l})$ *is at most*

$$\delta(m,n,p) = \sum_{\ell} \binom{2m-p-1}{n-\ell} \binom{n-1}{2m-2p-2+\ell} \binom{p}{\ell}$$

where $\ell \in \{\max\{0, n-2m+p+1\}, \dots, \min\{p, n-2m+2p+1\}\}$.

PROOF. By [20, Proposition 11.1], this degree is bounded by the multilinear Bézout bound $\delta(m,n,p)$ which is the sum of the coefficients of

$$(s_x+s_y)^{2m-p-1}(s_y+s_z)^{n-1}(s_x+s_z)^p \in \mathbb{Q}[s_x,s_y,s_z]$$

modulo $I = \left\langle s_x^{n+1}, s_y^{p+1}, s_z^{2m-p-1} \right\rangle$. The conclusion comes straightforwardly by technical computations. □

With input $\mathbf{l}$, the homotopy system $\mathbf{t}$ is constituted by $2m-p-1$, $n-1$ and p polynomials of multidegree respectively bounded by $(1,1,0,1)$, $(0,1,1,1)$ and $(1,0,1,1)$ with respect to $(\mathbf{x},\mathbf{y},\mathbf{z},t)$. Technical but conceptually simple computations show the following.

Lemma 6 $\deg \mathsf{Z}(\mathbf{t}) \in O(pn(2m-p)\delta(m,n,p))$.

Estimates.
We provide the whole complexity of ZeroDimSolveMaxRank.

Theorem 7 *Let* $\delta = \delta(m,n,p)$ *be given by Lemma 5. Then* ZeroDimSolveMaxRank *with input* $\mathbf{l}(H^M,\mathbf{u}_p,\mathbf{v}_p)$ *computes a rational parametrization within*

$$\widetilde{O}(pn(2m-p)(pn(2m-p)(n+2m)^2 + (n+2m)^4)\delta^2),$$

arithmetic operations over $\mathbb{Q}$.

PROOF. A bound for δ' is given in Lemma 6. By [15, Prop.6.2] the complexity is $\widetilde{O}((\tilde{n}N + \tilde{n}^4)\delta\delta')$ where $\tilde{n} \in O(n+2m)$ and N is the sum of cardinalities of supports of polynomials in $\mathbf{l}$. We conclude by a straightforward computation. □

From Lemma 5, one deduces that for all $0 \leq p \leq r$, the maximum number of complex solutions computed by ZeroDimSolveMaxRank is bounded above by $\delta(m,n,p)$. We deduce the following result.

Proposition 8 *Let* H *be a* $m \times m$, $n-$*variate linear Hankel matrix, and let* $r \leq m-1$. *The maximum number of complex solutions computed by* LowRankHankel *with input* (H,r) *is*

$$\binom{2m-r-1}{r} + \sum_{k=2m-2r}^{n} \sum_{p=0}^{r} \delta(m,k,p).$$

PROOF. The maximum number of complex solutions computed by ZeroDimSolve is the degree of $\mathsf{J}(H, \mathbf{u}, r)$. Using, the multilinear Bézout bounds, this is bounded by the coefficient of the monomial $s_x^n s_y^r$ in the expression $(s_x + s_y)^{2m-r-1}$, that is exactly $\binom{2m-r-1}{r}$. The proof is now straightforward, since ZeroDimSolveMaxRank runs $r+1$ times at each recursive step of LowRankHankel, and since the number of variables decreases from n to $2m-2r$. □

5. PROOF OF PROPOSITION 2

We start with a local description of the algebraic sets defined by our Lagrange systems. This is obtained from a local description of the system defining $\mathsf{J}(H, \mathbf{u}, p)$. Without loss of generality, we can assume that $\mathbf{u} = (0, \ldots, 0, 1)$ in the whole section: such a situation can be retrieved from a linear change of the $\mathbf{y}$-variables that leaves invariant the $\mathbf{x}$-variables.

5.1 Local equations

Let $(\mathbf{x}, \mathbf{y}) \in \mathsf{K}(H, \mathbf{u}, p)$. Then, by definition, there exists a $p \times p$ minor of $\tilde{H}(\mathbf{x})$ that is non-zero. Without loss of generality, we assume that this minor is the determinant of the upper left $p \times p$ submatrix of $\tilde{H}$. Hence, consider the following block partition

$$\tilde{H}(\mathbf{x}) = \begin{bmatrix} N & Q \\ P & R \end{bmatrix} \quad (1)$$

with $N \in \mathbb{Q}[\mathbf{x}]^{p \times p}$, and $Q \in \mathbb{Q}[\mathbf{x}]^p$, $P \in \mathbb{Q}[\mathbf{x}]^{(2m-2p-1)\times p}$, and $R \in \mathbb{Q}[\mathbf{x}]^{2m-2p-1}$. We are going to exhibit suitable local descriptions of $\mathsf{K}(H, \mathbf{u}, p)$ over the Zariski open set $O_N \subset \mathbb{C}^{n+p+1}$ defined by $\det N \neq 0$; we denote by $\mathbb{Q}[\mathbf{x}, \mathbf{y}]_{\det N}$ the local ring of $\mathbb{Q}[\mathbf{x}, \mathbf{y}]$ localized by $\det N$.

Lemma 9 *Let N, Q, P, R be as above, and $\mathbf{u} \in \mathbb{Q}^{p+1} - \{\mathbf{0}\}$. Then there exist $\{q_i\}_{1 \le i \le p} \subset \mathbb{Q}[\mathbf{x}]_{\det N}$ and $\{\tilde{q}_i\}_{1 \le i \le 2m-2p-1} \subset \mathbb{Q}[\mathbf{x}]_{\det N}$ such that the constructible set $\mathsf{K}(H, \mathbf{u}, p) \cap O_N$ is defined by the equations*

$$\begin{aligned} y_i - q_i(\mathbf{x}) &= 0 \qquad 1 \le i \le p \\ \tilde{q}_i(\mathbf{x}) &= 0 \qquad 1 \le i \le 2m-2p-1 \\ y_{p+1} - 1 &= 0. \end{aligned}$$

PROOF. Let $c = 2m-2p-1$. The proof follows by the equivalence

$$\begin{bmatrix} N & Q \\ P & R \end{bmatrix} \mathbf{y} = 0 \text{ iff } \begin{bmatrix} \mathrm{I}_p & 0 \\ -P & \mathrm{I}_c \end{bmatrix} \begin{bmatrix} N^{-1} & 0 \\ 0 & \mathrm{I}_c \end{bmatrix} \begin{bmatrix} N & Q \\ P & R \end{bmatrix} \mathbf{y} = 0$$

in the local ring $\mathbb{Q}[\mathbf{x}, \mathbf{y}]_{\det N}$, that is if and only if

$$\begin{bmatrix} \mathrm{I}_p & N^{-1}Q \\ 0 & R - PN^{-1}Q \end{bmatrix} \mathbf{y} = 0$$

Recall that we have assumed that $\mathbf{u} = (0, \ldots, 0, 1)$; then the equation $\mathbf{u}\mathbf{y} = 1$ is $y_{p+1} = 1$. Denoting by q_i and $\tilde{q}_i$ respectively the entries of vectors $-N^{-1}Q$ and $-(R - PN^{-1}Q)$ ends the proof. □

The above local system is denoted by $\tilde{\mathbf{f}} \in \mathbb{Q}[\mathbf{x}, \mathbf{y}]_{\det N}^{2m-p}$. The Jacobian matrix of this polynomial system is

$$D\tilde{\mathbf{f}} = \begin{bmatrix} D_x \tilde{\mathbf{q}} & 0 \\ \star & \mathrm{I}_{p+1} \end{bmatrix}$$

with $\tilde{\mathbf{q}} = (\tilde{q}_1(\mathbf{x}), \ldots, \tilde{q}_{2m-2p-1}(\mathbf{x}))$. Its kernel defines the tangent space to $\mathsf{K}(H, \mathbf{u}, p) \cap O_N$. Let $\mathbf{w} = (\mathbf{w}_1, \ldots, \mathbf{w}_n) \in \mathbb{C}^n$ be a row vector; we denote by $\pi_{\mathbf{w}}$ the projection $\pi_{\mathbf{w}}(\mathbf{x}, \mathbf{y}) = \mathbf{w}_1 x_1 + \cdots + \mathbf{w}_n x_n$. Given a row vector $\mathbf{v} \in \mathbb{C}^{2m-p+1}$, we denote by $\mathsf{wlagrange}(\tilde{\mathbf{f}}, \mathbf{v})$ the following polynomial system

$$\tilde{\mathbf{f}}, \ (\tilde{\mathbf{g}}, \tilde{\mathbf{h}}) = [z_1, \ldots, z_{2m-p}, z_{2m-p+1}] \begin{bmatrix} D\tilde{\mathbf{f}} \\ \mathbf{w} \quad 0 \end{bmatrix}, \ \mathbf{v}'\mathbf{z} - 1. \quad (2)$$

For all $0 \le p \le r$, this polynomial system contains $n + 2m + 2$ polynomials and $n + 2m + 2$ variables. We denote by $\mathsf{L}_p(\tilde{\mathbf{f}}, \mathbf{v}, \mathbf{w})$ the set of its solutions whose projection on the $(\mathbf{x}, \mathbf{y})$-space lies in O_N.

Finally, we denote by $\mathsf{wlagrange}(\mathbf{f}, \mathbf{v})$ the polynomial system obtained when replacing $\tilde{\mathbf{f}}$ above with $\mathbf{f} = \mathbf{f}(H, \mathbf{u}, p)$. Similarly, its solution set is denoted by $\mathsf{L}_p(\mathbf{f}, \mathbf{v}, \mathbf{w})$.

5.2 Intermediate result

Lemma 10 *Let $\mathscr{H} \subset \mathbb{C}^{(2m-r)(n+1)}$ be the non-empty Zariski open set defined by Proposition 1, $H \in \mathscr{H}$ and $0 \le p \le r$. There exist non-empty Zariski open sets $\mathscr{V} \subset \mathbb{C}^{2m-p}$ and $\mathscr{W} \subset \mathbb{C}^n$ such that if $\mathbf{v} \in \mathscr{V}$ and $\mathbf{w} \in \mathscr{W}$, the following holds:*

(a) the set $\mathsf{L}_p(\mathbf{f}, \mathbf{v}, \mathbf{w}) = \mathsf{L}(\mathbf{f}, \mathbf{v}, \mathbf{w}) \cap \{(\mathbf{x}, \mathbf{y}, \mathbf{z}) \mid \operatorname{rank} \tilde{H}(\mathbf{x}) = p\}$ is finite and the Jacobian matrix of $\mathsf{wlagrange}(\mathbf{f}, \mathbf{v})$ has maximal rank at any point of $\mathsf{L}_p(\mathbf{f}, \mathbf{v}, \mathbf{w})$;

(b) the projection of $\mathsf{L}_p(\mathbf{f}, \mathbf{v}, \mathbf{w})$ in the $(\mathbf{x}, \mathbf{y})$-space contains the critical points of the restriction of $\pi_{\mathbf{w}}$ restricted to $\mathsf{K}(H, \mathbf{u}, p)$.

PROOF. We start with Assertion (a).

The statement to prove holds over $\mathsf{K}(H, \mathbf{u}, p)$; hence it is enough to prove it on any open set at which one $p \times p$ minor of $\tilde{H}$ is non-zero. Hence, we assume that the determinant of the upper left $p \times p$ submatrix N of $\tilde{H}$ is non-zero; $O_N \subset \mathbb{C}^{n+p+1}$ is the open set defined by $\det N \neq 0$, and we reuse the notation introduced in this section. We prove that there exist non-empty Zariski open sets $\mathscr{V}'_N \subset \mathbb{C}^{2m-p}$ and $\mathscr{W}_N \subset \mathbb{C}^n$ such that for $\mathbf{v} \in \mathscr{V}'_N$ and $\mathbf{w} \in \mathscr{W}_N$, $\mathsf{L}_p(\tilde{\mathbf{f}}, \mathbf{v}, \mathbf{w})$ is finite and that the Jacobian matrix associated to $\mathsf{wlagrange}(\tilde{\mathbf{f}}, \mathbf{v})$ has maximal rank at any point of $\mathsf{L}_p(\tilde{\mathbf{f}}, \mathbf{v}, \mathbf{w})$. The Lemma follows straightforwardly by defining $\mathscr{V}'$ (resp. $\mathscr{W}$) as the intersection of $\mathscr{V}'_N$ (resp. $\mathscr{W}_N$) where N varies in the set of $p \times p$ minors of $\tilde{H}(\mathbf{x})$.

Equations $\tilde{\mathbf{h}}$ yield $z_j = 0$ for $j = 2m-2p, \ldots, 2m-p$, and can be eliminated together with their $\mathbf{z}$ variables from the Lagrange system $\mathsf{wlagrange}(\tilde{\mathbf{f}}, \mathbf{v})$. It remains $\mathbf{z}$-variables $z_1, \ldots, z_{2m-2p-1}, z_{2m-p+1}$; we denote by $\Omega \subset \mathbb{C}^{2m-2p}$ the Zariski open set where they don't vanish simultaneously.

Now, consider the map

$$\begin{aligned} q: \quad O_N \times \Omega \times \mathbb{C}^n &\longrightarrow \mathbb{C}^{n+2m-p} \\ (\mathbf{x}, \mathbf{y}, \mathbf{z}, \mathbf{w}) &\longmapsto (\tilde{\mathbf{f}}, \tilde{\mathbf{g}}) \end{aligned}$$

and, for $\mathbf{w} \in \mathbb{C}^n$, its section map $q_{\mathbf{w}}(\mathbf{x}, \mathbf{y}, \mathbf{z}) = q(\mathbf{x}, \mathbf{y}, \mathbf{z}, \mathbf{w})$. We consider $\tilde{\mathbf{v}} \in \mathbb{C}^{2m-p}$ and we denote by $\tilde{\mathbf{z}}$ the remaining $\mathbf{z}-$variables, as above. Hence we define

$$\begin{aligned} Q: \quad O_N \times \Omega \times \mathbb{C}^n \times \mathbb{C}^{2m-2p} &\longrightarrow \mathbb{C}^{n+2m-p+1} \\ (\mathbf{x}, \mathbf{y}, \mathbf{z}, \mathbf{w}, \tilde{\mathbf{v}}) &\longmapsto (\tilde{\mathbf{f}}, \tilde{\mathbf{g}}, \tilde{\mathbf{v}}'\mathbf{z} - 1) \end{aligned}$$

and its section map $Q_{\mathbf{w}, \tilde{\mathbf{v}}}(\mathbf{x}, \mathbf{y}, \mathbf{z}) = q(\mathbf{x}, \mathbf{y}, \mathbf{z}, \mathbf{w}, \tilde{\mathbf{v}})$. We claim that $\mathbf{0} \in \mathbb{C}^{n+2m-p}$ (resp. $\mathbf{0} \in \mathbb{C}^{n+2m-p+1}$) is a regular value for q (resp. Q). Hence we deduce, by Thom's Weak Transversality Theorem, that there exist non-empty Zariski open sets $\mathscr{W}_N \subset \mathbb{C}^n$ and $\tilde{\mathscr{V}}_N \subset \mathbb{C}^{2m-2p}$ such that if $\mathbf{w} \in \mathscr{W}_N$ and $\tilde{\mathbf{v}} \in \tilde{\mathscr{V}}_N$, then $\mathbf{0}$ is a regular value for $q_{\mathbf{w}}$ and $Q_{\mathbf{w}, \tilde{\mathbf{v}}}$.

We prove now this claim. Recall that since $H \in \mathscr{H}$, the Jacobian matrix $D_{\mathbf{x}, \mathbf{y}} \tilde{\mathbf{f}}$ has maximal rank at any point $(\mathbf{x}, \mathbf{y}) \in \mathsf{Z}(\tilde{\mathbf{f}})$. Let $(\mathbf{x}, \mathbf{y}, \mathbf{z}, \mathbf{w}) \in q^{-1}(\mathbf{0})$ (resp. $(\mathbf{x}, \mathbf{y}, \mathbf{z}, \mathbf{w}, \tilde{\mathbf{v}}) \in Q^{-1}(\mathbf{0})$). Hence $(\mathbf{x}, \mathbf{y}) \in \mathsf{Z}(\tilde{\mathbf{f}})$. We isolate the square submatrix of $Dq(\mathbf{x}, \mathbf{y}, \mathbf{z}, \mathbf{w})$ obtained by selecting all its rows and

- the columns corresponding to derivatives of $\mathbf{x}, \mathbf{y}$ yielding a non-singular submatrix of $D_{\mathbf{x}, \mathbf{y}} \tilde{\mathbf{f}}(\mathbf{x}, \mathbf{y})$;
- the columns corresponding to the derivatives w.r.t. $\mathbf{w}_1, \ldots, \mathbf{w}_n$, hence this yields a block of zeros when applied to the lines corresponding to $\tilde{\mathbf{f}}$ and the block I_n when applied to $\tilde{\mathbf{g}}$.

For the map Q, we consider the same blocks as above. Moreover, since $(\mathbf{x}, \mathbf{y}, \mathbf{z}, \mathbf{w}, \tilde{\mathbf{v}}) \in Q^{-1}(\mathbf{0})$ verifies $\tilde{\mathbf{v}}'\mathbf{z} - 1 = 0$, there exists ℓ such that $z_\ell \neq 0$. Hence, we add the derivative of the polynomial $\tilde{\mathbf{v}}'\mathbf{z} - 1$ w.r.t. $\tilde{\mathbf{v}}_\ell$, which is $z_\ell \neq 0$. The claim is proved.

Note that $q_{\mathbf{w}}^{-1}(\mathbf{0})$ is defined by $n + 2m - p$ polynomials involving $n + 2m - p + 1$ variables. We deduce that for $\mathbf{w} \in \mathscr{W}_N$, $q_{\mathbf{w}}^{-1}(\mathbf{0})$ is either empty or it is equidimensional and has dimension 1. Using the homogeneity in the $\mathbf{z}$-variables and the Theorem on the Dimension of Fibers [21, Sect. 6.3, Theorem 7], we deduce that the projection on the $(\mathbf{x},\mathbf{y})$-space of $q_{\mathbf{w}}^{-1}(\mathbf{0})$ has dimension ≤ 0. We also deduce that for $\mathbf{w} \in \mathscr{W}_N$ and $\tilde{\mathbf{v}} \in \tilde{\mathscr{V}}_N$, $Q_{\mathbf{w},\tilde{\mathbf{v}}}^{-1}(\mathbf{0})$ is either empty or finite.

Hence, the points of $Q_{\tilde{\mathbf{v}},\mathbf{w}}^{-1}(\mathbf{0})$ are in bijection with those in $\mathsf{L}(\tilde{\mathbf{f}},\mathbf{v},\mathbf{w})$ forgetting their 0-coordinates corresponding to $z_j = 0$. We define $\mathscr{V}'_N = \tilde{\mathscr{V}}_N \times \mathbb{C}^p \subset \mathbb{C}^{2m-2p}$. We deduce straightforwardly that for $\mathbf{v} \in \mathscr{V}'_N$ and $\mathbf{w} \in \mathscr{W}_N$, the Jacobian matrix of $\mathsf{wlagrange}(\tilde{\mathbf{f}},\mathbf{v})$ has maximal rank at any point of $\mathsf{L}_p(\tilde{\mathbf{f}},\mathbf{v},\mathbf{w})$. By the Jacobian criterion, this also implies that the set $\mathsf{L}_p(\tilde{\mathbf{f}},\mathbf{v},\mathbf{w})$ is finite as requested.

We prove now Assertion (b).

Let $\mathscr{W} \subset \mathbb{C}^n$ and $\mathscr{V}' \subset \mathbb{C}^{2m-p}$ be the non-empty Zariski open sets defined in the proof of Assertion (a). For $\mathbf{w} \in \mathscr{W}$ and $\mathbf{v} \in \mathscr{V}'$, the projection of $\mathsf{L}_p(\tilde{\mathbf{f}},\mathbf{v},\mathbf{w})$ on the $(\mathbf{x},\mathbf{y})-$space is finite. Since $H \in \mathscr{H}$, $\mathsf{K}(H,\mathbf{u},p)$ is smooth and equidimensional.

Since we work on $\mathsf{K}(H,\mathbf{u},p)$, one of the $p\times p$ minors of $\tilde{H}(\mathbf{x})$ is non-zero. Hence, suppose to work in $O_N \cap \mathsf{K}(H,\mathbf{u},p)$ where $O_N \subset \mathbb{C}^{n+p+1}$ has been defined in the proof of Assertion (a). Remark that

$$\mathrm{crit}\,(\pi_{\mathbf{w}},\mathsf{K}(H,\mathbf{u},p)) = \bigcup_N \mathrm{crit}\,(\pi_{\mathbf{w}},O_N \cap \mathsf{K}(H,\mathbf{u},p))$$

where N runs over the set of $p\times p$ minors of $\tilde{H}(\mathbf{x})$. We prove below that there exists a non-empty Zariski open set $\mathscr{V} \subset \mathbb{C}^{2m-p}$ such that if $\mathbf{v} \in \mathscr{V}$, for all N and for $\mathbf{w} \in \mathscr{W}$, the set $\mathrm{crit}\,(\pi_{\mathbf{w}},O_N \cap \mathsf{K}(H,\mathbf{u},p))$ is finite and contained in the projection of $\mathsf{L}_p(\mathbf{f},\mathbf{v},\mathbf{w})$. This straightforwardly implies that the same holds for $\mathrm{crit}\,(\pi_{\mathbf{w}},\mathsf{K}(H,\mathbf{u},p))$.

Suppose w.l.o.g. that N is the upper left $p\times p$ minor of $\tilde{H}(\mathbf{x})$. We use the notation $\tilde{\mathbf{f}},\tilde{\mathbf{g}},\tilde{\mathbf{h}}$ as above. Hence, the set $\mathrm{crit}\,(\pi_{\mathbf{w}},O_N \cap \mathsf{K}(H,\mathbf{u},p))$ is the image by the projection $\pi_{\mathbf{x},\mathbf{y}}$ over the $(\mathbf{x},\mathbf{y})-$space, of the constructible set defined by $\tilde{\mathbf{f}},\tilde{\mathbf{g}},\tilde{\mathbf{h}}$ and $\mathbf{z} \neq 0$. We previously proved that, if $\mathbf{w} \in \mathscr{W}_N$, $q^{-1}(\mathbf{0})$ is either empty or equidimensional of dimension 1. Hence, the constructible set defined by $\tilde{\mathbf{f}},\tilde{\mathbf{g}},\tilde{\mathbf{h}}$ and $\mathbf{z}\neq 0$, which is isomorphic to $q^{-1}(\mathbf{0})$, is either empty or equidimensional of dimension 1.

Moreover, for any $(\mathbf{x},\mathbf{y}) \in \mathrm{crit}\,(\pi_{\mathbf{w}},O_N \cap \mathsf{K}(H,\mathbf{u},p))$, $\pi_{\mathbf{x},\mathbf{y}}^{-1}(\mathbf{x},\mathbf{y})$ has dimension 1, by the homogeneity of polynomials w.r.t. variables $\mathbf{z}$. By the Theorem on the Dimension of Fibers [21, Sect. 6.3, Theorem 7], we deduce that $\mathrm{crit}\,(\pi_{\mathbf{w}},O_N \cap \mathsf{K}(H,\mathbf{u},p))$ is finite.

For $(\mathbf{x},\mathbf{y}) \in \mathrm{crit}\,(\pi_{\mathbf{w}},O_N \cap \mathsf{K}(H,\mathbf{u},p))$, let $\mathscr{V}_{(\mathbf{x},\mathbf{y}),N} \subset \mathbb{C}^{2m-p}$ be the non-empty Zariski open set such that if $\mathbf{v} \in \mathscr{V}_{(\mathbf{x},\mathbf{y}),N}$ the hyperplane $\mathbf{v}'\mathbf{z}-1=0$ intersects transversely $\pi_{\mathbf{x},\mathbf{y}}^{-1}(\mathbf{x},\mathbf{y})$. Recall that $\mathscr{V}'_N \subset \mathbb{C}^{2m-p}$ has been defined in the proof of Assertion (a). Define

$$\mathscr{V}_N = \mathscr{V}'_N \cap \bigcap_{(\mathbf{x},\mathbf{y})} \mathscr{V}_{(\mathbf{x},\mathbf{y}),N}$$

and $\mathscr{V} = \bigcap_N \mathscr{V}_N$. This concludes the proof, since $\mathscr{V}$ is a finite intersection of non-empty Zariski open sets. □

5.3 Proof

We denote by $\mathscr{M}_1 \subset \mathrm{GL}(n,\mathbb{C})$ the set of non-singular matrices M such that the first row $\mathbf{w}$ of M^{-1} lies in the set $\mathscr{W}$ given in Lemma 10: this set is non-empty and Zariski open since the entries of M^{-1} are rational functions of the entries of M. Let $\mathscr{V} \subset \mathbb{C}^{2m-p}$ be the non-empty Zariski open set given by Lemma 10 and let $\mathbf{v} \in \mathscr{V}$. Let $\mathbf{e}_1$ be the row vector $(1,0,\ldots,0) \in \mathbb{Q}^n$ and for all $M \in \mathrm{GL}(n,\mathbb{C})$, let

$$\tilde{M} = \begin{bmatrix} M & 0 & 0 \\ 0 & \mathrm{I}_m & 0 \\ 0 & 0 & \mathrm{I}_{2m-p} \end{bmatrix}.$$

Remark that for any $M \in \mathscr{M}_1$ the following identity holds:

$$\begin{bmatrix} D\mathbf{f}(H^M,\mathbf{u},p) \\ \mathbf{e}_1 \quad 0\cdots 0 \end{bmatrix} = \begin{bmatrix} D\mathbf{f}(H,\mathbf{u},p)^M \\ \mathbf{w} \quad 0\cdots 0 \end{bmatrix} \begin{bmatrix} M & 0 \\ 0 & \mathrm{I}_m \end{bmatrix}.$$

We conclude that the set of solutions of the system

$$\left(\mathbf{f}(H,\mathbf{u},p), \quad \mathbf{z}' \begin{bmatrix} D\mathbf{f}(H,\mathbf{u},p) \\ \mathbf{w} \quad 0\cdots 0 \end{bmatrix}, \quad \mathbf{v}'\mathbf{z}-1\right) \tag{3}$$

is the image by the map $(\mathbf{x},\mathbf{y},\mathbf{z}) \mapsto \tilde{M}^{-1}(\mathbf{x},\mathbf{y},\mathbf{z})$ of the set S of solutions of the system

$$\left(\mathbf{f}(H,\mathbf{u},p), \quad \mathbf{z}' \begin{bmatrix} D\mathbf{f}(H,\mathbf{u},p) \\ \mathbf{e}_1 \quad 0\cdots 0 \end{bmatrix}, \quad \mathbf{v}'\mathbf{z}-1\right). \tag{4}$$

Now, let φ be the projection that eliminates the coordinate z_{2m-p+1}. Remark that $\varphi(S) = \mathsf{L}_p(\mathbf{f}^M,\mathbf{v},\mathbf{e}_1)$. Now, Lemma 10 concludes. □

6. PROOF OF PROPOSITION 3

The proof of Proposition 3 relies on results of [14, Section 5] and of [19]. We use the same notation as in [14, Section 5], and we recall them below.

Notations. For $\mathsf{Z} \subset \mathbb{C}^n$ of dimension d, we denote by $\Omega_i(\mathsf{Z})$ its $i-$equidimensional component, $i=0,\ldots,d$. We denote by $\mathscr{S}(\mathsf{Z})$ the union of $\Omega_0(\mathsf{Z}) \cup \cdots \cup \Omega_{d-1}(\mathsf{Z})$ and of the set $\mathrm{sing}\,(\Omega_d(\mathsf{Z}))$ of singular points of $\Omega_d(\mathsf{Z})$.

Let π_i be the map $(x_1,\ldots,x_n) \to (x_1,\ldots,x_i)$. We denote by $\mathscr{C}(\pi_i,\mathsf{Z})$ the Zariski closure of the union of $\Omega_0(\mathsf{Z}) \cup \cdots \cup \Omega_{i-1}(\mathsf{Z})$ and of the sets $\mathrm{crit}\,(\pi_i,\mathrm{reg}\,(\Omega_r(\mathsf{Z})))$ for $r \geq i$. For $M \in \mathrm{GL}(n,\mathbb{C})$ and Z as above, we define the collection of algebraic sets $\{\mathscr{O}_i(\mathsf{Z}^M)\}_{0\leq i\leq d}$ as follows: (1) $\mathscr{O}_d(\mathsf{Z}^M) = \mathsf{Z}^M$ and (2) $\mathscr{O}_i(\mathsf{Z}^M) = \mathscr{S}(\mathscr{O}_{i+1}(\mathsf{Z}^M)) \cup \mathscr{C}(\pi_{i+1},\mathscr{O}_{i+1}(\mathsf{Z}^M)) \cup \mathscr{C}(\pi_{i+1},\mathsf{Z}^M)$ for $i=0,\ldots,d-1$. We finally recall the two following properties:

Property $\mathsf{P}(\mathsf{Z})$. Let $\mathsf{Z} \subset \mathbb{C}^n$ be an algebraic set of dimension d. We say that $M \in \mathrm{GL}(n,\mathbb{C})$ satisfies $\mathsf{P}(\mathsf{Z})$ when for all $i=0,1,\ldots,d$:

1. *(i)* $\mathscr{O}_i(\mathsf{Z}^M)$ has dimension $\leq i$ and
2. *(ii)* $\mathscr{O}_i(\mathsf{Z}^M)$ is in Noether position with respect to $x_1,\ldots,x_i$.

Property Q. We say that an algebraic set Z of dimension d satisfies $\mathsf{Q}_i(\mathsf{Z})$ (for a given $1 \leq i \leq d$) if for any connected component C of $\mathsf{Z}\cap\mathbb{R}^n$ the boundary of $\pi_i(C)$ is contained in $\pi_i(\mathscr{O}_{i-1}(\mathsf{Z})\cap C)$. We say that Z satisfies Q if it satisfies $\mathsf{Q}_1,\ldots,\mathsf{Q}_d$.

Let $\mathsf{Z} \subset \mathbb{C}^n$ be an algebraic set of dimension d. By [14, Proposition 15], there exists a non-empty Zariski open set $\mathscr{M} \subset \mathrm{GL}(n,\mathbb{C})$ such that for $M \in \mathscr{M} \cap \mathrm{GL}(n,\mathbb{Q})$ Property $\mathsf{P}(\mathsf{Z})$ holds. Moreover, if $M \in \mathrm{GL}(n,\mathbb{Q})$ satisfies $\mathsf{P}(\mathsf{Z})$, then $\mathsf{Q}_i(\mathsf{Z}^M)$ holds for $i=1,\ldots,d$ [14, Proposition 16]. We use these results in the following proof of Proposition 3.

Proof. We start with assertion (a). Let $\mathscr{M}_2 \subset \mathrm{GL}(n,\mathbb{C})$ be the non-empty Zariski open set of [14, Proposition 17] for $\mathsf{Z} = \mathsf{H}_p$: for $M \in \mathscr{M}_2$, M satisfies $\mathsf{P}(\mathsf{H}_p)$. Remark that the connected components of $\mathsf{H}_p \cap \mathbb{R}^n$ and are in bijection with those of $\mathsf{H}_p^M \cap \mathbb{R}^n$ (given by $C \leftrightarrow C^M$).

Let $C^M \subset \mathsf{H}_p^M \cap \mathbb{R}^n$ be a connected component of $\mathsf{H}_p^M \cap \mathbb{R}^n$. Let π_1 be the projection on the first variable $\pi_1 : \mathbb{R}^n \to \mathbb{R}$, and consider its restriction to $\mathsf{H}_r^M \cap \mathbb{R}^n$. Since $M \in \mathscr{M}_2$, by [14, Proposition 16] the boundary of $\pi_1(C^M)$ is included in $\pi_1(\mathscr{O}_0(\mathsf{H}_p^M)\cap C^M)$ and in particular in $\pi_1(C^M)$. Hence $\pi_1(C^M)$ is closed.

We prove now assertion (b). Let $M \in \mathscr{M}_2$, C a connected component of $\mathsf{H}_p \cap \mathbb{R}^n$ and $\alpha \in \mathbb{R}$ be in the boundary of $\pi_1(C^M)$. By [14, Lemma 19] $\pi_1^{-1}(\alpha)\cap C^M$ is finite.

We claim that there exists a non-empty Zariski open set $\mathscr{U}_{C,\mathbf{x}} \subset \mathbb{C}^{p+1}$ such that if $\mathbf{u} \in \mathscr{U}_{C,\mathbf{x}} \cap \mathbb{Q}^{p+1}$, there exists $\mathbf{y} \in \mathbb{Q}^{p+1}$ such that $(\mathbf{x},\mathbf{y}) \in \mathsf{J}(H^M,\mathbf{u},p)$. One concludes by taking $\mathscr{U} = \bigcap_{C,\mathbf{x}} \mathscr{U}_{C,\mathbf{x}}$, where C varies in the finite set of connected components of $\mathsf{H}_p \cap \mathbb{R}^n$, and $\mathbf{x} \in \pi_1^{-1}(\alpha)\cap C^M$, which is also finite.

It remains to prove the claim we made. For $\mathbf{x} \in \pi_1^{-1}(\alpha)\cap C^M$, the matrix $\tilde{H}(\mathbf{x})$ is rank defective, and let $p' \leq p$ be its rank.

(m,r,n)	RAGlib	New	TotalDeg	MaxDeg
(3,2,2)	0.3	5	9	6
(3,2,3)	0.6	10	21	12
(3,2,4)	2	13	33	12
(3,2,5)	7	20	39	12
(3,2,6)	13	21	39	12
(3,2,7)	20	21	39	12
(3,2,8)	53	21	39	12
(4,2,3)	2	2.5	10	10
(4,2,4)	43	6.5	40	30
(4,2,5)	56575	18	88	48
(4,2,6)	∞	35	128	48
(4,2,7)	∞	46	143	48
(4,2,8)	∞	74	143	48
(4,3,2)	0.3	8	16	12
(4,3,3)	3	11	36	52
(4,3,4)	54	31	120	68
(4,3,5)	341	112	204	84
(4,3,6)	480	215	264	84
(4,3,7)	528	324	264	84
(4,3,8)	2638	375	264	84

(m,r,n)	RAGlib	New	TotalDeg	MaxDeg
(5,2,5)	25	4	21	21
(5,2,6)	31176	21	91	70
(5,2,7)	∞	135	199	108
(5,2,8)	∞	642	283	108
(5,2,9)	∞	950	311	108
(5,2,10)	∞	1106	311	108
(5,3,3)	2	2	20	20
(5,3,4)	202	18	110	90
(5,3,5)	∞	583	338	228
(5,3,6)	∞	6544	698	360
(5,3,7)	∞	28081	1058	360
(5,3,8)	∞	∞	-	-
(5,4,2)	1	5	25	20
(5,4,3)	48	30	105	80
(5,4,4)	8713	885	325	220
(5,4,5)	∞	15537	755	430
(5,4,6)	∞	77962	1335	580

(m,r,n)	RAGlib	New	TotalDeg	MaxDeg
(6,2,7)	∞	6	36	36
(6,2,8)	∞	matbig	-	-
(6,3,5)	∞	10	56	56
(6,3,6)	∞	809	336	280
(6,3,7)	∞	49684	1032	696
(6,3,8)	∞	matbig	-	-
(6,4,3)	3	5	35	35
(6,4,4)	∞	269	245	210
(6,4,5)	∞	30660	973	728
(6,4,6)	∞	∞	-	-
(6,5,2)	1	9	36	30
(6,5,3)	915	356	186	150
(6,5,4)	∞	20310	726	540
(6,5,5)	∞	∞	-	-

The linear system $\begin{bmatrix} \tilde{H}(\mathbf{x}) \\ \mathbf{u} \end{bmatrix} \cdot \mathbf{y} = \begin{bmatrix} \mathbf{0} \\ 1 \end{bmatrix}$ has a solution if and only if $\operatorname{rank} \begin{bmatrix} \tilde{H}(\mathbf{x}) \\ \mathbf{u} \end{bmatrix} = \operatorname{rank} \begin{bmatrix} \tilde{H}(\mathbf{x}) & \mathbf{0} \\ \mathbf{u} & 1 \end{bmatrix}$, and the rank of the second matrix is $p'+1$. Denoting by $\mathscr{U}_{C,\mathbf{x}} \subset \mathbb{C}^{p+1}$ the complement in $\mathbb{C}^{p+1}$ of the p'−dimensional linear space spanned by the rows of $\tilde{H}(\mathbf{x})$, proves the claim and concludes the proof. □

7. EXPERIMENTS

The implementation of LowRankHankel is under MAPLE, and it will be freely released as a MAPLE library and available at `http://homepages.laas.fr/henrion/software`. We use the FGB [8] library implemented by J.-C. Faugère for solving solving zero-dimensional polynomial systems using Gröbner bases. In particular, we used the new implementation of [9] for computing rational parametrizations. Our implementation checks the genericity assumptions on the input.

We test the algorithm with input $m \times m$ linear Hankel matrices $H(\mathbf{x}) = H_0 + x_1 H_1 + \ldots + x_n H_n$, where the entries of $H_0, \ldots, H_n$ are random rational numbers, and an integer $0 \leq r \leq m-1$. By randomness of such rational numbers we mean that they are generated as quotients of integers chosen with uniform distribution in a fixed interval. We are aware of the fact that this implies that the set of possible inputs is finite (in particular, not dense). On the other hand, this does not affect genericity and also the correctness of the algorithm since the requested properties are checked before its execution. We remark that none of the implementations of Cylindrical Algebraic Decomposition solved our examples involving more that 3 variables. Also, on all our examples, we found that Lagrange systems define finite algebraic sets.

We compare the practical behavior of LowRankHankel with the performance of the library RAGLIB, implemented by the third author (see [17]). Its function PointsPerComponents, with input the list of $(r+1)$−minors of $H(\mathbf{x})$, returns one point per connected component of the real counterpart of the algebraic set H_r, that is it solves the problem presented in this paper. It also uses critical point methods. The symbol ∞ means that no result has been obtained after 24 hours. The symbol matbig means that the standard limitation in FGB to the size of matrices for Gröbner bases computations has been reached.

We report on timings (given in seconds) of the two implementations in the table. The column New corresponds to timings of LowRankHankel. Both computations have been done on an Intel(R) Xeon(R) CPU $E7540$ @2.00GHz 256 Gb of RAM. We remark that RAGLIB is competetitive for problems of small size (e.g. $m=3$) but when the size increases LowRankHankel performs much better, especially when the determinantal variety has not co-dimension 1. It can tackle problems that are out reach of RAGLIB. Note that for fixed r, the algorithm seems to have a behaviour that is polynomial in nm (this is particularly visible when m is fixed, e.g. to 5). Finally, we report in column TotalDeg the degree of the rational parametrization obtained as output of the algorithm, that is the number of its complex solutions. We observe that this value is definitely constant when m, r are fixed and n grows, as for the maximum degree (column MaxDeg) appearing during the recursive calls. The same holds for the multilinear bound given in Section 4 for the total number of complex solutions.

8. REFERENCES

[1] B. Bank, M. Giusti, J. Heintz, M. Safey El Din, and É. Schost. On the geometry of polar varieties. *Applicable Algebra in Engineering, Communication and Computing*, 21(1):33–83, 2010.

[2] S. Basu, R. Pollack, and M.-F. Roy. *Algorithms in real algebraic geometry*, volume 10 of *Algorithms and Computation in Mathematics*. Springer-Verlag, second edition, 2006.

[3] G. Blekherman and R. Sinn. Extreme rays of the Hankel spectrahedra for ternary forms. *ArXiv e-prints arXiv:1406.1873v2*, October 2014.

[4] W. Bruns and U. Vetter. *Determinantal rings*, volume 1327. Springer-Verlag Berlin-Heidelberg, 1988.

[5] G. Collins. Quantifier elimination for real closed fields by cylindrical algebraic decompostion. In *Automata Theory and Formal Languages*, pages 134–183. Springer, 1975.

[6] A. Conca. Straightening law and powers of determinantal ideals of Hankel matrices. *Advances in Mathematics*, 138(2):263–292, 1998.

[7] D. Eisenbud. *Commutative algebra with a view toward algebraic geometry*, volume 150 of *Graduate Texts in Mathematics*. Springer-Verlag, 1995.

[8] J.-C. Faugère. Fgb: a library for computing Gröbner bases. In *Mathematical Software–ICMS 2010*, pages 84–87. Springer, 2010.

[9] J.-C. Faugère and C. Mou. Fast algorithm for change of ordering of zero-dimensional Gröbner bases with sparse multiplication matrices. In É. Schost and I. Z. Emiris, editors, *Symbolic and Algebraic Computation, International Symposium, ISSAC 2011 (co-located with FCRC 2011), San Jose (CA), USA, June 7-11, 2011, Proceedings*, pages 115–122. ACM, 2011.

[10] J-C. Faugère, M. Safey El Din, and P-J. Spaenlehauer. Critical points and Gröbner bases: the unmixed case. In Proceedings of *ISSAC '12*, Grenoble (France), pages 162–169. ACM, 2012.

[11] A. Greuet and M. Safey El Din. Probabilistic algorithm for polynomial optimization over a real algebraic set. *SIAM Journal on Optimization*, 24(3):1313–1343, 2014.

[12] D. Grigoriev and N. Vorobjov. Solving systems of polynomial inequalities in subexponential time. *Journal of Symbolic Computation*, 5:37–64, 1988.

[13] G. Heinig and K. Rost. *Algebraic methods for Toeplitz-like matrices and operators*. Springer, 1984.

[14] D. Henrion, S. Naldi, and M. Safey El Din. Real root finding for determinants of linear matrices. *ArXiv e-prints arXiv:1412.5873*, December 2014.

[15] G. Jeronimo, G. Matera, P. Solernó, and A. Waissbein. Deformation techniques for sparse systems. *Foundations of Computational Mathematics*, 9(1):1–50, 2009.

[16] I. Markovsky. *Low rank approximation: algorithms, implementation, applications*. Communications and Control Engineering. Springer, 2012.

[17] M. Safey El Din. RAGLib (Real Algebraic Geometry Library), Maple Package. http://www-polsys.lip6.fr/~safey.

[18] M. Safey El Din. Finding sampling points on real hypersurfaces is easier in singular situations. *MEGA (Effective Methods in Algebraic Geometry) Electronic proceedings*, 2005.

[19] M. Safey El Din and É. Schost. Polar varieties and computation of one point in each connected component of a smooth real algebraic set. In Proceedings of *ISSAC'03*, Philadelphia (PA), USA, pages 224–231. ACM, 2003.

[20] M. Safey El Din and É. Schost. A nearly optimal algorithm for deciding connectivity queries in smooth and bounded real algebraic sets. *arXiv preprint arXiv:1307.7836*, 2013.

[21] I. Shafarevich. *Basic Algebraic Geometry 1*. Springer Verlag, 1977.

[22] P.-J. Spaenlehauer. On the complexity of computing critical points with Gröbner bases. *SIAM Journal on Optimization*, 24(3):1382–1401, 2014.

[23] A. Tarski. *A decision method for elementary algebra and geometry*. University of California Press, 1951.

Constructing All Composition Series of a Finite Group

Alexander Hulpke
Department of Mathematics
Colorado State University
1874 Campus Delivery
Fort Collins, CO, 80523-1874, USA
hulpke@math.colostate.edu

ABSTRACT

This paper describes an effective method for enumerating all composition series of a finite group, possibly up to action of a group of automorphisms. By building the series in an ascending way it only requires a very easy case of complement computation and can avoid the need to fuse subspace chains in vector spaces.

As a by-product it also enumerates all subnormal subgroups.

Categories and Subject Descriptors

I.1.2 [**Symbolic and Algebraic Manipulation**]: Algebraic Algorithms

General Terms

Algorithms

Keywords

Finite Groups; Composition series; Subnormal subgroups; Enumeration

1. INTRODUCTION

A composition series, that is a series of subgroups each normal in the previous such that subsequent factor groups are simple, is one of the basic concepts in group theory. The aim of this paper is to describe an effective process for enumerating all composition series of a finite group, possibly up to the action of a group of automorphisms.

While the Jordan-Hölder theorem states that the collection of composition factors (with multiplicity) is an invariant of the group, groups can have a huge number of composition series (see the examples in Section 6.1 below) even when enumerating up to automorphisms. This shows that such an enumeration is a nontrivial task, producing useful information.

ISSAC'15, July 6–9, 2015, Bath, United Kingdom.

DOI: http://dx.doi.org/10.1145/2755996.2756642.

Subgroups that can occur in a composition series are called *subnormal*, thus a list of all subnormal subgroups will be a by-product of such an enumeration.

For solvable groups, the set of all composition series also parameterizes the set of polycyclic presentations, up to a choice of generators of cyclic groups. (A polycyclic presentation [11, Section 8.1] is the standard way of representing solvable groups on a computer.)

A naive approach to enumerating composition series would be to determine the maximal normal subgroups of the whole group and then for each such subgroup U calculate U's maximal normal subgroups in turn, iterating down. If there is a group action one would need to form orbits on each level.

This approach will quickly run into problems. For example consider the group $G = (3^5 \rtimes GL_5(3)) \times A_5^2$, classifying composition series up to conjugacy in G. For $N = 3^5$ there are 24 partial composition series that descend from G and contain N. The action of $GL_5(3)$ then implies that in each case there is one orbit of composition series through N. The naive approach however would first enumerate maximal subspaces and then fuse them back into one orbit each time, causing much redundancy and making this approach infeasible.

The approach we use instead will only determine the possible composition series in each chief factor once, and then combine these in all possible ways to series for the whole group. Furthermore, the combination step involves calculations that are far easier than the determination of maximal normal subgroups.

2. REDUCTION TO CHIEF FACTORS

We assume globally that G is a finite group, given in a representation that allows us to test membership in subgroups, compute subgroup orders (and their prime number factorizations), as well as compute a chief series for G. This certainly holds for permutation groups and groups given by a PC presentation, which are the cases for which the algorithm has been implemented. Using matrix group recognition [1] there is no fundamental obstacle to apply it also to matrix groups, though implementation would be harder.

This model allows for the test of subgroup membership and computation of subgroup orders in factor groups of G. In that it is nominally stronger than the model of a black-box group (in which it is only possible to test for element equality) that is sometimes used to describe computations in factor groups; however it models the main classes of representations of finite groups on a computer as used today,

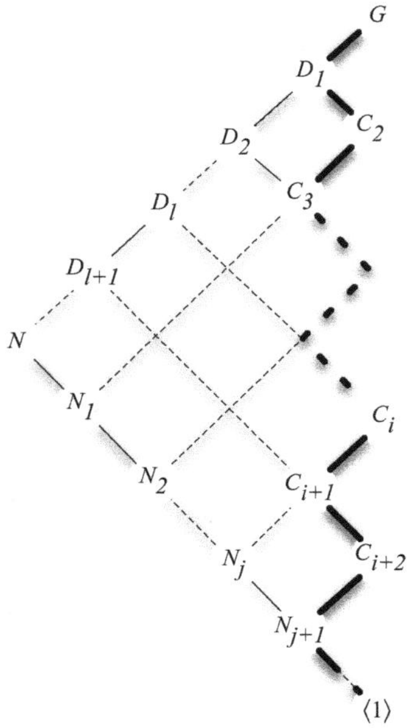

Figure 1: Relation to normal subgroup.

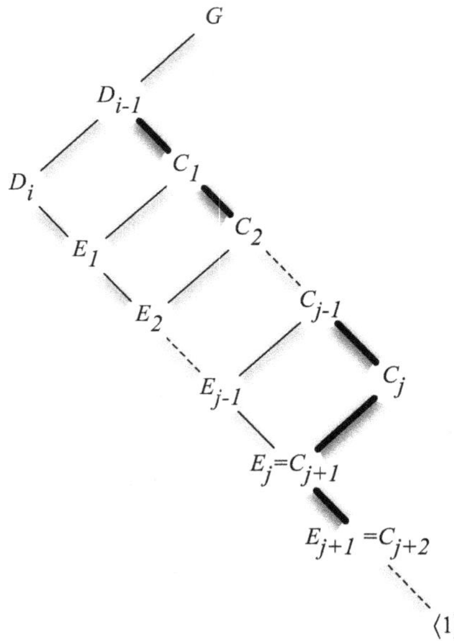

Figure 2: Extension to a single step in the factor group

and avoids technical assumptions (such as the existence of discrete logarithm or element order oracles, or the use of quantum algorithms) that are otherwise sometimes needed in the black-box model.

We identify a series of subgroups $G = C_0 \geq C_1 \geq \cdots \geq C_l = \langle 1 \rangle$ with the set $\{C_i\}$, inclusion providing a natural ordering. (We shall assume that indices are always chosen compatible with inclusion.)

Such a series $\{C_i\}$ is called a *subnormal series* if each subgroup is normal in the previous one, $C_i \lhd C_{i-1}$. It is called a *composition series* if furthermore each factor C_{i-1}/C_i is simple, that is the series is as fine as possible.

If we consider instead the case that all subgroups are normal in G, such a series $\{C_i\}$ is called a *normal series*; if it is maximally refined it is called a *chief series*. In a chief series the subsequent factors C_{i-1}/C_i do not have to be simple, but must be a isomorphic to a direct power of a simple group, that is $C_{i-1}/C_i \cong T_i \times \cdots \times T_i$ with T_i simple. (We say that C_{i-1}/C_i is *characteristically simple*.)

The standard reduction of algorithmic problems in group theory is to consider a normal subgroup $N \lhd G$ and recurse to N and G/N, combining the results in the end.

We now assume that $\{C_i\}$ is a composition series of G and that $N \lhd G$.

A standard exercise in abstract algebra shows that $\{C_i \cap N\}$ forms a composition series for N. (Note that there will be duplication of subgroups, i.e. for some i we have that $C_i \cap N = C_{i+1} \cap N$, though $C_i \neq C_{i+1}$. Considering a series as a set eliminates such duplicates.) Similarly, $\{NC_i/N\}_i$ is a composition series for G/N. As the concatenation of the series NC_i with the series $N \cap C_i$ yields a composition series for G, we easily see that for each i we have that either $NC_i = NC_{i+1}$, or $N \cap C_i = N \cap C_{i+1}$. (See Figure 1)

To see how the enumeration problem reduces, assume that we have classified all composition series for N and for G/N. (The base case of the reduction is that of a characteristically simple group, section 5 describes how to find composition series for these.)

Also assume that we have chosen a particular composition series $N = N_0 \rhd N_1 \rhd \cdots \rhd \langle 1 \rangle$ for N, as well as a particular series of subgroups $G = D_0 \rhd D_i \rhd \cdots \rhd D_k = N$ that induces a composition series for G/N. Our goal now is to determine all composition series $\{C_i\}$ of G such that $\{N \cap C_i\} = \{N_i\}$ and $\{NC_i\} = \{D_i\}$.

We shall construct all these series $\{C_i\}$ in a process of ascending over the series $\{D_i\}$. In each step we assume that the composition series for D_i are known; the base case being the series $\{N_i\}$ for $N = D_k$.

To describe a single step, assume that we have a particular composition series $\{E_j\}$ for D_i and want to find all series $\{C_j\}_j$ for D_{i-1} such that $\{C_j \cap D_i\}_j = \{E_j\}_j$. (Figure 2) As $D_{i-1} \rhd D_i$, the description above shows that there is exactly one step j such that $C_j \cap D_i = C_{j+1} \cap D_i$. We therefore have that $C_{m+1} = E_m$ for $m \geq j$.

For $m \leq j$ we have that $E_m = D_i \cap C_m$ and $C_m = \langle E_m, C_j \rangle$, implying that $E_m \lhd C_m$ and thus $E_m \lhd \langle E_{m-1}, C_m \rangle = C_{m-1}$. Thus in the factor C_{m-1}/E_m, the subgroup C_m/E_m is a normal (as $C_m \lhd C_{m-1}$) complement to E_{m-1}/E_m.

We thus can construct all possible series $\{C_i\}$ in a successive calculation of normal complements, in each step m constructing those series for which $C_m \cap D_i = C_{m+1} \cap D_i$.

We describe this construction in more detail:

Let $C_0 = D_{i-1}$ and take (this will be the series for $j = 0$) the concatenation $C_0 = D_{i-1} \rhd E_0 \rhd E_1 \rhd \cdots \rhd \langle 1 \rangle$. Next, test whether $E_1 \lhd C_0$, if not there are no series for $j > 0$. Otherwise determine all normal complements C_1/E_1 to E_0/E_1 in C_0/E_1. For each such subgroup C_1 we get a series

$C_0 \rhd C_1 \rhd E_1 \rhd \cdots \rhd \langle 1\rangle$; all series for $j = 1$ are obtained this way.

Next, for each of these series, test whether $E_2 \lhd C_1$ and if so determine normal complements C_2/E_2 to E_1/E_2. This yields the series $C_0 \rhd C_1 \rhd C_2 \rhd E_2 \rhd \cdots \rhd \langle 1\rangle$ for $j = 2$.

We continue in the same way for increasing j as long as $E_j \lhd C_{j-1}$, building series that coincide with $\{E_m\}$ for $m \geq j$.

All composition series for D_{i-1} that intersect with D_i in $\{E_j\}$ are obtained this way, iterating over all series for D_i thus yields all composition series for D_{i-1}.

The only task required for combining these series is the construction of normal complements in a factor group that has composition length two. We describe how to do this in section 3.

If we want to determine composition series only up to the action of some group $\leq \mathrm{Aut}(G)$ a further fusion becomes necessary. We shall describe how to do this in section 4.

3. NORMAL COMPLEMENTS

In this section we describe the required computation of normal complements. While this can be done by cohomological methods from [7], these become overly costly given the frequency of calculations required. Instead we shall describe direct methods for the required case of factor groups of composition length two.

For ease of description we denote this factor group by H and the normal subgroup to be complemented by $A \lhd H$ though in practice both are factors of subgroups of G and as described in [14] we work with representatives of elements and pre-images of subgroups.

THEOREM 1. *Let H be a finite group and $A \lhd H$ such that A and H/A are both nontrivial simple groups. Then normal complements to A in H are given by the following classification:*

a) *If A is not abelian there is at most one complement, namely $C_H(A)$ if this group is nontrivial. If H/A also is not abelian, such a complement always exists.*

b) *If A is abelian but H/A not, there is at most one complement, namely H', this group is a complement if and only if $H' \neq H$.*

(The remaining two cases now assume that both A and H/A are abelian, that is cyclic of prime order.)

c) *If $|A| \neq |H/A|$ there is exactly one complement and this is the case if and only if $[H, A] = \langle 1\rangle$.*

d) *Otherwise there are either 0, or q, normal complements (where $q = |A|$). The case of no complements occurring exactly when $|x| = q^2$ for one (and thus for all) $x \notin A$.*

PROOF. The existence of a normal complement B is equivalent to $H = A \times B$ (with $B \cong H/A$).
a) If A is not abelian we have that $C_H(A) \cap A = \langle 1\rangle$. If $C_H(A)$ is not trivial it thus is a complement (since $A \neq AC_H(A) \lhd H$ and H/A is simple). Vice versa, if a normal complement B exists, we must have that $B = C_H(A)$. By the proof of Schreier's conjecture (see [9]) the outer automorphism group $\mathrm{Out}(A)$ is solvable for a simple nonabelian A. Thus if H/A is nonsolvable, every element of H must induce an inner automorphism which shows that in this case $C_H(A)$ is not trivial.
In all other cases A is abelian, $|A| = q$ prime, and thus it is a necessary condition for the existence of a normal complement that $A \leq Z(H)$.
b) If H/A is simple nonabelian, then $AH' = H$. Thus if $H' \neq H$ we must have that $A \cap H' = \langle 1\rangle$ and H' is a normal complement to A. Vice versa if $B \cong H/A$ is a normal complement we have that $H' = (A \times B)' = B' = B$.
In the remaining cases we have that both A and H/A are abelian. Thus a necessary condition for the existence of normal complements is that $A \leq Z(H)$, that is $[H, A] = \langle 1\rangle$. But then $H/Z(H)$ is cyclic and thus H is abelian. We shall assume this now.
c) If $|A| \neq |H/A|$ the complements to A are simply p-Sylow subgroups for $p = |H/A|$. As H is abelian there is only one such subgroup.
d) Otherwise $|H| = q^2$ for q prime. If $H \cong C_{q^2}$ there is no complement, if $H \cong C_q \times C_q$ there are q complements, all normal. □

We give more details on how to find these complements in practice:

3.1 Nonabelian normal subgroup

In this section we assume that A is simple nonabelian. We may assume that we know the isomorphism type of A, for example from recognition performed when setting up the initial data structure for G, following [3, 16].

Assume initially that H is a direct product. Our task is to find a nontrivial element $c \in C_H(A)$. (One such element is sufficient, as $C_H(A) \cong H/A$ is assumed to be simple and thus minimally normal. Therefore $C_H(A) = \langle c\rangle_H$ will be the normal closure in H of $\langle c\rangle$.)

The basic process of decomposing a group into direct factors in a black-box context is already described in [2]. As we do not know whether the group is a direct product we describe a variant that also can prove the non-existence of a direct product decomposition. (Note that in some cases we know a priori that H must be a direct product, for example if $[H{:}A]$ is not prime, or if it does not divide $|\mathrm{Out}(A)|$.)

To find centralizing elements we set up the following probabilistic process: Choose one $x \in H$, $x \notin A$. By taking a suitable power of x we may assume without loss of generality that $x^p \in A$ for a prime $p \mid [H{:}A]$.

Now repeatedly choose (pseudo-)random elements $r \in A$ (using for example [6]) and test whether $|rx| = pq$ with $\gcd(p, q) = 1$. In this case, form $c = (rx)^q$ and test whether the nontrivial element c centralizes A. If so, it is a centralizing element as desired.

To see that this process is likely to succeed, write $x = (a, b)$ with $a \in A$, $b \in C_H(A)$. We know that $|b| = |Ax| = p$. If $r \in A$ is chosen randomly, then $rx = (ra, b)$ with ra ranging randomly over A.

But by [4] there is a fair probability w that a random element of A is of order coprime to p. (Concretely, [4] prove that $w \geq 2/29$ for a sporadic A; $w \geq 26/(27\sqrt{n})$ for $A \cong A_n$; $w \geq 1/(2n)$ if A is classical with a natural projective action in dimension $n - 1$; and $w \geq 1/15$ for sporadic A.)

Thus with probability w we have that $|ra| = q$ is coprime to p. In this case $|rx| = pq$ with $\gcd(p, q) = 1$ and

$c = (rx)^q = \left((ra)^q, b^b\right) = (1, b^q)$ is a nontrivial element of $C_H(A)$.

If $C_G(H)$ is not trivial, this test will succeed with probability $1-(1-w)^k$ after k iterations.

If this test fails, however, we need to prove that A has no normal complement in H. We may assume here that $[H{:}A] = p$ is prime, as otherwise the existence of a normal complement is guaranteed. What we have to show is that $H \cong A.C_p \leq \mathrm{Aut}(A)$.

Generically, this amounts to recognizing the structure of H: For example one could consider the conjugation action of H on A, and use black-box recognition to test whether the group is isomorphic to A. In practice one often can do much better:

The process of searching for a centralizing element described above produces elements rx that are chosen randomly over one coset of A. As we assume that H/A is of prime order, the orders of rx thus sample the element orders of H outside A.

If $|rx|$ is an order that does not arise in A, and the power $(rx)^q$ used above does not centralize A we can deduce that H is not a direct product. This is because $(a,b) \in A\times C_p$ has element order $|(a,b)| = \mathrm{lcm}(|a|, |b|)$. This differs from the order of a only if $|b| = p$ is coprime to $|a|$, but this is exactly the case in which the order-p power is $(1,b)$ and centralizes A.

An inspection of nonabelian simple groups up to order $2\cdot 10^{13}$ (i.e. groups smaller than $G_2(9)$) reveals that (excluding groups of the form $\mathrm{L}_2(q)$ which always have such elements) 104 of the 117 simple groups A have such elements in every extension in $\mathrm{Aut}(A)$, all with ratio at least 1/200. The only exceptions are (all for $p=2$): $U_3(3)$, $L_3(5)$, $U_3(7)$, $S_4(8)$, $L_3(17)$, $U_3(19)$, $U_5(3)$, $L_3(29)$, $U_3(31)$, $L_3(41)$, $O_8^-(3)$, and $PSU(3,43)$.

Even if element orders do not allow to recognize the case of not being a direct product, the group H arises in our situation not on its own, but as a subfactor of the larger group G. As part of the initial setup (section 6) we might have set up already (e.g. as in [12]) an epimorphism from G onto $G/\mathrm{Rad}(G)$ with the image that lies in (a direct product) of groups of type $\mathrm{Aut}(T)\wr S_m$ for T simple nonabelian. Then H is not to be a direct product if and only if the image of H under this homomorphism has order $|A|\cdot p$ and does not lie in the subgroup $T\wr S_m$. This is readily tested.

3.2 Abelian normal subgroup

If $A \cong C_p$ is abelian and H/A is simple nonabelian then A must be central, as H/A has no nontrivial representation in dimension 1. The two possible extensions thus are either the direct product, or (a quotient of) a covering group of H/A. The latter can only happen if $|A|$ divides the multiplier order $|M(H/A)|$. (Again we may assume we know the isomorphism type of H/A, thus we know this multiplier order.)

By theorem 1, we know that $H = A\times H'$ if it is a direct product. To find this decomposition (and test the condition) we form one nontrivial random commutator c and let $C = \langle c\rangle_H \leq H'$ be the normal closure of this commutator. If $A \leq C$ then no normal complement to A exists (as every commutator would have trivial A-part and thus lie in such a complement). Otherwise $C \lhd H$ with $AC = H$ and $A\cap C = \langle 1\rangle$, thus it is a normal complement.

To avoid calculating normal closures unnecessarily, we observe that many cases of not being a direct product can be deduced by element orders alone:

Definition 2. Let $A \leq Z(H)$. We call $x \in H$ *order-increasing* if $|Ax|$ is a multiple of $|A|$ and $|x| \neq |Ax|$.

Many covers of simple groups contain such elements, for example in $\mathrm{SL}_2(p)$ (cover of $\mathrm{PSL}_2(p)$) the element $\begin{pmatrix} 0 & 1 \\ -1 & 0 \end{pmatrix}$ is order-increasing.

LEMMA 3. *If $H = A\times B$ then H contains no order-increasing element.*

PROOF. Assume that if $x = (a,b) \in H$ fulfills that $|Ax| = |b|$ is a multiple of $|A|$. Then $|x| = |Ax|$, since $x^{|Ax|} = x^{|b|} = (a^{|b|}, b^{|b|}) = 1$, as by assumption $|b|$ is a multiple of $|a|$). □

We thus initially test the generators of H (and a couple of random elements) whether they are order-increasing. If such an element is found, H cannot be a direct product, and we do not need to calculate a normal closure of a commutator.

If both A and H/A are abelian but $|A| \neq [H{:}A]$ we first test that A is central in H (if not, H is not a direct product). If so, we obtain a complement by choosing $x \in H$, $x \notin A$ and forming $C = \langle x^{|A|}\rangle$.

Finally, if A and H/A are abelian and $|A| = [H{:}A]$ we take $x \in H$, $x \notin A$. If $|x| = p = |A|$ we have that H is a vector space with basis $\{x, a\}$ (where $A = \langle a\rangle$), The elements $x\cdot a^k$, $0 \leq k < p$ then are generators for the normal complements.

If on the other hand $|x| \neq p$, then $H \cong C_{p^2}$ is not a direct product.

3.3 Cost

The required computations for finding all normal complements are (in a Las Vegas model, i.e the calculation might fail with bounded probability, in which case it can be repeated with new random selections) one of the following:

- A constant number of element order computations in a factor group.
- Computation of a derived subgroup.
- Constructive recognition of black-box simple groups (in the fall-back case for identifying outer automorphism actions).

The first two are known to be polynomial time in the size of the input. The third is (possibly Monte-Carlo, possibly assuming a discrete logarithm oracle) polynomial time for most classes of simple groups groups [8, 15, 13], with the exception of composition factors of type ${}^2G_2(q)$. One can of course dispense with these qualifiers if the size of nonabelian composition factors is bounded.

4. ACTION ON SERIES

If we want to construct series only up to the action of a group A (for example the full, or the inner automorphism group) we associate with every (partial) series a stabilizer (namely the intersection of the A-normalizers of the subgroups in the series). We also replace chief factors by A-invariant normal factors. These still must be characteristically simple.

If the normal subgroup $N \lhd G$ is chosen to be invariant under A, then the stabilizer of a subgroup X also stabilizes NX and $N \cap X$, thus in the above construction process we may assume that the acting group is stabilizing the series $\{N_i\}$ in N and $\{D_i\}$ in the factor group. The construction process described above is thus compatible with maintaining series stabilizers.

Now consider the effect of a group action on the combination process. Its basic step is that, for a given j, we have a series (figure 2) $D_{i-1}, C_1, C_2, \ldots, C_j, E_j = C_{j+1}, E_{j+1}, \ldots$, with an associated stabilizer S, and we are looking for series that differ in the group E_j by classifying (normal) complements to E_j/E_{j+1} in C_j/E_{j+1}. The series stabilizer S will act on these complements. (In cases a,b,c) of Theorem 1 there is at most one complement, which automatically is stabilized if it exists. In case d) the action is a projective action on the vector space C_j/E_{j+1}.)

Representatives of the S-orbits then correspond to A-classes of series that arose from the prior series, with complement stabilizers becoming stabilizers for the new series.

5. ELEMENTARY FACTORS

To utilize the reduction of Section 2 we need to obtain the composition series of the chief factors of G (or, in the case of an A-action, A-invariant normal factors, up to A action). Such factors are characteristically simple, i.e. they are direct powers of simple groups of one isomorphism type.

Again for ease of description we describe the construction in a factor group, that is we consider $H \cong T \times \cdots \times T$ for T simple, possibly with a (possibly trivial) action of a group A on H.

5.1 Abelian Case

If T (and thus H) is abelian, a composition series for H is equivalent to a flag, i.e. a sequence of increasing subspaces of dimensions $1, 2, 3 \ldots$. We construct these flags in increasing dimension: First determine the A-orbits on 1-dimensional subspaces of H. For each such subspace U we consider recursively the factor space H/U with action of $S = \mathrm{Stab}_A(U)$ and determine S-representatives of the flags on H/U. For each such flag $U_2/U, U_3/U, \ldots$ for H/U we have that $U, U_2, U_3, \ldots$ is a flag for H. Collecting these flags for all representatives U produces representatives of the A-orbits on flags and thus of the A-orbits of composition series.

5.2 Nonabelian Case

If T is nonabelian then the only normal subgroups of $H = T^m$ are the obvious direct products of subsets of the copies of T. Applying the same statement to these normal subgroups we find that any subnormal subgroup of H must be one of these normal subgroups. Thus the composition series of H are parameterized (indicating in each step which direct factor is added to the subgroup) by the permutations of $\{1, \ldots, m\}$.

The action of A permutes the m direct factors, and thus their indices. Let $\varphi\colon A \to S_m$ be the corresponding homomorphism. On permutations, representing subnormal series, this action is by right multiplication by A^φ. Representatives of the orbits are obtained as representatives for the left cosets of A^φ in S_m, in each case the stabilizer of the series is the kernel of φ.

6. COMBINING THE STEPS

Assume that a group G as well as a group $A \leq \mathrm{Aut}(G)$ are given. To describe the A-orbits on composition series for G we adapt the standard "Trivial-Fitting" (or "Solvable Radical") method [2, 5]: Consider the series $G \rhd Pker \rhd S^* \rhd R\langle 1 \rangle$ of characteristic subgroups, where R is the solvable radical (the largest solvable normal subgroup), $S^*/R = \mathrm{Soc}(G/R)$ and $Pker$ is the kernel of the permutation action of G on the direct factors of S^*/R. We refine this series to a series of A-invariant normal subgroups $G = N_0 > N_1 > \cdots > N_{k-1} > N_k = \langle 1 \rangle$ with N_i/N_{i+1} elementary. As most calculations involving the action of A happen in elementary abelian factors, and as the composition process itself extends *up*, it seems to be most plausible to work *ascending* along this series with decreasing k, starting with $N_{k-1}/\langle 1 \rangle$.

In each step we assume we have all A-classes of composition series of N_i. For each such class we have a representative and a series stabilizer.

For each different N_i-series stabilizer S, we determine the S-classes of series through the elementary factor N_{i-1}/N_i. We then use the process from section 2 to form all combinations of these series with those N_i-series for which S is the stabilizer.

As the examples below show, the number of composition series can be easily exponential (or worse) in the size of the input. The algorithm therefore cannot be in polynomial time. However each new series is the result of one complement computation, and the total number of complement computations (including those that do not lead to new series) for each series is the number of composition steps. Since each complement calculation is (with qualifiers as given in section 3.3) polynomial time, the algorithm is therefore overall of polynomial delay.

6.1 Implementation and Examples

The algorithm has been implemented by the author in the system GAP [10].

Table 1 gives examples of calculations of series. Series were calculated under the action of the group itself (column **G-Orbits**), respectively under the full automorphism group (column **Aut(G)**). Timings are in seconds on a 3.7 GHz Quad-Core Intel Xeon E5 Mac Pro (Late 2013). Groups were represented by a PC presentation or as permutation group. Names $\mathrm{t}_d\mathrm{n}_x$ or $\mathrm{s}_d\mathrm{n}_x$ are from the transitive, respectively the small groups library. Using the indices of the stabilizers in the acting group, the total number of series **NrSeries** was computed. An arrow $\to$ indicates that the automorphism group provides no further fusion.

One notes that runtime is roughly proportional to the number of composition series representatives (which is as good as one might hope for). Calculations under the automorphism group take longer for the need to work with stabilizers that were represented as groups of automorphisms.

Group	Order	NrSeries	G-Orbits	time	Aut(G)-Orb.	time
$\mathrm{t}_{30}\mathrm{n}_{3000}$	$2^{10}3^{4}5^{3}$	318	53	0.5	49	3.2
$3^5 \rtimes \mathrm{GL}_5(3)$	$2^{10}3^{15}5 \cdot 11^{2}13$	503360	2	1.3	$\to$	
$3^5 \rtimes \mathrm{GL}_5(3) \times \mathrm{A}_5^2$	$2^{14}3^{17}5^{3}11^{2}13$	36241920	144	54	72	50
$3^6 \rtimes \mathrm{SP}_6(3)$	$2^{10}3^{15}5 \cdot 7 \cdot 13$	91611520	15	6.5	$\to$	
$\mathrm{Weyl}(\mathrm{F}_4)$	$2^{7}3^{2}$	13482	377	0.25	204	0.5
$\mathrm{s}_{1152}\mathrm{n}_{157000}$	$2^{7}3^{2}$	116802	24998	13.5	12000	17
$2^{4+1+1} \rtimes \mathrm{A}_5$	$2^{8}3 \cdot 5$	645435	12339	41	2214	15
$(3^5.2) : \mathrm{S}_5 = \mathrm{t}_{30}\mathrm{n}_{1254}$	$2^{4}3^{6}5$	1015040	13296	34	7816	34
$\mathrm{GL}_2(5) \wr \mathrm{S}_2$	$2^{11}3^{2}5^{2}$	2314	928	4	794	9
$\mathrm{SL}_2(5) \wr \mathrm{D}_8$	$2^{15}3^{4}5^{4}$	143160	17895	96	17641	504
$\mathrm{GU}_3(3) \wr \mathrm{S}_2$	$2^{15}3^{6}7^{2}$	890	388	7	257	75
$\mathrm{PGU}_3(3) \wr \mathrm{D}_8$	$2^{23}3^{12}7^{4}$	200	25	3.6	$\to$	
$\mathrm{s}_{256}\mathrm{n}_{100}$	2^8	22287	4124	3.5	3451	11
$\mathrm{s}_{256}\mathrm{n}_{6000}$	2^8	90651	17763	16	10042	37
$\mathrm{s}_{256}\mathrm{n}_{10000}$	2^8	429219	212661	226	94964	478
$\mathrm{s}_{256}\mathrm{n}_{20000}$	2^8	124875	57017	50	49749	147
$\mathrm{s}_{256}\mathrm{n}_{56000}$	2^8	14252283	5345253	42433[a]	621047	3216

[a] identifying duplicate subgroups, at extra cost, for memory reasons.

Table 1: Examples and Runtimes

7. ACKNOWLEDGMENTS

The author is would like to thank Hoon Hong for suggesting the problem.

The author's work has been supported in part by Simons Foundation Collaboration Grant 244502 which is gratefully acknowledged.

8. REFERENCES

[1] H. Bäärnhielm, D. Holt, C. R. Leedham-Green, and E. A. O'Brien. A practical model for computation with matrix groups. *J. Symbolic Comput.*, 68(part 1):27–60, 2015.

[2] L. Babai and R. Beals. A polynomial-time theory of black box groups. I. In C. M. Campbell, E. F. Robertson, N. Ruskuc, and G. C. Smith, editors, *Groups St Andrews 1997 in Bath*, volume 260/261 of *London Mathematical Society Lecture Note Series*, pages 30–64. Cambridge University Press, 1999.

[3] L. Babai, W. M. Kantor, P. P. Pálfy, and Á. Seress. Black-box recognition of finite simple groups of Lie type by statistics of element orders. *J. Group Theory*, 5(4):383–401, 2002.

[4] L. Babai, P. P. Pálfy, and J. Saxl. On the number of p-regular elements in finite simple groups. *LMS J. Comput. Math.*, 12:82–119, 2009.

[5] J. Cannon, B. Cox, and D. Holt. Computing the subgroup lattice of a permutation group. *J. Symbolic Comput.*, 31(1/2):149–161, 2001.

[6] F. Celler, C. R. Leedham-Green, S. H. Murray, A. C. Niemeyer, and E. A. O'Brien. Generating random elements of a finite group. *Comm. Algebra*, 23(13):4931–4948, 1995.

[7] F. Celler, J. Neubüser, and C. R. B. Wright. Some remarks on the computation of complements and normalizers in soluble groups. *Acta Appl. Math.*, 21:57–76, 1990.

[8] H. Dietrich, C. R. Leedham-Green, and E. A. O'Brien. Effective black-box constructive recognition of classical groups. *J. Algebra*, 421:460–492, 2015.

[9] W. Feit. Some consequences of the classification of finite simple groups. In *The Santa Cruz Conference on Finite Groups (Univ. California, Santa Cruz, Calif., 1979)*, volume 37 of *Proc. Sympos. Pure Math.*, pages 175–181. Amer. Math. Soc., Providence, R.I., 1980.

[10] The GAP Group, `http://www.gap-system.org`. *GAP – Groups, Algorithms, and Programming, Version 4.7.4*, 2014.

[11] D. F. Holt, B. Eick, and E. A. O'Brien. *Handbook of Computational Group Theory*. Discrete Mathematics and its Applications. Chapman & Hall/CRC, Boca Raton, FL, 2005.

[12] A. Hulpke. Computing conjugacy classes of elements in matrix groups. *J. Algebra*, 387:268–286, 2013.

[13] S. Jambor, M. Leuner, A. C. Niemeyer, and W. Plesken. Fast recognition of alternating groups of unknown degree. *J. Algebra*, 392:315–335, 2013.

[14] W. M. Kantor and E. M. Luks. Computing in quotient groups. In *Proceedings of the 22nd ACM Symposium on Theory of Computing, Baltimore*, pages 524–563. ACM Press, 1990.

[15] W. M. Kantor and K. Magaard. Black box exceptional groups of Lie type II. *J. Algebra*, 421:524–540, 2015.

[16] M. W. Liebeck and E. A. O'Brien. Finding the characteristic of a group of Lie type. *J. London Math. Soc. (2)*, 75(3):741–754, 2007.

Computing Hypergeometric Solutions of Second Order Linear Differential Equations using Quotients of Formal Solutions

Erdal Imamoglu*
Department of Mathematics
Florida State University
Tallahassee, FL 32306, USA
eimamogl@math.fsu.edu

Mark van Hoeij*
Department of Mathematics
Florida State University
Tallahassee, FL 32306, USA
hoeij@math.fsu.edu

ABSTRACT

Let L be a second order differential equation with coefficients in $\mathbb{C}(x)$. The goal of this paper is to find solutions of L in the form

$$\exp(\int r\,dx) \cdot {}_2F_1(a_1, a_2; b_1; f) \qquad (1)$$

where $r, f \in \overline{\mathbb{Q}(x)}$, and $a_1, a_2, b_1 \in \mathbb{Q}$.

Categories and Subject Descriptors

I.1.2 [**Symbolic and Algebraic Manipulation**]: Algorithms; G.4 [**Mathematics of Computing**]: Mathematical Software

General Terms

Algorithms

Keywords

Symbolic Computation, Differential Equations, Closed Form Solutions, Hypergeometric Solutions

1. INTRODUCTION

Consider a second order homogenous linear differential equation with rational function coefficients $A_i \in \mathbb{C}(x)$

$$A_2 y'' + A_1 y' + A_0 y = 0 \qquad (2)$$

which corresponds to the differential operator

$$L = A_2\partial^2 + A_1\partial + A_0 \in \mathbb{C}(x)[\partial]$$

where $\partial = \frac{d}{dx}$. Then (2) is the equation $L(y) = 0$.

This paper gives a (heuristic[1]) algorithm to find a solution of (2) in the form of (1). This form is both more and less general than in prior work. Less general in the sense that papers [2], [7] considered 3 transformations instead of the 2 in section 2.3 and more general in the sense that prior work was restricted to either a specific number of singularities (4 in [9] and 5 in [6]) or specific degrees (degree 3 in [7] and a degree-2 decomposition in [2]). Moreover, our program can also find algebraic functions f in (1) (although at the moment this requires additional user inputs).

We assume that (2) has no Liouvillian solutions (this implies it is irreducible), otherwise one can solve it with Kovacic's algorithm [5]. The goal of this paper is: *Given a second order operator $L_{inp} \in \mathbb{C}(x)[\partial]$, regular singular[2] without Liouvillian solutions, find a solution of form (1) if it exists.* This means finding $a_1, a_2, b_1 \in \mathbb{Q}$ and finding transformations (sections 2.3 and 3.2) that send L_B to the input equation L_{inp}, where L_B is the minimal operator of ${}_2F_1(a_1, a_2; b_1; x)$.

Two crucial steps of this task are: (1) find (candidates for) a_1, a_2, b_1 and (2) find the pullback function f (after that, finding r becomes easy). Given a_1, a_2, b_1 (or equivalently, L_B), by comparing *quotients of formal solutions* of L_B and L_{inp}, we can compute f *if we know the value of a certain constant* c. We have no direct formula for c; to obtain it with a finite computation, we take a prime number ℓ. Then, for each $c \in \{1, \ldots, \ell - 1\}$ we try to compute f modulo ℓ. If this succeeds, then we lift f modulo a power of ℓ, and try reconstruction.

Example 1. **Rational Pullback Function**

$$L = 21x(x-1)(x+1)\partial^2 + (38x^2 - 6x - 14)\partial + \frac{20x - 5}{7}$$

has a ${}_2F_1$-type solution

$$Y(x) = \exp\big(\int r\,dx\big) \cdot {}_2F_1\left(\frac{5}{42}, \frac{11}{42}; \frac{2}{3}; f\right)$$

where

$$\exp(\int r\,dx) = (x+1)^{-\frac{5}{21}} \quad \text{and} \quad f = \frac{4x}{(x+1)^2} \qquad (3)$$

Here the degree of the pullback function f is 2. We can find this solution with the quotient method in remark 1 below. In the quotient method, the parameters a_1, a_2, b_1 (here $\frac{5}{42}, \frac{11}{42}, \frac{2}{3}$) and the degree of f (here 2) are taken as an input. We implemented section 3.2 which computes candidates for

*Supported by NSF grant 1319547.

[1] For completeness we still need a theorem for "good primes" and address remark 2.

[2] For details see the section 2.1.

ISSAC'15, July 6–9, 2015, Bath, United Kingdom.

DOI: http://dx.doi.org/10.1145/2755996.2756651.

a_1, a_2, b_1 and $\deg(f)$ so that a_1, a_2, b_1, and $\deg(f)$ no longer need to be part of the input.

Remark 1. **The Quotient Method**

The hypergeometric function ${}_2F_1(\frac{5}{42}, \frac{11}{42}; \frac{2}{3}, x)$ is a solution of the operator

$$L_B = \partial^2 + \frac{(29\,x - 14)}{21x\,(x-1)}\partial + \frac{55}{1764\,x\,(x-1)}.$$

L_B has two solutions at $x = 0$:

$$y_1(x) = {}_2F_1\left(\frac{5}{41}, \frac{11}{42}; \frac{2}{3}, x\right) = 1 + \frac{55}{1176}x + \dots,$$

$$y_2(x) = x^{\frac{1}{3}}\left(1 + \frac{475}{2352}x + \frac{1941325}{19361664}x^2 + \dots\right).$$

The so-called *exponents* of L_B at $x = 0$ are the exponents of x in the dominant terms of y_1 and y_2, so the exponents are $e_{0,1} = 0$ and $e_{0,2} = \frac{1}{3}$. The minimal operator for $y(f)$ has these solutions at $x = 0$:

$$y_1(f) = 1 + \frac{55}{294}x - \frac{4939}{86436}x^2 + \frac{16135823}{304946208}x^3 + \dots,$$

$$y_2(f) = c_f \cdot x^{\frac{1}{3}}\left(1 + \frac{83}{588}x + \frac{6805}{1210104}x^2 + \dots\right)$$

for some constant c_f that depends on f. Here the exponents are again $0, \frac{1}{3}$. This is because $x = 0$ is a root of f with multiplicity $e = 1$. Let

$$Y_1(x) = \exp(\int r\,dx) y_1(f) = 1 - \frac{5}{98}x + \frac{439}{9604}x^2 + \dots, \quad (4)$$

$$Y_2(x) = \exp(\int r\,dx) y_2(f) = c_f \cdot x^{\frac{1}{3}}\left(1 - \frac{19}{196}x + \dots\right). \quad (5)$$

(4) and (5) form a basis of solutions of L. Here $\exp(\int r\,dx)$ is as the same as in (3). Denote the quotients of the formal solutions of L_B and L by

$$q = \frac{y_1(x)}{y_2(x)}, \qquad Q = \frac{Y_1(x)}{Y_2(x)} = \frac{y_1(f)}{y_2(f)} = q(f),$$

respectively. It follows that $q^{-1}(Q(x))$ gives an expansion of f at $x = 0$. Given enough terms we can reconstruct f. However, the following questions occur:

- Q1. How many terms are needed to reconstruct f? This is equivalent to finding a degree bound for f.
- Q2. How to find the parameters a_1, a_2, b_1?
- Q3. The exponents $0, \frac{1}{3}$ of L at $x = 0$ only determine $\frac{Y_1}{Y_2}$ up to a constant factor (see remark 3 in section 2.3). This means $\frac{y_1(f)}{y_2(f)}$ is only known up to a constant c_f. How to find this constant?
- Q4. What if L has logarithmic solutions at $x = 0$?
- Q5. What if f is an algebraic function?

We will address these questions in section 3, which contains the main new results in this paper (the method illustrated in this remark was already used in [9, section 5.1]).

Example 2. **Algebraic Pullback Function**

$$L = \partial^2 + \frac{1}{4}\frac{x^4 - 44\,x^3 + 1206\,x^2 - 44\,x + 1}{(x^2 - 34\,x + 1)^2\,x^2}$$

has a ${}_2F_1$-type solution

$$Y(x) = \exp(-\frac{1}{2}\int r\,dx)\,{}_2F_1(\frac{1}{3}, \frac{2}{3}; 1; f)$$

where $r =$

$$\frac{-x^5 + 22\,x^4 - 55\,x^3 - 343\,x^2 + 6\,x\left(x^2 - 7\,x + 1\right)\sqrt{x^2 - 34\,x + 1} + 58\,x - 1}{x\left(x^4 - 41\,x^3 + 240\,x^2 - 41\,x + 1\right)(x+1)}$$

and $f =$

$$-\frac{1}{2}\,\frac{-1 - 30\,x + 24\,x^2 - x^3 + (x^2 - 7\,x + 1)\sqrt{x^2 - 34\,x + 1}}{1 + 3\,x + 3\,x^2 + x^3}.$$

Here the pullback function f is an algebraic function. The algorithm given in this paper can find this solution.

Equations with such solutions are remarkably common, for instance in the OEIS, the *Online Encyclopedia of Integer Sequences* (`oeis.org`). The implementations of Fang [2] and Kunwar [6] solve many but not all such equations, which forms the motivation for this work.

Remark 2. Our current implementation of recovering pullback functions should terminate if there is a pullback function in $\mathbb{Q}(x)$. If there is a pullback in $\overline{\mathbb{Q}(x)}$ but not in $\mathbb{Q}(x)$, without additional inputs, the current version of our program may enter an infinite loop.

2. PRELIMINARIES

2.1 Differential Operators

Let $L = \sum_{i=0}^{n} a_i \partial^i \in \mathbb{C}(x)[\partial]$. A point $p \in \mathbb{C}$ is called a *singularity* of L if it is a zero of the leading coefficient of L or a pole of any other coefficients of L. The point $p = \infty$ is called a singularity if $p = 0$ is a singularity of $L_{1/x}$. Here $L_{1/x}$ is the differential operator obtained from L via a change of variables $x \mapsto \frac{1}{x}$ (note: $x \mapsto f$ sends ∂ to $\frac{1}{f'}\partial$). If $x = p$ is not a singularity, it is called a *regular point* of L. A singularity $p \in \mathbb{C}$ is called a *regular singularity* if $(x-p)^i \frac{a_{n-i}}{a_n}$ is analytic at $x = p$ for $1 \le i \le n-1$. The point $p = \infty$ is a regular singularity if $p = 0$ is a regular singularity of $L_{1/x}$. The differential operator L is said to be *regular singular* if all singularities of L are regular singular.

The *local parameter* of a point $p = x \in \mathbb{C} \cup \{\infty\}$ is defined by $t_p = x - p$ if $x \neq \infty$, and $t_p = \frac{1}{x}$ otherwise. The exponents $e_{p,1}$ and $e_{p,2}$ at $x = p$ are the powers of t_p in the dominant terms of the formal solutions at $x = p$, as illustrated in remark 1. In this paper we restrict to rational exponents. The *exponent difference* of L at $x = p$ is $\Delta(L, p) = |e_{p,1} - e_{p,2}|$. If a formal solution at $x = p$ involves a logarithm (a logarithmic singularity), then $\Delta(L, p)$ must be an integer [11, 12].

2.2 Gauss Hypergeometric Function

Let $a_1, a_2, b_1 \in \mathbb{Q}$. The operator $L_B = x(1-x)\partial^2 + (b_1 - (a_1 + a_2 + 1)x)\partial - a_1 a_2$ is called *Gauss hypergeometric differential operator (GHDO)*. The solution space has dimension 2 because the order is 2. One of the solutions at $x = 0$ is the *Gauss hypergeometric function*, denoted by ${}_2F_1$, defined by the Gauss hypergeometric series

$${}_2F_1(a_1, a_2; b_1; x) = \sum_{k=0}^{\infty} \frac{(a_1)_k (a_2)_k}{(b_1)_k k!} x^k.$$

Here $(\lambda)_k$ denotes the *Pochammer symbol*. It is defined as $(\lambda)_k = \lambda(\lambda+1)\ldots(\lambda+k-1)$ and $(\lambda)_0 = 1$. L_B has three regular singularities: $x=0$, $x=1$, and $x=\infty$ with exponents $\{0, 1-b_1\}$, $\{0, b_1-a_1-a_2\}$, and $\{a_1, a_2\}$ respectively. We denote the exponent differences as $\alpha_0 = |1-b_1|, \alpha_1 = |b_1-a_1-a_2|, \alpha_\infty = |a_1-a_2|$. Let d_i be ∞ if $\alpha_i \in \mathbb{Z}$, and the denominator of α_i if $\alpha_i \in \mathbb{Q}-\mathbb{Z}$. The so-called Schwarz list [8] classifies a_1, a_2, b_1 for which L_B has Liouvillian solutions. We will only consider a_1, a_2, b_1 for which L_B has no Liouvillian solutions. From the Schwarz list [8] one finds that this is equivalent to $\frac{1}{d_0}+\frac{1}{d_1}+\frac{1}{d_\infty}<1$.

2.3 Transformations and Singularities

Let $L_1, L_2 \in \mathbb{C}(x)[\partial]$ be two differential operators of order 2. We consider the following *transformations* that send solutions of L_1 to solutions of L_2.

1. Change of variables: $y(x) \longrightarrow y(f)$, $f \in \overline{\mathbb{Q}(x)}$. For L this means substituting $(x, \partial) \mapsto (f, \frac{1}{f'}\partial)$.
2. Exp-product: $y(x) \longrightarrow \exp\left(\int r\, dx\right) y(x)$, $r \in \overline{\mathbb{Q}(x)}$. For L this means $\partial \mapsto \partial - r$.

These transformations are denoted by $\xrightarrow{f}_C$ and $\xrightarrow{r}_E$ respectively. A third transformation, called gauge transformation, was allowed in the algorithms in [2] and [6]. We hope to use [4] to reduce an equation L that requires a gauge transformation to an equation $\tilde{L}$ that doesn't.

Transformations can affect singularities and exponents. If a transformation $\xrightarrow{r}_E$ can send a singular point $x=p$ to a regular point $x=p$, then we call $x=p$ a *false singularity*. We denote $\mathrm{Sing}(L_1)$ as the set of singularities of L_1 except these false singularities. A singularity $x=p$ is a false singularity if and only if $x=p$ is not logarithmic and the exponent difference is 1.

If $x=p$ is a singularity of L_1 and if transformation $\xrightarrow{r}_E$ can send L_1 to an equation L_2 for which all solutions of L_2 are analytic at $x=p$, then we call $x=p$ a *removable singularity*. A point $x=p$ is removable if and only if $x=p$ is not logarithmic and the exponent difference is an integer. Non-removable singularities are called *true singularities*. A point $x=p$ is a true singularity if and only if the exponent difference is not an integer *or* $x=p$ is logarithmic.

Remark 3. The quotient method (remark 1 in section 1) can only use true singularities, otherwise $\frac{Y_1}{Y_2}$ would only be known up to a Möbius transformation instead of a constant.

THEOREM 1. *[1] Let the GHDO L_B have exponent differences α_0 at $x=0$, α_1 at $x=1$, and α_∞ at $x=\infty$. Let $L_B \xrightarrow{f}_C L_{inp}$. If $f(p) \in \{0,1,\infty\}$, then L_{inp} has the following exponent difference at $x=p$:*

1. *$\alpha_0 \cdot e_p$ if f has a zero at $x=p$ with multiplicity e_p,*
2. *$\alpha_1 \cdot e_p$ if $f-1$ has a zero at $x=p$ with multiplicity e_p,*
3. *$\alpha_\infty \cdot e_p$ if f has a pole at $x=p$ with order e_p.*

If $f(p) \notin \{0,1,\infty\}$, then f maps p to a regular point of L_B (exponent difference 1). Then the exponent difference of L_{inp} at $x=p$ is $1 \cdot e_p$ where e_p is the ramification index of f at $x=p$ (i.e., $x=p$ is a root of $f(x)-f(p)$ with multiplicity e_p). The Riemann-Hurwitz formula (section 3.1) relates to the sum of all $e_p - 1$ to the degree of f.

3. ALGORITHM

Problem Description: Given a second order linear differential operator $L_{inp} \in \mathbb{C}(x)[\partial]$, irreducible and regular singular, we want to find a ${}_2F_1$-type solution of the differential equation $L_{inp}(y)=0$ of the form of (1). This is equivalent to finding transformations 1 and 2 from a GHDO L_B to L_{inp}. Therefore, we need to find

1. L_B (i.e., find a_1, a_2, b_1),
2. parameters f and r of the change of variables and exp-product transformations such that $L_B \xrightarrow{f}_C \xrightarrow{r}_E L_{inp}$.

The general outline is as follows.

Algorithm Outline: `find_2f1`

Input:

- L_{inp}, a second order differential operator.
- At the moment we only handle coefficients in $\mathbb{Q}(x)$. If f in (1) is algebraic, then our current implementation needs three more inputs which are
  - L_B, a candidate GHDO,
  - a_f, an algebraic degree bound for f,
  - d_f, degree bound for f.

Output:

- A list of basis elements of solutions of L_{inp} in form (1), or an empty list [ ].

1. Try Kovacic's algorithm [5]. If there exists Liouvillian solutions, then return them. The algorithm in [10] computes Liouvillian solutions in form (1) if L_{inp} is irreducible.
2. If L_B, a_f, d_f are not provided in the input, then use section 3.2 (at the moment this only covers rational f's, i.e., $a_f=1$) to compute candidates for L_B and d_f.
3. For a candidate GHDO L_B, compute formal solutions of L_B and L_{inp} at a non-removable singularity (see remark 3 in section 2.3) up to precision $a \geq 2(a_f+1)(d_f+1)+3$. Take the quotients of formal solutions and compute series expansions for q^{-1} and Q (in order to compute $f=q^{-1}(cQ(x))$ in the next step).
4. Choose a good prime number ℓ, and try to find c mod ℓ by looping $c=1,2,\ldots,\ell-1$ as in section 3.3. If no solution is found, then proceed with the next candidate GHDO (if any) in step 3. If no candidates remain, then return an empty list [ ].
5. Compute f mod (x^a, ℓ) and then use Hensel lifting to find f mod higher powers of ℓ. After each lifting try rational reconstruction. If it does not fail, then we have f.
6. Compute the parameter r of the exp-product transformation (section 3.5).
7. Return a basis of ${}_2F_1$-type solutions of L_{inp}.

Step 2 is explained in sections 3.1 and 3.2. Step 3 is the quotient method, see section 3.3 for more. Steps 5 and 6 are explained in sections 3.4 and 3.5 respectively.

Remark 5, section 3.2, section 3.4, and section 3.3.2 provide answers to Q1, Q2, Q3, and Q4 respectively. Remark 7 and section 3.4 answer Q5. Maple codes can be found at [3].

3.1 General Degree Bound

Let X and Y be two algebraic curves with genus g_X and g_Y, and let $f : X \longrightarrow Y$ be a non-constant analytic map. The *Riemann-Hurwitz* formula says

$$2g_X - 2 = \deg(f)(2g_Y - 2) + \sum_{p\in X}(e_p - 1). \quad (6)$$

Here p is a branching point and e_p is its ramification order. In this paper $f : \mathbb{P}^1 \longrightarrow \mathbb{P}^1$ so $g_X = g_Y = 0$ and

$$\sum_{p\in\mathbb{P}^1}(e_p - 1) = 2\deg(f) - 2. \quad (7)$$

In section 3.1.1 and 3.1.2 we compute a degree bound for a rational pullback function f from formula (7). In section 3.1.3 we use it to compute a formula for $\alpha_0 + \alpha_1 + \alpha_\infty$, the sum of the exponent differences of L_B.

3.1.1 Bound for Logarithmic Cases

Let L_B be a GHDO with at least one logarithmic singularity. Assume that $L_B \xrightarrow{f}_C \xrightarrow{r}_E L_{inp}$. Let $d_f = \deg(f)$. The number of elements in the set $T = f^{-1}(\{0, 1, \infty\})$ can be at most $3d_f$.

$$\#T = \sum_{p\in T} 1 = \sum_{p\in T} e_p - (e_p - 1) = 3d_f - \sum_{p\in T}(e_p - 1). \quad (8)$$

From (7), we have

$$0 \le \sum_{p\in T}(e_p - 1) \le \sum_{p\in\mathbb{P}^1}(e_p - 1) = 2d_f - 2$$

where the latter sum is taken over all branching points of f. Hence $d_f + 2 \le \#T \le 3d_f$.

The set of true singularities of L_{inp} is a subset of T and these two sets do not need to be equal. Points in T come from (p comes from s when $f(p) = s$) the singular points $\{0, 1, \infty\}$ of L_B. Such points need not be singular, for instance, if L_B has exponents $0, \frac{1}{3}$ at $x = 0$ and f has a root p of order $e_p = 3$, then the exponents at $x = p$ will be $3 \cdot \{0, \frac{1}{3}\} = \{0, 1\}$ and $x = p$ will be a regular point (a "disappeared singularity"). We define the set of *disappeared singularities* as $T - \mathrm{Sing}(L_{inp})$. Logarithmic singularities do not disappear; if $s \in \{0, 1, \infty\}$ is a logarithmic singularity of L_B, then every point p above s is a logarithmic singularity as well.

Let n_{diss} be the number of disappeared singularities of L_{inp}. For a GHDO with exponent differences $[0, \frac{1}{2}, \frac{1}{3}]$ at $0, 1, \infty$ respectively, $n_{diss} \le \frac{1}{2}d_f + \frac{1}{3}d_f$, with equality if and only if every point above s with exponent difference $\alpha = \frac{1}{2}$, respectively $\alpha = \frac{1}{3}$ disappears (i.e., $e_p = 2$, respectively $e_p = 3$). So, if the total number of true singularities of L_{inp} is n_{true}, then

$$\begin{aligned} n_{true} = \#T - n_{diss} &= \left(3d_f - \sum_{p\in S}(e_p - 1)\right) - n_{diss} \\ &\ge [3d_f - (2d_f - 2)] - n_{diss} = d_f + 2 - n_{diss} \\ &\ge d_f + 2 - \left(\frac{1}{2}d_f + \frac{1}{3}d_f\right) = \frac{1}{6}d_f + 2 \end{aligned}$$

and so

$$d_f \le 6(n_{true} - 2). \quad (9)$$

Inequality (9) is an upper bound for d_f in all cases with at least one logarithmic singularity. This is because $\frac{1}{2}d_f + \frac{1}{3}d_f$ is an upper bound for the number of disappeared singularities in the logarithmic case (the GHDO cannot have two singularities with exponent difference $\frac{1}{2}$ if it is irreducible, this makes $\frac{1}{2}d_f + \frac{1}{3}d_f$ the maximum possible value for n_{diss} in the logarithmic case).

3.1.2 Bound for Non-Logarithmic Cases

In the non-logarithmic case one could have disappeared singularities above all three singularities $\{0, 1, \infty\}$ of the GHDO. The maximal degree bound is achieved at exponent differences $[\frac{1}{2}, \frac{1}{3}, \frac{1}{7}]$. All L_B's with a higher bound such as $[\alpha_0, \alpha_1, \alpha_\infty] = [\frac{1}{2}, \frac{1}{3}, \frac{1}{6}]$, $[\frac{1}{2}, \frac{1}{3}, \frac{1}{5}]$, etc, are either reducible or appear in Schwarz's list [8], which means they have Liouvillian solutions.

The maximum number of disappeared singularities for $[\frac{1}{2}, \frac{1}{3}, \frac{1}{7}]$ is not $(\frac{1}{2} + \frac{1}{3} + \frac{1}{7})d_f$ because that contradicts the formula (7). The maximum number consistent with (7) is

$$\left(\frac{1}{2} + \frac{1}{3}\right)d_f + \frac{1}{7-1}\left(2d_f - 2 - \frac{2-1}{2}d_f - \frac{3-1}{3}d_f\right)$$

and it leads to

$$d_f \le 36\left(n_{true} - \frac{7}{3}\right). \quad (10)$$

We use inequality (10) as an a priori upper bound for d_f for all cases with no logarithmic singularity.

Therefore, an a priori degree bound for a rational pullback function f is

$$d_f \le \begin{cases} 6(n_{true} - 2), & \text{logarithmic case,} \\ 36\left(n_{true} - \frac{7}{3}\right), & \text{non-logarithmic case.} \end{cases} \quad (11)$$

Our algorithm uses this degree bound only as a starting point; additional restrictions are computed during the algorithm that may lower the degree.

3.1.3 Riemann-Hurwitz Type Formula

The differential operators L_B and L_{inp} are in $\mathbb{C}(x)[\partial]$, i.e., they are defined on $\mathbb{P}^1$. The function field of $\mathbb{P}^1$ is $\mathbb{C}(\mathbb{P}^1) \cong \mathbb{C}(x)$. Denote $D_{\mathbb{C}(\mathbb{P}^1)} = \mathbb{C}(x)[\partial]$. So $L_B, L_{inp} \in D_{\mathbb{C}(\mathbb{P}^1)}$.

In general, let X be any algebraic curve and $\mathbb{C}(X)$ be its function field. The ring $D_{\mathbb{C}(X)} := \mathbb{C}(X)[\partial_t]$ is the ring of differential operators on X. Here $t \in \mathbb{C}(X)$ with $t' \neq 0$. An element $L \in D_{\mathbb{C}(X)}$ is a differential operator defined on the algebraic curve X.

THEOREM 2. *Let X, Y be two algebraic curves with genus g_X, g_Y; and function fields $\mathbb{C}(X), \mathbb{C}(Y)$. Let $f : X \to Y$ be a non-constant morphism with $\deg(f) = d$. The morphism f corresponds a homomorphism $\mathbb{C}(Y) \to \mathbb{C}(X)$, which induces a homomorphism $D_{\mathbb{C}(Y)} \to D_{\mathbb{C}(X)}$. If $L_1 \in D_{\mathbb{C}(Y)}$ with $\mathrm{ord}(L_1) = 2$ and, L_2 is the corresponding element in $D_{\mathbb{C}(X)}$, then*

$$2 - 2g_X + \sum_{p\in X}(\Delta(L_2, p) - 1) = d(2 - 2g_Y + \sum_{s\in Y}(\Delta(L_1, s) - 1)).$$

PROOF. Let $S \subset Y$ be a finite set and $T = f^{-1}(S)$ such that $\mathrm{Sing}(L_1) \subseteq S$, $\mathrm{Sing}(L_2) \subseteq T$, and all branching points in X are in T. There are infinitely many points in $X \setminus T$ and for each $p \in X \setminus T$, we have $\Delta(L_2, p) = 1$ and $e_p = 1$. There are infinitely many points in $Y \setminus S$ and for each $s \in Y \setminus S$, we have $\Delta(L_1, s) = 1$.

$$\#T = \sum_{p\in T} 1 = \sum_{p\in T} e_p - \sum_{p\in T}(e_p - 1) \tag{12}$$
$$= d \cdot \#S - \sum_{p\in X}(e_p - 1) \tag{13}$$
$$= d \cdot \#S - (2g_x - 2 - d(2g_Y - 2)). \tag{14}$$

From (13) to (14) we used (6). Then,

$$\sum_{p\in X}(\Delta(L_2, p) - 1) = \sum_{p\in T}(\Delta(L_2, p) - 1) \tag{15}$$
$$= \sum_{p\in T}\Delta(L_2, p) - \sum_{p\in T} 1 \tag{16}$$
$$= d\sum_{s\in S}\Delta(L_1, s) - \#T. \tag{17}$$

Combine (14) and (17) to obtain

$$\sum_{p\in X}(\Delta(L_2, p) - 1)$$
$$= d\sum_{s\in S}\Delta(L_1, s) - d\cdot\#S + (2g_x - 2 - d(2g_Y - 2)).$$

Therefore,

$$2-2g_X+\sum_{p\in X}(\Delta(L_2, p) - 1) = d(2-2g_Y+\sum_{s\in Y}(\Delta(L_1, s) - 1)). \tag{18}$$

□

We use differential operators $L_B, L_{inp} \in \mathbb{C}(x)[\partial]$. So $X = Y = \mathbb{P}^1$ and $g_X = g_Y = g_{\mathbb{P}^1} = 0$. Suppose that

$$L_B \xrightarrow{f}_C \xrightarrow{r}_E L_{inp}$$

where $f : \mathbb{P}^1 \to \mathbb{P}^1$ and L_B is a GHDO with exponent differences $[\alpha_0, \alpha_1, \alpha_\infty]$ at $\{0, 1, \infty\}$. Since the exp-product transformation does not affect exponent differences, formula (18) gives us:

$$2+\sum_{p\in\mathbb{P}^1}(\Delta(L_{inp}, p)-1) = \deg(f)(2+\sum_{i\in\{0,1,\infty\}}(\alpha_i-1)). \tag{19}$$

We will use formula (19) in section 3.2.

3.2 Candidate Exponent Differences

This section explains a method of computing exponent differences for candidate GHDOs.

Remark 4. Consider the operator L_{inp} in example 1. It has 4 true singularities, so (11) gives us $d_f = 60$. For a candidate L_B having exponent differences $[\alpha_0, \alpha_1, \alpha_\infty]$, we have

$$\alpha_0, \alpha_1, \alpha_\infty \in \{\frac{a}{b} : a \in S_T \cup S_R \cup \{1\}, 1 \leq b \leq d_f\}. \tag{20}$$

Here S_T is the set of exponent differences of L_{inp} at its true singularities and S_R is the set of exponent differences of L_{inp} at its removable singularities. There are 176 elements in the set (20). This leaves too many candidates for $[\alpha_0, \alpha_1, \alpha_\infty]$. Algorithm **find_expdiffs** is designed to skip most combinations (formula (19) is particularly effective). In about 0.25 seconds **find_expdiffs** returns all different candidates: $[\frac{2}{7}, \frac{1}{3}, \frac{1}{7}, 2]$, $[\frac{1}{7}, \frac{1}{3}, \frac{1}{2}, 20]$. The first candidate gives a pullback function of degree 2 and the second candidate gives a pullback function of degree 20.

Algorithm: `find_expdiffs`

Input:

- e_{inp}, a list of exponent differences of L_{inp} at its true singularities.
- e_{rem}, a (possibly empty) list of exponent differences of L_{inp} at its removable singularities.

Output:

- List of candidate exponent differences for candidate GHDOs.

  Output is a list of all lists $e_B = [\alpha_0, \alpha_1, \alpha_\infty, d]$ of integers or rational numbers where $[\alpha_0, \alpha_1, \alpha_\infty]$ is a list of candidate exponent differences and d is a candidate degree for f such that:
  - For every exponent difference m in e_{inp} there exists $e \in \{1, 2, \ldots, d\}$ such that $m = e\alpha_i$ for some $i \in \{0, 1, \infty\}$.
  - The multiplicities e are consistent with (7), and their sums are compatible with d, see the last paragraph in step 2.

1. Let $\overline{\alpha}_1, \overline{\alpha}_2, \overline{\alpha}_3 = \alpha_0, \alpha_1, \alpha_\infty$. After reordering we may assume that $\overline{\alpha}_1, \ldots, \overline{\alpha}_k \in \mathbb{Z}$ and $\overline{\alpha}_{k+1}, \ldots, \overline{\alpha}_3 \notin \mathbb{Z}$ for $k \in \{0, 1, 2, 3\}$. For each $k \in \{0, 1, 2, 3\}$ we use `CoverLogs` in [3] to compute candidates for $\overline{\alpha}_1, \ldots, \overline{\alpha}_k \in \mathbb{Z}$. If $\overline{\alpha}_1 + \cdots + \overline{\alpha}_k \neq 0$ then algorithm `CoverLogs` also returns the exact degree d_f of f (theorem 1 shows that $d_f(\overline{\alpha}_1 + \cdots + \overline{\alpha}_k)$ must be the sum of the logarithmic exponent differences of L_{inp}). Otherwise, it uses (11) to compute a degree bound d_f for f.

2. We will explain only the case where $k = 1$, which is the case $[\overline{\alpha}_1, \overline{\alpha}_2, \overline{\alpha}_3] = [\alpha_0, \alpha_1, \alpha_\infty]$, where $\alpha_0 \in \mathbb{Z}$ and $\alpha_1, \alpha_\infty \notin \mathbb{Z}$. For other cases ($k = 0, 1, 3$) see [3].

   Let $k = 1$. So we have $\alpha_0 \in \mathbb{Z}$. We need to find rational numbers α_1 and α_∞.

   The logarithmic singularities of L_{inp} come from the point 0. Non-integer exponent differences of L_{inp} must be multiples of α_1 or α_∞. Let S_N be the set of non-logarithmic exponent differences of L_{inp} and S_R be the set of exponent differences of L_{inp} at its removable singularities. Consider the set

   $$\Gamma_1 = \begin{cases} \Gamma_A = \{\frac{\max(S_N)}{b} : b = 1, \ldots, d_f\} & \text{if } S_N \neq \emptyset, \\ \Gamma_B = \{\frac{a}{b} : a \in S_R \cup \{1\}, b = 1, \ldots, d_f\} & \text{otherwise.} \end{cases}$$

   α_1 (or α_∞, but if so, we may interchange them) must be one of the elements of Γ_1. We loop over all elements of Γ_1. Assume that a candidate for α_1 is chosen. Let $\Omega = S_N \setminus \alpha_1\mathbb{Z}$. Now consider the set

   $$\Gamma_\infty = \begin{cases} \Gamma_A \cup \Gamma_B & \text{if } \Omega = \emptyset, \\ \{\frac{g}{b} : g = \gcd(\Omega) : b = 1, \ldots, d_f\} & \text{otherwise.} \end{cases}$$

   Now take all pairs (α_∞, d) satisfying (19), $\alpha_\infty \in \Gamma_\infty$, $1 \leq d \leq d_f$, with additional restrictions on d, as follows:

   For every potential non-zero value v for one of the α_i's we pre-compute a list of integers N_v by dividing all exponent differences of L_{inp} by v and then selecting the quotients that are integers. Next, let D_v be the set of all $1 \leq d \leq d_f$ that can be written as the sum of a sublist of N_v. Each time a non-zero value v is taken for one of the α_i, it imposes the restriction $d \in D_v$. This means that we need not run a loop for $\alpha_\infty \in \Gamma_\infty$, instead, we run a (generally much shorter) loop for d (taking values in the intersection of the D_v's so far) and then for each such d compute α_∞ from (19). We also check if $d \in D_{\alpha_\infty}$.

3. Return the list of candidate exponent differences with a candidate degree, the list of lists $[\alpha_0, \alpha_1, \alpha_\infty, d]$, for candidate GHDOs.

Once we have the list of candidate exponent differences, then each of the elements of this list gives a candidate GHDO. If L_{inp} has a ${}_2F_1$-type solution in form (1), then it is among the candidate GHDOs that we computed, via a change of variables and exp-product transformations. This answers question Q2.

3.3 Quotient Method

In this section, we explain a method to recover the pullback function f, which is the most crucial part of our algorithm. We will explain our algorithm for rational pullback functions. For algebraic pullback functions, the only difference is the lifting algorithm, which is explained in section 3.4. Before starting this section, note that we can always compute the formal solutions of a given differential equation $L_{inp}(y) = 0$ up to a finite precision.

3.3.1 Non-Logarithmic Case

Let the second order differential equation $L_{inp}(y) = 0$ be given. Let L_B be a GHDO such that $L_B \xrightarrow{f}_C \xrightarrow{r}_E L_{inp}$. Let $f : \mathbb{P}^1_x \mapsto \mathbb{P}^1_z$ and $L_1 \xrightarrow{f}_C L_2$. If $x = p$ is a singularity of L_2 and $z = s$ is a singularity of L_1, then we say that p comes from s when $f(p) = s$.

After a change of variables we can assume that $x = 0$ is a singularity of L_{inp} that comes from the singularity $z = 0$ of L_B. This means $f(0) = 0$ and we can write $f = c_0 x^{v_0(f)}(1 + \dots)$ where $c_0 \in \mathbb{C}$, $v_0(f)$ is the multiplicity of 0, and the dots refer to an element in $x\mathbb{C}[[x]]$.

Let y_1 and y_2 be the formal solutions of L_B at $x = 0$. The following diagram shows the effects of the change of variables and exp-product transformations on the formal solutions of L_B,

$$y_1(x) \xrightarrow{f}_C y_1(f) \xrightarrow{r}_E Y_1(x) = \exp\left(\int r dx\right) y_1(f),$$

$$y_2(x) \xrightarrow{f}_C y_2(f) \xrightarrow{r}_E Y_2(x) = \exp\left(\int r dx\right) y_2(f),$$

where Y_1 and Y_2 are solutions of L_{inp}.

Let $q = \frac{y_1}{y_2}$ be a quotient of formal solutions of L_B. The change of variables transformation sends x to f, and so q to $q(f)$. Therefore, $q(f)$ will be a quotient of formal solutions of L_{inp}.

The effect of exp-product transformation disappears under taking quotients. In general, a quotient of formal solutions of L_B at a point $x = p$ is only unique up to Möbius transformations $\frac{y_1}{y_2} \mapsto \frac{\alpha y_1 + \beta y_2}{\gamma y_1 + \eta y_2}$.

If $x = p$ has a non-integer exponent difference, then we can choose q uniquely up to a constant factor c. So if we likewise compute a quotient Q of formal solutions of L_{inp}, then we have $q(f) = c \cdot Q(x)$ for some unknown constant c. Then

$$f(x) = q^{-1}\left(c \cdot Q(x)\right). \tag{21}$$

If we know the value of this constant c, then we can compute an expansion for the pullback function f from expansions of q and Q. To obtain c with a finite computation, we take a prime number ℓ. Then, for each $c \in \{1, \dots, \ell - 1\}$ we try to compute f modulo ℓ. If this succeeds, then we lift f modulo a power of ℓ, and try reconstruction. Details of lifting is explained in section 3.4.

Remark 5. Here we should compute the formal solutions up to a precision $a \geq (a_f + 1)(d_f + 1) + 3$. This precision is enough to recover the correct pullback function with a few extra terms for checking. This answers Q1.

Algorithm: `case1` (non-logarithmic case)
Input:
- L_{inp}, a second order differential operator with non-logarithmic solutions,
- L_B, a candidate GHDO,
- d_f, degree bound for f.

Output:
- The rational pullback function f, or 0 (in this case there is no rational pullback function).

1. Compute expansions of the formal solutions y_1, y_2 of L_B and Y_1, Y_2 of L_{inp} up to precision $a \geq 2d_f + 5$. Select a prime ℓ for which these expansions can be reduced mod ℓ.
2. $q \leftarrow \frac{y_2}{y_1}$, $Q \leftarrow \frac{Y_2}{Y_1}$, then compute q^{-1}.
3. Search for c_0 such that $c \equiv c_0 \mod \ell$ by looping over $c_0 = 1, \dots, \ell - 1$. If there is no such c_0, then return 0.
4. Compute $f_1 = q^{-1}(c_0 \cdot Q) \in \mathbb{Z}[x]/(\ell, x^a)$.
5. Lift[3] f_1 to $f_l \in \mathbb{Z}[x]/(\ell^l, x^a)$ for a suitable $l \in \mathbb{N}$, and then reconstruct the rational pullback function f from f_l (we still need to address remark 2).
6. Return f.

3.3.2 Logarithmic Case

A logarithm may occur in one of the formal solutions of L_{inp} at $x = p$ if exponents at $x = p$ differ by an integer. We may assume that L_{inp} has a logarithmic solution at the singularity $x = 0$.

Let y_1, y_2 be the formal solutions of L_B at $x = 0$. Let y_1 be the non-logarithmic solution (it is unique up to a multiplicative constant). Then $\frac{y_2}{y_1} = c_1 \cdot \log(x) + h$ for some $c_1 \in \mathbb{C}$ and $h \in \mathbb{C}[[x]]$. We can choose y_2 such that

$$c_1 = 1 \quad \text{and} \quad \text{constant term of } h = 0. \tag{22}$$

That makes $\frac{y_2}{y_1}$ unique. If h does not contain negative powers of x then define

$$g = \exp\left(\frac{y_2}{y_1}\right) = x \cdot (1 + \dots) \tag{23}$$

where the dots refer to an element of $x\mathbb{C}[[x]]$.

[3]For details see the section 3.4.

Remark 6. If we choose y_2 differently, then we obtain another $\tilde{g} = \exp\left(\frac{y_2}{y_1}\right)$ that relates to g in (23) by $\tilde{g} = c_1 g^{c_2}$ for some constants c_1, c_2. If h contains negative powers of x, then the formula for g is slightly different (we have not implemented this case yet).

We do likewise for the formal solutions Y_1, Y_2 of L_{inp} and denote

$$G = \exp\left(\frac{Y_2}{Y_1}\right) = x \cdot (1 + \dots). \tag{24}$$

Write $f \in \mathbb{C}(x)$ as $c_0 x^{v_0(f)} \cdot (1 + \dots)$. Then $g(f) = c \cdot x^{v_0(f)} (1 + \dots)$. Note that g, G are not intrinsically unique, the choices we made in (22) implies that

$$g(f) = c_1 \cdot G^{c_2} \tag{25}$$

for some constants c_1, c_2. Here $c_1 = c$ and $c_2 = v_0(f)$.

If $\Delta(L_{inp}, 0) \neq 0$, then find $v_0(f)$ from $\Delta(L_B, 0) v_0(f) = \Delta(L_{inp}, 0)$. Otherwise we loop over $v_0(f) = 1, 2, \dots, d_f$. That leaves one unknown constant c. We address this problem as before, choose a good prime number ℓ, try $c = 1, 2, \dots, \ell - 1$. Then calculate an expansion for f with the formula

$$f = g^{-1}\left(c \cdot G^{v_0(f)}\right). \tag{26}$$

Then we lift f modulo a power of ℓ, and try reconstruction. The discussion in this section answers Q4.

Algorithm: case2 (logarithmic case)

Input:

- L_{inp}, a second order differential operator with at least one logarithmic solution,
- L_B, a candidate GHDO,
- d_f, degree bound for f.

Output:

- The rational pullback function f, or 0 (in this case there is no rational pullback function).

1. Compute the exponents of L_{inp} and L_B.
2. Compute expansions of the formal solutions y_1, y_2 of L_B and Y_1, Y_2 of L up to precision $a \geq 2d_f + 5$. Select a prime ℓ for which these expansions can be reduced mod ℓ.
3. $q \leftarrow \frac{y_2}{y_1}$, $Q \leftarrow \frac{Y_2}{Y_1}$, and compute g and G from (23) and (24) respectively. Then compute g^{-1}.
4. Select (compute if $\Delta(L_{inp}, 0) \neq 0$, loop otherwise) $v_0(f)$ and search for c_0 such that $c \equiv c_0 \mod p$ by looping over $1, \dots, \ell - 1$. If there is no such c_0 (which means there is no rational pullback function for this candidate L_B), then return 0.
5. Compute $f_1 = g^{-1}\left(c_0 \cdot G^{v_0(f)}\right) \in \mathbb{Z}[x]/(\ell, x^a)$.
6. Lift[4] f_1 to $f_l \in \mathbb{Z}[x]/(\ell^l, x^a)$ for a suitable $l \in \mathbb{N}$, and reconstruct the rational pullback function f from f_l (we still need to address remark 2).
7. Return f.

[4]For details see the section 3.4.

Remark 7. **Algebraic Pullback Functions**
Let L_{inp} have a ${}_2F_1$-type solution in the form (1) where f is an algebraic function. We do not have a degree bound for this case, nor the analogue of the algorithm from section 3.2. Therefore, for this case, the current version of our implementation needs extra inputs: a candidate GHDO, a degree bound for f, and an algebraic degree bound for f. Then we can find the algebraic pullback function via the quotient method. The only difference is the lifting algorithm which is explained in section 3.4. An algebraic degree bound is needed for lifting. This remark together with section 3.4 answer question Q5.

3.4 Lifting: Recovering the Pullback Function

We introduce two lifting algorithms, one for rational functions, one for algebraic functions. We explain lifting by using the formula (21) for the pullback function, which occurs in the non-logarithmic case. The algorithm for the formula (26) in the logarithmic case is similar. The discussion in this section answers Q3.

3.4.1 Lifting for a Rational Pullback Function

By using the formula (21), which is $f(x) = q^{-1}(c \cdot Q(x))$, we can recover the rational pullback function f, if we know the value of the constant c. We do not have a direct formula for c. However, if we know c_0 such that $c \equiv c_0 \mod \ell$ for a good prime number ℓ, then we can recover the pullback function f. This can be done via *Hensel lifting techniques*.

Let ℓ be a good prime number and consider

$$h : \mathbb{Q} \longrightarrow \mathbb{Q}[x]/(x^a)$$
$$h(c) \equiv q^{-1}(c \cdot Q(x)) \mod x^a.$$

By looping on $c_0 = 1, \dots, \ell - 1$ and trying rational function reconstruction for $h(c_0) \mod (\ell, x^a)$, we can compute the image of f in $\mathbb{F}_\ell/(x^a)$. If a is high enough, then for correct value(s) of c_0, rational function reconstruction will succeed and return a rational function $\frac{A_0}{B_0} \mod (\ell, x^a)$. This c_0 is the one satisfying $c \equiv c_0 \mod \ell$.

Write $c \equiv c_0 + \ell c_1 \mod \ell^2$ for $0 \leq c_1 \leq \ell - 1$. Taylor series expansion of h gives us

$$h(c) = h(c_0 + \ell c_1) \equiv h(c_0) + \ell c_1 h'(c_0) \mod (\ell^2, x^a). \tag{27}$$

Substitute $c_1 = 0$, $c_1 = 1$, respectively, in (27) and compute

$$h(c_0) \mod (\ell^2, x^a), \tag{28}$$
$$h(c_0 + \ell) \equiv h(c_0) + \ell h'(c_0) \mod (\ell^2, x^a). \tag{29}$$

Subtracting (28) from (29) gives

$$\ell h'(c_0) \equiv [h(c_0 + \ell) - h(c_0)] \mod (\ell^2, x^a).$$

Let

$$S = \{h(c_0) + \ell c_1 h'(c_0) \, : \, c_1 = 0, \dots, \ell - 1\}. \tag{30}$$

Let $f = \frac{A}{B}$ in characteristic 0. We do not know what A and B are. However, from applying rational function reconstruction for $h(c_0)$, we obtain A_0, B_0 with $f \equiv \frac{A_0}{B_0} \mod (\ell, x^a)$. It follows that $f = \frac{A}{B} \equiv \frac{A_0}{B_0} \equiv E_{c_1} \mod (\ell, x^a)$ for an element $E_{c_1} \in S$ defined in (30). From this equation we have

$$A \equiv B E_{c_1} \mod (\ell, x^a). \tag{31}$$

Now let

$$f = \frac{A}{B} \equiv \frac{A_0 + \ell A_1}{B_0 + \ell B_1} \mod (\ell^2, x^a) \tag{32}$$

where $A_1 = a_0 + a_1 x + \cdots + a_{\deg(A_0)} x^{\deg(A_0)}$ and $B_1 = b_1 x + \cdots + b_{\deg(B_0)} x^{\deg(B_0)}$ are unknown polynomials. Here we are fixing the constant term of B. If we can find the unknowns $\{a_i, b_j\}$, then find $f \mod (\ell^2, x^a)$. Then, from (31), we have

$$(A_0 + \ell A_1) \equiv (B_0 + \ell B_1)[h(c_0) + \ell c_1 h'(c_0)] \mod (\ell^2, x^a). \quad (33)$$

Now, solve the linear equation (33) for unknowns $\{a_i, b_j, c_1\}$ in $\mathbb{F}_\ell$, and from (32) find $f \mod (\ell^2, x^a)$ and $c \equiv c_0 + \ell c_1 \mod \ell^2$. Then try rational number reconstruction. If it succeeds, then check if this rational function is the one that we are looking for or not (apply change of variables transformation and try to find the parameter of the exp-product transformation). If it is not, then use the same algorithm to lift $f \mod (\ell^2, x^a)$ to $\mod (\ell^3, x^a)$ (or (ℓ^4, x^a) if an implementation for solving linear equations $\mod \ell^n$ is available). After a (finite) (we still need to address remark 2) number of steps, we can recover the rational pullback function f.

3.4.2 Lifting for an Algebraic Pullback Function

We can also recover algebraic pullback functions with a very similar method as explained in the previous section. However, in the algebraic pullback case we need to know an algebraic degree bound for f. The idea here is *to recover the minimal polynomial of the algebraic pullback function f.*

Let d_f be a degree bound, and a_f be an algebraic degree bound for f. Consider the below polynomial in y,

$$\sum_{j=1}^{a_f} A_j y^j \mod (\ell, x^a), \quad (34)$$

with unknown polynomials $A_j = \sum_{i=0}^{d_f} a_{i,j} x^i$, $(j = 1, \ldots, a_f)$.

First we need to find the value of c_0 such that $c_0 \equiv c \mod \ell$. Similarly, by looping on $c_0 = 1, \ldots, \ell - 1$, we can compute the corresponding $f \equiv f_\ell \in \mathbb{F}_\ell/(x^a)$. For this f_ℓ, the polynomial (34) will be congruent to 0 mod (ℓ, x^a) if we plug f_ℓ in y. So, solve the equation

$$\sum_{j=1}^{a_f} A_j f_\ell^j \equiv 0 \mod (\ell, x^a)$$

in $\mathbb{F}_\ell$ and find the unknown polynomials A_j. After finding $c \equiv c_0 \mod \ell$ and polynomials A_j, then let $c \equiv c_0 + \ell c_1 \mod \ell^2$. Then f_ℓ also satisfies the polynomial

$$\sum_{j=1}^{a_f} (A_j + \ell \tilde{A}_j) y^j \mod (\ell^2, x^a).$$

in $\mathbb{F}_\ell$ for unknown polynomials $\tilde{A}_j$. Similarly, find the c_1 and unknown polynomials $\tilde{A}_j = \sum_{i=0}^{d_f} \tilde{a}_{i,j} x^i$, $(j = 1, \ldots, a_f)$. After a finite number of lifting steps, and rational reconstruction, we will have the minimal polynomial of an algebraic pullback function f.

3.5 Recovering the Parameter of Exp-product

After finding f, we can compute the differential operator M, such that $L_B \xrightarrow{f}_C M \xrightarrow{r}_E L_{inp}$. Then we can compare the second highest terms of M and L_{inp} to find the parameter r of the exp-product transformation: If $M = \partial^2 + B_1 \partial + B_0$ and $L_{inp} = \partial^2 + A_1 \partial + A_0$, then $r = \frac{B_1 - A_1}{2}$.

4. FUTURE WORK

We plan to work on finding a method to compute a degree bound and an algebraic degree bound for an algebraic pullback function as well as finding a method to compute candidate GHDOs for algebraic cases. We also plan to use [4] to find a method to reduce equations involving gauge transformation to equations involving only change of variables and exp-product transformations.

5. REFERENCES

[1] A. Bostan, F. Chyzak, M. van Hoeij, and L. Pech. Explicit Formula for Generating Series of Diagonal 3d Rook Paths. *Seminaire Lotharingien de Combinatorie*, (2011).

[2] T. Fang and M. van Hoeij. 2-Descent for Second Order Linear Differential Equations. *ISSAC'11 Proceedings*, pages 107–114, (2011).

[3] E. Imamoglu. Implementation of `find_2f1`. `www.math.fsu.edu/~eimamogl/issac15/codes/`.

[4] M. Kauers and C. Koutschan. Integral D-Finite Functions. `http://arxiv.org/abs/1501.03691`, (2015).

[5] J. Kovacic. An Algorithm for Solving Second Order Linear Homogeneous Equations. *J. Symb. Comput.*, 2(1):2–43, (1986).

[6] V. J. Kunwar. *Hypergeometric Solutions of Linear Differential Equations with Rational Function Coefficients.* PhD thesis, Florida State University, (2014).

[7] V. J. Kunwar and M. van Hoeij. Second Order Differential Equations with Hypergeometric Solutions of Degree Three. *ISSAC'13 Proceedings*, pages 235–242, June 26-29 (2013).

[8] H. A. Schwarz. Ueber diejenigen Fälle, in welchen die Gaussische hypergeometrische Reihe eine algebraische Function ihres vierten Elementes darstellt. *Journal für die Reine und Angewandte Mathematik*, 75:292 – 335, (1873).

[9] M. van Hoeij and R. Vidunas. Belyi Functions for Hyperbolic Hypergeometric-to-Heun Transformations. `http://arxiv.org/abs/1212.3803`, (2013).

[10] M. van Hoeij and J. A. Weil. Solving Second Order Linear Differential Equations with Klein's Theorem. *ISSAC'05 Proceedings*, pages 340–347, (2005).

[11] Z. X. Wang and D. R. Guo. *Special Functions.* World Scientific, (1989).

[12] Q. Yuan and M. van Hoeij. Finding All Bessel Type Solutions for Linear Differential Equations with Rational Function Coefficients. *ISSAC'10 Proceedings*, pages 37–44, (2010).

An Algorithm to Check Whether a Basis of a Parametric Polynomial System is a Comprehensive Gröbner Basis and the Associated Completion Algorithm*

Deepak Kapur
Department of Computer Science
University of New Mexico
Albuquerque, NM, USA
kapur@cs.unm.edu

Yiming Yang
Department of Computer Science
University of New Mexico
Albuquerque, NM, USA
yiming@cs.unm.edu

ABSTRACT

Given a basis of a parametric polynomial ideal, an algorithm is proposed to test whether it is a comprehensive Gröbner basis or not. A basis of a parametric polynomial ideal is a comprehensive Gröbner basis if and only if for every specialization of parameters in a given field, the specialization of the basis is a Gröbner basis of the associated specialized polynomial ideal. In case a basis does not check to be a comprehensive Gröbner basis, a completion algorithm for generating a comprehensive Gröbner basis from it that is patterned after Buchberger's algorithm is proposed. Its termination is proved and its correctness is established. In contrast to other algorithms for computing a comprehensive Gröbner basis which first compute a comprehensive Gröbner system and then extract a comprehensive Gröbner basis from it, the proposed algorithm computes a comprehensive Gröbner basis directly. Further, the proposed completion algorithm always computes a minimal faithful comprehensive Gröbner basis in the sense that every polynomial in the result is from the ideal as well as *essential* with respect to the comprehensive Gröbner basis. A prototype implementation of the algorithm has been successfully tried on many examples from the literature. An interesting and somewhat surprising outcome of using the proposed algorithm is that there are example parametric ideals for which a minimal comprehensive Gröbner basis computed by it is different from minimal comprehensive Gröbner bases computed by other algorithms in the literature.

Categories and Subject Descriptors

I.1.2 [**Symbolic and Algebraic Manipulation**]: Algorithms

*This work is supported by the National Science Foundation award DMS-1217054

ISSAC'15, July 6–9, 2015, Bath, United Kingdom.
Copyright © 2015 ACM. ISBN 978-1-4503-3435-8/15/07 ...$15.00.
DOI: http://dx.doi.org/10.1145/2755996.2756676.

General Terms

Algorithms

Keywords

minimal comprehensive Gröbner basis, parametric polynomial system, parametric S-polynomial, parametric specialization.

1. INTRODUCTION

The concept of a comprehensive Gröbner basis (CGB) was introduced by Weispfenning [18] to associate Gröbner basis like objects for parametric polynomial systems (see also the notion of a related concept of a parametric Gröbner basis independently introduced by Kapur [5]). For a specialization of parameters, a Gröbner basis of the specialized ideal is the specialized CGB. These properties of CGB make it very attractive in applications where a family of related problems can be parameterized and specified using a parametric polynomial system. For various specializations, they can be solved by specializing a parametric solution without having to repeat computations.

Because of their applications, these topics have been well investigated by researchers and a number of algorithms have been proposed to construct such objects for parametric polynomial systems ([11], [19],[15], [16], [17], [9], [4], [14], [20], [10], [12], [6], [7]). An algorithm for simultaneously generating a comprehensive Gröbner system (CGS) and a comprehensive Gröbner basis (CGB) by Kapur, Sun and Wang (KSW) [7] is particularly noteworthy because of its many nice properties: (i) fewer segments (branches) in the resulting CGS, (ii) all polynomials in the CGS and CGB are faithful meaning that they are in the input ideal, and more importantly, (iii) the algorithm has been found efficient in practice [13].

There is however no algorithm to directly compute a minimal faithful CGB of a parametric ideal. Weispfenning's paper [18] and Kapur's paper [5] appear to be the only attempts to compute a CGB directly but the outputs in both cases are polynomials relative to segments or constrained polynomials.[1] Since Suzuki and Sato's paper [17] where they showed

[1]In Section 4 entitled *Reduced Gröbner Systems* of his paper [18], Weispfenning discussed reduced comprehensive Gröbner basis as well as globally reduced comprehensive Gröbner basis which suggest that he was thinking along similar lines in defining minimal faithful comprehensive Gröbner basis. His notions were dependent upon *global reduction*

how reduced Gröbner basis construction over $K[X, U]$, where X and U are sets of variables and parameters respectively, could be effectively used to compute a CGS, all known algorithms for computing a comprehensive Gröbner basis of a parametric ideal, including Weispfenning's reduced Gröbner system [18], are indirect in the sense that they first compute a CGS and then extract from it an associated CGB by collecting all polynomials generated and ignoring segments.

In this paper we give the first completion algorithm for directly computing a minimal faithful CGB of a parametric polynomial. It is patterned after Buchberger's algorithm. A parametric polynomial f can be viewed as a family of specialized polynomials generated from it with different leading terms, $\{f_{\alpha_1}, f_{\alpha_2}, \ldots, f_{\alpha_n}\}$ with $\alpha_1, \alpha_2, \ldots, \alpha_n$ being the associated segments of specializations on parameters. The algorithm computes a set of parametric S-polynomials of two parametric polynomials f and g from the critical pairs between the specialized tuples of f and g for various segments.

Like Buchberger's algorithm, the proposed completion algorithm depends upon a direct CGB test. Each parametric S-polynomial of every pair of distinct polynomials in a given basis must be reduced to 0 in its associated segment for the test to succeed. When the test fails, new polynomials generated from parametric S-polynomials with non-zero normal forms are added to the current basis. An important distinction of this algorithm is that *reduction* of a parametric S-polynomial is performed under a given segment: the leading term of an S-polynomial under the segment is simplified by a given basis under the the same segment.

The proposed completion algorithm has another nice feature that its output is always a minimal faithful CGB, in the sense that every polynomial in it is *essential* for the basis to be a CGB as well as every polynomial is in simplified form and in the parametric ideal generated by the input basis. In other words, every polynomial is needed for some specialization to ensure that the specialized CGB is indeed a Gröbner basis of the associated specialized ideal.

More importantly, the completion algorithm can be used to generate minimal faithful CGB for certain parametric ideals which cannot be obtained using other indirect algorithms proposed in the literature for computing a CGB.

The paper is organized as follows. After an overview of basic definitions in the next section, a test for checking a CGB is presented in Section 3. Concepts of a family of parametric S-polynomials generated from a pair of parametric polynomials as well as reduction of a parametric polynomial by a finite basis of parametric polynomials are presented. They are closely related to the associated concepts discussed in [18] and [5]. Section 4 is a detailed discussion of the completion algorithm using concepts presented in Section 3. It is shown that the completion algorithm computes a minimal comprehensive Gröbner basis (MCGB). Section 5 is a detailed comparison with other algorithms proposed in the literature for computing a CGB. Section 6 presents some experimental observations from the prototypical implementation of the proposed algorithm. In particular, two illustrative examples are given for which the algorithm computes MCGBs different from those given by algorithms including another indirect algorithm [8]. Section 7 makes concluding remarks and discusses topics for future research.

algorithm which he never included in the paper but commented that it could be obtained by a slight modification of the usual non-parametric reduction algorithm by Buchberger. However, this algorithm turns out to be not easy to design.

2. PRELIMINARIES

Let K be a field, L an algebraically closed field extension of K, U and X are the sets of parameters and variables respectively. Let $>$ be an admissible total term order in which $X \gg U$. In a ring of parametric polynomials $K[U][X]$, where K is a field, for a polynomial $f \in K[U][X]$, $\mathrm{LC}(f)$, $\mathrm{LT}(f)$ and $\mathrm{LM}(f)$ are defined as its leading coefficient, leading term and leading monomial w.r.t. a given term order $>$ respectively. For example, let $f = 32(u-1)x^2 + 4uy$, where $U = \{u\}$, $X = \{x, y\}$, and $>$ is a lexicographic term order with $x > y \gg u$. Then $\mathrm{LC}(f) = 32(u-1)$, $\mathrm{LT}(f) = x^2$ and $\mathrm{LM}(f) = \mathrm{LC}(f) \cdot \mathrm{LT}(f) = 32(u-1)x^2$.

A specialization σ is a ring homomorphism from $K[U]$ to L, where L is usually an algebraically closed field extension of K. It can be canonically extended to $K[U][X] \to L[X]$ with the identity on variables. For a polynomial $f \in K[U][X]$, σ is given by $f \to f(v_1, v_2, \ldots, v_m)$, where $m = |U|$ and $v_1, \ldots, v_m \in L$. This image of f is denoted as $\sigma_{\overline{v}}(f)$ for brevity, where $\overline{v} = (v_1, \ldots, v_m) \in L^m$, or simply $\sigma(f)$ if it is clear from the context.

Definition 2.1 *Let E, N be subsets of $K[U]$, then the tuple (E, N) is called a* ***parametric segment*** *(or* ***segment****). An associated* ***constructible set*** *α is given by $\mathbb{V}(E) - \mathbb{V}(N)$, where $\mathbb{V}(E)$ is the algebraic variety (zero set) of E in L. (E, N) is consistent if $\alpha \neq \emptyset$.*

The concept of a Gröbner basis is generalized to the ring $K[U][X]$ as a CGB of a parametric ideal:

Definition 2.2 *Given an ideal $I \subseteq K[U][X]$, $S \subseteq L^m$ the parameter space, and an admissible term order $>$, a finite basis $\mathcal{G} \subseteq K[U][X]$ is called a* ***comprehensive Gröbner basis (CGB)*** *of I on S w.r.t. $>$ if for $\forall \sigma \in S$, $\sigma(\mathcal{G})$ is always a Gröbner basis of the ideal $\sigma(I)$ on $L[X]$. Specifically, if $S = L^m$, $\mathcal{G}$ is a CGB of I.*

Notice that the above definition of a CGB requires it to be *faithful*, i.e. $\mathcal{G} \subseteq I$.

2.1 Tuple Representation

Since computations in the proposed algorithm are done with respect to a segment, we adopt the tuple representation introduced in [7].

Given a a non-empty segment α, a parametric polynomial $f \in K[U][X]$ with respect to α, written as f_α, is represented by a tuple: $f_\alpha = ([\overline{f},\ \underline{f}],\ \alpha)$, where $\overline{f}$ and $\underline{f}$ are the non-zero and zero parts of f under α, and $f = \overline{f} + \underline{f}$. That is, every term in f with coefficient determined to be 0 under α is collected in $\underline{f}$. Such a polynomial f is called *unambiguous* under α, since $LC(\overline{f}) \neq 0$ under α. On the contrary, a polynomial is *ambiguous* under α if its leading coefficient under α is not determined. Since we need to compute the leading term and leading coefficient of a polynomial f under a segment α, we will abuse the terminology and denote them by $\mathrm{LT}(f, \alpha)$ and $\mathrm{LC}(f, \alpha)$ respectively.

From each polynomial f, we can construct a finite set of its specializations, each of which is represented by a tuple consisting of the specialized polynomial and the associated segment of specializations, such that the leading terms of the polynomials under the corresponding segments are distinct, and parametric segments are disjoint and non-empty. This can be easily done by considering terms in the parametric polynomials in descending order w.r.t. the given term order $>$, until all specializations have been accounted for. Let Φ_f be a finite set of such tuples $\{f_{\alpha_1}, f_{\alpha_2}, \dots, f_{\alpha_n}\}$ of f under nonempty and disjoint segments $\alpha_1, \alpha_2, \dots, \alpha_n$ respectively, where these segments form a partition of the parameter space. Related concepts were introduced in [18, 5].

3. TEST FOR A COMPREHENSIVE GRÖBNER BASIS

It is easy to see that a reduced Gröbner basis of a parametric ideal over $K[X, U]$ need not be its CGB. Different specializations of parameters can change the leading term, total degree and the kind of terms appearing in a specialization of a parametric polynomial. Consequently, concepts of S-polynomial and reduction used in Buchberger's algorithm must be adapted accordingly. This is first illustrated using a simple example below.

3.1 An Illustrative Example

Example 3.1 *Let $U = \{a, b\}$ be parameters, $X = \{x, y, z\}$ be variables. Consider a graded term order such that $x > y > z \gg a > b$. Given a basis*

$$\mathcal{F} = \{f_1 = ab^2y^2 + b^3 - 1,$$
$$f_2 = (a^3b^2 + b^3 - 1)x^2 + 3ab^2y - 3a^2b^2,$$
$$f_3 = a(a^3b^2 + b^3 - 1)x^4 - 6a^3b^2x^2 + 9a^2b^2\ \},$$

the goal is to check if $\mathcal{F}$ is a CGB for the whole space of specialization of parameters, i.e., the parametric segment $(\mathcal{E}, \mathcal{N}) = (\{\}, \{1\})$.

Step 1: Parametric Specializations of a Polynomial with different Leading Terms

$$\Phi_{f_1} = \{(f_{11} = [ab^2y^2 + b^3 - 1,\ 0],\ \alpha_1 = (\emptyset,\ \{ab^2\})),$$
$$(f_{12} = [b^3 - 1,\ ab^2y^2],\ \alpha_2 = (\ \{ab^2\},\ \{b^3 - 1\}\ ))\},$$

Notice that in the first tuple, the leading term is y^2 which is ensured by enforcing the leading coefficient of f_1 to be nonzero in the specializations. In the second tuple, the leading coefficient of f_1 is enforced to be 0 in specializations; so for these specializations, the leading term is not y^2 any more. The next possible leading term is 1. To enforce that, its leading coefficient should be made nonzero. Finally, when the coefficients of both the terms y^2 and 1 are 0 in f_1, then f_1 is specialized to 0, and hence the resulting tuple is omitted.

Similarly, for f_2, f_3, the associated finite sets of tuples are computed; let $\psi = a^3b^2 + b^3 - 1$.

$$\Phi_{f_2} = \{(f_{21} = [\psi x^2 + 3ab^2y - 3a^2b^2,\ 0],\ \beta_1 = (\ \emptyset,\ \{\psi\}\ )),$$
$$(f_{22} = [3ab^2y - 3a^2b^2,\ \psi x^2],\ \beta_2 = (\ \{\psi\},\ \{3ab^2\}))\};$$
$$\Phi_{f_3} = \{(f_{31} = [a\psi x^4 - 6a^3b^2x^2 + 9a^2b^2,\ 0],\ \gamma_1 = (\ \emptyset,\ \{a\psi\}\ )),$$
$$(f_{32} = [6a^3b^2x^2 - 9a^2b^2,\ a\psi x^4],\ \gamma_2 = (\{a\psi\}, \{6a^3b^2\}))\}.$$

Note that the number of tuples of a polynomial f is not necessarily equal to that of its terms. For example, f_2 above cannot have a specialization with the leading term of nonzero part being 1, since when term y vanishes by setting $a = b^2 = 0$, so does its constant term.

Step 2: Compute Parametric S-polynomials

For each pair of parametric polynomials, a set of S-polynomials is computed using their specialization. For example, for f_1 and f_2, construct all possible critical pairs as $(\Phi_{f_1} \times \Phi_{f_2}) = \{(f_{11}, f_{21}), (f_{11}, f_{22}), (f_{12}, f_{21}), (f_{12}, f_{22})\}$. By Buchberger's first criterion, we can ignore the unnecessary critical pairs with coprime leading terms as such an S-polynomial always reduces to 0. So among the above set, only (f_{11}, f_{22}) needs further consideration.

Parametric S-polynomial from (f_{11}, f_{22}): The segment $\delta_1 = \alpha_1 \cap \beta_2 = (\ \{\psi\},\ \{ab^2\}\ )$ is not empty. Under δ_1, the parametric S-polynomial is $h_1 = 3f_{11} - yf_{22} = [3a^2b^2y + 3b^3 - 3,\ -\psi x^2y]$. If a segment is empty for a critical pair, the associated S-polynomial is not considered.

Step 3: Reduction under Segment

Reduce h_1 by the basis $\mathcal{F}$ under segment δ_1. This reduction is defined in Section 3.3. For illustration, both h_1 and $\mathcal{F}$ are unambiguous under δ_1. So h_1 has a normal form $h_1' = h_1 - af_2 = [3\psi,\ -3\psi x^2y - a\psi x^2]$. So h_1 is reduced to 0 by $\mathcal{F}$ under δ_1, since $\overline{h_1} = 3\psi = 0$ under δ_1.

Repeat Step 2 and 3 for Other Pairs

We are done with the f_1 and f_2 pair. The other two pairs, (f_2, f_3) and (f_1, f_3), must be checked using steps 2 and 3.

For f_2 and f_3, after removing unnecessary critical pairs, there are two left: (f_{21}, f_{31}) and (f_{21}, f_{32}). Further, since $\beta_1 \cap \gamma_2 = \emptyset$, we only need to consider the first one:

The segment $\delta_2 = \beta_1 \cap \gamma_1 = (\emptyset,\ \{a\psi\}))$. Under δ_2, the S-polynomial is $h_2 = ax^2f_{21} - f_{31} = [3a^2b^2x^2y + 3a^3b^2x^2 - 9a^2b^2,\ 0]$. Reduce it by $\mathcal{F}$ under δ_2. h_2 is unambiguous, while $f_1 \in \mathcal{F}$ is ambiguous. So partition δ_2 into δ_{20} and δ_{21} to make $\mathcal{F}$ unambiguous:

- In $\delta_{20} = \delta_2 \cup \{ab^2 = 0\}$: $h_2 = [0,\ 3a^2b^2x^2y + 3a^3b^2x^2 - 9a^2b^2]$, which is already reduced to 0.
- In $\delta_{21} = \delta_2 \cup \{ab^2 \neq 0\}$: $h_2' = \psi h_2 + 2a^2b^2f_1 - (a^2b^2y + a^3b)f_2 = [0,\ 0]$.

So f_2 is also reduced to 0.

Finally, since all critical pairs from f_1 and f_3 are unnecessary, the algorithm terminates declaring $\mathcal{F}$ to be a CGB.

3.2 Parametric S-polynomial

Two key concepts are used to check for a CGB: *parametric S-polynomial* and *reduction under segment*, both of which are generalizations of S-polynomial and reduction in Buchberger's algorithm. They are also related to similar concepts introduced in [18, 5].

Since a parametric polynomial f stands for many specialized polynomials under various segments, denoted by Φ_f, a distinct pair of parametric polynomials can have multiple parametric S-polynomials for different segments, as illustrated above, in contrast to exactly one S-polynomial defined in Buchberger's algorithm.

Definition 3.2 *Given two distinct parametric polynomials $f, g \in K[U][X]$, let $f_\alpha = ([\overline{f}, \underline{f}], \alpha)$ and $g_\beta = ([\overline{g}, \underline{g}], \beta)$ be the forms of f under segment α and g under segment β respectively. Then a* ***parametric S-polynomial*** *of f and g under a non-empty segment $\alpha \cap \beta$ is*

$$\text{S-PolyP}_{\alpha\cap\beta}(f_\alpha, g_\beta) = \frac{\text{lcm}(\text{LM}(\overline{f}), \text{LM}(\overline{g}))}{\text{LM}(\overline{f})} f - \frac{\text{lcm}(\text{LM}(\overline{f}), \text{LM}(\overline{g}))}{\text{LM}(\overline{g})} g.$$

There are a lot more unnecessary S-polynomials which will trivially reduce to 0 especially for the parametric case. Many of them can be discarded by Buchberger's criterion if the leading terms of the polynomials are coprime (Proposition 4 in [2]), or if the segment in the associated critical pair is empty, or the leading term of one of the polynomials is 1. In Example 3.1, for instance, only h_1 and h_2 are necessary out of 12 possible parametric S-polynomials.

3.3 Reduction of a Parametric Polynomial by a Parametric Basis under a Segment

Given $f, p \in K[U][X]$ and a non-empty segment α such that $f_\alpha = ([\overline{f}, \underline{f}], \alpha)$ and $p_\alpha = ([\overline{p}, \underline{p}], \alpha)$. f reduces to f' by p under α in one step if there is a term t in $\overline{f}$ with coefficient c such that $\mathrm{LT}(\overline{p}) \mid t$, and

$$f' = \frac{\mathrm{lcm}(c, \mathrm{LC}(\overline{p}))}{c} \cdot f - \frac{\mathrm{lcm}(c, \mathrm{LC}(\overline{p}))}{\mathrm{LC}(\overline{p})} \cdot \frac{t}{LT(\overline{p})} \cdot p,$$

We write it as $f \xrightarrow{\alpha}_p f'$.

The reader should note that the above reduction differs from the normal reduction relation since f is being multiplied by a non-zero coefficient that can be a parametric polynomial, so that the resulting multiple of f is reducible by p. This definition is closer to the concept of pseudo-division (see [2]). For instance, in Example 3.1, the first step of the reduction of h_2 by $\mathcal{F}$ under δ_{21} has h_2 multiplied by ψ to make the leading coefficients of h_2 and f_2 divisible, where ψ is determined to be non-zero under δ_{21}.

Given a finite basis $\mathcal{B} \subseteq K[U][X]$ and a segment α, $f \xrightarrow{\alpha}_{\mathcal{B}} f'$ if there is an unambiguous polynomial $p \in \mathcal{B}$ under α such that $f \xrightarrow{\alpha}_p f'$. Then $f \xrightarrow{\alpha}{}^{*}_{\mathcal{B}} f'$ is the transitive closure of $\xrightarrow{\alpha}_{\mathcal{B}}$ such that $\forall p = [\overline{p}, \underline{p}] \in \mathcal{B}$, $\mathrm{LT}(\overline{p})$ cannot divide any term in $\overline{f'}$. f' is then a normal form of f w.r.t. $\mathcal{B}$ under α.

Proposition 3.3 *Given $f \xrightarrow{\alpha}_{\mathcal{B}} f'$, the followings are true:*

(i) $\overline{f'} < \overline{f}$ under α;

(ii) f' is in the ideal generated by $\mathcal{B} \cup \{f\}$;

(iii) $\xrightarrow{\alpha}_{\mathcal{B}}$ terminates for a fixed $\mathcal{B}$ and α.

Both f and $\mathcal{B}$ can be ambiguous under α. In such a case, to perform reduction, α is partitioned into a number of subsegments such that f and $\mathcal{B}$ are unambiguous under each of them. After that reduction is applied in each subsegment separately. The reduction of h_2 by $\mathcal{F}$ under δ_2 in Example 3.1 is such a case.

3.4 Algorithm

The algorithm below tests whether a given basis is a CGB or not.

Algorithm CGBTest($\mathcal{G}, \mathcal{E}, \mathcal{N}$)
Input: $\mathcal{G}$: a finite basis in $K[U][X]$; $(\mathcal{E}, \mathcal{N})$: the given parameter space, where $\mathcal{E}, \mathcal{N} \subseteq K[U]$.
Output: *True* if $\mathcal{G}$ is a CGB on $(\mathcal{E}, \mathcal{N})$; *False* otherwise.

```
if |G| ≤ 1 return True;
for each f ∈ G: { Compute Φ_f; }
for each f, g ∈ G where f ≠ g: {
    P := {(f_α, g_β, δ = α ∩ β) | (f_α, α) ∈ Φ_f,
                              (g_β, β) ∈ Φ_g, δ ≠ ∅};
    for each (f_i, g_j, δ_ij) ∈ P: {
        if necessary(f_i, g_j, δ_ij) then
            h_ij := S-PolyP_δij(f_i, g_j);
            h_ij --δij-->*_F h'_ij;
            if h'_ij ≠ 0 under δ_ij then
                return False; } }
return True;
```

Proposition 3.4 *Given a finite basis $\mathcal{F} \subseteq K[U][X]$ and a parameter space $S = (\mathcal{E}, \mathcal{N})$, the CGBTest algorithm terminates, and returns True iff $\mathcal{F}$ is a CGB on S.*

4. COMPLETION ALGORITHM

A completion algorithm for computing a comprehensive Gröbner basis of a parametric ideal is designed similar to Buchberger's completion algorithm for computing a Gröbner basis of a polynomial ideal. When the check for CGB (*CGBTest*) fails on a given basis of a parametric ideal, the current basis can be augmented with (normal forms of) S-polynomials that do not reduce to 0 during the CGB check. This process is repeated until a basis is obtained that passes the CGB check. The performance of the completion algorithm is governed by many factors including the order in which S-polynomials are processed, whether polynomials in the current basis are normalized using the new polynomial(s) generated and added to the basis including discarding polynomials in the current basis which become redundant (called *non-essential* below), as well as parametric S-polynomials are computed all at once.

Before discussing the details of the completion algorithm, we illustrate the key ideas using a simple example.

4.1 An Illustrative Example

Example 4.1 *Consider an ideal $I = \langle \mathcal{F} \rangle = \langle g_1 = ab^2y^2 + b^3 - 1,\ g_2 = ax^2y + a^2x^2 - 3a \rangle \subseteq K[a,b][x,y]$ on $(\emptyset,\ \{1\})$. Compute a CGB of I w.r.t. a graded lexicographic term order $x > y > z \gg a > b$.*

We start with the basis $\mathcal{G} = \{g_1, g_2\}$.

Step 1: Parametric Specializations of Polynomials and Redundancy Check

Compute Φ_{g_1} and Φ_{g_2} as the sets of all possible specializations of g_1 and g_2:

$$\Phi_{g_1} = \{(g_{11} = [ab^2y^2 + b^3 - 1, 0],\ \alpha_1 = (\emptyset,\ \{ab^2\})),$$
$$(g_{12} = [b^3 - 1,\ ab^2y^2],\ \alpha_2 = (\{ab\},\ \{b^3 - 1\}))\};$$
$$\Phi_{g_2} = \{(g_{21} = [ax^2y + a^2x^2 - 3a,\ 0],\ \beta_1 = (\emptyset,\ \{a\}))\}.$$

Neither of g_1, g_2 is redundant since each of them has a non-zero normal form after reduction by the other polynomial under some segment.

Step 2: Reduce Parametric S-polynomial

Let $\mathcal{P}$ be the set of critical pairs constructed from Φ_{g_1} and Φ_{g_2}; there is only one necessary pair: $(g_{11},\ g_{21},\ \delta_1 = \alpha_1 \cap \beta_1 = (\emptyset,\ \{a^2b^2\}))$. Under δ_1, the parametric S-polynomial is $h_1 = \text{S-PolyP}_{\delta_1}(g_{11}, g_{21}) = x^2 g_{11} - b^2 y g_{21} = [-a^2b^2x^2y + (b^3 - 1)x^2 + 3ab^2y,\ 0]$.

Both h_1 and the basis $\mathcal{G}$ are unambiguous under δ_1. h_1 can be reduced using $\mathcal{G}$ leading to its normal form: $h_1' = [\psi x^2 + 3ab^2y - 3a^2b^2,\ 0]$ under δ_1, where $\psi = a^3b^2 + b^3 - 1$. Since $\overline{h_1'} \neq 0$ under δ_1, $\mathcal{G}$ fails to be a CGB.

This normal form $g_3 = \psi x^2 + 3ab^2y - 3a^2b^2$ is added to $\mathcal{G}$, making it $\{g_1, g_3, g_2\}$, where $g_1 < g_3 < g_2$.

Step 3: Redundancy Check and Update

It is checked whether adding g_3 can make any of g_1, g_2 redundant, which is not the case. Note that in order to eventually achieve a smaller minimal CGB, polynomials are checked in a descending order, i.e. check g_2 first, then continue to g_1. g_3 contributes new critical pairs both with g_1 and g_2 using Φ_{g_3}:

$$\Phi_{g_3} = \{(g_{31} = [g_3,\ 0],\ \gamma_1 = (\emptyset,\ \{\psi\})),$$
$$(g_{32} = [3ab^2y - 3a^2b^2,\ \psi x^2],\ \gamma_2 = (\{\psi\},\ \{3ab^2\}))\}.$$

There are 3 new necessary critical pairs: $(g_{11}, g_{32}, \alpha_1 \cap \gamma_2)$, $(g_{31}, g_{21}, \gamma_1 \cap \beta_1)$ and $(g_{32}, g_{21}, \gamma_2 \cap \beta_1)$.

Repeat Step 2

(g_{11}, g_{32}, $\alpha_1 \cap \gamma_2$): $\delta_2 = (\{\psi\}, \{3a^2b^4\})$ gives $h_2 = \text{S-PolyP}_{\delta_2}(g_{11}, g_{32}) = [3a^2b^2y + 3b^3 - 3, -\psi x^2 y]$. Both h_2 and the basis $\mathcal{G}$ are unambiguous under δ_2. A normal form is $h_2' = h_2 - ag_{32} = [3\psi, -\psi x^2 y - a\psi x^2]$. Since $\overline{h_2'} = 3\psi = 0$ under δ_2, no new polynomial is added to $\mathcal{G}$.

The next critical pair is (g_{32}, g_{21}, $\gamma_2 \cap \beta_1$). $\delta_3 = (\{\psi\}, \{3a^2b^2\})$ resulting in $h_3 = \text{S-PolyP}_{\delta_3}(g_{32}, g_{21}) = x^2 g_{32} - 3b^2 g_{21} = [-6a^2b^2x^2 + 9ab^2, \psi x^4]$. Both h_3 and the basis $\mathcal{G}$ are unambiguous under δ_3. h_3 is already reduced, with $\overline{h_3} \neq 0$ under δ_3. So $h_3 = \psi x^4 - 6a^2b^2x^2 + 9ab^2$ is added as g_4 to the current basis: $\mathcal{G} = \{g_1, g_3, g_2, g_4\}$, where $g_1 < g_3 < g_2 < g_4$.

Repeat Step 3

It is checked whether adding g_4 can make polynomials g_1, g_2, g_3 in $\mathcal{G}$ redundant. First consider g_2, which has only one specialized tuple (g_{21}, β_1). $\mathcal{G} - \{g_2\}$ is ambiguous under $\beta_1 = (\emptyset, \{a\})$, so partition β_1 into β_{11}, β_{12} and β_{13}:

- Under $\beta_{11} = \beta_1 \cup \{ab^2 \neq 0, \psi \neq 0\}$: g_{21} has normal form $g_{21}' = \psi g_{21} + 3ag_1 - (ay + a^2)g_2 = [0, 0]$.
- Under $\beta_{12} = \beta_1 \cup \{ab^2 = 0\}$: Since $g_1 = [-1, ab^2y^2 + b^3]$, g_{21} can be fully reduced to 0 simply by g_1.
- Under $\beta_{13} = \beta_1 \cup \{\psi = 0, ab^2 \neq 0\}$: the reduction is $g_{21}'' = (-3b^2)g_{21} + x^2 g_3 - g_4$, where the non-zero part of g_{21}'' is 0.

So g_2 is reduced to 0 by $\mathcal{G} - \{g_2\}$ under any specialization. g_2 is redundant, and it is removed from $\mathcal{G}$.

Neither of the remaining polynomials g_1 and g_3 are redundant. The current basis is thus $\mathcal{G} = \{g_1, g_3, g_4\}$.

Since g_2 is no more in the current basis, all critical pairs due to g_2 are removed from $\mathcal{P}$ making $\mathcal{P} = \emptyset$.

Compute critical pairs due to Φ_{g_4}:

$\Phi_{g_4} = \{(g_{41} = [g_4, 0], \eta_1 = (\emptyset, \{\psi\}),$
$(g_{42} = [-6a^2b^2x^2 + 9ab^2, \psi x^4], \eta_2 = (\{\psi\}, \{6a^2b^2\}))\}$.

There is only one necessary pair: (g_{31}, g_{41}, $\gamma_1 \cap \eta_1$).

The segment associated with this critical pair is: $\delta_4 = \gamma_1 \cap \eta_1 = (\emptyset, \{\psi\})$, and $h_4 = \text{S-PolyP}_{\delta_4}(g_{31}, g_{41}) = x^2 g_{31} - g_{41} = 3ab^2x^2y + 3a^2b^2x^2 - 9ab^2$. Both h_4 and $\mathcal{G}$ are ambiguous under δ_4. So partition δ_4 as follows:

- Under $\delta_{40} = \delta_4 \cup \{ab^2 = 0\}$: h_4 already has non-zero part $\overline{h_4} = 0$.
- Under $\delta_{41} = \delta_4 \cup \{ab^2 \neq 0\}$: the reduction is $h_4' = \psi h_4 + 9ab^2 g_1 - (3ab^2y + 3a^2b^2)g_3$, where the non-zero part of h_4' is 0.

h_4 reduces to 0 by $\mathcal{G}$ under both the segments. Since that is the only critical pair in $\mathcal{P}$, the algorithm terminates with a CGB of I:$\mathcal{G} = \{g_1 : ab^2y^2 + b^3 - 1, g_3 : \psi x^2 + 3ab^2y - 3a^2b^2, g_4 : \psi x^4 - 6a^2b^2x^2 + 9ab^2\}$, where $\psi = a^3b^2 + b^3 - 1$.

4.2 Algorithm

As illustrated above, the *Completion* algorithm is patterned after Buchberger's algorithm for computing a Gröbner basis of a polynomial ideal. During the CGB check (*CGBTest*), if an S-polynomial does not reduce to 0 for the associated segment of specializations, its normal form is added to the current basis; this process is repeated until the CGB check succeeds implying that all S-polynomials generated from all distinct pairs of parametric polynomials in the current basis reduce to 0. The definitions of S-polynomials and reduction above ensure that every new polynomial added to the current basis in the completion algorithm is in the parametric ideal, thus ensuring faithfulness of the current basis as an invariant property of the completion algorithm. For more details about tuple operations, please see [7].

4.2.1 Minimality

In Buchberger's algorithm, a minimal Gröbner basis (MGB) is obtained by always using the newly added polynomial in normal form to simplify other polynomials in the current basis, by eliminating their leading terms. A reduced Gröbner basis (RGB) is achieved when full reduction is used for simplification and polynomials in the current basis are always kept in their normal forms. Such a minimal reduced Gröbner basis can be made unique for a given ideal I for a given term order $>$ by making the leading coefficient of every polynomial in the basis to be a unit.

For the parametric case, the properties of MGB and RGB are however a lot more difficult to achieve by *Completion* algorithm because of complications due to specializations. The normal form of a polynomial varies for different segments. In Example 4.1, g_4 can be reduced by $\mathcal{G} - \{g_4\}$ to 0 under η_1, but it is not even reducible under η_2. Removing g_4 from the basis would make $\mathcal{G} - \{g_4\}$ not a CGB; in fact, the parametric ideal generated without g_4 is a proper subideal of $\mathcal{G}$ for many specializations.

Algorithm Redundant($f, \mathcal{G}, \mathcal{E}, \mathcal{N}$)

Input: f: a parametric polynomial in $\mathcal{G}$; $\mathcal{G}$: a finite basis in $K[U][X]$; ($\mathcal{E}$,$\mathcal{N}$): the given parameter space, where $\mathcal{E}, \mathcal{N} \subseteq K[U]$.

Output: *True* if f is redundant in $\mathcal{G}$ on ($\mathcal{E}$,$\mathcal{N}$); *False* otherwise.

1. **if** $|\mathcal{G}| \leq 1$ **then return** *False*;
2. Compute Φ_f;
3. **for each** $(f_\alpha, \alpha) \in \Phi_f$: **{**
4. $\quad f \xrightarrow{\alpha}{}^{*}_{\mathcal{G}-\{f\}} f'$;
5. $\quad$ **if** $f' = 0$ under α **then**
6. $\quad\quad$ **continue**;
7. $\quad$ **else return** *False*; **}**
8. **return** *True*;

As illustrated above, the redundancy of polynomials in a basis is based relative to specializations (segments):

Definition 4.2 *Given a finite basis $\mathcal{F} \subseteq K[U][X]$, a polynomial $f \in \mathcal{F}$ is* **essential** *w.r.t. $\mathcal{F}$, if there is a non-empty segment α such that f is reduced by $\mathcal{F} - \{f\}$ to a non-zero normal form under α.*

Specifically, if the basis is a CGB, we have the following nice property which justifies the adjective "essential."

Proposition 4.3 *Given a CGB $\mathcal{G}$ of an ideal $I \subseteq K[U][X]$, a polynomial $f \in \mathcal{G}$ is essential w.r.t. $\mathcal{G}$, iff $\mathcal{G} - \{f\}$ is not a CGB of I.*

A minimal CGB (MCGB) can be defined as follows:

Definition 4.4 *A CGB $\mathcal{G}$ of an ideal $I \subseteq K[U][X]$ w.r.t. a term order $>$ is minimal, if the following conditions are satisfied –*

(1) No proper subset of $\mathcal{G}$ is a CGB of I w.r.t. $>$;

(2) For $\forall g \in \mathcal{G}$, $LC(g)$ is monic in $K[U]$.

The second requirement in Definition 4.4 enables the comparison among different minimal CGBs of the same ideal I using the extension of $>$ on polynomials to finite sets of polynomials, since I can have multiple minimal CGBs.

Essentiality can be used to characterize minimal CGBs as follows:

Corollary 4.5 *A CGB $\mathcal{G}$ of an ideal $I \subseteq K[U][X]$ is minimal, iff $\forall g \in \mathcal{G}$, g is essential w.r.t. $\mathcal{G}$ and monic w.r.t. $K[X, U]$.*

The above corollary motivates using *Redundant* algorithm below to achieve an MCGB. Assuming that every polynomial in the input basis is essential (which can be checked at the start of the algorithm) and by applying the *Redundant* algorithm on the basis every time a new polynomial is added to the basis, the *Completion* algorithm has another invariant property as stated below.

Proposition 4.6 *The basis $\mathcal{G}$ in the main loop of Completion algorithm (Line 8 to 21) contains only essential polynomials at the end of each iteration.*

Algorithm Completion($\mathcal{F},\mathcal{E},\mathcal{N}$)
Input: $\mathcal{F}$: a finite basis in $K[U][X]$; $(\mathcal{E},\mathcal{N})$: the given parameter space, where $\mathcal{E},\mathcal{N} \subseteq K[U]$.
Output: An MCGB $\mathcal{G}$ of ideal $I = \langle F \rangle$.

1. $\mathcal{G} := \mathcal{F}$;
2. **if** $|\mathcal{G}| \leq 1$ **then return** $\mathcal{G}$;
3. **for each** $f \in \mathcal{G}$: **{**
4.   **if** Redundant($f,\mathcal{G},\mathcal{E},\mathcal{N}$) **then**
5. $\mathcal{G} := \mathcal{G} - \{f\}$;
6.   **else** Compute Φ_f; **}**
7. $P := \{\pi = (f_\alpha, g_\beta, \alpha \cap \beta) \mid \alpha \cap \beta \neq \emptyset,\ f, g \in \mathcal{G},$ $(f_\alpha, \alpha) \in \Phi_f,\ (g_\beta, \beta) \in \Phi_g, \text{necessary}(\pi)\}$;
8. **while** $\mathcal{P} \neq \emptyset$ **{**
9.   Choose $\pi = (f_i, g_j, \delta_{ij}) \in \mathcal{P}$;
10. $h_{ij} = \text{S-PolyP}_{\delta_{ij}}(f_i, g_j)$;
11. $h_{ij} \xrightarrow{\delta_{ij}}{}^{*}_{\mathcal{G}}\ r = h'_{ij}$;
12.   **if** $r = 0$ under δ_{ij} **then**
13. $\mathcal{P} := \mathcal{P} - \{\pi\}$;
14.   **continue**;
  else
15.   **for each** $q \in \mathcal{G}$: **{**
16.   **if** Redundant($q, \mathcal{G} \cup \{r\}, \mathcal{E}, \mathcal{N}$) **then**
17. $\mathcal{G} := \mathcal{G} - \{q\}$;
18. $\mathcal{P} := \mathcal{P} - \{(\phi_\gamma, \psi_\eta, \gamma \cap \eta) \mid \phi = q \text{ or } \psi = q\}$; **}**
19.   Compute Φ_r;
20. $\mathcal{P} := \mathcal{P} \cup \{(r_\gamma, \phi_\eta, \gamma \cap \eta) \mid \gamma \cap \eta \neq \emptyset, \phi \in \mathcal{G},$ $(r_\gamma, \gamma) \in \Phi_r,\ (\phi_\eta, \eta) \in \Phi_\phi\}$;
21. $\mathcal{G} := \mathcal{G} \cup \{r\}$; **}**
22. **return** $\mathcal{G}$;

Invariant properties of a basis $\mathcal{G}$ at every iteration of the main loop of the *Completion* algorithm ensure that the basis always consists of faithful and essential polynomials.

The termination of the *Completion* algorithm on any given basis follows from (i) Dickson's Lemma, which is also needed for showing termination of Buchberger's completion algorithm and the fact that (ii) there are finitely many disjoint segments (Theorem 2.7 in [18]). and for each segment, the specialized ring is Noetherian, both of which follow from the Hilbert Basis Theorem. The correctness of the algorithm can be established by a proof similar to proofs of correctness of Buchberger's algorithms and algorithms given in [18, 5].

Theorem 4.7 *Given a finite basis $\mathcal{F} \subseteq K[U][X]$ and a parameter space $S = (\mathcal{E},\mathcal{N})$, the Completion algorithm terminates, and outputs a faithful minimal CGB of an ideal $I = \langle \mathcal{F} \rangle$ on S.*

In Example 4.1, the *Completion* algorithm indeed computes a minimal CGB $\mathcal{G} = \{g_1, g_3, g_4\}$ of I. Further, by performing the *Redundant* algorithm every time when adding a new polynomial to the basis, unnecessary critical pairs related to redundant polynomials are discarded. For example, after removing g_2 from the basis in Example 4.1, the pair $(g_{32},\ g_{21},\ \gamma_2 \cap \beta_1)$ in $\mathcal{P}$ is removed without consideration.

A normal selection strategy [1] is applied on triples in $\mathcal{P}$ to improve the efficiency. For instance, in Example 4.1, when $\mathcal{P}$ has 3 triples: $\pi_1 = (g_{11},\ g_{32},\ \alpha_1 \cap \gamma_2)$, $\pi_2 = (g_{31},\ g_{21},\ \gamma_1 \cap \beta_1)$ and $\pi_3 = (g_{32},\ g_{21},\ \gamma_2 \cap \beta_1)$, π_1 is chosen first, since $\text{lcm}(\text{LT}(g_{11}),\ \text{LT}(g_{32})) = y^2$ is the least, while those of the other two are both x^2y.

While the proposed completion algorithm is deterministic and computes a unique minimal CGB from a basis of any given ideal, different bases of the same ideal can lead the completion to generate different minimal CGBs. Further the order in which polynomials in the current basis are checked for redundancy can also lead to the completion algorithm producing different minimal CGBs. We have implemented a strategy in which polynomials in the current basis are checked for redundancy in descending order, with a purpose of removing larger redundant polynomials first and thus achieving a minimal CGB as small as possible.

5. RELATED WORKS

We have proposed a direct algorithm for computing a minimal faithful comprehensive Gröbner basis of a given parametric ideal. We are unaware of any other algorithm that computes a CGB directly from a given basis. All existing algorithms proposed in the literature instead first compute a comprehensive Gröbner system (CGS) of a given parametric ideal, which is a finite set of branches, with each branch consisting of a segment and a corresponding Gröbner basis under it. A CGB is then recovered from such a CGS by taking the union of these Gröbner bases. The resulting CGB is faithful only if branches in a CGS have faithful Gröbner bases; otherwise, the resulting CGB is not even faithful. Below we discuss other algorithms proposed in the literature from the stand point of whether they produce a minimal and/or faithful and/or unique comprehensive Gröbner basis.

Weispfenning's CGB and RGS (Reduced Gröbner System) algorithms in [18] and the parametric Gröbner basis (PGB) algorithm by Kapur in [5] are patterned after the Buchberger's algorithm much like the above proposed Completion algorithm. RGS is defined using S-polynomials and reduction relative to a condition γ (equivalent to a segment); similarly, PGB has constrained polynomials (γ, f), where f is a parametric polynomial and γ is a set of constraints, which is also equivalent to a segment. Both algorithms enforce the Gröbner basis under each segment to be reduced. Weispfenning's RGS looked similar to CGS. Weispfenning also defined a CGB to be the union of all polynomials generated during RGS computation after dropping the segments associated with the polynomials. The faithful CGS and CGB computed by the (KSW) algorithm proposed by Kapur, Sun and Wang in [7] have the property that under each segment γ, the corresponding Gröbner basis G_γ is minimal of the specialized ideal. The KSW algorithm thus computes a minimal CGS. However, the CGB recovered by taking the union of these corresponding Gröbner bases fails to be minimal [8]. That is despite the fact that all segments in the KSW are disjoint whereas that need not be the case for other algorithms. The RGS algorithm and the PGB algorithm do not have faithful polynomials in their bases; further, in the redundancy check, all specialized tuples of a polynomial f are used together for determining whether f is redundant, while they are considered independent of each other in RGS and PGB.

The Canonical Comprehensive Gröbner Basis (CCGB) algorithm [19] achieves the algorithm-dependent uniqueness of the resulting CGB, but it fails to be minimal or canonical in the sense that it is a unique minimal CGB associated with a parametric ideal for a given admissible term ordering. Consider Example 8.2 in [19], given a ring $\mathbb{Q}[v,u][z,y,x]$ and a lexicographic term order such that $z > y > x \gg v > u$, and an ideal $I = \langle f : uy + x,\ g : vz + x + 1\rangle$, CCGB algorithm computes CGB $\mathcal{G} = \{f, g, h, -h\}$, where $h = vz - uy + 1$. And it's easy to check that both $\{f, g, h\}$ and $\{f, g, -h\}$ are also CGBs of I, so $\mathcal{G}$ is neither minimal nor unique.

Algorithms proposed by Kapur, Sun and Wang in [6, 7] compute faithful CGSs, whereas algorithms of Suzuki and Sato [17] as well as the MCCGS [10] and Gröbner cover [12] algorithms of Montes and his collaborators do not compute faithful CGSs.

Montes' MCCGS algorithm also achieves an algorithm-dependent definition of uniqueness of CGS. It was later modified by Montes and Wibmer as the Gröbner Cover algorithm, in which the parametric coefficients are represented as regular functions rather than polynomials over $K[U]$. The modified algorithm computes a unique Gröbner cover for a given parametric ideal with a given admissible term ordering. It first homogenizes the given basis, then computes the canonical Gröbner Cover of this homogeneous ideal using [11, 6] as the first phase, and finally maps it back to the affine space. However, Gröbner cover is not faithful, thus no CGB emerges from it.

Suzuki and Sato's ACGB algorithm [15] over a von Neumann regular ring has a similar representation as Gröbner Cover algorithm. Its modified version [16] is patterned after Buchberger's algorithm and generates faithful CGBs, but they may still contain redundant polynomials.

6. EXPERIMENTAL EVALUATION

The proposed algorithm has been implemented on top of Singular system 4.0 [3]. Except for using basic polynomial operations of Singular, we had to implement S-polynomials and reduction of a polynomial with an associated segment by a basis of polynomials, from scratch since all computations must be done with respect to segments; we were thus unable to use any of the available infrastructure such as computing normal forms, reduction of a polynomial by a basis of polynomials, computing a Gröbner basis, etc. This has made our implementation slower compared to implementations for computing reduced Gröbner basis supported by Singular. Despite this disadvantage/handicap, we have successfully computed minimal CGBs of all examples of parametric ideals reported in [7, 10, 12, 13, 17, 19].

The efficiency and output of the Completion algorithm is compared with a two-phase algorithm of computing MCGBs proposed in [8]: first compute a faithful CGS and the associated CGB using the KSW algorithm, which is considered the fastest algorithm available for computing CGSs [13]; subsequently, an MCGB is generated from the CGB by removing redundant polynomials and simplifying non-redundant polynomials while the resulting set remains to be a CGB.

The Completion algorithm computes for most examples smaller minimal CGBs than the alternative approach. In simple small examples, the Completion algorithm is slower. But for complex examples, its performance is comparable to the above two-phase algorithm. A detailed comparison needs further inspection, especially after the Completion algorithm has been optimized using various heuristics.

The most surprising observation has been that using the proposed Completion algorithm, we are able to generate minimal faithful CGBs for some parametric ideals which cannot be obtained using any other algorithm. Below we give two such examples.

Example 6.1 *Consider Example 4.1. The KSW algorithm gives a CGB* $\mathcal{G} = \{g_1 : ab^2y^2 + b^3 - 1,\ g_2 : \psi x^2 + 3ab^2y - 3a^2b^2,\ g_3 : a^2\psi x^2 + 3a^3b^2y - 3a^4b^2,\ g_4 : a\psi x^4 - 6a^3b^2x^2 + 9a^2b^2\}$, *where* $\psi = a^3b^2 + b^3 - 1$.

The two-phase algorithm [8] however generates an MCGB $\mathcal{M}' = \{g_1, g_2, g_4\}$.

The Completion algorithm gives a smaller MCGB $\mathcal{M} = \{g_1, g_2, g_5\}$, *where* $g_5 = \psi x^4 - 6a^2b^2x^2 + 9ab^2$.

Example 6.2 *Given an ideal* $I = \langle (a-b)x^2 - by^2 + ay,\ axy - ay^2 - by\rangle \subseteq K[a,b][x,y]$ *and a graded lexicographic term order such that* $x > y \gg a > b$.

The KSW algorithm gives a CGB

$$\begin{aligned}
\mathcal{G} = \{\ & g_1 : axy - ay^2 - by,\\
& g_2 : (a-b)x^2 - by^2 + ay,\\
& g_3 : (a-b)x^2 - axy + (a-b)y^2 + (a+b)y,\\
& g_4 : (a^2 - 2ab)y^3 - b^2xy + (a^2 + 2ab - b^2)y^2 + b^2y,\\
& g_5 : axy^2 - ay^3 + (-a+b)x^2 - ay,\\
& g_6 : (a-2b)x^2y + (a-2b)y^3 + \frac{1}{2}(-a+2b)xy\\
& \quad + \frac{1}{2}(5a+2b)y^2 + \frac{1}{2}by,\\
& g_7 : (a-2b)x^2y + (a-2b)y^3 + \frac{1}{2}(5a+2b)xy\\
& \quad + \frac{1}{2}(-a+2b)y^2 - \frac{5}{2}by,\\
& g_8 : (a-2b)x^2y + (a-2b)y^3 + (6a-6b)x^2\\
& \quad + \frac{1}{2}(-a+2b)xy + \frac{1}{2}(5a-10b)y^2 + \frac{1}{2}(12a+b)y\ \}.
\end{aligned}$$

After removing redundant polynomials g_3, g_5, g_7, g_8, *the two-phase algorithm gives an MCGB* $\mathcal{M}_1 = \{g_1, g_2, g_4, g_6\}$.

Interestingly, the Completion algorithm gives an MCGB $\mathcal{M}_2 = \{g_1, g_2, g_9\}$, *where*
$g_9 = (a^3 - 2a^2b)y^3 + (a^3 + 2a^2b - 2ab^2)y^2 + (ab^2 - b^3)y$.

$\mathcal{M}_2$ *not only reduces the size of* $\mathcal{G}$ *by half, but it's the least MCGB with a smaller size and simpler polynomials than* $\mathcal{M}_1$.

7. CONCLUSION AND FUTURE WORK

We have presented a test for checking whether a basis of a parametric polynomial ideal is a comprehensive Gröbner basis or not. Further, we have also proposed a completion algorithm for computing a comprehensive Gröbner basis from a basis that fails the test of being a comprehensive Gröbner basis. The algorithm is patterned after Buchberger's algorithm in the sense that it uses S-polynomial construction as well as simplification/reduction. While the completion algorithm may have lots of similarities in using constructions proposed in [18] as well as [5], it is the first algorithm to compute a comprehensive Gröbner basis directly without having to go through a comprehensive Gröbner system. Other algorithms for computing a comprehensive Gröbner basis reported in the literature essentially compute a comprehensive Gröbner basis for various segments of specializations and then take the union of the results for each segment to get a comprehensive Gröbner basis for all specializations.

Depending upon an algorithm used for computing a comprehensive Gröbner basis for a segment, resulting comprehensive Gröbner basis for all specializations needs not be faithful in the sense that the polynomials in the basis may not be in the parametric ideal;

Many algorithms compute unfaithful comprehensive Gröbner systems and bases by keeping track of only the non-zero parts of polynomials under segments. KSW Algorithm differs from them in the sense that the results are faithful even though some of the polynomials in the output may not be essential. In contrast, an important feature of the completion algorithm proposed in this paper is that the output generated by it is a minimal comprehensive Gröbner basis of the input basis of the parametric polynomial ideal, consisting only of faithful polynomials. Because of this nice property, the completion algorithm has been able to generate minimal faithful CGBs for some parametric ideals which cannot be computed using any other algorithm for computing a CGB.

For future work, we plan to explore additional criteria for avoiding S-polynomials given that there are multiple S-polynomials generated from a pair of polynomials due to their different specializations. We plan to explore Buchberger's second criterion as well as possible criteria arising from considering various specializations arising from a single parametric polynomial. Different selection strategies for considering S-polynomials are also worth investigating in which it is not necessary to consider all S-polynomials arising due from a pair of polynomials due to different specializations. When reduction should be performed and interleaved with S-polynomial generation is another important research topic worth investigation for performance considerations. We are also interested in adapting signature-based algorithms for computing Gröbner basis to the parametric case. We however consider such an extension to be quite challenging.

As stated earlier, the proposed Completion algorithm is able to compute for certain parametric polynomial ideals, minimal CGBs which we are unable to generate using any other algorithm. This gives us hope that the Completion algorithm can perhaps be extended to generate a canonical CGB; a canonical CGB is a minimal CGB, which is like a reduced canonical Gröbner basis of a polynomial ideal, reduced and uniquely determined by a parametric ideal and an admissible term ordering on indeterminates and parameters, independent of any algorithm to compute it.

Acknowledgement

This research project is partially supported by an NSF award DMS-1217054. Some of this work was done during the first author's sabbatical at the Institute of Software, Chinese Academy of Sciences in Beijing, China, and was supported by the CAS/SAFEA Partnership Program for Creative Research Teams.

8. REFERENCES

[1] B. Buchberger, *A criterion for detecting unnecessary reductions in the construction of Gröbner-bases.* Symbolic and Algebraic Computation, Springer Berlin Heidelberg, 3-21, 1979.

[2] D. Cox, J. Little, and D. OSHEA. *Ideals, varieties, and algorithms: an introduction to computational algebraic geometry and commutative algebra*, Springer, 2007.

[3] W. Decker, G.-M. Greuel, G. Pfister, H. Schönemann, SINGULAR *3-1-6 — A computer algebra system for polynomial computations.* http://www.singular.uni-kl.de (2012).

[4] M. Kalkbrener, *On the stability of Gröbner bases under specializations*, Journal of Symbolic Computation 24.1: 51-58, 1997.

[5] D. Kapur, *An approach for solving systems of parametric polynomial equations*, In: Saraswat, Vijay, Van Hentenryck, Pascal (Eds.), Principles and Practices of Constraints Programming, MIT Press, pp. 217-224, 1995

[6] D. Kapur, Y. Sun, D. Wang, *An efficient algorithm for computing a comprehensive Gröbner system of a parametric polynomial system*, Journal of Symbolic Computation 49: 27-44, 2013

[7] D. Kapur, Y. Sun, D. Wang, *An efficient method for computing comprehensive Gröbner bases*, Journal of Symbolic Computation 52: 124-142, 2012

[8] D. Kapur, Y. Yang, *An algorithm for computing a minimal comprehensive Gröbner basis of a parametric polynomial system*, EACA 2014: 21, 2014

[9] M. Manubens, A. Montes, *Improving the DISPGB algorithm using the discriminant ideal*, Journal of Symbolic Computation 41.11: 1245-1263, 2006

[10] M. Manubens, A. Montes, *Minimal canonical comprehensive Gröbner systems*, Journal of Symbolic Computation 44.5: 463-478, 2009

[11] A. Montes, *A new algorithm for discussing Gröbner bases with parameters*, Journal of Symbolic Computation 33.2: 183-208, 2002

[12] A. Montes, M. Wibmer, *Gröbner bases for polynomial systems with parameters*, Journal of Symbolic Computation 45.12: 1391-1425, 2010

[13] A. Montes, *Using Kapur-Sun-Wang algorithm for the Gröbner cover*, In Proceedings of EACA 2012. Ed.: J.R. Sendra, C. Villarino. Universidad de Alcalá de Henares., pp. 135-138, 2012

[14] K. Nabeshima, *A speed-up of the algorithm for computing comprehensive Gröbner systems*, Proceedings of the 2007 international symposium on Symbolic and Algebraic Computation (pp. 299-306), ACM, 2007

[15] A. Suzuki, Y. Sato, *An alternative approach to comprehensive Gröbner bases*, Journal of Symbolic Computation 36.3: 649-667, 2003

[16] A. Suzuki, and Y. Sato, *Comprehensive Gröbner bases via ACGB*, ACA2004: 65-73, 2004.

[17] A. Suzuki, Y. Sato, *A simple algorithm to compute comprehensive Gröbner bases using Gröbner bases*, Proceedings of the 2006 international symposium on Symbolic and Algebraic Computation (pp. 326-331), ACM, 2006

[18] V. Weispfenning, *Comprehensive Gröbner bases*, Journal of Symbolic Computation 14.1: 1-29, 1992

[19] V. Weispfenning, *Canonical comprehensive Gröbner bases*, Journal of Symbolic Computation 36.3: 669-683, 2003

[20] M. Wibmer, *Gröbner bases for families of affine or projective schemes*, Journal of Symbolic Computation 42.8: 803-834, 2007

Integral D-Finite Functions

Manuel Kauers*
RISC / Johannes Kepler University
4040 Linz, Austria
mkauers@risc.jku.at

Christoph Koutschan†
RICAM / Austrian Academy of Sciences
4040 Linz, Austria
christoph.koutschan@ricam.oeaw.ac.at

ABSTRACT

We propose a differential analog of the notion of integral closure of algebraic function fields. We present an algorithm for computing the integral closure of the algebra defined by a linear differential operator. Our algorithm is a direct analog of van Hoeij's algorithm for computing integral bases of algebraic function fields.

Categories and Subject Descriptors

I.1.2 [**Computing Methodologies**]: Symbolic and Algebraic Manipulation—*Algorithms*

General Terms

Algorithms

Keywords

Integral Basis, D-finite Function, Differential Operator

1. INTRODUCTION

The notion of integrality is a classical concept in the theory of algebraic field extensions. If R is an integral domain, k the quotient field of R, and $K = k(\alpha)$ an algebraic extension of k of degree d, then an element of K is called *integral* if its monic minimal polynomial has coefficients in R. While K forms a k-vector space of dimension d, the set of all integral elements of K forms an R-module, called the *integral closure* (or *normalization*) of R in K, and commonly denoted by $\mathcal{O}_K$. A k-vector space basis of K which at the same time generates $\mathcal{O}_K$ as an R-module is called an *integral basis*. For example, when $R = \mathbb{Z}$, $k = \mathbb{Q}$, and $K = \mathbb{Q}(\alpha)$ with $\alpha = \sqrt[3]{4}$, then the canonical vector space basis $\{1, \alpha, \alpha^2\}$ of K is not an integral basis, because $\frac{1}{2}\alpha^2 = \sqrt[3]{2}$ is an integral element of K (its minimal polynomial is $x^3 - 2$) but not a $\mathbb{Z}$-linear combination of $1, \alpha, \alpha^2$. An integral basis in this example is $\{1, \alpha, \frac{1}{2}\alpha^2\}$.

The concept of integral closure has been studied in rather general domains [9, 6]. To compute an integral basis for an algebraic number field, special algorithms have been developed [7, 5]. At least two different approaches are known for algebraic function fields, i.e., the case when $R = C[x]$ for some field C, $k = C(x)$, and $K = k[y]/\langle M\rangle$ for some irreducible polynomial $M \in k[y]$. The algorithm derived by Trager [10] in his thesis is an adaption of an algorithm for number fields, and the algorithm by van Hoeij [12] is based on the idea of successively canceling lower order terms of Puiseux series.

The theory of algebraic functions parallels in many ways the theory of D-finite functions, i.e., the theory of solutions of linear differential operators. It is therefore natural to ask what corresponds to the notion of integrality in this latter theory. In the present paper, we propose such a definition and give an algorithm which computes integral bases according to this definition. Our algorithm and the arguments underlying its correctness are remarkably similar to van Hoeij's algorithm for computing integral bases of algebraic function fields.

In view of the key role that integral bases play for indefinite integration (Hermite reduction) of algebraic functions [10, 3, 2], we have hope that results presented below will help to develop new algorithms for indefinite integration of D-finite functions. An example pointing in this direction is given in the end.

Acknowledgment. We want to thank the anonymous referees for their detailed and valuable comments.

2. INTEGRAL FUNCTIONS, INTEGRAL CLOSURE, AND INTEGRAL BASES

Throughout this paper, let C be a computable field of characteristic zero, $\bar{C}$ an algebraically closed field containing C (not necessarily the smallest), and x transcendental over $\bar{C}$. When R is a subring of $\bar{C}(x)$, we write $R[D]$ for the algebra of differential operators with coefficients in R, i.e., the algebra of all (formal) polynomials $\ell_0 + \ell_1 D + \cdots + \ell_r D^r$ with $\ell_0, \ldots, \ell_r \in R$. This algebra is equipped with the natural addition and the unique noncommutative multiplication respecting the commutation rules $Dc = cD$ for all $c \in R \cap \bar{C}$ and $Dx = xD + 1$. Typical choices of R will be $C[x]$, $\bar{C}[x]$, $C(x)$, or $\bar{C}(x)$ in the following.

*Supported by the Austrian Science Fund (FWF): Y464.
†Supported by the Austrian Science Fund (FWF): W1214.

ISSAC'15, July 6–9, 2015, Bath, United Kingdom

ACM 978-1-4503-3435-8/15/07 ...$15.00.
DOI: http://dx.doi.org/10.1145/2755996.2756658

For an operator $L = \ell_0 + \ell_1 D + \cdots + \ell_r D^r \in \bar{C}[x][D]$ with $\ell_r \neq 0$ we denote by $\operatorname{ord}(L) = r$ the order of L. Recall that such an operator with $x \nmid \ell_r$ admits a fundamental system of formal power series solutions, i.e., the vector space $V \subseteq \bar{C}[[x]]$ consisting of all the power series f with $L \cdot f = 0$ has dimension r. When $x \mid \ell_r \neq 0$, there is still a fundamental system of generalized series solutions of the form $\exp(p(x^{-1/s}))x^\nu a(x^{1/s}, \log(x))$ for some $s \in \mathbb{N}$, $p \in \bar{C}[x]$, $\nu \in \bar{C}$, $a \in \bar{C}[[x]][y]$. (This notation is not meant to imply that a has a nonzero constant term, so the series in general does not start at x^ν but at some $x^{\nu+i}$ where $i \in \mathbb{N}$ is such that x^i is the lowest order term of a.) We restrict our attention here to the case where $p = 0$ and $s = 1$. Moreover, we want to assume that $\nu \in C$ (this can always be achieved by a suitable choice of C), to ensure that the output of our algorithm involves only coefficients in C. Hence we only consider operators L which admit a fundamental system in $\bigcup_{\nu \in C} x^\nu \bar{C}[[x]][\log x]$. It is well known [8] how to determine the first terms of a basis of such solutions for a given operator $L \in \bar{C}[x][D]$. By a linear change of variables, the same techniques can also be used to find the first terms of solutions in $\bigcup_{\nu \in C}(x-\alpha)^\nu \bar{C}[[x-\alpha]][\log(x-\alpha)]$, for any given $\alpha \in \bar{C}$. More precisely, if L belongs only to $C[x][D]$ and $\alpha \in \bar{C}$, then these solutions are actually linear combinations of elements of $\bigcup_{\nu \in C}(x-\alpha)^\nu C(\alpha)[[x-\alpha]][\log(x-\alpha)]$. For a field K with $C \subseteq K \subseteq \bar{C}$ we will use the notation

$$K[[[x-\alpha]]] := \bigcup_{\nu \in C} (x-\alpha)^\nu K[[x-\alpha]][\log(x-\alpha)].$$

Observe that this is not a ring or a K-vector space. Also observe that the exponents ν are restricted to the small field $C \subseteq K$, although the dependence on the choice of C is not reflected by the notation. We hope that the intended field C will always be clear from the context.

An operator $L \in \bar{C}[x][D]$ shall be considered integral if all the terms in all its series solutions remain above a certain threshold. In the algebraic case, where series solutions involve at worst only fractional exponents, the stipulation of having only nonnegative exponents in all the solutions happens to be equivalent to the requirement that the monic minimal polynomial has polynomial coefficients. In the differential case, solutions involving fractional exponents cause factors in the leading coefficient of L regardless of whether the exponents are positive or negative. Therefore it doesn't seem promising to use the leading coefficient of L for defining integrality. Instead, we will consider the exponents of its series solutions. These exponents ν may however belong to a field C which is not necessarily ordered, and there may be logarithmic terms. For our purposes we will use the following definition of integrality, depending on a function ι which can be chosen according to the needs of the user.

Definition 1. *Let $\iota\colon C/\mathbb{Z} \times \mathbb{N} \to C$ be a function such that*

1. *$\iota(\nu + \mathbb{Z}, j) \in \nu + \mathbb{Z}$ for every $\nu \in C$ and $j \in \mathbb{N}$,*
2. *$\iota(\nu_1 + \mathbb{Z}, j_1) + \iota(\nu_2 + \mathbb{Z}, j_2) - \iota(\nu_1 + \nu_2 + \mathbb{Z}, j_1 + j_2) \geq 0$ for every $\nu_1, \nu_2 \in C$ and $j_1, j_2 \in \mathbb{N}$,*
3. *$\iota(\mathbb{Z}, 0) = 0$.*

A series $f \in \bar{C}[[[x-\alpha]]]$ is called integral with respect to ι *if for all terms $(x-\alpha)^\mu \log(x-\alpha)^j$ occurring with a nonzero coefficient in f we have $\mu - \iota(\mu + \mathbb{Z}, j) \geq 0$. (For this to make sense the left-hand sides of the occurring inequalities have to be interpreted as integers, not as elements of C.)*

The function $\iota(\cdot, j)$ specifies for each element $\nu + \mathbb{Z}$ of $C/\mathbb{Z}$ the smallest element ν such that $x^\nu \log(x)^j$ should be considered integral. If $\iota(\nu + \mathbb{Z}, j) = \nu$, then $x^\nu \log(x)^j, x^{\nu+1}\log(x)^j, \ldots$ are integral and $x^{\nu-1}\log(x)^j, x^{\nu-2}\log(x)^j, \ldots$ are not. The condition $\iota(\mathbb{Z}, 0) = 0$ implies that formal Laurent series are integral if and only if they are in fact formal power series.

Example 2. *A natural choice for $C \subseteq \mathbb{C}$ is perhaps $\iota(z + \mathbb{Z}, 0) = z$ for all $z \in \mathbb{C}$ with $0 \leq \Re(z) < 1$, and $\iota(z + \mathbb{Z}, j) = z$ for all $z \in \mathbb{C}$ with $0 < \Re(z) \leq 1$ when $j \geq 1$. With this convention, a term $x^\nu \log(x)^j$ is integral if and only if the corresponding function is bounded in a small neighborhood of the origin. For example, 1, $x^{\sqrt{-1}}$, $x\log(x)$ all are integral, while x^{-1}, $x^{\sqrt{-1}-1}$, $\log(x)$ are not. Unless otherwise stated, we shall always assume this choice of ι in the examples given below.*

Proposition 3. *Let $\alpha \in \bar{C}$ and let R be the set of all $\bar{C}$-linear combinations of series in $(x-\alpha)^\nu \bar{C}[[x-\alpha]][\log(x-\alpha)]$, $\nu \in C$. Then:*

1. *In every series $f \in R$ there are at most finitely many terms $(x-\alpha)^\mu \log(x-\alpha)^j$ which are not integral.*
2. *The set R together with the natural addition and multiplication forms a ring, and $\{ f \in R \mid f \text{ is integral} \}$ forms a subring of R.*

Proof. 1. First consider the case when $f \in (x-\alpha)^\nu \bar{C}[[x-\alpha]][\log(x-\alpha)]$ for some $\nu \in C$. Let $\deg(f)$ denote the highest power of $\log(x-\alpha)$ in f. Then the only possible non-integral terms in f can be $(x-\alpha)^{\nu+i}\log(x-\alpha)^j$ for $j \in \{0, \ldots, \deg(f)\}$ and $i \in \{0, \ldots, \iota(\nu + \mathbb{Z}, j) - \nu - 1\}$. These are finitely many. In general, if f is a linear combination of some series in $(x-\alpha)^\nu \bar{C}[[x-\alpha]][\log(x-\alpha)]$ with possibly distinct $\nu \in C$, the set of all non-integral terms is still a finite union of finite sets of non-integral terms, and therefore finite.

2. It is clear that R is a ring. To see that the integral elements form a subring, let $f, g \in R$ be integral. Then the series $f + g$ cannot contain any term which is not present in at least one of the two summands, so all terms of $f + g$ are integral and $f + g$ as a whole is integral. Now consider multiplication: for any term $(x-\alpha)^\mu \log(x-\alpha)^j$ in $f \cdot g$ there must be some terms τ in f and σ in g such that $\sigma\tau = (x-\alpha)^\mu \log(x-\alpha)^j$, say $\tau = (x-\alpha)^{\mu_1}\log(x-\alpha)^{j_1}$ and $\sigma = (x-\alpha)^{\mu_2}\log(x-\alpha)^{j_2}$. Since f and g are integral, we have $\mu_1 - \iota(\mu_1 + \mathbb{Z}, j_1) \geq 0$ and $\mu_2 - \iota(\mu_2 + \mathbb{Z}, j_2) \geq 0$. The assumption on ι in Definition 1 implies that $(\mu_1 + \mu_2) - \iota(\mu_1 + \mu_2 + \mathbb{Z}, j_1 + j_2) = \mu - \iota(\mu + \mathbb{Z}, j) \geq 0$. Hence all terms of $f \cdot g$ are integral, so also the product of two integral elements is integral. ■

Definition 4. *Let $L \in \bar{C}(x)[D]$ and ι be as in Definition 1.*

1. *We call L* regular *if it has a fundamental system in $\bar{C}[[[x-\alpha]]]$ for every $\alpha \in \bar{C}$.*
2. *L is called* (locally) integral at α with respect to ι *if it admits a fundamental system in $\bar{C}[[[x-\alpha]]]$ whose elements all are integral.*
3. *L is called* (globally) integral with respect to ι *if it is locally integral at α in the sense of part 2 for every $\alpha \in \bar{C}$.*

Of course part 2 of this definition is independent of the choice of the fundamental system. In fact, L is locally integral at α iff all its series solutions in $x-\alpha$ are integral and form a $\bar{C}$-vector space of dimension $\operatorname{ord}(L)$.

Example 5. *1. The operator $(2-x)+2(2-2x+x^2)D+4(x-1)xD^2 \in \mathbb{Q}[x][D]$ is locally integral at $\alpha=0$, because its two linearly independent solutions*

$$1-\tfrac{1}{2}x-\tfrac{1}{24}x^3-\tfrac{7}{384}x^4-\tfrac{53}{3840}x^5+\mathrm{O}(x^6),$$
$$x^2+\tfrac{1}{6}x^3+\tfrac{1}{6}x^4+\tfrac{13}{120}x^5+\mathrm{O}(x^6)$$

are both integral. It is also locally integral at $\alpha=1$, because its two linearly independent solutions

$$(x-1)^{1/2}+\mathrm{O}((x-1)^6),$$
$$1-\tfrac{1}{2}(x-1)+\tfrac{1}{8}(x-1)^2-\tfrac{1}{48}(x-1)^3+\mathrm{O}((x-1)^4)$$

are integral as well.

The operator is also globally integral because at all $\alpha \in \mathbb{C}\setminus\{0,1\}$ it has a fundamental system of formal power series, and formal power series are always integral.

2. The operator $1+xD \in \mathbb{Q}[x][D]$ is not locally integral at $\alpha=0$, because it has the non-integral solution $\frac{1}{x}$. It is therefore also not globally integral.

3. The operator $(-1-2x)+(x+2x^2)D+(x^3+x^4)D^2 \in \mathbb{Q}[x][D]$ is not locally integral at $\alpha=0$ although all its series solutions are. The reason is that it has only one series solution in $\mathbb{C}[[[x]]]$ while our definition requires that the number of linearly independent series solutions must match the order of the operator. In other words, generalized series solutions involving exponential terms, like the solution $\exp(\frac{1}{x})$ in the present example, are always considered as not integral.

Let $L=\ell_0+\cdots+\ell_rD^r \in C[x][D]$ with $\ell_r \neq 0$ and consider the quotient algebra $\bar{C}(x)[D]/\langle L\rangle$, where $\langle L\rangle := \bar{C}(x)[D]L$ denotes the left ideal generated by L in $\bar{C}(x)[D]$. The algebra $\bar{C}(x)[D]/\langle L\rangle$ is generated as a $\bar{C}(x)$-vector space by the basis $\{1,D,\dots,D^{r-1}\}$. It is also a $\bar{C}(x)[D]$-left module, and we can interpret its elements as all those "functions" which can be reached by letting an operator $P \in \bar{C}(x)[D]$ act on a "generic solution" of L, very much like the elements of an algebraic extension field $\bar{C}(x)[y]/\langle M\rangle$ can be described as those objects which can be reached by applying a polynomial $P \in \bar{C}(x)[y]$ to a "generic root" of M. A difference in this analogy is that in the algebraic case there are only finitely many roots while in the differential case we have a finite dimensional $\bar{C}$-vector space of solutions.

Definition 6. *Let $L=\ell_0+\cdots+\ell_rD^r \in C[x][D]$ with $\ell_r \neq 0$ be a regular operator and let ι be as in Definition 1.*

1. An element $P \in A=\bar{C}(x)[D]/\langle L\rangle$ is called integral *(with respect to ι) if $P\cdot f$ is integral (with respect to ι) for every series solution f of L.*

2. The $\bar{C}[x]$-left module $\mathcal{O}_L$ of all integral elements of A is called the integral closure *of $\bar{C}[x]$ in A.*

3. A $\bar{C}(x)$-vector space basis

$$\{B_1,\dots,B_r\} \subseteq \bar{C}(x)[D]/\langle L\rangle$$

is called an integral basis *if it also generates $\mathcal{O}_L$ as $\bar{C}[x]$-left module.*

It is easy to see that $\mathcal{O}_L$ is a $\bar{C}[x]$-left module. Note however that $\mathcal{O}_L$ is in general not a $\bar{C}[x][D]$-left module, because the application of D may turn integral elements into non-integral ones (for example, $D\cdot x^{1/2}=\frac{1}{2}x^{-1/2}$ when $\iota(\frac{1}{2}+\mathbb{Z},0)=\frac{1}{2}$).

Example 7. *1. The operator $L=1-D \in \mathbb{Q}[x][D]$ has for every $\alpha \in \mathbb{C}$ one power series solution of the form $f=1+\mathrm{O}(x-\alpha)$. Since f is integral we have $1 \in \mathcal{O}_L$. Since $(x-\alpha)^{-1}f$ is not integral for any α, we have in fact that $\{1\}$ is an integral basis.*

2. The operator $L=1+xD$ has the solution $f=\frac{1}{x}$. It is integral for every $\alpha \neq 0$, but not integral at $\alpha=0$. However, $xf=1$ is integral, hence $x \in \mathcal{O}_L$, and in fact $\{x\}$ is an integral basis.

3. Whenever L has only power series solutions at every $\alpha \in \bar{C}$, we clearly have $\{1,D,\dots,D^{r-1}\} \subseteq \mathcal{O}_L$. However, there may still be integral elements that are not $C[x]$-linear combinations of these. For example, observe that for the operator $L=(x-1)+D-xD^2$, which has two solutions $\exp(x)=1+x+\frac{1}{2}x^2+\mathrm{O}(x^3)$ and $(2x+1)\exp(-x)=x^2+\mathrm{O}(x^3)$, we have the non-trivial element $\frac{1}{x}(1-D) \in \mathcal{O}_L$. Note that it is integral at all $\alpha \neq 0$ as well.

4. It can also happen that $1 \in \mathcal{O}_L$ but $D \notin \mathcal{O}_L$. For example, for $L=(-1+2x)+(1-4x)D+2xD^2$ we have two solutions $1+x+\frac{1}{2}x^2+\mathrm{O}(x^3)$ and $x^{1/2}+x^{3/2}+\frac{1}{2}x^{5/2}+\mathrm{O}(x^3)$ at $\alpha=0$. Since both are integral (and there are two linearly independent power series solutions for every $\alpha \neq 0$) we have $1 \in \mathcal{O}_L$. However, $D \notin \mathcal{O}_L$, because the derivative of the second solution is $\frac{1}{2}x^{-1/2}+\frac{3}{2}x^{1/2}+\frac{5}{4}x^{3/2}+\mathrm{O}(x^2)$, which is not integral since it involves the term $x^{-1/2}$. An integral basis in this case turns out to be $\{1,xD\}$.

5. We have produced a prototype implementation in Mathematica of the algorithm described below. The code is available on the homepage of the first author. For the operator $L=x^3D^3+xD-1$, it finds the integral basis $\{1,xD,xD^2-D+\frac{1}{x}\}$. A fundamental system of L is $\{x,x\log(x),x\log(x)^2\}$.

6. Let $L=24x^3D^3-134x^2D^2+373xD-450$. This operator has the solutions $x^{3/2}$, $x^{10/3}$, and $x^{15/4}$. Our code finds the integral basis

$$\Big\{\frac{1}{x},\frac{1}{x^2}D-\frac{3}{2x^3},\frac{1}{x}D^2-\frac{7}{2x^2}D+\frac{9}{2x^3}\Big\}.$$

In the analogy with algebraic functions, the integral operators from Definition 4 correspond to the monic minimal polynomials with coefficients in a ring, and the integral elements of Definition 6 correspond to integral elements of an algebraic function field. Definitions 4 and 6 are obviously connected as follows.

Proposition 8. *Let $L \in C[x][D]$ and $\tilde{L} \in \bar{C}(x)[D]$ be regular and assume that there exists $P \in \bar{C}(x)[D]$ such that for every $\alpha \in \bar{C}$ we have*

$$\{\,f \mid \tilde{L}\cdot f=0\,\}=\{\,P\cdot f \mid L\cdot f=0\,\}$$

where f runs over $\bar{C}[[[x-\alpha]]]$ on both sides. Then $P+\langle L\rangle \in \bar{C}(x)[D]/\langle L\rangle$ is integral in the sense of Definition 6 if and only if $\tilde{L}$ is integral in the sense of Definition 4.

Lemma 9. *Let $L = \ell_0 + \cdots + \ell_r D^r \in \bar{C}[x][D]$ with $\ell_r \neq 0$ be a regular operator. Let $p_0, \ldots, p_{r-1} \in \bar{C}(x)$ and let $p = x - \alpha \in \bar{C}[x]$ be a factor of the common denominator of $p_0, \ldots, p_{r-1}$. If $p_0 + \cdots + p_{r-1}D^{r-1} \in \mathcal{O}_L$ then $p \mid \ell_r$.*

Proof. After performing a change of variables, we may assume that $p = x$. By a classical result about linear differential equations (e.g., [8]), $x \nmid \ell_r$ implies that L admits a fundamental system $b_0, \ldots, b_{r-1}$ in $C[[x]]$ with $b_i = x^i + \mathrm{O}(x^r)$ for $i = 0, \ldots, r-1$. Then $D^j b_i = i(i-1)\cdots(i-j+1)x^{i-j} + \mathrm{O}(x^{r-j})$ for $i = 0, \ldots, r-1$ and $j = 0, \ldots, r-1$. Let e_i be the largest integer such that x^{e_i} divides the denominator of p_i, let $e = \max\{e_0, \ldots, e_{r-1}\}$, and let $i \in \{0, \ldots, r-1\}$ be some index with $e_i = e$. Then $p_i D^i b_i = i!x^{-e} + \mathrm{O}(x^{-e+1})$ and $p_j D^j b_i = \mathrm{O}(x^{-e+1})$ for all $j \neq i$. Hence $(p_0 + p_1 D + \cdots + p_{r-1}D^{r-1}) \cdot b_i = i!x^{-e} + \mathrm{O}(x^{-e+1})$ is not integral because $-e - \iota(-e + \mathbb{Z}, 0) = -e - \iota(\mathbb{Z}, 0) = -e < 0$, and hence $p_0 + p_1 D + \cdots + p_{r-1}D^{r-1} \notin \mathcal{O}_L$. ■

3. ALGORITHM OUTLINE

We shall now discuss how to construct an integral basis $\{B_0, \ldots, B_{r-1}\}$ for a given regular operator $L \in C[x][D]$. The key observation is that van Hoeij's algorithm for computing integral bases for algebraic function fields as well as the arguments justifying its correctness and termination carry over almost literally to the present setting. The remainder of this paper therefore follows closely the corresponding sections of van Hoeij's paper.

The algorithm computes the basis elements $B_0, \ldots, B_{r-1}$ in order, at each stage $d \in \{0, \ldots, r-1\}$ starting with an initial conservative guess for B_d and refining it repeatedly until an operator B_d is found which together with $B_0, \ldots, B_{d-1}$ generates the $\bar{C}[x]$-left module consisting of all the elements of $\mathcal{O}_L$ corresponding to operators of order d or less. Although parts of the calculation take place in the large field $\bar{C}$, it will be shown that the elements B_i in the resulting integral basis always have coefficients in the small field C, in which the coefficients of the input operator L live.

It is not hard to find a suitable B_0: For each root $\alpha \in \bar{C}$ of the leading coefficient ℓ_r of L, compute the first terms of a basis $\{b_1, \ldots, b_r\}$ of solutions in $\bar{C}[[[x-\alpha]]]$. Determine the smallest integer e_α such that $(x-\alpha)^{e_\alpha} b_i$ is integral for every i according to the chosen ι. Then B_0 can be set to the product of $(x-\alpha)^{e_\alpha}$ over all α. Since $e_\alpha = e_{\tilde{\alpha}}$ whenever $\tilde{\alpha}$ is a conjugate of α, it follows that B_0 belongs to $C(x)$.

The outline of the algorithm is now given on a conceptual level. In Section 5 a more detailed description of steps 5–7 will be given.

Algorithm 10.
INPUT: A regular operator $L = \ell_0 + \cdots + \ell_r D^r \in C[x][D]$ with $\ell_r \neq 0$
OUTPUT: $\{B_0, \ldots, B_{r-1}\} \subseteq C(x)[D]/\langle L\rangle$, an integral basis of $\bar{C}(x)[D]/\langle L\rangle$.

1 Set s to the squarefree part of ℓ_r.
2 Set B_0 to the zero-order operator described above.
3 For $d = 1, \ldots, r-1$, do the following:
4 Set $B_d = s\,D\,B_{d-1}$. (Also $B_d = s^d D^d B_0$ would work.) Consider

$$E = \{\, A \in \mathcal{O}_L : \mathrm{ord}(A) \leq d \,\} \setminus \big(\bar{C}[x]B_0 + \cdots + \bar{C}[x]B_d\big).$$

5 While $E \neq \emptyset$, do the following:
6 Construct $A \in E$ of the form

$$A = \frac{1}{p}\big(a_0 B_0 + \cdots + a_{d-1}B_{d-1} + B_d\big)$$

with $a_0, \ldots, a_{d-1}, p \in C[x]$.
7 We have

$$\bar{C}[x]B_0 + \cdots + \bar{C}[x]B_{d-1} + \bar{C}[x]B_d \subsetneq \bar{C}[x]B_0 + \cdots + \bar{C}[x]B_{d-1} + \bar{C}[x]A \subseteq \mathcal{O}_L.$$

Replace B_d by A. (This makes E strictly smaller.)
8 Return $\{B_0, \ldots, B_{r-1}\}$.

In the refined version of the algorithm, we will see that the set E is never explicitly constructed. Instead, it suffices to be able to solve the following subproblems. First, we need to decide whether $E = \emptyset$ for recognizing the termination of the loop in lines 5–7; this is discussed in Section 5. Second, we need to show the existence of an element $A \in E$ of the form required in step 6 whenever $E \neq \emptyset$; see Section 4. In Section 5 we explain how such an A is constructed. Finally, the termination of the loop in lines 5–7 is proved in Section 6. Except for these issues, the correctness of the algorithm is obvious.

4. EXISTENCE OF A IF $E \neq \emptyset$

The arguments in this section are almost identical to those in [12]. Nevertheless, for sake of completeness, we formulate them here for the differential case.

In the d-th iteration of the algorithm we can assume by induction that $B_0, \ldots, B_{d-1}$ with $\mathrm{ord}(B_i) = i$ for all i form a $\bar{C}[x]$-left module basis of all integral elements of order up to $d-1$. We consider the case where the current choice of B_d, together with $B_0, \ldots, B_{d-1}$, does not generate all integral elements of order up to d, i.e., $E \neq \emptyset$. Recall that

$$E = \{\, A \in \mathcal{O}_L : \mathrm{ord}(A) \leq d \,\} \setminus \big(\bar{C}[x]B_0 + \cdots + \bar{C}[x]B_d\big).$$

We need to show that there exists an integral element $A \in E$ which can be written in the form $\frac{1}{p}(a_0 B_0 + \cdots + a_d B_d)$ with $a_0, \ldots, a_d, p \in C[x]$ and $a_d = 1$. The idea is as follows: starting from an arbitrary element $A \in E$, we construct, in several steps, simpler elements in E until we obtain one with the desired properties.

Lemma 11. *If $E \neq \emptyset$, then there exists $A \in E$ of the form*

$$A = \frac{1}{x-\alpha}\big(a_0 B_0 + \cdots + a_{d-1}B_{d-1} + a_d B_d\big) \tag{1}$$

with $\alpha \in \bar{C}$, $a_0, \ldots, a_{d-1}, a_d \in \bar{C}[x]$.

Proof. Let $A \in E$, say $A = a_0 B_0 + \cdots + a_d B_d$ for some $a_i \in \bar{C}(x)$. Since $A \notin \bar{C}[x]B_0 + \cdots + \bar{C}[x]B_d$, at least one a_i must be in $\bar{C}(x) \setminus \bar{C}[x]$. Let $p \in \bar{C}[x]$ be the common denominator of all the a_i, and let $\alpha \in \bar{C}$ be a root of p. Then $\frac{p}{x-\alpha}A$ has the required form. To see that it belongs to E, notice that $\frac{p}{x-\alpha} \in \bar{C}[x]$ and $\mathcal{O}_L$ is a $\bar{C}[x]$-module, and that $\frac{p}{x-\alpha}A \notin \bar{C}[x]B_0 + \cdots + \bar{C}[x]B_d$. ■

Lemma 12. *If $A \in E$ and $P \in \bar{C}[x]B_0 + \cdots + \bar{C}[x]B_d$, then $A + P \in E$.*

Proof. $A \in E \subseteq \mathcal{O}_L$ and $P \in \bar{C}[x]B_0 + \cdots + \bar{C}[x]B_d \subseteq \mathcal{O}_L$ implies that $A+P \in \mathcal{O}_L$. It is also clear that $\mathrm{ord}(A+P) \leq d$, because $\mathrm{ord}(A) \leq d$ and $\mathrm{ord}(P) \leq d$. Finally, to show that

$A+P \notin \bar{C}[x]B_0+\cdots+\bar{C}[x]B_d$, assume otherwise. Then also $A=(A+P)-P \in \bar{C}[x]B_0+\cdots+\bar{C}[x]B_d$ in contradiction to $A \in E$. ∎

Lemma 13. *If E contains an element of the form (1), then it also contains such an element with $a_0,\dots,a_{d-1} \in \bar{C}$ and $a_d = 1$.*

Proof. Let $A = \frac{1}{x-\alpha}\big(a_0B_0+\cdots+a_dB_d\big) \in E$ be of the form (1). For each $i = 0,\dots,d$, write $a_i = (x-\alpha)p_i + a_i'$ with $p_i \in \bar{C}[x]$ and $a_i' \in \bar{C}$. By Lemma 12, $A \in E$ implies $A' \in E$ for $A' := \frac{1}{x-\alpha}\big(a_0'B_0+\cdots+a_{d-1}'B_{d-1}+a_d'B_d\big)$. Since $B_0,\dots,B_{d-1}$ are assumed to generate the submodule of all the elements of $\mathcal{O}_L$ of order at most $d-1$, we have $a_d' \neq 0$. Dividing A' by a_d' yields an element of E of the requested form. ∎

Lemma 14. *If E contains an element of the form (1) with $a_0,\dots,a_{d-1} \in \bar{C}$ and $a_d = 1$, then it also contains such an element with $a_0,\dots,a_{d-1} \in C(\alpha)$ and $a_d = 1$.*

Proof. Let $A \in E$ be of the form (1) with $a_0,\dots,a_{d-1} \in \bar{C}$ and $a_d = 1$. Since $\bar{C}$ is necessarily a $C(\alpha)$-vector space, there are some $C(\alpha)$-linearly independent elements $e_0,\dots,e_n$ of $\bar{C}$ such that $a_0,\dots,a_d$ all belong to $V = e_0C(\alpha)+\cdots+e_nC(\alpha)$. We may assume $e_0 = 1$. Consider a fundamental system $b_1,\dots,b_r \in C(\alpha)[[[x-\alpha]]]$ of L. Then each $A \cdot b_j$ has coefficients in V and, since $A \in E \subseteq \mathcal{O}_L$, only involves integral terms. For an element $v \in V$ let us write $[e_i]v$ for the coordinate of v with respect to e_i. By the linear independence of the e_i over $C(\alpha)$, the series $[e_i]\big(A \cdot b_j\big) = ([e_i]A)\cdot b_j$ obtained from $A \cdot b_j$ by replacing each coefficient by its e_i-coordinate will be integral. In particular, the operator $A_0 = [e_0]A \in C(\alpha)[x][D]$ must belong to E. Because of $[e_0]a_d = [e_0]1 = 1$, it meets all the requirements. ∎

Lemma 15. *If E contains an element of the form (1) with $a_0,\dots,a_{d-1} \in C(\alpha)$ and $a_d = 1$, then it also contains such an element with $a_0,\dots,a_{d-1} \in C[x]$ and $a_d = 1$.*

Proof. For every $n > 0$ we have $x-\alpha \mid x^n - \alpha^n$ in $\bar{C}[x]$, and thus also $x-\alpha \mid p(x)-p(\alpha)$ for $p \in \bar{C}[x] \setminus \bar{C}$. Therefore, if we view the $a_i \in C(\alpha)$ as polynomials in α, then replacing α in them by x amounts to adding some polynomial multiple of $(x-\alpha)$ to them. This change means for $A = \frac{1}{x-\alpha}(a_0B_0+\cdots+a_{d-1}B_{d-1}+B_d)$ that adding a suitable element $P \in C(\alpha)[x]B_0+\cdots+C(\alpha)[x]B_{d-1} \subseteq \mathcal{O}_L$ turns A into an operator of the requested form. By Lemma 12, this new operator also belongs to E. ∎

Theorem 16. *If $E \neq \emptyset$, then there exists an element $A \in E$ of the form*

$$A = \frac{1}{p}\big(a_0B_0+\cdots+a_{d-1}B_{d-1}+B_d\big)$$

with $p \in C[x]$ an irreducible factor of ℓ_r and $a_0,\dots,a_{d-1} \in C[x]$ such that $\deg(a_i) < \deg(p)$ for all i.

Proof. The assumption $E \neq \emptyset$ in combination with Lemmas 11, 13, 14, and 15 implies that E contains an element of the form (1) with $a_0,\dots,a_{d-1} \in C[x]$ and $a_d = 1$. Furthermore, Lemma 9 implies that α is a root of ℓ_r. Let $p \mid \ell_r$ be the minimal polynomial of α. We claim that $A := \frac{1}{p}B \in E$ where $B := a_0B_0+\cdots+a_{d-1}B_{d-1}+B_d$.

To prove this, we have to show that for every $\tilde{\alpha} \in \bar{C}$ and every solution $\tilde{b} \in C(\tilde{\alpha})[[[x-\tilde{\alpha}]]]$ of L we still have that $A \cdot \tilde{b}$ is integral. When $\tilde{\alpha}$ is not a root of p, this is clear because $1/p$ admits an expansion in $C[[x-\tilde{\alpha}]]$, and multiplication of the integral series $B \cdot \tilde{b}$ by a formal power series preserves integrality by Proposition 3. When $\tilde{\alpha} = \alpha$, write $p = (x-\alpha)q$ for some $q \in \bar{C}[x]$ with $x-\alpha \nmid q$ and note that $1/q$ admits an expansion in $\bar{C}[[x-\alpha]]$ and $\frac{1}{x-\alpha}B \cdot \tilde{b}$ is integral, so $\frac{1}{p}B \cdot \tilde{b}$ is integral too. When $\tilde{\alpha}$ is a conjugate of α, note that $\frac{1}{x-\tilde{\alpha}}B \cdot \tilde{b}$ must be integral, because if it were not, then for the series $b \in C(\alpha)[[[x-\alpha]]]$ obtained from $\tilde{b}$ via the conjugation map that sends $\tilde{\alpha}$ to α we would have that $\frac{1}{x-\alpha}B \cdot b$ is also not integral, in contradiction to our choice of $a_0,\dots,a_d$. Therefore the same argument as in the case $\tilde{\alpha} = \alpha$ applies.

This completes the proof of the claim. To complete the proof of the theorem, note that the claimed degree bounds on a_i can be ensured by Lemma 12. ∎

5. CONSTRUCTION OF A IN STEP 6

In the previous section we have demonstrated that in step 6 of the algorithm it suffices to search for an integral element A of the form

$$A = \frac{1}{p}\big(a_0B_0+\cdots+a_{d-1}B_{d-1}+B_d\big)$$

where $a_0,\dots,a_{d-1},p \in C[x]$, $p \mid \ell_r$ and $\deg(a_i) < \deg(p)$. Conversely, this means that if no such A exists, the set E is empty.

For each irreducible factor p of ℓ_r one can set up an ansatz for A with undetermined coefficients $a_0,\dots,a_{d-1}$. We want to find $a_0,\dots,a_{d-1}$ such that $A \cdot f$ is integral for all solutions f of L. Note that we need to enforce integrality only for series solutions in $x-\alpha$ where α is a root of p. Choosing a fundamental system $b_1,\dots,b_r$ of such solutions, computing the first terms of $B_j \cdot b_i$, plugging them into the ansatz, and equating the coefficients of all non-integral terms to zero yields a linear system for $a_0,\dots,a_{d-1}$. If this system does not admit a solution, one knows that no such A with denominator p exists.

In summary, the loop in lines 5–7 of Algorithm 10 can be described in more detail as follows.

5a Let $Q \subseteq \bar{C}$ be a set containing exactly one root $\alpha \in \bar{C}$ for each irreducible factor p of ℓ_r.
5b While $Q \neq \emptyset$, do the following:
5c   For all $\alpha \in Q$, do the following:
6a   Let $b_1,\dots,b_r$ be a fundamental system of L in $C(\alpha)[[[x-\alpha]]]$.
6b   With variables $a_0,\dots,a_{d-1}$, form the series

$$\big(a_0B_0+\cdots+a_{d-1}B_{d-1}+B_d\big)b_i$$

    for $i = 1,\dots,r$.
6c   Construct a linear system for $a_0,\dots,a_{d-1}$ by equating the coefficients of all the non-integral terms in these series to zero.
7a   If the system has a solution $(a_0,\dots,a_{d-1}) \in C(\alpha)^d$:
7b   Let p be the minimal polynomial of α over C.
7c   Replace each $a_i \in C(\alpha) = C[x]/\langle p\rangle$ by the corresponding polynomial in $C[x]$ of degree less than $\deg(p)$.

7d Replace B_d by $\frac{1}{p}(a_0B_0 + \cdots + a_{d-1}B_{d-1} + B_d)$.
7e Otherwise
7f discard α from Q.

Despite being more detailed than the listing given in Algorithm 10, these lines are still somewhat conceptual. An actual implementation cannot just "let" b_i be some infinite series object, and it does not need to. What we need are only the terms of b_i that give rise to some non-integral terms of $(a_0B_0+\cdots+a_{d-1}B_{d-1}+B_d)b_i$. These are only finitely many by Proposition 3. In Section 7 we address the question how many terms of b_i we need to compute.

6. TERMINATION

The termination of van Hoeij's algorithm [12] is established by the observation that the degree of a certain polynomial, starting with the discriminant $\operatorname{Res}_y\left(M, \frac{\partial M}{\partial y}\right)$, decreases in each iteration of the main loop. In the case of D-finite functions, the role of the discriminant is played by the *Wronskian* and a generalized version of it. Recall that the Wronskian of the functions $f_1(x), \dots, f_r(x)$ is defined as the determinant

$$W = \begin{vmatrix} f_1(x) & f_2(x) & \cdots & f_r(x) \\ f_1'(x) & f_2'(x) & \cdots & f_r'(x) \\ \vdots & \vdots & \ddots & \vdots \\ f_1^{(r-1)}(x) & f_2^{(r-1)}(x) & \cdots & f_r^{(r-1)}(x) \end{vmatrix}. \tag{2}$$

Definition 17. *Let $L \in \bar{C}[x][D]$ be regular and let $b_1, \dots, b_r$ be a fundamental system of L in $\bar{C}[[[x-\alpha]]]$ for some $\alpha \in \bar{C}$. For $B_0, \dots, B_{r-1} \in \bar{C}(x)[D]/\langle L\rangle$ we define the* generalized Wronskian at α, *as*

$$\operatorname{wr}_{L,\alpha}(B_0, \dots, B_{r-1}) := \begin{vmatrix} B_0 \cdot b_1 & \cdots & B_0 \cdot b_r \\ \vdots & \ddots & \vdots \\ B_{r-1} \cdot b_1 & \cdots & B_{r-1} \cdot b_r \end{vmatrix}.$$

Note that the generalized Wronskian $\operatorname{wr}_{L,\alpha}(B_0, \dots, B_{r-1})$ belongs to $\bar{C}[[[x-\alpha]]]$ and that the choice of a different fundamental system instead of $b_1, \dots, b_r$ only changes its value by a nonzero multiplicative constant, which will be irrelevant for our purpose.

For the special choice $B_i = D^i$, the generalized Wronskian $\operatorname{wr}_{L,\alpha}(1, D, \dots, D^{r-1})$ reduces to the Wronskian (2) with $f_i = b_i$. It is well-known and easy to check that the classical Wronskian (2) of $b_1, \dots, b_r$ satisfies the first-order equation $\ell_r D W + \ell_{r-1} W = 0$ and hence is hyperexponential. Since the generalized Wronskian can be obtained from the usual Wronskian by elementary row operations over $C(x)$, it is clear that also the generalized Wronskian is hyperexponential.

Theorem 18. *Algorithm 10 terminates.*

Proof. First observe that during the whole execution of the algorithm, $B_0, \dots, B_{r-1} \in C(x)[D]/\langle L\rangle$ are integral, i.e., $B_0 \cdot f, \dots, B_{r-1} \cdot f$ are integral for any series solution f of L according to Definition 6. (Actually, the B_d's are constructed one after the other, but they can be initialized with $B_d = s^d D^d B_0$.) This means that, at any time and for any $\alpha \in \bar{C}$, the generalized Wronskian $\operatorname{wr}_{L,\alpha}(B_0, \dots, B_{r-1})$ is integral, as it is the sum of products of integral series (see Proposition 3). Since it is hyperexponential, it follows that it has no logarithmic terms. Every nonzero term of $\operatorname{wr}_{L,\alpha}(B_0, \dots, B_{r-1})$ is therefore of the form $(x-\alpha)^\mu$ with $\mu = \iota(\mu + \mathbb{Z}, 0) + m$ for some nonnegative integer m. For each $\alpha \in \bar{C}$ let m_α be the smallest such integer. Now let $n = \sum_{\alpha \in Q} m_\alpha$ where Q is defined as in step 5a. Each time B_d is updated in the algorithm (either in step 4 or in step 7d), none of the m_α can increase and exactly one of them strictly decreases, so also n decreases. More precisely, if for example B_d is replaced by $\frac{1}{p}(a_0B_0 + \cdots + a_{d-1}B_{d-1} + B_d)$ in step 7, then $\operatorname{wr}_{L,\alpha}(B_0, \dots, B_d)$ is divided by p (recall that p is a non-constant polynomial in $C[x]$). But the m_α cannot become negative as this would violate the integrality of $\operatorname{wr}_{L,\alpha}(B_0, \dots, B_{r-1})$. Therefore the algorithm must terminate. ∎

7. BOUNDS

In the algebraic case, van Hoeij [12] gave a-priori bounds on the orders to which the b_i have to be calculated. His algorithm computes their terms at the very beginning once and for all in order to avoid their recomputation inside the loop. He also suggested that the terms of $B_j \cdot b_i$ for $j < d$ should not be recomputed but cached.

Nowadays, in an object-oriented programming environment, the algorithm can be implemented in such a way that recomputations of series terms are avoided even when no a-priori bound on the truncation order is available, via the paradigm of lazy series [4, 11].

Nevertheless it is desirable to have a-priori bounds available also in the D-finite case. A rough bound follows immediately from the discussion in Section 6: as we have seen, the Wronskian $\operatorname{wr}_{L,\alpha}\left(B_0, sDB_0, \dots, s^{r-1}D^{r-1}B_0\right)$ gives a denominator bound for the elements of the integral basis. More refined bounds are elaborated in the following.

Let $\alpha \in \bar{C}$ be a root of the leading coefficient ℓ_r and $\{b_1, \dots, b_r\} \subset C(\alpha)[[[x-\alpha]]]$ be a fundamental system of L:

$$b_i = \sum_{k=0}^{\infty} b_{i,k}\big(\log(x-\alpha)\big)\,(x-\alpha)^{\nu_i+k}, \quad b_{i,0} \neq 0, \tag{3}$$

where $b_{i,k} \in C(\alpha)[\log(x-\alpha)]$ are polynomials in $\log(x-\alpha)$ such that for each i the degrees of $b_{i,0}, b_{i,1}, \dots$ are bounded by some integer d_i. According to step 5c, we have to consider each $\alpha \in Q$ separately, so for the rest of this section we fix such an α.

In step 6a we want to replace $b_1, \dots, b_r$ by truncated series $t_1, \dots, t_r$ of the form

$$t_i = \sum_{k=0}^{N_i} b_{i,k}\big(\log(x-\alpha)\big)\,(x-\alpha)^{\nu_i+k} \text{ with } N_i \in \mathbb{N}. \tag{4}$$

The bounds N_i must be chosen such that this replacement does not change the result of the algorithm. The only critical step is when $b_1, \dots, b_r$ are used to test the integrality of certain elements from the algebra $C(x)[D]/\langle L\rangle$, which are not known in advance. Theorem 20 below gives a sufficient condition that allows us to use t_i instead of b_i in the integrality test, by asserting that its answer does not change, whatever element of $C(x)[D]/\langle L\rangle$ we consider. For brevity, let R denote the ring $C(\alpha)[[x-\alpha]][\log(x-\alpha)]$ in the subsequent reasoning.

Lemma 19. *Let $\{b_1, \dots, b_r\} \subset C(\alpha)[[[x-\alpha]]]$ be a fundamental system of the form (3) with ν_i as above, and let $W_b = (D^j \cdot b_i)_{1 \le i \le r, 0 \le j < r}$. Then we can find an $m \in \mathbb{N}$ such* *that*

$$\det(W_b) = \sum_{k=0}^{\infty} w_k \, (x-\alpha)^{\nu_1+\cdots+\nu_r-r(r-1)/2+m+k}$$

with $w_0 \neq 0$.

Proof. For the (i,j)-entry of W_b we have

$$(W_b)_{i,j} = D^{j-1} \cdot b_i \in (x-\alpha)^{\nu_i-j+1}R$$

and therefore

$$\det(W_b) \in (x-\alpha)^{\nu_1+\cdots+\nu_r-r(r-1)/2}R.$$

Note that $\det(W_b) \neq 0$ because it is precisely the Wronskian of $b_1,\ldots,b_r$. It follows that a unique $m \geq 0$ with the desired property exists. ∎

Theorem 20. *Let $L \in C(x)[D]$ be an operator of order r and $\{b_1,\ldots,b_r\} \subset C(\alpha)[[[x-\alpha]]]$ be a fundamental system of L with ν_i and d_i as above. Moreover, let $m \in \mathbb{N}$ be as in Lemma 19 and let $N_1,\ldots,N_r \in \mathbb{N}$ be given by*

$$N_i = m + \max_{\substack{1\leq j\leq r\\ 0\leq k<d_i+r}} \Big(\iota(\nu_i-\nu_j+\mathbb{Z},k) - (\nu_i-\nu_j)\Big).$$

If t_i is the truncation (4) of b_i at order N_i, for $1 \leq i \leq r$, then for all $B \in C(x)[D]/\langle L\rangle$ we have the equivalence:

$$\forall i\colon B\cdot b_i \text{ is integral} \iff \forall i\colon B\cdot t_i \text{ is integral.} \qquad (5)$$

Proof. We introduce the matrix $W_b = (D^j \cdot b_i)_{1\leq i\leq r, 0\leq j<r}$ as before, and the short notation $B\cdot b = (B\cdot b_1,\ldots,B\cdot b_r)$. Analogously we define W_t and $B\cdot t$. A vector resp. matrix is called integral if all its entries are integral. If c is the coefficient vector of B, i.e., $c\cdot(1,D,\ldots,D^{r-1}) = B$, then we have $B\cdot b = W_b\, c$ and $B\cdot t = W_t\, c$. Combining these two equations we get

$$B\cdot t = W_t W_b^{-1}(B\cdot b). \qquad (6)$$

Setting $Z = W_b - W_t$ yields

$$W_t W_b^{-1} = \mathrm{Id}_r - Z W_b^{-1}. \qquad (7)$$

The proof is split into two parts, according to the two directions of the equivalence (5).

Part 1: If we assume that $B\cdot b$ is integral, then (6) exhibits that the integrality of $W_t W_b^{-1}$ is a sufficient condition to conclude that also $B\cdot t$ is integral, using Proposition 3. By (7) it suffices to show that ZW_b^{-1} is integral. First of all we have to argue that $W_b^{-1} \in C(\alpha)[[[x-\alpha]]]^{r\times r}$ since otherwise Definition 1 would not be applicable. In Section 6 we have remarked that the Wronskian $\det(W_b)$ is hyperexponential. In particular, it involves no logarithmic terms and therefore is invertible in $C(\alpha)[[[x-\alpha]]]$. Using Cramer's rule we find that

$$\left(W_b^{-1}\right)_{i,j} = (-1)^{i+j}\frac{\det W_b^{[j,i]}}{\det W_b} \in (x-\alpha)^{i-\nu_j-m-1}R,$$

where $W_b^{[j,i]}$ is the matrix obtained by deleting row j and column i from W_b. So the entries of W_b^{-1} are series in $C(\alpha)[[[x-\alpha]]]$. The fact that $\det W_b^{[j,i]}$ satisfies a differential equation of order less than or equal to r implies that the highest power of $\log(x-\alpha)$ that can appear in the entries of W_b^{-1} is $r-1$. On the other hand, it is easy to see that $Z_{i,j} \in (x-\alpha)^{\nu_i+N_i-j+2}R$, so it follows that

$$\left(ZW_b^{-1}\right)_{i,j} \in (x-\alpha)^{\nu_i-\nu_j+N_i-m+1}R, \qquad (8)$$

and that herein $\log(x-\alpha)$ appears with exponent at most d_i+r-1. By our choice of N_i the series in (8) is integral for all $1\leq i,j\leq r$ and therefore the whole matrix ZW_b^{-1}.

Part 2: Now assume that $B\cdot b$ is not integral. Then from

$$B\cdot t = \left(\mathrm{Id}_r - ZW_b^{-1}\right)(B\cdot b) = B\cdot b - \left(ZW_b^{-1}\right)(B\cdot b)$$

it follows that $B\cdot t$ is non-integral as well. To see this, let n be the largest integer such that a term of the form $(x-\alpha)^{\iota(\mu+\mathbb{Z},k)-n}\log(x-\alpha)^k$ appears in $B\cdot b$ for some $\mu \in C$ and $k \in \mathbb{N}$. Let i be an index such that a term of the given form appears in $B\cdot b_i$ with nonzero coefficient. This term cannot be canceled in

$$B\cdot t_i = B\cdot b_i - \sum_{j=1}^{r}\left(ZW_b^{-1}\right)_{i,j}(B\cdot b_j)$$

because all terms of the series $\left(ZW_b^{-1}\right)_{i,j}$ are of the form $(x-\alpha)^{\iota(\nu_i-\nu_j+\mathbb{Z},k)+\ell}\log(x-\alpha)^k$ with $\ell \geq 1$ by our choice of N_i. So also $B\cdot t$ is not integral. ∎

8. COMPARISON WITH THE ALGEBRAIC CASE

We have shown that the underlying ideas of van Hoeij's algorithm for computing integral bases of algebraic function fields apply in a more general context. Indeed, it is fair to regard van Hoeij's algorithm as a special case of our algorithm, since every algebraic function is also D-finite. Recall that an algebraic function field $C(x)[y]/\langle M\rangle$ with some irreducible polynomial M of degree d becomes a differential field if we set $D\cdot c = 0$ for all $c \in C$, $D\cdot x = 1$, and

$$D\cdot y := -\frac{\frac{d}{dx}M}{\frac{d}{dy}M} \bmod M.$$

Since $C(x)[y]/\langle M\rangle$ is also a $C(x)$-vector space of dimension d, it is clear that any $d+1$ elements must be $C(x)$-linearly dependent. This implies the existence of an operator $L \in C(x)[D]$ of order at most d with $L\cdot y = 0$. Usually there is no such operator of lower order, which means that $y, D\cdot y,\ldots,D^{d-1}\cdot y$ are $C(x)$-linearly independent and thus a basis of $C(x)[y]/\langle M\rangle$. In this case, a vector space basis $\{B_1,\ldots,B_d\} \subseteq \mathbb{C}(x)[y]/\langle L\rangle$ is an integral basis in the sense of Definition 6 if and only if $\{B_1\cdot y,\ldots,B_d\cdot y\} \subseteq \mathbb{C}(x)[y]/\langle M\rangle$ is an integral basis of the algebraic function field in the classical sense.

When $y \in C(x)[y]/\langle M\rangle$ is annihilated by an operator L of order less than d, we can compute the minimal-order operators $L_0,\ldots,L_{d-1}$ which annihilate $y^0,\ldots,y^{d-1}$, respectively, and take $L = \mathrm{lclm}(L_0,\ldots,L_{d-1})$. Then the $C(x)$-vector space generated by all solutions of L is the whole field $C(x)[y]/\langle M\rangle$, and if $\{B_1,\ldots,B_n\}$ is an integral basis for L, then $\{B_i\cdot y^j : i=1,\ldots,n,\ j=0,\ldots,d-1\}$ generates the $C[x]$-module of all integral elements of $C(x)[y]/\langle M\rangle$.

As a less brutal approach, we can simply replace y by some other generator of the field. In practice, most field generators will have an annihilating operator of order d, but none of smaller order.

Example 21. *An integral basis for the field* $\mathbb{Q}(x)[y]/\langle M\rangle$ *with* $M = y^3 - x^2$ *is* $\{1, y, \frac{1}{x}y^2\}$. *The lowest-order differential operator annihilating* y *is* $L = 3xD - 2$, *which is not useful because its order is less than the degree of* M.

Instead, let us try $Z = 1 + y + y^2$ *as generator. We have* $\mathbb{Q}(x)[y]/\langle M\rangle = \mathbb{Q}(x)[Z]/\langle N\rangle$, *where* $N = Z^3 - 3Z^2 - 3(x^2-1)Z - x^4 + 2x^2 - 1$ *is the minimal polynomial of* Z. *Given* N *instead of* M *as input, van Hoeij's algorithm finds the following integral basis for* $\mathbb{Q}(x)[Z]/\langle N\rangle$:

$$\left\{1, Z, \frac{Z^2}{x(x-1)(x+1)} - \frac{(x^2+2)Z}{x(x-1)(x+1)} - \frac{1}{x}\right\}. \quad (9)$$

The lowest order annihilating operator of Z *is* $L = 9x^2D^3 + 9xD^2 - D$. *It has the right order and our Mathematica implementation returns the integral basis* $\{1, xD, xD^2 + \frac{1}{3}D\}$. *We can express its derivatives as polynomials in* Z, *using*

$$D \cdot Z = \frac{-2Z^2 + 2(2x^2+1)Z}{3x(x-1)(x+1)},$$

and obtain the following integral basis for $\mathbb{Q}(x)[Z]/\langle N\rangle$:

$$\left\{Z, \frac{-2Z^2 + 2(2x^2+1)Z}{3(x-1)(x+1)}, \frac{8(-Z^2 + (x^2+2)Z + x^2 - 1)}{9x(x-1)(x+1)}\right\}.$$

Applying a change of basis with the unimodular matrix

$$\frac{1}{8}\begin{pmatrix} 8 & -12 & 9x \\ 8 & 0 & 0 \\ 0 & 0 & -9 \end{pmatrix}$$

gives the integral basis (9) computed by Maple.

One of the features of integral bases for algebraic function fields is that they allow an extension of the classical Hermite reduction for integration of rational functions to the case of algebraic functions. This was observed by Trager [10]. In order to make this work, Trager requires that both the integral basis as well as the integrand should be "normal at infinity". This corresponds to the condition in the rational case that the rational function to be integrated must not have a polynomial part. Trager shows that normality of the integrand can always be achieved by applying a suitable change of variables, and he gives an algorithm that turns an arbitrary integral basis into one that is normal at infinity. After that, the Hermite reduction process looks very similar to the rational case. We give here an example for a non-algebraic D-finite function.

Example 22. *Let* $L = (2x+1) - (4x^2+1)D + 2(2x-1)xD^2$; *its solutions are* $\exp(x)$ *and* $\sqrt{x}$, *but we will not use this information. Let us just write* y *for a solution of* L. *An integral basis of* $\mathcal{O}_L$ *is given by* $\{1, \frac{1}{2x-1}(2xD-1)\}$. *Let* $\omega_0 := y$ *and* $\omega_1 := \frac{1}{2x-1}(2xD-1)\cdot y$ *and consider the function*

$$f = \frac{a_0\omega_0 + a_1\omega_1}{uv^m}$$

where $a_0 = 4x^2 + 37x - 11$, $a_1 = -28x^3 + 40x^2 - x - 1$, $u = 4$, $v = (x-1)x$, $m = 2$.

Hermite reduction consists in finding $b_0, b_1, c_0, c_1 \in \mathbb{Q}[x]$ *with*

$$\frac{a_0\omega_0 + a_1\omega_1}{uv^m} = \left(\frac{b_0\omega_0 + b_1\omega_1}{v^{m-1}}\right)' + \frac{c_0\omega_0 + c_1\omega_1}{uv^{m-1}}.$$

After working out the differentiation, multiplying by uv^m, *and taking the whole equation mod* v *we are left with the constraint*

$$a_0\omega_0 + a_1\omega_1 \equiv b_0uv^m\left(\frac{\omega_0}{v^{m-1}}\right)' + b_1uv^m\left(\frac{\omega_1}{v^{m-1}}\right)' \bmod v$$

For the derivatives of ω_0 *and* ω_1 *we have*

$$D\omega_0 = \frac{1}{2x}\omega_0 - \frac{1-2x}{2x}\omega_1, \quad D\omega_1 = \omega_1,$$

so that the previous constraint can be rewritten to

$$a_0\omega_0 + a_1\omega_1 \equiv -\tfrac{1}{2}b_0u(3\omega_0 + \omega_1) - 2b_1u\omega_1 \bmod v.$$

Plugging in a_0, a_1 *and* u *and comparing coefficients of* ω_i *leads to the linear system*

$$\begin{pmatrix} 41x - 11 \\ 11x - 1 \end{pmatrix} = \begin{pmatrix} 2-6x & 2-2x \\ 0 & 4-8x \end{pmatrix}\begin{pmatrix} b_0 \\ b_1 \end{pmatrix} \bmod v$$

which has the solution $b_0 = \frac{1}{2}(4x+11)$, $b_1 = \frac{5}{2}(2x-1)$. *Next we find that*

$$f - \left(\frac{b_0\omega_0 + b_1\omega_1}{v^{m-1}}\right)' = \frac{c_0\omega_0 + c_1\omega_1}{uv^{m-1}}$$

for $c_0 = 0$, $c_1 = 0$. *Consequently, we have found that*

$$\int f = \frac{(11+4x)\omega_0 + 5(2x-1)\omega_1}{8(1-x)^2x^2} = \frac{5}{x-1}y' - \frac{2x+3}{(x-1)x}y.$$

The same answer could have been found using an algorithm of Abramov and van Hoeij [1], using a different approach.

9. REFERENCES

[1] Sergei A. Abramov and Mark van Hoeij. Integration of solutions of linear functional equations. *Integral transforms and Special Functions*, 9:3–12, 1999.

[2] Manuel Bronstein. The lazy Hermite reduction. Technical Report 3562, INRIA, 1998.

[3] Manuel Bronstein. Symbolic integration tutorial. ISSAC'98, 1998.

[4] William H. Burge and Stephen M. Watt. Infinite structures in scratchpad II. In *Proceedings of the European Conference on Computer Algebra*, EUROCAL '87, pages 138–148, London, UK, 1989.

[5] Henri Cohen. *A Course in Computational Algebraic Number Theory.* Springer, 1993.

[6] Theo de Jong. An algorithm for computing the integral closure. *Journal of Symbolic Computation*, 26(3):273–277, 1998.

[7] David J. Ford. *On the Computation of the Maximal Order in a Dedekind Domain.* PhD thesis, Ohio State University, 1978.

[8] Edward L. Ince. *Ordinary Differential Equations.* Dover, 1926.

[9] Irena Swanson and Craig Huneke. *Integral closure of ideals, rings, and modules*, volume 336 of *London Mathematical Society Lecture Note Series.* Cambridge University Press, 2006.

[10] Barry M. Trager. *Integration of algebraic functions.* PhD thesis, Massachusetts Institute of Technology, 1984.

[11] Joris van der Hoeven. Relax, but don't be too lazy. *Journal of Symbolic Computation*, 34(6):479–542, 2002.

[12] Mark van Hoeij. An algorithm for computing an integral basis in an algebraic function field. *Journal of Symbolic Computation*, 18(4):353–363, 1994.

On the Sign of a Trigonometric Expression

Pierre-Vincent Koseleff
INRIA, Paris-Rocquencourt, Ouragan
UPMC-Sorbonne Universités
CNRS, UMR 7586, IMJ-PRG
pierre-vincent.koseleff@upmc.fr

Fabrice Rouillier
INRIA, Paris-Rocquencourt, Ouragan
UPMC-Sorbonne Universités
CNRS, UMR 7586, IMJ-PRG
fabrice.rouillier@inria.fr

Cuong Tran
UPMC-Sorbonne Universités
CNRS, UMR 7586, IMJ-PRG
cuong.tran@imj-prg.fr

ABSTRACT

We propose a set of simple and fast algorithms for evaluating and using trigonometric expressions in the form $F = \sum_{k=0}^{d} f_k \cos k\frac{\pi}{n}$, $f_k \in \mathbf{Z}$, $d < n$ for a fixed $n \in \mathbf{Z}_{>0}$: computing the sign of such an expression, evaluating it numerically and computing its minimal polynomial in $\mathbf{Q}[x]$. As critical byproducts, we propose simple and efficient algorithms for performing arithmetic operations (multiplication, division, gcd) on polynomials expressed in a Chebyshev basis (with the same bit-complexity as in the monomial basis) and for computing the minimal polynomial of $2\cos\frac{\pi}{n}$ in $\widetilde{\mathcal{O}}(n_0^2)$ bit operations with $n_0 \leq n$ is the odd squarefree part of n. Within such a framework, we can decide if $F = 0$ in $\widetilde{\mathcal{O}}(d(\tau+d))$ bit operations, compute the sign of F in $\widetilde{\mathcal{O}}(d^2\tau)$ bit operations and compute the minimal polynomial of F in $\widetilde{\mathcal{O}}(n^3\tau)$ bit operations, where τ denotes the maximum bitsize of the f_k's.

Categories and Subject Descriptors

I.1.4 [**Computing Methodologies**]: Symbolic and Algebraic Manipulation—*Applications*; F.2.1 [**Theory of Computation**]: Analysis Of Algorithms And Problem Complexity—*Computations on polynomials*

General Terms

Algorithms, Theory

Keywords

Chebyshev polynomial, minimal polynomial, cyclotomic polynomial, root isolation

1. INTRODUCTION

The present contribution was initially motivated by the computation of Chebyshev knots with the objective of decreasing the complexity bound of the algorithm proposed in [11]. The bottleneck for this algorithm was the computation of the sign of a multivariate polynomial at the zeroes of a zero-dimensional system. It has been shown later [10] that this problem finally reduces to the computation of the sign of a polynomial with rational coefficients at some particular real points in the form $\cos\frac{\pi}{n}$, $n \in \mathbf{Z}_{>0}$, which can easily be turned into the computation of the sign of an expression in the form $F = \sum_{k=0}^{d} f_k \cos k\frac{\pi}{n}$, $f_k \in \mathbf{Z}$ for a fixed n in $\mathbf{Z}_{>0}$.

Evaluating numerically such an expression can be done straightforwardly, but getting its sign (in particular deciding if it is null or not) or computing its minimal polynomial to use it for further exact computations needs some efforts to be done efficiently in practice.

As $F = f(2\cos\frac{\pi}{n})$ with $f(x) = f_0 + \sum_{k=1}^{d} f_k T_k(x)$, where $T_k(x) \in \mathbf{Z}[x]$ is the k-th monic Chebyshev polynomial, evaluating F can be seen as evaluating $f \in \mathbf{Q}[x]$ at the real value $2\cos\frac{\pi}{n}$, testing if $F = 0$ can resume to testing if the minimal polynomial $M_n \in \mathbf{Q}[x]$ of $2\cos\frac{\pi}{n}$ divides f and, finally, computing the minimal polynomial $M_F \in \mathbf{Q}[x]$ of F reduces to computing the minimal polynomial M_f of f in $\mathbf{Q}[x]/(M_n)$.

Our primary objective was thus to find a way for computing efficiently $M_n \in \mathbf{Q}[x]$, the minimal polynomial of $2\cos\frac{\pi}{n}$ in order, for example, to use state of the art algorithms for testing if $F = 0$ (which then resumes to a single polynomial division) or computing M_F (for example using [15]).

The algorithm we propose in section 4 for computing M_n is an adaptation of the algorithm from [1] that basically computes Φ_n, the minimal polynomial of the n-th primitive root of unity. The relation between Φ_n and M_n is simple: $\Phi_{2n} = \mathcal{D}(M_n)$, where $\mathcal{D}$ is the transformation $\mathbf{Q}[x]$ defined by $\mathcal{D}(P) = x^{\deg P} P(x + \frac{1}{x})$.

This simple transformation is also used in Section 2 to set simple and fast algorithms for multiplying, dividing, computing greatest common divisors for polynomials expressed in the Chebyshev basis. In particular, we provide, for the multiplication, a very simple alternative to [7] with an equivalent bit complexity. More generally, the complexity of these operations is the same as for polynomials in the monomial basis (see [16]).

It turns out that expressing the polynomials in the Chebyshev basis instead of in the usual monomial basis simplifies some parts of the algorithms and makes easier the computation of complexity bounds. For example, we show that the computation of M_n can be done in $\widetilde{\mathcal{O}}(n_0^2)$ bit operations where $n_0 \leq n$ is the odd squarefree part of n.

The efficiency of this algorithm depends also on the way the transformations from the Chebyshev basis to the monomial basis and vice-versa are computed. In order not to rein-

ISSAC'15, July 6–9, 2015, Bath, United Kingdom.

DOI: http://dx.doi.org/10.1145/2755996.2756664.

vent the wheel, we have considered these transformations as a particular case of the composition method developed in [8] with additional refinements linked to the properties of Chebyshev polynomials.

In section 3, we show that passing from the monomial basis to the Chebyshev basis consists essentially to inject in the algorithm from [8] the fast operations we have introduced in Section 2. For the reverse operation, we make use of the linear recurrence introduced in [4] and essentially keep the structure of the composition algorithm from [8], thanks to some remarkable properties of Chebyshev polynomials. We finally show that the two transformations we propose perform $\widetilde{\mathcal{O}}(d)$ arithmetic operations in $\mathbf{Z}$ and $\widetilde{\mathcal{O}}(d^2 + d\tau)$ bit operations if τ is the maximal bitsize of the f_k's.

In section 5, we first come back to our initial problem and propose some algorithms together with their complexity analysis. We show that we can test whether $F = 0$ in $\mathcal{O}(n^2 + n\tau)$ binary operations and can decide the sign of F in $\widetilde{\mathcal{O}}(n^2\tau)$ binary operations, using an algorithm of [6] for a fast evaluation of $\cos x$.

As F could also be used inside other algebraic expressions, we propose in section 6 an algorithm for computing efficiently the minimal polynomial of F in $\widetilde{\mathcal{O}}(n^3\tau)$ binary operations.

2. CHEBYSHEV POLYNOMIALS

As seen in the introduction, Chebyshev polynomials and their algebraic properties play a central role in the present contribution. We consider the *Chebyshev monic polynomials*[1] defined by

$$T_n(x) = 2\cos nt, \quad U_n(x) = \frac{\sin nt}{\sin t},$$

where $x = 2\cos t$. Both of them satisfy the linear recurrence relation:

$$P_{n+1}(x) = xP_n(x) - P_{n-1}(x), \tag{1}$$

but their first terms differ: $\{T_0(x) = 2, T_1(x) = x\}$,$\{U_0(x) = 0, U_1(x) = 1\}$. The roots of T_n and U_n are real roots and we have:

$$T_n(x) = \prod_{k=0}^{n-1}(x - 2\cos\tfrac{(2k+1)\pi}{2n}), \tag{2a}$$

$$U_n(x) = \prod_{k=1}^{n-1}(x - 2\cos\tfrac{k\pi}{n}). \tag{2b}$$

By derivating the relation $T_n(2\cos t) = 2\cos nt$, we obtain $\sin t\, T_n'(2\cos t) = n \sin nt$ that is

$$T_n' = nU_n. \tag{3}$$

By derivating once again we obtain

$$4(\sin t)^2\, T_n''(2\cos t) + 2\cos t\, T_n'(2\cos t) = 2n^2 \cos nt,$$

or, equivalently,

$$(4 - x^2)T_n''(x) - xT_n'(x) + n^2T_n(x) = 0. \tag{4}$$

[1]For getting simpler relations in the sequel, our notations differ from the usual definition of Chebyshev polynomials of first or second kind such as those from [12] where $T_n(\cos t) = \cos nt$ and $U_n(\cos t) = \dfrac{\sin(n+1)t}{\sin t}$.

It means that T_n is a hypergeometric function. By identifying the coefficients, we get

$$T_n(x) = \sum_{k=0}^{\lfloor \frac{n}{2} \rfloor}(-1)^k \tfrac{n}{n-k}\tbinom{n-k}{k}x^{n-2k}. \tag{5}$$

On the other hand, because $x = 2\cos t$ we get $x^n = \left(e^{it} + e^{-it}\right)^n$ whose expansion gives

$$x^n = \sum_{k=0}^{\lfloor \frac{n}{2} \rfloor - 1} \tbinom{n}{k}T_{n-2k}(x) + \tfrac{1+(-1)^n}{2}. \tag{6}$$

From Equation (3) and Formula (5), we also obtain

$$U_{n+1}(x) = \sum_{k=0}^{\lfloor \frac{n}{2} \rfloor}(-1)^k\tbinom{n-k}{k}x^{n-2k}. \tag{7}$$

The sequence $\mathcal{T} = (1, T_j, j \geq 1)$ is a basis of $\mathbf{Z}[x]$ and we denote by $\mathcal{X}$ the monomial basis $(x^n, n \geq 0)$. Given a basis $\mathcal{B} = (B_i)_{i\geq 0}$ of $\mathbf{Q}[x]$ and a polynomial P of degree d, we denote by $\tau_{\mathcal{B}}(P)$ the maximum bitsize of its coefficients in the basis $\mathcal{B}$.

Proposition 1. *We have $\tau_{\mathcal{X}}(T_n) \leq n$, $\tau_{\mathcal{X}}(U_n) \leq n - 1$, $\tau_{\mathcal{T}}(x^n) \leq n$.*

Proof. From $\binom{n-k}{k} \leq \frac{n}{n-k}\binom{n-k}{k}$, we obtain first that $\tau_{\mathcal{X}}(U_{n+1}) \leq \tau_{\mathcal{X}}(T_n)$, using Formulas (5) and (7). The sum of the absolute values of the coefficients of T_n is $\sum_k \frac{n}{n-k}\binom{n-k}{k} = (-i)^nT_n(i)$. The sequence $t_n = (-i)^nT_n(i)$ satisfies the relation $t_{n+1} = t_n + t_{n-1}$ and we easily deduce that $t_n < 2^n$ when $n \geq 1$ and $\tau_{\mathcal{X}}(T_n) \leq n$.

We get $\tau_{\mathcal{T}}(x^n) \leq n$ since $\sum_k \binom{n}{k} = 2^n$. □

A useful consequence for the next sections:

Corollary 2. *Let P be a polynomial of degree d. Then we have $\tau_{\mathcal{X}}(P) \leq \tau_{\mathcal{T}}(P) + d + \log_2 d$, and $\tau_{\mathcal{T}}(P) \leq \tau_{\mathcal{X}}(P) + d + \log_2 d$.*

Chebyshev forms

Let $f \in \mathbf{Q}[x]$. We will say that f is in *Chebyshev form* when it is expressed in the Chebyshev basis: $[\mathcal{T}]f = f_0 + \sum_{j=1}^{d} f_jT_j$. The set of Chebyshev forms with rational coefficients is a Euclidean ring and we focus on computing efficiently in this ring, starting with elementary operations.

Let us introduce a simple shortcut that will straightforwardly offer a simple link between basic operations in the Chebyshev basis and in the usual monomial basis:

Definition 3. *$\mathcal{D}$ is the transformation from $\mathbf{Q}[x]$ to the space of even degree self-reciprocal polynomials given by*

$$\mathcal{D}(P) = x^{\deg P}\, P(x + \tfrac{1}{x}).$$

Note that $\mathcal{D}$ satisfies the following relation:

$$\mathcal{D}(f \cdot g) = \mathcal{D}(f) \cdot \mathcal{D}(g), \tag{8}$$

so that, as $T_n(x + \frac{1}{x}) = x^n + \frac{1}{x^n}$, then

$$\mathcal{D}(a_0 + \sum_{j=1}^{n} a_jT_j) = a_0x^n + \sum_{j=1}^{n} a_j(x^{n-j} + x^{n+j}). \tag{9}$$

Note that Equation (9) shows that passing from $[\mathcal{X}]\mathcal{D}(P)$ to $[\mathcal{T}]P$ and vice versa is just a way of changing the numbering of the coefficients, having in mind that $[\mathcal{X}]\mathcal{D}(P)$ is a self-reciprocal polynomial. In particular, $\tau_{\mathcal{X}}(\mathcal{D}(P)) = \tau_{\mathcal{T}}(P)$ and $\deg \mathcal{D}(P) = 2\deg P$. Also, passing from $[\mathcal{X}]\mathcal{D}(P)$ to $[\mathcal{T}]P$ and vice-versa can be done in $\mathcal{O}(\deg(P))$ bit operations.

From this remark, it is then sufficient to apply the classical fast multiplication for polynomials in $\mathbf{Q}[x]$ after applying $\mathcal{D}$ on the operands. We will denote by $M(\delta,\tau) = \widetilde{\mathcal{O}}(\delta\tau)$ the number of bit operations for multiplying two polynomials of $\mathbf{Z}[x]$ with degrees at most δ and coefficients of bitsize at most τ with respect to the usual monomial basis $\mathcal{X}$ and by $M(\tau) = \widetilde{\mathcal{O}}(\tau)$ the cost of the multiplication of two integers of bitsize dominated by τ. We obtain

PROPOSITION 4. *Let $f, g \in \mathbf{Z}[x]$ given by their Chebyshev forms $[\mathcal{T}]f$ and $[\mathcal{T}]g$. Then we have $\tau_{\mathcal{T}}(f\cdot g) \le \tau_{\mathcal{T}}(f) + \tau_{\mathcal{T}}(g) + \log_2 \min(\deg f, \deg g) + 1$.*

Suppose that $\tau_{\mathcal{T}}(f)$, $\tau_{\mathcal{T}}(g) \le \tau$ and $\deg f, \deg g \le d$ then computing $[\mathcal{T}](f\cdot g)$ requires $M(2d,\tau) + \mathcal{O}(d)$ bit operations.

Note that this very simple algorithm might be replaced by the one from Giorgi [7] which requires the equivalence of two multiplications between polynomials of degree d with coefficients of bitsize in $\mathcal{O}(\tau)$.

Let us now extend these results to the division. Applying the transformation $\mathcal{D}$ on both sides of the relation $f = g\cdot q + r$, we then get:

$$\mathcal{D}(f) = \mathcal{D}(g)\mathcal{D}(q) + x^{\deg f - \deg r}\mathcal{D}(r). \tag{10}$$

In particular, Formulas (8) and (10) imply that $g \mid f$ iff $\mathcal{D}(g) \mid \mathcal{D}(f)$. Also, applying the same strategy as for the product of Chebyshev forms, we immediately get:

COROLLARY 5. *Let $f, g \in \mathbf{Z}[x]$ given by their Chebyshev forms $[\mathcal{T}]f$ and $[\mathcal{T}]g$. Suppose that $\deg f, \deg g \le d$ and $\tau_{\mathcal{T}}(f), \tau_{\mathcal{T}}(g) \le \tau$. Then,*

1. (a) *deciding if g divides f knowing $[\mathcal{T}]f$ and $[\mathcal{T}]g$ can be done in $\widetilde{\mathcal{O}}(d^2 + d\tau)$ bit operations;*
   (b) *if g divides f then computing $[\mathcal{T}]Quo(f,g)$ from $[\mathcal{T}]f$ and $[\mathcal{T}]g$ can be done in $\widetilde{\mathcal{O}}(d^2 + d\tau)$ bit operations;*
   (c) *computing $[\mathcal{T}]gcd(f,g)$ from $[\mathcal{T}]f$ and $[\mathcal{T}]g$ can be done in $\widetilde{\mathcal{O}}(d^2\tau)$ bit operations.*
2. (a) *if $g|f$ then $\tau_{\mathcal{T}}(g) = \mathcal{O}(\tau_{\mathcal{T}}(f) + d)$.*
   (b) *$\tau_{\mathcal{T}}(\gcd(f,g)) \le \mathcal{O}(\tau + d)$.*

PROOF. The first items are direct consequences of [16, exercise 9.14] while the third item is a direct consequence of [16, Corollary 11.14]. The two last items come from the Mignotte bound [16, p. 166]. □

3. BASES CHANGE

It is a classical result that $\mathcal{T}$ is an orthogonal basis. Bostan *et al.* (see [4]) give a fast general conversion method from the monomial basis to orthogonal bases. The alternatives we propose are based on the general method of Hart & Novocin for polynomial composition (see [8]) which lead to simpler descriptions and complexity analysis. Given $f = \sum_{i=0}^d a_i x^i$ in the monomial basis and $f = f_0 + \sum_{i=1}^d f_i T_i$ in the Chebyshev basis, in both cases, the method is based on the same divide and conquer principle as in [8]: splitting f into $\lceil \frac{d}{2} \rceil$ sub-polynomials of length 2.

Suppose that we have to evaluate the sum $S = \sum_{j=0}^d u_j v^j$. We first define:

$$d_0 = d,\ v_0 = v,\ S_{0,j} = u_j,\ j = 0,\dots,d.$$

Let $c = \lceil \log_2 d \rceil - 1$. Then we define for $k = 0,\dots,c$:

$$\begin{aligned} d_{k+1} &= \lceil \tfrac{d_k}{2} \rceil, v_{k+1} = v_k^2, \\ S_{k+1,j} &= S_{k,2j} + S_{k,2j+1}\cdot v_k,\ j = 0,\dots,d_{k+1}. \end{aligned}$$

Then, for $k = 0,\dots,c+1$, $S = \sum_{j=0}^{d_k} S_{k,j}\cdot v_k^j$. At the end, we get $S = S_{c+1,0}$ and Algorithm 1 is then a direct application of this strategy for the evaluation of $f = \sum_{j=1}^{d} a_j x^j$ in the Chebyshev basis $\mathcal{T}$.

Algorithm 1: From $\mathcal{X}$ to $\mathcal{T}$

```
Input: f = Σ_{i=0}^{n} a_i x^i
Output: [T]f = f_0 + Σ_{i=1}^{n} f_i T_i
begin
    d ← ⌊n/2⌋; c ← 0; v ← T_1 ;
    for j ← 0 to d do
        [T]S_{c,j} ← a_{2j} + a_{2j+1} · T_1
    [T]v ← ([T]v)^2;
    while d > 0 do
        d ← ⌊d/2⌋;
        for j ← 0 to d do
            [T]S_{c+1,j} ← [T]S_{c,2j} + [T]S_{c,2j+1} · [T]v
        c ← c + 1; [T]v ← ([T]v)^2;
    return [T]S_{c,0}
```

PROPOSITION 6. *Let $f = \sum_{i=0}^d a_i x^i$ be a polynomial with coefficients of bitsize τ. One can compute the Chebyshev form of f in $\widetilde{\mathcal{O}}(d)$ arithmetic operations, or in binary complexity $\widetilde{\mathcal{O}}(d^2 + d\tau)$. The Chebyshev form $[\mathcal{T}]f$ has bitsize $\tau + \mathcal{O}(d)$.*

PROOF. We use Algorithm 1. Let $c = \lceil \log_2 d \rceil$. We start with $v = [\mathcal{T}]x = T_1$, and compute successively $v = x^{2^k}$, $k = 0,\dots,c$. We know that x^{2^k} has size $\mathcal{O}(2^k)$ in the Chebyshev basis. From Proposition 4, one can compute $[\mathcal{T}]x^{2^{k+1}}$ from $[\mathcal{T}]x^{2^k}$ in $\widetilde{\mathcal{O}}(2^{2k})$ bit operations.

At each step, the bitsize τ_{k+1} of the Chebyshev form $[\mathcal{T}]S_{k+1,j} = [\mathcal{T}]S_{k,2j} + [\mathcal{T}]S_{k,2j+1}\cdot[\mathcal{T}]x^{2^k}$ satisfies $\tau_{k+1} \le \tau_k + 2^k + k + 1$. We therefore obtain $\tau_k = \tau + \mathcal{O}(2^k)$. One can compute the Chebyshev form $S_{k+1,j} = S_{k,2j} + S_{k,2j+1}\cdot x^{2^k}$ in $\widetilde{\mathcal{O}}(2^k\tau_k)$ binary operations by Proposition 4 and the total computing time is bounded by $\sum_{k=1}^c \tau_k 2^k = \widetilde{\mathcal{O}}(d^2 + d\tau)$. □

Conversely, given a Chebyshev form $f = f_0 + \sum_{j=1}^d f_j T_j$, we have to find the expression $f = \sum_{j=0}^d a_i x^i$. We use a key idea from the general method of [4], considering the characteristic matrix of the Chebyshev polynomials:

$$X = \begin{bmatrix} 0 & 1 \\ -1 & x \end{bmatrix}.$$

Using the recurrence (1), we get:

$$\begin{bmatrix} T_j \\ T_{j+1} \end{bmatrix} = X^j \begin{bmatrix} T_0 \\ T_1 \end{bmatrix}, \; j \geq 0.$$

Algorithm 2 computes the polynomial matrix

$$M(f) = \sum_{i=0}^{\lfloor \frac{d}{2} \rfloor} \begin{bmatrix} f_{2i} & f_{2i+1} \end{bmatrix} X^{2i}$$

using the composition method from [8]. Then, following [4], we get (because $T_0 = 2$)

$$f = -f_0 + M(f) \cdot \begin{bmatrix} T_0 \\ T_1 \end{bmatrix}.$$

Algorithm 2: From $\mathcal{T}$ to $\mathcal{X}$

Input: $f = \sum_{i=0}^{n} f_i T_i$
Output: $f = \sum_{i=0}^{n} a_i x^i$
begin
  $d \leftarrow \lfloor \frac{n}{2} \rfloor$; $c \leftarrow 0$; $V \leftarrow X^2$;
  for $j \leftarrow 0$ **to** d **do**
    $S_{c,j} \leftarrow [f_{2j} \; f_{2j+1}]$
  while $d > 0$ **do**
    $d \leftarrow \lfloor \frac{d}{2} \rfloor$;
    for $j \leftarrow 0$ **to** d **do**
      $S_{c+1,j} \leftarrow S_{c,2j} + S_{c,2j+1} \cdot V$
    $c \leftarrow c + 1$; $V \leftarrow V^2$;
  return $S_{c,0} \cdot \begin{bmatrix} 2 \\ x \end{bmatrix} - f_0$

PROPOSITION 7. *Let $f = f_0 + \sum_{i=1}^{d} f_i T_i$ be a Chebyshev form of bitsize τ. One can compute f in the monomial basis in $\widetilde{\mathcal{O}}(d)$ arithmetic operations, or a binary complexity $\widetilde{\mathcal{O}}(d^2 + d\tau)$. $[\mathcal{X}]f$ has bitsize $\tau + \mathcal{O}(d)$.*

PROOF. An induction shows that $X^n = \begin{bmatrix} -U_{n-1} & U_n \\ -U_n & U_{n+1} \end{bmatrix}$. Thus the bitsize of X^n is $\mathcal{O}(n)$, using Proposition 1.

Let $c = \lceil \log_2 d \rceil$ and $0 < k \leq c$. We compute X^{2^k} from $X^{2^{k-1}}$ in $\mathcal{O}(2^{2k})$ binary operations. We thus compute X^{2^k} for $k = 0, \ldots, c$ in $\mathcal{O}(d^2)$ binary operations.

The bitsize $\tau_{k+1,j}$ of the 1×2 matrix $S_{k+1,j} = S_{k,2j} + S_{k,2j+1} \cdot X^{2^k}$ is bounded by $\tau_{k,j} + \mathcal{O}(2^k)$. It follows that $\tau_{k,j} \leq \tau_k \leq \tau + \mathcal{O}(2^k)$. At the end the bitsize of $[\mathcal{X}]f$ is bounded by $\tau + \mathcal{O}(d)$.

S_{k+1} is derived from S_k by evaluating the $S_{k+1,j}$ for $j = 0, \ldots, \lfloor \frac{d}{2^k} \rfloor$. This requires $d/2^k \times \widetilde{\mathcal{O}}(\tau_k 2^k) = \widetilde{\mathcal{O}}(d(\tau + 2^k))$ binary operations.

At the end we compute $S_{c,0}$ in $\widetilde{\mathcal{O}}(d^2 + d\tau)$ binary operations. □

4. THE MINIMAL POLYNOMIAL

The degree of the minimal polynomial of $\cos \frac{2\pi}{n}$ is $\frac{1}{2}\varphi(n)$, where φ is the Euler function. (see Rivlin [14, Chapter 5] or Watkin & Zeitlin [17]). This minimal polynomial appears as a factor of the Chebyshev monic polynomials U_{n+1} in [14]. It is a factor of $T_{\lfloor \frac{n}{2} \rfloor + 1} - T_{\lfloor \frac{n}{2} \rfloor}$ in [17]. Bayard & Cangul ([3]) use this formula to get an induction formula for the minimal polynomial of $2\cos\frac{\pi}{n}$ with the help of the Möbius inversion formula.

Here, we will show that the minimal polynomial M_n of $2\cos\frac{\pi}{n}$ satisfies $\Phi_{2n} = \mathcal{D}(M_n)$. We will adapt the algorithm given in [1] for the computation of Φ_n to the computation of M_n in the Chebyshev basis.

DEFINITION 8. *Let $n > 2$, M_n denotes the minimal polynomial of $2\cos\frac{\pi}{n}$ in $\mathbf{Q}[x]$. We set $M_1 = 1$.*

Let ζ_n be a primitive n-th root of the unity, its minimal polynomial is the cyclotomic polynomial Φ_n. It is monic and of degree $\varphi(n)$. The roots of Φ_n are all the primitive n-th roots, hence $\Phi_n(1/\zeta_n) = 0$ and thus Φ_n is reversible. We have $\mathbf{Q}(\cos\frac{2\pi}{2n}) = \mathbf{Q}(\zeta_{2n}) \cap \mathbf{R}$ and the minimal polynomial over $\mathbf{Q}$ of $\cos\frac{2\pi}{2n}$ has degree $\frac{1}{2}\varphi(2n)$, when $n > 2$. Its roots are the $\cos\frac{k\pi}{n}$ where k and $2n$ are coprime. Note that the minimal polynomial of $2\cos 2\frac{\pi}{n}$ is $\pm M_n(-t)$.

LEMMA 9. *If $m \geq 3$ is odd, then $M_{2^k m} = M_m(T_{2^k})$.*

PROOF. As $M_m \circ T_{2^k}(\cos\frac{\pi}{2^k m}) = 0$ and $(2^k, m) = 1$, then $M_{2^k m} | M_m(T_{2^k})$. We conclude since $M_{2^k m}$ and $M_m(T_{2^k})$ have the same leading term. □

The number of factors of T_n is given in [9]. We give here the complete factorization of the Chebyshev polynomials T_n and U_n as products of polynomials M_n, see also [10]:

PROPOSITION 10. *We have*

$$U_{2^k(2m+1)} = (-1)^m \prod_{d|2m+1} \left(M_d(-t) \prod_{i=0}^{k} M_d(T_{2^i}) \right)$$

$$T_{2^k(2m+1)} = \prod_{d|2m+1} M_d(T_{2^{k+1}})$$

where M_n is the minimal polynomial of $2\cos\frac{\pi}{n}$.

PROOF. The factorization of U_n is obtained by comparing its roots with those of $M_d(\pm t)$, when $d | 2m+1$ and using the Euler identity $n = \sum_{d|n} \varphi(d)$.

Let d be an odd divisor of n. We write $n = 2^k \cdot d_1 \cdot d$, where d_1 is odd. $\cos\frac{d_1 \pi}{2n} = \cos\frac{\pi}{2^{k+1}d}$ is a root of T_n so $M_{2^{k+1}d} | T_n$. We conclude by comparing the leading terms. □

From $M_n(\zeta_{2n} + 1/\zeta_{2n}) = 0$ when $n > 2$, we deduce a relation between the Chebyshev form of M_n and Φ_{2n}, see also [14, Chapter 5]:

PROPOSITION 11. *We have $\Phi_{2n} = \mathcal{D}(M_n)$, for $n > 2$.*

Let $x = 2\cos t$ and $V_n(x) = \dfrac{\sin(n + \frac{1}{2})t}{\cos\frac{t}{2}}$ then $V_n = \prod_{d|2n+1} M_d$. This is an analogous formula to $X^n - 1 = \prod_{d|n} \Phi_d$, see [11].

Computation of M_n

The relation $T_n \circ T_m = T_n \circ T_m = T_{mn}$ makes the Chebyshev basis very convenient for the computation of the minimal polynomial M_n. Lemma 12 is a generalization of Lemma 9:

LEMMA 12. *Let $n = 2^\alpha p_1^{\alpha_1} \ldots p_k^{\alpha_k}$ where the p_i are distinct odd primes. Let $n_0 = p_1 \cdots p_k$. Then we have*

$$\begin{cases} M_n = M_{n_0}(T_{n/n_0}), & \textit{if } k \geq 1 \\ M_{2^\alpha} = T_{2^{\alpha-1}}, & \textit{if } n_0 = 1 \textit{ and } \alpha \geq 1. \end{cases}$$

PROOF. If $n = 2^\alpha > 1$ then $T_{n/2}(2\cos\pi/n) = 0$. On the other hand $T_{n/2}$ and M_n are monic with the same degree. Thus they are equal.

If $n_0 > 1$ then $M_{n_0}(T_{n/n_0}(2\cos\pi/n)) = M_{n_0}(2\cos\pi/n_0) = 0$. We thus have $M_n | M_{n_0}(T_{n/n_0})$. On the other hand, M_n and $M_{n_0}(T_{n/n_0})$ are monic with the same degree. Thus they are equal. □

Lemma 12 shows that the Chebyshev basis is particularly adapted for the computation of M_n.

LEMMA 13. *$n = 2^\alpha p_1^{\alpha_1}\dots p_k^{\alpha_k}$ where the p_i are distinct odd primes. Let $n_0 = p_1\cdots p_k$. Then the coefficients of M_n have bitsize $\mathcal{O}(n_0)$ in the Chebyshev basis and have bitsize $\mathcal{O}(n)$ in the monomial basis.*

PROOF. As $M_{n_0} | U_{n_0}$ the conclusion is a consequence of Corollary 5, because we derive from

$$U_n = \sum_{k=1}^{\lfloor \frac{n}{2}\rfloor} T_{n-2k-1} + \tfrac{1}{2}(1-(-1)^n),$$

that the Chebyshev form U_n has maximum bitsize 1. We use the Corollary 2 for the coefficients in the monomial basis. □

When n is an odd prime, we get :

LEMMA 14. *Let p a prime odd number, then*

$$M_p = T_k - T_{k-1} + \cdots + (-1)^{k-1}T_1 + (-1)^k,$$

where $k = (p-1)/2$.

PROOF. Let $p = 2k+1$ and $h = T_k - T_{k-1} + \cdots + (-1)^{k-1}T_1 + (-1)^k$. We have $\sin\frac{\pi}{2k+1}\cdot h(2\cos\frac{\pi}{2k+1}) = 0$.

But $\deg h = k = \frac{1}{2}\varphi(p)$ and thus $h = M_p$. □

LEMMA 15. *Let p be an odd prime and n such that $p \nmid n$, then $M_{np} = \dfrac{M_n(T_p)}{M_n}$.*

PROOF. We just need to show that both M_{np} and M_n divide $M_n(T_p)$ because these polynomials are monic and their degrees satisfy $2(\deg M_n + \deg M_{np}) = \varphi(2n) + \varphi(2pn) = p\varphi(n) = 2\deg M_n(T_p)$.

If $t = 2\cos\frac{\pi}{np}$ then $T_p(t) = 2\cos\frac{\pi}{n}$ and $M_n(T_p)(t) = 0$ so that $M_{np} | M_n(T_p)$. If $t = 2\cos\frac{\pi}{n}$ then $T_p(t) = 2\cos\frac{p\pi}{n}$ is a root of M_n. □

Following Arnold and Monagan in [1] for the computation of Φ_n, we derive Algorithm 3 to compute the Chebyshev form of M_n:

PROPOSITION 16. *Algorithm 3 computes M_n in the Chebyshev basis in complexity $\widetilde{\mathcal{O}}(n_0)$ or $\widetilde{\mathcal{O}}(n_0^2)$ bit operations.*

PROOF. The factorization of n requires $\widetilde{\mathcal{O}}(n_0^{1/4})$ binary operations, see [16, Corollary 19.4].

We have to compute successively $M_{q_{i+1}} = (M_{q_i}\circ T_{p_{i+1}})/M_{q_i}$, where $q_i = p_1\cdots p_i$.

We know that $\tau_{\mathcal{T}}(M_{q_i}) = \mathcal{O}(q_i)$, $\tau_{\mathcal{T}}(M_{q_i}(T_{p_{i+1}})) = \tau_{\mathcal{T}}(M_{q_i})$ and $\deg(M_{q_i}(T_{p_{i+1}})) = \varphi(2q_i)p_{i+1}/2 \le q_{i+1}$. By Proposition 4, we compute $M_{q_{i+1}}$ from M_{q_i} in $\widetilde{\mathcal{O}}(q_{i+1})$ arithmetic operations or $\widetilde{\mathcal{O}}(q_{j+1}^2)$ binary operations.

Finally we compute M_{n_0} in $\mathcal{O}(q_2 + \cdots + q_k) = \widetilde{\mathcal{O}}(n_0)$ arithmetic operations and $\widetilde{\mathcal{O}}(q_1^2 + \cdots + q_k^2) = \widetilde{\mathcal{O}}(n_0^2)$ binary operations. □

Algorithm 3: Compute $[\mathcal{T}]M_n$

Input: n
Output: $[\mathcal{T}]M_n$
begin
  Factorize $n = 2^{\alpha_0}p_1^{\alpha_1}\cdots p_k^{\alpha_k}$; $n_0 \leftarrow p_1\cdots p_k$;
  if $k = 0$ **then**
    if $\alpha_0 = 0$ **then**
      return 1
    else
      return $T_{2^{\alpha_0 - 1}}$
  $i \leftarrow \frac{1}{2}(p_1 - 1)$;
  $m \leftarrow T_i - T_{i-1} + \cdots + (-1)^{i-1}T_1 + (-1)^i$;
  for $j \leftarrow 2$ **to** k **do**
    $m \leftarrow [\mathcal{T}]\left(\dfrac{m(T_{p_j})}{m}\right)$
  return $m(T_{n/n_0})$

The analogy between M_n and the cyclotomic polynomial Φ_n allows us to derive the following complexity bound for the computation of Φ_n from the algorithm proposed by Arnold and Monagan in [1] :

COROLLARY 17. *One can compute Φ_n in the complexity $\widetilde{\mathcal{O}}(n_0)$ and in the running time $\widetilde{\mathcal{O}}(n_0^2)$, where n_0 is the odd squarefree part of n.*

Example

The minimal polynomial M_{1260} is

$$\begin{aligned} M_{105}(T_{12}) \;=\;& T_{288} - T_{276} + T_{264} + T_{228} - T_{216} + 2\,T_{204} \\ & -T_{192} + T_{180} + T_{144} - T_{132} + T_{120} - T_{108} \\ & +T_{96} - T_{84} - T_{48} - T_{24} - 1. \end{aligned}$$

The maximum bitsize of $[\mathcal{X}]M_{1260}$ is 197 while the total bitsize of its coefficients is 20329.

The minimal polynomial M_{936} is

$$\begin{aligned} M_{39}(T_{24}) \;=\;& T_{288} + T_{264} - T_{216} - T_{192} \\ & +T_{144} + T_{120} - T_{72} - T_{48} + 1. \end{aligned}$$

Its maximum bitsize of $[\mathcal{X}]M_{936}$ is 197 while the total bitsize of its coefficients is 20338.

5. SUM OF COSINES

The aim of this section is to give methods for determining the sign of $F = f(\gamma)$ where γ is one root of M_n, for evaluating F and for getting the minimal polynomial of F.

We consider here the expression

$$F = f_0 + 2\sum_{j=1}^{d} f_j \cos\tfrac{j\pi}{n}, \tag{11}$$

where $d \le n$ and $f_i \in \mathbf{Z}$. It is convenient to write F as $f(\gamma)$ where γ is the algebraic number $2\cos\frac{\pi}{n}$ and $f = f_0 + \sum_{k=1}^{d} f_k T_k \in \mathbf{Z}[x]$. For an arbitrary f with rational coefficients, we should consider the size of the common denominator of f and convert f into a polynomial with integral coefficients.

Evaluating the sum

The first step is the approximation of $\gamma = 2\cos k\frac{\pi}{n}$, using Brent's methods ([5, 6])

LEMMA 18. *Let $0 \le k \le n$ and $\gamma = 2\cos k\frac{\pi}{n}$. Let $\ell \in \mathbf{Z}_{>0}$. One can compute $c \in \mathbf{Q}$, of bitsize $\tau(c) \le \ell$ such that $|c-\gamma| \le 2^{-\ell}$ in $\widetilde{\mathcal{O}}(\ell + \log n)$ bit operations.*

PROOF. We first compute $r \in \mathbf{Q}$ of bitsize $2(\ell + 2\log n)$ such that $\left|r - k\frac{\pi}{n}\right| < 2^{-\ell-1}$. It requires $\widetilde{\mathcal{O}}(l + \log n)$ bit operations, using [5].

Then we compute c such that $|c - \cos r| < 2^{-\ell-1}$, using [6], in $\widetilde{\mathcal{O}}(\ell + \log n)$ binary operations. □

From the above results we then get

COROLLARY 19. *Let $0 \le k \le n$ and $\gamma = 2\cos k\frac{\pi}{n}$. Let $\ell \in \mathbf{Z}_{>0}$. Let f be the Chebyshev form $f_0 + \sum_{i=1}^{n-1} f_i T_i$ with $\tau_{\mathcal{T}}(f) \le \tau$. One computes $\widetilde{F} \in \mathbf{Q}$ of bitsize $\widetilde{\mathcal{O}}(n\tau + \ell)$ such that $\left|\widetilde{F} - f(\gamma)\right| \le 2^{-\ell}$ in $\widetilde{\mathcal{O}}(n\ell + n\tau)$ bit operations.*

One computes F^- and F^+ of bitsize $\widetilde{\mathcal{O}}(n\tau + \ell)$ such that $F^- \le F \le F^+$ and $F^+ - F^- \le 2^{-\ell}$ in $\widetilde{\mathcal{O}}(n\ell + n\tau)$ bit operations.

PROOF. Using Lemma 18, one can compute the rational numbers $c_i, i = 1, \ldots, n-1$ such that $\left|c_i - \cos ik\frac{\pi}{n}\right| \le 2^{-\ell-\tau}/n$. They are of bitsize $\mathcal{O}(\tau + \ell + \log n)$ and we can compute them in $\widetilde{\mathcal{O}}(n\tau + n\ell)$ bit operations.

If $\widetilde{F} = f_0 + 2\sum_{i=1}^{n-1} f_i c_i$, then

$$\left|\tilde{F} - F\right| \le 2\sum_{i=1}^{n-1} |f_i|\,\left|c_i - \cos ik\tfrac{\pi}{n}\right| \le 2^{-\ell}.$$

Here, the $f_i c_i$ have bitsize $\tau + \ell + \log n$ and each can be computed in $\widetilde{\mathcal{O}}(\tau + \ell + \log n)$ bit operations, using the fast multiplication described in [16, Chap. 8]. F has bitsize $\mathcal{O}(\tau + \ell + \log n)$ and can be computed in $\widetilde{\mathcal{O}}(n\tau + n\ell)$ bit operations. The proof of the second part of the Lemma is similar. □

Evaluating the sign of the sum

We now want to evaluate the sign of $f(\gamma)$ where $\gamma = 2\cos k\frac{\pi}{n}$ and f is the Chebyshev form $f_0 + \sum_{i=1}^{n-1} f_i T_i$ with $f_0, .., f_n \in \mathbf{Z}$. Without loss of generality, we can suppose that $(k, 2n) = 1$, that is to say that γ is a root of M_n. If $(k, n) = d > 1$, then we can change n by n/d. If k is even, then γ will be a root of $M_n(-t)$.

As M_n is the minimal polynomial of γ then $f(\gamma) = 0$ iff $M_n \mid f$. If M_n does not divide f then we have $|\mathrm{Res}\,(M_n, f)| \ge 1$. As M_n is monic, we have also

$$\mathrm{Res}\,(M_n, f) = \prod_{M_n(\gamma)=0} f(\gamma).$$

Let γ be a root of M_n, then we have $|f(\gamma)| \le ||f||_1$, where $||f||_1 = |f_0| + 2\sum_{i=1}^{d} |f_i|$. We thus obtain for every root γ of M_n:

$$|f(\gamma)| \ge (||f||_1)^{1-\deg M_n} = \delta. \qquad (12)$$

Then, it is then sufficient to compute an approximation $\tilde{F}$ of $f(\gamma)$ such that $\left|\tilde{F} - f(\gamma)\right| < \frac{\delta}{2}$ in order to ensure that this approximation has the same sign as $f(\gamma)$. We thus deduce

PROPOSITION 20. *Let f of degree $d < n$ with $\tau_{\mathcal{T}}(f) \le \tau$. Let $\gamma = 2\cos k\frac{\pi}{n}$ where $(k, 2n) = 1$.*

1. *we can decide whether $f(\gamma) = 0$ in $\widetilde{\mathcal{O}}(n^2 + n\tau)$ bit operations,*
2. *we can compute* sign $f(\gamma)$ *in $\widetilde{\mathcal{O}}(n^2\tau)$ bit operations,*
3. *we can evaluate $f(\gamma)$ with precision $2^{-\ell}$ in the complexity $\widetilde{\mathcal{O}}(n\ell + n\tau)$.*

PROOF. We first decide if $f(\gamma) = 0$ by testing if $M_n | f$. It requires $\widetilde{\mathcal{O}}(n^2 + n\tau)$ bit operations by Propositions 16 and 5.

If $f(\gamma) \ne 0$, then we compute an approximation F of $f(\gamma)$ with accuracy $\frac{1}{2}\delta$ where $\delta = (||f||_1)^{1-\deg M_n}$. But $-\log_2 \delta \le (\deg M_n - 1)(\log_2(2n+1) + \tau) = \widetilde{\mathcal{O}}(n\tau)$. We deduce, using Corollary 19, that F can be computed in $\widetilde{\mathcal{O}}(n^2\tau)$ bit operations. The last point of the Proposition is a consequence of Corollary 19. □

The estimate of δ in Inequality (12) may be too sharp. The alternative we propose is to explicitly compute $[\mathcal{T}]M_n$, then test if $[\mathcal{T}]M_n$ divides F using Corollary 5, and then compute $\tilde{F}$ using interval arithmetic, starting in low precision, and doubling the precision if the resulting interval contains 0. According to the above result, Algorithm 4 will terminate, performing $\widetilde{\mathcal{O}}(n^2\tau)$ bit operations in the worst case, but will use much less precision in generic situations.

Algorithm 4: Determine the sign of $f(\gamma)$

```
Input: f = f_0 + Σ_i^n f_i T_i, k such that (k, 2n) = 1
Output: sign f(γ) where γ = 2cos(kπ/n)
begin
    Compute [T]M_n ;
    if M_n | f then
        return f(2 cos kπ/n) = 0
    ℓ ← 1, F⁻ ← −1, F⁺ ← 1;
    while F⁺ · F⁻ < 0 do
        Compute [F⁻, F⁺] of length 2^(−ℓ), containing f(γ);
        ℓ ← 2ℓ;
return sign (F⁺)
```

Example

In [13], Myerson pointed out that

$$a = 16\,\sin\frac{\pi}{9}\,\sin\frac{5\pi}{18}\,\sin\frac{11\pi}{39}\,\sin\frac{3\pi}{8}$$

is very closed to 3. Combining the sine functions, we easily obtain $a = 2\,\cos 69\,X + 2\,\cos 243\,X - 2\,\cos 459\,X - 2\,\cos 771\,X - 2\,\cos 277\,X - 2\,\cos 451\,X + 2\,\cos 251\,X + 2\,\cos 979\,X$, where $X = \pi/936$. Using $-T_i \equiv T_{936-i} \equiv T_{936+i} \pmod{M_{936}}$, we can write a as $f(\gamma)$ where

$$f = -T_{43} + T_{69} + T_{165} + T_{243} + T_{251} - T_{277} - T_{451} - T_{459},$$

and $\gamma = 2\cos\frac{\pi}{936}$ is the biggest root of M_{936}. Inequality (12) asserts that

$$|f(\gamma) - 3| \ge ||f-3||_1^{-287} = 19^{-287} \ge 2^{-1220}.$$

Indeed, $\min_{M_{936}(x)=0} |f(x) - 3| \ge 2^{-29}$ and Algorithm 4 provides the value and the sign of $f(\gamma)$ after 5 iterations.

6. THE SUM'S MINIMAL POLYNOMIAL

We give an algorithm for the minimal polynomial of $F = f(\gamma)$. It is classical to consider the monic polynomial (because M_n is monic)

$$P_f(z) = \mathrm{Res}_x(z - f(x), M_n(x)) = \prod_{M_n(\gamma)=0} (z - f(\gamma)). \quad (13)$$

The roots of P_f are $z_k = f(2\cos k\frac{\pi}{n}) = f(T_k(2\cos\frac{\pi}{n}))$ where $(k, 2n) = 1$. We thus deduce that

PROPOSITION 21. *There exists $\nu \in \mathbf{Z}_{>0}$ such that $P_f = M_f^{\nu}$, where M_f is the minimal polynomial of $f(2\cos\frac{\pi}{n})$.*

PROOF. Let $\gamma_k = 2\cos k\frac{\pi}{n}$, be a root of M_n. The minimal polynomial μ_k of $f(\gamma_k)$ satisfies $\mu_k \circ f(\gamma_k) = 0$. Thus M_n divides $\mu_k \circ f$ and $\mu_k(f(\gamma_j)) = 0$ for every root γ_j of M_n. We thus deduce that μ_j divides μ_k and that $\mu_k = \mu_j = M_f$. P_f factorizes into $P_f = M_f^{\nu}$. □

We will first compute P_f and then $M_f = P_f / \gcd(P_f, P_f')$.

One might directly compute P_f using a general algorithm, following [16, Section 11.2]. It would then require $\widetilde{\mathcal{O}}(\delta\tau_s)$ bit operations where $\delta = \deg(f) + \deg(M_n)$ and τ_s is a bound on the total bitsize required to store any principal subresultant coefficient which are all polynomials of degree in $\mathcal{O}(\delta)$ in z with coefficients of bitsizes in $\widetilde{\mathcal{O}}(\delta\tau)$ (see Proposition 8.50 in [2]). Such an algorithm would then perform, in our case, $\widetilde{\mathcal{O}}(n^3\tau)$ bit operations, and we do not pretend to give a better theoretical upperbound. However, in pratice, this classical strategy is based on the *Half-Gcd* algorithm and makes use of fast operations on univariate polynomials, both starting to be efficient for rather high degrees (several hundred). The algorithm we propose in the sequel runs efficiently even for small degrees.

It is natural to consider P_f as a polynomial whose coefficients are in $\mathbf{Q}[x]/(M_n)$. As $T_{n+i}(\gamma) = 2\cos(n+i)k\frac{\pi}{n} = (-1)^k T_i(\gamma)$, then $T_{n+i} \equiv T_{n-i} \equiv -T_i \pmod{M_n}$. The Chebyshev basis $(1, T_1, \ldots T_{\lfloor\frac{n-1}{2}\rfloor})$ is then particularly adapted as generating family of $\mathbf{Q}[x]/(M_n)$:

LEMMA 22. *Let $f = f_0 + \sum_{i=1}^{\lfloor\frac{n-1}{2}\rfloor} f_i T_i$ and $g = g_0 + \sum_{i=1}^{\lfloor\frac{n-1}{2}\rfloor} g_i T_i$ be Chebyshev forms. Then one can compute $h = h_0 + \sum_{i=1}^{\lfloor\frac{n-1}{2}\rfloor} h_i T_i$ where $h \equiv f \cdot g \pmod{M_n}$ in $\widetilde{\mathcal{O}}(n\tau)$ bit operations and $\tau(h) \le \tau(f) + \tau(g) + \log_2 n + 1$.*

PROOF. We compute $h = [\mathcal{T}](f \cdot g)$ in $\widetilde{\mathcal{O}}(n\tau)$ bit operations. We obtain $h = h_0 + \sum_{i=1}^{n-1} h_i T_i = h_0 + \sum_{i=1}^{\lfloor\frac{n-1}{2}\rfloor}(h_i - h_{n-i})T_i$. □

Let $N = \frac{1}{2}\varphi(2n)$ be the degree of P_f. The N roots of P_f are the $f(T_k(x))$ where $(k, 2n) = 1$. We shall consider the i-th Newton sum:

$$S_i(P_f) = \sum_{\substack{1\le k\le n\\(k,2n)=1}} f(T_k(x))^i.$$

Consider first $f^i = f(x)^i = f_{i,0} + \sum_{j=1}^{\lfloor\frac{n-1}{2}\rfloor} f_{i,j} T_j$ in $\mathbf{Q}[x]/(M_n)$, then $f(T_k(x))^i \equiv f_{i,0} + \sum_{j=1}^{\lfloor\frac{n-1}{2}\rfloor} f_{i,j} T_{jk} \pmod{M_n}$ so that

$$S_i(P_f) \equiv N f_{i,0} + \sum_{j=1}^{\lfloor\frac{n-1}{2}\rfloor} f_{i,j}\Big(\sum_{\substack{1\le k\le n\\(k,2n)=1}} T_{jk}\Big) \pmod{M_n}.$$

LEMMA 23. *Let j and n be nonnegative integers, then*

$$\sum_{\substack{1\le k\le n\\(k,2n)=1}} T_{jk} \equiv 2S_j(\Phi_{2n}) \pmod{M_n}.$$

PROOF. Let $\gamma = 2\cos\frac{\pi}{n}$ then

$$\sum_{\substack{1\le k\le n\\(k,2n)=1}} T_{jk}(\gamma) = 2\,\mathrm{Re}\Big(\sum_{\substack{1\le k\le n\\(k,2n)=1}} e^{jki\frac{\pi}{n}}\Big) = 2S_j(\Phi_{2n}),$$

because $S_j(\Phi_{2n})$ is real. □

One can then obtain $S_j(P_f)$ from the coefficients $f_{i,j}$ of $f^j(x)$ in $\mathbf{Q}[x]/(M_n)$ with

$$S_i(P_f) = f_{i,0}N + 2\sum_{j=1}^{\lfloor\frac{n-1}{2}\rfloor} f_{i,j} S_j(\Phi_{2n}). \quad (14)$$

Note that $(f_{i,j})$ are not unique but the Formula (14) does not depend on them. Equation (14) gives a linear relation between the Newton sums of Φ_{2n} and the Newton sums of P_f and is the core of Algorithm 5.

Algorithm 5: Compute P_f

Input: $[\mathcal{T}]f = f_0 + \sum_{j=1}^{n-1} f_i T_i$
Output: $P_f = \mathrm{Res}_x(z - f(x), M_n(x))$

```
begin
    Compute [T]M_n = σ_0 + Σ_{i=1}^{N} σ_i T_i;
    for i ← 2 to N do
        Compute the Newton sums
        S_i = iσ_i − Σ_{j=1}^{i-1} σ_j S_{i-j}
    for i ← 2 to N do
        Compute f^i = f_{i,0} + Σ_{j=1}^{⌊(n-1)/2⌋} f_{i,j} T_j;
        Compute the Newton sums
        S_i(P_f) = f_{i,0} · N + 2 Σ_{j=1}^{⌊(n-1)/2⌋} f_{i,j} S_j;
        Compute
        σ_i(P_f) = −(1/i) (S_i(P_f) + Σ_{j=1}^{i-1} σ_{i-j}(P_f) S_j(P_f))
return z^N + Σ_{i=1}^{N} σ_i(P_f) z^{N-i}
```

PROPOSITION 24. *Algorithm 5 computes P_f in $\widetilde{\mathcal{O}}(n^3\tau)$ bit operations.*

PROOF. We first compute $[\mathcal{T}]M_n$ in $\widetilde{\mathcal{O}}(n^2)$ bit operations. We obtain $[\mathcal{T}]M_n = \sigma_0 + \sum_{i=1}^{N} \sigma_i T_i$. As $\Phi_{2n} = \mathcal{D}(M_n)$ we get $\Phi_{2n} = \sum_{i=0}^{2N} b_i x^i$ where $b_i = b_{2N-i} = \sigma_i$.
We then obtain the $S_i(\Phi_{2n})$ using the Newton relations:

$$S_k + \sigma_1 S_{k-1} + \cdots + \sigma_{k-1}S_1 + k\sigma_k = 0, \quad 1 \le k \le N. \quad (15)$$

Here the σ_i's have bitsize $\mathcal{O}(n)$. By induction, all the S_k's have bitsize $\mathcal{O}(n)$. Also, S_k is computed from $S_1, \ldots, S_{k-1}$ in $k\widetilde{\mathcal{O}}(n)$ bit operations. In conclusion $S_1, \ldots, S_N$ may be computed in $\widetilde{\mathcal{O}}(n^3)$ bit operations.

By induction, $f^i \pmod{M_n}$ has bitsize $\mathcal{O}(i\tau)$ and can be computed from $f^{i-1} \pmod{M_n}$ in $\widetilde{\mathcal{O}}(in\tau)$ bit operations, using Lemma 22. We can compute all $f_{i,j}$, $1 \le i \le N$, $1 \le j \le \lfloor \frac{n-1}{2} \rfloor$ in $\widetilde{\mathcal{O}}(n^3\tau)$ bit operations.

We then compute each $S_j(P_f)$ in $\widetilde{\mathcal{O}}(n^2\tau)$ bit operations, using Formula (14). It requires $\widetilde{\mathcal{O}}(n^3\tau)$ bit operations.

We then use the Newton formula (15) to get the coefficients $\sigma_1(P_f), \ldots, \sigma_N(P_f)$ of P_f:

$$k\sigma_k(P_f) = -\sum_{i=1}^{k-1} S_i(P_f)\sigma_{k-i}(P_f).$$

Also, all $k\sigma_k$ have bitsize $\mathcal{O}(n\tau)$ and may be computed in $\widetilde{\mathcal{O}}(n^3\tau)$ bit operations. As $\sigma_k \in \mathbf{Z}$ they can all be obtained in $\widetilde{\mathcal{O}}(n^3\tau)$ bit operations $\square$

Once P_f is computed, we can compute M_f as $P_f/\gcd(P_f, P_f')$. Here P_f has degree N and bitsize $\mathcal{O}(n\tau)$. Then $h = \gcd(P_f, P_f')$ is calculated in time $\widetilde{\mathcal{O}}(n^3\tau)$, using Proposition 5.

From Proposition 5, we know that $\tau_T(h) = \widetilde{\mathcal{O}}(n\tau)$ so that the last operation $M_f = P_f/h$ requires $\widetilde{\mathcal{O}}(n^2\tau)$ bit operations. We finally get

PROPOSITION 25. *We can compute the minimal polynomial M_f of $f(2\cos\frac{\pi}{n})$ in $\widetilde{\mathcal{O}}(n^3\tau)$ binary operations.*

Example

Consider $F = 2b\cos\frac{\pi}{7} + 2c\cos\frac{\pi}{5}$. We write $F = f(2\cos\frac{\pi}{35})$ where $f = bT_5 + cT_7$. The minimal polynomial of $2\cos\frac{\pi}{35}$ is

$$\begin{aligned} M_{35} &= T_{12} + T_{11} - T_7 - T_6 - T_5 - T_4 + T_2 + T_1 + 1 \\ &= t^{12} + t^{11} - 12\,t^{10} - 11\,t^9 + 54\,t^8 + 43\,t^7 \\ &\quad -113\,t^6 - 71\,t^5 + 110\,t^4 + 46\,t^3 - 40\,t^2 - 8\,t + 1. \end{aligned}$$

Computing $P_f = \mathrm{Res}\,(z - bT_5 - cT_7, M_{35})$ we obtain $P_f = M_f^2$ where

$$\begin{aligned} M_f &= z^6 - (3\,b + 2\,c)\,z^5 + c\,(-3\,c + 5\,b)\,z^4 \\ &\quad + \left(5\,b^3 + 6\,bc^2 + 6\,c^3\right)z^3 \\ &\quad -c\left(5\,b^3 + 7\,b^2c + 9\,bc^2 - 2\,c^3\right)z^2 \\ &\quad - \left(3\,b^5 - 4\,b^3c^2 - 7\,b^2c^3 + 2\,bc^4 + 4\,c^5\right)z \\ &\quad -b^6 + b^5c + 7\,c^2b^4 - 2\,b^3c^3 - 7\,b^2c^4 + 2\,bc^5 + c^6. \end{aligned}$$

7. CONCLUSION

This framework provides a set of simple and fast algorithms, dedicated to the computations in real cyclotomic extensions $\mathbf{Q}[\cos\pi/n]$. It allows us to achieve the computation of minimal Chebyshev parametrizations for the first two-bridge knots (see [11, 10]). Precisely, the original methods used in [11], based on straightforward resolutions of multivariate systems were not powerful enough to find the the minimal parameterizations, the ones proposed in the present contribution optimize those used in [10] and also allow a precise complexity study of the entire problem (finding minimal Chebyshev parameterizations).

8. REFERENCES

[1] ARNOLD, A., AND MONAGAN, M. A high-performance algorithm for calculating cyclotomic polynomials. In *Proceedings of the 4th International Workshop on Parallel and Symbolic Computation* (2010), pp. 112–120.

[2] BASU, S., POLLACK, R., AND ROY, F.-M. *Algorithms in Real Algebraic Geometry*, vol. 10 of *Algorithms and Computation in Mathematics*. Springer-Verlag, 2006.

[3] BAYAD, A., AND CANGUL, I. N. The minimal polynomial of $2\cos\frac{\pi}{q}$ and Dickson polynomials. *Applied Mathematics and Computation 218*, 13 (Mars 2012), 7014–7022.

[4] BOSTAN, A., SALVY, B., AND SCHOST, É. Fast conversion algorithms for orthogonal polynomials. *Linear Algebra and its Applications 431*, 1 (2010), 249–258.

[5] BRENT, R. Multiple precision zero-finding methods and the complexity of elementary function evaluation. *Analytic Computational Complexity (edited by J. F. Traub), Academic Press, New York* (1975), 151–176.

[6] BRENT, R. Fast multiple precision evaluation of elementary functions. *Journal of the Association for Computing Machinery 23*, 2 (1976), 242–251.

[7] GIORGI, P. On polynomial multiplication in Chebyshev basis. *IEEE Transactions on Computers 61*, 6 (2012), 780–789.

[8] HART, W. B., AND NOVOCIN, A. Practical divide-and-conquer algorithms for polynomial arithmetic. In *Lecture Notes in Computer Science* (september 2011), vol. 6885, CASC'11 Proceedings of the 13th international conference on Computer algebra in scientific computing, pp. 200–214.

[9] HSIAO, H. J. On factorization of Chebyshev's polynomial of the first kind. *Bulletin of the Institute of Mathematics Academia Sinica 12*, 1 (1984), 89–94.

[10] KOSELEFF, P.-V., PECKER, D., AND ROUILLIER, F. Computing Chebyshev knot diagrams. http://arxiv.org/abs/1001.5192.

[11] KOSELEFF, P.-V., PECKER, D., AND ROUILLIER, F. The first rational Chebyshev knots. *Journal of Symbolic Computation 45* (2010), 1341–1358.

[12] MASON, J. C., AND HANDSCOMB, D. C. *Polynomial Chebyshev.* Chapman and Hall/CRC, 2003.

[13] MYERSON, G. Rational products of cosine of rational angles. *Aequationes Mathematicae, Univ. of Waterloo 45* (1993), 70–82.

[14] RIVLIN, T. J. *Chebyshev Methods in Numerical Approximation.* John Wiley & Sons, Inc., 1990.

[15] SHOUP, V. Efficient computation of minimal polynomials in algebraic extensions of finite fields. In *Proceedings of the 1999 International Symposium on Symbolic and Algebraic Computation* (New York, NY, USA, 1999), ISSAC '99, ACM, pp. 53–58.

[16] VON JUR GATHEN, J., AND GERHARD, J. *Modern Computer Algebra*, 03 ed. Cambridge University Press, juin 2013.

[17] WATKINS, W., AND ZEITLIN, J. The minimal polynomial of $\cos\frac{2\pi}{n}$. *The American Mathematical Monthly 100*, 5 (May 1993), 471–474.

Implementation of the DKSS Algorithm for Multiplication of Large Numbers

Christoph Lüders
Universität Bonn
Institut für Informatik
Bonn, Germany
chris@cfos.de

ABSTRACT

The Schönhage-Strassen algorithm (SSA) is the de-facto standard for multiplication of large integers. For N-bit numbers it has a time bound of $O(N \cdot \log N \cdot \log\log N)$. De, Kurur, Saha and Saptharishi (DKSS) presented an asymptotically faster algorithm with a better time bound of $N \cdot \log N \cdot 2^{O(\log^* N)}$. For this paper, a simplified DKSS multiplication was implemented. Assuming a sensible upper limit on the input size, some required constants could be precomputed. This allowed to simplify the algorithm to save some complexity and run-time. Still, run-time is about 30 times larger than SSA, while memory requirements are about 2.3 times higher than SSA. A possible crossover point is estimated to be out of reach even if we utilized the whole universe for computer memory.

Categories and Subject Descriptors

G.1.0 [**Numerical Analysis**]: General—*Multiple precision arithmetic*; G.4 [**Mathematical Software**]: Algorithm design and analysis, Efficiency; I.1.2 [**Symbolic And Algebraic Manipulation**]: Algorithms—*Algebraic algorithms, Analysis of algorithms*

General Terms

Algorithms, Performance.

Keywords

Integer multiplication, multiprecision arithmetic, fast Fourier transform.

1. INTRODUCTION

Multiplication of integers is one of the most basic arithmetic operations. The naive method to multiply two N-bit integers requires $O(N^2)$ bit-operations. As numbers get larger, soon this process becomes too slow and faster means are desirable.

ISSAC'15, July 6–9, 2015, Bath, United Kingdom.

ACM 978-1-4503-3435-8/15/07 ...$15.00.
DOI: http://dx.doi.org/10.1145/2755996.2756643.

In the 1960s methods were discovered (cf. [14], [20], [3]) that lowered the number of bit-operations successively until in 1971 Schönhage and Strassen [19] presented their now well known algorithm (abbreviated as *SSA*). If $\log N$ denotes the logarithm to base 2, their algorithm has a time bound of

$$T(N) = O(N \cdot \log N \cdot \log\log N). \tag{1}$$

It uses a *fast Fourier transform* (FFT), a technique that was already known by Gauss, but rediscovered in 1965 by Cooley and Tukey [4].

SSA was the asymptotically fastest known method for multiplication until in 2007 Fürer [9] found an even faster way. Fürer's algorithm inspired De, Kurur, Saha and Saptharishi to their multiplication method [6] (see [7] for an expanded text), here called *DKSS multiplication* (or *DKSSA* for short). Both Fürer's and DKSS' algorithms require

$$T(N) = N \cdot \log N \cdot 2^{O(\log^* N)} \tag{2}$$

bit-operations, where $\log^* N$ is the number of times the logarithm function has to be applied to get a value ≤ 1.

However, Fürer conjectured that his method only becomes faster than SSA for "astronomically large numbers" [9, sec. 7]. Fürer's algorithm uses floating point operations, in contrast to SSA and DKSSA, which both use integer operations. To obtain a fair comparison, I implemented DKSSA and compared it to SSA.

The ability to multiply numbers with millions or billions of digits is not only academically interesting, but bears practical relevance. Number theoretical tasks like specialized primality tests require fast multiplication of potentially very large integers. Multiplication of dense polynomials with numerical coefficients can be reduced to one huge integer multiplication through Kronecker-Schönhage substitution [18, sec. 2]. Likewise, multiplication and factoring of multivariate polynomials [10] and calculation of π or e to billions of digits or computing billions of roots of Riemann's zeta function are other fields that require fast multiplication of large numbers [21, sec. 8.0]. Such calculations can be performed nowadays with general purpose computer algebra systems.

Fast multiplication is an important building block of a general library for arithmetic operations on large numbers like GMP, the GNU Multiple Precision Arithmetic Library [12] or MPIR, a popular GMP fork for Windows [11]. Many of the more complex tasks — like inversion, division, square root or greatest common divisor — revert back to multiplication, cf. [10].

The method of Schönhage and Strassen (we use the updated version from [18]) uses the ring $\mathbb{Z}/(2^K + 1)\mathbb{Z}$, where

2 is a primitive $2K$-th root of unity. It breaks numbers of N bits into pieces of $O(\sqrt{N})$ bits, which are in turn multiplied, maybe using the algorithm recursively. It is cleverly designed to take advantage of the binary nature of today's computers: multiplications by powers of 2 are particularly simple and fast to perform and this permits a crucial speed-up for the FFT. This is why it has not only held the crown of the asymptotically fastest multiplication algorithm for over 35 years, but is also in widespread practical use today.

DKSS multiplication has a better asymptotic time bound, but is more complicated. Its elaborate structure allows input numbers to be broken into pieces only $O(\log^2 N)$ bits small. However, its arithmetic operations are more costly.

We are investigating here if or when an implementation of DKSS multiplication becomes faster than one of Schönhage-Strassen multiplication. An expanded account on the theory, implementation and analysis can be found in [16].

1.1 Note on Asymptotics

We know from theory that DKSSA is asymptotically faster than SSA. Unfortunately, that doesn't tell us if a practical implementation will be faster for the range of input lengths it is used for.

Software that multiplies large numbers usually chooses the fastest algorithm for a given input bit-length N. In our case, the implementation was done with my own `BIGNUM` library [15] that features grade-school (or ordinary), Karatsuba, Toom-Cook 3-way and Schönhage-Strassen multiplication. Except for grade-school, all other methods are recursive schemes, that means, they reduce the input to multiple smaller multiplications that in turn are handled by the fastest algorithm for their length until, at the lowest level, grade-school multiplication is used.

This requires to find the *crossover points* between different algorithms, i.e. the bit-length N, where the more complex, yet asymptotically faster algorithm becomes just as fast as the simpler algorithm. Since these crossover points depend on several factors (many of them implementation details or rooted in code optimization), they are usually found by benchmarking, that is, measuring and comparing the runtime of the different algorithms. Figure 2 lists their values for `BIGNUM` and MPIR.

Since a practical implementation is limited by the hardware it's run on, this implies an upper limit on the bit-length N. Our implementation runs on a 64-bit CPU, so the length of input numbers is limited to $8 \cdot 2^{64}/4 = 2^{65}$ bits. This is not a serious limitation. According to `top500.org`, even the fastest supercomputers in 2015 are equipped with around $1 \text{ PB} = 2^{53}$ bits of memory.

This is only to show that for a practical application today a limitation of $N < 2^{65}$ bits is not very limiting. As we will see, the picture doesn't change much even if we assume $N < 2^{128}$ bits. If Moore's law holds, that limit will hardly be exceeded within this century.

2. (SIMPLIFIED) DKSS ALGORITHM

DKSS multiplication as laid our in [7] uses the polynomial quotient ring $\mathcal{R} = \mathcal{P}[\alpha]/(\alpha^m + 1)$. Since $\alpha^m \equiv -1$, α is a primitive $2m$-th root of unity and multiplications by powers of α can be done as cyclic shifts (where coefficients only change place and possibly their sign, but not their absolute value; hence a cyclic shift can be done in time linear to the number of coefficients). Underlying $\mathcal{R}$ is the ring $\mathcal{P} = \mathbb{Z}/p^c\mathbb{Z}$, where p is a prime number and c is a constant. This "double structure" can be exploited in the FFT and allows to break down an N-bit input number into numbers of $O(\log^2 N)$ bits.

In their paper, De, Kurur, Saha and Saptharishi describe the algorithm without any assumptions about the hardware, but as described in §1.1, we assume here that the length of input numbers is limited to 2^{65} bits.

DKSS go to great lengths to show that suitable primes p can be found at run-time. To facilitate that, the modulus p^c with $c > 1$ is used and numbers are encoded as k-variate polynomials, $k > 1$. Both c and k are constants that depend on Linnik's constant. Polynomials have a degree less than M in each variable, i.e. they have M^k coefficients. To calculate the modulus p^c, Hensel lifting is used. All of this is done to keep the time to find the prime p bounded, cf. [7, §4.2].

Instead, in our simplified DKSS, the needed constants (the prime p and a generator ζ of $\mathbb{F}_p^*$) can be precomputed, since an upper limit of input numbers is known. Therefore, our M is chosen as large as M^k in the original paper and our p as large as p^c in the original paper. There is no more need for Hensel lifting. This allows us to simplify the algorithm and to skip c and k from now on.

The computational cost can of course only be lower, since we leave out some steps (no searching for prime p or generator ζ, no Hensel lifting, no recursion to reduce the number of variables in multivariate polynomials). Between the genuine DKSS and our simplified version, the number of coefficients is chosen in the same way, whereas in the simplified case the ring $\mathcal{P}$ is even a field.

2.1 Short Description

Let $[a : b]$ denote the set $\{x \in \mathbb{Z} \mid a \le x \le b\}$.

Furthermore, for a ring R, a primitive n-th root of unity $\omega \in R$ is called *principal*, if and only if n is coprime to the characteristic of R and $\sum_{i=0}^{n-1} \omega^{ij} = 0$ for $j \in [1 : n-1]$.

To multiply two nonnegative integers a, $b < 2^N$, $N \in \mathbb{N}$ to obtain their product $c := ab < 2^{2N}$, we convert the numbers into polynomials over a ring $\mathcal{R}$, use the fast Fourier transform to transform their coefficients, then multiply the sample values and transform backwards to gain the product polynomial. From there, we can easily recover the resulting integer product.

Define $\mathcal{R} := \mathcal{P}[\alpha]/(\alpha^m + 1)$ and $\mathcal{P} := \mathbb{Z}/p\mathbb{Z}$. Polynomial coefficients are in $\mathcal{P}$ and are henceforth called *inner* coefficients.

Input numbers a and b are encoded as polynomials $a(x)$ and $b(x) \in \mathcal{R}[x]$ with degree less than M (M will be defined shortly). The coefficients are called *outer* coefficients.

We can multiply a and b as follows:

1. Choose integers $m \ge 2$ and $M \ge m$ as powers of 2, such that $m \approx \log N$ and $M \approx N/\log^2 N$. $2M$ will be the length of the FFTs, while m is the degree of elements of $\mathcal{R}$. For simplicity of notation, define $\mu := M/m$.

2. Let $u := \lceil 2N/Mm \rceil$ denote the number of input bits per inner coefficient. Find a prime p with $2M \mid p - 1$, i.e. $p := h \cdot 2M + 1$ for some $h \in \mathbb{N}$.

   Furthermore, the condition

   $$p \ge \frac{1}{2} M m 2^{2u} \qquad (3)$$

   must be met to ensure that the inner coefficients don't overflow.

3. From parameters M, m and p compute a principal $2M$-th root of unity $\rho \in \mathcal{R}$ with the additional property $\rho^\mu = \alpha$:

   A generator ζ of $\mathbb{F}_p^*$ has order $p - 1 = h \cdot 2M$ and is a principal $(p-1)$-th root of unity, making $\omega := \zeta^h$ a principal $2M$-th root of unity.

   Denote $\gamma := \omega^\mu$, a principal $2m$-th root of unity. Furthermore, let $i \in [1 : 2m - 1]$ be odd. Observe that γ^i is a root of $\alpha^m + 1 = 0$, since $(\gamma^i)^m = (\gamma^m)^i = (-1)^i = -1$. Now use Lagrange interpolation to find $\rho(\alpha)$ with $\rho(\gamma^i) = \omega^i$ for all i.

4. Encode a and b as polynomials $a(x), b(x) \in \mathcal{R}[x]$ with degree less than M by breaking them into M blocks with $um/2$ bits in each block. Each such block describes an outer coefficient. Furthermore, split each outer coefficient block into $m/2$ blocks of u bits each, where each block forms an inner coefficient in the lower-degree half of a polynomial. Set the upper $m/2$ inner coefficients to zero. Finally, set the upper M outer coefficients to zero.

5. Use root ρ to perform a length-$2M$ fast Fourier transform of $a(x)$ and $b(x)$ to obtain $\widehat{a}_i := a(\rho^i) \in \mathcal{R}$, likewise $\widehat{b}_i$. Use the special structure of $\mathcal{R}$ to speed up the FFT, see the next section.

6. Multiply pointwise $\widehat{a}_i\widehat{b}_i =: \widehat{c}_i$. Note that $\widehat{a}_i, \widehat{b}_i \in \mathcal{R}$ are themselves polynomials. Reduce their multiplication to integer multiplication by Kronecker-Schönhage substitution and multiply them recursively (with the fastest algorithm for their length). See below for details.

7. Perform a backwards transform of length $2M$ to obtain the product polynomial $c(x) := a(x)b(x)$. This includes the usual reordering of the resulting coefficients and dividing them by $2M$.

8. Evaluate the inner polynomials of the product polynomial $c(x)$ at $\alpha = 2^u$ and the outer polynomial $c(x)$ at $x = 2^{um/2}$ to recover the integer result $c = ab$.

To multiply two elements of $\mathcal{R}$ (which are themselves polynomials), we use Kronecker-Schönhage substitution, cf. [18, sec. 2] and [2, sec. 1.3 & 1.9]. This reduces polynomial multiplication to integer multiplication with $m(2\lceil \log p \rceil + \log m) = O(\log^2 N)$ bits. To do so, we use the fastest multiplication for that length, possibly recursing into DKSSA.

After that we still have to perform both modulo operations: mod $(\alpha^m + 1)$ on the product polynomial and mod p on its coefficients.

2.2 Performing the FFT

A Cooley-Tukey FFT [4] works for any length that is a power of 2. Here the length is $2M$ and it can be split as $2M = 2m \cdot \mu$, with $\mu = M/m$. The input vector can be organized as a matrix with $2m$ rows of μ columns each.

The DKSS algorithm uses a radix-μ decimation in time Cooley-Tukey FFT, cf. [8, sec. 4.1]. That is, it first does μ FFTs of length $2m$ on the columns of the matrix, then multiplies the results by twiddle factors (called *bad multiplications* by DKSS) and finally performs $2m$ FFTs of length μ on the rows of the matrix.

The length-$2m$ column FFTs use α as root of unity and since multiplications with powers of α can be performed as cyclic shifts, they can be done in linear time.

Let's see how this works in detail. The length-$2M$ DFT of $a(x)$ with ρ as root of unity can be computed in three steps:

1. Perform *inner DFTs.*

   Rewrite the input vector a as a matrix of $2m$ rows of μ columns (called e_ℓ) and perform FFTs on the columns.

   Let $v \in [0 : 2m - 1]$ and define polynomials $\bar{a}_v(x) \in \mathcal{R}[x]$ with degree less than μ as

   $$\bar{a}_v(x) := a(x) \bmod (x^\mu - \alpha^v). \qquad (4)$$

   Denote $\bar{a}_{v,\ell}$ the ℓ-th coefficient of $\bar{a}_v(x)$. Then it holds that

   $$\bar{a}_{v,\ell} = e_\ell(\alpha^v).$$

   So to find the ℓ-th coefficient of each $\bar{a}_v(x)$ perform a length-$2m$ DFT of $e_\ell(y)$, using α as root of unity. Call these the *inner DFTs.*

   Perform multiplications by powers of α as cyclic shifts. Since $\alpha^m \equiv -1$, coefficients of powers $\geq m$ wrap around with changed sign.

2. Perform *bad multiplications.*

   Let $[0 : 2M - 1] \ni i = 2m \cdot f + v$ with $f \in [0 : \mu - 1]$ and $v \in [0 : 2m - 1]$. Then it follows from (4) that

   $$a(\rho^i) = a(\rho^{2m \cdot f + v}) = \bar{a}_v(\rho^{2m \cdot f + v}). \qquad (5)$$

   In order to efficiently compute $\bar{a}_v(\rho^{2m \cdot f + v})$, define

   $$\widetilde{a}_v(x) := \bar{a}_v(x \cdot \rho^v). \qquad (6)$$

   Compute $\widetilde{a}_v(x)$ by computing its coefficients $\widetilde{a}_{v,\ell} = \bar{a}_{v,\ell} \cdot \rho^{v\ell}$, with $\ell \in [0 : \mu - 1]$.

3. Perform *outer DFTs.*

   Now all that is left is to evaluate the $\widetilde{a}_v(x)$, $v \in [0 : 2m - 1]$, at $x = \rho^{2m \cdot f}$, for $f \in [0 : \mu - 1]$. The $\widetilde{a}_v(x)$ are arranged in such a way that these evaluations are nothing but length-μ DFTs of $\widetilde{a}_v(x)$ with ρ^{2m} as root of unity, performed on the rows of the matrix. Call these the *outer DFTs.*

   If $M \geq m$, this is done by a *recursive* call to the FFT routine. According to (5) and (6) it computes $\widetilde{a}_v(\rho^{2m \cdot f}) = \bar{a}_v(\rho^{2m \cdot f + v}) = a(\rho^{2m \cdot f + v}) = a(\rho^i)$.

   If called recursively, $M < m$ might hold. Then, just computing an inner DFT with $\alpha^{m/M}$ as (m/M)-th root of unity is sufficient.

The source code of the whole FFT can be found as `dkss_fft()` in `BIGNUM`.

3. IMPLEMENTATION

3.1 Parameter Selection

There is some freedom on how exactly to select parameters M, m, u and p. It follows from (3) that

$$p \geq \frac{1}{2} M m 2^{2u} \approx \frac{1}{2} N^5 / \log N. \quad (7)$$

Both allocated memory and cost of division (for modular reductions) depend on the length of p or, more precisely, on its length in processor words. But the larger the value of p (which is the modulus of $\mathcal{P}$), the more bits we can encode in each coefficient. This is turn can lead to fewer coefficients and thus maybe to a shorter FFT length, which is desirable.

So we select a value for p that satisfies condition (7), but makes the most of the memory it occupies. That is, $\log p$ should be slightly less than a multiple of the processor word size in bits. Benchmarking showed that this leads to faster run-time than using (7) without rounding up, see [16, fig. 19].

The prime p is selected from a list of precomputed primes. I precomputed suitable primes for bit-lengths from 2 to 1704. According to (7) this allows DKSSA up to a bit-length of $N = 2^{342}$ bits. Since the implementation is running on a 64-bit machine, a shorter table would have done. And since we're rounding the length of p to multiples of 64 bit, the table of possible primes for p contains only 6 entries, listed in Figure 1.

Next, the largest u is selected that permits the polynomial to hold the whole $2N$ bits of the result. It follows from (3) that $\log p \geq \log(Mm) + 2u - 1$. Since $\log p$ is already fixed, maximize u. The larger u is, the less coefficients are needed.

After finding an u that fits, minimize the product Mm, because the smaller Mm is, the smaller the FFT length and memory requirements are.

Lastly, set M and m. Factors can be moved around between M and m, since until now only the product Mm was needed. To prove the time-bound for DKSSA it is only required that $M = O(N/\log^2 N)$ and $m = O(\log N)$, cf. [7, §4.2]. This means that their quotient $M/m \approx k \cdot N/\log^3 N$ can contain some arbitrary constant k.

Some short tests on selecting k indicated that $k = 1$ is overall a good choice, but more research should confirm this. This selection leads to the same values that DKSS use and that were already described in §2.1, Step 1.

This parameter selection was implemented in `BIGNUM` as `dkss_set_mmu()`.

3.2 Test Environment

The implementation was done with my own `BIGNUM` library [15] that is written in C++ with a few inner subroutines in assembly language. `BIGNUM` allows different multiplication algorithms and selects the fastest one, depending on the size of the operands. An extensive explanation of the algorithms and their implementation can be found in [16, ch. 2].

Prime p	Bit-length of p
$27 \cdot 2^{59} + 1$	64
$81 \cdot 2^{121} + 1$	128
$13 \cdot 2^{188} + 1$	192
$207 \cdot 2^{248} + 1$	256
$13 \cdot 2^{316} + 1$	320
$285 \cdot 2^{375} + 1$	384

Figure 1: Primes p used by `BIGNUM`

Algorithm	`BIGNUM`	MPIR
Karatsuba	≥ 28	≥ 14
Toom-Cook 3-way	≥ 152	≥ 98
Toom-Cook 4-way	—	≥ 154
Toom-Cook 8.5-way	—	≥ 270
Schönhage-Strassen	> 2464	≥ 2880

Figure 2: Crossover points in 64-bit words for `BIGNUM` and MPIR

Implementations of SSA and DKSSA are called `SMUL` and `DKSS_MUL`, respectively. The source code is available under LGPL.

In `BIGNUM`, I chose to implement everything from scratch, that is, I did not use any other large integer library or special hardware, so I would not be limited by someone else's design decisions. This implies that `BIGNUM` did not benefit from the large codebase that e.g. GMP [12] or MPIR [11] already offer.

Since DKSSA is compared to SSA, some work on `BIGNUM` went into fine-tuning SSA to make it faster, like "Mersenne transforms" and extensive "tuning" (to use the same names as in [10]). Missing is Bailey's 4-step transform (cf. [10, §2.2.3]), which explains most of why `BIGNUM` is slower than MPIR (see below).

To the best of my knowledge, GMP is the leading and fastest open-source large integer library. Its port for the Windows operating system is MPIR. Comparing SSA multiplication speed for `BIGNUM` and MPIR 2.6.0, `BIGNUM` is on average slower by a factor of about 1.30. As we will see, this factor is negligible when compared to the factor of slowness that `DKSS_MUL` vs. `SMUL` exhibits.

Tests were run on an Intel Core i7-3770 processor (Ivy Bridge microarchitecture) with 3.40 GHz clock rate and 32 GB memory. This CPU has level 1 caches per core of both 32 KB for data and 32 KB for instructions, unified level 2 caches of 256 KB per core and a unified level 3 cache of 8 MB for all cores.

The operating system was Windows 7 64-bit and the compiler was Visual Studio 2012 (C++ compiler v17). To improve cache performance, the process affinity was fixed to one processor. The same testing conditions were used both for `BIGNUM` and MPIR.

Correctness of the code was verified with Lucas-Lehmer tests of hundreds of Mersenne numbers (both prime and composite), including all Mersenne primes up to $2^{1398269} - 1$.

To measure speed, two operands of the same bit-length were multiplied. Both were properly aligned, filled with random words (generated with the C++ `mt19937_64` Mersenne Twister) and the average run-time of several tests was used.

Timings were taken by use of Windows' `QueryThreadCycleTime()` function that counts only CPU cycles spent by the thread in question. It queries the CPU's Time Stamp Counter and has clock-cycle resolution, i.e. 3.4 GHz, which is very accurate.

The benchmarks were done with input lengths of 237 to 169,869,312 words. The largest input number requires already temporary memory of about 26 GB. Because of memory limitations, I could not test larger inputs.

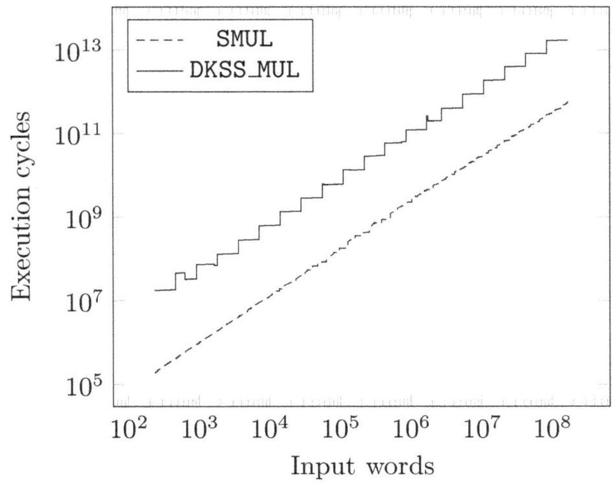

Figure 3: Execution time of DKSS_MUL

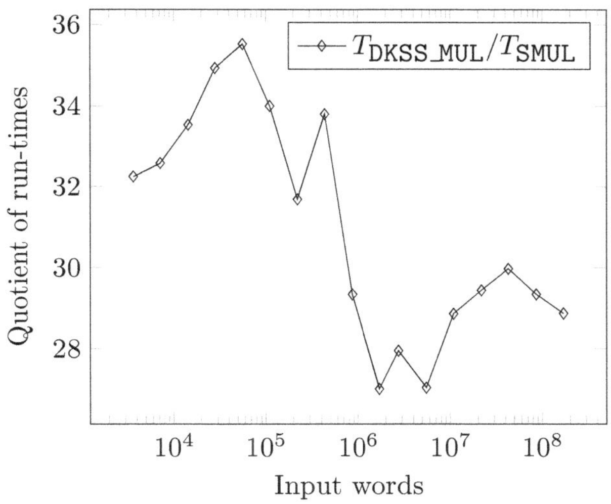

Figure 4: Quotient of DKSS_MUL and SMUL run-times vs. input length

3.3 Improvements

The implementation was improved over the simplified algorithm described in §2 in two respects:

In §2.2, Step 2 every coefficient is multiplied by some power of ρ. To calculate ρ^i, $i \in [0 : 2M - 1]$, set $r = \lfloor i/\mu \rfloor$ and $s = i \bmod \mu$. Since $\rho^\mu = \alpha$, it holds that $\rho^i = \rho^{\mu r + s} = \rho^{\mu r} \rho^s = \alpha^r \rho^s$. Because multiplications by powers of α can be done as cyclic shifts, we can save almost half of the bad multiplications by precomputing ρ^s, for $s \in [0 : \mu - 1]$. Doing so costs negligible memory (cf. §3.5) and saves almost half of execution time.

The FFT from §2.2 requires temporary memory of the size of a full input vector to store the $\bar{a}_v(x)$. By using an in-place matrix transposition the $\bar{a}_{v,\ell}$ can be reordered in such a way that the FFTs can be done in-place as well. This saves about one third of temporary memory. The FFT then works like Bailey's "six step" FFT algorithm [1], but with faster inner DFTs. Cache efficiency of the matrix transposition is not a concern here, since profiling showed that about 85 % of total run-time is spent with *bad multiplications*, cf. [16, sec. 4.7].

3.4 Execution Time

Figure 3 shows a double-logarithmic plot of the execution time of DKSS_MUL in comparison to SMUL. The stair-like graph of DKSS_MUL execution time stems from the fact that execution time almost totally depends on the FFT length $2M$ and the size of elements of $\mathcal{R}$. Since both M and m are powers of 2, many different input lengths lead to the same set of parameters and hence to the same FFT length.

In contrast, the SMUL execution time graph is much smoother. The reason for this is that SSA uses the ring $\mathbb{Z}/(2^K + 1)\mathbb{Z}$, where K does not have to be a power of 2, thus allowing a finer granularity.

The DKSS_MUL graph shows that execution time is almost the same for the beginning and the end of each step. The only part that depends directly on N is the encoding of the input numbers and decoding into the resulting product. The time needed to do the FFT clearly dominates overall execution time.

To compare run-times and memory consumption numerically, we pick the rightmost point for each step of the DKSS_MUL graph, because only then are all outer coefficients filled with bits from the input and not zero-padded.

As can be seen clearly, DKSS_MUL is much slower over the whole range of tested input lengths. From this graph it is hard to see if DKSS_MUL is gaining on SMUL. Figure 4 shows the quotient of run-times that is between 27 to 36 times slower at best. The location of a crossover point is discussed in §4.

In §2.1, Step 6 it is mentioned that DKSSA might be called recursively. In the tests, it never came to that. Even with maximal long inputs, the inner multiplications were just 195 words long and are thus still in the range for Toom 3-way multiplication. In fact, for recursion into DKSS_MUL to happen, DKSS_MUL would have to be faster than SMUL on the top level first.

3.5 Memory Requirements

DKSS_MUL memory requirements are dominated by two times the size of the polynomials: input $a(x)$ and $b(x) \in \mathcal{R}[x]$. The result $c(x)$ requires no further memory, since storage of one of the input polynomials can be reused.

Each polynomial has $2M$ coefficients and with (7) we estimate its memory requirement as $2Mm\lceil \log p \rceil \approx 10N$ bits.

To be exact, more memory, namely another $m \cdot \lceil \log p \rceil \approx 5 \log^2 N$ bits of temporary memory, is allocated in `dkss_fft()`, but that is of no big consequence compared to $10N$ bits for each polynomial. The same applies to the M/m precomputed powers of ρ, each with a length of $m\lceil \log p \rceil$ bits. Together, they only need $M\lceil \log p \rceil$ bits, that is, a $2m$-th part of the memory of one polynomial.

If we assume fully utilized outer coefficients and both input numbers have N bits, total memory needed by DKSS_MUL is

$$M_{\text{DKSS\_MUL}}(N) \approx 20N \text{ bits.}$$

The above memory requirements are a direct consequence of the algorithm, since they stem from the memory needed to store the encoded input numbers.

Compare this to the memory requirements of SMUL. According to [16, eq. (2.32)], the approximate amount of tem-

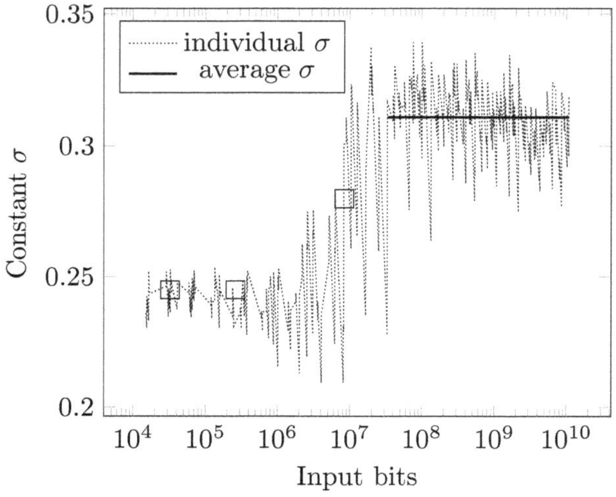

Figure 5: `SMUL` run-time constant σ

porary memory for SMUL is

$$M_{\texttt{SMUL}}(N) \approx 8N \text{ bits.}$$

Again, this is the memory needed to hold the encoded polynomials.

Measured memory consumption fitted theory nicely with an average $M_{\texttt{DKSS\_MUL}} \approx 18.88$ and $M_{\texttt{SMUL}} \approx 8.26$. The average quotient was $M_{\texttt{DKSS\_MUL}}/M_{\texttt{SMUL}} \approx 2.30$, which fits the theoretical $20/8 = 2.5$ well.

4. EXTRAPOLATION

Now that we have seen that in the ranges our tests have covered DKSS_MUL is still much slower than SMUL, we estimate the input length where DKSS_MUL starts to outperform SMUL.

To do that, we model the run-times for the algorithms, i.e. express them with explicit constants, then try to determine the constants from our measurements.

The formulas for run-times both contain terms that express the level of recursion: $\log\log N$ for SSA and $\log^* N$ for DKSSA, respectively. When it comes to recursion, the fastest algorithm for that length is used. For example, SSA calls itself only then for a second time if that would be faster than Toom-Cook. That leads to a relatively smooth run-time graph without large jumps.

To model that, we use the smooth function $\log\log N$ instead of $\lceil \log\log N \rceil$ for SSA and the super-logarithm $\operatorname{slog} N$ instead of $\log^* N$ for DKSSA, respectively.

4.1 Modeling SMUL Run-Time

Following (1) we model SMUL run-time, that is, rewrite it with an explicit constant as

$$T_\sigma(N) \le \sigma \cdot N \cdot \log N \cdot \log\log N. \quad (8)$$

Dividing measured execution cycles by $N \cdot \log N \cdot \log\log N$ to calculate σ leads to the graph depicted in Figure 5. Interestingly, this graph seems to have two plateau-like sections.

The plateaus correspond quite nicely with the cache sizes of the test machine, see §3.2. The three boxes indicate maximum input sizes that could still be calculated in the respective cache memory.

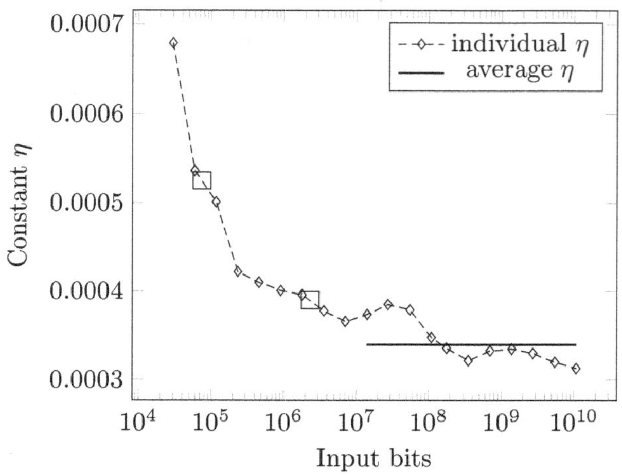

Figure 6: `DKSS_MUL` run-time constant η

After level 3 there is no further caching, hence when the required temporary memory is some orders larger there is no further visible influence on the run-time constant σ. Averaging from input sizes of 32 Mbits (this uses about 32 MB temporary memory) onwards leads to an average $\sigma \approx 0.311$.

4.2 Modeling DKSS_MUL Run-Time

Likewise, we use the measured run-times to model the run-time of DKSS_MUL. We write (2) with explicit constants and the smooth super-logarithm and get:

$$T_\eta(N) \le \eta \cdot N \cdot \log N \cdot 2^{\delta \cdot \operatorname{slog} N}. \quad (9)$$

Substitute $K := 2^\delta$ and we get

$$T_\eta(N) \le \eta \cdot N \cdot \log N \cdot K^{\operatorname{slog} N}.$$

The question is now: what is the value of K? The latest result on integer multiplication from 2014 by Harvey, van der Hoeven and Lecerf [13] suggests that DKSSA implies $K = 16$.

Unfortunately, with the few data points we have, any model of run-time is not very robust. As explained in §3.4, we get only one data point per step of the input bit-length N and since there is approximately one step per power of 2, we have only 20 measured run-time values to base our model on.

Figure 6 shows a graph of the constant η for each data point. The two boxes shown mark inputs that fit in level 2 and 3 caches, respectively. Like in Figure 5, we use only values of η where DKSS_MUL temporary memory has surely exceeded the level 3 cache size, that is, where is exceeds 12.8 Mbits (again, using 32 MB temporary memory).

To calculate the super-logarithm numerically, I used the linear approximation approach [17]. For $K = 16$ this leads to $\eta \approx 0.00034$. As we will see now, it leads to a crossover point that is extremely large.

4.3 When Will DKSS_MUL Trump SMUL?

Based on (8) and (9) we can solve

$$T_\eta(N) \le T_\sigma(N)$$
$$\eta \cdot N \cdot \log N \cdot K^{\operatorname{slog} N} \le \sigma \cdot N \cdot \log N \cdot \log\log N$$
$$K^{\operatorname{slog} N} \le (\sigma/\eta) \cdot \log\log N$$
$$\log K \cdot \operatorname{slog} N \le \log(\sigma/\eta) + \log\log\log N.$$

For large N substitute $\nu := \log\log N$ and get

$$\log K \cdot (\operatorname{slog} \nu + 2) \le \log(\sigma/\eta) + \log \nu. \qquad (10)$$

Solving (10) numerically yields the enormous solution of $\nu \ge 15934$ and hence $N \ge 10^{10^{4796}}$! An optimistic estimation of the number of bits for computer memory available in this universe is 10^{100}. So the estimations of the crossover point are *orders of orders* of magnitude higher than the largest machine we can build.

It should be mentioned here that SMUL is better optimized than DKSS_MUL. The reason for that is that SSA is now studied and in wide use for many years and its details are well understood. In contrast, DKSSA is still quite young and to my knowledge this is the first implementation of it. Still, in my appraisal none of the possible improvements to DKSS_MUL of §5.1 have the potential to speed it up so much that it becomes faster than SMUL.

Even if DKSS_MUL was only 1.5 times slower than SMUL, the crossover point would still be at least at $N \approx 10^{10^{99}}$ bits and thus unreachable.

5. CONCLUSION

De, Kurur, Saha and Saptharishi describe a new procedure to multiply large integers efficiently that was implemented as DKSS_MUL. The currently widely used algorithm by Schönhage and Strassen was implemented as SMUL. Both algorithms were compared for their run-time and memory consumption.

The results indicate that Schönhage and Strassen's algorithm is still the better choice for a variety of reasons:

1. SMUL is faster than DKSS_MUL.

   Benchmarks show that SMUL is at least between 27 to 36 times faster than DKSS_MUL, see Figure 3. The estimated input length where DKSS_MUL could become faster than SMUL is $N \ge 10^{10^{4796}}$ bits (which is larger than googolplex). But even if SMUL was only 1.5 times faster than DKSS_MUL, the crossover point would be so large that it could never be reached.

2. SMUL requires less memory than DKSS_MUL.

   If both input numbers are N bits long, DKSS_MUL requires about $20N$ bits of temporary memory, while SMUL requires only about $8N$ bits. In practice, the quotient is about 2.30.

3. SMUL is simpler to implement than DKSS_MUL.

   A simple implementation of SMUL needs about 550 lines of C++ code, where DKSS_MUL requires about 1000 lines plus more supporting routines, see [16, sec. 4.6] with more complex program code that is harder to test.

5.1 Future Work

Some possible improvements to DKSS_MUL are listed below. For more on profiling DKSS_MUL, see [16, sec. 4.7].

- Find optimum values of parameters M, m, u and p for any given N.

  Figure 3 shows some areas where longer input numbers lead to shorter execution times. Furthermore, profiling showed developments in percentages of run-times that suggest that a better choice of parameters is possible.

- Add support for "sparse integers" in the underlying multiplication.

  DKSSA reduces multiplication of large integers to multiplications in $\mathcal{R}$, a polynomial ring. To multiply two elements of $\mathcal{R}$, each is converted to one huge integer. About half of the words of it are zero and a future multiplication routine could exploit that. Profiling showed that up to 85 % of execution time is spent with multiplication of elements of $\mathcal{R}$ and a rising percentage of that is used by the underlying integer multiplication. I optimistically estimate the potential for speed up to be almost a factor of 2.

  Any other means of improving the speed of bad multiplications would be very beneficial, like speeding up Kronecker-Schönhage substitution.

- Exploit the structure of prime numbers p.

  The modulus of $\mathcal{P}$ is a prime number of the form $h \cdot 2M + 1$, where h is a small positive odd integer and M is a power of 2. Maybe modular reductions can be sped up by the technique listed in [5, p. 457]. This has the potential to save a great part of the cost of modular reductions, which showed to cost about 22 % of run-time in profiling.

If the potential savings listed above could be achieved, this would speed up DKSS_MUL by a factor of about 2.5. Not included in this factor is a better parameter selection. But even if that and other, yet unthought-of, improvements lead to another speed-up by a factor of 2, DKSS_MUL would still be at least about 5.4 times slower than SMUL.

Source Code

The full source code of of the implementation is available for evaluation as the BIGNUM library [15]. It is licensed under LGPL. Requirements are listed in §3.2.

Acknowledgments

I thank Andreas Weber for his support and advice with this paper. Furthermore, I am grateful to Michael Clausen for his help and advice with my diploma thesis which contains an earlier and expanded account on this topic. Last, but not least, I am thankful for the detailed feedback of the reviewers.

6. REFERENCES

[1] D. H. Bailey. FFTs in external or hierarchical memory. *Journal of Supercomputing*, 4:23–35, Dec. 1990.

[2] R. P. Brent and P. Zimmermann. *Modern Computer Arithmetic*. Cambridge University Press, 2011.

[3] S. A. Cook. *On the Minimum Computation Time of Functions*. PhD thesis, Harvard University, 1966.

[4] J. W. Cooley and J. W. Tukey. An algorithm for the machine calculation of complex Fourier series. *Mathematics of Computation*, 19:297–301, 1965.

[5] R. Crandall and C. Pomerance. *Prime numbers: A Computational Perspective.* Springer, 2nd edition, 2005.

[6] A. De, P. P. Kurur, C. Saha, and R. Saptharishi. Fast integer multiplication using modular arithmetic. In *Proceedings of the fortieth annual ACM symposium on Theory of computing*, pages 499–506, 2008.

[7] A. De, P. P. Kurur, C. Saha, and R. Saptharishi. Fast integer multiplication using modular arithmetic. *SIAM Journal on Compution*, 42(2):685–699, 2013.

[8] P. Duhamel and M. Vetterli. Fast Fourier transforms: A tutorial review and a state of the art. *Signal Processing*, 19:250 – 299, 1990.

[9] M. Fürer. Faster integer multiplication. In *Proceedings of the 39th ACM Symposium on Theory of Computing*, pages 57–66, June 2007.

[10] P. Gaudry, A. Kruppa, and P. Zimmermann. A GMP-based implementation of Schönhage-Strassen's large integer multiplication algorithm. In *Proceedings of the 2007 International Symposium on Symbolic and Algebraic Computation*, pages 167–174, 2007.

[11] T. Granlund, W. Hart, and the GMP and MPIR teams. The multiple precision integers and rationals library. `http://www.mpir.org/mpir-2.6.0.pdf`, Nov. 2012.

[12] T. Granlund and the GMP development team. The GNU multiple precision arithmetic library manual. `https://gmplib.org/gmp-man-6.0.0a.pdf`, Mar. 2014.

[13] D. Harvey, J. van der Hoeven, and G. Lecerf. Even faster integer multiplication. `http://arxiv.org/abs/1407.3360`, July 2014.

[14] A. Karatsuba and Y. Ofman. Multiplication of multidigit numbers on automata. *Soviet Physics — Doklady*, 7:595–596, 1963.

[15] C. Lüders. BIGNUM library for multiple precision arithmetic. `http://www.wrogn.com/bignum`.

[16] C. Lüders. Fast multiplication of large integers: Implementation and analysis of the DKSS algorithm. Diploma thesis, Universität Bonn, Apr. 2014. `http://arxiv.org/abs/1503.04955`.

[17] A. Robbins. Solving for the analytic piecewise extension of tetration and the super-logarithm. 2005. `http://iteror.org/big/Source/articles/TetrationSuperlog_Robbins.pdf`.

[18] A. Schönhage. Asymptotically fast algorithms for the numerical multiplication and division of polynomials with complex coefficients. In J. Calmet, editor, *European Computer Algebra Conference*, volume 144, pages 3–15, 1982.

[19] A. Schönhage and V. Strassen. Schnelle Multiplikation großer Zahlen. *Computing*, 7:281–292, 1971.

[20] A. L. Toom. The complexity of a scheme of functional elements realizing the multiplication of integers. *Soviet Mathematics — Doklady*, 3:714–716, 1963.

[21] J. von zur Gathen and J. Gerhard. *Modern Computer* Algebra. Cambridge University Press, 3rd edition, 2013.

Formulas for Continued Fractions
An Automated Guess and Prove Approach

Sébastien Maulat
ÉNS de Lyon
LIP (U. Lyon, CNRS, ENS Lyon, UCBL)
France
Sebastien.Maulat@ens-lyon.fr

Bruno Salvy
Inria
LIP (U. Lyon, CNRS, ENS Lyon, UCBL)
France
Bruno.Salvy@inria.fr

ABSTRACT

We describe a simple method that produces automatically closed forms for the coefficients of continued fractions expansions of a large number of special functions. The function is specified by a non-linear differential equation and initial conditions. This is used to generate the first few coefficients and from there a conjectured formula. This formula is then proved automatically thanks to a linear recurrence satisfied by some remainder terms. Extensive experiments show that this simple approach and its straightforward generalization to difference and q-difference equations capture a large part of the formulas in the literature on continued fractions.

Categories and Subject Descriptors:
I.1.2 [**Computing Methodologies**]: Symbolic and Algebraic Manipulations — *Algebraic Algorithms*

General Terms: Algorithms, Theory.

Keywords: continued fractions; special functions; P-recursive sequences.

1. INTRODUCTION

Continued fractions are well known for their approximation properties, their use in acceleration of convergence and analytic continuation, as well as their application in proofs of irrationality. Any formal power series can be converted into a *corresponding* continued fraction (C-fraction)

$$a_0 + \cfrac{a_1(z)}{1 + \cfrac{a_2(z)}{1 + \cfrac{a_3(z)}{1 + \cdots}}} \qquad (1)$$

classically denoted $a_0 + \mathcal{K}_{m=1}^{\infty} \frac{a_m(z)}{1}$ or $[a_0, a_1(z), a_2(z), \cdots]$, where a_0 is a constant and $a_i(z)$ are nonconstant monomials for $i > 0$ that are called *partial numerators*. In the frequent case when all the exponents are equal to 1, the C-fraction is called *regular*. Truncating a continued fraction after its nth term gives a rational function which is called its nth *convergent*. There is a one-to-one correspondence between power series and C-fractions. It is easily computed by a sequence of extractions of the constant coefficient, division by the variable and inversion. This conversion is available in the major computer algebra systems.

In several isolated cases, the coefficients a_m are known to possess a closed form, as in the following formula for $\exp(z)$:

$$\exp(z) = 1 + \cfrac{z}{1 - \cfrac{z/(2\cdot 1)}{1 + \cfrac{z/(2\cdot 3)}{1 - \cfrac{z/(2\cdot 3)}{1 + \cfrac{z/(2\cdot 5)}{1+\cdots}}}}},$$

or more compactly

$$a_1 = z, \quad a_{2k} = -z/(2(2k-1)), \quad a_{2k+1} = z/(2(2k+1)). \quad (2)$$

Such formulas are the object of this work. A number of them are listed in the classical handbook by Abramowitz and Stegun [1], or in its successor [15] and the most extensive list to date is the recent handbook by Cuyt *et alii* [10]. Our aim is to derive many of these formulas automatically, starting from a description of the function to be expanded in continued fraction.

We concentrate on functions that are given as solutions of ordinary differential equations with initial conditions (or difference or q-difference equations, see §6). Our approach can be summarized as follows. First, the differential equation and initial conditions are used to generate the first terms of the power series expansion of the function. This power series is then converted into a continued fraction. The coefficients of this continued fraction are then "guessed" by variants of rational interpolation. When this guessing phase is successful, a new power series is defined by this guessed continued fraction expansion. It remains to show that this power series satisfies the differential equation (the initial conditions being correct by construction). The key point in this proof is Theorem 4, stating that the (properly normalized) evaluations of the differential equation on the successive convergents to the continued fraction satisfy a linear recurrence, that can be computed. In all cases, after an operation we call "reduction of order", this recurrence exhibits a growth in the valuations that is sufficient to conclude the proof. A surprisingly large proportion of known explicit continued fractions are thus obtained completely automatically.

Classically, a very effective method due to Gauss derives formulas for continued fractions starting from the contiguity of hypergeometric series. Specialization of the parame-

ISSAC'15, July 6–9, 2015, Bath, United Kingdom..

ACM 978-1-4503-3435-8/15/07 ...$15.00.
DOI: http://dx.doi.org/10.1145/2755996.2756660.

ters then leads to formulas for elementary or special functions [12, §6.1]. This leads to explicit continued fraction expansions by recognizing the function to be expanded as a special case of a quotient of contiguous hypergeometric functions and then relying on a small table of such explicit formulas. These quotients satisfy Riccati equations, so that they are covered by our approach, which is not limited to them (see §6) and proves more suited to the targetted application to the *Dynamic Dictionary of Mathematical Functions* [5]. This is an online encyclopedia of special functions, where the formulas are all generated by computer algebra algorithms from differential equations, in many cases along with a human-readable proof. In this context, it makes sense to avoid any table lookup and generate formulas and proofs for continued fractions directly from the differential equation.

The work closer to ours is the investigation by Chudnovsky and Chudnovsky [8]. They used computer algebra in the study of formulas for continued fractions. Their aim was to classify all functions possessing continued fractions with explicit formulas of various types and relating them to Painlevé transcendents. In contrast, we focus on *one* function that is given as input, and heuristically produce a rational continued fraction expansion when possible.

This article is structured as follows. Section 2 gives an overview of our method on the example of the tangent function. Next, Section 3 presents a heuristic of independent interest that reduces the order of a recurrence given initial conditions. This plays a crucial role in the proving phase of our method. Section 4 is a brief account of what guessing means in this context, while Section 5 is the heart of this work and shows how proofs are achieved automatically. Finally, Section 6 presents experiments with this approach.

2. DETAILED EXAMPLE: TAN

The tangent function can be defined by the Riccati equation

$$y' = 1 + y^2, \quad y(0) = 0. \tag{3}$$

The first 15 coefficients of the unique power series solution are easily computed from the differential equation (see Proposition 3 below for existence and uniqueness). A conversion into a continued fraction gives the coefficients

$$[0, z, -z^2/3, -z^2/15, -z^2/35, -z^2/63, -z^2/99, -z^2/143].$$

The general formula can be deduced from these first terms by rational interpolation, which leads automatically to the (so far conjectural) formula

$$a_1(z) := z; \quad a_n(z) := -z^2/((2n-3)(2n-1)), n > 1. \tag{4}$$

Next, we turn to the automatic proof of this formula. The strategy is to prove that the sequence of rational functions defined by truncating (4) after the nth term for $n = 1, 2, \dots$ converges to the formal power series solution to the differential equation (3). More precisely, let f_n be defined by

$$f_n = \frac{P_n}{Q_n} := [0, z, -z^2/3, \dots, -z^2/((2n-3)(2n-1))],$$

where the rightmost term denotes the finite continued fraction. Then the proof will be completed by showing that $\operatorname{val}(\tan - f_n) \to \infty$ as $n \to \infty$, where val denotes the valuation of a power series:

$$\operatorname{val}\Big(\sum_{i\ge 0} c_i z^i\Big) := \min\{i \ge 0 \mid c_i \ne 0\},$$

with the convention $\operatorname{val}(0) = \infty$. Proposition 3 below shows that it is sufficient to prove that $\operatorname{val}(\mathcal{D}(f_n)) \to \infty$, where $\mathcal{D}(f_n) := f_n' - 1 - f_n^2$.

It is classical that the numerator and denominator of the convergents of a continued fraction are related to the coefficients a_n through a linear recurrence:

$$\begin{aligned} (P_{-1}, P_0) &= (1, 0), & P_n &= P_{n-1} + a_n P_{n-2}, & n &\ge 1, \\ (Q_{-1}, Q_0) &= (0, 1), & Q_n &= Q_{n-1} + a_n Q_{n-2}, & n &\ge 1. \end{aligned} \tag{5}$$

In view of (4), it follows that for all $n \ge 0$, $Q_n(0) = 1$. Thus, the valuation of $\mathcal{D}(f_n)$ is that of its numerator

$$H_n := P_n' Q_n - Q_n^2 - P_n^2 - P_n Q_n'. \tag{6}$$

Using (5) to rewrite P_{n+k} and Q_{n+k} in terms of $P_n, P_{n+1}, Q_n, Q_{n+1}$, it follows that any shift H_{n+k} ($k \in \{0, 1, 2, \dots\}$) can be rewritten as a linear combination of

$$P_{n+i}' Q_{n+j}, P_{n+i} Q_{n+j}', P_{n+i} P_{n+j}, Q_{n+i} Q_{n+j},$$

for i and j in $\{0, 1\}$. There are finitely many such terms, which implies that a linear dependency between $H_n, H_{n+1}, \dots$ (ie, a linear recurrence for H_n) can be computed directly from (5) by linear algebra. This computation produces a linear recurrence of order 4:

$$\begin{aligned} &(2n+7)z^8 H_n - z^4(2n+7)(2n+3)^2(2n+1)^2 H_{n+1} \\ &+ 2z^2(2n+5)(2n+3)^2(2n+1)^2(4n^2 - z^2 + 20n + 21) H_{n+2} \\ &\quad - (2n+5)^2(2n+1)^2(2n+7)^2(2n+3)^3 H_{n+3} \\ &\quad + (2n+5)^2(2n+1)^2(2n+7)^2(2n+3)^3 H_{n+4} = 0. \end{aligned} \tag{7}$$

This recurrence is satisfied by all sequences defined by (6), with P_n and Q_n arbitrary solutions of (5). Using the actual sequences P_n and Q_n provided by the continued fraction gives the first values of H_n:

$$-1, -z^2, -\frac{z^4}{9}, \frac{z^6}{225}, -\frac{z^8}{11025}, -\frac{z^{10}}{893025}.$$

From there, automatic guessing again suggests the following simpler recurrence for H_n:

$$(2n+1)^2 H_{n+1} - z^2 H_n = 0. \tag{8}$$

And again, this recurrence admits of an automatic proof: the right Euclidean division of the fourth order recurrence operator from (7) by this first order one has a remainder equal to 0. This shows that the solution of (8) with the initial conditions given above coincides with the solution of (7) with the same initial conditions, and thus the numerator of $\mathcal{D}(f_n)$ satisfies (8). On this last recurrence, the increase of the valuation with n is clear and this concludes the proof that f_n converges to tan and thus that the power series defined by the continued fraction (4) is that of tan.

In summary, starting with the differential equation (3), this method produces and proves automatically the general term of the famous continued fraction

$$\tan z = \cfrac{z}{1 - \cfrac{z^2/3}{\ddots\, 1 - \cfrac{z^2/((2n-3)(2n-1))}{1 - \ddots}}}$$

that was the basis of Lambert's proof that π is irrational.

3. REDUCTION OF ORDER BY GUESS AND PROVE

The transformation of the large recurrence (7) into the shorter one (8) makes it possible to prove automatically that the valuations $\operatorname{val} H_n(z)$ increase with n. This transformation turns out to play a role in most of the examples dealt with in our experiments. It is actually of more general interest: the closure properties enjoyed by the class of D-finite series or P-recursive sequences give rise to operators satisfied by products or sums of zeroes of such operators [17, 16]. These operators annihilate all possible cases and are potentially of large size, while operators of smaller order may exist for the specific solution of interest. Such an operator may be a right factor of the large one and could be searched for by factoring, but this is made difficult by the potentially infinite number of distinct factorizations [18].

Sequences. Let $\mathcal{A}$ be a recurrence operator with polynomial coefficients in n, of order denoted by $\operatorname{ord}\mathcal{A}$ and leading coefficient $\operatorname{lc}(\mathcal{A})(n)$. A sequence $(u_n)_{n\geq 0}$, abbreviated (u_n), is said to be *defined* by the operator $\mathcal{A}$ and the initial conditions $\mathcal{K} = (u_i)_{i\in\mathcal{I}}$, when the value u_n is given by $\mathcal{K}$ for $n \in \mathcal{I}$ and by the recurrence operator evaluated at $n - \operatorname{ord}\mathcal{A}$ otherwise. Note that the set $\mathcal{I}$ must contain

$$\{0, \dots, \operatorname{ord}\mathcal{A} - 1\} \cup \{i \in \mathbb{N} \mid \operatorname{lc}(\mathcal{A})(i - \operatorname{ord}\mathcal{A}) = 0\}.$$

Algorithm. We now detail an efficient heuristic approach finding such right factors, whose complexity is controlled with respect to the size of the large operator. The idea is to exploit the *initial values* of the sequence by a "guess and prove" approach. This is described in Algorithm 1. This algorithm takes as input a linear recurrence operator $\mathcal{A}$ and initial values, as well as an upper bound N on the number of coefficients used to find a right factor. It is described here in the case of recurrence operators; similar variants apply to differential or q-difference cases.

The search for a smaller order operator is performed in two main steps, "guessing" and "proving". First, the input recurrence of order M and its initial values are used to compute the first N terms of the sequence. Next, these N terms are used to "guess" a linear recurrence. This is done by linear algebra: we search successively for the existence of a linear recurrence operator $\mathcal{G}$ of order $1, 2, \dots, M$ with polynomial coefficients of degrees such that the sum of the numbers of undetermined coefficients of the recurrence is smaller than N. The structure of this linear algebra problem is exploited by computing matrix rational interpolants [4] (in the differential case, Hermite-Padé approximants are used [3]).

When N is sufficiently large, this linear algebra phase is always successful, since it can reconstruct $\mathcal{A}$. The next step is to prove that the recurrence $\mathcal{G}$ obtained from the first N terms of (u_n) defines the same sequence for all n. The operator $\mathcal{G}$ is not necessarily a right factor of $\mathcal{A}$, but could be merely a left multiple of such a right factor, the factor itself being too large to be found with N terms only. This is related to the typical shape of the order-degree curve [7]. Thus the algorithm next computes the greatest common right divisor of $\mathcal{G}$ and $\mathcal{A}$ and its numerator $\mathcal{R}$, obtained by left-multiplication with the least common multiple of the denominators of the coefficients.

At this stage, the algorithm has produced a right factor $\mathcal{R}$ of $\mathcal{A}$. It is then associated initial conditions $(u_i)_{i\in\mathcal{J}}$, with which $\mathcal{R}$ defines a sequence $(v_n)_{n\geq 0}$. We now prove that if

Algorithm 1 Reduction of Order

Input: $(\mathcal{A}, (u_n)_{n\in\mathcal{I}})$ defining $(u_n)_{n\geq 0}$, and $N > 0$.
Output: $(\mathcal{R}, (u_n)_{n\in\mathcal{J}})$ defining $(u_n)_{n\geq 0}$
  s.t. $\operatorname{ord}\mathcal{R} \leq \operatorname{ord}\mathcal{A}$.
  $\mathcal{U} \leftarrow (u_n)_{n=0,\dots,N-1}$, computed using $\mathcal{A}$ and $(u_n)_{n\in\mathcal{I}}$
  $\mathcal{G} \leftarrow \operatorname{guessrec}(\mathcal{U})$
  if $\mathcal{G} \neq \mathrm{FAIL}$ **then**
    $\mathcal{R} \leftarrow \operatorname{numer}(\gcd_{\mathrm{right}}(\mathcal{A}, \mathcal{G}))$
    $\mathcal{J} \leftarrow \mathcal{I} \cup \left(\operatorname{lc}(\mathcal{R})^{-1}(0) - \operatorname{ord}\mathcal{R}\right) \cap \mathbb{N}$
    $\mathcal{V} \leftarrow (v_n)_{n\in\mathcal{J}+\{1,\dots,\operatorname{ord}\mathcal{A}-\operatorname{ord}\mathcal{R}\}}$, using $(\mathcal{R}, (u_n)_{n\in\mathcal{J}})$
    $\mathcal{U}' \leftarrow (u_n)_{n\in\mathcal{J}+\{1,\dots,\operatorname{ord}\mathcal{A}-\operatorname{ord}\mathcal{R}\}}$, using $(\mathcal{A}, (u_n)_{n\in\mathcal{I}})$
    if $\mathcal{U}' = \mathcal{V}$ **then return** $(\mathcal{R}, (u_n)_{n\in\mathcal{J}})$ **end if**
  end if
  return $(\mathcal{A}, (u_n)_{n\in\mathcal{I}})$

$v_n = u_n$ for $n \in \mathcal{J} + \{1, \dots, \operatorname{ord}\mathcal{A} - \operatorname{ord}\mathcal{R}\}$, then $v_n = u_n$ for all n. The induction on n is based on the following.

Lemma 1. *If $u_n = v_n$ for $n \leq i + \operatorname{ord} A - 1$ and $i + j \notin \mathcal{J}$ for all $j \in \{\operatorname{ord}\mathcal{R}, \dots, \operatorname{ord}\mathcal{A}\}$ then $u_{i+\operatorname{ord} A} = v_{i+\operatorname{ord} A}$.*

Proof. The sequences $\{S^j\mathcal{R} \cdot v_n\}_{\operatorname{ord}\mathcal{R}\leq j\leq \operatorname{ord}\mathcal{A}}$ all cancel at $n = i$. The application of $\mathcal{A}$ at $(v_n)_{n\geq 0}$ is a linear combination of them with coefficients that are finite, as shown in the next lemma, so that $\mathcal{A} \cdot v_n$ is 0 at $n = i$. □

Lemma 2. *Let $\mathcal{A}$ and $\mathcal{C}$ be recurrence operators with polynomial coefficients, satisfying $\mathcal{A} = \mathcal{B}\mathcal{C}$ where $\mathcal{B}$ has rational coefficients. Then the denominator* $\operatorname{den}\mathcal{B}$ *satisfies:*

$$\operatorname{den}(\mathcal{B})^{-1}(0) \subseteq \operatorname{lc}(\mathcal{C})^{-1}(0) + \{0, -1, \dots, -\operatorname{ord}\mathcal{B}\}$$

where addition denotes the sumset.

Proof. This is seen by following the steps of a right Euclidean division. □

In practice, this algorithm is run for increasing values of $N = 4, 8, 16, \dots$ and stopped when either a factor is found or N is larger than the number of coefficients of $\mathcal{A}$. Note however that if $\mathcal{A}$ is not irreducible, then increasing N further is bound to find a nontrivial right factor.

4. GUESSING CONTINUED FRACTIONS

The first step of our approach to continued fractions is the automatic discovery of formulas for the partial numerators a_k. This section is very short since this part of the computation is straightforward.

Starting from the differential equation, a first method would be to produce the first terms of the series expansion of the function, convert them into the first terms of the continued fraction and then use the method of the previous section to look for a linear recurrence of size bounded by the number of terms that have been computed. It turns out that in most of the known examples, explicit formulas are of rational form (see Section 6). We therefore concentrate on rational coefficients, or on interlacing of rational coefficients as in the example of the exponential function. This means that the "guessing" stage of our approach relies simply on rational interpolation, problem for which efficient algorithms are known through its relation to the extended Euclidean algorithm [11, §5.7]. Moreover, the degrees of the numerator and denominator are generally low, so that a few terms of the expansion are sufficient for the computation.

5. PROVING CONTINUED FRACTIONS FOR SOLUTIONS OF ORDINARY DIFFERENTIAL EQUATIONS

The proving phase is the heart of our work. It is also where most of the computational work takes place. We consider first-order non-linear differential equations with rational coefficients, ie, $y' = p(y)$, with $p \in \mathbb{Q}(z)[Y]$ of degree d. In particular, the case $d \leq 2$ corresponds to the classical Riccati equations that are ubiquitous in the study of continued fractions, due to their stability under linear fractional transformations of the unknown function [2, 10.7]. Explicit solutions for restricted classes of equations have been provided by Euler and Lagrange and more recently by Khovanskii [13].

Our procedure goes in the reverse direction. The continued fraction with explicit rational coefficients that was found in the previous stage defines a power series. The aim is to show that it is a solution of the differential equation.

5.1 Valuations

The following proposition reduces the proof to that of the ultimate increase of a sequence of integers.

Proposition 3. *Let $F \in \mathbb{K}[[X,Y]]$ be a formal power series with coefficients in a field $\mathbb{K}$ and let $(f_n(X))$ be a sequence of power series in $\mathbb{K}[[X]]$. Then the differential equation $Y' = F(X,Y)$ with initial condition $Y(0) = 0$ admits a unique power series solution $S(X)$. Moreover, the sequence $(f_n(X))$ converges to $S(X)$ (ie $\operatorname{val}(f_n - S) \to \infty$) if and only if $f_n(0) = 0$ for n sufficiently large and $\operatorname{val}(f_n'(X) - F(X, f_n(X))) \to \infty$.*

Note that equations with an initial condition $Y(0) = a \neq 0$ can often be brought to this setting by changing the unknown function into $a + Y$.

Proof. Recall that the algebra of power series is a metric space for the distance induced by the valuation: if f and g are two power series, then $d(f,g) = 2^{-\operatorname{val}(f-g)}$, where val denotes the valuation (this distance does not derive from a norm). It is a simple consequence of the definition that Cauchy sequences for this distance converge in $\mathbb{K}[[X]]$.

The first part of the proposition is a variant of Cauchy's theorem, whose proof is straightforward thanks to Taylor expansions. In detail, the solutions of $Y' = F(X,Y)$ with initial condition $Y(0) = 0$ are the fixed points of the operator $\mathcal{G} : Y \mapsto \int F(X,Y)$; this operator is a contraction:

$$\begin{aligned}\operatorname{val}(\mathcal{G}(Y_1) - \mathcal{G}(Y_2)) &= \operatorname{val}\left(\int F(X,Y_1) - F(X,Y_2)\right)\\ &= \operatorname{val}\left(\int \frac{\partial F}{\partial Y}(X,Y_2)(Y_1 - Y_2) + O((Y_1-Y_2)^2)\right)\\ &> \operatorname{val}(Y_1 - Y_2);\end{aligned}$$

this shows both the existence of a solution (start from $Y = 0$, iterate $\mathcal{G}$ and use completeness) and its uniqueness.

Next, if $\operatorname{val}(f_n' - F(X, f_n)) = K$, while $f_n(0) = 0 = S(0)$, then

$$\begin{aligned}S - f_n &= S(0) - f_n(0) + \int (F(X,S) - F(X,f_n)) + O(x^{K+1})\\ &= (\mathcal{G}(S) - \mathcal{G}(f_n)) + O(x^{K+1}).\end{aligned}$$

The previous inequality with $Y_1 = S$ and $Y_2 = f_n$ shows that the valuation of the first term on the right-hand side is larger than that of the left-hand size and thus $\operatorname{val}(S - f_n) \geq K + 1$, which shows that $f_n \to S$. The converse implication follows from the continuity of the map $Y \mapsto Y' - F(X,Y)$. □

This proposition extends to more general equations of the type $P(z, y, y', \dots, y^{(n)}) = 0$, with natural assumptions on the initial and separant of the equation.

5.2 P-recursivity and Convergents

Recall that a sequence is called P-recursive when it satisfies a linear recurrence with coefficients that are polynomial in the index. P-recursive sequences are closed under sum and product and algorithms computing the corresponding recurrences are known and implemented [17, 16].

The key to our approach is the following.

Theorem 4. *Let $(P_k(z))$ and $(Q_k(z))$ be P-recursive sequences of rational functions in z and let $F \in \mathbb{K}(z)[Y]$ be a polynomial of degree $d > 0$ in Y. Then the sequence*

$$H_k := Q_k^{\max(2,d)}\left(\left(\frac{P_k}{Q_k}\right)' - F\left(z, \frac{P_k}{Q_k}\right)\right)$$

satisfies a linear recurrence with coefficients in $\mathbb{K}[z,k]$.

This theorem is used when (P_k) and (Q_k) are the sequences of numerators and denominators of the continued fraction supposed to converge to a solution of $y' = F(z,y)$. Its proof constructs a recurrence for H_k from which the increase of valuation will be obtained using the reduction of order of Section 3. This is sufficient thanks to Proposition 3 and the observation that $\operatorname{val} Q_k = 0$, which will follow by induction from Eq. (5) and the fact that $\operatorname{val} a_k > 0$ in applications to C-fractions.

Again, similar results can be stated for higher order differential equations, but they proved unnecessary for the continued fractions dealt with in our experiments.

Proof. Let M be the order of the recurrence satisfied by (P_k). Using this recurrence, all P_{k+i}, $i \in \mathbb{N}$ can be rewritten as linear combinations of P_{k+j} for $j = 0, \dots, M-1$, with coefficients in $\mathbb{Q}(k,z)$, while the polynomials P'_{k+i} rewrite as linear combinations of those same polynomials complemented by P'_{k+j} for $j = 0, \dots, M-1$. The same argument applies to the sequence (Q_k) and we denote by M' the order of the recurrence it satisfies.

The choice of the exponent of Q_k makes H_k a polynomial of degree d in P_k, Q_k, P_k' and Q_k'. Thus all the H_{k+i} for $i \in \mathbb{N}$ can be rewritten as linear combinations of monomials of degree d in P_{k+i}, Q_{k+j}, $i = 0, \dots, M-1$, $j = 0, \dots, M'-1$ and their derivatives. These monomials are in finite number N, whence a linear dependency between $H_k, \dots, H_{k+N}$ (ie, a linear recurrence of order at most N satisfied by (H_k)). It can be found by linear algebra. □

As exemplified by the computation in the example of tan in Section 2, the bound on the order on specific examples may not be as large as suggested by this proof. Our implementation thus proceeds by increasing the order one by one and looking for a linear dependency until one is found. The algorithm is outlined in Algorithm 2. Its termination is granted by the theorem.

We state a simple generalization of this result that could be useful in applications to continued fractions: if the partial

Algorithm 2 Recurrence for $(H_k)_{k\geq 0}$

Input: linear recurrences $\mathcal{L}_P$ and $\mathcal{L}_Q$ of order bounded by M for $(P_k)_{k\geq 0}$ and $(Q_k)_{k\geq 0}$
Output: a linear recurrence $\mathcal{L}_H$ for $(H_k)_{k\geq 0}$

```
T_0(k) ← H_k
for i = 1, 2, 3, ... do
  T_i(k) ← T_{i-1}(k+1) with P_{k+M}, P'_{k+M}, Q_{k+M}, Q'_{k+M}
  rewritten in terms of values of these sequences with
  smaller indices, using L_P, L_Q and their derivatives.
  if the linear equation Σ_{j=0}^{i-1} c_j T_j(k) + T_i(k) in the un-
  knowns c_0, ..., c_{i-1} has a solution then
    return H_{k+i} + c_{i-1} H_{k+i-1} + ··· + c_0 H_k = 0
  end if
end for
```

numerators in the continued fraction expansion (1) are of the form $r(k)z^{p(k)}$ with r rational and p polynomial, then again, the polynomials H_k defined in the theorem satisfy a linear recurrence, this time with coefficients that are polynomials in k, z and a finite number of z^{k^i}, with $i \leq \deg p$. The proof follows along the same lines.

5.3 Riccati Equations

The case when the polynomial F of Theorem 4 has degree 2 gives rise to Riccati equations that are ubiquitous in the theory of continued fractions [2, 10.7]. In this case, the computation of a recurrence of the form predicted by the theorem can be made explicit in full generality.

Proposition 5. *Let $\mathcal{K}_{k=1}^{\infty} \frac{a_k(z)}{1}$ be a solution of the Riccati differential equation $Y' = F(z, Y)$ where F is a polynomial in $\mathbb{K}(z)[Y]$ of degree 2 in Y, let (P_k) and (Q_k) be sequences obeying the linear recurrence $u_{k+2} = u_{k+1} + a_{k+2}(z)u_k$, with $a'_k(z) \neq 0$. Let finally H_k be defined by*

$$H_k = Q_k^2\left((P_k/Q_k)' - F(z, P_k/Q_k)\right).$$

Then the sequence (H_k) satisfies the following linear recurrence of order 4:

$$\frac{1}{a'_{k+1}}H_{k+1} + \left(\frac{a_k}{a'_k} - \frac{a_{k+1}+1}{a'_{k+1}}\right)H_k - \left(\frac{a_k(a_k+1)}{a'_k} + \frac{a_{k+1}(a_{k+1}+1)}{a'_{k+1}}\right)H_{k-1} - \left(\frac{a_k+1}{a'_k} - \frac{a_{k+1}}{a'_{k+1}}\right)a_k^2 H_{k-2} + \frac{a_{k-1}^2 a_k^2}{a'_k}H_{k-3} = 0.$$

The shift of the indices (from H_{k+1} to H_{k-3}) is only for readability. A nice property of this recurrence is that its coefficients do not depend on the differential equation, but only on the sequence a_k. This persists for higher degrees: a differential equation with a cubic right-hand side leads to a recurrence of order 6 that does not depend on the equation.

Proof. The formula is obtained automatically by the method from the proof of Theorem 4, on a differential equation with symbolic coefficients. It could also be derived by hand. However, once it is given, it is a simple matter to produce a proof: inject the definition of H_k into the recurrence, rewrite all the P_k's and Q_k's using the recurrence they satisfy in terms of $P_{k-3}, Q_{k-3}, P_{k-2}, Q_{k-2}$ and collect terms to observe that the left-hand side becomes 0. □

As an example, setting $a_k(z) = -z^2/((2k-1)(2k-3))$ recovers Eq. (7) obtained for tan.

Corollary 6. *If the sequences (P_k) and (Q_k) satisfy a linear recurrence of the form $u_{k+2} = b_{k+2}(z)u_{k+1} + a_{k+2}(z)u_k$, then the sequence (H_k) satisfies a fourth-order linear recurrence obtained by evaluating that of Prop. 5, replacing a_1 by a_1/b_1 and a_k by $a_k/(b_k b_{k-1})$ for $k \geq 2$.*

Proof. This is a classical transformation of continued fractions. Setting $\tilde{P}_k = P_k/(b_1 \cdots b_{k-1}b_k)$ and similarly for $\tilde{Q}_k$ and injecting into the recurrence equation shows that both sequences $(\tilde{P}_k)$ and $(\tilde{Q}_k)$ satisfy

$$u_{k+2} = u_{k+1} + \frac{a_{k+2}}{b_{k+2}b_{k+1}}u_k.$$

Since $\tilde{P}_k/\tilde{Q}_k = P_k/Q_k$, the proposition applies. □

5.4 Nonregularity and Periodicities

As the example of the continued fraction for the exponential function in Eq. (2) shows, not all common closed forms for continued fractions are given by one rational function. However, most C-fractions formulas in the literature appear to be "periodic", in the sense that there exists a period $\ell > 0$, and ℓ sequences $(a_k^0), \ldots, (a_k^{\ell-1})$, that alternately define the partial numerators a_k: $a_k = a_k^{(k \bmod \ell)}$. The case $\ell = 2$ encountered for exp is the most common, but higher values also happen (e.g., $\ell = 4$ for ψ'', where $\psi = \Gamma'/\Gamma$ is the logarithmic derivative of the Gamma function).

This is not a restriction in our approach, by the following.

Lemma 7. *Given a period $\ell > 0$, a sequence $(u_k)_{k\geq 0}$ is P-recursive if and only if all its subsequences $(u_{\ell k+j})_{k\geq 0}$ are P-recursive, for $j = 0 \ldots \ell - 1$.*

Proof. This lemma is classical. We give a constructive proof for completeness. If the sections $(u_{\ell k+j})_{k\geq 0}$ are P-recursive, then their generating series $s_j(z) = \sum_{k\geq 0} u_{\ell k+j}z^k$ are D-finite, then so is $s_0(z^\ell) + zs_1(z^\ell) + \cdots + z^{\ell-1}s_{\ell-1}(z^\ell)$ and therefore its sequence of coefficients $(u_k)_{k\geq 0}$ is P-recursive. Conversely, if $(u_k)_{k\geq 0}$ is P-recursive, then its generating series $s(z)$ is D-finite and so is its Hadamard product with $z^j/(1-z^\ell)$, then also its quotient by z^j evaluated at $z^{1/\ell}$ and this is precisely the generating series of $(u_{\ell k+j})_{k\geq 0}$. □

In cases like the exponential function, this lemma implies that the sequence of partial numerators $(a_k)_{k\geq 0}$ itself satisfies a linear recurrence. With the recurrences (5), this alone does not imply that (P_k) and (Q_k) are also P-recursive for in general, no such closure property exists. For instance, the sequence defined by $u_n := \prod_{k=1}^n k!$ satisfies a linear recurrence of order 1 with a coefficient $(k!)$ that is P-recursive, but (u_n) itself is not P-recursive, as can be seen from its asymptotic growth that is too fast. The crucial property in our application is that the sequences (a_k^i) are rational in k. This allows for the following.

Lemma 8. *Let $a_k^0, \ldots, a_k^{\ell-1}$ be rational functions of k and z, a_k be defined for $k \geq 0$ by $a_k := a_k^{(k \bmod \ell)}$ and let the sequences (P_k) and (Q_k) be defined by the recurrence (5). Then (P_k) and (Q_k) are P-recursive sequences.*

Proof. The proof is constructive. By the recurrences (5) and the definition of a_k, all $P_{\ell k+j}$ for $j = 1, \dots, 2\ell$ rewrite as linear combinations of $P_{\ell k+1}$ and $P_{\ell k}$ with coefficients that are rational functions of z and k. Thus $P_{\ell k} + j$, $P_{\ell(k+1)+j}$ and $P_{\ell(k+2)+j}$ are linearly dependent for $j = 0, \dots, d-1$.

The same reasoning applies to $(P_{\ell k+j})_{k\geq 0}$ for any $j \in \{0, \dots, \ell-1\}$ and shows that it is a P-recursive sequence and thefore that so is (P_k) by the previous lemma. By construction, (Q_k) satisfies the same recurrence as (P_k). □

Example. The special case $\ell = 2$ is important in applications. Starting from $P_{2k} = P_{2k-1} + a_{2k}P_{2k-2}$ and its first two shifts, the linear combination $P_{2k+2} + P_{2k+1} - a_{2k+1}P_{2k}$ gets rid of the terms with odd index, leaving:

$$P_{2k+2} = (1 + a_{2k+1} + a_{2k+2})P_{2k} - a_{2k}a_{2k+1}P_{2k-2}. \quad (9)$$

A similar computation would give a recurrence between the terms with odd index.

The proof of Lemma 8 leads to an algorithm in two steps: compute a recurrence for (P_k) and (Q_k) and then appeal to Lemma 7. A simpler and faster computation proceeds directly from a recurrence for $(P_{\ell k})$, thanks to the following.

Proposition 9. *Let $F(X,Y)$ be a rational function, that is regular at $X = Y = 0$. Let a_k^i, $i = 1, \dots, \ell$ be rational functions in X and k with positive valuation in X. Let (a_k), (P_k) and (Q_k) be defined as in the previous lemma and (H_k) as in Theorem 4. If $\operatorname{val} H_{k\ell} \to \infty$ as $k \to \infty$, then the continued fraction $\mathcal{K}_{m=1}^{\infty} \frac{a_k}{1}$ is the solution of $Y' = F(X,Y)$ with $Y(0) = 0$.*

Here again, other values for $Y(0)$ are obtained by a change of unknown function.

Proof. Since the denominator of F does not vanish at 0, F admits an expansion in power series and thus by Proposition 3, the differential equation $Y' = F(X,Y)$ with $Y(0) = 0$ possesses a formal power series solution $S(X)$.

The condition on the valuations of the sequences (a_k^i) makes the continued fraction well-defined, in the sense that the sequence of power series (P_k/Q_k) converges to a power series $G(X)$. Thus if its subsequence $f_k = P_{k\ell}/Q_{k\ell}$ converges to $S(X)$, then we have $G(X) = S(X)$. Induction from Eq. (5) shows that $Q_k(0) = 1$ for all $k \geq 0$ and that $P_k(0) = 0$ (by the positive valuation of a_1^1). This gives $f_k(0) = 0$ and $\operatorname{val} H_{k\ell} = \operatorname{val}(f_k' - F(X, f_k))$. Thus by Proposition 3, the sequence (f_k) converges to S. □

Example. The proof for the continued fraction for exp from the introduction goes as follows. Starting from the recurrences for (P_k) when k is even and when k is odd and proceeding as for Eq. (9) yields

$$P_{2k+2} = P_{2k} + \frac{z^2}{4(4k^2-1)}P_{2k-2},$$

which is also satisfied by Q_{2k} since this computation does not depend on the initial conditions.

Next, turn to the numerator of the evaluation of $y' - y - 1$ at $y = P_{2k}/Q_{2k}$, namely

$$H_{2k} = P_{2k}'Q_{2k} - P_{2k}Q_{2k}' - P_{2k}Q_{2k} - Q_{2k}^2.$$

Using Proposition 5, or directly as in Section 2, leads to a recurrence of order 4, on which reduction of order yields $H_{2k+2} = -z^2 H_{2k}/(4(2k+1)^2)$, which concludes the proof.

Algorithm 3 Discovery and proof of continued fractions

Input: $Y' = F(z,Y)$ with $F \in \mathbb{K}(z)[Y]$;
a bound N on the number of coefficients to guess from;
a bound L on the period to be found.

Output: In case of success, an explicit expression for the continued fraction expansion of the solution such that $Y(0) = 0$.

Compute the first coefficients $a_1, \dots, a_N$ of the continued fraction expansion of the power series solution of $Y' = F(z,Y)$ with $Y(0) = 0$.
for $\ell = 1, 2, 3, \dots, L$ **do**
  Use rational interpolation to compute a_i^j interpolating the subsequences $(a_{\ell i+j})_i$, $j = 0, \dots, \ell-1$.
  if this has been successful **then**
    compute a recurrence $\mathcal{R}$ for $H_{k\ell}$, with H_k defined in Theorem 4
    compute a new recurrence $\mathcal{R}'$ from $\mathcal{R}$ and the initial conditions for (H_k) using Algorithm 1
    if $\mathcal{R}'$ exhibits the increase of $(\operatorname{val} H_{\ell k})$ **then**
      return the rational functions a_i^j
    end if
  end if
end for
return FAIL

6. EXPERIMENTS

An overview of the whole approach is given in Figure 3. In practice, $N = 20$ and $L = 2$ have proved sufficient in our experiments except for one case of period 4. For the computation of the first terms of the continued fraction, one can either compute a power series expansion first, e.g., by Newton iteration [6], or use techniques for continued fraction expansions of solutions of Riccati equations [9].

Our main experimental result is the following.

Empirical Observation. *All the 53 explicit C-fractions formulas of the compendium by Cuyt et alii [10] can be guessed and proved by our approach and its variants below. Among them the vast majority (44) are solutions of Riccati equations, 2 satisfy q-Riccati equations and the remaining 7 satisfy difference equations.*

We now give more detail on the calculations in the differential case and then outline the variants of our method in the q-difference and difference cases. An implementation in the differential case is available under the form of a submodule `gfun:-ContFrac` of the package `gfun` (for versions $\geq$ 3.70). It can be downloaded from our web pages. All the examples of solutions of Riccati equations from [10] are provided through the associated help pages.

6.1 C-fractions from Differential Equations

In our experiment, the Riccati equations were themselves found by a guessing approach on power series expansions to small order (less than 30). Depending on how one decides to define the power series from the computer algebra point of view, these Riccati equations can also be automatically proved to hold.

Gauss's continued fraction. The classical hypergeometric series is

$${}_2F_1(a,b;c;z) := \sum_{n\geq 0} \frac{(a)_n(b)_n}{(c)_n}\frac{z^n}{n!},$$

where $(a)_n$ is the Pochhammer symbol $(a)_n = a(a+1)\cdots(a+n-1)$. Gauss proved the following identity

$$\frac{{}_2F_1(a,b;c;z)}{{}_2F_1(a,b+1;c+1;z)} = 1 + \overset{\infty}{\underset{m=1}{\mathcal{K}}} \frac{a_m z}{1},$$

$$a_{2k} = -\frac{(k+b)(k+c-a)}{(2k+c)(2k-1+c)}, a_{2k+1} = -\frac{(k+a)(k+c-b)}{(2k+c)(2k+1+c)},$$

for the quotient of two contiguous hypergeometric series. This is the source of many continued fractions for special functions by specialization of the parameters. If $y = 1 + F$ is the function on the left-hand side, then elementary properties of the ${}_2F_1$ that can be derived from the first order recurrences satisfied by its coefficients show that

$$cz(z-1)y' = a(c-b)z + (c(a-b)z + c^2)y + c^2y^2.$$

This is our starting point. From there, it is easy to compute the first 20 coefficients and conjecture the formulas for a_{2k} and a_{2k+1} by rational interpolation. As in Eq. (9), a recurrence for even indices follows. From Corollary 6, a linear recurrence of order 4 follows for the remainder H_{2k}, that can be either obtained by hand from Proposition 5, or by a generic code that searches for linear dependency. Next, reduction of order gives a two-term linear recurrence within a couple of seconds:

$$H_{2(n-2)} = z^2 \frac{(n+a)(n-a+c)(n+b)(n-b+c)}{(2n+c)^2(2n+c-1)^2} H_{2(n-3)}$$

and this concludes the automatic proof.

More parameters. Khovanskii [13, p. 85] gives an explicit continued fraction with 5 parameters for the power series solution of the differential equation

$$(1+\alpha z)zy' + (\beta+\gamma z)y + \delta y^2 = \epsilon z, \; y(0) = 0$$

(an extra parameter k is obtained by changing z into z^k and adjusting the coefficient of y'; we have relabeled the parameters). This contains the equation for Gauss's continued fraction above as a special case.

From there again rational formulas for a_{2k} and a_{2k+1} are obtained by guessing on the first 20 values; a recurrence of order 4 can be found for the remainders H_{2k}; Algorithm 1 reduces it to the conclusive recurrence:

$$(2n+\beta)^2(2n+\beta-1)^2H_{2(n-2)} =$$
$$-(\alpha n^2+(\alpha\beta+\gamma)n+\beta\gamma+\delta\epsilon)(\alpha n^2+(\alpha\beta-\gamma)n+\delta\epsilon)z^2H_{2(n-3)}.$$

Other examples. We also applied our method to a few functions not mentioned by Cuyt *et alii* [10] and in particular found (and proved) experimentally the following nice C-fraction for the Airy function:

$$z\frac{\mathrm{Ai}'}{\mathrm{Ai}}(1/z^2) = -1 - \frac{z^3}{4} \Big/ \left(1 + \overset{\infty}{\underset{m=2}{\mathcal{K}}} \frac{a_m(z)}{1}\right),$$

$$a_{2k} = (6k-1)z^3/8, \quad a_{2k+1} = (6k+1)z^3/8.$$

It also follows from known C-fractions for the divergent ${}_2F_0$.

6.2 q-analogues

The method used in this article also applies to q-analogues. We outline the very simple example of the q-exponential:

$$e_q(z) := \sum_{m\geq 0} \frac{(1-q)^m}{(1-q)(1-q^2)\cdots(1-q^m)} z^m,$$

which satisfies the q-differential equation

$$\frac{e_q(qz) - e_q(z)}{(q-1)z} - e_q(z) = 0. \tag{10}$$

The classical exponential is obtained as the limit when $q \to 1$. The first coefficients of the continued fraction expansion let one guess $a_1 = z$,

$$a_{2k} = -\frac{q^{k-1}(1-q)z}{(1+q^k)(1-q^{2k-1})}, \quad a_{2k+1} = \frac{q^{2k}(1-q)z}{(1+q^k)(1-q^{2k+1})},$$

a clear generalization of the continued fraction (2) for exp. In order to prove this continued fraction, the recurrence for (P_{2k}) is computed as in Section 5.4, which gives

$$P_{2k+2} = \left(1 - \frac{(1-q)q^k z}{(1+q^k)(1+q^{k+1})}\right) P_{2k}$$
$$+ \frac{q^{3k-1}(1-q)^2z^2}{(1+q^k)^2(1-q^{2k+1})(1-q^{2k-1})} P_{2k-2}.$$

The sequence H_k is defined as the numerator of the evaluation of (10), namely

$$\frac{P_k(qz)Q_k(z) - P_k(z)Q_k(qz)}{(q-1)z} - P_k(z)Q_k(qz) - Q_k(z)Q_k(qz).$$

Next, we compute a linear dependency between $H_{2k}, H_{2k+2}, \ldots$, which is still of order 4 (but significantly bigger than its limit as $q \to 1$). The q-analogue of reduction of order then proves

$$H_{2k+2} = -\frac{q^{3k+2}(1-q)^2z^2}{(1+q^{k+1})^2(1-q^{2k+1})^2} H_{2k},$$

which concludes the proof, providing with a generalization of the expression for exp that is recovered by letting $q \to 1$.

Using the same steps leads to an automatic proof of Heine's q-analogue of Gauss's continued fraction [10, 19.2.1]: the q-hypergeometric series is defined by

$${}_2\phi_1(a,b;c;q;z) = \sum_{n\geq 0} \frac{(a;q)_n(b;q)_n}{(c;q)_n} \frac{z^n}{(q;q)_n},$$

where $(a;q)_n$ is the q-Pochhammer symbol

$$(a;q)_n = (1-a)(1-aq)\cdots(1-aq^{n-1}).$$

Heine's continued fraction is

$$\frac{{}_2\phi_1(a,b;c;q;z)}{{}_2\phi_1(a,bq;cq;q;z)} = 1 + \overset{\infty}{\underset{m=1}{\mathcal{K}}} \frac{a_m z}{1},$$

$$a_{2k+1} = \frac{(1-aq^k)(cq^k-b)q^k}{(1-cq^{2k})(1-cq^{2k+1})},$$

$$a_{2k} = \frac{(1-bq^k)(cq^k-a)q^{k-1}}{(1-cq^{2k-1})(1-cq^{2k})}.$$

We sketch the main steps of the computation. The q-Riccati equation is

$$(1-c)^2F(z)F(qz) + (1-c)(bz-c)F(qz)$$
$$+ (1-z)(1-az)F(z) - z(a-1)(b-c) = 0.$$

The sequence H_k of interest is therefore the numerator of the evaluation of this left-hand size at $F(z) = P_k(z)/Q_k(z)$. The continued fraction being periodic of period 2, a recurrence for H_{2k} (or order 4) is computed. Reduction of order yields

$$\frac{H_{2k+2}}{z^2H_{2k}} = \frac{(1-aq^{k+1})(1-bq^{k+1})(a-cq^{k+1})(b-cq^{k+1})q^{2k+1}}{(1-cq^{2k+1})(1-cq^{2k+2})},$$

which concludes the proof. This automates 2 more of the formulas in [10].

6.3 Difference Equations

The same method applies to difference equations. For instance, it results in one of the classical proofs [14, chap. 3] of Brouncker's continued fraction for

$$b(s) := \left(\frac{\Gamma\left(\frac{s+1}{4}\right)}{\Gamma\left(\frac{s+3}{4}\right)} \right)^2,$$

where Γ is Euler's Gamma function. Using the functional equation $\Gamma(s+1) = s\Gamma(s)$, it follows that $b(s)$ satisfies

$$b(s)b(s+2) = 16/(s+1)^2.$$

Looking for a formal power series solution in inverse powers of s (and nonnegative leading term) leads to a unique solution $b(s) = 4/s - 2/s^3 + \cdots$ This is then converted into a continued fraction expansion with coefficients (a_k) given by

$$\frac{4}{s}, \frac{1}{2s^2}, \frac{9}{4s^2}, \frac{25}{4s^2}, \frac{49}{4s^2}, \frac{81}{4s^2}, \ldots$$

from which it is easy to conjecture $a_k = (2k-3)^2/(4s^2)$ for $k \geq 3$. The analogue of H_k in this context is

$$H_k = (s+1)^2 P_k(s) P_k(s+2) - 16 Q_k(s) Q_k(s+2),$$

for which the same approach as above produces a linear recurrence of order 4 which is not sufficient to conclude that the valuations increase. From there, reduction of order with Algorithm 1 yields the shorter

$$H_{k+1} = -\frac{(2k+1)^2}{4s(s+2)} H_k, \quad k \geq 1,$$

which exhibits the required increase of valuations.

The same technique has been applied to all the explicit C-fractions concerning the ψ function in [10], thereby completing the experiment on this book.

7. CONCLUSION

In a simple and unified way, our approach to continued fractions recovers an unexpectedly large number of explicit C-fractions from the literature. One miracle that takes place is that in all cases, the sequence of remainder polynomials turns out to be hypergeometric or q-hypergeometric. We are currently exploring this phenomenon in more detail.

Acknowledgements

This work was supported in part by the project FastRelax ANR-14-CE25-0018-01.

References

[1] M. Abramowitz and I. A. Stegun, editors. *Handbook of mathematical functions with formulas, graphs, and mathematical tables.* Dover Publications Inc., New York, 1992.

[2] G. A. Baker, Jr. and P. Graves-Morris. *Padé approximants*, volume 59 of *Encyclopedia of Mathematics and its Applications.* Cambridge University Press, Cambridge, second edition, 1996.

[3] B. Beckermann and G. Labahn. A uniform approach for the fast computation of matrix-type Padé approximants. *SIAM Journal on Matrix Analysis and Applications*, 15(3):804–823, July 1994.

[4] B. Beckermann and G. Labahn. Recursiveness in matrix rational interpolation problems. *Journal of Computational and Applied Mathematics*, 77(1-2):5–34, 1997.

[5] A. Benoit, F. Chyzak, A. Darrasse, S. Gerhold, M. Mezzarobba, and B. Salvy. The dynamic dictionary of mathematical functions (DDMF). In K. Fukuda, J. van der Hoeven, M. Joswig, and N. Takayama, editors, *ICMS 2010*, volume 6327 of *LNCS*, pages 35–41, 2010.

[6] R. P. Brent and H. T. Kung. Fast algorithms for manipulating formal power series. *J. ACM*, 25(4):581–595, 1978.

[7] S. Chen, M. Jaroschek, M. Kauers, and M. F. Singer. Desingularization explains order-degree curves for ore operators. In *ISSAC'13*, pages 157–164, New York, NY, USA, 2013. ACM.

[8] D. Chudnovsky and G. Chudnovsky. Classical constants and functions: Computations and continued fraction expansions. In D. Chudnovsky, G. Chudnovsky, H. Cohn, and M. Nathanson, editors, *Number Theory*, pages 13–74. Springer New York, 1991.

[9] K. D. Cooper, S. C. Cooper, and W. B. Jones. More on C-fraction solutions to Riccati equations. In *Proceedings of the U.S.-Western Europe Regional Conference on Padé Approximants and Related Topics (Boulder, CO, 1988)*, volume 21, pages 139–158, 1991.

[10] A. Cuyt, V. B. Petersen, B. Verdonk, H. Waadeland, and W. B. Jones. *Handbook of continued fractions for special functions.* Springer, New York, 2008.

[11] J. v. z. Gathen and J. Gerhard. *Modern Computer Algebra.* Cambridge University Press, Cambridge u.a., 3 edition edition, June 2013.

[12] W. B. Jones and W. J. Thron. *Continued fractions*, volume 11 of *Encyclopedia of Mathematics and its Applications.* Addison-Wesley Publishing Co., Reading, Mass., 1980.

[13] A. N. Khovanskii. *The application of continued fractions and their generalizations to problems in approximation theory.* P. Noordhoff N. V., 1963.

[14] S. Khrushchev. *Orthogonal polynomials and continued fractions*, volume 122 of *Encyclopedia of Mathematics and its Applications.* Cambridge University Press, Cambridge, 2008.

[15] F. W. J. Olver, D. W. Lozier, R. F. Boisvert, and C. W. Clark, editors. *NIST Handbook of Mathematical Functions.* Cambridge University Press, 2010.

[16] B. Salvy and P. Zimmermann. Gfun: a Maple package for the manipulation of generating and holonomic functions in one variable. *ACM Trans. Math. Softw.*, 20(2):163–177, 1994.

[17] R. P. Stanley. *Enumerative combinatorics*, volume 2. Cambridge University Press, 1999.

[18] S. P. Tsarev. An algorithm for complete enumeration of all factorizations of a linear ordinary differential operator. In *ISSAC '96*, pages 226–231. ACM Press, 1996.

De Nugis Groebnerialium 4: Zacharias, Spears, Möller

Ferdinando Mora
DIMA Università di Genova
Via Dodecaneso 35
I-16100 Genova, Italy
theomora@disi.unige.it

ABSTRACT

It is well-known that each effective associative ring with identity is endowed with a Buchberger Theory, *id est* a notion of Gröbner bases and related algorithms. This note is a sort of Do-It-Yourself manual for setting a Gröbner bases approach to such a ring.

The extension of Buchberger Theory and Algorithm from the classical case of polynomial rings over a field to the case of (non necessarily commutative) monoid rings over a (non necessarily free) monoid and a principal ideal ring was immediately performed by a series of milestone papers: Zacharias' approach to canonical forms, Spear's theorem which extends Buchberger Theory to each effectively given rings, Möller's reformulation of Buchberger Algorithm in terms of lifting.

Since the universal property of the free monoid ring $\mathcal{Q} := \mathbb{Z}\langle\overline{\mathbf{Z}}\rangle$ over $\mathbb{Z}$ and the monoid $\langle\overline{\mathbf{Z}}\rangle$ of all words over the alphabet $\overline{\mathbf{Z}}$ grants that each ring with identity $\mathcal{A}$ can be presented as a quotient $\mathcal{A} = \mathcal{Q}/\mathcal{I}$ of a free monoid ring $\mathcal{Q}$ modulo a bilateral ideal $\mathcal{I} \subset \mathcal{Q}$, in order to impose a Buchberger Theory over any effective associative ring it is sufficient to reformulate it in filtration-valuation terms and apply the results quoted above; in particular Zacharias canonical forms allow to effectively present $\mathcal{A}$ and its elements, Spear's theorem describes how $\mathcal{Q}$ imposes its $\langle\overline{\mathbf{Z}}\rangle$-filtration on $\mathcal{A}$ and a direct application of Möller's lifting theorem to such filtration allows to characterize the required S-polynomials.

Categories and Subject Descriptors

I.1.2 [**Symbolic and Algebraic Manipulation**]: Algorithms—*Algebraic algorithms*

General Terms

Algorithms

Keywords

Associative rings, Buchberger theory, Gröbner bases, Gebauer–Möller set, pseudovaluation, Spear's Theorem

ISSAC'15, July 6–9, 2015, Bath, United Kingdom.

ACM 978-1-4503-3435-8/15/07 ...$15.00.
DOI: http://dx.doi.org/10.1145/2755996.2756640.

1. INTRODUCTION

Möller's intuition [6] that the crucial test/completion of Buchberger Algorithm, namely *S-polynomial reduction* can be easily reformulated as "lifting syzygies from monomials to basis elements" gave not only a strong improvement in Buchberger Algorithm in the classical cases of polynomial rings and free associative algebra, but provided a scheme which allows to export a Buchberger Theory *id est* a notion of Gröbner bases and related algorithms in more generally setting.

In fact, the reformulation in the language of filtration of Möller's Lifting Theorem and of Spear's [13] intuition that a Buchberger Theory defined in a ring can be exported to its quotients, allowed [7] to provide a framework in which Buchberger Theory may be cast in a general setting that specializes nicely to useful cases such as monoid rings [5], solvable polynomial rings [4] and Ore extensions [2].

The weakness of the proposal put forward in [7] was that it was applicable only to rings and modules presented as vector-spaces over a field, while the universal property grants to a ring a representation as quotient of a monoid ring over the integers. However Buchberger Theory of monoid rings over the integers is strongly established [6] and Zacharias' Thesis [16] provides the natural setting for describing canonical forms of the elements of each ring which can be presented as quotient $\mathcal{A} = \mathcal{Q}/\mathcal{I}$ of a free monoid ring $\mathcal{Q} := \mathbb{Z}\langle\overline{\mathbf{Z}}\rangle$ over $\mathbb{Z}$ and the monoid $\langle\overline{\mathbf{Z}}\rangle$ of all words over the alphabet $\overline{\mathbf{Z}}$ modulo a bilateral ideal $\mathcal{I} \subset \mathcal{Q}$ of which a Gröbner basis is available.

2. BUCHBERGER THEORY

2.1 Effectiveness

Let R be a (not necessarily commutative) ring with identity $\mathbf{1}_R$ and $\mathcal{A}$ another (not necessarily commutative) ring with identity $\mathbf{1}_\mathcal{A}$ which is a left module on R.

Recalling that the universal property of the free monoid ring $\mathcal{Q} := \mathbb{Z}\langle\overline{\mathbf{Z}}\rangle$ over $\mathbb{Z}$ and the monoid $\langle\overline{\mathbf{Z}}\rangle$ of all words over the alphabet $\overline{\mathbf{Z}}$ grants that, for each unitary ring $\mathcal{A}$, there is a (not necessarily finite nor necessarily countable) set $\overline{\mathbf{Z}}$ and a projection $\Pi : \mathbb{Z}\langle\overline{\mathbf{Z}}\rangle \twoheadrightarrow \mathcal{A}$ so that, denoting $\mathcal{I}$ the bilateral ideal $\mathcal{I} := \ker(\Pi)$, we have $\mathcal{A} = \mathcal{Q}/\mathcal{I}$, we can state:

DEFINITION 1. *[8] We consider $\mathcal{A}$ to be* effectively given *when we are given*

- *sets* $\overline{\mathbf{v}} := \{x_1, \dots, x_j, \dots\}$, $\overline{\mathbf{V}} := \{X_1, \dots, X_i, \dots\}$, *which are* countable *and*
- $\overline{\mathbf{Z}} := \overline{\mathbf{v}} \sqcup \overline{\mathbf{V}} = \{x_1, \dots, x_j, \dots, X_1, \dots, X_i, \dots\}$;

– *rings* $\mathcal{R} := \mathbb{Z}\langle\overline{\mathbf{v}}\rangle \subset \mathcal{Q} := \mathbb{Z}\langle\overline{\mathbf{Z}}\rangle$;

– *projections* $\pi : \mathcal{R} = \mathbb{Z}\langle x_1, \ldots, x_j, \ldots\rangle \twoheadrightarrow R$ *and*

– $\Pi : \mathcal{Q} := \mathbb{Z}\langle x_1, \ldots, x_j, \ldots, X_1, \ldots, X_i, \ldots\rangle \twoheadrightarrow \mathcal{A}$ *which satisfies*

$$\Pi(x_j) = \pi(x_j)\mathbf{1}_{\mathcal{A}}, \text{ for each } x_j \in \overline{\mathbf{v}},$$

so that $\Pi(\mathcal{R}) = \{r\mathbf{1}_{\mathcal{A}} : r \in R\} \subset \mathcal{A}$.

Thus denoting

– $\mathcal{I} := \ker(\Pi) \subset \mathcal{Q}$ *and*

– $I := \mathcal{I} \cap \mathcal{R} = \ker(\pi) \subset \mathcal{R}$,

we have $\mathcal{A} = \mathcal{Q}/\mathcal{I}$ *and* $R = \mathcal{R}/I$; *moreover we can wlog assume that* $R \subset \mathcal{A}$.

Further, when considering $\mathcal{A}$ *as effectively given in this way, we explicitly require that*

$$X_i x_j \equiv \sum_{l=1}^{i} \pi(a_{lij})X_l + \pi(a_{0ij}) \bmod \mathcal{I}, a_{lij} \in \mathbb{Z}\langle\overline{\mathbf{v}}\rangle, \quad (1)$$

for all $X_i \in \overline{\mathbf{V}}, x_j \in \overline{\mathbf{v}}$.

If we impose on $\langle\overline{\mathbf{Z}}\rangle$ a total ordering $<$, then each $f \in \mathcal{Q}$ has a unique representation as an ordered linear combination of terms $t \in \langle\overline{\mathbf{Z}}\rangle$ with coefficients in $\mathbb{Z}$:

$$f = \sum_{i=1}^{s} c(f, t_i)t_i : c(f, t_i) \in \mathbb{Z} \setminus \{0\}, t_i \in \langle\overline{\mathbf{Z}}\rangle, t_1 > \cdots > t_s.$$

The *support* of f is the set $\text{supp}(f) := \{t : c(f, t) \neq 0\}$; we further denote $\mathbf{T}(f) := t_1$ the *maximal term* of f, $\text{lc}(f) := c(f, t_1)$ its *leading coefficient* and $\mathbf{M}(f) := c(f, t_1)t_1$ its *maximal monomial*.

For a set G of a module, $\mathbb{I}_L(G), \mathbb{I}_R(G), \mathbb{I}_2(G)$ denotes the left (resp. right, bilateral) module generated by G the index being dropped when there is no need of specification.

2.2 Zacharias: canonical representation

Zacharias approach [16] to Buchberger Theory consisted in remarking that, if each module $\mathsf{I} \subset R\langle\overline{\mathbf{X}}\rangle^m$ has a groebnerian property, necessarily the same property must be satisfied at least by the modules $\mathsf{I} \subset R^m \subset R\langle\overline{\mathbf{X}}\rangle^m$ and thus such property in R is available and can be used to device a procedure granting the same property in $R\langle\overline{\mathbf{X}}\rangle^m$. The most elementary applications of Zacharias approach is the generalization (up to membership test and syzygy computation) of the property of canonical forms from the case in which $R = \mathbb{K}$ is a skew field to the general case: all we need is an effective notion of canonical forms for modules in R.

In our setting, where $R = \mathbb{Z}$, for each $m \in \mathbb{Z}$, a reasonable set A_m of the canonical representatives of the residue classes of $\mathbb{Z}_m = \mathbb{Z}/\mathbb{I}(m)$ is $A_m = \{z \in \mathbb{Z} : -\frac{m}{2} < z \leq \frac{m}{2}\}$ and we denote $\pi_m : \mathbb{Z} \to A_m$ the related canonical projection.

If we fix

– a term-ordering $<$ on $\langle\overline{\mathbf{Z}}\rangle$

we can assume $\mathcal{I}$ to be given via

– its bilateral Gröbner basis G w.r.t. $<$

and, if $<$ satisfies

$$X_i > t \text{ for each } t \in \langle\overline{\mathbf{v}}\rangle \text{ and } X_i \in \overline{\mathbf{V}}, \quad (2)$$

also I is given via

– its bilateral Gröbner basis $G_0 := G \cap \mathcal{R}$ w.r.t. $<$.

Since condition (1) implies that, for each $X_i \in \overline{\mathbf{V}}, x_j \in \overline{\mathbf{v}}$,

$$f_{ij} := X_i x_j - \sum_{l=1}^{i} a_{lij}X_l - a_{0ij} \in \mathcal{I} \subset \mathcal{Q},$$

if we further require that $<$ satisfies

$$X_i x_j = \mathbf{T}(f_{ij}) \text{ for each } X_i \in \overline{\mathbf{V}}, x_j \in \overline{\mathbf{v}}, \quad (3)$$

and denote $C := \{f_{ij} : X_i \in \overline{\mathbf{V}}, x_j \in \overline{\mathbf{v}}\}$ we have

- $G_0 \sqcup C \subset G$,
- $\mathcal{A}$ is generated as R-module by $\Pi(\langle\overline{\mathbf{V}}\rangle)$ and,
- as $\mathbb{Z}$-module, by a subset of $\left\{v\omega : v \in \langle\overline{\mathbf{v}}\rangle, \omega \in \langle\overline{\mathbf{V}}\rangle\right\}$.

Thus, $\mathcal{A}$ can be described via its Zacharias canonical representation w.r.t. $<$ [16, 8] as

$$\mathcal{A} = \mathcal{Q}/\mathcal{I} \cong \bigoplus_{\omega \in \langle\overline{\mathbf{V}}\rangle} \left(\bigoplus_{v \in \langle\overline{\mathbf{v}}\rangle} A_{c_{v\omega}} v\right) \omega =: \mathbf{Zach}_<(\mathcal{A}) \subset \mathcal{Q} \quad (4)$$

EXAMPLE 2. *W.r.t. the ideal* $\mathsf{I} := \mathbb{I}(2X, 3Y) \in \mathbb{Z}[X, Y]$ *whose strong Gröbner basis is* $\{2X, 3Y, XY\}$, *the ring*

$$\mathcal{A} := \mathbb{Z}[X, Y]/\mathsf{I} \cong \mathbb{Z}\langle X, Y\rangle/\mathbb{I}_2(2X, 3Y, XY, YX)$$

has the canonical representation

$$\mathcal{A} \cong \mathbb{Z} + \mathbb{Z}_2[X]X + \mathbb{Z}_3[Y]Y;$$

thus the underline $\mathbb{Z}$*-module has the structure*

$$\mathcal{A} \cong \mathbb{Z} \bigoplus \left(\bigoplus_{i \in \mathbb{N}\setminus\{0\}} \mathbb{Z}_2\right) \bigoplus \left(\bigoplus_{i \in \mathbb{N}\setminus\{0\}} \mathbb{Z}_3\right)$$

and the ring structure is defined by

$$(a, \ldots d_i, \ldots g_i, \ldots) \star (b, \ldots e_i, h_i, \ldots) = (c, \ldots f_i, \ldots, l_i, \ldots)$$

where $a, b, c \in \mathbb{Z}, d_i, e_i, f_i \in \mathbb{Z}_2 \cong \{0, 1\}, g_i, h_i, l_i \in \mathbb{Z}_3 \cong \{-1, 0, 1\}$ *and*

$$\begin{aligned} c &:= ab, \\ f_i &:= \pi_2(a)e_i + \sum_{j=1}^{i-1} d_j e_{i-j} + d_i\pi_2(b), i \in \mathbb{N} \setminus \{0\}, \\ l_i &:= \pi_3(a)h_i + \sum_{j=1}^{i-1} g_j h_{i-j} + g_i\pi_3(b), i \in \mathbb{N} \setminus \{0\}. \end{aligned}$$

In the present setting, we can further consider, for each $\omega \in \langle\overline{\mathbf{V}}\rangle$, the left Szekeres ideal [15, 8]

$$\mathcal{I}_\omega := \{r \in \mathcal{R} : \exists h \in \mathcal{Q}, \mathbf{T}(h) < \omega, r\omega + h \in \mathcal{I}\} \supset I = \mathcal{I} \cap \mathcal{R}$$

and the ring $R_\omega = \mathcal{R}/\mathcal{I}_\omega$, having the Zacharias canonical representation

$$\mathbf{Zach}_<(R_\omega) \cong \bigoplus_{v \in \langle\overline{\mathbf{v}}\rangle} A_{c_{v\omega}} v \subset \mathcal{R}$$

so that we have

$$\mathbf{Zach}_<(\mathcal{R}/\mathcal{I}_\omega) \subset \mathbf{Zach}_<(\mathcal{R}/I) = \mathbf{Zach}_<(R)$$

and

$$\mathcal{A} \cong \bigoplus_{\omega\in\langle\overline{\mathbf{V}}\rangle} \left(\bigoplus_{\upsilon\in\langle\overline{\mathbf{v}}\rangle} A_{c_{\upsilon\omega}} \upsilon \right) \omega = \bigoplus_{\omega\in\langle\overline{\mathbf{V}}\rangle} R_\omega \omega \subset \mathcal{R}\langle\overline{\mathbf{V}}\rangle \subset \mathcal{Q}. \tag{5}$$

More precisely, denoting

- $\mathbf{N}(\mathcal{I}) := \{\omega \in \langle\overline{\mathbf{V}}\rangle : \mathcal{I}_\omega = I\}$,
- $\mathbf{L}(\mathcal{I}) := \{\omega \in \langle\overline{\mathbf{V}}\rangle : \mathcal{I}_\omega = R\}$,
- $\mathbf{R}(\mathcal{I}) := \{\omega \in \langle\overline{\mathbf{V}}\rangle : \mathcal{I}_\omega \notin \{I, R\}\}$

we have the partition $\langle\overline{\mathbf{V}}\rangle = \mathbf{L}(\mathcal{I}) \sqcup \mathbf{R}(\mathcal{I}) \sqcup \mathbf{N}(\mathcal{I})$ and, denoting

- $\mathcal{B} = \mathbf{R}(\mathcal{I}) \sqcup \mathbf{N}(\mathcal{I}) = \langle\overline{\mathbf{V}}\rangle \setminus \mathbf{L}(\mathcal{I}) \subset \langle\overline{\mathbf{V}}\rangle$,

we obtain

1. $\mathcal{B} \subset \langle\overline{\mathbf{V}}\rangle$ is an order module *i.e.* $\lambda\tau\rho \in \mathcal{B} \implies \tau \in \mathcal{B}$ for each $\lambda, \tau, \rho \in \langle\overline{\mathbf{V}}\rangle$;
2. $\mathcal{A}$ is both a left $\mathcal{R}$-module and a left R-module with generating set $\mathcal{B}$;
3. If R is a field, we further have $\mathbf{R}(\mathcal{I}) = \emptyset, \mathcal{B} = \mathbf{N}(\mathcal{I})$, and
$$\mathcal{A} \cong \bigoplus_{\omega\in\mathcal{B}} R\omega = R[\mathcal{B}].$$

REMARK 3. *1. We must stress that all inclusions — $A_{c_{\upsilon\omega}} \subset \mathbb{Z}$, $\mathbf{Zach}_<(R_\omega) \subset \mathcal{R} = \mathbb{Z}\langle\overline{\mathbf{v}}\rangle$, $\mathbf{Zach}_<(\mathcal{A}) \subset \mathcal{R}[\mathcal{B}] \subset \mathcal{R}\langle\overline{\mathbf{V}}\rangle$ — must be understood as set inclusions only and do not preserve the module structure and the notation $\mathcal{R}\langle\overline{\mathbf{V}}\rangle$ does not denote the canonical monoid ring but, as the notation $\mathcal{R}[\mathcal{B}]$, only the underlying free left $\mathcal{R}$-modules with bases $\langle\overline{\mathbf{V}}\rangle$ and $\mathcal{B}$.*

2. Note that Zacharias' approach holds for any effective unitary ring R with canonical representations; thus of course the rôle of $\mathbb{Z}$ can be assumed on one side by each effectively given domain/field, on the other side by, say, $\mathbb{Z}(\overline{\mathbf{x}})$, $\mathbb{Q}(\overline{\mathbf{x}})$,.... Actually, if we are interested in polynomial rings with coefficients in $\mathbb{R}$ or in a ring of analytical functions, since a given finite basis has a finite number of coefficients $c_i \in R$, the requirement that the data are effectively given essentially means that we need to provide the algebraically dependencies among such c_i.

Each free $\mathcal{A}$-module $\mathcal{A}^m, m \in \mathbb{N}$, — the canonical basis of which will be denoted by $\{\mathbf{e}_1, \ldots, \mathbf{e}_m\}$ — is an R-module with basis the set of *terms*

$$\mathcal{B}^{(m)} := \{t\mathbf{e}_i : t \in \mathcal{B}, 1 \le i \le m\}$$

and the projection $\Pi : \mathcal{Q} \twoheadrightarrow \mathcal{A}$, $\mathcal{I} = \ker(\Pi)$, $\mathcal{A} = \mathcal{Q}/\mathcal{I}$, extends to each canonical projection, still denoted Π,

$$\Pi : \mathcal{Q}^m \twoheadrightarrow \mathcal{A}^m, \ker(\Pi) = \mathcal{I}^m = \mathbb{I}_2(G^{(m)})$$

where G is the Gröbner basis w.r.t. $<$ of $\mathcal{I}$ and

$$G^{(m)} := \{g\mathbf{e}_i, g \in G, 1 \le i \le m\}$$

is the Gröbner basis of $\mathcal{I}^m$ w.r.t. any term-ordering on $\langle\overline{\mathbf{Z}}\rangle^{(m)}$ — which we still denote $<$ with a slight abuse of notation — satisfying, for each $t_1, t_2 \in \langle\overline{\mathbf{Z}}\rangle, \tau_1, \tau_2 \in \langle\overline{\mathbf{Z}}\rangle^{(m)}$,

$$t_1 \le t_2, \tau_1 \le \tau_2 \implies t_1\tau_1 \le t_2\tau_2, \tau_1 t_1 \le \tau_2 t_2.$$

Thus, w.r.t. a term-ordering $<$ satisfying Eqs. (2) and (3), each non-zero element $f \in \mathcal{A}^{(m)}$ has, in $\mathbf{Zach}_<(\mathcal{A})^m$, its canonical representation

$$f := \sum_{j=1}^{s} c_j t_j \mathbf{e}_{\iota_j}, t_j \in \mathcal{B}, c_j \in R_{t_j} \setminus \{0\}, 1 \le \iota_j \le m,$$

with $t_1\mathbf{e}_{\iota_1} > t_2\mathbf{e}_{\iota_2} > \cdots > t_s\mathbf{e}_{\iota_s}$ and we denote $\mathbf{T}_<(f) := t_1\mathbf{e}_{\iota_1}$ the *maximal term* of f, $\mathrm{lc}_<(f) := c_1$ its *leading coefficient* and $\mathbf{M}_<(f) := c_1 t_1 \mathbf{e}_{\iota_1}$ its *maximal monomial.*

2.3 Apel: pseudovaluation

Denoting, for a semigroup $(\Gamma, \circ)$, $\Gamma^{(u)}$ the sets

$$\Gamma^{(u)} := \{\gamma e_i, \gamma \in \Gamma, 1 \le i \le u\}, u \in \mathbb{N},$$

endowed with no operation except the natural action of Γ

$$\Gamma \times \Gamma^{(u)} \times \Gamma \to \Gamma^{(u)} : (\delta_l, \gamma, \delta_r) \mapsto \delta_l \circ \gamma \circ \delta_r,$$

recall [1, 7, 14, 9] that a Γ-pseudovaluation $v : \mathcal{A} \setminus \{0\} \mapsto \Gamma$ on $\mathcal{A}$ and a related v-compatible $\Gamma^{(u)}$-pseudovaluation $w : \mathcal{A}^u \setminus \{0\} \mapsto \Gamma^{(u)}$ on the free $\mathcal{A}$-module $\mathcal{A}^u$, with canonical basis $\{e_1, \ldots, e_u\}$, are functions satisfying, $\forall a, a_1, a_2 \in \mathcal{A} \setminus \{0\}$, $m, m_1, m_2 \in \mathcal{A}^u \setminus \{0\}$,

1. $v(a_1 - a_2) \le \max(v(a_1), v(a_2))$,
2. $v(a_1 a_2) \le v(a_1) \circ v(a_2)$,
3. $v(r) = \mathbf{1}_\Gamma$ for each $r \in R \subset \mathcal{A}$;
4. $w(m_1 - m_2) \le \max(w(m_1), w(m_2))$,
5. $w(am) \le v(a) \circ w(m)$ and $w(ma) \le w(m) \circ v(a)$,

which allow to deduce the *associated* Γ*-graded ring* $G(\mathcal{A})$ and the related associated $\Gamma^{(u)}$-graded modules $G(\mathcal{A}^u) = (G(\mathcal{A}))^u$, which are all left R-modules.

When the ring $\mathcal{A}$ is explicitly given via the Zacharias representation (5) we cannot use the function

$$\mathbf{T}(\cdot) : \mathcal{A} \mapsto \mathcal{B} : f \to \mathbf{T}(f)$$

as a natural pseudovaluation because, in general, either $\mathcal{B}$ is not a semigroup or, at least, $<$ is not a semigroup ordering on it.

Thus we consider a semigroup Γ, $\mathcal{B} \subset \Gamma \subset \langle\overline{\mathbf{V}}\rangle$, such that the restriction of $<$ on Γ is a semigroup ordering. In this way, the function $\mathbf{T}(\cdot) : \mathcal{A} \mapsto \mathcal{B} \subset \Gamma : f \to \mathbf{T}(f)$ is a Γ-pseudovaluation, which we will call its *natural* Γ*-pseudovaluation* and the free $\mathcal{A}$-module $\mathcal{A}^m$ has the *natural* $\mathbf{T}(\cdot)$*-compatible pseudovaluation*

$$\mathbf{T}(\cdot) : \mathcal{A}^m \mapsto \mathcal{B}^{(m)} \subset \Gamma^{(m)} : f \to \mathbf{T}(f).$$

The crucial rôle of filtration/graduation theory in Buchberger Theory, as realized in [7], is that in the classical setting (polynomial rings, free associative algebras) and, more in general in a monoid ring $R[\mathsf{S}]$ [8] where $\mathcal{A} = R[\mathsf{S}]$ and its associated S-graded ring $G(\mathcal{A})$ under the S-pseudovaluation $\mathbf{T}(\cdot)$ coincide, is that Buchberger test/completion can be smoothly formalized as Möller Lifting Theorem and (following the intuition of Spear) to be exported to each quotient rings.

The central point is that, even when $\mathcal{A}$ and $\mathcal{G} = G(\mathcal{A})$ do not coincide as rings (thus the multiplication $\star$ of $\mathcal{A}$ does not coincide with the one, $*$, of $\mathcal{G}$) and even as modules but just as sets, both Möller Lifting Theorem and Speer's Theorem can be reformulated and provide a complete Buchberger Theory. For instance, if we consider the Weyl algebra,

$$\mathcal{A} = \mathbb{Q}\langle D, X\rangle / \mathbb{I}(DX - XD - 1)$$

where

$$\mathcal{G} = \mathbb{Q}[D, X], D \star X = XD - 1, D * X = XD,$$

an old slogan stated that in order to provide a Buchberger Algorithm on $\mathcal{A}$, one just needs to modify, in the algorithm for $\mathcal{G}$, the multiplication procedure!

2.4 Gröbner bases

Let $\mathcal{A} = \mathcal{Q}/\mathcal{I}$ be an effectively given left R-module, endowed with its natural Γ-pseudovaluation $\mathbf{T}(\cdot)$ where the semigroup $(\Gamma, \circ)$ satisfies

- $\mathcal{B} \subset \Gamma \subset \langle \overline{\mathbf{V}} \rangle$;
- the restriction of $<$ on Γ is a semigroup ordering.

We denote $\mathcal{G} = G(\mathcal{A})$ and by $\star$ the multiplication of $\mathcal{A}$ and by $*$ the one of $\mathcal{G}$.

For any set $F \subset \mathcal{A}^m$ we denote, in function of $<$:

- $\mathbf{T}\{F\} := \{\mathbf{T}(g) : g \in F\} \subset \mathcal{B}^{(m)}$,
- $\mathbf{M}\{F\} := \{\mathbf{M}(g) : g \in F\} \subset \mathcal{G}^m$,
- $\mathbf{M}(F) := \{a\lambda * \mathbf{M}(g) * b\rho : \lambda, \rho \in \mathcal{B}, a \in R_\lambda \setminus \{0\}, b \in R_\rho \setminus \{0\}, g \in F\}$.

DEFINITION 4. *Let* $\mathsf{M} \subset \mathcal{A}^m$ *be a (left, right, bilateral)* $\mathcal{A}$*-module.* $F \subset \mathsf{M}$ *will be called*

- *a (left, right, bilateral)* Gröbner basis *of* M *if* F *satisfies the following condition:*
  - *for each* $f \in \mathsf{M}$*, there are* $g_i \in F$*,* $\lambda_i, \rho_i \in \mathcal{B}, a_i \in R_{\lambda_i} \setminus \{0\}, b_i \in R_{\rho_i} \setminus \{0\}$ *such that*
    - $\mathbf{T}(f) = \lambda_i \circ \mathbf{T}(g_i) \circ \rho_i$ *for all* i,
    - $\mathbf{M}(f) = \sum_i a_i\lambda_i * \mathbf{M}(g_i) * b_i\rho_i$;
- *a (left, right, bilateral)* strong Gröbner basis *of* M *if* F *satisfies the following equivalent conditions*
  - *for each* $f \in \mathsf{M}$ *there is* $g \in F$ *s.t.* $\mathbf{M}(g) \mid \mathbf{M}(f)$,
  - *for each* $f \in \mathsf{M}$ *there are* $g \in F$*,* $\lambda, \rho \in \mathcal{B}, a \in R_\lambda \setminus \{0\}, b \in R_\rho \setminus \{0\}$*, such that*

    $\mathbf{T}(f) = \lambda \circ \mathbf{T}(g) \circ \rho$ *and* $\mathbf{M}(f) = a\lambda * \mathbf{M}(g) * b\rho$.

DEFINITION 5. *Let* $\mathsf{M} \subset \mathcal{A}^m$ *be a (left, right, bilateral)* $\mathcal{A}$*-module and* $F \subset \mathsf{M}$*. We say that* $f \in \mathcal{A}^m \setminus \{0\}$ *has*

- *a left* (weak) Gröbner representation *in terms of* F *if it can be written as* $f = \sum_{i=1}^{\mu} a_i\lambda_i \star g_i$*, with* $\lambda_i \in \mathcal{B}, a_i \in R_{\lambda_i} \setminus \{0\}, g_i \in F$ *and* $\mathbf{T}(f) \geq \lambda_i \circ \mathbf{T}(g_i) \forall i$;
- *a left* strong Gröbner representation *in terms of* F *if it can be written as* $f = \sum_{i=1}^{\mu} a_i\lambda_i \star g_i$*, with* $\lambda_i \in \mathcal{B}, a_i \in R_{\lambda_i} \setminus \{0\}, g_i \in F$*, and*

  $$\mathbf{T}(f) = \lambda_1 \circ \mathbf{T}(g_1) > \lambda_i \circ \mathbf{T}(g_i) \forall i, 1 < i \leq \mu;$$
- *right weak/strong Gröbner representations are dually defined;*
- *a bilateral (weak)* Gröbner representation *in terms of* F *if it can be written as* $f = \sum_{i=1}^{\mu} a_i\lambda_i \star g_i \star b_i\rho_i$*, with* $\lambda_i, \rho_i \in \mathcal{B}, a_i \in R_{\lambda_i} \setminus \{0\}, b_i \in R_{\rho_i} \setminus \{0\}, g_i \in F$*, and* $\mathbf{T}(f) \geq \lambda_i \circ \mathbf{T}(g_i) \circ \rho_i \forall i$;
- *a bilateral* strong Gröbner representation *in terms of* F *if it can be written as* $f = \sum_{i=1}^{\mu} a_i\lambda_i \star g_i \star b_i\rho_i$*, with* $\lambda_i, \rho_i \in \mathcal{B}, a_i \in R_{\lambda_i} \setminus \{0\}, b_i \in R_{\rho_i} \setminus \{0\}, g_i \in F$*, and* $\mathbf{T}(f) = \lambda_1 \circ \mathbf{T}(g_1) \circ \rho_1 > \lambda_i \circ \mathbf{T}(g_i) \circ \rho_i \forall i, 1 < i \leq \mu$.

For $f \in \mathcal{A}^m \setminus \{0\}, F \subset \mathcal{A}^m$*, an element* $g \in \mathcal{A}^m$ *is called a*

- *(left, right, bilateral)* (weak) normal form *of* f *w.r.t.* F*, if*

  $f - g \in \mathbb{I}(F)$ *has a weak Gröbner repr. wrt* F*, and*
  $g \neq 0 \implies \mathbf{M}(g) \notin \mathbf{M}\{\mathbb{I}(\mathbf{M}\{F\})\}$;
- *(left, right, bilateral)* strong normal form *of* f *w.r.t.* F*, if*

  $f - g \in \mathbb{I}(F)$ *has a strong Gröbner repr. wrt* F*, and*
  $g \neq 0 \implies \mathbf{M}(g) \notin \mathbf{M}(F)$.

THEOREM 6. *For any set* $F \subset \mathcal{A}^m \setminus \{0\}$*, among the following conditions:*

1. $f \in \mathbb{I}(F) \iff$ *it has a (left,right,bilateral) strong Gröbner representation* $f = \sum_{i=1}^{\mu} a_i\lambda_i \star g_i \star b_i\rho_i$ *in terms of* F *which further satisfies* $\mathbf{T}(f) = \lambda_1 \circ \mathbf{T}(g_1) \circ \rho_1$ *and* $\lambda_i \circ \mathbf{T}(g_i) \circ \rho_i > \lambda_{i+1} \circ \mathbf{T}(g_{i+1}) \circ \rho_{i+1} \forall i$;
2. $f \in \mathbb{I}(F) \iff$ *it has a (left,right,bilateral) strong Gröbner representation in terms of* F*;*
3. F *is a (left,right,bil.) strong Gröbner basis of* $\mathbb{I}(F)$*;*
4. *for each* $f \in \mathcal{A}^m \setminus \{0\}$ *and any strong normal form* h *of* f *w.r.t.* F *we have* $f \in \mathbb{I}(F) \iff h = 0$;
5. $f \in \mathbb{I}(F) \iff$ *it has a (left,right,bilateral) weak Gröbner representation in terms of* F*;*
6. F *is a (left,right,bilateral) weak Gröbner basis of* $\mathbb{I}(F)$*;*
7. *for each* $f \in \mathcal{A}^m \setminus \{0\}$ *and any weak normal form* h *of* f *w.r.t.* F *we have* $f \in \mathbb{I}(F) \iff h = 0$;

there are the implications

$$\begin{array}{ccccccc} (1) & \iff & (2) & \iff & (3) & \iff & (4) \\ & & \Downarrow & & \Downarrow & & \Downarrow \\ & & (5) & \iff & (6) & \iff & (7) \end{array}$$

If R *is a skew field we have also the implication* $(5) \implies (2)$ *and as a consequence also* $(6) \implies (3)$ *and* $(7) \implies (4)$.

2.5 Möller: Lifting Theorem

Let us now consider the ring $\mathcal{A}$ endowed with its natural Γ-pseudovaluation $\mathbf{T}(\cdot)$ and denote $\mathcal{G} := G(\mathcal{A})$ its associated graded ring, by $\star$ the multiplication of $\mathcal{A}$, by $*$ the one of $\mathcal{G}$ and by $\circ$ that of Γ.

Given a finite set

$$F := \{g_1, \ldots, g_u\} \subset \mathcal{A}^m, g_i = \mathbf{M}(g_i) - p_i =: a_i\tau_i\mathbf{e}_{\iota_i} - p_i,$$

we denote M the (left/right/bilateral) module $\mathsf{M} := \mathbb{I}(F)$ endowed with its natural pseudovaluation.

Consider the morphisms

$$\mathfrak{s}_L : \mathcal{G}^u \to \mathcal{G}^m \text{ and } \mathfrak{S}_L : \mathcal{A}^u \to \mathcal{A}^m$$

defined as

$$\mathfrak{s}_L\left(\sum_{i=1}^{u}\left(\sum_{\omega\in\mathcal{B}} a_{i\omega}\omega\right)e_i\right) := \sum_{i=1}^{u}\sum_{\omega\in\mathcal{B}} a_{i\omega}\omega * \mathbf{M}(g_i),$$
$$\mathfrak{S}_L\left(\sum_{i=1}^{u}\left(\sum_{\omega\in\mathcal{B}} a_{i\omega}\omega\right)e_i\right) := \sum_{i=1}^{u}\sum_{\omega\in\mathcal{B}} a_{i\omega}\omega \star g_i,$$

where the symbols $\{e_1,\dots,e_u\}$ denote the common canonical basis of $\mathcal{A}^u$ and $\mathcal{G}^u$, which, as sets, coincide and which satisfy $\mathcal{G}^u = G(\mathcal{A})^u = G(\mathcal{A}^u)$ under the pseudovaluation $w : \mathcal{A}^u \to \Gamma^{(m)}$ defined, for each

$$\sigma := \sum_{i=1}^{u}\left(\sum_{\omega\in\mathcal{B}} a_{i\omega}\omega\right)e_i \in \mathcal{A}^u \setminus \{0\}$$

by

$$w(\sigma) := \max_{<}\{\omega \circ \mathbf{T}(g_i) : a_{i\omega} \neq 0\} \in \Gamma^{(m)};$$

the corresponding $\Gamma^{(m)}$-homogeneous —of $\Gamma^{(m)}$-degree $w(\sigma)$ — *leading form* is

$$\mathcal{L}_L(\sigma) := \sum_{i=1}^{u}\left(\sum_{\omega\in B_i} a_{i\omega}\omega\right)e_i \in \mathcal{G}^u$$

where, for each i we set $B_i := \{\omega \in \mathcal{B} : \omega \circ \mathbf{T}(g_i) = w(\sigma)\}$.

The morphisms $\mathfrak{s}_R$ are $\mathfrak{S}_R$ are defined in the obvious way; the bilateral version requires a further refinement. Denoting

$$\hat{R} := \{a \in R : ah = a \star h = h \star a, \text{ for each } h \in \mathcal{A}\}$$

the commutative subring $\hat{R} \subset R$ of R consisting of the elements belonging to the center of $\mathcal{A}$, remarking that the subring of R generated by $\mathbf{1}_R$ is a subring of $\hat{R}$ and that $\hat{R}$ is also a subring of the center of $\mathcal{G}$, and considering both the $\mathcal{A}$-bimodule $\mathcal{A} \otimes_{\hat{R}} \mathcal{A}^{\mathrm{op}}$ and the $\mathcal{G}$-bimodule $\mathcal{G} \otimes_{\hat{R}} \mathcal{G}^{\mathrm{op}}$, which, as sets, coincide, we impose on the bilateral $\mathcal{A}$-module $(\mathcal{A} \otimes_{\hat{R}} \mathcal{A}^{\mathrm{op}})^u$, whose canonical basis is denoted $\{e_1,\dots,e_u\}$ and whose generic element has the shape

$$\sum_i a_i\lambda_i e_{l_i} b_i\rho_i, \lambda_i, \rho_i \in \mathcal{B}, a_i \in R_{\lambda_i} \setminus \{0\}, b_i \in R_{\rho_i} \setminus \{0\}, l_i \leq u,$$

the $\Gamma^{(m)}$-pseudovaluation $w : (\mathcal{A} \otimes_{\hat{R}} \mathcal{A}^{\mathrm{op}})^u \to \Gamma^{(m)}$ defined for each $\sigma := \sum_i a_i\lambda_i e_{l_i} b_i\rho_i \in (\mathcal{A} \otimes_{\hat{R}} \mathcal{A}^{\mathrm{op}})^u \setminus \{0\}$ as

$$w(\sigma) := \max_{<}\{\lambda_i \circ \mathbf{T}(g_{l_i}) \circ \rho_i\} \in \Gamma^{(m)}$$

so that $G((\mathcal{A} \otimes_{\hat{R}} \mathcal{A}^{\mathrm{op}})^u) = (G(\mathcal{A} \otimes_{\hat{R}} \mathcal{A}^{\mathrm{op}}))^u = (\mathcal{G} \otimes_{\hat{R}} \mathcal{G}^{\mathrm{op}})^u$ and its corresponding $\Gamma^{(m)}$-homogeneous *leading form* is

$$\mathcal{L}_2(\sigma) := \sum_{h\in H} a_h\lambda_h e_{l_h} b_h\rho_h \in (\mathcal{G} \otimes_{\hat{R}} \mathcal{G}^{\mathrm{op}})^u$$

where $H := \{h : \lambda_h \circ \tau_{l_h} \circ \rho_h \mathbf{e}_{\iota_{l_h}} = v(\sigma)\}$.

We can therefore consider the morphisms

$$\mathfrak{s}_2 : (\mathcal{G} \otimes_{\hat{R}} \mathcal{G}^{\mathrm{op}})^u \to \mathcal{G}^m \text{ and } \mathfrak{S}_2 : (\mathcal{A} \otimes_{\hat{R}} \mathcal{A}^{\mathrm{op}})^u \to \mathcal{A}^m$$

defined as

$$\mathfrak{s}_2\left(\sum_i a_i\lambda_i e_{l_i} b_i\rho_i\right) := \sum_i a_i\lambda_i * \mathbf{M}(g_{l_i}) * b_i\rho_i,$$
$$\mathfrak{S}_2\left(\sum_i a_i\lambda_i e_{l_i} b_i\rho_i\right) := \sum_i a_i\lambda_i \star g_{l_i} \star b_i\rho_i.$$

REMARK 7. *The point of Möller Theorem is a reformulation (and a more efficient procedure) of the classical Buchberger test-completion, which states that "a basis F is Gröbner if and only if each S-polynomial reduces to 0". The new formulation states, with the current notation, that "a basis F is Gröbner if and only if each element u in a minimal basis of the module* $\ker(\mathfrak{s})$ *of the syzygies among the leading monomials* $\mathbf{M}(g_i)$ *lifts, via Buchberger reduction of* $\mathfrak{S}(u)$*, to a syzygy* $U \in \ker(\mathfrak{S})$ *among the* g_i*". More precisely we have*

$$U = \mathfrak{S}(u) - \sum_{i=1}^{\mu} a_i\lambda_i \star e_i \star b_i\rho_i$$

where $\sum_{i=1}^{\mu} a_i\lambda_i \star g_i \star b_i\rho_i$ *is the Gröbner representation of* $\mathfrak{S}(u)$ *modulo* F.

In connection Janet and Schreier proved that such syzygies are a basis of the module $\ker(\mathfrak{S})$

This formulation allowed to easily and efficiently provide a Buchberger Theory at least in $\mathbb{F}\langle\overline{\mathbf{X}}\rangle$ *and in the monoid rings* $R[\mathsf{S}]$*,* R *a PIR, and (via Spear's Theorem) in their quotients.*

The point here is that the theorem naturally extends Buchberger Theory to all rings which have such a ring as is associated graded ring. Thus, to each effectively given ring.

DEFINITION 8. *If* $u \in \ker(\mathfrak{s})$ *is* $\Gamma^{(m)}$*-homogeneous and* $U \in \ker(\mathfrak{S})$ *is such that* $u = \mathcal{L}(U)$*, we say that* u lifts *to* U*, or* U *is a* lifting *of* u*, or simply* u has a lifting.

A (left/right/bilateral) Gebauer–Möller set *for* F *is any* $\Gamma^{(m)}$*-homogeneous basis of* $\ker(\mathfrak{s})$.

For each $\Gamma^{(m)}$*-homogeneous element* $\sigma \in \mathcal{A}^u$*, we say that* $\mathfrak{S}_L(\sigma)$ *has a (left)* quasi-Gröbner representation *in terms of* F *if it can be written as* $\mathfrak{S}_L(\sigma) = \sum_{l=1}^{\mu} a_l\lambda_l \star g_{i_l}$ *with* $\lambda_l \in \mathcal{B}, a_l \in R_{\lambda_l} \setminus \{0\}, 1 \leq i_l \leq u$*, and*

$$w(\sigma) > \mathbf{T}(a_l\lambda_l \star g_{i_l}) = \lambda_l \circ \mathbf{T}(g_{i_l}) \text{ for each } l.$$

For each $\Gamma^{(m)}$*-homogeneous element* $\sigma \in (\mathcal{A} \otimes_{\hat{R}} \mathcal{A}^{\mathrm{op}})^u$*, we say that* $\mathfrak{S}_2(\sigma)$ *has a (bilateral)* quasi-Gröbner representation *in terms of* F *if it can be written as*

$$\mathfrak{S}_2(\sigma) = \sum_{l=1}^{\mu} a_l\lambda_l \star g_l \star b_l\rho_l$$

with $\lambda_l, \rho_l \in \mathcal{B}, a_l \in R_{\lambda_l} \setminus \{0\}, b_l \in R_{\rho_l} \setminus \{0\}, g_l \in F$ *and* $w(\sigma) > \mathbf{T}(a_l\lambda_l \star g_l \star b_l\rho_l) = \lambda_l \circ \mathbf{T}(g_l) \circ \rho_l$ *for each* l.

Denoting for each set $S \subset \mathsf{M}$*,* $\mathcal{L}\{S\} := \{\mathcal{L}(g) : g \in S\}$*, a set* $B \subset \mathsf{M}$ *is called a (left/right/bilateral)* standard basis *of* M *if* $\mathbb{I}(\mathcal{L}\{B\}) = \mathbb{I}(\mathcal{L}\{\mathsf{M}\})$.

THEOREM 9 (MÖLLER–PRITCHARD). *[6, 11] With the present notation and denoting* $\mathfrak{GM}(F)$ *any (left/right/bilateral) Gebauer–Möller set for* F*, the following conditions are equivalent:*

1. *F is a (left/right/bilateral) Gröbner basis of* M*;*
2. $f \in \mathsf{M} \iff f$ *has a (left/right/bilateral) Gröbner representation in terms of* F*;*
3. *for each* $\sigma \in \mathfrak{GM}(F)$*, the (left/right/bilateral) S-polynomial* $\mathfrak{S}(\sigma)$ *has a (left/right/bilateral) quasi-Gröbner representation in terms of* F*;*
4. *each* $\sigma \in \mathfrak{GM}(F)$ *has a lifting* $\mathrm{lift}(\sigma)$*;*
5. *each* $\Gamma^{(m)}$*-homogeneous element* $u \in \ker(\mathfrak{s})$ *has a lifting* $\mathrm{lift}(u)$*;*

THEOREM 10 (JANET—SCHREIER). *[3, 12]* *With the same notation the equivalent conditions (1-5) imply that*

6. $\{\text{lift}(\sigma) : \sigma \in \mathfrak{GM}(F)\}$ *is a (left/right/bilateral) standard basis of* $\ker(\mathfrak{S})$.

2.6 Spear's Theorem

Recall that for each free $\mathcal{A}$-module $\mathcal{A}^m, m \in \mathbb{N}$, endowed with its natural pseudovaluation and whose canonical basis we denote by $\{\mathbf{e}_1, \dots, \mathbf{e}_m\}$, the projection

$$\Pi : \mathcal{Q} := \mathbb{Z}\langle\overline{\mathbf{Z}}\rangle \twoheadrightarrow \mathcal{A}, \mathcal{I} := \ker(\Pi), \mathcal{A} = \mathcal{Q}/\mathcal{I},$$

extends to the canonical projections, still denoted Π,

$$\Pi : \mathcal{Q}^m \twoheadrightarrow \mathcal{A}^m, \ker(\Pi) = \mathcal{I}^m = \mathbb{I}_2(G^{(m)})$$

where G is the (left/right/bilateral) Gröbner basis w.r.t. $<$ of $\mathcal{I}$ and $G^{(m)} := \{g\mathbf{e}_j, g \in G, 1 \leq j \leq m\}$.

Let $\mathsf{M} \subset \mathcal{A}^m$ be a (left/right/bilateral) module and denote $\mathsf{M}' := \Pi^{-1}(\mathsf{M}) = \mathsf{M} + \mathcal{I}^m$.

REMARK 11. *As for the Lifiting Theorem, filtration/graduation theory is the most natural setting [7] for formalizing Spear's [13] intuition that a Buchberger Theory defined in a ring can be exported to its quotients. In our setting this grants us that at least the $\mathbb{Z}$-valuation $\mathbf{T}(\cdot)$ of $\mathcal{Q}$ is surely available in $\mathcal{A}$. In our setting, moreover, it allows to deduce the required Gebauer–Möller set of S-polynomials from the well-known and classical result describing the S-polynomials in $\mathcal{Q}$.*

LEMMA 12. *Assume $F \subset \mathsf{M}'$ is a Gröbner basis of M' and denote*

$$\bar{F} := \{\text{Can}(g, \mathcal{I}^m) : g \in F, \mathbf{T}(g) \notin \mathbf{T}(\mathcal{I}^m)\} \subset \mathbf{Zach}_<(\mathcal{A})^m$$

where $\text{Can}(g, \mathcal{I}^m) \in \mathbf{Zach}_<(\mathcal{A})^m$ denotes the canonical form of $g \in \mathcal{Q}^m$ w.r.t. $G^{(m)}$ so that in particular $g = \Pi(g)$ for each $g \in \bar{F}$. Then $\bar{F} \sqcup G^{(m)}$ is a Gröbner basis of M'.

THEOREM 13 (SPEAR). *With the present notation, the following holds:*

1. *if F is a reduced Gröbner basis of M', then*

$$\begin{aligned}\{g \in F : g = \Pi(g)\} &= \{\Pi(g) : g \in F, \mathbf{T}(g) \in \mathcal{B}^{(m)}\} \\ &= F \cap \mathbf{Zach}_<(\mathcal{A})^m\end{aligned}$$

   is a reduced Gröbner basis of M.

2. *Assume each $m' \in \mathsf{M}'$ has a Gröbner representation in terms of $F \subset \mathsf{M}'$. Set*

$$\bar{F} := \{\text{Can}(g, \mathcal{I}^m) : g \in F, g \notin \mathcal{I}^m\} \subset \mathbf{Zach}_<(\mathcal{A})^m$$

   where $\text{Can}(g, \mathcal{I}^m) \in \mathbf{Zach}_<(\mathcal{A})^m$ denotes the canonical form of $g \in \mathcal{Q}^m$ w.r.t. $G^{(m)}$ so that in particular $g = \Pi(g)$ for each $g \in \bar{F}$. Then each $m \in \mathsf{M}$ has a Gröbner representation in terms of $\bar{F}$.

3. *If $F \subset \mathbf{Zach}_<(\mathcal{A})^m$, so that in particular $\Pi(f) = f$ for each $f \in F$, is the Gröbner basis of M, then $F \sqcup G^{(m)}$ is a Gröbner basis of M'.*

   Moreover, if each $m \in \mathsf{M}$ has a Gröbner representation in terms of F, then each $m' \in \mathsf{M}'$ has a Gröbner representation in terms of $F \sqcup G^{(m)}$.

COROLLARY 14. *With the present notation and denoting*

- *for each bilateral module $A^{|H|}$ over a ring A indexed by a set $H \subset A$, its canonical basis by $\{\mathsf{e}(h) : h \in H\}$,*
- $\mathfrak{S}_2 : (\mathcal{A} \otimes_{\hat{R}} \mathcal{A}^{\text{op}})^{|F|} \to \mathcal{A}^m : \mathsf{e}(f) \mapsto f = \Pi(f), f \in F,$
- $\hat{\mathfrak{S}}_2 : (\mathcal{Q} \otimes_{\hat{R}} \mathcal{Q}^{\text{op}})^{|F|+m|G|} \to \mathcal{Q}^m : \mathsf{e}(h) \mapsto h$, *for each* $h \in F \cup G^{(m)}$;
- *and $\bar{\Pi} : (\mathcal{Q} \otimes_{\hat{R}} \mathcal{Q}^{\text{op}})^{|F|+m|G|} \to (\mathcal{A} \otimes_{\hat{R}} \mathcal{A}^{\text{op}})^{|F|}$ the map (where $\lambda_i, \rho_i \in \langle\overline{\mathbf{V}}\rangle, \bar{\upsilon}_i, \varpi_i \in \langle\overline{\mathbf{v}}\rangle, a_i, b_i \in \mathbb{Z} \setminus \{0\}$)*

$$\begin{aligned}&\bar{\Pi}\left(\sum_i a_i\bar{\upsilon}_i\lambda_i\mathsf{e}(h_i)b_i\varpi_i\rho_i\right) \\ = &\sum_{i:h_i \in F} \pi(a_i\bar{\upsilon}_i)\Pi(\lambda_i)\mathsf{e}(h_i)\pi(b_i\varpi_i)\Pi(\rho_i),\end{aligned}$$

if $\Sigma \subset (\mathcal{Q} \otimes_{\hat{R}} \mathcal{Q})^{|F|+m|G|}$ is a bilateral standard basis of $\ker(\hat{\mathfrak{S}}_2)$, then $\bar{\Pi}(\Sigma)$ is a bilateral standard basis of $\ker(\mathfrak{S}_2)$.

In principle, effectively given a left R-module ring $\mathcal{A}$ and a set $B \subset \mathcal{A}^m$, a Gröbner basis of $\mathsf{M} := \mathbb{I}(B) \subset \mathcal{A}^m$ could be obtained, via Spear's Theorem 13(1), by applying in $\mathcal{Q}^m$ Buchberger algorithm to $B \cup G^{(m)}$, where G denotes the Gröbner basis of $\mathcal{I}$ whose knowledge is required by the effectiveness of $\mathcal{A}$.

If G is finite and $\mathcal{A}$ is noetherian so that there is a finite set $F \subset \mathbf{Zach}_<(\mathcal{A})^m$ which is a Gröbner basis of M, then, according Spear's Theorem 13(3), M' has the finite Gröbner basis $F \sqcup G^{(m)}$ and, if moreover R is a field and M is an ideal, then a direct application of Kandri-Rody–Weispfenning completion [4] or (better) Pritchard's Algorithm [11] grants that Buchberger algorithm terminates returning such finite Gröbner basis $F \sqcup G^{(m)}$.

On the other side, already in the easiest cases where $\mathcal{A}$ is either the commutative polynomial ring or Weyl algebra, while G is finite when we are considering bilateral modules, G is instead infinite for left/right modules. Thus our approach requires infinite computations.

Thus, in general, the approach consisting into applying Buchberger algorithm to $B \cup G^{(m)}$ and deducing the Gröbner basis of M via Spear's Theorem 13(1) does not seem to be helpful for a computation of Gröbner bases, while it can help in understanding the structure of $\mathcal{A}$ and the underlying Zacharias representation.

3. BUCHBERGER ALGORITHM

It seems in principle more effective a reformulation in the line of Möller Lifting Theorem of Buchberger Algorithms both for computing normal forms and Gröbner Bases. We will sketch both **NormalForm** (Figure 1) and **GroebnerBasis** (Figure 2) Algorithms under suitable effectiveness assumptions which should be granted by a careful choice of a pseudovaluation and of an R-module structure providing an effective Zacharias representation.

3.1 Buchberger Reduction

It is sufficient to adapt the classical Buchberger Reduction algorithm, in order to obtain an algorithm for computing left, right and bilateral (cf. Figure 1) (weak) normal forms provided that in $\mathcal{A}$ it is possible to solve the following problem:

(Z1). Given $g \in \mathcal{A}^m \setminus \{0\}$ and $F \subset \mathcal{A}^m \setminus \{0\}$ decide whether

$$\mathbf{M}(g) \in \mathbf{M}\{\mathbb{I}_2(\mathbf{M}\{F\})\} \subset \mathcal{G}^m$$

in which case return $g_i \in F$, $\lambda_i, \rho_i \in \mathcal{B}, a_i \in R_{\lambda_i} \setminus \{0\}, b_i \in R_{\rho_i} \setminus \{0\}$ such that

- $\mathbf{T}(g) = \lambda_i \circ \mathbf{T}(g_i) \circ \rho_i$ for all i and
- $\mathbf{M}(g) = \sum_i a_i\lambda_i * \mathbf{M}(g_i) * b_i\rho_i$.

For the computation of *strong* normal forms, this problem must be formulated requiring $\nu = 1$ as follows:

(Z1s). Given $g \in \mathcal{A}^m \setminus \{0\}$ and $F \subset \mathcal{A}^m \setminus \{0\}$ decide whether $\mathbf{M}(f) \in \mathbf{M}(F)$ in which case return $h \in F$, $\lambda, \rho \in \mathcal{B}, a \in R_\lambda \setminus \{0\}, b \in R_\rho \setminus \{0\}$ such that

- $\mathbf{T}(g) = \lambda \circ \mathbf{T}(h) \circ \rho$ and
- $\mathbf{M}(g) = a\lambda * \mathbf{M}(h) * b\rho$;

and the instructions $\diamond$ must be substituted with $a_{\mu+1} := a, b_{\mu+1} := b, \lambda_{\mu+1} := \lambda, \rho_{\mu+1} := \rho, g_{\mu+1} := h$, $g := g - a_{\mu+1}\lambda_{\mu+1} \star g_{\mu+1} \star b_{\mu+1}\rho_{\mu+1}$, $\mu := \mu + 1$.

3.2 Buchberger Completion

DEFINITION 15. *For a finite set $F \subset \mathcal{A}^m \setminus \{0\}$, a subset $\mathfrak{GM}(F) \subset \ker(\mathfrak{s})$ of $\Gamma^{(m)}$-homogeneous elements is called a* non-trivial *Gebauer–Möller set for F iff there is a set $\mathrm{triv}(F) \subset \ker(\mathfrak{s})$ of $\Gamma^{(m)}$-homogeneous elements for which it is known that*

- *for each $\sigma \in \mathrm{triv}(F)$, $\mathfrak{S}(\sigma)$ has a quasi-Gröbner representation in terms of F,*
- *$\mathfrak{GM}(F) \cup \mathrm{triv}(F)$ is a Gebauer–Möller set for F.* □

If $\mathcal{A}$ has the following effectiveness properties:

- for any finite set $F \subset \mathcal{A}^m \setminus \{0\}$, there is a finite non-trivial Gebauer–Möller set $\mathfrak{GM}(F)$ and, more important,
- there is an algorithm **SyzBasis**$(F, \mathfrak{GM}(F), g)$ which,

(Z2). given a finite set $F \subset \mathcal{A}^m \setminus \{0\}$, a non-trivial Gebauer–Möller set $\mathfrak{GM}(F)$ of F and an element $g \in \mathcal{A}^m \setminus \{0\}$, return a finite set

$$S(F, g) := \mathbf{SyzBasis}(F, \mathfrak{GM}(F), g)$$

such that $\mathfrak{GM}(F) \cup S(F, g)$ is a non-trivial Gebauer–Möller set for $F \cup \{g\}$,

adapting the classical Buchberger test-completion Algorithm to this setting (and removing trivial, *i.e.* useless, S-polynomials) we obtain the procedure (a procedure, not an algorithm!) presented in Figure 2 which, under the application of a fair strategy [10] in the **FairChoose**-instruction, terminates returning a finite Gröbner basis of $\mathbb{I}_2(F)$ if and only if such finite basis exists.

If R is a field and $m = 1$, a direct application of Buchberger's First Criterion implies that each finite set $F \subset \mathcal{A} \setminus \{0\}$, has a finite non-trivial Gebauer–Möller set $\mathfrak{GM}(F)$.

Of course, if $\mathcal{G}$ is noetherian any Gebauer–Möller set of a finite set F is finite and, in this setting, triviality of syzygies is needed only for improving the computation.

If R is not a field and $\mathcal{G}$ is not noetherian, examples show that in general the procedure of Figure 2 does not necessarily terminate.

EXAMPLE 16. *Let $\mathcal{G} = \mathcal{Q}/\mathcal{I}, \mathcal{Q} = \mathbb{Z}\langle X_1, X_2, X_3\rangle$, $\mathcal{I} = \mathbb{I}_2(X_2X_1 - 2X_1X_2, X_3X_1 - 3X_1X_3, X_3X_2 - 5X_2X_3)$,* **Zach**$_<(\mathcal{G}) = \mathbb{Z}[X_1, X_2, X_3]$.

Denoting $\mathcal{T} = \{X_1^{a_1}X_2^{a_2}X_3^{a_3}, (a_1, a_2, a_3) \in \mathbb{N}^3\}$. For any elements $p_i \in \mathrm{Span}_\mathbb{Z}(1, X_1, X_2, X_3), 1 \le i \le 3$, $\mathcal{G}$ is the associated $\mathcal{T}$-graded ring of $\mathcal{A} = \mathcal{Q}/\mathcal{J}$, where $\mathcal{J}$ is generated by $\{X_2X_1 - 2X_1X_2 - p_1, X_3X_1 - 3X_1X_3 - p_2, X_3X_2 - 5X_2X_3 - p_3\}$ if and only if they satisfy the Jacobi identity

$$p_1X_1 + 5X_2p_2 + 15p_3X_3 = X_3p_3 + 2p_2X_2 + 6X_1p_1.$$

We begin by remarking that the monomial arithmetic is described by

$$\begin{aligned} & aX_1^{a_1}X_2^{a_2}X_3^{a_3} * bX_1^{b_1}X_2^{b_2}X_3^{b_3} * cX_1^{c_1}X_2^{c_2}X_3^{c_3} \\ = \; & abc3^{a_3b_1+a_3c_1+b_3c_1}2^{a_2b_1+a_2c_1+b_2c_1}5^{a_3b_2+a_3c_2+b_3c_2}\tau \end{aligned}$$

with $\tau = X_1^{a_1+b_1+c_1}X_2^{a_2+b_2+c_2}X_3^{a_3+b_3+c_3}$.

As a consequence, for each $(b_1, b_2, b_3), (j_1, j_2, j_3) \in \mathbb{N}^3$

$$cX_1^{b_1+j_1}X_2^{b_2+j_2}X_3^{b_3+j_3} \in \mathbb{I}_L(bX_1^{b_1}X_2^{b_2}X_3^{b_3})$$

if and only if $b3^{j_3b_1}2^{j_2b_1}5^{j_3b_2} \mid c$.

An element

$$\sigma := \left(\alpha X_1^{\alpha_1}X_2^{\alpha_2}X_3^{\alpha_3}, \beta X_1^{\beta_1}X_2^{\beta_2}X_3^{\beta_3}, \gamma X_1^{\gamma_1}X_2^{\gamma_2}X_3^{\gamma_3}\right) \in \mathcal{G}^3$$

is homogeneous of $\mathcal{T}$-degree $X_1^{a+2}X_2^{b+2}X_3^{c+2}$ iff $\alpha_1 - 1 = \beta_1 = \gamma_1 =: a$, $\alpha_2 = \beta_2 - 1 = \gamma_2 =: b$, $\alpha_3 = \beta_3 = \gamma_3 - 1 =: c$.

Moreover, for $f_1, f_2, f_3 \in \mathcal{A}$ with

$$\mathbf{M}(f_1) = X_1X_2^2X_3^2, \mathbf{M}(f_2) = X_1^2X_2X_3^2, \mathbf{M}(f_3) = X_1^2X_2^2X_3,$$

σ is a syzygy in $\ker(\mathfrak{s}_L)$ iff

$$0 = \left(\alpha 3^c 2^b 5^{2c} + 2^2\beta 3^{2c}2^{2b}5^c + 3^2 5^2\gamma 3^{2c}2^{2b}5^{2c}\right).$$

A minimal Gebauer-Möller set for $\ker(\mathfrak{s}_L)$ consists of

$$\sigma_1 := (-4X_1, X_2, 0) \text{ and } \sigma_2 := (-15^2X_1, 0, X_3).$$

A Gebauer-Möller set for $\ker(\mathfrak{s}_2) \subset (\mathcal{G} \otimes \mathcal{G})^3$ is obtained by including

$$\begin{aligned} & \{X_1e_1 - e_3X_3, 5^2X_2e_1 - 2e_1X_2\} \\ \cup \; & \{X_3e_1 - 3 \cdot 5^2e_1X_3, e_1X_1 - 2^23^2e_3X_3\} \\ \cup \; & \{X_3e_2 - 3^25e_2X_3, e_2X_1 - 3^22X_1e_2, e_2X_2 - 5^2X_1e_1\} \\ \cup \; & \{5X_2e_3 - 4e_3X_2\}. \end{aligned}$$

Note that, for instance, $X_1X_2^{2+i}X_3^2 \in \mathbb{I}_2(\mathbf{M}(f_1))$ since $\gcd(2^i, 5^i) = 1$; similarly $X_1^2X_2^{2+i}X_3 \in \mathbb{I}_2(\mathbf{M}(f_3))$.

Thus if each listed elements lift, $\{f_1, f_2, f_3\}$ is a (weak) Gröbner bases; the strong one is infinite containing at least all terms $X_1^{a_1+1}X_2^{a_2+2}X_3^{a_3+1}$ provided $a_1 + a_3 > 0$.

4. REFERENCES

[1] J. Apel. Computational ideal theory in finitely generated extension rings. *Th. Comp. Sci.*, 224:1–33, 2000.

[2] J. Bueso, J. Gomez-Torrecillas, and A. Verschoren. *Methods in Non-Commutative Algebra*. Kluwer, 2003.

[3] M. Janet. Sur les systèms d'equations aux dérivées partialles. *J. Math. Pure et Appl.*, 3:65–151, 1920.

[4] A. Kandri-Rody and W. Weispfenning. Non-commutativer Gröbner Bases in Algebras of Solvable Type. *J. Symb.Comp.*, 9:1–26, 1990.

Figure 1: Normal Form Algorithms

$(g, \sum_{i=1}^{\mu} a_i\lambda_i \star g_i \star b_i\rho_i) :=$ **BilateralNormalForm**(f, F)

where

$f \in \mathcal{A}^m$, $F \subset \mathcal{A}^m$,

$g \in \mathcal{A}^m$ is a bilateral normal form of f w.r.t. F.

$g_i \in F$, $\lambda_i, \rho_i \in \mathcal{B}, a_i \in R_{\lambda_i} \setminus \{0\}, b_i \in R_{\rho_i} \setminus \{0\}$,

$f - g = \sum_{i=1}^{\mu} a_i\lambda_i \star g_i \star b_i\rho_i$ is a bilateral Gröbner representation in terms of F,

$g := f, \mu := 0$,

While $\mathbf{M}(g) \in \mathbf{M}\{\mathbb{I}_2(\mathbf{M}\{F\})\}$ **do**

Let $g_i \in F, \lambda_i, \rho_i \in \mathcal{B}, a_i \in R_{\lambda_i} \setminus \{0\}, b_i \in R_{\rho_i} \setminus \{0\}$:

$\mathbf{T}(f) = \lambda_i \circ \mathbf{T}(g_i) \circ \rho_i, \mu < i \leq \nu$,

$\mathbf{M}(g) = \sum_{i=\mu+1}^{\nu} a_i\lambda_i * \mathbf{M}(g_i) * b_i\rho_i$,

$\diamond$ $g := g - \sum_{i=\mu+1}^{\nu} a_i\lambda_i \star g_i \star b_i\rho_i$, $\mu := \nu$.

Figure 2: Buchberger Procedure

$G :=$ **BilateralGroebnerBasis**(F)

where

$F := \{g_1, \ldots, g_s\} \subset \mathcal{A}^m \setminus \{0\}$,

$\mathsf{M} := \mathbb{I}_2(F)$ is the bilateral module generated by F,

G is a bilateral Gröbner basis of M;

$B := \emptyset$, $G := \emptyset$, $\mathfrak{GM}(G) := \emptyset$

For each $r, 1 \leq r \leq s$ **do**

$S :=$ **SyzBasis**$(G, \mathfrak{GM}(G), g_r)$, $B := B \cup S$, $\mathfrak{GM}(G \cup \{g_r\}) := \mathfrak{GM}(G) \cup S$, $G := G \cup \{g_r\}$

While $B \neq \emptyset$ **do**

FairChoose $\sigma \in B$

$B := B \setminus \{\sigma\}$, $h := \mathfrak{S}_2(\sigma)$, $(h, \sum_{i=1}^{\mu} a_i\lambda_i \star g_i \star b_i\rho_i) :=$ **BilateralNormalForm**(h, G)

If $h \neq 0$ **then**

$s := s + 1, g_s := h$,

$S :=$ **SyzBasis**$(G, \mathfrak{GM}(G), g_s)$, $B := B \cup S$, $\mathfrak{GM}(G \cup \{g_s\}) := \mathfrak{GM}(G) \cup S$, $G := G \cup \{g_s\}$

[5] K. Madlener and B. Reinert. Computing Gröbner bases in monoid and group rings. In *Proc.ISSAC '93*, pages 254–263. ACM, 1993.

[6] H. Möller. On the construction of Gröbner bases using syzygies. *J. Symb.Comp.*, 6:345–359, 1988.

[7] T. Mora. Seven variations on standard bases, www.dima.unige.it/ morafe/publications/7variations.pdf.gz. *Preprint. DIMA Univ. Genova*, 45, 1988.

[8] T. Mora. Zacharias representeation of effective associative rings. *J. Symb.Comp. (submitted)*, 2014.

[9] E. Mosteig and M. Sweedler. Valuations and filtrations. *J. Symb.Comp.*, 34:399–435, 2002.

[10] F. Ollivier. Canonical bases: relations with standard bases, finiteness conditions and application to tame automorphisms. *Progress in Mathematics*, 94:379–400, 1990.

[11] F. L. Pritchard. The ideal membership problem in non-commutative polynomial rings. *J. Symb.Comp.*, 22:27–48, 1996.

[12] F. Schreyer. *Die Berechnung von Syzygien mit dem verallgemeinerten Weierstrass'schen Divisionsatz,Diplomarbait.* Hamburg Univ., 1980.

[13] D. Spear. A constructive approach to commutative ring theory. In *Proc. of the 1977 MACSYMA Users' Conference*, pages 369–376. NASA CP-2012, 1977.

[14] M. Sweedler. Ideal bases and valuation rings `http://math.usask.ca/fvk/Valth.html`. *Manuscript*, 1986.

[15] L. Szekeres. A canonical basis for the ideals of a polynomial domain. *Am. Math. Monthly*, 59:379–386, 1952.

[16] G. Zacharias. *Generalized Gröbner bases in commutative polynomial rings. Bachelor's thesis.* M.I.T., 1978.

Computing Logarithmic Vector Fields associated with Parametric semi-quasihomogeneous Hypersurface isolated Singularities

Katsusuke Nabeshima
Institute of Socio-Arts and Sciences,
Tokushima University,
1-1 Minamijosanjima, Tokushima, JAPAN
nabeshima@tokushima-u.ac.jp

Shinichi Tajima
Graduate School of Pure and Applied Sciences,
University of Tsukuba,
1-1-1 Tennoudai, Tsukuba, JAPAN
tajima@math.tsukuba.ac.jp

ABSTRACT

Logarithmic vector fields associated with parametric semi-quasihomogeneous hypersurface isolated singularities are considered in the context of symbolic computation. A new algorithm for computing the logarithmic vector fields is introduced. The keys of this approach are the concept of a polar variety and parametric local cohomology systems. The resulting algorithm also provides a decomposition of the parameter space depending on the structure of the logarithmic vector fields.

Categories and Subject Descriptors

I.1.2 [**Computing Methodologies**]: Symbolic and Algebraic Manipulation

General Terms

Algorithms

Keywords

logarithmic vector fields, algebraic local cohomology, singularities, parametric standard bases

1. INTRODUCTION

The concept of logarithmic vector fields along a hypersurface, introduced by K. Saito [28], is of considerable importance in singularity theory. Logarithmic vector fields have been extensively studied and utilized by several authors [4, 5, 8, 11, 12, 26, 27, 28, 29]. A. G. Aleksandrov [2] and J. Wahl [37] considered quasihomogeneous complete intersection cases and gave independently, among other things, a closed formula of generators of logarithmic vector fields. However, there is no closed formula for generators of logarithmic vector fields, even for semi-quasihomogeneous hypersurface isolated singularity cases. Many problems related with logarithmic vector fields remain still unsolved, especially for non-quasihomogeneous cases.

In this paper, we consider logarithmic vector fields associated with semi-quasihomogeneous hypersurface isolated singularities. We present a new method to study complex analytic properties of logarithmic vector fields and illustrate an algorithm for computing logarithmic vector fields.

To be more precise, let f be a semi-quasihomogeneous polynomial with parameters. Assume that the weighted homogeneous part of f has an isolated singularity at the origin. Then, f can be regarded as a μ-constant deformation where μ is the Milnor number of the singularity. Each hypersurface defined by f is topologically equivalent to the hypersurface defined by the weighted homogeneous part of f. These hypersurfaces are not in general analytically equivalent. The complex analytic structure of the sheaf of logarithmic vector fields along these hypersurfaces also depends on deformation parameters.

We consider the parameter dependency of logarithmic vector fields by using local cohomology classes with parameters. We describe how to compute completely the structure of logarithmic vector fields. The keys of our approach are the concept of a polar variety [17, 18, 36] and parametric local cohomology systems associated with the polar variety [31]. In [21], an algorithm has been introduced for computing parametric local cohomology systems associated with the Jacobi ideal of f. We adapt the algorithm for computing parametric local cohomology systems associated with a polar variety. Moreover, we show that logarithmic vector fields with parameters can be computed by using the parametric local cohomology systems. The resulting algorithm has been implemented in the computer algebra system `Risa/Asir` [25].

This paper is organized as follows. Section 2 quickly reviews algebraic local cohomology, and gives notation and definitions that will be used in this paper. Section 3 discusses an algorithm for computing parametric local cohomology systems associated with a polar variety. Section 4 studies relations between logarithmic vector fields and local cohomology classes. Section 5 provides a new computational method of logarithmic vector fields with parameters.

2. PRELIMINARIES

In this section, we briefly review local cohomology classes, semi-quasihomogeneity, weighted degrees and strata. The details are in [9, 10, 24, 32, 34, 35]. Throughout this paper, we use the notation x as the abbreviation of n variables

ISSAC'15, July 6–9, 2015, Bath, United Kingdom.

DOI: http://dx.doi.org/10.1145/2755996.2756641.

$x_1, \ldots, x_n$. The set of natural numbers $\mathbb{N}$ includes zero. $\mathbb{C}$ is the field of complex numbers.

2.1 Algebraic Local Cohomology

Let $S = \{x \in X | f(x) = 0\}$ be a hypersurface with an isolated singularity at the origin O in $\mathbb{C}^n$, where X is an open neighborhood of the origin O and f is a holomorphic defining function. Let $\mathcal{O}_X$ be the sheaf of holomorphic functions and $\mathcal{O}_{X,O}$ the stalk at the origin of the sheaf $\mathcal{O}_X$. Let $\mathcal{H}^n_{\{O\}}(\mathcal{O}_X)$ be the local cohomology supported at O. Consider the pair $(X, X-O)$ and its relative Čech covering. Then, any section of $\mathcal{H}^n_{\{O\}}(\mathcal{O}_X)$ can be represented as an element of relative Čech cohomology. All local cohomology classes we handle in this paper are actually algebraic local cohomology classes that belong to the set defined by

$$H^n_{[O]}(\mathcal{O}_X) := \lim_{k\to\infty} \mathrm{Ext}^n_{\mathcal{O}_X}(\mathcal{O}_{X,O}/\langle x_1, x_2, \ldots, x_n\rangle^k, \mathcal{O}_X),$$

where $\langle x_1, \ldots, x_n\rangle$ is the maximal ideal generated by $x_1, \ldots, x_n$. We represent an algebraic local cohomology class, given by a finite sum of the form $\sum c_\lambda \left[\frac{1}{x^{\lambda+1}}\right]$, as a polynomial in n variables $\sum c_\lambda \xi^\lambda$ called "polynomial representation", where $c_\lambda \in \mathbb{C}$, $\lambda \in \mathbb{N}^n$ and $\xi = (\xi_1, \xi_2, \ldots, \xi_n)$. The multiplication by x^α for polynomial representation is defined as

$$x^\alpha * \xi^\lambda = \begin{cases} \xi^{\lambda-\alpha}, & \lambda_i \geq \alpha_i, i = 1, \ldots, n, \\ 0, & \text{otherwise}, \end{cases}$$

where $\alpha = (\alpha_1, \ldots, \alpha_n) \in \mathbb{N}^n, \lambda = (\lambda_1, \ldots, \lambda_n) \in \mathbb{N}^n$, and $\lambda - \alpha = (\lambda_1 - \alpha_1, \ldots, \lambda_n - \alpha_n)$. (We use " $*$ " for polynomial representation.) Hereafter, we adopt polynomial representation to represent an algebraic local cohomology class.

Let Ψ be a set of algebraic local cohomology classes and $\psi \in \Psi$. Then, we define the set of terms of ψ as $\mathrm{Term}(\psi) = \{\xi^\lambda | \psi = \sum_{\lambda\in\mathbb{N}^n} c_\lambda \xi^\lambda, c_\lambda \neq 0, c_\lambda \in \mathbb{C}\}$. Moreover, for the set Ψ, $\mathrm{Term}(\Psi) = \bigcup_{\psi\in\Psi} \mathrm{Term}(\psi)$.

2.2 Semi-quasihomogeneity and term orders

Let $\mathbf{w} = (w_1, w_2, \ldots, w_n) \in \mathbb{N}^n$ be a weight vector with positive entries (i.e., $w_i > 0$ for all i) for a given coordinate system $x = (x_1, x_2, \ldots, x_n)$ and $\xi = (\xi_1, \xi_2, \ldots, \xi_n)$. The weighted degree of a term $x^\alpha = x_1^{\alpha_1} x_2^{\alpha_2} \cdots x_n^{\alpha_n}$, with respect to $\mathbf{w}$ is defined to be $|x^\alpha|_{\mathbf{w}} = \sum_{i=1}^n w_i \alpha_i$.

DEFINITION 1 ([1]).

(i) A nonzero polynomial f in $\mathbb{C}[x]$ is **quasihomogeneous of type** $(d; \mathbf{w})$ if all terms of f have the same weighted degree d with respect to $\mathbf{w}$, i.e., $f = \sum_{|x^\alpha|_{\mathbf{w}}=d} c_\alpha x^\alpha$ where $c_\alpha \in \mathbb{C}$. We define a weighted degree of f by $\deg_{\mathbf{w}}(f) = \max\{|x^\alpha|_{\mathbf{w}} \mid x^\alpha \text{ is a term of } f\}$.

(ii) Let $f \in \mathbb{C}[x]$ be a polynomial. We define $\mathrm{ord}_{\mathbf{w}}(f) = \min\{|x^\alpha|_{\mathbf{w}} \mid x^\alpha \text{ is a term of } f\}$ ($\mathrm{ord}_{\mathbf{w}}(0) = -1$). The polynomial f is called semi-quasihomogeneous of type $(d; \mathbf{w})$ if f is of the form $f = f_0 + g$ where f_0 is a quasihomogeneous polynomial of type $(d; \mathbf{w})$ with an isolated singularity at the origin, $f = f_0$ or $\mathrm{ord}_{\mathbf{w}}(f - f_0) > d$.

DEFINITION 2 (A WEIGHTED TERM ORDER). For two multi-indices $\lambda = (\lambda_1, \lambda_2, \ldots, \lambda_n)$ and $\lambda' = (\lambda'_1, \lambda'_2, \ldots, \lambda'_n)$ in $\mathbb{N}^n$, we denote $\xi^{\lambda'} \prec \xi^\lambda$ or $\lambda' \prec \lambda$ if $|\xi^{\lambda'}|_{\mathbf{w}} < |\xi^\lambda|_{\mathbf{w}}$, or if $|\xi^{\lambda'}|_{\mathbf{w}} = |\xi^\lambda|_{\mathbf{w}}$ and there exists $j \in \mathbb{N}$ so that $\lambda'_i = \lambda_i$ for $i < j$ and $\lambda'_j < \lambda_j$, where $|\xi^\lambda|_{\mathbf{w}} = \sum_{i=1}^n w_i \lambda_i$.

DEFINITION 3 (INVERSE ORDERS). Let $\prec$ be a local or global term order. Then, the **inverse order** $\prec^{-1}$ of $\prec$ is defined by $x^\alpha \prec x^\beta \iff x^\beta \prec^{-1} x^\alpha$ where $\alpha, \beta \in \mathbb{N}^n$.

If $\prec$ is a global term order (1 is the minimal term), then $\prec^{-1}$ is the local term order (1 is the maximal term). Conversely, if $\prec$ is a local term order, then $\prec^{-1}$ is the global term order.

2.3 Strata and specialization

Let $t = (t_1, t_2, \ldots, t_m)$ denote parameters in $\mathbb{C}^m$. For $g_1, \ldots, g_q \in \mathbb{C}[t]$, $\mathbb{V}(g_1, \ldots, g_q) \subseteq \mathbb{C}^m$ denotes the affine variety of $g_1, \ldots, g_q$, i.e., $\mathbb{V}(g_1, \ldots, g_q) := \{\bar{a} \in \mathbb{C}^m \mid g_1(\bar{a}) = \cdots = g_q(\bar{a}) = 0\}$ and $\mathbb{V}(0) := \mathbb{C}^m$. We call an algebraically constructible set of a form $\mathbb{V}(g_1, \ldots, g_q) \setminus \mathbb{V}(g'_1, \ldots, g'_{q'}) \subseteq \mathbb{C}^m$ with $g_1, \ldots, g_q, g'_1, \ldots, g'_{q'} \in \mathbb{C}[t]$, a **stratum**. (Notation $\mathbb{A}, \mathbb{A}', \mathbb{A}'', \mathbb{A}_1, \ldots, \mathbb{A}_l, \mathbb{B}_1, \ldots, \mathbb{B}_k$ are frequently used to represent strata.)

We define the localization of $\mathbb{C}[t]$ w.r.t. a stratum $\mathbb{A} \subseteq \mathbb{C}^m$ as follows: $\mathbb{C}[t]_{\mathbb{A}} = \{\frac{c}{b} \mid c, b \in \mathbb{C}[t], b(t) \neq 0 \text{ for } t \in \mathbb{A}\}$. Then for every $\bar{a} \in \mathbb{A}$, the specialization homomorphism $\sigma_{\bar{a}} : \mathbb{C}[t]_{\mathbb{A}}[x] \to \mathbb{C}[x]$ (or $\sigma_{\bar{a}} : \mathbb{C}[t]_{\mathbb{A}}[\xi] \to \mathbb{C}[\xi]$) is defined as a map that substitutes $\bar{a}$ into m variables t. When we say that $\sigma_{\bar{a}}(h)$ makes sense for $h \in \mathbb{C}(t)[x]$, it has to be understood that $h \in \mathbb{C}[t]_{\mathbb{A}}[x]$ for some $\mathbb{A}$ with $\bar{a} \in \mathbb{A}$ and for $F \subset \mathbb{C}[t]_{\mathbb{A}}[x]$, $\sigma_{\bar{a}}(F) = \{\sigma_{\bar{a}}(h) | h \in F\}$.

3. PARAMETRIC LOCAL COHOMOLOGY SYSTEMS

Here, we illustrate an algorithm for computing a parametric local cohomology system of the vector space $H_{\Gamma(f)}$ associated with a polar variety $\Gamma(f)$ of a hypersurface S.

Let $f = f_0 + g$ be a semi-quasihomogeneous polynomial of type $(d; \mathbf{w})$ in $\mathbb{C}[x]$, where $\mathbf{w}$ is a weight vector. Let $\Gamma(f)$ be a polar variety [17, 36] of the hypersurface S defined to be

$$\Gamma(f) = \left\{x \in X \,\middle|\, \frac{\partial f}{\partial x_2}(x) = \frac{\partial f}{\partial x_3}(x) = \cdots = \frac{\partial f}{\partial x_n}(x) = 0\right\},$$

and set

$$H_{\Gamma(f)} = \left\{\psi \in \mathcal{H}^n_{\{O\}}(\mathcal{O}_X) \,\middle|\, f * \psi = \frac{\partial f}{\partial x_2} * \psi = \frac{\partial f}{\partial x_3} * \psi = \cdots \right.$$
$$\left. \cdots = \frac{\partial f}{\partial x_n} * \psi = 0\right\}.$$

Here, the system of coordinates $(x_1, x_2, \ldots, x_n)$ is assumed to be generic in a sence that the sequence $(f, \frac{\partial f}{\partial x_2}, \frac{\partial f}{\partial x_3}, \ldots, \frac{\partial f}{\partial x_n})$ is a regular sequence ([17, 18]). Note that $H_{\Gamma(f)}$ becomes a finite-dimensional subspace of $H^n_{[O]}(\mathcal{O}_X)$.

In the following definition, we recall a Poincaré polynomial for the ideal $\langle f, \frac{\partial f}{\partial x_2}, \frac{\partial f}{\partial x_3}, \ldots, \frac{\partial f}{\partial x_n}\rangle$ which plays an important role for computing a basis of $H_{\Gamma(f)}$.

DEFINITION 4 ([3]). Let $f = f_0 + g$ be a semi-quasihomogeneous polynomial of type $(d; \mathbf{w})$. Then, the **Poincaré polynomial** of the ideal $\langle f, \frac{\partial f}{\partial x_2}, \frac{\partial f}{\partial x_3}, \ldots, \frac{\partial f}{\partial x_n}\rangle$ is defined by

$$P_{\Gamma(f)}(s) = \frac{(s^d - 1)(s^{d-w_2} - 1)(s^{d-w_3} - 1)\cdots(s^{d-w_n} - 1)}{(s^{w_1} - 1)(s^{w_2} - 1)(s^{w_3} - 1)\cdots(s^{w_n} - 1)}.$$

Let $P_{\Gamma(f)}(s) = \sum_{i=1}^{p} m_i s^{d_i}$ be the Poincaré polynomial of the ideal $\langle f, \frac{\partial f}{\partial x_2}, \frac{\partial f}{\partial x_3}, \ldots, \frac{\partial f}{\partial x_n}\rangle$ for $f = f_0 + g$. We introduce the multiset $D_{P_{\Gamma(f)}}$ of weighted degrees as

$$D_{P_{\Gamma(f)}} = \bigcup_{i=1}^{p} \{\underbrace{d_i, d_i, \ldots, d_i}_{m_i \text{ elements}}\}.$$

The following two results are essentially same to our previous results presented in [21, 24].

PROPOSITION 5. Using the same notation as above, there exists a basis Ψ_0 of $H_{\Gamma(f_0)}$ that satisfies the following conditions

(i) Ψ_0 consists of quasihomogeneous polynomials.

(ii) $D_{P_{\Gamma(f)}} = \{\deg_{\mathbf{w}}(\psi) | \psi \in \Psi_0\}$.

The following theorem shows the relations between a basis of $H_{\Gamma(f_0)}$ and that of $H_{\Gamma(f)}$.

THEOREM 6. Let $\Psi_0 = \{\rho_1, \ldots, \rho_{r_0}\}$ be a basis of the vector space $H_{\Gamma(f_0)}$ that satisfies Proposition 5. Then, for each $i \in \{1, \ldots, r_0\}$, there exists ν_i such that $\deg_{\mathbf{w}}(\rho_i) > \deg_{\mathbf{w}}(\nu_i)$ and $\psi_i := \rho_i + \nu_i$ is an element of the vector space $H_{\Gamma(f)}$. That is, the set $\Psi = \{\psi_1, \ldots, \psi_{r_0}\}$ is a basis of the vector space $H_{\Gamma(f)}$ w.r.t. the weighted term order.

The theorem says that, in semi-quasihomogeneous case, the weighted degree of the basis of $H_{\Gamma(f)}$ is completely determined by the Poincaré polynomial $P_{\Gamma(f)}(s)$ associated with the ideal $\langle f, \frac{\partial f}{\partial x_2}, \ldots, \frac{\partial f}{\partial x_n}\rangle$.

In [21], by exploiting a notion of Poincaré polynomial, an efficient algorithm has been introduced for computing a basis of $H_{J(f)} = \{\psi \in \mathcal{H}^n_{\{O\}}(\mathcal{O}_X) \mid h * \psi = 0, h \in J(f)\}$, the space of local cohomology classes annihilated by the Jacobi ideal $J(f) = \langle \frac{\partial f}{\partial x_1}, \ldots, \frac{\partial f}{\partial x_n}\rangle$. The use of the Poincaré polynomial reduces the cost of computation considerably. We are able to adapt, by using the Poincaré polynomial $P_{\Gamma(f)}(s)$, the algorithm mentioned above to compute efficiently a basis of $H_{\Gamma(f)}$. Let us remark that the Poincaré polynomial $P_{\Gamma(f)}(s)$ (Definition 4) is different from the Poincaré polynomial of $J(f)$.

We turn to the parametric case. Let $f = f_0 + g$ be a semi-quasihomogeneous polynomial of type $(d; \mathbf{w})$ with **parameters** $t = (t_1, \ldots, t_m) \in \mathbb{C}^m$, where f_0 is the quasihomogeneous part. We assume that for generic values of the parameters t, f_0 has an isolated singularity at the origin.

As f has parameters, the structure of the vector spaces $H_{\Gamma(f)}$ depends on the values of parameters t. In order to deal with this issue, we introduce now a notion of parametric local cohomology system of $H_{\Gamma(f)}$.

DEFINITION 7. Let $\mathbb{A}_i$, $\mathbb{B}_j$ be strata in $\mathbb{C}^m$ and S_i a subset of $(\mathbb{C}[t]_{\mathbb{A}_i})[\xi]$ where $1 \leq i \leq l$ and $1 \leq j \leq k$. Set $\mathcal{S} = \{(\mathbb{A}_1, S_1), \ldots, (\mathbb{A}_l, S_l)\}$ and $\mathcal{D} = \{\mathbb{B}_1, \ldots, \mathbb{B}_k\}$. Then, a pair $(\mathcal{S}, \mathcal{D})$ is called a **parametric local cohomology system** of $H_{\Gamma(f)}$ on $\mathbb{A}_1 \cup \cdots \cup \mathbb{A}_l \cup \mathbb{B}_1 \cup \cdots \cup \mathbb{B}_k$, if for all $i \in \{1, \ldots, l\}$ and $\bar{a} \in \mathbb{A}_i$, $\sigma_{\bar{a}}(S_i)$ is a basis of the vector space $H_{\Gamma(\sigma_{\bar{a}}(f))}$, and for all $j \in \{1, \ldots, k\}$ and $\bar{b} \in \mathbb{B}_j$, $\{x \in X | \sigma_{\bar{b}}(f)(x) = \sigma_{\bar{b}}(\frac{\partial f}{\partial x_2})(x) = \cdots = \sigma_{\bar{b}}(\frac{\partial f}{\partial x_n})(x) = 0\}$ is not zero-dimensional for any sufficiently small neighborhood X of O, where $H_{\Gamma(\sigma_{\bar{a}}(f))} = \{\psi \in \mathcal{H}^n_{\{O\}}(\mathcal{O}_X) | \sigma_{\bar{a}}(f) * \psi = \sigma_{\bar{a}}(\frac{\partial f}{\partial x_2}) * \psi = \cdots = \sigma_{\bar{a}}(\frac{\partial f}{\partial x_n}) * \psi = 0\}$.

As in the non-parametric case, an algorithm for computing parametric local cohomology system of $H_{\Gamma(f)}$ can be devised by adapting the method presented in [21]. The resulting algorithm has been already implemented in the computer algebra system `Risa/Asir`. We refer the reader to [21] for the detail of the algorithm.

We illustrate a parametric local cohomology system of $H_{\Gamma(f)}$ with the following examples. In the examples, variables ξ_1, ξ_2 are corresponding to variables x_1, x_2.

EXAMPLE 8. A polynomial $f = x_1^4 + x_2^5 + t x_1 x_2^4 \in (\mathbb{C}[t])[x_1, x_2]$ is semi-quasihomogeneous of type $(20; (5, 4))$ where x_1, x_2 are variables and t is a parameter. (A weight vector is $\mathbf{w} = (5, 4)$.) Then, a parametric local cohomology system of $H_{\Gamma(f)} = \{\psi \in \mathcal{H}^2_{\{O\}}(\mathcal{O}_X) | f * \psi = \frac{\partial f}{\partial x_2} * \psi = 0\}$ w.r.t. the weighted term order, is the following;
if the parameter t belongs to $\mathbb{C}$, then the set

$\Psi = \{1, \xi_2, \xi_2^2, \xi_2^3, \xi_2, \xi_1\xi_2, \xi_1\xi_2^2, \xi_1^2, \xi_1^2\xi_2, \xi_1^2\xi_2^2, \xi_1^3, \xi_1^3\xi_2, \xi_1^3\xi_2, \frac{4}{25}t^2\xi_1^5 - \frac{16}{125}t^3\xi_2\xi_1^4 + \xi_2^3\xi_1^3 - \frac{4}{5}t\xi_2^4\xi_1^2 + \frac{16}{25}t^2\xi_2^5\xi_1 - \frac{64}{125}t^3\xi_2^6, \frac{4}{25}t^2\xi_1^4 + \xi_2^3\xi_1^2 - \frac{4}{5}t\xi_2^4\xi_1 + \frac{16}{25}t^2\xi_2^5, \xi_2^3\xi_1 - \frac{4}{5}t\xi_2^4\}$

is a basis of $H_{\Gamma(f)}$. In this case, the parameter space $\mathbb{C}$ has not been decomposed.

EXAMPLE 9. A polynomial $f = x_1^3 + x_2^9 + t x_1^2 x_2^3 \in (\mathbb{C}[t])[x_1, x_2]$ is quasihomogeneous of type $(9; (3, 1))$ where x_1, x_2 are variables and t is a parameter. (A weight vector is $\mathbf{w} = (3, 1)$.) Then, a parametric local cohomology system of $H_{\Gamma(f)} = \{\psi \in \mathcal{H}^2_{\{O\}}(\mathcal{O}_X) | f * \psi = \frac{\partial f}{\partial x_2} * \psi = 0\}$ w.r.t. the weighted term order, is the following;

- if parameter t belongs to $\mathbb{V}(4t^3 + 27)$, then f has non-isolated singularity,
- if parameter t belongs to $\mathbb{V}(t)$, then $\{1, \xi_2, \xi_2^2, \xi_2^3, \xi_2^4, \xi_2^5, \xi_2^6, \xi_2^7, \xi_1, \xi_1\xi_2, \xi_1\xi_2^2, \xi_1\xi_2^3, \xi_1\xi_2^4, \xi_1\xi_2^5, \xi_1\xi_2^6, \xi_1\xi_2^7, \xi_1^2, \xi_1^2\xi_2, \xi_1^2\xi_2^2, \xi_1^2\xi_2^3, \xi_1^2\xi_2^4, \xi_1^2\xi_2^5, \xi_1^2\xi_2^6, \xi_1^2\xi_2^7\}$ is a basis of $H_{\Gamma(f)}$, and
- if parameter t belongs to $\mathbb{C} \setminus \mathbb{V}(4t^4 + 27t)$, then $\{1, \xi_2, \xi_2^2, \xi_2^3, \xi_2^4, \xi_2^5, \xi_2^6, \xi_2^7, \xi_1, \xi_1\xi_2, \xi_1\xi_2^2, \xi_1\xi_2^3, \xi_1\xi_2^4, \xi_1\xi_2^5, \xi_1\xi_2^6, \xi_1\xi_2^7, \xi_1^2, \xi_1^2\xi_2, \xi_2\xi_1^4 - \frac{3}{2t}\xi_2^4\xi_1^3 + \frac{9}{4t^2}\xi_2^7\xi_1^2 + \frac{1}{2}\xi_2^{10}\xi_1 - \frac{3}{4t}\xi_2^{13}, \xi_1^4 - \frac{3}{2t}\xi_2^3\xi_1^3 + \frac{9}{4t^2}\xi_2^6\xi_1^2 + \frac{1}{2}\xi_2^9\xi_1 - \frac{3}{4t}\xi_2^12, \xi_2^2\xi_1^3 - \frac{3}{2t}\xi_2^5\xi_1^2 - \frac{t}{3}\xi_2^8\xi_1 + \frac{1}{2}\xi_2^{11}, \xi_2\xi_1^3 - \frac{3}{2t}\xi_2^4\xi_1^2 + \frac{1}{2}\xi_2^{10}, \xi_1^3 - \frac{3}{2t}\xi_2^3\xi_1^2 + \frac{1}{2}\xi_2^9, \xi_2^2\xi_1^2 - \frac{1}{3}t\xi_2^8\}$ is a basis of $H_{\Gamma(f)}$.

4. LOGARITHMIC VECTOR FIELDS AND LOCAL COHOMOLOGY

Here, first, we show the relations between logarithmic vector fields and local cohomology classes. Second, we describe a method to compute a parametric standard basis of the annihilator ideal of a certain subspace of $H_{\Gamma(f)}$, which will be exploited to construct an algorithm for computing logarithmic vector fields.

4.1 Logarithmic vector fields

DEFINITION 10 ([28]). A holomorphic vector field

$$v = a_1(x)\frac{\partial}{\partial x_1} + a_2(x)\frac{\partial}{\partial x_2} + \cdots + a_n(x)\frac{\partial}{\partial x_n},$$

$a_i(x) \in \mathcal{O}_X, i = 1, \ldots, n$, is **logarithmic** along S if $v(f)$ belongs to the ideal $\langle f \rangle$ generated by f in $\mathcal{O}_X$.

Let $\mathcal{D}er_X(-\log S)$ denote the sheaf of logarithmic vector fields along S.

Let $\pi_\Gamma : H_{\Gamma(f)} \to H_{\Gamma(f)}$ be the map defined by $\pi_\Gamma(\psi) = \frac{\partial f}{\partial x_1} * \psi$ and let $H_{\Phi(f)}$ denote the image of the map π_Γ:

$$H_{\Phi(f)} = \left\{ \frac{\partial f}{\partial x_1} * \psi \middle| \psi \in H_{\Gamma(f)} \right\}.$$

Let $\mathrm{Ann}_{\mathcal{O}_{X,O}}(H_{\Gamma(f)})$ denote the annihilator ideal in $\mathcal{O}_{X,O}$ of $H_{\Gamma(f)}$:

$$\mathrm{Ann}_{\mathcal{O}_{X,O}}(H_{\Gamma(f)}) = \{a(x) \in \mathcal{O}_{X,O} \mid a(x)*\psi = 0, \forall \psi \in H_{\Gamma(f)}\}.$$

The following theorem is of basic importance.

THEOREM 11 ([31]). Let $a(x) \in \mathcal{O}_{X,O}$. Then, the following conditions are equivalent.

(i) $a(x) \in \mathrm{Ann}_{\mathcal{O}_{X,O}}(H_{\Phi(f)})$.

(ii) There exists a logarithmic vector field v along S ($v \in \mathcal{D}er_{X,O}(-\log S)$) such that

$$v = a(x)\frac{\partial}{\partial x_1} + a_2(x)\frac{\partial}{\partial x_2} + \cdots + a_n(x)\frac{\partial}{\partial x_n}$$

where $a_2(x), \ldots, a_n(x) \in \mathcal{O}_{X,O}$.

PROOF. It is sufficient to show that the annihilator ideal, in the local ring $\mathcal{O}_{X,O}$, of $H_{\Phi(f)}$ is the ideal quotient $\langle f, \frac{\partial f}{\partial x_2}, \ldots, \frac{\partial f}{\partial x_n}\rangle : \langle \frac{\partial f}{\partial x_1}\rangle$. Let $a(x) \in \mathcal{O}_{X,O}$. Then, $a(x)$ is in the annihilator ideal $\mathrm{Ann}_{\mathcal{O}_{X,O}}(H_{\Phi(f)})$ if and only if

$$a(x) * \left(\frac{\partial f}{\partial x_1} * \psi\right) = \left(a(x)\frac{\partial f}{\partial x_1}\right) * \psi = 0, \ \forall \psi \in H_{\Gamma(f)}.$$

The Grothendieck local duality theorem on residue ([9]) implies that $\mathrm{Ann}_{\mathcal{O}_{X,O}}(H_{\Gamma(f)}) = \langle f, \frac{\partial f}{\partial x_2}, \frac{\partial f}{\partial x_3}, \ldots, \frac{\partial f}{\partial x_n}\rangle$. Therefore the condition above is equivalent to the following.

$$a(x) \in \left\langle f, \frac{\partial f}{\partial x_2}, \frac{\partial f}{\partial x_3}, \ldots, \frac{\partial f}{\partial x_n} \right\rangle : \left\langle \frac{\partial f}{\partial x_1} \right\rangle.$$

Namely $\mathrm{Ann}_{\mathcal{O}_{X,O}}(H_{\Phi(f)}) = \langle f, \frac{\partial f}{\partial x_2}, \frac{\partial f}{\partial x_3}, \ldots, \frac{\partial f}{\partial x_n}\rangle : \langle \frac{\partial f}{\partial x_1}\rangle$, which completes the proof. □

A logarithmic vector field v generated over $\mathcal{O}_{X,O}$ by $f\frac{\partial}{\partial x_1}, \ldots, f\frac{\partial}{\partial x_n}$ and $\frac{\partial f}{\partial x_j}\frac{\partial}{\partial x_i} - \frac{\partial f}{\partial x_i}\frac{\partial}{\partial x_j}$, $(1 \le i < j \le n)$, is called trivial. Note that M. Kersken showed that, for isolated and quasihomogeneous cases, $\mathcal{D}er_{X,O}(-\log S)$ is generated as an $\mathcal{O}_{X,O}$ module by the Euler vector field and trivial logarithmic vector fields [15].

Since $(f, \frac{\partial f}{\partial x_2}, \frac{\partial f}{\partial x_3}, \ldots, \frac{\partial f}{\partial x_n})$ is a regular sequence, we have the following.

LEMMA 12. Let $v' = a_2(x)\frac{\partial}{\partial x_2} + \cdots + a_n(x)\frac{\partial}{\partial x_n}$ be a germ of holomorphic vector field. If v' is a logarithmic vector field along S, then v' is trivial.

This yields the following.

PROPOSITION 13. Let $v = a(x)\frac{\partial}{\partial x_1} + a_2(x)\frac{\partial}{\partial x_2} + \cdots + a_n(x)\frac{\partial}{\partial x_n}$ be a logarithmic vector field along S. Then, the following conditions are equivalent.

(i) v is trivial.

(ii) $a(x) \in \langle f, \frac{\partial f}{\partial x_2}, \frac{\partial f}{\partial x_3}, \ldots, \frac{\partial f}{\partial x_n}\rangle$.

In the next subsection, we consider an algorithm for computing a standard basis of the ideal $\mathrm{Ann}_{\mathcal{O}_{X,O}}(H_{\Phi(f)})$ which is utilized to reveal the structure of logarithmic vector fields along S.

4.2 Local cohomology and standard bases

In [21], a method, that utilizes parametric local cohomology system, is described for computing standard bases of Jacobi ideals with parameters w.r.t. a local term order. We extend the method and derive an algorithm of computing standard bases of the annihilator ideal $\mathrm{Ann}_{\mathcal{O}_{X,O}}(H_{\Phi(f)})$.

In order to treat standard bases with parameters, we introduce now a notion of parametric standard basis.

DEFINITION 14. Let F be a subset of $(\mathbb{C}[t])[x]$, $\mathbb{A}_1, \ldots, \mathbb{A}_l$ strata in $\mathbb{C}^m$, $S_1, \ldots, S_l$ subsets of $\mathbb{C}(t)\{x\}$ and $\prec$ a local term order. A finite set $\mathcal{S} = \{(\mathbb{A}_1, S_1), \ldots, (\mathbb{A}_l, S_l)\}$ of pairs is called a **parametric standard basis** on $\mathbb{A}_1 \cup \cdots \cup \mathbb{A}_l$ of $\langle F\rangle$ w.r.t. $\prec$ if $S_i \subset (\mathbb{C}[t]_{\mathbb{A}_i})[x]$ and $\sigma_{\bar{a}}(S_i)$ is a standard basis of the ideal $\langle \sigma_{\bar{a}}(F)\rangle$ in $\mathbb{C}\{x\}$ w.r.t. $\prec$ for each $i = 1, \ldots, l$ and $\bar{a} \in \mathbb{A}_i$ where $\mathbb{C}(t)$ is the field of rational functions and $\mathbb{C}\{x\}$ is the ring of power series.

Let f be a semi-quasihomogeneous polynomial of type $(d; \mathbf{w})$ with parameters t. Assume that the parametric local cohomology system $(\mathcal{S}, \mathcal{D})$ of $H_{\Gamma(f)}$ is given by the algorithm described in section 3. For each $(\mathbb{A}, \Psi) \in \mathcal{S}$, where $\mathbb{A}$ is a stratum in $\mathbb{C}^m$ and Ψ is a basis on $\mathbb{A}$ of $H_{\Gamma(f)}$, we consider a set Φ of local cohomology classes with parameters defined by $\Phi = \{\frac{\partial f}{\partial x_1} * \psi \mid \psi \in \Psi\}$. Since Φ is a set of generators of the vector space $H_{\Phi(f)}$, all the information on the structure of the space $H_{\Phi(f)}$ in question is encoded in the set Φ.

In order to handle parametric cases, we have extended the Gaussian elimination method with parameters ([30]) and implemented an algorithm for computing local cohomology bases with parameters. Notably the algorithm also performs simultaneously a decomposition of a given stratum into finer strata according to the structure of resulting vector spaces.

By executing the extended Gaussian elimination algorithm, we can compute the local cohomology system $\mathcal{S}'$ of $H_{\Phi(f)}$ from the set Φ on each stratum $\mathbb{A}$. In fact, in our implementation, the algorithm computes a basis Φ' of the vector space $H_{\Phi(f)}$ on a (finer) stratum $\mathbb{A}'$ where $(\mathbb{A}', \Phi') \in \mathcal{S}'$, that satisfies the following conditions :

(1) the set Φ' is a maximal linearly independent subset of $H_{\Phi(f)}$ on $\mathbb{A}'$, and

(2) the coefficient matrix of Φ', w.r.t. the vector ${}^t(\xi^{\alpha_1}, \ldots, \xi^{\alpha_u})$, is the row reduced echelon matrix on $\mathbb{A}'$ where $\mathrm{Term}(\Phi') = \{\xi^{\alpha_1}, \ldots, \xi^{\alpha_u}\}$, $\xi^{\alpha_u} \prec \cdots \prec \xi^{\alpha_1}$ and ${}^t(\xi^{\alpha_1}, ..., \xi^{\alpha_u})$ is the transposed matrix of $(\xi_1^{\alpha}, ..., \xi^{\alpha_u})$.

As a parametric local cohomology system of $H_{\Phi(f)}$ is computable, by the algorithm of our recent results [21, 23], one can obtain a reduced standard basis of the annihilator ideal $\mathrm{Ann}_{\mathcal{O}_{X,O}}(H_{\Phi(f)})$ w.r.t. the inverse order of $\prec$ on $\mathbb{A}'$. Notably, it is possible to compute a standard basis of the annihilator ideal w.r.t. "*any given local term order*" from a set Φ of local cohomology classes. The details are in [21, 22, 23].

We sketch the algorithm for computing a parametric standard basis of $\mathrm{Ann}_{\mathcal{O}_{X,O}}(H_{\Phi(f)})$ in Algorithm 1.

The correctness and termination of Algorithm 1 follow from [21]. We have implemented the algorithm for computing parametric standard bases of $\mathrm{Ann}_{\mathcal{O}_{X,O}}(H_{\Phi(f)})$, in the computer algebra system `Risa/Asir`.

We illustrate parametric standard bases of $\mathrm{Ann}_{\mathcal{O}_{X,O}}(H_{\Phi(f)})$ with Example 15.

Algorithm 1. Parametric standard bases

Input: f : a semi-quasihomogeneous polynomial of type $(d; \mathbf{w})$ with parameters t. $\prec$: a local term order.
Output: $(\mathcal{P}, \mathcal{D})$:

$\mathcal{P} = \{(\mathbb{A}_1, P_1), \dots, (\mathbb{A}_l, P_l)\}$ is a parametric standard basis on $\mathbb{A}_1 \cup \cdots \cup \mathbb{A}_l$, for $\mathrm{Ann}_{\mathcal{O}_{X,O}}(H_{\Phi(f)})$ w.r.t. $\prec$. For all $\bar{a} \in \mathbb{A}_i$, $\sigma_{\bar{a}}(P_i)$ is the **reduced standard basis** of $\mathrm{Ann}_{\mathcal{O}_{X,O}}(H_{\Phi(f)})$ w.r.t. $\prec$, $1 \le i \le l$.

$\mathcal{D} = \{\mathbb{B}_1, \dots, \mathbb{B}_k\}$ is a set of strata s.t. the quasihomogeneous part of f does not define an isolated singularity at the origin on $\mathbb{B}_i$ for $1 \le i \le k$.

BEGIN
$(\mathcal{S}, \mathcal{D}) \leftarrow$ Compute a parametric local cohomology system of $H_{\Gamma(f)}$;
$\mathcal{S}' \leftarrow \{(\mathbb{A}, \Phi) \mid \Phi = \{\frac{\partial f}{\partial x_1} * \psi \neq 0 \mid \psi \in \Psi\}, (\mathbb{A}, \Psi) \in \mathcal{S}\}$;
$\mathcal{P} \leftarrow \emptyset$;
while $\mathcal{S}' \neq \emptyset$ **do**
Select $(\mathbb{A}', \Phi')$ from $\mathcal{S}'$; $\mathcal{S}' \leftarrow \mathcal{S}' \setminus \{(\mathbb{A}', \Phi')\}$;
$v \leftarrow {}^t(\xi^{\alpha_1}, \dots, \xi^{\alpha_u})$ where $\mathrm{Term}(\Phi') = \{\xi^{\alpha_1}, \dots, \xi^{\alpha_u}\}$, $\xi^{\alpha_u} \prec \cdots \prec \xi^{\alpha_1}$;
$\mathcal{H} \leftarrow$ Compute a maximal linearly independent subset of Φ whose coefficient matrix is the row reduced echelon matrix w.r.t. v on $\mathbb{A}$;
while $\mathcal{H} \neq \emptyset$ **do**
Select $(\mathbb{A}'', \Phi'')$ from $\mathcal{H}$; $\mathcal{H} \leftarrow \mathcal{H} \setminus \{(\mathbb{A}'', \Phi'')\}$;
$(\mathbb{A}'', P) \leftarrow$Compute the reduced standard basis P of the ideal $\mathrm{Ann}_{\mathcal{O}_{X,O}}(H_{\Phi(f)})$ on $\mathbb{A}''$ by Φ'' and Theorem 15 of [21];
$\mathcal{P} \leftarrow \mathcal{P} \cup \{(\mathbb{A}'', P)\}$;
end-while
end-while
return$(\mathcal{P}, \mathcal{D})$;
END

EXAMPLE 15. Let us consider Example 8, again. As we have a basis Ψ of the vector space $H_{\Gamma(f)}$, the set $\Phi = \{\frac{\partial f}{\partial x_1} * \psi | \psi \in \Psi\}$ is $\{-\frac{4}{5}t^2, -\frac{4}{25}t^2\xi_1 + \frac{16}{25}t^3\xi_2, -\frac{4}{25}t^2\xi_1^2 + \frac{16}{125}t^3\xi_1\xi_2 + 4\xi_2^3 - \frac{64}{125}t^4\xi_2^2, 4, 4\xi_2, 4\xi_2^2\}$. Hence, we can obtain a parametric local cohomolgy system of $H_{\Phi(f)}$ from the set Φ. The maximal linearly independent subset of $H_{\Phi(f)}$ whose coefficient matrix is a row reduced echelon matrix w.r.t. the total degree lexicographic term order $\prec$ s.t. $\xi_2 \prec \xi_1$, is the following;

- if parameter t belongs to $\mathbb{V}(t)$, then $\{\xi_2^3, \xi_2^2, \xi_2, 1\}$ is a basis of $H_{\Phi(f)}$,

and

- if parameter t belongs to $\mathbb{C} \setminus \mathbb{V}(t)$, then $\{\xi_2^3 - \frac{1}{25}t^2\xi_1^2 + \frac{4}{125}t^3\xi_1\xi_2, \xi_2^2, \xi_2, \xi_1, 1\}$ is a basis of $H_{\Phi(f)}$.

By Algorithm 1, the reduced standard basis of the annihilator ideal $\mathrm{Ann}_{\mathcal{O}_{X,O}}(H_{\Phi(f)})$ w.r.t. $\prec^{-1}$ is easily obtained from a parametric local cohomolgy system of $H_{\Phi(f)}$, that is as follows;

- if parameter t belongs to $\mathbb{V}(t)$, then $\{x_1, x_2^4\}$ is the reduced standard basis,

and

- if parameter t belongs to $\mathbb{C} \setminus \mathbb{V}(t)$, then $\{x_1^2 + \frac{1}{25}t^2x_2^3, x_1x_2 - \frac{4}{125}t^3x_2^3, x_2^4\}$ is the reduced basis.

5. A COMPUTATIONAL METHOD

This is the main section of this paper. Here we present a new algorithm for computing logarithmic vector fields along S.

In order to explain the main ideas of the algorithm, let us consider first, for simplicity, the case where f does not contain parameters. Assume that the reduced standard basis $\{q_1, q_2, \dots, q_r\}$ of the annihilating ideal $\mathrm{Ann}_{\mathcal{O}_{X,O}}(H_{\Phi(f)})$ w.r.t. a local term order $\prec$ and a standard basis M_j of the module of syzygies with respect to the generators $q_j\frac{\partial f}{\partial x_1}, \frac{\partial f}{\partial x_2}, \dots, \frac{\partial f}{\partial x_n}, f$ in $\mathcal{O}_X$ for each $j = 1, 2, \dots, r$, are given. Note that, the module order is POT ("top down" order, see [6]) with $\prec$. Then, we have the following theorem.

THEOREM 16. Under the setup above, there exists a vector $(c_{j_1}, c_{j_2}, \dots, c_{j_n}, c_{j_{n+1}}) \in M_j$ such that c_{j_1} contains a term of degree 0, i.e., a non-zero constant term is in c_{j_1}. A holomorphic vector field

$$v_j = q_j \frac{\partial}{\partial x_1} + \frac{c_{j_2}}{c_{j_1}} \frac{\partial}{\partial x_2} + \cdots + \frac{c_{j_n}}{c_{j_1}} \frac{\partial}{\partial x_n}$$

is logarithmic along S, for each $j \in \{1, \dots, r\}$. Moreover, $v_1, v_2, .., v_r$ and trivial vector fields generate $\mathcal{D}er_{X,O}(-\log S)$.

PROOF. As the coefficients of $\frac{\partial}{\partial x_1}$ are generated by the reduced standard basis $\{q_1, \dots, q_r\}$ (by Theorem 11) w.r.t. $\prec$, there exists a $(c_{j_1}, c_{j_2}, \dots, c_{j_n}, c_{j_{n+1}}) \in M_j$ that satisfies the property because M_j is a standard basis w.r.t. POT with $\prec$. Since $(c_{j_1}, c_{j_2}, \dots, c_{j_n}, c_{j_{n+1}})$ is a syzygy,

$$c_{j_1} q_j \frac{\partial f}{\partial x_1} + c_{j_2} \frac{\partial f}{\partial x_2} + \cdots + c_{j_n} \frac{\partial f}{\partial x_n} = -c_{j_{n+1}} f.$$

Hence, $v_j(f) \in \langle f \rangle$ holds. Therefore, by Proposition 13, $v_1, v_2, \dots, v_r$ and trivial vector fields generate $\mathcal{D}er_{X,O}(-\log S)$ over $\mathcal{O}_{X,O}$. $\square$

Remark: If we construct logarithmic vector fields directly by computing standard basis of the module of syzygies with respect to the generators $\frac{\partial f}{\partial x_1}, \frac{\partial f}{\partial x_2}, .., \frac{\partial f}{\partial x_n}, f$ in $\mathcal{O}_{X,O}$, then the output of the computation are, in general, not suitable to know the local analytic properties of logarithmic vector fields. In contrast, the proposed method that utilize the standard basis $\{q_1, q_2, .., q_r\}$ gives a nice set of generators of $\mathcal{D}er_{X,O}(-\log S)$ for analyzing complex analytic properties, near the singular point in question, of logarithmic vector fields.

In the non-parametric case, it is possible to compute a standard basis of a module of syzygies w.r.t. a given local term order in $\mathcal{O}_{X,O}$. In fact, the computer algebra system SINGULAR [7] has a command of computing them.

Now we turn to the parametric case. It is easy to see that Theorem 16 can be generalized to the parametric case. The outline of the algorithm for computing logarithmic vector fields is therefore the following.

Step 1. Compute a parametric standard basis of the annihilator ideal $\mathrm{Ann}_{\mathcal{O}_{X,O}}(H_{\Phi(f)})$ by Algorithm 1.

Step 2. Compute a basis of the module of parametric syzygies of $(q_j\frac{\partial f}{\partial x_1}, \frac{\partial f}{\partial x_2}, \dots, \frac{\partial f}{\partial x_n}, f)$ where q_j is an element of the standard basis of $\mathrm{Ann}_{\mathcal{O}_{X,O}}(H_{\Phi(f)})$.

Step 3. Select an element $(c_1, c_2, \dots, c_n, c_{n+1})$ from a set of parametric syzygies, whose first component has a non-zero constant term.

Step 4. Set $v_j = q_j \frac{\partial}{\partial x_1} + \frac{c_2}{c_1}\frac{\partial}{\partial x_2} + \cdots + \frac{c_n}{c_1}\frac{\partial}{\partial x_n}$.

In step 2, it is necessary to compute syzygies of "*parametric polynomials*" $q_j \frac{\partial f}{\partial x_1}, \frac{\partial f}{\partial x_2}, \dots, \frac{\partial f}{\partial x_n}, f$ in the rings of power series. However, to the best of our knowledge, there is currently no implementation of such syzygy computation. Thus, we provide a new alternative efficient algorithm for computing the syzygies of parametric polynomials in the rings of power series.

In [19], an efficient algorithm for computing parametric syzygies in a "polynomial ring", has been introduced. One can generalize the algorithm to a local ring by using Lazard's homogenization technique [16]. The complete algorithm of parametric syzygies is in Appendix[1].

Note that as we apply Lazard's homogenization technique, we obtain a standard basis of the module of syzygies w.r.t. a local "*total degree*" term order $\prec$. Thus, we have to compute, beforehand in Step 1, a parametric standard basis of $\mathrm{Ann}_{\mathcal{O}_{X,O}}(H_{\Phi(f)})$ w.r.t. the same term order $\prec$. If there exists an efficient algorithm for computing a parametric syzygy w.r.t. any given local term order, we will be free from this restriction on term orders.

The complete algorithm for computing logarithmic vector fields along S with parameters, is Algorithm 2.

The correctness clearly follows from Algorithm 1 and Theorem 16. As we use the Lazard's homogenization technique, it follows from [19] and Algorithm 1 that the algorithm for computing a parametric syzygy basis, at $(*)$, terminates (See Appendix). Since the set $\mathcal{P}$ and $\mathcal{M}$ have only finite number of pairs, the algorithm terminates.

We illustrate the algorithm with the following examples.

EXAMPLE 17. A polynomial $f = x_1^2 + x_2^5 + x_1 x_2^3 \in \mathbb{C}[x_1, x_2]$ is semi-quasihomogeneous of type $(10; (5, 2))$ and $\prec$ is a total degree lexicographic order s.t. $x_2 \prec x_1$. By the algorithm 1, the reduced standard basis of $\mathrm{Ann}_{\mathcal{O}_{X,O}}(H_{\Phi(f)})$ w.r.t. $\prec^{-1}$ is $\{x_2^4, x_1 - \frac{1}{10}x_2^3\}$. We compute a syzygy basis of $(x_2^4 \frac{\partial f}{\partial x_1}, \frac{\partial f}{\partial x_2}, f)$. Then we get as a syzygy basis the following: $\{(6x_2 - 25, (-3x_2+10)x_1 - 3x_2^4 + 11x_2^3, 9x_2^3 - 30x_2^2), (-18x_1 - 125x_2, 9x_1^2 + (9x_2^3 - 3x_2^2 + 50x_2)x_1 + 55x_2^4, -27x_2^2 x_1 - 150x_2^3), (3x_1 + 5x_2^2, -2x_2^2 x_1 - x_2^5, 0)\}$.
We take $(6x_2 - 25, (-3x_2+10)x_1 - 3x_2^4 + 11x_2^3, 9x_2^3 - 30x_2^2)$ (because the first component has a non-zero constant term) and set

$$v_1 = x_2^4 \frac{\partial}{\partial x_1} + \frac{(3x_2 - 10)x_1 + 3x_2^4 - 11x_2^3}{25 - 6x_2}\frac{\partial}{\partial x_2}.$$

[1]It is possible to extend a normal algorithm for computing syzygies, to parametric cases like Weispfenning comprehensive Gröbner bases' algorithm [38] (discussing whether a leading coefficient is zero or nonzero). However, if we adopt this approach, a number of strata becomes big and the computational complexity becomes also big. Nowadays, the major way to compute parametric Gröbner bases is using the theory of stability of ideals [13, 14, 20] which outputs a small numbers of strata and is more efficient than the classical Weispfenning's one. We apply the efficient method for computing parametric syzygies by using Lazard's technique in a local ring. In the appendix of the paper, we introduce the algorithm for computing syzygies in a "local ring".

Algorithm 2. Logarithmic vector fields

Input: f: a semi-quasihomogeneous polynomial of type $(d; \mathbf{w})$ with parameters t. $\prec$: a local term order.
Output: $(\mathcal{V}, \mathcal{D})$:
$\mathcal{V} = \{(\mathbb{A}_1, V_1), \dots, (\mathbb{A}_l, V_l)\}$, V_i is a set of logarithmic vector fields along S on $\mathbb{A}_i$ for each $i \in \{1, \dots, l\}$.
$\mathcal{D} = \{\mathbb{B}_1, \dots, \mathbb{B}_k\}$ is a set of strata s.t. the quasihomogeneous part of f does not define an isolated singularity at the origin on $\mathbb{B}_i$ for $1 \le i \le k$.
BEGIN
$(\mathcal{P}, \mathcal{D}) \leftarrow$Compute a parametric standard basis of the ideal $\mathrm{Ann}_{\mathcal{O}_{X,O}}(H_{\Phi(f)})$ w.r.t. $\prec$ by Algorithm 1;
$\mathcal{V} \leftarrow \{(\mathbb{C}^m, \emptyset)\}$;
while $\mathcal{P} \neq \emptyset$ **do**
  Select $(\mathbb{A}, \{q_1, \dots, q_r\})$ from $\mathcal{P}$; $\mathcal{P} \leftarrow \mathcal{P} \backslash \{(\mathbb{A}, \{q_1, \dots, q_r\})\}$;
  `/*`$\{q_1, \dots, q_r\}$ `is the reduced standard basis*/`
  for each j from 1 to r **do**
    $\mathcal{M} \leftarrow$ Compute a basis of the module of syzygies of $(q_j \frac{\partial f}{\partial x_1}, \frac{\partial f}{\partial x_2}, \dots, \frac{\partial f}{\partial x_n}, f)$ with $\prec$ in $\mathcal{O}_X$ on $\mathbb{A}$; $(*1)$
    $\mathcal{S} \leftarrow \emptyset$;
    while $\mathcal{M} \neq \emptyset$ **do**
      Select $(\mathbb{A}', M)$ from $\mathcal{M}$; $\mathcal{M} \leftarrow \mathcal{M} \backslash \{(\mathbb{A}', M)\}$;
$(c_1, .., c_{n+1}) \leftarrow$ Select an element from M whose first component has a non-zero constant term;
      $v \leftarrow q_j \frac{\partial}{\partial x_1} + \frac{c_2}{c_1}\frac{\partial}{\partial x_2} + \cdots + \frac{c_n}{c_1}\frac{\partial}{\partial x_n}$;
      while $\mathcal{V} \neq \emptyset$ **do**
        Select $(\mathbb{A}'', V)$ from $\mathcal{V}$; $\mathcal{V} \leftarrow \mathcal{V} \backslash \{(\mathbb{A}'', V)\}$;
        if $\mathbb{A}' \cap \mathbb{A}'' \neq \emptyset$ **then**
        $\mathcal{S} \leftarrow \mathcal{S} \cup \{(\mathbb{A}' \cap \mathbb{A}'', V \cup \{v\})\}$;
        end-if
      end-while
    end-while
    $\mathcal{V} \leftarrow \mathcal{S}$;
  end-for
end-while
return $(\mathcal{V}, \mathcal{D})$;
END

As $\frac{1}{25 - 6x_2} = \sum_{i=0}^{\infty} \left(\frac{6^i}{25^{i+1}}\right) x_2^i$, v_1 is a holomorphic vector field

$$x_2^4 \frac{\partial f}{\partial x_1} + ((3x_2 - 10)x_1 + 3x_2^4 - 11x_2^3) \sum_{i=0}^{\infty} \left(\frac{6^i}{25^{i+1}}\right) x_2^i \frac{\partial}{\partial x_2}.$$

Likewise, we take the following vector from a syzygy basis of $((x_1 - \frac{1}{10})x_2^3 \frac{\partial f}{\partial x_1}, \frac{\partial f}{\partial x_2}, f)$;
$(60x_2 - 250, 3x_1 + 3x_2^3 + 19x_2^2 - 100x_2, -9x_2^2 - 120x_2 + 500)$.
Hence, we have the following as a non-trivial logarithmic vector field

$$v_2 = \left(x_1 - \frac{1}{10}x_2^3\right)\frac{\partial}{\partial x_1} + \frac{-3x_1 - 3x_2^3 + 19x_2^2 + 100x_2}{10(25 - 6x_2)}\frac{\partial}{\partial x_2}$$
$$= \left(x_1 - \frac{1}{10}x_2^3\right)\frac{\partial}{\partial x_1}$$
$$+(-3x_1 - 3x_2^3 - 19x_2^2 + 100x_2)\left(\frac{1}{10}\sum_{i=0}^{\infty}\left(\frac{6^i}{25^{i+1}}\right)x_2^i\right)\frac{\partial}{\partial x_2}.$$

Thus, v_1, v_2 and trivial vector fields generate the sheaf of logarithmic vector fields along S.

Note that since every plane curve is a Saito free divisor ([28]), the sheaf of logarithmic vector fields can be generated by two vector fields for plane curve cases.

The next example handles a parametric case.

EXAMPLE 18. Let us consider Example 8 and Example 15, again. From Example 15, we know a parametric standard basis of the annihilator ideal $\mathrm{Ann}_{\mathcal{O}_{X,O}}(H_{\Phi(f)})$ w.r.t. $\prec^{-1}$ where $\prec$ is the local total degree lexicographic term order s.t. $x_2 \prec x_1$.

- If parameter t belongs to $\mathbb{V}(t)$, then $\{x_1, x_2^4\}$ is the reduced standard basis. Compute a parametric syzygy basis of $(x_1\frac{\partial f}{\partial x_1}, \frac{\partial f}{\partial x_2}, f)$. Then, $\{(-5, 4x_2, 20), (5x_2^4, -4x_1^4, 0)\}$ is the syzygy basis w.r.t. $\prec^{-1}$. Select $(-5, 4x_2, 20)$ and set $v_1 = x_1\frac{\partial}{\partial x} - \frac{4}{5}x_2\frac{\partial}{\partial x_2}$ which is an Euler logarithmic vector field. Next, we compute a parametric syzygy basis of $\langle x_2^4\frac{\partial f}{\partial x_1}, \frac{\partial f}{\partial x_2}, f\rangle$. Then, $\{(0, -x_1^4 - x_2^5, 5x_2^4), (-5, 4x_1^3, 0)\}$ is the syzygy basis. Select $(-5, 4x_1^3, 0)$ and set $v_2 = x_2^4\frac{\partial}{\partial x} - \frac{4}{5}x_1^3\frac{\partial}{\partial x_2}$ which is a trivial logarithmic vector field. Therefore, in this case, v_1 and trivial vector fields generates $\mathcal{D}er_{X,O}(-\log S)$.
- If parameter t belongs to $\mathbb{C} \setminus \mathbb{V}(t)$, then $\{x_1^2 + \frac{1}{25}t^2x_2^3, x_1x_2 - \frac{4}{125}t^3x_2^3, x_2^4\}$ is the reduced standard basis. By the same way, we can obtain the following three non-trivial logarithmic vector fields u_1, u_2, u_3;

$$u_1 = (x_1^2 + \tfrac{1}{25}t^2x_2^3)\frac{\partial}{\partial x_1} + \frac{1}{25}\left((64t^6x_1^3 - (16t^5x_2 + 625t)x_1^2 -(1180t^4x_2^2 - 12500x_2)x_1 + 64t^7x_2^4 - 125t^3x_2^3)/(625- 64t^4x_2)\right)\frac{\partial}{\partial x_2},$$

$$u_2 = (x_1x_2 - \tfrac{4}{125}t^3x_2^3)\frac{\partial}{\partial x_1} + \frac{1}{125}\left((-256t^7x_1^3 + (64t^6x_2+ 2500t^2)\, x_1^2 - (80t^5x_2^2 + 3125tx_2)x_1 - 256t^8x_2^4 - 5900t^4x_2^3 +62500x_2^2)/(625 - 64t^4x_2)\right)\frac{\partial}{\partial x_2},$$

$$u_3 = x_2^4\frac{\partial}{\partial x_1} + \left(((64t^4x_2 - 500)x_1^3 - 16t^3x_2^2x_1^2 + 20t^2x_2^3x_1 +64t^5x_2^5 - 525tx_2^4)/(625 - 64t^4x_2)\right)\frac{\partial}{\partial x_2}.$$

All algorithms of this paper have been implemented in the computer algebra system `Risa/Asir`[2].

The expansion of a polynomial $(10x_1 - x_2^3)(25 - 6x_2)$, that is from Example 17, is $250x_1 - 60x_1x_2 - 25x_2^3 + 6x_2^4$. If the expansion of a polynomial is given, then we cannot obtain the really important factor $(10x_1 - x_2^3)$. If we compute logarithmic vector fields with expanded polynomials in coefficients (for example the command "syz" of SINGULAR [7]), then as, in general, a coefficient polynomial cannot be factored into polynomials, we cannot get really important information as outputs and we need further computation to find the essential factor. In contrast, our algorithm tells us the essential information on coefficients $a_1(x)$'s, at the isolated singularity, by computing a standard basis of an annihilating ideal $\mathrm{Ann}_{\mathcal{O}_{X,O}}(H_{\Phi(f)})$. That is, $a_1(x) = q(x) \times c(x)$, where $q(x)$ is an element of a standard basis of the annihilating ideal and $c(x)$ is a polynomial that do not vanish at the singular point. This is the most different point and big advantage.

[2] One can get our implementation from `http://www-math.ias.tokushima-u.ac.jp/~nabesima/softwares.html`.

Acknowledgments

This work has been partly supported by JSPS Grant-in-Aid for Young Scientists (B) (No.15K17513) and Grant-in-Aid for Scientific Research (C) (No. 2454016201).

6. REFERENCES

[1] V. I. Arnold, Normal forms of functions in neighbourhoods of degenerate critical points, Russian Math. Survey **29**, pages 10–50, 1974.

[2] A. G. Aleksandrov, Cohomology of a quasihomogeneous complete intersection. *Math. USSR Izvestiya*, **26**, pages 437–477, 1986.

[3] W. Bruns and J. Herzog, *Cohen-Macaulay rings, revised edition.* Cambridge Univ. Press, 1998.

[4] F. J. Calderón-Moreno, D. Mond, L. Narváez-Macarro and F. J. Castro-Jiménez, Logarithmic cohomology of the complement of a plane curve. *Comment. Math. Helv.* **77**, pages 24–38, 2002.

[5] F. J. Castro-Jiménez and J. M. Ucha-Enríquez, Gröbner bases and logarithmic D-modules. *J. Symb. Comp.* **41**, pages 317–335, 2006.

[6] D. Cox, J. Little and D. O'Shea, *Using Algebraic Geometry.* Springer, 1998.

[7] W. Decker, G.-M. Greuel, G. Pfister and H. Schönemann, SINGULAR 3-1-6 - A computer algebra system for polynomial computations. 2012. `http://www.singular.uni-kl.de`

[8] M. Granger and M. Schulze, Quasihomogeneity of isolated hypersurface singularities and logarithmic cohomology. *Manuscripta Math.*, **121**, pages 411–416, 2006.

[9] A. Grothendieck, Théorèmes de dualité pour les faisceaux algébriques cohérents, *Séminaire Bourbaki.* **149**, 1957.

[10] A. Grothendieck, Local Cohomology, notes by R. Hartshorne. *Lecture Notes in Math.* **41**, Springer, 1967.

[11] H. Hauser and G. Müller, Affine varieties and Lie algebras of vector fields, *Manuscripta Math.*, **80-2**, pages 309–337, 1993.

[12] H. Hauser and G. Müller, On the Lie algebra $\Theta(X)$ of vector fields on a singularity. *J. Math. Sci. Univ. Tokyo*, **1**, pages 239–250, 1994.

[13] M. Kalkbrener, On the stability of Gröbner bases under specializations. *J. Symb. Comp.*, **24**, pages 51–58, 1997.

[14] D. Kapur, Y. Sun and D. Wang, A new algorithm for computing comprehensive Gröbner systems. *Proc. ISSAC2010*, pages 29–36. ACM-Press, 2010.

[15] M. Kersken, Reguläre Differentialformen. *Manuscripta Math.* , **46**, pages 1–26, 1984.

[16] D. Lazard, Gröbner bases, Gaussian elimination, and resolution of systems of algebraic equations. *Proc. EUROCAL '83, Lecture Note in Computer Science*, **162**, pages 146–156, Springer, 1983.

[17] D. T. Lê, Calcul du nombre de cycles évanouissants d'une hypersueface complexe, *Ann. Inst. Fourier, Grenoble*, **23**, pages 261–270, 1973.

[18] D. T. Lê et B. Teissier, Variétés polaires locales et classes de Chern des variétés singulières. *Annals of Mathematics*, **114**, pages 457–491, 1981.

[19] K. Nabeshima, On the computation of parametric Gröbner bases for modules and syzygies. *Japan Journal of Industrial and Applied Mathematics*, **27**, No.2, pages 217–238, 2010.

[20] K. Nabeshima, Stability conditions of monomial bases and comprehensive Gröbner systems. *Proc. CASC2012, Lecture Notes in Computer Science*,**7442**, pages 248–259, Springer, 2012.

[21] K. Nabeshima and S. Tajima, On efficient algorithms for computing parametric local cohomology classes associated with semi-quasihomogeneous singularities and standard bases. *Proc. ISSAC2014*, pages 351–358. ACM-Press, 2014.

[22] K. Nabeshima and S. Tajima, An algorithm for computing standard bases by changer of ordering via algebraic local cohomology (Extended Abstract), *Lecture Notes in Computer Science*, **8592**, pages 414–418. Springer, 2014.

[23] K. Nabeshima and S. Tajima, Algebraic local cohomology with parameters and parametric standard bases for zero-dimensional ideals, submitted.

[24] Y. Nakamura and S. Tajima, On weighted-degrees for algebraic local cohomologies associated with semiquasihomogeneous singularities, *Advanced Studies in Pure Mathematics*, **46**, pages 105 – 117, 2007.

[25] M. Noro and T. Takeshima, `Risa/Asir`- A computer algebra system. *Proc. ISSAC1992*, pages 387–396, ACM-Press, 1992. `http://www.math.kobe-u.ac.jp/Asir/asir.html`

[26] J.J. Nuño-Ballesteros, B. Oréfice and J.N. Tomazella, The Bruce-Roberts number of a function on a weighted homogeneous hypersurface. *The Quarterly J. Math.*, **64**, pages 269 – 280, 2013.

[27] B. Oréfice, O número de Milnor de uma singularidade isolada. *Ph.D. thesis*, Federal University of São Carlos (Brazil), 2011.

[28] K. Saito, Theory of logarithmic differential forms and logarithmic vector fields. *J. Fac. Sci. Univ. Tokyo, Sect. IA Math*, **27**, pages 265–291, 1980.

[29] E. Sernesi, The local cohomology of the Jacobian ring. arXiv:1306.3736v4 [math.AG] 2 may 2014.

[30] W. Sit, An algorithm for solving parametric linear systems. *J. Symb. Comp.*, **13**, pages 353–394, 1992.

[31] S. Tajima, On polar varieties, logarithmic vector fields and holonomic D-modules. *RIMS Kôkyûroku Bessatsu* **B40**, pages 41–51, 2013.

[32] S. Tajima and Y. Nakamura, Algebraic local cohomology class attached to quasi-homogeneous isolated hypersurface singularities. *Publications of the Research Institute for Mathematical Sciences*, **41**, pages 1–10, 2005.

[33] S. Tajima and Y. Nakamura, Annihilating ideals for an algebraic local cohomology class. *J. Symb. Comput.*, **44**, pages 435–448, 2009.

[34] S. Tajima and Y. Nakamura , Algebraic local cohomology classes attached to unimodal singularities. *Publications of the Research Institute for Mathematical Sciences*, **48**, pages 21–43. 2012.

[35] S. Tajima, Y. Nakamura and K. Nabeshima, Standard bases and algebraic local cohomology for zero dimensional ideals, *Advanced Studies in Pure Mathematics*, **56**, pages 341–361, 2009.

[36] B. Teissier, Cycles évanescents, sections planes et conditions de Whitney, Singularités à Cargèse, *Astérisque*, **7-8**, pages 285–362, 1973.

[37] J. Wahl, Automorphisms and deformations of quasi-homogeneous singularities, *Proc. Sympos. Pure. Math.*, **40-2**, pages 613–624, Amer. Math. Soc., Providence, RI, 1983.

[38] V. Weispfenning, Comprehensive Gröbner bases. *J. Symb. Comput.*, **36**, pages 669–683, 1992.

APPENDIX

PARAMETRIC SYZYGIES

Here, we describe how to compute parametric syzygies in a local ring. Our main idea is to combine the algorithm for computing parametric syzygies in a polynomial ring [19] with Lazard's homogenization technique [16].

DEFINITION 19. Let $g = \sum_{i=0}^{d} g_i \in \mathbb{C}[x]$ be a polynomial of total degree d where g_i is a homogeneous polynomial of degree i. Then, $g^h(x_0, x) = \sum_{i=0}^{d} g_i(x)x_0^{d-i}$ is a homogeneous polynomial of total degree d in $\mathbb{C}[x_0, x]$ where x_0 is the extra variable. We call g^h the homogenization of g. Let q be a homogenization of g, i.e., $q = g^h$. The dehomogenization of q is $q^e := q(1, x)$, i.e., $q^e = g^h(1, x) = g(x)$.

We generalize the algorithm of [19] to compute parametric syzygies in a local ring by using Lazard's homogenization technique [16]. The following algorithm outputs parametric syzygies.

Algorithm 3. Parametric syzygies

Input: $f_1, \ldots, f_s$: polynomials with parameters t.
Output: $\{(\mathbb{A}_1, G'_1), \ldots, (\mathbb{A}_l, G'_l)\}$: For all $\bar{a} \in \mathbb{A}'_i$, $\sigma_{\bar{a}}(G'_i)$ is a standard basis of a syzygy module of $f_1, \ldots, f_s$ in $\mathbb{C}\{x\}$ where G_i is a subset of $((\mathbb{C}[t])\{x\})^s$ and $1 \leq i \leq l$.
BEGIN
Step 1. $f_1^h, \ldots, f_s^h$ ←Homogenize $f_1, \ldots, f_s$.
Step 2. $\{(\mathbb{A}_1, G_1), .., (\mathbb{A}_l, G_l)\}$ ← Compute parametric syzygies of $f_1^h, \ldots, f_s^h$ w.r.t. a total degree term order s.t. $x_0 \gg x$ in a polynomial ring, by [19]. (For all $\bar{a}$, $\sigma_{\bar{a}}(G_i)$ is a Gröbner basis of a syzygy module where $1 \leq i \leq l$.)
Step 3. $\{(\mathbb{A}_1, G'_1), \ldots, (\mathbb{A}_l, G'_l)\}$ ←For each stratum, dehomogenize G_i for each $1 \leq i \leq l$. $G'_i = \{q^e | q \in G_i\}$.
return$\{(\mathbb{A}_1, G'_1), \ldots, (\mathbb{A}_l, G'_l)\}$
END

The correctness and termination follow from [16] and [19].

Let us remark that as we apply the homogenization technique [16] in the algorithm, the outputs of the implementation often have redundant elements.

If we apply the SINGULAR [7] approach, then a number of strata of parametric syzygies becomes big and the computational complexity becomes also big. As we adapt the Lazard's technique, we can use the efficient algorithm for computing parametric Gröbner bases [14, 20] and its implementation to compute parametric syzygies without any modification. Thus, the presented algorithm is easily implemented.

Improving Complexity Bounds for the Computation of Puiseux Series over Finite Fields

Adrien Poteaux
CRISTAL
UMR 9189 Université de Lille 1 - CNRS
Bâtiment M3
59655 Villeneuve d'Ascq, France
adrien.poteaux@univ-lille1.fr

Marc Rybowicz
XLIM-DMI
UMR 7252 Université de Limoges - CNRS
123 avenue Albert Thomas
87060 Limoges Cedex
marc.rybowicz@unilim.fr

ABSTRACT

Let L be a field of characteristic p with $\mathfrak{q}$ elements and $F \in L[X,Y]$ be a polynomial with $p > \deg_Y(F)$ and total degree d. In [40], we showed that rational Puiseux series of F above $X = 0$ could be computed with an expected number of $\mathcal{O}\tilde{}(d^5 + d^3 \log \mathfrak{q})$ arithmetic operations in L. In this paper, we reduce this bound to $\mathcal{O}\tilde{}(d^4 + d^2 \log \mathfrak{q})$ using Hensel lifting and changes of variables in the Newton-Puiseux algorithm that give a better control of the number of steps. The only asymptotically fast algorithm required is polynomial multiplication over finite fields. This approach also allows to test the irreducibility of F in $\overline{L}[[X]][Y]$ with $\mathcal{O}\tilde{}(d^3)$ operations in L. Finally, we describe a method based on structured bivariate multiplication [34] that may speed up computations for some input.

Categories and Subject Descriptors

I.1.2 [**Symbolic and Algebraic Manipulation**]: Algorithms—*Analysis of algorithms*

General Terms

Algorithms, Performance

Keywords

Puiseux series, Finite Fields, Algebraic Curves, Algebraic Functions, Genus, Complexity

1. INTRODUCTION

Let L be a field of characteristic p with $\mathfrak{q}$ elements, $\overline{L}$ be an algebraic closure of L and F be a polynomial in $L[X,Y]$ with partial degrees $\deg_X(F) = d_X > 0$, $\deg_Y(F) = d_Y > 0$ and total degree $\deg(F) = d$. We assume that F, considered as a polynomial in Y, is separable and primitive, hence squarefree and without non trivial factor in $L[X]$.

We also assume in the sequel that $p > d_Y$. Therefore, for any $x_0 \in \overline{L}$, it is well-known that the roots of F may be expressed as fractional Laurent power series in $(X - x_0)$ with coefficients in $\overline{L}$, called *(classical) Puiseux series of F above x_0* (CPS in the sequel). Terms written *in italics* in this introduction will be defined in section 2. If $p \leq d_Y$, CPS may not exist and other types of expansions are necessary: generalized Puiseux series, see [29] and references therein, or Hamburger-Noether expansions [10, 43].

CPS are an important tool to study singularities of the curve $F(X,Y) = 0$ [9, 52], to determine the genus of the curve via Riemman-Hurwitz's formula, to determine bases of Riemann-Roch spaces [22, 7], to compute integral bases of the function field $L(X)[Y]/(F)$ [50], etc. Code for computing CPS is available for instance in Maple [36] (implemented by Van Hoeij [50]), Magma [8] (see Beck [4]) or Singular [19] (implemented by Lamm and Lossen, see [26]).

Our interest in the finite field case stemmed from a modular reduction method that we proposed to avoid coefficient swell in the number field case [39, 41]. In this context, the condition $p > d_Y$ may always be enforced and is part of our good reduction criterion. Our goal is to compute *singular parts* of CPS since they contain the arithmetic and geometric information required for most applications. When singular parts are known, subsequent terms of CPS may be efficiently computed using quadratic Newton iterations [31].

It is however more convenient to compute singular parts of *rational Puiseux expansions* (RPE) of F rather than CPS. Introduced by Duval [22, 23], RPEs allow to work in the *residue fields* of the *places* of the function field $L(X)[Y]/(F)$ (or the product of function fields if F is not irreducible in $L[X,Y]$). Computations therefore take place in optimal degree extensions of L and RPEs provide arithmetical insight. CPS may easily be recovered from RPEs; see Section 2.

In [40], we studied how to truncate coefficients throughout the computations and gave a detailed count of the number of arithmetic operations in L required by Duval's version of the Newton-Puiseux algorithm to compute RPEs.

Inspired by a proof by Abhyankar of Newton-Puiseux's Theorem [1, Chapter 12], we show herein that it is possible to improve this result using Hensel-like factorizations and simple, but essential, substitutions.

We explain precisely our goal in Section 2 and recall main features of the Rational Newton-Puiseux algorithm in Section 3. We describe the improved algorithm in Section 4 and study its worst case complexity in Section 5. Finally, we show that if a fast multiplication algorithm for bivariate polynomials with support in a lattice is given (see [34, Theorem 12]), then the input polynomials may be factorized at an acceptable cost. This modification may lead to improved performances for some families of input, but does not reduce worst case asymptotic complexity.

The main contributions of this paper are Theorem 1 and 2 below. Notation $\mathcal{O}\tilde{}$ hides logarithmic factors of the degrees:

ISSAC'15, July 6–9, 2015, Bath, United Kingdom.

DOI: http://dx.doi.org/10.1145/2755996.2756650.

THEOREM 1. *There is an algorithm to compute singular parts of a system of RPEs above 0 of F with an expected number of $\mathcal{O}^{\sim}(d_X {d_Y}^3 + {d_Y}^2 \log \mathfrak{q}) \subset \mathcal{O}^{\sim}(d^4 + d^2 \log \mathfrak{q})$ field operations in L.*

This result should be compared with the bound $\mathcal{O}^{\sim}(d^5 + d^3 \log \mathfrak{q})$ given in [40], where we also derived an $\mathcal{O}^{\sim}(d^5 \log \mathfrak{q})$ bound for the computation of the genus of the curve defined by F and new complexity results for the number field case. Unfortunately, the improvement given by Theorem 1 does not propagate to genus computation; we will discuss this issue in the conclusion.

THEOREM 2. *There is an algorithm to decide whether F is irreducible in $\overline{L}[[X]][Y]$ performing $\mathcal{O}^{\sim}(d_X {d_Y}^2) \subset \mathcal{O}^{\sim}(d^3)$ operations in L.*

Related works. The complexity of the Newton-Puiseux algorithm, in its classical or rational form, has been investigated by Chistov [12], Duval [23], and Walsh [54, 53]. Other approaches to compute CPS have been proposed: linear algebra [21] (following [15]) and differential equations [16, 13, 14, 47, 49, 17], notably. Merle and Henry [27], then Teitelbaum [46] studied the arithmetic complexity of the resolution of the singularity at the origin defined by $F(X, Y) = 0$, a process tightly related to Puiseux series [9]. We have commented on these works and explained why we prefer to stick to the Newton-Puiseux algorithm in [40, 41].

Sasaki and als. use generalizations of Hensel's lifting to compute Puiseux series [45] or for polynomial factorization in $\overline{L}[[X]][Y]$ [44, 28], but no complexity analysis is given. In [32], Kuo revisited the theory of algebroids in $\mathbb{C}[[X, Y]]$, avoiding CPS and singularity resolution processes, and gave an irreducibility test in $\mathbb{C}[[X, Y]]$ [33] that could probably be extended to finite fields, but did not demonstrate that his approach is competitive. More recently, Berthomieu, Lecerf and Quintin [5, Section 3] proposed a Hensel-like factorization method to speed up the computation of roots of F in $L[[X]]$; with our notations, they obtain an $\mathcal{O}^{\sim}(d^3)$ algorithm, thus gaining an order of magnitude.

Factorization of F in $L[[X]][Y]$ or $\overline{L}[[X]][Y]$ is closely related to CPS since minimal polynomials over L or $\overline{L}$ of CPS are the irreducible factors of F. The factorization of univariate polynomials over local fields, such as $L((X))$, has been studied intensively; see [37, 38, 25, 3] and references therein. In particular, the Montes algorithm has received a lot of attention recently. Bauch, Nart and Stainsby [3] have proved that the factorization of a monic F over $L[[X]][Y]$ up to precision μ can be achieved in $\mathcal{O}^{\sim}({d_Y}^2 + d_Y \mathcal{V}_F^2 + d_Y(1 + \mathcal{V}_F) \log \mathfrak{q} + {d_Y}^2 \mu)$ operations in L, where $\mathcal{V}_F = v_X(\Delta_F)$ is the valuation of the discriminant of F. In our context, we may set $\mu = \mathcal{V}_F$ (see [40, Section 4]) and remark that $\mathcal{V}_F \in O(d_X d_Y)$. This yields $\mathcal{O}^{\sim}(d^5 + d^3 \log \mathfrak{q})$, as in [40]. They also provide an irreducibility test that runs in $\mathcal{O}^{\sim}({d_Y}^2 + d_Y(1 + \mathcal{V}_F) \log \mathfrak{q} + \mathcal{V}_F^2) \subset \mathcal{O}^{\sim}(d^4 + d^3 \log \mathfrak{q})$. For genus computation, [2] proposed a method with an $\mathcal{O}^{\sim}(d^7 \log \mathfrak{q})$ complexity bound, but more promising experimental results. Algorithms derived from Montes' method have so far not demonstrated a better asymptotic complexity than the classical Newton-Puiseux approach for $L((X))$. Besides, they are significantly more involved.

Additional notations and definitions.

- For $S \in \overline{L}[[X]]$, we denote by $v_X(S)$ the X-adic valuation of S and extend this notation to fractional power series.
- For $t \in \mathbb{N}^*$, L_t is the degree t extension of L in $\overline{L}$.
- If $S = \sum_k \alpha_k X^{k/e}$ is a fractional power series in $\overline{L}((X^{1/e}))$ and r is a rational number, $\lceil S \rceil^r$ denotes the truncated series $\lceil S \rceil^r = \sum_{k \le N} \alpha_k X^{k/e}$ where $N = \max\{k \in \mathbb{N} \mid \frac{k}{e} \le r\}$. It is extended to elements of $\overline{L}((X^{1/e}))[Y]$ coefficient-wise.
- For $e \in \mathbb{N}^*$, ζ_e is a primitive e-th root of unity.
- For a polynomial $H = \sum a_{ij} X^j Y^i \in \overline{L}[X, Y]$:
  - $d_Y(H)$ is its degree with respect to Y,
  - Δ_H is its discriminant with respect to Y,
  - $\mathcal{V}_H = v_X(\Delta_H)$,
  - $\mathcal{I}(H) = v_Y(H(0, Y))$,
  - $\mathrm{Supp}(H) = \{(i, j) \in \mathbb{N}^2 \mid a_{ij} \neq 0\}$ is the *support of* H,
  - H is called Y*-monic* if it is monic in the variable Y.

Complexity model and arithmetic cost. To estimate algorithm complexity, we just count the number of operations (addition, multiplication, division) in L. Multiplying by the binary cost of operations in L should give realistic bounds for running times of a careful implementation. Our algorithm is deterministic and we consider worst case estimates. However, it makes use of sub-algorithms for factoring polynomials in $L[T]$ and computing primitive elements in finite fields that are probabilistic of Las Vegas type. For them, we use upper bounds for average arithmetic complexity that propagate to Theorem 1.

Our complexity results require asymptotically fast algorithms for polynomial arithmetic and we will use bounds below for basic task arithmetic complexity. When no specific reference is given, the result may be found in [51]. Integers n_X and n_Y are bounds for degrees in X and Y of input polynomials.

- Multiplication of two polynomials in $L[X]$: $\mathcal{O}^{\sim}(n_X)$.
- Multiplication of two polynomials in $L[X, Y]$: $\mathcal{O}^{\sim}(n_X n_Y)$.
- Operations in L_t: $\mathcal{O}^{\sim}(t)$ with primitive representation.
- Factorization of a polynomial in $L[X]$: $\mathcal{O}^{\sim}(n_X^2 + n_X \log \mathfrak{q})$.
- Computation of Δ_H: $\mathcal{O}^{\sim}(n_X n_Y^2)$.
- Y-shift, i.e. computation of $H(X, Y + B) \mod X^{n_X+1}$ where $H \in L[X, Y]$ is Y-monic and B is in $L[X]$: $\mathcal{O}^{\sim}(n_X n_Y)$ if $n_X > 0$ and $\mathcal{O}^{\sim}(n_Y)$ if $n_X = 0$. Indeed, if $p > n_Y$, [6, Problem 2.6] shows how to perform a shift in a univariate polynomial of degree n_Y with coefficients in a commutative ring $\mathbb{A}$ with $\mathcal{O}^{\sim}(n_Y)$ operations in $\mathbb{A}$. Taking $\mathbb{A} = L[X]/(X^{n_X+1})$ gives the above bounds.

2. RATIONAL PUISEUX EXPANSIONS

In this section, we precisely set our goal and recall useful properties. Let L and $F = \sum_{l=0}^{d_Y} A_l(X) Y^l$ be as in Section 1. Up to a change of variable $X \mapsto X + x_0$ and an extension of the ground field L, it is sufficient to give definitions and properties for the case $x_0 = 0$. Following Duval [23], we consider decompositions into irreducible elements:

$$F = \prod_{i=1}^{\rho} F_i \text{ with } F_i \text{ irreducible in } L[[X]][Y]$$

$$F_i = \prod_{j=1}^{f_i} F_{ij} \text{ with } F_{ij} \text{ irreducible in } \overline{L}[[X]][Y]$$

$$F_{ij} = A_{d_Y} \prod_{k=0}^{e_i - 1} \left(Y - S_{ij}(X^{1/e_i} \zeta_{e_i}^k)\right) \text{ with } S_{ij} \in \overline{L}[[X]]$$

DEFINITION 1. *The series $S_{ijk}(X) = S_{ij}(X^{1/e_i} \zeta_{e_i}^k)$ are the classical Puiseux series (CPS) of F above 0.*

PROPOSITION 1. *The $\{F_{ij}\}_{1 \le j \le f_i}$ have coefficients in a finite extension K_i of L and $f_i = [K_i : L]$. They are conjugated by the action of the Galois group of K_i/L.*

DEFINITION 2. *A system of rational Puiseux expansions over L (L-RPE) of F above 0 is a set* $\{R_i\}_{1\le i\le\rho}$ *such that:*

- $R_i(T) \in K_i((T))^2$,
- $R_i(T) = (X_i(T), Y_i(T)) = \left(\gamma_i T^{e_i}, \sum_{l=n_i}^{\infty} \beta_{il} T^l\right)$, $\gamma_i \neq 0$,
- R_i *is a parametrization of* F_i, *i.e.* $F_i(X_i(T), Y_i(T)) = 0$,
- *the parametrization is irreducible, i.e.* e_i *is minimal.*

If $Y_i(0)$ *is defined,* $(X_i(0), Y_i(0))$ *is called the center of* R_i.

Duval [23] showed that there is a canonical bijection between the R_i and the *places over L* (see [11, 24] for a definition) of the algebraic function fields defined by the irreducible factors of F in $L[X,Y]$. Under this correspondence, residue fields of the places are isomorphic to the coefficient fields of the R_i and ramifications indices of the places are equal to the e_i. This leads to the following terminology:

DEFINITION 3. *The integer* e_i *is the ramification index of* R_i, K_i *is its residue field and* f_i *its residual degree.*

PROPOSITION 2. $\sum_{i=1}^{\rho} e_i f_i = d_Y$.

From a system of L-RPEs, CPS can easily be recovered:

1. R_i has f_i conjugates $R_{ij}(T) = (X_{ij}(T), Y_{ij}(T))$ over L:

$$X_{ij} = \gamma_{ij} T^{e_i} \text{ and } Y_{ij} = \sum_{l=n_i}^{\infty} \beta_{ijl} T^l \ ; \ 1 \le j \le f_i$$

2. The CPS are $S_{ijk}(X) = Y_{ij}\left(\zeta_{e_i}^k X^{1/e_i}/\gamma_{ij}^{1/e_i}\right)$, where γ_{ij}^{1/e_i} denotes any e_i-th root of γ_{ij} and $0 \le k \le e_i - 1$.

DEFINITION 4. *Define* $s_i = \min\{0, n_i\}$. *The regularity index* r_i *of* S_{ijk} *in F is the least integer* $N \ge s_i$ *such that* $\lceil S_{ijk} \rceil^{\frac{N}{e_i}} = \lceil S_{uvw} \rceil^{\frac{N}{e_i}}$ *implies* $(u,v,w) = (i,j,k)$. *The truncated series* $\lceil S_{ijk} \rceil^{\frac{r_i}{e_i}}$ *is the singular part of* S_{ijk} *in F.*
The regularity index r_i *of* R_i *in F is that of* S_{ijk} *in F, for any j, k. The singular part of* R_i *is* $\left(\gamma_i T^{e_i}, \sum_{l=n_i}^{r_i} \beta_{ik} T^l\right)$.

In other words, the regularity index of S_{ijk} is the smallest truncation order that allows to distinguish S_{ijk} from other CPS of F; see [40, page 194]. Singular parts contain arithmetic and geometric information necessary for many applications: ramification indices, residual degrees, Puiseux exponents, etc. We aim at computing them efficiently.

3. NEWTON-PUISEUX ALGORITHM

This work improves a version of Duval's rational Newton-Puiseux algorithm presented in [40], called `RNPuiseux`. In this section, we introduce some notations and recall useful facts regarding `RNPuiseux`. Because of space constraints, the reader is referred to [40, Section 3] for a detailed description of this algorithm.

DEFINITION 5. *The* Newton polygon $\mathcal{N}(H)$ *of a polynomial H in* $L_t[X,Y]$ *is the lower part of the convex hull of its support.*

If $\mathrm{Supp}(H)$ is a vertical line, $\mathcal{N}(H)$ is reduced to a point. Otherwise, $\mathcal{N}(H)$ is a sequence of (non degenerate) edges with increasing slopes. In order to get exactly singular parts of RPEs and no superfluous terms, it is convenient to modify slightly this definition (see examples of Figure 1):

DEFINITION 6. *Let* $H = \sum_i A_i(X) Y^i$ *be squarefree, primitive, with* $d_Y(H) > 0$. *The* modified Newton polygon[1] $\mathcal{N}^\star(H)$ *is constructed as follow: If* $A_0 = 0$ *(resp.* $A_0 \neq 0$ *and the first edge, starting from the left, ends at* $(1, v_X(A_1))$*), add to* $\mathcal{N}(H)$ *(resp. replace the first edge by) a fictitious edge joining the vertical axis to* $(1, v_X(A_1))$ *such that its slope is the largest (negative or null) integer less than or equal to the slope of the next edge.*

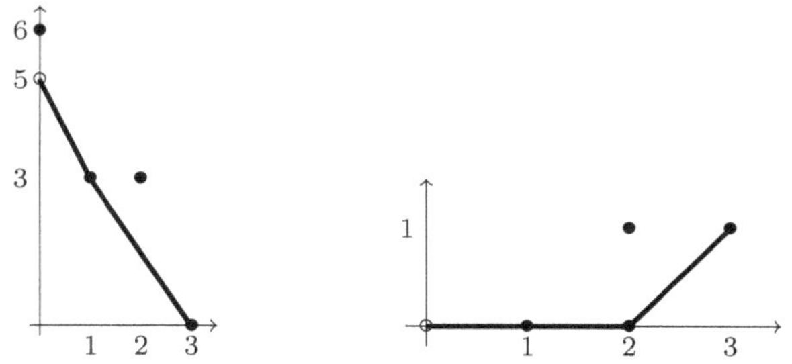

Figure 1: $\mathcal{N}^\star(H)$ **for** $(Y - X^3)(Y^2 - X^3)$ **and** $Y(Y-1)(XY-1)$

The introduction of $\mathcal{N}^\star$ is motivated by the next example:

Example 1. Consider $F(X,Y) = (Y - X^k)(Y^2 - X^3)$ with $k \ge 3$. CPS of F are $S_1 = X^k$, $S_{2,j} = (-1)^j X^{3/2}$, $j = 1, 2$. According to Definition 4, regularity indices are respectively $r_1 = 2$ and $r_{2,j} = 3$. Using $\mathcal{N}(F)$ would cause the algorithm to return X^k for the singular part of S_1, instead of the expected value $\lceil S_1 \rceil^2 = 0$. If a dense representation is used for the output, returning X^k would not allow to bound running times in terms of $\mathcal{V}_F$ (see Proposition 9) because $\mathcal{O}(k)$ operations would be required to build the result, while $\mathcal{V}_F = 9$ for any $k > 1$.

Each edge Δ of $\mathcal{N}^\star(H)$ corresponds to three integers q, m and l with $q > 0$, q and m coprime, such that Δ is on the line $q\,j + m\,i = l$. If Δ is an horizontal edge, $m = l = 0$ and we choose $q = 1$.

DEFINITION 7. *If* $H = \sum a_{ij} X^j Y^i$, *then the* characteristic polynomial ϕ_Δ *of* Δ *is* $\phi_\Delta(T) = \sum_{(i,j)\in\Delta} a_{ij} T^{\frac{i-i_0}{q}}$ *where* i_0 *is the smallest value such that* (i_0, j_0) *belongs to* Δ *for some* j_0. *In particular,* $\phi_\Delta(T) = T$ *if* Δ *is a fictitious edge.*

When applied to $(L, F, \mathcal{V}_F)$, `RNPuiseux` returns a set of pairs[2] $\mathcal{R}_t(F) = \{(P_i, Q_i)\}_{1\le i\le\rho}$ representing singular parts of L-RPEs of F above 0. More precisely:

- $P_i \in \overline{L}[X]$ is a monomial of the form $\lambda_i X^{e_i}$,
- $Q_i(X,Y) = Q_{i0}(X) + c_i Y X^{r_i}$, where $(P_i(T), Q_{i0}(T))$ is the singular part of an RPE of F, r_i its regularity index, and $c_i \in K_i$.

Starting at $H = F$, algorithm `RNPuiseux` consists in recursive applications of transformations:

$$H_{\Delta,\xi}(X,Y) = H(\xi^b X^q, X^m(\xi^a + Y))/X^l \qquad (1)$$

where integers (q, m, l) are determined by an edge Δ of $\mathcal{N}^\star(H)$, ξ is a root of ϕ_Δ and a and b are integers satisfying $aq - bm = 1$ and $0 \le b < q$. These transformations are applied for each relevant pair (Δ, ξ) and the algorithm is called recursively on $H_{\Delta,\xi}$ until $\mathcal{I}(H) = 1$, yielding a computation tree whose nodes and leaves are `RNPuiseux` function calls. It is shown in [40] that the expected number of operations in L required by `RNPuiseux` is in $\mathcal{O}(d_X{}^2 d_Y{}^3 + d_Y{}^2 d_X \log q)$.

The following remark and lemma are essential for understanding the next sections:

Remark 1. To compute all RPEs of H above 0, it is sufficient to compute RPEs centered at $(0,0)$ of the $H_{\Delta,\xi}$. Consequently, for the initial call, (i.e. $H = F$) all edges Δ are considered, but recursive calls of `RNPuiseux` treats only edges with negative slopes.

[1] $\mathcal{N}^\star(H)$ is more convenient herein than the generic Newton polygon used in [40] and yields essentially the same output.
[2] In [40], `RNPuiseux` actually returns triplets (G_i, P_i, Q_i) but G_i is useless for our purpose.

4. IMPROVING `RNPuiseux`

To simplify the exposition, from now on, we assume that **the input polynomial F is Y-monic**, but this section may easily be adapted to non monic F as in [40].

Our improvements rely on the following observations:

• Consider first the obvious following consequence of Weierstrass Preparation Theorem:

PROPOSITION 3. *If $G \in L_t[X,Y]$ satisfies $\mathcal{I}(G) > 0$, then there exist unique $\widehat{G}$ and U in $L_t[[X]][Y]$ such that:*
- $G = \widehat{G}\, U$
- $U(0,0) \neq 0$, i.e. U is a unit in $L_t[[X,Y]]$,
- $\widehat{G}$ is monic, with $d_Y(\widehat{G}) = \mathcal{I}(G)$,
Moreover, RPEs of G and $\widehat{G}$ centered at $(0,0)$ are the same.

Polynomial $\widehat{G}$ is called the *distinguished polynomial* associated with G. In view of Remark 1, we can replace $H_{\Delta,\xi}$ in `RNPuiseux` by an approximation $\widetilde{H}_{\Delta,\xi}$ of its distinguished polynomial $\widehat{H}_{\Delta,\xi}$, provided that we can compute an approximation that preserves singular parts of RPEs at a sufficiently low cost; see Proposition 4 below. This will ensure that the input polynomial H of our algorithm is always monic with $d_Y(H) = \mathcal{I}(H)$ and that edges of $\mathcal{N}^\star(H)$ have negative slopes, except maybe for the initial function call. Moreover, degrees of input polynomials for recursive function calls will be lower.

• Assuming that the above factorization step is performed, it is possible to get a better control on the number of recursive calls and, in particular, to ensure that the sequence of integers $d_Y(H)$ along a branch of the computation tree is strictly decreasing. Degrees are stationary, i.e. $d_Y(H) = d_Y(\widetilde{H}_{\Delta,\xi})$, if and only if H has a single edge Δ with $\phi(\Delta) = (T-\xi)^{d_Y(H)}$. In this case, Δ has integer slope (i.e. $q=1$) and all Puiseux series of H have a first term equal to $\xi X^m \in L_t[X]$. Following Abhyankar [1, Chapter 12], we propose to use a simple trick to avoid this case: just remove at once all common polynomial terms of Puiseux series by replacing H with $\overline{H} = H(X, Y - A_{n_Y-1}/n_Y)$, where $n_Y = d_Y(H)$. Then, if $\mathcal{N}^\star(\overline{H})$ still has a unique edge $\overline{\Delta}$ with integer slope, $\phi_{\overline{\Delta}}$ cannot be of the form $(T-\overline{\xi})^{d_Y(H)}$ because its monomial of degree $d_Y(H)-1$ is null and $p > d_Y(H)$. Therefore, the algorithm will always split $\overline{H}$ and degrees will be reduced for subsequent recursive calls.

Remark 2. It is worth noting the following: factorization steps alone do not suffice to reduce `RNPuiseux` complexity, but they allow to apply the method above to decrease the number of recursive calls and get a more accurate count of arithmetic operations.

We now specify sub-algorithms and describe a recursive version of the main algorithm `ARNP`, wherein we emphasize simplicity rather than efficiency. The first one is just an application of Hensel lifting as described in [51, Chapter 15] to get an effective version of Weierstrass Preparation Theorem.

PROPOSITION 4. *Let $G \in L_t[X,Y]$ be a polynomial satisfying hypotheses of Proposition 3, N be in $\mathbb{N}$ and $\widehat{G}$ denote the distinguished polynomial of G. There exists an algorithm* `WPT` *such that* `WPT`(L_t, G, N) *computes $\widetilde{G} = \lceil \widehat{G} \rceil^N$ with $\mathcal{O}\tilde{}(N d_Y(G))$ operations in L_t.*

PROPOSITION 5. *Let ϕ be in $L_t[T]$ with $n = d_T(\phi)$. There exists an algorithm* `Oneroot` *such that* `Oneroot`(L_t,ϕ) *decides if $\phi(T) = c(T-\xi)^n$ for some $c, \xi \in L_t$ and computes ξ if the answer is positive using $\mathcal{O}\tilde{}(n)$ operations in L_t.*

`Bézout`(q,m)
`Input:` $(q,m) \in \mathbb{Z}^2$ with $q > 0$.
`Output:` *$(a,b) \in \mathbb{Z}^2$ such that $a\,q - b\,m = 1$ and $0 \leq b < q$.*

`Factor`(L_t,ϕ)
`Input:` L_t, *a field*, and $\phi \in L_t[T]$, with $d_T(\phi) > 0$.
`Output:` *A set $\{(\phi_i, M_i)\}_i$ with ϕ_i monic, irreducible in $L_t[T]$ and $\phi = c \prod_i \phi_i^{M_i}$ for some $c \in L_t$.*

`ARNP`(L_t,H,N)
`Input:` L_t, a field, $H = \sum_i A_i(X) Y^i \in L_t[X,Y]$, separable, Y-monic, with $\deg_Y(H) > 0$, $N \in \mathbb{N}$ (truncation order).
`Output:` If N is large enough, $\mathcal{R}_t(H)$.

1. If $d_Y(H) = 1$ then Return $\{[X,Y]\}$
2. If $\mathcal{N}^\star(H)$ is made of a unique edge Δ with integer slope and `Oneroot`(L_t, ϕ_Δ) then
3. $\quad B \leftarrow A_{d_y(H)-1}/d_y(H)$ *// Abhyankar's trick*
4. $\quad \overline{H} \leftarrow \lceil H(X, Y-B) \rceil^N$
5. else $B \leftarrow 0$; $\overline{H} \leftarrow \lceil H \rceil^N$
6. $\mathcal{R} \leftarrow \{\}$
7. For Δ in $\mathcal{N}^\star(\overline{H})$ do
8. $\quad$ Compute q, m, l, and ϕ_Δ
9. $\quad (a,b) \leftarrow$ `Bézout`(q,m)
10. $\quad$ For (ϕ, M) in `Factor`(L_t,ϕ) do
11. $\quad\quad$ Let ξ be any root of ϕ
12. $\quad\quad \widetilde{N} \leftarrow N/[L_t(\xi) : L_t]$ *// Update truncation order*
13. $\quad\quad \overline{H}_{\Delta,\xi} \leftarrow \lceil \overline{H}(\xi^b X^q, X^m(\xi^a + Y))/X^l \rceil^{\lfloor \widetilde{N} \rfloor}$
14. $\quad\quad \widetilde{H}_{\Delta,\xi} \leftarrow$ `WPT`$(\overline{H}_{\Delta,\xi}, \lfloor \widetilde{N} \rfloor)$
15. $\quad\quad$ For each (P,Q) in `ARNP`$(L_t(\xi), \widetilde{H}_{\Delta,\xi}, \widetilde{N})$ do
16. $\quad\quad\quad C \leftarrow -\lceil B(\xi^b P^q) \rceil^{m\, d_X(P)+r}$ *// $Q = Q_0 + X^r Y$*
17. $\quad\quad\quad \mathcal{R} \leftarrow \mathcal{R} \cup \{(\xi^b P^q, C + P^m(\xi^a + Q))\}$
18. Return $\mathcal{R}$.

Remark 3. At line 11, if ξ has multiplicity one in ϕ, there is no need to execute lines 13 and 14 because the expected output for the recursive call is just $[X,Y]$. Similarly, if $\lfloor \widetilde{N} \rfloor = 0$, we must have $\mathcal{I}(\widetilde{H}_{\Delta,\xi}) = 1$ and ξ must have multiplicity one. For the sake of clarity, we have not included this optimization in the description of `ARNP`, but we will take it into account in our complexity analysis because it will simplify intermediate results. For instance, if $H(0,Y)$ is squarefree, there is no cost for lines ≥ 11.

PROPOSITION 6. `ARNP`$(L, F, \mathcal{V}_F)$ *returns $\mathcal{R}_t(F)$.*

PROOF. (sketch) Truncation orders of line 4, 5 and 13 preserve singular parts because they are the same as in [40]. We just need to check that the two modifications introduced in `RNPuiseux` do not alter the output.

• Consider first Abhyankar's trick. If S is a Puiseux series for H and $(P', Q' = Q'_0 + cX^{r'}Y)$ is the corresponding output of `ARNP`, then $Q'_0(X) = \lceil S(P') \rceil^{r'}$. Obviously $S + B$ is a Puiseux series for $H(X, Y-B)$, with regularity index r' in $H(X, Y-B)$ and singular part $\lceil S + B \rceil^{r'}$. Moreover $H(X, Y-B)$ and $\overline{H}$ have the same singular parts. Hence the expected RPE for $\overline{H}$ is $(P', \lceil B(P') \rceil^{r'} + Q')$. But the pair (P,Q) in line 15 is an RPE for $\widetilde{H}_{\Delta,\xi}$ and $(P', \lceil B(P') \rceil^{r'} + Q') = (\xi^b P^q, P^m(\xi^a + Q))$ is an RPE for $\overline{H}$

with regularity index $r' = m\, d_X(P) + r$. Therefore, line 16 correctly compensates line 4.

- For line 14, $\overline{H}_{\Delta,\xi}$ and its distinguished polynomial $\widehat{H}_{\Delta,\xi} \in L_t(\xi)[[X]][Y]$ have the same RPEs centered at $(0,0)$. At recursive calls, we are only concerned with RPEs centered at $(0,0)$ and we are allowed to discard the other factor. It is shown in [40] that truncation at order $\lfloor \widetilde{N} \rfloor$ preserves singular parts centered at $(0,0)$. We may thus continue the computation with $\widetilde{H}_{\Delta,\xi}$ instead of $\overline{H}_{\Delta,\xi}$. $\square$

Example 2. If $F \in \mathbb{F}_{29}[X,Y]$ is defined by $F = \prod_{i=1}^{3}(Y - S_i(X)) + X^{19}Y$ with $S_i = X + X^2 + X^3 + 17\,X^4 + X^5 + X^6 + X^7 + (-1)^i\, X^{15/2}$, $1 \le i \le 2$ and $S_3 = X + X^2 + X^3 + X^4$. We have $\mathcal{V}_F = 94$ and ARNP runs as follow:

- $\mathcal{N}^\star(F)$ has a single edge with a unique root. Abhyankar's trick is applied with $-B = X + X^2 + X^3 + 2\,X^4 + 20\,X^5 + 20\,X^6 + 20\,X^7$.
- $\mathcal{N}^\star(\overline{H})$ has a single edge Δ $4\,i + j = 12$ with $\phi_\Delta = (T-28)\,(T-15)^2$. We obtain two factors $H_1 = \widetilde{H}_{\Delta,28}$ and $H_2 = \widetilde{H}_{\Delta,15}$, with respective Y-degree 1 and 2.
- The recursive call for H_1 returns $[X, Y]$.
- Since $\mathcal{N}^\star(H_2)$ has once again a single edge with a unique root, the recursive call for H_2 applies Abhyankar's trick again with $-B = 10\,X + 10\,X^2 + 10\,X^3 + \ldots$.
- $\mathcal{N}^\star(\overline{H}_2)$ has a single edge $7\,i + 2\,j = 14$ and $\phi_\Delta = T - 1$. Since $\mathcal{I}(\overline{H}_2) = 1$, execution stops at the next recursive call.

Let us now illustrate the reconstruction of RPEs for S_1 and S_2 (lines 16 and 17):

- The terminal call returns $(P,Q) = [X,Y]$. Since $m = 7$, $d_X(P) = 1$, $r = 0$ and $\xi^b = 1$, this gives $C = 10\,X^2 + 10\,X^4 + 10\,X^6$ and a RPE $[X^2, 10\,X^2 + 10\,X^4 + 10\,X^6 + (Y+1)\,X^7]$
- Coming back to the initial call, we have $r = 7$, $m = 4$, $d_X(P) = 2$, and $\xi^b = 1$. This time we have $C = X^2 + X^4 + X^6 + 2\,X^8 + 20\,X^{10} + 20\,X^{12} + 20\,X^{14}$, which provides the RPE $[X^2, S_2(X^2) + X^{15}Y]$. As for S_3, we have $r = 0$ and $d_X(P) = 1$, which leads to $C = X + X^2 + X^3 + 2\,X^4$, and to the RPE $[X, S_3(X) + X^4Y]$ ($\xi = 28$ here).

5. COMPLEXITY

In this section, our goal is to prove Theorem 1 and 2. We recall that F is assumed Y-monic. The following relations are useful and easy to prove:

LEMMA 1. *Consider a function call* ARNP$(L, F, \mathcal{V}_F)$. *For any input* (L_t, H, N) *in the computation tree, we have:*

1. $d_Y(H) = \sum_{\Delta,\xi} d_Y(\widetilde{H}_{\Delta,\xi}) q_\Delta [L_t(\xi) : L_t]$.

2. $N\,t = \mathcal{V}_F$.

3. $d_Y(H)\, t \le d_Y = d_Y(F)$.

We recall that ρ denotes the number of L-RPEs above 0.

PROPOSITION 7. *The expected number of operations in L required to factor all characteristic polynomials during the execution of* ARNP$(L, F, \mathcal{V}_F)$ *is in* $\mathcal{O}\tilde{}(\rho\, d_Y{}^2 + d_Y{}^2 \log \mathfrak{q})$.

PROOF. We first estimate the cost of a single function call with input (L_t, H, N), forgetting for a moment recursive calls. Since $\texttt{Factor}(L_t, \phi_\Delta)$ requires an expected number of $\mathcal{O}\tilde{}(\deg(\phi_\Delta)^2 + \deg(\phi_\Delta) \log \mathfrak{q}^t)$ operations in L_t, summing over Δ, we get $\mathcal{O}\tilde{}(d_Y(H)^2 + d_Y(H) \log \mathfrak{q}^t)$ operations in L_t, hence $\mathcal{O}\tilde{}(d_Y(H)^2 t + d_Y(H)\, t^2 \log \mathfrak{q})$ operations in L. By Lemma 1, this is in $\mathcal{O}\tilde{}(d_Y{}^2 + t\, d_Y \log q)$. In order to conclude, we must estimate the sum of these quantities over the computation tree $\mathcal{T}$. Let R_i denote the RPE corresponding to a branch $\mathcal{B}_i$ of $\mathcal{T}$. There are three types of function calls, corresponding to three types of vertices of $\mathcal{T}$:

- Type (I): $\mathcal{N}^\star(\overline{H})$ has a single edge with slope m/q and $\phi_\Delta = \phi^M$, with ϕ irreducible in $L_t[T]$. Two sub-cases may occur:

– Type (I.a): $d_T(\phi) = 1$. In this case, thanks to Abhyankar's trick, we must have $q > 1$. Since the product of all integers q along $\mathcal{B}_i$ is e_i, this situation happens at most $\log_2 e_i$ times along $\mathcal{B}_i$.

– Type (I.b): $d_T(\phi) > 1$. The product of the degrees of all polynomials ϕ along $\mathcal{B}_i$ is f_i, hence this case may occur at most $\log_2 f_i$ times along $\mathcal{B}_i$.

From Proposition 2, we deduce that type (I) calls may occur at most $\log_2 e_i f_i \le \log_2(d_Y)$ times along $\mathcal{B}_i$. Along $\mathcal{B}_i$, all integers t that occur satisfy $t \le f_i$. Summing costs of type (I) along $\mathcal{B}_i$, we get $\log_2(d_Y) \times \mathcal{O}\tilde{}(d_Y{}^2 + f_i d_Y \log q) = \mathcal{O}\tilde{}(d_Y{}^2 + f_i d_Y \log q)$. Summing over i, we obtain $\mathcal{O}\tilde{}(\rho\, d_Y{}^2 + d_Y{}^2 \log \mathfrak{q})$ using Proposition 2.

- Type (II): $\mathcal{N}^\star(\overline{H})$ has several edges, or the characteristic polynomial of the unique edge has several irreducible factors in $L_t[T]$. Since algorithm ARNP then separates two groups of RPEs, this can happen at most $(\rho - 1)$ times. Since these nodes have at least two subtrees, there exists an injective map j from these nodes to leaves of $\mathcal{T}$ such that node c is mapped to leaf $R_{j(c)}$ of a subtree rooted at c. With this construction, integer t associated with c is at most $f_{j(c)}$. Summing costs over all such nodes and using Proposition 2 yields again the expected result.
- Type (III): $d_Y(H) = 1$. Those are the leaves of $\mathcal{T}$and induce no operations in L. $\square$

For Theorem 1 to hold, arithmetic operations in a subfield L_t of a residue field must be performed in $\mathcal{O}\tilde{}(t)$ operations in L. Unfortunately, ARNP builds residue fields by adding step by step roots ξ_j of characteristic polynomials and no $\mathcal{O}\tilde{}(t)$ algorithm is known if L_t is represented as a tower of extensions over L [35, 42]. Following [40], we propose to compute a primitive element and to change the coefficient field representation whenever a new root of a characteristic polynomial is required. To simplify the exposition, transformations related to coefficients fields are not explicitly described in algorithm ARNP, but their complexity must be taken into account. The analysis of [40, Section 5.1] applies to ARNP:

PROPOSITION 8. *The number of operations in L required by changes of representation to execute* ARNP$(L,F,\mathcal{V}_F)$ *is in* $\mathcal{O}\tilde{}(\mathcal{V}_F d_Y{}^2)$.

PROPOSITION 9. *Not taking into account univariate factorizations and changes of representation,* ARNP$(L, F, \mathcal{V}_F)$ *requires at most* $\mathcal{O}\tilde{}(\rho\, d_Y\, (\mathcal{V}_F + 1))$ *operations in L.*

PROOF. Consider first the execution of one function call, ignoring for now recursive calls.

By Proposition 5, line 2 requires $\mathcal{O}\tilde{}(d_Y(H))$ operations in L_t, hence $\mathcal{O}\tilde{}(t d_Y(H)) \subset \mathcal{O}\tilde{}(d_Y)$ operations in L.

Shift of line 4 may be performed with $\mathcal{O}\tilde{}((N+1) d_Y(H))$ operations in L_t, hence $\mathcal{O}\tilde{}(t\,(N+1) d_Y(H)) \subset \mathcal{O}\tilde{}(d_Y(\mathcal{V}_F + 1))$ operations in L; see Lemma 1.

Define $d_{t\xi} = [L_t(\xi) : L_t]$ and consider one execution of line 13. If $\lfloor \widetilde{N} \rfloor > 0$, then [40, Lemma 2] indicates that it requires $\mathcal{O}\tilde{}(\widetilde{N} d_Y(H))$ operations in $L_t(\xi)$, hence $\mathcal{O}\tilde{}(\widetilde{N}\, d_Y(H)\, t\, d_{t\,\xi})$ operations in L. Lemma 1 and line 12 gives $\mathcal{O}\tilde{}(N d_Y) \subset \mathcal{O}\tilde{}(d_Y \mathcal{V}_F)$. If $\lfloor \widetilde{N} \rfloor = 0$, Remark 3 indicates that there is no cost at all. If s denotes the number of pairs (Δ, ξ), total cost for line 13 is thus in $\mathcal{O}\tilde{}(s\, d_Y \mathcal{V}_F)$.

For line 14, the operation count is the same as for line 13.

As for line 16, we denote by $(P = \lambda X^e, Q)$ an $L_t(\xi)$-RPE of $\widetilde{H}_{\Delta,\xi}$ computed recursively and r (resp. f) its regularity index (resp. its residual degree over L). Setting $r' = m\,e + r$, the computation of $\xi^b \lambda^q$ requires less than $\mathcal{O}(f \log d_Y)$ operations in L and the cost of computing C is in $\mathcal{O}((r'+1)\,f)$ operations in L. Since f is the residual degree over L of an RPE of H, $r'f \leq \mathcal{V}_F$; see [40, Proposition 5]. Moreover, $\sum_{(P,Q)} f \leq t d_Y(H) \leq d_Y$ by Proposition 2. Total cost is thus in $\mathcal{O}(\mathcal{V}_F + d_Y)$.

Line 17 needs no arithmetic in L if the output is returned without expanding expressions, except for the computation of ξ^a and ξ^b, which can be done in $O(f \log d_Y(H))$ operations in L. Summing over (P,Q) as above, we obtain $\mathcal{O}(d_Y)$. If an output in expanded form is expected, computations may also be done with $\mathcal{O}((\mathcal{V}_F + 1)d_Y)$ operations in L.

Altogether, we have shown that a single call to **ARNP** performs $\mathcal{O}(s\,d_Y\,(\mathcal{V}_F + 1))$ operations in L. We now sum this cost over all nodes of the computation tree $\mathcal{T}$ following the proof of Proposition 7.

For type (I) function calls, $s = 1$. There are at most $\rho \log_2 d_Y$ of those and the total cost is in $\mathcal{O}(\rho\, d_Y(\mathcal{V}_F + 1))$.

For type (II) calls, $s > 1$ and such a call separate RPEs into s groups. Consider the tree $\mathcal{T}'$ where nodes of type (I) are ignored. We set $s = 0$ for leaves and show by induction on the depth $\mathcal{D}$ of $\mathcal{T}'$ that $\sum_{s\in\mathcal{T}'} s \leq 2\rho - 2$ (with equality when $\mathcal{T}'$ is a binary tree). For $\mathcal{D}$=0, $\mathcal{T}'$ is just a leaf and the formula is correct because $\rho = 1$. Assume $\mathcal{D} > 0$ and let s_0 be the value associated with the root of $\mathcal{T}'$ (initial call). Removing the root gives $s_0 \geq 2$ subtrees of lower depth, having respectively $\rho_1, \ldots, \rho_{s_0}$ leaves. The induction hypothesis yields:

$$\sum_{s\in\mathcal{T}'} s = s_0 + \sum_{s\in\mathcal{T}'\setminus\{s_0\}} s \leq s_0 + \sum_{i=1}^{s_0}(2\rho_i - 2) = 2\rho - s_0 \leq 2\rho - 2,$$

and the proposition is proved. □

Proof of Theorem 1. The bound $\mathcal{V}_F$ can be computed with $\mathcal{O}(d_X {d_Y}^2)$ operations in L. Since $\rho \leq d_Y$ and $\mathcal{V}_F \leq d_X(2d_Y - 1)$, the monic case is a direct consequence of Proposition 7, 8 and 9. For non monic F we follow [40]: algorithm **ARNP** returns the expected output provided that the truncation bound $\mathcal{V}_F$ is replaced by $\mathcal{V}_F + v_X(A_{d_Y})$, where $A_{d_Y}(X)$ is the leading coefficient of F. The complexity analysis must be sligtly adapted, but yields the same result.

Proof of Theorem 2. The polynomial F is irreducible in $\overline{L}[[X]][Y]$ if and only if $\rho = 1$ and the corresponding RPE has coefficients in L. This condition is equivalent to the following one: each Newton polygon encountered by **ARNP** has a unique edge Δ and $\phi_\Delta(T) = (T - \xi)^{d_T(\phi_\Delta)}$. The latter condition may be tested with the **Oneroot** function at a cost of $\mathcal{O}(d_T(\phi_\Delta)) \subset \mathcal{O}(d_Y)$ operations in L; see Proposition 5. Hence, it is easy to modify **ARNP** to abort and return **False** whenever any of these two conditions is not satisfied. The **Oneroot** test will be repeated at most $\log_2 d_Y$ times, thanks to Abhyankar's trick. There will be no factorization cost, nor change of representation cost. By Proposition 9, execution of the modified algorithm requires $\mathcal{O}(d_Y(\mathcal{V}_F + 1))$ operations in L because $\rho = 1$; thus Theorem 2 holds.

6. FURTHER FACTORIZATION

In this section, we present a technique that may reduce running times in some cases, but does not improve the worst case complexity bound of Theorem 1. Due to space constraints, all proofs are omitted. The method is based on the following well-known result, that can easily be justified:

PROPOSITION 10. *Consider $H \in L_t[X,Y]$, a Y-monic polynomial with $d_Y(H) > 0$ and $H(X,0) \neq 0$. Denote $\{\Delta_i\}_{1\leq i\leq u}$ the edges of $\mathcal{N}(H)$, $-m_i/q_i$ the slope of Δ_i (with $\gcd(m_i,q_i) = 1$) and $\phi_{\Delta_i} = \prod_{j=1}^{c_i} \phi_{ij}^{M_{ij}}$ the factorization ϕ_{Δ_i} into irreducible elements of $L_t[T]$. Then there exists a unique set of Y-monic $G_{ij} \in L_t[[X]][Y]$ such that:*

1. *$H = \prod_{i=1}^{u}\prod_{j=1}^{c_i} G_{ij}$.*
2. *$d_Y(G_{ij}) = q_i \deg(\phi_{ij}) M_{ij}$*
3. *$\gcd(G_{ij}, G_{i'j'}) = 1$ if $(i,j) \neq (i',j')$*
4. *$\mathcal{N}(G_{ij})$ has a unique edge with slope $-m_i/q_i$,*
5. *The characteristic polynomial of $\mathcal{N}(G_{ij})$ is $\phi_{ij}^{M_{ij}}$.*

Applying line 13 of **ARNP** to each factor $\lceil G_{ij} \rceil^N$ for a well-chosen N instead of $\overline{H}$ may save useless computations since $d_Y(G_{ij}) < d_Y(H)$, provided that an approximate factorization of $\overline{H}$ that preserves singular parts can be computed at a sufficiently low cost. Since $\overline{H}(0,Y) = Y^{\deg(\overline{H})}$, there is no initial factorization that allows to directly construct approximations of the G_{ij} via Hensel lifting. Algorithm **Split** below explains how to alleviate the problem. But to stay within the complexity bound of Theorem 1, we must first reduce the complexity of Hensel lifting for polynomials with support in a lattice.

Structured Hensel Lifting. Let $(q,m) \in \mathbb{Z}^2$ with $q > 0$ and $\gcd(m,q) = 1$ and denote $\Gamma_{q,m}$ the lattice of $\mathbb{Z}^2$ generated by $(0,q)$ and $(1,m)$. We also introduce $L_t[X,Y]_{\Gamma_{q,m}}$, the ring of polynomials with support in $\Gamma_{q,m}$.

LEMMA 2. *$L_t[X,Y]_{\Gamma_{q,m}} \cap L_t[Y] = L_t[Y^q]$.*

Complexity results in Section 6 are subject to the following hypothesis:

HYPOTHESIS 1. *It is possible to multiply two polynomials in $L_t[X,Y]_{\Gamma_{q,m}}$ with degrees less than n_X and $n_Y \geq q$ using at most $\mathcal{O}(n_X n_Y/q)$ operations in L_t.*

By notation $\mathcal{O}(n_X n_Y/q)$, we mean that, for all $q \geq 1$ and all $n_Y \geq q$, with n_Y and n_X sufficiently large, the function is bounded by $n_X n_Y/q$ times logarithmic factors of n_X and n_Y. If L_t contains sufficiently many roots of unity, the existence of such a multiplication algorithm might be deduced from [34, Section 4.3]. Assuming Hypothesis 1, we get:

PROPOSITION 11. *Let $A, B \in L_t[X,Y]_{\Gamma_{q,m}}$ with $d_Y(B) \leq d_Y(A) = n_Y$, $q \leq n_Y$, B is Y-monic and let N be in $\mathbb{N}^*$. There exists an algorithm to compute $Q, R \in L[X,Y]$ such that $A = QB + R \mod X^N$ with $d_Y(R) < d_Y(B)$ requiring no more than $\mathcal{O}(n_Y N/q)$ operations in L. Moreover, Q and R are in $L_t[X,Y]_{\Gamma_{q,m}}$.*

PROPOSITION 12. *Let $H \in L_t[X,Y]_{\Gamma_{q,m}}$ be Y-monic, assume $n_Y = d_Y(H) \geq q$ and let N be in $\mathbb{N}^*$. Suppose that $H(0,Y) = \prod_i h_i(Y)$ with $h_i \in L_t[Y^q]$ and $\gcd(h_i,h_j) = 1$ for $i \neq j$. Then there exist unique $H_i \in L_t[X,Y]_{\Gamma_{q,m}}$ such that $H = \prod_i H_i \mod X^N$ and $H_i(0,X) = h_i(Y)$. Moreover, there exists an algorithm* **SHensel** *such that the function call* **SHensel**$(H,\{h_i\}_i,q,N)$ *computes the (ordered) set $\{H_i\}_i$ with no more than $\mathcal{O}(n_Y N/q)$ operations in L_t.*

Factorization of $\overline{H}$. We can now describe algorithm **Split** to compute an approximate factorization of H in $L_t[[X]][Y]$ corresponding to Proposition 10. The following points are essential:

• To get sufficient approximation for the factors, we must start from the edge with greatest slope, i.e., the rightmost edge. Therefore, the classical dichotomic approach used in multi-factor Hensel lifting cannot be applied to reduce complexity further. During a function call, other edges are grouped together and treated recursively; see lines 5 and 9.
• If $-m/q$ is the slope of the rightmost edge, we use at line 6 a transformation similar to (1) to obtain a polynomial in $L_t[X,Y]_{\Gamma_{q,m}}$ that allows to use structured Hensel lifting. All factors corresponding to the rightmost edge are computed, together with a factor H_0 corresponding to other edges.
• To get an order N approximation, we must lift factors up to order qN; see [40, Figure 2]. The key point is that the extra factor q is compensated by the gain given by Proposition 12. Otherwise, this factorization step would worsen our complexity bound because q may be as large as d_Y.

Split(L_t, H, N)

Input: L_t, *a field,* $H \in L_t[X,Y]$, Y*-monic, with* $d_Y(H) > 0$ *and* $H(X,0) \neq 0$, N *an integer with* $N > v_X(H(X,0))$.
Output: *A set* $\{(m_i, q_i, H_{ij}, \phi_{ij}, M_{ij})\}_{i,j}$ *with* $1 \leq i \leq u$, $1 \leq j \leq c_i$ *such that* $H_{ij} = \lceil G_{ij} \rceil^N$ *where* m_i, q_i, G_{ij}, ϕ_{ij} *and* M_{ij} *are defined in Proposition 10.*

1. Compute the quantities m, q, l, ϕ_Δ associated with the rightmost edge Δ of $\mathcal{N}(H)$.
2. $\{(\phi_j, M_j)\}_{j=1}^{c} \leftarrow$ **Factor**(L_t, ϕ_Δ)
3. Let (i_0, j_0) be the leftmost point of Δ.
4. If $i_0 = 0$ and $c = 1$ then Return $\{(m, q, H, \phi_1, M_1)\}$.
5. If $i_0 > 0$ then // *There is more than one edge.*
   Write $i_0 = (a-1)q + b$ with $0 < b \leq q$ and set $r = q - b$.
   $(\phi_0, M_0) \leftarrow (T^a, 1)$
6. $\widehat{H}(X,Y) \leftarrow Y^r H(X^q, X^m Y)/X^l \in L[X,Y]$.
7. $\{\widehat{H}_j\}_j \leftarrow$ **SHensel**$(\widehat{H}, \{\phi_j(Y^q)^{M_j}\}_j, q, qN+1)$
8. For j from 1 to c do // $\widehat{H}_j$ *corresponds to* ϕ_j.
   $H_j(X,Y) \leftarrow \widehat{H}_j(X^{1/q}, X^{-m/q}Y)X^{m\deg(\phi_j)M_j}$
9. If $i_0 > 0$ then // *Treat remaining edges.*
   $H_0(X,Y) \leftarrow \widehat{H}_0(X,Y)X^{ma}Y^{-r}$
   $\mathcal{S} \leftarrow$ **Split**(L_t, H_0, N)
10. Return $\mathcal{S} \cup \{(m, q, H_j, \phi_j, M_j)\}_{1 \leq j \leq c}$

Note that at line 7, index j ranges from 0 to c if $i_0 > 0$ and from 1 to c if $i_0 = 0$.

Proposition 13. *Algorithm* **Split** *returns the expected output. Not taking into account operations induced by sub-algorithm* **Factor**, *it requires at most* $\tilde{\mathcal{O}}(uNd_Y(H))$ *operations in* L_t, *where* u *is the number of edges of* $\mathcal{N}(H)$.

Function **ARNP** may be easily modified to include this factorization step: After line 5, include a line

5b. $\{(m_k, q_k, H_k, \phi_k, M_k)\}_{1 \leq k \leq s} \leftarrow$ **Split**$(L, \overline{H}, \lfloor N \rfloor)$,

then replace the nested "For" loops over Δ and ξ by a loop over the $(m_k, q_k, H_k, \phi_k, M_k)$ for $1 \leq k \leq s$, and continue the processing as before. The modified algorithm must also take a special care of the first edge of $\overline{H}$, if the corresponding H_k has degree 1, otherwise it may return expansions with superfluous terms. This causes no significant problem and has no impact on the complexity, hence we omit these technical details.

From the proof of Proposition 9, cost for lines 13 and 14 of one function call is $\tilde{\mathcal{O}}(s\,Nd_Y(H))$ operations in L_t, where s is the number of pairs (Δ, ξ). With the above modifications, this becomes $\tilde{\mathcal{O}}(u\,Nd_Y(H)) + \sum_{k=1}^{s} \tilde{\mathcal{O}}(Nd_Y(H_k)) \subset \tilde{\mathcal{O}}(u\,Nd_Y(H))$ because $\sum_k d_Y(H_k) = d_Y(H)$. This factorization step is thus worthwhile if u/s is sufficiently small to compensate larger factors hidden by the notation $\tilde{\mathcal{O}}$.

7. CONCLUSION

Theorem 1 reduces by one order of magnitude the bound of [40] for the computation of RPEs of F above 0. Example 3 below shows that our operation count is sharp because Algorithm **ARNP** requires $\Theta(d^4)$ operations in L for this case.

Example 3. Define $S_k = 2X^k + \sum_{l=1}^{k-1} X^l$ and $F(X,Y) = \prod_{k=1}^{N}(Y - S_k)$. At each call of **ARNP**, H has single edge $i + j = d_Y(H)$, with $\phi_\Delta = (T-2)(T-1)^{d_Y(H)-1}$ and Abhyankar's trick does not save any function call. We have $d_Y = N$, $d_X = \frac{N(N+1)}{2}$ and $\mathcal{V}_F = \frac{(N-1)N(N+1)}{3} \in \Theta(d_X d_Y)$. Moreover, **ARNP** will execute $\rho - 2 = d_Y - 2$ recursive calls; this leads to a complexity in $\Theta(d_X {d_Y}^3)$.

It turns out that the $\tilde{\mathcal{O}}(d^5 \log \mathfrak{q})$ complexity bound derived in [40] using the Riemann-Hurwitz formula for the computation of the genus of the curve $F(X,Y) = 0$ cannot be decreased by a mere application of Theorem 1. Indeed, suppose that Δ_F has a large irreducible factor D in $L[X]$ of degree t_0 close to $d_X d_Y$. In order to apply the Riemann-Huwitz formula, we need to compute RPEs above 0 of $F_c(X,Y) = F(X+c, Y) \in L_{t_0}[X,Y]$ where c is a root of D. When applying **ARNP** to F_c, if a characteristic polynomial ϕ of degree close to d_Y is encountered, the factorization of ϕ in $L_{t_0}[T]$ alone will require $\tilde{\mathcal{O}}({d_Y}^2 + d_Y \log \mathfrak{q}^{t_0})$ operations in L_{t_0} with standard factorization algorithms, thus $\tilde{\mathcal{O}}(d^5 \log \mathfrak{q})$ operations in L. Unless a univariate factorization algorithm with a drastically reduced running time is discovered, there is no hope to get an $\tilde{\mathcal{O}}(d^4 \log q)$ bound with this method (the recent algorithm of [30] is not even sufficient). However, following [40], we obtain:

Proposition 14. *Not taking into account univariate factorizations, there exists an algorithm to compute the genus of the curve* $F(X,Y) = 0$ *with* $\tilde{\mathcal{O}}(d_X {d_Y}^2 (d_X + d_Y)) \subset \tilde{\mathcal{O}}(d^4)$ *operations in* L.

This result suggests to use the D5 technique [20, 18] to avoid the univariate factorization bottleneck; this will the topic of forthcoming investigations.

A prototype for **ARNP** has been implemented in Maple to validate the algorithm, but a significant amount of work is still necessary to develop efficient code. In fact, the technique introduced in this paper give better asymptotic operation counts and better upper complexity bounds, but it is not even clear that **ARNP** can be made to run faster than other implementations for reasonable input size. In particular, the truncation bound $\mathcal{V}_F$ is usually not sharp (as demonstrated by Example 2 where the value $\mathcal{V}_F = 94$ is far from optimal) and calls to **WPT** artificially increase X-degree. Finer bounds, or/and a "relaxed" approach [48] could prove useful.

As for Section 6, we consider it for now as a motivation for studying further structured multiplication algorithms [34]. No implementation of those is known to the authors and this would be a significant contribution in itself.

Acknowledgments. We are grateful to Eric Schost for useful input about [34]. We thank anonymous referees for their contribution to the clarity of the paper.

8. REFERENCES

[1] S. Abhyankar. *Algebraic Geometry for Scientists and Engineers*, volume 35 of *Mathematical surveys and monographs*. Amer. Math. Soc., 1990.

[2] J.-D. Bauch. Genus computation of global function fields. *Journal of Symbolic Computation*, 66:8–20, 2015.

[3] J.-D. Bauch, E. Nart, and H. Stainsby. Complexity of the OM factorizations of polynomials over local fields. *LMS Journal of Computation and Mathematics*, 16:139–171, 2013.

[4] T. Beck. Formal desingularization of surfaces: The Jung method revisited. *J. Symb. Comp.*, 44(2):131–160, 2009.

[5] J. Berthomieu, G. Lecerf, and G. Quintin. Polynomial root finding over local rings and application to error correcting codes. *Applicable Algebra in Engineering, Communication and Computing*, 24(6):413–443, 2013.

[6] D. Bini and V. Y. Pan. *Polynomial and Matrix Computations*, volume 1 of *Progress in Theoretical Computer Science*. Birkhäuser, Saarbrücken, 1994.

[7] G. A. Bliss. *Algebraic functions*. AMS, 1933.

[8] W. Bosma, J. Cannon, and C. Playoust. The Magma Algebra System I : The user language. *J. Symb. Comp.*, 24(3-4):235–265, 1997.

[9] E. Brieskorn and H. Knörrer. *Plane Algebraic Curves*. Birkhaüser, 1986.

[10] A. Campillo. *Algebroid Curves in Positive Characteristic*, volume 378 of *LNCS*. Springer-Verlag, 1980.

[11] C. Chevalley. *Introduction to the Theory of Algebraic Functions of One Variable*, volume 6 of *Mathematical Surveys*. AMS, 1951.

[12] A. L. Chistov. Polynomial complexity of the Newton-Puiseux algorithm. In *Mathematical Foundations of Computer Science 1986*, pages 247–255, London, UK, 1986. Springer-Verlag.

[13] D. V. Chudnovsky and G. V. Chudnovsky. On expansion of algebraic functions in power and puiseux series. I. *Journal of Complexity*, 2(4):271–294, 1986.

[14] D. V. Chudnovsky and G. V. Chudnovsky. On expansion of algebraic functions in power and puiseux series. II. *Journal of Complexity*, 3(1):1–25, 1987.

[15] P. M. Cohn. Puiseux's Theorem revisited. *Journal of Pure and Applied Algebra*, 24:1–4, 1984.

[16] L. Comtet. Calcul pratique des coefficients de Taylor d'une fonction algébrique. *L'Enseignement Mathématique*, 2(10):267–270, 1964.

[17] O. Cormier, M. F. Singer, B. M. Trager, and F. Ulmer. Linear differential operators for polynomial equations. *J. Symb. Comp.*, 34(5):355–398, 2002.

[18] X. Dahan, E. Schost, M. M. Maza, W. Wu, and Y. Xie. On the complexity of the D5 principle. *SIGSAM Bull.*, 39(3):97–98, 2005.

[19] W. Decker, G.-M. Greuel, G. Pfister, and H. Schönemann. SINGULAR 3-1-6 — A computer algebra system for polynomial computations. http://www.singular.uni-kl.de, 2012.

[20] J. Della Dora, C. Dicrescenzo, and D. Duval. About a new method for computing in algebraic number fields. In *EUROCAL 85*. Springer-Verlag LNCS 204, 1985.

[21] G. Diaz-Toca and L. Gonzalez-Vega. Determining puiseux expansions by hensel's lemma and dynamic evaluation. In V. Ganzha, E. Mayr, and E. Vorozhtsov, editors, *Computer Algebra in Scientific Computing, CASC 2002*. Technische Universität München, Germany, Sept. 2002.

[22] D. Duval. Diverses questions relatives au calcul formel avec des nombres algébriques. Université de Grenoble, Thèse d'État, 1987.

[23] D. Duval. Rational Puiseux expansions. *Compositio Math.*, 70(2):119–154, 1989.

[24] M. Eichler. *Introduction to the Theory of Algebraic Numbers and Functions*. Academic Press, 1966.

[25] D. Ford and O. Veres. On the complexity of the Montes ideal factorization. In Springer, editor, *ANTS IX*, volume 6197, pages 174–185. Lecture Notes in Computer Science, 2010.

[26] G.-M. Greuel, C. Lossen, and M. Schulze. Three algorithms in Algebraic Geometry, Coding Theory and Singularity Theory. In Kluwer, editor, *Application of Algebraic Geometry to Coding Theory, Physics and Computation*, pages 161–194, 2001.

[27] J.-P. Henry and M. Merle. Complexity of computation of embedded resolution of algebraic curves. In *Proceedings Eurocal 87*, number 378 in Lecture Notes in Computer Science, pages 381–390. Springer-Verlag, 1987.

[28] D. Inaba. Factorization of multivariate polynomials by extended hensel construction. *SIGSAM Bull.*, 39(1):142–154, 2005.

[29] K. S. Kedlaya. The algebraic closure of the power series fields in positive characteristic. *Proc. Amer. Math. Soc.*, 129:3461–3470, 2001.

[30] K. S. Kedlaya and C. Umans. Fast polynomial factorization and modular composition. *SIAM J. Computing*, 40(6):1767–1802, 2011.

[31] H. T. Kung and J. F. Traub. All algebraic functions can be computed fast. *J. ACM*, 25(2):245–260, 1978.

[32] T.-C. Kuo. Generalized Newton-Puiseux Theory and Hensel's Lemma in $c[[x, y]]$. *Can. J. of Math.*, XLI:1101–1116, 1989.

[33] T.-C. Kuo. A simple algorithm for deciding primes in $k[[x, y]]$. *Can. J. of Math.*, 47(4):801–816, 1995.

[34] J. Lebreton, E. Schost, and J. V. der Hoeven. Structured FFT and TFT: symmetric and lattice polynomials. In ACM, editor, *Proc. ISSAC '13*, pages 355–362, 2013.

[35] X. Li, M. M. Maza, and E. Schost. Fast arithmetic for triangular sets: from theory to practice. In *Proc. ISSAC '07*, pages 269–276, New York, NY, USA, 2007. ACM.

[36] M. B. Monagan, K. O. Geddes, K. M. Heal, G. Labahn, S. M. Vorkoetter, J. McCarron, and P. DeMarco. *Maple 10 Programming Guide*. Maplesoft, Waterloo ON, Canada, 2005.

[37] S. Pauli. Factoring polynomials over local fields. *J. Symb. Comp.*, 32(533-547), 2001.

[38] S. Pauli. Factoring polynomials over local fields ii. In Springer, editor, *ANTS IX*, volume 6197 of *Lecture Notes in Computer Science*, pages 301–315, 2010.

[39] A. Poteaux and M. Rybowicz. Good reduction of puiseux series and complexity of the Newton-Puiseux algorithm. In *Proc. ISSAC '08*, pages 239–246, New-York, 2008. ACM.

[40] A. Poteaux and M. Rybowicz. Complexity Bounds for the Rational Newton-Puiseux Algorithm over Finite Fields. *Applicable Algebra in Engineering, Communication and Computing*, 22(3):187–217, 2011.

[41] A. Poteaux and M. Rybowicz. Good reduction of Puiseux series and applications. *J. Symb. Comp.*, 47(1):32–63, 2012.

[42] A. Poteaux and E. Schost. On the complexity of computing with zero-dimensional triangular sets. *J. Symb. Comp.*, 50:110–138, 2013.

[43] M. Rybowicz. An algorithm for computing an integral basis in an algebraic function field. In *Proc. ISSAC '91*. ACM Press, 1991.

[44] T. Sasaki and D. Inaba. Hensel construction of $f(x, u_1, \ldots, u_l)$ at a singular point and its application. *SIGSAM Bull.*, 1:9–17, 2000.

[45] T. Sasaki and F. Kako. Solving multivariate algebraic equations by Hensel construction. *Japan J. of Industrial and Applied Math.*, 16:257–285, 1999.

[46] J. Teitelbaum. The computational complexity of the resolution of plane curve singularities. *Math. Comp.*, 54(190):797–837, 1990.

[47] J. van der Hoeven. Fast evaluation of holonomic functions. *Theoretical Computer Science*, 210(1):199–215, 1999.

[48] J. van der Hoeven. Relax, but don't be too lazy. *J. Symb. Comp.*, 34:479–542, 2002.

[49] J. van der Hoeven. Effective analytic functions. *J. Symb. Comp.*, 39(3-4):433–449, 2005.

[50] M. van Hoeij. An algorithm for computing an integral basis in an algebraic function field. *J. Symb. Comp.*, 18:353–363, 1994.

[51] J. von zur Gathen and J. Gerhard. *Modern Computer Algebra*. Cambridge University Press, third edition, 2013.

[52] R. J. Walker. *Algebraic Curves*. Springer Verlag, Berlin-New York, 1978.

[53] P. G. Walsh. On the complexity of rational Puiseux expansions. *Pacific J. of Math.*, 188:369–387, 1999.

[54] P. G. Walsh. A polynomial-time complexity bound for the computation of the singular part of an algebraic function. *Math. of Comp.*, 69:1167–1182, 2000.

Data-Discriminants of Likelihood Equations *

Jose Israel Rodriguez[†]
University of Notre Dame
Department of Applied and Computational Mathematics and Statistics
Notre Dame, IN 46556
jo.ro@nd.edu

Xiaoxian Tang[‡]
CAMP, National Institute for Mathematical Sciences
Daejeon, Republic of Korea 305-811
tangxiaoxian@nims.re.kr

ABSTRACT

Maximum likelihood estimation (MLE) is a fundamental computational problem in statistics. The problem is to maximize the likelihood function with respect to given data on a statistical model. An algebraic approach to this problem is to solve a very structured parameterized polynomial system called likelihood equations. For general choices of data, the number of complex solutions to the likelihood equations is finite and called the ML-degree of the model.

The only solutions to the likelihood equations that are statistically meaningful are the real/positive solutions. However, the number of real/positive solutions is not characterized by the ML-degree. We use discriminants to classify data according to the number of real/positive solutions of the likelihood equations. We call these discriminants data-discriminants (DD). We develop a probabilistic algorithm for computing DDs. Experimental results show that, for the benchmarks we have tried, the probabilistic algorithm is more efficient than the standard elimination algorithm. Based on the computational results, we discuss the real root classification problem for the 3 by 3 symmetric matrix model.

Categories and Subject Descriptors

G.3 [**Probability and Statistics**]: Statistical Computing; I.1.2 [**Computing Methodologies**]: Algorithms—*Algebraic Algorithms*

General Terms

Theory, Algorithms

*This research paper is partly supported by 2014 NIMS Thematic Program on Applied Algebraic Geometry.

†This material is based upon work supported by the National Science Foundation under Award No. DMS-1402545, as well as the hospitality of the Simons Institute.

‡Corresponding Author

ISSAC'15, July 6–9, 2015, Bath, United Kingdom.

DOI: http://dx.doi.org/10.1145/2755996.2756649.

Keywords

Maximum likelihood estimation, Likelihood equation, Data-Discriminant, Real root classification

1. INTRODUCTION

We begin the introduction with an illustrative example. Suppose we have a weighted four-sided die such that the *probability* p_i of observing side i $(i = 0, 1, 2, 3)$ of the die satisfies the constraint $p_0 + 2p_1 + 3p_2 - 4p_3 = 0$. We toss the die 1000 times and record a 4-dimensional *data* vector (u_0, u_1, u_2, u_3), where u_i is the number of times we observe the side i. We want to determine the probability distribution $(p_0, p_1, p_2, p_3) \in \mathbb{R}^4_{>0}$ that best explains the data subject to the constraint. One approach is by *maximum likelihood estimation* (MLE):

Maximize the *likelihood function* $p_0^{u_0}p_1^{u_1}p_2^{u_2}p_3^{u_3}$ subjected to

$$p_0 + 2p_1 + 3p_2 - 4p_3 = 0, p_0 + p_1 + p_2 + p_3 = 1,$$
$$p_0 > 0, p_1 > 0, p_2 > 0, \text{and } p_3 > 0.$$

For some statistical models, the MLE problem can be solved by well known *hill climbing* algorithms such as the EM-algorithm. However, the hill climbing method can fail if there is more than one local maximum. Fortunately, it is known that the MLE problem can be solved by solving the system of *likelihood equations* [15, 2]:

$$\begin{aligned} F_0 &= p_0\lambda_1 + p_0\lambda_2 - u_0 & F_3 &= p_3\lambda_1 - 4p_3\lambda_2 - u_3 \\ F_1 &= p_1\lambda_1 + 2p_1\lambda_2 - u_1 & F_4 &= p_0 + 2p_1 + 3p_2 - 4p_3 \\ F_2 &= p_2\lambda_1 + 3p_2\lambda_2 - u_2 & F_5 &= p_0 + p_1 + p_2 + p_3 - 1 \end{aligned}$$

where λ_1 and λ_2 are newly introduced indeterminates (Lagrange multipliers) for formulating the likelihood equations. More specifically, for given (u_0, u_1, u_2, u_3), if (p_0, p_1, p_2, p_3) is a critical point of the likelihood function, then there exist complex numbers λ_1 and λ_2 such that $(p_0, p_1, p_2, p_3, \lambda_1, \lambda_2)$ is a solution of the polynomial system. For randomly chosen data u_i, the likelihood equations have 3 complex solutions. However, only solutions with positive coordinates p_i are statistically meaningful. A solution with all positive p_i coordinates is said to be a positive solution. So an important problem is *real root classification* (RRC):

For which u_i, the polynomial system has $1, 2$ and 3 real/positive solutions?

According to the theory of computational (real) algebraic geometry [26, 20], the number of (real/positive) solutions only changes when the data u_i goes across some "special" values (see Theorem 2). The set of "special" u_i is a *(projective) variety* (see Lemma 4 in [20]) in (3 dimensional complex projective space) 4-dimensional complex space. The number of real/positive solutions is uniform over each open connected component determined by the variety. In other words, the "special" u_i plays the similar role as the *discriminant* for univariate polynomials. The first step of RRC is calculating the "special" u_i, leading to the discriminant problem:

How to effectively compute the "special" u_i?

Geometrically, the "special" u_i is a projection of a variety. So in principle, it can be computed by *elimination* (see Chapter 3, page 115–128 in [6]). For instance, by the command `eliminate` in `Macaulay2` [10], we compute that the "special" u_i in the illustrative example form a hypersurface defined by a homogenous polynomial in (u_0, u_1, u_2, u_3) (see Example 1). However, for most MLE problems, due to the large size of likelihood equations, the elimination computation is too expensive. In this paper, we discuss the "discriminant" problem for the likelihood equations. The contributions of the paper are listed as follows.

• For likelihood equations, we show that the "special" u_i form a projective variety. We call the homogenous polynomial that generates the codimension 1 component of the projective variety the *data-discriminant.* This name distinguishes it from the *weight-discriminant* for the likelihood equations (which replaces the condition $p_0 + \cdots + p_n = 1$ with the condition $h_0p_0 + \cdots + h_np_n = 1$ with parameters $h_0, \ldots, h_n$).

• For algebraic statistical models, we develop a probabilistic algorithm to compute data-discriminants. We implement the algorithm in `Macaulay2`. Experimental results show that the probabilistic algorithm is more efficient than the standard elimination algorithm.

• We discuss the real root classification for the 3×3 symmetric matrix model, which inspire future work.

We remark that our work can be viewed as following the numerous efforts in applying computational algebraic geometry to tackle MLE and critical points problems [15, 2, 1, 16, 25, 12, 8, 13, 18, 14, 21].

The paper is organized as follows. The formal definition of the data-discriminant is introduced in Section 2. The standard elimination algorithm and the probabilistic algorithm are presented in Section 3. Experimental results comparing the two algorithms are shown in Section 4. The real root classification of the 3×3 symmetric matrix model and conclusion are given in Section 5.

2. DEFINITION

In this section, we discuss how to define "data-discriminant". We assume the readers are familiar with elimination theory (see Chapter 3 in [6]).

Notation 1. *Let* $\mathbb{P}$ *denote the* projective closure *of the complex numbers* $\mathbb{C}$. *For homogeneous polynomials* $g_1, \ldots, g_s$ *in* $\mathbb{Q}[p_0, \ldots, p_n]$, $\mathcal{V}(g_1, \ldots, g_s)$ *denotes the* projective variety *in* $\mathbb{P}^n$ *defined by* $g_1, \ldots, g_s$. *Let* Δ_n *denote the n-dimensional* probability simplex $\{(p_0, \ldots, p_n) \in \mathbb{R}^{n+1} | p_0 > 0, \ldots, p_n > 0, p_0 + \cdots + p_n = 1\}$.

Definition 1. *[15]***(Algebraic Statistical Model and Model Invariant)** *The set* X *is said to be an* algebraic statistical model *if* $X = \mathcal{V}(g_1, \ldots, g_s) \cap \Delta_n$ *where* $g_1, \ldots, g_s$ *define an irreducible generically reduced projective variety. Each* g_k $(1 \le k \le s)$ *is said to be a* model invariant *of* X.

For a given algebraic statistical model, there are several different ways to formulate the likelihood equations [15]. In this section, we introduce the Lagrange likelihood equations and define the data-discriminant for this formulation. One can similarly define data-discriminants for other formulations of the likelihood equations.

Notation 2. *For any* $f_1, \ldots, f_m$ *in the polynomial ring* $\mathbb{Q}[x_1, ..., x_k]$, $\mathcal{V}_a(f_1, \ldots, f_m)$ *denotes the* affine variety *in* $\mathbb{C}^k$ *defined by* $f_1, \ldots, f_m$ *and* $\langle f_1, \ldots, f_m \rangle$ *denotes the* ideal *generated by* $f_1, \ldots, f_m$. *For an ideal* I *in* $\mathbb{Q}[x_1, \ldots, x_k]$, $\mathcal{V}_a(I)$ *denotes the* affine variety *defined by* I.

Definition 2. *[13]***(Lagrange Likelihood Equations and Correspondence)** *Given an algebraic statistical model* X. *The system of polynomial equations below is said to be the* Lagrange likelihood equations *of* X:

$$F_0 = \quad p_0(\lambda_1 + \frac{\partial g_1}{\partial p_0}\lambda_2 + \cdots + \frac{\partial g_s}{\partial p_0}\lambda_{s+1}) - u_0 = 0$$

$$\cdots$$

$$F_n = \quad p_n(\lambda_1 + \frac{\partial g_1}{\partial p_n}\lambda_2 + \cdots + \frac{\partial g_s}{\partial p_n}\lambda_{s+1}) - u_n = 0$$

$$F_{n+1} = \quad g_1(p_0, \ldots, p_n) = 0$$

$$\cdots$$

$$F_{n+s} = \quad g_s(p_0, \ldots, p_n) = 0$$

$$F_{n+s+1} = \quad p_0 + \cdots + p_n - 1 = 0$$

where $g_1, \ldots, g_s$ *are the model invariants of* X *and* $u_0, \ldots, u_n$, $p_0, \ldots, p_n$, $\lambda_1, \ldots, \lambda_{s+1}$ *are indeterminates (also denoted by* $\mathbf{u}$, $\mathbf{p}$, Λ*). More specifically,*

– $p_0, \ldots, p_n, \lambda_1, \ldots, \lambda_{s+1}$ *are unknowns,*

– $u_0, \ldots, u_n$ *are parameters.*

$\mathcal{V}_a(F_0, \ldots, F_{n+s+1})$, *namely the set*

$$\{(\mathbf{u}, \mathbf{p}, \Lambda) \in \mathbb{C}^{n+1} \times \mathbb{C}^{n+1} \times \mathbb{C}^{s+1} | F_0 = 0, \ldots, F_{n+s+1} = 0\},$$

is said to be the Lagrange likelihood correspondence *of* X *and denoted by* $\mathcal{L}_X$.

Notation 3. *Let* π *denote the* canonical projection *from the ambient space of the Lagrange likelihood correspondence to the* $\mathbb{C}^{n+1}$ *associated to the* $\mathbf{u}$ *indeterminants* π: $\mathbb{C}^{n+1} \times \mathbb{C}^{n+s+2} \to \mathbb{C}^{n+1}$.

Given an algebraic statistical model X and a data vector $\mathbf{u} \in \mathbb{R}^n_{>0}$, the *maximum likelihood estimation* (MLE) problem is to **maximize the** *likelihood function* $p_0^{u_0} \cdots p_n^{u_n}$ **subject to** X. The MLE problem can be solved by computing $\pi^{-1}(\mathbf{u}) \cap \mathcal{L}_X$. More specifically, if $\mathbf{p}$ is a regular point of $\mathcal{V}(g_1, \ldots, g_s)$, then $\mathbf{p}$ is a critical point of the likelihood function if and only if there exist $\Lambda \in \mathbb{C}^{s+1}$ such that $(\mathbf{u}, \mathbf{p}, \Lambda) \in \mathcal{L}_X$. Theorem 1 states that for a general data vector $\mathbf{u}$, $\pi^{-1}(\mathbf{u}) \cap \mathcal{L}_X$ is a finite set and the cardinality of $\pi^{-1}(\mathbf{u}) \cap \mathcal{L}_X$ is constant over a dense Zariski open set, which inspires the definition of ML-degree. For details, see [15].

Theorem 1. *[15] For an algebraic statistical model* X, *there exist an affine variety* $V \subset \mathbb{C}^{n+1}$ *and a non-negative integer* N *such that for any* $\mathbf{u} \in \mathbb{C}^{n+1} \backslash V$,

$$\#\pi^{-1}(\mathbf{u}) \cap \mathcal{L}_X = N.$$

Definition 3. *[15]*(**ML-Degree**) *For an algebraic statistical model X, the non-negative integer N stated in Theorem 1 is said to be the* ML-degree *of X.*

Notation 4. *For any S in $\mathbb{C}^{n+1}$, $\mathcal{I}(S)$ denotes the ideal*

$$\{D \in \mathbb{Q}[\mathbf{u}] | D(a_0, \ldots, a_n) = 0, \forall (a_0, \ldots, a_n) \in S\}.$$

$\overline{S}$ denotes the affine closure *of S in $\mathbb{C}^{n+1}$, namely $\mathcal{V}_a(\mathcal{I}(S))$.*

Definition 4. *For an algebraic statistical model X, suppose $F_0, \ldots, F_{n+s+1}$ are defined as in Definition 2. Let J denote*

$$\det \begin{bmatrix} \frac{\partial F_0}{\partial p_0} & \cdots & \frac{\partial F_0}{\partial p_n} & \frac{\partial F_0}{\partial \lambda_1} & \cdots & \frac{\partial F_0}{\partial \lambda_{s+1}} \\ \vdots & \ddots & \vdots & \vdots & \ddots & \vdots \\ \frac{\partial F_{n+s+1}}{\partial p_0} & \cdots & \frac{\partial F_{n+s+1}}{\partial p_n} & \frac{\partial F_{n+s+1}}{\partial \lambda_1} & \cdots & \frac{\partial F_{n+s+1}}{\partial \lambda_{s+1}} \end{bmatrix}.$$

Then, we have the following:

- *$\mathcal{L}_{X_\infty}$ denotes the* set of non-properness *of π, i.e., the set of the $u \in \overline{\pi(\mathcal{L}_X)}$ such that there does not exist a compact neighborhood U of u where $\pi^{-1}(U) \cap \mathcal{L}_X$ is compact;*
- *$\mathcal{L}_{X_J}$ denotes $\overline{\pi(\mathcal{L}_X \cap \mathcal{V}_a(J))}$;*
- *$\mathcal{L}_{X_p}$ denotes $\overline{\pi(\mathcal{L}_X \cap \mathcal{V}_a(\Pi_{k=0}^n p_k))}$.*

The geometric meaning of $\mathcal{L}_{X_p}$ and $\mathcal{L}_{X_J}$ are as follows. The first, $\mathcal{L}_{X_p}$, is the projection of the intersection of the Lagrange likelihood correspondence with the coordinate hyperplanes. The second, $\mathcal{L}_{X_J}$, is the projection of the intersection of the Lagrange likelihood correspondence with the hypersurface defined by J. Geometrically, $\mathcal{L}_{X_J}$ is the closure of the union of the projection of the singular locus of $\mathcal{L}_X$ and the set of critical values of the restriction of π to the regular locus of $\mathcal{L}_X$ (see Definition 2 in [20]).

The Lagrange likelihood equations define an affine variety. As we continuously deform the parameters u_i, coordinates of a solution can tend to infinity. Geometrically, $\mathcal{L}_{X_\infty}$ is the set of the data $\mathbf{u}$ such that the Lagrange likelihood equations have some solution $(\mathbf{p}, \Lambda)$ at infinity; this is the closure of the set of "non-properness" as defined in the page 1, [19] and page 3, [23]. It is known that the set of non-properness of π is closed and can be computed by Gröbner bases (see Lemma 2 and Theorem 2 in [20]).

The ML-degree encaptures geometry of the likelihood equations over the complex numbers. However, statistically meaningful solutions occur over real numbers. Below, Theorem 2 states that $\mathcal{L}_{X_\infty}$, $\mathcal{L}_{X_J}$ and $\mathcal{L}_{X_p}$ define open connected components such that the number of real/positive solutions is uniform over each open connected component. Theorem 2 is a corollary of *Ehresmann's theorem* for which there exists semi-algebraic statements since 1992 [5].

Theorem 2. *For any algebraic statistical model X,*

- *if $\mathcal{C}_1, \ldots, \mathcal{C}_t$ are the open connected components of*
$$\mathbb{R}^{n+1} \backslash (\mathcal{L}_{X_\infty} \cup \mathcal{L}_{X_J}),$$
then for each k $(1 \le k \le t)$, for any $\mathbf{u} \in \mathcal{C}_k$,
$$\# \pi^{-1}(\mathbf{u}) \cap \mathcal{L}_X \cap \mathbb{R}^{n+s+2}$$
is a constant;
- *if $\mathcal{C}_1, \ldots, \mathcal{C}_t$ are the open connected components of*
$$\mathbb{R}^{n+1} \backslash (\mathcal{L}_{X_\infty} \cup \mathcal{L}_{X_J} \cup \mathcal{L}_{X_p}),$$
then for each k $(1 \le k \le t)$, for any $\mathbf{u} \in \mathcal{C}_k$,
$$\# \pi^{-1}(\mathbf{u}) \cap \mathcal{L}_X \cap (\mathbb{R}_{>0}^{n+1} \times \mathbb{R}^{s+1})$$
is a constant.

Before we give the definition of data-discriminant, we study the structures of $\mathcal{L}_{X_\infty}$, $\mathcal{L}_{X_J}$, and $\mathcal{L}_{X_p}$ below.

- Proposition 1 shows that the structure of the likelihood equations forces $\mathcal{L}_{X_p}$ to be contained in the union of coordinate hyperplanes defined by $\prod_{k=0}^n u_k$.
- Proposition 2 shows that the structure of the likelihood equations forces $\mathcal{L}_{X_J} \backslash \{\mathbf{0}\}$ to be a projective variety.
- Similarly as the proof of Proposition 2, we can also show that the structure of the likelihood equations forces $\mathcal{L}_{X_\infty} \backslash \{\mathbf{0}\}$ to be a projective variety.

Proposition 1. *For any algebraic statistical model X,*

$$\mathcal{L}_{X_p} \subset \mathcal{V}_a(\Pi_{k=0}^n u_k).$$

Proof. By Definition 2, for any k $(0 \le k \le n)$,

$$u_k = p_k(\lambda_1 + \frac{\partial g_1}{\partial p_1} \lambda_2 + \cdots + \frac{\partial g_s}{\partial p_1} \lambda_{s+1}) - F_k.$$

Hence,

$$u_k \in \langle F_k, p_k \rangle \cap \mathbb{Q}[u_k] \subset \langle F_0, \ldots, F_{n+s+1}, p_k \rangle \cap \mathbb{C}[\mathbf{u}]$$

So

$$\mathcal{V}_a(\langle F_0, \ldots, F_{n+s+1}, p_k \rangle \cap \mathbb{C}[\mathbf{u}]) \subset \mathcal{V}_a(u_k)$$

By the Closure Theorem [6],

$$\mathcal{V}_a(\langle F_0, \ldots, F_{n+s+1}, p_k \rangle \cap \mathbb{C}[\mathbf{u}]) = \overline{\pi(\mathcal{L}_X \cap \mathcal{V}_a(p_k))}$$

Therefore,

$$\begin{aligned} \mathcal{L}_{X_p} &= \overline{\pi(\mathcal{L}_X \cap \mathcal{V}_a(\Pi_{k=0}^n p_k))} \\ &= \overline{\pi(\mathcal{L}_X \cap \cup_{k=0}^n \mathcal{V}_a(p_k))} \\ &= \cup_{k=0}^n \overline{\pi(\mathcal{L}_X \cap \mathcal{V}_a(p_k))} \\ &\subset \cup_{k=0}^n \mathcal{V}_a(u_k) \\ &= \mathcal{V}_a(\Pi_{k=0}^n u_k). \square \end{aligned}$$

Remark 1. *Generally, $\mathcal{L}_{X_p} \neq \mathcal{V}_a(\Pi_{k=0}^n u_k)$. For example, suppose the algebraic statistical model is $\mathcal{V}_a(p_0 - p_1) \cap \Delta_1$. Then $\mathcal{L}_{X_p} = \emptyset \neq \mathcal{V}_a(u_0 u_1)$.*

Notation 5. *$\mathcal{D}_{X_p}$ denotes the product $\Pi_{k=0}^n u_k$.*

Proposition 2. *For an algebraic statistical model X, we have $\mathcal{L}_{X_J} \backslash \{\mathbf{0}\}$ is a projective variety in $\mathbb{P}^n$, where $\mathbf{0}$ is the zero vector $(0, \ldots, 0)$ in $\mathbb{C}^{n+1}$.*

Proof. By the formulation of the Lagrange likelihood equations, we can prove that $\mathcal{I}(\pi(\mathcal{L}_X \cap \mathcal{V}_a(J))$ is a homogeneous ideal by the two basic facts below, which can be proved by Definition 2 and basic algebraic geometry arguments.

C1. For every $\mathbf{u}$ in $\pi(\mathcal{L}_X \cap \mathcal{V}_a(J))$, each scalar multiple $\alpha \mathbf{u}$ is also in $\pi(\mathcal{L}_X \cap \mathcal{V}_a(J))$.

C2. For any $S \subset \mathbb{C}^{n+1}$, if for any $\mathbf{u} \in S$ and for any scalar $\alpha \in \mathbb{C}$, $\alpha \mathbf{u} \in S$, then $\mathcal{I}(S)$ is a homogeneous ideal in $\mathbb{Q}[\mathbf{u}]$.

That means the ideal $\mathcal{I}(\pi(\mathcal{L}_X \cap \mathcal{V}_a(J))$ is generated by finitely many homogeneous polynomials $D_1, \ldots, D_m$. Therefore, $\mathcal{L}_{X_J} = \mathcal{V}_a(\mathcal{I}(\pi(\mathcal{L}_X \cap \mathcal{V}_a(J))) = \mathcal{V}_a(D_1, \ldots, D_m)$. So $\mathcal{L}_{X_J} \backslash \{\mathbf{0}\} = \mathcal{V}(D_1, \ldots, D_m) \subset \mathbb{P}^n$. $\square$

Notation 6. *For an algebraic statistical model X, we define the notation $\mathcal{D}_{X_J}$ according to the codimension of $\mathcal{L}_{X_J} \backslash \{\mathbf{0}\}$ in $\mathbb{P}^n$.*

• *If the codimension is 1, then assume $\mathcal{V}(D_1), \ldots, \mathcal{V}(D_K)$ are the codimension 1 irreducible components in the minimal irreducible decomposition of $\mathcal{L}_{X\,J} \backslash \{\mathbf{0}\}$ in $\mathbb{P}^n$ and $\langle D_1 \rangle, \ldots, \langle D_K \rangle$ are radical. $\mathcal{D}_{X\,J}$ denotes the homogeneous polynomial $\Pi_{j=1}^{K} D_j$.*

• *If the codimension is greater than 1, then our convention is to take $\mathcal{D}_{X\,J} = 1$.*

Similarly, we use the notation $\mathcal{D}_{X\,\infty}$ to denote the projective variety $\mathcal{L}_{X\,J} \backslash \{\mathbf{0}\}$. Now we define the "data-discriminant" of Lagrange likelihood equations.

Definition 5. **(Data-Discriminant)** *For a given algebraic statistics model X, the homogeneous polynomial $\mathcal{D}_{X\,\infty} \cdot \mathcal{D}_{X\,J} \cdot \mathcal{D}_{X\,p}$ is said to be the* data-discriminant *(DD) of Lagrange likelihood equations of X and denoted by $\mathcal{D}_X$.*

Remark 2. *Note that DD can be viewed as a generalization of the "discriminant" for univariate polynomials. So it is interesting to compare DD with border polynomial (BP) [26] and discriminant variety (DV) [20]. DV and BP are defined for general parametric polynomial systems. DD is defined for the likelihood equations but can be generalized to any square and generic zero-dimensional system. Generally, for any square and generic zero-dimensional system, $\mathcal{V}_a(DD) \subset DV \subset \mathcal{V}_a(BP)$. Note that due to the special structure of likelihood equations, DD is a homogenous polynomial despite being an affine system of equations. However, generally, DV is not a projective variety and BP is not homogenous.*

Example 1 (Linear Model). The algebraic statistic model for the four sided die story in Section 1 is given by

$$X = \mathcal{V}(p_0 + 2p_1 + 3p_2 - 4p_3) \cap \Delta_3.$$

The Langrange likelihood equations are the $F_0 = 0, \ldots, F_5 = 0$ shown in Section 1. The Langrange likelihood correspondence is $\mathcal{L}_X = \mathcal{V}_a(F_0, \ldots, F_5) \subset \mathbb{C}^{10}$. If we choose generic $(u_0, u_1, u_2, u_3) \in \mathbb{C}^4$, $\pi^{-1}(u_0, u_1, u_2, u_3) \cap \mathcal{L}_X = 3$, namely the ML-degree is 3. The data-discriminant is the product of $\mathcal{D}_{X\,\infty}$, $\mathcal{D}_{X\,p}$ and $\mathcal{D}_{X\,J}$, where

$\mathcal{D}_{X\,\infty} = u_0 + u_1 + u_2 + u_3$, $\mathcal{D}_{X\,p} = u_0 u_1 u_2 u_3$, and

$\mathcal{D}_{X\,J} = 441u_0^4 + 4998u_0^3u_1 + 20041u_0^2u_1^2 + 33320u_0u_1^3 + 19600u_1^4 - 756u_0^3u_2 + 20034u_0^2u_1u_2 + 83370u_0u_1^2u_2 + 79800u_1^3u_2 - 5346u_0^2u_2^2 + 55890u_0u_1u_2^2 + 119025u_1^2u_2^2 + 4860u_0u_2^3 + 76950u_1u_2^3 + 18225u_2^4 - 1596u_0^3u_3 - 11116u_0^2u_1u_3 - 17808u_0u_1^2u_3 + 4480u_1^3u_3 + 7452u_0^2u_2u_3 - 7752u_0u_1u_2u_3 + 49680u_1^2u_2u_3 - 17172u_0u_2^2u_3 + 71460u_1u_2^2u_3 + 27540u_2^3u_3 + 2116u_0^2u_3^2 + 6624u_0u_1u_3^2 - 4224u_1^2u_3^2 - 9528u_0u_2u_3^2 + 15264u_1u_2u_3^2 + 14724u_2^2u_3^2 - 1216u_0u_3^3 - 512u_1u_3^3 + 3264u_2u_3^3 + 256u_3^4$.

By applying the well known partial cylindrical algebraic decomposition (PCAD) [4] method to the data-discriminant above, we get that for any $(u_0, u_1, u_2, u_3) \in \mathbb{R}^4_{>0}$,

• if $\mathcal{D}_{X\,J}(u_0, u_1, u_2, u_3) > 0$, then the system of likelihood equations has 3 distinct real solutions and 1 of them is positive;

• if $\mathcal{D}_{X\,J}(u_0, u_1, u_2, u_3) < 0$, then the system of likelihood equations has exactly 1 real solution and it is positive.

The answer above can be verified by the `RealRootClassification` [26, 3] command in `Maple 17`. In this example, the $\mathcal{D}_{X\,\infty}$ does not effect the number of real/positive solutions since it is always positive when each u_i is positive. However, generally, $\mathcal{D}_{X\,\infty}$ plays an important role in real root classification. Also remark that the real root classification is equivalent to the positive root classification for this example but it is not true generally (see Example 6).

3. ALGORITHM

In this section, we discuss how to compute $\mathcal{D}_X$. We assume that X is a given statistical model, $F_0, \ldots, F_{n+s+1}$ are defined as in Definition 2, and J is defined as in Definition 4. We rename $F_0, \ldots, F_{n+s+1}$ as $F_0, \ldots, F_m$. Subsection 3.1 presents the standard elimination algorithm for reference and Subsection 3.2 presents our main algorithm (Algorithm 2).

3.1 Standard Elimination Algorithm

Considering the data-discriminant as a projection drives a natural algorithm to compute it. This is the standard elimination algorithm in symbolic computation:

• we compute the $\mathcal{L}_{X\,J}$ by *elimination* and then get $\mathcal{D}_{X\,J}$ by the *radical equidimensional decomposition* (see Definition 3 in [20]). The algorithm is formally described in the Algorithm 1;

Algorithm 1: DX-J

input : $F_0, \ldots, F_m, J$
output: $\mathcal{D}_{X\,J}$
1 $\mathcal{G}_{\mathbf{u}} \leftarrow$ the generator polynomial set of the elimination ideal $\langle F_0, \ldots F_m, J \rangle \cap \mathbb{Q}[\mathbf{u}]$
2 $\mathcal{D}_{X\,J} \leftarrow$ the codimension 1 component of the equidimensional radical decomposition of $\langle \mathcal{G}_{\mathbf{u}} \rangle$
3 **return** $\mathcal{D}_{X\,J}$

• we compute $\mathcal{L}_{X\,\infty}$ by the Algorithm `PROPERNESSDEFECTS` presented in [20] and then get $\mathcal{D}_{X\,\infty}$ by the radical equidimensional decomposition. We omit the formal description of the algorithm.

The previous algorithms in this subsection can not be used to compute DDs of algebraic statistical models in a reasonable time, see Tables 1–2 in Section 4. This motivates the exploration of a more practical method found in the next subsection.

3.2 Probabilistic Algorithm

First, we prepare the lemmas, then we present the main algorithm (Algorithm 2).

• Lemma 1 is used to linearly transform parameter space.

• Corollary 1 and Lemma 2 are used to compute the totally degree of $\mathcal{D}_{X\,J}$.

• Corollary 2 is used in the sampling for interpolation.

Lemma 1. *For any $G \in \mathbb{Q}[\mathbf{u}]$, there exists an affine variety V in $\mathbb{C}^n$ such that for any $(a_1, \ldots, a_n) \in \mathbb{C}^n \backslash V$, the total degree of G equals the degree of $B(t_0, t_1, \ldots, t_n)$ w.r.t. to t_0, where*

$$B(t_0, t_1, \ldots, t_n) = G(t_0, a_1 t_0 + t_1, \ldots, a_n t_0 + t_n)$$

Proof. Suppose the total degree of G is d and G_d is the homogeneous component of G with total degree d. For any $(1, a_1, \ldots, a_n) \in \mathbb{C}^{n+1} \backslash \mathcal{V}_a(G_d)$, let $B(t_0, t_1, \ldots, t_n) = G(t_0, a_1 t_0 + t_1, \ldots, a_n t_0 + t_n)$. It is easily seen that the degree of B *w.r.t.* t_0 equals d. □

Corollary 1. *For any $G \in \mathbb{Q}[\mathbf{u}]$, there exists an affine variety V in $\mathbb{C}^{2n+2}$ such that for any*

$$(a_0, b_0, \ldots, a_n, b_n) \in \mathbb{C}^{2n+2} \backslash V,$$

the total degree of G equals the degree of $B(t)$ where

$$B(t) = G(a_0 t + b_0, \ldots, a_n t + b_n).$$

Lemma 2. *There exists an affine variety V in $\mathbb{C}^{2n+2}$ such that for any $(a_0, b_0, \dots, a_n, b_n) \in \mathbb{C}^{2n+2} \backslash V$, if*

$$\langle A(t) \rangle = \langle F_0(t), \dots, F_n(t), F_{n+1}, \dots, F_m, J \rangle \cap \mathbb{Q}[t]$$

where $F_i(t)$ is the polynomial by replacing u_i with $a_i t + b_i$ in F_i $(i = 0, \dots, n)$ and

$$B(t) = \mathcal{D}_{X\,J}(a_0 t + b_0, \dots, a_n t + b_n),$$

then $\langle B(t) \rangle = \sqrt{\langle A(t) \rangle}$.

Proof. By the definition of $\mathcal{D}_{X\,J}$ (Notation 6), there exists an affine variety V_1 such that for any $(a_0, b_0, \dots, a_n, b_n) \in \mathbb{C}^{2n+2} \backslash V_1$, $\langle B(t) \rangle$ is radical. Thus, we only need to show that there exists an affine variety V_2 in $\mathbb{C}^{2n+2}$ such that for any $(a_0, b_0, \dots, a_n, b_n) \in \mathbb{C}^{2n+2} \backslash V_2$, $\mathcal{V}_a(\langle B(t) \rangle) = \mathcal{V}_a(\langle A(t) \rangle)$.

Suppose π_t is the canonical projection: $\mathbb{C} \times \mathbb{C}^{m+1} \to \mathbb{C}$. For any

$$t^* \in \pi_t(\mathcal{V}_a(F_0(t), \dots, F_n(t), F_{n+1}, \dots, F_m, J)),$$

let $u_i^* = a_i t^* + b_i$ (for $i = 0, \dots, n$), then $(u_0^*, \dots, u_n^*) \in \pi(\mathcal{L}_X \cap \mathcal{V}_a(J))$. Hence $\mathcal{D}_{X\,J}(u_0^*, \dots, u_n^*) = 0$ and so $B(t^*) = 0$. Thus

$$B(t) \in \mathcal{I}(\pi_t(\mathcal{V}_a(F_0(t), \dots, F_n(t), F_{n+1}, \dots, F_m, J)).$$

Therefore,

$$\begin{aligned} \mathcal{V}_a(A(t)) &= \mathcal{V}_a(\mathcal{I}(\pi_t(\mathcal{V}_a(F_0(t), \dots, F_n(t), F_{n+1}, \dots, F_m, J))) \\ &\subset \mathcal{V}_a(B(t)). \end{aligned}$$

For any $t^* \in \mathcal{V}_a(\langle B(t) \rangle)$, let $u_i^* = a_i t^* + b_i$ for $i = 0, \dots, n$, then $(u_0^*, \dots, u_n^*) \in \mathcal{V}_a(\mathcal{D}_{X\,J}) \subset \mathcal{L}_{X\,J}$. By the Extension Theorem [6], there exists an affine variety $V_2 \subset \mathbb{C}^{2n+2}$ such that if $(a_0, b_0, \dots, a_n, b_n) \notin V_2$, then $(u_0^*, \dots, u_n^*) \in \pi(\mathcal{L}_X \cap \mathcal{V}_a(J))$, thus

$$t^* \in \pi_t(\mathcal{V}_a(F_0(t), \dots, F_n(t), F_{n+1}, \dots, F_m, J)) \subset \mathcal{V}_a(A(t)). \square$$

Corollary 2. *There exists an affine variety V in $\mathbb{C}^n$ such that for any $(a_1, \dots, a_n) \in \mathbb{C}^n \backslash V$, if*

$$\langle A(u_0) \rangle = \langle F_0, F_1^* \dots, F_n^*, F_{n+1}, \dots, F_m, J \rangle \cap \mathbb{Q}[u_0]$$

where F_i^* is the polynomial by replacing u_i with a_i in F_i $(i = 1, \dots, n)$ and

$$B(u_0) = \mathcal{D}_{X\,J}(u_0, a_1, \dots, a_n),$$

then $\langle B(u_0) \rangle = \sqrt{\langle A(u_0) \rangle}$.

We show an example to explain the basic idea of the probabilistic algorithm and how the lemmas work in the algorithm.

Example 2 (Toy Example for Interpolation Idea). Suppose the radical of the elimination ideal $\langle F, J \rangle \cap \mathbb{Q}[\mathbf{u}]$ is generated by $D(u_0, u_1, u_2)$, where $F = u_0 p^2 + u_1 p + u_2$ and $J = 2u_0 p + u_1$. We already know that D is homogenous and equals $u_1^2 - 4u_0 u_2$. Rather than by the standard elimination algorithm, we compute D by the steps below.

- First, we substitute $u_0 = t + 11, u_1 = 3t + 2$ and $u_2 = 5t + 6$ into F and J (the integers $1, 11, 3, 2, 5$ and 6 are randomly chosen). We compute the radical of the elimination ideal $\langle F(t,p), J(t,p) \rangle \cap \mathbb{Q}[t]$ and get $\langle 11t^2 + 232t + 260 \rangle$. By Lemma 2, $D(t + 11, 3t + 2, 5t + 6) = 11t^2 + 232t + 260$. By Corollary 1, the total degree of D is 2 (it geometrically means the random line $u_0 = t + 11, u_1 = 3t + 2, u_2 = 5t + 6$ intersect our desired hypersurface at 2 points in the parameter space and it is exactly the definition of the degree of hypersurface). Similarly, we compute the degree of D *w.r.t* u_0, u_1 and u_2 and get $1, 2$ and 1, respectively. So all the possible monomials in D are $u_1^2, u_0 u_1, u_1 u_2$ and $u_0 u_2$.
- Assume $D = u_1^2 + (C_1 u_0 + C_2 u_2) u_1 + C_3 u_0 u_2$. We first substitute $u_0 = 13$ and $u_2 = 4$ into F and J. We compute the radical of the elimination ideal $\langle F(u_1, p), J(u_1, p) \rangle \cap \mathbb{Q}[u_1]$ and get $\langle u_1^2 - 208 \rangle$. By Corollary 2, $D(13, u_1, 4)$ equals $u_1^2 - 208$. Hence, $13C_1 + 4C_2 = 0$ and $52C_3 = -208$. Therefore, $C_3 = -4$. We need one more evaluation to solve C_1 and C_2. So we substitute $u_0 = 7$ and $u_2 = 3$ into F and J. Similarly, we get $7C_1 + 3C_2 = 0$ and thus $C_1 = C_2 = 0$. Therefore, $D = u_1^2 - 4u_0 u_2$ (the integers $13, 4, 7, 3$ are randomly chosen).

This example is "nice". Because the degree of D *w.r.t* u_1 equals the total degree of D. In general case, if there is no u_i such that the degree of D *w.r.t* u_i equals the total degree, then we should apply the linear transformation to change the parameter coordinates before interpolation. Lemma 1 guarantees the linear transformation makes sense.

Algorithm 2: (Main Algorithm) InterpolationDX-J

input : $F_0, \dots, F_m, J$
output: $\mathcal{D}_{X\,J}$
$a_1, \dots, a_n \leftarrow$LinearOperator$(F_0, \dots, F_m, J)$
for i **from** 1 **to** n **do**
  $F_i' \leftarrow$ replace u_i in F_i with $a_i u_0 + u_i$
$NewSys \leftarrow F_0, F_1' \dots, F_n', F_{n+1}, \dots, F_m, J$
$d, d_0, \dots, d_n \leftarrow$Degree$(NewSys)$
for j **from** 1 **to** d **do**
  Rename all the monomials of the set
  $$\{u_1^{\alpha_1} \cdots u_n^{\alpha_n} | \alpha_1 + \ldots + \alpha_n = j, 0 \le \alpha_i \le d_i\}$$
  as $U_{j,1}, \dots, U_{j,N_j}$
$N \leftarrow \max(N_1, \dots, N_d)$
for k **from** 1 **to** N **do**
  $b_{k,1}, \dots, b_{k,n} \leftarrow$ random integers
  $A(u_0) \leftarrow$Intersect$(NewSys, b_{k,1}, \dots, b_{k,n})$
  $C_{d,k}^*, \dots, C_{1,k}^* \leftarrow$ the coefficients of $A(u_0)$ *w.r.t* $u_0^0, \dots, u_0^{d-1}$
for j **from** 1 *to* d **do**
  $\mathcal{M}_j \leftarrow N_j \times N_j$ matrix whose (k, r)-entry is $U_{j,r}(b_{k,1}, \dots, b_{k,n})$
  $C_j \leftarrow (U_{j,1}, \dots, U_{j,N_j}) \mathcal{M}_j^{-1} (C_{j,1}^*, \dots, C_{j,N_j}^*)^T$
$\mathcal{D}_{X\,J} \leftarrow$ replace $u_1, \dots, u_n$ in $u_0^d + \Sigma_{i=0}^{d-1} C_{d-i} u_0^i$ with $u_1 - a_1 \cdot u_0, \dots, u_n - a_n \cdot u_0$
Return $\mathcal{D}_{X\,J}$

Algorithm 3: Intersect

input : $F_0, \dots, F_m, J$ and integers $b_1, \dots, b_n$
output: $\mathcal{D}_{X\,J}(u_0, b_1, \dots, b_n)$
for i **from** 1 **to** n **do**
  $F_i^* \leftarrow$ replace u_i in F_k with b_i
$A(u_0) \leftarrow$ the generator of the elimination ideal $\langle F_0, F_1^*, \dots, F_n^*, F_{n+1}, \dots F_m, J \rangle \cap \mathbb{Q}[u_0]$
$A(u_0) \leftarrow$ the monic generator of $\sqrt{\langle A(u_0) \rangle}$
return $A(u_0)$

Now we are prepared to introduce the probabilistic algorithm for computing the $\mathcal{D}_{X\,J}$. We explain the main algorithm (Algorithm 2) and all the sub-algorithms (Algorithms 4–6) below.

Algorithm 5 (Degree). The probabilistic algorithm terminates correctly by Corollary 1 and Lemma 2.

Algorithm 4: LinearOperator

input : $F_0, \ldots, F_m, J$
output: $a_1, \ldots, a_n$ such that the total degree of $\mathcal{D}_{XJ}$ equals the degree of $\mathcal{D}_{XJ}(u_0, a_1 \cdot u_0 + u_1, \ldots, a_n \cdot u_0 + u_n)$ $w.r.t$ u_0

$d, d_0, \ldots, d_n \leftarrow$Degree$(F_0, \ldots, F_m, J)$
if $d = d_0$ **then**
  return $0, \ldots, 0$
else
  repeat
    for i **from** 1 **to** n **do**
      $a_i \leftarrow$ a random integer
      $F_i' \leftarrow$ replace u_i in F_i with $a_i \cdot u_0 + u_i$
    $NewSys \leftarrow F_0, F_1' \ldots, F_n', F_{n+1}, \ldots, F_m, J$
    $d, d_0, \ldots, d_n \leftarrow$Degree$(NewSys)$
  until $d = d_0$
return $a_1, \ldots, a_n$

Algorithm 5: Degree

input : $F_0, \ldots, F_m, J$
output: $d, d_0, \ldots d_n$, where d is the total degree of $\mathcal{D}_{XJ}$ and d_i is the degree of $\mathcal{D}_{XJ}$ $w.r.t$ each u_i $(i = 0, \ldots, n)$

1 **for** i **from** 0 **to** n **do**
2   $F_0^*, \ldots, F_n^* \leftarrow$ replace $u_0, \ldots, u_{i-1}, u_{i+1}, \ldots, u_n$ in $F_0, \ldots, F_n$ with random integers
3   $A(u_i) \leftarrow$ the generator of the elimination ideal $\langle F_0^*, \ldots, F_n^*, F_{n+1}, \ldots F_m, J\rangle \cap \mathbb{Q}[u_i]$
4   $A(u_i) \leftarrow$ the generator of $\sqrt{\langle A(u_i)\rangle}$
5   $d_i \leftarrow$ degree of $A(u_i)$
6   $a_i, b_i \leftarrow$ random integers
7 $F_0(t), \ldots, F_n(t) \leftarrow$ replace $u_0, \ldots, u_n$ with $a_0 \cdot t + b_0, \ldots, a_n \cdot t + b_n$ in $F_0, \ldots, F_n$
8 $A(t) \leftarrow$ the generator of the elimination ideal $\langle F_0(t), \ldots, F_n(t), F_{n+1}, \ldots F_m, J\rangle \cap \mathbb{Q}[t]$
9 $A(t) \leftarrow$ the generator of $\sqrt{\langle A(t)\rangle}$
10 $d \leftarrow$ degree of $A(t)$
11 **return** $d, d_0, \ldots, d_n$

Algorithm 4 (LinearOperator). The probabilistic algorithm terminates correctly by Lemma 1.

Algorithm 3 (Intersect). The probabilistic algorithm terminates correctly by Corollary 2.

Algorithm 2 (InterpolationDX-J).

Lines 1–5. We compute the total degree of $\mathcal{D}_{XJ}$ and the degrees of $\mathcal{D}_{XJ}$ $w.r.t$ $u_0, \ldots, u_d$: $d, d_0, \ldots, d_n$ by Algorithm 5. Algorithm 4 guarantees that $d_0 = d$ by applying a proper linear transformation $u_1 = a_1 \cdot u_0 + u_1, \ldots, u_n = a_n \cdot u_0 + u_n$.

Lines 6–7. Suppose $\mathcal{D}_{XJ} = u_0^d + C_1 u_0^{d-1} + \ldots + C_{d-1} u_0 + C_d$ where $C_1, \ldots, C_d \in \mathbb{Q}[u_1, \ldots, u_n]$ and the total degree of C_j is j. For $j = 1, \ldots, n$, we estimate all the possible monomials of C_j by computing the set

$$\{u_1^{\alpha_1} \cdots u_n^{\alpha_n} | \alpha_1 + \ldots + \alpha_n = j, 0 \leq \alpha_i \leq d_i\}$$

Assume the cardinality of the set is N_j and rename these monomials as $U_{j,1}, \ldots, U_{j,N_j}$. Then we assume

$$C_j = c_{j,1} U_{j,1} + \ldots + c_{j,N_j} U_{j,N_j}$$

where $c_{j,1}, \ldots, c_{j,N_j} \in \mathbb{Q}$. The rest of the algorithm is to compute $c_{j,1}, \ldots, c_{j,N_j}$.

Lines 8–12. For each j, for $k = 1, \ldots, N_j$, for a random integer vector $\mathbf{b}_k = (b_{k,1}, \ldots, b_{k,n})$, we compute $\mathcal{D}_{XJ}(u_0, \mathbf{b}_k)$ by Algorithm 3. That means to compute the function value $C_j(\mathbf{b}_k)$ without knowing $\mathcal{D}_{XJ}$.

Lines 13–15. For each j, we solve a square linear equation system for the unknowns $c_{j,1}, \ldots, c_{j,N_j}$:

$$c_{j,1} U_{j,1}(\mathbf{b}_k) + \ldots + c_{j,N_j} U_{j,N_j}(\mathbf{b}_k) = C_j(\mathbf{b}_k), \quad (k = 1, \ldots, N_j)$$

It is known that we can choose nice $\mathbf{b}_k$ probabilistically such that the coefficient matrix of the linear equation system is non-singular.

Lines 16. We apply the inverse linear transformation in the parameter space to get the $\mathcal{D}_{XJ}$ for the original $F_0, \ldots, F_m$.

We can also apply the interpolation idea to Algorithm PROPERNESSDEFECTS [20] and get a probabilistic algorithm to compute the $\mathcal{D}_{X\infty}$. We omit the formal description of the algorithm.

Remark 3. *According to the Notation 6, when the codimension of* $\mathcal{L}_{XJ}\backslash\{\mathbf{0}\}$ *(*$\mathcal{L}_{X\infty}\backslash\{\mathbf{0}\}$*) is greater than* 1*, we define* $\mathcal{D}_{XJ}$ *(*$\mathcal{D}_{X\infty}$*) is* 1*. Therefore, it is no more true that the number of real/positive solutions still remains constant over the region determined by the data-discriminant. That means if the output of the Algorithm 2 is* 1*, we should use the standard method (elimination or computing Gröbner base).*

4. EXPERIMENTAL TIMINGS

We have implemented the probabilistic algorithm in `Macaulay2`. We have also implemented the standard algorithm in `Macaulay2` to do comparisons (Tables 1 and 2). Some of the necessary implementation details are shown below.

- In the Algorithm 1. Line 1, Algorithm 3. Line 3 and Algorithm 5. Lines 3 and 8, we use the `Macaulay2` command **`eliminate`** to compute the elimination ideals.
- The probabilistic algorithm is implemented in two different ways. The first implementation is to interpolate at once, which is exactly the same as the Algorithm 2. The second implementation is to interpolate step by step. For example, suppose the $\mathcal{D}_{XJ}$ is a polynomial in u_0, u_1, u_2 and u_3, we first compute $\mathcal{D}_{XJ}(u_0, u_1, u_2^*, u_3^*)$ by interpolation for some chosen integers u_2^* and u_3^*. And then we compute $\mathcal{D}_{XJ}(u_0, u_1, u_2, u_3^*)$ by interpolation. At this time, it is easy to recover $\mathcal{D}_{XJ}$ since $\mathcal{D}_{XJ}$ is homogeneous. The algorithm is naive to describe so we omit the formal description.

We run Algorithms 1 and 2 for many examples to set benchmarks by a 3.2 GHz Inter Core i5 processor (8GB total memory) under OS X 10.9.3. There are two kinds of benchmarks, the random models and literature models.

- We generate 2 groups of "random models". The first group of random models are generated as follows. We first generate a random homogenous polynomial in 3 variables p_0, p_1 and p_2 with total degree 2. Suppose this homogenous polynomial is a model variant. We repeat the process for 10 rounds and get 10 random models. We call this group of 10 models 2 deg-models. Similarly, we generate the group of 3 deg-models. The Table 1 provides the timings of Algorithm 1 and Algorithm 2 (with two different implementations) for 2 deg-models and 3 deg-models.
- The literature models are the examples presented in the literatures [15, 7, 13]. Table 2 provides the timings of Algorithm 1 and Algorithm 2 (with two different implementations) for the literature models. For Examples 3–5 in the Table 2, the model invariants for these models are list below. Example 6 is given in Section 5.1.

Example 3 (Random Censoring (Ex. 2.2.2 in [7])).

$$2p_0p_1p_2 + p_1^2p_2 + p_1p_2^2 - p_0^2p_{12} + p_1p_2p_{12}$$

Table 1: Timings of Computing $\mathcal{D}_{XJ}$ for Random Models (s: seconds; h: hours; S1: Strategy 1; S2: Strategy 2)

2deg-models			3deg-models		
Algorithm 1	Algorithm 2		Algorithm 1	Algorithm 2	
	S1	S2		S1	S2
4.9s	0.8s	0.6s	>2h	800.4s	901.2s
3.0s	0.7s	0.6s	>2h	777.3s	871.5s
5.0s	0.8s	0.6s	>2h	1428.9s	1499.5s
5.4s	0.8s	0.7s	>2h	1118.9s	1192.9s
6.3s	0.8s	0.7s	>2h	448.9s	489.8s
3.9s	0.7s	0.6s	>2h	1279.6s	1346.1s
2.0s	0.7s	0.5s	>2h	1286.5s	1409.0s
1.7s	0.7s	0.5s	>2h	1605.9s	1620.9s
3.8s	0.8s	0.6s	>2h	1099.4s	1242.6s
5.8s	0.8s	0.7s	>2h	1229.0s	1288.7s

Table 2: Timings of Computing $\mathcal{D}_{XJ}$ for Literature Models (s: seconds; h: hours; d: days; S1: Strategy 1; S2: Strategy 2)

Models	Algorithm 1	Algorithm 2	
		S1	S2
Example 3	11.1s	5.3s	6.4s
Example 4	36446.4s	360.2s	56.3s
Example 5	>16h	>16h	2768.2s
Example 6	>12d	>30d	30d

Example 4 (3×3 Zero-Diagonal Matrix [13]).

$$\det \begin{bmatrix} 0 & p_{12} & p_{13} \\ p_{21} & 0 & p_{23} \\ p_{31} & p_{32} & 0 \end{bmatrix}$$

Example 5 (Grassmannian of 2-planes in $\mathbb{C}^4$ [15, 13]).

$$p_{12}p_{34} - p_{13}p_{24} + p_{14}p_{23}$$

In the Tables 1–2, the columns "Algorithm 1" give the timings of Algorithm 1. The columns "Algorithm 2" give the timings of Algorithm 2, where "S1" and "S2" means the first and second implementations, respectively. The red data means the computation has not finished and received no output. It is seen from the tables that

- for all the benchmarks we have tried, the Algorithm 2 is more efficient than Algorithm 1;
- for the random models and Example 3, the two implementations of Algorithm 2 have almost the same efficiency;
- for Examples 4–6, the second implementation (interpolation step by step) of Algorithm 2 is more efficient than the first implementation (interpolation at once). In fact, it takes the same time for the two implementations to get sample points. But it takes more time for the first implementation to compute the inverse of $\mathcal{M}_j$ in Algorithm 2. Line 13, which is a large size matrix with rational entries.
- for Example 6, with the standard elimination algorithm, our computer runs out of memory after 12 days.

Note that for each benchmark, the output of Algorithm 2 is the same as Algorithm 1 when both algorithms terminate.

5. CONCLUSIONS AND LAST EXAMPLE

In order to classify the data according to the number of real/positive solutions of likelihood equations, we study the data-discriminant and develop a probabilistic algorithm to compute it. Experiments show that the probabilistic algorithm is more practical than the standard elimination algorithm. This is our first application of real root classification method on the MLE/likelihood equations problem. Our future work aims to

- improve Algorithm 2 (note that Algorithm 2 is applying evaluation/interpolation technique to the standard method. It is not the first time that such an approach is investigated. In [9, 24], Newton–Hensel lifting has been applied to compute (parametric) geometric resolutions. It is hopeful that Algorithm 2 will be more powerful if we apply the Newton-Hensel lifting techniques to balance the time consuming of the evaluation and lifting steps);
- study the data-discriminants of different formulations of likelihood equations for the same algebraic statistical model
- develop algorithms for computing real root classification for likelihood equations.

More broadly, the ideas in Subsection 3.2 and Algorithm 2 can be applied to compute discriminants when the Newton polytope is known.

5.1 3×3 symmetric matrix model

We end the paper with the discussion of real root classification on the 3×3 symmetric matrix model.

Consider the following story with dice. A gambler has a coin, and two pairs of three-sided dice. The coin and the dice are all unfair. However, the two dice in the same pair have the same weight. He plays the same game 1000 rounds. In each round, he first tosses the coin. If the coin lands on side 1, he tosses the first pair of dice. If the coin lands on side 2, he tosses the second pair of dice. After the 1000 rounds, he records a 3×3 data matrix $[\overline{u}_{ij}]$ $(i, j = 1, 2, 3)$ where $\overline{u}_{ij}$ is the the number of times for him to get the sides i and j with respect to the two dice. By the matrix $[\overline{u}_{ij}]$, he is trying to estimate the probability $\overline{p}_{ij}$ of getting the sides i and j with respect to the two dice.

It is easy to check that the matrix

$$\begin{bmatrix} \overline{p}_{11} & \overline{p}_{12} & \overline{p}_{13} \\ \overline{p}_{21} & \overline{p}_{22} & \overline{p}_{23} \\ \overline{p}_{31} & \overline{p}_{32} & \overline{p}_{33} \end{bmatrix}$$

is symmetric and has at most rank 2. Let

$$p_{ij} = \begin{cases} \overline{p}_{ij} & i = j \\ \frac{1}{2}\overline{p}_{ij} & i < j \end{cases}, \quad u_{ij} = \begin{cases} \overline{u}_{ij} & i = j \\ \overline{u}_{ij} + \overline{u}_{ji} & i < j \end{cases}.$$

We have an algebraic statistical model below.

Example 6 (3×3 Symmetric Matrix Model). The algebraic statistical model for the dice story is given by

$$X = \mathcal{V}(g) \cap \Delta_5,$$

where

$$g = \det \begin{bmatrix} 2p_{11} & p_{12} & p_{13} \\ p_{12} & 2p_{22} & p_{23} \\ p_{13} & p_{23} & 2p_{33} \end{bmatrix},$$

$$\Delta_5 = \{(p_{11}, \ldots, p_{33}) \in \mathbb{R}^6_{>0} | p_{11}+p_{12}+p_{13}+p_{22}+p_{23}+p_{33} = 1\}.$$

The gambler's problem is equivalent to **maximizing the likelihood function** $\frac{\Pi p_{ij}^{u_{ij}}}{(\Sigma p_{ij})^{\Sigma u_{ij}}}$ $(i \leq j)$ **subjected to** $\mathcal{V}(g) \cap \Delta_5$. According to the Definition 2, we present the Langrange likelihood equations below.

$$F_0 = p_{11}\lambda_1 + (8p_{22}p_{33} - 2p_{23}^2)p_{11}\lambda_2 - u_{11} = 0$$
$$F_1 = p_{12}\lambda_1 + (2p_{13}p_{23} - 4p_{12}p_{33})p_{12}\lambda_2 - u_{12} = 0$$
$$F_2 = p_{13}\lambda_1 + (2p_{12}p_{23} - 4p_{13}p_{22})p_{13}\lambda_2 - u_{13} = 0$$
$$F_3 = p_{22}\lambda_1 + (8p_{11}p_{33} - 2p_{13}^2)p_{22}\lambda_2 - u_{22} = 0$$
$$F_4 = p_{23}\lambda_1 + (2p_{12}p_{13} - 4p_{11}p_{23})p_{23}\lambda_2 - u_{23} = 0$$
$$F_5 = p_{33}\lambda_1 + (8p_{11}p_{22} - 2p_{12}^2)p_{33}\lambda_2 - u_{33} = 0$$
$$F_6 = g(p_{11}, p_{12}, p_{13}, p_{22}, p_{23}, p_{33}) = 0$$
$$F_7 = p_{11} + p_{12} + p_{13} + p_{22} + p_{23} + p_{33} - 1 = 0$$

where $p_{11}, p_{12}, p_{13}, p_{22}, p_{23}, p_{33}, \lambda_1$ and λ_2 are unknowns and u_{11}, u_{12}, u_{13}, u_{22}, u_{23} and u_{33} are parameters.

We have 8 equations in 8 unknowns with 6 parameters and the ML-degree is 6 [15]. By the Algorithm 2, we have computed $\mathcal{D}_{X\,J}$, which has 1307 terms with total degree 12. By a similar computation, we get $\mathcal{D}_{X\,\infty}$ [1] whose last factor is exactly $g(u_{11}, \ldots, u_{33})$ and all the other factors are positive when each u_i is positive.

For the data-discriminant $\mathcal{D}_X$ we have computed above, we have also computed[2] at least one rational point (sample point) from each open connected component of $\mathcal{D}_X \neq 0$ using `RAGlib`[22, 17, 11]. With these sample points we can solve the real root classification problem on the open cells. By testing all 236 sample points, we see that if $g(u_{11}, \ldots, u_{33}) \neq 0$, then[3]

– if $\mathcal{D}_{X\,J}(u_{11}, \ldots, u_{33}) > 0$, then the system has 6 distinct real solutions and there can be 6 positive solution or 2 positive solutions;

– if $\mathcal{D}_{X\,J}(u_{11}, \ldots, u_{33}) < 0$, then the system has 2 distinct real (positive) solutions.

With 2 of these sample points, we see that the sign of $\mathcal{D}_X$ is not enough to classify the positive solutions. For example, for the sample point ($u_{11} = 1, u_{12} = 1, u_{13} = \frac{280264116870825}{2951479051793528258856}, u_{22} = 1, u_{23} = \frac{340890092055929220385535}{14108069867573065075 9168}$, $u_{33} = \frac{32898355113670387769001}{1410806986757306507591 68}$), the system has 6 distinct positive solutions. While for the sample point ($u_{11} = 1, u_{12} = 1, u_{13} = 199008, u_{22} = 30, u_{23} = 2022, u_{33} = 1$), the system has also 6 real solutions but only 2 positive solutions[4].

6. ACKNOWLEDGMENTS

We thank Professors Bernd Sturmfels, Hoon Hong, Jonathan Hauenstein and Frank Sottile for their valuable advice. We also thank Professors Mohab Safey El Din and Jean-Charles Faugere for their software advice on `RAGlib` and `FGb` respectively. We also especially thank the anonymous referees for their insightful suggestions to greatly improve the paper.

7. REFERENCES

[1] M.-L. G. Buot, S. Hoşten, and D. Richards. Counting and locating the solutions of polynomial systems of maximum likelihood equations, ii: The behrens-fisher problem. *Statistica Sinica*, 17:1343–1354, 2007.

[2] F. Catanese, S. Hoşten, A. Khetan, and B. Sturmfels. The maximum likelihood degree. *Amer. J. Math.*, 128(3):671–697, 2006.

[3] C. Chen, J. H. Davemport, J. P. May, M. M. Maza, B. Xia, and R. Xiao. Triangular decomposition of semi-algebraic systems. In *Proceedings of ISSAC'10*, pages 187–194. ACM New York, 2010.

[4] G. E. Collins and H. Hong. *Partial Cylindrical Algebraic Decomposition for Quantifier Elimination.* Springer, 1998.

[5] M. Coste and M. Shiota. Nash triviality in families of nash manifolds. *Inventiones Mathematicae*, 108(1):349–368, 1992.

[6] D. A. Cox, J. Little, and D. Oshea. *Ideals, varieties, and algorithms: an introduction to computational algebraic geometry and commutative algebra.* Springer, 2007.

[7] M. Drton, B. Sturmfels, and S. Sullivant. *Lectures on algebraic statistics.* Springer, 2009.

[8] J.-C. Faugère, M. Safey El Din, and P.-J. Spaenlehauer. Gröbner bases and critical points: the unmixed case. In *Proceedings of ISSAC'12*, pages 162–169. ACM New York, 2012.

[9] M. Giusti, G. Lecerf, and B. Salvy. A Gröbner free alternative for polynomial system solving. *Journal of Complexity*, 17:154–211, 2001.

[10] D. R. Grayson and M. E. Stillman. *Macaulay2, a software system for research in algebraic geometry.*

[11] A. Greuet and M. Safey El Din. Probabilistic algorithm for the global optimization of a polynomial over a real algebraic set. *SIAM Journal on Optimization*, 24(3):1313–1343, 2014.

[12] E. Gross, M. Drton, and S. Petrović. Maximum likelihood degree of variance component models. *Electronic Journal of Statistics*, 6:993–1016, 2012.

[13] E. Gross and J. I. Rodriguez. Maximum likelihood geometry in the presence of data zeros. In *Proceedings of ISSAC'14*, pages 232–239. ACM New York, 2014.

[14] J. Hauenstein, J. I. Rodriguez, and B. Sturmfels. Maximum likelihood for matrices with rank constraints. *Journal of Algebraic Statistics*, 5:18–38, 2014.

[15] S. Hoşten, A. Khetan, and B. Sturmfels. Solving the likelihood equations. *Foundations of Computational Mathematics*, 5(4):389–407, 2005.

[16] S. Hoşten and S. Sullivant. The algebraic complexity of maximum likelihood estimation for bivariate missing data. In *Algebraic and geometric methods in statistics*, pages 123–133. Cambridge University Press, 2009.

[17] H. Hong and M. Safey El Din. Variant quantifier elimination. *Journal of Symbolic Computation*, 47(7):883–901, 2012.

[18] J. Huh and B. Sturmfels. *Likelihood geometry*, pages 63–117. Springer International Publishing, 2014.

[19] Z. Jelonek. Testing sets for properness of polynoimal mappings. *Mathematische Annalen*, 315:1–35, 1999.

[20] D. Lazard and F. Rouillier. Solving parametric polynomial systems. *Journal of Symbolic Computation*, 42(6):636–667, 2005.

[21] J. I. Rodriguez. Maximum likelihood for dual varieties. In *Proceedings of the 2014 Symposium on Symbolic-Numeric Computation*, SNC '14, pages 43–49, New York, NY, USA, 2014. ACM.

[22] M. Safey El Din and E. Schost. Polar varieties and computation of one point in each connected component of a smooth real algebraic set. In *Proceedings of ISSAC'03*, pages 224–231. ACM Press, 2003.

[23] M. Safey El Din and E. Schost. Properness defects of projections and computaion of in each connected component of a real algebraic set. *Discrete and Computational Geometry*, 32(3):417–430, 2004.

[24] E. Schost. Computing parametric geometric resolutions. *Applicable Algebra in Engineering, Communication and Computing*, 13(5):349–393, 2003.

[25] C. Uhler. Geometry of maximum likelihood estimation in gaussian graphical models. *Annals of Statistics*, 40(1):238–261, 2012.

[26] L. Yang, X. Hou, and B. Xia. A complete algorithm for automated discovering of a class of inequality-type theorems. *Science in China Series F Information Sciences*, 44(1):33–49, 2001.

[1] See $\mathcal{D}_{X\,J}$ and $\mathcal{D}_{X\,\infty}$ on the second author's website: sites.google.com/site/rootclassificaiton/publications/DD

[2] The sample points were first successfully computed by one of the anonymous referees.

[3] This proves the real version of the RRC conjecture in the previous version of this manuscript.

[4] This disproves the positive version of the RRC conjecture in the previous version of this manuscript.

Green's Functions for Stieltjes Boundary Problems

Markus Rosenkranz
School of Mathematics, Statistics & Act. Sci.
University of Kent
Canterbury CT2 7NF
United Kingdom
M.Rosenkranz@kent.ac.uk

Nitin Serwa
School of Mathematics, Statistics & Act. Sci.
University of Kent
Canterbury CT2 7NF
United Kingdom
ns512@kent.ac.uk

ABSTRACT

Stieltjes boundary problems generalize the customary class of well-posed two-point boundary value problems in three independent directions, regarding the specification of the boundary conditions: (1) They allow more than two evaluation points. (2) They allow derivatives of arbitrary order. (3) Global terms in the form of definite integrals are allowed. Assuming the Stieltjes boundary problem is regular (a unique solution exists for every forcing function), there are symbolic methods for computing the associated Green's operator.

In the classical case of well-posed two-point boundary value problems, it is known how to transform the Green's operator into the so-called Green's function, the representation usually preferred by physicists and engineers. In this paper we extend this transformation to the whole class of Stieltjes boundary problems. It turns out that the extension (1) leads to more case distinction, (2) implies ill-posed problems and hence distributional terms, (3) has apparently no effect on the structure of the Green's function.

Categories and Subject Descriptors

I.1.2 [**Symbolic and Algebraic Manipulation**]: Algorithms—*algebraic algorithms*

General Terms

Differential algebra.

Keywords

Green's functions and Green's operators; integro-differential algebras; noncommutative Gröbner bases; linear boundary value problems.

1. INTRODUCTION

Boundary problems for linear ordinary differential equations (LODEs) or partial differential equations (LPDEs) are certainly among the most important model types in the engineering sciences. Interestingly, their systematic treatment in Symbolic Computation started rather recently [17]. For handling the central problems of solving and factoring boundary problems, a *differential algebra setting* for LODEs is employed in [20, 19] and for LPDEs in [21, 18]. An overarching abstract framework based only on Linear Algebra is developed in [15]. For the classical treatment of boundary problems in Analysis, we refer to [7, 10, 22, 24].

In this paper we restrict ourselves to LODEs, where the "industrial standard" for solving boundary problems is their so-called *Green's function*. This is in stark contrast to the operator-based methodology used in the above references. In fact, given a fundamental system, the algorithm of [17, 20] computes the solution of a boundary problem in the form of its *Green's operator*. In the classical setting of well-posed two-point boundary value problems (see Section 2), this algorithm admits an optional extra step for extracting the corresponding Green's function. Our goal here is to extend this postprocessing step to the considerably larger class of Stieltjes boundary problems (see Section 2).

One way to understand the relationship between Green's operators and functions is to view the latter as a certain canonical form. For making this precise we equip the ring of integro-differential operators with a slightly different set of reduction rules favoring multiply initialized integrals, leading to the ring of *equitable integro-differential operators* (Section 3).

A *simple example* will make this clear—in fact the simplest of all honest boundary problems [17, §3.2]. Given a forcing function $f \in C^\infty[0,1]$, we want to find $u \in C^\infty[0,1]$ such that

$$\boxed{\begin{array}{l} u'' = f, \\ u(0) = u(1) = 0. \end{array}}$$

The Green's operator $G\colon C^\infty[0,1] \to C^\infty[0,1]$ of this problem is defined by $Gf = u$. Using the standard reduction system of [20], we would distinguish one integral like $\textstyle\int f := \int_0^x f(\xi)\,d\xi$ and then obtain the Green's operator in the canonical form

$$G = x{\textstyle\int} - {\textstyle\int} x + x\lfloor 1\rfloor {\textstyle\int} x - x\lfloor 1\rfloor {\textstyle\int}, \tag{1}$$

where $\lfloor\alpha\rfloor$ denotes the evaluation functional $f \mapsto f(\alpha)$ for any real number $\alpha \in \mathbf{R}$, in analogy to the multiplier notation of [17]. For extracting the Green's function, however, it is more useful to use the alternative canonical form

$$G = x{\textstyle\int_0} x - x{\textstyle\int_1} x - {\textstyle\int_0} x + x{\textstyle\int_1} \tag{2}$$

where $\textstyle\int_\alpha f := \int_\alpha^x f(\xi)\,d\xi$ now denotes the integral initialized

ISSAC'15, July 6–9, 2015, Bath, United Kingdom.

DOI: http://dx.doi.org/10.1145/2755996.2756681.

at the point $\alpha \in \{0, 1\}$. In fact, this is the form given in [17], and we shall see in Section 3 that the setting of biintegro-differential operators used there is essentially a special case of the equitable operator ring employed in this paper. The point of the canonical form (2) is that it allows us to apply the defining relation $Gf(x) = \int_0^1 g(x,\xi)\, f(\xi)\, d\xi$ of the Green's function directly to obtain the latter as

$$g(x,\xi) = \begin{cases} (x-1)\xi & \text{for } 0 \le \xi \le x \le 1, \\ x(\xi-1) & \text{for } 0 \le x \le \xi \le 1. \end{cases} \tag{3}$$

Heuristically speaking, one moves the $\int_0$ terms to the upper and the $\int_1$ terms to the lower branch, at the same time translating the "x" after the integrals into ξ. Note incidentally that $g(x,\xi) = g(\xi,x)$ in the above Green's function (3). As is well known in Analysis [5, §7] [24, §5], this is a consequence of the self-adjoint nature of this boundary problem—a topic that we would wish to investigate in the future for the more general class of Stieltjes boundary Problems (Section 6).

We will elaborate on the above principles to *generalize* it in three "orthogonal directions": (1) We allow more than two evaluation points, leading to an increased number of case branches. (2) Using derivatives of arbitrary order in the boundary conditions leads to distributional terms. (3) Boundary conditions with integral terms (so-called "nonlocal problems") are also included; they do not lead to further complications.

2. STIELTJES BOUNDARY PROBLEMS

For giving a precise definition of the class of admissible boundary problems, we follow the setting of [20]. We fix an ordinary integro-differential K-algebra $(\mathcal{F}, \partial, \int)$, where ordinary here means $\ker \partial = K$). Later we shall specialize this to $\mathcal{F} = C^\infty(\mathbf{R})$, the real- or complex-valued smooth function. This is theoretically convenient but of course needs to be replaced by a suitable constructive subalgebra for actual computations.

The *ring of integro-differential operators* over $\mathcal{F}$, introduced in [20, §3], will be denoted here by $\mathcal{F}_\Phi[\partial, \int]$ to emphasize its dependence of the chosen set of characters Φ, and also to mark the contrast to the equitable operator ring $\mathcal{F}[\partial, \int_\Phi]$ to be introduced in Section 3, where the integral operators are parametrized by Φ. In the case of $\mathcal{F} = C^\infty(\mathbf{R})$, these characters will be evaluations at given points of $\mathbf{R}$ so that we may take $\Phi \subseteq \mathbf{R}$.

We recall the *standard decomposition*

$$\mathcal{F}_\Phi[\partial, {\textstyle\int}] = \mathcal{F}[\partial] \dotplus \mathcal{F}[{\textstyle\int}] \dotplus (\Phi), \tag{4}$$

where $\mathcal{F}[\partial]$ denotes the subalgebra of differential operators (the K-subalgebra of $\mathcal{F}_\Phi[\partial, \int]$ generated by $\mathcal{F}$ and ∂), $\mathcal{F}[\int]$ the nonunital subalgebra of integral operators (the nonunital K-subalgebra of $\mathcal{F}_\Phi[\partial, \int]$ generated by $\mathcal{F}$ and $\int$), and (Φ) the two-sided ideal of $\mathcal{F}_\Phi[\partial, \int]$ generated by the characters in Φ. The corresponding *right* ideal $|\Phi) = \Phi \cdot \mathcal{F}_\Phi[\partial, \int]$ is known as the ideal of *Stieltjes conditions*, and one may check that (Φ) is in fact the left $\mathcal{F}$-module generated by the Stieltjes conditions.

From the viewpoint of applications, Stieltes conditions $\beta \in (\Phi)$ are easier to comprehend in terms of their $\mathcal{F}_\Phi[\partial, \int]$-normal form: They can be described uniquely as sums

$$\beta = \sum_{\varphi \in \Phi} \sum_{i \ge 0} a_{\varphi,i} \varphi \partial^i + \sum_{\varphi \in \Phi} \varphi {\textstyle\int} f_\varphi \tag{5}$$

with only finitely many $a_{\varphi,i} \in K$ and $f_\varphi \in \mathcal{F}$ nonzero. The double sum in (5) is called the *local part* of β, the subsequent sum its *global part*. In the important $C^\infty(\mathbf{R})$ case with distinguished integral $\int = \int_0^x$, this yields

$$\beta(u) = \sum_{\varphi,i} a_{\varphi,i} u^{(i)}(\varphi) + \sum_{\varphi} \textstyle\int_0^\varphi f_\varphi(\xi)\, u(\xi)\, d\xi,$$

for certain $a_{\varphi,i} \in \mathbf{R}$ and $f_\varphi \in C^\infty(\mathbf{R})$.

An n-th order *Stieltjes boundary problem* is a pair $(T, \mathcal{B})$ with a monic differential operator $T \in \mathcal{F}[\partial]$ of order n and a boundary space $\mathcal{B} \le \mathcal{F}^*$ given as linear span $\mathcal{B} = [\beta_1, \dots, \beta_n]$ of n linearly independent Stieltjes conditions. In traditional representation, such a boundary problem is displayed as

$$\boxed{\begin{array}{l} Tu = f, \\ \beta_1 u = \dots = \beta_n u = 0, \end{array}} \tag{6}$$

with the understanding that $u \in \mathcal{F}$ is desired for any prescribed forcing function $f \in \mathcal{F}$. For the (usual) Green's operator to be well-defined, we need the boundary problem (6) to be *regular* in the sense that $\ker T \dotplus \mathcal{B}^\perp = \mathcal{F}$, where $\mathcal{B}^\perp = \{u \in \mathcal{F} \mid \beta(u) = 0 \text{ for all } \beta \in \mathcal{B}\}$ is the corresponding space of admissible functions. Regularity is equivalent to the requirement that (6) has a unique solution $u \in \mathcal{F}$ for every given $f \in \mathcal{F}$. An algorithmic method for testing regularity starts from a fundamental system $u_1, \dots, u_n \in \mathcal{F}$ for T, meaning a K-basis of $\ker T$. Then (6) is regular iff the evaluation matrix

$$\beta(u) = \begin{pmatrix} \beta_1(u_1) & \cdots & \beta_1(u_n) \\ \vdots & \ddots & \vdots \\ \beta_n(u_1) & \cdots & \beta_n(u_n) \end{pmatrix} \in K^{n \times n} \tag{7}$$

is regular; see (15) of [20]. For a given system of fundamental solutions $u_1, \dots, u_n$ for T, the solution algorithm of [20] computes the Green's operator of any regular Stieltjes boundary problem as an integro-differential operator $G \in \mathcal{F}_\Phi[\partial, \int]$.

Within the class of Stieltjes boundary problems, we make the following distinctions in order to characterize the *classical scenario* as a certain special case.

Definition 1. A Stieltjes boundary problem $(T, \mathcal{B})$ of order n with $\mathcal{B} = [\beta_1, \dots, \beta_n]$ is called *well-posed* if the β_i can be chosen with all derivatives having order below n; otherwise it is called *ill-posed*. Furthermore, we call $(T, \mathcal{B})$ an *m-point boundary problem* if the maximal number of evaluation points occurring in any K-basis (β_i) of $\mathcal{B}$ is m, and we call $(T, \mathcal{B})$ *local* if the β_i can be chosen without global parts.

Let us digress a bit on the notion of ill-posed boundary problems. Following Hadamard, a problem is generally called *well-posed* [8, p. 86] if it is regular (meaning its solution u exists and is unique for all given data f) as well as stable (meaning u depends continuously on f). Otherwise, one speaks of an *ill-posed* problem. In the case of boundary problems (6), we search for $u \in C^\infty(\mathbf{R})$, and the data is given by the forcing function $f \in C^\infty(\mathbf{R})$. Stability—and hence well-posedness—depends on the topology chosen for the function space $C^\infty(\mathbf{R})$. Using the L^2 norm as in many application problems, the distinction between well- and ill-posed boundary problems coincides with the one given above.

Since local boundary problems involve only evaluations of the unknown function (rather than definite integrals), we also call them "boundary *value* problems". We can now characterize the classical case, described for example in [5, §7], by the following three-fold restriction: They are the well-posed two-point boundary value problems. (Sometimes one meets the further restriction to self-adjoint boundary problems.)

The classical case (in the above sense) is clearly the most frequent case in the applications (but this could also be due to a selection bias: having a well-equipped toolbox for classical problems might tempt engineers to restrict their attention to classical problems). Nevertheless, *multi-point boundary value problems* are also important for some applications [1, Ex. 1.6], [23], [13], [14], [3]. Boundary problems with nonlocal conditions are more seldom, they are usually studied for nonlinear equations [4], [11]; the linear case serves as the initial approximation. Finally, the case of ill-posed boundary problems is—for obvious reasons—mostly avoided when engineering problems are modelled. However, there are cases where their treatment is inevitable, typically in the context of inverse problems [9]. Since the numerical treatment of such problems is very delicate, it is of paramount importance to have exact symbolic algorithms wherever this is possible.

We will lift all three of these restrictions for the algorithm of *extracting Green's functions*, which will be given below (Section 4). As indicated in the Introduction, the crucial tool for this purpose—even in the classical case—is the ring of equitable integro-differential operators with its alternative canonical forms.

3. EQUITABLE OPERATORS

The passage from the usual integro-differential operator ring $\mathcal{F}_\Phi[\partial, \int]$ to its equitable clone $\mathcal{F}[\partial, \int_\Phi]$ is based on the *fundamental theorem of calculus* $\int_\varphi^x f'(\xi)\, d\xi = f(x) - f(\varphi)$ for any function $f \in C^\infty(\mathbf{R})$ and initialization point $\varphi \in \mathbf{R}$. Likewise, if $(\mathcal{F}, \partial, \int)$ is an arbitary integro-differential K-algebra and φ a character (multiplicative linear functional), one can use the definition $\int_\varphi := (\mathrm{id} - \varphi) \int$ to obtain the corresponding relation $\int_\varphi \partial = \mathrm{id} - \varphi$. In some contexts (especially in the presence of several integral operators like $\int^x$ and $\int^y$ on bivariate functions), it may be useful to write the integral $\int_\varphi$ as $\int_\varphi^x$. If ψ is another character, one observes the relation $\psi \int_\varphi = \int_\psi - \int_\varphi$, and it is natural to write $\int_\varphi^\psi$ for both expressions.

Note that $(\mathcal{F}, \partial, \int_\varphi)$ is also an ordinary integro-differential K-algebra, and the preference of $\int$ over $\int_\varphi$ can appear arbitrary in certain settings. Accordingly, one may build the ring of integro-differential operators by adjoining *all* $\int_\varphi$ while the characters φ themselves are now redundant due to the above fundamental relation. The precise formulation of the resulting ring $\mathcal{F}[\partial, \int_\Phi]$ as a quotient is described in [16, §5.1]. For our present purposes, we shall only list its relations (see Table 1 where $\cdot$ denotes the natural action of the operators), which are an easy consequence of the relations of the standard integro-differential operator ring $\mathcal{F}_\Phi[\partial, \int]$.

Similar to the standard decomposition (4), we have also the *equitable decomposition* $\mathcal{F}[\partial, \int_\Phi] = \mathcal{F}[\partial] + \mathcal{F}[\int_\Phi] + \mathcal{F}[\int_\Phi \partial]$ where $\mathcal{F}[\int_\Phi]$ is the nonunital subalgebra of equitable integral operators $\sum_{i=0}^n f_i \int_\varphi^x g_i$ and $\mathcal{F}[\int_\Phi \partial]$ the $\mathcal{F}$-submodule consisting of $\sum_{i=0}^n f_i \int_\varphi^x \partial^i$; this leads to the obvious normal forms in $\mathcal{F}[\partial, \int_\Phi]$.

fg	$\to$	$f \cdot g$	∂f	$\to$	$\partial \cdot f + f\partial$	$\partial \int_\varphi^x$	$\to$	1
$\int_\varphi^x f \int_\psi^x$	$\to$	$(\int_\varphi^x \cdot f) \int_\psi^x - \int_\varphi^x (\int_\varphi^x \cdot f)$						
$\int_\varphi^x f \partial$	$\to$	$f - \int_\varphi^x (\partial \cdot f) - \varphi \cdot f + (\varphi \cdot f) \int_\varphi^x \partial$						

Table 1: Equitable Integro-Differential Relations

We introduce now the so-called *translation isomorphism* $\iota \colon \mathcal{F}_\Phi[\partial, \int] \to \mathcal{F}[\partial, \int_\Phi]$ that fixes $f \in \mathcal{F}$ and ∂ while using the above fundamental relation in the form $\iota(\varphi) = \mathrm{id} - \int_\varphi \partial$ and $\iota^{-1}(\int_\varphi) = (\mathrm{id} - \varphi) \int$. Note that this includes also the character $\text{€} := \mathrm{id} - \int \partial$ associated to the distinguished integral $\int = \int_{\text{€}}$ underlying $\mathcal{F}_\Phi[\partial, \int]$.

Specializing to $\mathcal{F} = C^\infty(\mathbf{R})$ and $\Phi = \{0, 1\}$, we can deal with the *example* in the Introduction, where we have the normal form $G \in \mathcal{F}_\Phi[\partial, \int]$ in (1) along with its equitable variant $\iota(G) \in \mathcal{F}[\partial, \int_\Phi]$ in (2). In such two-point cases with characters $\Phi = \{\alpha, \beta\}$, the equitable operator ring $\mathcal{F}[\partial, \int_\Phi]$ is essentially the same as the ring of *biintegro-differential operators*. More precisely, we obtain a biintegro-differential algebra $(\mathcal{F}, \partial, \int^*, \int_*)$ with integral $\int^* := \int_\alpha$ and cointegral $\int_* := -\int_\beta$ in the sense of [16, Def. 3.23]. Note that $\int^*$ and $\int_*$ are adjoint with respect to the inner product defined by $\langle f | g \rangle := (\int^* + \int_*)(fg) = \int_\alpha^\beta fg$. Incidentally, the notion of biintegro-differential algebra coincides with the (badly named) notion of "analytic algebra" introduced in [17, Def. 2] and replicated in [20, Ex. 5]. Clearly, the operator ring resulting from $\mathcal{F}[\partial]$ by adjoining $\int^*$ and $\int_*$ is the same as $\mathcal{F}[\partial, \int_\Phi]$, modulo the sign change in the cointegral.

Note that also $\int_\varphi \in \mathcal{F}_\Phi[\partial, \int]$ and $\varphi \in \mathcal{F}[\partial, \int_\Phi]$ are legitimate expressions via the above translation isomorphism. They are not in canonical form but we may think of them as a kind of *abbreviation* for the corresponding canonical expression.

In fact, the extraction of Green's functions is based on the following slight variation of the equitable integro-differential operator ring $\mathcal{F}[\partial, \int_\Phi]$. Writing any element $U \in \mathcal{F}_\Phi[\partial, \int]$ in the form $U = T + K + B$ with $T \in \mathcal{F}[\partial]$, $K \in \mathcal{F}[\int]$ and $B \in (\Phi)$ according to (4), we let $T \in \mathcal{F}[\partial, \int_\Phi]$ and $K \in \mathcal{F}[\int_{\text{€}}] \subseteq \mathcal{F}[\int_\Phi]$ invariant while translating $B \in (\Phi)$ as follows. Since (Φ) is the left $\mathcal{F}$-module generated by Stieltjes conditions (5), we may split $B = \lambda + \gamma$ into a left $\mathcal{F}$-linear combination λ of local Stieltjes conditions and a left $\mathcal{F}$-linear combination γ of global Stieltjes conditions. It turns out to be expedient to keep λ in this form, without eliminating the characters via $\varphi = \mathrm{id} - \int_\varphi \partial$, but to translate γ via $\varphi \int_{\text{€}} = \int_{\text{€}} - \int_\varphi =: \int_{\text{€}}^\varphi$. This is what we mean when referring in the sequel to the *equitable form* of an integro-differential operator U.

4. EXTRACTING GREEN'S FUNCTIONS

We now turn to the central task of this paper, the extraction of the Green's function $g(x, \xi)$ corresponding to the Green's operator $G \in \mathcal{F}[\partial, \int_\Phi]$ computed by the algorithm of [20] and converted to equitable form as described in Section 3. Hence we specialize now to $\mathcal{F} = C^\infty(\mathbf{R})$. Note that we may think of $g(x, \xi)$ as a kind of *coordinate representation* of the induced operator action $G \colon \mathcal{F} \to \mathcal{F}$; in quantum mechanics this would correspond to the "position basis" (as opposed to the "momentum basis" in the Pontryagin dual reached via the Fourier transform). Hence we will use the notation $g(x,\xi) = G_{x\xi}$, thinking of the x, ξ rather like continuous indices similar to the discrete indices i, j in the matrix elements A_{ij} of some $A \in K^{n\times n}$.

In fact, we will use this notation $G_{x\xi}$ for any equitable integro-differential operator $G \in \mathcal{F}[\partial, \textstyle\int_\Phi]$. Its result will in general contain Dirac distributions [22, §2] and their derivatives but nothing beyond that. Since all boundary problems considered in this paper have only finitely many evaluation points $\alpha \in \Phi \subset \mathbf{R}$, one may choose an interval $J \subset \mathbf{R}$ containing all the α. Hence the $C(J^2)$-module $\mathcal{G} \subset \mathcal{D}'(J^2)$ generated by the *Dirac distributions* δ_α and their derivatives will be sufficient to capture all Green's "functions" $G_{x\xi} \in \mathcal{G}$. Here and in the sequel we shall follow the common engineering (and also applied maths) practice of referring to distributions like δ_α as functions. In the same vein, we shall also write $\delta(\xi - \alpha)$ in place of δ_α, in view of the defining property $\int_J \delta(\xi-\alpha)\, f(\xi)\, d\xi = f(\alpha)$.

The transformation from Green's operators to Green's functions

$$\mathcal{F}[\partial, \textstyle\int_\Phi] \to \mathcal{G},\ G \mapsto G_{x\xi}$$

is clearly an $\mathbf{R}$-linear map, hence it will be sufficient to define it on the *canonical* $\mathbf{R}$*-basis* of $\mathcal{F}_\Phi[\partial, \textstyle\int] \cong \mathcal{F}[\partial, \textstyle\int_\Phi]$. Following the strategy of the example in the Introduction, the easiest part is $\mathcal{F}[\textstyle\int] \subseteq \mathcal{F}_\Phi[\partial, \textstyle\int]$, which is handled by setting

$$(f \textstyle\int g)_{x\xi} = f(x)\, g(\xi)\, [0 \le \xi \le x] - f(x)\, g(\xi)\, [x \le \xi \le 0],$$

where we use the Iverson bracket notation $[P]$ signifying 1 if the property P is true and zero otherwise. Note that at most one of the two summands above is nonzero for fixed (x, ξ). Since $(\Phi) \subset \mathcal{F}_\Phi[\partial, \textstyle\int]$ is a left $\mathcal{F}$-module over $|\Phi)$, we settle this part via

$$(f\, \lfloor\alpha\rfloor \partial^i)_{x\xi} = (-1)^i f(x)\, \delta^{(i)}(\xi - \alpha),$$
$$(f\, \lfloor\alpha\rfloor \textstyle\int g)_{x\xi} = \operatorname{sgn}(\alpha)\, f(x)\, g(\xi)\, [0 \le \xi \le \alpha].$$

Finally, on $\mathcal{F}[\partial]$ we define

$$(f\partial^i)_{x\xi} = (-1)^i\, f(x)\, \delta^{(i)}(x - \xi),$$

and the definition is complete in view of (4). Moreover, it is easy to check that the assignment $G \mapsto G_{x\xi}$ is correct in the sense that $Gf = \int_J G_{x\xi}\, f(\xi)\, d\xi$. The isomorphism ι of Section 3 may now be employed to obtain the required transformation $\mathcal{F}[\partial, \textstyle\int_\Phi] \to \mathcal{G}$. In fact, the above case $f \textstyle\int g \in \mathcal{F}[\textstyle\int]$ generalizes immediately to

$$(f \textstyle\int_\alpha g)_{x\xi} = f(x)\, g(\xi)\, [\alpha \le \xi \le x] - f(x)\, g(\xi)\, [x \le \xi \le \alpha],$$

which will turn out to be the essential clause for extracting Green's functions of (well-posed) multi-point boundary problems. For seeing this, we need a more detailed description of the underlying Green's operators.

We turn first to the easy case of a one-point boundary problem, more appropriately known under the name of *initial value problems* $(T, [\unicode{x20AC}, \dots, \unicode{x20AC}\partial^{n-1}])$ for $T \in \mathcal{F}[\partial]$ of order n. The corresponding Green's operator is called the fundamental right inverse $T^\diamond$ and can be computed easily via the well-known "variation of constants" formula [16, Thm. 6.4]: If $u_1, \dots, u_n$ is a fundamental system for T with Wronskian matrix W, the fundamental right inverse is given by the operator expression

$$T^\diamond = \sum_{j=1}^n u_j \textstyle\int \dfrac{d_j}{d}.$$

Here $d = \det(W)$ and $d_i = \det(W_i)$, where W_i denotes the matrix resulting from W when replacing the i-th column by the n-th unit vector of K^n.

What we shall need in the sequel is how $T^\diamond$ reacts to left multiplication by $\mathcal{F}[\partial]$.

Lemma 1. *Let $T \in \mathcal{F}[\partial]$ be any monic differential operator of order n, and choose a fundamental system $u_1, \dots, u_n$ for T with Wronskian matrix W. Then we have*

$$\partial^k T^\diamond = \sum_{j=1}^n u_j^{(k)} \textstyle\int \dfrac{d_j}{d} + \displaystyle\sum_{j=1}^k \partial^{k-j} \rho_j \tag{8}$$

$$\textit{with} \qquad \rho_k := \frac{1}{d} \sum_{j=1}^n u_j^{(k-1)} d_j \in \mathcal{F},$$

where d and d_i are as above.

Note that $\rho_1 = \dots = \rho_{n-1} = 0$ by the definition of the d_j; hence the second sum in $\partial^k T^\diamond$ is only present for $k \ge n$, and we may equivalently write its range as $j = n, \dots, k$. Furthermore, we have $\rho_n = 1$ from the definition of d. For $k > n$, however, the ρ_k are functions of $\mathcal{F}$, so in general they *do not commute* with the ∂^{k-j} in the second summand of (8).

Proof. We use induction on k. In the base case $k = 0$, this is the usual variation-of-constants formula as given in [5, p. 74]; see [20, Prop. 22] and [16, Thm. 6.4] for its operator formulation. Now assume (8) for fixed $k \ge 0$; we show it for $k+1$. By the induction hypothesis we obtain

$$\partial^{k+1} T^\diamond = \sum_{j=1}^n u_j^{(k+1)} \textstyle\int \dfrac{d_j}{d} + \dfrac{1}{d} \displaystyle\sum_{j=1}^n u_j^{(k)} d_j + \sum_{j=1}^k \partial^{k-j+1} \rho_j,$$

which is just (8) for $k+1$ since the middle sum is ρ_{k+1} and can be absorbed into the third. □

Lemma 2. *The Green's operator of any regular Stieltjes boundary problem is contained in $\mathcal{F}[\textstyle\int_\Phi] + \mathcal{L}$, where $\mathcal{L}$ denotes the left $\mathcal{F}$-module generated by the local Stieltjes conditions.*

Proof. Assume $(T, \mathcal{B})$ is any regular Stieltjes boundary problem of order n with Green's operator G, and let P be the projector onto $\ker T$ along $\mathcal{B}^\perp$. By the proof of [20, Thm. 26] we have $G = (1 - P)T^\diamond$, and we know that P is an $\mathcal{F}$-linear combination of Stieltjes conditions by [20, (16)] in that same proof. From (8) it is clear that $T^\diamond \in \mathcal{F}[\textstyle\int_\Phi]$, so it suffices to show $PT^\diamond \in \mathcal{F}[\textstyle\int_\Phi] + \mathcal{L}$. Each summand of P is either of the form $f \lfloor\alpha\rfloor\, \partial^k$ or $f \lfloor\alpha\rfloor \textstyle\int g = f \textstyle\int_\unicode{x20AC} g - f \textstyle\int_\alpha g \in \mathcal{F}[\textstyle\int_\Phi]$. In the latter case we obtain an expression in $\mathcal{F}[\textstyle\int_\Phi]$ since $\mathcal{F}[\textstyle\int_\Phi]$ is a (nonunital) subalgebra of $\mathcal{F}[\partial, \textstyle\int_\Phi]$. It remains to prove $f \lfloor\alpha\rfloor\, \partial^k T^\diamond \in \mathcal{F}[\textstyle\int_\Phi] + \mathcal{L}$. From (8) we see that

$$f \lfloor\alpha\rfloor\, \partial^k T^\diamond = \sum_{j=1}^n f u_j^{(k)}(\alpha) \textstyle\int_\unicode{x20AC}^\alpha \dfrac{d_j}{d} + \displaystyle\sum_{j=1}^k f \lfloor\alpha\rfloor\, \partial^{k-j} \rho_j.$$

The first sum is clearly contained in $\mathcal{F}[\textstyle\int_\Phi]$, while the second is in $\mathcal{L}$ because $\partial^{k-j}\rho_j \in \mathcal{F}[\partial]$ may be rewritten in canonical form as a sum of terms $g_i \partial^i$ so that $\lfloor\alpha\rfloor\, \partial^{k-j} \rho_j$ is a sum of local conditions $\alpha(g_i)\, \lfloor\alpha\rfloor\, \partial^i$ and hence itself local. □

We are now ready to state the main *structure theorem for Green's functions* of regular Stieltjes boundary problems.

THEOREM 1. *The Green's function of any regular Stieltjes boundary problem with m evaluations $\alpha_1, \dots, \alpha_m$ has the form $g(x,\xi) = \tilde{g}(x,\xi) + \hat{g}(x,\xi)$, where the functional part $\tilde{g} \in C(J^2)$ is defined by the $2(m-1)$ case branches*

$$\xi \in [\alpha_i, \alpha_{i+1}]\ (0 < i < m), x \le \xi;$$
$$\xi \in [\alpha_i, \alpha_{i+1}]\ (0 < i < m), \xi \le x,$$

while the distributional part $\hat{g}(x,\xi)$ is an $\mathcal{F}$-linear combination of the $\delta(\xi - \alpha_i)$ and their derivatives.

PROOF. If G is the Green's operator of the given Stieltjes boundary problem, Lemma 2 says that $G = \tilde{G} + \hat{G}$ with $\tilde{G} \in \mathcal{F}[\textstyle\int_\Phi]$ and $\hat{G} \in \mathcal{L}$. We will show that $\tilde{g}(x,\xi) = \tilde{G}_{x\xi}$ and $\hat{g}(x,\xi) = \hat{G}_{x\xi}$ are as described in the theorem. Starting with the former, we may write

$$\tilde{G} = \sum_{i=1}^{r} f_i \textstyle\int_{\alpha_i} g_i,$$

where $\alpha_i = \alpha_j$ is possible for $i \ne j$. Using the transformation $\mathcal{F}[\partial, \textstyle\int_\Phi] \to \mathcal{G}$, we obtain $\tilde{g}(x,\xi)$ as

$$\begin{aligned}
&\sum_{i=1}^{r} \Big(f_i(x)\, g_i(\xi)\, [\alpha_i \le \xi][\xi \le x] - f_i(x)\, g_i(\xi)\, [\xi \le \alpha_i][x \le \xi] \Big) \\
&\quad = \sum_{i=1}^{r} \Big(\sum_{\alpha_j \le \alpha_i} f_j(x)\, g_j(\xi) \Big) [\alpha_{j-1} \le \xi \le \alpha_j][\xi \le x] \\
&\quad\quad - \sum_{i=1}^{r} \Big(\sum_{\alpha_j \ge \alpha_i} f_j(x)\, g_j(\xi) \Big) [\alpha_j \le \xi \le \alpha_{j+1}][x \le \xi],
\end{aligned}$$

where the two inner sums are restricted by $j > 0$ and $j < n$. Collecting terms, this is a sum of $2(m-1)$ characteristic functions over disjoint domains in $\mathbf{R}^2$, hence one may also write $\tilde{g}(x,\xi)$ in terms of a corresponding case distinction with $2(m-1)$ branches.

The distributional part $\hat{g}(x,\xi)$ is even easier. Writing $\hat{G}$ as an $\mathcal{F}$-linear combination of local conditions we obain $\hat{g}(x,\xi)$ via

$$\hat{G}_{x\xi} = \Big(\sum_{\alpha,i} f_{i,\alpha} \alpha \partial^i \Big)_{x\xi} = \sum_{\alpha,i} (-1)^i f_{i,\alpha}(x)\, \delta^{(i)}(\xi - \alpha),$$

which is clearly of the stated form. □

The above theorem is constructive, and we plan to implement the underlying algorithm on top of the `Maple` package `IntDiffOp` [12].

Remark 1. If the distinguished character $€ = \lfloor 0 \rfloor$ is not used in the boundary conditions, a straightforward translation of the Green's operator G may introduce two spurious extra case branches in the Green's function $G_{x\xi}$ since $\int_0^x$ occurs in the formula for G. For avoiding this, one has to use a different version of $T^\diamond$ that replaces $\lfloor 0 \rfloor$ by any one of the characters $\lfloor \alpha_i \rfloor$ used in the boundary conditions.

5. EXAMPLES

Our first example (in addition to the minimal one from the Introduction) is a four-point boundary value problem

Case	Term
$0 \le \xi \le 1/3, \xi \le x$	$(3/4)x\xi - (5/8)\xi$
$0 \le \xi \le 1/3, x \le \xi$	$(3/4)x\xi + (3/8)\xi - x$
$1/3 \le \xi \le 2/3, \xi \le x$	$(3/2)x\xi - (5/4)\xi - (1/4)x + 5/24$
$1/3 \le \xi \le 2/3, x \le \xi$	$(3/2)x\xi - (1/4)\xi - (5/4)x + 5/24$
$2/3 \le \xi \le 1, \xi \le x$	$(3/4)x\xi - (9/8)\xi + (1/4)x + 1/8$
$2/3 \le \xi \le 1, x \le \xi$	$(3/4)x\xi - (1/8)\xi - (3/4)x + 1/8$

Table 2: Green's Function for (9)

taken from [2, (2.1,2.2)], where we have specialized the parameters and rescaled the interval to $J = [0,1]$ for the sake of simplicity. Hence we are dealing with the boundary problem

$$\boxed{\begin{aligned} &-u'' = f, \\ &u(0) + u(1/3) = u(1) + u(2/3) = 0, \end{aligned}} \tag{9}$$

where we may assume $u, f \in C^\infty[-2,2]$. Note that this is a well-posed boundary problem, so the Green's function will not have a distributional part. Computing the Green's operator with the `IntDiffOp` package yields after some rearrangements the result

$$\begin{aligned}
G = {} & x\textstyle\int - \int x + (-5/24 + x/4)\lfloor 1/3 \rfloor \int \\
& + (5/8 - 3x/4)\lfloor 1/3 \rfloor \textstyle\int x + (1/8 - 3x/4)\lfloor 1 \rfloor \int x \\
& + (1/12 - x/2)\lfloor 2/3 \rfloor \textstyle\int + (-1/8 + 3x/4)\lfloor 2/3 \rfloor \int x
\end{aligned}$$

Transforming G to equitable form is simple, via $\lfloor \alpha \rfloor \int \rightsquigarrow \int_0^x - \int_\alpha^x$. We can then determine the corresponding Green's function $g(x,\xi) = \tilde{g}(x,\xi)$ with 6 cases, and its terms may be computed according to Theorem 1. The result for $g(x,\xi)$ is summarized in Table 2.

Our second example is, as it were, totally unclassical: It is ill-posed, has nonlocal conditions and contains three evaluation points $-1, 0, 1$. In our standard notation, we write this boundary problem as

$$\boxed{\begin{aligned} &u'' - u = f, \\ &u'''(-1) - \textstyle\int_0^1 u(\xi)\, \xi\, d\xi = 0, \\ &u'(-1) - u''(1) + \textstyle\int_{-1}^1 u(\xi)\, d\xi = 0, \end{aligned}} \tag{10}$$

where we assume now $u, f \in C^\infty[-1,1]$. Using the method of [20], it is straightforward to compute the Green's operator G. In fact, the `IntDiffOp` package yields the result

$$\begin{aligned}
\sigma G = {} & \sigma/2\, (e^x \textstyle\int e^{-x} - e^{-x} \int e^x) \\
& + 2(-e^{x+3} + e^{x+2} - e^{x+1} + e^{-x+2} - e^{-x+1})(\lfloor -1 \rfloor \partial + \lfloor 1 \rfloor \textstyle\int x) \\
& + (e-1)(-e^{x+2} - 2e^{x+1} + e^{-x+1})(\lfloor -1 \rfloor \textstyle\int + \lfloor 1 \rfloor \int) \\
& + (3e^{x+2} - e^{x+1} - 3e^{-x+1} + 3e^{-x})\lfloor 1 \rfloor \textstyle\int e^x \\
& + (2e^{x+2} - 3e^{x+1})(e^{-1}\lfloor -1 \rfloor \textstyle\int e^{-x} + e\lfloor -1 \rfloor \int e^x) \\
& + (-e^{x+3} - e^{x+2} + 2e^{x+1} + e^{-x+2} - e^{-x+1})\lfloor 1 \rfloor
\end{aligned}$$

using the abbreviation $\sigma := 2(2e-3)(e-1)$ while collecting and factoring some terms for enhanced readability. After transforming this to equitable form (which is again straightforward), we can apply Theorem 1 to extract the Green's function $g(x,\xi) = \tilde{g}(x,\xi) + \hat{g}(x,\xi)$ with the distributional part

$$\begin{aligned}
\sigma\, \hat{g}(x,\xi) = {} & (-e^{x+3} - e^{x+2} + 2e^{x+1} + e^{-x+2} - e^{-x+1})\, \delta(\xi - 1) \\
& + 2\, (-e^{x+3} + e^{x+2} - e^{x+1} + e^{-x+2} - e^{-x+1})\, \delta'(\xi - 1)
\end{aligned}$$

coming from the $(\dots)\lfloor 1 \rfloor$ and $(\dots)\lfloor 1 \rfloor \partial$ terms, and with the functional part defined by the case distinction for $\sigma\, \tilde{g}(x,\xi)$ as given in Table 3.

Case	Term
$-1 \le \xi \le 0$, $\xi \le x$	$3e^{x+2+\xi} + 3e^{x-\xi} - 2e^{x+1-\xi} - 2e^{3+x+\xi}$ $+e^{3+x} + e^{-x+1} + e^{x+2} - e^{-x+2} - 2e^{x+1}$
$-1 \le \xi \le 0$, $x \le \xi$	$-2e^{x+1} + 2e^{-x+2+\xi} - 5e^{-x+1+\xi} - 2e^{x+2-\xi}$ $-2e^{3+x+\xi} + 3e^{-x+\xi} + e^{-x+1} + e^{x+2}$ $+e^{3+x} + 3e^{x+1-\xi} + 3e^{x+2+\xi} - e^{-x+2}$
$0 \le \xi \le 1$, $\xi \le x$	$-2e^{3+x}\xi - 2e^{-x+1}\xi + 2e^{x+2}\xi + 2e^{-x+2}\xi$ $-2e^{x+1}\xi + 3e^{x+2+\xi} + 3e^{x-\xi} - 5e^{x+1-\xi}$ $+2e^{-x+1+\xi} - e^{x+1+\xi} - 2e^{-x+2+\xi} + 2e^{x+2-\xi}$ $-e^{3+x} - e^{-x+1} - e^{x+2} + e^{-x+2} + 2e^{x+1}$
$0 \le \xi \le 1$, $x \le \xi$	$-2e^{3+x}\xi - 2e^{-x+1}\xi + 2e^{x+2}\xi + 2e^{-x+2}\xi$ $-2e^{x+1}\xi + 3e^{-x+\xi} + 3e^{x+2+\xi} - e^{3+x}$ $-e^{-x+1} - e^{x+2} + e^{-x+2} + 2e^{x+1}$ $-3e^{-x+1+\xi} - e^{x+1+\xi}$

Table 3: Green's Function for (10)

Incidentally, this example shows also that the *representation of Green's operators* in terms of Green's functions—despite its long tradition in engineering and physics—is not always the most useful and economical way of representing the Green's operator. For many purposes it is better to take the Green's operator just as an element of the operator ring $\mathcal{F}_\Phi[\partial, \textstyle\int]$ or $\mathcal{F}[\partial, \textstyle\int_\Phi]$.

6. CONCLUSION AND FUTURE WORK

While we have focused in this paper to the case of semi-inhomogeneous boundary problems (those with an inhomogeneous differential equation and homogeneous boundary conditions), one may also consider the opposite case of semi-homogeneous boundary problems—this is especially important in the case of LPDEs. The so-called semi-homogeneous Green's operator maps the prescribed boundary values to the solution [18]. In the case of LODEs, one often restricts attention to well-posed two-point boundary value problems (in the sense of Definition 1). Writing the two evaluations as $\lfloor a \rfloor$ and $\lfloor b \rfloor$ and their action on u as $u(a)$ and $u(b)$, one may consider the extended evaluation matrix

$$\lfloor a, b \rfloor(u) := \begin{pmatrix} u_1(a) & \cdots & u_n(a) \\ \vdots & \ddots & \vdots \\ u_1^{(n-1)}(a) & \cdots & u_n^{(n-1)}(a) \\ u_1(b) & \cdots & u_n(b) \\ \vdots & \ddots & \vdots \\ u_1^{(n-1)}(b) & \cdots & u_n^{(n-1)}(b) \end{pmatrix} \in K^{2n \times n}$$

which is similar to (7) except that it is rectangular since we consider more boundary functionals than we could possibly impose for one regular boundary problem. If we do prescribe all $2n$ boundary derivatives, they must satisfy n relations given by the kernel of the map $\mathbf{R}^{2n} \to \mathbf{R}^n, X \mapsto X \cdot \lfloor a, b \rfloor(u)$. For the simple example in Section 1, the extended evaluation matrix for the fundamental system $u_1 = 1, u_2 = x$ is

$$\lfloor 0, 1 \rfloor(u) = \begin{pmatrix} 1 & 0 \\ 0 & 1 \\ 1 & 1 \\ 0 & 1 \end{pmatrix}$$

whose kernel has basis $(-1, 1, 1, 0), (0, -1, 0, 1)$. Written in terms of the boundary functionals, they encode the two relations $u(1) - u(0) = u'(0)$ and $u'(0) = u'(1)$. The analogous case for LPDEs gives rise to the interesting notion of universal boundary problem [25].

There is another, more fundamental, way of extending the results in this paper: Currently our method for extracting Green's functions works for arbitrary Stieltjes boundary problems $(T, \mathcal{B})$, but only in the *standard integro-differential algebra* $\mathcal{F} = C^\infty(\mathbf{R})$. Of course, it requires a Green's operator $G \in \mathcal{F}_\Phi[\partial, \textstyle\int] \cong \mathcal{F}[\partial, \textstyle\int_\Phi]$ and hence a fundamental system for T.

It would be interesting to extend the concept of Green's function and the corresponding extraction method to arbitrary ordinary integro-differential algebras $(\mathcal{F}, \partial, \textstyle\int)$. For the functional part $\tilde{g}(x, \xi)$, it is clear how to achieve this since one sees from the structure of Green's operators that necessarily $\tilde{g} \in \mathcal{F} \otimes \mathcal{F}$. The ring $\mathcal{F} \otimes \mathcal{F}$ has the structure of a partial integro-differential algebra with derivations and integrals

$$\partial_x(f \otimes g) = (\partial f) \otimes g \quad \text{and} \quad \partial_y(f \otimes g) = f \otimes (\partial g),$$
$$\textstyle\int^x(f \otimes g) = (\textstyle\int f) \otimes g \quad \text{and} \quad \textstyle\int^y(f \otimes g) = f \otimes (\textstyle\int g).$$

This structure will be useful for studying various properties of Green's function, in particular their symmetry: For well-posed two-point boundary value problems $(T, \mathcal{B})$ it is known [22, §3.3] that the Green's function $g(x, \xi)$ is symmetric whenever $(T, \mathcal{B})$ is *self-adjoint*. Otherwise one may associate to $(T, \mathcal{B})$ an *adjoint boundary value problem* whose Green's function is then $g(\xi, x)$. It would be useful to know how these results generalizes to arbitrary Stieltjes boundary problems.

Having an abstract integro-differential algebras $(\mathcal{F}, \partial, \textstyle\int)$, the other problem is Green's function will in general have a distributional part $\hat{g}(x, \xi)$ that does not fit into $\mathcal{F} \otimes \mathcal{F}$. For accommodating distributions into the setting of integro-differential algebras, it is probably necessary to construct a integro-differential module generated over $\mathcal{F} \otimes \mathcal{F}$ by a suitable notion of *abstract Dirac distributions.* (It is well known that distributions do not enjoy a convenient ring structure, hence it seems to be more reasonable to go for a module. This is also the path followed in the algebraic analysis of $\mathcal{D}$-modules; see [6, §6.1] for example.)

Acknowledgments

We would like to thank the referees for their diligent work and their crucial suggestions. In particular, the reference on the universal boundary value problem (see first paragraph of Section 6) is of considerable interest.

7. REFERENCES

[1] R. Agarwal. *Boundary value problems for higher order differential equations.* World Scientific Publishing Co., Teaneck, NJ, 1986.

[2] Z. Bai, W. Ge, and Y. Wang. Multiplicity results for some second-order four-point boundary value problem. *Nonlinear Analysis*, 60:491–500, 2005.

[3] P. R. Beesack. On the Green's function of an N-point boundary value problem. *Pacific J. Math.*, 12:801–812, 1962.

[4] M. Benchohra, J. Henderson, R. Luca, and A. Ouahab. Boundary data smoothness for solutions of second order ordinary differential equations with

integral boundary conditions. *Dynam. Systems Appl.*, 23(2-3):133–143, 2014.

[5] E. A. Coddington and N. Levinson. *Theory of ordinary differential equations.* McGraw-Hill Book Company, Inc., New York-Toronto-London, 1955.

[6] S. C. Coutinho. *A primer of algebraic D-modules*, volume 33 of *London Mathematical Society Student Texts.* Cambridge University Press, Cambridge, 1995.

[7] D. G. Duffy. *Green's functions with applications.* Studies in Advanced Mathematics. Chapman & Hall, Boca Raton, FL, 2001.

[8] H. W. Engl. *Integralgleichungen.* Springer Lehrbuch Mathematik. Springer-Verlag, Vienna, 1997.

[9] H. W. Engl, M. Hanke, and A. Neubauer. *Regularization of inverse problems*, volume 375 of *Mathematics and its Applications.* Kluwer Academic Publishers Group, Dordrecht, 1996.

[10] A. S. Fokas. *A unified approach to boundary value problems*, volume 78 of *CBMS-NSF Regional Conference Series in Applied Mathematics.* Society for Industrial and Applied Mathematics (SIAM), Philadelphia, PA, 2008.

[11] T. Jankowski. Differential equations with integral boundary conditions. *J. Comput. Appl. Math.*, 147(1):1–8, 2002.

[12] A. Korporal, G. Regensburger, and M. Rosenkranz. A Maple package for integro-differential operators and boundary problems, 2010. Also presented as a poster at ISSAC '10.

[13] W. S. Loud. Self-adjoint multi-point boundary value problems. *Pacific J. Math.*, 24:303–317, 1968.

[14] C. Pang, W. Dong, and Z. Wei. Green's function and positive solutions of nth order m-point boundary value problem. *Appl. Math. Comput.*, 182(2):1231–1239, 2006.

[15] G. Regensburger and M. Rosenkranz. An algebraic foundation for factoring linear boundary problems. *Ann. Mat. Pura Appl. (4)*, 188(1):123–151, 2009. DOI:10.1007/s10231-008-0068-3.

[16] G. Regensburger and M. Rosenkranz. Symbolic integral operators and boundary problems. Lecture Notes, available at `http://www.risc.jku.at/education/courses/ws2009/SioBp2/siobp.pdf`, 2009.

[17] M. Rosenkranz. A new symbolic method for solving linear two-point boundary value problems on the level of operators. *J. Symbolic Comput.*, 39(2):171–199, 2005.

[18] M. Rosenkranz and N. Phisanbut. A symbolic approach to boundary problems for linear partial differential equations. In V. Gerdt, W. Koepf, E. Mayr, and E. Vorozhtsov, editors, *Computer Algebra in Scientific Computing*, volume 8136 of *Lecture Notes in Computer Science*, pages 301–314. Springer, 2013.

[19] M. Rosenkranz and G. Regensburger. Integro-differential polynomials and operators. In D. Jeffrey, editor, *ISSAC'08: Proceedings of the 2008 International Symposium on Symbolic and Algebraic Computation.* ACM Press, 2008.

[20] M. Rosenkranz and G. Regensburger. Solving and factoring boundary problems for linear ordinary differential equations in differential algebras. *Journal of Symbolic Computation*, 43(8):515–544, 2008.

[21] M. Rosenkranz, G. Regensburger, L. Tec, and B. Buchberger. A symbolic framework for operations on linear boundary problems. In V. P. Gerdt, E. W. Mayr, and E. H. Vorozhtsov, editors, *Computer Algebra in Scientific Computing. Proceedings of the 11th International Workshop (CASC 2009)*, volume 5743 of *LNCS*, pages 269–283, Berlin, 2009. Springer.

[22] I. Stakgold and M. Holst. *Green's functions and boundary value problems.* Pure and Applied Mathematics (Hoboken). John Wiley & Sons, Inc., Hoboken, NJ, third edition, 2011.

[23] J.-P. Sun and Q.-Y. Ren. Existence of solution for third-order m-point boundary value problem. *Applied Mathematics E-Notes*, 10:268–274, 2010.

[24] G. Teschl. *Ordinary differential equations and dynamical systems*, volume 140 of *Graduate Studies in Mathematics.* American Mathematical Society, Providence, RI, 2012.

[25] I. Volovich and V. Sakbaev. Universal boundary value problem for equations of mathematical physics. *Proceedings of the Steklov Institute of Mathematics*, 285(1):56–80, 2014. Preprint version at `http://arxiv.org/abs/1312.4302`.

Matrices with Two Nonzero Entries per Row

B.D. Saunders
University of Delaware
Newark, DE, USA
saunders@udel.edu

ABSTRACT

Matrices with two nonzero entries per row (or per column) occur in many contexts. For example, edge-vertex incidence matrices of graphs have this form. Also, the boundary matrix for the highest dimensional simplices in a simplicial complex sometimes has this form as well. In particular, the homology of a triangulation of a 2 dimensional non-self-intersecting surface is obtained from the Smith forms of 2 two-per-row matrices (the edge-vertex and triangle-edge boundary matrices).

For an n by n matrix having just two nonzero entries per row, we show that rank, determinant, LU decomposition, and linear system solution can all be done in $\mathcal{O}(n)$ arithmetic operations (algebraic complexity). In the LU decomposition, U is bidiagonal and L, generally dense, is represented as a blackbox occupying $O(n)$ space and such that matrix vector product with L and with its inverse can both be performed in $\mathcal{O}(n)$ arithmetic operations.

If the nonzero entries are restricted to one and minus one then rank, LU decomposition, and Smith normal form can be computed in essentially $\mathcal{O}(n)$ bit operations (ignoring log factors). In this limited situation, Smith form is meaningfully defined over any ring. Determinant and linear system solution can each be performed with $\mathcal{O}(n)$ additions and negations in the entry ring.

For integer two-per-row matrices with the nonzeros not limited to one and minus one, the methods here can be combined with standard techniques for algorithms of bit complexity greater than $\mathcal{O}(n)$ but less than the complexity for general matrices.

ISSAC'15, July 6–9, 2015, Bath, United Kingdom.

DOI: http://dx.doi.org/10.1145/2755996.2756679.

Categories and Subject Descriptors

I.1.2 [**Symbolic and Algebraic Manipulation**]: Algorithms—*algebraic algorithms*; F.2.2 [**Theory of Computation**]: Analysis of Algorithms and Problem ComplexityNonnumerical Algorithms and Problems; G.4 [**Mathematics of Computing**]: Mathematical Software

General Terms

{0,1,-1}-matrix, linear system solving

Keywords

Homology, sparse matrix, Smith form

1. INTRODUCTION

We will call a matrix having two nonzero entries in each row a *tupero* matrix. Tupero is close to Tupelo, the name of a species of tree native to Southeastern North America whose fruits commonly appear in clusters of two. Please indulge the name whimsy.

The results may be succinctly expressed in terms of the concept of a FIBB (Fast Inverse Black Box). An matrix representation is an $f(n)$-FIBB if it has functions for rank, determinant, matrix vector product, linear system solving, and nullspace sampling, all of which operate in $\mathcal{O}(f(n))$ algebraic operations, in the worst case on $n \times n$ instances.For example, triangular matrices are n^2-FIBBs, permutations and diagonal matrices are n-FIBBs. Furthermore a product of FIBBs is a FIBB if either of the factors is nonsingular. The purpose of the many variants of LU decomposition may be seen as to create a product FIBB. The FIBB concept, primarily a software design device, is further developed in section 3.

The main result of this paper, in section 4, is that tupero matrices are n-FIBBs. A corollary, in section 5 is that {1,0,-1}-tupero matrices have Smith normal form, $A = USV$, computable in $\mathcal{O}^{\sim}(n)$ bit operations, including n-FIBBs for the unimodular transform matrices, U, V. $\mathcal{O}^{\sim}()$ means we ignore logarithmic factors. Applications to algebraic graph theory and simplicial homology are also discussed in section 5.

The central observation for the results reported here is simply that Gaussian elimination can be performed on a tupero without fill-in. With care to the details, this leads to linear time algorithms for the FIBB functions (rank, det, solve, nullspace sampling). First we give an example to show that care really is necessary to achieve linear time.

2. TUPERO SLOW LU DECOMPOSITION

Consider the matrix

$$\begin{pmatrix} 1 & -1 & 0 & 0 & 0 & 0 \\ 1 & 0 & -1 & 0 & 0 & 0 \\ 1 & 0 & 0 & -1 & 0 & 0 \\ 1 & 0 & 0 & 0 & -1 & 0 \\ 1 & 0 & 0 & 0 & 0 & -1 \\ 1 & 0 & 0 & 0 & 0 & 0 \end{pmatrix}.$$

If elimination is done by subtracting the first row from the others, one obtains

$$\begin{pmatrix} 1 & -1 & 0 & 0 & 0 & 0 \\ 0 & 1 & -1 & 0 & 0 & 0 \\ 0 & 1 & 0 & -1 & 0 & 0 \\ 0 & 1 & 0 & 0 & -1 & 0 \\ 0 & 1 & 0 & 0 & 0 & -1 \\ 0 & 1 & 0 & 0 & 0 & 0 \end{pmatrix}.$$

Continuing recursively with row operations on the lower right block, yields an $\Theta(n^2)$ algorithm for producing an upper triangular matrix, U. Furthermore the lower triangular matrix, L, representing the row operations will be dense, thus the elimination costs $\Theta(n^2)$ time and space. We will overcome the time cost with a spanning tree guided elimination and we will overcome the space issue by designing a compact representation for L.

3. FIBB: FAST INVERSE BLACK BOX

Over the past 3 decades or so a large number of iterative methods for problems in exact linear algebra have been developed. These methods exploit a separation of concerns between how matrix vector product, $Ax \to y$ is performed and how a linear algebra problem may be solved with the use of matrix vector products in which the matrix is applied to a succession of vectors.

These solvers are then indifferent to the nature of the blackbox. They perform the same. For example on a Toeplitz matrix and on a sparse matrix having the same matrix vector product cost. The Toeplitz is exploiting FFT while the sparse matrix object is organized to avoid storing zeroes of the matrix or or multiplying by them. These two matrix times vector operations are very different indeed.

The C++ exact linear algebra library `LinBox`(found at `linalg.org`) is designed to provide blackbox matrices and algorithms like these. There the matrix is represented by an object with member function `apply`, and the product $y = Ax$ is written $A.apply(y, x)$, with vector object reference y being an argument for memory management reasons. Here we are going to compromise between full programming language usage and mathematical usage. We'll use the member function dot and write $y \leftarrow A.\mathrm{mv}(x)$ for the matrix vector product $y = Ax$. An important property of the blackbox representation is that blackboxes can be composed, thus the matrix vector product of AB is $AB.\mathrm{mv}(x) := A.\mathrm{mv}(B.\mathrm{mv}(x))$. The cost is the sum of the costs for A and B. Ordinarily this is vastly less than the cost of first doing a matrix product. This convenience of forming products of blackboxes is used widely to *precondition* so that, say, Wiedemann's algorithm on a preconditioned A (product involving A) serves the purpose where direct application to A would not. For example, blackbox rank and determinant algorithms work like this [13, 7].

Here we extend the notation of blackbox to that of FIBB, where the main point is that a blackbox should be a FIBB if its structure is such that solving a linear system is fast, as well as mv product (solve $Ax = y$ for x given y as well as for y given x. For example, a Toeplitz matrix is a good candidate to be a FIBB, with the solver implementing a "superfast" method [14]. Secondarily, we will ask our FIBBs to also provide fast rank and determinant functions. As with blackboxes, a key point is that products of FIBBs can be FIBBs. Indeed, the main point here is separation of concerns between forming matrix factorizations and using them.

Definition: For $n \in \mathcal{O}(m)$, a $f(m)$-FIBB A is an object representing a linear transformation T_A in $\mathbb{F}^{m\times n}$ by implementing the following functions in such a way that each has $\mathcal{O}(f(m))$ worst case algebraic cost.

- Rank: $r \leftarrow A.\mathrm{rank}()$ returns $r = \mathrm{rank}(T_A)$.
- Determinant: $d \leftarrow A.\det()$ returns d, the determinant of T_A if $m = n$. For the convenience of defining a total function, we use the convention $A.\det() = 0$ if T_A is not square.
- Matrix vector product: $y \leftarrow A.\mathrm{mv}(x)$. For $x \in \mathbb{F}^n$, $A.\mathrm{mv}(x)$ returns $y \in \mathbb{F}^m$ such that $T_A x = y$.
- Linear system solution (arbitrary): $x \leftarrow A.\mathrm{solve}(y), x \in \mathbb{F}^n$. For $y \in \mathrm{Im}(T_A) \subset \mathbb{F}^m$, A.solve returns x such that $T_A x = y$. If T_A is singular, *any* arbitrary solution is acceptable. If the system is inconsistent, $y \notin \mathrm{Im}(T_A)$, the result is not specified.

In the sequel we will generally use the same symbol to denote a FIBB and to denote the linear operator it represents.

Again, the main advantage of FIBBs from the point of view of software design is a separation of concerns, resulting in more compact and flexible code. If you can factor a matrix as a product of $f(m)$-FIBBs then you have made a $f(m)$-FIBB for the matrix without having to individually specify the functions rank, det, mv, and solve for your specific product form. Primitive examples of n-FIBBs are permutation matrices and diagonal matrices. Triangular matrices are m^2-FIBBS. From the point of view of software design, the power of the FIBB concept is that we have a generic way to build a FIBB for a product of other FIBBs (primitive, or themselves products), per the next lemma. Thus the many standard matrix factorizations each produce a product FIBB for a given matrix without having to provide custom implementations of the functions rank, det, mv, solve. For example, the many factorizations PLUQ, LQUP, PLE, CUP, etc. discussed in [12, 5] are all FIBBs as is decomposition with unit triangular matrices and a diagonal, $PLDUQ$, or Cholesky decomposition of a symmetric matrix, LDL^T, etc., ad infinitum. (Here P, Q are permutations, L, U are triangular, C, E are (triangular) echelon forms, D is diagonal.) In these factorizations, for a square matrix, the most common complexity result is that a n^2-FIBB is produced at construction cost of $\mathcal{O}(n^\omega)$ for $\omega < 3$, the matrix multiplication exponent.

For another context, a FIBB may be made from a blackbox matrix. Suppose a $m \times m$ matrix, A, has a cost $\mathcal{O}(m^\alpha)$ mv product. Using Wiedemann's algorithm we may produce a rank revealing minimal polynomial for a preconditioning $B = LAR$ at $\mathcal{O}\tilde{}(m^{1+\alpha})$ cost. Here the preconditioners L and R are chosen at random but nonsingular and with fast mv product. See [16, 13, 1] for some preconditioner choices. The matrix together with preconditioners and minpoly forms a $m^{1+\alpha}$-FIBB for A because the FIBB functions rank, det, solve may be implemented using the minpoly [1]. In this case the rank, det, mv are much faster than the solve, which has essentially the same asymptotic complexity as constructing the FIBB (computing the minpoly). Nonetheless, forming and using the FIBB is as fast for a single solve and a constant factor faster for repeated solves than independent solves would be.

Finally, the point of this paper is to provide, for extremely sparse matrices (tupero), factorizations which are product FIBBs whose functions use linear time and space.

LEMMA 1. *Let positive integers r, s, t be given and $n = \max(r, s, t)$. If $A \in \mathbb{F}^{s\times r}$ and $B \in \mathbb{F}^{r\times t}$ are $f(n)$-FIBBs and*

1. *$r = s$ and A is nonsingular, or*
2. *$r = t$ and B is nonsingular, or*
3. *A and B both have rank r,*

then AB is an $f(n)$-FIBB.

PROOF. In all cases, the functions

$AB.\text{mv}(x) := A.\text{mv}(B.\text{mv}(x))$, and

$AB.\text{det}() := A.\text{det}()B.\text{det}()$

evidently have $\mathcal{O}(f(n))$ cost. We will show that the definition

$AB.\text{solve}(y) := B.\text{solve}(A.\text{solve}(y))$

works correctly, albeit with different explanation in each case. AB.rank() is defined differently for each case.

(1) If A is square nonsingular then $AB.\text{rank}() := B.\text{rank}()$. Let $z = A.\text{solve}(y), (A^{-1}y)$. The system $ABx = y$ is consistent if and only if $Bx = z = A^{-1}y$. Thus the composition $B.\text{solve}(A.\text{solve}(y))$ works correctly.

(2) Similarly, if B is square nonsingular then $AB.\text{rank}() := A.\text{rank}()$ and $AB.\text{solve}(y)$ is correct because $\text{Im}(AB) = \text{Im}(A)$.

(3) For consideration of the product of full column rank A and full row rank B, let I, J, and $R = (1, 2, \ldots, r)$ be sequences of r indices. Denote by $A_{I,R}$ the minor of A in rows I, columns R, and denote by $B_{R,J}$ the minor of B in rows R, columns J. Note that, by the Cauchy-Binet theorem [9], the I, J minor of AB is $A_{I,R}B_{R,J}$. Because A has full column rank r, for some I we have $A_{I,R} \neq 0$. Similarly some $B_{R,J} \neq 0$. Thus r is a lower bound for the rank of AB. On the other hand the rank of a factor is an upper bound for the rank of the product, so the rank is r. Define $AB.\text{rank}() := r$.

For consideration of solving, let I be an index set as above that identifies a full rank nonzero minor of A. Let A_1, A_2 denote the $r \times r$ matrix consisting of the I-rows of A and the $(m - r) \times r$ matrix consisting of the remaining rows, respectively. Let $y = y_1 + y_2$ be a corresponding vector decomposition. Finally, let $z = A.solve(y) \in \mathbb{F}^r$. Then z is uniquely determined by $z = A_1^{-1}y_1$ (with $A_2z = y_2$ being a consistency condition). A solution to $Bx = z$ exists; in more detail it is $x_1 = B_1^{-1}(z - B_2x_2)$, where B and x are decomposed conformally such that B_1 is the full rank submatrix in columns J, and x_2 is chosen arbitrarily. It follows that the overall system has solution $B.\text{solve}(z)$, justifying the definition $AB.\text{solve}(y) := B.\text{solve}(A.\text{solve}(y))$. □

3.1 Nullspace: sample and basis

For any FIBB over a finite field, we have a fast random nullspace sampler by solving $Ax = Ay$ for x with uniformly random $y \in \mathbb{F}^n$ and returning $x - y$. In turn, for a nullspace of dimension k, a random nullspace sampler may be used to generate a probabilistic nullspace basis constructor by sampling $\mathcal{O}(k)$ times. However, it can be more efficient to use the structure of the matrix explicitly for nullspace construction. For instance if A is diagonal with some zero diagonal entries we know exactly how to describe a nullspace basis. Or consider $A = \begin{pmatrix} I & B \\ 0 & 0 \end{pmatrix}$. The nullspace is

$$\{x = \begin{pmatrix} x_1 \\ x_2 \end{pmatrix} | x_2 \text{ is arbitrary, and } Ix_1 = -Bx_2\}.$$

A basis is derived from the unit vectors among the x_2. Products of FIBBs with efficient nullspace basis generation have efficient nullspace basis as well, as we show next.

For $n \in \mathcal{O}(m)$, let us call a $m \times n$ $f(m)$-FIBB A an $f(m)$-FIBB *with efficient nullspace basis*, if it has function $N \leftarrow A.\text{nsb}()$ which, for k being the (right) nullspace dimension, costs $\mathcal{O}(kf(m))$ arithmetic operations and returns $N \in F^{n\times k}$ such that the columns of N are a (right) nullspace basis for A.

LEMMA 2. *Let positive integers r, s, t be given and $n = \max(r, s, t)$. If $A \in \mathbb{F}^{s\times r}$ and $B \in \mathbb{F}^{r\times t}$ are $f(n)$-FIBBs with efficient nullspace basis and*

1. *$r = s$ and A is nonsingular, or*
2. *$r = t$ and B is nonsingular, or*
3. *A and B both have rank r,*

then AB is an $f(n)$-FIBB with efficient nullspace basis.

PROOF. (1) $AB.\text{nsb}() := B.\text{nsb}()$.

(2) $AB.\text{nsb}() := B^{-1}(A.\text{nsb}())$, where we mean that B's solver is applied to each column of $N = A.\text{nsb}()$. By hypothesis on B's solver, the cost with B is evidently $k\mathcal{O}(f(m, n))$, while the cost of A's nsb producing N, by hypothesis, is another $\mathcal{O}(kf(m, n))$.

For (3), note that a column full rank A acts bijectively: $\mathbb{F}^r \to \text{Im}(A)$, so that we may define $AB.\text{nsb}() := B.\text{nsb}()$. □

Parts (3) of the lemmas (about full rank rectangular products) and nullspace basis computation will not play a role in the sequel. We have included this for the sake of completeness regarding the FIBB construct.

3.2 Specific linear cost FIBBs

We focus next on some extremely fast n-FIBBs which *are* needed in the sequel. For better motivation of the next construction, the reader may prefer to skip the remainder of this section and return to it later after seeing how it arises in the context of tupero decomposition.

The factorization of tupero matrices will involve a lower triangular $m \times n$ matrix, each row of which has (at most) 3 distinct entry values. The i-th row consists of some 0's followed by some 1's followed by repetitions of the value e_i specific to the given row. Let j_i denote the position of the first 1 and k_i denote the position of the first e_i. Furthermore, the matrix is lower triangular, specifically with

$k_i = i + 1$ and $e_i = 0$ for $i \in 1..n-1$, so that the e's figure nontrivially only in rows $n..m$ and the diagonal entries are 1's except possibly in the last column. We will further require (for later notational simplicity) that the number of rows is at least one less than the number of columns, i.e. $m \geq n-1$. We call such a matrix, which can be represented by storing the 3 m-vectors j, k, e, a *ZOE* matrix (ZOE is for "Zero, One, E"). For example, $j = (1,1,3,2,1,3), k = (2,3,4,5,5,4), e = (0,0,0,0,e_5,e_6)$ describe this ZOE matrix:

$$\begin{pmatrix} 1 & 0 & 0 & 0 & 0 \\ 1 & 1 & 0 & 0 & 0 \\ 0 & 0 & 1 & 0 & 0 \\ 0 & 1 & 1 & 1 & 0 \\ 1 & 1 & 1 & 1 & e_5 \\ 0 & 0 & 1 & e_6 & e_6 \end{pmatrix}.$$

LEMMA 3.

1. *The $m \times m$ permutation, diagonal, and bidiagonal matrices are m-FIBBs.*
2. *For $n-1 \leq m$, the $m \times n$ ZOE matrices are m-FIBBs.*

PROOF. Part (1) is straightforward and left as an exercise.

For part (2), a ZOE matrix A, consider first $A.\text{mv}(x)$. Let vector p be the prefix sums of x, $p_i = \sum_{k=1}^{i-1} x_k$, $p_1 = 0$. These prefix sums up to p_{n+1} are computed in $\mathcal{O}(n)$. Then for i-th row of the form $(0,\ldots,0,1,\ldots,1,e_i,\ldots,e_i)$ with first 1 in position j and first e in position k we have

$$y_i = \sum_{j=j_i}^{k_i-1} x_j + \sum_{j=k_i}^{n} e_i x_j = p_{k_i} - p_{j_i} + e_i(p_{n+1} - p_{k_i}).$$

Since this has constant cost for each y_i once the prefix sums are at hand, the overall cost for mv is $\mathcal{O}(m)$. The prefix sums will also be used in the solver. We remark that the triangularity is not needed for mv.

To solve: $x \leftarrow A.\text{solve}(y)$, we may use standard lower triangular solving technique, with fast row vector times partial solution using the prefix sum approach of the mv function. Let the prefix sums of the solution vector x be vector p, as before. But here the p_i will be computed incrementally along with the x_i. Start with $x_1 := y_1, p_1 := 0, p_2 = x_1$. For rows 2 through $n-1$, at the i-th stage, set $x_i := y_i - (p_i - p_{j_i})$ and then $p_{i+1} := p_i x_i$. The term $p_i - p_{j_i}$ captures multiplying the below diagonal portion of row i of A by x. For the last entry, x_n, we have, for $i \in n..m$, the requirements $e_i x_n = y_n - (p_{k_i} - p_{j_i}) - e_i(p_n - p_{k_i})$. Thus x_n will be determined by a row in which e_i is nonzero, the other rows serving as consistency requirements. In case all e_i are zero, the solution space is one dimensional and x_n may be chosen arbitrarily. The overall cost is n times a constant for each x_i (and p_i) plus the cost of a search for a nonzero among $e_n..e_m$, totaling $\mathcal{O}(m)$.

Since the diagonal is of the form $(1,\ldots,1,e_n)$ and the matrix is lower triangular, we have

$$A.\text{det}() = \begin{cases} e_n, & \text{if } m = n, \\ 0, & \text{if } m \neq n. \end{cases}$$

Noting also that the last column is of the form $(0,\ldots,0,e_n,e_{n+1},\ldots,e_m)^T$, we have

$$A.\text{rank}() = \begin{cases} n-1, & \text{if } m < n \text{ or } e_n = 0,\ldots,e_m = 0, \\ n, & \text{if } m \geq n \text{ and some } e_i \neq 0. \end{cases}$$

Evidently the cost of determinant is constant and of rank is $\mathcal{O}(\max(1, m-n))$. □

We'll use these definitions to indicate the construction of a primitive n-FIBB of the specified type. For index vectors j, k, and entry vectors c, d, e,

- ZOE(m,n,j,k,e) is the ZOE matrix with parameters j, k, e,
- Diag(n,d) is the square diagonal matrix with (i,i) entry d_i,
- Bidiag(n,c) is the square bidiagonal matrix with (i,i) entry 1 and $(i,i+1)$ entry c_i in all but the last row.

Beyond these primitives, that for permutations (which we don't detail here, but is obvious), and the product construction of lemma 1, we need one more tool, namely direct sum FIBB construction.

LEMMA 4. *A direct sum of $f(m)$-FIBBs is an $f(m)$-FIBB, provided $f(m)$ is convex: $f(a+b) \geq (f(a)+f(b))/2$.*

PROOF. Consider $m \times n$ matrix $C = A \oplus B$, where A is $p \times q$ and B is $s \times t$. Because of the independent action of the blocks on conformally blocked vectors, plainly we have

$$C.\text{mv}(\begin{pmatrix} x_1 \\ x_2 \end{pmatrix}) := \begin{pmatrix} A.\text{mv}(x_1) \\ B.\text{mv}(x_2) \end{pmatrix},$$

$$C.\text{solve}(\begin{pmatrix} y_1 \\ y_2 \end{pmatrix}) := \begin{pmatrix} A.\text{solve}(y_1) \\ B.\text{solve}(y_2) \end{pmatrix},$$

$$C.\text{rank}() := A.\text{rank}() + B.\text{rank}(),$$

$$C.\text{det}() := A.\text{det}() \times B.\text{det}().$$

A word about the deteminant which only "makes sense" if the matrix is square: By our convention determinant is extended to be zero on rectanglar matrices. Note that a rectangular direct product has at least one rectangular factor, hence the definition just given correctly returns zero. On the other hand, if the direct sum is square, it may have non-square factors, but we are also ok in this (more sensible) situation since the correct determinant, zero, will be returned.

Each of these functions does a constant amount of work plus calls to the factor functions so runs in time $C + f(p,q) + f(s,t) \leq C + f(p+s, q+t) \in \mathcal{O}(f(m,n))$ by the convexity assumption. □

Of course, then, direct sums of any fixed number of f-FIBB factors are f-FIBBs.

4. TUPERO FAST LU DECOMPOSITION

Let F be a field and let $A \in F^{m \times n}$ be a matrix with nonzero entries a_i, b_i in row i, located in columns j_i, k_i respectively. The pattern of the matrix is the incidence matrix of an undirected graph whose vertices are labeled by the column indices and whose edges are $(j_i, k_i), i \in 1..m$. Through permutations, the rows and columns may be ordered according to the components of this graph, making a block diagonal matrix. We focus first on the base case of a single block corresponding to a connected graph. In section 4.2 we discuss the straightforward extension to multi-component graphs.

4.1 Single component tupero

Order the vertices of the connected graph (columns of the matrix) according to a depth first traversal of a spanning tree of the graph, numbering each vertex at the first visit in the traversal. Likewise list the tree edges ($n-1$ matrix rows) according to the order traversed. These $n-1$ first rows we will call the tree rows. The non-tree edges (rows) may follow in any order. Thus the tree rows have their second nonzero entry, b_i, in the first superdiagonal ($k_i = i+1$). We perform LU decomposition on the matrix resulting from these row and column permutations to achieve a PLUQ factorization of the original matrix. Our LU decomposition of the permuted matrix will have a bidiagonal U and a representation for L which uses linear space. An example will illustrate.

$$B = PAQ = \begin{pmatrix} a_1 & b_1 & \cdot & \cdot & \cdot & \cdot & \cdot \\ \cdot & a_2 & b_2 & \cdot & \cdot & \cdot & \cdot \\ \cdot & \cdot & a_3 & b_3 & \cdot & \cdot & \cdot \\ \cdot & a_4 & \cdot & \cdot & b_4 & \cdot & \cdot \\ \cdot & \cdot & \cdot & \cdot & a_5 & b_5 & \cdot \\ a_6 & \cdot & \cdot & \cdot & \cdot & \cdot & b_6 \\ \cdot & a_7 & \cdot & \cdot & \cdot & b_7 & \cdot \\ a_8 & \cdot & \cdot & b_8 & \cdot & \cdot & \cdot \end{pmatrix} = DC,$$

with $D = \text{diag}(a_1, \dots, a_8)$ and

$$C = \begin{pmatrix} 1 & c_1 & \cdot & \cdot & \cdot & \cdot & \cdot \\ \cdot & 1 & c_2 & \cdot & \cdot & \cdot & \cdot \\ \cdot & \cdot & 1 & c_3 & \cdot & \cdot & \cdot \\ \cdot & 1 & \cdot & \cdot & c_4 & \cdot & \cdot \\ \cdot & \cdot & \cdot & \cdot & 1 & c_5 & \cdot \\ 1 & \cdot & \cdot & \cdot & \cdot & \cdot & c_6 \\ \cdot & 1 & \cdot & \cdot & \cdot & e_7 & \cdot \\ 1 & \cdot & \cdot & e_8 & \cdot & \cdot & \cdot \end{pmatrix},$$

for $c_i = b_i/a_i$ in the tree rows, $i = 1..n-1$ and for $e_i = b_i/a_i$ in the following non-tree rows.

C then has LU factorization with this pattern:

$$\begin{pmatrix} 1 & \cdot & \cdot & \cdot & \cdot & \cdot & \cdot \\ \cdot & 1 & \cdot & \cdot & \cdot & \cdot & \cdot \\ \cdot & \cdot & 1 & \cdot & \cdot & \cdot & \cdot \\ \cdot & * & * & * & \cdot & \cdot & \cdot \\ \cdot & \cdot & \cdot & \cdot & 1 & \cdot & \cdot \\ * & * & * & * & * & * & \cdot \\ \cdot & * & * & * & * & + & + \\ * & * & * & + & + & + & + \end{pmatrix} \begin{pmatrix} 1 & c_1 & \cdot & \cdot & \cdot & \cdot & \cdot \\ \cdot & 1 & c_2 & \cdot & \cdot & \cdot & \cdot \\ \cdot & \cdot & 1 & c_3 & \cdot & \cdot & \cdot \\ \cdot & \cdot & \cdot & 1 & \hat{c}_4 & \cdot & \cdot \\ \cdot & \cdot & \cdot & \cdot & 1 & c_5 & \cdot \\ \cdot & \cdot & \cdot & \cdot & \cdot & 1 & \hat{c}_6 \\ \cdot & \cdot & \cdot & \cdot & \cdot & \cdot & 1 \end{pmatrix}.$$

For the 4th row of L, a tree row, we have

$$\begin{pmatrix} 0 & 1 & -c_2 & c_2c_3 & 0 & 0 \end{pmatrix}$$

with $\hat{c}_4 = c_4/(c_2c_3)$ and for the 6th tree row it is

$$\begin{pmatrix} 1 & -c_1 & c_1c_2 & -c_1c_2c_3 & c_1c_2c_3\hat{c}_4 & -c_1c_2c_3\hat{c}_4c_5 & 0 \end{pmatrix}$$

with $\hat{c}_6 = c_6/(c_1c_2c_3\hat{c}_4c_5)$. A strong pattern of prefix products emerges, which we will later exploit for a compact representation of L. Observe that, in the index range j_i to k_i, the entries are the prefix products of the $-c$'s divided by prefix product of the first j_i of them.

Finishing, we examine the form of the last two (non-tree) rows of L, which are the last two rows of C times the inverse of U,

$$\begin{pmatrix} \cdot & 1 & \cdot & \cdot & \cdot & e_7 & \cdot \\ 1 & \cdot & \cdot & e_8 & \cdot & \cdot & \cdot \end{pmatrix} U^{-1} =$$

$$\begin{pmatrix} \cdot & 1 & -c_2 & c_2c_3 & -c_2c_3\hat{c}_4 & \hat{e}_7c_2c_3\hat{c}_4c_5 & -\hat{e}_7\hat{c}_6 \\ 1 & -c_1 & c_1c_2 & -\hat{e}_8 & \hat{e}_8\hat{c}_4 & -\hat{e}_8\hat{c}_4c_5 & \hat{e}_8\hat{c}_4c_5\hat{c}_6 \end{pmatrix},$$

where $\hat{e}_7 = e_7/(c_2c_3\hat{c}_4c_5) + 1$ and $\hat{e}_8 = e_8/(-c_1c_2c_3) + 1$. We have eliminated in the same row oriented style as for the tree rows, but in two stages, one to pass from the column of the first nonzero to that of the second and one to continue to the last column. Letting $p_i = \prod_{j=1}^{i-1} -c_i$, with $p_1 = 1$, L has the pleasant form:

$$\text{diag}(p_{j_1}^{-1}, \dots, p_{j_m}^{-1}) \begin{pmatrix} p_1 & \cdot & \cdot & \cdot & \cdot & \cdot & \cdot \\ \cdot & p_2 & \cdot & \cdot & \cdot & \cdot & \cdot \\ \cdot & \cdot & p_3 & \cdot & \cdot & \cdot & \cdot \\ \cdot & p_2 & p_3 & p_4 & \cdot & \cdot & \cdot \\ \cdot & \cdot & \cdot & \cdot & p_5 & \cdot & \cdot \\ p_1 & p_2 & p_3 & p_4 & p_5 & p_6 & \cdot \\ \cdot & p_2 & p_3 & p_4 & p_5 & \hat{e}_7p_6 & \hat{e}_7p_7 \\ p_1 & p_2 & p_3 & \hat{e}_8p_4 & \hat{e}_8p_5 & \hat{e}_8p_6 & \hat{e}_8p_7 \end{pmatrix}.$$

In the tree rows, the p_i's begin in column j_i and continue to the diagonal. In the non-tree rows, the p_i's begin in column j_i and continue to the last column, being multiplied by $\hat{e}_i$ beginning in column k_i. Thus we have full information about L and from the vectors p, e, j, k, and about U from c, where the vector c, e store the updated values $\hat{c}_i, \hat{e}_i$, for those rows in which elimination occurred.

Note that we may further factor as $L = DME$, where $D = \text{diag}(p_{j_1}^{-1}, \dots, p_{j_m}^{-1})$, $E = \text{diag}(p_1, \dots, p_n)$, and M is the ZOE matrix,

$$\begin{pmatrix} 1 & \cdot & \cdot & \cdot & \cdot & \cdot & \cdot \\ \cdot & 1 & \cdot & \cdot & \cdot & \cdot & \cdot \\ \cdot & \cdot & 1 & \cdot & \cdot & \cdot & \cdot \\ \cdot & 1 & 1 & 1 & \cdot & \cdot & \cdot \\ \cdot & \cdot & \cdot & \cdot & 1 & \cdot & \cdot \\ 1 & 1 & 1 & 1 & 1 & 1 & \cdot \\ \cdot & 1 & 1 & 1 & 1 & \hat{e}_7 & \hat{e}_7 \\ 1 & 1 & 1 & \hat{e}_8 & \hat{e}_8 & \hat{e}_8 & \hat{e}_8 \end{pmatrix}.$$

Next we give the algorithm for LU factorization motivated by this example. It produces a product of FIBB's.

Tupero-component-LU-algorithm

Input: An $m \times n$ matrix A with two nonzero entries per row and whose pattern is the incidence matrix of a connected graph.

Output: A product m-FIBB representation of A formed from permutations P, Q, diagonal matrices D, E, ZOE matrix M (lower triangular), and upper bidiagonal matrix U such that $A = PDMEUQ$. We also may put the factorization in the familiar $A = PLUQ$ form, with lower triangular $L = DME$. We have decomposed L only to facilitate the discussion of expressing it as an m-FIBB.

Method:

1. Compute permutations P, Q and tupero matrix B such that $A = PBQ$ and the first $n-1$ rows of B have their second nonzero entry in the first superdiagonal. Specifically:

   (a) Compute the graph of which A's pattern is the incidence matrix, each row corresponding to an edge.

(b) Compute a spanning tree of the graph and then reorder the columns of the matrix according to the order that vertices are first visited in a depth-first traversal of the graph. This defines permutation Q.

(c) Order the rows according to the order in which edges are first visited in the same depth-first traversal. Follow with the rows corresponding to non-tree edges in any order. This defines permutation P.

(d) Let $B = P^{-1}AQ-1$. We call B a *normalized* tupero.

2. [initial D] Denote the first nonzero in row i of B as a_i and the second as b_i and define vectors j, k of column indices such that a_i is in position (i, j_i) and b_i is in position (i, k_i). Let $D = \text{Diag}(m, d)$, where $d = (a_1, \ldots, a_m))$. Factor B as $B = DC$. C is characterized by vector c in which $c_i = b_i/a_i$, for $i = 1..m$. Thus $C_{i,j_i} = 1$ and $C_{i,k_i} = c_i$, with all other entries zero.

3. [tree rows: compute p and update c, d]
$p_0 = 1$.
For row index i from 1 through $n-1$ do:
if $j_i < i$ then $c_i = c_i / \prod_{j=j_i}^{i-1} c_j$.
$p_{i+1} = -p_i c_i$.
$d_i = d_i p_{j_i}^{-1}$.

4. [non-tree rows, update c, d, e]
For row index i from n through m do:
$e_i = e_i/p_i$.
$d_i = d_i p_{j_i}^{-1}$.

5. Return the FIBB product PDMEUQ, where
$D = \text{Diag}(m, d), M = \text{ZOE}(m, n, j, k, e)$,
$E = \text{Diag}(n, p), U = \text{Bidiag}(n, c)$.

THEOREM 1. *Algorithm Tupero component LU is correct and costs $\mathcal{O}(m)$ arithmetic steps applied to an $m \times n$ matrix with two nonzero entries in each row, incidence pattern of a connected graph. The resulting factorization is a (m)-FIBB, so that matrix vector product, linear system solving, rank, and determinant all run at cost linear in the dimensions.*

PROOF. Connectedness implies existence of a spanning tree so that $n - 1 \leq m$ and we can replace n by m in cost expressions.

We leave correctness to the reader, guided by the example, and observe that each step of the algorithm plainly uses a linear number of arithmetic operations.

The decomposition product $PDMEUQ$ is a m-FIBB by repeated application of lemma 1 since each factor is an m-FIBB, and only M may be nonsquare or nonsingular. □

4.2 Multiple component tupero

If the graph for which a $m \times n$ tupero matrix is the edge-vertex incidence matrix has multiple components, we may apply the LU decomposition of the preceeding section to each component, noting that the permutations are driven only by the graph structure and thus done once and for all, placing the rows and columns in order of depth first search of a spanning forest, traversing first one tree then another in arbitrary order. We have $PAQ =: B = \oplus B_i$ where each B_i is a block corresponding to the edges (rows) and vertices (columns) in a single component of the graph, already in normalized form. Factor the B_i as $L_i U_i$ with $(L_i = D_i M_i E_i)$ by algorithm 4 (skipping step 1). By lemma 4, B is then a FIBB. We have proven:

THEOREM 2. *For a two nonzero entry per row $m \times n$ matrix, the problems of rank, determinant, and solution of linear system (nonsingular or singular consistent) are all solvable in $O(m+n)$ arithmetic time.*

5. {1,-1}-TUPERO MATRICES

In many incidence relation situations the matrix entries are 1's and -1's. This is the case for a basic graph incidence matrix in which both entries in a row may be 1 (undirected graph) or each row may have exactly a 1 and a -1 (directed graph). Also the boundary matrices in simplicial homology are {1, -1}-matrices, with two entries per row in the (transposed) vertex-edge boundary and also in the face-facet boundary in the case of a triangulated surface. By facet we refer to the simplices of the dimension of the surface. In triangulating a surface they share each face with exactly one other facet. In such situations the Smith normal form is of interest [2, 11, 4].

Recall some basic properties of the Smith form of $A \in R^{m \times n}$, where R is a principal ideal ring [9]:

- A is equivalent to a unique matrix in Smith form $= \text{diag}(s_1, \ldots, s_k)$, where $k = \min(m, n)$ and $s_i | s_{i+1}, i \in 1..k-1$.
- $s_i = D_i / D_{i-1}$, where the i-th determinantal divisor D_i is the greatest common divisor of all the $i \times i$ minors of A. Let $D_0 = 1$.

As before we will consider first a single component matrix and then the general case of a direct sum of such blocks. Most of the values we manipulated in our tupero LU decomposition algorithm were products and quotients of the original nonzero entries. In the {1,-1} situation all such values are also ± 1. The exception is the single addition by 1 that occurs in the elimination on a non-tree row (computation of the e_i). In the {1,-1} situation, that addition can yield ± 2 or 0 and only those values. Inspecting the Tupero-LU-decomposition algorithm further we see the resulting value affects only M and is not used as a divisor or in any other addition/subtraction. In this case the P, D, E, U, Q matrices are unimodular. This the Smith form of A is that of the ZOE matrix factor M.

LEMMA 5. *The Smith form of a $m \times n$ {1,-1}-tupero matrix A, with connected underlying graph is*

$$s = \begin{pmatrix} I_{n-1} & 0 \\ 0 & e \\ 0 & 0 \end{pmatrix},$$

where $e = 0$ or 2 and the bottom two zeroes represent $m - n$ rows. Only the first block row is present if $m = n - 1$. The Smith form and m-FIBBs for unimodular cofactors U, V such that $A = USV$ may be computed in $\mathcal{O}^{\sim}(m)$ bit operations.

PROOF. We remark that the ring of the entries plays a very weak role here. The only values that are manipulated in constructing the factorization are {-2, 1, 0, 1, 2}, which can be done without resort to ring operations. It is for this reason that we speak of bit operations. Soft $\mathcal{O}$ is used simply to account for the $\mathcal{O}(m)$ manipulations of indices which are of size $\mathcal{O}(\log(m))$. We remark that the mv and solve operations of the FIBBs only involve multiplications by elements of the same limited set. Thus mv and solve of all these FIBBs can be performed using only addition/subtraction of the ring.

We have seen that it suffices to compute the Smith factorization of $M = \mathrm{ZOE}(m, n, j, k, e)$, where the entries of e are in {0,2}.

When $m = n - 1$, we have

$$M = \begin{pmatrix} M_1 & 0 \end{pmatrix} = M_1 \begin{pmatrix} I_{n-1} & 0 \end{pmatrix},$$

where 0 denotes a zero column. The Smith form is the second factor and the Smith invariants on the diagonal are $n-1$ 1's. M_1, the first $n-1$ columns of M, is unit lower triangular and is a ZOE matrix, an m-FIBB.

When $m \geq n$ and the last column is zero (all $e_i = 0$), we may write, for $k = m - n + 1$,

$$M = \begin{pmatrix} M_1 & 0 \\ M_2 & 0_{k,1} \end{pmatrix} = \begin{pmatrix} M_1 & 0_{n-1,k} \\ M_2 & I_k \end{pmatrix} \begin{pmatrix} I_{n-1} & 0 \\ 0 & 0_{k,1} \end{pmatrix}.$$

Here M_2 is the lower left $k \times n - 1$ block of M. We see that the first factor is unimodular and the second is a Smith form with the diagonal Smith invariants consisting of $n - 1$ 1's and a single zero. The first factor is a slight variation of a ZOE matrix and easily implemented as an m-FIBB.

Finally, when $m \geq n$ and the last column contains some $e_i \neq 0$), we may transpose row i and row n so that the n-th row ends in a nonzero (which is 2). Assuming $e_n \neq 0$ for notational simplicity, we may write, for $k = m - n$,

$$M = \begin{pmatrix} M_1 & 0 \\ M_2 & 2 \\ M_3 & m_3 \end{pmatrix} = \begin{pmatrix} M_1 & 0 & 0 \\ M_2 & 1 & 0 \\ M_3 & m_3/2 & I_k \end{pmatrix} \begin{pmatrix} I_{n-1} & 0 \\ 0 & 2 \\ 0 & 0 \end{pmatrix}.$$

Here M_2 is the first part of row n, M_3 is the lower left $k \times n - 1$ block of M, and m_3 is the bottom of column n and consists of zeroes and twos. We see that the first factor is unimodular, an m-FIBB, and the second is a Smith form with the diagonal Smith invariants consisting of $n - 1$ 1's and a single 2. □

THEOREM 3. *Let R any ring and $A \in R^{m \times n}$ be a matrix which has two nonzero entries per row, each of which is ± 1, A diagonal matrix S, and m-FIBBs for the unimodular transition matrices U, V such that $A = USV$ can be computed in $\mathcal{O}\tilde{}(m)$ bit-complexity. S is a Smith form in which the diagonal entries are in {1,2,0} in the order 1's followed by 2's followed by 0's. The number of 1's is n minus the number of components in the underlying graph.*

PROOF. As discussed for any tupero in section 4.2, A may be permuted to a block diagonal form $A = PBQ$, where $B = \oplus_i B_i$ with each B_i a {1,-1}-tupero with connected graph. We may factor B as UTV Here $U = \oplus_i U_i$, $T = \oplus_i S_i$, and $V = \oplus_i V_i$, with $B_i = U_i S_i V_i$, where this is the factorization of lemma 5. By lemma 4, U and V are unimodular m-FIBBs. However T is not yet diagonal, since the blocks S_i may be rectangular.

T has the property that each row and column has at most one nonzero entry, a 1 or a 2. Permute the rows so that the rows with 1 preceed the rows with 2, which preceed the zero rows. Similarly permute the columns. Suppose there are a 1's and b 2's in T. We have $T = PSQ$, where

$$S = \begin{pmatrix} I_a & 0 & 0 \\ 0 & 2I_b & 0 \\ 0 & 0 & 0_{c,d} \end{pmatrix},$$

for $m = a + b + c, n = a + b + d$.

Thus the cofactors UP and QV are unimodular m-FIBBs and S is in the desired diagonal (Smith) form. □

6. CONCLUSIONS AND FUTURE WORK

We have given optimal algorithms for solution of linear systems, rank, and determinant over a field (using $\mathcal{O}(n)$ algebraic complexity). This is for matrices with two nonzero entries per row. When the nonzeros are restricted to ± 1, we go further and present an optimal algorithm for the Smith form factorization. The transform matrices are fast black boxes, so individual rows or columns may be explicitly exposed by multiplication with a unit vector, useful for some applications. This may have some practical use in algebraic graph studies or low dimensional simplicial homology, e.g., incremental homology computations.

The essence of the approach is to use elimination steps which cause no fill-in and to do a LU factorization in which the rows of L involve strings of successive prefix products. On top of that, prefix sums of the argument vector are also used so as to have a constant time dot product for each matrix row times vector.

It may be interesting to find other problems which have fast solutions for this extremely sparse situation. For example, rational solution of an integer linear system with constant bounded entries can be done in $O(n^2)$ using Dixon's algorithm [3]. The initial modular solution and each lifting step runs in $\mathcal{O}(n)$. There is no log factor in the Hadamard bound for tupero matrices, so the number of lifting steps needed is $\mathcal{O}(n)$.

On the other hand, I do not know how to get a Smith form algorithm for general (not ± 1) integer tupero matrices that is faster in the worst case than the best general purpose sparse Smith form algorithms [10, 6, 8]. The rational solution for largest invariant factor and modular rank computations of Wan's approach [15] are fast, but the local Smith forms are an issue. To compute by integral unimodular row operations either directly on integers or locally modulo a prime power involves fill in. Consider the step to eliminate b by use of the extended gcd cofactors of $g = \gcd(a, b)$:

$$\begin{pmatrix} s & t \\ u & v \end{pmatrix} \begin{pmatrix} a & 0 & c \\ b & d & 0 \end{pmatrix} = \begin{pmatrix} g & * & * \\ 0 & * & * \end{pmatrix}.$$

Unfortunately we have fill-in. It is not clear if two entries per row is a sufficient condition to have a Smith form speedup over the general case.

7. REFERENCES

[1] L. Chen, W. Eberly, E. Kaltofen, W. J. Turner, B. D. Saunders, and G. Villard. Efficient matrix preconditioners for black box linear algebra. *Linear Algebra and Applications*, 343-344:119–146, 2002.

[2] R. Diestel. *Graph Theory*, volume 173 of *Graduate Texts in Mathematics*. Springer-Verlag, 2005.

[3] J. D. Dixon. Exact solution of linear equations using p-adic expansion. *Numer. Math.*, pages 137–141, 1982.

[4] J-G. Dumas, B. D. Saunders, and G. Villard. Integer Smith form via the valence: Experience with large sparse matrices from homology. In *ISSAC 00 Proc. 2000 Internat. Symp. Symbolic Algebraic Comput.*, pages 95–105. ACM Press, 2000.

[5] Jean-Guillaume Dumas, Clément Pernet, and Ziad Sultan. Simultaneous computation of the row and column rank profiles. In *Proceedings of the 38th International Symposium on Symbolic and Algebraic Computation*, ISSAC '13, pages 181–188, New York, NY, USA, 2013. ACM.

[6] Jean-Guillaume Dumas, B. David Saunders, and Gilles Villard. On efficient sparse integer matrix Smith normal form computations. *Journal of Symbolic Computation*, 32:71–99, 2001.

[7] W. Eberly, M. Giesbrecht, and G. Villard. On computing the determinant and Smith form of an integer matrix. *41st IEEE Symposium on Foundations of Computer Science*, pages 675–687, 2000.

[8] Mustafa ElSheik, Mark Giesbrecht, Andrew Novocin, and B. D. Saunders. Fast computation for Smith forms of sparse matrices over local rings. In *Proc. 2012 Internat. Symp. Symbolic Algebraic Comput. ISSAC'12*, pages 146–153. ACM Press, 2012.

[9] F. R. Gantmacher. *The Theory of Matrices*. Chelsea, New York, NY, 1959.

[10] Mark Giesbrecht. Probabilistic computation of the smith normal form of a sparse integer matrix. In *Proceedings of the Second International Symposium on Algorithmic Number Theory*, ANTS-II, pages 173–186, London, UK, UK, 1996. Springer-Verlag.

[11] Allen Hatcher. *Algebraic Topology*. Cambridge University Press, Cambridge, UK, 2002.

[12] Claude-Pierre Jeannerod, Clément Pernet, and Arne Storjohann. Rank-profile revealing gaussian elimination and the CUP matrix decomposition. *Journal of Symbolic Computation*, 56(0):46 – 68, 2013.

[13] E. Kaltofen and B. D. Saunders. On Wiedemann's method of solving sparse linear systems. In H. F. Mattson, T. Mora, and T. R. N. Rao, editors, *Proc. AAECC-9*, volume 539 of *Lect. Notes Comput. Sci.*, pages 29–38, Heidelberg, Germany, 1991. Springer Verlag.

[14] Victor Y. Pan. *Structured Matrices and Polynomials: Unified Superfast Algorithms*. Springer-Verlag New York, Inc., New York, NY, USA, 2001.

[15] B. D. Saunders and Z. Wan. Smith normal form of dense integer matrices, fast algorithms into practice. In *ISSAC 04 Proc. 2004 Internat. Symp. Symbolic Algebraic Comput.*, pages 274–281. ACM Press, 2004.

[16] D. Wiedemann. Solving sparse linear equations over finite fields. *IEEE Trans. Inf. Theory*, IT-32:54–62, 1986.

Near Optimal Subdivision Algorithms for Real Root Isolation

Vikram Sharma
Institute of Mathematical Sciences
Chennai, India 600113
vikram@imsc.res.in

Prashant Batra
Technische Universität Hamburg-Harburg
Hamburg, Germany
batra@tuhh.de

ABSTRACT

Isolating real roots of a square-free polynomial in a given interval is a fundamental problem. Subdivision based algorithms are a standard approach to solve this problem. E.g., Sturm's method, or various algorithms based on the Descartes's rule of signs. For isolating all the real roots of a degree n polynomial with root separation σ, the subdivision tree size of most of these algorithms is bounded by $O(\log 1/\sigma)$ (assume $\sigma < 1$). Recently Sagraloff (2012) and Sagraloff-Mehlhorn (2013) have developed algorithms that combine subdivision with Newton iteration to reduce the size of the subdivision tree to $O(n(\log(n \log 1/\sigma)))$. Their algorithms and analysis crucially depend on the terminating predicates. We describe a subroutine that improves the running time of any subdivision algorithm for real root isolation. The subdivision tree size of our algorithm using predicates based on the Descartes's rule of signs is bounded by $O(n \log n)$. Our analysis differs in two key aspects from earlier approaches. First, we use the general technique of continuous amortization from Burr-Krahmer-Yap (2009), and hence the analysis extends to other predicates; and second, we use the geometry of clusters of roots instead of root bounds.

Categories and Subject Descriptors

F.2.1 [**Analysis of Algorithms and Problem Complexity**]: Numerical Algorithms and Problems—*Computations on polynomials*; G.1.5 [**Numerical Analysis**]: Roots of Nonlinear Equations—*Methods for polynomials*

General Terms

Algorithms, Theory.

Keywords

Real root isolation, Subdivision algorithms, Newton diagram, Continuous amortization, Integral analysis.

ISSAC'15, July 6–9, 2015, Bath, United Kingdom.

ACM 978-1-4503-3435-8/15/07 ...$15.00.
DOI: http://dx.doi.org/10.1145/2755996.2756656.

1. INTRODUCTION

Given a square-free polynomial $f \in \mathbb{R}[x]$ of degree n, the problem is to isolate the real roots of f in an input interval I_0, i.e., compute disjoint intervals which contain exactly one real root of f, and together contain all roots of f in I_0. Subdivision based algorithms have been successful in addressing the problem; for other optimal approaches see [9]. A general subdivision algorithm uses two predicates, given an interval I: an exclusion predicate $C_0(I)$, which if true means I has no roots; an inclusion predicate $C_1(I)$, which if true means I has exactly one root. The algorithm outputs a **root-partition** $\mathcal{P}$ of I_0, i.e., a set of pairwise disjoint open intervals such that for each interval either C_0 or C_1 holds, and $I_0 \setminus \mathcal{P}$ contains no roots of f. To compute isolating intervals for roots of f, check the sign of f at the endpoints of the intervals in $\mathcal{P}$. The following generic subdivision algorithm constructs a root-partition:

```
Isolate(f, I_0)
0. Preprocessing step.
1. Initialize a queue Q with I_0, and P ← ∅.
2. While Q is not empty
       Remove an interval I = (a, b) from Q.
       If C_0(I) ∨ C_1(I) then add I to P.
       else  ◁ Subdivide I
           Let m ← (a + b)/2.
           Push (a, m) and (m, b) into Q.
3. Output P.
```

The algorithm is guaranteed to terminate for square-free polynomials; otherwise we get an infinite sequence of intervals converging to a multiple root. Some standard choices of the predicates and the corresponding algorithms are: Sturm sequences and Sturm's method [5], Descartes's rule of signs and the Descartes method [6], and interval-arithmetic based approaches and `Eval` [3]. One measure of complexity is the size of the subdivision tree constructed by the algorithm for isolating all real roots of a square-free polynomial. We express the bounds in terms of n and the root separation σ of f. For the first two algorithms a bound of $O(\log 1/\sigma)$ is known ([5],[6] respectively); for `Eval` a weaker bound of $O(n^2 + \log 1/\sigma)$ is known [15]. It is also known that this is essentially tight for any algorithm doing uniform subdivision, i.e., the width of the interval decreases by a constant (in our case, by half) at each subdivision step [6]. Uniform subdivision cannot improve on $O(\log 1/\sigma)$ because it only gives linear convergence to a "root cluster", i.e., roots which are relatively closer to each other than to any other root. But it is known that from points sufficiently far away from the cluster, variants of Newton iteration for multiple roots converge quadratically to the cluster. This has been an underlying idea in improving the linear convergence of subdivision algorithms for root isolation [10, 12, 13]. The subdivision tree size of these improvements is bounded by $O(n \log(n \log 1/\sigma))$. Given C_0 and C_1, our algorithm can be succinctly described as follows (see §3 for complete details):

Newton-Isol(I_0)

...
If $C_0(I) \vee C_1(I)$ then add I to $\mathcal{P}$.
else if a cluster $\mathcal{C}$ of roots is detected in I then
  Apply Newton iteration to approximate $\mathcal{C}$ while quadratic convergence holds.
  Estimate an interval J containing $\mathcal{C}$.
  Push J into Q.
else $\triangleleft$ *Subdivide I*
...

For detecting clusters, we use a result of Ostrowski based on the Newton diagram of a polynomial [8]; other choices are a generalization of Smale's α-theory (see [7] and the references therein), or Pellet's test (see §2.1). These tools have been used earlier (e.g., in [10]) but we have some key differences:

(i) The tools used to detect and estimate the size of a cluster are independent of the particular choice of the exclusion-inclusion predicates (cf. [12]). This way we obtain a general approach to improve any subdivision algorithm.

(ii) Another difference is the method that is combined with bisection to improve convergence. In [12], Abbott's QIR method [1] is combined with the Schröder operator [7], whereas we apply standard Newton iteration to a suitable derivative of f. The former combination is a backtracking approach to get quadratic convergence; the latter gives quadratic convergence right away. This separates the Newton iteration steps from the subdivision tree, which is reflected in the bounds on the subdivision tree size: $O(n \log(n \log 1/\sigma))$ for the former, and $O(n \log n)$ for the latter. The bound on the number of Newton iterations remains the same.

(iii) Our approach can be modified to isolate complex roots; replace binary subdivision with a quad-tree subdivision, and choose appropriate predicates (e.g., Ostrowski's result above, or the argument principle). The results required by such an algorithm are developed in §2.1 and hold in $\mathbb{C}$.

We assume the Real RAM model and bound the arithmetic complexity of `Newton-Isol`. An important component of the bound is the size of subdivision tree constructed by the algorithm. Our key contributions are as follows:

(i) Theorem 10 gives a bound of $O(n \log n)$ on the size of the subdivision tree of `Newton-Isol` when C_0, C_1 are based on the Descartes's rule of signs. This is the first application of the continuous amortization framework [3, 4] to a non-uniform subdivision algorithm. Using this framework we directly obtain bounds on the tree size of `Newton-Isol` combined with either Sturm sequences or interval-arithmetic based predicates, unlike the known analyses in the literature that crucially depend on the predicates or the structure of the subdivision tree (cf. [10, 13]).

(ii) We show that if the distance of the cluster center to the nearest root outside the cluster exceeds roughly n^3 times the diameter of the cluster, then Ostrowski's criterion (which implies Pellet's test) for cluster detection works, and we obtain quadratic convergence to the cluster center (see Lemma 6). In the absence of such strongly separated clusters, our analysis shows that the size of the subdivision tree using only subdivision and the Descartes's rule of signs is bounded by $O(n \log n)$. Thus, Graeffe iteration, which is used to detect ordinary clusters by converting them to strongly separated clusters is not required (as in [10]).

(iii) Our analysis crucially uses the cluster tree of the polynomial (see Proposition 1). We derive an integral bound on the size of the subdivision tree (see Theorem 9). Instead of the usual approach to upper bound this integral by breaking it over the (real) Voronoi regions of the roots [4], we break the integral over the Voronoi regions corresponding to the cluster centers in an inductive manner based on the cluster tree. For the internal nodes of the cluster tree, the integral is bounded using known techniques. At the leaves, we devise an amortized bound on the integral (see Lemma 13). This is of independent interest, as it highlights a property of a pointset $P \subset \mathbb{C}$ that does not contain a sub-cluster: the integral of the inverse of the distance function P over the (real) Voronoi regions of the points in P is $O(|P| \log |P|)$. It is this result that underlies the $O(n \log n)$ improvement.

2. NOTATION AND BASIC RESULTS

Let $f \in \mathbb{R}[x]$ be a square-free polynomial of degree $n \geq 2$ and $Z(f) \subset \mathbb{C}$ be its set of roots. Given a finite pointset $S \subseteq \mathbb{C}$, let D_S be the closed disc $D(m_S, r_S) \subseteq \mathbb{C}$, where m_S is the centroid of the points in S, and r_S is the least radius such that $S \subseteq D(m_S, r_S)$; let $I_S := D_S \cap \mathbb{R}$. For $\lambda \in \mathbb{R}_{>0}$, define $\lambda D_S := D(m_S, \lambda r_S)$. For an interval I, let $m(I)$ be its midpoint and $w(I)$ its width. We often use the shorthand $I = [m(I) \pm w(I)/2]$, and for $\lambda > 0$, $\lambda I := [m(I) \pm \lambda w(I)/2]$.

Following [14], we call a subset $\mathcal{C} \subseteq Z(f)$ a (root) **cluster** if the only roots in $3D_{\mathcal{C}}$ are from $\mathcal{C}$; individual roots are trivial clusters. The notation $|\mathcal{C}|$ denotes the size of the cluster. Define $R_{\mathcal{C}}$ as the distance from $m_{\mathcal{C}}$ to the nearest point in the set $Z(f) \setminus \mathcal{C}$. A **conjugate-cluster** is a cluster $\mathcal{C}$ in which the non-real roots come in conjugate pairs; therefore, the center $m_{\mathcal{C}}$ of $D_{\mathcal{C}}$ will always be in $\mathbb{R}$. From the definition of clusters and the fact that the non-real roots of f come in conjugate pairs, it follows that $Z(f)$ is a conjugate-cluster and $R_{Z(f)} = \infty$. An **interval I contains a cluster** $\mathcal{C}$ if $\mathcal{C} \subseteq D(m(I), w(I)/2)$. We introduce the following notation that is convenient in the subsequent definitions: for $x, y \in \mathbb{R}_{\geq 0}$, if $x \geq cy$, for some constant $c \geq 1$, then we express it as "$x \gtrsim y$".

A **strongly separated cluster (ssc)** is a *conjugate-cluster* $\mathcal{C}$ for which $R_{\mathcal{C}}/r_{\mathcal{C}} \gtrsim n^3$ (the exact constant is in the proof of Corollary 7). With a ssc $\mathcal{C}$, we also associate the following quantities: (i) $\mathbb{I}_{\mathcal{C}} := [m_{\mathcal{C}} \pm c \cdot |\mathcal{C}| r_{\mathcal{C}}]$, for a fixed $c \geq 1$; (ii) $\mathcal{I}_{\mathcal{C}} := \{x \in \mathbb{R} : |x - m_{\mathcal{C}}| \lesssim R_{\mathcal{C}}/n^2\}$; and (iii) the "annulus" $\mathcal{A}_{\mathcal{C}} := \mathcal{I}_{\mathcal{C}} \setminus \mathbb{I}_{\mathcal{C}}$. The exact constants in these definitions are given in Lemma 6. If $\mathcal{C}$ is not a ssc, then we define $\mathbb{I}_{\mathcal{C}} := I_{\mathcal{C}} = [m_{\mathcal{C}} \pm r_{\mathcal{C}}]$ and $\mathcal{I}_{\mathcal{C}} := 1.5 \mathbb{I}_{\mathcal{C}}$. Note that for all clusters $\mathcal{C}$, $I_{\mathcal{C}} \subseteq \mathbb{I}_{\mathcal{C}} \subset \mathcal{I}_{\mathcal{C}}$. We need the following result:

PROPOSITION 1 ([14, LEMMA 2.1]). *Given a root cluster $\mathcal{C}$ of f. There is a unique unordered tree $T'_{\mathcal{C}}$ rooted at $\mathcal{C}$ whose set of nodes are the clusters contained in $\mathcal{C}$, and the parent-child relation is subset inclusion.*

The result originally is stated for root clusters of $f \in \mathbb{C}[x]$. But observe that $3D_{\mathcal{C}}$ contains the union of $D_{\mathcal{C}}$ with the set

$D(m_\mathcal{C} + 2r_\mathcal{C}\sqrt{-1}, r_\mathcal{C}) \cup D(m_\mathcal{C} - 2r_\mathcal{C}\sqrt{-1}, r_\mathcal{C})$. This implies that the parent in $T'_\mathcal{C}$ of a conjugate-cluster will also be a conjugate-cluster. Therefore, when $\mathcal{C}$ is a conjugate-cluster, we can define $T_\mathcal{C}$ as the subtree of $T'_\mathcal{C}$ whose internal nodes consists of only conjugate-clusters contained in $\mathcal{C}$, and the leaves are the roots in $\mathcal{C}$; note that the non-real roots come as conjugate pairs. We call $T_\mathcal{C}$ the **conjugate-cluster tree** of $\mathcal{C}$. Let $T_f := T_{Z(f)}$, i.e., the conjugate-cluster tree where the parent is the cluster $Z(f)$.

2.1 Cluster Detection and Approximation

The literature on detection and approximation of root clusters is vast (see [ ] and the references therein). One approach is based on Pellet's test: if for a complex polynomial $f(x) = \sum_{i=0}^n a_i x^i$ there is an $r > 0$ such that $|a_k| r^k > \sum_{i \neq k} |a_i| r^i$ then the disc $D(0, r)$ contains exactly k roots of f. A point $z \in \mathbb{C}$ is said to satisfy Pellet's test, if there is a k and r for which the test holds with the coefficients of $f(x + z)$. Results in [ ] generalize Smale's α-theory and relate it to Pellet's test. We instead use a result by Ostrowski [ ]. We need the following definitions. Let $f(x) = \sum_{i=0}^n a_i x^i$, where $a_i \in \mathbb{C}$. With each index i, $a_i \neq 0$, associate the point $P_i := (i, -\ln|a_i|) \in \mathbb{R}^2$. The lower-hull of the convex-hull of these points is called the **Newton diagram** of f. Given an index $k \in \{0, \ldots, n\}$, let $y_k \in \mathbb{R}$ be such that (k, y_k) is on the diagram. Define $\rho_k := e^{y_k - y_{k-1}}$, for $1 \leq k \leq n$, $\rho_{n+1} := \infty$, and the kth **deviation** $\Delta_k := \rho_{k+1}/\rho_k$, for $0 < k < n$. Let $\alpha_1, \ldots, \alpha_n \in \mathbb{C}$ be the roots of f ordered such that $|\alpha_1| \leq |\alpha_2| \leq \cdots \leq |\alpha_n|$. Ostrowski showed the following fundamental relation [, p. 143]:

$$\frac{1}{2k} < \frac{|\alpha_k|}{\rho_k} < 2(n - k + 1). \tag{1}$$

Given $z \in \mathbb{C}$, we will be interested in the Newton diagram of $f(x+z)$. If $f_j(z) := f^{(j)}(z)/j!$, then from a result of Ostrowski [, p. 128] we get:

$$\rho_k(z) = \max_{j<k} \left| \frac{f_j(z)}{f_k(z)} \right|^{\frac{1}{(k-j)}}, \quad \rho_{k+1}(z) = \min_{j>k} \left| \frac{f_k(z)}{f_j(z)} \right|^{\frac{1}{(j-k)}}. \tag{2}$$

The RHS of both equations above are defined for any k such that $f_k(z) \neq 0$, but we are only interested in those k for which P_k is on the diagram. Let $\Delta_k(z) := \rho_{k+1}(z)/\rho_k(z)$, the kth deviation. The following result for detecting clusters can be derived similar to [, Thm. 1.5]:

LEMMA 2. *If $\Delta_k(z) \geq 27$, for some index $0 < k < n$, then there are exactly k roots in $D(z, 3\rho_k(z))$ and $D(z, \rho_{k+1}(z)/3)$. Moreover, as $\rho_{k+1}(z)/3 \geq 9\rho_k(z)$, these roots form a cluster.*

The proof idea is to show that $\Delta_k(z) \geq 27$ implies that Pellet's test holds for $D(z, r)$, $3\rho_k(z) \leq r \leq D(z, \rho_{k+1}(z)/3)$. Note that the ρ_k's can be computed using, e.g., Graham's scan for convex hull computation, which takes $O(n)$ operations, since the P_i's are ordered by x-coordinate.

Once a cluster $\mathcal{C}$ is detected near z, we want a good approximation to $m_\mathcal{C}$. One approach is to do the iteration $z_{i+1} = z_i - kf(z_i)/f'(z_i)$, starting from z, but this may not be numerically desirable, as both f and f' are small near $\mathcal{C}$. We use the standard Newton iteration applied to $f^{(k-1)}$. The following result is crucial for the correctness of the algorithm. The proof uses standard bounds and analysis from the theory of approximate zero that is developed in Smale et al. [ ], and generalized in [ ].

LEMMA 3. *There is a constant c_0, such that if $\Delta_k(z) \geq c_0$, for $z \in \mathbb{C}$ and some $k \geq 2$, and $\mathcal{C}$ is the cluster in $D(z, 3\rho_k(z))$ then, for $D' := D(z, \frac{3\rho_k(z)}{2k})$, the following hold:*

- (i) *z is an approximate zero to the root z^* of $f^{(k-1)}$ in D' and the Newton iterates starting from z are in D'*
- (ii) *For all $z' \in D'$, $\Delta_k(z') \geq 27$, and $\mathcal{C}$ is the cluster in $D(z', 3\rho_k(z'))$.*
- (iii) *If $\Delta_k(z), \Delta_k(w) \geq 27$, for $z, w \in \mathbb{C}$, and $D(z, 3\rho_k(z))$, and $D(w, 3\rho_k(w))$ intersect, then both the discs contain the same cluster.*

We define $c_0 := 27 \times 6e^6$. Given $z \in \mathbb{C}$, a value of k satisfying the condition $\Delta_k(z) \geq c_0$ is called an **admissible value** for z, with the corresponding **inclusion disc** $D(z, 3\rho_k(z))$. Note that there can be more than one admissible value for a point z corresponding to clusters of different sizes. *In the rest of the paper, a cluster would always mean a conjugate-cluster unless mentioned otherwise.*

3. THE ALGORITHM

Let C_0 and C_1 be some exclusion and inclusion predicate respectively. The following algorithm takes as input f and an interval I_0 and outputs a root-partition of I_0.

```
Newton-Isol(f, I_0)
1    Initialize P ← ∅, Φ ← ∅; let Q be an empty queue.
1.a. If this is a recursive call then subdivide I_0 and
     push the two halves into Q; else Q ← {I_0}.
2.   While Q is not empty do
         Remove an interval I from Q.
2.a.     If C_0(I) ∨ C_1(I) then add I to P.
         else if Newton-Incl-Exc(I) then
             Let (J, k) be the pair returned.
2.b.         If ∀J' ∈ Φ, J ∩ J' = ∅ and J ∩ I_0 ≠ ∅ then
2.c.             ∀ I' ∈ Q, I' ← I' \ D(m(J), (ρ_{k+1}(m(J)))/3).
2.d.             Add J ∩ I_0 to Φ.
         else subdivide I and push the two halves into Q.
3.   Return P ∪_{J∈Φ} Newton-Isol(f, J).
```

If Newton-Incl-Exc does not return failure, i.e., is successful, then it returns an interval J containing a cluster such that $w(J) < w(I)/2$, and an admissible value k for $m(J)$.

```
Newton-Incl-Exc (f, I)
1.   Let m := (a + b)/2.
2.   For p ∈ {a, m, b}, let k_p ≥ 2 be the smallest admissible value k for p such that I ⊆ D(p, (ρ_{k+1}(p))/3).
3.   If k_a = k_m = k_b and the three inclusion discs
     are contained in D(m, (ρ_{k_m+1}(m))/3) then:
3.a.     z_0 := m, k := k_m, g := f^{(k-1)}, i := 0.
4.       While ρ_k(z_i) ≤ 2^{5-2^i} ρ_k(z_0)
             z_{i+1} := z_i - g(z_i)/g'(z_i); i := i + 1.
         J := [z_{i-1} ± 3ρ_k(z_{i-1})]
5.       If w(J) ≥ w(I)/2 then return failure
6.       else return (J, k).
7.   Return failure.
```

We first explain some steps in the subroutine above:

Step 2. A point p in I can have more than one admissible value associated with it. The right admissible value is governed by $w(I)$, since we should only consider those clusters $\mathcal{C}$ for which $r_\mathcal{C} \lesssim w(I) \lesssim R_\mathcal{C}$.

Step 3. As $D(m, \rho_{k_m+1}(m)/3)$ contains all the three inclusion discs, they all contain the same cluster $\mathcal{C}$. Otherwise, it is possible that the three inclusion discs contain different clusters but of the same size.
Step 4. This ensures that as z_i converges to the root of $f^{(k-1)}$, the distance to $m_\mathcal{C}$ decreases quadratically; this fails when we are near $\mathcal{C}$, or the root of $f^{(k-1)}$ is not near $m_\mathcal{C}$.
Step 5. Required to ensure linear convergence to $\mathcal{C}$.
Step 6. The interval J contains the cluster $\mathcal{C}$. Moreover, as $I \subseteq D(m, \rho_{k+1}(m)/3)$, we know that if the roots in I are a subset of $\mathcal{C}$, and hence are inside J. By now $w(J) < w(I)/2$, therefore, it suffices to return J.

We now comment on some steps in `Newton-Isol`:

Step 1.a. Ensures that a successful call to the subroutine `Newton-Incl-Exc` is followed by a subdivision step. Thus the recursion tree of `Newton-Isol` is a binary tree. The subroutine can be successful on an interval J returned by an earlier successful call. But the convergence in this case would only be linear, and so we prefer subdivision instead of Newton iteration, though in practice one can continue with the latter.
Step 2.b. Checks if $\mathcal{C}$ has not been found before (see Lemma 3(iii)), and that J is inside I_0; if either of this test fails, then I contains no roots and can be excluded.
Step 2.c. As the only cluster in $D(m(J), \frac{\rho_{k+1}(m(J))}{3})$ is $\mathcal{C}$, we can remove this disc from the intervals in Q. It is this exclusion step that significantly contributes to the improvement of the subdivision algorithm.
Step 2.d. This step adds the interval $J \cap I_0$ containing the newly discovered cluster $\mathcal{C}$ to the set Φ.

There are only two loops in the algorithm where termination is unclear: first, the while-loop in step 2 of the algorithm, and second, the Newton iteration in step 4 of `Newton-Incl-Exc`. The argument for the termination of the first loop is the same as that for `Isolate`. The termination of the second loop is guaranteed, because if $\rho_k(z_i)$ keeps decreasing, then in the limit it converges to zero. As the disc $D(z_i, 3\rho_k(z_i))$ contains exactly k roots, and, in the limit, z_i's tend to a root z^* of $f^{(k-1)}$, this implies that z^* is a k-fold root of f, which is a contradiction as f is square-free.

The following is a proof of correctness of the algorithm.

THEOREM 4. *Given a polynomial f and an interval I_0, `Newton-Isol`(f, I_0) outputs a root partition $\mathcal{P}$ of I_0.*

PROOF. We need to show the following claims:
1. $I_0 \setminus \mathcal{P}$ contains no real roots of f.
2. $\mathcal{P}$ contains (interior) pairwise disjoint intervals.
3. For all $I \in \mathcal{P}$, C_0 or C_1 holds (follows from step 2.a.).

Lemma 3 gives us the correctness of `Newton-Incl-Exc`(I), i.e., if the subroutine is successful then it returns an interval J such that any roots in I are contained in J. We only argue for the first claim. For every interval J returned by a successful call of `Newton-Incl-Exc` define

$$A_J := \left[m(J) \pm \frac{\rho_{k+1}(m(J))}{3}\right] \setminus J \qquad (3)$$

i.e., the annulus around J that does not contain any roots. We exclude intervals if step (2.b) fails for the interval J, or a portion of an interval is removed in step (2.c.). In the former case, either the cluster contained in J was already detected, or it is outside I_0. In the latter case, we do not loose any roots since A_J has no roots. So $I_0 \setminus \mathcal{P}$ contains no roots. □

4. COMPLEXITY ANALYSIS

We first show that `Newton-Incl-Exc` will hold near a ssc $\mathcal{C}$. Let $c_0 > 20$ be the constant in Lemma 3, and $\mathcal{C}$ a ssc throughout this section. Our first claim is that $|\mathcal{C}|$ is an admissible value for all points in $\mathcal{I}_\mathcal{C}$.

LEMMA 5. *If $|z - m_\mathcal{C}| \le R_\mathcal{C}/(8c_0n^2)$ then $\Delta_{|\mathcal{C}|}(z) \ge c_0$.*

PROOF. Let $\alpha_1, \dots, \alpha_k \in \mathcal{C}$ and $\alpha_{k+1}, \dots, \alpha_n \in Z(f) \setminus \mathcal{C}$. Moreover, assume that they are ordered in increasing distance from z. From (1), we know that $2k|z - \alpha_{k+1}| > \rho_{k+1}(z) > |z - \alpha_{k+1}|/(2(n-k+1))$. Moreover, $|z - \alpha_{k+1}| > R_\mathcal{C} - |z - m_\mathcal{C}| \ge R_\mathcal{C}/2$; similarly, $|z - \alpha_{k+1}| < 3R_\mathcal{C}/2$. Therefore,

$$\frac{R_\mathcal{C}}{4n} \le \rho_{k+1}(z) \le 3|\mathcal{C}|R_\mathcal{C}. \qquad (4)$$

From (1), we again have $\rho_k(z) < 2k|z - \alpha_k|$. But as $|z - \alpha_k|$ is smaller than $|z - m_\mathcal{C}| + r_\mathcal{C}$, we obtain

$$\rho_k(z) \le 2k(|z - m_\mathcal{C}| + r_\mathcal{C}). \qquad (5)$$

Since $|z - m_\mathcal{C}|, r_\mathcal{C} \le R_\mathcal{C}/(8c_0n^2)$, we get $\rho_k(z) \le kR_\mathcal{C}/(2c_0n^2)$. Combining this with (4), and the observation that $(n-k)k \le n^2/4$, we obtain that $\Delta_k \ge 2c_0n^2/(8(n-k)k) \ge c_0$. □

Recall the definition of the intervals $\mathbb{I}_\mathcal{C}$, $\mathcal{I}_\mathcal{C}$ and the annulus $\mathcal{A}_\mathcal{C}$ from §2, and A_J from (3).

LEMMA 6. *If an interval I is such that*

$$I \subseteq \mathcal{I}_\mathcal{C} = [m_\mathcal{C} \pm R_\mathcal{C}/(8c_0n^2)] \text{ and } w(I) > 72|\mathcal{C}|r_\mathcal{C}$$

then the pair (J, k) returned by `Newton-Incl-Exc`(I) is such that $k = |\mathcal{C}|$, $J \subseteq \mathbb{I}_\mathcal{C} = [m_\mathcal{C} \pm 20kr_\mathcal{C}]$, and $A_J \supseteq \mathcal{A}_\mathcal{C}$.

PROOF. We show that the conditions on I above imply that `Newton-Incl-Exc`(I) reaches step 6 (all the steps below refer to the subroutine). This requires showing the following: (i) all the conditions in step 3 hold; (ii) Newton iteration in step 4 converges quadratically and terminates with an interval J with $w(J) < w(I)/2$; (iii) $J \subseteq \mathbb{I}_\mathcal{C}$. The following claims provide the proof. Let $I = [a, b]$ and $m = m(I)$.
Claim 1: For all $p \in \{a, m, b\}$, $k_p = |\mathcal{C}|$. Recall from Step 2 that k_p is defined as the *smallest* admissible value k for which $I \subset D(p, \rho_{k+1}(p)/3)$. From Lemma 5, we have $k_p \le |\mathcal{C}|$. Since the roots in I can only come from $\mathcal{C}$, any smaller admissible value corresponds to a subcluster $\mathcal{C}'$ of $\mathcal{C}$, which implies $R_{\mathcal{C}'} \le r_\mathcal{C}$. From (4) we know that $\rho_{|\mathcal{C}'|+1}(p) \le 3(|\mathcal{C}'|+1)R_{\mathcal{C}'} \le 3|\mathcal{C}|r_\mathcal{C}$. Since $w(I) \ge 72|\mathcal{C}|r_\mathcal{C}$, clearly $I \not\subseteq D(p, \rho_{|\mathcal{C}'|+1}(p)/3)$ for any subcluster $\mathcal{C}' \subset \mathcal{C}$. Thus $k_p \ge |\mathcal{C}|$.
Claim 2: For all $p \in I$, $I \subseteq D(p, \rho_{k+1}(p)/3)$. This will follow from the more general claim that

$$D_1 := D(m_\mathcal{C}, R_\mathcal{C}/(8c_0n^2)) \subseteq D(z, \rho_{|\mathcal{C}|+1}(z)/3) =: D_2,$$

for all $z \in D_1$; since $a, m, n \in I \subseteq D_1$, the claim holds. But for any $z \in D_1$, we know from (4) that $\frac{\rho_{|\mathcal{C}|+1}(z)}{3} \ge \frac{R_\mathcal{C}}{12n}$ which is greater than $\frac{R_\mathcal{C}}{4c_0n^2}$, the diameter of D_1, for $c_0 \ge 3$.
Claim 3: For all $z, w \in D_1$, the disc $D(z, 3\rho_k(z)) \subseteq D(w, \frac{\rho_{k+1}(w)}{3})$. This follows if

$$|z - w| + 3\rho_k(z) \le \frac{\rho_{k+1}(w)}{3}. \qquad (6)$$

But $|z - w|, r_\mathcal{C} \le R_\mathcal{C}/(8c_0n^2)$, which along with (5) implies that $3\rho_k(z) \le 6kR_\mathcal{C}/(4c_0n^2)$. Therefore, LHS of (6) is smaller than $13kR_\mathcal{C}/(8c_0n^2)$, which is smaller than $R_\mathcal{C}/(12n)$ for $c_0 \ge 20$, but from (4) we know that the latter is smaller than the RHS of (6).

Claim 4: Let z_i be the sequence of iterates computed in the while-loop in Step 4. If $z_i \in D(m_\mathcal{C}, \frac{R_\mathcal{C}}{8c_0n^2}) \setminus D(m_\mathcal{C}, 2r_\mathcal{C})$, then $\rho_k(z_i) < 2^{5-2^i}\rho_k(z_0)$. Since $z_i \notin 2D_\mathcal{C}$, $r_\mathcal{C} \le |z_i - m_\mathcal{C}|$, and hence from (5) we obtain $\rho_k(z_i) \le 4k|z_i - m_\mathcal{C}|$. From [11, Thm. 2.2] we know that there is a unique root z^* of $f^{(k-1)}$ in $D_\mathcal{C}$. Therefore, $|z_i - m_\mathcal{C}| \le |z_i - z^*| + r_\mathcal{C}$. But as $z_i \notin 2D_\mathcal{C}$ and $z^* \in D_\mathcal{C}$, we have $r_\mathcal{C} \le |z_i - z^*|$, and hence $|z_i - m_\mathcal{C}| \le 2|z_i - z^*|$. Thus, $\rho_k(z_i) \le 8k|z_i - z^*|$. As z_0 is an approximate zero to z^* (see Lemma 3(i)), we know $|z_i - z^*| \le 2^{1-2^i}|z_0 - z^*|$, which implies that $\rho_k(z_i) \le 2^{4-2^i}k|z_0 - z^*|$. Furthermore, from Lemma 3(i) we know $k|z_0 - z^*| < 2\rho_k(z_0)$. Hence $\rho_k(z_i) < 2^{5-2^i}\rho_k(z_0)$.

Claim 5: The interval $J \subseteq \mathbb{I}_\mathcal{C}$ and $w(J) < w(I)/2$. The previous claim shows that if $z_i \notin 2D_\mathcal{C}$, then we will obtain quadratically decreasing values of $\rho_k(z_i)$. Thus when the iteration stops $z_i \in 2D_\mathcal{C}$, and it follows from (5) that $\rho_k(z_i) \le 6kr_\mathcal{C}$. Hence the interval $J = z_i \pm 3\rho_k(z_i)$ is contained in $\mathbb{I}_\mathcal{C}$, for $k \ge 2$. Moreover, $w(J) \le 36kr_\mathcal{C} < w(I)/2$, and hence the condition in Step 5 fails and we return J. The claim on the annulus follows from (4).

□

COROLLARY 7. *Let $\mathcal{C}$ be a ssc such that $\mathcal{I}_\mathcal{C} \subseteq I_0$. If I is the first interval such that* `Newton-Incl-Exc`(I) *is successful and the interval returned contains $\mathcal{C}$, then $\mathcal{I}_\mathcal{C} \subseteq I' \cup I''$, where I' is the parent-interval of I and I'' is one of I''s neighbors.*

PROOF. We claim that if I is the first interval in the subdivision tree such that $I \subseteq \mathcal{I}_\mathcal{C}$ then $\mathcal{C}$ will be detected. Given Lemma 6, it suffices to show that for such an I, $w(I) \gtrsim |\mathcal{C}|r_\mathcal{C}$. Since I is the first interval to be contained in $\mathcal{I}_\mathcal{C}$, both I' and I'' have endpoints outside $\mathcal{I}_\mathcal{C}$, thus $\mathcal{I}_\mathcal{C} \subseteq I' \cup I''$. So $2w(I) \ge R_\mathcal{C}/(16c_0n^2) > 72|\mathcal{C}|r_\mathcal{C}$, as $\mathcal{C}$ is ssc. Therefore, the first time `Newton-Incl-Exc` is successful in detecting $\mathcal{C}$ it must be either at I or at an ancestor of I. □

Remark: The proof gives the explicit constant in the definition of ssc, namely, we require $R_\mathcal{C}/r_\mathcal{C} > 16c_0 \times 72n^3$. A careful analysis shows that the weaker inequality $R_\mathcal{C}/r_\mathcal{C} > 4c_0 \times 72(n - |\mathcal{C}|)|\mathcal{C}|^2$ (or $50c_0n^3$) is sufficient.

Recall that the set of all roots $Z(f)$ is a cluster. As a consequence of Corollary 7, we assume that $I_0 \subseteq 1.5\mathbb{I}_{Z(f)}$; otherwise `Newton-Incl-Exc` will be successful right away and the interval returned will satisfy this property.

4.1 An Integral Bound on the Subdivision Tree

Let $\mathcal{N}(I_0)$ be the set of leaves in the subdivision tree of `Newton-Isol`(f, I_0). Step 1.a. of the algorithm ensures that the subdivision tree is a binary tree. Therefore, it suffices to bound $|\mathcal{N}(I_0)|$. To achieve this, we use the general framework of continuous amortization [3, 4]. The idea is to bound $|\mathcal{N}(I_0)|$ by an integral and then derive an upper bound on this integral. For this purpose, we need the following notion: Given a choice of predicates C_0, C_1, a function $G : \mathbb{R} \to \mathbb{R}_{\ge 0}$ is called a **stopping function** corresponding to C_0 and C_1 if for every interval I, if there is an $x \in I$ such that $w(I)G(x) \le 1$, then either $C_0(I)$ or $C_1(I)$ holds. Stopping functions, corresponding to different predicates, are provided in [4]. They have the following property:

LEMMA 8. *If $C_0(I)$ and $C_1(I)$ fail for an interval I, then for all $J \subseteq I$, such that $2w(J) \ge w(I)$, $2\int_J G(x)dx \ge 1$.*

PROOF. From the definition of $G(x)$, we have for all $x \in I$, $G(x)w(I) \ge 1$. As $J \subseteq I$, $\forall x \in J$, $2G(x)w(J) \ge G(x)w(I) \ge 1$. Thus $2\int_J G(x)dx \ge 2w(J)\min_{x\in J} G(x) \ge 1$. □

The main result of this section is the following:

THEOREM 9.

$$|\mathcal{N}(I_0)| \le 4n + 2\int_{I_0 \setminus \cup_\mathcal{C} \mathcal{A}_\mathcal{C}} G(x)dx,$$

where the union is over all ssc $\mathcal{C}$ in T_f.

We bound $\mathcal{N}(I_0)$ recursively. The leaves in $\mathcal{N}(I_0)$ correspond to three types of intervals: (i) intervals in the root partition $\mathcal{P}$, (ii) intervals that were discarded in step 2.c., and (iii) intervals for which condition 2.b fails to hold (either cluster already found, or $J \cap I_0 = \emptyset$). We will bound each of these three types. We analyse what happens before the first set of recursive calls.

Let Φ be the set of intervals collected in Step 2.d. of the algorithm, A_J be as defined in (3), and $\mathbb{I}_J := J \cup A_J$. From the construction of Φ, we know that all the intervals $J \in \Phi$ are contained in I_0 and each contains a unique cluster. For each $J \in \Phi$, let L_J be the set of *parent-intervals* of intervals in the subdivision tree that intersect $\mathbb{I}_J$; the type (ii) intervals are children of intervals in L_J. Let M be the set of intervals that do not intersect $\cup_{J\in\Phi}\mathbb{I}_J$ and are of type (iii). Note that if $I \in L_J$ contains an endpoint of $\mathbb{I}_J$, then $I \setminus \mathbb{I}_J$ can be of type (i) or (iii); but there can be at most two such intervals for each J on either side of $\mathbb{I}_J$. We abuse notation and use L_J to represent a set and also the union of the intervals in it; similarly for M.

For an $I \in M$, both C_0 and C_1 failed. Therefore, from Lemma 8 we get $|M| \le 2\sum_{I\in M}\int_I G(x)dx = 2\int_M G(x)dx$. As C_0 and C_1 also fail for the intervals in L_J, we can similarly bound $|L_J|$, but this will fail to give the desired improvement as it amounts to doing subdivision on J. Instead we do the following: since the width of the intervals in L_J is more than $w(J)$, we know that there are at most two neighboring intervals I'_J and I''_J that contain J. We count them separately, and for the rest we use Lemma 8 to get $|L_J| \le 2 + 2\int_{L_J \setminus (I'_J \cup I''_J)} G(x)dx$. For an interval $I \in \mathcal{P}$, we expect $2\int_I G(x)dx \ge 1$, as the predicates must have failed for the parent I' of I. However, Lemma 8 requires that $w(I') \le 2w(I)$. This can fail to happen near the boundary of $\mathbb{I}_J$, as noted earlier. But then there are at most two such intervals. Therefore, the number of intervals in $\mathcal{P}$ coming from the non-recursive calls is at most $2|\Phi| + 2\int_{I_0 \setminus \cup_J (L_J \cup M)} G(x)dx$. Combining this with the bounds on $|L_J|$ and $|M|$ we get

$$|\mathcal{N}(I_0)| \le 4|\Phi| + 2\int_{I_0 \setminus \cup_J (I'_J \cup I''_J)} G(x)dx + \sum_{J\in\Phi} |\mathcal{N}(J)|. \quad (7)$$

To expand the RHS inductively, we introduce the **cluster tree T_{I_0} with respect to an interval** I_0: It is the smallest subtree $T_\mathcal{C}$ of T_f rooted at a cluster $\mathcal{C}$ such that $I_0 \subseteq 1.5\mathbb{I}_\mathcal{C}$; since by assumption $I_0 \subseteq 1.5\mathbb{I}_{Z(f)}$, in the worst case, T_{I_0} is T_f. As enlarging I_0 increases the integral in (7), we make the simplifying assumption that $I_0 = 1.5\mathbb{I}_{\mathcal{C}_0}$, where $\mathcal{C}_0$ is the root of T_{I_0} [1]. To simplify (7), consider a cluster $\mathcal{C}$ associated with a node u in T_{I_0}. Let $J_u \in \Phi$ be the interval returned the first time $\mathcal{C}$ is detected by `Newton-Incl-Exc` ; let $A_u := (I'_{J_u} \cup$

[1]The factor 1.5 because $R_\mathcal{C}/2 \ge 1.5r_\mathcal{C}$, for any cluster $\mathcal{C}$.

$I''_{J_u}) \setminus J_u$; if $\mathcal{C}$ is not detected, then $A_u = J_u{:=}\emptyset$. Induction gives the following from (7):

$$|\mathcal{N}(I_0)| \leq 4|T_{I_0}| + 2\int_{I_0 \setminus \cup_{u \in T_{I_0}} A_u} G(x)dx. \quad (8)$$

For a ssc $\mathcal{C} \in T_{I_0}$, the assumption $I_0 = 1.5\mathbb{I}_{\mathcal{C}_0}$ ensures that $\mathcal{I}_\mathcal{C} \subseteq I_0$. So Corollary 7 implies that $I'_u \cup I''_u \supseteq \mathcal{I}_\mathcal{C}$, and Lemma 6 implies that $J_u \subseteq \mathbb{I}_\mathcal{C}$; hence, $A_u \supseteq \mathcal{A}_\mathcal{C}$. Considering only the ssc in T_{I_0} on the RHS of (8), and as $|T_{I_0}| \leq n$, we obtain Theorem 9.

4.2 Bound for the Descartes's rule of signs

In this section, we bound the integral on the RHS of Theorem 9, where the predicate is based on the Descartes's rule of signs [6] and the corresponding stopping function given in [4]. We derive the following bound:

THEOREM 10. *Given a square-free polynomial $f \in \mathbb{R}[x]$ of degree n, the size of the subdivision tree constructed by* `Newton-Isol`*(f, I_0) using predicates based on the Descartes's rule of signs is bounded by $O(n \ln n)$.*

Given a pointset $S \subset \mathbb{C}$ and $x \in \mathbb{C}$, define $d(x, S)$ as the distance from x to the closest point in S, and $d_2(x, S)$ as the distance to the second closest point in S. Let $V{:=}Z(f)$, the set of roots of f. The crucial idea in [4] is to partition the integral over the (real) Voronoi region of each root α. In [4], this integral is $O(|\log d_2(\alpha, V)|)$, which can be $(\log 1/\sigma)$; e.g., if $\alpha \in \mathbb{R}$ and all the other roots are of the form $\alpha \pm it$, for increasing values of t, such that $d_2(\alpha, V) = \sigma$.

Our idea is based on the following observation: for non-ssc clusters, the integral in Theorem 9 is bounded by the ratio $R_\mathcal{C}/r_\mathcal{C} = O(n^3)$, therefore, the number of subdivisions needed to converge to the cluster center is $O(\log n)$; for a ssc, because of `Newton-Incl-Exc`, the integral is restricted to the sets $[m_\mathcal{C} \pm R_\mathcal{C}] \setminus [m_\mathcal{C} \pm R_\mathcal{C}/n^2]$ and $[m_\mathcal{C} \pm |\mathcal{C}| r_\mathcal{C}] \setminus [m_\mathcal{C} \pm r_\mathcal{C}]$, and is again bounded by $O(\log n)$. The stopping function $G(x)$ is $1/d(x, V)$ almost everywhere except near real roots where it is $1/d_2(x, V)$.

A pointset $P \subseteq \mathbb{C}$ is a **conjugate pointset** if all non-real points in P also have their complex conjugates in P. A conjugate pointset is λ**-dense**, for $\lambda \geq 2$, if for all conjugate pointset $S \subset P$, where $|S| > 1$, the disc λD_S contains a point from $P \setminus S$. A **collection** $\mathcal{M}$ is a set $\{\mathcal{C}_1, \ldots, \mathcal{C}_k, Q\}$, where $\mathcal{C}_i$'s are pairwise disjoint clusters and Q is a conjugate pointset; let $\mathcal{M}$ also stand for the pointset $\cup_i \mathcal{C}_i \cup Q$, so that $D_\mathcal{M}$ is well-defined. A non-trivial **sub-collection** of $\mathcal{M}$ is a subset S of $\mathcal{M}$ such that $|S| > 1$. A collection $\mathcal{M}$ is λ-dense, for $\lambda \geq 2$, if for all non-trivial sub-collections $S \subseteq \mathcal{M}$, $\lambda D_S \cap (\mathcal{M} \setminus S) \neq \emptyset$. The **pointset corresponding to a collection** $\mathcal{M}$ is defined as the conjugate pointset $\mathcal{M}'$ obtained from $\mathcal{M}$ by replacing each $\mathcal{C}_i$ by its centroid m_i. Then we have the following relation:

LEMMA 11. *If $\mathcal{M}$ is a λ-dense collection then its corresponding pointset $\mathcal{M}'$ is 5λ-dense.*

PROOF. We claim $r_\mathcal{M} < 3r_{\mathcal{M}'}$. As $m_\mathcal{M}$ is a convex combination of the points in $\mathcal{M}'$, $m_\mathcal{M} \in D_{\mathcal{M}'}$. For any $\mathcal{C}_i$, the disc $D_{\mathcal{M}'}$ contains m_i and a point in $\mathcal{M} \setminus \mathcal{C}_i$, so, $2r_{\mathcal{M}'} \geq R_{\mathcal{C}_i} \geq 3r_{\mathcal{C}_i}$, for $i = 1, \ldots, k$. Suppose $q \in \mathcal{M}$ is farthest from $m_\mathcal{M}$ and $q \in \mathcal{C}_i$, then $|m_\mathcal{M} - q| = r_\mathcal{M} \leq |m_\mathcal{M} - m_i| + r_{\mathcal{C}_i}$; but as $m_\mathcal{M}, m_i \in D_{\mathcal{M}'}$, we have $r_\mathcal{M} \leq 2r_{\mathcal{M}'} + r_{\mathcal{C}_i} < 3r_{\mathcal{M}'}$; if $q \in Q$ then $q, m_\mathcal{M} \in D_{\mathcal{M}'}$ and so $r_\mathcal{M} \leq 2r_{\mathcal{M}'}$. Let $S \subset \mathcal{M}$ be a sub-collection and S' be the corresponding subset in $\mathcal{M}'$. If λD_S contains a point q from a $\mathcal{C}$ outside S (the case when $q \in Q \setminus S$ is similar), then as $3D_\mathcal{C}$ contains no points except $\mathcal{C}$, we obtain $m_S \notin 3D_\mathcal{C}$. Since $q \in \lambda D_S$, we have $\lambda r_s \geq 2r_\mathcal{C}$. Hence, $|m_S - m_\mathcal{C}| \leq \lambda r_S + r_\mathcal{C} \leq 1.5\lambda r_S$, which implies $|m_{S'} - m_\mathcal{C}| \leq 5\lambda r_{S'}$, as $r_S < 3r_{S'}$ and $\lambda \geq 2$. $\square$

We will need the following result from [4, 15] later:

LEMMA 12. *Let $\gamma \in \mathbb{C}$ and $J = [r, s]$.*
(Re) *If $\gamma \in \mathbb{R} \setminus J$, then*

$$\int_J \frac{dx}{|\gamma - x|} = \ln \left|\frac{\gamma - s}{\gamma - r}\right|^{\delta(J > \gamma)}, \quad (9)$$

where $\delta(J > \gamma) = +1$ if $r > \gamma$ and -1 if $s < \gamma$.
(Im) *If $\gamma \in \mathbb{C} \setminus \mathbb{R}$ then, say $\gamma = \Re(\gamma) + \sqrt{-1}\Im(\gamma)$,*

$$\int_J \frac{dx}{|\gamma - x|} \leq O\left(\ln \frac{\max\{|s - \gamma|, |r - \gamma|\}}{|\Im(\gamma)|}\right). \quad (10)$$

We now give the proof of Theorem 10.

PROOF. The proof is by induction on $|T_{I_0}|$. We claim that

$$\int_{I_0 \setminus \cup_\mathcal{C} \mathcal{A}_\mathcal{C}} G(x)dx = O(|T_{I_0}| \ln n). \quad (11)$$

Let $\mathcal{C}_0$ be the root of T_{I_0}, and $\mathcal{M}$ be the collection formed by its children. By assumption, $I_0 = 1.5\mathbb{I}_{\mathcal{C}_0}$. Consider a ssc $\mathcal{C} \in \mathcal{M}$. Then $I_0 \setminus \mathcal{A}_\mathcal{C} = I_0 \setminus (\mathcal{I}_\mathcal{C} \setminus \mathbb{I}_\mathcal{C}) \subseteq (I_0 \setminus \mathcal{I}_\mathcal{C}) \cup 1.5\mathbb{I}_\mathcal{C}$. If $\mathcal{C}'$ is a ssc contained in $\mathcal{C}$, we can inductively remove $\mathcal{A}_{\mathcal{C}'}$ from $\mathbb{I}_\mathcal{C}$. This also applies to non-ssc clusters in $\mathcal{M}$, since by definition $\mathcal{I}_\mathcal{C} = 1.5\mathbb{I}_\mathcal{C}$. Therefore,

$$I_0 \setminus \cup_\mathcal{C} \mathcal{A}_\mathcal{C} \subseteq (I_0 \setminus \cup_{\mathcal{C} \in \mathcal{M}} \mathcal{I}_\mathcal{C}) \cup (\cup_{\mathcal{C} \in \mathcal{M}} (1.5\mathbb{I}_\mathcal{C} \setminus \cup_{\mathcal{C}' \subset \mathcal{C}} \mathcal{A}_{\mathcal{C}'})).$$

We claim that

$$\int_{I_0 \setminus \cup_{\mathcal{C} \in \mathcal{M}} \mathcal{I}_\mathcal{C}} G(x)dx = O(|\mathcal{M}| \ln n). \quad (12)$$

As $|T_\mathcal{C}| < |T_{I_0}|$, for $\mathcal{C} \in \mathcal{M}$, by induction we obtain

$$\int_{1.5\mathbb{I}_\mathcal{C} \setminus \cup_{\mathcal{C}' \subset \mathcal{C}} \mathcal{A}_{\mathcal{C}'}} G(x)dx = O(|T_\mathcal{C}| \ln n).$$

This bound along with (12) and the observation that $|\mathcal{M}| + \sum_{\mathcal{C} \in \mathcal{M}} |T_\mathcal{C}| < |T_{I_0}|$ gives us (11). The base case is when $\mathcal{M}$ contains only leaves, in which case (11) reduces to (12).

We next claim that

$$\int_{I_0 \setminus \cup_{\mathcal{C} \in \mathcal{M}} \mathcal{I}_\mathcal{C}} G(x)dx = O(\ln n) + \int_{I'_0 \setminus \cup_{\mathcal{C} \in \mathcal{M}} \mathcal{I}_\mathcal{C}} G(x)dx,$$

where $I'_0{:=}1.5I_{\mathcal{C}_0}$. If $\mathcal{C}_0$ is not a ssc, then this is clear as $I'_0 = 1.5I_{\mathcal{C}_0} = I_0$. If $\mathcal{C}_0$ is a ssc, then $I_0 = 1.5\mathbb{I}_{\mathcal{C}_0} = [m_{\mathcal{C}_0} \pm 1.5|\mathcal{C}_0| r_{\mathcal{C}_0}]$. Break it as I'_0, $[m_{\mathcal{C}_0} + 1.5r_{\mathcal{C}_0}, m_{\mathcal{C}_0} + 1.5|\mathcal{C}_0| r_{\mathcal{C}_0}]$ and $[m_{\mathcal{C}_0} - 1.5r_{\mathcal{C}_0}, m_{\mathcal{C}_0} - 1.5|\mathcal{C}_0| r_{\mathcal{C}_0}]$. The closest root to any x in these intervals is from $\mathcal{C}_0$. Moreover, as $|x - m_{\mathcal{C}_0}| \geq 1.5r_{\mathcal{C}_0}$, we get $G(x){:=}1/d(x, V) \leq 3/|x - m_{\mathcal{C}_0}|$. Therefore, from Lemma 12(Re) it follows that $\int_{m_{\mathcal{C}_0}+1.5r_{\mathcal{C}_0}}^{m_{\mathcal{C}_0}+|\mathcal{C}_0| r_{\mathcal{C}_0}} \frac{2}{|x - m_{\mathcal{C}_0}|} = O(\ln |\mathcal{C}_0|)$. Similarly for the other interval. Hence to prove (12), it suffices to show

$$\int_{I'_0 \setminus \cup_{\mathcal{C} \in \mathcal{M}} \mathcal{I}_\mathcal{C}} G(x)dx = O(|\mathcal{M}| \ln n). \quad (13)$$

Let $\mathcal{M}'$ be the pointset corresponding to the collection $\mathcal{M}$. Since the points in any sub-collection S of $\mathcal{M}$ do not form a cluster (as $3D_S$ contains a point from $\mathcal{M}\setminus S$) from Lemma 11 it follows that $\mathcal{M}'$ is 15-dense. To apply Lemma 13 to $\mathcal{M}'$, we remove an interval around every $p \in \mathcal{M}' \cap \mathbb{R}$: define $J_p := [p \pm d_2(p, \mathcal{M}')/2]$; for $p \in P \setminus \mathbb{R}$, $J_p := \emptyset$. Further, if $p = m_\mathcal{C}$, for some $\mathcal{C} \in \mathcal{M}$, then define $\mathcal{I}_p := \mathcal{I}_\mathcal{C} \subseteq J_p$; otherwise, $\mathcal{I}_p := \emptyset$. From this notation, it follows that $I_0' \setminus \cup_{p\in\mathcal{M}'} \mathcal{I}_p = I_0' \setminus \cup_{\mathcal{C}\in\mathcal{M}} \mathcal{I}_\mathcal{C}$ is the union of $I_0' \setminus (\cup_{p\in\mathcal{M}'\cap\mathbb{R}} J_p)$ and $\cup_{p\in\mathcal{M}'\cap\mathbb{R}}(J_p \setminus \mathcal{I}_p)$. We bound the integral on these two sets. On $I_0' \setminus (\cup_{p\in\mathcal{M}'\cap\mathbb{R}} J_p)$, $G(x) := 1/d(x, V)$. But for x in this set $d(x, V) \geq d(x, \mathcal{M}')/3$. Moreover, from Lemma 11, we get $I_0' \subseteq [m_{\mathcal{M}'} \pm 5r_{\mathcal{M}'}]$. So applying Lemma 13 to $\mathcal{M}'$ with $\lambda = 15$ and the interval $[m_{\mathcal{M}'} \pm 5r_{\mathcal{M}'}]$ gives us

$$\int_{I_0' \setminus \cup_{p\in\mathcal{M}'} J_p} G(x)dx = O(|\mathcal{M}| \ln n).$$

This bound and the following claim proves (13):

$$\int_{\cup_{p\in\mathcal{M}'\cap\mathbb{R}}(J_p\setminus\mathcal{I}_p)} G(x)dx = O(|\mathcal{M}| \ln n). \qquad (14)$$

To prove (14), we show that $\int_{J_p\setminus\mathcal{I}_p} G(x)dx = O(\ln n)$, for all $p \in \mathcal{M}' \cap \mathbb{R}$. There are three cases to consider:

(i) $p = m_\mathcal{C}$ for some non-ssc $\mathcal{C} \in \mathcal{M}$. Then $J_p = [m_\mathcal{C} \pm d_2(m_\mathcal{C}, \mathcal{M}')/2]$ and $\mathcal{I}_p = \mathcal{I}_\mathcal{C} = 1.5I_\mathcal{C}$. If the point $q \in \mathcal{M}'$ nearest to $m_\mathcal{C}$ is a root then $d_2(m_\mathcal{C}, \mathcal{M}') = R_\mathcal{C}$; otherwise, if $q = m_{\mathcal{C}'}$, for some $\mathcal{C}' \in \mathcal{M}$, then $R_\mathcal{C} \geq 2\max\{r_\mathcal{C}, r_{\mathcal{C}'}\}$, and hence $d_2(m_\mathcal{C}, \mathcal{M}') = R_\mathcal{C} + r_{\mathcal{C}'} \leq 3R_\mathcal{C}/2$. In either case, $J_p \subseteq [m_\mathcal{C} \pm 3R_\mathcal{C}/4]$. Consider the interval $[m_\mathcal{C} + 1.5r_\mathcal{C}, m_\mathcal{C} + 3R_\mathcal{C}/4]$, which is one of the two in $J_p \setminus \mathcal{I}_p$; the argument is same for the other interval. For all x in this interval $d(x, V) \geq |x - m_\mathcal{C}|/4$; therefore, $G(x) := \frac{1}{d(x,V)} \leq 4/|x - m_\mathcal{C}|$. From Lemma 12(Re), we get $\int_{m_\mathcal{C}+1.5r_\mathcal{C}}^{m_\mathcal{C}+3R_\mathcal{C}/4} G(x)dx = O(\ln R_\mathcal{C}/r_\mathcal{C})$. Since $\mathcal{C}$ is not a ssc, $R_\mathcal{C}/r_\mathcal{C} = O(n^3)$, which gives us the desired bound.

(ii) $p = m_\mathcal{C}$, where $\mathcal{C} \in \mathcal{M}$ is a ssc. The argument is similar to the one above, except $\mathcal{I}_p = \mathcal{I}_\mathcal{C} = [m_\mathcal{C} \pm R_\mathcal{C}/n^2]$.

(iii) $p \in V \cap \mathbb{R}$. This is essentially the argument in [4]. *For $x \in J_p$, $G(x) := 1/d_2(x, V)$, i.e., corresponding to the inclusion predicate.* The integral $\int_{J_p} \frac{dx}{d_2(x,V)} = O(1)$.

□

The proof can be carried out with the exact constants involved in the definitions of $\mathbb{I}_\mathcal{C}$, $\mathcal{I}_\mathcal{C}$ and $\mathcal{A}_\mathcal{C}$ (see Lemma 6), but they will be absorbed by the big-O notation. Note that $G(x) = 1/d(x, V)$ almost everywhere, except in a certain neighborhood of each real root. This corresponds to the exclusion predicate C_0, and so $O(n \ln n)$ bounds the number of calls to C_0; the calls to C_1 are $O(n)$. For Sturm sequences, the corresponding choice for C_0 is $G(x) := 1/d(x, V \cap \mathbb{R}) \leq 1/d(x, V)$. Therefore, $O(n \ln n)$ holds for `Newton-Isol` combined with Sturm sequences. For `Eval`, one choice of $G(x)$ for C_0 is $n/d(x, V)$, which immediately gives an $O(n^2 \ln n)$ bound for `Newton-Isol` combined with `Eval`. Whether it can be improved using $\sum_{\alpha\in V} \frac{1}{|x-\alpha|}$ remains open.

Let P be a λ-dense conjugate pointset; recall that $I_P = [m_P \pm r_P]$. Given a point $p \in P$, define $\sigma_p := d_2(p, P)$, and $J_p := [p \pm \sigma_p/2]$. We want to bound $\int_{cI_P\setminus\cup_p J_p} dx/d(x, P)$, for $c \geq 1.5$. We first show an $O(|P|^2 \log \lambda)$ bound, essentially following [4]. Let $\mathcal{V}_p$ be the set of points in cI_P closer to p than to any other point in P; clearly, these sets are disjoint and partition cI_P. It is also clear that $J_p \subseteq \mathcal{V}_p$. From Lemma 12 we obtain $\int_{\mathcal{V}_p\setminus J_p} dx/d(x, P) = O(\ln r_P/\sigma_p)$. The density of P implies that $r_P \leq \lambda^{O(|P|)}\sigma_p$, for all $p \in P$. Therefore, $\sum_{p\in P} \int_{\mathcal{V}_p\setminus J_p} \frac{dx}{d(x,P)} = O(|P|^2 \ln \lambda)$. The improvement in Theorem 10 is based on the intuition that if σ_p is very small then the density of P implies that there is a set S of points close to p; for $x \in \mathcal{V}_p$ sufficiently far from m_S, say outside $1.5D_S$, $|x - p| \sim |x - m_S|$; as $\mathcal{V}_p$ are all disjoint, the integral over all $p \in S$ can be collectively charged to the centroid m_S. The challenge is to get an "almost cluster-like" decomposition of P. We construct a tree $\mathcal{T}_P$ with leaves from P that gives us this decomposition. With every node u of $\mathcal{T}_P$ we associate the following parameters: $P_u \subseteq P$ a conjugate pointset; $\mathbb{D}_u$ a set of closed discs with centers in P_u all having radius $\mu_u/2$; $D_u := D_{P_u}$ (similarly, define m_u, r_u), and $\Im_u := \min_{p\in P_u} |\Im(p)|$, where $\Im(p)$ is the imaginary part of p. A leaf of $\mathcal{T}_P$ is either a real point or *a pair of complex conjugates* in P. At a leaf, $\mu_u := 0$; the remaining parameters are obvious. Given $u \in \mathcal{T}_P$, its separation is defined as $\min\{|p - q|; p \in P_u, q \in P \setminus P_u\}$; if u is a leaf then the minimum also includes $\Im_u$.

We describe an iterative bottom-up procedure to construct $\mathcal{T}_P$. Let $\mathcal{U}$ be the set of leaves of $\mathcal{T}_P$, and μ be the minimum separation over all the nodes in $\mathcal{U}$, i.e., $\mu = \min_{p\in P} \sigma_p$. Draw the disc $D(p, \mu/2)$, for $p \in P$. Two such discs can at most touch each other. The discs touching each other form a connected component. The set of maximal connected components partitions P; if two components in this set are conjugates of each other but are not connected, then we conceptually consider them as a single component. For each such component $\mathbb{D}$ containing more than one disc we introduce an internal node u in $\mathcal{T}_P$, with children as those nodes in $\mathcal{U}$ whose components connected to form $\mathbb{D}_u$. Define $\mathbb{D}_u := \mathbb{D}$, $\mu_u := \mu$, and P_u as the set of centers of the discs in $\mathbb{D}_u$. Now redefine $\mathcal{U}$ as the set of newly created internal nodes and the remaining leaves, and continue as above starting with redefining μ. The procedure terminates when $\mathcal{U}$ is a singleton containing the root of $\mathcal{T}_P$ with associated pointset P.

Let $u, v \in \mathcal{T}_P$ be such that v is a child of u. We have the following properties of $\mathcal{T}_P$:

(R1) $\mu_u \leq \lambda r_v$. From the λ-density of P, we know that the separation of v is at most λr_v, and from the construction of $\mathcal{T}_P$ it follows that the separation of v is at least μ_u.

(R2) $r_u \leq (|P_u| - 1)\mu_u + 2\Im_u$. We use the observation that $2r_u$ is smaller than diameter of P_u, and bound the latter. If $\mathbb{D}_u$ is connected then diameter of P_u is $\leq (|P_u| - 1)\mu_u$. Otherwise, $\mathbb{D}_u$ consists of two connected components each of size $|P_u|/2$ that are conjugate of each other (since $P_u \cap \mathbb{R} = \emptyset$); the minimum distance between these components is $2\Im_u$, and their diameter is smaller than $(|P_u|/2 - 1)\mu_u$.

(R3) $\Im_u \leq \min\{r_u, \Im_v\}$. If $\Im_u = 0$ then this is trivial. If $p, \overline{p} \in P_u$ are such that $\Im(p) = \Im_u > 0$, then as $p, \overline{p} \in D_u$, $2r_u \geq |p - \overline{p}| = 2\Im_u$. Since $P_v \subseteq P_u$, $\Im_v \geq \Im_u$.

(R4) If v is a leaf and $p \in P_v$ then $\mu_u = \sigma_p$. The first time $D(p, r) \cap D(q, r) \neq \emptyset$, where $q \neq p$, is when $2r = \sigma_p$; as v is a child of u, $\mu_u = \sigma_p$. If $p \in \mathbb{C} \setminus \mathbb{R}$, then $|\Im(p)| \geq \sigma_p \geq \mu_u$.

LEMMA 13. *Given a λ-dense conjugate pointset P and $c \geq 1.5$*

$$\int_{cI_P\setminus\cup_{p\in P} J_p} \frac{dx}{d(x, P)} = O(|P| \ln(c\lambda|P|)), \qquad (15)$$

where for $p \in P \cap \mathbb{R}$, $J_p := [p \pm \sigma_p/2]$ and $J_p := \emptyset$ otherwise.

PROOF. If u is an internal node of $\mathcal{T}_P$, then we show the following stronger claim:

$$\int_{I_u \setminus \cup_{p \in P_u} J_p} \frac{dx}{d(x,P)} = O(|\mathcal{T}_u| \ln(\lambda |P_u|)), \tag{16}$$

where $\mathcal{T}_u$ is the subtree rooted at u and $I_u := [m_u \pm 1.5r_u]$. Applying (16) to the root of $\mathcal{T}_P$ almost gives the bound in (15), except the integral on $cI_P \setminus 1.5I_P$, which will be bounded separately. For $p \in P$, recall that $\mathcal{V}_p$ is the Voronoi region of p inside cI_P, and $J_p \subseteq \mathcal{V}_p$. For a child v of u, there are following cases to consider:

Case 1. v is a leaf corresponding to $p \in \mathbb{R}$. We bound the integral on $I_p := \mathcal{V}_p \cap I_u$. For all $x \in I_p \subseteq \mathcal{V}_p$, $d(x,P) = |x - p|$. Lemma 12(Re) implies $\int_{I_p \setminus J_p} \frac{dx}{|x-p|} = O\left(\ln \frac{w(I_p)}{\sigma_p}\right)$. As $I_p \subseteq I_u$, $w(I_p) \leq 3r_u$. From (R4), we know that $\sigma_p = \mu_u$. Therefore, $\int_{I_p \setminus J_p} \frac{dx}{|x-p|} = O(\ln r_u/\mu_u) = O(\ln |P_u|)$, from (R2); note that $\Im_u = 0$ as $P_u \cap \mathbb{R} \neq \emptyset$.

Case 2. v is a leaf corresponding to a pair of complex conjugate $p, \overline{p}$. Again let $I_p := \mathcal{V}_p \cap I_u$; in this case $J_p = \emptyset$. For $x \in I_p$, $d(x,P) = |x-p|$. Moreover, as $\{p\}, I_p \subseteq 1.5D_u$, the distance from p to either endpoint of I_p is at most $3r_u$. Therefore, from Lemma 12(Im) we have $\int_{I_p} \frac{dx}{d(x,P)} = O\left(\ln \frac{r_u}{|\Im(p)|}\right) = O(\ln |P_u|)$, from (R4), (R3) and (R2).

Case 3. v is an internal node. From induction we obtain that $\int_{I_v \setminus \cup_{p \in P_v} J_p} \frac{dx}{d(x,P)}$ is $O(|\mathcal{T}_v| \ln(\lambda |P_v|))$. If $p \in P_v$ is such that that $\mathcal{V}_p$ extends beyond I_v, then for $x \in W_p := \mathcal{V}_p \cap (I_u \setminus I_v)$, $|x - p| \geq |x - m_v|/3$. Since $\cup_{p \in P_v} W_p \subseteq I_u \setminus I_v$, $\sum_{p \in P_v} \int_{W_p} \frac{dx}{|x-p|} \leq \int_{I_u \setminus I_v} \frac{3dx}{|x-m_v|}$. This equation captures the amortization of the integral over the Voronoi regions. As $2w(I_u) = 3r_u$, from Lemma 12(Re), we get that $\int_{I_u \setminus I_v} \frac{3dx}{|x-m_v|} = O(\ln r_u/r_v)$. From (R2), (R1), (R3) and as $\lambda \geq 2$, we obtain $\sum_{p \in P_v} \int_{W_p} \frac{dx}{d(x,P)} = O(\ln(\lambda |P_u|))$.

Summing these bounds along with the inductive bound gives (16). To complete the proof, apply Case 3 to the root of $\mathcal{T}_P$ over $cI_P \setminus 1.5I_P$ to get the term $\ln(c\lambda |P|)$ in (15). □

5. CONCLUDING REMARKS

We propose a general approach to improve any subdivision based algorithm for real root isolation. The crucial component is the `Newton-Incl-Exc` subroutine, which gives quadratic convergence to a strongly separated cluster and reduces the number of subdivisions to approximate the cluster from $O(\log \frac{R_\mathcal{C}}{r_\mathcal{C}})$ to $O(\log n)$. For non-ssc clusters, we show that standard subdivision takes $O(\log n)$ steps. These two results give us the overall bound on the size of the subdivision tree of our approach. The main ingredient for detecting clusters is Ostrowski's criterion based the Newton diagram of a polynomial. The criterion works for polynomials in $\mathbb{C}[x]$, so we expect an analogue of `Newton-Isol` for isolating complex roots that is conceptually simpler than the existing approaches. We think that our analysis based on continuous amortization and the geometry of root clusters provides tools and techniques for an alternate and uniform approach to analyzing existing algorithms. The arithmetic complexity of `Newton-Isol` can be bounded as follows. The Newton diagram computation takes $O(n)$, and the Taylor shift $O(n \log n)$ operations. The number of Newton steps to approximate $\mathcal{C}$ is bounded by $O(\log \log \frac{R_\mathcal{C}}{r_\mathcal{C}})$, which is $O(\log |\log \sigma|)$, where σ is the root separation. Therefore, the arithmetic complexity, ignoring poly-log factors, is bounded by $\widetilde{O}(n^2)$. The extension to the bitstream model requires a robust version of Ostrowski's result and bounds on precision requirements. The latter will be governed by perturbation bounds for clusters: we expect that an ϵ-perturbation in the coefficients should perturb the roots in a cluster of size k by $O(\epsilon^{1/k})$. This would give an $O(|\log \sigma|)$ bound on the precision, and $\widetilde{O}(n^2 |\log \sigma|)$ bound on the overall bit-complexity.

6. REFERENCES

[1] John Abbott. Quadratic interval refinement for real roots. *ACM Commun. Comput. Algebra*, 48(1/2):3–12, 2014.

[2] L. Blum, F. Cucker, M. Shub, and S. Smale. *Complexity and Real Computation*. Springer, 1998.

[3] M. Burr, F. Krahmer, and C. Yap. Continuous amortization: A non-probabilistic adaptive analysis technique. *Elec. Colloq. Comp. Compl.*, 16:136, 2009.

[4] M. Burr. Applications of continuous amortization to bisection-based root isolation. *CoRR*, abs/1309.5991 (2013).

[5] J. H. Davenport. Computer algebra for cylindrical algebraic decomposition. Tech. Report 88-10 , School of Math. Sci., U. of Bath, Bath, England.

[6] A. Eigenwillig, V. Sharma, and C. Yap. Almost tight complexity bounds for the Descartes method. In *Proc. 31st ISSAC*, pp. 71–78, 2006.

[7] M. Giusti, G. Lecerf, B. Salvy, and J.-C. Yakoubsohn. On location & approximation of clusters of zeros of analytic functns. *Fnd. Comp. Math.*, 5(3):257–311, '05.

[8] A. Ostrowski. Recherches sur la méthode de Graeffe et les zéros des polynomes et des séries de Laurent. *Acta Mathematica*, 72:99–155, 1940.

[9] V.Y. Pan. Optimal and nearly optimal algorithms for approximating polynomial zeros. *Computers Math. Applic.*, 31(12):97–138, 1996.

[10] V. Y. Pan. Approximating complex polynomial zeros: Modified Weyl's quadtree construction and improved Newton's iteration. *J. Complexity*, 16(1):213–264, '00.

[11] P. Pawlowski. The location of the zeros of the higher order derivatives of a polynomial. *Proc. AMS*, 127(5):1493–1497, 1999.

[12] M. Sagraloff. When Newton meets Descartes: a simple and fast algorithm to isolate the real roots of a polynomial. In *Proc. Intl. Symp. Symb. & Algb. Comp (ISSAC)*, pp. 297–304, 2012.

[13] M. Sagraloff and K. Mehlhorn. Computing real roots of real polynomials *CoRR*, abs/1308.4088 (2013). To appear in *J. of Sym. Comp. (JSC)*.

[14] M. Sagraloff, V. Sharma, and C. Yap. Analytic root clustering: A complete algorithm using soft zero tests. In P. Bonizzoni *et al.*, eds., *In Proc. CiE 2013.*, vol. 7921 of *LNCS*, pp. 434–444. Springer, 2013.

[15] V. Sharma and C.-K. Yap. Near optimal tree size bounds on a simple real root isolation algorithm. In *Proc. 37th ISSAC*, pp. 319–326. ACM, 2012.

A Relaxed Algorithm for Online Matrix Inversion

Arne Storjohann
astorjoh@uwaterloo.ca
David R. Cheriton School of Computer Science
University of Waterloo, Ontario, Canada
N2L 3G1

Shiyun Yang
shiyyang@amazon.com
Amazon Canada Fullfillment Services Inc
1071 Mainland St, Vancouver, BC, Canada
V6B 5P9

ABSTRACT

We consider a variation of the well known problem of computing the unique solution to a nonsingular system $Ax = b$ of n linear equations over a field K. The variation assumes that A has generic rank profile and requires as output not only the single solution vector $A^{-1}b \in \mathsf{K}^{n\times 1}$, but rather the solution to all leading principle subsystems. Most importantly, the rows of the augmented system $[\ A \parallel b\ ]$ are given one at a time from first to last, and as soon as the next row is given the solution to the next leading principal subsystem should be produced. We call this problem OnlineSystem. The obvious iterative algorithm for OnlineSystem has a cost in terms of field operations that is cubic in the dimension of A. In this paper we introduce a relaxed representation for the inverse and show how to obtain an algorithm for OnlineSystem that allows us to incorporate matrix multiplication. As an application we show how to introduce fast matrix multiplication into the inherently iterative algorithm for row rank profile computation presented previously by the authors.

Categories and Subject Descriptors

I.1.2 [**Symbolic and Algebraic Manipulation**]: Algorithms—*algebraic algorithms, analysis of algorithms*; G.4 [**Mathematical Software**]: Algorithm Design and Analysis; F.2.1 [**Analysis of Algorithms and Problem Complexity**]: Numerical Algorithms and Problems—*computations in finite fields, computations on matrices*

General Terms

Algorithms

Keywords

Linear system; finite field; relaxed algorithm; rank profile

1. INTRODUCTION

Consider the well known problem of computing the solution to a nonsingular system of linear equations over a finite field K. The problem takes as input a nonsingular matrix $A \in \mathsf{K}^{n\times n}$ together with a right hand side vector $b \in \mathsf{K}^{n\times 1}$, and requires as output the solution $x := A^{-1}b \in \mathsf{K}^{n\times 1}$ to the linear system $Ax = b$. For an unstructured and dense input matrix A, the fastest known solutions (in terms of asymptotic complexity [1,8] and in practice [2,4,5]) all reduce the problem to matrix multiplication by computing a decomposition of A or the inverse of A as the product of structured matrices, typically upper / lower triangular and permutation matrices (see [9] for a survey).

In this paper we consider an online version of the nonsingular linear system solving problem. Consider the augmented linear system $[\ A \parallel b\ ] \in \mathsf{K}^{n\times(n+1)}$. We can decompose this augmented system for $s = 1, 2, \ldots, n$ as

$$[\ A \parallel b\ ] = \left[\begin{array}{c|c||c} A_s & * & b_s \\ \hline * & * & * \end{array}\right] \in \mathsf{K}^{n\times(n+1)},$$

where $A_s \in \mathsf{K}^{s\times s}$ is the principal leading $s\times s$ submatrix of A and $b_s \in \mathsf{K}^{s\times 1}$ is the first s entries of b. Moreover, we assume that A has generic rank profile, that is, all of $A_1, A_2, \ldots, A_n$ are nonsingular. In this paper we show how to compute the sequence of solutions $A_1^{-1}b_1, A_2^{-1}b_2, \ldots, A_n^{-1}b_n$ in an *online* fashion in time $O(n^\omega)$, where $2 < \omega \le 3$ is the exponent of matrix multiplication. By online we mean that the rows of the augmented system are given one at a time, from first to last: as soon as row s is given, the solution to $A_s^{-1}b_s$ should be produced. We call this problem OnlineSystem. Online algorithms for computer algebra were popularized by van der Hoeven with the introduction of online algorithms for formal power series multiplication [7,13]. Recently, an online algorithm for polynomial matrix order basis computation has been proposed [6].

Our interest in studying problem OnlineSystem is motivated by the following two problems that take as input an $A \in \mathsf{K}^{n\times m}$ of arbitrary rank.

- MaxIndependentRowSet: Compute the rank r and a list of r row indices such that these rows are linearly independent.
- RowRankProfile: Compute the rank r and the lexicographically minimal list $[i_1, i_2, \ldots, i_r]$ of row indices of A such that these rows are linearly independent.

In a surprising result, Cheung, Kwok and Lau [3] give a Monte Carlo algorithm for MaxIndependentRowSet with running time only $(r^\omega + n + m + |A|)^{1+o(1)}$ field operations in K. Here, $|A|$ denotes the number of nonzero entries of A and ω is the exponent for matrix multiplication. The following year, using an alternative technique [12], a Monte

ISSAC'15, July 6–9, 2015, Bath, United Kingdom.

DOI: http://dx.doi.org/10.1145/2755996.2756672.

Carlo algorithm for RowRankProfile was presented that has running time $(r^3 + n + m + |A|)^{1+o(1)}$ operations in K. The algorithm for RowRankProfile is inherently iterative: the indices $i_1, i_2, \ldots, i_r$ are computed in succession, and each iteration requires the solution of the next principal subsystem of a linear system comprised of rank profile rows of A found so far. The main bottleneck to introduce matrix multiplication into the algorithm for RowRankProfile is to find a solution to problem OnlineSystem that allows the use of fast matrix multiplication; this paper presents such an algorithm.

The rest of the paper is organized as follows. In Section 2 we show how problem OnlineSystem can be reduced to problem OnlineInverse: computing a representation of A_s^{-1} as the product of $2s$ structured matrices, with the decomposition of A_s^{-1} being produced as soon as row s of A is given, $s = 1, 2, \ldots, n$. Both problem OnlineSystem and OnlineInverse are defined precisely in Section 2. In Section 3 we recall the obvious iterative algorithm for OnlineInverse that has cost $O(n^3)$. In Section 4 we propose a relaxed representation of the inverse of a matrix. Instead of representing A_s^{-1} as the product of $2s$ structured matrices, we define a compressed representation of A_s^{-1} as the product of $O(\log s)$ structured matrices. Finally, Section 5 designs the algorithm for solving problem OnlineInverse in time $O(n^\omega)$. Our analysis assumes $\omega > 2$. Section 6 shows how to incorporate the fast algorithm for OnlineSystem to obtain a fast algorithm for rank profile computation. Section 7 concludes.

Following [12], throughout the paper we use the following notation. For a list $\mathcal{P} = [i_1, i_2, \ldots, i_k]$ of distinct row indices and $\mathcal{Q} = [j_1, j_2, \ldots, j_\ell]$ of distinct column indices, we write $A^{\mathcal{P}}$ to denote the submatrix of A consisting of rows $\mathcal{P}$, $A_{\mathcal{Q}}$ to denote the submatrix consisting of columns $\mathcal{Q}$, and $A^{\mathcal{P}}_{\mathcal{Q}}$ to denote the submatrix consisting of the intersection of rows $\mathcal{P}$ and columns $\mathcal{Q}$ of A.

2. INVERSE DECOMPOSITION

Let $A \in \mathsf{K}^{n\times n}$ and $b \in \mathsf{K}^{n\times 1}$ be given. Let A_s denote the leading $s \times s$ submatrix of A and $b_s \in \mathsf{K}^{s\times 1}$ be the vector containing the first s elements of b as shown in the following augmented system.

$[\ A \parallel b\ ] =$ 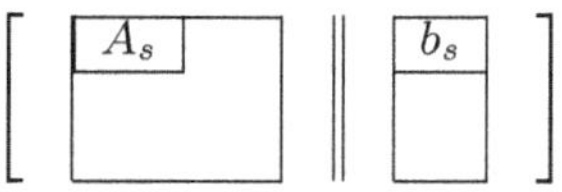

Assume A has generic rank profile, that is, A_s is nonsingular for $1 \le s \le n$. In this section we consider the following problem.

- OnlineSystem: Let $A \in \mathsf{K}^{n\times n}$ with generic rank profile and $b \in \mathsf{K}^{n\times 1}$ be given. Suppose the rows of the augmented system $[\ A \parallel b\ ]$ are given one at a time, from first to last. As soon as rows $1, 2, \ldots, s$ of $[\ A \parallel b\ ]$ are given, produce the subsystem solution $A_s^{-1} b_s$, for $s = 1, 2, \ldots, n$.

Because A is assumed to have generic rank profile, Gaussian elimination without pivoting produces a unique decomposition $A^{-1} = P_n \cdot P_{n-1} \cdots P_1$, where $P_s = R_s \cdot L_s$ can be represented as the product of the pair of structured matrices R_s and L_s, $1 \le s \le n$. The matrices R_s and L_s will be defined precisely in the next section. For now, consider the following example which shows the structure of matrices in the decomposition for $n = 6$.

$$A^{-1} = \underbrace{\overset{R_6}{\begin{bmatrix} 1 & & & & & * \\ & 1 & & & & * \\ & & 1 & & & * \\ & & & 1 & & * \\ & & & & 1 & * \\ & & & & & * \end{bmatrix}} \overset{L_6}{\begin{bmatrix} 1 & & & & & \\ & 1 & & & & \\ & & 1 & & & \\ & & & 1 & & \\ & & & & 1 & \\ * & * & * & * & * & 1 \end{bmatrix}}}_{P_6} \underbrace{\overset{R_5}{\begin{bmatrix} 1 & & & & * & \\ & 1 & & & * & \\ & & 1 & & * & \\ & & & 1 & * & \\ & & & & * & \\ & & & & & 1 \end{bmatrix}} \overset{L_5}{\begin{bmatrix} 1 & & & & & \\ & 1 & & & & \\ & & 1 & & & \\ & & & 1 & & \\ * & * & * & * & 1 & \\ & & & & & 1 \end{bmatrix}}}_{P_5} \cdots \tag{1}$$

Moreover, $P_s P_{s-1} \cdots P_1 = \operatorname{diag}(A_s^{-1}, I_{n-s})$ for $1 \le s \le n$. Thus, computing the sequence

$$A_1^{-1}b_1,\ A_2^{-1}b_2,\ A_3^{-1}b_3, \ldots, A_n^{-1}b_n \tag{2}$$

can be accomplished by computing the sequence

$$P_1 b,\ P_2P_1 b,\ P_3P_2P_1 b, \ldots,\ P_n \cdots P_3P_2P_1 b. \tag{3}$$

This motivates the definition of the following problem.

- OnlineInverse: Suppose the rows of an $A \in \mathsf{K}^{n\times n}$ with generic rank profile are given one at a time, from first to last. As soon as rows $1, 2, \ldots, s$ of A are given, the matrix $P_s = R_s \cdot L_s$ should be produced, for $s = 1, 2, \ldots, n$. Note that P_s should be represented as the unevaluated product of the two structured matrices R_s and L_s.

On the one hand, if the representation of $P_1, P_2, \ldots, P_n$ as the pairs of multiplicands $R_1 \cdot L_1, R_2 \cdot L_2, \ldots, R_n \cdot L_n$ is known, the sequence shown in (3) can be computed in $O(n^2)$ field operations. On the other hand, a lower bound on the cost of solving OnlineInverse is $\Omega(n^2)$ since this a lower bound for the total size (number of field elements) to write down the sequence $P_1, P_2, \ldots, P_n$. It follows that any algorithm for OnlineInverse immediately gives an algorithm for OnlineSystem that supports the same running time bound. For the rest of this paper, we consider algorithms to solve OnlineInverse.

3. FULL DECOMPOSITION

For $1 \le s \le n$, let

$$A_s = \left[\begin{array}{c|c} A_{s-1} & u_s \\ \hline v_s & d_s \end{array}\right] \in \mathsf{K}^{s\times s},$$

where $u_s \in \mathsf{K}^{(s-1)\times 1}$, $v_s \in \mathsf{K}^{1\times(s-1)}$, and $d_s \in \mathsf{K}$. Suppose we have computed a decomposition of A_{s-1}^{-1} for some $s > 0$. Then Gaussian elimination produces a pair of $s \times s$ matrices $\bar{L}_s$ and $\bar{R}_s$ such that A_s^{-1} is equal to

$$\overset{\bar{R}_s}{\left[\begin{array}{c|c} I_{s-1} & -A_{s-1}^{-1}u_s \\ \hline & (d_s - v_sA_{s-1}^{-1}u_s)^{-1} \end{array}\right]} \overset{\bar{L}_s}{\left[\begin{array}{c|c} I_{s-1} & \\ \hline -v_s & 1 \end{array}\right]} \left[\begin{array}{c|c} A_{s-1}^{-1} & \\ \hline & 1 \end{array}\right]. \tag{4}$$

The exact formula for A_s^{-1} could be derived by multiplying together the expression for A_s^{-1} in (4). However, the algorithms we describe in this paper do not compute A_s^{-1} explicitly at each stage, but rather keep it as the product of structured matrices. For example, applying (4) for $s = 1, 2, \ldots, n$ gives the following full decomposition for the inverse of $A = A_n$.

$$\begin{aligned} A_n^{-1} &= P_n \cdot \left[\begin{array}{c|c} A_{n-1}^{-1} & \\ \hline & 1 \end{array}\right] \\ &= P_n \cdot P_{n-1} \cdot \left[\begin{array}{c|c} A_{n-2}^{-1} & \\ \hline & I_2 \end{array}\right] \\ &\vdots \\ &= P_n \cdot P_{n-1} \cdots P_1, \end{aligned}$$

where $P_s \in \mathsf{K}^{n \times n}$, $1 \le s \le n$, is the product of two structured matrices:

$$\begin{aligned} P_s &= R_s \cdot L_s \\ &= \left[\begin{array}{c|c} \bar{R}_s & \\ \hline & I_{n-s} \end{array}\right] \cdot \left[\begin{array}{c|c} \bar{L}_s & \\ \hline & I_{n-s} \end{array}\right] \\ &= \begin{bmatrix} I_{s-1} & \Box & \\ & & I_{n-s} \end{bmatrix} \cdot \begin{bmatrix} I_{s-1} & & \\ \Box & 1 & \\ & & I_{n-s} \end{bmatrix}, \end{aligned} \quad (5)$$

with $\bar{R}_s$ and $\bar{L}_s$ as in (4). Thus R_s and L_s are the identity matrices, except for possibly the column vector and row vector indicated by the rectangles in R_s and L_s, respectively.

Naturally, equation (4) gives an iterative approach to solve problem OnlineInverse. Once the matrix×vector product $A_{s-1}^{-1} u_s$ has been computed, the representation $P_s = R_s \cdot L_s$ can be computed in a further $O(s)$ field operations. Computing $A_{s-1}^{-1} u_s$ is equivalent to premultiplying u_s by the leading principal $(s-1) \times (s-1)$ submatrices of $P_1, P_2, \cdots, P_{s-1}$ sequentially at a cost of $4s^2 + O(s)$ field operations. Overall, all the pairs of multiplicands $P_s = R_s \cdot L_s$, $1 \le s \le n$, can be computed sequentially in $2n^3 + O(n^2)$ field operations. In the next two sections we show how to incorporate matrix multiplication to solve problem OnlineInverse in overall time $O(n^\omega)$.

4. RELAXED DECOMPOSITION

To store each A_s^{-1} explicitly as a dense $s \times s$ matrix at each stage is too expensive, but the representation

$$\mathrm{diag}(A_s^{-1}, I_{n-s}) = P_s \cdot P_{s-1} \cdots P_1$$

as the product of s pairs of structured multiplicands is too lazy: both of these approaches lead to an algorithm with running time $\Omega(n^3)$. In this section, we present a relaxed inverse decomposition for A_s^{-1} such that, at stage s, after the first s rows of A are given, A_s^{-1} is represented as the product of HammingWeight$(s) \le \lceil \log s \rceil$ pairs of structured multiplicands, where HammingWeight(s) is the number of 1s in the binary representation of s.

Lemma 1. *$(R_j \cdot L_j) \cdot (R_{j-1} \cdot L_{j-1}) \cdots (R_i \cdot L_i)$ can be expressed as the product $R_{j\sim i} \cdot L_{j\sim i}$ of two structured matrices with the shape*

$$R_{j\sim i} = \begin{bmatrix} I_{i-1} & \Box \cdots \Box & \\ & & I_{n-j} \end{bmatrix} \quad (6)$$

and

$$L_{j\sim i} = \begin{bmatrix} I_{i-1} & & & \\ \Box & 1 & & \\ \vdots & & \ddots & \\ \Box & & & 1 \\ & & & & I_{n-j} \end{bmatrix}, \quad (7)$$

where the column dimension of the submatrix indicated by the rectangle in $R_{j\sim i}$ and the row dimension of the submatrix indicated by the rectangle in $L_{j\sim i}$ are both $j - i + 1$.

Proof. Decompose

$$A_j = \left[\begin{array}{c|c} A_{i-1} & U \\ \hline V & D \end{array}\right]$$

where $U \in \mathsf{K}^{(i-1)\times(j-i+1)}$, $V \in \mathsf{K}^{(j-i+1)\times(i-1)}$, and $D \in \mathsf{K}^{(j-i+1)\times(j-i+1)}$, and consider the block case of (4). Block Gaussian elimination produces a pair of $j \times j$ matrices $\bar{R}_{j\sim i}$ and $\bar{L}_{j\sim i}$ such that

$$A_j^{-1} = \bar{R}_{j\sim i} \bar{L}_{j\sim i} \left[\begin{array}{c|c} A_{i-1}^{-1} & \\ \hline & I_{j-i+1} \end{array}\right],$$

where

$$\bar{R}_{j\sim i} = \left[\begin{array}{c|c} I_{i-1} & -A_{i-1}^{-1} U \\ \hline & (D - V A_{i-1}^{-1} U)^{-1} \end{array}\right]$$

and

$$\bar{L}_{j\sim i} = \left[\begin{array}{c|c} I_{i-1} & \\ \hline -V & I_{j-i+1} \end{array}\right].$$

The augmented matrices

$$R_{j\sim i} = \mathrm{diag}(\bar{R}_{j\sim i}, I_{n-j})$$

and

$$L_{j\sim i} = \mathrm{diag}(\bar{L}_{j\sim i}, I_{n-j})$$

have the shape shown in (6) and (7), respectively. Finally, note that both

$$(R_{j\sim i} \cdot L_{j\sim i}) \left[\begin{array}{c|c} A_{i-1}^{-1} & \\ \hline & I_{n-i+1} \end{array}\right]$$

and

$$(R_j \cdot L_j) \cdot (R_{j-1} \cdot L_{j-1}) \cdots (R_i \cdot L_i) \left[\begin{array}{c|c} A_{i-1}^{-1} & \\ \hline & I_{n-i+1} \end{array}\right]$$

are the inverse of

$$\left[\begin{array}{c|c} A_j & \\ \hline & I_{n-j} \end{array}\right].$$

The result follows by the uniqueness of the inverse. □

Remark 2. Lemma 1 does not hold for general matrices $(R_* \cdot L_*)$ of the shape shown in (5). But it does hold in the case where the pairs of multiplicands $(R_* \cdot L_*)$ are arising from Gaussian elimination of the same matrix A.

Definition 3. *$P_{j\sim i}$ denotes the unevaluated product of the pair of matrices $R_{j\sim i} \cdot L_{j\sim i}$ with the shape as shown in (6) and (7). The size of $P_{j\sim i}$ is $j - i + 1$, the number of pairs of multiplicands in the product.*

Lemma 1 defines $P_{j\sim i}$ in terms of the input matrix A_j. But since $P_{j\sim i} = (R_j \cdot L_j) \cdot (R_{j-1} \cdot L_{j-1}) \cdots (R_i \cdot L_i)$ it is possible to define $P_{j\sim i}$ in terms of the pairs of structured multiplicands $R_j \cdot L_j, R_{j-1} \cdot L_{j-1}, \ldots, R_i \cdot L_i$. We do not give such a formula for general $P_{j\sim i}$, but we will give the formula for a special case later. To have a basic idea we remark that the submatrix indicated by the rectangle in $L_{j\sim i}$ is equal to $-A^{[i,\ldots,j]}_{[1\ldots,i-1]}$. The following example gives the formula for a $P_{j\sim i}$ of size 2.

EXAMPLE 4. Let $\bar{P}_j$ and $\bar{P}_{j-1}$ be the leading $j \times j$ principal submatrix of P_j and P_{j-1}. Let

$$\bar{P}_j = \begin{bmatrix} I_{j-2} & & \boxed{\begin{matrix} a \\ b \\ c \end{matrix}} \\ & 1 & \\ & & \end{bmatrix} \cdot \begin{bmatrix} I_{j-2} & & \\ & 1 & \\ \boxed{d \quad e} & & 1 \end{bmatrix},$$

$$\bar{P}_{j-1} = \begin{bmatrix} I_{j-2} & \boxed{\begin{matrix} f \\ g \end{matrix}} & \\ & & \\ & 1 & \end{bmatrix} \cdot \begin{bmatrix} I_{j-2} & & \\ \boxed{h} & 1 & \\ & & 1 \end{bmatrix},$$

and

$$M = \begin{bmatrix} d & e \end{bmatrix} \begin{bmatrix} f \\ g \end{bmatrix}.$$

Then $\bar{P}_{j\sim j-1}$ can be expressed as the product of two structured matrices as follows:

$$\bar{P}_{j\sim j-1} = \begin{bmatrix} I_{j-2} & \overbrace{\boxed{\begin{matrix} aM+f & a \\ bM+g & b \\ cM & c \end{matrix}}}^{\bar{R}_{j\sim j-1}} \end{bmatrix} \cdot \overbrace{\begin{bmatrix} I_{j-2} & & \\ \boxed{\begin{matrix} h \\ d \end{matrix}} & 1 & \\ & & 1 \end{bmatrix}}^{\bar{L}_{j\sim j-1}}.$$

As shown in Section 3, $\mathrm{diag}(A_s^{-1}, I_{n-s})$ can be expressed as the product of s pairs of structured multiplicands of size 1:

$$\mathrm{diag}(A_s^{-1}, I_{n-s}) = P_s \cdot P_{s-1} \cdots P_1.$$

Based on Lemma 1, we now introduce a relaxed/lazy representation for $\mathrm{diag}(A_s^{-1}, I_{n-s})$, denoted by $(A_s)_L^{-1}$, that expresses A_s^{-1} as the product of at most $\log s$ pairs of structured multiplicands. We first give a few examples of the relaxed representation before giving a precise definition.

EXAMPLE 5. The relaxed representation of A_s^{-1} for $1 \leq s \leq 8$.

s	$(A_s)_L^{-1}$
$1 = (1)_2$	$P_{1\sim 1}$
$2 = (10)_2$	$P_{2\sim 1}$
$3 = (11)_2$	$P_{3\sim 3} \cdot P_{2\sim 1}$
$4 = (100)_2$	$P_{4\sim 1}$
$5 = (101)_2$	$P_{5\sim 5} \cdot P_{4\sim 1}$
$6 = (110)_2$	$P_{6\sim 5} \cdot P_{4\sim 1}$
$7 = (111)_2$	$P_{7\sim 7} \cdot P_{6\sim 5} \cdot P_{4\sim 1}$
$8 = (1000)_2$	$P_{8\sim 1}$

The relaxed inverse decomposition for $s = 6, 7, 8$ are shown below. Note that for each of these examples we assume $n = s$, to avoid having to augment with I_{n-s}.

$$(A_6)_L^{-1} = \underbrace{\overbrace{\begin{bmatrix} 1 & & & & * & * \\ & 1 & & & * & * \\ & & 1 & & * & * \\ & & & 1 & * & * \\ & & & & * & * \\ & & & & * & * \end{bmatrix}}^{R_{6\sim 5}} \cdot \overbrace{\begin{bmatrix} 1 & & & & & \\ & 1 & & & & \\ & & 1 & & & \\ & & & 1 & & \\ * & * & * & * & 1 & \\ * & * & * & * & & 1 \end{bmatrix}}^{L_{6\sim 5}}}_{P_{6\sim 5}} \times \underbrace{\overbrace{\begin{bmatrix} * & * & * & * & & \\ * & * & * & * & & \\ * & * & * & * & & \\ * & * & * & * & & \\ & & & & 1 & \\ & & & & & 1 \end{bmatrix}}^{R_{4\sim 1}} \cdot \overbrace{\begin{bmatrix} 1 & & & & & \\ & 1 & & & & \\ & & 1 & & & \\ & & & 1 & & \\ & & & & 1 & \\ & & & & & 1 \end{bmatrix}}^{L_{4\sim 1}}}_{P_{4\sim 1}}$$

$$(A_7)_L^{-1} = \underbrace{\overbrace{\begin{bmatrix} 1 & & & & & & * \\ & 1 & & & & & * \\ & & 1 & & & & * \\ & & & 1 & & & * \\ & & & & 1 & & * \\ & & & & & 1 & * \\ & & & & & & * \end{bmatrix}}^{R_7} \cdot \overbrace{\begin{bmatrix} 1 & & & & & & \\ & 1 & & & & & \\ & & 1 & & & & \\ & & & 1 & & & \\ & & & & 1 & & \\ & & & & & 1 & \\ * & * & * & * & * & * & 1 \end{bmatrix}}^{L_7}}_{P_7} \times \underbrace{\overbrace{\begin{bmatrix} 1 & & & & * & * & \\ & 1 & & & * & * & \\ & & 1 & & * & * & \\ & & & 1 & * & * & \\ & & & & * & * & \\ & & & & * & * & \\ & & & & & & 1 \end{bmatrix}}^{R_{6\sim 5}} \cdot \overbrace{\begin{bmatrix} 1 & & & & & & \\ & 1 & & & & & \\ & & 1 & & & & \\ & & & 1 & & & \\ * & * & * & * & 1 & & \\ * & * & * & * & & 1 & \\ & & & & & & 1 \end{bmatrix}}^{L_{6\sim 5}}}_{P_{6\sim 5}} \times \underbrace{\overbrace{\begin{bmatrix} * & * & * & * & & & \\ * & * & * & * & & & \\ * & * & * & * & & & \\ * & * & * & * & & & \\ & & & & 1 & & \\ & & & & & 1 & \\ & & & & & & 1 \end{bmatrix}}^{R_{4\sim 1}} \cdot \overbrace{\begin{bmatrix} 1 & & & & & & \\ & 1 & & & & & \\ & & 1 & & & & \\ & & & 1 & & & \\ & & & & 1 & & \\ & & & & & 1 & \\ & & & & & & 1 \end{bmatrix}}^{L_{4\sim 1}}}_{P_{4\sim 1}}$$

$$(A_8)_L^{-1} = \underbrace{\overbrace{\begin{bmatrix} * & * & * & * & * & * & * & * \\ * & * & * & * & * & * & * & * \\ * & * & * & * & * & * & * & * \\ * & * & * & * & * & * & * & * \\ * & * & * & * & * & * & * & * \\ * & * & * & * & * & * & * & * \\ * & * & * & * & * & * & * & * \\ * & * & * & * & * & * & * & * \end{bmatrix}}^{R_{8\sim 1}} \cdot \overbrace{\begin{bmatrix} 1 & & & & & & & \\ & 1 & & & & & & \\ & & 1 & & & & & \\ & & & 1 & & & & \\ & & & & 1 & & & \\ & & & & & 1 & & \\ & & & & & & 1 & \\ & & & & & & & 1 \end{bmatrix}}^{L_{8\sim 1}}}_{P_{8\sim 1}}$$

To understand the following formal definition of the relaxed inverse, consider the case $s = 7$ and $\mathrm{diag}(A_7^{-1}, I_{n-7})$. The full inverse decomposition is

$$\mathrm{diag}(A_7^{-1}, I_{n-7}) = P_7 \cdot P_6 \cdot P_5 \cdot P_4 \cdot P_3 \cdot P_2 \cdot P_1$$

while the relaxed/lazy representation is

$$\mathrm{diag}(A_7^{-1}, I_{n-7}) = P_{7\sim 7} \cdot P_{6\sim 5} \cdot P_{4\sim 1}.$$

The structure of the relaxed decomposition is determined as follows. The largest power of 2 that is less than or equal to 7 is 4, and thus in the relaxed representation the rightmost four pairs $P_4 \cdot P_3 \cdot P_2 \cdot P_1$ of multiplicands of size 1 are compressed into the single pair of multiplicands $P_{4\sim 1}$ of size 4. Continuing, the largest power of 2 that is less than or equal to $7 - 4$ is 2, so $P_6 \cdot P_5$ is compressed to $P_{6\sim 5}$. Finally, the largest power of 2 that is less than or equal to $7 - 4 - 2$ is 1, so $P_7 = P_{7\sim 7}$ is left alone.

DEFINITION 6. *Decompose a positive integer* $s = 2^{i_1} + 2^{i_2} + \cdots + 2^{i_\ell}$ *in binary representation with* $i_1 > i_2 >$

$\cdots > i_\ell \geq 0$. The relaxed/lazy representation of the inverse $(A_s)^{-1}$ is defined as

$$(A_s)_L^{-1} = \left(P_{s \sim 2^{i_1} + 2^{i_2} + \cdots + 2^{i_{\ell-1}} + 1} \right) \cdot \cdots$$
$$\cdots \left(P_{2^{i_1} + 2^{i_2} \sim 2^{i_1} + 1} \right) \cdot \left(P_{2^{i_1} \sim 1} \right).$$

Note that when s is a power of two, we have $s = 2^{i_1}$ and

$$(A_s)_L^{-1} = P_{2^{i_1} \sim 1} = R_{2^{i_1} \sim 1} \cdot L_{2^{i_1} \sim 1} = R_{2^{i_1} \sim 1},$$

so A_s^{-1} is explicitly computed in this case. Otherwise, the relaxed representation $(A_s)_L^{-1}$ is comprised of the product of a sequence of pairs of structured multiplicands $P_{* \sim *}$. Observe that according to Definition 6 the sizes of the $P_{* \sim *}$ from right to left are $2^{i_1} > 2^{i_2} > \cdots > 2^\ell$.

In the next section we will give algorithms for the online algorithm that starts with $\mathcal{R} = (A_0)_L^{-1}$ (which trivially consists of zero pairs of structured multiplicands) and updates $\mathcal{R}$ so that

$$\mathcal{R} = (A_1)_L^{-1}, \mathcal{R} = (A_2)_L^{-1}, \mathcal{R} = (A_3)_L^{-1}, \ldots.$$

It turns out — and may already be clear from Example 5 — that the construction of $(A_s)_L^{-1}$ from $(A_{s-1})_L^{-1}$ and $P_{s \sim s}$ may require the combinations of two adjacent $(P_{* \sim *})$ of equal size. In particular, we will need to compute the compression

$$P_{j \sim j - 2m + 1} = P_{j \sim j - m + 1} \cdot P_{j - m \sim j - 2m + 1}, \quad (8)$$

where both $P_{j \sim j - m + 1}$ and $P_{j - m \sim j - 2m + 1}$ are of size m. Since this computation is important in deriving the cost of the relaxed approach, we give the formula and derive the cost for computing the left hand side of (8) given the two pairs of multiplicands on the right. For brevity, let $P_2 = R_2 \cdot L_2$, $P_1 = R_1 \cdot L_1$ and $P = R \cdot L$ denotes the leading $j \times j$ principal submatrix of $P_{j \sim j - m + 1}$, $P_{j - m \sim j - 2m + 1}$ and $P_{j \sim j - 2m + 1}$ respectively. (Note that we are "overloading" the notation $P_2, R_2, L_2, \ldots$, but only temporarily in this example.) Then equation (8) is the block case of Example 4. We have

$$P = \begin{bmatrix} I_{j-2m} & & \\ & R & \\ & & \end{bmatrix} \cdot \begin{bmatrix} I_{j-2m} & & \\ & L & 1 \\ & & \ddots \\ & & 1 \end{bmatrix}$$

$$= \begin{bmatrix} I_{j-m} & & \\ & \bar{R}_2 & \\ & & \end{bmatrix} \cdot \begin{bmatrix} I_{j-m} & & \\ & L_2 & 1 \\ & & \ddots \\ & & 1 \end{bmatrix}$$
$$\underbrace{\hspace{6cm}}_{P_2}$$

$$\times \begin{bmatrix} I_{j-2m} & & \\ & R_1 & \\ & & I_i \end{bmatrix} \cdot \begin{bmatrix} I_{j-2m} & & \\ & L_1 & 1 \\ & & \ddots \\ & & 1 & I_i \end{bmatrix}$$
$$\underbrace{\hspace{6cm}}_{P_1}$$

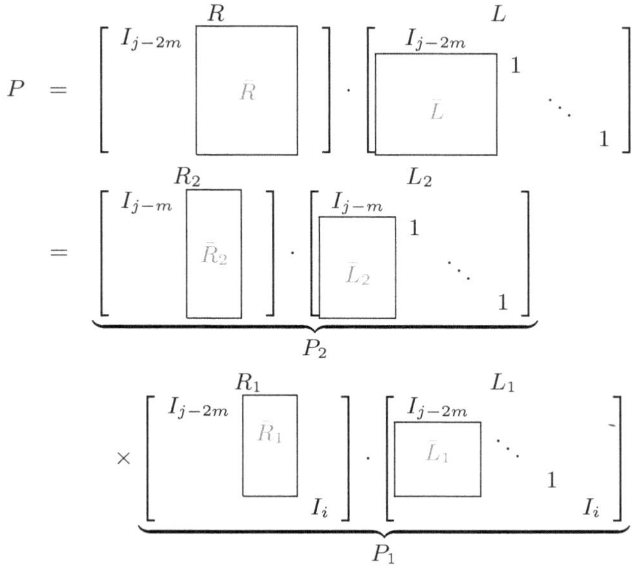

where

$$\bar{L} = \begin{bmatrix} \bar{L}_1 \\ (\bar{L}_2)_{[1,\ldots,j-2m]} \end{bmatrix} \in \mathsf{K}^{2m \times (j-2m)} \quad (9)$$

and $\bar{R} \in \mathsf{K}^{j \times 2m}$ can be computed by solving

$$R = (R_2 L_2 R_1 L_1) L^{-1}$$

to obtain

$$\bar{R} = \begin{bmatrix} \bar{R}_2 (\bar{L}_2 \bar{R}_1) + \begin{bmatrix} \bar{R}_1 \\ 0 \end{bmatrix} \mid \bar{R}_2 \end{bmatrix}. \quad (10)$$

THEOREM 7. *There exists an algorithm* EqualSizeCompress *that takes as input the two pairs of multiplicands* $P_{j \sim j - m + 1}, P_{j - m \sim j - 2m + 1} \in \mathsf{K}^{n \times n}$, *both with size* m, *and returns as output the single pair of multiplicands* $P_{j \sim j - 2m + 1} \in \mathsf{K}^{n \times n}$ *of size* $2m$ *such that*

$$P_{j \sim j - 2m + 1} = P_{j \sim j - m + 1} \cdot P_{j - m \sim j - 2m + 1}.$$

The cost of the algorithm is $O(nm^{\omega - 1})$ *field operations in* K.

PROOF. See (9) and (10) for the formula for computing the pair of multiplicands $P_{j \sim j - 2m + 1}$. Computing L is free since $\bar{L}$ can be read off from $\bar{L}_2$ and $\bar{L}_1$ directly. The dominating cost of computing R is to compute $\bar{R}_2(\bar{L}_2 \bar{R}_1)$, where $\bar{R}_2 \in \mathsf{K}^{j \times m}$, $\bar{L}_2 \in \mathsf{K}^{m \times (j-m)}$ and $\bar{R}_1 \in \mathsf{K}^{(j-m) \times m}$. The product of two $m \times m$ matrix can be computed in cm^ω field operations, for some fixed constant c. Dividing $\bar{R}_2, \bar{L}_2$, and $\bar{R}_1$ into at most $\lceil j/m \rceil$ blocks of dimension bounded by $m \times m$, $\bar{L}_2 \bar{R}_1$ can be computed in $\lceil j/m \rceil cm^\omega + O(mj)$ field operations and $\bar{R}_2(\bar{L}_2 \bar{R}_1)$ takes another $\lceil j/m \rceil cm^\omega + O(mj)$ field operations. The result now follows by noting that $j \leq n$. □

5. RELAXED ONLINE INVERSION

The iterative approach to solve problem ONLINEINVERSE has overall cost $2n^3 + O(n^2)$. In this section we show how to incorporate matrix multiplication to solve the problem ONLINEINVERSE in $O(n^\omega)$ field operations in K. We adopt two ideas used in relaxed [7] and online [6] algorithms.

The first idea is to *relax*, that is, to use the relaxed representation $(A_s)_L^{-1}$ for A_s^{-1} as in Definition 6. The representation $(A_s)_L^{-1}$ for $s = 1, 2, \ldots, n$ is constructed in an incremental fashion. Let $s > 0$ and suppose $(A_{s-1})_L^{-1}$ and P_s are known. Since $(A_s)^{-1} = P_s(A_{s-1})_L^{-1}$, the relaxed representation $(A_s)_L^{-1}$ is computed by compressing the pair of multiplicands P_s (of size one) and the first pair of multiplicands of $(A_{s-1})_L^{-1}$ into a single pair if they have equal size, repeating if required. Algorithm 1 outlines the algorithm that starts with $\mathcal{R} = (A_{s-1})_L^{-1}$ and P_s and updates $\mathcal{R}$ so that $\mathcal{R} = (A_s)_L^{-1}$.

Algorithm 1 UpdateRelaxedInverse[$\mathcal{R}$](P_s)

Require: $\mathcal{R} = (A_{s-1})_L^{-1}$, $P_s \in \mathsf{K}^{n \times n}$
Ensure: $\mathcal{R}$ is updated so that $\mathcal{R} = (A_s)_L^{-1}$
1: $P := P_s$;
2: $P_l :=$ first pair of multiplicands in $\mathcal{R}$;
3: **while** (size of P = size of P_l) **do**
4: $\quad P := $ EqualSizeCompress(P, P_l);
5: $\quad$ Remove P_l from $\mathcal{R}$;
6: $\quad P_l :=$ first pair of multiplicands in $\mathcal{R}$;
7: **end while**
8: $\mathcal{R} := P \cdot \mathcal{R}$;

Note that when s is odd, then by Definition 6 the first pair of multiplicands in $(A_{s-1})_L^{-1}$ has size greater than one, so the while loop is never executed. For even values of s

the while loop is executed at least once, possibly as many as $\log s$ times.

EXAMPLE 8. If $\mathcal{R} = (A_7)_L^{-1}$, the steps to update to $\mathcal{R} = (A_8)_L^{-1}$ are as follows.

$$
\begin{aligned}
(A_8)_L^{-1} &= P_8 \cdot (A_7)_L^{-1} \\
&= P_8 \cdot (P_7 \cdot P_{6\sim5} \cdot P_{4\sim1}) \\
&= P_{8\sim7} \cdot P_{6\sim5} \cdot P_{4\sim1} \quad\quad (11) \\
&= P_{8\sim5} \cdot P_{4\sim1} \quad\quad\quad\quad (12) \\
&= P_{8\sim1} \quad\quad\quad\quad\quad\quad\quad (13)
\end{aligned}
$$

Three compressions are required:

- $P_{8\sim7} := \texttt{EqualSizeCompress}(P_{8\sim8}, P_{7\sim7})$ of size 1 to 2 in (11),

- $P_{8\sim5} := \texttt{EqualSizeCompress}(P_{8\sim7}, P_{6\sim5})$ of size 2 to 4 in (12), and

- $P_{8\sim1} := \texttt{EqualSizeCompress}(P_{8\sim5}, P_{4\sim1})$ of size 4 to 8 in (13).

The second idea is to *anticipate* computations. To make it clear that rows of A are given one at a time, we use a work matrix B for the anticipated computations. B is initialized to be the $n \times n$ zero matrix. At stage $s > 0$, row $A^{[s]}$ is copied to row $B^{[s]}$. At stage s the first s rows of the input matrix A are defined, and the (untransformed) input matrix can be decomposed as

$$
A = \left[\begin{array}{cc|c}
A_{s-1} & u_s & A_{[s+1\ldots n]}^{[1\ldots s-1]} \\
\hline
v_s & d_s & A_{[s+1\ldots n]}^{[s]} \\
\hline
\multicolumn{3}{c}{0}
\end{array} \right] \in \mathsf{K}^{n\times n}. \quad (14)
$$

Recall that the dominant cost of computing the pair of multiplicands $P_s = R_s \cdot L_s$ arises from computing the matrix $\times$ vector product $A_{s-1}^{-1} u_s$ as shown in (5). At stage $s-1$, when $(A_{s-1})_L^{-1}$ has been computed, we do not apply A_{s-1}^{-1} to the single column u_s of A, which would be sufficient to compute the pair of multiplicands P_s at the next stage. Rather, we anticipate computations by applying the first element $P_{s\sim*}$ of the lazy representation $(A_{s-1})_L^{-1}$ to m columns of the work matrix B, where m is the size of $P_{s\sim*}$. This effectively incorporates matrix multiplication, and ensures that at the beginning of stage s we have $B_{[s]}^{[1,\ldots,s-1]} = (A_{s-1})^{-1} u_s$. Algorithm 2 computes P_s given row s of A using the work matrix B and $\mathcal{R} = (A_{s-1})_L^{-1}$. As a side effect, the algorithm updates the work matrix B as described above and updates $\mathcal{R}$ so that $\mathcal{R} = (A_s)_L^{-1}$. The algorithm first checks whether P_s exists, and reports "FAIL" if not. Detection is simple: if $d_s - v_s(A_{s-1})^{-1} u_s = 0$ then P_s does not exist.

EXAMPLE 9. We consider the computations of the first four stages of the relaxed online inverse update for $A \in \mathsf{K}^{8\times8}$. The following shows the work matrix B with certain

---

Algorithm 2 $\texttt{ComputeP}[\mathcal{R}, B](A^{[s]})$

Require: $\mathcal{R} = (A_{s-1})_L^{-1}$ and $B \in \mathsf{K}^{n\times n}$ with $B_{[s]}^{[1,\ldots,s-1]} = (A_{s-1})^{-1} u_s$

Require: row $A^{[s]}$ of nonsingular $A \in \mathsf{K}^{n\times n}$

Ensure: $\mathcal{R}$ is updated so that $\mathcal{R} = (A_s)_L^{-1}$

Ensure: B is updated by copying row $A^{[s]}$ to row $B^{[s]}$ and applying the first element $P_{s\sim*}$ of $(A_s)_L^{-1}$ to columns $s+1, s+2, \ldots, \min(s+m, n)$ of B, where m is the size of $P_{s\sim*}$.

Ensure: $P_s \in \mathsf{K}^{n\times n}$

1: Copy $A^{[s]}$ to row $B^{[s]}$;
2: **if** $(d_s - v_s B_{[s]}^{[1,\ldots,s-1]} = 0)$ **then**
3:   **return** "FAIL";
4: **end if**
5: Compute $P_s := R_s \cdot L_s$ using Equation (5);
6: **if** $(s < n)$ **then**
7:   $\texttt{UpdateRelaxedInverse}[\mathcal{R}](P_s)$;
8:   Let $P_{s\sim*}$ be the first element of $(A_s)_L^{-1}$;
9:   Let m be the size of $P_{s\sim*}$;
10:   $B_{[s+1,\ldots,\min(s+m,n)]} := P_{s\sim*} B_{[s+1,\ldots,\min(s+m,n)]}$;
11: **end if**;
12: **return** P_s;

---

submatrices highlighted.

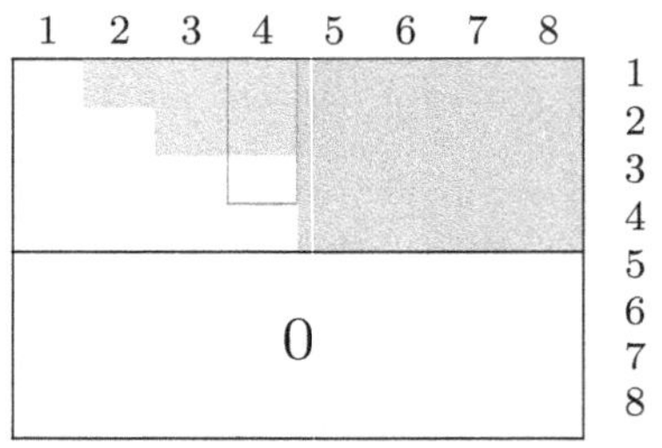

At stage $s = 0$, B is initialized to be the 8×8 zero matrix. For $s = 1, 2, 3, 4$, the computations done at each stage are summarized below.

1. Copy row $A^{[1]}$ to row $B^{[1]}$ and compute $P_1 = R_1 \cdot L_1$. Apply P_1 to column 2 of B (area).

2. Copy row $A^{[2]}$ to row $B^{[2]}$ and compute $P_2 = R_2 \cdot L_2$. Compress $P_2 \cdot P_1 = P_{2\sim1}$. Apply $P_{2\sim1}$ to columns 3, 4 of B (area).

3. Copy row $A^{[3]}$ to row $B^{[3]}$ and compute $P_3 = R_3 \cdot L_3$. Apply P_3 to column 4 of B (area).

4. Copy row $A^{[4]}$ to row $B^{[4]}$ and compute $P_4 = R_4 \cdot L_4$. Compress $P_4 \cdot P_3 = P_{4\sim3}$. Compress $P_{4\sim3} \cdot P_{2\sim1} = P_{4\sim1}$. Apply $P_{4\sim1}$ to columns 5,6,7,8 of B (area).

At stages $2^k = 1, 2, 4, \ldots$ the explicit inverse has been computed since $L_{2^k\sim1} = I_n$ and $R_{2^k\sim1} = \operatorname{diag}(A_{2^k}^{-1}, n - 2^k)$. At the end of stage 3, though, we only have the relaxed representation $\operatorname{diag}(A_3^{-1}, n - 3) = P_3 \cdot P_{2\sim1}$.

The relaxed algorithm to solve problem ONLINEINVERSE is thus to initialize $\mathcal{R} = (A_0)_L^{-1}$, initialize B to be the $n \times n$

zero matrix, and call Algorithm 2 ComputeP$[\mathcal{R}, B](A^{[s]})$ for $s = 1, 2, \ldots, n$.

THEOREM 10. *There exists a relaxed algorithm to solve problem* ONLINEINVERSE *in* $O(n^\omega)$ *field operations in* K.

PROOF. For simplicity, assume n is a power of two; otherwise, we can augment A as $\text{diag}(A, I_*)$. There are two parts of the cost: (1) computing P_s and updating B; (2) updating $(A_{s-1})_L^{-1}$ to $(A_s)_L^{-1}$ using P_s.

For part (1), the dominant cost is to perform the update to B according to step 10 of Algorithm 2. At each stage s, step 10 costs $O(s \cdot m^{w-1})$ field operations in K, where m is the size of the first element of $(A_s)_L^{-1}$. From Definition 6, m is the highest power of 2 that is less than or equal to s. Note that for $s = n$ no update to B is required. The sequence of sizes m for stages $s = 1, 2, \ldots, n-1$ stages are given by

$$(2^{\nu_2(s)})_{s=1}^{n-1} = 1, 2, 1, 4, 1, 2, 1, 8, 1, 2, 1, 4, 1, 2, 1, 16, \ldots, 2, 1,$$

where $\nu_2(s)$ is the highest power of two dividing s (sequence A00659 [11]). Note that the number 2^i in the sequence appears $n/2^{i+1}$ times. For instance, 1 appears every other number, 2 appears every four numbers, etc. For some absolute constant c, the total cost of all the updates to B is thus bounded by

$$\begin{aligned}
&\sum_{i=0}^{(\log n)-2} \frac{n}{2^{i+1}} \left(cn(2^i)^{\omega-1}\right) \\
&= \frac{cn^2}{2} \sum_{i=0}^{(\log n)-2} 2^{i(\omega-2)} \\
&= \frac{cn^2}{2} \left(1 + 2^{\omega-2} + 4^{(\omega-2)} + \cdots + (n/4)^{\omega-2}\right) \\
&= \frac{cn^2}{2} \left(\frac{2^{(\omega-2)(\log n-1)} - 1}{2^{\omega-2} - 1}\right) \\
&= \frac{cn^2}{2} \left(\frac{(n/2)^{\omega-2} - 1}{2^{\omega-2} - 1}\right) \\
&= \frac{cn^2}{2} O(n^{\omega-2}) \\
&= O(n^\omega).
\end{aligned}$$

Now consider part (2). The number of compressions done at stage s is equal to the maximal $t \in \mathbb{Z}$ such that $2^t \mid s$. Thus some stages are more costly than others. For example, when s is odd, $t = 0$ and no compressions are performed. When s is a power of 2, $t = \log_2 s$ compressions are required (see Figure 1, where compressions performed are highlighted in dashed lines).

We consider the overall cost for $1 \le s \le n$ as shown in Figure 2. Nodes in the inverse tree are computed in a bottom-up fashion. We label level $l = 0, 1, \ldots, \log n$ from leaf up to root level. For $l > 0$, nodes at level l can be computed using Theorem 7 with $m = 2^{l-1}$. The number of nodes at level l is $n/2^l$. Overall, the cost of constructing the whole inverse tree is

$$\sum_{l=1}^{\log n} \left(cn(2^{l-1})^{w-1}\right) \frac{n}{2^l} = O(n^\omega).$$

The derivation of the closed form for this summation are omitted since it is similar to the previous summation. The result follows by adding the cost of both parts. □

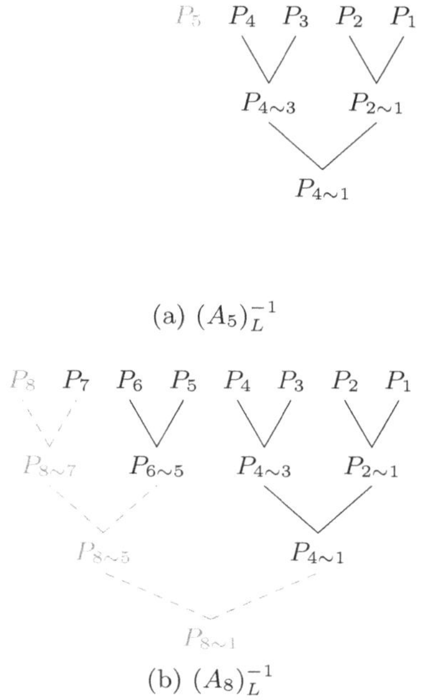

Figure 1: Examples of relaxed representation update

COROLLARY 11. *There exists an algorithm to solve problem* ONLINESYSTEM *in* $O(n^\omega)$ *field operations in* K.

6. APPLICATION TO RANK PROFILE

The algorithm for ONLINEINVERSE allows matrix multiplication to be incorporated in the algorithm for row rank profile presented in [12]. A complete exposition can be found in [14, Chapter 8] but we sketch the approach here.

- **Reduction to matrix of full column rank:** Use the Monte Carlo rank algorithm in [3, Theorem 2.11] to find a submatrix B of A that consists of $s \le r$ linearly independent columns of A in time

$$(r^\omega + n + m + |A|)^{1+o(1)}.$$

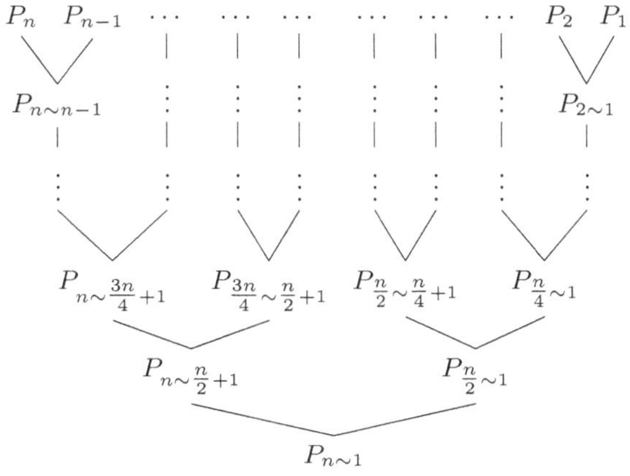

Figure 2: Online inverse tree

The algorithm should return $s = r$ with probability at least $3/4$. Provided $r = s$, the column space of the resulting matrix is equal to that of A so they must have the same row rank profile.

- **Reduction to matrix generic rank profile:** Let L be a lower triangular Toeplitz matrix L with entries chosen uniformly and randomly from K. Work with the unevaluated pair of matrices $B \cdot L$. With probability at least $1-m(m+1)/(2\#\mathsf{K})$ the matrix obtained from the submatrix comprised of the rank profile columns of B postmultiplied by L will have generic rank profile [10, Theorem 2].

- Use a modification of the Monte Carlo rank profile algorithm supporting [12, Theorem 19] to compute the row rank profile of $B \cdot L$, where $B \cdot L$ is kept unevaluated. The key observation is that, if v is a linear combination of the rows of B, and we need to compute the dot product vLu for a column vector u, we can compute $v(Lu)$ instead of $(vL)u$: the latter expression implies we can construct a linear independence oracle from the rows of the (possibly sparse) B instead of the (probably dense) BL.

The above approach gives a Monte Carlo algorithm to compute the row rank profile of an arbitrary input matrix in time $(r^{\omega} + n + m + |A|)^{1+o(1)}$ field operations in K.

7. CONCLUSIONS

Our online algorithm for OnlineInverse assumed that at stage s the first s rows of A comprising the submatrix $A^{[1\cdots s]}$ be produced, $s = 1, 2, \ldots, n$. The requirement that the entire row be produced at each stage can be weakened somewhat. For example, at stage s, it suffices that the first $2 \cdot 2^{\lfloor \log_2 s \rfloor} \leq 2s$ entries of $A^{[1\cdots s]}$ be produced. In other words, at stage 1 the first 2 entries of the row is required, at stages 2–3 the first 4 entries of the rows are required, at stages 4–7 the first 8 entries of the rows are required, etc.

8. REFERENCES

[1] J. Bunch and J. Hopcroft. Triangular factorization and inversion by fast matrix multiplication. *Mathematics of Computation*, 28:231–236, 1974.

[2] Z. Chen and A. Storjohann. A BLAS based C library for exact linear algebra on integer matrices. In M. Kauers, editor, *Proc. Int'l. Symp. on Symbolic and Algebraic Computation: ISSAC'05*, pages 92–99. ACM Press, New York, 2005.

[3] H. Y. Cheung, T. C. Kwok, and L. C. Lau. Fast matrix rank algorithms and applications. *Journal of the ACM*, 60(5):733–751, 2013. Article No. 31.

[4] J.-G. Dumas, T. Gautier, M. Giesbrecht, P. Giorgi, B. Hovinen, E. Kaltofen, B. D. Saunders, W. J. Turner, and G. Villard. LinBox: A generic library for exact linear algebra. In A. J. Cohen and N. Gao, X.-S. andl Takayama, editors, *Proc. First Internat. Congress Math. Software ICMS 2002, Beijing, China*, pages 40–50, Singapore, 2002. World Scientific.

[5] J.-G. Dumas, T. Gautier, and C. Pernet. Finite field linear algebra subroutines. In T. Mora, editor, *Proc. Int'l. Symp. on Symbolic and Algebraic Computation: ISSAC'02*, pages 63–74. ACM Press, New York, 2002.

[6] P. Giorgi and R. Lebreton. Online order basis algorithm and its impact on block Wiedemann algorithm. In *Proc. Int'l. Symp. on Symbolic and Algebraic Computation: ISSAC'14*. ACM Press, New York, 2014.

[7] J. van der Hoeven. Relax, but don't be too lazy. *Journal of Symbolic Computation*, 36(6):479–542, 2002.

[8] O. Ibarra, S. Moran, and R. Hui. A generalization of the fast LUP matrix decomposition algorithm and applications. *Journal of Algorithms*, 3:45–56, 1982.

[9] C.-P. Jeannerod, C. Pernet, and A. Storjohann. Rank-profile revealing Gaussian elimination and the CUP matrix decomposition. *Journal of Symbolic Computation*, 56:56–58, 2013.

[10] E. Kaltofen and B. D. Saunders. On Wiedemann's method of solving sparse linear systems. In *Proc. AAECC-9, Lecture Notes in Comput. Sci., vol. 539*, pages 29–38, 1991.

[11] N. J. A. Sloane. The on-line encyclopedia of integer sequences. *Notices of the American Mathematical Society*, 50(8):912–915, 2003.

[12] A. Storjohan and S. Yang. Linear independence oracles and applications to rectangular and low rank linear systems. In *Proc. Int'l. Symp. on Symbolic and Algebraic Computation: ISSAC'14*. ACM Press, New York, 2014.

[13] J. van der Hoeven. Lazy multiplication of formal power series. In W. W. Küchlin, editor, *Proc. Int'l. Symp. on Symbolic and Algebraic Computation: ISSAC'97*, pages 17–20. ACM Press, New York, 1997.

[14] S. Yang. Algorithms for fast linear system solving and rank profile computation. Master's thesis, David R. Cheriton School of Computer Science, University of Waterloo, 2014.

Subtropical Real Root Finding

Thomas Sturm
Max Planck Institute for Informatics
Saarbrücken, Germany
sturm@mpi-inf.mpg.de

ABSTRACT

We describe a new incomplete but terminating heuristic method for real root finding for large multivariate polynomials. We take an abstract view of the polynomial as the set of exponent vectors associated with sign information on the coefficients. Then we employ linear programming to heuristically find roots. There is a specialized variant for roots with exclusively positive coordinates, which is of considerable interest for applications in chemistry and systems biology. An implementation of our method combining the computer algebra system Reduce with the linear programming solver Gurobi has been successfully applied to input data originating from established mathematical models used in these areas. We have solved several hundred problems with up to more than 800 000 monomials in up to 10 variables with degrees up to 12. Our method has failed due to its incompleteness in only 10 percent of the cases.

Categories and Subject Descriptors

I.1 [**Symbolic and Algebraic Manipulation**]: Algorithms

General Terms

Algorithms, Experimentation, Performance

Keywords

large polynomial; linear programming; real root

1. INTRODUCTION

Our work discussed here is motivated by our studies of Hopf bifurcations [16, 15] for reaction systems in chemistry and gene regulatory networks in systems biology, which are originally given by systems of ordinary differential equations. Hopf bifurcations can be described algebraically [7, 34, 12, 11], resulting in one very large multivariate polynomial equation $f = 0$ subject to few much simpler polynomial side conditions $g_1 > 0, \ldots, g_n > 0$. For such systems one is interested in feasibility over the reals and, in the positive case, in at least one feasible point. It turns out that, generally, scientifically meaningful information can be obtained already by checking only the feasibility of $f = 0$, which is the focus of this article. For further details on the scientific background, we refer the reader to our publications [30, 31, 35, 10, 8, 9].

With one of our models, viz. *Mitogen-activated protein kinase (MAPK)*, we obtain and solve polynomials of considerable size. Our currently largest instance `mapke5e6` contains 863438 monomials in 10 variables. One of the variables occurs with degree 12, all other variables occur with degree 5. Such problem sizes are clearly beyond the scope of classical methods in symbolic computation. To give an impression, the size of an input file with `mapke5e6` in infix notation is 30 MB large. LaTeX-formatted printing of `mapke5e6` would fill more than 3000 pages in this document. The MAPK model actually yields even larger instances, which we, unfortunately, cannot generate at present, because in our toolchain Maple cannot produce polynomials larger than 32 MB.

This article introduces an incomplete but terminating algorithm for finding real roots of large multivariate polynomials. The principle idea is to take an abstract view of the polynomial as the set of its exponent vectors supplemented with sign information on the corresponding coefficients. To that extent, our approach is quite similar to tropical algebraic geometry [32]. However, after our abstraction we do not consider tropical varieties but employ linear programming to determine certain suitable points in the Newton polytope, which somewhat resembles successful approaches to sum-of-square decompositions [27].

We have implemented our algorithm in Reduce [17] using direct function calls to the dynamic library of the LP solver Gurobi [14]. In practical computations on several hundred examples, our method has failed do to its incompleteness in only 10 percent of the cases. The longest computation time observed was around 16 s. As mentioned above, the limiting factor at present is the technical generation of even larger input.

In Section 2 we introduce a specialization of our method that only finds roots with all positive coordinates. This is highly relevant in our context of reaction networks, where typically all variables are known to be positive. We also discuss an illustrating example in detail. Section 3 generalizes our method to arbitrary roots. In Section 4 we discuss issues and share experiences related to a practical implementation of our method. In Section 5 we evaluate the performance

ISSAC'15, July 6–9, 2015, Bath, United Kingdom.

ACM 978-1-4503-3435-8/15/07 ...$15.00.
DOI: http://dx.doi.org/10.1145/2755996.2756677.

of our method with respect to efficiency and to its incompleteness on several hundred examples originating from four different chemical and biological models.

2. FINDING ROOTS WITH STRICTLY POSITIVE COORDINATES

Denote $\mathbb{N}_1 = \mathbb{N} \setminus \{0\}$, and let $d \in \mathbb{N}_1$. For $a \in \mathbb{R}$, vectors $\mathbf{x} = (x_1, \dots, x_d)$ of either indeterminates or real numbers, and $\mathbf{p} = (p_1, \dots, p_d) \in \mathbb{N}^d$, we use the notations $a^{\mathbf{p}} = (a^{p_1}, \dots, a^{p_d})$ and $\mathbf{x}^{\mathbf{p}} = x_1^{d_1} \cdots x_d^{p_d}$. We will, however, never consider a vector to the power of a number. Our notations are compatible with the standard scalar product as follows:

$$(a^{\mathbf{p}})^{\mathbf{q}} = (a^{p_1}, \dots, a^{p_d})^{\mathbf{q}} = a^{p_1 q_1} \cdots a^{p_d q_d} = a^{\mathbf{p}\mathbf{q}}.$$

Consider a multivariate integer polynomial

$$f = \sum_{\mathbf{p} \in \operatorname{supp}(f)} \operatorname{coeff}(f, \mathbf{p}) \cdot \mathbf{x}^{\mathbf{p}} \in \mathbb{Z}[\mathbf{x}],$$

where $\operatorname{coeff}(f, \mathbf{p}) \neq 0$ for $\mathbf{p} \in \operatorname{supp}(f)$, which is called the *support* of f.

2.1 Finding a Point with Positive Value

The *Newton polytope* of f is the convex hull of $\operatorname{supp}(f)$. It forms a polyhedron in $\mathbb{R}^d$, which we identify with its vertices, formally $\operatorname{newton}(f) \subseteq \operatorname{supp}(f)$. The following lemma is a straightforward consequence of the convex hull property.

Lemma 1 Let $f = \operatorname{coeff}(f, \mathbf{p}) \cdot \mathbf{x}^{\mathbf{p}} + f' \in \mathbb{Z}[\mathbf{x}]$. Assume that $\mathbf{p} \notin \operatorname{newton}(f)$. Then $\operatorname{newton}(f) = \operatorname{newton}(f')$. □

For $\mathbf{p} \in \operatorname{supp}(f)$ we define $\operatorname{sign}(f, \mathbf{p}) = \operatorname{sign}(\operatorname{coeff}(f, \mathbf{p}))$. We partition the support of f as follows:

$$\begin{aligned}
\operatorname{supp}(f) &= \operatorname{supp}^+(f) \,\dot\cup\, \operatorname{supp}^-(f) \,\dot\cup\, \operatorname{supp}^0(f),\\
\operatorname{supp}^+(f) &= \{\, \mathbf{p} \in \operatorname{supp}(f) \mid \operatorname{sign}(f, \mathbf{p}) > 0 \wedge \mathbf{p} \neq \mathbf{0} \,\},\\
\operatorname{supp}^-(f) &= \{\, \mathbf{p} \in \operatorname{supp}(f) \mid \operatorname{sign}(f, \mathbf{p}) < 0 \wedge \mathbf{p} \neq \mathbf{0} \,\},\\
\operatorname{supp}^0(f) &= \operatorname{supp}(f) \cap \{\mathbf{0}\}.
\end{aligned}$$

Let $\operatorname{supp}^+(f) = \{\mathbf{p}_1, \dots, \mathbf{p}_r\}$, $\operatorname{supp}^-(f) = \{\mathbf{p}_{r+1}, \dots, \mathbf{p}_s\}$, and fix any order on $\operatorname{supp}(f)$. The *basic LP matrix* $B(f)$ is composed as follows, where the last row is present if and only if $\operatorname{supp}^0(f) \neq \emptyset$:

$$B(f) = \left[\begin{array}{c} B^+(f) \\ \hline B^-(f) \\ \hline (\mathbf{0}, -1) \end{array}\right] = \left[\begin{array}{cccc} p_{11} & \cdots & p_{1d} & -1 \\ \vdots & \ddots & \vdots & \vdots \\ p_{rd} & \cdots & p_{rd} & -1 \\ \hline p_{r+1,1} & \cdots & p_{r+1,d} & -1 \\ \vdots & \ddots & \vdots & \vdots \\ p_{s,d} & \cdots & p_{s,d} & -1 \\ \hline 0 & \cdots & 0 & -1 \end{array}\right].$$

Considering matrices concatenations of their rows, we write this also as $B(f) = B^+(f) \circ B^-(f) \circ (\mathbf{0}, -1)^*$. Whenever we write for a given matrix $B \in \mathbb{Z}^{m \times n}$ a product $N^* B$, then we implicitly agree that

$$N^* = \begin{bmatrix} -1 & 0 & 0 & 0 & \cdots \\ 0 & 1 & 0 & 0 & \cdots \\ 0 & 0 & 1 & 0 & \cdots \\ \vdots & \vdots & \ddots & \ddots & \ddots \end{bmatrix} \in \mathbb{Z}^{m \times m}.$$

That is, the multiplication $N^* B$ replaces the elements of the first row of B with their additive inverses. Similarly, $-\mathbf{1} = (-1, \dots, -1)^T$ is generally a column matrix of suitable length. In these terms, we are going to consider systems

$$N^* \cdot B(f) \cdot \mathbf{x}^T \leq -\mathbf{1}, \quad \text{where} \quad \mathbf{x} = (\mathbf{n}, c) \in \mathbb{R}^{d+1},$$

which can be rewritten as follows:

$$\begin{aligned}
\mathbf{p}_1 \mathbf{n} - c &\geq 1 \\
\mathbf{p}_i \mathbf{n} - c &\leq -1, \qquad i \in \{2, \dots, s\}.
\end{aligned}$$

Lemma 2 Let $f \in \mathbb{Z}[\mathbf{x}]$. Let $\mathbf{n} \in \mathbb{R}^d$, and let $c \in \mathbb{R}$. Then the following are equivalent:

(i) The hyperplane $H(\mathbf{x})$ defined by $\mathbf{n}\mathbf{x} = c$ strictly separates $\mathbf{p}_1$ from $\operatorname{supp}(f) \setminus \{\mathbf{p}_1\}$, and the normal vector $\mathbf{n}$ is pointing from $H(\mathbf{x})$ in direction $\mathbf{p}_1$. In particular, $\mathbf{p}_1 \in \operatorname{newton}(f)$.

(ii) There is $0 < \lambda \in \mathbb{R}$ s.t. $N^* \cdot B(f) \cdot (\lambda \mathbf{n}, \lambda c)^T \leq -\mathbf{1}$.

PROOF. Assume that (i) holds. The orientation of $\mathbf{n}$ is chosen such that $\mathbf{n} \cdot \mathbf{p}_1 > c$ and $\mathbf{n} \cdot \mathbf{p}_i < c$ for $i \in \{2, \dots, s\}$. Define $\delta = \min_{i \in \{1,\dots,s\}} |\operatorname{dist}(\mathbf{p}_i, H)| > 0$. Then

$$\begin{aligned}
\mathbf{p}_1 \cdot \mathbf{n} - c &\geq \delta \|\mathbf{n}\|, \\
\mathbf{p}_i \cdot \mathbf{n} - c &\leq -\delta \|\mathbf{n}\|, \qquad i \in \{2, \dots, s\},
\end{aligned}$$

and we can choose $\lambda = (\delta \|\mathbf{n}\|)^{-1}$.

Vice versa, assume that (ii) holds. It follows that

$$\begin{aligned}
\mathbf{p}_1 \cdot \mathbf{n} &\geq c + 1/\lambda, \\
\mathbf{p}_i \cdot \mathbf{n} &\leq c - 1/\lambda, \qquad i \in \{2, \dots, s\}.
\end{aligned}$$

Hence $H(\mathbf{x})$ defined by $\mathbf{n}\mathbf{x} = c$ is a hyperplane separating $\mathbf{p}_1$ from $\operatorname{supp}(f) \setminus \{\mathbf{p}_1\}$, where the distance between $H(\mathbf{x})$ and $\operatorname{supp}(f)$ is at least $\|\mathbf{n}\|/\lambda > 0$. Furthermore, $\mathbf{n}$ is oriented as required in (i). □

Lemma 3 Let $0 \neq f \in \mathbb{Z}[\mathbf{x}]$. Then the following are equivalent:

(i) There is $(\mathbf{n}, c) \in \mathbb{R}^{d+1}$ s.t. $N^* \cdot B(f) \cdot (\mathbf{n}, c)^T \leq -\mathbf{1}$.

(ii) There is $(\mathbf{n}, c) \in \mathbb{Q}^{d+1}$ s.t. $N^* \cdot B(f) \cdot (\mathbf{n}, c)^T \leq -\mathbf{1}$.

(iii) There is $\mathbf{n} \in \mathbb{Z}^d$, $c \in \mathbb{Q}$ s.t. $N^* \cdot B(f) \cdot (\mathbf{n}, c)^T \leq -\mathbf{1}$.

PROOF. The existence of a real solution in (i) and a rational solution in (ii) coincide due to the Linear Tarski Principle: Ordered fields admit quantifier elimination for linear formulas [22, 29]. Given a solution $(n_1, \dots, n_d, c) \in \mathbb{Q}^{d+1}$ in (ii), we can use the principal denominator $m \in \mathbb{N}_1$ of n_1, $\dots$, n_d to obtain a solution $(mn_1, \dots, mn_d, mc + m - 1) \in \mathbb{Z}^d \times \mathbb{Q}$ in (iii). The implication from (iii) to (i) is trivial. □

Lemma 4 Let $f \in \mathbb{Z}[\mathbf{x}] \setminus \mathbb{Z}$. Let $(\mathbf{n}, c) \in \mathbb{R}^{d+1}$ such that $N^* \cdot B(f) \cdot (\mathbf{n}, c)^T \leq -\mathbf{1}$. Then there is $a_0 \in \mathbb{N}$ such that for all $a \in \mathbb{N}$ with $a \geq a_0$ the following hold:

(i) $|\operatorname{coeff}(f, \mathbf{p}_1) \cdot a^{\mathbf{n}\mathbf{p}_1}| > \left| \sum_{i=2}^{s} \operatorname{coeff}(f, \mathbf{p}_i) \cdot a^{\mathbf{n}\mathbf{p}_i} \right|$,

(ii) $\operatorname{sign}\big(f(a^{\mathbf{n}})\big) = \operatorname{sign}(f, \mathbf{p}_1)$.

PROOF. (i) From $f \notin \mathbb{Z}$ it follows that $\mathbf{p}_1 \neq \mathbf{0}$. By Lemma 2 we know $\mathbf{n}\mathbf{p}_1 > c$ and $\mathbf{n}\mathbf{p}_i < c$ for $i \in \{2, \dots, s\}$. It follows that there is $0 < \delta \in \mathbb{R}$ such that

$$\begin{aligned} \mathbf{n}\mathbf{p}_1 &\geq c + \delta, & (1)\\ \mathbf{n}\mathbf{p}_i &\leq c - \delta \quad i \in \{2, \dots, s\}. & (2) \end{aligned}$$

We are going to show that $a_0 = \lceil \max\{2, (b \cdot (k-1))^{\frac{1}{\delta}}\} \rceil$ is a suitable choice, where

$$b = |\mathrm{coeff}(f, \mathbf{p}_1)|^{-1} \cdot \max_{i \in \{2,\dots,s\}} |\mathrm{coeff}(f, \mathbf{p}_i)| .$$

For $a \geq a_0 \geq 2$ and for all $i \in \{2, \dots, s\}$, the inequalities (1) and (2) and monotony yield

$$a^{\mathbf{n}\mathbf{p}_1} \geq a^{\delta} a^{c} > a^{\delta} a^{c} a^{-\delta} \geq a^{\delta} a^{\mathbf{n}\mathbf{p}_i} \geq b \cdot (k-1) \cdot a^{\mathbf{n}\mathbf{p}_i}.$$

Using the triangle inequality it follows that

$$a^{\mathbf{n}\mathbf{p}_1} > b \sum_{i=2}^{s} a^{\mathbf{n}\mathbf{p}_i} \geq |\mathrm{coeff}(f, \mathbf{p}_1)|^{-1} \cdot \left| \sum_{i=2}^{s} \mathrm{coeff}(f, \mathbf{p}_i) \cdot a^{\mathbf{n}\mathbf{p}_i} \right| ,$$

which straightforwardly implies

$$|\mathrm{coeff}(f, \mathbf{p}_1) \cdot a^{\mathbf{n}\mathbf{p}_1}| > \left| \sum_{i=2}^{s} \mathrm{coeff}(f, \mathbf{p}_i) \cdot a^{\mathbf{n}\mathbf{p}_i} \right| .$$

(ii) It follows from (i) that for $a \geq a_0$ the sign of the monomial $\mathrm{coeff}(f, \mathbf{p}_1) \cdot a^{\mathbf{n}\mathbf{p}_1}$ determines the sign of $f(a^{\mathbf{n}})$. Since $a > 0$, we obtain

$$\mathrm{sign}(f(a^{\mathbf{n}})) = \mathrm{sign}(\mathrm{coeff}(f, \mathbf{p}_1) \cdot a^{\mathbf{n}\mathbf{p}_1}) = \mathrm{sign}(f, \mathbf{p}_1). \quad \square$$

After these preparations we can state our first subalgorithm as Algorithm 1.

function `find-positive`(f)
  data : $f \in \mathbb{Z}[x_1, \dots, x_d]$
  result: $\mathbf{p} \in (\mathbb{Q}^+)^d$ or `"failed"`
1 $B^+ := B^+(f)$
2 $B^- := B^-(f)$
3 $h :=$ `"infeasible"`
4 **while** $h =$ `"infeasible"` *and* $B^+ \neq [\,]$ **do**
5   $h :=$ `lpsolve`$(B^+ \circ B^- \circ (\mathbf{0}, -1)^*)$
6   delete the first row from B^+
7 **if** $h =$ `"infeasible"` **then**
8   **return** `"failed"`
9 $(\mathbf{n}, c) := h$
10 $t := 2$
11 **while** $f(t^{\mathbf{n}}) \leq 0$ **do**
12   $t := 2t$
13 **return** $t^{\mathbf{n}}$

function `lpsolve`(B)
  data : a matrix B with $d+1$ columns
  result: $(\mathbf{n}, c) \in \mathbb{Z}^d \times \mathbb{Q}$ or `"infeasible"`
14 $\Pi :=$ LP problem given by $N^* B$ and $-\mathbf{1}$
15 $h :=$ a solution $(\mathbf{n}, c) \in \mathbb{Q}^{d+1}$ of Π or `"infeasible"`
16 **if** $h =$ `"infeasible"` **then**
17   **return** `"infeasible"`
18 $m :=$ principal denominator of the coordinates of $\mathbf{n}$
19 $\mathbf{n} := m \cdot \mathbf{n}$
20 $c := mc + m - 1$
21 **return** $(\mathbf{n}, c)$

Algorithm 1: Functions `find-positive` and `lpsolve`

Theorem 5 (Correctness of `find-positive`) *Consider $f \in \mathbb{Z}[\mathbf{x}]$. Then the following hold:*

(i) The function `find-positive` terminates.

(ii) The function `find-positive` returns either `"failed"` or $\mathbf{p} \in (\mathbb{Q}^+)^d$ with $f(\mathbf{p}) > 0$.

PROOF. (i) The termination of `lpsolve` follows from the existence of terminating algorithms for linear programming in line 15, including the Simplex algorithm [5], the ellipsoid method [20], and the interior point method [18]. For the function `find-positive` itself, the number of iterations of the while-loop in line 3 is bounded by the number of rows of B^+, which is in turn bounded by the finite cardinality of $\mathrm{supp}(f)$. The termination of the while-loop in line 11 will be discussed with the correctness in (ii).

(ii) To start with, the subroutine `lpsolve` solves the LP problem Π defined in line 14 and, in the feasible case, $(\mathbf{n}, c)$ in line 15 is a feasible point in $\mathbb{Q}^{d+1}$. The return value $(\mathbf{n}, c) \in \mathbb{Z}^d \times \mathbb{Q}$ in line 21 is a feasible point for Π as well. Its construction in lines 18–20 follows the proof step from (ii) to (iii) in Lemma 3.

Next, the while-loop in line 3 has the following loop invariants. Consider $f_{(n)} = f - \sum_{i=1}^{n-1} \mathrm{coeff}(f, \mathbf{p}_i)\mathbf{x}^{\mathbf{p}_i}$ before the n-th iteration:

(I_1) $\mathrm{newton}(f_{(n)}) = \mathrm{newton}(f)$,

(I_2) $B(f_{(n)}) = B^+_{(n)} \circ B^- \circ (\mathbf{0}, -1)^*$.

Invariant (I_2) is easy to see. Consider (I_1). For $n = 1$ this is trivial. Before the $n+1$-st iteration we know that $h =$ `"infeasible"`, which means that the LP problem given by

$$N^* \cdot ((\mathbf{p}_n) \circ B^+_{(n+1)} \circ B^- \circ (\mathbf{0}, -1)^*) \quad \text{and} \quad -\mathbf{1}$$

was infeasible at the n-th iteration. By Lemma 2 it follows that $\mathbf{p}_n \notin \mathrm{newton}(f_{(n)})$. Using Lemma 1 and the induction hypothesis we conclude $\mathrm{newton}(f_{(n+1)}) = \mathrm{newton}(f_{(n)} - \mathrm{coeff}(f, \mathbf{p}_n)\mathbf{x}^{\mathbf{p}_n}) = \mathrm{newton}(f_{(n)}) = \mathrm{newton}(f)$.

The function `find-positive` has two possible exit points at lines 8 and 13 corresponding to its two possible return values. Assume we are in line 13. We have to show that $t^{\mathbf{n}} \in (\mathbb{Q}^+)^d$ with $f(t^{\mathbf{n}}) > 0$. The while-loop in line 3 has terminated after n iterations, and the if-condition in line 7 is false. In line 9 we know by (I_1), (I_2), and Lemma 2 that the feasible regions for $N^* \cdot (B^+ \circ B^- \circ (\mathbf{0}, -1)^*) \cdot \mathbf{v} \leq -\mathbf{1}$ and $N^* \cdot B(f) \cdot \mathbf{v} \leq -\mathbf{1}$ are identical. This allows us to use $B^+ \circ B^- \circ (\mathbf{0}, -1)^*$ instead of $B(f)$ for applying Lemma 4 to the original f, and our $\mathbf{n} \in \mathbb{Z}^d$ has the property described there. In line 11, at the beginning of the k-th iteration of the while-loop we have $t = 2^k$. By Lemma 4 we know that we will eventually have $t \geq a_0$ and thus $\mathrm{sign}(f(t^{\mathbf{n}})) = \mathrm{sign}(f, \mathbf{p}_n) > 0$. $\square$

2.2 Finding a Zero

We have discussed how to heuristically find $\mathbf{p} \in (\mathbb{Q}^+)^d$ such that $f(\mathbf{p}) > 0$ for our given $f \in \mathbb{Z}[\mathbf{x}]$. On that basis Algorithm 2 computes $\mathbf{z} \in (\bar{\mathbb{Q}}^+)^d$ such that $f(\mathbf{z}) = 0$, where $\bar{\mathbb{Q}}$ denotes the algebraic closure of $\mathbb{Q}$.

function find-zero(f)
data : $f \in \mathbb{Z}[x_1, \dots, x_d]$
result: $\mathbf{z} \in (\mathbb{Q}^+)^d$ or "failed"

1 $y := f(\mathbf{1})$
2 **if** $y = 0$ **then**
3 **return 1**
4 **if** $y > 0$ **then**
5 $f := -f$
6 $\mathbf{p}$:= find-positive(f)
7 **if** $\mathbf{q}$ = "failed" **then**
8 **return** "failed"
9 $\mathbf{z}$:= construct-zero(f, $\mathbf{p}$, $\mathbf{1}$)
10 **return z**

function construct-zero(f, $\mathbf{p}$, $\mathbf{q}$)
data : $f \in \mathbb{Z}[x_1, \dots, x_d]$, $\mathbf{p}, \mathbf{q} \in \mathbb{Q}^d$
result: $\mathbf{z} \in \mathbb{Q}^d$ or "failed"

11 $\mathbf{b} := \mathbf{p} + y \cdot (\mathbf{q} - \mathbf{p})$, where y is a new variable
12 $g := f(\mathbf{b})$
13 isolate $r \in]0, 1[$ with $g(r) = 0$
14 $\mathbf{z} := \mathbf{b}(r)$
15 **return z**

Algorithm 2: Functions find-zero and construct-zero

Lemma 6 (Correctness of construct-zero) Consider $f \in \mathbb{Z}[\mathbf{x}]$, and let $\mathbf{p}, \mathbf{q} \in \mathbb{Q}^d$ such that $f(\mathbf{p})f(\mathbf{q}) < 0$. Then the following hold:

(i) The function construct-zero terminates.

(ii) The function construct-zero returns either "failed" or $\mathbf{z} \in \bar{\mathbb{Q}}^d$ with $f(\mathbf{z}) = 0$. If $\mathbf{p}, \mathbf{q} \in (\mathbb{Q}^+)^d$, then $\mathbf{z} \in (\bar{\mathbb{Q}}^+)^d$.

PROOF. (i) The termination of construct-zero follows from the existence of terminating algorithms for univariate real root isolation including Sturm sequences [28] and more efficient algorithms [4, 1] based on Vincent's Theorem [33].

(ii) Since f is continuous and $f(\mathbf{p})f(\mathbf{q}) < 0$, the intermediate value theorem guarantees the existence of $\mathbf{z} \in \overline{\mathbf{pq}}$ with $f(\mathbf{z}) = 0$. Formally, $\mathbf{z} \in \bar{\mathbb{Q}}^d$ is a solution for $\mathbf{x}$ of the following nonlinear system with indeterminates $x_1, \dots, x_d, y$:

$$f = 0 \tag{3}$$

$$x_1 = p_1 + y \cdot (q_1 - p_1) \tag{4}$$

$$\vdots$$

$$x_d = p_d + y \cdot (q_d - p_d) \tag{5}$$

$$y > 0 \tag{6}$$

$$y < 1. \tag{7}$$

In line 11, $\mathbf{b}$ is assigned the vector of the right hand sides of the d equations (4)–(5). In line 12, these are plugged into the left hand side of equation (3) yielding a nonlinear univariate polynomial equation in y. Using any of the methods mentioned in (i), we obtain in line 13 a solution $r \in \bar{\mathbb{Q}}$ for y of that equation subject to the constraints (6)–(7). That solution r is a real algebraic number in some suitable representation [24]. In line 14 we substitute r back into the equations (4)–(5) to finally obtain $\mathbf{x} = \mathbf{z} \in \bar{\mathbb{Q}}$, also as a real algebraic number.

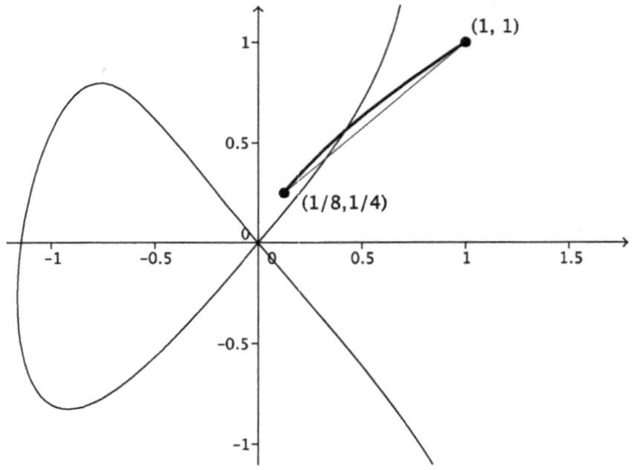

Figure 1: The variety of $f = -2x_1^5 + x_1^2x_2 - 3x_1^2 - x_2^3 + 2x_2^2$ and the segment given by $t \in [0, 2]$ of the moment curve (t^{-3}, t^{-2}) corresponding to the normal vector $(-3, -2)$ of the separating hyperplane in Figure 2.

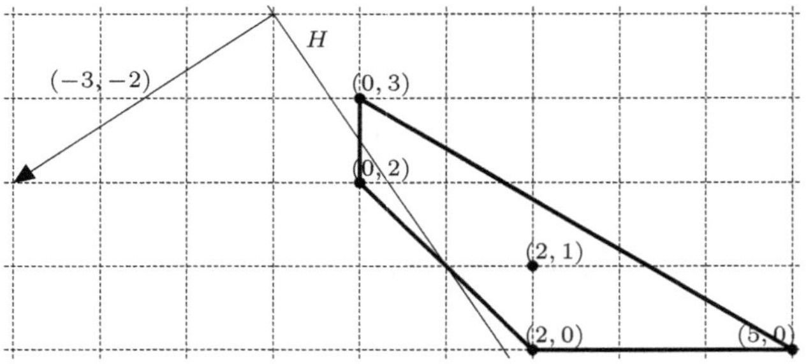

Figure 2: A subtropical view on the polynomial $f = -2x_1^5 + x_1^2x_2 - 3x_1^2 - x_2^3 + 2x_2^2$ from Figure 1. We see a hyperplane separating $(0, 2) \in \text{newton}(f)$ from $\text{supp}(f) \setminus \{(0, 2)\}$ together with its normal vector $\mathbf{n} = (-3, -2)$.

Since $\mathbf{z} \in \overline{\mathbf{pq}}$, it follows from $\mathbf{p}, \mathbf{q} \in (\mathbb{Q}^+)^d$ that also $\mathbf{z} \in (\mathbb{Q}^+)^d$. □

On the basis of Lemma 6 the following theorem is straightforward.

Theorem 7 (Correctness of find-zero) *Let $f \in \mathbb{Z}[\mathbf{x}]$. Then the function* find-zero *terminates and returns either* "failed" *or $\mathbf{z} \in (\bar{\mathbb{Q}}^+)^d$ with $f(\mathbf{z}) = 0$.* □

When one is interested only in the *existence* of a zero of f, then one can, in the positive case, obviously skip construct-zero and exit from find-zero after line 8. Notice that, in addition, one can then also exit early from find-positive after line 8 in Algorithm 1.

2.3 An Illustrating Example

Consider $f = -2x_1^5 + x_1^2x_2 - 3x_1^2 - x_2^3 + 2x_2^2 \in \mathbb{Z}[x_1, x_2]$. We apply find-zero to find a point on the variety of f. Figure 1 pictures the variety. We obtain $f(1, 1) = -3 < 0$, and apply find-positive to f.

Figure 2 pictures the support of f and indicates the Newton polytope. We split into $\text{supp}^+(f) = \{(2, 1), (0, 2)\}$,

$\text{supp}^-(f) = \{(2,0),(5,0),(0,3)\}$, and $\text{supp}^0(f) = \emptyset$, and we construct

$$B^+ = \begin{bmatrix} 2 & 1 & -1 \\ 0 & 2 & -1 \end{bmatrix}, \quad B^- = \begin{bmatrix} 2 & 0 & -1 \\ 5 & 0 & -1 \\ 0 & 3 & -1 \end{bmatrix}.$$

Our first LP problem

$$\begin{bmatrix} -2 & -1 & 1 \\ 0 & 2 & -1 \\ 2 & 0 & -1 \\ 5 & 0 & -1 \\ 0 & 3 & -1 \end{bmatrix} \cdot (\mathbf{n}, c)^T \le \begin{bmatrix} -1 \\ -1 \\ -1 \\ -1 \\ -1 \end{bmatrix}$$

is infeasible, which confirms the observation in Figure 2 that $(2,1) \notin \text{newton}(f)$. Our next LP problem

$$\begin{bmatrix} 0 & -2 & 1 \\ 2 & 0 & -1 \\ 5 & 0 & -1 \\ 0 & 3 & -1 \end{bmatrix} \cdot (\mathbf{n}, c)^T \le \begin{bmatrix} -1 \\ -1 \\ -1 \\ -1 \end{bmatrix}$$

is feasible with $\mathbf{n} = (-3,-2)$ and $c = 5$. Figure 2 shows the corresponding hyperplane H given by $-3x_1 - 2x_2 + 5 = 0$. It strictly separates $(0,2) \in \text{newton}(f)$ from $\text{supp}(f) \setminus \{(0,2)\}$, and its normal vector $\mathbf{n} = (-3,-2)$ is oriented towards $(0,2)$. We now know that $f(t^{-3}, t^{-2}) > 0$ for sufficiently large positive t. In fact, already

$$f(2^{-3}, 2^{-2}) = f\left(\tfrac{1}{8}, \tfrac{1}{4}\right) = \tfrac{1087}{16384}.$$

The relevant part of the moment curve (t^{-3}, t^{-2}) for $t \in [1,2]$ is pictured in Figure 1. Since both coordinates of $\mathbf{n}$ happen to be negative, the curve will for $t \to \infty$ not extend to infinity but converge to the origin. In particular, the curve will not leave the sign invariant region containing $\left(\frac{1}{8}, \frac{1}{4}\right)$.

Finally, we call `construct-zero` with $\left(\frac{1}{8}, \frac{1}{4}\right)$ and $(1,1)$ to solve the system

$$\begin{aligned} -2x_1^5 + x_1^2 x_2 - 3x_1^2 - x_2^3 + 2x_2^2 &= 0 \\ x_1 &= \tfrac{1}{8} + y \cdot \left(1 - \tfrac{1}{8}\right) \\ x_2 &= \tfrac{1}{4} + y \cdot \left(1 - \tfrac{1}{4}\right) \\ y &> 0 \\ y &< 1. \end{aligned}$$

Dropping a positive integer denominator, we obtain the univariate polynomial

$$\bar{g} = -16807y^5 - 12005y^4 - 934y^3 - 20778y^2 + 285y + 1087$$

and an isolating interval $y \in \,]0.2, 0.3[$. Substitution of the real algebraic number $\langle \bar{g},]0.2, 0.3[\rangle$ into the equations for x_1 and x_2 yields an exact solution

$$\begin{aligned} x_1 &= \langle 686x^5 - 78x^3 + 584x^2 - 150x - 13,]0.32, 0.33[\rangle, \\ x_2 &= \langle 16807x^5 - 12005x^4 + \\ &\qquad 2026x^3 + 9122x^2 - 4609x + 323,]0.42, 0.43[\rangle, \end{aligned}$$

where the intervals can, of course, be refined to arbitrary precision. Geometrically, our solving has intersected the variety with the line segment connecting the end points of our moment curve segment, which is also indicated in Figure 1.

2.4 Why Strictly Positive Coordinates?

In the present section, we have focused on roots with strictly positive coordinates. This not only slightly simplifies the presentation. In fact, it is an important feature of our algorithm to be able to perform such a directed search.

To start with, the research presented here was originally motivated by questions on the stability of chemical and biological reaction networks, where the variables of the models typically are strictly positive. Our practical computations in Section 5 are taken from those areas. For details on the theoretical background we refer the reader to [3, 30, 31, 35, 10, 8].

Furthermore, the concept of positive feasible points is well-known from linear programming. Techniques used there can be straightforwardly transfered to our situation: Consider $f \in \mathbb{Z}[x_1, \dots, x_d]$. For finding zeros $(z_1, \dots, z_d)$ with $\text{sign}(z_i) = s_i \in \{-1, 1\}$ consider $f(s_1 x_1, \dots, s_d x_d)$, for $z_1 \in \,]\alpha, \infty[$ consider $f(x_1 + \alpha, x_2, \dots, x_d)$, for $z_1 \in \,]-\infty, \beta[$ consider $f(-x_1 - \beta, x_2, \dots, x_d)$, and for x_1 unbounded consider $f(x_1 - x_1', x_2, \dots, x_d)$ introducing a new variable x_1'.

3. FINDING ARBITRARY ROOTS

3.1 Using a Transformation

Consider $f \in \mathbb{Z}[x_1, \dots, x_d]$. At the end of the previous section we have addressed a technique for turning a real feasibility test based on positive variables into a general one. Using the observation that every real number is a difference of two positive real numbers, on introduces additional variables x_1', $\dots$, x_d' and transforms f into $f(x_1 - x_1', \dots, x_d - x_d')$. That transformation is ubiquitous in linear programming, if not explicitly then implicitly within the solvers.

From an efficiency point of view our procedure is clearly dominated by the LP solving steps, where we have $d+1$ variables and $|\text{supp}(f)|$ many constraints. Thinking in terms of state-of-the-art LP solvers [14, 23] and the Simplex method with the option of dualization [2, 21], the crucial complexity parameter is $\min\{d, |\text{supp}(f)|\}$. With our considered transformation the cardinality of the support increases exponentially in d in the worst case, but the number of variables only doubles from d to $2d$.

Recall that our incomplete method relies on finding some $\mathbf{p} \in \text{newton}(f)$ with $\text{coeff}(f, \mathbf{p}) > 0$. We would like to point out that, doubling the dimension d with the transformation, the ratio $|\text{newton}(f)| \,/\, |\text{supp}(f)|$ will in general increase for geometric reasons [6]. Furthermore the exponential increase of $|\text{supp}(f)|$ increases the absolute number of candidates for a suitable $\mathbf{p}$. On the other hand, the transformation does not add points to $\text{supp}(f)$ but exchanges it entirely. It would require either comprehensive empirical studies or a thorough average-case analysis to make a precise statement about the quality of the transformation in terms of incompleteness.

3.2 A Genuine Generalization

We are now going to describe a generalization of the function `find-positive` in Algorithm 1, which searches for a suitable $\mathbf{p}$ not only in $\text{supp}^+(f)$ but also in a subset of $\text{supp}^-(f)$. Recall that in case of success, `find-positive` identifies the first row of B^+ as corresponding to the exponent vector of a monomial with positive coefficient that dominates f in the sense of Lemma 4. Then it constructs a point $\mathbf{p}$ with large suitably balanced positive coordinates. The key idea for our generalization is the following: If the

function `find-positive-general`(f)
data : $f \in \mathbb{Z}[x_1, \dots, x_d]$
result: $\mathbf{p} \in \mathbb{Q}^d$ or `"failed"`

1 $B := B^+(f) \circ B^{w-}(f)$
2 $B^{s-} := B^{s-}(f)$
3 $\mu := \infty$
4 $h :=$ `"infeasible"`
5 **while** $h =$ `"infeasible"` *and* $B \neq [\,]$ **do**
6   **if** *the first row of* B *is in* $B^{w-}(f)$ **then**
7         $\mu := \mathrm{moc}(B)$
8     $h :=$ `lpsolve`$(B^+ \circ B \circ (\mathbf{0}, -1)^*)$
9   delete the first row from B
10 **if** $h =$ `"infeasible"` **then**
11   **return** `"failed"`
12 $(n_1, \dots, n_d, c) := h$
13 $t := 2$
14 $(t_1 \dots, t_d) := (t^{n_1}, \dots, t^{n_d})$
15 **if** $\mu < \infty$ **then**
16     $t_\mu := -t_\mu$
17 **while** $f(t_1, \dots, t_d) \leq 0$ **do**
18     $t := 2t$
19     $(t_1 \dots, t_d) := (t^{n_1}, \dots, t^{n_d})$
20   **if** $\mu < \infty$ **then**
21         $t_\mu := -t_\mu$
22 **return** $(t_1, \dots, t_d)$

Algorithm 3: Function `find-positive-general`

coefficient of an otherwise suitable monomial is negative but there is at least one odd exponent in the exponent vector, then we can correct the "wrong" sign of the coefficient by replacing the respective coordinate in the constructed point $\mathbf{p}$ with its additive inverse.

For $\mathbf{p} = (p_1, \dots, p_d) \in \mathrm{supp}(f)$ define the *minimal odd coordinate*

$$\mathrm{moc}(\mathbf{p}) = \min\{\, i \in \{1, \dots, d\} \mid 2 \nmid p_i \},$$

where $\min \emptyset = \infty$. We use the minimal odd coordinate to partition $\mathrm{supp}^-(f) = \mathrm{supp}^{w-}(f) \,\dot\cup\, \mathrm{supp}^{s-}$, where

$$\begin{aligned} \mathrm{supp}^{w-}(f) &= \{\mathbf{p} \in \mathrm{supp}^- \mid \mathrm{moc}(\mathbf{p}) < \infty \}, \\ \mathrm{supp}^{s-}(f) &= \{\mathbf{p} \in \mathrm{supp}^- \mid \mathrm{moc}(\mathbf{p}) = \infty \}. \end{aligned}$$

The elements of $\mathrm{supp}^{w-}(f)$ are called *weakly negative*. They have at least one odd coordinate. The elements of $\mathrm{supp}^{s-}(f)$ are called *strongly negative*. They have exclusively even coordinates. We furthermore define $B^{w-}(f)$ and $B^{s-}(f)$ corresponding to $\mathrm{supp}^{w-}(f)$ and $\mathrm{supp}^{s-}(f)$, respectively, and we obtain

$$B(f) = B^+(f) \circ B^{w-}(f) \circ B^{s-}(f) \circ (\mathbf{0}, -1)^*.$$

Consider a matrix B obtained from $B(f)$ by deleting rows. Then we define $\mathrm{moc}(B) = \mathrm{moc}(B_{11}, \dots, B_{1d})$, i.e., the minimal odd coordinate of $\mathbf{p} \in \mathrm{supp}(f)$ corresponding to the first row of B.

After these preparations we can state our function `find-positive-general` in Algorithm 3. A corresponding function `find-zero-general` is obtained by replacing in `find-zero` in Algorithm 2 the call to `find-positive` with a call to `find-positive-general`. Everything else remains unchanged.

For showing the correctness of `find-positive-general` we are going to use the following variant of Lemma 4:

Lemma 8 Let $f \in \mathbb{Z}[\mathbf{x}] \setminus \mathbb{Z}$. Let $(\mathbf{n}, c) \in \mathbb{R}^{d+1}$ such that $N^* \cdot B(f) \cdot (\mathbf{n}, c)^T \leq -\mathbf{1}$, and let $\mu = \mathrm{moc}(B(f)) < \infty$. Then there is $a_0 \in \mathbb{N}$ such that for all $a \in \mathbb{N}$ with $a \geq a_0$ the following holds: Define $\mathbf{t} = (t_1, \dots, t_d) \in \mathbb{N}^d$ with $t_j = a^{n_j}$ for $j \in \{1, \dots, d\} \setminus \{\mu\}$ and $a_\mu = -t^{n_\mu}$. Then

$$\mathrm{sign}\big(f(\mathbf{t})\big) = -\,\mathrm{sign}(f, \mathbf{p}_1).$$

PROOF. We have $t_j = a^{n_j} > 0$ for $j \in \{1, \dots, d\} \setminus \{\mu\}$, $t_\mu = -a^{n_\mu} < 0$, and $p_{1\mu}$ is odd by definition of the minimal odd coordinate. It follows that

$$0 < a^{\mathbf{n}\mathbf{p}_1} = -\mathbf{t}^{\mathbf{p}_1}. \qquad (8)$$

For $i \in \{2, \dots, s\}$ we have at least $|a^{\mathbf{n}\mathbf{p}_i}| = |\mathbf{t}^{\mathbf{p}_i}|$. This allows us to conclude from Lemma 4 (i) that

$$|\mathrm{coeff}(f, \mathbf{p}_1) \cdot \mathbf{t}^{\mathbf{p}_1}| > \left| \sum_{i=2}^{s} \mathrm{coeff}(f, \mathbf{p}_i) \cdot \mathbf{t}^{\mathbf{p}_i} \right|.$$

Hence $\mathrm{coeff}(f, \mathbf{p}_1) \cdot \mathbf{t}^{\mathbf{p}_1}$ determines the sign of $f(\mathbf{t})$. Using the inequality in (8) we obtain

$$\mathrm{sign}\big(f(\mathbf{t})\big) = \mathrm{sign}\big(\mathrm{coeff}(f, \mathbf{p}_1) \cdot \mathbf{t}^{\mathbf{p}_1}\big) = -\,\mathrm{sign}(f, \mathbf{p}_1). \quad \square$$

Theorem 9 (Correctness of `find-positive-general`) *Consider $f \in \mathbb{Z}[\mathbf{x}]$. Then the following hold:*

(i) If the function `find-positive` *in Algorithm 1 does not fail on f, then* `find-positive-general`(f) = `find-positive`(f).

(ii) The function `find-positive-general` *terminates.*

(iii) The function `find-positive-general` *returns either* `"failed"` *or $\mathbf{p} \in \mathbb{Q}^d$ with $f(\mathbf{p}) > 0$.*

PROOF. (i) The function `find-positive-general` operates on $B^+(f) \circ B^{w-}(f) \circ B^{s-}(f) \circ (\mathbf{0}, -1)^*$ while `find-positive` operates on $B^+(f) \circ B^- \circ (\mathbf{0}, -1)^*$ so that there is possibly a different order of rows lying below $B^+(f)$. However, when `find-positive` does not fail, then the same feasible solution is found in both functions before touching anything outside B^+, and in line 10 of `find-positive-general` we have exited the while-loop with $\mu = \infty$. It follows that the if-conditions in lines 15 and 20 of `find-positive-general` are always false, and the rest of the code after the while-loop is computationally equivalent to the corresponding part of `find-positive` except for an expanded notation.

Accordingly, a proof of parts (ii) and (iii) can be straightforwardly derived from the proof of (i) and (ii) of Theorem 5, respectively: If the function `find-positive` in Algorithm 1 does not fail on f, then there is nothing else to do. Otherwise we always reach lines 15 and 20 with $\mu < \infty$, replace t_μ with its additive inverse, and apply Lemma 8 instead of Lemma 4 (ii), where we know that that $\mathrm{sign}(f, \mathbf{p}_n) < 0$. $\square$

4. PRACTICAL ISSUES

In this section we would like to discuss issues and share experiences related to a practical implementation of our method.

One major benefit of our approach is the reduction of an algebraic problem to linear programming (LP). Linear programming is a field with more than 50 years of active algorithmic research, strongly driven by practical applicability and aiming at robust implementations. Our own implementation combines the the Codemist Standard Lisp (CSL)-based version of the computer algebra system Reduce [17, 25, 26] with the Gurobi Optimizer [14]. Technically, CSL provides a foreign function interface that allows us to dynamically load the Gurobi C-library at runtime and call its functions from within symbolic mode Reduce functions. Gurobi uses the Simplex algorithm. So far we have got no experience with the use of implementations of polynomial methods for LP, like the interior point method [18].

Gurobi uses floating point arithmetic with a limited precision. We want to adress some issues related to this, which we consider of general inteterst, because that floating point approach is typical for Simplex-based LP software.

On the one hand, LP solvers are quite good at controlling numerical stability. With our comprehensive computations we have never encountered any problems with false results due to LP rounding errors. On the other hand, in line 15 of Algorithm 1 we obtain $n_1, \dots, n_d$, c as floats with small rounding errors. These rounding errors do not affect correctness but cause a subtle problem: Converting $n_1, \dots, n_d$ into fractions, the GCD of their denominators will typically be 1 so that the principal denominator m computed in line 18 becomes the very large product of those denominators. Consequently, in line 19 we obtain our final $\mathbf{n}$ with very large relatively prime integer coordinates. This, in turn, renders infeasible the exponentiation of increasing powers of 2 with those integer coordinates and substitution of the result into f in line 11 of Algorithm 1 or in lines 14, 17, and 19 of Algorithm 3. There are two principle ways out, which we call the *pure LP approach* and the *MIP approach*, respectively. Of course, the single design decisions made with these approaches can be recombined to yield further, mixed, approaches.

The Pure LP Approach.

The pure LP approach tries to get along with the delivered floats. Specifically, lines 18–20 in Algorithm 1 are skipped, and a floating point vector is returned. The while-loops in line 11 of Algorithm 1 and line 17 of Algorithm 3 remain correct with floating point exponents $\mathbf{n}$. Later, in lines 11–12 of Algorithm 2 it is important to convert to rationals. In particular the substitution of floats into a high-degree polynomial f in line 12 could cause considerable numerical instabilities. Subsequent root isolation to floating point precision in line 13 and back-substitution of the obtained floats in line 14 worked well with all our computations.

The MIP Approach.

MIP stands for *mixed integer (linear) programming.* Our Lemma 3 allows us to declare $n_1, \dots, n_d$ as integers to the LP solver right away, while c remains real. As MIP is NP-hard [19], the MIP approach is considerably harder than the pure LP approach in terms of theoretical complexity. In practice there are several advanced algorithms for Simplex-based MIP solving, which rely in some way on considering an *LP relaxation*, i.e., considering integer variables as real variables, and, in the feasible case, trying to construct a mixed real integer feasible point on the basis of an LP solution. The Gurobi solver specifically uses advanced *cutting plane* [13] methods for that construction. For the largest

```
13  (y_1, ..., y_d) = (y^{n_1}, ..., y^{n_d}) for a new variable y
14  if μ < ∞ then
15  └ y_μ = −y_μ
16  f_1 := f(y_1, ..., y_d) ∈ Z(y)
17  t := 2
18  while f_1(t) ≤ 0 do
19  └ t := 2t
20  return (y_1(t), ..., y_d(t))
```

Algorithm 4: Code to replace lines 13–22 in Algorithm 3

problems discussed with our practical computations in Section 5 below, we have observed factor of about 3 for MILP solving compared to LP solving.

There is an interesting optimization with the MIP approach: Since in our situation MIP feasibility is equivalent to LP feasibility by Lemma 3, one can generally first check the latter in lines 14–15 of Algorithm 1, and in the feasible case rerun for the corresponding MIP problem. Using this strategy, there is always at most one MIP solving step per root finding problem. Furthermore, one runs MIP solving only on feasible instances. This excludes the really problematic cases, which are LP feasible but not MIP feasible problems.

In rare cases one obtains integer solutions which are so large that they render exponentiation and substitution in line 11 of Algorithm 1 or in lines 14, 17, and 19 of Algorithm 3 infeasible. One can impose a suitable bound on the absolute values of the solutions, and in case of exceeding that bound treat the problem as infeasible, and proceed to the next candidate.

Another noteworthy optimization is the symbolic precomputation of a univariate rational function for the while-loop in line 17 of Algorithm 3. See Algorithm 4 for details. A corresponding simpler variant, of course, works also for lines 10–12 in Algorithm 1.

For root isolation in line 13 of Algorithm 2 we use the *Vincent–Collins–Akritas* method [4]. We obtain a real algebraic number encoded by a univariate defining polynomial and an open isolating interval, which is back-substituted in line 14, yielding a vector of such real algebraic numbers as the final solution $\mathbf{z}$.

5. SOME PRACTICAL COMPUTATIONS

We consider input polynomials originating from 4 different chemical and biological models. This yields 929 instances altogether. For all of these instances we are checking for zeros with strictly positive coordinates. It turns out that for 640 of the instances we find $B^+ = [\ ]$ in line 1 of Algorithm 1, which tells us that the corresponding polynomial is positive definite (on the interior of the first hyperoctant). Running our method on the 289 remaining instances, it fails in only 7.3 percent of the cases. The following table shows detailed information for the single models. It also shows size (number of monomials), dimension (number of variables), and the largest degree of an occurring variable for the respective largest instance. It furthermore shows the maximal computation time for a single instance and the sum of computation times.[1] All computations have been carried out on

[1]All input and log files are available at **http://research-data.redlog.eu/ISSAC2015/**.

a 2.8 GHz Xeon E5-4640 with the MIP approach, yielding exact algebraic number solutions:

	METH	OMBO	MBO	MAPK	Total
instances	7	496	405	21	**929**
definite	3	338	283	16	**640**
remaining	4	158	122	5	**289**
found zero	4	144	107	5	**260**
failed	0	14	15	0	**29**
failed (%)	0	8.9	12.3	0	**10.0**
size max	347	9787	9706	863438	**863438**
dim max	7	7	7	10	**10**
deg max	6	10	9	12	**12**
max time (s)	0.16	4.68	10.00	15.87	**15.87**
total time (s)	0.21	199.91	162.88	15.92	**379.92**

Notice that for our particular application the detection of definiteness by our implementation establishes a perfect result. From that point of view, one could argue that our method fails in only 3 percent of the cases.

Acknowledgments

We would like to thank D. Grigoriev, H. Errami, W. Hagemann, M. Košta, and A. Weber for valuable discussions. A. Norman realized a robust foreign function interface for CSL Reduce. We are also grateful to Gurobi Optimization Inc. and to the GeoGebra Institute for making their excellent software free for academic purposes. This research was supported in part by the German Transregional Collaborative Research Center SFB/TR 14 AVACS and by the ANR/DFG project STU 483/2-1 SMArT.

6. REFERENCES

[1] A. G. Akritas and A. W. Strzebonski. A comparative study of two real root isolation methods. *Nonlinear Analysis: Modelling and Control*, 10(4):297–304, 2005.

[2] E. M. L. Beale. An alternative method for linear programming. *Mathematical Proceedings of the Cambridge Philosophical Society*, 50:513–523, 1954.

[3] F. Boulier, M. Lefranc, F. Lemaire, P.-E. Morant, and A. Ürgüplü. On proving the absence of oscillations in models of genetic circuits. In H. Anai, K. Horimoto, and T. Kutsia, editors, *Proceedings of Algebraic Biology 2007*, volume 4545 of *LNCS*, pages 66–80. Springer, 2007.

[4] G. E. Collins and A. G. Akritas. Polynomial real root isolation using Descarte's rule of signs. In *Proceedings of the SYMSAC '76*, pages 272–275, ACM Press, 1976.

[5] G. B. Dantzig. Linear programming and extensions. Princeton University Press, Princeton, NJ, 1963.

[6] R. A. Dwyer. On the convex hull of random points in a polytope. *Journal of Applied Probability*, 25(4):688–699, 1988.

[7] M. El Kahoui and A. Weber. Deciding Hopf bifurcations by quantifier elimination in a software-component architecture. *J. Symb. Comput.*, 30(2):161–179, 2000.

[8] H. Errami, M. Eiswirth, D. Grigoriev, W. M. Seiler, T. Sturm, and A. Weber. Efficient methods to compute Hopf bifurcations in chemical reaction networks using reaction coordinates. In *Proceedings of the CASC 2013*, volume 8136 of *LNCS*, pages 88–99. Springer, 2013.

[9] H. Errami, M. Eiswirth, D. Grigoriev, W. M. Seiler, T. Sturm, and A. Weber. Detection of Hopf bifurcations in chemical reaction networks using convex coordinates. *Journal of Computational Physics*, 291:279–302, 2015.

[10] H. Errami, W. M. Seiler, T. Sturm, and A. Weber. On Muldowney's criteria for polynomial vector fields with constraints. In *Proceedings of the CASC 2011*, volume 6885 of *LNCS*, pages 135–143. Springer, 2011.

[11] K. Gatermann, M. Eiswirth, and A. Sensse. Toric ideals and graph theory to analyze Hopf bifurcations in mass action systems. *J. Symb. Comput.*, 40:1361–1382, 2005.

[12] K. Gatermann and S. Hosten. Computational algebra for bifurcation theory. *J. Symb. Comput.*, 40(4–5):1180–1207, 2005.

[13] R. Gomory. An algorithm for integer solutions to linear programs. In R. L. Graves and P. Wolfe, editors, *Recent Advances in Mathematical Programming*, pages 269–302. McGraw-Hill, 1963.

[14] Gurobi Optimization, Inc. *Gurobi Optimizer Reference Manual*, 2014.

[15] E. Hairer, S. P. Norsett, and G. Wanner. *Solving Ordinary Differential Equations I. Nonstiff Problems*, volume 8 of *Series in Computational Mathematics*. Springer, 1993.

[16] J. K. Hale and H. Kocak. *Dynamics and Bifurcations*, volume 3 of *Texts in Applied Mathematics*. Springer, 1991.

[17] A. C. Hearn and R. Schöpf. *Reduce User's Manual, Free Version*, Oct. 2014.

[18] N. Karmakar. A new polynomial-time algorithm for linear programming. *Combinatorica*, 4(4):373–395, 1984.

[19] R. M. Karp. Reducibility among combinatorial problems. In R. E. Miller, J. W. Thatcher, and J. D. Bohlinger, editors, *Complexity of Computer Computations*, The IBM Research Symposia Series, pages 85–103. Springer, 1972.

[20] L. G. Khakhiyan. A polynomial algorithm in linear programming. *Soviet Mathematics Doklady*, 20(1):191–194, 1979.

[21] C. E. Lemke. The dual method of solving the linear programming problem. In *Naval Research Logistics Quarterly*, volume 1, pages 36–47. 1954.

[22] R. Loos and V. Weispfenning. Applying linear quantifier elimination. *The Computer Journal*, 36(5):450–462, 1993.

[23] A. Makhorin. *GNU Linear Programming Kit*. Department for Applied Informatics, Moscow Aviation Institute, Moscow, Russia, Aug. 2014.

[24] B. Mishra. *Algorithmic Algebra*. Texts and Monographs in Computer Science. Springer, New York, 1993.

[25] A. C. Norman. Codemist Standard Lisp (CSL) technical overview and details, July 1991.

[26] A. C. Norman. Thirty years of Lisp support for REDUCE. In *Proceedings of the A3L 2005*. BOD, Norderstedt, Germany, 2005.

[27] H. Peyrl and P. A. Parrilo. Computing sum of squares decompositions with rational coefficients. *Theoretical Computer Science*, 409(2):269–281, 2008.

[28] J. C. F. Sturm. Mémoire sur la résolution des équations numériques. In *Mémoires présentés par divers Savants étrangers à l'Académie royale des sciences, section Sc. math. phys.*, volume 6, pages 273–318, 1835.

[29] T. Sturm. *Real Quantifier Elimination in Geometry*. Doctoral dissertation, Universität Passau, Germany, 1999.

[30] T. Sturm and A. Weber. Investigating generic methods to solve Hopf bifurcation problems in algebraic biology. In K. Horimoto, editor, *Proceedings of Algebraic Biology 2008*, volume 5147 of *LNCS*, pages 200–215. Springer, 2008.

[31] T. Sturm, A. Weber, E. O. Abdel-Rahman, and M. El Kahoui. Investigating algebraic and logical algorithms to solve Hopf bifurcation problems in algebraic biology. *Mathematics in Computer Science*, 2(3):493–515, 2009.

[32] B. Sturmfels. *Solving Systems of Polynomial Equations*. AMS, Providence, RI, 2002.

[33] A. J. H. Vincent. Sur la résolution des équations numériques. *Journal de Mathématiques Pures et Appliquées*, 1:341–372, 1836.

[34] D. Wang and B. Xia. Stability analysis of biological systems with real solution classification. In *Proceedings of the ISSAC 2005*, pages 354–361. ACM Press, 2005.

[35] A. Weber, T. Sturm, and E. O. Abdel-Rahman. Algorithmic global criteria for excluding oscillations. *Bulletin of Mathematical Biology*, 73(4):899–916, 2011.

Matrix-F5 Algorithms and Tropical Gröbner Bases Computation

Tristan Vaccon
Université de Rennes 1
tristan.vaccon@univ-rennes1.fr

ABSTRACT

Let K be a field equipped with a valuation. Tropical varieties over K can be defined with a theory of Gröbner bases taking into account the valuation of K. Because of the use of the valuation, this theory is promising for stable computations over polynomial rings over a p-adic fields.

We design a strategy to compute such tropical Gröbner bases by adapting the Matrix-F5 algorithm. Two variants of the Matrix-F5 algorithm, depending on how the Macaulay matrices are built, are available to tropical computation with respective modifications. The former is more numerically stable while the latter is faster.

Our study is performed both over any exact field with valuation and some inexact fields like $\mathbb{Q}_p$ or $\mathbb{F}_q[[t]]$. In the latter case, we track the loss in precision, and show that the numerical stability can compare very favorably to the case of classical Gröbner bases when the valuation is non-trivial. Numerical examples are provided.

Categories and Subject Descriptors

I.1.2 [**Computing Methodologies**]: Symbolic and Algebraic Manipulations—*Algebraic Algorithms*

Keywords

Gröbner bases; tropical geometry; F5 algorithm; p-adic precision; p-adic algorithm

1. INTRODUCTION

Despite its young age, tropical geometry has revealed to be of significant value, with applications in algebraic geometry, combinatorics, computer science, and non-archimedean geometry (see [11], [5]).

Effective computation over tropical varieties make decisive usage of Gröbner bases, but before Chan and Maclagan's definition of tropical Gröbner bases taking into account the valuation in [3], [4], computations were only available over fields with trivial valuation where standard Gröbner bases

ISSAC'15, July 6–9, 2015, Bath, United Kingdom.
Copyright is held by the owner/author(s). Publication rights licensed to ACM.
ACM 978-1-4503-3435-8/15/07 ...$15.00.
DOI: http://dx.doi.org/10.1145/2755996.2756665

techniques applied. In this document, we show that following this definition, Matrix-F5 algorithms can be performed to compute tropical Gröbner bases.

Our motivations are twofold. Firstly, our result bears promising application for computation over fields with valuation that are not effective, such as $\mathbb{Q}_p$ or $\mathbb{Q}[[t]]$. Indeed, in [14], the author studies computation of Gröbner bases over such fields and proves that for a regular sequence and under some regularity assumption (whose genericity is at best conjectural) and with enough initial entry precision, approximate Gröbner bases can be computed. Thank to the study of Matrix-F5 algorithms, we prove that to compute a tropical Gröbner basis of the ideal generated by $F = (f_1, \ldots, f_s)$, F being regular and known with enough initial precision is sufficient. Hence, generically, approximate tropical Gröbner bases can be computed. Moreover, for a special choice of term order, the smallest loss in precision that can be obtained by linear algebra is attained: tropical Gröbner bases then provide a generically numerically stable alternative to Gröbner bases.

Secondly, Matrix-F5 algorithms allow an easy study of the complexity of the computation of tropical Gröbner bases and are a first step toward a tropical F5 algorithm.

Related works on tropical Gröbner bases: We refer to the book of Maclagan and Sturmfels [11] for an introduction to computational tropical algebraic geometry.

The computation of tropical varieties over $\mathbb{Q}$ with trivial valuation is available in the Gfan package by Anders Jensen (see [9]), by using standard Gröbner basis computation. Yet, for computation of tropical varieties over general fields, with non-trivial valuation, such techniques are not readily available. This is why Chan and Maclagan have developed in [4] a way to extend the theory of Gröbner bases to take into account the valuation and allow tropical computation. Their theory of tropical Gröbner bases is effective and allows, with a suitable division algorithm, a Buchberger algorithm.

Main results: Let K be a field equipped with a valuation val. Let $\geq$ be an order on the terms of $K[X_1, \ldots, X_n]$ as in Definition 2.3, defined with $w \in Im(val)^n$ and a monomial ordering $\geq_1$. Following [4], we define tropical D-Gröbner bases as for classical Gröbner bases.

Then, we provide with Algorithm 1 a tropical row-echelon form computation algorithm for Macaulay matrices. We show that the F5 criterion still holds in a tropical setting. We therefore define the tropical Matrix-F5 algorithm (Algorithm 2) as an adaptation of a *naïve* Matrix-F5 algorithm with the tropical row-echelon form computation. We then have the following result :

Proposition 1.1. *Let $(f_1, \dots, f_s) \in K[X_1, \dots, X_n]^s$ be a sequence of homogeneous polynomials. Then, the tropical Matrix-F5 algorithm computes a tropical D-Gröbner basis of $\langle f_1, \dots, f_s \rangle$. Time-complexity is in $O\left(s^2 D \binom{n+D-1}{D}^3\right)$ operations in K, as $D \to +\infty$.*[1] *If $(f_1, \dots, f_s)$ is regular, time-complexity is in $O\left(sD\binom{n+D-1}{D}^3\right)$.*

The Macaulay bound is also available. Furthermore, not only does the tropical Matrix-F5 algorithm computes tropical D-Gröbner bases, but it is compatible with finite-precision coefficients, under the assumption that the entry sequence is regular. Let us assume that $K = \mathbb{Q}_p$, $\mathbb{F}_q[\![t]\!]$ or $\mathbb{Q}[\![t]\!]$. Let $(f_1, \dots, f_s) \in K[X_1, \dots, X_n]^s$. We define a bound on the precision, $prec_{MF5trop}((f_1, \dots, f_s), D, \geq)$, and one on the loss in precision, $loss_{MF5trop}((f_1, \dots, f_s), D, \geq)$, which depend explicitly on the coefficients of the f_i's. Then we have the following proposition regarding to numerical stability of tropical Gröbner bases :

Proposition 1.2. *Let $F = (f_1, \dots, f_s) \in K[X_1, \dots, X_n]^s$ be a regular sequence of homogeneous polynomials.*

Let $(f'_1, \dots, f'_s)$ be some approximations of F, with precision l on their coefficients better than $prec_{MF5trop}(F, D, \geq)$. Then, with the tropical Matrix-F5 algorithm, one can compute an approximation $g'_1, \dots, g'_t$ of a Gröbner basis of $\langle F \rangle$, up to precision $l - loss_{MF5trop}(F, D, \geq)$.

This contrasts with the case of classical Gröbner bases, for a monomial order ω, over p-adics (or complete discrete valuation fields) considered in [14]. Indeed, the structure hypothesis **H2** which requires that the ideals$\langle f_1, \dots, f_i \rangle$ are weakly-ω is no longer necessary (see Subsection 4.6). It is only replaced by the (possibly stronger) assumption that the initial precision is better than $prec_{MF5trop}(F, D, \geq)$. In the special case of a weight $w = (0, \dots, 0)$, the loss in precision is the smallest linear algebra on the Macaulay matrices can provide, and numerical evidences show that it is in average rather low.

Finally, we show that a faster variant of Matrix-F5 algorithm, where one use the Macaulay matrices in degree d to build the Macaulay matrices in degree $d+1$, can be adapted to compute tropical Gröbner bases. We first provide a tropical LUP-form computation for Macaulay matrices that is compatible with signatures, and then what we call the tropical signature-based Matrix-F5 algorithm (algorithms 3 and 4). We prove the following result :

Proposition 1.3. *Let $(f_1, \dots, f_s) \in K[X_1, \dots, X_n]^s$ be a sequence of homogeneous polynomials. Then, the tropical signature-based Matrix-F5 algorithm computes a tropical D-Gröbner basis of $\langle f_1, \dots, f_s \rangle$.*

Time-complexity is then in $O\left(sD\binom{n+D-1}{D}^3\right)$ operations in K, as $D \to +\infty$ and $O\left(D\binom{n+D-1}{D}^3\right)$ when the input polynomials form a regular sequence.

Structure of the paper: Section 2 is devoted to provide a tropical setting and definitions for tropical Gröbner bases. In Section 3, we show that matrix algorithms can be performed to compute such bases. To that intent, after an introduction to matrix algorithms for Gröbner bases, we provide a row-reduction algorithm that will make a first *naïve* Matrix-F5 algorithm available. We then prove and analyze this tropical Matrix-F5 algorithm. In Section 4 we analyze the stability of this algorithm over inexact fields with valuations, such as $\mathbb{Q}_p$. Section 5 is devoted to numerical examples regarding the loss in precision in the computation of tropical Gröbner bases. In Section 6, we prove that the classical signature-based Matrix-F5 algorithm is available, along with an adapted tropical LUP algorithm for row-reduction of Macaulay matrices. Finally, Section 7 is a glance at some future possible developments for tropical Gröbner bases.

[1] One could also write $O\left(s^2\binom{n+D}{D}^3\right)$.

2. CONTEXT AND MOTIVATIONS

From now on, let K be a field equipped with a valuation $val : K^* \to \mathbb{R}$. Let R be the ring of integers of K, m its maximal ideal, k_K its residue field and let $\Gamma = Im(val)$. An example of such a field is $\mathbb{Q}_p$ with p-adic valuation. In that case, $R = \mathbb{Z}_p$, $m = p\mathbb{Z}_p$, $k_K = \mathbb{Z}/p\mathbb{Z}$ and $\Gamma = \mathbb{Z}$.

Let also $n \in \mathbb{Z}_{>0}$, $A = K[X_1, \dots, X_n]$, $B = R[X_1, \dots, X_n]$ and $C = k_K[X_1, \dots, X_n]$. We write $|f|$ for the degree of a homogeneous polynomial $f \in A$, and $A_d = K[X_1, \dots, X_n]_d$ for the K-vector space of degree d homogeneous polynomials.

2.1 Tropical varieties, tropical Gröbner bases

If I is an homogeneous ideal in A, and $V(I) \subset \mathbb{P}_K^{n-1}$ is the projective variety defined by I. Then the tropical variety defined by I, or the tropicalization of $V(I)$, is $Trop(I) = \overline{val\left(V(I) \cap (K^*)^n\right)}$ (closure in $\mathbb{R}^n$). $Trop(I)$ is a polyhedral complex and acts as a combinatorial shadow of $V(I)$: many properties of $V(I)$ can be recovered combinatorially from $Trop(I)$.

If $w \in \Gamma^n$, we define an order on the terms of $K[X_1, \dots, X_n]$.

Definition 2.1. If $a, b \in K$ and x^α, x^β are two monomials in A, $ax^\alpha \geq_w bx^\beta$ if $val(a) + w \cdot \alpha \leq val(b) + w \cdot \beta$. Naturally, it is possible that $ax^\alpha \neq bx^\beta$ and $val(a) + w \cdot \alpha = val(b) + w \cdot \beta$.

For any $f \in A$, we can define $LT_{\geq_w}(f)$, and then $LT_{\geq_w}(I)$, for $I \subset A$ an ideal, accordingly.

We remark that $LT_{\geq_w}(f)$ might be a polynomial (with more than one term). For example, if we take $w = [1, 2, 3]$ in $\mathbb{Q}_2[x, y, z]$ (with 2-adic valuation), then

$$LT_{\geq_w}\left(x^4 + x^2y + 2y^4 + 2^{-8}z^4\right) = x^4 + x^2y + 2^{-8}z^4.$$

$Trop(I)$ is then connected to $LT_{\geq_w}(I)$:

Theorem 2.2 (Fundamental th. of tropical geometry). *If K is algebraically closed with non-trivial valuation, Trop(I) is the closure in $\mathbb{R}^n$ of those $w \in \Gamma^n$ such that $LT_{\geq_w}(I)$ does not contain a monomial.*

Proof. See Theorem 3.2.5 of [11]. □

To compute $LT_{\geq_w}(I)$ one can add a (classical) monomial order in order to break ties when $LT_{\geq_w}(f)$ has more than one monomial.

Definition 2.3. Let us take $\geq_1$ a monomial order on A.

Given $a, b \in K$ and x^α and x^β two monomials in A, we write $ax^\alpha \geq bx^\beta$ if $val(a) + w \cdot \alpha < val(b) + w \cdot \beta$, or $val(a) + w \cdot \alpha = val(b) + w \cdot \beta$ and $x^\alpha \geq_1 x^\beta$.

Let $f \in A$ and A be an ideal of A. We define $LT(f)$ and $LT(I)$ accordingly. We remark that $LT(I) = LT_{\geq_1}(LT_w(I))$. We define $LM(f)$ to be the monomial of $LT(f)$, and $LM(I)$

accordingly. If $G = (g_1, \dots g_s) \in A^s$ is such that its leading monomials $(LM(g_1), \dots, LM(g_s))$ generate $LM(I)$, we say that G is a **tropical Gröbner basis** of I.

We can finally remark that to compute a generating set of $LM_{\geq_w}(I)$, it is enough to compute a tropical Gröbner basis of I.

Comparison with notations in previous works: In [4], K is such that there is a group homomorphism $\phi : \Gamma \to K$ such that for any $w \in \Gamma$, $val(\phi(w)) = w$. If $x \in R$, its reduction modulo m is denoted by $\overline{x}$. We define $\rho : K^* \to k_K$ to be defined by $\rho(x) = \overline{x\phi(val(x))}$. ρ extends naturally to $A \setminus \{0\}$ with $\rho(\sum_u a_u x^u) = \sum_u \rho(a_u)x^u$. $\geq_1$ extends naturally to C. Let $w \in \Gamma^n$, then, in [3], the author defines for any $f \in A$, $in_w = \rho(LT_{\geq_w}(f))$ and $lm(f) = LM_{\geq_1}(in_w)$. Let $G = (g_1, \dots, g_s) \in A^s$. Then G is a tropical Gröbner basis of $I = \langle G \rangle$ for the term order $\leq$ if and only if $(in_w(g_1), \dots, in_w(g_s))$ is a Gröbner basis of $in_w(I)$ for $\leq_1$. As a consequence, computing $LM(I)$ and $in(I)$ yields the same monomials. Nevertheless, we prefer working with LM since computations over (inexact) fields with valuations are among our motivations.

2.2 The algorithm of Chan and Maclagan

A Buchberger-style algorithm: in their article [4], Chan and Maclagan have proved that if one modifies the classical division algorithm of a polynomial by a finite family of polynomials with a variant of Mora's tangent cone algorithm, then one can get a division algorithm suited to the computation of tropical Gröbner bases. Indeed, they proved that Buchberger's algorithm using this division algorithm computes tropical Gröbner bases of ideals generated by homogeneous polynomials. The main ideas of their division algorithm is to allow division by previous partial quotients, and choose the divisor polynomial with a suited *écart* function.

Precision issues: Polynomial computation over (inexact) fields such as $\mathbb{Q}_p$ or $\mathbb{F}_p[\![t]\!]$ is our main motivation. To compute tropical Gröbner bases in such a setting, one may want to apply Chan and Maclagan's algorithm. Unfortunately, Buchberger-style algorithms rely on zero-testing: the termination criterion is Buchberger's. This is definitely not suited to finite precision. For instance, let F be $(x^2 + xy + y^2 + (1+O(p^N))t^2, x^2 + 2xy + 4y^2 + (1+O(p^N))t^2, t^4) \in \mathbb{Q}_p[x, y, t]^3$, for some $N \in \mathbb{N}$. Then the application of Chan and Maclagan's algorithm (*e.g.* for $w = (0, 0, 0)$ and grevlex) lead to S-polynomials that reduce to quantity of the form $O(\pi^{N'})xyt^2$, *i.e.* such that it is not possible to decide whether the polynomial in remainder is zero or not. Such issues appear even with the usage of Buchberger's criteria. Hence, they exclude the usage of Buchberger-style algorithms for most of the computations of Gröbner bases over fields such as $\mathbb{Q}_p$.

3. A TROPICAL MATRIX-F5 ALGORITHM

3.1 Matrix algorithm

Here we show that to compute a tropical Gröbner basis of an ideal given by a finite sequence of homogeneous polynomials, a matrix algorithm can be written. The first main idea is due to Daniel Lazard in [10], who remarked that for an homogeneous ideal $I \subset A$, generated by homogeneous polynomials $(f_1, \dots, f_s)$, for $d \in \mathbb{N}$, then as K-vector space: $I \cap A_d = \langle x^\alpha f_i, \ |\alpha| + |f_i| = d \rangle$. One of the main features of this property is that it can be given in term of matrices. First, we define the matrices of Macaulay :

Definition 3.1. Let $B_{n,d}$ be the basis of the monomials of degree d, ordered decreasingly according to $\geq$. Then for $f_1, \dots, f_s \in A$ homogeneous polynomials, $|f_i| = d_i$, $d \in \mathbb{N}$, we define $Mac_d(f_1, \dots, f_s)$ to be the matrix with coefficients in K and whose rows are $x^{\alpha_{1,1}} f_1, \dots, x^{\alpha_{1,\binom{n+d-d_1-1}{n-1}}}$, $x^{\alpha_{2,1}} f_2, \dots, x^{\alpha_{s,\binom{n+d-d_s-1}{n-1}}} f_s$, written in the basis $B_{n,d}$. The $x^{\alpha_{i,1}} < \dots < x^{\alpha_{i,\binom{n+d-d_i-1}{n-1}}}$'s are the monomials of degree $n + d - d_i - 1$. The i-th column of this matrix corresponds to the i-th monomial of $B_{n,d}$.

If we identify naturally the rows vectors of $k^{\binom{n+d-1}{n-1}}$ with homogeneous polynomials of degree d, then

$$Im(Mac_d(f_1, \dots, f_s)) = I \cap A_d,$$

with Im being the left image of the matrix.

When performing classical matrix algorithms to compute Gröbner bases (see [1]), the idea is then to compute row-echelon forms of the $Mac_d(f_1, \dots, f_s)$ up to some D: if D is large enough, the reduced rows forms a Gröbner basis of I. Though, it is not easy to guess in advance up to which D we have to perform row-reductions of Macaulay matrices. This is why the idea of tropical D-Gröbner bases can be introduced.

Definition 3.2. Let I be an ideal of A, Then $(g_1, \dots, g_l)$ is a D-Gröbner basis of I for $\geq$ if for any $f \in I$, homogeneous of degree less than D, there exists $1 \leq i \leq l$ such that $LT(g_i)$ divides $LT(f)$.

3.2 Tropical row-echelon form computation

This Subsection is devoted to provide an algorithm that can compute $LM(\langle f_1, \dots, f_i \rangle) \cap A_d$ by computing echelonized bases of the $Mac_d(f_1, \dots, f_i)$. To track what the leading term of a row is, we add a label of monomials to the matrices:

Definition 3.3. We define a Macaulay matrix of degree d in A to be a couple (M, mon) where $M \in K^{r \times \binom{n+d-1}{n-1}}$ is a matrix, and mon is the list of the $\binom{n+d-1}{n-1}$ monomials of degree d of A, in decreasing order according to $\geq$. If mon is not ordered, (M, mon) is only called a labeled matrix.

Algorithm 1 over Macaulay matrices computes by pivoting the leading terms of their rows:

Definition 3.4. We define the tropical row-echelon form of a Macaulay matrix M as the result of the previous algorithm, and denote it by $\widetilde{M}$. $\widetilde{M}$ is indeed in row-echelon form.

Correctness: $\widetilde{Mac_d(f_1, \dots, f_i)}$ provides exactly the leading terms of $\langle f_1, \dots, f_i \rangle \cap A_d$:

Proposition 3.5. *Let $F = (f_1, \dots, f_s)$ be homogeneous polynomials in A. Let $d \in \mathbb{Z}_{>0}$ and $M = Mac_d(f_1, \dots, f_s)$.. Let $I = \{F\}$ be the ideal generated by the f_i's.*

Let $\widetilde{M}$ be the tropical row-echelon form of M. Then the rows of $\widetilde{M}$ form a basis of $I \cap A_d$ such that their LT's corresponds to $LT(I) \cap A_d$.

Algorithm 1: The tropical row-echelon algorithm

input : M, a Macaulay matrix of degree d in $A = K[X_1, \dots, X_n]$, with n_{row} rows and n_{col} columns.
output: $\widetilde{M}$, the tropical row-echelon form of M

$\widetilde{M} \leftarrow M$;
if $n_{col} = 1$ *or* $n_{row} = 0$ *or* M *has no non-zero entry* **then**
  Return $\widetilde{M}$;
else
  Find i, j such that $\widetilde{M}_{i,j}$ has the greatest term $\widetilde{M}_{i,j} x^{mon_j}$ (with smallest i in case of tie);
  Swap the columns 1 and j of $\widetilde{M}$, and the 1 and j entries of *mon*;
  Swap the rows 1 and i of $\widetilde{M}$;
  By pivoting with the first row, eliminate the first-column coefficients of the other rows ;
  Proceed recursively on the submatrix $\widetilde{M}_{i \geq 2, j \geq 2}$;
  Return $\widetilde{M}$;

The fact that the rows of $\widetilde{M}$ form a basis of $I \cap A_d$ is clear, it forms an echelonized basis (considering the basis *mon* of A_d). Considering the initial terms of $I \cap A_d$, the result is a direct consequence of the following lemma:

Lemma 3.6. *if* $ax^\alpha > b_1 x^\beta$ *and* $ax^\alpha > b_2 x^\beta$, *then* $ax^\alpha > (b_1 + b_2) x^\beta$.

Consequence: We can find all the polynomials of a tropical D-Gröbner basis of $\langle f_1, \dots, f_s \rangle$ by computing the tropical row-echelon forms of the $Mac_d(f_1, \dots, f_s)$ for d from 1 to D. Nevertheless, there is room for improvement: those matrices are huge and most of the time not of full rank.

3.3 The F5 criterion

We introduce here Faugère's F5 criterion that is enough to discard most of the rows of the $Mac_d(f_1, \dots, f_s)$'s that do not yield any meaningful information for the computation of $LT(I)$. For any $j \in [\![1, s]\!]$, we denote by I_j the ideal $\langle f_1, \dots, f_j \rangle$. Then, Faugère proved in [7] that for a classical monomial ordering, if we know which monomials x^α are in $LM(I_{i-1})$, we are able to discard corresponding rows $x^\alpha f_i$ of the Macaulay matrices. This criterion is compatible with our definition of LM:

Theorem 3.7 (F5-criterion). *For any* $i \in [\![1, s]\!]$,

$$I_i \cap A_d = Span(\{x^\alpha f_k, \text{ s.t. } 1 \leq k \leq i, |x^\alpha f_k| = d \text{ and } x^\alpha \notin LM(I_{k-1})\}).$$

To prove this result, one can rely on the following fact, which can be proved inductively. Let $(f_1, \dots, f_i)$ be homogeneous polynomials of A of degree $d_1, \dots, d_i$. Let $a_{\alpha_1} x^{\alpha_1}, \dots, a_{\alpha_u} x^{\alpha_u}$ be the initial terms of the rows of $\widetilde{Mac_{d-d_i}}(f_1, \dots, f_{i-1})$, ordered by decreasing order (regarding the initial term). Let x^{β_j} denote the remaining monomials of degree $d - d_i$ (*i.e.* the monomials that are not an initial monomial of $\langle f_1, \dots, f_{i-1} \rangle \cap A_{d-d_i}$). Then, for any k, the row $x^{\alpha_k} f_i$ of $Mac_d(f_1, \dots, f_i)$ is a linear combination of some rows of the form $x^{\alpha_{k+k'}} f_i$ ($k' > 0$), $x^{\beta_j} f_i$ and $x^\gamma f_j$ ($j < i$) of $Mac_d(f_1, \dots, f_i)$.

Thus, it is now clear which rows we can remove with the F5 criterion. The following subsection provides an effective way of taking advantage of this criterion.

3.4 A first Matrix-F5 algorithm

The tropical MF5 algorithm: We apply Faugère's idea (see [1],[2], [7]) to the tropical setting and therefore provide a tropical Matrix-F5 algorithm:

Algorithm 2: A tropical Matrix-F5 algorithm

input : $F = (f_1, \dots, f_s) \in A^s$, homogeneous with respective degrees $d_1 \leq \dots \leq d_s$, and $D \in \mathbb{N}$
output: $(g_1, \dots, g_k) \in A^k$, a D-tropical Gröbner basis of $\{F\}$.

$G \leftarrow F$
for $d \in [\![0, D]\!]$ **do**
  $\widetilde{\mathscr{M}_{d,0}} := \emptyset$
  for $i \in [\![1, s]\!]$ **do**
    $\mathscr{M}_{d,i} := \widetilde{\mathscr{M}_{d,i-1}}$
    for α *such that* $|\alpha| + d_i = d$ **do**
      if x^α *is not the leading term of a row of* $\widetilde{\mathscr{M}_{d-d_i,i-1}}$ **then**
        Add $x^\alpha f_i$ to $\mathscr{M}_{d,i}$
    Compute $\widetilde{\mathscr{M}_{d,i}}$, the tropical row-echelon form of $\mathscr{M}_{d,i}$
    Add to G all the rows with a new leading monomial.
Return G

Correctness: What we have to show is that for any $d \in [\![0, D]\!]$ and $i \in [\![1, s]\!]$, $Im(\mathscr{M}_{d,i}) = I_i \cap A_d$. This can be proved by induction on d and i. We remark that there is nothing to prove for $i = 1$ and any d. Now let us assume that there exists some $i \in [\![1, s]\!]$ such that for any j with $1 \leq j < i$ and for any d, $0 \leq d \leq D$, $Im(\mathscr{M}_{d,j}) = I_j \cap A_d$. Then, i being given, the first d such that $\mathscr{M}_{d,i} \neq \mathscr{M}_{d,i-1}$ is d_i. Let d be such that $d_i \leq d \leq D$. Then, with the induction hypothesis and corollary 3.7 :

$$I_i \cap A_d = Im(\mathscr{M}_{d,i-1}) + Span\left(\{x^\alpha f_i, \text{ s.t. } x^\alpha \notin LM(I_{i-1})\}\right). \tag{1}$$

Besides, by the induction hypothesis and the correctness of the row-echelon algorithm (see Proposition 3.5), the leading terms of $I_{i-1} \cap A_{d-d_i}$ are exactly the leading terms of rows of $\widetilde{\mathscr{M}_{d-d_i,i-1}}$. Thus, the rows that we add to $\widetilde{\mathscr{M}_{d,i-1}}$ in order to build $\mathscr{M}_{d,i}$ are exactly the $x^\alpha f_i$, such that $x^\alpha \notin LM(I_{i-1})$. Finally, we remark that $Im(\mathscr{M}_{d,i}) = Im(\widetilde{\mathscr{M}_{d,i-1}})$. Therefore, $Im(\mathscr{M}_{d,i})$ contains both summands of (1), and since it is clearly included in $I_i \cap A_d$, we have proved that $I_i \cap A_d = Im(\mathscr{M}_{d,i})$. To conclude the correctness of the tropical MF5 algorithm, we point out that the correctness of the tropical row-echelon computation (see prop 3.5) show that the leading terms of rows of $\widetilde{\mathscr{M}_{d,i}}$ indeed correspond to the leading terms of $I_i \cap A_d$.

3.5 Regular sequences and complexity

Principal syzygies and regularity: The behavior of this algorithm with respect to principal syzygies is the same as the classical Matrix-F5 algorithm. See [1] for a precise description of the link between syzygies and row-reduction. We instead only prove the main result connecting principal syzygies and tropical row-reduction of Macaulay matrices.

Proposition 3.8. *If a row reduces to zero during the tropical row-echelon form computation of the tropical MF5 algorithm, then the syzygy it yields is not in the module of principal syzygies.*

Proof. Let $\sum_{j=1}^{i} a_j f_j$ with $a_j \in A$ be a syzygy of $(f_1, \dots, f_i)$. If $a_j \neq 0$ and if this this syzygy is principal, then $a_i \in I_{i-1}$ and $LM(a_i) \in LM(I_{i-1})$. Since because of the F5 criterion, there is no row of the form $x^\alpha f_i$ with $x^\alpha \in LM(I_{i-1})$ in the operated $\mathscr{M}_{d,i}$, then no such syzygy can be produced during the reduction of $\mathscr{M}_{d,i}$. □

Corollary 3.9. *If the sequence $(f_1, \dots, f_s)$ is regular, then no row of a Macaulay matrix in the tropical MF5 algorithm reduces to zero. In other words, the $\mathscr{M}_{d,i}$ are all injective, and have non-strictly less rows than columns.*

Proof. For a regular sequence of homogeneous polynomials, all syzygies are principal. See [6] page 69. □

Complexity: The complexity to compute tropical row-echelon form of a matrix of rank r with n_{rows} rows and n_{cols} columns can be expressed as $O(r \times n_{rows} \times n_{cols})$ operations in K. This yields the following complexities for Algorithm 2:

- $O\left(s^2 D \binom{n+D-1}{D}^3\right)$ operations in K, as $D \to +\infty$.
- $O\left(s D \binom{n+D-1}{D}^3\right)$ operations in K, as $D \to +\infty$, in the special case where $(f_1, \dots f_s)$ is regular, because of corollary 3.9.

Compared to the classical case, for which we refer to [2], complexity gets essentially an extra factor s. This comes from the fact that we need to compute the tropical row-echelon form from start for each new $\mathscr{M}_{d,i}$. In other words, we do not take into account the fact that, after building $\mathscr{M}_{d,i}$, $\widetilde{\mathscr{M}}_{d,i-1}$ was already under row-echelon form.

Bound on D: Regarding bounds on a sufficient D for D-Gröbner bases to be Gröbner bases, we might not hope better bounds than in the classical case (*i.e.* with trivial valuation) exist. Chan has proved in [3] (Theorem 3.3.1) that $D = 2(d^2/2 + d)^{2^{n-2}}$, with $d = \max_i d_i$, is enough. If $(f_1, \dots, f_n)$ is a regular sequence, we remark that all monomials of degree greater than the Macaulay bound $\sum_i (d_i - 1) + 1$ are in $LM(I)$. This is a consequence of the fact that we know what is the Hilbert function of a regular sequence. Hence,

Proposition 3.10. *If $(f_1, \dots, f_n) \in A^n$ is a regular sequence of homogeneous polynomials, all D-Gröbner bases are Gröbner bases for $D \geq \sum_i (|f_i| - 1) + 1$.*

4. THE CASE OF FINITE-PRECISION CDVF

4.1 Setting

Throughout this section, we further assume that K is a complete discrete valuation field. We refer to Serre [13] for an introduction to such fields. Let $\pi \in R$ be a uniformizer for K and let $S_K \subset R$ be a system of representatives of $k_K = R/m$. All numbers of K can be written uniquely under its π-adic power series development form : $\sum_{k \geq l} a_k \pi^k$ for some $l \in \mathbb{Z}$, $a_k \in S_K$. We assume that K is not an exact field, but k_K is, and symbolic computation can only be performed on truncation of π-adic power series development. We denote by finite-precision CDVF such a field. An example of such a CDVF is $K = \mathbb{Q}_p$, with p-adic valuation. We are interested in the computation of tropical Gröbner bases over finite-precision CDVF and its comparison with that of classical Gröbner bases.

4.2 Precision issues with leading terms

For any $m \in \mathbb{Z}$, let $O(\pi^m) = \pi^m R$. In a finite-precision CDVF K, we are interested in computation over approximations x of elements of K which take the form $x = \sum_{k \geq l}^{m-1} a_k \pi^k + O(\pi^m)$. m is called the precision over x.

If the precision on the coefficients of $f \in A$ is not enough, then one can not determine what the leading term of f is. For example, on $\mathbb{Q}_p[X_1, X_2]$, with $w = (0, 4)$ and lexicographical order, then one can not compare $O(p^2) X_1$ and X_2. Yet, with enough precision, such an issue does not occur when computing tropical row-echelon form. The following proposition provides a bound on the precision needed on f to determine its leading term.

Proposition 4.1. *Let $f \in A$ be an homogeneous polynomial, and let aX^α be its leading term.*

Then precision $val(a) + \max_{|\beta|=d} ((\alpha - \beta) \cdot w)$ on the coefficients of f is enough to determine which term of f is $LT(f)$.

Proof. We only have to remark that $O(p^n) X^\beta < a X^\alpha$ if and only if $n > val(a) + (\alpha - \beta) \cdot w$. □

4.3 Row-echelon form computation

Regular sequences: As we have already seen, when dealing with finite-precision coefficients, a crucial issue is that one can not decide whether a coefficient $O(\pi^k)$ is zero or not. Fortunately, thanks to Corollary 3.9, when the input polynomials form a regular sequence, all matrices in the tropical MF5 algorithm are injective. It means that if the precision is enough, the tropical row-echelon form computation performed over these matrices will have no issue with finding pivots and deciding what the leading terms of the rows are. In other words, if the precision is enough, **there is no zero-testing issue**.

We then estimate which precision is enough in order to be able to compute D-Gröbner bases of such a sequence.

A sufficient precision:

Proposition 4.2. *Let M be an injective tropical Macaulay matrix with coefficients in R, of degree d. Let $a_1, \dots, a_u$ be the pivots chosen during the computation of its tropical row-echelon form. Let x^{α_k} be the corresponding monomials. Let prec be :*

$$prec = \sum_k val(a_k) + \max_k val(a_k) + \max_{k, |\beta|=d} (\alpha_k - \beta) \cdot w.$$

Then, if the coefficients of the rows are known up to the same precision $O(\pi^{prec})$, the tropical row-echelon form computation of M can be computed, and the loss in precision is $\sum_k val(a_k)$.

Proof. We begin with a matrix M with coefficients all known with precision $O(\pi^l)$, and we first assume that there is no issue with finding the pivots. Thus, we first analyze what the loss in precision is when we pivot. That is, we wish to put a "real zero" on the coefficient $M_{i,j} = \varepsilon\pi^{n_1} + O(\pi^n)$, by pivoting with a pivot $piv = \mu\pi^{n_0} + O(\pi^n)$ on row L, with $n_0, n_1 < n$ be integers, and $\varepsilon = \sum_{k=0}^{n-n_1-1} a_k\pi^k$, $\mu = \sum_{k=0}^{n-n_0-1} b_k\pi^k$, with $a_k, b_k \in S_K$, and $a_0, b_0 \neq 0$. We remark that by definition of the pivot, necessarily, $n_0 \leq n_1$. Now, this can be performed by the following operation on the i-th row L_i :

$$L_i \leftarrow L_i - \frac{M_{i,j}}{piv} L = L_i + (\varepsilon\mu^{-1}\pi^{n_1-n_0} + O(\pi^{n-n_0}))L,$$

along with the symbolic operation $M_{i,j} \leftarrow 0$. Indeed, $\frac{M_{i,j}}{piv} = \frac{\varepsilon\pi^{n_1}+O(\pi^n)}{\mu\pi^n+O(\pi^{m_0})}$, therefore $\frac{M_{i,j}}{piv} = \varepsilon\mu^{-1}\pi^{n_1-n_0} + O(\pi^{n-n_0})$. As a consequence, after the first pivot is chosen and other coefficient of the first column have been reduced to zero, the coefficients of the submatrix $\widetilde{M}_{i\geq 2, j\geq 2}$ are known up to $O(\pi^{l-val(a_1)})$. We can then proceed inductively to prove that after the termination of the tropical row-echelon form computation, coefficients of $\widetilde{M}$ are known up to $O(\pi^{l-val(a_1\times\cdots\times a_u)})$. Since we have to be able to determine what the leading terms of the rows are in order to determine what the pivots are, then, with Proposition 4.1, it is enough that $l - val(a_1 \times \cdots \times, a_u)$ is bigger than $\max_{k,|\beta|=d} (\alpha - \beta) \cdot w$, which concludes the proof. □

4.4 Tropical MF5 algorithm

We apply this study of the row-echelon computation to prove Proposition 1.2 concerning the tropical Matrix-F5 algorithm over CDVF. To facilitate this investigation, and only for section 4, the step $\mathscr{M}_{d,i} := \widetilde{\mathscr{M}_{d,i-1}}$ in algorithm 2 is replaced with $\mathscr{M}_{d,i} := \mathscr{M}_{d,i-1}$. This is harmless since both matrices have same dimension and image. We first define bounds on the initial precision and loss in precision. Let $(f_1, \ldots, f_s) \in B^s$ be a regular sequence of homogeneous polynomials.

Definition 4.3. Let $d \geq 1$ and $1 \leq i \leq s$. Let $x^{\alpha_1}, \ldots, x^{\alpha_u}$ be the monomials of the leading terms of $\langle f_1, \ldots, f_i \rangle \cap A_d$.

Let $\Delta_{d,i}$ be the minor over the columns corresponding to the x^{α_l} that achieves smallest valuation. Let

$$\square_{d,i} = 2\Delta_{d,i} + \max_{k,|\beta|=d} (\alpha_k - \beta) \cdot w.$$

We define $prec_{MF5trop}((f_1, \ldots, f_s), D, \geq) = \max_{d \leq D, i} \square_{d,i}$, and $loss_{MF5trop}((f_1, \ldots, f_s), D, \geq) = \max_{d \leq D, i} \Delta_{d,i}$.

As a consequence of Proposition 4.2, these bounds are enough for Proposition 1.2.

Furthermore, we can precise the special case of $w = 0$:

Proposition 4.4. *If $w = 0$, then the loss in precision corresponds to the maximal minors of the $\mathscr{M}_{d,i}$ with the smallest valuation. In particular, $w = 0$ corresponds to the smallest $loss_{MF5trop}$ and a straight-forward $prec_{MF5trop}$.*

4.5 Precision versus time-complexity

We might remark that if one want to achieve a smaller loss in precision, one might want to drop the F5 criterion and use the tropical row-reduction algorithm on the whole Macaulay matrices until enough linearly-free rows are found. The required number of rows can be computed thanks to the F5-criterion and corollary 3.7 if Macaulay matrices are operated iteratively in d and i. This way, one would be assured that its pivots will yield the smallest loss of precision possible over $Mac_d(f_1, \ldots, f_s)$. Yet, such an algorithm would be more time-consuming because of the huge number of useless rows, and would be in $O\left(s^2 D \binom{n+D-1}{D}^3\right)$ operations in K even for regular sequences.

4.6 Comparison with classical Gröbner bases

We compare here the results over finite-precision CDVF for computation of tropical Gröbner bases and for computation of classical Gröbner bases, as it was performed in [14].

We recall the main result of [14] :

Definition 4.5. Let ω be a monomial order on A. Let $F = (f_1, \ldots, f_s) \in B^s$ be homogeneous polynomials. Let $\mathscr{M}_{d,i}$ be the Macaulay matrix in degree d for $(f_1, \ldots, f_i)$, without the rows discarded by the F5-criterion. Let $l_{d,i}$ be the maximum of the $l \in \mathbb{Z}_{\geq 0}$ such that the l-first columns of $\mathscr{M}_{d,i}$ are linearly free. We define

$$\Delta_{d,i} = \min\left(val\left(\{\text{minor over the } l_{d,i}\text{-first columns of } \mathscr{M}_{d,i}\}\right)\right).$$

We define the Matrix-F5 precision of F regarding to ω and D as :

$$prec_{MF5}(F, D, \omega) = \max_{d \leq D,\ 1 \leq i \leq s} val\left(\Delta_{d,i}\right).$$

Then, $prec_{MF5}(F, D, \omega)$ is enough to compute approximate D-Gröbner bases :

Theorem 4.6. *Let $(f'_1, \ldots, f'_s)$ be approximations of the homogeneous polynomials $F = (f_1, \ldots, f_s) \in B^s$, with precision better than $prec_{MF5} = prec_{MF5}(F, D, w)$. We assume that $(f_1, \ldots, f_s)$ is a regular sequence **(H1)** and all the $\langle f_1, \ldots, f_i \rangle$ are weakly-ω-ideals **(H2)**. Then, the weak Matrix-F5 algorithm computes an approximate D-Gröbner basis of $(f'_1, \ldots, f'_s)$, with loss in precision upper-bounded by $prec_{MF5}$. The complexity is in $O\left(sD\binom{n+D-1}{D}^3\right)$ operations in K, as $D \to +\infty$.*

We remark that for tropical Gröbner bases, the structure hypothesis **H2** is compensated by the precision requirement for the tropical row-echelon computation : $\max_k val(a_k) + \max_{k,|\beta|=d} (\alpha_k - \beta) \cdot w$ so that there is no position problem for the leading terms when a tropical Gröbner basis is computed. This leads to a bound on the required precision, $prec_{MF5trop}(F, D, \geq)$, that might be bigger than $prec_{MF5}$ but with no position problem and no requirement for **H2**.

Thus, for tropical Gröbner bases over a CDVF (where the valuation is non-trivial), the only structure hypothesis is the regularity **H1**, and is clearly generic, whereas for classical Gröbner bases, **H1** and **H2** might be generic only in special cases, like for the grevlex ordering if Moreno-Socias' conjecture holds. Therefore, tropical Gröbner bases computation may require a bigger precision on the input than classical Gröbner bases, but it can be performed generically, while it is not clear for classical Gröbner bases.

Finally, when the weight w is zero, thanks to Proposition 4.4, the smallest loss in precision defined by minors of Macaulay matrices is attained.

5. IMPLEMENTATION

A toy implementation in Sage [12] of the previous algorithm is available at `http://perso.univ-rennes1.fr/tristan.vaccon/toy_F5.py`. The purpose of this implementation was the study of the precision. It is therefore not optimized regarding to time-complexity. We have applied the tropical Matrix-F5 algorithm to homogeneous polynomials with varying degrees and random coefficients in $\mathbb{Z}_p$ (regarding to the Haar measure): $f_1, \dots, f_s$, of degree $d_1, \dots, d_s$ in $\mathbb{Z}_p[X_1, \dots, X_s]$, known up to initial precision 30, with a given weight w and the grevlex ordering to break the ties, and up to D the Macaulay bound. We have done this experiment 20 times for each setting and noted maximal loss, mean loss in precision and the number of failures (*i.e.* the computation can not be completed due to precision). We have compared with the weak-MF5 of [14] with grevlex on the same setting (the "grevlex" cases in the array). We present the results in the following array :

$d=$	w	D	p	maximal loss	mean loss	failure
[3,4,7]	grevlex	12	2	9	0.1	0
[3,4,7]	[1,-3,2]	12	2	11	0.1	0
[3,4,7]	[0,0,0]	12	2	0	0	0
[3,4,7]	[1,-3,2]	12	7	3	.02	0
[3,4,7]	[0,0,0]	12	7	0	0	0
[2,3,4,5]	grevlex	11	2	9	1.6	2
[2,3,4,5]	[1,4,1,-1]	11	2	13	0.2	0
[2,3,4,5]	[0,0,0,0]	11	2	0	0	0
[2,3,4,5]	[1,4,1,1]	11	7	5	0.02	0

These results suggest that the loss in precision is less when working with bigger primes. It seems reasonable since the loss in precision comes from pivots with positive valuation, whereas the probability that $val(x) = 0$ for $x \in \mathbb{Z}_p$ is $\frac{p-1}{p}$. Those results also corroborate the facts that $w = [0, \dots, 0]$ lead to significantly smaller loss in precision.

6. A FASTER TROPICAL MF5 ALGORITHM

In this section, we show that one can perform in a tropical setting an adaptation of the classical, signature-based, Matrix-F5 algorithm presented in [2]. This variant of the Matrix-F5 algorithm is characterized by the usage of the fact that $\widetilde{\mathscr{M}_{d,i}}$ is under echelon form to build a $\mathscr{M}_{d,i}$ closer to its echelon-form.

To that intent, we introduce labels and signatures for polynomials, and a tropical LUP-form computation.

6.1 Label and signature

Definition 6.1. Given $(f_1, \dots, f_s) \in A^s$, a *labeled polynomial* is a couple (u, p) with $u = (l_1, \dots, l_s) \in A^s$, $p \in A$ and $\sum_{i=1}^s l_i f_i = p$.
u is called the *label* of the labeled polynomial. We write $(e_1, \dots, e_s)$ to be the canonical basis of A^s.

If $u = (l_1, \dots, l_i, 0, \dots, 0)$ with $l_i \neq 0$, then the *signature* of the labeled polynomial (u, p), denoted by $sign((u,p))$, is $(HM(l_i), i)$, with the following definition : $HM(l_i)$ is the highest monomial, regarding to $\leq$, that appears in l_i with a non-zero coefficient.

Remark 6.2. We must point out that in the definition of the signature, we *do not* take into account the valuations of the coefficients in the label, hence the $HM(l_i)$ instead of $LT(l_i)$ or $LM(l_i)$. $HM(l_i)$ is not, in general, the monomial of the leading term of l_i.

Definition 6.3. We define a total order on the set of signatures {monomials in R} $\times \{1, \dots, s\}$ with the following definition : $(x^\alpha, i) \leq (x^\beta, k)$ if $i < k$, or $x^\alpha \leq x^\beta$ and $i = k$.

Signatures are compatible with operations over labeled polynomials :

Proposition 6.4. *Let (u, p) be a labeled polynomial, $(x^\alpha, i) = sign((u,l))$ and let x^β be a monomial in A. Then*

$$sign((x^\beta u, x^\beta p)) = (x^\alpha x^\beta, i).$$

If (v, q) is another labeled polynomial such that $sign((v,q)) < sign((u,p))$, and if $\mu \in K$, then $sign((u + \mu v, p + \mu q)) = sign((u,p))$.

6.2 Signature-preserving LUP-form computation

From now on throughout this subsection, an additional datum will be attached to the rows of the Macaulay matrices: its label and signature. We make the further assumption that the rows are ordered with increasing signature. Such a matrix will be called a labeled Macaulay matrix. When adding a row, both its label and its signature will be noted, and all the operations on the rows are carried on to the labels of these rows.

The algorithm: We provide a tropical LUP algorithm for labeled Macaulay matrices to compute the leading term of the Macaulay matrices while preserving signatures.

Algorithm 3: The tropical LUP algorithm

input : M, a labeled Macaulay matrix of degree d in A, with n_{row} rows and n_{col} columns.
output: $\widetilde{M}$, the U of the tropical LUP-form of M
$\widetilde{M} \leftarrow M$;
if $n_{col} = 1$ *or* $n_{row} = 0$ *or* M *has no non-zero entry* **then**
  Return $\widetilde{M}$;
else
  for $i = 1$ *to* n_{row} **do**
    Find j such that $\widetilde{M}_{i,j}$ has the greatest term $\widetilde{M}_{i,j} x^{mon_j}$ over the row;
    Swap the columns 1 and j of $\widetilde{M}$, and the 1 and j entries of mon;
    By pivoting with the first row, eliminates the coefficients of the other rows on the first column;
    Proceed recursively on the submatrix $\widetilde{M}_{i \geq 2, j \geq 2}$;
  Return $\widetilde{M}$;

We remark that at the end of the algorithm, there exists a unipotent lower-triangular matrix L, a permutation matrix P, such that $\widetilde{M} = LMP$, $\widetilde{M}$ is under row-echelon form up to permutation, and since we only add to a row L_i a linear combination of rows that are above L_i, those rows have a strictly lower signature than L_i, and therefore the operations performed on the rows (and on the columns) preserve the signature. Furthermore,

Proposition 6.5. *For any $1 \leq i \leq n_{row}(M)$, if j is the index of the i-th row of $\widetilde{M}$, then $\widetilde{M}_{i,j} x^{mon_j}$ is the leading term of the polynomial corresponding to this row.*

Those remarks justify the name of tropical LUP algorithm, and the facts that this algorithm computes the leading terms of $Span(rows(M))$. Finally, since signature remains unchanged throughout the tropical LUP reduction, we can omit the labels and only handle Macaulay matrices on which the signatures of the rows are marked.

6.3 A signature-based tropical MF5 algorithm

We show that with LUP-reduction we can adapt the classical Matrix-F5 algorithm.

The signature-based F5 criterion is still available:

Proposition 6.6. *Let (u, f) be a labeled homogeneous polynomial of degree d, such that $sign(u) = x^\alpha e_i$, with $1 < i \leq s$ and $x^\alpha \in I_{i-1}$. Then,*

$$x^\alpha \in Span\left(\left\{x^\beta f_k, |x^\beta f_k| = d, \text{ and } (x^\beta, k) < (x^\alpha, i)\right\}\right).$$

As a consequence, if (u, f) is a labeled homogeneous polynomial of degree d with $sign(u) = x^\alpha e_i$ and $x^\alpha \notin LM(I_{i-1})$. Then f can be written $f = x^\alpha f_i + g$, with

$$g \in Span\left(\left\{x^\beta f_k, |x^\beta f_k| = d, \text{ and } (x^\beta, k) < (x^\alpha, i)\right\}\right).$$

A faster tropical Matrix-F5 algorithm:

Algorithm 4: The tropical signature-based Matrix-F5 algorithm

---

input : $F = (f_1, \dots, f_s) \in A^s$, with respective degrees $d_1, \dots, d_s$, and $D \in \mathbb{N}$
output: $(g_1, \dots, g_k) \in A^k$, a D-tropical Gröbner basis of $\langle F \rangle$, if D is large enough.

$G \leftarrow F$
for $d \in [\![0, D]\!]$ **do**
  $\widetilde{\mathcal{M}_{d,0}} := \emptyset$
  for $i \in [\![1, s]\!]$ **do**
    $\mathcal{M}_{d,i} := \widetilde{\mathcal{M}_{d,i-1}}$
    for L *a row of* $\widetilde{\mathcal{M}_{d-1,i}}$ **do**
      for $x \in \{X_1, \dots, X_n\}$ **do**
        $x^\alpha e_k := sign(xL)$
        if $k = i$, x^α *is not the leading term of a row of* $\widetilde{\mathcal{M}_{d-d_i,i-1}}$, *and* $\mathcal{M}_{d,i}$ *has not already a row with signature* $x^\alpha e_i$ **then**
          Add xL to $\mathcal{M}_{d,i}$.
    Compute $\widetilde{\mathcal{M}_{d,i}}$, the tropical LUP-form of $\mathcal{M}_{d,i}$.
    Add to G all the rows with a new leading monomial.
Return G

Correctness: This algorithm indeed computes a tropical D-Gröbner basis. The first thing to prove is that with the building of the Macaulay matrices suggested in the algorithm, the two following properties are satisfied : $Im(\mathcal{M}_{d,i}) = I_i \cap A_d$ and for any monomial x^α of degree $d - d_i$ such that $x^\alpha \notin LM(I_{i-1})$, $\mathcal{M}_{d,i}$ has a row with signature $x^\alpha e_i$. This can be proved by induction on d and i.

Now, since the tropical LUP reduction indeed computes an echelon-basis of the $\mathcal{M}_{d,i}$, as in the previous tropical MF5 algorithm, the signature-based tropical MF5 algorithm computes tropical D-Gröbner bases.

Complexity: The main difference in complexity between Algorithm 2 and Algorithm 4 is that for the latter, the computation of the tropical LUP-form of the $\mathcal{M}_{d,i+1}$ takes into account the fact that it was previously done on $\mathcal{M}_{d,i}$, *i.e.* the first rows of $\mathcal{M}_{d,i+1}$ are already under row-echelon form with the right leading terms. As a consequence, the complexity to compute a tropical D-Gröbner basis of $(f_1, \dots, f_s)$ is the same as in the classical case, that is to say, $O\left(sD\binom{n+D-1}{D}^3\right)$ operations in K, as $D \to +\infty$. If $(f_1, \dots, f_s)$ is a regular sequence, then the complexity is in $O\left(D\binom{n+D-1}{D}^3\right)$.

7. FUTURE WORKS

Since both Buchberger and Matrix-F5 algorithms are available, we conjecture that the F5 algorithm can be adapted to the tropical setting. It would probably reduce to adapt properly the TopReduction of [7].

The numerical stability of Proposition 1.2 and the fact that tropical Gröbner bases provide normal forms, suggest investigating the FGLM ([8]) algorithm to pass from a tropical order (with $w = (0, \dots, 0)$) to a classical one, with a view toward stable computations over finite-precision CDVF.

8. REFERENCES

[1] BARDET, MAGALI "Étude des systèmes algébriques surdéterminés. Applications aux codes correcteurs et à la cryptographie", thèse de doctorat, Université Paris VI, Décembre 2004.

[2] BARDET, MAGALI, FAUGÈRE, JEAN-CHARLES & SALVY, BRUNO On the Complexity of the F5 Gröbner basis Algorithm, Journal of Symbolic Computation, pages 1-24, September 2014.

[3] CHAN, ANDREW J. Gröbner bases over fields with valuations and tropical curves by coordinate projections, PhD Thesis, University of Warwick, August 2013.

[4] CHAN, ANDREW J. & MACLAGAN, DIANE Gröbner bases over fields with valuations, arxiv:1303.0729

[5] EINSIEDLER, M., LIND, D. & KAPRANOV, M. Non-Archmidean Amoebas and Tropical Varieties.J. Reine Angew. Math. 601 (2006)

[6] ELKADI, MOURRAIN Introduction à la résolution des systèmes polynomiaux (Springer, 2007)

[7] FAUGÈRE, JEAN-CHARLES A new efficient algorithm for computing Gröbner bases without reduction to zero (F5). In Proceedings of the 2002 international symposium on Symbolic and algebraic computation, ISSAC '02, pages 75-83, New York, NY, USA, 2002. ACM.

[8] FAUGÈRE, GIANI, LAZARD, MORA Efficient Computation of Zero-Dimensional Gröbner Bases by a Change of Ordering, Journal of Symbolic Computation, 16(4), 1993.

[9] JENSEN, ANDERS Gfan, a software system for Gröbner fans and tropical varieties, available at http://home.imf.au.dk/jensen/software/gfan/gfan.html

[10] LAZARD, DANIEL Gaussian Elimination and Resolution of Systems of Algebraic Equations, in Proc. EUROCAL 83, volume 162 of LNCS, p.146-157, 1983

[11] MACLAGAN, DIANE & STURMFELS, BERND Introduction to Tropical Geometry, Book in preparation.

[12] STEIN, W.A. ET AL. Sage Mathematics Software (Version 4.7.2), The Sage Development Team, 2011, http://www.sagemath.org.

[13] SERRE, J.-P. Local Fields, Graduate Texts in Mathematics, 67, Springer-Verlag, 1995

[14] VACCON, TRISTAN Matrix-F5 algorithms over finite-precision complete discrete valuation fields, Proceedings of the 39th International Symposium on Symbolic and Algebraic Computation, ISSAC '14, pages 397-404, Kobe, Japan, ACM.

Author Index